"Rich continues to be one of the foremost authorities on tuning [...] and tricks is a must-have for any database professional."

"Another 'must have' technical reference for the Oracle professi[...] allow you to get the most out of Oracle and push it to the limit [...]
—Matt Swann, Vice President of Software Development, [...]

"This is a timely update of Rich's classic book on Oracle Database performance tuning to cover hot new topics like Database 11g Release 2 and Exadata. This is a must-have for DBAs moving to these new products."
—Andrew Mendelsohn, Senior Vice President, Oracle Database Server Technologies

"Packed with tips and tuning tricks, Rich draws from a lifetime of Oracle experience. This book is essential reading for every Oracle DBA who wants to stay current with the nuances of Oracle Database performance tuning."
—Sohan DeMel, Vice President of Product Strategy, Oracle Corporation

"Rich makes most complex concepts in Oracle simple and interesting. His deep passion to educate everybody is unique in all his books. I remember 12 years back when I started learning Oracle reading Rich Niemiec books, and even today I consider his books the most reliable source in decision making. No DBA library in this world is complete without Rich Niemiec books."
—Shiv Iyer, Founder & CEO, Ask DB Experts, Bangalore, India

"When I was a junior DBA in Chicago sixteen years ago, Rich Niemiec's brilliant and unique DBA/developer topics exposed me to the wonderful world of performance tuning. In today's era of Oracle Exadata when hardware and software are engineered to work together, I find Rich still at the forefront of this technology."
—Steven Xueyong Lu, iTech Consultant Lead, Oracle China

"Tuning Oracle Databases is a science. When I need to have an answer to any tuning issue, I always turn to Rich's Oracle Tuning Books. Whether it is 9i, 10g, or 11g, I know I can find the correct solution to the problem."
—Stan Novinsky, Senior Oracle DBA/VMware Engineer, The Johns Hopkins University Applied Physics Laboratory

"To every difficult problem exists a simple solution; this is what I've learned from Rich's books"
—Ghazi Ben Youssef, MBA, Senior Oracle DBA, Sogique, Canada

"If you could buy only one book on Oracle 11gR2 this is the one to have in your DBA arsenal. If it's not on your shelf, consider yourself unarmed. Rich does an excellent job of piecing the puzzle of performance tuning in an easy to follow outline."
—Jerry D. Robinson Jr., Sr. DBA, Northrop Grumman

"I admire Rich for his knowledge on Oracle Technology. This book from him is another masterpiece useful for anyone who would like to excel in Oracle Performance Tuning. The book encompasses Rich's rich Oracle expertise and experience and is a must read for all Oraclelites."
—Hardik Bhatt, Chief Information Officer, City of Chicago

"If you need the best tuning DBA: call Rich Niemiec! Or get his Oracle tuning book"
—Julian Dontcheff, Senior Oracle Database Administrator, Nokia Corporation, Finland

"There is nothing more rewarding than to see someone from your family succeed in life. Rich being from our Purdue Upward Bound Family has brought much pride to us with not only with his expert Oracle technology knowledge but also with his caring attitude and dedication to help others!"
—Joseph Flores, Director Upward Bound, Purdue University Calumet

"Rich Niemiec is a phenomenal entrepreneur with incredible depth of knowledge regarding Oracle applications."
—Prof. Gerald Hills, Coleman Chair of Entrepreneurship, University of Illinois at Chicago

"We have learned much from Rich."
—Nguyen Hoang, Information Expert, Ministry of Finance, Viet Nam

"Rich Niemiec had the courage to make his dreams come true. Through hard work and determination he overcame obstacles and serves as a role model for all students in TRiO Pre-College Programs. His knowledge and passion go beyond computers; he seeks to inspire others to have the courage to make their dreams come true too!"
—Bobbi Jo Johnson, Upward Bound Advisor, UW-Sheboygan

Oracle Press™

Oracle Database 11g Release 2 Performance Tuning Tips & Techniques

Richard J. Niemiec

New York   Chicago   San Francisco
Lisbon   London   Madrid   Mexico City   Milan
New Delhi   San Juan   Seoul   Singapore   Sydney   Toronto

Oracle Database 11*g* Release 2 Performance Tuning Tips & Techniques

1234567890 DOC DOC 1098765432

ISBN   978-0-07-178026-1
MHID   0-07-178026-2

Sponsoring Editor Paul Carlstroem	**Copy Editor** LeeAnn Pickrell	**Illustration** Cenveo Publisher Services
Editorial Supervisor Jody McKenzie	**Proofreader** Susie Elkind	**Art Director, Cover** Jeff Weeks
Project Editor LeeAnn Pickrell	**Indexer** Rebecca Plunkett	**Cover Designer** Pattie Lee
Acquisitions Coordinator Stephanie Evans	**Production Supervisor** George Anderson	
Technical Editors Janet Stern, Michelle Malcher	**Composition** Cenveo Publisher Services	

"We've all been touched by the hand of God and Greatness is within us."

To Regina, the love of my life...

There it was, the most beautiful rose, and God unveiled it to me one day! Regina, you are the light that glows within my heart on a cold winter night. You are the sweetness on my lips that brings me true happiness. You are that wonderful secret of my success that brings out the best in me. The world, Wall Street, big companies, and get-rich-quick manuals, are filled with broad yellow brick roads that lead to diamond-studded dreams and the Emerald City; Regina never wanted to follow this path. With Regina, life is a long

ride, with its thrills and a touch of danger on Space Mountain as well as pleasant walks along the West Lake. But the journey has always been a journey, not a sprint, not a power lunch, just a beautiful, wonderful ride with Regina at my side. It's never the same, never boring, sometimes tough, often challenging, but she's always been *just right* for me!

Slowing down when your world races at the NASCAR speeds of Oracle can be difficult, but together Regina and I have navigated a road from paltry meals and rented flowers (at our wedding) to pleasant dreams and calm nights. But we also wanted others to know the path to happiness. That path is filled with kindness toward others, simple pleasures, and even difficult times that challenge. God leads, you follow, and what's ahead is rarely what you had in mind. Sometimes pushing others to change and succeed is the toughest job of all, but where perfection is elusive, we do our best. Regina always had that vision for a better future through education for those who grew up a little tougher, as we did at times. She recognized that as a key to success in our life. As we did better and things slowed down, she started working to help others visualize that same path. Education is more than power: it's dynamic, it's insightful, and it provides a future. Most of all, it doesn't just help you succeed now; it helps you succeed when the world changes, as it will certainly do throughout your lifetime. So goodbye to the wide gate and the

Emerald City; Regina turned out to be the true Wizard of OZ (her license plate even starts with OZ!). We would rather sit on the front porch and watch the leaves change on our Cracker Barrel rockers than be front row at the Sidney Opera (although the people of Australia are great!).

The simple things in life are often the most wonderful things in life. Regina taught me that over time. She would always take

- Breakfast at Main Street Diner over breakfast at Tiffany's
- A handful of peppermints over chocolate truffles
- Pumpkin spice coffee over Dom Perignon
- A trip to Oberweis for a fantastic vanilla shake over Tiramisu (who wouldn't?)
- A box of Bic pens over a diamond cluster Mont Blanc
- Too many kittens and one big dog (Spartacus) over no pets allowed on 5th Avenue
- A morning drive with the kids, KLOVE, and coffee over a chauffeured limousine
- Mrs. Anderson's Village Courtyard for apple pie over a business power lunch
- Homemade pumpkin pie with whipped cream over Crème brûlée
- A fall day with the leaves changing and the crisp air over a crowded hot sunny beach
- A St. Mary's crowning on a sunny day over the 5K Chili Chase (but the chili is great!)
- A carriage ride on Michigan Avenue over the cab ride
- Walking across the top arches of the Sidney Bridge (bridge climb) over driving over it on the roadway
- Snorkeling the great barrier reef and surfing Hawaii over sitting by the pool
- A walk on the beach to a Luau (in Kauai) over dinner at Chez Paul's
- A pleasant walk on West Lake over the sightseeing cab ride to the hotel
- A brisk walk in Millennium Park to see the fireworks over a chair at North Beach
- A trip to the Bears-Packers game in –20 degree weather (okay that was my idea)
- A ride on the Zipper, or at least the Tilt-a-Whirl (or not … my idea again)
- A trip to Wildfire's after a Bears-Packers sub-zero game over watching it on TV
- The trip to the Sweet Shop at Purdue was, of course, priceless!

I thought Oracle was complex, hard, and enigmatic. But the real excitement began when our first child started talking and walking and then three more children quickly followed. Regina's love as a wife is only exceeded by her commitment to give our children a better life deeply rooted in good ethics, the promise of education, and a kind nature toward others. We've all been touched by the hand of God, and greatness lies within the reach of each of us. Regina has always focused on what's deep inside people waiting to be pulled out. Most of all, Regina, you do it with love and understanding as that guiding light only a mother can provide. Jacob, Lucas, Hollyann, and Melissa have always made us proud.

Regina's not perfect, but to me, she is indeed the Uncommon Leader. With every trait she demonstrates

- **Integrity**   She has a deep love and commitment to others and to her faith.

- **Physical courage**   She's a wonderful mother in the toughest of times (all parents deserve so much help and praise for what they go through these days).

- **Initiative**   She created something from nothing (www.cornerstonewomen.org) in the entrepreneurial spirit, but also out of love for others in need.

- **Mental courage**   Her courage to withstand the political objections to build Cornerstone was amazing.

- **Unselfishness**   She shares all she has—and both the first and last of what she has at times.

- **Tact**   She always tries to meet objections with kindness and desire to move forward.

- **Tenacity**   She finds a way above, below, around, through, and beyond when there seems to be no way. (Her parents passed on to her an incredibly rare tenacity.)

- **Respect**   She shows respect for everyone she works with and for those around her.

- **Humility**   She lived in the shadows for many years; few know how much she has helped me in building TUSC to be an Inc. 500 company.

- **Fortitude**   She built something on a belief and a vision, despite the obstacles that confronted her, and she's had the fortitude to move through the worst of situations with courage and character. She has also helped me to do the same.

The Purdue Sweet Shop led me to the sweetest sweet—Regina. She gives hope to those around her and lights a path to a better future. She's a keeper!

About the Author

Rich Niemiec is a world-renowned IT Expert. Rich is an Oracle Ace Director, Oracle Certified Master, and was a cofounder and the CEO of TUSC: a Chicago-based, Inc. 500, systems integrator with ten U.S. offices focused on Oracle-based business solutions. TUSC was started in 1988. Rich currently serves as an Executive Advisor to Rolta International Board of Directors and has served as President of Rolta TUSC and Rolta EICT International. TUSC was the Oracle Partner of the Year in 2002, 2004, 2007, 2008, 2010, and 2011 (Rolta TUSC). Rolta is an international market leader in IT-based geospatial solutions and caters to industries as diverse as infrastructure, telecom, electric, airports, defense, homeland security, urban development, town planning, and environmental protection. Rich is the past president of the International Oracle Users Group (IOUG) and the current president of the Midwest Oracle Users Group (MOUG). Rich has spoken in virtually every major U.S. city and many major international cities over the past three decades and has been named by attendees as the Top Speaker at Collaborate/IOUG (six times), MOUG (ten times), as well as at Oracle OpenWorld. Rich has architected and tuned many Fortune 500 systems over the past 25 years. Some Fortune 500 accounts he has managed and tuned include ACT, M&M Mars, McDonald's Corp., Nokia, Navteq (MapQuest), University of Michigan, AT&T, and PepsiCo. His experience in data processing ranges from teaching to consulting, with an emphasis on executive direction, database administration and architecture, performance tuning, project management, and technical education. Rich is one of six Oracle Certified Masters originally honored worldwide and works cooperatively with Oracle development from time to time especially during the beta process. In 2007, he authored the Oracle bestseller *Oracle10g Performance Tuning Tips & Techniques* (McGraw-Hill), an update of his previous two Oracle best sellers on Oracle8*i* and Oracle9*i* performance tuning. Rich was inducted into the Entrepreneurship Hall of Fame in 1998. He was awarded the National Trio Achiever Award in 2006 and the Purdue Outstanding Electrical & Computer Engineer award in 2007.

About the Technical Reviewers

Janet Stern has spent the last 15 years in various positions with Oracle Corporation, focused on training and most recently creating documentation for Oracle's most advanced features, including Streams, Real Application Clusters (RAC), and Quality of Service Management for Exadata. This gives her unique insight into performance tuning of Oracle databases. When she is not creating documentation for Oracle, she spends time taking care of her three children, her husband, two cats, and her dog, Jeb.

Michelle Malcher is a DBA Team Lead with several years of experience in database development, design, and administration. She has expertise in security, performance tuning, data modeling, and database architecture of very large database environments. As an Oracle ACE Director, she enjoys sharing knowledge about best practices involving database environments. Her experience is focused on designing, implementing, and maintaining stable, reliable, and secure database environments to support business and important business processes. She is on the IOUG Board of Directors and currently serves as Director of Education. She has authored articles for the IOUG *Select Journal* and a book, *Oracle Database Administration for the Microsoft SQL Server DBA* (McGraw-Hill/Oracle Press, 2010) and is a co-author of *Oracle Database 11g Beginner's Guide* (McGraw-Hill/Oracle Press, 2008).

Contents

Acknowledgments

"Perhaps, in order to really become free, we have to move from struggling to hear God's Voice to letting God's Voice speak through us."
—Rabbi Jonathan Kraus

The goal of this book is primarily focused on helping beginner and intermediate Oracle professionals understand and better tune Oracle systems. Many expert topics are also covered, but the objective is primarily to assist professionals who are frustrated and looking for simple tips to help improve database performance. This book has one simple aim: to provide an arsenal of tips you can use in various situations to make your system faster.

I would like to thank Janet Stern of Oracle for her absolutely wonderful technical editing. Janet is an absolutely fantastic tech guru, and I could not have asked for a better person to be my tech editor! She has added valuable content to every chapter and meticulously combs through every detail. She's one of the most dedicated and talented Oracle professionals who I know. I also want to thank Michelle Malcher for helping tech edit some of the later chapters in the book; we couldn't have completed things as fast or as well without Michelle's great work. I would like to thank Paul Carlstroem, Senior Acquisitions Editor at McGraw-Hill, for both his wonderful demeanor and great direction in taking me through every step of this project (he is *always* there when you need him!); Stephanie Evans, Acquisitions Coordinator at McGraw-Hill, for keeping us on the right track through the very end. Ian Au, Senior Marketing Manager at McGraw-Hill, is wonderful to work with and a great promoter, and Melinda Lytle does a great job coordinating all art production. Thank you Lisa McClain for getting me started on this and setting the course early. Thanks to LeeAnn Pickrell, my copyeditor, who really took this book to the next level. LeeAnn made sure the book was easier to understand by using standards that make the book more intuitive, improving the flow of the book, and making the sentences clearer and a little more Shakespeare-worthy. She really made this a better book for you, the reader! Lastly, thanks to Scott Rogers and Jeremy Judson for getting me through the first book after I'd let you guys know it would be done in a few weeks (and it took two years)!

Thanks to the following people who helped with the following chapters:

- Mike Messina—thanks for your work in updating much of Chapter 1 and also testing queries and updating the b-level section in Chapter 2. You were invaluable, and you are an incredible Oracle talent!

■ Kevin Loney—thanks for your work in previously updating Chapter 2.

■ Sridhar Avantsa for updates and many additions to Chapter 3. Also, both Bill Callahan and Nitin Vengurlekar for previous updates to Chapter 3.

■ Lucas Niemiec for testing scripts in Chapter 4. Craig Shallahamer, Randy Swanson, and Jeff Keller for previous notes and updates.

■ Anil Khilani, Prabhaker Gongloor (GP), David LeRoy, Martin Pena, Valerie Kane, and Mughees Minhas—thanks for your help with Enterprise Manager screen shots and information for Chapter 5.

■ Warren Bakker—thanks for the great update and additions to Chapter 6. Thanks to Mark Riedel and Greg Pucka for previous help on this chapter.

■ Mark Riedel did a great update of Chapter 7. Thanks to Lucas Niemiec for additional hint research.

■ Rama Balaji helped with the update to Chapter 8. Connor McDonald and Rob Christensen helped with previous notes and versions.

■ Mike Messina helped by adding Real Applications Testing and SQL Performance Analyzer to Chapter 9 and Joe Holmes of Canada helped with advanced information in Chapter 9. Francisco Javier Moreno, Guillermo L. Ospina Romero, and Rafael I. Larios Restrepo from the University Nacional in Medellín, Colombia, helped with Chapter 9 testing. Roger Schrag provided some of original information on joins in Chapter 9.

■ Bob Taylor—another great job updating Chapter 10. Joe Trezzo and Dave Ventura helped with previous versions.

■ Richard Stroupe made some great additions to Chapter 11, along with contributions from Madhu Tumma, Brad Nash, Jake Van der Vort, and Kevin Loney.

■ Rama Balaji helped update much of Chapter 12. Kevin Gilpen, Bob Yingst, and Greg Pucka made contributions as well.

■ Graham Thornton—thanks for your updates and excellent additions to Chapter 13; Kevin Gilpen helped in previous versions. Steve Adams of Australia was a technical editor in the past and a great contributor to the X$ scripts.

■ Hollyann Niemiec for quotes in Chapter 14. Robert Freeman and Kevin Loney for previous sections of Chapter 14.

■ Brad Nash for previous updates to Chapter 15 and Lucas Niemiec for testing the queries in 11*g*R2.

■ Doug Freyburger for the excellent update of Chapter 16. Judy Corley, Mike Gallagher, and Jon Vincenzo for previous updates.

■ Lucas Niemiec for testing all of the queries in Appendix A and updating them for 11*g*R2.

- Jacob Niemiec for testing all of the queries in Appendix C and updating them for 11gR2.

- Melissa Niemiec for thoughts, quotes, and suggestions for the introduction.

Thanks to those from Oracle who have made a big difference in my life:

- Thanks Larry Ellison, Bob Miner, Bruce Scott, and Ed Oates for the great database and future thinking, and for creating the most innovative company in history!

- The IOUG for making my Oracle life easier over the years.

- Andy Mendelsohn—thanks for getting answers to some of the really tough questions and driving this incredible Oracle database to the next level.

- Judith Sim—you are one the Oracle leaders who puts Oracle at the top. Thanks for all your help!

- Thomas Kurian—thanks for putting Fusion Middleware on the map and taking Oracle Applications to the next level.

- Mary Ann Davidson—thanks for your leadership and keeping Oracle secure.

- Ted Bereswill—you have made us true partners in the Oracle Partner Program!

- Tom Kyte—you are the ultimate Oracle tech guru!

- Angelo Pruscino, Kirk McGowan, and Erik Peterson—without you three, there would be no RAC; without Angelo, RAC would be a mess. Dan Norris and Phil Stephenson for their help with Exadata.

- Justin Kestelyn—you educate the world with OTN.

- Tirthankar Lahiri—what a job on the buffer cache!

- Bruce Scott—thanks for taking the time to do the *Select* article interview and for sending me the rare Oracle founders picture.

Thanks to the following people who in some way have contributed to this version of the book (in addition to those above):

David Anstey, Eyal Aronoff, Mike Ault, Janet Bacon, Kamila Bajaria, Roger Bamford, Greg Bogode, Mike Broullette, Don Burleson, Bill Burke, Rachel Carmichael, Tony Catalano, Rob Christensen, Craig Davis, Sergio Del Rio, Dr. Paul Dorsey, Kim Floss, Mark Greenhalgh, K. Gopalakrishnan, Tim Gorman, Kent Graziano, Damon Grube, Roman Gutfraynd, Vinod Haval, Gerry Hills, Steven Hirsch, Nguyen Hoang, Pat Holmes, Scott Heaton, Jeff Jacobs, Tony Jambu, Tony Jedlinski, Ron Jedlinski, Zhigang Ji, Jeremy Judson, Dave Kaufman, Mike Killough, Peter Koletzke, Tom Kyte,

Mike La Magna, Vinoy Lanjwal, Steve Lemme, Jonathan Lewis, Bill Lewkow, Kevin Loney, Steven Lu, Scott Martin, Connor McDonald, Sean McGuire, Ronan Miles, Cary Milsap, Ken Morse, Shankar Mukherjee, Ken Naim, Arup Nanda, Frank Naude, Pradeep Navalkar, Albert Nashon, Aaron Newman, Dan Norris, Stanley Novinsky, Cetin Ozbutun, Tanel Poder, Venkatesh Prakasam, Greg Pucka, Heidi Ratini, Steve Rubinow, Chuck Seaks, Bert Spencer, Craig Shallahamer, Burk Sherva, Judy Sim, Richard Stroupe, Felipe Teixeira de Souza, Randy Swanson, Megh Thakkar, George Trujillo, Madhu Tumma, Gaja Krishna Vaidyanatha, Jake Van der Vort, Murali Vallath, Shyam Varan Nath, Dave Ventura, Sandra Vucinic, Lyssa Wald, Milton Wan, Graham Wood, Tom Wood, Zhong Yang, Pedro Ybarro, Ghazi Ben Youssef, and Dr. Oleg Zhooravlev.

I want to thank the two best partners a person can ever have in Brad Brown and Joe Trezzo.

We make a great band of brothers! I would like to thank all of the people at TUSC, Rolta, Piocon, and WhittmanHart (all now one global Rolta company), who work hard every day and are dedicated to excellence. Thanks Barb, Karen, Sandy, Kim, and Amy for keeping us sane. Thanks Tony, Dave, Barry, Burk, Bill, Bob, Janet, Terry, Heidi, John, Matt, and Mike for the leadership and memories. Thanks KK, Ben, Mark, Sohrab, Vinay, Blane, Jack, Dave, and Rif for taking us into that global world. Thanks Sanjay, Narendra, Nimesh, and all of the others for keeping us sane on the other side of the world. I also want to thank Eric Noelke and Mike Simmons personally for giving my first job at Oracle and Matt Vranicar for helping me understand indexes when I got there. Although I can't thank the almost 4000 people at Rolta individually, thanks for all you do every day to improve the world!

I do want to thank those from Rolta TUSC who assisted during the writing of the book (since it's a smaller list of superstars):

Barbara Allen, Stacy Allen, Ravishankar Ananthanarayana, Lalit Anapu, Andy Anastasi, Nilton Aquino, Jyotin Arora, Manu Arora, Hiranya Ashar, Sridhar Avantsa, Steve Babin, Rohit Badiyani, Warren Bakker, Rama Balaji, Mathi Balasubramaniam, Bruce M. Bancroft, Bill Banze, Otis Barr, Roger Baroutjian, Chris Baumgartner, Roger Behm, Vinny Belanger, Matthew Berrisford, Bobby Bhandari, Sohrab Bhot, Donald Bieger, Paul Bobak, John Bogdue, Greg Bogode, Keith Braley, Jessica Brandenburg, Christopher Brinkman, Bob Britton, Bradley David Brown, Deborah Bryda, Mike Butler, Eric Kamplin, Alain Campos, Bolton Carroll, Tony Catalano, Matthew Chance, Bharat

Chitnavis, Bob Christensen, John Clark, James Clarke, Mike Cochran, Liz Coffee, Randy Cook, Judy Corley, Joselle Cortez, Dick Coulter, Matt Cox, Janeen Coyle, Darrel Craig, Keith D'agostino, Janet Dahmen, Terry Daley, Prithis Das, Don Davis, David deBoisblanc, Brian Decker, Hank Decker, Mario Desiderio, Dinesh De Silva, Ernie DiLegge, Robert Donahue, Dan Dosmann, Melloney Douce, Barb Dully, Brian Dunnells, Christopher Dupin, Ben Eazzetta, Melissa Eazzetta, Marcus Eidson, Phillip Ellington, Reida Elwannas, Phil Estep, Mark Fate, Andy Fiesman, Robert Filtzkowski, Robin Fingerson, Newton "Fletch" Fletcher, Yvonne Formel, Dave Fornalsky, Joshua Forrest, Stacie Forrester, Sergio Frank "Power Surge", George Frederick, Doug Freyburger, Jan Gabelev, Steve Galassini, John Gallacher, Chris Gamble, David Gannon, Laxmidhar Gaopande, Michael Garcia, Nimesh Gawad, Biju George, Santhosh George, Brad Gibson, Brad Gillespie, Kevin Gilpin, Agenor Gnanzou, Martin Goodfriend, MK Govind, Chelsea Graylin, Dexter Greener, John Griebel, Ignacio Guerrero, Narendra Gupta, Brian Hacker, John Halsema, Scott Heaton, Andrew Henderson, Katy Heng, Kristina Henning, Allwyn Henry, Mark Heyvaert, Karen Hollomon, Amy Horvat, Vijayashankar Hosahalli, Sharon Howard, Thomas Huelsman, Mohammad Jamal, Cyndi Jensen, Rif Jiwani, Shafik Jiwani, Benjamin Johnson, Kimberly Johnson, Cristin Jones, Monica Jones, Kimberly Joyce, William Kadlec, Sudhir Kalavagunta, Joanna Kalgreen, Sandeep Ohri, Anil Kalra, Palaniappan "Palani" Kasiviswanathan, Dave Kaspar, Dorraine Keim, Karen King, Nicholas King, Bruce Kissinger, Robert Koester, Kirby Kraft, Kiran Kulkarni, Sampath Kumar, Matthew Kundrat, Thomas Kuruvilla, Deborah Kuznik, Felix LaCap, Lynn Lafleur, Wendy Lamar, Bob Landgren, Bob Landgridge, Randy Lawson, Bill Lewkow, Jack Leahey, Brad Linnell, Lawrence Linnemeyer, Paul LoBue, Scott Lockhart, George Loewenthal, Steven Lu, Andy Mackintosh, Dana MacPhail, Chris Madding, Tim Mahoney, Gregory Mancuso, Suganya Manoharan, Claude Mariottini, Donald Martin, Daniel Martino, Chip Mason, Grant Materna, Joe Mathew, Chris McElroy, Brendan McGettigan, Patrick McGovern, Kamlesh Mehta, Carlos Mendez, Rey Mendez, Subodh Mendhurwar, Prakash Menon, Andy Merrett, Mike Messina, Matt Metrik, Brian Michael, Eric Mies, Melissa Miller, Michael Milner, Quadeerullah Mohammed, John Molinaro, Patrick Monahan, Albert Moreno, Sanjay Narkar, Ravishankar Narayanan, James Nash, Eric Noelke, Mark O'Dwyer, Gary Ohmstede, Sandeep Ohri, Steven Ostendorf, James Owen, David Pape, Breanne Parker, John Parker, Mohan Parna, Charlotte Partridge, Amit Haresh Patel, Ashvinkumar Patel, Jitendra Patibandla, Reggie Peagler, Vishnuvardhan Reddy Peddamaru, Mark Pelzel, Gregg Petri, Greg Pike, Caleb Pingelton, Eric Potts, James Powell, Lynne Preston, Preetha Pulusani, Mohammed Quadeer, Karen Quandt, Kathleen Quinn, Sriram Rajagopalan, Aakash Rami, Samir Rane, Heidi Ratini "Trinity", Douglas Resler, Aleksandr Reyderman, Mark Riedel, Holly Robinson, Jeremy Rogers, Randy Rogers, Rob Rolek, Sean Ryan, Sherry Safranski, Mirinda Sandoval, Alwyn Santos "The Machine", Satinath Sarkar, John Sasser, Leon Saverus, Vinay Sawarkar, Blane Schertz, Louis Schoeller, Steven Schuld, Chad Scott, John A. Senatore, Ahsan Shah, Girishan Shanmugam, David R. Shearin, Sharon Sherley, Burk Sherva, Makarand Shete, Jeremy Simmons, A.P. Singh, Aditya Singh, KK Singh, Karan Singh, Ronak Sitafalwalla, Dave Sligting, David Smith, Molly Smith, Karen Smudde, Patrick Spaulding, Laura Sprowls, Stephanie Spurrier, Ed Stayman, Jack Stein, Michael Stevenson, Cheryl Stewart, Jerzy Suchodolski, Sreedhar Swayampakula, Srikalyan Swayampakula, Michael Tarka, William Tate, Atul Tayal, Bob Taylor, Sameer Satish Thawani, Chris Thoman, Leo Thomas, Bryan Thompson, Graham Thornton, Thomas Tisdale, Bill Toebbe, Renee Townsend, Joseph Conrad Trezzo, Dave Trch "Torch", Joel Tuisl, Tom Usher, Amit Vaidya, Hiten Valia, Lynne VanArsdale, Chandrasekar Vellala, Dave Ventura, Tejinder Vohre, Matthew G. Vranicar, Ashrith R. Vuyyuru, Sandra Wade, Randy Warner, John Watson, John Weicher, Joyce Wheeler, John Whitaker, Barry Wiebe, James Williams, Nicole Wilson, Mark Wittkopp, Mark Woelke, Gary Wojda, Lisa Wright, Bob Yingst, James Zadrovicz, and Julian Zambra.

I would also like to thank all of the people who make a difference in my life (in addition to those above and from the previous books):

Sandra Hill, Floyd & Georgia Adams, Kristen Brown, Lori Trezzo, Sohaib Abbasi, Michael Abbey, Ian Abramson, Jeff & Donna Ackerman, Steve & Becky Adams, Keith Altman, Judson Althoff, Joe Anzell, Joe Arozarena, Ian Au, Mike Ault, Paster James C. Austin, Jim Basler, Nicholas Bassey, John Beresniewicz, Hardik Bhatt, Ronny Billen, Jon & Linda Bischoff, Keith Block, George Bloom, Melanie Bock, Mike Boddy, David Bohan, A.W. Bolden, Rep. Henry Bonilla, Rene Bonvanie, Stephen Boyle, Gary Bradshaw, Ted Brady, Barry Brasseaux, Aldo Bravo, J. Birney & Julia Brown, John Brown, Karen Brownfield, Sam & Rhonda Bruner, Bill Burke, Ashley Burkholder, Lillian Buziak, Dan Cameron, Bogdan Capatina, Rachel Carmichael, Monty Carolan, Christina Cavanna, Sheila Cepero, Edward Chu, Sonia Cillo, Dr. Ken Coleman, Margarita Contreni, Mike Corey, Peter Corrigan, Jason Couchman, Stephen Covey, Shanda Cowan, Richard Daley, Sharon Daley, Nancy Daniel, Barb Darrow, Jeb Dasteel, Mary Ann Davidson, Tom Davidson, Elaine DeMeo, Tony DeMeo, Sohan DeMel, Jose DiAvilla, Julian Dontcheff, Mary Lou Dopart, Joe Dougherty Jr., Bob & Lori Dressel, Carl Dudley, Carlos Duchicela, Ben & Melissa Eazzetta, Matt Eberz, Jeff Ellington, Lisa Elliot, Brian Embree, Buff Emslie, Dan Erickson, Chick Evans Jr., Lisa Evans, Dr. Tony Evans, Mark Farnham, Tony Feisel, Dick Fergusun, Julie Ferry, Stephen Feurenstein, Ted & Joan File, Caryl Lee Fisher, Lee Fisher, Charlie Fishman, Tim & Jan Fleming, Flip, Joe Flores, Andy Flower, Mark Fontechio, Heidi Fornalsky, Vicky Foster, Rita Franov, Kate Freeman, Doug Freud, Mike Frey, Dr. Susan Friedberg, Sylvain Gagne, Karen Gainey, Mike Gangler, Fred Garfield, Charles Gary, Sharon Gaudet, Julie Geer-Brown, Jenny Gelhausen, Len Geshan, George Gilbert, Tom Goedken, Mark Gokman, Alex Golod, Laverne Gonzales, John Goodhue, Ellen Gordon, Kevin Gordon, Greg Gorman, Dennis Gottlieb, Joe Graham Jr., Cammi Granato, Tony Granato, John Gray, Kent Graziano, Alan Greenspan, Carrie Greeter, Sarah Grigg, Ken Guion, Mark Gurry, Eric Guyer, Pasi Haapalainen, Steve Hagan, Rebecca Hahn, John Hall, Don Hammer, Rick & Tammy Hanna, Robert Hanrahan, Bob Hausler, Jim Hawkins, Marko Hellevaara, Jeff Henley, John Hernandez, Bob Hill, James Hobbs, Stacy Hodge, Kristin Hollins, Pat Holmes, Napoleon Hopper Jr., Howard Horowitz, Jerry Horvath, Dan Hotka, Rich Houle, Maureen Hoyler, Ellie Hurley, Laura Hurley, Jerry Ireland, Shiv Iyer, Suman Iyer, Roger Jackson, Jeff Jacobs, Ken Jacobs "Dr. DBA", Tony Jambu, Don & Dianne Jaskulske, Amit Jasuja, Corey Jenkins, Bobbi Jo Johnson, Steve Johnson, Jeff Jonas, Shawn Jones, Michael Jordan, Michael Josephson, Jeremy Judson, Mark Jungerman, Valerie Kane, Emily Kao, Ari Kaplan, Stephen Karniotis, Tom Karpus, Dr. Ken & Cathy Kavanaugh, Maralynn Kearney, John Kelly, Robert Kennedy, Kate Kerner, Anil Khilani, Ann Kilhoffer-Reichert, John & Peggy King, Martin Luther King Jr., Jan Klokkers, George Koch, Jodi Koehn-Pike, Fran Koerner, Sergey Koltakov, Larry Kozlicki, Mark & Sue Kramer, Paul C. Krause, Mark Krefta, Ron Krefta, Dave Kreines, Thomas Kurian, John Krasnick, Mark Kwasni, Paul Lam, Donald Lamar, Marva Land, Ray Lane, Karen Langley, Jari Lappalainen, Carl Larson, John Lartz, Brian Laskey, Deb LeBlanc, Margaret Lee, Sami Lehto, Herve Lejeune, Steve Lemme, Coleman Leviter, Troy Ligon, Cheng Lim, Victoria Lira, Juan Loaiza, Quan Logan, Jeff London, Xavier Lopez, Bob Love, Senator Dick Lugar, Dave

Luhrsen, James Lui, Lucas Lukasiak, Barb Lundhild, Liz Macin, Tony Mack, Ann Mai, Tom Manzo, Paul Massiglia, Lisa McClain, Donna McConnell, Stephen McConnell, Kirk McGowan, Carol McGury, Dennis McKinnon, Amanda McLafferty, Mary Elizabeth McNeely, Gail McVey, Ehab & Andrea Mearim, Margaret Mei, Sara Mejia, Kuassi Mensah, Scott Messier, Kelly Middleton, Regina Midkiff, Debbie Migliore, Mary Miller, Jeff Mills, Mary Miner, Justine Miner, Jal Mistri, Dr. Arnold Mitchem, John Molinaro, Congresswoman Gwen Moore, Matt Morris, Ken Morse, Solveig Morkeberg, Bill Moses, Jane Mott, Steve Muench, Brad Musgrave, Francisco Munez, Minelva

Munoz, Scott Myers, Ken Naim, Shyam Nath, Cassie Naval, Bill Nee, Paul Needham, Marie-Anne Neimat, Scott Nelson, Phil Newlan, Olli Niemi, Cindy Niemiec, Dr. Dave & Dawn Niemiec, Mike Niemiec, Regina Sue Elizabeth Niemiec, Robert & Cookie Niemiec, Dr. Ted & Paula Niemiec, Merrilee Nohr, Robin North, Rick Norris, Stan Novinsky, Perttu Nuija, Cheryl Nuno, Julie O'Brian, Shaun O'Brien, Jon O'Connell, Barb O'Malley, Anne O'Neill, Mike Olin, Francisco Martinez Oviedo, Rita Palanov, Jeri Palmer, Bharat Patel, Jignesh Patel, Arlene Patton, Ray Payne, Steve Pemberton, Monica Penshorn, Dr. Mary Peterson, Michael Pettigrew, Elke Phelps, Chuck Phillips, Mary Platt, Lisa Price, Megan Price, John Quinones, John Ramos, Gautham Ravi, Sheila Reiter, Frank Ress, Denise Rhodes, Elizabeth Richards, Aisha Richardson, Dennis Richter, Arnold Ridgel, Wendy Rinaldi, Anne Ristau, Tom Roach, George Roberts, Jerry D. Robinson Jr., Mike Rocha, Ulka Rodgers, Charlie Rose, Chuck Rozwat, Leslie Rubin, Steve Rubin, Mike Runda, Joe Russell, Mike Russell, Katy Ryan, Theresa Rzepnicki, Stan Salett, David Saslav, Terry Savage, Rami Savila, Nanak Sawlani, Ed Schalk, Ed Scheidt, Douglas Scherer, Scott Schmidt, Jeff Schumaker, David Scott, Kevin Scruggs, Mike Serpe, Guner Seyhan, Allen Shaheen, Lewei Shang, Smiti Sharma, Dr. Austin Shelley, Muhammad Shuja, Julie Silverstein, Judy Sim, Mike Simpson, Angela Sims, Sinbad, David Sironi, Dinu Skariah, Linda Smith, Mark Smith, Mary Ellen Smith, Peter Smith, Congressman Mike & Keta Sodrel, Peter Solomon, Marc Songini, Julie Sowers, Anthony Speed, Jeff Spicer, Rick Stark, Cassandra Staudacher, Bill Stauffer, Leslie Steere, Phil Stephenson, Thomas Stickler, Bob Stoneman, Bob Strube Sr., Bob Strube Jr., Olaf Stullich, Burt & Dianna Summerfield, Cyndie Sutherland, Inna Suvorov, Matt Swann, Mary Swanson, Michael Swinarski, Matt Szulik, Vijay Tella, David Teplow, Marlene Theriault, Margaret Tomkins, Susan Trebach, Eugene (EGBAR) & Adrienne (Sky's the Limit) Trezzo, Sean Tucker, David Tuson, Vicky Tuttle, Razi Ud-Din, Paul Ungaretti, Pete Unterlander, Lupe Valtierre, Petri Varttinen, Angelica Vialpando, Jussi Vira, Jarmo Viteli, Matt Vranicar, Oleg Wasynczuk, Lori Wachtman, Bill Weaver, Jim Weber, Mike Weber, Huang Wei, Dale Weideling, Erich Wessner, Steve Wilkenson, Dennie Williams, Donna Williams, Sherry Williams, John Wilmott, Marcus Wilson, Jeremiah Wilton, Greg Witek, Wayne Wittenberger, Ron Wohl, Marty Wolf, Randy Womack, Marcia Wood, Chris Wooldridge, Don Woznicki, David Wright, Lv Xueyong, Stan Yellott, Janet Yingling Young, Ron Yount, Ji Zhigang, Tony Ziemba, Mary Ann Zirelli, Edward Zhu, Chris Zorich and Andreas Zwimpfer.

Lastly, thanks to (*your name goes here*) for buying this book and being dedicated to improving your own skills (or if I forgot your name above). Father Tony once told me everything you need to know in life: ***"Nothing in life is so big that God can't handle it and nothing is so small that God doesn't notice it."*** Thanks to all of those above who have made and continue to make both big and small differences in my life and in this book!

In Memory:

Finally, I would like to remember a few of our friends in the Oracle world who we've lost over the past couple of years. Chris "Bubba" Madding was a wonderful manager and salesperson, but an even better humanitarian. He worked tirelessly creating and running the Just a Little Faith Foundation to help young children with special needs. He will always be a missing part of our team! We also lost four giants of the tech world. Steve Jobs was always the most innovative visionary, a man who helped create some of the most amazing devices on earth. Every time you thought you knew what was coming next from Apple, they would again exceed your expectations. Ken Olsen launched DEC in 1957. How important was DEC? Oracle was first written for the DEC PDP-11; Microsoft wrote its first version of BASIC on the DEC PDP-10. At its peak, DEC was the second largest technology company behind IBM. Dennis Richie brought us both C and UNIX (part of the Bell Labs duo with Ken Thomson). Jim Gray who wrote *Transaction Processing: Concepts & Techniques* (with Andreus Reuter) was a genius in explaining how to build a database. We'll also miss Bobby Patton.

God takes us home one day when our work is done; we'll be with them soon enough to "*run with angels on streets made of gold.*" I look forward to that day, but until that day, let's continue to make a difference and ensure that God speaks through us by our wonderful actions toward one another! By always looking to improve our integrity, knowledge, physical courage, loyalty, self-control, enthusiasm, unselfishness, tact, moral courage, respect, humility, and initiative, we will ensure that we have the fortitude to face any tough challenge ahead. And, of course, never forget, faith, hope, and love… "and the greatest of these is Love." To make a difference in the world with character and with a heart that always brings out the best in others—this is my goal in life!

Introduction

"Only a life lived for others is worth living."
—**Albert Einstein**

There is a fifth dimension that is as vast as Exadata disk space and as untimely as an infinite loop for those who fail to embrace this future. This future dimension was once the dimension of imagination only, where we could dream of a single database filled with millions of terabytes of data and media. A wonderland where developers could write any query without penalty of being timed out or being the victim of an anonymous kill –9; it's a place where speed and disk space no longer matter (as much). This future has now become a reality, and I call it the "Exabyte Zone!"

A brave new world is coming quickly, whether we like it or not, and whether we are ready for it or not. We saw the first faint lights of this world with 8 bits and access to 256 bytes of memory, and then more of a glow with 16 bits and Windows with 64K of memory and 1M of extended memory. We then saw highways with streams of lights with the advent of the Internet age, as we boldly headed into the gigabyte SGA world that 32 bits brought us. Now technology has grown to 64 bits and moves from the burdens of 4G max, which the 32-bit Internet world gave us. With 64 bits, the theoretical limit of addressable memory (2 to the power of 64) has become 16E (Exabytes) or 18,446,744,073,709,551,616 bytes (2^{64} bytes) of directly addressable memory. Today, 16 Exabytes—18 with 18 zeros—is staring at us, waiting for us to leverage its incredible power in every aspect of our lives. Instead of terabyte databases, we now have Exabyte databases (an Exabyte is one million terabytes); an 11g database is capable of being a full 8 Exabytes in size. Instead of gigabyte SGAs, enter petabyte SGAs (a petabyte is 1,000 terabytes). This jump is not just a step up on the stairs; no longer are we simply doubling power every 18 months (Moore's law). We're not jumping from the earth to the moon, we're jumping from the earth to the heavens to the distant stars—to terabytes times a million.

	Address Direct	**Indirect/Extended**
4 bit	16	640
8 bit	256	65,536
16 bit	65,536	1,048,576
32 bit	4,294,967,296	
64 bit	18,446,744,073,709,551,616	

Oracle led us into the Exabyte world with Oracle10g and a database capable of growing to 8E (8 Exabytes or 8 million terabytes), but there were no takers at that time. Nobody could find the financial resources to buy the hardware that would hold even 1E. There were those that, with video, found their way into the early petabytes, some Wall Street firms spent their terabytes on short-term gains, but buying Exabytes of hardware was too costly; it was flying too close to the *sun* to survive. The real fact is that hardware companies just haven't kept pace with Oracle over the past two decades.

Enter Oracle's acquisition of Sun Microsystems, which has Oracle changing the game forever! You can now fly closer to the sun without worry of getting burned. Grid computing molds the DBA into Iron Man. (Larry was in *Iron Man 2* in case you missed it, and Robert Downey, Jr., even accesses the Oracle Grid from his workstation to locate the bad guys.) Once again, the Hollywood fantasy is not as far away from reality as we think. Even the final battle is in the Oracle dome, with Iron Man triumphant over the bad guys (we've seen this movie in the computer world before, where Oracle excels again and again). Exadata and other Oracle hardware (see Chapter 1 for a peek and Chapter 11 for the details) are now engineered with the Oracle database to provide unbelievable capacity and performance. Your future has no limit, neither does the world's! The sky is no longer the limit; you are way past that with Oracle11g.

How did Oracle do it, and can they ever be caught up to as a company? Let's say you start a company in 1977 using the relational database and Codd's best nonpatentable idea (software patents were not allowed back then) that he ever came up with at IBM in 1977 and beat IBM to market with the first commercial database ever. You start hiring the best talent on earth, from the best universities, and you work them as hard as they've ever worked in their life. You give them twice the annual income of any other company (three times if you're a salesperson), but only if they put in the time and deliver stellar results. You first client is noncommercial; it's the CIA, so security is a hallmark of everything you ever do. You wire security into every avenue the product takes and into the mindset of every developer who works on the product. Every neuron in the Oracle brain-trust fires off with security as a redundant connection. Your first commercial clients are Bank of America and Wright Patterson Air Force Base, so you immediately know how to build things for big companies. You go public eight days after Sun and get out of the gate one day before Microsoft (they've always followed in your wake) to challenge the mighty IBM, whose middle name is Business. At that time, IBM owns the Fortune 1000; it owns IT; it owns the corner office with every C-level executive (the relationship firmly resting with a senior salesperson at IBM). But the winds shift, and new companies start to rise up to the challenge with new IT power on their side. The four horsemen of the Internet arise: Oracle, Cisco, EMC, and Sun. The four are now three and perhaps they will soon be one once again. Oracle acquired Sun and a new paradigm shift has begun. Moore's law gave us hardware capacity that doubled every 18 months, but Larry's law is "You're not going fast enough." So Oracle buys Sun and comes out with faster hardware in two years than Sun came out with in its entire lifetime. The new Sun multithreaded T4 chip is 5× faster than the T3 was (as is the new Sun employee), but that's only the beginning of increasing hardware speed (the Oracle SuperCluster Machine has 4 servers, each with 4 T4s; each T4 has 8 cores; each core has 8 threads, with 1200 total threads). The new SuperCluster Machine, along with Oracle's Exadata line, clearly looks like it will move us thousands of times faster at a minimum—so much for doubling capacity every 18 months. With the Exadata expansion rack and compression, you can now get to 8E by stringing a few hundred of these together (with compression, of course). But is Oracle just starting with Sun? With a new T4 Sparc chip, Exadata, Exalogic, Exalytics, StorageTek, PeopleSoft, Hyperion, TimesTen, MySQL, Java, JD Edwards, Tangosol, BEA, and all the others, perhaps we're only at the beginning.

Oracle RDBMS History Over the Years

1970   Dr. Edgar Codd publishes his theory of relational data modeling.

1977   Software Development Laboratories (SDL) is formed by Larry Ellison, Bob Miner, Ed Oates, and Bruce Scott with $2,000 of startup cash. Larry and Bob come from Ampex where they were working on a CIA project code-named "Oracle." Bob and Bruce begin work on the database.

1978   The CIA is SDL's first customer, yet the product is not released commercially. SDL changes its name to Relational Software Inc. (RSI)

1979   RSI ships the first commercial version, Version 2 of the database, written in Assembler Language (no V1 is shipped based on fears that people won't buy a first version of software). The first commercial version of the software is sold to Wright-Patterson Air Force Base. It is the first commercial RDBMS on the market.

1981   The first tool, Interactive Application Facility (IAF), which is a predecessor to Oracle's future SQL*Forms tool, is created.

1982   RSI changes its name to Oracle Systems Corporation (OSC) and then simplifies the name to Oracle Corporation.

1983   Version 3, written in C (which makes it portable) is shipped. Bob Miner writes half, while also supporting the Assembler-based V2, and Bruce Scott writes the other half. It is the first 32-bit RDBMS.

1984   Version 4 is released, along with some first tools (IAG-genform, IAG-runform, RPT). Version 4 is the first database with read consistency. Oracle is ported to the PC.

1985   Version 5 is released, first Parallel Server database on VMS/VAX.

1986   Oracle goes public March 12 (the day before Microsoft and eight days after Sun). The stock opens at $15 and closes at $20.75. Oracle Client/Server is introduced, which is the first client/server database. Oracle 5.1 is released.

1987   Oracle is the largest DBMS company. Oracle Applications group started. First symmetrical multiprocessing (SMP) database introduced.

1987   Rich Niemiec along with Brad Brown and Joe Trezzo while working at Oracle implement the first production client/server application running Oracle on a souped-up 286 running 16 concurrent client/server users for NEC Corporation.

1988   Oracle V6 released. First row-level locking. First hot database backup. Oracle moves from Belmont to Redwood Shores. PL/SQL introduced.

1992   Oracle V7 is released.

1993   Oracle GUI client/server development tools introduced. Oracle Applications moved from character mode to client/server.

1994   Bob Miner, the genius behind the Oracle database technology, dies of cancer.

1995   First 64-bit database developed.

1996   Oracle 7.3 released.

1997   Oracle 8 is introduced. Oracle Application Server is introduced. Applications for the Web are introduced. Oracle is the first Web database. Oracle BI tools like Discoverer are introduced for data warehousing. Tools have native Java support.

1998   First major RDBMS (Oracle 8) ported to Linux. Applications 11 shipped. Oracle is the first database with XML support.

1999   Oracle 8*i* released. Integrates Java/XML into development tools. Oracle is the first database with native Java support.

2000   Oracle9*i* Application Server released. It becomes the first database with middle-tier cache. Launches E-Business Suite, wireless database with OracleMobile, Oracle9*i* Application Server Wireless, and Internet File System (iFS).

2001   Oracle9*i* (9.1) released. Oracle is the first database with Real Application Clusters (RAC).

2002   Oracle9*i* Release 2 (9.2) released.

2003   Oracle at France Telecom is #1 on Winter Group's Top Ten in DB size at 29T.

2003   Oracle10*g* comes out, with grid focus, encrypted backups, auto-tuning, and ASM.

2005   Oracle RAC at Amazon hits the Winter Group's Top Ten in DB size at 25T.

2005   Oracle acquires PeopleSoft (includes JD Edwards), Oblix (Identity Management), Retek (Retail) for $630M, TimesTen (in memory DB), and Innobase (InnoDB Open Source).

2006   Oracle buys Siebel for $5.8B, Sleepycat Software (Open Source), and Stellant (Content Management). Oracle with an open source push offers "unbreakable" support for Red Hat Linux.

2006   Oracle10*g* Release2 comes out in fall (the previous edition of this book was based on that version).

2007   Oracle buys Hyperion for $3.3B. Oracle 11*g* comes out (2009 was the first release of 11gR2)

2008   Oracle Exadata announced; Oracle buys BEA.

2009   Oracle releases 11gR2. Oracle buys Sun (which includes Java, MySQL, Solaris, hardware, OpenOffice, StorageTek).

2010   Oracle announces MySQL Cluster 7.1, Exadata 2-8, Exalogic, and 11.2.0.2 released.

2011   Oracle 11gR2 (11.2.0.4) terminal release (all Exadata line is 11gR2) and Oracle 11g Express Edition Released (September 24, 2011). Oracle announces Exalytics, SuperCluster, Oracle Data Appliance, Exadata Expansion Rack, and Oracle Cloud 12c.

2014   12cR2 database prediction.

Clearly Oracle is a company that has matured in breadth, ability, and character over the years, and Oracle's leaders don't really need any more money (they've made enough along the way). Oracle's leaders have the ability to innovate, and they've always hired for that next leader and visionary like Larry Ellison, or the next quietly driven Bob Miner, that next superstar developer Bruce Scott. Somehow they find that creative/innovative special something in every employee they hire. Oracle hires unique, incredibly intelligent, intensely driven, and innovative people! Starting with the attitude of Larry, and his ability to get more out of people than they are aware they have within them, and his ability to reward them when they deliver. Oracle also has the genius, spirit, and "blue collar–like" hard-working drive of a Bob Miner in all of those in the development world who have followed him. Oracle is well run because they have leaders in Safra Catz and Mark Hurd balancing out operations; a Judith Sim driving marketing at an always "catch us if you can," too-fast speed; and delivery on products due to Andy Mendelsohn and his tremendously intelligent team inventing the next bend in the road. Thomas Kurian and his ever-growing, over-achieving team are always finding new ways to integrate applications and make businesses even more successful. Then there's Mary Ann Davidson's silent warriors in security, and many more who I don't know or don't remember anymore (and don't forget the superglue—Jenny, Mary Ann, and Tania and her team who hold it all together).

Before the Web took off, Oracle banked everything on the Web and rewrote all of their applications to run on the Web and on application servers running on Linux well before Linux was fashionable. The press had a field-day quoting Larry Ellison: "If the Web isn't the next best thing, then we're toast, but if it is the next best thing, then we're golden." The gold came fast with the Internet boom bringing a new California gold rush to Silicon Valley and Oracle selling all the tools needed for mining. But the bust came a decade later for many. With broken companies all around for the taking after the 1929 crash, it was GE, buying up all the bankrupt dreams and cash-strapped companies only to emerge as a giant for the next eight decades and counting. In our current combination of recessions, pseudo-depression, and stagflation, it is Oracle buying up the likes of Sun ($7.4B, hardware, Solaris, SPARC, Java, OpenOffice, StorageTek), Hyperion ($3.3B EPM software with dashboards tailor-made for the CFO, and the Essbase database), PeopleSoft ($10.3B, financials and other enterprise software), Siebel ($5.85B, CRM), JD Edwards (manufacturing), BEA ($8.5B middleware), Sleepycat Software (BerkeleyDB open source database), Innobase (ultra-fast database engine), TimesTen (in-memory database), Tangosol (coherence in-memory database and data grid software), AmberPoint (SOA), Stellant ($440M, digital rights management and document management), Pillar Data (intelligent hardware), TripleHop

(context-sensitive search), Fat Wire, Relsys (drug safety and risk management), Bharosa (online identity theft and fraud protection), Demantra (demand-driven planning), Retek (retail solutions), Art Technology ($1B, e-commerce software), IRI Software (OLAP), Rdb (division of DEC, database), Oblix (identity management solutions), G-log (transportation management), i-flex banking ($500M), Convergin (telecom service broker), Loadstar (utilities applications software), SPL WorldGroup (utility billing and customer services systems), and many more (I've listed less than half). You should learn something from this paragraph: *Teach your kids Oracle* as it is prevalent in pretty much every sector of business on earth.

Will Oracle use these acquisitions to unite media, knowledge, and education? Perhaps Oracle will touch the consumer even more with Java innovation growing at the same Oracle-pace at which they drove the database (there are 9M Java developers worldwide and 5B Java cards in use); perhaps only through a larger Microsoft or Apple acquisition. Will SAP, HP, or even IBM be next to get consolidated into an ever-shrinking large IT company world? Perhaps an Oracle acquisition of Yahoo! could lead to the race with Google, making both stronger (or will Google or Microsoft get Yahoo! first)? Whoever or whatever Oracle touches next will surely accelerate! My hope is that perhaps the Oracle Public Cloud and corporate internal clouds will transition life to a better plateau for all of us. With Oracle's Exadata, Exalogic, Exalytics, SuperCluster, and all the rest, things are sure to accelerate for those who can effectively leverage these tools. If you want to know where the gold is today: "X marks the spot." Start with Exadata and see what you can do with 8E!

I learned that I had a different gear when I worked at Oracle. From the first day, I walked in, I understood that nothing short of 10× faster would do (later I learned 100× faster was required). I taught and wrote my first Oracle classes within weeks of starting. I didn't even know how to spell Oracle when I started, but enough sleepless nights brought me success and a gear I didn't know that I had. In the introduction to my first book, around two decades ago (this book is part of the best-selling tuning book series over these past two decades), I wrote about always moving faster personally—the new gear—and I wrote about how I thought the world would start to move into this gear as well. The technological acceleration is beginning to hit a level even I didn't see possible two decades ago.

TUSC

Lastly, I want to provide a quick note on TUSC, The Ultimate Software Consultants. At TUSC, I was blessed to work with the best of the best. We were often called the Navy Seals or the Marines of the

Oracle world (being a former Marine, I like the latter description). We were called into Fortune 500 companies across the globe to solve various complex problems, and we always delivered!

With globalization, it became harder to grow, harder to compete at unseen lower offshore rates, and even harder to stay relevant. We saw the need for a partner or to be a part of something bigger that was globalized to be relevant and competitive. So we searched for a similar global company with the breadth to span the globe and the ability to drive growth for us both here at home and globally even in tough times. We were lucky enough to be bought in January 2008 by Rolta International (out of Atlanta). Rolta International oversees the U.S., Europe, and most of Asia for their parent company—a global company and defense engineering and GIS contractor out of Mumbai, Rolta India Limited. Rolta brought us relevance, a global reach, competitive rates, and a future in the global economy. With Rolta, we found a company where people truly cared about what they did and the people around them, where excellence was paramount, and where their work mattered. Soon I was promoted to running International EITS (Enterprise IT Solutions) for Rolta. The International EITS group had approximately 1000 people working in that group companywide, although I found myself primarily helping drive the Oracle message for others around the globe and focusing on leveraging the Rolta TUSC brand. After acquiring two more companies over the next year, WhittmanHart Consulting and Piocon, we inherited many new great employees. In fact, WhittmanHart Consulting had acquired several gems over the years and had several Oracle professionals in Oracle Applications, Fusion, and Database Administration. They also bought a company called Infinis, a truly great Hyperion EPM company (Hyperion Partner of the year), which gave us experience in an area that Oracle had acquired. Piocon was also a company among Oracle leaders in the BI world. Piocon had won the Oracle Partner of the Year award two times to go with our four times (at Rolta, we are now at eight awards as of 2011). While we continued to change (which is always painful), we also became stronger and broader in our Oracle scope. However, my international travels would wear on me over the years. I've travelled to Australia, Austria, Belgium, Canada, China, the Czech Republic, Denmark, Finland, India, Ireland, Germany, Luxembourg, Mexico, Poland, Slovakia, Spain, Sweden, the U.A.E., and the United Kingdom. So I recently moved on to being an advisor to the Rolta International Board in Atlanta instead. I get a lot more tech and presentation hands-on time in this role (and less international travel :)).

To my fellow Marines, Semper Fi, and to all servicemen and women, government workers and agencies that protect freedom, thanks for making the world a safer and better place. The Marines always taught me God, Family, Country, and Corps. Add to that, the golden rule, not the version that goes "He who has the gold makes the rules," but the true golden rule: "To love your neighbor as yourself." Somehow, these two versions of the golden rule contrast the worst values on Wall Street with the best values on Main Street. Although it's tough to do, *love your neighbor as yourself* will take you a whole lot further in life, and even if it leads you to a tough life, it will certainly lead you to a better place just after life. That's the best advice I could give you to prepare for the challenging future ahead!

How This Book Is Organized and Changes in This Version

If you read this entire book and apply it, you will be in the top 1 percent of Oracle Tuning professionals. Over 400 Tuning experts have added to this book in some manner. For those who read the last version of the book, here are some changes and/or additions for each of the chapters:

- **Chapter 1**   Rewritten completely for basic Oracle11gR2 new features
- **Chapter 2**   Expanded to cover all of the index types and tested for 11gR2

- **Chapter 3**   Updated for 11gR2: ASM, LMT, Auto UNDO, and improved I/O sections

- **Chapter 4**   Added MEMORY_TARGET and updated initialization parameters for 11gR2

- **Chapter 5**   Added 11g screen shots, Grid Control, and some Exadata

- **Chapter 6**   Updated EXPLAIN, SQL Plan Management, DBMS_MONITOR, and TRCSESS

- **Chapter 7**   Added new hints and updated others—the best resource for hints!

- **Chapter 8**   Updated for 11gR2; added Result Cache and SQL Performance Analyzer

- **Chapter 9**   Updated and tested for 11gR2; updated block tuning and added DB Replay

- **Chapter 10**   Expanded again as PL/SQL tuning expands; added 11gR2 changes

- **Chapter 11**   Added Exadata, improved RAC, and updated Parallel Query operations

- **Chapter 12**   Expanded again to show more V$ view queries, especially those new in 11gR2

- **Chapter 13**   Expanded X$ view queries, trace section, and X$ naming conventions

- **Chapter 14**   Updated AWR, Statspack for 11gR2; added mutexes and block tuning

- **Chapter 15**   Updated for 11gR2 and for much larger systems

- **Chapter 16**   Unix chapter updated to include more commands

- **Appendix A**   Updated queries for 11gR2 and new Top 25 initialization parameters

- **Appendix B**   Updated for 11gR2 with updated V$ view queries

- **Appendix C**   Updated for 11gR2 with updated X$ queries

References

Mark Harris, "Wish you were here," Daywind, 2006.

Donita Klement, *History of Oracle,* 1999.

Rich Niemiec, "Retrospective: Still Growing After All These Years," *Oracle Magazine,* 2001.

Rich Niemiec, "Rich Niemiec Interviews Bruce Scott," *Select Magazine,* 2001.

Rich Niemiec, "64-Bit Computing," *Oracle Magazine,* 2004.

Lee Strobel, *The Case for a Creator,* Illustra Media, 2006.

Wikipedia website: en.wikipedia.com (Googol, Exabyte).

Mike Wilson, *The Difference between God and Larry Ellison,* William Morrow, November 1998.

Websites: www.oracle.com, www.tusc.com, www.rolta.com.

CHAPTER
1

Introduction to 11g
R1 & R2 New Features
(DBA and Developer)

First, I want to note that this book is primarily focused on helping beginner and intermediate Oracle professionals understand and better tune Oracle systems. Many expert topics are also covered in the later chapters, but the objective is primarily to assist professionals who are frustrated and looking for simple tips to help improve performance. This book has one simple goal: to provide an arsenal of tips you can use in various situations to make your system faster.

Since the 9*i* edition of this book, Chapter 1 is a new features chapter (covering many of the most-used features focused on tuning), which many people have liked. The new features chapter has been so popular I am going to continue and make the Oracle 11*g* new features the first chapter of this book (starting out with the Exadata paradigm shift). The rest of the chapters gradually increase in complexity and provide a plethora of tips to help you in your tuning adventures. I am sure that you will encounter at least some information that you won't find elsewhere.

If you want a single method or an all-encompassing way of tuning a database (in a single chapter), I provide two such chapters for those who don't have the time to read the whole book. The first is Chapter 14 on Statspack and AWR Report (Statspack is free, but AWR is better): two incredible tools that include most of the common scripts the majority of experts use to tune a system using V$ views and X$ tables (covered in Chapters 12 and 13). Chapter 14 took a long time to write to update things like latches and the new mutexes. The second all-encompassing tuning chapter is Chapter 5 on Enterprise Manager (includes Database Control and Grid Control), a tool of the future that provides a graphical way to tune your system, including many features for both RAC systems and large-scale grid control. Enterprise Manager gives you the incredible ability to view and tune multiple systems through one single interface.

This first chapter will discuss, briefly, some of the more interesting new features that are included in Oracle's 11*g* release 1 and 2. Many new and improved features are included in this version. Oracle's goal in 11*g* was not only to create a more robust database management system but also to simplify the installation and administration activities, thereby enhancing availability. This continues a trend that began with Oracle 9*i*, continued with 10*g*, and is furthered in 11*g*. Oracle's strategic direction is to provide a fully integrated set of features that replaces the third-party software that DBAs typically use to help them manage their environments. Not all features listed in this chapter are detailed in the book (since they are not *directly* tuning related and the size of the book needs to be limited), yet I wanted a chapter to mention some of the good features whether directly tuning related or not to give you an overview of 11*g*R2.

The new features covered in this chapter include:

- Exadata is what's next!
- Advanced Compression
- Automatic Diagnostic Repository
- Automatic Shared Memory Management (ASMM) improvements
- Automatic Storage Management (ASM) improvements
- Automatic SQL tuning
- Data Guard enhancements
- Data Pump enhancements (compression, encryption, Legacy Mode)

- Enhanced statistics
- Flashback Data Archive
- Health Monitor
- Incident Packaging Service (IPS)
- Invisible indexes
- New Partitioning features (Interval, REF, System, Virtual Column, Partition Advisor)
- Read Only Tables
- Real Application Clusters (RAC) One Node and RAC Patching
- Real Application Testing
- SQL Performance Analyzer
- Result Cache
- RMAN new features
- SecureFiles
- Enhancements to Streams (XStream In, XStream Out, Advanced Compression Support)
- Shrink Temporary Tablespace
- Transparent Data Encryption (TDE) improvements
- New background processes in 11*g*
- Version 11*g* Feature Comparison Chart

CAUTION
Because these features are new, you should use them cautiously and test them completely until you are sure they work without causing your database problems. If you have access to My Oracle Support, I strongly advise you to determine whether any known problems exist with the feature you are preparing to use. Google.com (although quite broad) is another good place to search for current information on Oracle features and functionality.

Exadata Is What's Next!

With the acquisition of Sun, a paradigm shift occurred in the database market, the hardware world, and the IT industry. While this shift is just beginning, the early tremors are showing that the major shift is coming and will be big over the next decade. Here are a few points about what is coming, but please refer to the Exadata chapter (Chapter 11), which has a lot more detail. Exadata is hardware that combines the power of the database, while leveraging features Oracle added at the hardware level that other hardware providers will not be able to replicate easily (or at all). Some of the topics included in Chapter 11 include expanded details on some major Exadata benefits:

- **Flash Cache** The Flash Cache is comprised of solid-state disks (information stored on chips—over 5 terabytes in a full rack), which is around 20x to 50x faster than disks (depending on the disks). The Flash Cache caches *hot* data (data frequently used). It does this as the *last* step (so it returns data to the user *first* and then caches it for the next time based on the settings you give it).

NOTE
The Flash Cache memory (hardware/chips) is not the same as the Database Flash Cache. You can use Database Flash Cache with the Oracle Database 11g and Oracle RAC 11g. The Database Flash Cache is an optional area that you can add if your database is running on Solaris or Oracle Linux. It is a file-based extension of the SGA-resident buffer cache (similar to a swap area), providing a level-2 cache for database blocks. The file is used as the database is aged out of the SGA. To get more information, see the initialization parameter DB_FLASH_CACHE_SIZE.

- **Storage index** A storage index utilizes minimum/maximum (min/max) values to help queries run faster. A performance gain of 10x is common with storage indexes. They primarily maintain summary information about the data (like metadata in a way). The memory structure resides at the *cell level* (disk/storage cell). For a *cell* (a unit of storage), the min/max values for up to eight queried table columns are stored in that Exadata storage cell and in the storage index. So a storage index is an index of how the data is stored across cells (like the min/max values for partitions). When a query is run against a table, the storage index is checked to see which cells need to be accessed to retrieve the data. Oracle searches data based on the min/max for various columns and eliminates I/Os where there is no match. The process is 100 percent transparent to the user. It is performed at the hardware level and typically has one index for every 1M of disk. No setup is required; Oracle does this internally and automatically. Storage indexes can also provide a huge benefit for highly skewed data. The storage index offers quick access to the highly selective values, whereas the normal Exadata offloading handles the nonselective values.

- **Smart scans** Smart scans are performed internally at the hardware level by Oracle and 10x savings are common. Oracle filters things based on the WHERE clause (predicates) and filters on row/column/join condition. No setup is required; Oracle does this internally and automatically.

- **Hybrid Columnar Compression (HCC)** Hybrid Columnar Compression (HCC), also known as *Exadata Hybrid Columnar Compression (EHCC),* is data that is organized by a hybrid of column and row formats and then compressed. A performance gain anywhere from 10x to 30x is common. The tables are organized in Compression Units (CU), which contain around 1000 rows (more or less depending on the amount of data in the rows). CUs span many blocks. HCC is good for data that is bulk loaded, but it's not built for OLTP or single block-read operations. It is primarily built for Data Warehouses and Queried Data and *not* for frequently updated data. Compared to Gzip/Bzip2, HCC typically has 2× the compression and is 10× faster.

- **Enterprise Manager Grid Control**   Oracle Enterprise Manager Grid Control has a specific plug-in for Exadata, which allows you to manage and view many of the advantages that Oracle provides with Exadata easily. It is also a good way to ensure things are working properly and efficiently (this is covered in Chapter 5 as well as Chapter 11).

- **Enterprise Manager Exadata Simulation**   This allows you to check the benefits of Exadata before implementing it by running a simulation on your current system. This feature is a part of SQL Performance Analyzer, which is a part of Oracle Real Application Testing. Additional licensing is required.

- **I/O Resource Manager**   Oracle's latest I/O Resource Management (IORM) tool can be used with Exadata to manage multiple workloads and set resources as you deem necessary for each database, user, or task. IORM gives you the capability to manage many systems easily with a single machine.

- **Security**   Secure encrypted backup with change tracking file (which is much faster), in which the storage nodes offer hardware decryption acceleration. Exadata takes advantage of CPU hardware decryption acceleration with AES-NI, so you can encrypt and decrypt even when using TDE tablespace or column encryption (encrypted data is now decrypted before Smart-Scan is applied).

- **Utilities**   Cellcli is a command-line interface for queries at the hardware level and for monitoring various health metrics for individual cells; DCLI is for querying multiple cells, and ADR Command Interpreter (ADRCI) is for diagnostics.

Many best practices will help you get the most out of Exadata. I'll start with a list of *must haves* and *don't do's* and then list some best practices! Note that these can change at any time (check Oracle's documentation for the latest as these are subject to change).

- Must have Bundle Patch 5. (See Note: 888828.1 for latest patch.)

- Must have ASM to use Exadata; Automatic Storage Management (ASM) serves as the filesystem and volume manager for Exadata.

- Must have the correct data center cooling! This is *very* important (I suggest doing some research on this).

- Must have three floor tiles on a raised floor (must support 2219 lbs./964 kg) with holes (cooling) for a full rack (between 1560 CFM and 2200 CFM front to back). You don't want to melt it! All of this is subject to change so please check the latest specifications.

- Must have the correct power needs.

- Must have Oracle Linux 5.3 (x86_64) and Oracle DB 11.2 (currently).

- Must have RMAN for backups.

- Consider StorageTek SL500 Tape backup (many positive reviews but pricey).
- Don't add any foreign hardware or … *no support!*
- Don't change BIOS/firmware or … *no support!*

Here are some other best practices:

- Use an ASM allocation unit (AU) size of 4M (currently).
- "CREATE ALL" celldisk and griddisks.
- Use DCLI to run on *all* storage servers at once (this is both helpful and saves time).
- Use IORM for resource management.
- Decide your Fast Recovery Area (FRA) and MAA needs before you install.
- Use Database 11.2.0.1+ (11.2.1.3.1) and ASM 11.2.0.1+ (minimums currently).
- Must be compatible with 11.2.0.1+ (current minimum).
- Has a logfile size of 32G (Whoa!).
- Use Locally Managed Tablespaces (LMT) with 4M uniform extents.
- Move data with Data Pump (usually, but you have many other options).
- Start with the default initialization parameters for tuning and then adjust as needed for your workload.

At the time of writing, the following database machines were available and Oracle had already sold their 1000th Exadata machine in June 2011. The Exadata machine now delivers 1.5M Flash IOPS (I/O's per second). This figure is sure to change as you read this. Oracle is accelerating the hardware world as they did the software world. The world depicted in the popular movie *Iron Man* may not be as far away as you think if Oracle continues this acceleration. In the movie, Iron Man even "accesses the Oracle Grid." Larry Ellison is also in the movie in case you didn't notice. Engineering the hardware and software together is a game changer!

The *Version 2 (V2-2) Exadata Machine,* which is only manufactured by Oracle (Sun) includes:

- 8 compute servers (x4170 M2's)
  - 8 servers × 2 CPU sockets × 6 cores = 96 cores
  - 8 servers × 4 disks × 300G (10K RPM) each (9.6T SAS on server)
- 8 compute servers × 96G DRAM = 768G DRAM
- 3 InfiniBand switches (40Gb/s) ×36 ports = 108 ports
- 14 storage servers with 168 CPU cores & Flash Cache
  - 96G × 4 banks = 394G DRAM per storage server
  - 14 storage servers × 394G = 5.376T Flash Cache

- 12 disks per storage server × 14 servers = 168 disks
- 168 disks × 600G SAS = 101T SAS (15K RPM) or...
- 168 disks × 2T SATA = 336T SATA (7.2K RPM)

The *Version 2 (V2-8) Exadata Machine,* which is only manufactured by Oracle (Sun), includes:

- 2 compute servers (7560 CPU at 2.26 GHz and 5T SAS)
  - 2 servers (x4800's) × 8 CPU sockets × 8 cores = 128 cores
  - 2 servers × 8 disks × 300G (10K RPM) each (4.8T SAS on server)
- 2 compute servers × 1T DRAM = 2T DRAM
- 3 InfiniBand switches (40Gb/s) × 36 ports = 108 ports
- 14 storage servers with 168 CPU cores and Flash Cache
  - 96G × 4 banks = 394G DRAM per storage server
  - 14 storage servers × 394G = 5.376T Flash Cache
  - 12 disks per storage server × 14 servers = 168 disks
  - 168 disks × 600G SAS = 101T SAS (15K RPM) or...
  - 168 disks × 2T SATA = 336T SAS (7.2K RPM)

As of July 2011, Oracle added an *Exadata Storage Expansion Rack,* which allows you to grow the storage capacity of the X2-2 and X2-8 by connecting to it via InfiniBand. It has 18 additional storage servers with 216 CPU cores; 6.75T of Flash Cache (around 1.9M flash IOPS); and 216 of the 2T 7.2K RPM SAS drives (432T of raw disk space, roughly 194T of mirrored uncompressed usable capacity). Using this for an on-disk backup gives you a speed of around 27T/hour. There is also an Exalytics Machine Business Intelligence Machine, the Oracle Data Appliance for small businesses, and a SPARC SuperCluster machine with the new T4 processor (discussed in Chapter 11). The paradigm shift in the hardware world is just beginning!

Following are some quick stats on *Exalogic Elastic Cloud,* which is a machine geared to run applications (and other middleware software) fast on the Web (Amazon, Facebook, Google, Twitter, Yahoo!, Apple, Salesforce.com, EBay, and anyone else who's going to be an Internet commerce player need to get one or two of these if they haven't already).

An Exalogic Elastic Cloud (X2-2) includes (serves 1M HTTP requests per second):

- **EL X2-2**   30 compute servers, 360 CPU cores, 2.9T DRAM, 4T SSD Read Cache, 40T SAS. Will help Fusion Apps smoke!

- **1M HTTP/sec**   I heard that you could fit Facebook on two of these even though there are over 500M people on Facebook.

Here's what makes Exadata fast: Fast hardware, many CPUs, fast Flash Cache, lots of DRAM on database servers and storage, compression (save 10x–70x), partition pruning (save 10x–100x), Storage Indexes (save 5x–10x), Smart-Scan (save 4x–10x), and other features not covered (see Oracle

Docs for more information). Exadata is the best way to turn a 1T search into a 500M search or even a 50M search. I believe Exadata is *the real deal* and will drive accelerated hardware innovation by all major hardware vendors. It's smokin' fast!

Advanced Compression

Oracle 11g introduces a new feature called Advanced Compression that offers organizations the promise of tables that take up less space, therefore, equaling a smaller database. A smaller database taking up less disk space also equals a lower cost for disk storage for databases. With database sizes continuing to grow at an alarming rate, the ability to increase the amount of data stored per gigabyte is exciting. There is also the potential performance benefits from large read operations like full table scans, where Oracle would need to read fewer physical blocks to complete a full table scan, as well as the potential buffer cache memory savings by allowing more data to be stored in the SGA with the compressed blocks.

Oracle first introduced compression in 8i with index key compression, and then in 9i Oracle added compression for tables. Oracle 9i table compression was limited as compression could be used only upon creation via operations like CREATE TABLE AS SELECT, direct loads, or INSERT with APPEND. This compression was well suited for initial loads of data, but over time the table had to be reorganized to recompress, which required maintenance and downtime to maintain compression over time. With pressure to increase availability of database table, compression was not well suited for normal OLTP systems since most data was not direct loaded. Oracle's introduction of Advanced Compression changes that and allows a table to maintain compression as data is updated and inserted into a table, as shown in the CREATE TABLE:

```
create table emp_compressed
(EMPNO              NUMBER(4),
 ENAME              VARCHAR2(10),
 JOB                VARCHAR2(9),
 MGR                NUMBER(4),
 HIREDATE           DATE,
 SAL                NUMBER(7,2),
 COMM               NUMBER(7,2),
 DEPTNO             NUMBER(2))
COMPRESS FOR OLTP;
```

Consider the following Advanced Compression settings:

- **NOCOMPRESS**   The table or partition is not compressed. This is the default action.

- **COMPRESS**   Suitable for data warehouses. Compression enabled during direct-path inserts only.

- **COMPRESS FOR DIRECT_LOAD OPERATIONS**   Same effect as the simple COMPRESS.

- **COMPRESS FOR ALL OPERATIONS**   Suitable for OLTP systems. Compression for all operations, including regular DML statements. Requires COMPATIBLE to be set to 11.1.0 or higher.

- **COMPRESS FOR OLTP**   Suitable for OLTP systems. Enables compression for OLTP operations, including regular DML statements. Requires COMPATIBLE to be set to 11.1.0 or higher and, in 11.2, replaces the COMPRESS FOR ALL OPERATIONS syntax, but COMPRESS FOR ALL OPERATIONS syntax still exists and is still valid.

Automatic Diagnostic Repository

Oracle 11g introduces the Automatic Diagnostic Repository (ADR), which provides a uniform and consistent mechanism to store, format, and locate all database diagnostic information (an easy-to-use file structure). The ADR correlates errors across various components such as Oracle RAC, Oracle Clusterware, OCI, Net, processes, and so on, and automatically generates incidents for serious errors and provides incident management functionality. The ADR can significantly reduce the time to incident/problem resolution.

Typically with the traditional BACKGROUND_DUMP_DEST, CORE_DUMP_DEST, and USER_DUMP_DEST initialization parameters, you had to purge the files manually with custom processes if you wanted the clean-up of files to be automated. With ADR and the ADR command-line interface (ADRCI),you can set policies that control how long files are kept:

```
adrci> set control (SHORTP_POLICY = 360 )
adrci> set control (LONGP_POLICY = 4380 )
```

With ADR, the traditional CORE_DUMP_DEST, BACKGROUND_DUMP_DEST, and USER_DUMP_DEST locations change to a DIAGNOSTIC_DEST, as shown in the table. Therefore, when DIAGNOSTIC_DEST is specified, the original parameter locations are ignored.

Original Location	New Location
CORE_DUMP_DEST	DIAGNOSTIC_DEST/diag/rdbms/<DBNAME>/<INSTANCENAME>/cdump
BACKGROUND_DUMP_DEST (Alert Log text) (Alert Log XML)	DIAGNOSTIC_DEST/diag/rdbms/<DBNAME>/<INSTANCENAME>/trace DIAGNOSTIC_DEST/diag/rdbms/<DBNAME>/<INSTANCENAME>/alert
BACKGROUND_DUMP_DEST	DIAGNOSTIC_DEST/diag/rdbms/<DBNAME>/<INSTANCENAME>/trace
USER_DUMP_DEST	DIAGNOSTIC_DEST/diag/rdbms/<DBNAME>/<ENAME>/trace

The following is an abbreviated list of ADR file locations:

- DIAGNOSTIC_DEST/diag/rdbms/<DBNAME>/<INSTANCENAME>/trace
- DIAGNOSTIC_DEST/diag/rdbms/<DBNAME>/<INSTANCENAME>/alert
- DIAGNOSTIC_DEST/diag/rdbms/<DBNAME>/<INSTANCENAME>/cdump

- DIAGNOSTIC_DEST/diag/rdbms/<DBNAME>/<INSTANCENAME>/incident
- DIAGNOSTIC_DEST/diag/rdbms/<DBNAME>/<INSTANCENAME>/hm
- DIAGNOSTIC_DEST/diag/rdbms/<DBNAME>/<INSTANCENAME>/incpkg
- DIAGNOSTIC_DEST/diag/rdbms/<DBNAME>/<INSTANCENAME>/ir
- DIAGNOSTIC_DEST/diag/rdbms/<DBNAME>/<INSTANCENAME>/lck
- DIAGNOSTIC_DEST/diag/rdbms/<DBNAME>/<INSTANCENAME>/metadata
- DIAGNOSTIC_DEST/diag/rdbms/<DBNAME>/<INSTANCENAME>/sweep
- DIAGNOSTIC_DEST/diag/rdbms/<DBNAME>/<INSTANCENAME>/stage
- ** By default, the location of DIAGNOSTIC_DEST is $ORACLE_HOME/log

However, if ORACLE_BASE is set in the environment, then DIAGNOSTIC_DEST is set to $ORACLE_BASE. See Chapter 4 for additional information on this topic and setting initialization parameters.

Automatic Shared Memory Management (ASMM) Improvements

Oracle 9*i* implemented the PGA to manage SORT_AREA_SIZE, HASH_AREA_SIZE, bitmap merge area, and the create bitmap area together. Oracle 10*g* gave us the first step toward automatic memory management through SGA memory management to manage the shared pool, large pool, java pool, and buffer cache together. Oracle 11*g* has improved Automatic Shared Memory Management even more so you can automatically manage SGA + PGA memory together. To use Automatic Memory Management (AMM) to manage both the SGA and PGA, Oracle has introduced two new database parameters: MEMORY_TARGET and MEMORY_MAX_TARGET.

So how does Oracle handle the use of the prior automatic memory management parameters? The SGA_TARGET and PGA_AGGREGATE_TARGET will simply be used to indicate minimum memory settings when you set MEMORY_TARGET. To allow Oracle the greatest flexibility to manage memory (not advised; I suggest setting minimums), you can set the SGA_TARGET and PGA_AGGREGATE_TARGET to 0.

Here are some important notes:

- It is incompatible to set MEMORY_TARGET when using Linux Huge Pages. See Metalink note 749851.1 for further detail.

- Use a value for MEMORY_TARGET that is less than the size of the shared memory filesystem (dev/shm). On Oracle Linux systems, /dev/shm free will need to be larger than the MEMORY_TARGET setting when starting the database or an "ORA-00845: MEMORY_TARGET not supported on this system" will result.

- You cannot enable automatic memory management with MEMORY_TARGET if the LOCK_SGA database initialization parameter is TRUE.

Please see Chapter 4 for a large amount of additional information on this topic and on setting initialization parameters.

Automatic Storage Management (ASM) Improvements

Oracle 11g has greatly improved Oracle ASM to improve scalability, availability, performance, and file management. Oracle 11g ASM improvements reduce database startup time and memory requirements, allowing support of larger ASM files and providing the ability to implement several hundred terabyte (T) or even petabyte (P = 1000T) databases on ASM. To improve scalability, ASM increases support for very large datafile sizes. Oracle Database limits any single datafile to 128T (if DB_BLOCK_SIZE = 32K)—far less than the new ASM file-size limits.

Following are the new ASM limits:

- 40 exabytes maximum storage with Oracle Exadata (otherwise 20 petabytes)
- Each ASM disk is 4P with Oracle Exadata (otherwise 2T)
- 1 million files per diskgroup
- 10,000 ASM disks
- 63 diskgroups per ASM instance
- Maximum file sizes for diskgroups with AU_SIZE = 1M and compatible.rdbms =>11.1
  - External redundancy: 140P
  - Normal redundancy: 23P
  - High redundancy: 15P

NOTE
The maximum size of the Oracle database is 65,533 (maximum number of datafiles) ×128T (maximum size of a datafile on 64-bit systems) = 8 exabytes when using big file tablespaces (8P when using small file tablespaces). Maximum addressable memory in a 64-bit system is 16 exabytes (roughly 18 with 18 zeros of bytes). So you can make that 8E database memory resident in the future and still have 8E of memory to spare!

Other sizing notes include:

- **Variable Size Extent**   Allows for much larger ASM files, reduces SGA memory requirements for very large databases (VLDB), and improves performance of file creation and file open.
- **Allocation Unit (AU)**   Minimum segment of a disk that can be assigned to a file that can be sized at 1, 2, 4, 8, 18, 32, and 64MB; default is 1MB.

- **Striping**   Coarse stripe size = 1 AU, fine stripe size = 128K

- **Larger allocation units**   For large sequential reads and writes, larger AUs have shown significant performance gains.

- **Extent size**   In 11.1, an ASM file can start with 1M extents assuming a 1M AU and gradually increase by a factor of 8 to 8M and 64M at a predetermined number of extents as the ASM file grows. In 11.2, the extent size of a file varies as follows:

  - Extent size always equals the diskgroup AU size for the first 20,000 extent sets (0–19,999).

  - Extent size equals 4xAU size for the next 20,000 extent sets (20,000–39,999).

  - Extent size equals 16xAU size for the next 20,000 and higher extent sets (40,000+).

- **MAXIO buffersize**   Beneficial to increase MAXIO buffersize to 4M and create the ASM diskgroup with a 4M allocation unit for optimal performance for large sequential I/O.

ASM Preferred Mirror Read

With Oracle 11*g*, and when Oracle ASM is managing the redundancy, an ASM instance on a host can be configured to read from a "preferred mirror" copy; the default is to read from the primary group. This provides the most benefit to an Oracle RAC environment where ASM fail groups are on separate sites. In cases where ASM fail group is at a different site from the primary group, RAC instances can be configured to read from a local mirror copy rather than from the remote primary group, thus eliminating potential network latencies. The ASM preferred mirror read is controlled with the initialization parameter ASM_PREFERRED_READ_FAILURE_GROUPS for each ASM instance. For example, say you have two sites you are calling site1 and site2, an ASM diskgroup named DATA1 with failure groups SITE1 and SITE2 (please read appropriate Oracle documentation thoroughly before using this):

For site1:

```
ASM_PREFERRED_READ_FAILURE_GROUP=DATA1.SITE1
```

For site2

```
ASM_PREFERRED_READ_FAILURE_GROUP=DATA1.SITE2
```

Rolling Upgrades/Patching

To improve availability, Oracle 11*g* has added the capability to perform rolling upgrades for the ASM instances within an Oracle RAC environment, by allowing the ASM cluster to be put in a "rolling migration" mode. The rolling migration mode allows an ASM instance to operate temporarily in a multiversion ASM environment. It is recommended that before starting an ASM rolling migration that all Oracle software installation is complete on the cluster before starting the rolling upgrades/migration to keep the time in rolling migration to a minimum, as most ASM operations are not allowed once the ASM cluster is in a rolling migration mode (please read appropriate Oracle documentation thoroughly before attempting this).

To start rolling migration:

```
ALTER SYSTEM START ROLLING MIGRATION TO <ver_number>;
```

To stop rolling migration or downgrade if issues arise during migration:

```
ALTER SYSTEM STOP ROLLING MIGRATION;
```

Faster Rebalance

Oracle 11*g* improves the performance of ASM rebalance operations, which significantly reduces the time to recover from offline disks due to a transient failure such as a loose cable, power loss, bus adapter, or disk controller. ASM will track the extents modified during the outage. Once the transient failure is repaired, and assuming the content of the disks are intact, ASM can quickly resynchronize the ASM mirror extents that missed modifications during the outage. This can make a difference of hours or even days to bring the disk back online and in sync.

The new DISK_REPAIR_TIME attribute allows a time window to be defined in which a failure repair or sync operation can occur and the mirror disk can be brought back on line. The DISK_REPAIR_TIME defaults to 3.6 hours, but can be changed for a diskgroup through the ALTER DISKGROUP command (please read appropriate Oracle documentation thoroughly before using this):

```
ALTER DISKGROUP <DiskGroupName> SET ATTRIBUTE 'DISK_REPAIR_TIME'= '24H';
```

To bring the all diskgroups back online (you can bring specific ones by using DISK <*disk name*> instead of ALL) and start the resynchronization process:

```
ALTER DISKGROUP DISK ONLINE ALL;
```

NOTE
Oracle 11g allows diskgroups to be mounted in restricted mode, eliminating the need for lock and unlock messages between ASM instances during a rebalance operation. This greatly improves the performance of a rebalance operation in a RAC environment. Here is a sample of the series of commands you would use:
ALTER DISKGROUP <diskgroup> DISMOUNT ;
ALTER DISGROUP <diskgroup> MOUNT RESTRICTED ;

Perform maintenance activity (rebalance/add/drop/online/offline disks, etc.):
ALTER DISKGROUP <diskgroup> DISMOUNT ;
ALTER DISKGROUP <diskgroup> MOUNT ;

ASM Diskgroup Compatibility

Oracle 11*g* introduces two new diskgroup compatibility attributes that determine the minimum version of ASM instances and database instances that can use a specific ASM diskgroup. The new attributes compatible.asm and compatible.rdbms are set at the diskgroup level and are valuable in cases where downgrades could be necessary (see example):

```
CREATE DISKGROUP DATA1 NORMAL REDUNDANCY DISK '/dev/raw/raw1',
'/dev/raw/raw2' ATTRIBUTE 'compatibile.asm'='11.1' ;

ALTER DISKGROUP DATA1 SET ATTRIBUTE 'compatible.rdbms'='11.1' ;

select group_number GN, name, compatibility COMPAT,
       database_compatibility DCOMPAT
from   v$asm_diskgroup;

GN NAME COMPAT     DCOMPAT
-- ---- ---------- ----------
1  DG1  11.1.0.0.0 11.1.0.0.0
2  DG2  10.1.0.0.0 10.1.0.0.0
```

ASMCMD Extensions

To better manage ASM diskgroups, Oracle 11*g* adds some great new commands to the ASMCMD utility. Several of these are listed here:

- **CP**   Copies ASM files between diskgroups and OS filesystems.

  ```
  ASMCD> cp +ASM1/ system.dbf /backups/orcl/system.dbf
  ```

- **MD_BACKUP**   Backs up diskgroup metadata.

  ```
  ASMCMD> md_backup -b /backups/orcl/asmbackupfile.md -g ASM1
  ```

- **MD_RESTORE**   Restores diskgroup metadata.

  ```
  ASMCMD> md_restore -b /backups/orcl/asmbackupfile.md -t full -g ASM1
  ```

- **LSDSK**   Lists ASM disk information.

  ```
  ASMCMD> lsdsk
  ```

- **REMAP**   Invokes bad block remapping for specified blocks.

  ```
  ASMCMD> remap <diskgroup name> <disk name> <block range>
  ```

- **SYSASM** privileges   Assigns new role like SYSDBA for ASM.

  ```
  SQL> GRANT SYSASM TO <username> ;
  SQL> CONNECT <username> AS SYSASM ;
  ```

Automatic SQL Tuning

Oracle 11g introduces Automatic SQL Tuning. Many chapters in this book cover this topic in detail, so this section only serves as an overview. Oracle 11g runs the SQL Tuning Advisor against SQL statements determined to be of high impact based on statistics from the Automatic Workload Repository (AWR). The AWR statistics are used to make a list of SQL statements and orders them based on their greatest performance impact on the system during the past week. The SQL list will automatically exclude all SQL statements determined to be less tunable, such as parallel queries, DML, DDL, and any SQL statements where performance problems are determined to be caused by concurrency issues. The SQL Tuning Advisor generates recommendations to tune SQL that may include SQL profiles (using statistical information). When SQL profiles are recommended, the SQL profiles are performance tested, and if the result is at least a threefold improvement, they are *accepted* when the SQL Tuning Task parameter ACCEPT_SQL_PROFILES is set to TRUE and *reported* when ACCEPT_SQL_PROFILES is set to FALSE. You can also perform any of these steps individually for any query.

The ENABLE and DISABLE procedures of the DBMS_AUTO_TASK_ADMIN package control the execution of the Automatic SQL Tuning Tasks. When enabled, the SQL Tuning Advisor is run during the defined maintenance windows; the default maintenance windows are shown in Table 1-1.

To enable and disable automatic SQL Tuning:

```
EXEC DBMS_AUTO_TASK_ADMIN.ENABLE(client_name => 'sql tuning advisor',operation =>
  NULL, window_name => NULL);

EXEC DBMS_AUTO_TASK_ADMIN.DISABLE(client_name => 'sql tuning advisor', operation
  => NULL,window_name => NULL);
```

Window Name	Description
MONDAY_WINDOW	Starts at 10 p.m. on Monday to 2 a.m.
TUESDAY_WINDOW	Starts at 10 p.m. on Tuesday to 2 a.m.
WEDNESDAY_WINDOW	Starts at 10 p.m. on Wednesday to 2 a.m.
THURSDAY_WINDOW	Starts at 10 p.m. on Thursday to 2 a.m.
FRIDAY_WINDOW	Starts at 10 p.m. on Friday to 2 a.m.
SATURDAY_WINDOW	Starts at 6 a.m. on Saturday and is 20 hours long.
SUNDAY_WINDOW	Starts at 6 a.m. on Sunday and is 20 hours long.

TABLE 1-1.   *Oracle 11g Default Maintenance Windows*

To configuring automatic SQL Tuning:

```
EXEC DBMS_SQLTUNE.SET_TUNING_TASK_PARAMETER (task_name =>
 'SYS_AUTO_SQL_TUNING_TASK', parameter => 'ACCEPT_SQL_PROFILES', value => 'TRUE');
```

The following are the DBMS_SQLTUNE options for controlling Automatic SQL Tuning tasks:

- **INTERRUPT_TUNING_TASK** To interrupt a task while executing, causing a normal exit with intermediate results

- **RESUME_TUNING_TASK** To resume a previously interrupted task

- **CANCEL_TUNING_TASK** To cancel a task while executing, removing all results from the task

- **RESET_TUNING_TASK** To reset a task while executing, removing all results from the task and returning the task to its initial state

- **DROP_TUNING_TASK** To drop a task, removing all results associated with the task

Chapter 5 will show how to use Automatic SQL Tuning features using Enterprise Manager for easy "click and run" ease.

Data Guard Enhancements

Oracle 11g includes several enhancements to Oracle Data Guard to improve its capabilities and its usability. The following sections detail a few of these enhancements.

Snapshot Standby

With the Oracle11g new feature Snapshot Standby, you can now temporarily open a physical standby to utilize it for read/write activity, allowing for activities such as reporting and load testing. The physical standby database opened in a read/write mode still receives redo data from its primary database, so it continues to provide protection against primary failure while allowing the standby to be used for other activities. This improves the value of a physical standby database by allowing it to serve more purposes for the enterprise and further justifying the costs associated with maintaining a physical standby. Keep in mind that the Snapshot Standby Database receives and archives the redo data from the primary database but does not apply it until the Snapshot Standby Database is converted back into a physical standby database.

Oracle 11g also improved the speed of role transitions between primary and standby databases.

Active Data Guard

The Active Data Guard is an optional feature introduced with the release of Oracle Database 11g for a physical standby database. This optional feature requires additional licensing from Oracle Corporation; therefore, you'll have to obtain the license for this feature prior to implementing in your environment. This feature allows a physical standby database to be open in read-only mode while the redo apply processing that keeps the physical standby database up to date with the primary database continues. Both the primary and physical standby database must have their compatible database initialization parameter set to 11.0 (11*g* compatibility mode). Note that Oracle Active Data Guard requires a separate license and can only be used with Oracle Database Enterprise Edition. You can purchase it as the Active Data Guard Option for Oracle Database Enterprise Edition. It is also included with Oracle GoldenGate.

In 11*g*R2, Oracle improved the Active Data Guard option by adding lag history through a query of the V$STANDBY_EVENT_HISTOGRAM view (see example query).

```
select *
from   v$standby_event_histogram
where  name = 'APPLY LAG';
```

Also, 11*g*R2 added a database initialization parameter that helps control how far behind the standby database can get before query activity starts being controlled. You can use the STANDBY_MAX_DATA_DELAY parameter to specify a session-specific apply lag tolerance, measured in seconds, for queries issued by nonadmin users on the physical standby database with Active Data Guard on. This capability allows queries to be offloaded from the primary database's resources onto a physical standby database's resources safely because it is possible to know if the standby database has become unacceptably stale prior to query execution. The STANDBY_MAX_DATA_DELAY default value is NONE, which means that queries issued to a physical standby database will be executed regardless of the apply lag on that database. Other valid values are an integer value >0 (indicating the number of seconds of tolerable lag time). A value of 0 indicates that all queries issued against the physical standby will return the exact same result as if it was executed against the primary, whereas a value >0 indicates a query issued against the physical standby database will be executed only if the apply lag is less than or equal to STANDBY_MAX_DATA_DELAY (otherwise an ORA-3172 error is returned to alert that the apply lag is too large). A couple of helpful queries are listed next.

To check the status of the physical standby to ensure that the database role is physical standby and the open mode is read only, you can run the query shown here. *Note that 11gR2 will show the open mode as "read only with apply."*

```
select db_unique_name, database_role, open_mode
from   v$database;

DB_UNIQUE_NAME                      DATABASE_ROLE     OPEN_MODE
------------------------------      ----------------  ----------
TESTSB                              PHYSICAL STANDBY  READ ONLY
```

To check the lag time of the physical standby database from the primary database, you can run the following:

```
SELECT name, value, unit, time_computed,
       to_char(sysdate, 'DD-MON-YY HH24:MI:ss')
FROM   V$DATAGUARD_STATS
WHERE  name like 'apply lag';

NAME
-------------------------------------------------------------------
```

```
VALUE
---------------------------------------------------------------
UNIT                           TIME_COMPUTED
TO_CHAR(SYSDATE,'D
------------------------------ ------------------------------
------------------
apply lag
+00 00:00:00
day(2) to second(0) interval   20-MAY-2009 19:04:17            20-MAY-09 19:04:44
```

Mixed Platform Support

Oracle11g expands the capability to have a physical standby database on an O/S that differs from the primary. Oracle11g now allows Linux and Windows combinations as well as Solaris/IBM AIX (in 11.2.0.2; see bug 12702521 for additional restrictions). While other platform combinations were supported in 10g, this is the first time that complete operating system differences are supported.

NOTE
For a complete list of supported platform/OS combinations, see Metalink Note 413484.1. See My Oracle Support (Metalink) Notes 395982.1 and/or 414043.1 for more exact restrictions and further details.

Advanced Compression for Logical Standby (11gR2)

Oracle Database 11gR1 introduced Advanced Compression; however, advanced compression could not be utilized for objects that were subject to streams or a logical standby database. With 11gR2, Advanced Compression is supported and works with streams and a logical standby database.

Transparent Data Encryption Support for Logical Standby

Oracle 11g introduces support for Transparent Data Encryption for logical standby databases. The SQL Apply also supports the use of Transparent Data Encryption, further enhancing the capabilities and utilization of logical standby databases.

Data Pump Compression Enhancements

Oracle10g Data Pump can compress metadata from a Data Pump export via the COMPRESSION parameter with a value of METADATA_ONLY (which can yield up to 15 percent smaller dump file sizes). In 11g, Data Pump can now compress not only the metadata but also the database data. Compression is specified for metadata, row data, or entire dump file set via the COMPRESSION parameter with valid values now being ALL, METADATA_ONLY, DATA_ONLY, NONE.

Data Pump Encrypted Dump File Sets

Oracle 11*g* adds the capability for Data Pump to encrypt the dump files. Data Pump can now encrypt metadata and database data in the dump files. Oracle 11*g* Data Pump adds new parameters to control the encryption:

- **ENCRYPTION**   Sets encryption for the dump file or dump file set; valid values are ALL, DATA_ONLY, METADATA_ONLY, ENCRYPTED_COLUMNS_ONLY, or NONE.

- **ENCRYPTION_ALGORITHM**   Specify how encryption should be done for the dump file or dump file set; valid values are AES128, AES192, and AES256.

- **ENCRYPTION_MODE**   Method of generating encryption key for the encrypted dump file or dump file set; valid values are DUAL, PASSWORD, and TRANSPARENT.

I highly recommend that you consider many levels of encryption in your systems. You should develop a comprehensive security plan that includes encryption at every needed level (especially encrypting your backup). Security is beyond the scope of this book, but should be very high on your list!

Data Pump Legacy Mode

With 11*g*R2, Data Pump now has a Legacy Mode. The Legacy Mode provides backward compatibility for scripts and parameter files created for the original Export and Import Utilities, allowing users and processes from the original Export and Import Utilities to continue to work with the new Data Pump Export and Import without needing to change and/or update the processes. This enhancement simplifies and eases the migration to the new Data Pump Utility.

Enhanced Statistics

Oracle 11*g* has improved statistics in several ways through enhanced I/O statistics, statistics collection on partitioned objects, pending statistics, multicolumn statistics, and expression statistics.

Enhanced I/O Statistics

Oracle 11*g* collects I/O statistics for all I/O calls for a consumer group, database file, and database function. When the Resource Manager is enabled, I/O statistics are gathered for each consumer group that is part of the enabled resource plan. These statistics can be viewed via V$IOSTAT_CONSUMER_GROUP. The database file statistics are gathered on database files that have been accessed. These statistics indicate large and small read and write requests, service time, and small read latency. They can be viewed via the V$IOSTAT_FILE dictionary view. The gathered database function I/O statistics are based on database functions such as LGWR and DBWR and show small and large read and write requests, number of waits, and wait time. They can be viewed via the V$IOSTAT_FUNCTION dictionary view.

Reducing the Gathering of Partitioned Objects Statistics

Oracle 11g has the ability to configure improved statistics collection on partitioned objects by only gathering statistics on partitions that have had write activity, thereby eliminating the processing required to gather statistics on partitions for an object that has not changed. This increases the speed at which statistics are gathered on large partitioned objects when some partitions contain static data.

Pending Statistics

Oracle 11g has a new feature called pending statistics. Pending statistics adds the capability of keeping newly gathered statistics in a pending state until you choose to publish them. However, the default is to publish statistics automatically upon completion of the gather operation. The pending statistics are controlled via the DBMS_STATS package and the database initialization parameter, OPTIMIZER_USE_PENDING_STATISTICS.

To see pending statistics settings:

```
SQL> SELECT DBMS_STATS.GET_PREFS('PUBLISH') PUBLISH FROM DUAL;
```

To set global pending statistics to auto publish (default):

```
SQL> exec dbms_stats.SET_GLOBAL_PREFS ('PUBLISH', 'TRUE');
```

To set global pending statistics to not auto publish:

```
SQL> exec dbms_stats.SET_GLOBAL_PREFS ('PUBLISH', 'FALSE') ;
```

A great feature of pending statistics is that it allows the testing of unpublished statistics before publishing them by using the OPTIMIZER_USE_PENDING_STATISTICS initialization parameter. This parameter can be set at a system or session level; when used at a session level, it allows a session to test the optimizer statistics prior to publishing:

```
SQL> alter session set OPTIMIZER_USE_PENDING_STATISTICS=TRUE;
```

Multicolumn Statistics

Oracle 11g introduces multi-column statistics, which is a powerful feature when multiple columns from a single table are used in the WHERE clause of SQL statements. Multi-column statistics allows the optimizer to identify the relationship between the two columns, therefore, treating them as a "column group." An example of this would be items sold in a given season; there is a relationship between items sold (winter parka vs. swim suit) and the season (winter vs. summer). Oracle 11g will gather multi-column statistics automatically based on workload analysis, much in the same way histograms are done, but they can also be created manually using the DBMS_STATS package:

```
Exec DBMS_STATS.gather_table_stats( 'SCOTT', 'EMP', method_opt => 'for columns
(job,deptno)');
```

You can query settings using DBA / ALL / USER_STAT_EXTENSIONS.

Expression Statistics

Oracle 11*g* *expression statistics* help the cost-based optimizer know the effect of applying a function to a column, based on the selectivity of the column. This allows the optimizer to make better decisions when applying a function to a column as it will be able to better predict the number of rows returned.

```
Exec DBMS_STATS.gather_table_stats( 'SCOTT', 'EMP', method_opt => 'for columns
  (upper(ename))');
```

You can query settings using DBA / ALL / USER_STAT_EXTENSIONS.

Flashback Data Archive

Flashback Data Archive (FBDA) is a powerful new feature of Oracle Database 11*g*. Flashback Data Archive can transparently track in a secure and efficient manner all data stored in database with no limit on the retention period. Easily configured, FBDA is efficient on storage as well as performance. FBDA protects from accidental updates and deletes (user error) or malicious data destruction (hacker intrusion) by providing the functionality to view data at a prior point in time via the "AS OF" flashback SQL clause without dependency on UNDO.

The FBDA requires a Flashback Data Archive tablespace and collects its data via the new FBDA background process. The FBDA process writes to the Flashback Data Archive in the FDBA tablespace. FBDA is set per table, and there are some limitations as to the type of changes that you can perform on the table such as ALTER TABLE using the UPGRADE TABLE clause, moving or exchanging a partition or subpartition, and dropping the table. Although this might sound great for protection, FBDA does not record who made changes; therefore, it will not assist in forensic operations. This feature is now part of an extra cost option—Oracle Total Recall.

The following is a Flashback Data Archive example (please consult Oracle docs before using):

To create a Flashback Data tablespace, call it fbda1:

```
create tablespace fbda1 datafile 'c:\oracle\oradata\db\fbda1.dbf' size 500M;
```

To create a Flashback Data Archive:

```
create flashback archive default dbda1 tablespace fbda1 retention 1 year;
```

To create tables with the Flashback Data Archive:

```
create table a (n number) flashback archive;
```

To alter a table to use Flashback Data Archive:

```
alter table xyz flashback archive;
```

To alter a table to not use Flashback Data Archive:

```
alter table xyz no flashback archive;
```

To select from a table using AS OF Flashback SQL clause:

```
select * from a as of timestamp to_timestamp('19-SEP-2008 11:59:32','dd-mon-yyyy
  hh24:mi:ss') where table_name = 'EMP';
```

Health Monitor

Oracle 11*g* introduces a free database Health Monitor using the DBMS_HM package. The Health Monitor is manually executed and can run the following checks:

- DB Structure Integrity Check
- Data Block Integrity Check
- Redo Integrity Check
- Undo Segment Integrity Check
- Transaction Integrity Check
- Dictionary Integrity Check

To execute a health check using DBMS_HM:

```
SQL> exec dbms_hm.run_check ('Dictionary Integrity Check', 'HM_TEST') ;
PL/SQL procedure successfully completed.
```

Run the Healthcheck Report from a Healthcheck Run with the DBMS_HM package, GET_RUN_REPORT. This is a PL/SQL function that returns a Character Large OBject (CLOB) to extract the report. This example shows extracting the report to a file using a PL/SQL script that is run via SQL Plus.

To execute the example report:

```
$ sqlplus sysorcl11g as sysdba

SQL*Plus: Release 11.1.0.6.0 - Production on Thu Oct 2 09:08:55 2008
Copyright (c) 1982, 2007, Oracle.  All rights reserved.
Enter password:
Connected to:
Oracle Database 11g Enterprise Edition Release 11.1.0.6.0 - Production
With the Partitioning, OLAP, Data Mining and Real Application Testing options

SET LONG 100000
SET LONGCHUNKSIZE 1000
SET PAGESIZE 1000
SET LINESIZE 512
select DBMS_HM.GET_RUN_REPORT('HM_TEST')
from    dual;
```

Here's the example report:

```
Basic Run Information
  Run Name                    : HM_TEST
  Run Id                      : 966
  Check Name                  : Dictionary Integrity Check
  Mode                        : MANUAL
  Status                      : COMPLETED
  Start Time                  : 2008-10-02 08:59:50.734000 -04:00
  End Time                    : 2008-10-02 08:59:57.296000 -04:00
  Error Encountered           : 0
  Source Incident Id          : 0
  Number of Incidents Created : 0

Input Parameters for the Run
  TABLE_NAME=ALL_CORE_TABLES
  CHECK_MASK=ALL

Run Findings And Recommendations
  Finding
  Finding Name : Dictionary Inconsistency
  Finding ID   : 967
  Type         : FAILURE
  Status       : OPEN
  Priority     : CRITICAL
  Message      : SQL dictionary health check: dependency$.dobj# fk 126 on
                 object DEPENDENCY$ failed
  Message      : Damaged rowid is AAAABnAABAAAO2GAB3 - description: No further
                 damage description available
  Finding
  Finding Name : Dictionary Inconsistency
  Finding ID   : 970
  Type         : FAILURE
  Status       : OPEN
  Priority     : CRITICAL
  Message      : SQL dictionary health check: dependency$.dobj# fk 126 on
                 object DEPENDENCY$ failed
  Message      : Damaged rowid is AAAABnAABAAAQtpABQ - description: No further
                 damage description available
```

Following is the example script:

```
-------------------------------------------------------------------------------
-- Script: run_health_check_report.sql
-------------------------------------------------------------------------------
-- Create a directory where we are going to write out report file to
create directory healthcheck as '&u_name';

-- Get Database Instance Name to build file name to be used to put report into
column database_name noprint new_value i_name
SELECT UPPER(name) || '_healthcheck_report.lst' database_name
FROM v$database ;
```

```
declare
   v_rpt              CLOB ;
   buffer             VARCHAR2(32767);
   buffer_size        CONSTANT BINARY_INTEGER := 32767;
   amount             BINARY_INTEGER;
   offset             NUMBER(38);
   file_handle        UTL_FILE.FILE_TYPE;
   directory_name     CONSTANT VARCHAR2(80) := 'HEALTHCHECK';
   v_filename         CONSTANT VARCHAR2(80) := '&i_name';

begin
   -- Run the Report
   v_rpt := dbms_hm.GET_RUN_REPORT ('&HNAME') ;

   -- OPEN NEW FILE IN WRITE MODE
   file_handle := UTL_FILE.FOPEN(
        location      => directory_name,
        filename      => v_filename,
        open_mode     => 'w',
        max_linesize  => buffer_size);

   amount := buffer_size;
   offset := 1;

    WHILE amount >= buffer_size
    LOOP
        DBMS_LOB.READ(
           lob_loc     => v_rpt,
           amount      => amount,
           offset      => offset,
           buffer      => buffer);

        offset := offset + amount;

        UTL_FILE.PUT(file => file_handle, buffer    => buffer);
        UTL_FILE.FFLUSH(file => file_handle);
    END LOOP;

    UTL_FILE.FCLOSE(file => file_handle);
END;
/
```

Incident Packaging Service (IPS)

Oracle 11g, as part of the Automatic Diagnostic Repository (ADR), has the ability to gather incident information that can be sent to Oracle Support. When an incident occurs, the database makes an entry in the alert log, sends an incident alert to Oracle Enterprise Manager, gathers diagnostic data about the incident in the form of dump files (incident dumps), tags the incident dumps with an incident ID number, and stores the incident dumps in an ADR subdirectory created for that incident. The Incident Packaging Service allows the gathering and packaging of all diagnostic files related to specific problems. This can greatly reduce the amount of time needed to gather required diagnostic files, therefore, improving the turnaround time when sending diagnostic information to Oracle Support (a brief example is listed next). After creating a package, you can add external files to the package, remove selected files from the package, or scrub (edit) selected files in the package to remove sensitive data.

NOTE
The easier and recommended way to manage diagnostic data is with the Oracle Enterprise Manager Support Workbench.

```
$ adrci
adrci> help ips

adrci> show incident
```

(This example shows incident No. 9817 for ORA-600 [XYZ].)

```
adrci> ips create package incident 9817
Created package 4 based on incident id 9817, correlation level typical

adrci> ips add incident 9817 package 4
Added incident 9817 to package 4

adrci> ips add file
/opt/oracle/diag/rdbms/orcl/orcl/trace/alert_orcl.log package 4
Added file /opt/oracle/diag/rdbms/orcl/orcl/trace/alert_orcl.log to package 4

adrci> ips generate package 4 in /tmp
Generated package 4 in file /tmp/ORA600kci_20100514184516_COM_1.zip, mode complete
```

Invisible Indexes

Oracle has now taken, in my opinion, a huge step forward in the tuning of third-party applications. Oracle now allows users to hide indexes from the optimizer without having to drop them (they continue to be maintained) with the introduction of a feature called *invisible indexes* (invisible indexes are covered in detail in Chapter 2). If you have ever tuned queries of very large tables and had to drop and/or re-create indexes during your query tuning testing, then you realize the impact of this new feature. Invisible indexes will also be helpful in batch process tuning. There are numerous situations in which an index could really help your batch process, but would hurt OLTP transaction query performance. Now, however, you can hide the index from OLTP but allow your batch processes to see it.

To use an invisible index (force it to be used even when invisible), you can set the parameter OPTIMIZER_USE_INVISIBLE_INDEXES to TRUE. This parameter's default is false and can be set via an ALTER SESSION or ALTER SYSTEM command. Otherwise, invisible indexes are completely ignored by the optimizer even through hints. Another important note about invisible indexes is that optimizer statistics are not gathered on them while they are in an invisible state. To maintain statistics, the index has to be made visible by altering the index or setting the OPTIMIZER_USE_INVISIBLE_INDEXES parameter to true (be careful setting the parameter; see Chapter 4, Appendix A, and Oracle docs for more information). The following commands show the creation of an invisible index and altering of the index to be made visible for an individual session:

```
SQL> create index my_index on my_table (ename) invisible;
Index Created.

SQL> alter session set optimizer_use_invisible_indexes = true;
Session altered.
```

New Partitioning Features

Oracle 11g has added several partitioning capabilities that improve the manageability of partitioned tables as well as partitioning capabilities that greatly improve performance. The following sections cover interval partitioning, REF partitioning, system partitioning, virtual column-based partitioning, and the Partition Advisor.

Interval Partitioning

One of my favorite new features in Oracle 11g is *interval partitioning*. The reason that it's one of my favorites is because it solves a long-standing issue. Previously an Oracle error occurred if you didn't have a partition range specified that matched the value to be inserted. This new feature extends the functionality of range partitioning so you can define equal-sized (future) partitions using an interval definition. When using interval partitioning, Oracle automatically creates new partitions as they are needed. Oracle creates the new partition at the time of the first record insert for the new partition. This greatly helps with the manageability of partitioned tables by saving the DBA from having to create new partitions manually, while also preventing Oracle user errors. The valid combinations for the new interval partitioning are Interval, Interval-List, Interval-Hash, and Interval-Range. Interval partitioning will work especially well for range partitioning, where partitioning was done based on date ranges. Consider this example that shows this new functionality when creating a table. Future chapters will explore this in detail.

```
CREATE TABLE emp
   (EMPNO              NUMBER(4),
    ENAME              VARCHAR2(30),
    JOB                VARCHAR2(20),
    MGR                NUMBER(4),
    HIREDATE           DATE,
    SAL                NUMBER(7,2),
    COMM               NUMBER(7,2),
    DEPTNO             NUMBER(2))
PARTITION BY RANGE (hiredate)
INTERVAL (NUMTOYMINTERVAL(1,'YEAR'))
(PARTITION part_1999 values LESS THAN
(TO_DATE('01-JAN-2000','DD-MON-YYYY')));
```

A related feature is deferred segment creation for partitions (introduced in 11.2.0.2). With this feature, on-disk segments are not created for a subpartition and its dependent objects until the first row is inserted.

REF Partitioning

Oracle REF partitioning is a new partitioning feature with Oracle Database 11g. REF partitioning is the ability to partition a table based on the foreign key parent-child relationship. In REF partitioning, the partitioning key of the child table is inherited from the parent table. REF partitioning also duplicates all partition maintenance operations that change the logical shape of the parent table on the child table. REF partitioning also improves performance for joins between the parent and child table by enabling partition-wise joins. REF partitioning cannot be used when the parent table is partitioned using interval partitioning or virtual column-based partitioning. The following message will appear when you attempt to create the partitioned table with REF partitioning:

```
CREATE TABLE order_items
*
ERROR at line 1:
ORA-14659: Partitioning method of the parent table is not supported
```

Another oddity found in this test was that if you create a partitioned index on the parent table with parallel, you could not create the child table with REF partitioning as it caused an ORA-0600. If you create the index without parallel, the child table with REF partitioning is created. To get around this issue, you can create the partitioned index on the parent table after creating the child table with the REF partitioning.

The following example shows how to do this. Note the PARTITION BY REFERENCE in the second table creation (which references the primary key in the first table).

```
CREATE TABLE orders
( order_id       NUMBER(12)    CONSTRAINT orders_order_id_nn    NOT NULL,
  order_date     DATE          CONSTRAINT orders_order_date_nn  NOT NULL,
  order_mode     VARCHAR2(8),
  customer_id    NUMBER(6)     CONSTRAINT orders_customer_id_nn NOT NULL,
  order_status   VARCHAR2(2),
  order_total    NUMBER(8,2),
  sales_rep_id   NUMBER(6),
  promotion_id   NUMBER(6),
 CONSTRAINT orders_order_id_pk PRIMARY KEY (order_id))
PARTITION BY RANGE (order_date)
( PARTITION p_pre_1999 VALUES LESS THAN
(TO_DATE('01-JAN-1999','dd-MON-yyyy')),
  PARTITION p_JAN_1999 VALUES LESS THAN
(TO_DATE('01-FEB-1999','dd-MON-yyyy')),
  PARTITION p_FEB_1999 VALUES LESS THAN
(TO_DATE('01-MAR-1999','dd-MON-yyyy')),
  PARTITION p_MAR_1999 VALUES LESS THAN
(TO_DATE('01-APR-1999','dd-MON-yyyy')),
  PARTITION p_APR_1999 VALUES LESS THAN
(TO_DATE('01-MAY-1999','dd-MON-yyyy')),
  PARTITION p_MAY_1999 VALUES LESS THAN
```

```
(TO_DATE('01-JUN-1999','dd-MON-yyyy')),
   PARTITION p_JUN_1999 VALUES LESS THAN
(TO_DATE('01-JUL-1999','dd-MON-yyyy')),
   PARTITION p_JUL_1999 VALUES LESS THAN
(TO_DATE('01-AUG-1999','dd-MON-yyyy')),
   PARTITION p_AUG_1999 VALUES LESS THAN
(TO_DATE('01-SEP-1999','dd-MON-yyyy')),
   PARTITION p_SEP_1999 VALUES LESS THAN
(TO_DATE('01-OCT-1999','dd-MON-yyyy')),
   PARTITION p_OCT_1999 VALUES LESS THAN
(TO_DATE('01-NOV-1999','dd-MON-yyyy')),
   PARTITION p_NOV_1999 VALUES LESS THAN
(TO_DATE('01-DEC-1999','dd-MON-yyyy')),
   PARTITION p_DEC_1999 VALUES LESS THAN
(TO_DATE('01-JAN-2000','dd-MON-yyyy')),
   PARTITION p_JAN_2000 VALUES LESS THAN
(TO_DATE('01-FEB-2000','dd-MON-yyyy')),
   PARTITION p_FEB_2000 VALUES LESS THAN
(TO_DATE('01-MAR-2000','dd-MON-yyyy')),
   PARTITION p_MAR_2000 VALUES LESS THAN
(TO_DATE('01-APR-2000','dd-MON-yyyy')),
   PARTITION p_APR_2000 VALUES LESS THAN
(TO_DATE('01-MAY-2000','dd-MON-yyyy')),
   PARTITION p_MAY_2000 VALUES LESS THAN
(TO_DATE('01-JUN-2000','dd-MON-yyyy')),
   PARTITION p_JUN_2000 VALUES LESS THAN
(TO_DATE('01-JUL-2000','dd-MON-yyyy')),
   PARTITION p_JUL_2000 VALUES LESS THAN
(TO_DATE('01-AUG-2000','dd-MON-yyyy')),
   PARTITION p_AUG_2000 VALUES LESS THAN
(TO_DATE('01-SEP-2000','dd-MON-yyyy')),
   PARTITION p_SEP_2000 VALUES LESS THAN
(TO_DATE('01-OCT-2000','dd-MON-yyyy')),
   PARTITION p_OCT_2000 VALUES LESS THAN
(TO_DATE('01-NOV-2000','dd-MON-yyyy')),
   PARTITION p_NOV_2000 VALUES LESS THAN
(TO_DATE('01-DEC-2000','dd-MON-yyyy')),
   PARTITION p_DEC_2000 VALUES LESS THAN
(TO_DATE('01-JAN-2001','dd-MON-yyyy')))
PARALLEL ;

CREATE TABLE order_items
( order_id     NUMBER(12)   CONSTRAINT oitems_order_id_nn     NOT NULL,
  line_item_id NUMBER(3)    CONSTRAINT oitems_line_item_id_nn NOT NULL,
  product_id   NUMBER(6)    CONSTRAINT oitems_product_id_nn   NOT NULL,
  unit_price   NUMBER(8)    CONSTRAINT oitems_unit_price_nn   NOT NULL,
  quantity     NUMBER(8,2)  CONSTRAINT oitems_quantity_nn     NOT NULL,
  sales_amount NUMBER(12,2) CONSTRAINT oitems_sales_amount_nn NOT NULL,
  CONSTRAINT order_items_orders_fk
  FOREIGN KEY (order_id) REFERENCES orders(order_id))
```

```
PARTITION BY REFERENCE (order_items_orders_fk)
PARALLEL ;
```

System Partitioning

Oracle introduces the system partitioning option to allow manual control of which partitions of a table the rows will reside in. This provides an additional option that allows *full* control of which partitions the data will reside in. Creating a local index partitions the index with the table automatically. When inserting data, you have to tell Oracle *exactly* what partition you want to use. If you don't specify a partition, you receive an error (ORA-14701: partition-extended name or bind variable must be used for DMLs on tables partitioned by the System method).

While updating or deleting the data stored in the partitions, you *do not* have to provide the partition-aware syntax—but remember, there is no concept of partition boundaries. So when you issue a statement, Oracle has to scan all the partitions to see where the row resides unless you provide the partition using partition-aware syntax. A big mess results if you are not careful! Examples of creating, inserting, delete, and creating an index follow.

```
create table sales
(sales_id number,
product_code number,
state_code number)
partition by system
( partition p1 tablespace users,
  partition p2 tablespace users);

create index in_sales_state on sales (state_code) local;
insert into sales partition (p1) values (1,101,1);
delete sales partition (p1) where state_code = 1;
```

Virtual Column-based Partitioning

Oracle Database 11*g* introduces virtual column-based partitioning. This feature is very powerful as it extends partitioning past physical columns that exist in the table. The virtual column looks just like a regular column and allows you to base the partition keys on an expression using one or more physical columns of the table, thus storing the new virtual column information as metadata and making a "virtual column." For instance, if you have a table with MONTHLY_SALARY, you could add a virtual column that multiplies that column by 12 (for yearly salary); the actual data is not stored for the virtual column (a physical index can be created though—it's a function-based index). Additionally, virtual column-based partitioning supports all basic partitioning strategies; therefore, the virtual columns can partition using range, list, and hash partitioning.

In the following example, for all account numbers, the first two numbers represent the bank's branch. Let's say I want to partition based on the branch. With virtual column-based partitioning that is not only possible but also easy to do.

```
CREATE TABLE accounts
 (acc_no     number(10)    not null,
  acc_name   varchar2(50)  not null,
```

```
acc_branch number(2) generated always as
(to_number(substr(to_char(acc_no),1,2))))
partition by list (acc_branch)
  (partition main_branch values (1),
   partition NY_branch values(2),
   partition chicago_branch values (4),
   partition miami_branch values (11));
```

Partition Advisor

Oracle Database 11g provides the Partition Advisor as part of the SQL Access Advisor. The Oracle 11g Partition Advisor generates partitioning recommendations. The Partition Advisor assists by generating recommendations that show the expected performance gains resulting from implementing partitioning recommendations. It also generates a script for implementing the partitioning recommendations. The script can then be manually executed using SQL*Plus or Oracle Enterprise Manager (Oracle Enterprise Manager is covered in Chapter 5).

Read-Only Tables

Prior to Oracle Database 11g, you could make an entire tablespace read-only, which meant you had to group all the tables that you wanted to be read-only into a common tablespace or set of tablespaces, or you had to create a trigger that would cause an error, preventing data from being inserted. Oracle Database 11g now allows you to make a single table read-only without affecting the other tables in the tablespace, which helps save the overhead of having to move tables to read-only tablespaces when you are ready to make the table read-only. Not only can you modify the table to be read-only, but also you can change it back to read-write to allow inserts and updates when needed. The read-only designation for a table will stop all DML (truncate/insert/update/delete/etc.) operations and *certain* DDL operations as well, such as ALTER TABLE to add/modify/rename/drop columns, ALTER TABLE drop/truncate/exchange (SUB)PARTITION, ALTER TABLE upgrade (see the Oracle docs for all restrictions). Some DDL operations can still be performed on a table designated read-only, such as DROP TABLE, ALTER TABLE add/coalesce/merge/modify/move/rename/split (SUB)PARTITION, ALTER TABLE rename/move/add supplemental log/drop supplemental log/deallocate unused.

To identify if a table is read-only, a new column called READ_ONLY has been added to DBA_TABLES, USER_TABLES, and ALL_TABLES. This column is set to YES if the table is read-only and NO when the table is not read-only. Unfortunately, at this time, Oracle does not allow you just to take a table partition and make it read-only. To make a table partition read-only, the partition must be moved to a tablespace that can be marked read-only.

To put a table into read-only:

```
alter table big_emp2 read only ;
```

To take a table out of read-only:

```
alter table big_emp2 read write ;
```

Real Application Clusters (RAC) One Node and RAC Patching

RAC One Node represents an Oracle RAC database that runs only one active Oracle database and can be managed using Server Control Utility (SVRCTL) as any Oracle RAC database. You can add nodes that can be used for failover, but you cannot add additional *instances* without first converting Oracle RAC One Node to Oracle RAC. You can convert from single instance to RAC One Node or RAC using Oracle's Database Configuration Assistant (DBCA) at any time. The RAC One Node database can give you the High-Availability (HA) benefits of failover protection. Oracle uses Online Database Relocation using SVRCTL, which you can use to perform a live migration of database instances and connections to the other available cluster nodes. Please see the documentation for full details and use. Another benefit is if a node becomes overloaded, you can move the database to another node in the cluster using the simple relocation command listed here (rac10 is the unique name for this database and node17 is the target node; see documentation before using this and ensure you test things fully):

```
srvctl relocate database -d rac10 -n node17
```

Consider a RAC One Node use case. Let's say you're consolidating many small to medium databases into a smaller number (N) of servers. While these databases may be mission-critical, they are small and can comfortably run on a single node. So they don't need the scalability of RAC, but they do need the High Availability (HA) and flexibility that RAC provides. You can create a cluster of N or N+1 servers. You then create as many single-node RAC databases on the servers as you need (in this case, N of them). You can also use the new 11.2 instance caging, which limits the number of cores that each database can utilize on a server. Here are some use cases for RAC One Node:

- **Failover**   If a server fails, use cluster failover to switch to an idle server in the cluster (your N+1 server or one of the extra ones). This server is like a spare disk, but instead, it's a spare node.

- **Live migration**   If a server needs maintenance, temporarily add a second node to the RAC database during the high-use timeframe. While the application is live, move the users via standard load balancing to the second node. Then shut down (transactional) the first node to move over the remaining users. Do your maintenance, and then perform the same procedure in reverse to move the users back to the first node if desired.

- **Rolling upgrade**   If you want to upgrade your database software, temporarily add a second node to the RAC cluster that already has the new version of the database software. Then move users to the second node using live migration and upgrade the first node using RAC rolling upgrade. Move users back to first node if desired.

- **Scale out**   If your database load grows beyond one server, add a node and run full RAC (of course, then and only then, you must license RAC).

On the application side, the 11gR2 release has a new feature called *Edition-based Redefinition*. This is a huge feature that allows developers to implement online upgrades for their applications (think Siebel 8.0 to 8.1 upgrade). Oracle uses private *editions* (for the developers) of the application, which can be published when developers are fully ready. See the documentation for more information on these features, but for availability, they are both huge!

Lastly, Oracle Database 11gR2 Real Application Clusters has been improved to offer zero downtime patching. The patching of Oracle Clusterware and Oracle Real Application Clusters can now be accomplished without taking the cluster down. This improvement is huge for overall database availability and offering further capability for keeping critical database environments up to date.

Real Application Testing

Real Application Testing (using Database Capture/Replay) is an optional feature introduced with Oracle Database 11g, which offers the most promise in change, release, and performance management. Real Application Testing allows a DBA to utilize real workloads to judge the impact of application changes or new releases on a database environment. This feature does such a thorough job of predicting the impact of environment, OS, application, and database changes that the days of system changes triggering a surprise impact on performance due to unexpected errors, software bugs, or upgrades could be behind us.

Database Replay

Oracle Database 11g has introduced probably the most significant enhancement of any database vendor to date with Database Replay (this is covered in detail in Chapter 9, complete with examples). This feature will do more to ensure stability, availability, and scalability than any other tool. Database Replay captures an actual database workload from a production database. It then allows you to take that workload to a test system and replay it exactly as it occurred on the production system (allows synchronized—where the timing of statements is exactly at the same time as the original and preserves the commit order—or unsynchronized and compresses operations where possible; see the docs for all variables). It also allows application changes and upgrades, as well as database changes and upgrades, significantly reducing application upgrade performance issues, database upgrade performance issues, and application/database error testing.

Database Replay captures database requests made by external clients and stores them in *capture files*. Capture files are binary files stored on a local filesystem in a user-specified location using an Oracle Database directory. An important point to note is that a workload from an Oracle database prior to 11g is possible (as early as 9.2 as of this writing); see Oracle My Oracle Support Note: 560977.1 for further details. Keep in mind the following are unsupported workloads at the current time: direct path load, import/export, OCI-based object navigation (ADTs) and REF binds, streams, non-PL/SQL-based AQ, distributed transactions, remote describe/commit operations, Flashback, and Shared Server. After you complete the capture, the "capture files" can be moved to a test system and *prepared* to be replayed. Preparing the "capture files," known as *processing the workload*, transforms captured workload files into Replay files. It creates the necessary metadata for Replay and only needs to be done once for each captured workload. Because this process can be resource-intensive, Oracle recommends not processing the workload on a production system. When processing a workload, ensure that the workload processing is done on the exact same version of the database where the replay will need to occur. See Chapter 9 for a complete example, and see Chapter 5 for options to run this within Oracle Enterprise Manager.

SQL Performance Analyzer (SPA)

Oracle 11g SQL Performance Analyzer (SPA) is great for looking at the impact of changes on SQL execution plans and SQL execution statistics. This is covered in detail in Chapter 9, and in Chapter 5 for use with Enterprise Manager. Using SPA, Oracle examines the SQL before and after a change and then it shows a comparison and generates a report detailing the improvements, generating a list of improved/degraded SQL as well as the SQL execution plans with recommendations for improving the degraded SQL. SPA helps reduce the time spent identifying SQL regression due to a change by allowing a SQL workload to be captured and analyzed prior to a change and then executing that same SQL after the change by automating the SQL capture, SQL execution, and the comparison for identifying the degraded SQL. SPA is well integrated with SQL Tuning Advisor and SQL Plan Management (also covered for Enterprise Manager in Chapter 5) features where SQL Plan baselines and SQL Tuning Advisor can be utilized to address degraded SQL. This new feature is great for measuring the impact of database initialization parameter changes, database patches, database upgrades, as well as OS and hardware changes on a set of SQL statements.

The basic steps are to capture a SQL workload into a SQL Tuning Set. You can create the SQL Tuning Set in a number of ways—from the cursor cache, the Automatic Workload Repository (AWR), existing SQL Tuning Sets, or custom SQL provided by a user or DBA. You can also capture a SQL workload via what is called an *incremental capture*. The incremental capture polls the cursor cache over a period of time and updates the workload data in a SQL Tuning Set. The time period is configurable for as long a period as you want the polling to occur. The incremental capture collects data during the specified period and only for SQL statements that meet certain criteria, such as user, service, action, module, and so on. Oracle indicates that the overhead for this incremental capture is less than 1 percent; therefore, the use of the incremental capture should not have a significant negative affect on the overall database performance. Lastly, with SQL Performance Analyzer, the SQL Tuning Sets are transportable across databases. Therefore, a SQL Tuning Set can be captured in your production database, exported, and then imported into a test database for diagnostic tuning. See Chapters 5 and 9 for in-depth examples.

Result Cache

Oracle Database11g provides a new, separate shared memory pool to store query results. This *Result Cache* is allocated directly from the shared pool but is maintained separately. This is a great new feature for performance improvement and tuning. The Result Cache allows a query's result (for example, a sum of all salaries after being calculated) to be cached in memory, allowing for significant performance improvements for future queries that are executed multiple times and require the same results. The Result Cache works best for tables with mostly static data (if the data changes, it has to be recalculated); that is, the Result Cache works well for queries executed that return the same results over and over (great for data warehouses and batch queries). There is also a RESULT_CACHE hint to force its use (an example is shown here); see Chapter 7 for additional information. The first query computes the sum of all salaries grouped by department; the second query checks to see what's stored in the Result Cache:

```
select /*+ result_cache */ deptno, sum(sal)
from   scott.emp
group  by deptno;
```

```
select *
from    v$result_cache_memory;
```

Note that the Result Cache does not work when you are logged in as sysdba.

RMAN New Features

RMAN has several new features. Although RMAN has only a little to do with tuning (faster RMAN is great—means more time for everything else), here are just a few new features you may want to investigate.

Optimized Backups

Backup optimization is improved with Undo Optimization. Now RMAN no longer backs up the undo tablespace that is not needed for recovery (which is faster). As the majority of the undo tablespace is filled with undo data generated for transactions that have subsequently been committed, this can represent a substantial savings. This functionality is not configurable and, therefore, not affected by the CONFIGURE BACKUP OPTIMIZATION {ON | OFF} command.

Improved Handling of Long-term Backups

In Oracle Database 11g, RMAN now has the ability to mark a backup for long-term retention (which overrides the default retention policy). Using the KEEP option with the RMAN BACKUP command creates an all-inclusive backup much like an archive backup; see the brief syntax examples here:

```
RMAN> BACKUP DATABASE KEEP UNTIL TIME "TO_DATE('31-DEC-2018','dd-mon-yyyy')" NOLOGS;

RMAN> BACKUP TABLESPACE users KEEP FOREVER NOLOGS;
(note that RMAN catalog needs to be used with KEEP FOREVER)
```

Parallel Backup of Very Large Datafiles

Prior to Oracle Database 11g, RMAN parallelized the backup by allocating more than one channel so that each channel became a RMAN session; however, each channel could only back up one datafile at a time. This meant that even though there were several channels, each datafile was backed up by only one channel. In Oracle Database 11g RMAN, the allocated channels can break a datafile into chunks also called *sections*. You can indicate the size of each section:

```
RMAN> run {
2>        allocate channel c1 type disk format '/backup1/%U';
3>        allocate channel c2 type disk format '/backup2/%U';
4>        backup
5>        section size 50m
6>        datafile 4;
7> }
```

This RMAN command allocates two channels and backs up the datafile assigned the ID number 4 using two channels in parallel. Each channel takes a 50MB section of the datafile and backs that up in parallel. This makes backing up larger files faster. When backed up this way, the backups show up as sections as well.

Here's an example of the datafile 4 backup in sections:

```
RMAN> list backup of datafile 4;

    List of Backup Pieces for backup set 901 Copy #1
    BP Key   Pc#  Status      Piece Name
    ----     ---  ------      ----------
    2007      1   AVAILABLE   /backup1/9dhk7os1_1_1
    2008      2   AVAILABLE   /backup2/9dhk7os1_1_1
    2009      3   AVAILABLE   /backup1/9dhk7os1_1_3
    2009      3   AVAILABLE   /backup2/9dhk7os1_1_4
```

Faster Backup Compression (Improved Compression)

In Oracle Database 10g, RMAN compressed backups to conserve network bandwidth. Third-party compression utilities provided faster alternatives to RMAN's own, but RMAN's 10g compression provided some features that the third-party ones did not. For example, when RMAN 10g restored datafiles, it did not need to uncompress the files first. This approach offered significant bandwidth savings during restores. In Oracle Database 11g, RMAN offers another algorithm, ZLIB, in addition to the previously available BZIP2. ZLIB is a much faster algorithm, but it does not compress as much. However, it does not consume nearly as much CPU. Therefore, if you need to reduce CPU consumption, ZLIB compression offers you some compression at a lower CPU cost.

NOTE
BZIP2 is the default in version 11.1.x; if you want to use the new ZLIB compression, you will need to license a new option called Advanced Compression Option.

To use ZLIB compression, just set the RMAN configuration parameter:

```
RMAN> configure compression algorithm 'ZLIB' ;
```

To change it to BZIP2:

```
RMAN> configure compression algorithm 'bzip2';
```

Active Database Duplication

Oracle Database 11g has added a great capability to duplicate a database without using or having to use an existing RMAN backup or manual file copy. Those who do not use RMAN for their backups now have the ability to utilize the RMAN duplicate functionality for creating standby databases, a test environment, or development environment without first having to create a RMAN backup. This feature utilizes the network and is also referred to as a Network-enabled Database Duplication or Active database duplication.

The RMAN active database duplication automatically performs the following:

- Copies the spfile to the destination server.

- Starts the auxiliary instance with the SPFILE.

- Copies relevant database files and archived redo logs over the network to the destination server.

- Recovers the database.

- Opens the database with the RESETLOGS option.

```
RMAN> duplicate target database to newdb
2>      from active database
3>      db_file_name_convert '/nf/','/duptest/'
4>      spfile
5>      parameter_value_convert '/db/','/newdb/'
6>      set log_file_name_convert '/db/','/newdb/' ;
```

Better Recovery Catalog Management

In Oracle Database 11g, RMAN has been improved to allow better catalog management. You can now move a catalog to another database or merge catalogs via the import catalog functionality.

To move a catalog to another catalog/database:

```
$ sqlplus / as sysdba
SQL> CREATE USER rman2 IDENTIFIED BY rman2 QUOTA UNLIMITED ON rman_ts;
SQL> GRANT RECOVERY_CATALOG_OWNER TO rman2;
SQL> EXIT;
$ rman catalog=rman2/rman2
RMAN> CREATE CATALOG;
RMAN> IMPORT CATALOG rmandb11g;
```

To merge a database catalog data from another catalog (two separate examples are shown here):

```
RMAN> IMPORT CATALOG rman@db11g DBID=1423241 ;
RMAN> IMPORT CATALOG rman@db11g DB_NAME=prod3 ;
```

Archived Log Deletion Policy Enhancements

Oracle Database 11g has improved RMAN's ability to manage archive logs through improved archive log deletion policies. The policy improvements are to improve the flexibility and protection for Data Guard (standby) environments. Consider the following options with Oracle 10g/11g:

In Oracle 10g:

```
CONFIGURE ARCHIVELOG DELETION POLICY {CLEAR | TO {APPLIED ON STANDBY | NONE}}
```

In Oracle 11g:

```
CONFIGURE ARCHIVELOG DELETION POLICY {CLEAR | TO {APPLIED ON [ALL] STANDBY |
    BACKED UP integer TIMES TO DEVICE TYPE deviceSpecifier | NONE | SHIPPED TO [ALL]
    STANDBY} [ {APPLIED ON [ALL] STANDBY | BACKED UP integer TIMES TO DEVICE TYPE
    deviceSpecifier | NONE | SHIPPED TO [ALL] STANDBY}]...}
```

Also, in Oracle Database 11.1 RMAN archivelog deletion has been improved to ensure that archive logs are deleted only when not needed by required components (for example, Data Guard, Streams, and Flashback).

Data Recovery Advisor

The *Data Recovery Advisor* helps simplify recoveries and allows the DBA to check failures, obtain additional details and repair advice, as well as execute the advised repair. The Data Recovery Advisor has two flavors: command line and Oracle Enterprise Manager Database Control. The Data Recovery Advisor simplifies the diagnosis, analysis, and recovery steps for a database failure that requires media recovery via RMAN. Keep in mind, however, if you are not using RMAN for your backups, this feature will not be available to you.

The Data Recovery Advisor command-line utility is used via the RMAN command line. When a situation is encountered that requires a recovery operation, you can list the failure (LIST FAILURE), list the failure detail (LIST FAILURE *<failure id>* DETAIL), get advice on the failure, preview the failure repair action (REPAIR FAILURE PREVIEW), and then actually perform the data repair (REPAIR FAILURE). Consider the following error on startup and ability of RMAN with these new enhancements.

```
ORACLE instance started.

Total System Global Area    535662592 bytes
Fixed Size                    1334380 bytes
Variable Size               209716116 bytes
Database Buffers            318767104 bytes
Redo Buffers                  5844992 bytes
Database mounted.
ORA-01157: cannot identify/lock data file 4 - see DBWR trace file
ORA-01110: data file 4: 'C:\ORACLE\ORADATA\ORCL11G\USERS01.DBF'

RMAN> list failure ;
using target database control file instead of recovery catalog
List of Database Failures
=========================

Failure ID Priority Status    Time Detected Summary
---------- -------- --------- ------------- -------
222        HIGH     OPEN      27-NOV-10     One or more non-system datafiles are
 missing
```

```
RMAN> list failure 222 detail ;
List of Database Failures
=========================


Failure ID Priority Status    Time Detected Summary
---------- -------- --------- ------------- -------
222        HIGH     OPEN      27-NOV-10     One or more non-system datafiles are
 missing
  Impact: See impact for individual child failures
  List of child failures for parent failure ID 222
  Failure ID Priority Status    Time Detected Summary
  ---------- -------- --------- ------------- -------
   225       HIGH     OPEN      27-NOV-10     Datafile 4: 'C:\ORACLE\ORADATA\ORC
L11G\USERS01.DBF' is missing
     Impact: Some objects in tablespace USERS might be unavailable

RMAN> advise failure ;
List of Database Failures
=========================


Failure ID Priority Status    Time Detected Summary
---------- -------- --------- ------------- -------
222        HIGH     OPEN      27-NOV-10     One or more non-system datafiles are
 missing
  Impact: See impact for individual child failures
  List of child failures for parent failure ID 222

  Failure ID Priority Status    Time Detected Summary
  ---------- -------- --------- ------------- -------
   225       HIGH     OPEN      27-NOV-10     Datafile 4: 'C:\ORACLE\ORADATA\ORC
L11G\USERS01.DBF' is missing
     Impact: Some objects in tablespace USERS might be unavailable

analyzing automatic repair options; this may take some time
allocated channel: ORA_DISK_1
channel ORA_DISK_1: SID=152 device type=DISK
analyzing automatic repair options complete

Mandatory Manual Actions
========================
no manual actions available

Optional Manual Actions
========================
1. If file C:\ORACLE\ORADATA\ORCL11G\USERS01.DBF was unintentionally renamed or moved, restore
it

Automated Repair Options
========================
Option Repair Description
------ -------------------
1      Restore and recover datafile 4
  Strategy: The repair includes complete media recovery with no data loss
  Repair script: c:\oracle\diag\rdbms\orcl11g\orcl11g\hm\reco_1022222764.hm

RMAN> repair failure preview;
Strategy: The repair includes complete media recovery with no data loss
Repair script: c:\oracle\diag\rdbms\orcl11g\orcl11g\hm\reco_1022222764.hm

contents of repair script:
   # restore and recover datafile
   restore datafile 4;
   recover datafile 4;
```

```
RMAN> repair failure;
Strategy: The repair includes complete media recovery with no data loss
Repair script: c:\oracle\diag\rdbms\orcl11g\orcl11g\hm\reco_1022222764.hm

contents of repair script:
   # restore and recover datafile
   restore datafile 4;
   recover datafile 4;

Do you really want to execute the above repair (enter YES or NO)? YES
executing repair script

Starting restore at 27-NOV-10
using channel ORA_DISK_1

channel ORA_DISK_1: starting datafile backup set restore
channel ORA_DISK_1: specifying datafile(s) to restore from backup set
channel ORA_DISK_1: restoring datafile 00004 to C:\ORACLE\ORADATA\ORCL11G\USERS0
1.DBF
channel ORA_DISK_1: reading from backup piece C:\ORACLE\FLASH_RECOVERY_AREA\ORCL
11G\BACKUPSET\2010_11_27\O1_MF_NNNDF_TAG20101127T144712_3NRX264W_.BKP
channel ORA_DISK_1: piece handle=C:\ORACLE\FLASH_RECOVERY_AREA\ORCL11G\BACKUPSET
\2010_11_27\O1_MF_NNNDF_TAG20101127T144712_3NRX264W_.BKP tag=TAG20101127T144712
channel ORA_DISK_1: restored backup piece 1
channel ORA_DISK_1: restore complete, elapsed time: 00:00:25
Finished restore at 27-NOV-10

Starting recover at 27-NOV-10
using channel ORA_DISK_1

starting media recovery
media recovery complete, elapsed time: 00:00:01

Finished recover at 27-NOV-10
repair failure complete
```

Virtual Private Catalog

Oracle Database 11g adds improved security for the RMAN catalog by enabling multiple
"virtual" catalogs within the main RMAN catalog by allowing the owner of the main catalog to
grant access on individual databases to other users. This allows the separation of databases or
groups of databases within the RMAN catalog. Setting up and using a virtual private catalog is
fairly simple and straightforward, as outlined here:

```
SQL> CREATE USER vpc1 IDENTIFIED BY vpc_a QUOTA UNLIMITED ON users; SQL> GRANT
   RECOVERY_CATALOG_OWNER TO vpc1 ;
```

To grant access on the relevant databases to the virtual private catalog user on RMAN:

```
$ rman
RMAN> CONNECT CATALOG rman/rman@rman ;
RMAN> GRANT CATALOG FOR DATABASE db11g TO vpc1;
Grant succeeded.
```

To log into RMAN using the virtual private catalog owner and issue the CREATE VIRTUAL CATALOG command:

```
$ rman
RMAN> CONNECT CATALOG vpc1/vpc_a@rman ;
RMAN> CREATE VIRTUAL CATALOG;
```

If the catalog is going to be used for a database release prior to Oracle Database 11g, connect to the recovery catalog database as the virtual catalog owner using SQL*Plus and execute the CREATE_VIRTUAL_CATALOG procedure in the DBMS_RCVCAT package where <rman> represents the name of the base catalog owner in the RMAN database:

```
SQL> CONN vpc1/vpc_a@rman
SQL> EXEC rman.DBMS_RCVCAT.CREATE_VIRTUAL_CATALOG;
```

You can connect to the virtual private catalog using the virtual private catalog owner instead of the main catalog owner (use RMAN normally as you would a RMAN catalog):

From RMAN:

```
RMAN> CONNECT CATALOG vpc1/vpc_a@rman ;
```

From the O/S:

```
$ rman target / catalog vpc1/vpc_a@rman
```

Proactive Health Check

Oracle Database 11g enhances RMAN and provides the ability to check your database proactively for corrupt blocks. The check can be performed for the entire database, a tablespace, or a specific datafile or a specific block of a datafile. The DBA then has the capability to check the database periodically for corruption through a scheduled process, or to check a part of the database for corruption when he or she suspects corruption might exist. The health check reports the number of blocks examined, the number of empty blocks, and the number of corrupt blocks on a per datafile basis:

```
RMAN> validate database ;
RMAN> validate tablespace users ;
RMAN> validate datafile 4 block 1 ;
```

Here's some example output:

```
Starting validate at 27-NOV-10
using target database control file instead of recovery catalog
allocated channel: ORA_DISK_1
channel ORA_DISK_1: SID=128 device type=DISK
channel ORA_DISK_1: starting validation of datafile
channel ORA_DISK_1: specifying datafile(s) for validation
input datafile file number=00004 name=C:\ORACLE\ORADATA\ORCL11G\USERS01.DBF
channel ORA_DISK_1: validation complete, elapsed time: 00:00:15
```

```
List of Datafiles
=================
File Status Marked Corrupt Empty Blocks Blocks Examined High SCN
---- ------ -------------- ------------ --------------- ---------
4    OK     0                 51199         64000        13457224
   File Name: C:\ORACLE\ORADATA\ORCL11G\USERS01.DBF
   Block Type Blocks Failing Blocks Processed
   ---------- -------------- ----------------
   Data       0               12357
   Index      0               33
   Other      0               411

Finished validate at 27-NOV-10
```

Block Recovery (Flashback Logs)

Flashback Logging, which was introduced in Oracle 10g, records the before-images of changed blocks into Flashback logs that are generated in the Fast Recovery Area (FRA) when Flashback is enabled in the database. The logs help you flash the database back to a previous point in time without having to do a point-in-time recovery from your backups.

Since the Flashback logs have the past images of the blocks, why can't you use them for block-level recovery as well? Oracle Database 11g allows exactly that. When you recover the specific block (or blocks), Oracle now looks in the Flashback logs to find a good copy of a past block image and then applies archived redo logs to roll the block forward. This saves you a lot of time since you no longer have to go to the backups, especially when the backups are on tape.

Block Recovery (Physical Standby)

Automatic Block Recovery has been enhanced to execute a block recovery using a physical standby database when a physical standby database is available.

SecureFiles

Oracle SecureFiles, also known as *Fast Files*, are Oracle's improvement to storage of large object (LOBs) types. SecureFiles offers comparable performance to a filesystem for LOBs, and LOBs can store many types of data from images, large amounts of text, Word documents, Excel spreadsheets, XML, HTML, as well as DICOM-formatted medical images.

SecureFiles is a step forward in helping manage unstructured data with the Oracle database by not only boosting performance but also improving security. SecureFiles extends Transparent Data Encryption to LOBs; this not only makes storing and managing unstructured content easier, but also improves the security of the unstructured content. SecureFiles also offers advanced filesystem features such as compression and data deduplication and is 100 percent backward compatible with LOB interfaces. Data deduplication is when duplicate objects in LOBs, tied to many records within the database, are stored only once rather than as a copy for each record. This not only increases storage space, but also offers performance improvements. Compression like this compresses LOB data transparently, offering storage savings and a potential performance boost. But Oracle has taken it a step further and automatically determines if the data is able to be compressed and, if so, if the space savings from the compression are beneficial.

By default, normal LOB storage, called BASIC file, is used. To employ SecureFile for LOB storage, the SECUREFILE LOB storage keyword must be used. The default behavior for SecureFile usage can be changed via the DB_SECUREFILE initialization parameter:

```
db_securefile={ALWAYS | FORCE | PERMITTED | NEVER | IGNORE}

ALWAYS - Always attempts to create all LOBs as SECUREFILE LOBs
FORCE - all LOBs created in the system will be created as SECUREFILE LOBs.
PERMITTED - Allows LOBs to be created as SecureFiles.
NEVER - Never Allows LOBs that use SecureFiles, they will always be BASICFILE LOBs
IGNORE - Ignore errors that otherwise would be raised by forcing LOBs as SECUREFILE
LOBs and causes the SECUREFILE keyword and all SecureFile options to be ignored
(careful!).
```

This parameter can also be set dynamically via an ALTER SYSTEM command:

```
SQL> ALTER SYSTEM SET db_securefile = 'ALWAYS' ;
```

SecureFiles offers many benefits over the old LOB storage method, such as deduplication capability, compression, and encryption.

Compression

Compression has two forms: *medium,* which is the default, and *high.* Keep in mind this high level of compression has a larger resource impact on the database.

```
CREATE TABLE t1 ( a CLOB)
    LOB(a) STORE AS SECUREFILE (
        COMPRESS
        CACHE
        NOLOGGING);

CREATE TABLE t1 ( a CLOB)
    LOB(a) STORE AS SECUREFILE (
        COMPRESS HIGH
        CACHE
        NOLOGGING);
```

Encryption

Encryption for SecureFiles is implemented via Transparent Data Encryption (TDE), and SecureFiles extends that TDE for LOB data types. Encryption is performed at the block level and uses the following valid encryption levels: 2DES168, AES128, AES192 (default), and AES256. Keep in mind that for SecureFiles the NO SALT option is not supported.

```
CREATE TABLE t1 ( a CLOB ENCRYPT USING 'AES128')
LOB(a) STORE AS SECUREFILE (
        CACHE);
```

Deduplication

Deduplication can be a powerful feature that can reduce the amount of storage space needed for LOBs, as all duplicated LOBs are only stored once. If you need to reduce database disk space, SecureFiles compression and deduplication can provide significant cost savings for storage.

```
CREATE TABLE t1 ( REGION VARCHAR2(20), ID NUMBER, a BLOB)
     LOB(a) STORE AS SECUREFILE (
          DEDUPLICATE
          CACHE);

CREATE TABLE t1 ( a CLOB)
     LOB(a) STORE AS SECUREFILE (
        COMPRESS HIGH
        DEDUPLICATE
        CACHE);
```

Oracle SecureFiles utilizes memory in the form of a shared IO pool. The shared IO pool is used from the SGA and allocations are always for a specific session; therefore, the data is specific to the session. You can view the shared IO pool by querying both the V$SGAINFO and the V$SGA_DYNAMIC_COMPONENTS V$ views (see Chapter 12 for detailed V$ view information). If you examine the memory structures of the SGA, you can see what the shared IO pool max size is in relationship to the other database memory structures:

```
select name, bytes
from    v$sgainfo ;

NAME                                    BYTES
------------------------------- ----------
Fixed SGA Size                        1334380
Redo Buffers                          5844992
Buffer Cache Size                   268435456
Shared Pool Size                    239075328
Large Pool Size                       4194304
Java Pool Size                       12582912
Streams Pool Size                     4194304
Shared IO Pool Size                         0
Granule Size                          4194304
Maximum SGA Size                    535662592
Startup overhead in Shared Pool      46137344
Free SGA Memory Available                   0

select *
from    v$sga_dynamic_components
where   component='Shared IO Pool';
```

```
COMPONENT                                                        CURRENT_SIZE
-------------------------------------------------------------- ------------
 MIN_SIZE   MAX_SIZE USER_SPECIFIED_SIZE OPER_COUNT LAST_OPER_TYP LAST_OPER
---------- ---------- ------------------- ---------- ------------- ---------
LAST_OPER GRANULE_SIZE
--------- ------------
Shared IO Pool                                                            0
         0          0                              0          0 STATIC
                 4194304
```

When a session is unable to find free memory in the shared IO pool, PGA memory is used. To see PGA memory allocations, you can use the V$SECUREFILE_TIMER view, which receives an entry each time memory is allocated out of the PGA:

```
select *
from    v$securefile_timer
where   name like '%PGA%';

NAME                          LAYER_ID  OWNTIME MAXTIME MINTIME INVOCATIONS
LAYER_NAME
----------------------------- ---------- ------- ------- ------- -----------
-------------------------------------------------
kdlw kcbi PGA alloc timer  2          0       0       0       0
Write gather cache
kdlw kcbi PGA free timer   2          0       0       0       0
Write gather cache
kdlw kcb PGA borrow timer  2          0       0       0       0
Write gather cache
kdlw kcb PGA free timer    2          0       0       0       0
Write gather cache
```

Enhancements to Streams (Golden Gate Is the Future of Streams)

Oracle Database 11*g* R2 introduces Oracle Extended Streams (XStreams), which supplies an API for applications to be able to send and receive data changes between an Oracle database and a non-Oracle data source. This allows the sharing of data and data changes between Oracle and non-Oracle-based applications. XStreams supports all the same data types and capabilities of Oracle Streams, making it effective for the data sharing process. Oracle XStream contains two main components for handling the data sent and received between Oracle and non-Oracle-based applications: XStream In and XStream Out.

XStream In

The primary purpose of Extended Streams Inbound (XStream In) is to provide a high-performance, transaction-based interface to Oracle Streams for non-Oracle client applications. It allows non-Oracle clients to send data to Oracle, acting as an information exchange from non-Oracle databases or filesystems using an OCI or Java interface.

XStream Out

The primary purpose of Extended Streams Outbound (XStream Out) is to extract transactions from the Oracle database redo logs and send them to a non-Oracle client applications, using an OCI or Java interface, which acts as the interface to the non-Oracle data source.

Advanced Compression Support for Streams (I IgR2)

Oracle Database 11*g* R1 introduced advanced compression, however, advanced compression could not be utilized for objects that were subject to Streams or a logical standby database. With 11*g*R2, advanced compression is supported and works with Streams and a logical standby database.

Shrink Temporary Tablespace

Oracle Database 11*g* adds the ability to *shrink* the locally managed temporary tablespace. This eliminates the need to *rebuild* temporary tablespaces to reduce a temporary tablespace where the size has grown too large.

The following example will shrink the temporary tablespace to 20M:

```
ALTER TABLESPACE temp SHRINK SPACE KEEP 20M;
```

The following example shrinks the tempfile `temp01.dbf` temp tablespace. Due to the omission of the KEEP clause, the database will attempt to shrink the tempfile to the minimum possible size.

```
ALTER TABLESPACE temp SHRINK TEMPFILE 'c:\oracle\oradata\db\temp01.dbf';
```

Transparent Data Encryption (TDE) Improvements

Oracle Database 11*g* extends transparent data encryption (a part of the Oracle Advanced Security Option) to be able to encrypt by tablespace. This allows you to set transparent encryption for all objects and all columns of those objects for a specified tablespace. This simplifies encryption for a large number of tables and columns by allowing you to set encryption at a tablespace level rather than having to encrypt columns individually.

Oracle Database 11*g* also adds the Hardware-based Master Key Protection using the Hardware Security Module (HSM), which allows the Transparent Data Encryption (TDE) master key to be stored in an external HSM for even stronger security instead of using a wallet file. This feature is for customers who want even more security for the Transparent Data Encryption (TDE) master key and are concerned about storing the master key on the operating system in a wallet file.

```
SQL> CREATE TABLESPACE encrypted_ts
DATAFILE 'c:\oracle\oradata\DB\encrypted_ts01.dbf' SIZE 128K
ENCRYPTION USING 'AES256'
DEFAULT STORAGE(ENCRYPT);
```

New Background Processes in 11g

According to Oracle's documentation, 56 background processes were added in Oracle Database 11g. The following are the more important and noticeable new background processes as well as a process that has gotten an update:

- **ACMS** *The Atomic Control file to Memory Server process:* This Oracle RAC process ensures that SGA memory updates are applied to all nodes or to none.

- **DBRM** The Database Resource Manager process handles setting resource plans and other tasks related to the Database Resource Manager feature. It is responsible for the management and enforcement of resource plans.

- **DIA[0-9]** These processes are for hang detection and deadlock resolution.

- **DIAG** While this process is not exactly new, its responsibilities have changed a little. This diagnostic process was seen in RAC environments prior to 11g, and now in 11g, it manages the Automatic Diagnostic Repository (ADR) by monitoring the instance health and the capturing and processing of information on instance failures.

- **EMNC** The Event Monitor coordinator process handles database events and notifications. The Event Monitor launches automatically in response to the first issue of a notification for an instance.

- **FBDA** *The Flashback Data Archiver process:* This process manages the Flashback Data Archive by storing pre-images of rows for tracked tables and tracking the metadata for those rows in the Flashback Data Archive.

- **GTX[0-j]** The Global Transaction processes in an Oracle RAC environment handle XA global transactions. The number of these processes varies depending on the current workload.

- **KATE** This process performs a proxy I/O to an ASM metafile when an ASM disk goes offline.

- **MARK** This process marks, on a failed or missed write, ASM allocation units as stale.

- **PING** In a RAC environment, this process is focused on measuring interconnect latency; it accesses latencies for each pair of RAC clustered instances.

- **RCBG** *Result Cache BackGround process:* This process handles the management of the new query result cache.

- **SMCO** *Space Management COordinator:* This process handles the coordination as well as the execution of tasks related to space management. This process will start *Wnnn* processes to actually do the tasks.

- **VKTM** *Virtual Keeper of Time Management* process to keep track of wall clock time. This process is used as a time reference counter.

NOTE
The EMN0 background process has been removed in 11g as it appeared on the list of background processes for 10g and no longer appears on the process list for 11g.

Some important background processes that were new in Oracle 10*g* and are still worth mentioning:

- **ARB***x*   These processes are managed by the RBAL process and are used for the actual rebalancing of ASM-controlled disk resources (balances data extents within diskgroups). The number of ARBx processes invoked is directly influenced by the ASM_POWER_LIMIT parameter.

- **ASMB**   The ASMB process is used to provide information to and from the Cluster Synchronization Services used by ASM to manage the disk resources. It is also used to update statistics and provide a heartbeat mechanism.

- **CTWR**   *Change Tracking Writer* is a process that works with the block change tracking features in 10*g* for fast RMAN incremental backups.

- **M000**   These are MMON background slave (m000) processes.

- **MMNL**   *Manageability Monitor Light* is a process that works with the Automatic Workload Repository (AWR) features to write out full statistics buffers to disk as needed.

- **MMON**   *Memory Monitor process* is associated with the Automatic Workload Repository features used for automatic problem detection and self-tuning. Manageability Monitor Process (MMON) writes out the required statistics for AWR on a scheduled basis.

- **RBAL**   The *Rebalancing Daemon* is the ASM-related process that performs rebalancing of disk resources controlled by ASM.

- **RVWR**   *Recovery Writer* supports the Flashback database; this process is responsible for writing Flashback logs that store pre-image(s) of data blocks.

Version Comparison Chart

The following chart shows which components or options are available in the various editions of Oracle 11*g*. Note that a free version of Oracle called Oracle 11*g* Express Edition is also available; it has a 4GB database, 1 CPU, and 1GB of memory (subject to change). Please check with Oracle to verify *any* features as this is subject to change at any time. If you can afford it, you definitely want the Enterprise Edition! This chart shows features that are available for a given version of Oracle, but keep in mind, some cost extra to add (i.e., RAC, Oracle Tuning Pack, advanced compression … etc.). Consult with your salesperson for pricing and licensing and see http://www.oracle.com/us/products/database/index.html for the latest information.

Option or Feature	11g Standard Edition One	11g Standard Edition	11g Enterprise Edition	11g Express Edition
Advanced security	N	N	Y	N
Advanced compression	N	N	Y	N
Database Vault	N	N	Y	N
Change Mgt Pack	N	N	Y	N
Data mining	N	N	Y	N
Diagnostic Pack	N	N	Y	N
Label security	N	N	Y	N
Oracle OLAP	N	N	Y	N
Partitioning	N	N	Y	N
Oracle RAC	N	Y	Y	N
Oracle RAC One Node	N	N	Y	N
Oracle Spatial	N	N	Y	N
Real Application Testing	N	N	Y	N
Total Recall	N	N	Y	N
Active Data Guard	N	N	Y	N
In-Memory Database Cache	N	N	Y	N
Tuning Pack	N	N	Y	N
CM Pack	N	N	Y	N
DB Resource Manager	N	N	Y	N
VLDB, Data Warehousing, Business Intelligence				
Data compression	N	N	Y	N
OLTP compression (Advanced compression Option)	N	N	Y	N
Bitmapped index	N	N	Y	N
Export transp ts	N	N	Y	N
Import transp ts	Y	Y	Y	Y
Async change data capture	N	N	Y	N
Summary Management	N	N	Y	N
Analytic functions	Y	Y	Y	Y
Automated parallel query	N	N	Y	N
Descending indexes	Y	Y	Y	Y

Option or Feature	11g Standard Edition One	11g Standard Edition	11g Enterprise Edition	11g Express Edition
Direct Path Load API	Y	Y	Y	Y
External tables	Y	Y	Y	Y
Function-based indexes	Y	Y	Y	Y
Long operations monitor	Y	Y	Y	Y
Materialized views	Y	Y	Y	Y
MERGE	Y	Y	Y	Y
Optimizer stats mgt	Y	Y	Y	Y
Pipelined table functions	Y	Y	Y	Y
Sample scan	Y	Y	Y	Y
Star query optimization	Y	Y	Y	PL/SQL Only
Parallel Operations				
Parallel query	N	N	Y	N
Parallel DML	N	N	Y	N
Parallel index build	N	N	Y	N
Parallel stats gathering	N	N	Y	N
Parallel Data export and Data Pump	N	N	Y	N
Parallel text index creation	N	N	Y	N
Parallel backup & recovery	N	N	Y	N
Parallel analyze	N	N	Y	N
Parallel bitmap star query	N	N	Y	N
Parallel index scans	N	N	Y	N
Parallel load	Y	Y	Y	Y
High Availability				
Oracle Data Guard	N	N	Y	N
Integrated Clusterware	Y	Y	Y	N
Fast-start fault recovery	N	N	Y	N
Online operations	N	N	Y	N
Backup and recovery	N	N	Y	N
Oracle Flashback features (Table, Database, Transaction, Total Recall)	N	N	Y	N

Option or Feature	11g Standard Edition One	11g Standard Edition	11g Enterprise Edition	11g Express Edition
Automatic Storage Management (ASM)	Y	Y	Y	N
Content Management				
Dynamic Services	Y	Y	Y	Y
Multimedia	Y	Y	Y	N
Workspace Manager	Y	Y	Y	Y
Oracle Text	Y	Y	Y	Y
XML DB	Y	Y	Y	Y
Information Integration				
Oracle Streams	N	N	Y	Y
Advanced Queuing	Y	Y	Y	Y
Oracle Messaging Gateway	N	N	Y	Y
Database Features				
Database event triggers	Y	Y	Y	Y
DBMS_REPAIR package	Y	Y	Y	Y
Drop column	Y	Y	Y	Y
Flashback Query	Y	Y	Y	Y
Globalization	Y	Y	Y	Y
Index coalesce	N	N	Y	N
Invisible index	Y	Y	Y	Y
Query result cache	Y	Y	Y	Y
Index-organized tables	Y	Y	Y	Y
Instead-of Triggers	Y	Y	Y	Y
LOB (large object) support	Y	Y	Y	Y
Locally managed tablespaces	Y	Y	Y	Y
LogMiner	Y	Y	Y	Y
Plan stability	Y	Y	Y	Y
Quiesce database	N	N	Y	N
Reverse key indexes	Y	Y	Y	Y
SQL Plan Management	N	N	Y	N
Temporary tables	Y	Y	Y	Y

Option or Feature	IIg Standard Edition One	IIg Standard Edition	IIg Enterprise Edition	IIg Express Edition
		Development		
AppWizard for Virt Studio	Y	Y	Y	Y
Autonomous transactions	Y	Y	Y	Y
Client Side Query Cache	N	N	Y	N
COM cartridge	Y	Y	Y	Y
Java support	Y	Y	Y	N
JDBC drivers	Y	Y	Y	Y
MS Trans Server	Y	Y	Y	Y
Object/Relational Ext	Y	Y	Y	Y
PL/SQL native compilation	Y	Y	Y	Y
PL/SQL Function Result Cache	N	N	Y	N
PL/SQL stored procedures in triggers	Y	Y	Y	Y
PL/SQL Server embedded	Y	Y	Y	Y
SQL*Plus	Y	Y	Y	Y
User-defined aggregates	Y	Y	Y	Y
XML	Y	Y	Y	Y
		Distributed		
Advanced replication	N	N	Y	N
Basic replication	Y	Y	Y	Y
Distributed queries	Y	Y	Y	Y
Distributed transactions	Y	Y	Y	Y
Heterogeneous services	Y	Y	Y	Y
		Networking		
Connection Manager	N	N	Y	N
Multiprotocol	N	N	Y	N
SDP for InfiniBand	N	N	Y	N
Connection pooling	Y	Y	Y	Y
Oracle Net services	Y	Y	Y	Y
		System Management		
Basic standby database	Y	Y	Y	Y
Global index maintenance - DDL	Y	Y	Y	Y

Option or Feature	11g Standard Edition One	11g Standard Edition	11g Enterprise Edition	11g Express Edition
Legato Storage Manager	Y	Y	Y	Y
Multiple block size	Y	Y	Y	Y
Online backup & recovery	Y	Y	Y	Y
Standard Management Pack	N	N	Y	N
Oracle Enterprise Manager	Y	Y	Y	N
Oracle Fail Safe	Y	Y	Y	N
strightOracle Managed Files	Y	Y	Y	N
Recovery Manager	Y	Y	Y	N
Resumable Space Allocation	Y	Y	Y	Y
Standby database GUI	N	N	Y	N
Transparent Application Failover	Y	Y	Y	Y
Identify unused index	Y	Y	Y	Y
Security				
Virtual private database	N	N	Y	N
Fine-grained auditing	N	N	Y	N
Enterprise security	N	N	Y	N
N-tier authentication	N	N	Y	N
Password management	Y	Y	Y	Y
Encryption Toolkit	Y	Y	Y	Y
Proxy authentication	Y	Y	Y	N

This is by no means a complete list of new features in Oracle Database 11g. Overall, Oracle has made major strides in providing enhanced functionality and automating many administrative tasks, reducing the total cost of ownership. RAC and Grid Computing are now mature technologies. Oracle is leading the effort at integrating this technology and engineering it together with their Exadata, Exalogic, and other acquired hardware.

TIPS & REVIEW

New Features Review

- What makes Exadata fast is: fast hardware, many CPUs, Fast Flash Cache, lots of DRAM on database servers and storage, compression (save 10x–70x), partition pruning (save 10x–100x), storage indexes (save 5x–10x), Smart Scan (save 4x–10x), and other features.

- Exadata is the best way to turn a 1T search into a 500M search or even a 50M search. It's smokin' fast!

- Oracle's compression features will save you money on disk space and, in many cases, improve performance.

- The new ASM storage limit is 40 exabytes of storage (an exabyte is a million terabytes)! *The Oracle database limit is 8 exabytes.*

- Oracle has improved rolling patches and upgrades.

- ASM rebalance operations are faster in 11*g*.

- With the Oracle11*g* new feature Snapshot Standby Database, a physical standby can now be opened temporarily and utilized for read/write activity, allowing for activities such as reporting and load testing.

- With Oracle 11*g*R2, Advanced Compression is supported and works with Streams and a logical standby database.

- Oracle 11*g*R2 improves the Active Data Guard option by adding a lag history that can be viewed in the V$STANDBY_EVENT_HISTOGRAM view.

- Statistics may now be gathered and made PENDING until tested.

- Oracle 11*g* has multicolumn statistics that consider the relationships between various columns.

- Oracle 11*g* introduces a free database "health monitor" using the DBMS_HM package.

- Oracle 11*g* now allows you to hide indexes from the optimizer without having to drop them (they continue to be maintained) by a feature called invisible indexes.

- Oracle 11*g* enhanced portioning with interval, REF, system, and virtual-based column partitioning.

- Oracle 11*g* now allows a single table to be made read-only without affecting the other tables in the tablespace.

- Real Application Testing allows a DBA to utilize real workloads to judge the impact of application changes or releases on a database environment.

- Oracle 11*g* provides a new separate shared memory pool to store query results. This Result Cache is allocated directly from the shared pool but is maintained separately. A RESULT_CACHE hint allows you to direct a query to use the cache in addition to setting it at the database and table level.

- RMAN is much faster now that UNDO is not written and there is better compression. The Data Recovery Advisor helps simplify RMAN recoveries and allows the DBA to check failure, obtain additional details, obtain repair advice, as well as execute the advised repair. There are also catalog enhancements as well as a proactive health check (for corrupt blocks).

- Oracle SecureFiles, also known as Fast Files, are Oracle's improvement to storage of large object types (LOBs). SecureFiles gives comparable performance to a filesystem for LOBs, and LOBs can store many types of data from images, large amounts of text, Word documents, Excel spreadsheets, XML, HTML, as well as DICOM-formatted medical images.

- Oracle 11g adds the ability to *shrink* the locally managed temporary tablespace.

- Oracle 11gR2 is now engineered with the Oracle Exadata and Exalogic hardware. Oracle's hardware dramatically improves performance.

References

Many thanks to Mike Messina who did most of the upgrade of this chapter to Oracle11g!
My Oracle Support documents (several listed in the chapter).
Rich Niemiec, *11gR2 New Features, 2011.*
Rich Niemiec, *Exadata 101, 2011.*
Rich Niemiec, *Exadata for the Executive, 2011.*
Oracle11gR1, Administrators Guide.
Oracle11gR1, New Features Guide.
Oracle11gR2, New Features Guide.
Oracle 11gR2, SQL Language Reference.
Oracle11gR1, Utilities.
Oracle Database 11g Product Family, www.oracle.com.
Oracle Database 11g, ASM, An Oracle Technical White Paper, June 2007.
SQL Performance Analyzer, An Oracle White Paper, November 2007.

CHAPTER
2

Basic Index Principles
(Beginner Developer
and Beginner DBA)

This chapter is neither for the experts nor for those looking for fast answers. This is a chapter (maybe the only one) that looks at very basic indexing theory, including some new features in version 11gR2. The toughest part of being a beginner is finding information that will fill in the most basic gaps and enable visualization of Oracle's indexing capabilities. This chapter is intended to serve that purpose. While a considerable amount of material is published at the intermediate and advanced level, the beginner's information is usually scarce, yet highly desirable. Chapter 5 has additional index information on query tuning and the Access Advisor, which suggests indexes. Indexes related solely to Exadata are located in Chapter 11.

Oracle offers a variety of indexing options. Knowing which option to use in a given situation can be crucial to an application's performance. A wrong choice may cause performance to come to a grinding halt or cause processes to be terminated because of deadlock situations. By taking processes that previously took large amounts of resources and hours or even days to run and having them finish in minutes can make you an instant hero. This chapter will discuss each of the indexing options and point out the benefits and limitations of each. The introduction of the Invisible Index in Oracle Database 11g adds a new way to turn off unused or potentially harmful indexes before you delete them (when you are sure that you don't need them). Tips covered in this chapter include the following:

- Basic index concepts
- Leveraging invisible indexes
- Finding which tables are indexed and which have concatenated indexes
- How concatenated indexes are used
- The Oracle ROWID
- Using functions and indexes
- How to avoid comparing unmatched data types, causing index suppression
- Cluster factors as an index strategy
- Using the INDEX_STATS view
- The binary height of an index
- About histograms
- Fast full scans
- How to use the index skip-scan feature
- Explanation of b-tree indexes
- When to use bitmap indexes
- When to use hashing
- When to use the index-organized table
- When to use reverse key indexes
- When to use function-based indexes
- Local and global partitioned indexes

Basic Index Concepts

When accessing data from tables, Oracle has two options: to read every row in the table (also referred to as a *full table scan*) or to access a single row at a time via ROWID. When accessing a small percentage of the rows of a large table, you would want to use an index. For example, if you only wanted to select 5 percent of the rows in a large table, you would do fewer I/Os if you used the index to identify which blocks to read. If you don't use an index, you will read all of the blocks in the table.

The degree to which indexes help performance depends partly on the selectivity of the data and the way in which the data is distributed among the table's blocks. If the data is very selective, there will be few rows in the table that match the indexed value (such as a passport number). Oracle will be able to query the index quickly for the ROWIDs that match the indexed value, and the small number of related table blocks can be quickly queried. If the data is not very selective (such as the country name), then many ROWIDs may be returned by the index, resulting in many separate blocks being queried from the table.

If the data is selective but the related rows are not stored near each other in the table, then the benefit of indexing is further reduced. If the data that matches the indexed value is scattered throughout the table's blocks, then you may have to select many individual blocks from the table to satisfy your query. In some cases, you will find that when the data is dispersed throughout the table's blocks you are better off bypassing the index and performing a full table scan instead. When doing a full table scan, Oracle uses a multiblock read, enabling it to scan a table quickly. Index-based reads are single-block reads, so your goal when using an index should be to reduce the number of single blocks needed to resolve the query.

With some of the options available in Oracle, such as partitioning, parallel DML, parallel query operations, and larger I/O using the DB_FILE_MULTIBLOCK_READ_COUNT, the balance point between full table scans and index lookups is changing. Hardware is getting faster, disks cache more information in on-disk caching, and memory continues to get cheaper. At the same time, Oracle has enhanced the indexing features to include skip-scan indexes and other internal operations that reduce the time needed to retrieve your data.

TIP
As you upgrade Oracle versions, be sure to test your application's queries to determine whether the execution paths for your queries still use the indexes that were used prior to the upgrade. See if the execution plan has changed and if it is better or worse.

Indexes will generally improve performance for queries. SELECT, the WHERE clauses of UPDATE commands, and the WHERE clauses of DELETE statements (when few rows are accessed) can benefit from indexes. In general, adding indexes will decrease performance for INSERT statements (since INSERTs to both the table and the index must be performed). UPDATEs of indexed columns will be slower than if the columns were unindexed because the database has to manage the changes to both the table and the index. Additionally, DELETEs of large numbers of rows will be slowed by the presence of indexes on the table.

A DELETE statement deleting half of a table will also need to delete half of the rows for the index (very costly for this specific situation). In general, every index on a table slows INSERTs into the table by a factor of 3. Two indexes generally make the INSERT twice as slow; however, a two-column single index (either concatenated index or two-part single index) is not much worse than a one-column single index (a one-part single index). UPDATEs of the indexed columns and DELETEs may be similarly slowed. You need to balance the query performance benefits of indexes against their impact on your data manipulation performance.

To get a listing of all of the indexes on a table, query the DBA_INDEXES view. Also, note that you can retrieve the indexes for your schema by accessing USER_INDEXES. To see the indexes on all tables to which you have access, query ALL_INDEXES.

Shown here, for example, is a creation of indexes on the EMP table owned by SCOTT from the original Oracle demo tables provided as part of the product. You can use any of the old or new demo tables to test queries:

```
create index emp_id1 on emp(empno, ename, deptno);
create index emp_id2 on emp (sal);
```

When you issue those commands, the database creates two separate indexes on the EMP table. Each of the indexes contains the specified values from the EMP table along with the ROWID values for the rows that match them. If you want to find an EMP record that has a Sal value of 1000, the optimizer could use the EMP_ID2 index to find that value, find the related ROWID in the index, and then use that ROWID to find the right row(s) in the table.

The following USER_INDEXES query shows the new indexes on the EMP table:

```
select table_name, index_name
from    user_indexes
where   table_name = 'EMP' ;

TABLE_NAME                        INDEX_NAME
--------------------------------  ----------------------------
EMP                               EMP_ID1
EMP                               EMP_ID2
```

The output shows the two indexes, but it does not show the columns in each index. To get the specific columns that are indexed for a given table for the current user, access the USER_IND_COLUMNS view. Also note that DBAs can retrieve the columns that are indexed for all schemas by accessing DBA_IND_COLUMNS, and you can see the indexed columns for all of the tables you can access via ALL_IND_COLUMNS. To get the specific columns that are indexed for a given table, access the USER_IND_COLUMNS view, shown next.

```
column index_name format a12
column column_name format a8
column table_name format a8
select table_name, index_name, column_name, column_position
from    user_ind_columns
order   by table_name, index_name, column_position;

TABLE_NA INDEX_NAME    COLUMN_N COLUMN_POSITION
-------- ------------- -------- ---------------
EMP       EMP_ID1       EMPNO                  1
EMP       EMP_ID1       ENAME                  2
EMP       EMP_ID1       DEPTNO                 3
EMP       EMP_ID2       SAL                    1
```

The EMP table has two indexes. The first, EMP_ID1, is a concatenated index that indexes the EMPNO, ENAME, and DEPTNO columns. The second, EMP_ID2, indexes the SAL column only. The COLUMN_POSITION displayed in the listing shows the order of columns in a concatenated index—in this case, the EMPNO, then the ENAME, then the DEPTNO.

TIP
Query DBA_INDEXES and DBA_IND_COLUMNS to retrieve a list of the indexes on a given table. Use USER_INDEXES and USER_IND_COLUMNS to retrieve information for only your schema.

Invisible Indexes

Deciding which columns to index is hard. The primary key is automatically indexed, the foreign keys *should* also be indexed, but then what? Even more difficult is deciding which index to remove that might be a bad index. Every time a record is inserted, all of the indexes have to be updated. If the column of an index is updated, the index has to be updated. Deciding which index to drop without causing a slew of full table scans or Cartesian joins for subsequent user queries is difficult, especially when tuning third-party applications where the code cannot be changed. The solution just might be the invisible index. Oracle allows you to turn off the index (make it invisible), yet continue to maintain the index (during any DML—INSERT/UPDATE/DELETE) in case you need to turn it back on quickly. You can do this by making the index visible or invisible:

- ALTER INDEX *idx1* INVISIBLE;

- ALTER INDEX *idx1* VISIBLE;

- CREATE INDEX . . . INVISIBLE;

The following query shows the creation of a new invisible index on the DEPTNO column of the EMP table and subsequent query where the index is not seen:

```
create index dept_rich_inv_idx on dept_rich(deptno) invisible;
Index created.

select count(*)
from   dept_rich
where  deptno = 30; (doesn't see the index)

COUNT(*)
-------------
        512

Execution Plan
----------------------------------------------------------
Plan hash value: 3024595593

---------------------------------------------------------------------
| Id  | Operation      | Name     | Rows  | Bytes | Cost (%CPU)| Time     |
---------------------------------------------------------------------
```

```
|   0 | SELECT STATEMENT   |                |   1 |    2 |    4   (0)| 00:00:01 |
|   1 |  SORT AGGREGATE    |                |   1 |    2 |        |          |
|*  2 |   TABLE ACCESS FULL| DEPT_RICH  |  512 | 1024 |    4   (0)| 0:00:01 |
------------------------------------------------------------------------------
```

I can still force the use of the index if I use a hint. This only worked in the earliest versions of 11*g* with an INDEX hint; in 11*g*R2, with a USE_INVISIBLE_INDEXES hint—or by setting the initialization parameter OPTIMIZER_USE_INVISIBLE_INDEXES to TRUE (see Appendix A):

```
select /*+ USE_INVISIBLE_INDEXES */ count(*)
from    dept_rich
where   deptno = 30;    (forces the index with hint)

COUNT(*)
--------
     512

Execution Plan
--------------------------------------------------------------
Plan hash value: 3699452051
--------------------------------------------------------------------------------
| Id  | Operation          | Name              | Rows  | Bytes | Cost (%CPU)| Time       |
--------------------------------------------------------------------------------
|   0 | SELECT STATEMENT   |                   |     1 |     2 |    1   (0)| 00:00:01 |
|   1 |  SORT AGGREGATE    |                   |     1 |     2 |        |          |
|*  2 |   INDEX RANGE SCAN| DEPT_RICH_INV_IDX |   512 |  1024 |    1   (0)| 00:00:01 |
--------------------------------------------------------------------------------
```

If I make the index visible, I no longer need to use the INDEX hint:

```
alter index dept_rich_inv_idx visible;
Index altered.

select count(*)
from    dept_rich
where   deptno = 30;    (it does see the index)

COUNT(*)
--------
     512

Execution Plan
--------------------------------------------------------------
Plan hash value: 3699452051
--------------------------------------------------------------------------------
| Id  | Operation          | Name              | Rows  | Bytes | Cost (%CPU)| Time       |
--------------------------------------------------------------------------------
|   0 | SELECT STATEMENT   |                   |     1 |     2 |    1   (0)| 00:00:01 |
|   1 |  SORT AGGREGATE    |                   |     1 |     2 |        |          |
|*  2 |   INDEX RANGE SCAN| DEPT_RICH_INV_IDX |   512 |  1024 |    1   (0)| 00:00:01 |
--------------------------------------------------------------------------------
```

I can also use the NO_INDEX hint to turn off an index (before making it invisible) to see if another index (or no other index) will be used, other than the one that I intend to make invisible. In other words, use any index *except* the one listed in the NO_INDEX hint. Here is an example:

```
select /*+ no_index(dept_rich dept_rich_inv_idx) */ count(*)
from    dept_rich
where   deptno = 30; (forces not using the index with hint)
```

```
COUNT(*)
--------
    512

Execution Plan
----------------------------------------------------------
Plan hash value: 3024595593


---------------------------------------------------------------------------
| Id | Operation        | Name      | Rows | Bytes | Cost (%CPU)| Time     |
---------------------------------------------------------------------------
|  0 | SELECT STATEMENT |           |    1 |     2 |    4   (0)| 00:00:01 |
|  1 |  SORT AGGREGATE  |           |    1 |     2 |           |          |
|* 2 |   TABLE ACCESS FULL| DEPT_RICH |  512 |  1024 |    4   (0)| 0:00:01 |
---------------------------------------------------------------------------
```

I can make the index invisible again at any time:

```
alter index dept_rich_inv_idx invisible;
Index altered.
```

I can check visibility by querying USER_INDEXES or DBA_INDEXES:

```
select index_name, visibility
from   dba_indexes   (or go to USER_INDEXES)
where  index_name = 'DEPT_RICH_INV_IDX';

INDEX_NAME                          VISIBILITY
---------------------------------   ------------------
DEPT_RICH_INV_IDX                   INVISIBLE
```

TIP
By using invisible indexes, you can "turn off" indexes temporarily (make them invisible) to check how queries perform without them. Because invisible indexes continue to be maintained while invisible, turning them back on (making them visible again), if needed, is easy.

Concatenated Indexes

When a single index has multiple columns that are indexed, it is called a *concatenated* or *composite* index. While Oracle 9*i*'s introduction of skip-scan index access has increased the optimizer's options when using concatenated indexes, you should be careful when selecting the order of the columns in the index. In general, the leading column of the index should be the one most likely to be used in WHERE clauses and also the most selective column of the set.

Prior to the introduction of skip-scan functionality, queries could only use the index if the leading column of the index was in the WHERE clause. Consider the example in the following listing where the EMP table has a concatenated index on EMPNO, ENAME, and DEPTNO. Note that EMPNO is the first part; ENAME is the second part; and DEPTNO is the third part. If you are not making use of the skip-scan functionality, Oracle will generally not use this index unless your WHERE clause specifies a value for the leading column (EMPNO).

```
select  job, empno
from    emp
where   ename = 'RICH';
```

Since ENAME is not the leading column of the index, the optimizer may elect not to use the index. Starting with the introduction of the skip-scan functionality in Oracle 9*i*, the optimizer may choose to use the index, even though an EMPNO value is not specified in the WHERE clause. Instead, the optimizer could choose to perform a fast full scan of the index or a full scan of the table.

The same holds true if the third column of the index is used in the WHERE clause:

```
select  job, empno
from    emp
where   deptno = 30;
```

In this listing, the WHERE clause specifies a value for the third column in the index. The optimizer may select to perform an index skip-scan access, an index fast full scan, or a full table scan. By creating the index, you have given the database more choices to consider when executing the query, hopefully improving overall performance. Note that the user's code does not change; the optimizer is aware of the index and bases its decisions on the anticipated cost of each alternative.

In the following example, a part of the index is used. The leading column, EMPNO, is used as a limiting condition in the WHERE clause so that Oracle can use the index.

```
select  job, empno
from    emp
where   empno = 'RICH';
```

The two most common types of index scans are unique scans and range scans. In a *unique* scan, the database knows that the index contains a list of unique values. In a *range* scan, the database returns multiple values from the index according to the query criteria. In this example, the EMP_ID1 and EMP_ID2 indexes were not created as unique indexes. Oracle will perform a range scan when retrieving their data. To create a unique index, use the CREATE UNIQUE INDEX command when creating the index.

When you create a primary key or a UNIQUE constraint, Oracle automatically creates a unique index based on the columns you specify (unless the constraint is created with the DISABLE clause). If you create a multicolumn primary key, Oracle creates a concatenated index with the columns in the same order in which you specified them when creating the primary key.

Indexes like EMP_ID1 and EMP_ID2 provide Oracle with the ability to access a single row of data by supplying the ROWID of the individual row. The ROWID is a pointer directly to the physical location of the individual row.

TIP
Avoid hard-coding Oracle's ROWID into specific code. The ROWID structure in the past has changed from version to version and will probably change again in future releases. I recommend never hard-coding a ROWID.

Suppressing Indexes

Suppressing indexes is one of the most common mistakes made by an inexperienced developer. SQL contains many traps that cause indexes not to be used. Some of the most common problems are discussed in the following sections.

The Oracle optimizer works behind the scenes to choose and exploit the most effective methods possible for retrieving your data. For example, there are multiple cases in which you don't need to specify a WHERE clause for Oracle to use an index. If you query the MIN or MAX value of an indexed column, Oracle retrieves that value from the index rather than from the table. Similarly, if you perform a COUNT function on an indexed column, Oracle can use the index instead of the column. In the following sections, you will see situations in which the logic of the WHERE clause prevents Oracle from using an index.

Using the NOT EQUAL Operators: <>, !=

Indexes can only be used to find data that exists within a table. Whenever the NOT EQUAL operators are used in the WHERE clause, indexes on the columns being referenced cannot be used. Consider the following query on the CUSTOMERS table, which has an index on the CUST_RATING column. The following statement would result in a full table scan (since most records would *usually* be retrieved) even though the CUST_RATING column has an index:

```
select  cust_id, cust_name
from    customers
where   cust_rating <> 'aa';
```

When you analyze your tables, Oracle collects statistics about the distribution of data within the table. Using that analysis, the cost-based optimizer may decide to use the index for some values in your WHERE clause but not for other values. During application development and testing, you should use a representative set of rows so you can simulate the actual distribution of data values in the production environment.

TIP
You can create your indexes and analyze them in a single step by using the COMPUTE STATISTICS clause of the CREATE INDEX command. You can also import statistics from a production database to test out execution paths (refer to the Oracle 11.2 Database Performance Tuning Guide).

Using IS NULL or IS NOT NULL

When you use IS NULL or IS NOT NULL in your WHERE clauses, index usage is suppressed because the value of NULL is undefined. There is no value in the database that will equal a NULL value; not even NULL equals a NULL.

NULL values pose several difficulties for SQL statements. Indexed columns that have rows containing a NULL value do not have an entry in the index (except for bitmapped indexes—which is why bitmap indexes are usually fast for NULL searches). Under normal circumstances, the following statement would cause a full table scan to be performed, even if the SAL column is indexed:

```
select empno, ename, deptno
from   emp
where  sal is null;
```

To disallow NULL values for the columns, use NOT NULL when creating or altering the table. Note that if the table already contains data, you can only set a column to NOT NULL if it has a non-NULL value for every row or if you use the DEFAULT clause of the ALTER TABLE command. The following listing shows the modification of the EMP table's SAL column to disallow NULL values:

```
alter table emp modify
(sal not null);
```

Note that an error will be returned if insertion of a NULL value is attempted for the SAL column.

TIP
Creating a table specifying NOT NULL for a column causes NULL values to be disallowed and eliminates the performance problems associated with querying NULL values.

The following table creation statement provides a default value for the DEPTNO column. When a value for the column is not specified during INSERTs, the default value is used. If a default value is specified and you *do* want a NULL value, then you need to insert a NULL into the column.

```
create table employee
(empl_id number(8) not null, first_name varchar2(20) not null,
 last_name varchar2(20) not null, deptno number(4) default 10);

insert into employee(empl_id, first_name, last_name)
values (8100, 'REGINA', 'NIEMIEC');
1 row created.

select *
from   employee;

  EMPL_ID FIRST_NAME           LAST_NAME                DEPTNO
---------- -------------------- -------------------- ----------
     8100 REGINA               NIEMIEC                      10

insert into employee
values (8200, 'RICH', 'NIEMIEC', NULL);

1 row created.
```

```
select *
from    employee;
```

EMPL_ID	FIRST_NAME	LAST_NAME	DEPTNO
8100	REGINA	NIEMIEC	10
8200	RICH	NIEMIEC	

TIP
NULL values often cause indexes to be suppressed. Create a table specifying NOT NULL and DEFAULT for an unspecified column to help avoid a potential performance issue.

Using LIKE

LIKE, in some cases, uses an index, while in others, it does not. The most common uses of LIKE are LIKE '%*somevalue*%' or LIKE '*somevalue*%' (where the % is only at the end of the search string). Only one of these cases uses the index—the case where the value is first, LIKE '*somevalue*%'.

Let's examine this using a set of examples. First, create an index on the SCOTT.EMP table for the ENAME column so you can use an index when looking up employee names. This allows you to see when the index is used with a LIKE and when it is not.

```
SQL> create index emp_ename_nu on emp (ename) ;
Index created.
```

Now let's examine what happens when using LIKE with '%*somevalue*%':

```
SQL> set autotrace traceonly
SQL> select empno, ename, hiredate
  2  from    scott.emp
  3  where   ename like '%BLAKE%';
```

```
Execution Plan
-------------------------------------------------------------
Plan hash value: 3956160932
-----------------------------------------------------------------------------
| Id | Operation          | Name | Rows | Bytes | Cost (%CPU)| Time     |
-----------------------------------------------------------------------------
|  0 | SELECT STATEMENT   |      |    1 |   18 |    3   (0)| 00:00:01 |
|* 1 |  TABLE ACCESS FULL| EMP  |    1 |   18 |    3   (0)| 00:00:01 |
```

Now let's put the value first, before the '%':

```
SQL> set autotrace traceonly
SQL> select empno, ename, hiredate
  2  from    scott.emp
  3  where   ename like 'BLAKE%' ;
```

```
Execution Plan
```

```
-------------------------------------------------------------
Plan hash value: 3445075938
-------------------------------------------------------------------
| Id  | Operation                    | Name         | Rows  | Bytes | Cost (%CPU)| Time     |
-------------------------------------------------------------------
|   0 | SELECT STATEMENT             |              |    1  |  18   |    2   (0)|00:00:01 |
|   1 |  TABLE ACCESS BY INDEX ROWID| EMP          |    1  |  18   |    2   (0)|00:00:01 |
|*  2 |   INDEX RANGE SCAN           | EMP_ENAME_NU |    1  |       |    1   (0)|00:00:01 |
-------------------------------------------------------------------
```

Notice that when the '%' appears first, the index is not used, but when you put the value first, Oracle is able to utilize the index.

Using Functions

Unless you are using function-based indexes, applying functions on indexed columns in the WHERE clause of a SQL statement causes the optimizer to bypass indexes. Some of the most common functions are TRUNC, SUBSTR, TO_DATE, TO_CHAR, and INSTR. All of these functions alter the value of the column. Therefore, the indexes and the columns being referenced are not used. The following statement causes a full table scan to be performed, even if there is an index on the HIRE_DATE COLUMN (as long as it wasn't a function-based index):

```
select empno, ename, deptno
from    emp
where   trunc(hiredate) = '01-MAY-01';
```

Changing the statement to the following would allow for an index lookup:

```
select empno, ename, deptno
from    emp
where   hiredate > '01-MAY-01'
and     hiredate < (TO_DATE('01-MAY-01') + 0.99999);
```

TIP
By altering the values being compared to the column, and not the columns themselves, the indexes become available. Use this to eliminate full table scans.

For further details on function-based indexes, see the "Function-based Indexes" section later in this chapter.

Comparing Mismatched Data Types

One of the more difficult performance issues to resolve is caused by comparing differing data types. Oracle does not complain about the types being incompatible—quite the opposite. For example, Oracle implicitly converts the data in the VARCHAR2 column to match the numeric data type that it is being compared to. Consider the following example where ACCOUNT_NUMBER is a VARCHAR2.

If the ACCOUNT_NUMBER column uses a VARCHAR2 data type, the following statement may cause a full table scan to be performed, even if the ACCOUNT_NUMBER column is indexed:

```
select bank_name, address, city, state, zip
from   banks
where  account_number = 990354;
```

Oracle internally changes the WHERE clause to be:

```
to_number(account_number)=990354
```

which suppresses the index. An EXPLAIN PLAN of this query only shows that the table was accessed using a "FULL SCAN" (usually to coder's bewilderment). To some DBAs and developers, this appears to be a rare situation, but in many systems, numeric values are zero-padded and specified as VARCHAR2. Rewrite the preceding statement as follows to use the index on the account number by correctly including the single quote marks for the field:

```
select bank_name, address, city, state, zip
from   banks
where  account_number = '000990354';
```

Alternatively, the ACCOUNT_NUMBER column could be defined to use the NUMBER data type, providing the leading zeros are not critical information for the column.

TIP

Comparing mismatched data types can cause Oracle to suppress an index internally. Even an EXPLAIN PLAN on the query will not help you understand why a full table scan is being performed. Only knowing your data types can help you solve this problem.

Selectivity

Oracle offers several methods to determine the benefit of using an index. The method you choose depends upon both the query and the data. First, determine the number of unique or distinct keys in the index. You can determine the number of distinct values by analyzing the table or the index. You can then query the DISTINCT_KEYS column of the USER_INDEXES view to examine the results of the analysis. By comparing the number of distinct keys to the number of rows in the table (as shown in the NUM_ROWS column of USER_INDEXES), you can determine the index's selectivity. The greater the selectivity, the better an index will be for returning small numbers of rows.

TIP

An index's selectivity is what helps the cost-based optimizer determine an execution path. The more selective the index is, the fewer the number of rows that are returned, on average, for each distinct value. For concatenated indexes, the additional columns added to the index do not improve the selectivity greatly, and the cost of the additional columns may outweigh the gain.

The Clustering Factor

The *clustering factor* is a measure of the ordered-ness of an index in comparison to the table that it is based on. It is used to check the cost of a table lookup following an index access (multiplying the clustering factor by index's selectivity gives you the cost of the operation). The clustering factor records the number of blocks that will be read when scanning the index. If the index being used has a *large* clustering factor, then more table data blocks have to be visited to get the rows in each index block (because adjacent rows are in different blocks). If the clustering factor is close to the number of *blocks* in the table, then the index is well ordered, but if the clustering factor is close to the number of *rows* in the table, then the index is *not* well ordered. The clustering factor is computed by the following (explained briefly):

1. The index is scanned in order.

2. The block portion of the ROWID pointed at by the current indexed valued is compared to the previous indexed value (comparing adjacent rows in the index).

3. If the ROWIDs point to different TABLE blocks, the clustering factor is incremented (this is done for the entire index).

The CLUSTERING_FACTOR column in the USER_INDEXES view gives an indication as to how organized the data is compared to the indexed columns. If the value of the CLUSTERING_FACTOR column value is close to the number of leaf blocks in the index, the data is well ordered in the table. If the value is *not* close to the number of leaf blocks in the index, then the data in the table is not well ordered. The *leaf blocks* of an index store the indexed values as well as the ROWIDs to which they point.

For example, say the CUSTOMER_ID for the CUSTOMERS table is generated from a sequence generator, and the CUSTOMER_ID is the primary key on the table. The index on CUSTOMER_ID would have a clustering factor very close to the number of leaf blocks (well ordered). As the customers are added to the database, they are stored sequentially in the table in the same way the sequence numbers are issued from the sequence generator (well ordered). An index on the CUSTOMER_NAME column would have a very high clustering factor, however, because the arrangement of the customer names is random throughout the table.

The clustering factor can impact SQL statements that perform range scans. With a low clustering factor (relative to the number of leaf blocks), the number of blocks needed to satisfy the query is reduced. This increases the possibility that the data blocks are already in memory. A high clustering factor relative to the number of leaf blocks may increase the number of data blocks required to satisfy a range query based on the indexed column.

TIP
The clustering of data within the table can be used to improve the performance of statements that perform range scan–type operations. By determining how the column is being used in the statements, indexing these column(s) may provide a great benefit.

The Binary Height

The binary height of an index plays a major role in the amount of I/O that needs to be performed to return the ROWID to the user process. Each level in the binary height adds an extra block that needs to be read, and because the blocks are not being read sequentially, they each require a separate I/O operation. In Figure 2-1, an index with a binary height of three returning one row to the user would require four blocks to be read: three from the index and one from the table. As the binary height of an index increases, so does the amount of I/O required to retrieve the data.

After analyzing an index, you can query the BLEVEL column of DBA_INDEXES to see its binary height:

```
EXECUTE DBMS_STATS.GATHER_INDEX_STATS ('SCOTT','EMP_ID1');
PL/SQL procedure successfully completed.

select blevel, index_name
from   dba_indexes
where  index_name = 'EMP_ID1';
```

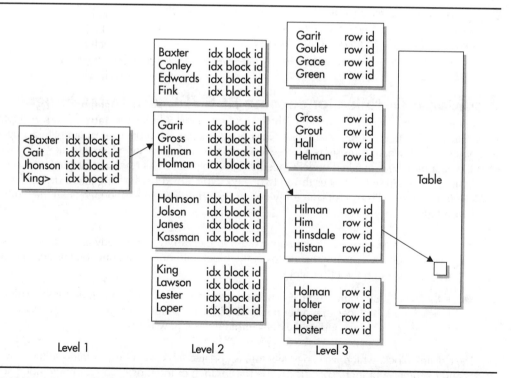

FIGURE 2-1.   *Index with binary height or BLEVEL = 3 (Level 3 is where the leaf blocks reside.)*

```
BLEVEL INDEX_NAME
---------- -----------------------------
         0 EMP_ID1
```

TIP
Analyzing the index or the table will provide the binary height of the index. Use the BLEVEL column in the USER_INDEXES view to check the binary height of the indexes.

The binary height increases mainly because of the number of non-NULL values for the indexed column in the table and the narrowness of the range of values in the indexed columns. Having a large number of deleted rows in the index can also increase the height. Rebuilding the index may help to decrease the height. While these steps reduce the number of I/Os performed against the index, the performance benefits may be small. If the number of deleted rows within an index approaches 20–25 percent, then rebuild the indexes to help reduce the binary height and the amount of empty space that is being read during an I/O.

TIP
In general, the larger the database block size, the smaller the binary height of the index. Each additional level in binary height (BLEVEL) adds additional performance costs during DML.

Additional Details Concerning BLEVEL and Index Height

The b-tree level (BLEVEL) is the depth of the index from its *root block* to its *leaf blocks*. A depth of 0 indicates that the root block and leaf block are the same. All indexes start out with a single leaf node (block), which represents a b-tree level of 0. As rows are added to the index, Oracle puts the data into the block/leaf node. Once the initial block fills as rows are inserted, two new blocks are created. Oracle handles this in two ways, typically known as a *90-10 index split* or a *50-50 index split*. Each type of split (only one or the other is executed) depends on the value being inserted:

- If the new value is greater than any values already in the index, then Oracle executes a 90-10 split by copying the values of the block into one of the new blocks and placing the new value in the other block.

- If the new value being inserted is not the maximum indexed value, then Oracle splits the block 50-50. It places the lower half of the indexed values in one of the new blocks and the higher half of the indexed values into the other new block.

The existing block, which was originally full, is updated to contain only pointers to the new leaf nodes and becomes a branch, specifically the root branch of the index. The resulting index now has a branch level of 1. As rows continue to be inserted into the index, when a leaf node fills, Oracle creates a new leaf block. If the value being inserted is greater than any value currently in the leaf node block, then Oracle places the new value into the new block. If the value is not max value, then Oracle splits the values of the block in half (50-50) by value, keeping the lower values in the current block and placing the higher values in the new block. Then the branch block for these leaf nodes is updated with the pointer for the new block and existing block. This continues until the branch node/block fills. When the branch node fills, the same block-split operation is performed. A new branch block is added and half the block is copied to the new block and the other half remains in the existing branch block. This does not increase either the height or BLEVEL of the index; it simply provides a new branch for a query to take when traversing the index. Only when a root branch block fills and splits does the height of the index increase.

NOTE
The only time two new blocks are created for an index is when the root branch block splits. The content in the current root block is split between the two new branch blocks, which form the top level of a higher index tree. The root block does not change its block address, and by adding two blocks when the split occurs at the root, the index tree is always balanced.

Effects on Index from Update Operations

The index is only affected by an UPDATE if the columns in the table that make up the index are updated. Therefore, in many cases, update operations do not affect an index at all. When the table columns that make up the index are updated, the operation within the index is a DELETE and INSERT. The old value is marked as deleted, and a new value for the entry is inserted. Therefore, no true "update" is performed within the index, in the way you would typically think of an update being performed. Index entries are also cleaned out by Oracle's delayed block cleanout feature. Only after the index entry is deleted and the block cleaned can the space in the index block be reused by new entries.

Effects on Index from DELETE Operations

DELETE operations for an index do not really remove the entry from the index to create empty space. When a DELETE operation occurs on a row in the table, the corresponding index entry is marked as deleted but remains in the index until it is cleaned out. The most common way to clean out an index entry is during an INSERT operation on that block. Index entries are also cleaned out by Oracle's delayed block cleanout feature (this happens on a subsequent query, which could be a SELECT statement). After the index entry is deleted and the block cleaned, the space in the index block can be reused by new entries.

Effects on Index of UPDATE and DELETE Operations

There has been much debate and many myths about indexes regarding the effects DELETES and UPDATES have on them. I have explained how basic DELETES and UPDATES work in Oracle indexes, so let's examine the true effect in detail. In DELETE operations, deletes are done by marking the index entry as deleted in the index, meaning that DELETE operations leave behind data in the leaf blocks that needs to be cleaned up. An INSERT operation in a leaf block, with rows marked for deletion, forces the cleanout of these rows, allowing the space to be "reused" by further inserts in that leaf block. Are there circumstances when that insert will not occur? Yes, but the index block is eventually cleaned out by the delayed block cleanout process.

UPDATE operations, along with DELETES/INSERTS within the same transaction, tend to increase the size of an index greatly, but only if you perform these operations in large numbers within the same transaction (which is not recommended anyway). DELETES in and of themselves do not cause higher index heights or BLEVELs, but are merely a symptom of the larger issue of reusing delete row areas. This means that a high number of DELETE operations or UPDATE operations, or a large number of deleted/updated entries in a single transaction, can potentially cause the size, height, and BLEVEL to increase (but Oracle does not recommend you perform lots and lots of DML operations within the same transaction). The solution for this is to break up your transactions with commits, effectively creating multiple transactions for larger numbers of DELETE+INSERT operations. This helps reuse space and does not cause the index to grow artificially larger than it needs to be. This also explains why large DELETE operations that contain large INSERTS within the same transaction usually cause index growth.

In the useful asktom.oracle.com blog, Tom Kyte puts it this way:

Well, the fact is that indexes, like people, have a certain "weight" they like to be at. Some of us are chubby—some skinny—some tall—some short. Sure, we can go on a diet — but we tend to gravitate BACK to the weight we were. The same is true for indexes — what happened to this person is their index wanted to be wide and fat and EVERY MONTH they rebuilt it (put it on a diet). It would spend the first half of the month then getting fat again and generating gobs of redo due to the block splits it was undergoing to get there…

The moral of the story is to use locally managed tablespaces to avoid fragmentation and to rebuild indexes rarely (build them right the first time and only rebuild when performance degrades versus on a regular basis).

Effects on Blocksize

As just covered, the height and branch level of a block only increase when a block split occurs and causes all the branch blocks up to the root block to also be split. The number of block splits, or more specifically, branch block splits, can be minimized by using larger block sizes for indexes. This is a reason why some experts believe that indexes should be created in larger block size tablespaces. If each block can hold more data, the need to split would occur far less frequently. Therefore, the overall number of branches and leafs could be reduced. This greatly depends on the size of the data for the indexed values—old block size versus new block size. Be careful when measuring the impact of a higher block size tablespace on an index. Moving an index to a larger block size tablespace involves rebuilding the index, which removes all entries marked for deletion and compresses space within the index, reclaiming the space of not only entries marked for deletion, but also entries deleted where space was not reclaimed or reused. Therefore, the full impact of a larger block size may not be as expected or as impressive when you consider what is truly going to occur.

Using Histograms

Histograms record the distribution of data when you analyze a table or index. With this information in hand, the cost-based optimizer can decide to use an index for conditions it knows will return a small number of rows and bypass the index when the condition will return many rows based on the limiting condition. The use of histograms is not limited to indexes. Any column of a table can have a histogram built on it.

The main reason for generating histograms is to help the optimizer plan properly if the data in a table is heavily skewed. For example, if one or two values make up a large percentage of a table, the related indexes may not help to reduce the number of I/Os required to satisfy the query. Creating a histogram lets the cost-based optimizer know when using the index is appropriate, or when 80 percent of the table is going to be returned because of the value in the WHERE clause.

When creating histograms, specify a size. This size relates to the number of buckets for the histogram. Each bucket will contain information about the value of the column(s) and the number of rows.

```
EXECUTE DBMS_STATS.GATHER_TABLE_STATS
('scott','company', METHOD_OPT => 'FOR COLUMNS SIZE 10 company_code');
PL/SQL procedure successfully completed.
```

The preceding query creates a ten-bucket histogram on the COMPANY table, as shown in Figure 2-2. The values for the COMPANY_CODE column are divided into the ten buckets as displayed in the figure. This example shows a large number (80 percent) of the COMPANY_CODE is equal to 1430. As is also shown in the figure, most of the width-balanced buckets contain only 3 rows; a single bucket contains 73 rows. In the height-balanced version of this distribution, each bucket has the same number of rows and most of the bucket endpoints are 1430, reflecting the skewed distribution of the data.

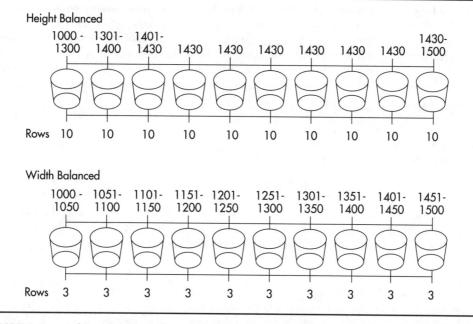

FIGURE 2-2. *A histogram is built on a COMPANY_CODE field with a size of 10 (buckets).*

Oracle's histograms are height-balanced as opposed to width-balanced. Consequently, all of the buckets in the histogram contain the same number of rows. The starting and ending points for a bucket are determined by the number of rows containing those values. The width-balanced histogram specifies the range values for each bucket and then counts the number of rows within that range, not an ideal option.

TIP
If the data in a table is skewed, histograms will provide the cost-based optimizer with a balanced picture of the distribution (by balancing it into buckets). Using the histograms on columns that are not skewed will not provide an increase in performance.

TIP
By default, Oracle creates 75 buckets in a histogram. You can specify SIZE values ranging from 1 to 254.

Fast Full Scans

During a fast full scan of an index, Oracle reads all of the leaf blocks in a b-tree index. The index is being read sequentially, so multiple blocks can be read at once. The DB_FILE_MULTIBLOCK_READ_COUNT parameter in the initialization file controls the number of blocks that can be read simultaneously. The fast full scan usually requires fewer physical I/Os than a full table scan, allowing the query to be resolved faster.

The fast full scan can be used if all of the columns in the query for the table are in the index with the leading edge of the index not part of the WHERE condition (you may need to specify the INDEX_FFS hint as detailed in Chapter 7). In the following example, the EMP table is used. As shown earlier in this chapter, it has a concatenated index on the columns EMPNO, ENAME, and DEPTNO.

```
select empno, ename, deptno
from    emp
where   deptno = 30;
```

Because all of the columns in the SQL statement are in the index, a fast full scan is available. Index fast full scans are commonly performed during joins in which only the indexed join key columns are queried. As an alternative, Oracle may perform a skip-scan access of the index; the optimizer should consider the histogram for the DEPTNO column (if one is available) and decide which of the available access paths yields the lowest possible performance cost.

TIP
If the indexes are relatively small in comparison to the overall size of the table, the fast full scan may provide the performance burst necessary for the application. With concatenated indexes that contain most of the columns of a table, the index may be larger than the actual table and the fast full scan could cause performance degradation.

Skip-Scans

As discussed in the section "Concatenated Indexes" earlier in this chapter, the index skip-scan feature enables the optimizer to use a concatenated index even if its leading column is not listed in the WHERE clause. Index skip-scans are faster than full scans of the index, requiring fewer reads to be performed. For example, the following queries show the difference between a full index scan and a skip-scan. See Chapter 6 to better understand the execution plan or the statistics displayed in the following listing. In this listing, the EMP5 table has many hundreds of thousands of rows.

Following the execution of the queries, the listing shows the time the query took, its execution path within the database, and statistics showing the number of logical reads (consistent gets) and physical reads required to resolve the query:

```
create index skip1 on emp5(job,empno);
Index created.
(you'll also need to gather statistics)

select count(*)
from    emp5
where   empno = 7900;
Elapsed: 00:00:03.13 (Result is a single row…not displayed)


Execution Plan
   0        SELECT STATEMENT Optimizer=CHOOSE (Cost=4 Card=1 Bytes=5)
   1     0    SORT (AGGREGATE)
   2     1      INDEX (FAST FULL SCAN) OF 'SKIP1' (NON-UNIQUE)

Statistics
6826  consistent gets
6819  physical reads

select /*+ index(emp5 skip1) */ count(*)
from    emp5
where   empno = 7900;
Elapsed: 00:00:00.56


Execution Plan
   0        SELECT STATEMENT Optimizer=CHOOSE (Cost=6 Card=1 Bytes=5)
   1     0    SORT (AGGREGATE)
   2     1      INDEX (SKIP SCAN) OF 'SKIP1' (NON-UNIQUE)

Statistics
21  consistent gets
17  physical reads
```

As shown in the listing, the second option used an INDEX (SKIP SCAN) operation to read the index. That execution path required 21 logical reads, which, in turn, required 17 physical I/Os. The first option performed an INDEX (FAST FULL SCAN) operation, which required a significantly greater number of logical and physical I/Os.

To influence the optimizer to choose a skip-scan, you may need to use a hint in the query as shown in the listing. The hint influences the optimizer and biases it toward the execution path you specify.

TIP
For large tables with concatenated indexes, the index skip-scan feature can provide quick access even when the leading column of the index is not used in a limiting condition.

Types of Indexes

The following is a list of indexes discussed in this section:

- B-tree
- Bitmap
- Hash
- Index-organized table
- Reverse key
- Function-based
- Partitioned (local and global)
- Bitmap join indexes

B-Tree Indexes

B-tree indexes are the general-purpose indexes in Oracle. They are the default index types created when creating indexes. B-tree indexes can be single-column (simple) indexes or composite/concatenated (multicolumn) indexes. B-tree indexes can have up to 32 columns.

In Figure 2-3, a b-tree index is created on the LAST_NAME column of the EMPLOYEE table. This index has a binary height of three; consequently, Oracle must go through two branch blocks to get to the leaf block containing the ROWID. Within each branch block, there are branch rows containing the block ID of the next block ID within the chain.

A leaf block contains the index values, the ROWID, and pointers to the previous and next leaf blocks. Oracle has the ability to transverse the binary tree in both directions. B-tree indexes contain the ROWIDs for every row in the table that has a value in the indexed column. Oracle does not index rows that contain NULL values in the indexed column. If the index is a concatenation of

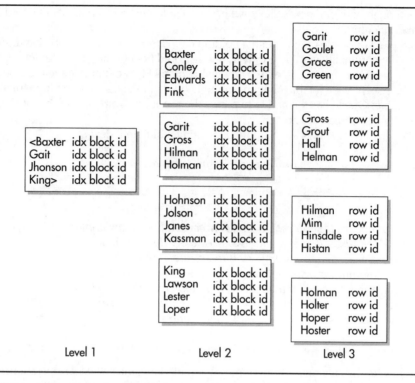

| | Level 1 | | Level 2 | | Level 3 |

FIGURE 2-3.   *B-tree index creation*

multiple columns and one of the columns contains a NULL value, the row will be in the index and the column containing the NULL value will be left empty.

TIP
The values of the indexed columns are stored in an index. For this reason, you can build concatenated (composite) indexes that can be used to satisfy a query without accessing the table. This eliminates the need to go to the table to retrieve the data, reducing I/O.

Bitmap Indexes

Bitmap indexes are ideal for decision support systems (DSS) and data warehouses. They should not be used for tables accessed via transaction-processing applications. Bitmap indexes provide fast access to very large tables using low to medium cardinality (number of distinct values) columns. Although bitmap indexes can have up to 30 columns, they are generally used for a small number of columns.

For example, your table may contain a column called SEX with two possible values: male and female. The cardinality would be only 2, and it would be a prime candidate for a bitmap index if users frequently query the table by the value of the SEX column. The real power of the bitmap index is seen when a table contains multiple bitmap indexes. With multiple bitmap indexes available, Oracle has the ability to merge the result sets from each of the bitmap indexes to eliminate the unwanted data quickly.

The following listing shows an example of creating a bitmap index:

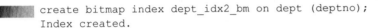

```
create bitmap index dept_idx2_bm on dept (deptno);
Index created.
```

TIP
Use bitmap indexes for columns with a low cardinality. An example would be a column called SEX with two possible values of "male" or "female" (the cardinality is only 2). Bitmaps are very fast for low cardinality columns (few distinct values) because the size of the index is substantially smaller than a b-tree index. Since they are very small when compared to a low-cardinality b-tree index, you can often retrieve over half of the rows in the table and still use a bitmap index.

Bitmap indexes usually outperform b-trees when loading tables (INSERT operations) in batch (single-user) operations when the bulk of the entries do not add new values to the bitmap. You should not use bitmap indexes when multiple sessions will be concurrently inserting rows into the table, as occurs in most transaction-processing applications.

Bitmap Index Example

Consider a sample table called PARTICIPANT that contains surveys from individuals. Each of the columns AGE_CODE, INCOME_LEVEL, EDUCATION_LEVEL, and MARITAL_STATUS has a separate bitmap index built on it. The balance of the data in each histogram and the execution path for a query accessing each of the bitmap indexes are displayed in Figure 2-4. The execution path in the figure shows how the multiple bitmap indexes have been merged, creating a significant performance gain.

As shown in Figure 2-4, the optimizer uses each of the four separate bitmap indexes whose columns were referenced in the WHERE clause. Each bitmap contains binary values (like 1 or 0) that indicate which rows contain the indexed value. Given that, Oracle then performs a BITMAP AND operation on the table containing the indexed value. Given that, Oracle then performs another BITMAP AND operation to find which rows would be returned from all four of the bitmaps. That value is then converted into a ROWID value and the query proceeds with the rest of the

AGE_CODE	INCOME_LEVEL	EDUCATION_LEVEL	MARITAL_STATUS
18-22 A	10,000 - 14,000 AA	High School HS	Single S
23-27 B	14,001 - 18,000 BB	Bachelor BS	Married M
28-32 C	18,001 - 22,000 CC	Masters MS	Divorced D
33-37 D	22,001 - 26,000 DD	Doctorate PhD	Widowed W
...	...	...	...

```
Select …
From Participant
Where Age_code = 'B'
  And Income_Level = 'DD'
  And Education_Level = 'MS'
  And Marital_Status = 'M'

SELECT STAEMENT Optimizer=CHOOSE
  SORT (AGGREGATE)
   BITMAP CONVERSION (RowID)
    BITMAP AND
        BITMAP INDEX (SINGLE VALUE) of 'PART_INCOME_LEVEL'
        BITMAP INDEX (SINGLE VALUE) of 'PART_AGE_CODE'
        BITMAP INDEX (SINGLE VALUE) of 'PART_EDUCATION_LEVEL'
        BITMAP INDEX (SINGLE VALUE) of 'PART_MARITAL_STATUS'
```

FIGURE 2-4. *Bitmap index creation*

processing. Note that all four of the columns had very low cardinality, yet the index allowed the matching rows to be returned very quickly.

TIP
Merging multiple bitmap indexes can lead to significant performance improvement when combined in a single query. Bitmap indexes also work better with fixed-length data types than they do with variable-length data types. Large block sizes improve the storage and read performance of bitmap indexes.

The following query displays index types. B-tree indexes are listed as 'NORMAL'; bitmap indexes will have an INDEX_TYPE value of 'BITMAP'.

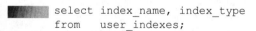

```
select index_name, index_type
from   user_indexes;
```

TIP
To query a list of your bitmap indexes, query the INDEX_TYPE column in the USER_INDEXES view.

Bitmap indexes are not recommended for online transaction processing (OLTP) applications. B-tree indexes contain a ROWID with the indexed value. So, when updating tables and their indexes, Oracle has the ability to lock individual rows. Bitmap indexes are stored as compressed indexed values, which can contain a range of ROWIDs. Therefore, Oracle has to lock the entire range of the ROWIDs for a given value. This type of locking has the potential to cause deadlock situations with certain types of DML statements. SELECT statements are not affected by this locking problem.

Bitmap indexes have several restrictions:

- Bitmap indexes are not considered by the rule-based optimizer.

- Performing an ALTER TABLE statement and modifying a column that has a bitmap index built on it invalidates the index.

- Bitmap indexes do not contain any of the data from the column and cannot be used for any type of integrity checking.

- Bitmap indexes cannot be declared as unique.

- Bitmap indexes have a maximum length of 30 columns.

TIP
Don't use bitmap indexes in heavy OLTP environments.

Hash Indexes

Using *hash* indexes requires the use of hash clusters. When you create a cluster or hash cluster, you define a cluster key. The cluster key tells Oracle how to store the tables in the cluster. When data is stored, all the rows relating to the cluster key are stored in the same database blocks, regardless of what table they belong to. With the data being stored in the same database blocks, using the hash index for an exact match in a WHERE clause enables Oracle to access the data by performing one hash function and one I/O—as opposed to accessing the data by using a b-tree index with a binary height of three, where potentially four I/Os would need to be performed to retrieve the data. As shown in Figure 2-5, the query is an equivalence query, matching the hashed column to an exact value. Oracle can quickly use that value to determine where the row is physically stored, based on the hashing function.

Hash indexes can potentially be the fastest way to access data in the database, but they do come with their drawbacks. The number of distinct values for the cluster key needs to be known before creating the hash cluster. This value needs to be specified at the time of creation. Underestimating the number of distinct values can cause *collisions* (two cluster key values with the same hash value) within the cluster, which are very costly. Collisions cause overflow buffers to be used to store the additional rows, thus causing additional I/O. If the number of distinct hash values has been underestimated, the cluster will need to be re-created to alter the value. An ALTER CLUSTER command cannot change the number of HASHKEYS.

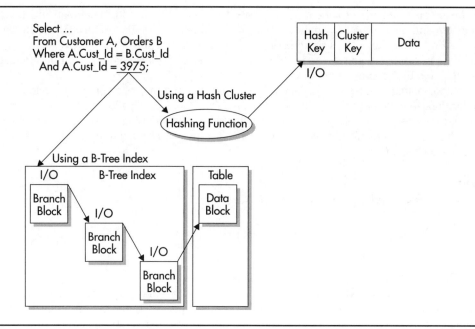

FIGURE 2-5. *Using hash indexes*

Hash clusters have a tendency to waste space. If it is not possible to determine how much space is required to hold all of the rows for a given cluster key, space may be wasted. If it is not possible to allocate additional space within the cluster for future growth, then hash clusters may not be the best option.

If the application often performs full table scans on the clustered table(s), hash clusters may not be the appropriate option. Because of the amount of empty space within the cluster to allow for future growth, full table scans can be very resource-intensive.

Caution should be taken before implementing hash clusters. Revise the application fully to ensure that enough information is known about the tables and data before implementing this option. Generally, hashing is best for static data with primarily sequential values.

TIP
Hash indexes are most useful when the limiting condition specifies an exact value rather than a range of values.

Index-Organized Tables

An *index-organized table* alters the storage structure of a table to that of a b-tree index, sorted on the table's primary key. This unique type of table is treated like any other table—all DML and DDL statements are allowed. ROWIDs are not associated with the rows in the table because of the structure of the table.

Index-organized tables provide faster key-based access to the data for statements involving exact match and range searches on the primary key columns. UPDATE and DELETE statements based on the primary key values should perform better because the rows are physically ordered. The amount of storage required is reduced because values of the key columns are not duplicated in the table and then again in an index.

If you do not frequently query the data by the primary key column, then you will need to create secondary indexes on other columns in the index-organized table. Applications that do not frequently query tables by their primary keys do not realize the full benefits of using index-organized tables. Consider using index-organized tables for tables that are always accessed using exact matches or range scans on the primary key.

TIP
You can create secondary indexes on index-organized tables.

Reverse Key Indexes
When sequential data is loaded, the index may encounter I/O-related bottlenecks. During the data loads, one part of the index, and one part of the disk, may be used much more heavily than any other part. To alleviate this problem, you should store your index tablespaces on disk architectures that permit the files to be physically striped across multiple disks.

Oracle provides reverse key indexes as another solution to this performance problem. When data is stored in a *reverse key* index, its values are reversed prior to being stored in the index. Thus, the values 1234, 1235, and 1236 are stored as 4321, 5321, and 6321. As a result, the index may update different index blocks for each inserted row.

TIP
If you have a limited number of disks and large concurrent sequential loads to perform, reverse key indexes may be a viable solution.

You cannot use reverse key indexes with bitmap indexes or index-organized tables.

Function-Based Indexes
You can create *function-based* indexes on your tables. Without function-based indexes, any query that performed a function on a column could not use that column's index. For example, the following query could not use an index on the JOB column unless it is a function-based index:

```
select  *
from    emp
where   UPPER(job) = 'MGR';
```

The following query *could* use an index on the JOB column, but it would not return rows where the job column had a value of 'Mgr' or 'mgr':

```
select *
from    emp
where   job = 'MGR';
```

You can create indexes that allow function-based columns or data to be supported by index accesses. Instead of creating an index on the JOB column, you can create an index on the column expression UPPER(job), as shown in the following listing:

```
create index EMP$UPPER_JOB on
emp(UPPER(job));
```

Although function-based indexes can be useful, be sure to consider the following questions when creating them:

- Can you restrict the functions that will be used on the column? If so, can you restrict all functions from being performed on the column?

- Do you have adequate storage space for the additional indexes?

- How will the increased number of indexes per column impact the performance of DML commands against the table?

Function-based indexes are useful, but you should implement them sparingly. The more indexes you create on a table, the longer all INSERTs, UPDATEs, and DELETEs will take.

NOTE
For function-based indexes to be used by the optimizer, you must set the QUERY_REWRITE_ENABLED initialization parameter to TRUE.

To see the magnitude of the benefit of function-based indexes, consider the following example that queries a table named SAMPLE that contains 1.4 million rows (note that you must first create the RATIO function; it is not built in).

```
select count(*)
from    sample
where   ratio(balance,limit) >.5;

Elapsed time: 3.61 seconds

create index ratio_idx1 on
sample (ratio(balance, limit));

select count(*)
from    sample
where   ratio(balance,limit) >.5;

Elapsed time: 0.07 seconds (over 50x faster)!!!
```

Partitioned Indexes

A *partitioned* index is simply an index broken into multiple pieces. By breaking an index into multiple physical pieces, you are accessing much smaller pieces (faster), and you may separate the pieces onto different disk drives (reducing I/O contention). Both b-tree and bitmap indexes can be partitioned. Hash indexes cannot be partitioned. Partitioning can work several different ways. The tables can be partitioned and the indexes are not partitioned; the table is not partitioned but the index is; or both the table and index are partitioned. Either way, the cost-based optimizer must be used. Partitioning adds many possibilities to help improve performance and increase maintainability.

There are two types of partitioned indexes: local and global. Each type has two subsets, prefixed and non-prefixed. A table can have any number or combination of the different types of indexes built on its columns. If bitmap indexes are used, they must be local indexes. The main reason to partition the indexes is to reduce the size of the index that needs to be read and to enable placing the partitions in separate tablespaces to improve reliability and availability.

Oracle also supports parallel query and parallel DML when using partitioned tables and indexes (see Chapter 11 for more information), adding the extra benefit of multiple processes helping to process the statement faster.

Local (Commonly Used Indexes)

Local indexes are indexes that are partitioned using the same partition key and same range boundaries as the partitioned table. Each partition of a local index will only contain keys and ROWIDs from its corresponding table partition. Local indexes can be b-tree or bitmap indexes. If they are b-tree indexes, they can be unique or nonunique.

Local indexes support partition independence, meaning that individual partitions can be added, truncated, dropped, split, taken offline, etc., without dropping or rebuilding the indexes. Oracle maintains the local indexes automatically. Local index partitions can also be rebuilt individually while the rest of the partition is unaffected.

Prefixed   *Prefixed* indexes are indexes that contain keys from the partitioning key as the leading edge of the index. For example, let's take the PARTICIPANT table again. Say the table was created and range-partitioned using the SURVEY_ID and SURVEY_DATE columns and a local prefixed index is created on the SURVEY_ID column. The partitions of the index are *equipartitioned,* meaning the partitions of the index are created with the same range boundaries as those of the table (see Figure 2-6).

TIP
Local prefixed indexes allow Oracle to prune unneeded partitions quickly. The partitions that do not contain any of the values appearing in the WHERE clause will not need to be accessed, thus improving the statement's performance.

Non-prefixed   *Non-prefixed* indexes are indexes that do not have the leading column of the partitioning key as the leading column of the index. Using the same PARTICIPANT table with the same partitioning key (SURVEY_ID and SURVEY_DATE), an index on the SURVEY_DATE column

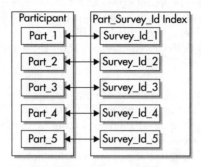

FIGURE 2-6.   *Partitioned, prefixed indexes*

would be a local non-prefixed index. A local non-prefixed index can be created on any column in the table, but each partition of the index only contains the keys for the corresponding partition of the table (see Figure 2-7).

For a non-prefixed index to be unique, it must contain a subset of the partitioning key. In this example, you would need a combination of columns, including the SURVEY_DATE and/or the SURVEY_ID columns (as long as the SURVEY_ID column was not the leading edge of the index, in which case it would be a prefixed index).

TIP
For a non-prefixed index to be unique, it must contain a subset of the partitioning key.

Global
Global partitioned indexes contain keys from multiple table partitions in a single index partition. The partitioning key of a global partitioned index is different or specifies a different range of values from the partitioned table. The creator of the global partitioned index is responsible for

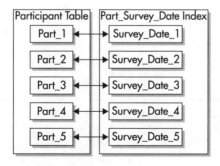

FIGURE 2-7.   *Partitioned, non-prefixed indexes*

defining the ranges and values for the partitioning key. Global indexes can only be b-tree indexes. Global partitioned indexes are not maintained by Oracle by default. If a partition is truncated, added, split, dropped, etc., the global partitioned indexes need to be rebuilt unless you specify the UPDATE GLOBAL INDEXES clause of the ALTER TABLE command when modifying the table.

Prefixed Normally, global prefixed indexes are not equipartitioned with the underlying table. Nothing prevents the index from being equipartitioned, but Oracle does not take advantage of the equipartitioning when generating query plans or executing partition maintenance operations. If the index is going to be equipartitioned, it should be created as a local index to allow Oracle to maintain the index and use it to help prune partitions that will not be needed (see Figure 2-8). As shown in the figure, the three index partitions each contain index entries that point to rows in multiple table partitions.

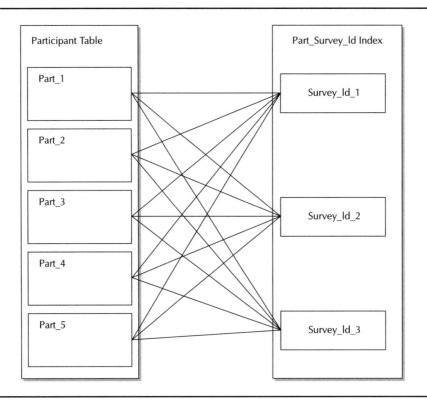

FIGURE 2-8. *Partitioned, global prefixed index*

TIP
If a global index is going to be equipartitioned, it should be created as a local index to allow Oracle to maintain the index and use it to help prune partitions, or exclude those partitions that are not needed by the query.

Non-prefixed Global non-prefixed indexes should not be used as Oracle does not support them. They do not provide any benefits over normal B-tree indexes on the same columns, so they have no value.

Bitmap Join Indexes

A *bitmap join* index is a bitmap index based on the join of two tables. Bitmap join indexes are used in data warehousing environments to improve the performance of queries that join dimension tables to fact tables. When creating a bitmap join index, the standard approach is to join a commonly used dimension table to the fact table within the index. When a user queries the fact table and the dimension table together in a query, the join does not need to be performed because the join results are already available in the bitmap join index. Further performance benefits are gained from the compression of ROWIDs within the bitmap join index, reducing the number of I/Os required to access the data.

When creating a bitmap join index, you specify both tables involved. The syntax should follow this model:

```
create bitmap index FACT_DIM_COL_IDX
    on FACT(DIM.Descr_Col)
  from FACT, DIM
 where FACT.JoinCol = DIM.JoinCol;
```

The syntax for bitmap joins is unusual in that it contains both a FROM clause and a WHERE clause, and it references two separate tables. The indexed column is usually a description column within the dimension table—that is, if the dimension is CUSTOMER and its primary key is Customer_ID, you would normally index a column such as CUSTOMER_NAME. If the FACT table is named SALES, you might create an index using the following command:

```
create bitmap index SALES_CUST_NAME_IDX
    on SALES(CUSTOMER.Customer_Name)
  from SALES, CUSTOMER
 where SALES.Customer_ID=CUSTOMER.Customer_ID;
```

If a user then queries the SALES and CUSTOMER tables with a WHERE clause that specifies a value for the CUSTOMER_NAME column, the optimizer can use the bitmap join index to return the rows quickly that match both the join condition and the CUSTOMER_NAME condition.

The use of bitmap join indexes is restricted; you can only index the columns in the dimension tables. The columns used for the join must be primary key or unique constraints in the dimension tables, and if it is a composite primary key, you must use each of the columns in your join. You cannot create a bitmap join index on an index-organized table, and the restrictions that apply to regular bitmap indexes also apply to bitmap join indexes.

Fast Index Rebuilding

The REBUILD option of the ALTER INDEX statement is executed to rebuild an index quickly using the existing index instead of the table:

```
alter index cust_idx1 rebuild parallel
tablespace cust_tblspc1
storage (pctincrease 0);
Index altered.
```

Modifications to the STORAGE clause can be made at this time and the parallel option may also be used.

TIP
Use the REBUILD option of the ALTER INDEX statement for quickly rebuilding an index using the existing index instead of the table. You must have enough space to store both indexes during this operation.

Rebuilding Indexes Online

You can create or rebuild indexes even when doing DML (INSERT/UPDATE/DELETE) statements on the base table. However, rebuilding during low DML activity is *still* better. Prior to Oracle 11g, this required an exclusive lock at the beginning and end of the rebuild. This lock could cause DML delays and a performance spike. This lock is no longer required for this operation and rebuilding indexes online is now much faster!. Rebuilding is also faster than a DROP and CREATE index.

Here's the basic syntax:

```
CREATE INDEX index_name ON table (col1,...) ONLINE;
Index created.

ALTER INDEX index_name REBUILD ONLINE;
Index altered.
```

Note that rebuilding an index is not the same as coalescing an index. A nice comparison is shown here:

Rebuild	Coalesce
Quickly move index to another tablespace	Can't move index to another tablespace
Requires more disk space	Requires much less disk space than rebuild
Creates new index tree and shrinks heights	Coalesces leaf blocks that are in the same branch
Change storage/tablespace without dropping	Quickly frees index leaf blocks for use

TIP

You can use the REBUILD ONLINE option to allow DML operations on the table or partition during the index rebuild. You cannot specify REBUILD ONLINE for bitmap indexes or for indexes that enforce referential integrity constraints.

TIP

Rebuilding indexes online during high levels of DML activity in 11g is much faster than it was in 10g.

Tips Review

- As you upgrade Oracle versions, be sure to test your application's queries to determine whether the execution paths for your queries still use the indexes that were used prior to the upgrade. See if the execution plan has changed and if it is better or worse.

- Query DBA_INDEXES and DBA_IND_COLUMNS to retrieve a list of the indexes on a given table. Use USER_INDEXES and USER_IND_COLUMNS to retrieve information for only your schema.

- By using *invisible indexes,* you can "turn off" indexes temporarily (make them invisible) to check how queries will perform without them. Since invisible indexes continue to be maintained while invisible, turning them back on (making them visible again) if needed is fast and simple.

- Avoid hard-coding Oracle's ROWID into specific code. The ROWID structure in the past has changed from version to version, and it will probably change again in future releases. I recommend against *never* hard-coding a ROWID.

- You can create your indexes and analyze them in a single step by using the COMPUTE STATISTICS clause of the CREATE INDEX command.

- Using the default values clause for a table column causes NULL values to be disallowed and eliminates the performance problems associated with using NULL values.

- By using functions (such as a TO_DATE or TO_CHAR) that alter the values being compared to a column and not the columns themselves, the indexes are used. The indexes might have been suppressed had you used the function on the column itself.

- Comparing mismatched data types can cause Oracle to suppress an index internally. Even an EXPLAIN PLAN on the query will not help you understand why a full table scan is being performed.

- An index's selectivity is what helps the cost-based optimizer determine an execution path. The more selective, the fewer number of rows will be returned. Improve selectivity by creating concatenated/composite (multicolumn) indexes.

- In general, the larger the database block size, the smaller the binary height of the index.

- Each additional level in the BLEVEL adds additional performance costs during DML.

- Clustering data within the table can be used to improve the performance of statements that perform range scan–type operations. By determining how the column is being used in the statements, indexing these column(s) may be a great benefit.

- Analyzing the index or the table provides the binary height of the index. Use the BLEVEL column in the USER_INDEXES view to check the binary height of the index.

- If the number of deleted rows within an index approaches 20–25 percent, rebuild the index to help reduce the binary height and the amount of empty space that is being read during an I/O.

- If the data in a table is skewed, histograms provide the cost-based optimizer with a picture of the distribution. Using the histograms on columns that are not skewed will not provide a performance increase but will probably degrade it.

- By default, Oracle creates 75 buckets in a histogram. You can specify SIZE values ranging from 1 to 254.

- For large tables with concatenated indexes, the index skip-scan feature provides quick access even when the leading column of the index is not used in a limiting condition.

- The values of the indexed columns are stored in an index. For this reason, you can build concatenated (composite) indexes that can be used to satisfy a query without accessing the table. This eliminates the need to go to the table to retrieve the data, reducing I/O.

- Use bitmap indexes for columns with a low cardinality. An example is a column called SEX with two possible values of 'male' or 'female' (the cardinality is only 2).

- To query a list of your bitmap indexes, query the USER_INDEXES view.

- Don't use bitmap indexes where many inserts occur on tables, such as heavy OLTP environments; learn the restrictions associated with bitmap indexes.

- Take caution before implementing hash clusters. Review the application carefully to ensure that enough information is known about the tables and data before implementing this option. Generally speaking, hashing is best for static data with primarily sequential values.

- Hash indexes are most useful when the limiting condition specifies an exact value rather than a range of values.

- Consider using index-organized tables for tables that are always accessed using exact matches or range scans on the primary key.

- If you have a limited number of disks and large concurrent sequential loads to perform, reverse key indexes may be a viable solution.

- For function-based indexes to be used by the optimizer, you must set the QUERY_REWRITE_ENABLED initialization parameter to TRUE.

- Local prefixed indexes allow Oracle to prune unneeded partitions quickly. The partitions that do not contain any of the values appearing in the WHERE clause will not need to be accessed, thus improving the statement's performance.

- For a non-prefixed index to be unique, it must contain a subset of the partitioning key.

- Specify the UPDATE GLOBAL INDEXES clause of the ALTER TABLE command when modifying a partitioned table. By default, you need to rebuild global indexes when altering a partitioned table.

- If a global index is going to be equipartitioned, create it as a local index to allow Oracle to maintain the index and use it to help prune partitions that will not be needed.

- Use bitmap join indexes to improve the performance of joins within data warehousing environments.

- Use the REBUILD option of the ALTER INDEX statement for quickly rebuilding an index using the existing index instead of the table.

- You can use the REBUILD ONLINE option to allow DML operations on the table or partition during the index rebuild. You cannot specify REBUILD ONLINE for bitmap indexes or for indexes that enforce referential integrity constraints. This option has been improved and is faster and better in 11*g*.

References

Ask Tom Blog, asktom.oracle.com.

"B-tree," http://www.wikipedia.org/wiki/B-tree#Insertion.

Kevin Loney and Bob Bryla, *Oracle Database 11g DBA Handbook* (Oracle Press, 2007).

Metalink note: 39836.1.

Rich Niemiec, "Expert Tuning Tips: Beginners Will Be Toast!", IOUG Conference Paper, 2005.

Oracle Server Tuning (Oracle Corporation).

Greg Pucka, *Oracle Indexing* (TUSC), Conference Paper, 2003.

Server Concepts (Oracle Corporation).

Server Reference (Oracle Corporation).

   Greg Pucka contributed a major portion of this original chapter. Kevin Loney contributed the major portion of the 10*g* update to this chapter. Rich Niemiec added 11*g* new content and Mike Messina tested queries and added BLEVEL detail for the 11*g* version.

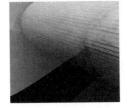

CHAPTER
3

Disk Implementation Methodology and ASM (DBA)

Oracle changed the landscape of disk access in Oracle 10g with the release of Automatic Storage Management (ASM). With the release of Oracle 11g, more features have been added to ASM to make it even more robust. ASM is now the standard for Oracle databases! This chapter will focus heavily on ASM in addition to the non-ASM-specific disk implementation methodology in Oracle.

In the last several years, disk configuration techniques seemed to be reaching the point where you couldn't do much more to improve the performance of your system without greatly complicating your life as a DBA. If your system operated with some unique qualities, or you chose to review the I/O activity on your tablespaces on a frequent basis, you might be able to achieve slightly better performance than simply mashing all your disk use into a single logical device, but for most people, this just wasn't worth it. If you used RAW partitions and were diligent, you could get some performance advantages from using that "technology," but again, it didn't simplify your life as a DBA. Then with the enormous leap in the capacity of single devices, even in the high-end Fibre Channel sector, things were further complicated; restricting yourself to only four or six very large disks was simple, whereas before you may have had a full array or multiple arrays of disks. In the most recent releases of the Oracle Database, you have been given a whole new toolbox.

More features are now available for managing how the data resides on disk. And more have been released in the last 24 months with Exadata. To make it even better, almost anyone running an Oracle database can use these new features. Don't worry; this chapter will still talk about balancing your disk and eliminating fragmentation, but it will also discuss the new features you can utilize to rid yourselves of the repeated effort these activities required in the past or, very possibly, prevent you from having to do them altogether.

To keep your system running at its peak, this chapter offers the following tips:

- Understanding storage hardware and its performance implications
- Understanding RAID levels
- Distributing "key" datafiles across filesystems to minimize contention
- Moving datafiles to balanced file I/O
- Using locally managed tablespaces (LMT) vs. dictionary-managed tablespaces
- Understanding bigfile tablespaces and getting to the 8-exabyte Oracle 11g database
- Viewing file and tablespace information to determine problem areas
- Understanding ASM instances, installation, and SGA parameter sizing
- Understanding ASM disks, diskgroups, and multipathing
- Understanding ASM best practices and rebalancing practices
- Avoiding disk contention and managing large tables by using partitions
- Sizing extents properly to eliminate fragmentation, reduce chaining, and keep performance optimal
- Managing redo and rollbacks in the database for speed
- Using UNDO management

- Sorting only in a TEMPORARY tablespace

- Having multiple control files on different disks and controllers

- Understanding issues to consider in the planning stages of your system

Disk Arrays: Not a Choice Anymore

Configuring disks with RAID (Redundant Array of Independent/Inexpensive Disks) is now the norm. RAID is here to stay, and one would be hard pressed to buy even a midrange system without it. Later in this chapter, you'll see that ASM also provides levels of redundancy. Even in the personal computing area, using some hardware-based configuration of redundant disks has become more commonplace. For the DBA, this means that more than ever, care must be taken to ensure that the disk array configuration used enhances I/O while also providing appropriate protection against drive failure. Regardless of whether the RAID configuration is hardware- or software-based (hardware-based is usually faster), the configuration should be configured properly for best performance, without sacrificing protection.

Use Disk Arrays to Improve Performance and Availability

A RAID logical unit number (LUN) is created by grouping several disks in such a way that the individual disks act as one logical disk (grouped into a volume or virtual disk). Prior to the advent of the storage area network (SAN), a LUN was the address (number) for the disk drive. During normal operation, a single logical device now gets the benefit of having multiple physical devices behind it, which means faster access to data (when configured properly) and the ability to have storage volumes that are significantly greater than the physical limit of an individual device. If a disk fails and all the data on the disk is destroyed, the group of disks can be structured so the data exists in more than one place. The system never goes down because of the failure of a single disk (when the proper RAID level is employed). Users continue to operate as if nothing has happened. The system alerts the system administrator that a specific disk has failed. The administrator pulls out the disk and slides in a new disk. The hardware controller or operating system automatically writes the missing information on the new disk. The system goes on without missing a beat.

How Many Disks Do You Need?

I know the hardware vendors out there are going to love me for this, but it is true. A good rule of thumb on buying disks in today's market is "Don't buy disks on the basis of capacity alone." If you have a moderately sized database at 10T, where performance is very important, why would you buy 600G SAS disks instead of 2TB SATA disks to run it? Speed and data distribution—that's why. SAS disks at 15,000 RPMs are much faster than SATA at 7,200 RPM's, but the infrastructure and tools surrounding SAS are also faster. With disk capacities hovering between 300G to 2T, this choice can be hard to rationalize, but too often lately I have seen people make disk purchase choices on capacity alone. This leaves them with inadequate redundancy (when they forget about mirroring costs), poor performance (using slower disks), or both. You can certainly still use the slower 2T disks for online backups, archived information, or very old information.

Remember, after you configure that 2T disk properly, you may have only less than 1T of usable storage (after mirroring, etc.). Whatever you do, try to use the high-speed 15,000 RPM SAS disks for your most important databases.

What Are Some of the RAID Levels Available?

Almost every midrange to enterprise-class server today offers a hardware RAID solution either built into the server or as an attached storage device. Using the various available RAID levels is pretty much standard, regardless of the type of array you buy. The following list describes some of the more common options that Oracle database administrators will want to consider:

- **RAID 0 (Striped Set)**   Automatic disk striping means that the Oracle datafiles are automatically spread across multiple disks. The tablespace's corresponding datafile pieces can be spread across and accessed from many disks at the same time instead of from one (a large savings in disk I/O). Just be wary; this isn't a solution for high availability or fault tolerance, as a loss of one disk in the group means all the data needs to be recovered.

- **RAID 1 (Mirrored Set)**   Automatic disk mirroring is available on most systems today. It's generally used for the operating system itself but can be used with the Oracle database for higher availability. You need twice the storage compared to the amount of data that you have for RAID 1.

- **RAID 5 (Striped Set with Parity)**   This level carries the parity on an extra disk, which allows for media recovery. Heavy read applications get the maximum advantage from this disk array distribution. This solution is low-cost and generally very bad for write-intensive Oracle applications. I will discuss improvements to this more in the next section.

- **RAID 1+0 (RAID 10, a Stripe of Mirrors)**   Mirrored disks that are then striped. This level is the most common Oracle OLTP production RAID level, also known as *"RAID TEN."* RAID 1+0 incorporates the advantages of the first two RAID levels by adding the disk I/O striping benefit of RAID 0 to the mirroring provided by RAID 1. For high read/write environments such as OLTP, where sporadic access to data is the norm, this RAID level is highly recommended.

- **RAID 0+1 (RAID 01, a Mirror of Stripes)**   Striped disks that are then mirrored. Often confused with RAID 10 or thought not to exist, this level incorporates the advantages of the first two RAID levels by providing the disk I/O striping benefit of RAID 0 to the mirroring provided by RAID 1. For high read/write environments such as OLTP, where sporadic access to data is the norm, this RAID level is good, but it is *not* as robust as RAID 10, and it cannot tolerate two disk failures if they are from different stripes. Also, in a rebuild after failure, all the disks in the array must participate in the rebuild, which is also not as favorable as RAID 10.

- **RAID 1+0+0 (RAID 100, a Stripe of RAID 10s)**   Mirrored disks that are then striped and then striped again (usually with software, the top-level stripe is a MetaLun or soft stripe). The advantages are mainly for random read performance improvement and the elimination of hotspots.

The Newer RAID 5

Many hardware vendors configure systems with a RAID 5 configuration to maximize the utilization of available space on disk and reduce the overall cost of the array. Although RAID 5 is a good choice for inexpensive redundancy, it is usually a poor choice for write-intensive performance. At the most general level, when a write request is made to a RAID 5 array, the modified block must be changed on disk; a "parity" block is read from disk; and using the modified block, a new parity block is calculated and then written to disk. This process, regardless of the size of the write request, can limit throughput because for every write operation, there are at least two more I/O operations. I recommend RAID 5 only for mostly read or read-only filesystems. Most storage vendors realize that this parity write is a penalty and have come up with various solutions to reduce the impact of this additional operation. The most common solution is to implement a memory cache on the array to speed up the write performance of all I/O on the array. For periodic or light write activity, this solution may be completely suitable for your system, but you need to remember that eventually those write operations need to make it to disk. If you overload that disk cache with heavy write activity, you may produce what is often referred to as a "serialized I/O" condition. This is where the array can't write to disk fast enough to clear the cache, essentially neutralizing the benefit of your cache. Be sure to check out other solutions that your vendor may have implemented. Don't be afraid to ask them how they handle heavy I/O. Some solutions to look for are

- **Dynamic cache management** This is the ability for the array to adjust the way that the cache is being used. Some vendors simply split the cache down the middle—if you have 1GB of cache, 500MB is for read and 500MB is for write. Because the Oracle buffer cache is essentially already a read cache, being able to adjust the array cache so it is primarily a write cache can give you some flexibility. This ability to adjust the array cache to be primarily a write cache goes for other configurations other than just RAID 5.

- **Bundled writes** Generally, the maximum size of a write operation is larger than an Oracle block. Some vendors have implemented intelligence into their arrays that allows them to group multiple parity operations into a single I/O operation. Because this requires fewer round trips to the physical disk, it can greatly improve the performance and effectiveness of the cache when running RAID 5.

RAID 6 is another variant of RAID 5 that you may also see advertised. RAID 6 behaves just like RAID 5, except it utilizes corresponding parity blocks for every set of data block stripes. While this does carry the added benefit of more fault tolerance, because you can lose two disks, it also brings with it even lower performance.

I still prefer to see RAID 1+0 (mirroring and then striping). RAID 1+0 (also known as *RAID TEN*) is generally going to be faster or at least as fast as RAID 5 and natively more fault tolerant to multiple device failures. Because you may be in a situation where you have multiple physical enclosures for your disk, using striping and mirroring allowed you to build fault tolerance between enclosures too.

Setup and Maintenance of the Traditional Filesystem

Using RAID-configured groups of physical devices and traditional filesystems makes Oracle datafile setup and maintenance *much* easier for the DBA because manually balancing disks is not as arduous. With the large disk sizes in today's storage systems, dissecting filesystem configuration between 4 or 6 devices quickly becomes an exercise in splitting hairs. Unless you are utilizing a system where 12 or more physical disks are involved, dividing these up into more than one logical disk device provides only a small benefit. Even if you have a case where two datafiles are heavily utilized, the cache or host bus adapter (HBA) that they share on the array may be a common avenue to the disk. Finally, depending on your expected growth, the number of filesystems you end up managing could, in time, make keeping all of this in balance a frustrating exercise.

TIP
Try to avoid splitting a logical device in a disk array into more than one filesystem. Splitting may seem to give you flexibility, but it can also increase the number of datafile locations you have to manage.

What Is the Cost?

To support disk arrays that mirror data, you need more—sometimes much more—raw disk storage (for RAID 1, you need double the space). While this requirement can increase the price of your initial system, the benefits are usually well worth it. For these reasons, while you are deciding how to configure the new storage system you are going to buy, think about the return on investment (ROI) for keeping the system up and running and also the value of great performance.

This leads me to another class of storage system that is becoming more popular. With the rising capacity of even the most basic storage array, companies are looking to leverage that storage space with *multinode* access technologies. Whether the implementation is as a storage area network (SAN) or network-attached storage (NAS), the initial investment and added benefit of being able to "plug in" another server to your storage system is often well worth it. So when you are faced with the dilemma of having a 4 Gbit/sec Fibre Channel (Exadata has 40Gb/sec each direction with InfiniBand) storage array with four disks and are feeling a bit like you aren't utilizing the resource to its maximum, consider expanding that purchase into an infrastructure decision that allows your enterprise to grow and share that resource among all your important systems.

TIP
Use disk arrays to improve performance and protect your data against disk failure. Choose the proper RAID level and technology solutions that enable you to maintain the availability your organization needs. Don't go "good enough," because you will regret it at 2 A.M. when you lose a disk.

Distributing "Key" Datafiles Across Hardware Disks

To operate the Oracle database efficiently on traditional filesystems, take special care to distribute "key" datafiles across available filesystems. For example, heavily accessed tables should be located on filesystems separate from corresponding indexes. In addition, online redo logs and archive logs should be stored separately from datafiles for recovery purposes when the disk configuration allows. The reality is, in most cases with the hardware available today, you want to make sure you aren't compromising the ability to use your disk effectively by resorting to overkill in dividing it up. Unless you have many devices under those filesystems, you are just making more work for yourself. The files associated with the following elements should be separated when possible:

- The SYSTEM tablespace

- The TEMPORARY tablespace

- The UNDO tablespace

- The online redo log files (try to put these on your fastest disks)

- The operating system disk

- Key Oracle files located in the ORACLE_HOME directory

- Datafiles for heavily accessed tables

- Datafiles for heavily accessed indexes

- Archive area (should always be separated from the data to be recovered)

The following example illustrates file distribution across 11*g* filesystems in a Unix environment:

```
/: Operating System
/u01: Oracle software
/u02: Temporary Tablespace, Control File 1
/u03: Undo Segments, Control File 2
/u04: Redo Logs, Archive Logs, Control File 4
/u05: System and SYSAUX Tablespaces
/u06: Data1, Control File 3
/u07: Redo Log Mirror, Index3
/u08: Data2
/u09: Index2
/u10: Data3
/u11: Index1
```

Storing Data and Index Files in Separate Locations

Tables that are joined (simultaneously accessed during a query) often could also have their data and index tablespaces separated. The following example shows a table join and one possible solution for managing the data:

```
select   COL1, COL2, ....
from     CUST_HEADER, CUST_DETAIL
where    ...;
```

Here is a data management solution:

```
Disk1:  CUST_HEADER Table
Disk5:  CUST_HEADER Index
Disk8:  CUST_DETAIL Table
Disk12: CUST_DETAIL Index
```

This solution allows the table join to be done while accessing four different disks and controllers. Separate data and index files onto different physical disk devices and controllers; consequently, when tables and indexes are accessed at the same time, they will not be accessing the same physical devices. You could expand this to involve a larger number of disks. You will see later in the chapter that table and index partitioning will help you to accomplish this more easily. Oracle's ASM does a great job of assisting with this when you set it up, but it also has ways of moving *hot* data to a different part of a disk.

TIP
Separate key Oracle datafiles to ensure that disk contention is not a bottleneck. By separating tables and indexes of often-joined tables, you can ensure that even the worst of table joins do not result in disk contention. In 11g Enterprise Manager, Oracle makes it easy to move data to a hotter *or* colder *region of a disk.*

Avoiding I/O Disk Contention

Disk contention occurs when multiple processes try to access the same physical disk simultaneously. Disk contention can be reduced, thereby increasing performance, by distributing the disk I/O more evenly over the available disks. Disk contention can also be reduced by decreasing disk I/O. To monitor disk contention, review the Database Files Metrics in Database Control. This Metric group contains two sets of metrics. The *Average File Read Time* and *Average File Write Time* apply to all datafiles associated with your database. If you find that one or two datafiles seem to have especially high values, you click one and then use the Compare Objects File Name link to view collected statistics between them. If they are both busy at the same time and are on the same disk, you may choose to relocate one datafile to another filesystem, if you are concerned about performance during that time.

You can also determine file I/O problems by running a query:

```
col PHYRDS   format 999,999,999
col PHYWRTS  format 999,999,999
ttitle  "Disk Balancing Report"
col READTIM   format 999,999,999
col WRITETIM   format 999,999,999
col name format a40
spool fio1.out

select  name, phyrds, phywrts, readtim, writetim
from    v$filestat a, v$datafile b
where   a.file# = b.file#
order   by readtim desc
/
spool off
```

Here is a partial query output:

```
Fri Mar 24                                          page 1
                   Disk Balancing Report
```

NAME	Phyrds	Phywrts	ReadTim	WriteTim
/d01/psindex_1.dbf	48,310	51,798	200,564	903,199
/d02/psindex_02.dbf	34,520	40,224	117,925	611,121
/d03/psdata_01.dbf	35,189	36,904	97,474	401,290
/d04/undotbs01.dbf	1,320	11,725	1,214	39,892
/d05/system01.dbf	1,454	10	10	956

. . .

NOTE
You may also have SYSAUX01.DBF, USERS01.DBF, and EXAMPLE01.DBF.

A large difference in the number of physical writes and reads between disks may indicate that a disk is being overburdened. In the preceding example, filesystems 1–3 are heavily used whereas filesystems 4–5 are only lightly used. To get a better balance, you'll want to move some of the datafiles. Splitting datafiles across multiple disks or using partitions would also help move access to a table or an index to an additional disk.

TIP
Query V$FILESTAT and V$DATAFILE to see how effectively datafiles have been balanced. Note that temporary tablespaces are monitored using V$TEMPFILE and V$TEMPSTAT.

Moving Datafiles to Balance File I/O

To physically move a datafile that is causing file contention, follow these steps:

1. Take the tablespace corresponding to the datafile offline:

   ```
   ALTER TABLESPACE ORDERS OFFLINE;
   ```

2. Copy the datafile to the new location on disk:

   ```
   $cp /disk1/orders1.dbf /disk2/orders1.dbf   (UNIX copy command)
   ```

3. Rename the datafile to the new datafile location for the tablespace:

   ```
   ALTER DATABASE orcl
   RENAME FILE '/disk1/orders1.dbf' to '/disk2/orders1.dbf';
   ```

4. Bring the tablespace back online:

   ```
   ALTER TABLESPACE ORDERS ONLINE;
    Delete the old data file (when sure the moved data file can be accessed):
   $rm /disk1/orders1.dbf   (UNIX delete command)
   ```

TIP
Solve disk contention problems by moving datafiles to disks that are not as heavily accessed.

Another method, useful for very large, critical files, is the following:

1. Put the tablespace in READ ONLY mode and verify the status by querying DBA_TABLESPACES.

2. Copy the datafiles at the OS level. Compare files sizes after the copy to make sure they are the same.

3. Alter the tablespace offline.

4. Use the ALTER TABLESPACE command to rename the datafile.

5. Alter the tablespace back ONLINE.

6. Alter the tablespace to READ WRITE.

7. Verify the control file was updated by querying V$DATAFILE.

8. Remove the old datafile at the OS level.

TIP
Use the Database Files Metrics in Enterprise Manager to determine the I/O that is taking place on each database file. Move heavily used datafiles to separate filesystems to distribute I/O.

Locally Managed Tablespaces

Prior to Oracle 8*i*, all tablespace extent information for segments was maintained by the Oracle data dictionary. As a result, any operations that occurred against segments in the database that related to extent allocation, such as extending or truncating a table, would incur operations against the data dictionary. These operations could become very expensive from a database management point of view since the data dictionary could become a bottleneck for these operations when many tables with many extents were involved. With Oracle 8*i*, a new extent management option was provided called *locally managed* extents. With locally managed extents, these extent management operations are relocated to a bitmap block in the header of the datafile itself. This allows for improved performance because each tablespace in the database contains only its own extent information that can be accessed using a fast hashing process instead of the slower table-based query.

When using the locally managed tablespace feature, Oracle provides two options for extent allocation to segments in addition to the traditional "user" "-managed extent definition available in dictionary-managed tablespaces. These two options are "*autoallocate*" and "*uniform.*" In an autoallocate management scheme, the database uses an internal algorithm to increase extent sizes for segments as they grow. With autoallocate, as a segment grows in a tablespace, the database determines the appropriate next extent size by using an internal algorithm that factors in, among other things, the number of extents and the rate of extension. The advantage here is that the database increases the next extent size of a table automatically and should, therefore, reduce the overall number of extents that the table would have had, if it had been defined with an inappropriately small extent size. If you are working with a new application and are unsure of how segments may grow, you may find using autoallocate to assure extent counts don't get out of hand advantageous.

In uniform extent management, all extents in a tablespace are allocated with an equal size that is specified when the tablespace is created, regardless of the storage clause specified in the segment CREATE statement. When possible, employing uniform extents is the preferred method. The principle reason is that when segments are moved or dropped, reusing freed extents in the tablespace can be achieved more efficiently because they are already the appropriate size for the remaining segments. I'll discuss this further in "Eliminating Fragmentation," later in the chapter.

Creating Tablespaces as Locally Managed

To create a tablespace as locally managed, use the extent management clause on the CREATE TABLESPACE statement to set the mode in which extents will be allocated:

```
CREATE TABLESPACE USER_256K_DAT datafile '/u01/user_256k_dat_01.dbf' SIZE 100M
extent management local uniform size 256K;
```

A good practice when creating locally managed tablespaces with uniform extents is to specify the extent size in the tablespace name. Doing this allows you to more easily track the tablespace extent sizes you have defined and makes determining which tablespace a segment should be moved to or created in easier.

When creating segments in a locally managed tablespace, do not specify a storage clause to define parameters such as INITIAL, NEXT, and PCTINCREASE. These parameters can lead to confusion, since they are traced in the DBA_SEGMENTS dictionary table, but ignored with respect to how extents are allocated. The following query shows how to get more information about the extent management of tablespaces in the database, which can be helpful in documenting what you have:

```
SELECT tablespace_name, extent_management, allocation_type
from   dba_tablespaces;
```

```
TABLESPACE_NAME      EXTENT_MAN ALLOCATION
-------------------- ---------- ----------
SYSTEM               LOCAL      SYSTEM
SYSAUX               LOCAL      SYSTEM
UNDOTBS1             LOCAL      SYSTEM
TEMP                 LOCAL      UNIFORM
USERS                LOCAL      SYSTEM
EXAMPLE              LOCAL      SYSTEM
```

The default database install has ALLOCATION_TYPE set to SYSTEM for the following tablespaces: SYSTEM, USERS, SYSAUX, EXAMPLE, and UNDOTBS1. Locally managed SYSTEM tablespaces became possible in 9.2. In 11g, if you manually create a database using the CREATE DATABASE command, the default is to create a dictionary-managed tablespace for SYSTEM. If you use DBCA to create a new database using a template, the LOCALLY MANAGED value is the default setting on the Storage tab for all tablespaces, including the SYSTEM tablespace.

Migrating Dictionary-Managed Tablespaces to Locally Managed

You can migrate dictionary-managed tablespaces to locally managed tablespaces, but this is not recommended. When a tablespace is migrated to locally managed, the extent map is moved into the tablespace datafile header. The second benefit, however, autoallocate or uniform extent size management, is not available. As a result, any benefit to reducing fragmentation is decreased because you must now specify storage clauses for each tablespace segment. The extent bitmap is located at the point previously occupied by the start of the first free extent in the file. The user does not get the policy benefits from migration but can still get performance benefits: no space transaction (ST) enqueue contention and more efficient extent operations.

Whenever possible, rebuild dictionary-managed tablespaces to a locally managed uniform extent mode by exporting segments in the tablespace, dropping and re-creating the tablespace, and then importing the segments back into the tablespace. Be sure to check your segment sizes before you perform this process. You might find it more beneficial to split the single tablespace into several different tablespaces with differently sized extents to accommodate segments of vastly different sizes.

The only exception to the rule with regard to tablespaces that you should migrate from dictionary-managed to locally managed is the SYSTEM tablespace. Although rebuilding your database using Data Pump expdp/impdp (or exp/imp) is still preferred, this may not always be possible. As of Oracle 11g/10g, you now have the ability to migrate the SYSTEM tablespace using the DBMS_SPACE_ADMIN.TABLESPACE_MIGRATE_TO_LOCAL procedure. Before you can perform this operation, there are several restrictions:

- The default TEMPORARY tablespace for all users in the database must be a tablespace other than SYSTEM.

- You must migrate or convert all of the tablespaces you intend to have read/write to locally managed tablespaces.

- The database must be started in restricted mode.

- You must have all tablespaces, other than undo, in read-only mode for the conversion or have an online rollback segment defined in a locally managed tablespace. In 11*g*, you should be using locally managed tablespaces (LMTs).

Oracle Bigfile Tablespaces

Oracle 10*g* (and continuing into 11*g*) introduced a new locally managed tablespace type for extreme-size databases: *Bigfile tablespaces* allow for the creation of tablespaces with one file where the size of that datafile fully incorporates the power of 64-bit systems. When implemented with Oracle Managed Files or Automatic Storage Management (ASM), bigfile tablespaces can greatly simplify the management of your storage system. Additionally, because you should have fewer datafiles, performance of database management operations such as checkpoints should improve, but be aware that recovery operation times are likely to increase in the event of datafile corruption.

Now you be may asking, "Then what is the benefit of bigfile tablespaces?" A bigfile tablespace with a typical 8K block can contain a single 32-terabyte datafile. If you're using a 32K block, it can contain a 128-terabyte datafile. This is achieved by changing the way ROWIDs are managed within the tablespace. In a traditional tablespace, three positions in the ROWID are used to identify the relative file number of the row. Because you only have one datafile in bigfile tablespaces, these three positions are instead used to lengthen the data block number for the row, thereby allowing for a much larger number of ROWIDs from traditional smallfile tablespaces.

NOTE
To have the largest Oracle 11g database possible—8 exabytes—you must use 128T datafiles.

To use bigfile tablespaces, you must be using locally managed tablespaces with Automatic Segment Space Management (ASSM). Also, you cannot use bigfile tablespaces for UNDO, TEMP, or SYSTEM. If you are thinking of using bigfile tablespaces to reduce the amount of management needed for your system, consider also using Oracle Managed Files (OMF) and ASM (covered later in this chapter). Also, if you are using traditional filesystems, make sure you are using a logical volume manager that provides the flexibility to map out your storage system appropriately so the single datafile can grow as needed.

Oracle Managed Files

Oracle Managed Files (OMF) was first introduced in version 9*i* of the database. The purpose of OMF is to eliminate the need for the DBA to manage directly the names of the datafiles that belong to the database. If you have a big filesystem for all your database-related files, OMF may be for you. To implement it, you first need to specify some initialization parameters for your database.

This parameter defines the default location of new datafiles, tempfiles, redo log files, control files, and any block change-tracking files:

```
DB_CREATE_FILE_DEST
```

These parameters define the default location and size of redo logs, control files, RMAN backup files, archived logs, and flashback logs. These parameters override the previous parameter for those common file types.

```
DB_RECOVERY_FILE_DEST
DB_RECOVERY_FILE_DEST_SIZE
```

This parameter defines the default location of redo log files and control files and overrides the previous two parameters for those types of files. As usual, specify two locations to make sure you have multiple copies of your archive logs and control files. You specify this parameter multiple times (using a value for *n* that is between 1 and 5) to set mirror locations.

```
DB_CREATE_ONLINE_LOG_DEST_n
```

Now when you need to add a datafile, you can simply run an "ALTER TABLESPACE...ADD DATAFILE" command. If you want to create a new tablespace, you can just run a "CREATE TABLESPACE..." command, all without specifying the actual datafiles involved because the database will do that for you.

For example, if you have six filesystems for the database, to use each of them for different files, you need to identify the filesystem when adding a datafile to a particular tablespace, as shown here:

```
SQL> ALTER SYSTEM SET DB_CREATE_FILE_DEST = '/u01/oradata';
SQL> CREATE TABLESPACE tbs_1;
```

This gives you the advantage of not needing to worry about creating a file that already exists, but it doesn't provide any advantage for capacity management or balancing I/O. To get this balance with OMF, you need to look at another technology that Oracle has provided: ASM.

ASM Introduction

Before diving into the intricacies of ASM, I want to first take a moment to thank Nitin Vengurlekar from Oracle, who provided this excellent addition to this chapter.

In Oracle Database 10g Release 2, storage management and provisioning for the database has been greatly simplified using *Automatic Storage Management (ASM)*. ASM provides filesystem and volume manager capabilities built into the Oracle database kernel. In Oracle Database 11g, Oracle ASM as a technology is the best of all worlds, combining the benefits of using RAW devices with the ease of management as seen with standard volume managers in UNIX. With this capability, ASM simplifies storage management tasks, such as creating/laying out databases and disk space management. Because ASM allows you to manage disks using familiar CREATE/ALTER/DROP SQL statements, DBAs do not need to learn a new skill set or make crucial provisioning decisions. ASM is basically built on RAW devices; therefore, it is also inherently CLUSTER aware. The initial release of ASM was first built for a clustered database and then made available for nonclustered databases. An Enterprise Manager interface (see Chapter 5 for additional information), as well as a new command-line utility (new in Oracle Database 10g Release 2 and available in 11g), asmcmd, is also available for those ASM administrators who are not familiar with SQL.

ASM is a management tool specifically built to simplify the DBA's job. It provides a simple storage management interface across all server and storage platforms. ASM provides the DBA with flexibility to manage a dynamic database environment with increased efficiency. This feature is a key component of grid computing and database storage consolidation.

The following are some of ASM's key benefits:

- As good as raw devices from a performance perspective.

- An extremely simple, but powerful, volume manager toolkit/utility for managing the space from a database perspective.

- Spreads I/O evenly across all available disk drives to prevent hot spots and maximize performance.

- Eliminates the need for over provisioning and maximizes storage resource utilization facilitating database consolidation.

- Inherently supports large files.

- Performs automatic online redistribution after the incremental addition or removal of storage capacity.

- Maintains redundant copies of data to provide high availability or leverage third-party RAID functionality.

- Supports Oracle Database 11g as well as Oracle Real Application Clusters (RAC).

- The OCR and voting disk can be on the ASM diskgroup and cluster filesystem with ASM in 11gR2.

- Can leverage third-party multipathing technologies.

- Inherently capable of supporting ASYNC I/O as well as DIRECT I/O.

- Fully integrated into Oracle Managed Files (OMF), thereby reducing complexity without comprising performance.

- Exadata only allows ASM.

For simplicity and easier migration to ASM, an Oracle 10gR2 and above database can contain ASM and non-ASM files. You can use the RMAN COPY command move datafiles from the filesystem to an ASM diskgroup.

Additionally, ASM is completely storage agnostic; therefore, ASM works with a wide spectrum of storage arrays from high-end storage arrays, such as EMC DMX and HDS, to low-cost commodity storage, such as Apple XServe. ASM was built primarily to resolve database configuration and layout issues and communication across IT roles.

DBAs have much to consider before they deploy and create a database. They must consider and determine the following:

- Plan filesystem layout and device usage

- Determine application workload characteristics (random read/write for OLTP versus sequential I/O for DSS systems)

- Calculate storage capacity and sizing for the database

ASM addresses these concerns in the following ways:

- Traditionally, DBAs would create filesystems to store their database files, and then create additional filesystems as needed. Doing this can become a manageability and provisioning nightmare since DBAs also have to manage the I/O load on each filesystem. ASM presents a single storage pool (*diskgroup*), so there is no need to maintain several filesystem containers and no need to worry about the placement of the next datafile.

- One of the core benefits of ASM is the ability to expand storage to meet an application's capacity needs. Thus, the ASM diskgroup that houses the database can be expanded without worrying excessively about storage capability management.

- Using ASM and applying the defined general best practices, ASM-based databases should be able to handle any workload. Additionally, because ASM inherently uses raw devices, considerations such as async I/O and direct I/O become nonissues.

Communication Across IT Roles

Sometimes there is a disconnect among the DBA, system admin, and storage admin. The DBA asks for a 200GB filesystem, the storage/system admin provides a 200GB RAID 5 device or RAID 10 device that has an improper or inefficient stripe size and performance starts to suffer. Later, the DBA finds out what was actually provisioned and isn't very happy.

DBAs and other technical IT roles will always experience some inherent level of disconnect because these groups think and operate differently. As this disconnect is mostly a communication issue, ASM doesn't necessarily fix it. However, several things come into play with ASM that have lessened this communication issue. First, Oracle published a paper called Optimal Storage Configuration Made Easy (available on technet.oracle.com). This paper proposed a stripe-and-mirror-everything (SAME) methodology. With this paper came a standard methodology for database deployment, which made DBA-storage admin communication much simpler because DBAs had a way to express what they needed.

NOTE
You can get more information at Technet:
http://www.oracle.com/technetwork/database/focus-areas/performance/
opt-storage-conf-130048.pdf.

ASM incorporates all the essentials of SAME methodology. ASM also offers a streamlined approach to storage capacity management. With ASM, database storage can be expanded as business or capacity plans dictate, all with no application downtime.

ASM Instances

Starting with Oracle Database 10*g* (and continuing through 11*g*R2), there are two types of instances: database and ASM instances. The ASM instance, which is generally named +ASM, is started with the INSTANCE_TYPE=ASM initialization parameter. This parameter, when set, signals the Oracle initialization routine to start an ASM instance, not a standard database instance. Unlike the standard database instance, the ASM instance contains no physical files, such as log files, control files, or datafiles, and requires only a few initialization parameters for startup.

Upon startup, an ASM instance will spawn all the basic background processes, plus some new ones that are specific to the operation of ASM. The STARTUP clauses for ASM instances are similar to those for database instances. For example, NOMOUNT starts up an ASM instance without mounting any diskgroup. The MOUNT option simply mounts all defined diskgroups.

ASM is the volume manager for all databases that employ ASM on a given node or server. Therefore, only one ASM instance is required per node, regardless of the number of database instances on the server. Additionally, ASM seamlessly works with the RAC architecture to support clustered storage environments. In RAC environments, there is one ASM instance per clustered node, and the ASM instances communicate with each other on a peer-to-peer basis using the interconnect.

Here is an example to query for the instance name that you are connected to:

```
select  instance_name
from    v$instance;


INSTANCE_NAME
----------------
+ASM
```

Below is a list of the various views that you can query to see the ASM configuration:

```
select name, type
from    v$fixed_table
where name like 'GV$%ASM%'
SYS@+ASM> /


NAME                              TYPE
--------------------------------- -----
GV$ASM_TEMPLATE                   VIEW
GV$ASM_ALIAS                      VIEW
GV$ASM_FILE                       VIEW
GV$ASM_VOLUME                     VIEW
```

```
GV$ASM_FILESYSTEM                    VIEW
GV$ASM_ACFSVOLUMES                   VIEW
GV$ASM_ACFSSNAPSHOTS                 VIEW
GV$ASM_ACFS_SECURITY_INFO            VIEW
GV$ASM_ACFS_ENCRYPTION_INFO          VIEW
GV$ASM_VOLUME_STAT                   VIEW
GV$ASM_CLIENT                        VIEW
GV$ASM_DISKGROUP                     VIEW
GV$ASM_DISKGROUP_STAT                VIEW
GV$ASM_DISK                          VIEW
GV$ASM_DISK_STAT                     VIEW
GV$ASM_DISK_IOSTAT                   VIEW
GV$ASM_OPERATION                     VIEW
GV$ASM_ATTRIBUTE                     VIEW
GV$ASM_USER                          VIEW
GV$ASM_USERGROUP                     VIEW
GV$ASM_USERGROUP_MEMBER              VIEW
```

These views are also available under the database that is using ASM sometimes with slightly different information, such as V$ASM_CLIENT

ASM Initialization Parameters

The list that follows shows some of the basic initialization parameters required to start ASM. Observe that all ASM processes begin with *asm,* as opposed to the database processes, whose names begin with *ora.*

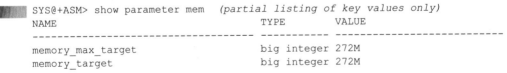

```
*.instance_type=asm
*.asm_diskgroups=DATA
*.large_pool_size=12M
*.asm_diskstring='/dev/rdsk/c3t19d*s4'        #
*.remote_login_passwordfile='SHARED'
*.diagnostic_dest='/u01/app/oracle'  -- 11g and higher
```

In 11*g,* DBAs that use ASM tend to use AUTOMATIC MEMORY MANAGEMENT, so it uses the initialization parameters MEMORY_TARGET and MAX_MEMORY_TARGET:

```
SYS@+ASM> show parameter mem   (partial listing of key values only)
NAME                                 TYPE        VALUE
------------------------------------ ----------- ---------------------------
memory_max_target                    big integer 272M
memory_target                        big integer 272M
```

ASM Installation

In Oracle 11gR1 and prior, Oracle ASM and the actual database instance could run from the same ORACLE_HOME. Where a single ASM instance is managing only one database instance, you may find it sufficient to maintain a single ORACLE_HOME for ASM and the database. For systems that have an ASM instance managing the storage for several database instances and require higher availability, however, it is recommended that the ASM instance be installed in a separate ORACLE_HOME (ASM_HOME) rather than the database ORACLE_HOME. This setup also gives you the ability to patch ASM separately from the Oracle Database.

Oracle Database 11gR2 represents a significant conceptual shift for the installation and infrastructure of the Oracle software stack. With Oracle 11gR2, you now

1. First install the Oracle Grid Infrastructure (GI) ORACLE HOME.

2. Second install the DB ORACLE_HOME.

From the GI ORACLE HOME, run the basic CRS components, the ASM instance, and the basic listener for the ASM instance. If installing in a single instance mode, the CRS components are run in what is known as "LOCAL" mode. All of this is done seamlessly via the Oracle Universal Installer (OUI), which now includes all the steps required to set up ASM. The databases run out of their respective DB ORACLE_HOMEs. The Database Configuration Assistant (DBCA), therefore, needs to be invoked out of the appropriate DB ORACLE_HOME. You could also choose to have OUI start DBCA to create a database as the last installation step.

Additionally, with Oracle Database 11gR2, ASM transparently provides file storage for both older and newer software versions of the database, ranging from version 10gR1 to 11gR2. This new feature provides higher availability as well as the foundation for the database storage consolidation feature.

ASM Parameters and SGA Sizing

With 11gR2, when you install ASM, OUI creates a server parameter file (SPFILE) for the ASM instance and stores it in a diskgroup. Enabling the ASM instance requires configuring only a handful of initialization parameters. The parameter file for ASM can be a Pfile or an SPFILE. However, if you use an SPFILE in clustered ASM environments, then you must put on a shared raw device or within an ASM diskgroup (which is the default). The initialization parameters specified next are the essential parameters required to start up ASM.

The following describes the usage of SGA components for an ASM instance:

- **DB_CACHE_SIZE** This value determines the size of the cache. This buffer cache area is used to cache metadata blocks. The default value suits most implementations, and in such cases, you do not even need to supply a value. With 11gR2, ASM now uses automatic memory management (AMM) *out of the box*. With 11gR2, this is now controlled via MEMORY_TARGET/MEMORY_MAX_TARGET VALUE (minimum values can be set, however; see Chapter 4 for additional details).

- **SHARED_POOL** Used for standard memory usage (control structures, etc.) to manage the instance. Also used to store extent maps. The default value suits most implementations. With 11gR2, the SHARED_POOL is now controlled via MEMORY_TARGET/MEMORY_MAX_TARGET VALUE (a minimum value can be set).

- **LARGE_POOL** Used for large allocations. The default value suits most implementations.

The "PROCESSES" initialization parameter for ASM may need to be modified from the default value. The following recommendation is for 11*g* (and also works with 10*g*) and will work for RAC and non-RAC systems. This formula can be used to determine an optimal value for this parameter:

25 + 15n, where *n* is the number of databases using ASM for their storage

ASM and Privileges

Access to the ASM instance is comparable to a standard instance; i.e., SYSDBA and SYSOPER. Note, however, that since there is no data dictionary, authentication is done from an operating system level and/or an Oracle password file. Typically, the SYSDBA privilege is granted through the use of an operating system group. On Unix, this is typically the dba group, also referred to as the OSDBA group. With Oracle 10*g*, members of the dba group have SYSDBA privileges on all instances on the node, including the ASM instance. Users who connect to the ASM instance with the SYSDBA privilege have complete administrative access to all diskgroups in the system.

In 11*g*, Oracle has modified this concept and introduced the concept of ASMDBA, as well as the role of SYSASM. This role is tied to the OS level group, logically called OSASM. This continues support for the separation of duties concept between system administrators and DBAs. The SYSDBA role can still be used when connecting to an ASM instance but this role is not the all powerful user. It has access capabilities to all the V$ views but does not have administrative privileges on ASM instances.

See table and example showing the various roles:

OS Level Logical Group	DBA Privilege Level
OSOPER	SYSOPER
OSDBA	SYSDBA
OSASM	SYSASM

```
SYS@+ASM> desc v$pwfile_users
 Name                                      Null?    Type
 ----------------------------------------- -------- ----------------
 USERNAME                                           VARCHAR2(30)
 SYSDBA                                             VARCHAR2(5)
 SYSOPER                                            VARCHAR2(5)
 SYSASM                                             VARCHAR2(5)

SYS@+ASM> select * from v$pwfile_users;

USERNAME                        SYSDB SYSOP SYSAS
------------------------------- ----- ----- -----
SYS                             TRUE  TRUE  TRUE
ASMSNMP                         TRUE  FALSE FALSE
```

The SYSOPER privilege is supported in ASM instances and limits the set of allowable SQL commands to the minimum required for basic operation of an already-configured system.

The SYSASM privileges permit mounting and dismounting diskgroups and other storage administration tasks. SYSASM privileges provide no access privileges on an RDBMS instance. The following commands are available to SYSASM users:

■ STARTUP/SHUTDOWN

■ ALTER DISKGROUP MOUNT/DISMOUNT

■ ALTER DISKGROUP ONLINE/OFFLINE DISK

■ ALTER DISKGROUP REBALANCE

■ ALTER DISKGROUP CHECK

■ Access to all V$ASM_* views

All other commands, such as CREATE DISKGROUP, ADD/DROP/RESIZE DISK, and so on, require the SYSDBA privilege and are not allowed with the SYSOPER privilege.

ASM Disks

The first task in building the ASM infrastructure is to discover and associate (add) disks under ASM management. This step is best done with the coordination of storage and systems administrators. The storage administrator identifies a set of disks from the storage array that will be presented to the host. The term *disk* may be used loosely. A disk can be a partition of a physical spindle, the entire spindle, or a RAID group set (defined in the storage array); usage depends on how the storage array presents the logical unit number (LUN) to the operating system (OS). In this chapter, I refer generically to LUNs or disks presented to the OS as simply *disks*. On Solaris systems, disks generally have the following SCSI name format: *CwTxDySz,* where *C* is the controller number, *T* is the target, *D* is the LUN/disk number, and *S* is the partition. Note that each OS has its own unique representation of SCSI disk naming.

ASM must use only character devices as disks, not block devices. However, on Linux, you can use ASMLib to access block devices. According to the Oracle docs: "The purpose of ASMLib, which is an optional add-on to ASM, is to provide an alternative interface for the ASM-enabled kernel to discover and access block devices."

On most Unix systems, character devices are shown as /dev/rdsk (or /dev/raw/raw on Linux). The only exception to this case is when ASM uses NAS file-system files as disks. ASMLib allows an Oracle database using ASM more efficient and capable access to the diskgroups it is using.

For example, it is a best practice on a Solaris system to create a partition on the disk, such as slice 4 or 6, that skips the first 1M into the disk. Creating a partition serves several purposes. A partition creates a placeholder to identify that the disk is being used. An unpartitioned disk could be accidentally misused or overwritten. Skipping 1M into the disk is done to skip the OS label/VTOC (volume table of contents), as well as to preserve alignment between ASM striping and storage array internal striping. Different operating systems have varying requirements for the OS label; some may require an OS label before it is used whereas others do not. The same principles apply for different operating systems, although the procedures may differ.

SAN environments assume the disks are identified and configured—that they are appropriately zoned or LUN-masked within the SAN fabric and can be seen by the OS. Once the disks are identified, they need to be discovered by ASM, which requires that the disk devices (Unix filenames) have their ownership changed from root to the OS user that owns the ASM software, for example, Oracle.

Throughout this chapter, a running example consisting of diskgroup DATA is used to outline the procedural steps for creating a diskgroup and other ASM objects. In this example, disks c3t19d5s4, c3t19d16s4, c3t19d17s4, and c3t19d18s4 are identified, and their ownership set to the correct "*ORACLE:DBA*" ownership. Now, you can configure the INIT.ORA parameter, ASM_DISKSTRING, to enable discovery of these disks. In this example, I use the following wildcard setting:

```
*.asm_diskstring='/dev/rdsk/c3t19d*s4'
```

When ASM scans for disks, it uses that string and finds any devices that it has permission to open. Upon successful discovery, the V$ASM_DISK view on the ASM instance now reflects which disks were discovered. Note, henceforth, all views, unless otherwise stated, are examined from the ASM instance and not from the database instance. In the example that follows, notice that the NAME column is empty and the GROUP_NUMBER is set to 0. Disks that are discovered but not yet associated with a diskgroup have a null name and a group number of 0.

```
select name, path, group_number
from    v$asm_disk;
```

NAME	PATH	GROUP_NUMBER
	/dev/rdsk/c3t19d5s4	0
	/dev/rdsk/c3t19d16s4	0
	/dev/rdsk/c3t19d17s4	0
	/dev/rdsk/c3t19d18s4	0

Disks have various *header statuses* that reflect their membership state with a diskgroup. Disks can have the following header statuses:

- **Former**   This state declares that the disk was formerly part of a diskgroup.
- **Candidate**   When a disk is in this state, it indicates it is available to be added to a diskgroup.
- **Member**   This state indicates that a disk is already part of a diskgroup.
- **Provisioned**   This state is similar to candidate, in that it is available to diskgroups.

However, the provisioned state indicates that this disk has been configured or made available using ASMLib. ASMLib is a support library for ASM. Cases may exist in RAC environments where disk paths are not identical on all nodes. For example, node1 will have /dev/rdsk/c3t1d4s4 that points to a disk, and node2 will present /dev/rdsk/c4t1d4s4 for the same device. This is typical and should not be considered an issue. ASM does not require the disks have the same names on every node. However, ASM does require that the same disks are visible to each ASM instance via that instance's discovery string. The instances can have different discovery strings if necessary.

ASM and Multipathing

An I/O path generally consists of an initiator port, a fabric port, a target port, and an LUN. Each permutation of this I/O path is considered an independent path. Dynamic multipathing/failover tools aggregate these independent paths into a single logical path. This path abstraction provides I/O load balancing across the host bus adapters (HBA), as well as nondisruptive failovers on I/O path failures. Multipathing (MP) software requires all the required disks to be visible on each available and eligible HBA. An MP driver detects multipaths by performing a SCSI inquiry command. Multipathing software also provides multipath software drivers. To support multipathing, a physical HBA driver must comply with the multipathing services provided by this driver. Please ensure that the configuration that you are considering is certified by the vendor. A multipathing tool provides the following benefits:

■ Provides a single block device interface for a multipathed LUN.

■ Detects any component failures in the I/O path, for example, fabric port, channel adapter, or HBA.

■ When a loss of path occurs, ensures that I/Os are rerouted to the available paths with no process disruption.

■ Reconfigures the multipaths automatically when events occur.

■ Ensures that failed paths get revalidated as soon as possible and provides auto-failback capabilities.

■ Configures the multipaths to maximize performance using various load-balancing methods, for example, round robin, least I/Os queued, or least service time.

Examples of multipathing software include EMC PowerPath, Veritas DMP, Sun Traffic Manager, Hitachi HDLM, and IBM SDDPCM. Linux 2.6 has a kernel-based multipathing driver called Device Mapper. Additionally, some HBA vendors also provide multipathing solutions. Oracle Corporation does not certify or qualify these multipathing tools.

TIP
Although ASM does not provide multipathing capabilities, ASM does leverage multipathing tools, as long as the path or device produced by the multipathing tool returns a successful return code from an FSTAT system call. My Oracle Support note 294869.1 provides more details on ASM and multipathing.

TIP
To ensure that ASM is using the multipath device names and not the regular device, set the "ASM_DISKSTRING" parameter to look for the multipath device names. For example, if you are using EMC PowerPath, then set the disk string to "/dev/emcpower." The only exception is when you are using Linux and the disk string is set to "ORCL:*". In such cases, you would configure ASMLib to give preference to saved multipath devices.*

ASM *Diskgroups*

Once the disks are discovered, you can create a diskgroup that will encapsulate one or more of these disks. A diskgroup, which is the highest-level data structure in ASM, is comparable to a LVM's volume group. However, there are differences between typical LVM volume groups and ASM diskgroups. An ASM file-system layer is implicitly created within a diskgroup. This filesystem is transparent to users and only accessible through ASM, interfacing databases, and the 10.2 ASM command-line tool. There are inherent automatic file-level striping and mirroring capabilities. A database file created within an ASM diskgroup will have its file extents (not to be confused with its database extents) distributed equally across all online disks in the diskgroup, which provides an even I/O load.

Creating a diskgroup involves validating the disks to be added. These disks must have the following attributes:

- Cannot already be in use by another diskgroup

- Must not have a preexisting ASM header

- Cannot have an Oracle file header

This check and validation prevents ASM from destroying any in-use data device. Disks with a valid header status—candidate, former, or provisioned—are the only ones allowed to be diskgroup members. The diskgroup is created using SQL commands. Oracle ASM Configuration Assistant enables you to configure or create Oracle ASM diskgroups on the Configure ASM Disk Groups tab. With `asmcmd`, you can use the `mkdg` command to create a new diskgroup with an XML configuration file that specifies the diskgroup name, redundancy, attributes, and paths of the disks that form the diskgroup. You can also use Enterprise Manager (EM) as well. The following diskgroup creation is issued from within the Oracle ASM instance and not from a normal database instance (using EM may be much easier):

```
create diskgroup DATA external redundancy disk
'/dev/rdsk/c3t19d5s4',
'/dev/rdsk/c3t19d16s4',
'/dev/rdsk/c3t19d17s4',
'/dev/rdsk/c3t19d18s4';
```

The output that follows, from V$ASM_DISKGROUP, shows the newly created diskgroup:

```
select name, state, type, total_mb, free_mb
from    v$asm_diskgroup;
```

NAME	STATE	TYPE	TOTAL_MB	FREE_MB
DATA	MOUNTED	EXTERN	34512	34101

In the preceding example, a DATA diskgroup is created using four disks, which reside in a storage array, with the redundancy being handled externally via the storage array. The query that follows shows how the V$ASM_DISK view reflects the disk state change after being incorporated into the diskgroup:

```
select name, path, mode_status, state, disk_number
from    v$asm_disk;

NAME          PATH                    MODE_ST STATE     DISK_NUMBER
-----------   ----------------------  ------- --------  -----------
DATA_0000     /dev/rdsk/c3t19d5s4     ONLINE  NORMAL              0
DATA_0001     /dev/rdsk/c3t19d16s4    ONLINE  NORMAL              1
DATA_0002     /dev/rdsk/c3t19d17s4    ONLINE  NORMAL              2
DATA_0003     /dev/rdsk/c3t19d18s4    ONLINE  NORMAL              3
```

ASM generates and assigns a disk name with a sequence number to each disk added to the diskgroup. However, if you omit the NAME clause and assign a label to a disk through ASMLib, then that label is used as the disk name. If you omit the NAME and you did not assign a label through ASMLib, then ASM creates a default name of the form DISKGROUP_NAME_####, where #### is the disk number. The disk name is used when performing any disk management activities. The ASM disk name is different from the disk/device name, which allows for consistent naming across RAC nodes and protects from disk/device name changes due to array reconfigurations. Disk names are unique only within diskgroups, whereas prior to 10.2, disk names were unique to an ASM instance (or clustered ASM instances in RAC).

After the diskgroup is successfully created, metadata information, which includes creation date, diskgroup name, and redundancy type, is stored in the SGA of the ASM instance and in the disk header of each disk in the DATA diskgroup. The V$ASM_DISK view will now reflect this disk header information. Once these disks are under ASM management, all subsequent mounts of the diskgroup cause ASM to reread and validate the ASM disk headers. When mounting diskgroups, either at ASM startup or for subsequent mounts, it is advisable to mount all required diskgroups at once. This minimizes the overhead of multiple ASM disk discovery scans. When a diskgroup becomes mounted, ASM registers the diskgroup name, the instance name, and the corresponding ORACLE_HOME path name with Cluster Synchronization Services (CSS). This registered data is then used by the database instance to build the TNS connect string. This connect string is subsequently used by the database instance to connect to the ASM instance for volume management activities.

The ASM instance also houses I/O statistics in the V$ASM_DISK and V$ASM_DISK_STAT views. These views include reads/writes processed, read/write blocks handled, and read/write errors incurred. An ASM-based utility similar to *iostat,* called *asmiostat,* can be used to show I/O statistics for ASM-based disks (this is an Oracle provided script; see Doc ID 437996.1). This script can be copied into a file and executed against any 10.2 or higher ASM instance.

Prior to 10.2, querying V$ASM_DISK and V$ASM_DISKGROUP was an expensive operation because each execution involved a disk discovery. To minimize overhead and allow lightweight access to this dataset, ASM now includes two views: V$ASM_DISK_STAT and V$ASM_DISKGROUP_STAT. These two views are identical to V$ASM_DISK and V$ASM_DISKGROUP; however, V$ASM_DISK_STAT and V$ASM_DISKGROUP_STAT views are polled from memory and, therefore, do not require disk discovery. Since these views provide efficient lightweight access, Enterprise Manager can periodically query performance statistics at the disk level and aggregate space-usage statistics at the diskgroup level, without incurring significant overhead.

Important Performance Notes

■ To ensure best performance, all disks in a diskgroup should have the same characteristics, such as disk size, speed, and response times. The diskgroup is as fast as the *slowest* disk in the diskgroup.

■ For high-volume and performance-sensitive databases using ASM, create separate diskgroups based on function, with each diskgroup configured to meet certain specifications. For example, use two diskgroups for online redo logs, one diskgroup for data, and one diskgroup for the ARCHIVE LOG and FLASHBACK (fast recovery) area.

■ In 11g, ASM supports different "AU" (Allocation Unit) sizes at a diskgroup level. For datafiles, use an AU size of 4M. For small diskgroups, use an AU size of 1M.

■ Add space to the diskgroup well before reaching 100 percent total used; a best practice is to ensure you have 25 percent free to allow Oracle to complete the auto rebalance effectively.

■ During high I/O volumes time slots, set the rebalance power down to 1 by altering the ASM_POWER_LIMIT initialization parameter. During off-peak hours, the value for this parameter can be raised to as high as 11 (or 1024 for diskgroups with COMPATIBLE.ASM = 11.2.0.2 or higher) so rebalancing can be performed at a faster speed.

TIP
To get accurate real-time statistics, it may be prudent to query the V$ASM_DISK and V$ASM_DISKGROUP views, but exercise caution when running queries against these views during peak workloads.

ASM Diskgroups and Databases

A single ASM instance can service one or more single-instance databases on a stand-alone server. Each ASM diskgroup can be shared among all the databases on the server. Thus, the databases cannot reside on different servers (although you could have databases on different servers if you have a clustered ASM installation). Disks and database files can be part of only one diskgroup. A single Oracle database can store its files in multiple diskgroups managed by the same ASM instance. Allowing multiple databases to share a diskgroup provides greater potential for improved disk utilization and greater overall throughput.

The database area is where active database files such as datafiles, control files, online redo logs, and change tracking files used in incremental backups are stored. The *fast recovery area* (FRA) is where recovery-related files are created, such as multiplexed copies of the current control file and online redo logs, archived redo logs, backup sets, and flashback log files. To provide higher availability for the database, when a fast recovery area is chosen at database creation time, an active copy of the control file and one member set of the redo log group is stored in the fast recovery area. (In 11gR2, the flash recovery area was renamed to the fast recovery area or FRA.)

NOTE
Additional copies of the control file or extra redo log files can be created and placed in either diskgroup as desired. Also note that these "areas" are really diskgroups.

ASM Redundancy and Failure Groups

For systems that do not use external redundancy, ASM provides its own internal redundancy mechanism and additional high availability by way of *failure groups.* A failure group, which is a subset of a diskgroup, is, by definition, a collection of disks that can become unavailable due to a failure of one of its associated components, for example, controllers or entire arrays. Thus, disks in two separate failure groups (for a given diskgroup) must not share a common failure component. If you define failure groups for your diskgroup, ASM can tolerate the simultaneous failure of multiple disks in a single failure group.

ASM uses a unique mirroring algorithm. ASM does not mirror disks; rather, it mirrors extents. As a result, to provide continued protection in event of failure, you need only spare capacity in your diskgroup rather than having to provision a hot spare disk. Creating failure groups of different sizes is not advisable, as this creates problems when allocating secondary extents. When ASM allocates a primary extent of a file to one disk in a diskgroup, it allocates a mirror copy of that extent to another disk in the diskgroup. Primary extents on a given disk will have their respective mirror extents on one of several partner disks in the diskgroup. ASM ensures that a primary extent and its mirror copy never reside in the same failure group. Redundancy for diskgroups can be either *normal redundancy* (the default), where files are two-way mirrored (requiring at least two failure groups), or *high redundancy,* which provides a higher degree of protection using three-way mirroring (requiring at least three failure groups). Once you've created a diskgroup, you can't change its redundancy level. To change the redundancy of a diskgroup, you must create another diskgroup with the appropriate redundancy desired and then move the datafiles (using RMAN restore or DBMS_FILE_TRANSFER) to this newly created diskgroup.

The following example shows how to create a diskgroup using failure groups. In this example, ASM normal redundancy is being deployed over a storage array that has four internal trays, with each tray having four disks. The failing component to isolate is the storage tray, and thus the failure group boundary is the storage tray; i.e., each storage tray will be associated with a failure group.

```
SQL> create diskgroup DATA_NRML normal redundancy
FAILGROUP flgrp1 disk
'/dev/rdsk/c3t19d3s4','/dev/rdsk/c3t19d4s4','/dev/rdsk/c3t19d5s4',
'/dev/rdsk/c3t19d6s4'
FAILGROUP flgrp2 disk
```

```
'/dev/rdsk/c4t20d3s4','/dev/rdsk/c4t20d4s4','/dev/rdsk/c4t20d5s4',
'/dev/rdsk/c4t19ds4'
FAILGROUP flgrp3 disk
/dev/rdsk/c5t21d3s4','/dev/rdsk/c5t21d4s4','/dev/rdsk/c5t21d5s4',
'/dev/rdsk/c5t21ds4'
FAILGROUP flgrp4 disk
/dev/rdsk/c6t22d3s4','/dev/rdsk/c6t22d4s4','/dev/rdsk/c6t22d5s4',
'/dev/rdsk/c6t22ds4';
```

Diskgroups created with normal or high redundancy contain files that are double or triple mirrored, respectively. The first file extent allocated is chosen as primary extent, and the mirrored extent is called the *secondary extent.* In the case of high redundancy, there are two secondary extents. This logical grouping of primary and secondary extents is called an *extent set.* An extent set always contains the exact same data because they are mirrored versions of each other. Thus when a block is written to a file, each extent in the extent set is written in parallel. However, when a block is read from disk, it is almost always read from the primary extent, unless the primary extent cannot be read. (With 11gR2, you can configure Oracle ASM to read from a secondary extent if that extent is closer to the node instead of Oracle ASM reading from the primary copy, which might be farther from the node. Using the *preferred read failure groups* feature is most useful in extended clusters.) Keep in mind that each disk in a diskgroup (and failure groups) contains nearly the same number of primary and secondary extents. This provides an even distribution of read I/O activity across all the disks and is different than most logical volume managers, which have primary and mirrored disksets.

As stated previously, failure groups are used to isolate component failures. Therefore, you must understand failing components. If a failing component cannot be determined or the failing component is the disk itself (as opposed to the array controller or storage tray), then it may be advisable *not* to specify any failure groups when defining normal or high redundancy diskgroups. This results in every ASM disk being in its own failure group, with ASM internally determining the disk mirroring partnership. If the storage array has fully redundant components with dual paths to the disk, it is best not to specify failure groups but to let ASM manage the disk mirroring partnerships.

In the previous example, consider the event of a disk failure in failure group FLGRP1, which will induce a rebalance—the contents (data extents) of the failed disk are reconstructed using the redundant copies of the extents from the partnered disk. This partnered disk can be from either failure group FLGRP2 or FLGRP3. Let's say that the partnered disk is c5t21d3s4 from failure group 3. During the rebalance, if the database instance needs to access an extent whose primary extent was on the failed disk, then the database reads the mirror copy from the appropriate disk in failure group FLGRP3. Once the rebalance is complete, and the disk contents fully reconstructed, the database instance returns to reading primary copies only.

Disk drives are mechanical devices, so they have a tendency to fail. As drives begin to fail or have sporadic I/O errors, the probability for database corruption increases. ASM takes proactive measures with regard to I/O errors. ASM does this irrespective of using failure groups. A permanent I/O error is only signaled to the caller (Oracle I/O process) after several retries in the device driver. If a permanent disk I/O error is incurred during an Oracle WRITE operation, then ASM removes the affected disk from the diskgroup, preventing more application failures. If the loss of a disk results in data loss, ASM automatically dismounts the diskgroup to protect the integrity of the diskgroup data.

TIP
In 11gR2, ASM uses failure groups to perform read I/O (given that you've set the ASM_PREFERRED_READ_FAILURE_GROUPS initialization parameter to specify a list of failure group names as preferred read disks), thus relieving I/O pressure on the primary failure group.

New Space-Related Columns

ASM has two new columns that provide accurate information on free-space usage.

■ **USABLE_FREE_SPACE** In 10.1, the FREE_MB value that is reported in V$ASM_DISKGROUP does not take mirroring into account. A new column in V$ASM_DISKGROUP called USABLE_FREE_MB indicates the amount of free space that can be "safely" utilized, taking mirroring into account. The column provides a more accurate view of usable space in the diskgroup. When this value is negative, a disk failure could be critical for the system because it means you do not have sufficient free space to tolerate a disk failure. If a disk were to fail, the subsequent rebalance would run out of space before full redundancy could be restored to all files. As such, this negative value is not a bug; it is just a signal that the diskgroup's failure groups need more space in order to tolerate a possible disk failure.

Also, note how to interpret the FREE_MB column values:

Total free megabytes in an ASM diskgroup is reported in the FREE_MB column, but the maximum space that can be allocated actually changes with the type of redundancy, as summarized here:

```
Redundancy type        Max. Space
--------------         -------------------------
External               FREE_MB of diskgroup
Normal                 1/2 FREE_MB of diskgroup
High                   1/3 FREE_MB of diskgroup
```

(Source: **Doc ID 371573.1 and Doc ID 460155.1**)

■ **REQUIRED_MIRROR_FREE_MB** Along with USABLE_FREE_MB, this column in V$ASM_DISKGROUP more accurately indicates the amount of space that is required to be available in a given diskgroup in order to restore redundancy after one or more disk failures. The amount of space displayed in this column takes mirroring into account. If a disk fails, ASM performs a rebalance of the surviving disks (including the surviving disks in the failed failure group) to restore redundancy for the data in the failed disks This parameter, therefore, indicates the amount of space that must be available in the diskgroup to restore full redundancy after the worst failure that can be tolerated by the diskgroup. (Oracle Doc ID 578606.1)

Cluster Synchronization Services

ASM was designed to work with single instances as well as with RAC 11g or 10g clusters. ASM, even in single-instance form, requires that Cluster Synchronization Services (CSS) be installed and started before ASM becomes available. In a single instance, CSS maintains synchronization between the ASM and database instances. CSS, which is a component of Oracle's Cluster Ready Services (CRS), is automatically installed on every node that runs Oracle Database 11g or 10g ASM and launches automatically on server boot-up. In RAC 11g and 10g environments, the full Oracle Clusterware is installed on every RAC node.

Since CSS provides cluster management and node monitor management, it inherently monitors ASM and its shared storage components (disks and diskgroups). Upon startup, ASM will register itself and all diskgroups it has mounted with CSS. This allows CSS to keep diskgroup metadata in sync across all RAC nodes. Any new diskgroups that are created are also dynamically registered and broadcast to other nodes in the cluster. As with the database, internode communication is used to synchronize activities in ASM instances. CSS is used to heartbeat the health of the ASM instances. ASM internode messages are initiated by structural changes that require synchronization, e.g., adding a disk. Thus, ASM uses the same integrated lock management infrastructure that is used by the database for efficient synchronization.

Database Instances and ASM

A database instance is the standard Oracle instance and is the client of the ASM instance. Database-to-ASM communication is always intranode; that is, the database will not contact the remote (in case of RAC) ASM instance for servicing database requests. After the ASM diskgroup is created, DBCA can now be used to create the database. DBCA has three options for database file structures: local filesystem, cluster or shared filesystem (for RAC databases), or ASM.

If ASM is selected, then all available diskgroups, if already created for that ASM instance, will be listed. Selecting ASM and a diskgroup tells DBCA to create a database with the datafiles stored in ASM. If no diskgroups exist or a new diskgroup is desired, then DBCA offers the opportunity to create a new diskgroup.

NOTE
An ASM diskgroup can house all of the Oracle database files, ranging from control files, datafiles, SPFILEs, and RMAN backup files. However, Oracle executables, CRS files (OCR and voting disks), and nondatabase files cannot be housed in ASM diskgroups. In 11gR2, OCR and voting disks can be housed in ASM diskgroups. The executables can also be on a cluster filesystem.

An active database instance that uses ASM storage can operate just like a typical database instance; all file access is directly performed without extensive ASM intervention. Database instances interact with the ASM instance when files are created, deleted, or opened. At this time, the file layout is read from the ASM instance and all subsequent I/Os are done using the extent map stored in the database instance. ASM and DB instances also interact if the storage configuration changes, for example, when disks are added, dropped, or fail.

Although the ASM layer is transparent to the database clients and users on the server, all datafile access can only be done via the database instance and its utilities. For example, database backups of ASM-based files can only be performed with RMAN. Note, utilities like the Unix dd command are not recommended for backing up or restoring ASM diskgroups.

The database file-level access (read/write) for ASM files is similar to non-ASM storage, except that any database filename that begins with a "+" will automatically be handled and managed using the ASM code path. With ASM files, the database file access inherently has the characteristics of raw devices—i.e., unbuffered (direct I/O) with kernelized asynchronous I/O (KAIO).

Database Consolidation and Clustering with ASM

In Oracle Database 10*g* Release 1, RAC and single-instance databases could not be managed by the same ASM instance. This created challenges in implementing storage grid architectures and consolidated database solutions. Oracle Database 10*g* Release 2 enhanced the ASM functionality in a clustered environment, allowing one ASM instance per node to manage all database instances in the cluster (this is also true in 11*g*). Therefore, an ASM instance on a given node can now manage storage simultaneously for a single instance or many RAC database instances and one or more single-instance databases. This feature relieves DBAs from maintaining more than one ASM instance needed to serve the different database types that might exist in the cluster, thus relieving DBAs of the need to manage separate storage pools. This feature leverages Oracle Clusterware to consolidate multiple islands of databases economically into a single clustered pool of storage managed by ASM. This essentially allows DBAs to optimize their storage utilization by eliminating wasted, overprovisioned storage and to save money by reducing their overall footprint of database storage.

Once the database is created and the instance is active, the database instance becomes a client of ASM. This is reflected in the V$ASM_CLIENT view. V$ASM_CLIENT contains one row for every ASM diskgroup that is opened by a database instance. The following note is from the Oracle ASM doc:

In an ASM instance, V$ASM_CLIENT identifies databases using diskgroups managed by the ASM instance. In a database instance, V$ASM_CLIENT displays information about the ASM instance if the database has an open ASM file.

In the example that follows, in the ASM instance, V$ASM_CLIENT displays two databases connected to ASM, with each instance using two diskgroups.

NOTE
Instance CUBS1 is a 11gR2 RAC–enabled database and SOX1 is a 11gR1 single instance.

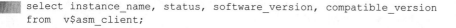
```
select instance_name, status, software_version, compatible_version
from  v$asm_client;
```

```
INSTANCE STATUS        SOFTWARE_VRSN COMPATIBLE_VRSN
-------- ------------  ------------- ---------------
cubs1    CONNECTED     11.2.0.1.0    11.2.0.1.0
cubs1    CONNECTED     11.2.0.1.0    11.2.0.1.0
sox1     CONNECTED     11.1.0.3.0    11.1.0.2.0
sox1     CONNECTED     11.1.0.3.0    11.1.0.2.0
```

Database Processes to Support ASM

In a database instance, three sets of processes are added to support the ASM diskgroups and infrastructure:

- **RBAL**   This process performs global opens of all the disks in the diskgroup. This process also manages the ASM diskgroups used by the database instance (not to be confused with the RBAL process for an ASM instance, which coordinates rebalance activity for all diskgroups).

- **ASMB**   This process contacts CSS using the diskgroup name and acquires the associated ASM connect string. This connect string is then used to connect into the ASM instance. Using this persistent connection, periodic messages are exchanged to update statistics and provide a heartbeat mechanism. During operations that require ASM intervention, such as a file creation by a database foreground process, the database foreground process connects directly to the ASM instance to perform the operation. Upon successful completion of file creation, database file extent maps are sent by ASM to ASMB. Additionally, ASMB also sends database I/O statistics to the ASM instance.

- **O00x**   A group of slave processes establish connections to the ASM instance, where *x* is a number from 1 to 10. Through this connection pool, database processes can send messages to the ASM instance. The slave (pool) connections eliminate the overhead of logging in to the ASM instance for short requests. For example, opening a file sends the open request to the ASM instance via a slave. However, slaves are not used for long-running operations such as creating a file. These slaves are shut down when not in use.

Bigfile and ASM

The bigfile feature (as stated earlier in this chapter) is a perfect fit for VLDB (very large databases) and ASM. Instead of managing several hundred datafiles, using bigfiles reduces the number of datafiles significantly. This improves checkpointing, and the time to open the database become significantly faster, as fewer file opens have to be performed. Using bigfiles reduces the internal overhead needed to manage large number of datafiles. With ASM, bigfiles can be 32T for external redundancy and 12T for normal/high redundancy. This is based on an 8K block size. When using bigfiles, you have to review your backup and recovery strategy carefully. Obviously, you can't do full datafile backup for a 36T datafile, so things like RMAN incremental and cumulative backups become an integral part of bigfile management.

Database Initialization Parameters to Support ASM

The SGA parameters for a database instance need slight modifications to support ASM extent maps and other ASM information. If the Automatic Memory Management feature is being used on the database instance, then the following sizing data can be treated as informational only or as supplemental data in gauging appropriate minimum values for the SGA. The following are guidelines for SGA sizing on the database instance:

- **Processes** Add 16.

- **LARGE_POOL** Add an additional 600K.

- **SHARED_POOL** Additional memory is required to store extent maps. Add the values from the following queries to obtain the current database storage size either already on ASM or that will be stored in ASM. Then determine the redundancy type used (or that will be used) and calculate the SHARED_POOL, using the total value as input:

```
connect user/pass<SID> as sysdba
select sum(bytes)/(1024*1024*1024)
from   v$datafile;

select sum(bytes)/(1024*1024*1024)
from   v$logfile a, v$log b
where  a.group#=b.group#;

select sum(bytes)/(1024*1024*1024)
from   v$tempfile
where  status='ONLINE';
```

- **For diskgroups using external redundancy** Every 100GB of space needs 1MB of extra shared pool + 2M.

- **For diskgroups using normal redundancy** Every 50GB of space needs 1MB of extra shared pool + 4M.

- **For diskgroups using high redundancy** Every 33GB of space needs 1MB of extra shared pool + 6M.

ASM and Database Deployment Best Practices

ASM enables redundancy and optimal performance out-of-the-box. However, consider the following items as they improve performance and/or increase availability:

- Implement multiple access paths to the storage array using two or more HBAs (host bus adaptors) or initiators.

- Deploy multipathing software over these multiple HBAs to provide I/O load-balancing and failover capabilities.

■ Use diskgroups with disks of similar size and performance. A diskgroup containing a large number of disks provides a wide distribution of data extents, thus allowing greater concurrency for I/O and reducing the occurrences of hotspots. Because a large diskgroup can easily sustain various I/O characteristics and workloads, a single (database area) diskgroup can be used to house database files, log files, and control files.

■ Use diskgroups with four or more disks, and make sure these disks span several backend disk adapters.

As stated earlier, Oracle generally recommends no more than two diskgroups. For example, a common deployment can include four or more disks in a database diskgroup (DATA diskgroup, for example) spanning all backend disk adapters/directors and eight to ten disks for the fast recovery area diskgroup. The size of the fast recovery area depends on what is stored and how much—full database backups, incremental backups, flashback database logs, and archive logs. An active copy of the control file and one member of each of the redo log groups are stored in the fast recovery area. See Oracle's *High Availability Architecture and Best Practices Manual* for more details on these topics.

ASM Storage Management and Allocation

A database created under the constructs of ASM will be striped by default and mirrored as specified in the SAME methodology (i.e., the I/O load is evenly distributed and balanced across all disks within the diskgroup). The striping is done on a file-by-file basis, using a 1MB stripe size, as opposed to other logical volume managers (LVMs) that perform striping and mirroring at a disk-volume level. Oracle states that an ASM 1MB stripe depth has proved to be the best stripe depth for Oracle databases. This optimal stripe depth, coupled with even distribution of extents in the diskgroup, reduces the occurrence of hot spots.

ASM allocates space in units called *allocation units (AUs)*. ASM always creates one-AU extents (not the same as tablespace extents) across all of the disks in a diskgroup. For diskgroups with similarly sized disks, there should be an equal number of AU extents on every disk. A database file is broken up into file extents. There are two types of AU extent distributions: coarse and fine. For coarse distribution, each coarse-grain file extent is mapped to a single allocation unit. With fine-grain distribution, each grain is interleaved 128K across groups of eight AUs. Fine distribution breaks up large I/O operations into multiple 128K I/O operations that can execute in parallel, benefiting sequential I/Os. Coarse- and fine-grain attributes are predefined, as part of system templates, for all system-related files.

TIP
Redo and archive log files are defined as fine-grained, whereas datafiles are coarse.

ASM Rebalance and Redistribution

With traditional volume managers, expansion/growth or shrinkage of striped filesystems has typically been difficult. With ASM, these disk/volume changes now include seamless redistribution (rebalancing) of the striped data that can be performed online. Any change in the storage configuration triggers a rebalance. The main objective of the rebalance operation is always to provide an even distribution of file extents and space usage across all disks in the diskgroup. Rebalancing is performed on all database files on a per file basis; however, some files may not require a rebalance.

The Oracle background process, RBAL, from the ASM instance manages this rebalance. The rebalance process examines each file extent map, and the new AU extents are replotted on to the new storage configuration. For example, consider an eight-disk diskgroup, with a datafile with 40 AU extents (each disk will house 5 AU extents). When two new drives of the same size are added, that datafile is rebalanced and spread across ten drives, with each drive containing 4 AU extents. Only 8 AU extents need to move to complete the rebalance. In other words, a complete redistribution of AU extents is not necessary; only the minimum number of AU extents are moved to reach equal distribution. The following is a typical process flow for ASM rebalancing:

1. On the ASM instance, a DBA adds (or drops) a disk to (from) a diskgroup.

2. This invokes the RBAL process to create the rebalance plan and then begin coordination of the redistribution.

3. RBAL will calculate estimation time and work required to perform the task and then message the ARB*x* processes actually to handle the request. The number of ARB*x* processes invoked is directly determined by the ASM_POWER_LIMIT parameter.

4. The Continuing Operations Directory (metadata) is updated to reflect rebalance activity.

5. Each extent to be relocated is assigned to an ARB*x* process.

6. ARB*x* performs rebalance on these extents. Each extent is locked, relocated, and unlocked. This is seen as a REBAL for the Operation column in the V$ASM_OPERATION view.

Rebalancing involves physically moving AU extents. The impact is generally low because the rebalance is done one AU extent at a time; therefore, only one outstanding I/O is present at any given time, per ARB*x* processes. This should not adversely affect online database activity. However, it is generally advisable to schedule the rebalance operation during off-peak hours.

TIP
The ASM instance parameter ASM_POWER_LIMIT is used to influence the throughput and speed of the rebalance operation. The range of values for the ASM_POWER_LIMIT is 0 to 11, where a value of 11 is full throttle and a value of 1 is low speed. A value of 0, which turns off automatic rebalance, should be used with caution. For diskgroups that have the diskgroup ASM compatibility set to 11.2.0.2 or greater (for example, COMPATIBLE.ASM = 11.2.0.2), the operational range of values is 0 to 1024 for rebalance power.

The power limit value can also be set for a specific rebalance activity using the ALTER DISKGROUP command. This value is only effective for the specific rebalance task. In the example that follows, using a *power limit value of 0* would indicate that no rebalance should occur for this rebalance, but I will use 11, which is full-throttle rebalancing. This setting is particularly important when adding or removing storage (that has external redundancy) and then deferring the rebalance to a later scheduled time.

```
"Session1 SQL"> alter diskgroup DATA add disk '/dev/rdsk/c3t19d39s4' rebalance
power 11;

From another session:
"Session2 SQL"> select * from v$asm_operation;

GROUP OPERA STAT      POWER    ACTUAL     SOFAR   EST_WORK   EST_RATE EST_MINUTES
----- ----- ----      ----------  ----------  ----------  ----------  ----------  -----------
1 REBAL WAIT      11         0          0          0          0          0
1 DSCV  WAIT      11         0          0          0          0          0

time passes..............)

OPERA STAT      POWER    ACTUAL     SOFAR   EST_WORK   EST_RATE EST_MINUTES
----------- -----   ----   ----------  ----------  ----------  ----------  ----------
1 REBAL REAP      11         2         25        219        485          0
```

TIP
If removing or adding several disks with ASM, best practice is to add or remove drives all at once. This reduces the number rebalance operations that are needed for storage changes.

An ASM diskgroup rebalance is an asynchronous operation, in that control is returned immediately to DBA after the operation is started in the background, with the status of the ongoing operation queryable from V$ASM_OPERATION. However, there are situations in which the diskgroup operation needs to be synchronous, for instance, when you need to wait until rebalance is completed. In Oracle Database 11g, you can now specify the option to wait with ALTER DISKGROUP commands that result in a rebalance. Waiting allows for accurate (sequential) scripting that may rely on the space change from a completed rebalance before any subsequent action is taken. For example, if you add 100GB of storage to a completely full diskgroup, you won't be able to use all 100GB of storage until the rebalance completes. If a new rebalance command is entered while one is already in progress in wait mode, the prior command will not return until the diskgroup is in a balanced state or the rebalance operation encounters an error.

The example that follows illustrates how the WAIT option can be used in SQL scripting. The script adds a new disk, /dev/raw/raw6, and waits until the ADD and REBALANCE operations complete, only then returning control back to the script. The subsequent step adds a large tablespace.

```
#An example script to test WAIT option
alter diskgroup data add disk '/dev/raw/raw6' rebalance power 2 wait;
#login into database and create a tablespace for the next month's Order Entry
data
sqlplus  oe_dba/oe1proddb  << EOF
create BIGFILE tablespace May_OE  datafile size 800 Gb;
<< EOF
```

With external redundancy, the dropping and adding of disks in the diskgroup is seamless and becomes more of an exercise in scheduling the rebalancing. However, with failure groups, some planning and forethought is required with respect to how disks are removed and added.

Avoiding Disk Contention by Using Partitions

Partitioning is probably the single best option available for increasing the performance related to large tables. *Partitioning* is a way to increase efficiency by accessing smaller pieces of a table or index instead of accessing the full table or index. This can be particularly useful when one or more users are accessing multiple parts of the same table. If these partitions (pieces) of the table reside on different devices, the throughput is greatly increased. Partitions can also be backed up and recovered independently of each other (even while they are in use), eliminating potential disk I/O issues during backup times. Only when partitions are properly implemented are Oracle's best performance-enhancing features realized. The best way to understand partitioning is to look at an example. Consider the following simple example, where you partition the DEPT table into three partitions (pieces) using the DEPTNO column.

The TABLE DEPT is created with three partitions:

```
create table dept
  (deptno      number(2),
   dept_name   varchar2(30))
   partition   by range(deptno)
  (partition d1 values less than (10) tablespace dept1,
   partition d2 values less than (20) tablespace dept2,
   partition d3 values less than (maxvalue) tablespace dept3);
```

This example builds three distinct partitions on the DEPT table. The key to getting better throughput is to ensure that each partition is placed on a different physical disk so that all three partitions can be accessed simultaneously if you are not using ASM. The tablespaces DEPT1, DEPT2, and DEPT3 must have physical files that are located on different physical disks. Remember that the tablespace is the logical holder of information where the datafile is the physical disk. You can have one tablespace that includes multiple datafiles, but a datafile can only relate to a single tablespace. The key to partitioning to improve disk I/O is to ensure that the partitions that will be accessed simultaneously are either located on different physical disks or use ASM.

Data is then entered into all three table partitions:

```
insert into dept values (1, 'ADMIN');
insert into dept values (7, 'MGMT');
insert into dept values (10, 'MANUF');
insert into dept values (15, 'ACCT');
insert into dept values (22, 'SALES');
```

The DEPT table still looks like a single table when you select from it:

```
select  *
from    dept;
```

DEPTNO	DEPT_NAME
1	ADMIN
7	MGMT
10	MANUF
15	ACCT
22	SALES

Here you selected all records from all of the partitions in the preceding example. In the next three examples, you select individually from each partition.

In this instance, you select from a single partition and access only a *single* partition:

```
select    *
from      dept partition (d1);
```

DEPTNO	DEPT_NAME
1	ADMIN
7	MGMT

```
select    *
from      dept partition (d2);
```

DEPTNO	DEPT_NAME
10	MANUF
15	ACCT

```
select    *
from      dept partition (d3);
```

DEPTNO	DEPT_NAME
22	SALES

```
select    *
from      dept
where     deptno = 22;
```

DEPTNO	DEPT_NAME
22	SALES

Note that in the final example, you eliminate the need to access the first or second partition (partition elimination). Partitioning indexes and using the parallel option along with partitions make partitioning even more powerful.

TIP
To minimize disk I/O on a single large table, you can break the table into multiple partitions that reside in tablespaces on different physical disks.

Getting More Information About Partitions

You can retrieve the information regarding partitions by accessing USER_TABLES, DBA_PART_TABLES, and USER_SEGMENTS. Example queries to these three tables are displayed next with corresponding output for the examples in the preceding section.

```
select   table_name, partitioned
from     dba_tables
where    table_name in ('DEPT','EMP');


TABLE_NAME    PAR
DEPT          YES
EMP           NO
```

In the preceding example, the PAR (partitioned) column indicates whether a table is partitioned.

```
select   owner, table_name, partition_count
from     dba_part_tables
where    table_name = 'DEPT';


OWNER     TABLE_NAME    PARTITION_COUNT
KEVIN     DEPT          3
```

In the preceding and following examples, there are three partitions on the DEPT table:

```
select   segment_name, partition_name, segment_type, tablespace_name
from     user_segments;


SEGMENT_NAME   PARTITION_NAME   SEGMENT_TYPE       TABLESPACE_NAME
EMP                             TABLE              USER_DATA
DEPT           D1               TABLE PARTITION    DEPT1
DEPT           D2               TABLE PARTITION    DEPT2
DEPT           D3               TABLE PARTITION    DEPT3
```

TIP
Tables can be easily partitioned for individual pieces to be accessed and/or manipulated; you can still access the entire table of a partitioned table. Accessing the tables DBA_TABLES, DBA_PART_TABLE, and DBA_SEGMENTS provides additional information concerning tables that have been partitioned. See Chapter 13 for more information on table and index partitioning.

Other Types of Partitioning

There are several types of partitioning. The main types are range, hash, composite, and list partitioning. There are also multiple index types associated with partitions. I covered range partitioning in the preceding section, but another partitioning option is multicolumn range partitioning.

Multicolumn Range Partitioning

Multicolumn range partitioning is the same as range partitioning except when using multiple columns to define the ranges. In the following example, the data is segmented into quarters so you can eliminate the quarters that are not needed when a single quarter is accessed, but also so the data can be archived one quarter at a time without interfering with another quarter. The data can also be segmented into multiple tablespaces so better I/O is achieved.

```
create table cust_sales
(acct_no      number(5),
 cust_name    char(30),
 item_id      number(9),
 sale_day     integer not null,
 sale_mth     integer not null,
 sale_yr      integer not null)
partition by range (sale_yr, sale_mth, sale_day)
(partition cust_sales_q1 values less than (2011, 04, 01) tablespace users,
 partition cust_sales_q2 values less than (2011, 07, 01) tablespace users2,
 partition cust_sales_q3 values less than (2011, 10, 01) tablespace users,
 partition cust_sales_q4 values less than (2012, 01, 01) tablespace users2,
 partition cust_sales_qx values less than (maxvalue, maxvalue, maxvalue)
 tablespace users2);
```

TIP
You can also partition tables using multiple columns as the criteria. You must specify "MAXVALUE" for all columns that are part of the partition key except for interval partitioning. This is new in 11g and covered in "New Partitioning Options in Oracle 11gR2."

Hash Partitioning

Hash partitioning is generally used when you are unsure where to put the breakpoints as you would in range partitioning. Hash partitioning breaks up data into the number of partitions specified based on the hash of the partition key specified. To get an even distribution, you should always specify a power of 2 (2^n) as the number of hash partitions. Hash partitioning only supports local indexes and range- or hash-partitioned global indexes. You can specify the names of the index and table partition, and you can later add or reduce the number of partitions if you find you have too many or too few. The following example shows a table with four hash partitions that is built on the partitioning key ACCT_NO and distributed across four tablespaces:

```
create table cust_sales_hash (
 acct_no     number(5),
 cust_name char(30),
 sale_day  integer not null,
 sale_mth  integer not null,
 sale_yr   integer not null)
partition by hash (acct_no)
partitions 4
store in (users1, users2, users3, users4);
```

TIP
*When you don't know how to break up a table, but you know that it
needs to be partitioned and spread out, use hash partitioning.*

Composite Partitioning

Sometimes a table is so large and accessed so frequently that you need a much better way to
"slice and dice it." *Composite partitioning* combines range and hash partitioning. You use range
partitioning to allow partition elimination and then hash the partitions further to distribute I/O.
Composite partitioning supports local indexes and range- or hash-partitioned global indexes. The
following is an example of composite partitioning that could lead to incredible job security due
to its nonintuitive complexity:

```
create table orders(
ordid      number,
acct_no    number(5),
cust_name char(30),
orderdate date,
productid number)
 partition by range(orderdate)
 subpartition by hash(productid) subpartitions 8
   (partition q1 values less than  (to_date('01-APR-2011', 'dd-mon-yyyy')),
    partition q2 values less than  (to_date('01-JUL-2011', 'dd-mon-yyyy')),
    partition q3 values less than  (to_date('01-OCT-2011', 'dd-mon-yyyy')),
    partition q4 values less than(maxvalue));
```

This example build partitions based on the range of values listed for the ORDERDATE column
and puts them into partitions Q1, Q2, Q3, and Q4. It then subpartitions each of these range
partitions into eight subpartitions based on a hash of the PRODUCTID column.

Here is an example of a hash-partitioned global index created on this table:

```
CREATE INDEX orders_acct_global_ix
ON orders (acct_no, ordid)
GLOBAL PARTITION BY HASH (acct_no)
partitions 4;
```

List Partitioning

Oracle added *list partitioning* for the DBA or developer who really knows his or her data well.
List partitioning allows you to assign the individual column values associated with each of the
partitions. Several restrictions on list partitioning are displayed after the following code listing.

```
create table dept_part
 (deptno     number(2),
  dname      varchar2(14),
  loc        varchar2(13))
partition by list (dname)
(partition d1_east  values ('BOSTON', 'NEW YORK', 'KANSAS CITY'),
```

```
partition d2_west  values ('SAN FRANCISCO', 'LOS ANGELES'),
partition d3_south values ('ATLANTA', 'DALLAS'),
partition d4_north values ('CHICAGO', 'DETROIT'));
```

Restrictions on list partitioning are as follows:

- You can specify only one partitioning key in the column list, and it cannot be a LOB column. If the partitioning key is an object-type column, you can partition on only one attribute of the column type.

- Each partition value in the VALUES clause must be unique among all partitions of the table.

- If you specify the literal NULL for a partition value in the VALUES clause, then to access data in that partition in subsequent queries, you must use an IS NULL condition in the WHERE clause, rather than a comparison condition.

- You cannot list partition an index-organized table.

- The string comprising the list of values for each partition can be up to 4K.

- The total number of partition values for all partitions cannot exceed 64K–1.

New Partitioning Options in Oracle 11gR2

Oracle 11gR2 has added four new partitioning options:

- Reference partitioning
- Interval partitioning
- Virtual column Partitioning
- System partitioning

Interval Partitioning

Interval partitioning is a long overdue enhancement to range partitioning that provides automation around the process of pre-creating partitions when an INSERT statement is looking for a partition that does not exist. Interval partitioning does support composite partitioning of the following types: interval-range, internal-list and interval-hash.

The following is an example of using interval partitioning:

```
CREATE TABLE DEPT_NEW2
(DEPTNO      NUMBER(2),
 DEPT_NAME   VARCHAR2(30))
PARTITION BY RANGE(DEPTNO)
INTERVAL(10)
      (PARTITION D1 VALUES    LESS THAN (10),
       PARTITION D2 VALUES    LESS THAN (20),
       PARTITION D3 VALUES    LESS THAN (30));
```

Now let's insert some values that don't fall into the partitions created. In previous versions, this would result in an "ORA-14400: inserted partition key does not map to any partition." With interval partitioning, the three records are successfully inserted and three new partitions are created:

```
insert into dept_new2 values(40,null);
insert into dept_new2 values(50,null);
insert into dept_new2 values(99,null);

select segment_name, partition_name
from   dba_segments
where  segment_name = 'DEPT_NEW2';

SEGMENT_NAME                   PARTITION_NAME
----------------------------   ----------------------------------
DEPT_NEW2                      D1
DEPT_NEW2                      D2
DEPT_NEW2                      D3
DEPT_NEW2                      SYS_P41
DEPT_NEW2                      SYS_P42
DEPT_NEW2                      SYS_P43
```

Some restrictions apply to the use of interval partitioning as well:

- You can only specify one table column in the partitioning key.

- Partitioning key can only be a NUMBER or DATE type column.

- Interval partitioning does not support index-organized tables.

- It does not support the creation of a domain index.

- Note that in 11*g*, you can use Data Pump to load or unload individual partitions for all partitioning types so there is no longer a restriction in this regard.

Reference Partitioning

Oracle 11*g*R2 has added reference partitioning where a child table derives its partitioning information from the parent table, and the relationship is defined based on existing Primary Key (PK)/Foreign Key (FK) relationships between the parent and child. The partitioning key is resolved through an existing parent-child relationship, enforced by enabled and active primary key and foreign key constraints. Tables with a parent-child relationship can be logically equipartitioned by inheriting the partitioning key from the parent table without duplicating the key columns. The logical dependency also automatically cascades partition maintenance operations, thus making application development easier and less error-prone.

For example, consider the simple case of the ORDERS (parent) and LINEITEMS (child) tables, which are joined based on the PK/FK relationship on the ORDER_ID column in both tables. The ORDERS table also has an ORDER_DATE column, which is used to partition and prune the ORDERS table (there is range partitioning on the ORDER_DATE). The LINEITEMS table does not have any such column (so it's not duplicated), and, therefore, there's not an easy way to partition this table, and it can't take advantage of partition pruning or partition-wide joins based on the ORDER_DATE column.

With reference partitioning, however, the ORDERS table is range-partitioned on ORDER_DATE, for a month at a time, and the LINETEMS table also now automatically has one partition for each partition of the parent table (given that a reference partition is created using the PARTITION BY REFERENCE clause). The partitioning key is *inherited* through the PK/FK relationship. Please see the *Oracle VLDB (Very Large Database) and Partitioning Guide* for more information.

TIP
Reference partitioning is tailor made for the partitioning of OLTP systems and those systems that tend to be far more normalized than the rest.

Partitionwise Joins
Oracle also allows a query against two partitioned tables to join on only the needed partitions. Instead of joining many rows to many rows, you can now perform partition elimination on each table and then join the results. To join on partitions, the tables must be equipartitioned tables, which means

- Tables are partitioned using the same partition key.
- Tables must be partitioned with the same partition breakpoints.

System Partitions
System partitions are used to break data into many smaller partitions, but not grouped into any particular groupings other than whatever you decide. System partitions are great to use when you are inserting large amounts of data and want to break it into smaller pieces, but using the same table. You decide exactly what data goes where. Yes, this is as powerful and as dangerous as it sounds; things go exactly where you want them! You can't forget to specify the partition or you will get an "ORA-14701: Partition-extended name or bind variable must be used for DMLs on tables partitioned by System method."

System partitions have the following restrictions:

- Can*not* be used with index-organized tables
- Can*not* play a part in composite partitioning
- Can*not* split
- Can*not* be used with CREATE TABLE AS SELECT…
- Can*not* be used with INSERT INTO *table* AS…

The basic syntax is:

CREATE TABLE ...**PARTITION BY SYSTEM** *PARTITIONS n*

(where *n* is 1 to 1024K–1)

```
CREATE TABLE DEPT
   (DEPTNO    NUMBER(2),
    DEPT_NAME VARCHAR2(30))
  PARTITION BY SYSTEM
  (PARTITION D1,
   PARTITION D2,
   PARTITION D3);

INSERT INTO DEPT  PARTITION (D1) VALUES (1, 'DEPT 1');
INSERT INTO DEPT  PARTITION (D1) VALUES (22, 'DEPT 22');
INSERT INTO DEPT  PARTITION (D1) VALUES (10, 'DEPT 10');
INSERT INTO DEPT  PARTITION (D2) VALUES (15, 'DEPT 15');
INSERT INTO DEPT  PARTITION (D3) VALUES (7, 'DEPT 7');
```

The partition clause is optional for UPDATE and DELETES, but more efficient if you can use it (*be very careful* to ensure that what you are doing is what you want to do).

Other Partitioning Options

This section covers some of the many options that you can use when managing partitions. You will see that many of these options that are available for operations on tables are also available for partitions:

- **MODIFY PARTITION** *partition_name*   Modifies the real physical attributes of a table partition. You can specify any of the following as new physical attributes for the partition: LOGGING, PCTFREE, PCTUSED, INITRANS, STORAGE (note MAXTRANS is deprecated and defaults to 255 concurrent update transactions for a given data block, if there is enough available space in the block).

- **RENAME PARTITION** *partition_name TO new_partition_name*   Renames table partition PARTITION_NAME to NEW_PARTITION_NAME.

- **MOVE PARTITION** *partition_name*   Moves a table partition to another segment. You can move partition data to another tablespace, recluster data to reduce fragmentation, or change a create-time physical attribute:

```
alter table dept move partition d3 tablespace dept4 nologging;
```

In this example, the D3 partition with all corresponding data is moved from the DEPT3 tablespace, where it originally resided, to the DEPT4 tablespace; NOLOGGING disables redo generation during the MOVE operation and is not the same as the LOGGING or NOLOGGING attribute of the partition or table.

TIP
When moving a partition, use the NOLOGGING option (if possible)
for speed.

- **ADD PARTITION *new_partition_name* VALUES LESS THAN (*value_list*)**   Adds a new partition to the "high" end of a partitioned table. You can specify any of the following as new physical attributes for the partition: LOGGING, PCTFREE, PCTUSED, INITRANS, and STORAGE. The VALUES clause specifies the upper bound for the new partition. The VALUE_LIST is a comma-separated, ordered list of literal values corresponding to partition key values. The VALUE_LIST must contain values that are greater than the partition bound for the highest existing partition in the table.

- **EXCHANGE PARTITION**   This powerful option allows you to convert a partition or subpartition into a nonpartitioned table or convert a nonpartitioned table into a partition. This option is very useful if you are archiving old range partitions and want to export them as stand-alone tables before you drop them. Also, it can be useful for quickly loading incremental data into an already-existing partitioned table.

- **DROP PARTITION *partition_name***   Removes a partition and the data in that partition from a partitioned table:

```
alter table dept drop partition d3;
```

TIP
Dropping a table partition causes its local index (but not the other
local partition indexes) to be dropped and a global index (one that
exists on the entire table) to be unavailable (unless you're willing to
rebuild the indexes afterward). Don't use global indexes if you plan to
drop table partitions.

- **TRUNCATE PARTITION *partition_name***   Removes all rows from a partition in a table. The example that follows shows the truncation of the D1 partition. For each partition or subpartition truncated, Oracle Database also truncates corresponding local index partitions and subpartitions. If those index partitions or subpartitions are marked UNUSABLE, then the database truncates them and resets the UNUSABLE marker to VALID.

```
Alter table dept truncate partition d1;
```

- **SPLIT PARTITION *partition_name_old***   Creates two new partitions, each with a new segment, new physical attributes, and new initial extents. The segment associated with the old partition is discarded. The example that follows shows *splitting* the D1 partition into a D1A partition and D1B partition at DEPTNO=5. Note that you must also rebuild the indexes after this operation.

```
Alter table dept split partition d1 at (5) into
   (partition d1a tablespace dept1,
    partition d1b tablespace dept2);
```

```
SEGMENT_NAME  PARTITION_NAME  SEGMENT_TYPE
------------  --------------  ----------------
DEPT          D1A             TABLE PARTITION
DEPT          D1B             TABLE PARTITION
DEPT          D2              TABLE PARTITION

Alter index dept_idx rebuild partition d1a;
Alter index dept_idx rebuild partition d1b;
```

- **MERGE PARTITIONS *partition_list* INTO PARTITION *new_name***   Takes two partitions and combines them into one partition. The next example shows *merging* the D1A and D1B partition back into the partition named D1. Note that you must also rebuild the indexes after this operation.

```
Alter table dept merge partitions d1a, d1b
into partition d1;

SEGMENT_NAME  PARTITION_NAME  SEGMENT_TYPE
------------  --------------  ----------------
DEPT          D1              TABLE PARTITION
DEPT          D2              TABLE PARTITION

Alter index dept_idx rebuild partition d1;
```

The following bullet points are no longer commands, but options you can use with the (ALTER TABLE PARTITION *name* MODIFY or the ALTER INDEX) partition maintenance commands:

- **UNUSABLE LOCAL INDEXES**   Marks all the local index partitions associated with the specified partition as unusable.

- **REBUILD UNUSABLE LOCAL INDEXES**   Rebuilds the unusable local index partitions associated with the named partition.

- **ALTER INDEX .. MODIFY PARTITION .. UNUSABLE**   Marks the index or index partition(s) as unusable. An unusable index must be rebuilt or dropped and re-created before it can be used. While one partition is marked unusable, the other partitions of the index are still valid, and you can execute statements that require the index if the statements do not access the unusable partition. You can also split or rename the unusable partition before rebuilding it.

- **ALTER INDEX .. REBUILD PARTITION**   Rebuilds one partition of an index. You can also use this option to move an index partition to another tablespace or to change a create-time physical attribute.

Index Partitioning

Partitioned indexes have the same advantages as partitioned tables. Accessing smaller pieces instead of one index on the entire table increases performance when properly executed. There are local and global indexes, and prefixed or nonprefixed indexes. A *local index* has been partitioned;

each piece is a local index. A *global index* is just a regular nonpartitioned index. A *prefixed index* is when the leftmost part of the index is the partition key, whereas a *nonprefixed index* can be costly to access because the partition key is not indexed. If a partition of a table with a global index is dropped, then the corresponding global index is invalidated. If a partition of a table with a local prefixed index is dropped, then the local index is also dropped.

The initialization parameter SKIP_UNUSABLE_INDEXES allows the user to disable error reporting of indexes and index partitions marked unusable. If you do not want the database to choose a new execution plan to avoid using unusable segments, you should set this parameter to FALSE (the default value is TRUE).

The following is an example of a local prefixed partitioned index (the most common type). The index name is DEPT_INDEX, and the index is on the DEPTNO column of the DEPT table. The index is split into three pieces (D1, D2, and D3) that are located in three tablespaces (DEPT1, DEPT2, and DEPT3) that are striped differently from the location of the corresponding table data. This ensures that accessing information from a table partition and its corresponding index partition will result in accessing two physical disk drives instead of one—given that DEPT1–DEPT3 are tablespaces that correspond to datafiles on different physical disks.

```
create index dept_index on dept (deptno)
   local
 (partition d1 tablespace dept2,
  partition d2 tablespace dept3,
  partition d3 tablespace dept1);


Index Created.
```

You can get the information regarding partitioned indexes by accessing DBA_INDEXES:

```
select     index_name, partition_name, tablespace_name
from       dba_ind_partitions
where      index_name = 'DEPT_INDEX'
order by   partition_name;


INDEX_NAME    PARTITION_NAME    TABLESPACE_NAME
DEPT_INDEX              D1            DEPT2
DEPT_INDEX              D2            DEPT3
DEPT_INDEX              D3            DEPT1
```

TIP
Indexes that are partitioned (local indexes) should also be prefixed, meaning the partitioning key is the leading edge of the index.

Exporting Partitions

Partitions can be effortlessly exported. If the data in your table is segmented carefully, it is possible to keep all new information in a single partition to export. This is only true for certain datasets, which use some sort of increasing column value for the partition key. For example, if you partition on date, all new data goes into the latest partition. However, if your data is partitioned by username, or some other generic identifier, then this is not always true. By using a partition key of increasing values, you could potentially eliminate the need to export data from partitions that have not changed and have been previously exported. By using the EXPORT command and giving the *owner.table.partition_name* for the table to be exported, only the partition is exported:

```
expdp user/pass file=tab.dmp tables=(owner.table:partition_name)
```

Here's a simple example using the DEPT table:

```
expdp scott/tiger file=dept_d1.dmp tables=(dept:d1) directory=dpump_dir
```

TIP
If you are archiving old data, consider exchanging the partition for a table name that is more verbose before exporting it. This way, you could import just that table back for reference later and potentially avoid even having to return it to the partitioned table.

Eliminating Fragmentation

Fragmentation can hamper space management operations in the database, but it is a long-enduring myth that overall the number of extents in a segment *always* impacts performance against the database. It is an equally long-enduring myth that the number of extents *never* impacts performance. Bitmap indexes with many noncontiguous extents spanning multiple datafiles can cause a big performance problem. Generally, locally managed tablespaces can minimize most extent-related issues. The need for repeated reorganizations should be a thing of the past for most DBAs (but not all DBAs), if you have set up your storage properly. Fortunately, if you do still need to deal with the occasional reorganization, you now have several ways to perform this activity while minimizing downtime.

To avoid performance issues with extent management, you can do the following:

- Use locally managed uniform-extent tablespaces when you know how big a segment will grow or the rate at which it will grow.

- Use extent sizes that are multiples of the database block size.

- Move tables to tablespaces with an appropriate extent size when they grow too large.

- Avoid row chaining by using Automatic Segment Space Management (ASSM).

I recommend that you regularly monitor your database to find segments that are growing to extreme numbers of extents (over a thousand) and then manage those segments appropriately:

```
select    segment_name, segment_type, extents, bytes
from      dba_segments a, dba_tablespaces b
where     a.extents > 1000;
```

SEGMENT_NAME	SEGMENT_TYPE	EXTENTS	BYTES
ORDER	TABLE	2200	220000000
ORDER_IDX1	INDEX	1200	120000000
CUSTOMER	TABLE	7000	70000000

TIP
Query DBA_SEGMENTS on a regular basis to ensure that objects are not building up too many extents (when not using ASM). Catching problems early is the key to avoiding performance issues later. The goal is to place objects correctly in tablespaces with uniform extent sizes that are appropriate for the expected growth of the objects.

Using the Correct Extent Size

When data is read from a table, it is either accessed by a ROWID operation via an index or by a full table scan (except for index-organized tables). In most cases, access by ROWID is the preferred method. The ROWID method allows the database to determine the exact block that a record resides in and, therefore, bypasses any extent allocation information in the segment. The short answer is that ROWID operations do not care how many extents are in the segment. Database block sizes generally range from 4K to 32K. So, regardless of the number of extents in a segment, a full table scan always performs the same number of reads as long as the extent size is a multiple of the database block size.

Do you still need to worry about extent counts if you are using extents that are multiples of the block size? Yes you do, but you aren't as driven by it as you used to be. Think of it this way, the more extents you have, the more you have to manage, even if it is managed via faster methods. Therefore, my rule of thumb is if you have a segment growing over 4096 extents (assuming you are using locally managed tablespaces), consider moving it to a tablespace where the extent size is more appropriate for the size of the segment. If you have a 15GB table, using a 200M extent size is probably more efficient than using a 1M extent size. For the purposes of loading data alone, you will save backend processing time because the database does not have to allocate as many extents during the load process.

Create a New Tablespace and Move the Segments to It

If a table is getting very large, you can reduce the number of extents by creating a new tablespace and moving the data to the new location. In this example, the CUSTOMER table is fragmented into 100 extents of 1M each, which can be found by querying the DBA_EXTENTS view:

```
select    SEGMENT_NAME, BYTES
from      DBA_EXTENTS
where     SEGMENT_NAME = 'CUSTOMER';

SEGMENT_NAME          BYTES
CUSTOMER              1048576
CUSTOMER              1048576
CUSTOMER              1048576
CUSTOMER              1048576
..etc.
```

First, create a tablespace and then create a new CUSTOMER table called CUSTOMER1 in the new tablespace, for example, NEW_10M_DAT (this tablespace has 10M extents that will better accommodate its growth):

```
CREATE TABLE CUSTOMER1
TABLESPACE NEW_10M_DAT
AS SELECT * FROM CUSTOMER;
```

After ensuring that the CUSTOMER1 table has been created and the data copied completely, drop the original table and all of its indexes:

```
DROP TABLE CUSTOMER;
```

You can now rename your new table and build its corresponding indexes (rebuilding indexes can be time consuming depending on the size of the table):

```
RENAME CUSTOMER1 TO CUSTOMER;
```

The new CUSTOMER table now occupies only 10 extents that are 10M in size. If the customer table is growing even faster, you want to move it to a tablespace with an even larger uniform extent size to accommodate this growth. Although you still have to rebuild the indexes on the CUSTOMER table (one of the drawbacks to this method), this method ensures that the table is never physically gone from the database until the new table is created. You can also use the COPY command to avoid the rollback segment requirements. And you can use the NOLOGGING option to avoid redo issues. An example of using the NOLOGGING feature is displayed in the two examples listed next.

The following is an example of creating a table with NOLOGGING:

```
create table orders_temp
as select * from orders
nologging;

Table created.
```

Here's an example of creating an index with NOLOGGING:

```
Create index ot_idx1 on orders_temp (order_no) nologging;

Index created.
```

TIP
Use the NOLOGGING option when rebuilding a problem table to avoid generating large amounts of redo.

CAUTION
When you create a table or index as NOLOGGING, the database does not generate redo log records for the operation. Therefore, you cannot recover objects created with NOLOGGING, even if you are running in ARCHIVELOG mode. If you cannot afford to lose tables or indexes created with NOLOGGING, then make a backup after the unrecoverable table or index is created.

Exporting and Then Reimporting the Table

You can also relocate the table by exporting, manually creating the table in the new tablespace, and then reimporting the table with the IGNORE=Y option. Don't forget to include your indexes, grants, and constraints (set their import parameters to Y when you export and import), and, if not using automatic undo management, make sure you create a large enough rollback segment for the import. You can also use this method to move your indexes to tablespaces with a larger extent size by creating an indexfile and modifying it to change the tablespace location. You can minimize the rollback or undo area needed by setting COMMIT=Y (to commit during the table import), and you can set the buffer setting higher to increase the import speed. The following procedure describes the operation:

```
Export the CUSTOMER Table
Import the CUSTOMER table with indexfile=[file_name]
Modify indexfile file to create table in new location. (Optional: Modify index locations also)

Drop the CUSTOMER Table

Create the table from the modified script.
Import the CUSTOMER Table (Ignore=y)
```

Note that the INDEXFILE clause means that the command only generates a file containing the import actions, it does not actually import anything.

Using Data Pump (`expdp/impdp`) is faster than re-creating the table using SQL as described in the preceding section, but it could be a problem if something were to happen to the export file before you have a chance to do the import. Precreating the table in the new tablespace is a critical step because the import normally wants to put the table back where you exported it. Using `expdp/impdp` is a lot safer than using NOLOGGING, in which case the table is at risk until a backup is made. Data Pump is also easier because it manages all the index rebuilds, table constraints, and so on, for you.

Data Pump Import parameters SQLFILE={directory-object:}filename and INCLUDE=INDEX parameters are used. If the original import used INDEXES=*n*, then Data Pump Import uses the EXCLUDE=INDEX parameter.

TIP
To speed up the actual table import, use the INDEXES=N option to not create the indexes at import time. Since you have the indexfile script created for changing the table location, you can run this script after the import to re-create the indexes.

To Avoid Chaining, Set PCTFREE Correctly

When a row is created in a table, the data is written to a block and is given a ROWID. The ROWID identifies the data's location on disk. If a row is updated, the changes are written to the same location on disk. The ROWID for the row does not change. Row chaining can occur when there isn't enough room in the data blocks to store a single row or the most recent changes made to a row. A chained row is one that exists in multiple blocks instead of a single block. Accessing multiple blocks for the same row can be costly in terms of performance. To see if you have chaining problems, run the utlchain.sql script that Oracle provides to create the CHAINED_ROWS table. The utlchain.sql file is a file that comes with Oracle and is in the /rdbms/admin subdirectory of your ORACLE_HOME. You can also use Enterprise Manager or look for "*Fetch By Continued Row*" in STATSPACK or AWR Report to detect chained rows. You should check for chaining on a weekly basis and fix any problems immediately. To analyze the amount of chaining in a table (CUSTOMER in this example), run the following query:

```
ANALYZE TABLE CUSTOMER
LIST CHAINED ROWS;
```

Then, run the following query accessing the CHAINED_ROWS table to check the CUSTOMER table for chaining:

```
select    HEAD_ROWID
from      CHAINED_ROWS
where     TABLE_NAME = 'CUSTOMER';
```

If no rows are returned, then you don't have a chaining problem. If there is a chaining problem, then the query will return the HEAD_ROWID for all chained rows. You can also use SELECT "COUNT(*)" against the CHAINED_ROWS table to find the number of chained rows. In V$SYSSTAT, "*table fetch continued row*" is an indicator of chained rows as well.

To avoid row chaining, set PCTFREE (the amount of space reserved in a block for updates) correctly (don't set this when using ASSM). This parameter is set when the table is created. The default value is set to 10 (10 percent free for updates), but this needs to be much higher in a table where there is a large frequency of update activity to rows in the table.

Incidentally, if you have a table where update activity will be very low to nonexistent, you can set the PCTFREE to a slightly lower value to assure more rows will fit into the block and, therefore, conserve space in your table.

TIP
Find chaining problems by accessing the CHAINED_ROWS table.
Avoid chaining problems by correctly setting PCTFREE or choosing
the correct size for your database.

Automatic Segment Space Management

Automatic Segment Space Management in locally managed tablespaces is an alternative to using free lists. This system of managing free space in segments utilizes bitmaps to track the amount of free space in blocks that is available for inserting rows. Because free lists are no longer used when ASSM is enabled, the overall time and resources needed by the database are greatly minimized.

In the latest version of the database, Oracle has further expanded the feature set of ASSM and provided a new clause to the ALTER TABLE and ALTER INDEXES statements. The "SHRINK SPACE" clause essentially coalesces the free space in the segment, releasing unused space so the segment can be smaller. This improves the performance of queries on this segment, and it is much easier to implement than to reduce a segment size through EXPORT/IMPORT or MOVE/RENAME operations. Refer to the documentation on this feature for restrictions and limitations.

ASSM should improve overall performance of block management within segments, but there is a circumstance where the architecture of using a free space bitmap for the block usage can slow performance. Full table scans of small tables (<1000 rows) in an ASSM-enabled tablespace will actually require more buffer gets than a non-ASSM tablespace. Therefore, if you have your tablespaces organized by segment size, ASSM should probably be used only on those tablespaces with medium to large segments.

ASSM has the potential to make a dramatic improvement to block management performance, but do your research, as there are several bugs scattered across different versions of the database that can affect you in specific situations. Before implementing ASSM on your system, be sure to research the types of segments you will have in your tablespace and check for issues related to operations against those types of segments for your version of the database. Most of these bugs have patches that can be applied to resolve the issues.

TIP
Improve performance and segment management by using ASSM, or use separate tablespaces for smaller segments.

Rebuilding the Database

While you should rarely need to do this, it seems that more and more people are looking to this as a necessary step to move forward. Sometimes it is because they have decided to move the database to a new platform like Linux. In other cases, there are new features in release 11*g* that are best implemented in a "new" database. However, be aware that this is a very large step to take and can be very time-consuming (e.g., take up an entire weekend) and should be done only by an advanced DBA. Rebuilding is not guaranteed to bring you any performance benefit. Therefore, it should be planned in advance, tested, and done only when absolutely necessary. To rebuild the database, an advanced DBA should complete the following steps in the order presented:

1. Complete a full-database export (`expdp`).

2. Complete a full-image backup, which includes the following:

   ■ The database files

   ■ The control files

   ■ The online redo log files

   ■ The init.ora(s)

3. Run a rebuild on the database by using the CREATE DATABASE command. *(You could also use a script that was created previously (or generate one using DBCA), and then modify the script as needed to create the new database.)*

4. Make sure you have a enough undo space and a large enough temporary tablespace to handle importing the database and the creation of indexes.

5. Import the entire database (`impdp`).

Refer to the *DBA Administrators Guide* for a more detailed approach.

Increasing the Log File Size and LOG_CHECKPOINT_INTERVAL for Speed

If you want to speed up large numbers of INSERTs, UPDATEs, and DELETEs, increase the sizes of your log files and make sure they are on the fastest disk. Previously, you could also increase the LOG_CHECKPOINT_INTERVAL if it was set such that it would checkpoint prior to a log switch, and this currently defaults to zero (which means switching based on the redo log being full). The LOG_CHECKPOINT_INTERVAL determines the length of time between checkpoints. Therefore, any recovery that involves applying the online redo logs is affected—meaning complete database recovery or instance recovery. Increasing the size of your log files can increase the time needed for media recovery.

Oracle relies on online redo log files to record transactions. Each time a transaction takes place in the database, an entry is added to the online redo log file. If you increase the size allocated for the redo log files, you can increase performance by decreasing the overall number of required log switches and checkpoints. Uncommitted transactions generate redo entries, too, because they generate undo records and these undo records are also written to the redo logs. You can watch the logs spin during a large batch transaction. But keep the following characteristics in mind when you make modifications to the size of your log files:

■ A log file must be online and available while the database is up or the database will halt (one of the few things that stops the database immediately).

■ Online redo log files are recycled and offline redo log files are written to archived log files automatically (if archiving is activated).

■ Minimum is two online redo log files. Online redo log file multiplexing (additional copies) is recommended to provide redundancy in case an online redo log file is lost.

■ The number of initial log files and their sizes are determined automatically when the database is created.

■ Archive logging can be turned on and off by restarting the database in MOUNT mode and then using the ALTER DATABASE command.

■ Checkpoints occur when committed transactions in redo logs get written to the database. Checkpoints also update the datafile headers to set the checkpoint SCN, which is used during the rolling back phase of recovery. If the current SCN for the database at the time of failure was 234578, and the datafiles have a checkpoint SCN of 234500, then only the changes in the redo logs from 234500 to 234578 need to be rolled back. Checkpoints are basically consistency markers for the database—a way of saying everything is in sync at this point.

Determining If Redo Log File Size Is a Problem

Two potential problems are possible that should be addressed. The first concerns batch jobs that do not have enough total redo space to complete or are so fast that the online redo logs wrap (cycle through all the logs and start writing to the first one again) before they are archived to the offline redo logs. Because an online redo log cannot be overwritten until it is archived (when archiving is enabled), DML and DDL activity has to wait until an online log becomes available. By listing the online redo logs with their last update date and time at the operating system level, you can determine how often they are switching. You can also query V$LOG_HISTORY for the last 100 log switches. If you increase the size of the online redo logs, it may provide the space for large batch jobs doing large INSERT, UPDATE, and DELETE transactions. A better solution may be to increase the number of online redo logs so the additional space is provided while also having a frequent log switch (smaller but more online redo logs).

The second potential problem concerns long-running jobs that are spending a large amount of time switching online redo logs. Long-running jobs are often much faster when the entire job fits into a single online redo log. For the online transaction processing (OLTP) type of environment, smaller online redo logs are usually better. My rule of thumb is for online redo logs to switch every half hour (not counting the long-running batch jobs that shorten this time). By monitoring the date and time of the online redo logs at the operating system level (or querying V$LOG_HISTORY), you can determine whether to increase the size or number of online redo logs to reach an optimum switching interval.

Here is a query that shows you the time between log switches. It can be handy in determining if you have a problem:

```
select  b.recid,
        to_char(b.first_time,'dd-mon-yy hh:mi:ss') start_time, a.recid,
        to_char(a.first_time,'dd-mon-yy hh:mi:ss') end_time,
        round(((a.first_time-b.first_time)*25)*60,2) minutes
from    v$log_history a, v$log_history b
where   a.recid = b.recid+1
order   by a.first_time asc
/
```

Determining the Size of Your Log Files and Checkpoint Interval

You can determine the size of your online redo log files by checking the size at the operating system level or querying the V$LOG and V$LOGFILE tables. Displaying information about redo logs is shown in the query listed here:

```
select    a.member, b.*
from      v$logfile a, v$log b
where     a.group# = b.group#;
```

```
MEMBER                GRP#   THRD#   BYTES      MEMBERS   STATUS
/disk1/log1a.ora      1      1       2048000    2         INACTIVE
/disk1/log2a.ora      2      1       2048000    2         CURRENT
/disk2/log1b.ora      1      1       2048000    2         INACTIVE
/disk2/log2b.ora      2      1       2048000    2         CURRENT
(partial columns listed only...)
```

The query output shows two groups of redo logs. Each group has two redo log files in it (one primary file and one multiplexed file). The data in /disk1/log1a.ora and in /disk2/log1b.ora is exactly the same (multiplexing redo log files is for availability and recoverability purposes).

TIP
Increase the size of your log files to increase the rate at which large INSERTS, DELETES, and UPDATES (DMLs) are processed.

Other Helpful Redo Log Commands

You can add additional redo logs by using the ALTER DATABASE ADD LOGFILE command to create larger redo logs and then to drop the smaller ones.

To multiplex online redo log files (creating a mirrored copy), use this command to add a log file to an existing group:

```
alter database add logfile member '/disk2/log1b.ora' to group 1;
alter database add logfile member '/disk2/log2b.ora' to group 2;
```

To drop an online redo log member, use this command:

```
alter database drop logfile member '/disk2/log2b.ora';
```

To add a new online redo log group, use this command:

```
alter database add logfile group 3 ('/disk1/log3a.ora') size 10M;
```

To drop an entire online redo log group (all copies), use this command:

```
alter database drop logfile group 1;
```

NOTE
You cannot drop a redo log file group if doing so would cause the redo thread to contain less than two redo log file groups. You cannot also drop the redo log file group if it contains the current online redo log (ORA-01623). In this case, you need to switch log groups first and then you can drop the redo log group.

To switch log files (change the current redo log group to the next redo log group), use this command:

```
alter system switch logfile;
```

TIP
Put the redo logs on the fastest disk if you plan to write a lot of information. Try to use the outer edge of the disk (the fastest part on many disk types) for the redo logs. Better yet, there is an ASM feature that does this: The Intelligent Data Placement feature enables you to specify disk regions on Oracle ASM disks to ensure that frequently accessed data is placed on the outermost (hot) tracks, which provide higher performance.

TIP
Increase the size of online redo logs if log switches are occurring less than every half hour during normal business conditions (excluding infrequent large batch jobs). Increase the number of online redo logs if you are wrapping during large batch jobs.

Additional Instance Parameters

These further instance parameters can have an effect on the performance of your online redo log files:

- **LOG_ARCHIVE_DUPLEX_DEST** Directory location with archive prefix (arch). This is a location to write an additional copy of archive logs (as redo logs are filled and are archived in ARCHIVELOG mode only). If you have the space, this safety net can save you if archiving errors occur. For EE databases, this parameter is deprecated in favor of the LOG_ARCHIVE_DEST_n parameters. If Oracle Enterprise Edition is not installed or it is installed but you have not specified any LOG_ARCHIVE_DEST_n parameters, this parameter is valid.

- **LOG_ARCHIVE_MIN_SUCCEED_DEST** Can be set to 1 to 10 if you are using LOG_ARCHIVE_DEST_n, or to values of 1 or 2 if you are using LOG_ARCHIVE_DEST and LOG_ARCHIVE_DUPLEX_DEST. This is the minimum number of successful archives written for a redo log. If you set it to 2, then you have two mandatory archiving destinations, similar to setting LOG_ARCHIVE_DEST1 and LOG_ARCHIVE_DEST2 and mandatory archive sites. If you set any LOG_ARCHIVE_DEST_n parameter where n > 3, then those sites are treated as optional archive sites. If you set LOG_ARCHIVE_MIN_SUCCEED_DEST to 1, then the LOG_ARCHIVE_DUPLEX_DEST or LOG_ARCHIVE_DEST_*n* (*n* > 1) sites are optional best-effort archive sites, not mandatory sites.

■ **DB_WRITER_PROCESSES**   This is the number of database writers to write data from the SGA to disk when one database writer isn't enough.

■ **DBWR_IO_SLAVES**   If you can't use multiple processes (or if you don't have asynchronous I/O and want to emulate it), then you can use DBWR_IO_SLAVES to distribute the load of the ARCH and LGWR processes over multiple I/O slaves. This can't be used if DB_WRITER_PROCESSES > 1.

Fast Recovery Area

The fast recovery area (as of 11*g*R2, it was previously the flash recovery area) is a new mechanism for maintaining recovery information on disk to improve recovery time. This feature greatly improves the ability to recover more quickly from an issue in your database (especially user or DBA error), but it can take a lot of extra disk space to implement. For this reason, many people may be inclined to utilize slower, less-expensive storage for maintaining the fast recovery area (FRA). This introduces some potential performance implications into your environment, depending on how you implement it. Oracle suggests you have an equal size group of disks on another disk array for your FRA:

■ If you are using a slower-performing disk for your FRA, redo performance will be negatively affected because all redo log files are stored in the FRA and are governed by the slowest performing device.

■ Consider whether you want to have a very large FRA, and find out what size is the most appropriate for your recovery needs or budget.

■ A large FRA can slow down your write performance when backups and other activities utilize the FRA.

■ Because the FRA is most often used only for archive and Flashback Database writes, it doesn't overburden the disk.

■ This configuration still maintains redundant redo areas.

Increasing Chances of Recovery: Committing After Each Batch

To increase your chances of recovering large batch processes, COMMIT more frequently during a batch process. Although doing this could slow processing, it will save time if a recovery is necessary. Determining what defines a large batch process really depends on how large your system is, but a job that takes several hours to complete should be broken into smaller jobs that have periodic COMMITs so the entire job doesn't need to be rerun in its entirety in the event of a failure during the job.

Isolating Large Transactions to Their Own Rollback Segments

When using rollback segments, keep in mind that batch processes may require a single large rollback segment. Use SET TRANSACTION USE ROLLBACK SEGMENT *rb_big* for large transactions (you can't do this if you are using automatic undo mode). An example is displayed next. Also, note that you must precode the SET TRANSACTION with a COMMIT even if it is the first command for your session.

```
commit;
set transaction use rollback segment rb_big;
Transaction set.

delete from big_table;
commit;
```

TIP
Failure to use the SET TRANSACTION USE ROLLBACK SEGMENT
rb_big *command for a given UPDATE, INSERT, DELETE, or batch program could cause the rollback segments to become fragmented and potentially too large for the corresponding tablespace. The SET TRANSACTION… command must be reissued after each COMMIT or rollback process.*

A rollback segment is dynamically extended as needed by a transaction up to the total available space in the tablespace (transactions cannot span rollback segments) in which it resides. The OPTIMAL storage option for a rollback segment dynamically shrinks extended rollback segments to a specified size. Although large transactions should be preceded with the SET TRANSACTION… statement, it is still a good idea to set the OPTIMAL option so that rollback segments that have been extended are returned to their original size, releasing the disk space. Use this statement to alter a rollback segment to OPTIMAL:

```
alter rollback segment rb1
storage (optimal 15M);
```

Note that you may also use the OPTIMAL storage setting at rollback creation time.
You can also force a rollback segment to shrink to its OPTIMAL setting or a specified size using these commands:

```
alter rollback segment rb1 shrink;
alter rollback segment rb1 shrink to 15M;
```

TIP
Do not depend on the OPTIMAL setting to shrink rollback segments as this is a costly process in terms of performance. The OPTIMAL setting should be activated infrequently. Also, note that you cannot shrink a rollback segment to a size that is less than the combined value of its first two extents.

Using the UNDO Tablespace

Since 9i, Oracle allows UNDO tablespaces in the database, which greatly simplifies the management of large transactions. With rollback segments, UNDO blocks are overwritten by newer transactions as required. This leads to the DBA having to "juggle" to ensure that large-enough rollback segments are available for large transactions to avoid a "snapshot too old" error as well as to ensure that enough rollback segments are available for regular database activity.

To utilize Automatic Undo Management, create a tablespace in the database of type UNDO.

```
create undo tablespace UNDOTBS1 datafile
'/u01/oradata/prod/undotbs1_01.dbf'
extent management local uniform size 256k;
```

Next, modify your initialization file to specify three new parameters:

- UNDO_MANAGEMENT=AUTO (the default value)
- UNDO_TABLESPACE=UNDOTBS1
- UNDO_RETENTION = <# of minutes> (default value is 900, or 15 minutes)

CAUTION
If UNDO_MANAGEMENT is set to AUTO (it is AUTO by default) and the UNDO_TABLESPACE is not set, then the SYSTEM tablespace is used—so don't do this! According to the Oracle Administrators Guide: "If the UNDO_TABLESPACE parameter is omitted, the first available undo tablespace in the database is chosen. If no undo tablespace is available, the instance will start without an undo tablespace. In such cases, user transactions will be executed using the SYSTEM rollback segment."

The initialization parameter UNDO_RETENTION is used to specify the amount of time (in seconds) that UNDO data is retained in the UNDO tablespace after it is committed. This is the real advantage of using UNDO tablespaces because, unlike traditional rollback segments, the database will at least make an attempt to maintain the older version of the data for long-running queries. Another advantage is that if you are running into issues where you aren't maintaining enough UNDO information, you can simply add more space to the tablespace and increase the value of UNDO_RETENTION.

Be aware, though, that if the tablespace does not have enough room for all of the UNDO records, it will reuse unexpired UNDO space as necessary regardless of the UNDO_RETENTION setting. One thing that you can't do if you are using Automatic Undo Management is to use a particular rollback segment (but that really isn't an issue anymore with Automatic Undo Management).

Monitoring UNDO Space

You can use the V$UNDOSTAT view to monitor the UNDO space used by current transactions in the instance. The view contains a total of 576 rows, spanning a 4-day cycle. Each row in this view lists statistics collected in the instance for ten-minute intervals. Each row represents one snapshot of the statistics for UNDO space utilization, transaction volume, and query length, taken every 10 minutes for the last 24 hours.

A database can have either UNDO segments or rollback segments. The V$ROLLSTAT view will show information on the UNDO segments in the UNDO tablespace when in Automatic Undo Management mode. Information on the actual extents for the UNDO tablespace can be retrieved from the DBA_UNDO_EXTENTS view in the database.

If you set UNDO_MANAGEMENT to AUTO, DBAs cannot manage UNDO segments at all. If you create an UNDO tablespace, you can create rollback segments in UNDO tablespaces, but it is strongly recommended that you *not* do it. UNDO segments are implemented as rollback segments in the UNDO tablespace. This is why V$ROLLSTAT works.

Killing Problem Sessions

If the demand for resources on your system is at a temporary peak, you can stop a low priority, problem session by using the operating system KILL command (using Enterprise Manager is easier). But first, you must find the user who's running the job that is draining system resources.

The following commands will help you find and KILL the problematic users:

```
select   sid, serial#
from     v$session
where    username = 'BADUSER'
```

Here is the query output:

```
SID __ SERIAL#
5       33
```

The following command is used to KILL the session:

```
alter system kill session '5,33';
```

You can also use the following code to determine which rollback segment is processing each transaction, along with the corresponding user and SQL statement. The output has been slightly modified for readability:

```
select   a.name, b.xacts, c.sid, c.serial#, c.username, d.sql_text
from     v$rollname a, v$rollstat b, v$session c, v$sqltext d,
         v$transaction e
where    a.usn = b.usn
```

```
and        b.usn = e.xidusn
and        c.taddr = e.addr
and        c.sql_address = d.address
and        c.sql_hash_value = d.hash_value
order by a.name, c.sid, d.piece;
```

name	xacts	sid	serial#	username	sql_text
RB1	1	5	33	USER1	delete from test1;
RB2	1	7	41	USER9	update orders
					set items = 5
					where orderno = 555;

The preceding output shows which users are currently using UNDO segments. This query could also show how many users are utilizing or waiting for the same UNDO segment if the V$ROLLSTAT.WAITS column is also selected.

If you just want the active transactions, then use this query:

```
select     a.name, b.xacts, c.sid, c.serial#, c.username
from       v$rollname a, v$rollstat b, v$session c,
           v$transaction e
where      a.usn = b.usn
and        b.usn = e.xidusn
and        c.taddr = e.addr
order by a.name, c.sid;
```

```
NAME                 XACTS SID  SERIAL# USERNAME
-------------------- ----- ---  -------- --------
SYSSMU10_378818850$      1  15       687 JANET
```

TIP
Isolate large transactions to their own rollback segment, but in 11g, use UNDO tablespaces (Automatic Undo management) to simplify your undo management.

Have Multiple Control Files on Different Disks and Controllers

Control files store information regarding startup, shutdown, and archiving. Because your system is useless without at least one good control file, you should store three copies of the control files on separate disks and controllers (if possible). If you do happen to remove *all* the control files while the database is open, you can use the ALTER DATABASE BACKUP CONTROLFILE command to generate a new one. If the database is closed and the control file is missing, you can use the CREATE CONTROLFILE statement to re-create a control file. However, re-creating the control file from scratch is a lot of work and prone to error. And lots of valuable, possibly critical, information is lost (for example, the most recent backup information for RMAN backups).

To view current control files, run the following query:

```
select   name, value
from     v$parameter
where    name = 'control_files';


NAME                    VALUE
control_files           /disk1/ora10/ctl1.ora, /disk2/ora10/ctl2.ora,
                        /disk3/ora10/ctl3.ora
```

Another suggestion is to create a text copy of the control file at regular intervals, or at least after any database architectural change (at the file or tablespace level). This helps if you lose all copies and have to re-create the control file from scratch.

Other Disk I/O Precautions and Tips

Here are a few further miscellaneous notes pertaining to disk I/O:

- Heavy batch processing may need much larger UNDO, REDO, and TEMP tablespace sizes.

- Heavy DML (INSERT, UPDATE, and DELETE) processing may need much larger UNDO, REDO, and TEMP tablespace sizes.

- Heavy user access to large tables will require more CPU and memory, and larger temporary tablespace sizes.

- Poorly tuned systems will require more CPU and memory and larger temporary tablespace sizes.

- A greater number of well-balanced disks and controllers will always increase performance (by reducing I/O contention).

- If you increase disk capacity, you can speed backup and recovery time by keeping a copy of the backup on disk instead of tape.

- Finally, if you can afford it, Exadata, Violin Memory, EMC, and/or solid state or flash disk solutions are some of the absolute best ways to improve Oracle I/O performance.

Issues to Consider in the Planning Stages

If you're planning a new system or an upgrade, here are some things you'll want to consider:

- What is the maximum possible disk capacity for the hardware?

- What disk sizes are available?

- What will be the initial size of the database?

- What will be the future size of the database and what is the rate of growth?

- Will there be a RAID (striping) level for database files or the OS?

- What recovery methods will be employed?

- What archiving methods will be used to store historical information?

- How often will report output be kept on the system?

- What development space will be needed?

- What software will be installed, and how much space will it need to function efficiently?

- What system utilities will be installed, and how much space will they need to function efficiently?

- What type of mail system is going to be installed?

- What data transfer methods are going to be employed?

- Is ASM installed? Learn and plan for it if it is.

- What are the batch processing requirements, and will there be ad hoc user queries?

- How will the data be accessed that may cause potential hot spots?

Finally, it's worth mentioning the product "Oracle Orion" here. Oracle Orion is a tool for predicting the performance of an Oracle database without having to install Oracle or create a database. Unlike other I/O calibration tools, Oracle Orion is expressly designed for simulating Oracle database I/O workloads using the same I/O software stack as Oracle. Orion can also simulate the effect of striping performed by Oracle Automatic Storage Management

TIP
When you are in the system planning stage, ensure that you find out all of the information related to the current and future use of the system. Don't just think about the Oracle database needs—investigate the other software and applications that affect the performance of your Oracle database.

Tips Review

- Try to avoid splitting a logical device in a disk array into more than one filesystem. This action may seem to give you flexibility, but it can also increase the number of datafile locations you have to manage.

- Use disk arrays to improve performance and protect your data against disk failure. Choose the proper RAID level and technology solutions that enable you to maintain the availability your organization needs. Don't just go "good enough," because you will regret it at 2 A.M. when you lose a disk.

- Separate key Oracle datafiles to ensure that disk contention is not a bottleneck. By separating tables and indexes of often-joined tables, you can ensure that even the worst of table joins do not result in disk contention. In 11*g* Enterprise Manager, Oracle makes it easy to move data to a *hotter* or *colder* region of a disk.

- Query V$FILESTAT and V$DATAFILE to see how effectively datafiles have been balanced. Temporary tablespaces are monitored using V$TEMPFILE and V$TEMPSTAT.

- Solve disk contention problems by moving datafiles to disks that are not as heavily accessed or moving tables to different tablespaces on different disks.

- Use the Database Files Metrics in Enterprise Manager to determine the I/O that is taking place on each database file. Move heavily used datafiles to separate filesystems to distribute I/O. See Chapter 5 for addition information.

- Although ASM does not provide multipathing capabilities, ASM does leverage multipathing tools, as long as the path or device produced by the multipathing tool returns a successful return code from an fstat system call. Metalink Note 294869.1 provides more details on ASM and multipathing.

- To get accurate real-time statistics, it may be prudent to query the V$ASM_DISK and V$ASM_DISKGROUP views, but exercise caution when running queries against these views during peak workloads.

- In 11gR2, ASM uses the failure groups to perform read I/O (given that you've set the ASM_PREFERRED_READ_FAILURE_GROUPS initialization parameter to specify a list of failure group names as preferred read disks), thus relieving I/O pressure from the primary failure group.

- Redo and archive log files are defined as fine-grained, whereas datafiles are coarse.

- The init.ora parameter ASM_POWER_LIMIT is used to influence the throughput and speed of the rebalance operation. The range of values for ASM_POWER_LIMIT is 0 to 11, where a value of 11 is full throttle and a value of 1 is low speed. Use a value of 0, which turns off automatic rebalance, with caution. For diskgroups that have the diskgroup ASM compatibility set to 11.2.0.2 or greater (for example, COMPATIBLE.ASM = 11.2.0.2), the operational range of values is 0 to 1024 for the rebalance power.

- If removing or adding several disks with ASM, best practice is to add or remove drives all at once. This reduces the number of rebalance operations that are needed for storage changes.

- Tables can be easily partitioned for individual pieces to be accessed and/or manipulated; you can still access the entire table of a partitioned table. Accessing the tables DBA_TABLES, DBA_PART_TABLE, and DBA_SEGMENTS provides additional information concerning tables that have been partitioned.

- You can also partition tables using multiple columns as the criteria. You must specify "MAXVALUE" for all columns that are part of the partition key except for interval partitioning (new in 11g and covered in this chapter).

- Reference partitioning is tailor made for the partitioning of OLTP systems and those systems that tend to be far more normalized than the rest.

- Use the NOLOGGING option when rebuilding a problem table to avoid generating large amounts of redo.

CAUTION
When you create a table or index as NOLOGGING, the database does not generate redo log records for the operation. Thus, you cannot recover objects created with NOLOGGING, even if you are running in ARCHIVELOG mode. If you cannot afford to lose tables or indexes created with NOLOGGING, then make a backup after the unrecoverable table or index is created.

- Find chaining problems by accessing the CHAINED_ROWS table. Avoid chaining problems by correctly setting PCTFREE or choosing the correct size for your database.

- Improve performance and segment management by using ASSM, or use separate tablespaces for smaller segments.

- Increase the size of your log files to increase the rate at which large INSERTS, DELETES, and UPDATES (DMLs) are processed.

- Put redo logs on the fastest disks (or flash or solid-state disks) if you plan to write a lot of information. Try to use the outer edge of the disk (the fastest part on many disk types) for the redo logs. Better yet, an ASM feature is available for doing this: The Intelligent Data Placement feature lets you specify disk regions on Oracle ASM disks to ensure that frequently accessed data is placed on the outermost (hot) tracks, which provide higher performance.

- When you are in the system planning stage, ensure that you find out all of the information related to the current and future use of the system. Don't just think about the Oracle database needs, investigate the other software and applications that impact performance of your Oracle database.

References

Oracle 11g Concepts Guide.
Oracle 11g DBA Administrators Guide.
Oracle 11g DBA Reference Guide (Oracle Corporation).
Oracle VLDB (Very Large Database) and Partitioning Guide.
TUSC DBA Guide, 1988–2006.
    Many thanks to Sri Avantsa, who did most of the updates for this chapter, and to Bill Callahan, who did the previous update of this chapter. Thanks to Nitin Vengurlekar who contributed a large amount of ASM knowledge to this chapter originally.

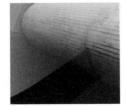

CHAPTER
4

Tuning the Database with Initialization Parameters (DBA)

The Oracle initialization files (SPFILE or a PFILE such as initSID.ora) determine many Oracle operating system environment attributes, such as memory allocated for data, memory allocated for statements, resources allocated for I/O, and other crucial performance-related parameters. Each version of Oracle continues to add to the total number of initialization parameters. Oracle 11g Release 2 now has 2394 (341 documented and 2053 hidden) initialization parameters (these numbers vary slightly on different versions of Oracle and platforms). As you might expect, an entire book could be written on how to set and tune each parameter; this book focuses on the key parameters that affect database performance. Consider reading or referencing Appendix A after this chapter, as it contains a list of all documented initialization parameters, obsolete and deprecated parameters, my Top 25 (many covered in this chapter), my Top 20 not-to-forget parameters (things like AUDIT_TRAIL for auditing and CELL_OFFLOAD_PROCESSING for smart scans in Exadata), my Top 13 undocumented parameters (many for recovery and corruption), my bonus Top 10 undocumented new parameters (such as the Exadata parameter _KCFIS_STORAGEIDX_DISABLED to turn off storage indexes for tuning/testing), and lastly, a section containing recommendations from the Oracle Applications Development team for 11i and Release 12.

The key to an optimized Oracle database is often the architecture of the system and the parameters that set the environment for the database. Setting key initialization parameters (MEMORY_TARGET, MEMORY_MAX_TARGET, SGA_MAX_SIZE, PGA_AGGREGATE_TARGET, DB_CACHE_SIZE, and SHARED_POOL_SIZE) can be the difference between subsecond queries and queries that take several minutes. A new MEMORY_TARGET parameter in 11g can replace some of the key parameters that are covered in this chapter. This chapter focuses on the crucial initialization parameters, but also lists the top 25 initialization parameters near the end of the chapter. The chapter concludes with a look at the *always growing* typical server configurations for various database sizes.

This chapter contains the following tips and techniques designed to achieve the greatest performance gain with the least effort by focusing on the parameters that yield the biggest impact:

- Crucial initialization parameters in Oracle including MEMORY_TARGET
- Parameters to consider when upgrading to 11gR2
- Using SEC_CASE_SENSITIVE_LOGON and case-sensitive passwords
- Modifying the initialization parameter file without a restart
- Working with the SPFILE and creating a readable PFILE (`init.ora`)
- Viewing the initialization parameters via Enterprise Manager
- Tuning DB_CACHE_SIZE
- Tuning the SHARED_POOL_SIZE
- Checking library cache and dictionary cache
- Querying the X$KSMSP table to get another picture of SHARED_POOL_SIZE
- Using multiple buffer pools

- Tuning the PGA_AGGREGATE_TARGET
- User, session, and system memory use
- Working with the OPTIMIZER_MODE parameter
- Two important Exadata initialization parameters
- The top 25 performance-related initialization parameters to consider
- Undocumented initialization parameters (more in Appendix A)
- Typical server setups with different size databases
- Oracle Applications recommendations (more in Appendix A)

When Upgrading to Oracle 11gR2

When upgrading to 11gR2, you need to consider many parameters for your unique system. Please check Appendix A for obsolete (removed) and deprecated (discouraged, although still okay to use for backward compatibility) parameters. I cover a few parameters that are both important and common to most systems. For single-instance databases, an Oracle Database Upgrade Assistant configuration utility includes a command-line option to auto extend system files, the ability to upgrade from Oracle Express Edition (XE or free edition) to others (the XE datafiles reside in ORACLE_BASE/oradata/XE and must be copied *prior* to the upgrade as the installer may remove them upon upgrade). There is also integration with the Oracle Database 11g pre-upgrade tool, the ability to move data files into ASM, and the ability to set the Oracle Base and Diagnostic Destination Configuration. The Database Upgrade Assistant (DBUA) is extremely helpful and shows that Oracle truly wants to assist you in the upgrade process. The DBUA uses pre-upgrade scripts that check the following before the upgrade:

- Invalid user accounts or roles
- Invalid data types or invalid objects
- Desupported character sets
- Statistics gathering (recommendation not a check)
- Adequate resources (UNDO/ROLLBACK segments, tablespaces, and free disk space)
- Missing SQL scripts needed for the upgrade
- Listener running (if Oracle Enterprise Manager Database Control upgrade or configuration is requested)
- Oracle Database software linked with Database Vault option (If Database Vault is enabled, disable Database Vault before upgrade.)

When you specify the ORACLE_BASE environment variable during install, Oracle also uses this value to set the DIAGNOSTIC_DEST (required for upgrade from previous version) parameter, which includes all ADR directories (alert, trace, incident, cdump, hm (health monitor), etc.). As of Oracle11gR1, CORE_DUMP_DEST, BACKGROUND_DUMP_DEST, and USER_DUMP_DEST have been replaced with DIAGNOSTIC_DEST. In the following output, ORACLE_BASE is set to *u01/app/oracle* and DIAGNOSTIC_DEST is set to */u01/app/oracle/diag*:

```
select name, value
from   v$diag_info;

NAME                      VALUE
--------------------      ----------------------------------------------
Diag Enabled              TRUE
ADR Base                  /u01/app/oracle
ADR Home                  /u01/app/oracle/diag/rdbms/o11gb/O11gb
Diag Trace                /u01/app/oracle/diag/rdbms/o11gb/O11gb/trace
Diag Alert                /u01/app/oracle/diag/rdbms/o11gb/O11gb/alert
Diag Incident             /u01/app/oracle/diag/rdbms/o11gb/O11gb/incident
Diag Cdump                /u01/app/oracle/diag/rdbms/o11gb/O11gb/cdump
Health Monitor            /u01/app/oracle/diag/rdbms/o11gb/O11gb/hm
Default Trace File        /u01/app/oracle/diag/rdbms/o11gb/O11gb/trace/O11gb_ora_17776.trc
Active Problem Count      0
Active Incident Count     0

11 rows selected.
```

A key new parameter as of Oracle11g is the MEMORY_TARGET parameter that enables you to set memory allocated to Oracle with *one* easy parameter (although you'll shortly see that setting some minimums for other values is recommended). MEMORY_TARGET is used by Oracle's Automatic Memory Management to set other memory settings, such as the memory allocated to *both* the Program Global Area (PGA) and SGA (System Global Area) combined. Setting this parameter enables Automatic Memory Management, an Oracle feature that allocates memory for you based on system needs, but you can also set minimum values for key parameters. MEMORY_TARGET is used for everything that SGA_TARGET covers, but also now includes the PGA (especially important since this covers PGA_AGGREGATE_TARGET, an important area). Key parameters such as DB_CACHE_SIZE, SHARED_POOL_SIZE, PGA_AGGREGATE_TARGET, LARGE_POOL_SIZE, and JAVA_POOL_SIZE are all set automatically when MEMORY_TARGET is set. Setting minimum values for important initialization parameters in your system is also a *very* good idea. The MEMORY_MAX_TARGET parameter is optional and is the maximum memory allocated for Oracle and the maximum value allowed for MEMORY_TARGET.

In Oracle9i, you saw the beginning of Oracle's Automated Memory Management with the SGA_MAX_SIZE (no more setting buffers, just DB_CACHE_SIZE and granule size: _KSMG_GRANULE_SIZE). In Oracle 10g, the SGA_TARGET parameter was introduced (still recommended by Oracle Applications even in 11g). In the 10g version of this book, however, I recommended that you still set minimums for the key memory areas such as the Data Cache (DB_CACHE_SIZE) and shared pool (SHARED_POOL_SIZE). In Oracle 11g, you now have MEMORY_TARGET, which combines the SGA and PGA into one setting, making life easy, especially for smaller, less complex systems. For larger, well-tuned, complex systems, you should certainly still set minimums as described in this chapter. Some parameters are automatically sized (this chapter details the use of many of these parameters in the coming pages). Also note that MEMORY_TARGET (Automatic Memory Management, or AMM) manages SGA_TARGET and PGA_TARGET. It is one level above Automatic Shared Memory Management (SGA_TARGET) and Automatic PGA Memory Management (PGA_AGGREGATE_TARGET).

These parameters are automatically sized when you use MEMORY_TARGET or SGA_TARGET (unless you set minimums):

Component	Initialization Parameter
Buffer cache	DB_CACHE_SIZE (usually set minimum value also)
Shared Pool	SHARED_POOL_SIZE (usually set minimum value)
Large Pool	LARGE_POOL_SIZE (usually set minimum value)
Java Pool	JAVA_POOL_SIZE (usually set minimum value)
Streams Pool	STREAMS_POOL_SIZE

These are manually sized SGA components that also use MEMORY_TARGET:

Component	Initialization Parameter
Log buffer	LOG_BUFFER (can only set in PFILE, since 10g)
Keep Pool	DB_KEEP_CACHE_SIZE (major benchmarks use this cache too)
Recycle Pool	DB_RECYCLE_CACHE_SIZE (major benchmarks use this cache too)
Block caches	DB_nK_CACHE_SIZE (major benchmarks use these caches too)

As stated earlier, the PGA is now managed by MEMORY_TARGET as well. This includes the PGA_AGGREGATE_TARGET parameter. You should also set a minimum for PGA_AGGREGATE_TARGET. To move from the SGA_TARGET to MEMORY_TARGET, set the MEMORY_TARGET and MEMORY_MAX_TARGET. To determine what value to use, run the following query and ensure that you add the values for SGA_TARGET and PGA_AGGREGATE_TARGET to estimate MEMORY_TARGET (the following outputs are limited to key values):

```
SQL> sho parameter target

NAME                                 TYPE            VALUE
------------------------------------ --------------- -----
memory_max_target                    big integer         0
memory_target                        big integer         0
pga_aggregate_target                 big integer      110M
sga_target                           big integer      250M

ALTER SYSTEM SET MEMORY_MAX_TARGET=360M SCOPE=SPFILE;
(shutdown/startup)
ALTER SYSTEM SET MEMORY_TARGET=360M SCOPE=SPFILE;
ALTER SYSTEM SET SGA_TARGET=0; (or set a minimum)
ALTER SYSTEM SET PGA_AGGREGATE_TARGET=0; (or set a minimum)
(shutdown/startup)
```

```
SQL> sho parameter target

NAME                                   TYPE            VALUE
------------------------------------   -------------   -----
memory_max_target                      big integer     360M
memory_target                          big integer     360M
pga_aggregate_target                   big integer     0
sga_target                             big integer     0

ALTER SYSTEM SET SGA_TARGET=200M;
ALTER SYSTEM SET PGA_AGGREGATE_TARGET=100M;
(you can do this with DB_CACHE_SIZE and SHARED_POOL_SIZE as needed)

SQL> sho parameter target

NAME                                   TYPE            VALUE
------------------------------------   -------------   -----
memory_max_target                      big integer     360M
memory_target                          big integer     360M
pga_aggregate_target                   big integer     100M
sga_target                             big integer     200M
```

Using SEC_CASE_SENSITIVE_LOGON (new in 11g)

With a new installation, be aware that passwords are now case sensitive. A new and important parameter in 11g is SEC_CASE_SENSITIVE_LOGON. The default is TRUE, which makes passwords case sensitive by default. Set this to FALSE to disable this feature. You can also lock an account if a user fails to enter the correct password a specified number of times, using the SEC_MAX_FAILED_LOGIN_ATTEMPTS parameter (the default is 10). Based on your security needs, you may consider changing this value.

Once locked, the DBA must issue the following command to unlock an account:

```
SQL> ALTER USER username ACCOUNT UNLOCK;
```

Identifying Crucial Initialization Parameters

Although tuning specific queries individually can lead to performance gains, the system will still be slow if the parameters for the initialization file are not set correctly because the initialization file plays such an integral role in the overall performance of an Oracle database. While you can spend time setting all the initialization parameters, there are a few main parameters that need to be set correctly to realize significant performance gains:

- MEMORY_TARGET

- MEMORY_MAX_TARGET

- SGA_TARGET

- SGA_MAX_SIZE

- PGA_AGGREGATE_TARGET
- DB_CACHE_SIZE
- SHARED_POOL_SIZE

TIP
The key initialization parameters in Oracle are MEMORY_TARGET, MEMORY_MAX_TARGET, SGA_TARGET, SGA_MAX_SIZE, PGA_AGGREGATE_TARGET, DB_CACHE_SIZE, and SHARED_POOL_SIZE.

As stated previously, if you use MEMORY_TARGET (and optionally MEMORY_MAX_TARGET), Oracle will use Automatic Memory Management (AMM) for the rest (Metalink note 443746.1 describes this in detail). In 10g, SGA_TARGET and SGA_MAX_SIZE can also be set so Oracle manages the shared memory on your system with Automatic Shared Memory Management (ASMM) (Metalink Note 295626.1 describes this in detail). The Oracle Applications Development team recommends using SGA_TARGET and SGA_MAX_SIZE for both 10g and 11g in 11i Apps (Metalink note 216205.1) and for 11g in Release 12 Apps (Metalink note 396009.1). I've included the Oracle Applications Development team's recommendations at the end of this chapter. I would like to see MEMORY_TARGET mature a bit more before I hand the "keys to the car" to Oracle, but I like the approach to simplicity, especially for beginners. The following query can be used to find the current settings of the key initialization parameters on your database (if SGA_TARGET is set to a non-zero value, then some of these parameters are set to zero, which means Oracle sets it). For this example, I manually set the shared pool:

```
Col name for a25
Col value for a50

select   name, value
from     v$parameter
where    name in ('sga_max_size', 'pga_aggregate_target',
                  'db_cache_size', 'shared_pool_size');

NAME                    VALUE
--------------------    --------------------
shared_pool_size        1073741824
sga_max_size            6878658560
db_cache_size           0
pga_aggregate_target    0
```

Changing the Initialization Parameters Without a Restart

With each version of Oracle, you can alter more and more parameters without needing to restart the database, greatly reducing the need for scheduled downtime to implement system tuning changes.

The next example shows changing the SHARED_POOL_SIZE to 128M while the database is running:

```
SQL> ALTER SYSTEM SET SHARED_POOL_SIZE = 128M;
```

In addition to being able to change parameters dynamically, you can now use a SPFILE to store dynamic changes persistently to the instance parameters. Prior to Oracle 9*i*, any dynamic changes were lost when the database was restarted unless the parameters were added to the initialization parameter file manually. As of Oracle 9*i*, and continuing through Oracle 11*g* Release 2, dynamic changes can be stored in a server parameter file (SPFILE). The default order of precedence when an instance is started is to read parameter files in the following order:

1. spfile<SID>.ora

2. spfile.ora

3. init<SID>.ora

Parameters can be dynamically modified at a system-wide or session-specific scope. In addition, parameters can be changed in memory only or persistently across restarts via an SPFILE. In the first example, I change the SHARED_POOL_SIZE and also write it to the SPFILE. Note that you can use K (kilobytes), M (Megabytes), G (Gigabytes), but not T (Terabytes), P (Petabytes), or E (Exabytes) yet (even though in 64-bit, an Oracle database can be 8E and you can directly address 16E). Also, note that 1G = 1024*1024*1024 = 1,073,741,824. In the second example, I write SHARED_POOL_SIZE to both the SPFILE and the MEMORY:

```
SQL> ALTER SYSTEM SET SHARED_POOL_SIZE = 128M SCOPE=SPFILE;
```

I can set both the SPFILE and MEMORY using this:

```
SQL> ALTER SYSTEM SET SHARED_POOL_SIZE = 1G SCOPE=BOTH;
SQL> SHOW PARAMETER SHARED_POOL_SIZE
```

NAME	TYPE	VALUE
shared_pool_size	big integer	1G

I can also create a PFILE from the SPFILE (since the SPFILE is nonreadable):

```
SQL> CREATE PFILE='C:\APP\USER\PRODUCT\11.2.0\DBHOME_2\DATABASE\INITORCL.ORA'
FROM SPFILE;
```

Or, as shown here, it checks default location and writes it to the default location:

```
SQL> CREATE PFILE FROM SPFILE;
```

If my SPFILE is deleted for some reason (don't ever do this), I can also re-create the SPFILE from the PFILE (if I've created one), as shown here, or from MEMORY:

```
SQL> CREATE SPFILE='C:\APP\USER\PRODUCT\11.2.0\DBHOME_2\DATABASE\SPFILEORCL.ORA'
     FROM PFILE='C:\APP\USER\PRODUCT\11.2.0\DBHOME_2\DATABASE\INITORCL.ORA';

SQL> CREATE SPFILE='C:\APP\USER\PRODUCT\11.2.0\DBHOME_2\DATABASE\SPFILEORCL.ORA' FROM MEMORY;
```

When you look at PFILE's output, other than the parameters I've physically set, it has limited information. It also has all of the settings for key memory parameters that have been set for me since I only set MEMORY_TARGET. Consider what happens if I run this:

```
SQL> CREATE PFILE='C:\APP\USER\INITORCL.ORA' FROM SPFILE;
```

TIP
If you use the ALTER SYSTEM commands to write to the SPFILE only, and then on startup realize you have set them incorrectly, the database will not start, and you cannot use an ALTER SYSTEM command to fix the problem. You can, however, create a PFILE from the SPFILE, modify the PFILE, and then use that to start the database. Afterward you need to create the SPFILE again and restart the database with the SPFILE.

Here is a listing of the INITORCL.ORA file (note that my MEMORY_TARGET was 6.56G):

```
orcl.__db_cache_size=2315255808
orcl.__java_pool_size=16777216
orcl.__large_pool_size=33554432
orcl.__oracle_base='C:\app\User'#ORACLE_BASE set from environment
orcl.__pga_aggregate_target=2399141888
orcl.__sga_target=4479516672
orcl.__shared_io_pool_size=973078528
orcl.__shared_pool_size=1073741824
orcl.__streams_pool_size=16777216
*.audit_file_dest='C:\app\User\admin\orcl\adump'
*.audit_trail='db'
*.compatible='11.2.0.0.0'
*.control_files='C:\app\User\oradata\orcl\control01.ctl','C:\app\User\flash_recovery_area\orcl\
control02.ctl'
*.db_block_size=8192
*.db_domain=''
*.db_name='orcl'
*.db_recovery_file_dest='C:\app\User\flash_recovery_area'
*.db_recovery_file_dest_size=4102029312
*.diagnostic_dest='C:\app\User'
*.dispatchers='(PROTOCOL=TCP) (SERVICE=orclXDB)'
*.local_listener='LISTENER_ORCL'
*.log_buffer=4931584#  log buffer update
*.max_dump_file_size='UNLIMITED'
*.memory_max_target=6871318528
*.memory_target=6871318528
*.open_cursors=300
*.optimizer_dynamic_sampling=2
*.optimizer_mode='ALL_ROWS'
```

```
*.processes=150
*.remote_login_passwordfile='EXCLUSIVE'
*.shared_pool_size=1073741824
*.undo_tablespace='UNDOTBS1'
```

You can get a better listing by dumping the MEMORY to a PFILE so you can see everything set:

```
SQL> CREATE PFILE='C:\APP\USER\TEST_BIGDUMP.ORA' FROM MEMORY;
```

This shows every parameter set for the database instance (whether you set them or Oracle did):

```
# Oracle init.ora parameter file generated by instance orcl on 04/25/2011 10:47:43
__db_cache_size=2208M
__java_pool_size=16M
__large_pool_size=32M
__oracle_base='C:\app\User' # ORACLE_BASE set from environment
__pga_aggregate_target=2288M
__sga_target=4272M
__shared_io_pool_size=928M
__shared_pool_size=1G
__streams_pool_size=16M
_aggregation_optimization_settings=0
_always_anti_join='CHOOSE'
_always_semi_join='CHOOSE'
_and_pruning_enabled=TRUE
_b_tree_bitmap_plans=TRUE
_bloom_filter_enabled=TRUE
_bloom_folding_enabled=TRUE
_bloom_pruning_enabled=TRUE
_complex_view_merging=TRUE
_compression_compatibility='11.2.0.0.0'
_connect_by_use_union_all='TRUE'
_convert_set_to_join=FALSE
_cost_equality_semi_join=TRUE
_cpu_to_io=0
_dimension_skip_null=TRUE
_eliminate_common_subexpr=TRUE
_enable_type_dep_selectivity=TRUE
_fast_full_scan_enabled=TRUE
_first_k_rows_dynamic_proration=TRUE
_gby_hash_aggregation_enabled=TRUE
_generalized_pruning_enabled=TRUE
_globalindex_pnum_filter_enabled=TRUE
_gs_anti_semi_join_allowed=TRUE
_improved_outerjoin_card=TRUE
_improved_row_length_enabled=TRUE
_index_join_enabled=TRUE
_ksb_restart_policy_times='0'
_ksb_restart_policy_times='60'
_ksb_restart_policy_times='120'
_ksb_restart_policy_times='240' # internal update to set default
_left_nested_loops_random=TRUE
_local_communication_costing_enabled=TRUE
_minimal_stats_aggregation=TRUE
_mmv_query_rewrite_enabled=TRUE
```

```
_new_initial_join_orders=TRUE
_new_sort_cost_estimate=TRUE
_nlj_batching_enabled=1
_optim_adjust_for_part_skews=TRUE
_optim_enhance_nnull_detection=TRUE
_optim_new_default_join_sel=TRUE
_optim_peek_user_binds=TRUE
_optimizer_adaptive_cursor_sharing=TRUE
_optimizer_better_inlist_costing='ALL'
_optimizer_cbqt_no_size_restriction=TRUE
_optimizer_coalesce_subqueries=TRUE
_optimizer_complex_pred_selectivity=TRUE
_optimizer_compute_index_stats=TRUE
_optimizer_connect_by_combine_sw=TRUE
_optimizer_connect_by_cost_based=TRUE
_optimizer_connect_by_elim_dups=TRUE
_optimizer_correct_sq_selectivity=TRUE
_optimizer_cost_based_transformation='LINEAR'
_optimizer_cost_hjsmj_multimatch=TRUE
_optimizer_cost_model='CHOOSE'
_optimizer_dim_subq_join_sel=TRUE
_optimizer_distinct_agg_transform=TRUE
_optimizer_distinct_elimination=TRUE
_optimizer_distinct_placement=TRUE
_optimizer_eliminate_filtering_join=TRUE
_optimizer_enable_density_improvements=TRUE
_optimizer_enable_extended_stats=TRUE
_optimizer_enable_table_lookup_by_nl=TRUE
_optimizer_enhanced_filter_push=TRUE
_optimizer_extend_jppd_view_types=TRUE
_optimizer_extended_cursor_sharing='UDO'
_optimizer_extended_cursor_sharing_rel='SIMPLE'
_optimizer_extended_stats_usage_control=224
_optimizer_false_filter_pred_pullup=TRUE
_optimizer_fast_access_pred_analysis=TRUE
_optimizer_fast_pred_transitivity=TRUE
_optimizer_filter_pred_pullup=TRUE
_optimizer_fkr_index_cost_bias=10
_optimizer_group_by_placement=TRUE
_optimizer_improve_selectivity=TRUE
_optimizer_interleave_jppd=TRUE
_optimizer_join_elimination_enabled=TRUE
_optimizer_join_factorization=TRUE
_optimizer_join_order_control=3
_optimizer_join_sel_sanity_check=TRUE
_optimizer_max_permutations=2000
_optimizer_mode_force=TRUE
_optimizer_multi_level_push_pred=TRUE
_optimizer_native_full_outer_join='FORCE'
_optimizer_new_join_card_computation=TRUE
_optimizer_null_aware_antijoin=TRUE
_optimizer_or_expansion='DEPTH'
_optimizer_order_by_elimination_enabled=TRUE
_optimizer_outer_to_anti_enabled=TRUE
```

```
_optimizer_push_down_distinct=0
_optimizer_push_pred_cost_based=TRUE
_optimizer_rownum_bind_default=10
_optimizer_rownum_pred_based_fkr=TRUE
_optimizer_skip_scan_enabled=TRUE
_optimizer_sortmerge_join_inequality=TRUE
_optimizer_squ_bottomup=TRUE
_optimizer_star_tran_in_with_clause=TRUE
_optimizer_system_stats_usage=TRUE
_optimizer_table_expansion=TRUE
_optimizer_transitivity_retain=TRUE
_optimizer_try_st_before_jppd=TRUE
_optimizer_undo_cost_change='11.2.0.2'
_optimizer_unnest_corr_set_subq=TRUE
_optimizer_unnest_disjunctive_subq=TRUE
_optimizer_use_cbqt_star_transformation=TRUE
_optimizer_use_feedback=TRUE
_or_expand_nvl_predicate=TRUE
_ordered_nested_loop=TRUE
_parallel_broadcast_enabled=TRUE
_partition_view_enabled=TRUE
_pga_max_size=468580K
_pivot_implementation_method='CHOOSE'
_pre_rewrite_push_pred=TRUE
_pred_move_around=TRUE
_push_join_predicate=TRUE
_push_join_union_view=TRUE
_push_join_union_view2=TRUE
_px_minus_intersect=TRUE
_px_pwg_enabled=TRUE
_px_ual_serial_input=TRUE
_query_rewrite_setopgrw_enable=TRUE
_remove_aggr_subquery=TRUE
_replace_virtual_columns=TRUE
_right_outer_hash_enable=TRUE
_selfjoin_mv_duplicates=TRUE
_smm_max_size=234290
_smm_min_size=1024
_smm_px_max_size=1171456
_sql_model_unfold_forloops='RUN_TIME'
_sqltune_category_parsed='DEFAULT' # parsed sqltune_category
_subquery_pruning_enabled=TRUE
_subquery_pruning_mv_enabled=FALSE
_table_scan_cost_plus_one=TRUE
_union_rewrite_for_gs='YES_GSET_MVS'
_unnest_subquery=TRUE
_use_column_stats_for_function=TRUE
audit_file_dest='C:\APP\USER\ADMIN\ORCL\ADUMP'
audit_trail='DB'
compatible='11.2.0.0.0'
control_files='C:\APP\USER\ORADATA\ORCL\CONTROL01.CTL'
control_files='C:\APP\USER\FLASH_RECOVERY_AREA\ORCL\CONTROL02.CTL'
core_dump_dest='c:\app\user\diag\rdbms\orcl\orcl\cdump'
db_block_size=8192
```

```
db_domain=''
db_name='orcl'
db_recovery_file_dest='C:\app\User\flash_recovery_area'
db_recovery_file_dest_size=3912M
diagnostic_dest='C:\APP\USER'
dispatchers='(PROTOCOL=TCP) (SERVICE=orclXDB)'
local_listener='LISTENER_ORCL'
log_buffer=16785408 # log buffer update
max_dump_file_size='UNLIMITED'
memory_max_target=6560M
memory_target=6560M
open_cursors=300
optimizer_dynamic_sampling=2
optimizer_mode='ALL_ROWS'
plsql_warnings='DISABLE:ALL' # PL/SQL warnings at init.ora
processes=150
query_rewrite_enabled='TRUE'
remote_login_passwordfile='EXCLUSIVE'
result_cache_max_size=16800K
shared_pool_size=1G
skip_unusable_indexes=TRUE
undo_tablespace='UNDOTBS1'
```

TIP
If you can't figure out why your system isn't using the value in your
`init.ora` *file, an SPFILE is probably overriding it. And, don't forget,*
you can also use a hint to override parameters at the query level in
11gR2.

Finally, in a Real Application Cluster (RAC/Grid) environment, parameters can be changed for a single instance or for all clustered database instances in a cluster.

There are two key fields in the V$PARAMETER view (V$PARAMETER shows the parameter in effect for the session. V$SYSTEM_PARAMETER shows the parameters in effect for the entire instance):

- **ISSES_MODIFIABLE**   Indicates if a user with the ALTER SESSION privilege can modify this initialization parameter for his or her session.

- **ISSYS_MODIFIABLE**   Indicates if someone with ALTER SYSTEM privilege can modify this particular parameter.

The following query illustrates a list of initialization parameters that can be set without shutting down and restarting the database.

This query displays the initialization parameters that can be modified with an ALTER SYSTEM or ALTER SESSION command (partial result displayed):

```
select    name, value, isdefault, isses_modifiable, issys_modifiable
from      v$parameter
where     issys_modifiable <> 'FALSE'
or        isses_modifiable <> 'FALSE'
order by  name;
```

The result of the query (partial listing only) is all of the initialization parameters that may be modified:

```
NAME                            VALUE                            ISDEFAULT ISSES ISSYS_MOD
------------------------------  -------------------------------  --------- ----- ---------
aq_tm_processes                 0                                TRUE      FALSE IMMEDIATE
archive_lag_target              0                                TRUE      FALSE IMMEDIATE
asm_diskgroups                                                   TRUE      FALSE IMMEDIATE
asm_diskstring                                                   TRUE      FALSE IMMEDIATE
asm_power_limit                 1                                TRUE      TRUE  IMMEDIATE
asm_preferred_read_failure_groups                               TRUE      FALSE IMMEDIATE
audit_file_dest                 C:\APP\USER\ADMIN\ORCL\ADUMP     FALSE     FALSE DEFERRED
background_dump_dest            c:\app\user\diag\rdbms\orcl\
                                orcl\trace                       TRUE      FALSE IMMEDIATE
backup_tape_io_slaves           FALSE                            TRUE      FALSE DEFERRED
```

Be careful granting the ALTER SESSION privilege to users, as knowledgeable developers can set individual parameters that positively affect their session at the expense of others on the system. A user could run the following command with the ALTER SESSION privilege:

```
SQL> ALTER SESSION SET SORT_AREA_SIZE=100000000;
```

TIP
Changing initialization parameters dynamically is a powerful feature for both developers and DBAs. Consequently, a user with the ALTER SESSION privilege is capable of irresponsibly allocating 100M+ for the SORT_AREA_SIZE for a given session, if it is not restricted.

Insight into the Initialization Parameters from Oracle Utilities

You can gain some insight into how Oracle balances some of these SGA parameters by crawling through the utility upgrade information and other scripts Oracle has published as guidelines. An interesting find is listed here, showing various size caches for different versions of Oracle, as well as 32- vs. 64-bit that Oracle included in the scripts as minimum values (given you have the memory). These guidelines can be nice, but I think the DB_CACHE_SIZE is a bit too low for all of these. There are some great examples at the end of this chapter as well.

PARAMETER	64-bit/11g	64-bit/10g	64-bit/9.2
MEMORY_TARGET	844M	N/A	N/A
SGA_TARGET	744M	744M	N/A
DB_CACHE_SIZE	48M	48M	48M
SHARED_POOL	596M	596M	448M
PGA_AGGREGATE_TARGET	24M	24M	24M
JAVA_POOL_SIZE	128M	128M	128M

PARAMETER	32-bit/11g	32-bit/10g	32-bit/9.2
MEMORY_TARGET	628M	N/A	N/A
SGA_TARGET	528M	528M	N/A
DB_CACHE_SIZE	48M	48M	48M
SHARED_POOL	298M	298M	224M
PGA_AGGREGATE_TARGET	24M	24M	24M
JAVA_POOL_SIZE	64M	64M	64M

Viewing the Initialization Parameters with Enterprise Manager

You can also use Enterprise Manager to view the initialization parameter settings by going to the Database home page, selecting the server, and then selecting Initialization Parameters under the Database Configuration heading. The section of Enterprise Manager displayed in Figure 4-1 shows the initialization parameters. It shows the current settings for the parameters and also shows if the parameters can be modified (dynamic=✓) without shutting down the database. Oracle Enterprise Manager is covered in detail in Chapter 5.

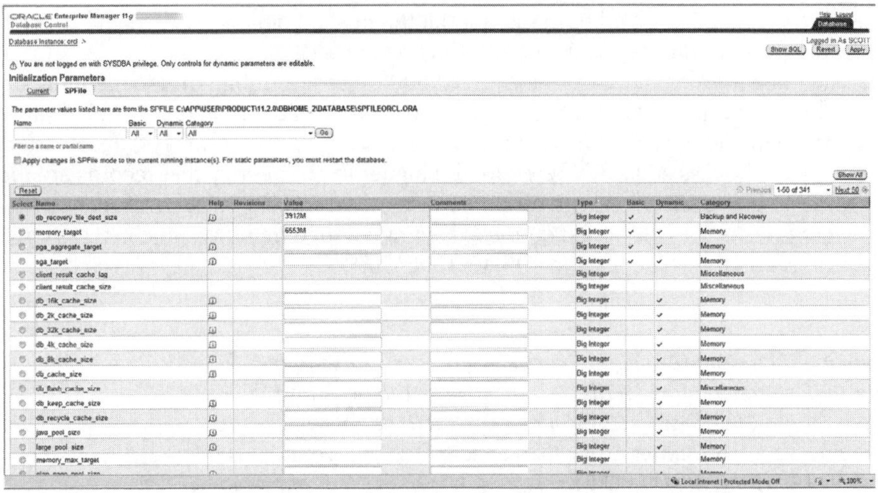

FIGURE 4-1. *Enterprise Manager—initialization parameters in the SPFILE*

Increasing Performance by Tuning the DB_CACHE_SIZE

Long-time users of Oracle and readers of prior editions of this book will notice that some familiar parameters have not been mentioned. In 10g, parameters such as DB_BLOCK_BUFFERS were deprecated (a parameter _DB_BLOCK_BUFFERS was set behind the scenes for backward compatibility). In 11g, DB_BLOCK_BUFFERS is back, but set to 0 (default), which means it's not used unless you set it (use DB_CACHE_SIZE instead). While many of the familiar parameters from prior versions of Oracle are still valid, using them may disable many Oracle 11g Release 2 features, including Automatic Memory Management (AMM). This chapter focuses on the Oracle 11g Release 2 parameters for tuning your system.

The DB_CACHE_SIZE is the initial memory allocated to the main data cache or the memory used for the data itself. This parameter doesn't need to be set if you set MEMORY_TARGET or SGA_TARGET, but it is a good idea to set a value for this as a minimum setting. Your goal should always be getting toward a memory resident database or at least getting all data that will be queried in memory. After MEMORY_TARGET (or SGA_TARGET) and MEMORY_MAX_TARGET, DB_CACHE_SIZE is the first parameter to look at in the initialization parameter file because it's the most crucial parameter in Oracle for retrieving data. If the DB_CACHE_SIZE is set too low, Oracle won't have enough memory to operate efficiently and the system may run poorly, no matter what else you do to it. If DB_CACHE_SIZE is too high, your system may begin to swap and may come to a halt. DB_CACHE_SIZE makes up the area of the SGA that is used for storing and processing data in memory initially and for subsequent queries to access. As users request information, data is put into memory. If the DB_CACHE_SIZE parameter is set too low, then the least recently used data is flushed from memory. If the flushed data is recalled with a query, it must be reread from disk (consuming I/O and CPU resources).

Retrieving data from memory can be over 10,000 times faster than disk (depending on the speed of memory and disk devices). Even if you take into consideration disk caching (memory on disk) and Oracle inefficiencies, retrieving data from memory is still about 100 times faster than reading data from the fastest disks. Therefore, the higher the frequency that records are found in memory (without being retrieved from disk), the faster the overall system performance (usually at least 100+ times faster for well-tuned queries). Having enough memory allocated to store data in memory depends on the value used for DB_CACHE_SIZE.

TIP
Retrieving data from physical memory is generally substantially faster than retrieving it from disk, so make sure the SGA and PGA are large enough. One Oracle study showed Oracle memory access as averaging about 100 times faster than disk access. However, this takes into account disk-caching advances, which you may or may not have on your system. The same study also showed an individual case where Oracle memory access was well over 10,000 times faster than disk (which was hard for me to believe), but it shows how important it is to measure this on your own unique system.

MEMORY_TARGET, SGA_SIZE (if used), and DB_CACHE_SIZE (if a minimum is set) are the key parameters to use when tuning the data cache hit ratio. The data cache hit ratio is the percentage of the data block accesses that occur without requiring a physical read from disk. While several situations can artificially inflate or deflate the data cache hit ratio, this ratio is a key indicator of system efficiency.

You can use the following query to view the data cache hit ratio (the first output is one with a lot of full table scans, the second a simple index scan):

```
column phys              format 999,999,999    heading 'Physical Reads'
column gets              format 999,999,999    heading ' DB Block Gets'
column con_gets          format 999,999,999    heading 'Consistent Gets'
column hitratio format 999.99 heading ' Hit Ratio '
 select    sum(decode(name,'physical reads',value,0)) phys,
           sum(decode(name,'db block gets',value,0)) gets,
           sum(decode(name,'consistent gets', value,0)) con_gets,
           (1 - (sum(decode(name,'physical reads',value,0)) /
           (sum(decode(name,'db block gets',value,0)) +
           sum(decode(name,'consistent gets',value,0))))) * 100 hitratio
 from      v$sysstat;
```

Physical Reads	DB Block Gets	Consistent Gets	Hit Ratio
32,895,507	23,959,814	59,387,065	60.53

Physical Reads	DB Block Gets	Consistent Gets	Hit Ratio
1,671	39,561	71,142	98.49

While every application has exceptions, a data cache hit ratio of 95 percent or greater should be achievable for a well-tuned transactional application with the appropriate amount of memory. Because there is such a performance difference between some disk devices and memory access, improving the data cache hit ratio from 90 to 95 percent can nearly double system performance when reading disk devices that are extremely slow. Improving the cache hit ratio from 90 to 98 percent could yield nearly a 500 percent improvement where disks are extremely slow and under the right (or should I say wrong) architectural setup. However, with the advent of more flash cache on storage servers, this continues to be something you have to look at in depth to understand what is appropriate for your particular hardware and application *load profile* (what's running through the system on a regular basis). If the load profile stays the same, but the hit ratio radically changes, you should investigate why it happened immediately (don't wait for system users to complain). In the first output just shown, I was aware of many full table scans that were not an issue, so the low hit ratio was not an issue.

Poor joins and poor indexing can also yield very high hit ratios due to reading many index blocks, so make sure your hit ratio isn't high for a reason other than a well-tuned system. An unusually high hit ratio may indicate the introduction of code that is poorly indexed or includes join issues. If the hit ratio goes much higher (bad query that might have over-indexing or poor use of indexes in joins) or much lower than normal (someone may have dropped an index or altered it to be invisible), you should investigate why it happened immediately (don't wait for system users to complain).

TIP
Hit ratios are useful to experienced DBAs but can be misleading or of little use for inexperienced DBAs. The best use of hit ratios is still to compare them over time to help alert you to a substantial change to a system on a given day. While some people have deprecated hit ratios from their tuning arsenal, they are usually tool vendors who don't see the value of tracking hit ratios over time because their tools are point-in-time or reactive-based tuning solutions. Hit ratios should never be your only tool, but they should definitely be one of many proactive tools in your arsenal (especially with the advent of the invisible index in 11g).

Oracle continues to downplay the importance of hit ratios by reducing the discussions on hit ratio tuning. Oracle is beginning to focus on analyzing system performance in terms of work done (CPU or service time) versus time spent waiting for work (wait time). Areas where hit ratios are still the primary tuning method are library cache and dictionary cache. See Chapter 14 on the AWR Report for more information on balancing the entire tuning arsenal, including hit ratios.

Using V$DB_CACHE_ADVICE in Tuning DB_CACHE_SIZE

V$DB_CACHE_ADVICE is a view introduced in Oracle 9i to assist in tuning DB_CACHE_SIZE. The view can be queried directly, and the data in the view is used by the Oracle kernel (or database engine) to make automatic cache management decisions.

Here is a query to view the effect of changing DB_CACHE_SIZE on the data cache hit ratio:

```
select name, size_for_estimate, size_factor, estd_physical_read_factor
from   v$db_cache_advice;
```

NAME	SIZE_FOR_ESTIMATE	SIZE_FACTOR	ESTD_PHYSICAL_READ_FACTOR
DEFAULT	4	.1667	1.8136
DEFAULT	8	.3333	1.0169
DEFAULT	12	.5	1.0085
DEFAULT	16	.6667	1
DEFAULT	20	.8333	1
DEFAULT	24	1	1

Reading these simple results from this very small SGA, you see the following:

- The current cache size in this example was 24M (size_factor = 1).

- You can decrease the cache size to be 16M and maintain the current cache hit ratio, since the PHYSICAL_READ_FACTOR remains at 1 up to a decrease to 16M.

Although this view provides an estimate of the effect of changing the cache size on the cache hit ratio, test any changes to validate that the results are as forecasted. Oracle Enterprise Manager provides a graphical view of the data in V$DB_CACHE_ADVICE. Enterprise Manager is covered in Chapter 5. To populate V$DB_CACHE_ADVICE, you have to enable the Dynamic Buffer Cache Advisory feature, and it is not recommended to have this feature enabled on production systems all the time.

Keeping the Hit Ratio for the Data Cache Above 95 Percent

The hit ratio for the data cache should generally be greater than 95 percent for transactional systems. The best use for a hit ratio, however, is to study your system over time to see major changes that should warrant further investigation. Usually, if your hit ratio is less than 95 percent, you may need to increase the value of DB_CACHE_SIZE. In some instances, you can increase performance substantially by increasing the hit ratio from 95 to 98 percent—especially if the last 5 percent of the hits going to disk are the main lag on the system or the disk cache gets flooded (full with cached data).

Monitoring the V$SQLAREA View to Find Bad Queries

Although hit ratios less than 95 percent are usually a sign that your DB_CACHE_SIZE is set too low or that you have poor indexing, hit ratio numbers can be distorted and this should be taken into account while tuning (note that Exadata works differently and is covered in the Chapter 11). Hit ratio distortion and non-DB_CACHE_SIZE issues include the following:

- Recursive calls
- Missing or suppressed indexes
- Data sitting in memory
- UNDO/ROLLBACK segments
- Multiple logical reads
- Physical reads causing the system to use CPU

To avoid being misled, locate bad queries by monitoring the V$SQLAREA view or use Enterprise Manager. Once you isolate the queries that are causing performance hits, tune the queries or modify how the information is stored to solve the problem. Using the Performance page of Enterprise Manager Grid Control or Database Control, a DBA can generate a report of the Top Activity for his or her system. The Top Activity section of Enterprise Manager Database Control (Figure 4-2) displays a list of the worst SQL statements in the current cache based on Activity and also the Top Sessions by Activity. The graph at the top of Figure 4-2 shows increasing performance issues. The graphs on the left and right show the problem SQL (left) and users (right). The DBA can then click the problem SQL to begin the process of analyzing and tuning the SQL statement. Chapter 5 discusses the benefits of Oracle's Enterprise Manager in detail and how to tune the SQL statements using Enterprise Manager. Also note that Database Control is installed with the Oracle Database software. Grid Control is a separate product.

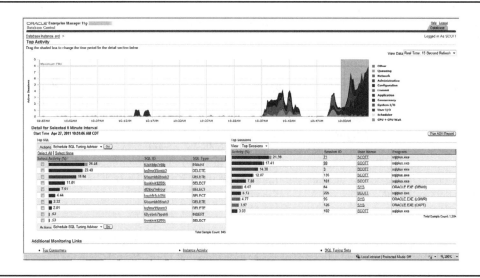

FIGURE 4-2. *Use Oracle's Enterprise Manager Database Control to find problem queries.*

TIP
In Oracle 11g Release 2, use the Enterprise Manager Grid Control or Database Control to find problem queries.

Bad Hit Ratios Can Occur When an Index Is Suppressed

Consider the following query where the CUSTOMER table is indexed on the unique CUSTNO column. It is *not* optimal to have this index suppressed by using the NVL because it results in a poor hit ratio.

```
select      custno, name
from        customer
where       nvl(custno,0)  = 5789;

Db block gets: 1
Consistent gets: 194
Physical reads: 184
Hit ratio = 1 - [184 / (194+1)] = 1 - 184/195 = 0.0564, or 5.64%
```

If you are looking at this in Enterprise Manager, you'll see an index missing on a query that is being executed at the current time. Focus on the query that is causing this problem and fix the query. The query can be found by accessing the V$SQLAREA view, as shown in Chapter 8. You could build a function-based index (see Chapter 2) to solve this problem as well. For Exadata, this might be fine if all of the data is in the Flash Cache on a cell or if the query brings back fewer blocks of data based on features like the Smart Scan or Storage Index (more in Chapter 11).

TIP
A low hit ratio for a query could be an indication of a missing or suppressed index.

Getting Good Hit Ratios with Well-Indexed Queries

Consider the following query, where the CUSTOMER table is indexed on the unique CUSTNO column. In this situation, it is optimal to utilize the CUSTNO index because it results in an excellent hit ratio.

```
select      custno, name
from        customer
where       custno = 5789;

Db block gets: 0
Consistent gets: 192
Physical reads: 0
Hit ratio = 100%
```

If you are looking at this in Enterprise Manager, there is usually an index on the query that is being executed or the table could be cached in memory.

Bad Queries Executing a Second Time Can Result in Good Hit Ratios

When a full table scan is completed for the second time and the data is still in memory, you may see a good hit ratio even though the system is trying to run a bad query:

```
Db block gets: 1
Consistent gets: 105
Physical reads: 1
Hit ratio = 99% (A very high/usually good hit ratio)
```

If you are looking at this in the Enterprise Manager, it appears that there is an index on the query being executed when, in fact, the data is in memory from the last time it was executed. The result is that you are "hogging up" a lot of memory even though it appears that an indexed search is being performed. Since 10*g*, you can flush the buffer cache to clear it (similar to flushing the shared pool if you are familiar with that). It is *not* intended for production use, but rather for system testing purposes. This can help with your tuning needs or as a Band-Aid if you have "free buffer" waits (there are better ways to fix free buffer waits, such as writing more often or increasing the DB_CACHE_SIZE). Note that any Oracle I/O not done in the SGA counts as a physical I/O. If your system has O/S caching or disk caching, the actual I/O that shows up as physical may indeed be a memory read outside of Oracle.

To flush the buffer cache, perform the following:

```
SQL> ALTER SYSTEM FLUSH BUFFER_CACHE;
```

TIP
*Bad (slow) queries show in the V$SQLAREA or
V$SESSION_LONGOPS (under certain conditions) views with poor
hit ratios the first time they are executed. You can also use Enterprise
Manager to see statistical information. Make sure you tune them at
that time. The second time that they execute, they may not show a
poor hit ratio. Flushing the buffer cache for testing can help you get
accurate results.*

Other Hit Ratio Distortions

You should consider several other hit distortions:

- **Oracle Developer distortion**   Systems that use Oracle Developer tools, JDeveloper
  (screens), or Application Express (APEX) to retrieve single rows of data frequently use the
  same information over and over. This reuse by some users of the system will drive up
  the hit ratio. Other users on the system may not be experiencing hit ratios that are as
  good as these users, yet the overall system hit ratio may look very good. The DBA must
  take into consideration that these users can be boosting the hit ratio to an artificially
  high level.

- **UNDO/ROLLBACK segment distortion**   Because the header block of the
  UNDO/ROLLBACK segment is usually cached, the activity to the UNDO/ROLLBACK
  segment gives a falsely high hit ratio impact when truly there is no significant impact
  on the hit ratio.

- **Index distortion**   An index range scan results in multiple logical reads on a very small
  number of blocks. I've seen hit ratios as high as 86 percent be recorded when none of
  the blocks are cached prior to the query executing. Make sure you monitor the hit ratio
  of individual, poorly tuned queries in addition to monitoring the big picture (overall hit
  ratio). You can also check bad indexes by making them invisible (see Chapter 2 for more
  information).

- **I/O distortion**   Physical reads that appear to be causing heavy disk I/O may be actually
  causing you to be CPU bound. In tests, the same amount of CPU was used for 89 logical
  reads as was used to process 11 physical reads. The result is that the physical reads are
  CPU costly because of buffer management. Fix the queries causing the disk I/O
  problems and you will usually free up a large amount of CPU as well. Performance
  degradation can be exponentially downward spiraling, but the good news is that when
  you begin to fix your system, it is often an exponentially upward-spiraling event. It's
  probably the main reason why some people live to tune; tuning can be exhilarating.

Setting DB_BLOCK_SIZE to Reflect
the Size of Your Data Reads

The DB_BLOCK_SIZE is the size of the default data block size when the database is created.
Since Oracle 10g Release 2, each tablespace can have a different block size, thus making block
size selection a *less* critical selection before the database is created. That said, a separate cache

memory allocation must be made for each different database block size. But it is still very important to choose wisely. Although you can have different block-size tablespaces, this is not truly a performance feature, as the nondefault buffer caches are not optimized for performance. You still want to put the bulk of your data in the default buffer cache. You must rebuild the database if you want to increase the DB_BLOCK_SIZE. The block size for data warehouses is often 32K (you want many rows to be read at a time) and OLTP systems are often 8K. Most experts recommend an 8K block size.

The data block cache for the default block size is set using the DB_CACHE_SIZE initialization parameter. Cache is allocated for other database block sizes by using the DB_*n*K_CACHE_SIZE, where *n* is the block size in KB. The larger the DB_BLOCK_SIZE, the more that can fit inside a single block and the more efficiently large amounts of data can be retrieved. A small DB_BLOCK_SIZE actually lets you retrieve single records faster and saves space in memory. In addition, a smaller block size can improve transactional concurrency and reduce log file generation rates. As a rule of thumb, a data warehouse should use the maximum block size available for your platform (either 16K or 32K) as long as no bugs exist for the given block size (check Metalink to make sure), whereas a transaction-processing system should use an 8K block size. Rarely is a block size smaller than 8K beneficial, but I've used a 2K block size for a stock exchange application and I've seen a 4K block size in benchmarks. If you have an extremely high transaction rate system or very limited system memory, you might consider a block size smaller than 8K.

Full table scans are limited to the maximum I/O of the box (usually 64K, but as high as 1M on many systems). Most systems support 1M I/O rates now. You can up the amount of data read into memory in a single I/O by increasing the DB_BLOCK_SIZE to 8K or 16K. You can also increase the DB_FILE_MULTIBLOCK_READ_COUNT to a maximum value of (max I/O size)/DB_BLOCK_SIZE.

Environments that run many single queries to retrieve data could use a smaller block size, but "hot spots" in those systems will still benefit from using a larger block size. Sites that need to read large amounts of data in a single I/O read should increase the DB_FILE_MULTIBLOCK_READ_COUNT. This may not be necessary with a parameter set, by default, to be much larger in 11g. My default for DB_FILE_MULTIBLOCK_READ_COUNT was 128, but check your system for variations to the default. The default value Oracle uses corresponds to the maximum I/O size that can be efficiently performed and is platform-dependent (according to Oracle docs). Setting the DB_FILE_MULTIBLOCK_READ_COUNT higher is especially important for data warehouses that retrieve lots of records. If the use of DB_FILE_MULTIBLOCK_READ_COUNT starts to cause many full table scans (since the optimizer now decides it can perform full table scans much faster and decides to do more of them), then set OPTIMIZER_INDEX_COST_ADJ between 1 and 10 (I usually use 10) to force index use more frequently.

TIP
The database must be rebuilt if you increase the DB_BLOCK_SIZE.
Increasing the DB_FILE_MULTIBLOCK_READ_COUNT allows more
block reads in a single I/O, giving a benefit similar to a larger block size.

Setting SGA_MAX_SIZE to 25 to 50 Percent of the Size Allocated to Main Memory

If you use it, the general rule of thumb is to start with an SGA_MAX_SIZE parameter of 20 to 25 percent of the size allocated to your main memory. A large number of users (300+) or a small amount of available memory may force you to make this 15 to 20 percent of physical memory. A small number of users (less than 100) or a large amount of physical memory may allow you to make this 30 to 50 percent of physical memory. In 11gR2, if you set the SGA_MAX_SIZE less than 1G, then the _KSM_GRANULE_SIZE is 4M. If the SGA_MAX_SIZE is greater than 1G and less than 8G, then the _KSM_GRANULE_SIZE is 16M; from there, up to 16G is 32M, up to 32G is 64M, up to 64G is 128M, up to 128G is 256M, and if your SGA_MAX_SIZE is greater than 256G, then the _KSM_GRANULE_SIZE is 512M. This granule size determines the multiples for other initialization parameters. A granule size of 4M means that certain initialization parameters are rounded up to the nearest 4M. Therefore, if I set SGA_MAX_SIZE to 64M and DB_CACHE_SIZE to 9M, then the DB_CACHE_SIZE is rounded to 12M (since the granule size is 4M). If I set SGA_MAX_SIZE to 200M and DB_CACHE_SIZE to 9M, then the DB_CACHE_SIZE is rounded to 16M (since the granule size is 16M). The V$SGA_DYNAMIC_COMPONENTS view allows you to see the sizes used for each SGA component (such as shared pool, buffer caches, etc.) and the granule size used.

TIP
The SGA_MAX_SIZE determines the granule size for other parameters. An SGA_MAX_SIZE < 1G means a 4M granule, whereas an SGA_MAX_SIZE >= 256G means a 512M granule size. Some benchmarks have the granule size as high as 256M.

Tuning the SHARED_POOL_SIZE for Optimal Performance

Sizing the SHARED_POOL_SIZE correctly makes sharing identical SQL statements possible. Getting the statement parsed is your first priority. If the query never makes it into memory, it can never request the data to be accessed; that's where the SHARED_POOL_SIZE comes in. SHARED_POOL_SIZE specifies the memory allocated in the SGA for data dictionary caching and shared SQL statements.

The data dictionary cache is very important because that's where the data dictionary components are buffered. Oracle references the data dictionary several times when a SQL statement is processed. Therefore, the more information (database and application schema and structure) that's stored in memory, the less information that has to be retrieved from disk. While the dictionary cache is part of the shared pool, Oracle also caches SQL statements and their corresponding execution plans in the library cache portion of the shared pool (see the next section for how the shared SQL area works).

The data dictionary cache portion of the shared pool operates in a manner similar to the DB_CACHE_SIZE when caching information. For the best performance, it would be great if the entire Oracle data dictionary could be cached in memory. Unfortunately, this generally is not feasible, so Oracle uses a least recently used algorithm for deciding what gets to stay in the cache.

Lastly, the Result Cache (11*g* only) is now part of the shared pool (allocated from the shared pool, but a separate area) as well, if you use it. Query function results and query fragments can be cached in memory for future executions. Choose calculations that frequently run over and over again. You should also choose data that does *not* frequently change. To use the Result Cache, set the RESULT_CACHE_SIZE=*amount* and the RESULT_CACHE_MODE=*force* parameters (set to *force* to automatically use it). The Result Cache takes its memory from the Shared Pool. You can use DBMS_RESULT_CACHE.FLUSH to clear the Result Cache. Note that anything cached is *not* passed between RAC/Grid nodes in 11*g*R1 (stays local to each instance), but data from the Result Cache is transferred over the interconnect to other RAC instances in 11*g*R2. Each Result Cache is local to each instance, as is the buffer cache, but can be shared over the interconnect in 11*g*R2. There is no global Result Cache. Please check the documentation for other restrictions and rules.

Using Stored Procedures for Optimal Use of the Shared SQL Area

Each time a SQL statement is executed, the statement is searched for in the shared SQL area and, if found, used for execution. This saves parsing time and improves overall performance. Therefore, to ensure optimal use of the shared SQL area, use stored procedures as much as possible since the SQL parsed is exactly the same every time and, therefore, shared. However, keep in mind, that the only time the SQL statement being executed can use a statement already in the shared SQL area is if the statements are identical (meaning they have the same content exactly—the same case, the same number of spaces, etc.). If the statements are not identical, the new statement is parsed, executed, and placed in the shared SQL area (exceptions to this are possible when the initialization parameter CURSOR_SHARING has been set to SIMILAR or FORCE).

In the following example, the statements are identical in execution, but the word *from* causes Oracle to treat the two statements as if they were different, thus *not* reusing the original cursor that was located in the shared SQL area:

```
SQL>     select name, customer from customer_information;
SQL>     select name, customer FROM customer_information;
```

TIP
SQL must be written exactly the same to be reused. Case differences and any other differences will cause a reparse of the statement.

In the following example, I am using different values for ENAME, which is causing multiple statements to be parsed:

```
declare
      temp VARCHAR2(10);
begin
      select ename into temp
      from    rich
      where   ename = 'SMITH';
```

```
      select ename into temp
      from   rich
      where  ename = 'JONES';
end;
```

A query of V$SQLAREA shows that two statements were parsed even though they were very close to the same thing. Note, however, that PL/SQL converted each SQL statement to uppercase *and* trimmed spaces *and* carriage returns (which is a benefit of using PL/SQL):

```
select sql_text
from   v$sqlarea
where  sql_text like 'SELECT ENAME%';

SQL_TEXT
------------------------------------------------
SELECT ENAME    FROM RICH   WHERE ENAME = 'JONES'
SELECT ENAME    FROM RICH   WHERE ENAME = 'SMITH'
```

In the following example, there is a problem with third-party applications that do not use bind variables (they do this to keep the code "vanilla" or capable of working on many different databases without modification). The problem with this code is that the developer has created many statements that fill the shared pool and these statements can't be shared (since they're slightly different). You can build a smaller shared pool so there is less room for cached cursors and thus fewer cursors to search through to find a match (this is the Band-Aid inexperienced DBAs use). If the following is your output from V$SQLAREA, you may benefit from lowering the SHARED_POOL_SIZE, but using CURSOR_SHARING is a better choice.

```
SQL_TEXT
------------------------------------------------
select empno from rich778 where empno =451572
select empno from rich778 where empno =451573
select empno from rich778 where empno =451574
select empno from rich778 where empno =451575
select empno from rich778 where empno =451576
etc. . .
```

Setting CURSOR_SHARING=FORCE and the query to V$SQLAREA will change to the one listed next because Oracle builds a statement internally that can be shared by all of the preceding statements. Now the shared pool is not inundated with all of these statements, but only one simple statement that can be shared by all users:

```
SQL_TEXT
------------------------------------------------
select empno from rich778 where empno =:SYS_B_0
```

Setting the SHARED_POOL_SIZE High Enough to Fully Use the DB_CACHE_SIZE

If the SHARED_POOL_SIZE is set too low, then you will not get the full advantage of your DB_CACHE_SIZE (since statements that can't be parsed can't be executed). The queries that can be performed against the Oracle V$ views to determine the data dictionary cache hit ratio and the shared SQL statement usage are listed in the sections that follow. These will help you determine if increasing the SHARED_POOL_SIZE will improve performance.

The SHARED_POOL_SIZE parameter is specified in bytes. The default value for the SHARED_POOL_SIZE parameter varies per system but is generally lower than necessary for large production applications.

Keeping the Data Dictionary Cache Hit Ratio at or above 95 Percent

The data dictionary cache is a key area to tune because the dictionary is accessed so frequently, especially by Oracle's internals of Oracle. At startup, the data dictionary cache contains no data. But as more data is read into cache, the likelihood of cache misses decreases. For this reason, monitoring the data dictionary cache should be done only after the system has been up for a while and stabilized. If the dictionary cache hit ratio is less than 95 percent, then you'll probably need to increase the size of the SHARED_POOL_SIZE parameter in the initialization parameter file. Implementing locally managed tablespaces (LMT) can also help your dictionary cache (see Metalink note 166474.1, "Can We Tune the Row Cache!"). However, keep in mind that the shared pool also includes the library cache (SQL statements), and Oracle decides how much of the distribution is for the library cache versus the row cache.

Use the following query against the Oracle V$ view to determine the data dictionary cache hit ratio:

```
select     ((1 - (Sum(GetMisses) / (Sum(Gets) + Sum(GetMisses)))) * 100) "Hit Rate"
from       V$RowCache
where      Gets + GetMisses <> 0;

  Hit Rate
----------
98.6414551
```

TIP
Measure hit ratios for the row cache (data dictionary cache) of the shared pool with the V$ROWCACHE view. A hit ratio of greater than 95 percent should be achieved. However, when the database is initially started, hit ratios will be around 85 percent.

Using Individual Row Cache Parameters to Diagnose Shared Pool Use

To diagnose a problem with the shared pool or overuse of the shared pool, use a modified query to the V$ROWCACHE view. This shows how each individual parameter makes up the data dictionary cache, also referred to as the row cache (partial listing):

```
column parameter        format a20        heading 'Data Dictionary Area'
column gets             format 999,999,999 heading 'Total|Requests'
column getmisses        format 999,999,999 heading 'Misses'
column modifications    format 999,999    heading 'Mods'
column flushes          format 999,999    heading 'Flushes'
column getmiss_ratio    format 9.99       heading 'Miss|Ratio'
set pagesize 50
ttitle 'Shared Pool Row Cache Usage'

select  parameter, gets, getmisses, modifications, flushes,
        (getmisses / decode(gets,0,1,gets)) getmiss_ratio,
        (case when (getmisses / decode(gets,0,1,gets)) > .1 then '*' else ' ' end) " "
from    v$rowcache
where   Gets + GetMisses <> 0;
```

```
Tue Aug 27                                              page    1
                      Shared Pool Row Cache Usage
                      Total                              Miss
                      Requests      Misses   Mods  Flushes Ratio
Data Dictionary Area
-------------------- ------------  ------------ -------- -------- ----- -
dc_segments                  637           184        0        0   .29 *
dc_tablespaces                18             3        0        0   .17 *
dc_users                     126            25        0        0   .20 *
dc_rollback_segments         235            21       31       30   .09
dc_objects                   728           167       55        0   .23 *
dc_global_oids                16             6        0        0   .38 *
dc_object_ids                672           164       55        0   .24 *
dc_sequences                   1             1        1        1  1.00 *
dc_usernames                 193            10        0        0   .05
dc_histogram_defs             24            24        0        0  1.00 *
dc_profiles                    1             1        0        0  1.00 *
dc_user_grants                24            15        0        0   .63 *
```

This query places an asterisk (*) for any query that has misses greater than 10 percent. It does this by using the CASE expression to limit the miss ratio to the tenth digit and then analyzes that digit for any value greater than 0 (which would indicate a hit ratio of 10 percent or higher). A 0.1 miss or higher returns an *. Explanations of each of the columns are listed in the next section.

Keeping the Library Cache Reload Ratio at 0 and the Hit Ratio Above 95 Percent

For optimal performance, you'll want to keep the library cache reload ratio [sum(reloads) / sum(pins)] at zero and the library cache hit ratio greater than 95 percent. If the reload ratio is not zero, then statements are being "aged out" that are later needed and brought back into memory. If the reload ratio is zero (0), it means items in the library cache were never aged or invalidated. If the reload ratio is greater than 1 percent, the SHARED_POOL_SIZE parameter should probably be increased. Likewise, if the library cache hit ratio comes in less than 95 percent, then the SHARED_POOL_SIZE parameter may need to be increased. Also, if you are using ASMM, the SGA_TARGET includes both auto-tuned and manual parameters. When you decide to raise a parameter specifically (such as SHARED_POOL_SIZE), it influences the auto-tuned part. (Other parameters are affected; see Metalink notes 443746.1 and 295626.1, "How to Use Automatic Shared Memory (AMM) in 11*g* and How to Use Automatic Shared Memory Management (ASMM) in Oracle 10*g*.")

You can monitor the library cache in a couple of ways. The first method is to execute the STATSPACK report (STATSPACK is covered in detail in Chapter 14). The second is to use the V$LIBRARYCACHE view.

The following query uses the V$LIBRARYCACHE view to examine the reload ratio in the library cache:

```
select     Sum(Pins) "Hits",
           Sum(Reloads) "Misses",
           ((Sum(Reloads) / Sum(Pins)) * 100)"Reload %"
from       V$LibraryCache;

     Hits     Misses   Reload %
---------- ---------- ----------
  1032669        441 .042704874
```

This next query uses the V$LIBRARYCACHE view to examine the library cache's hit ratio in detail:

```
select     Sum(Pins) "Hits",
           Sum(Reloads) "Misses",
           Sum(Pins) / (Sum(Pins) + Sum(Reloads)) "Hit Ratio"
from       V$LibraryCache;

     Hits     Misses  Hit Ratio
---------- ---------- ----------
  1033760        441 .999573584
```

This hit ratio is excellent (greater than 99 percent) and does not require any increase in the SHARED_POOL_SIZE parameter.

Using Individual Library Cache Parameters to Diagnose Shared Pool Use

Using a modified query on the same table, you can see how each individual parameter makes up the library cache. This may help diagnose a problem or reveal overuse of the shared pool.

```
set numwidth 3
set space 2
set newpage 0
set pagesize 58
set linesize 80
set tab off
set echo off
ttitle 'Shared Pool Library Cache Usage'
column namespace    format a20              heading 'Entity'
```

```
column pins          format 999,999,999    heading 'Executions'
column pinhits       format 999,999,999    heading 'Hits'
column pinhitratio   format 9.99           heading 'Hit|Ratio'
column reloads       format 999,999        heading 'Reloads'
column reloadratio   format .9999          heading 'Reload|Ratio'
spool cache_lib.lis
select   namespace, pins, pinhits, pinhitratio, reloads, reloads
         /decode(pins,0,1,pins) reloadratio
from     v$librarycache;
```

```
Sun Mar 19                                              page    1
                     Shared Pool Library Cache Usage
                                        Hit                Reload
Entity          Executions      Hits    Ratio    Reloads   Ratio
SQL AREA         1,276,366   1,275,672   1.00          2   .0000
TABLE/PROC         539,431     539,187   1.00          5   .0000
BODY                     0           0   1.00          0   .0000
TRIGGER                  0           0   1.00          0   .0000
INDEX                   21           0    .00          0   .0000
CLUSTER                 15           5    .33          0   .0000
OBJECT                   0           0   1.00          0   .0000
PIPE                     0           0   1.00          0   .0000
JAVA SRCE                0           0   1.00          0   .0000
JAVA RES                 0           0   1.00          0   .0000
JAVA DATA                0           0   1.00          0   .0000
```

```
11 rows selected.
```

Use the following list to help interpret the contents of the V$LIBRARYCACHE view:

- **namespace**   The object type stored in the library cache. The values SQL AREA, TABLE/PROCEDURE, BODY, and TRIGGER show the key types.

- **gets**   Shows the number of times an item in library cache was requested.

- **gethits**   Shows the number of times a requested item was already in the library cache.

- **gethitratio**   Shows the ratio of gethits to gets.

- **pins**   Shows the number of times an item in the library cache was executed.

- **pinhits**   Shows the number of times an item was executed when that item was already in the library cache.

- **pinhitratio**   Shows the ratio of pinhits to pins.

- **reloads**   Shows the number of times an item had to be reloaded into the library cache because it aged out or was invalidated.

Keeping the Pin Hit Ratio for Library Cache Items Close to 100 Percent

The pin hit ratio for all library cache items—*sum(pinhits)/sum(pins*—should be close to 1 (or a 100 percent hit ratio). A pin hit ratio of 100 percent means that every time the system needs to execute something, it is already allocated and valid in the library cache. Although you will always experience some misses the first time a request is made, misses can be reduced by writing identical SQL statements.

TIP
Measure hit ratios for the library cache of the shared pool with the V$LIBRARYCACHE view. A hit ratio of greater than 95 percent should be achieved. However, when the database is initially started, hit ratios are around 85 percent.

Keeping the Miss Ratio Less Than 15 Percent

The miss ratio for data dictionary cache *sum(getmisses)/sum(gets)* should be less than 10 to 15 percent. A miss ratio of zero (0) means that every time the system went into the data dictionary cache, it found what it was looking for and did not have to retrieve the information from disk. If the miss ratio "*sum(getmisses)/sum(gets)*" is greater than 10–15 percent, the initialization SHARED_POOL_SIZE parameter should be increased.

Using Available Memory to Determine If the SHARED_POOL_SIZE Is Set Correctly

Here's the main question that people usually want answered: "Is there any memory left in the shared pool?" To find out how fast memory in the shared pool is being depleted (made noncontiguous or in use) and also what percent is unused (and still contiguous), run the following query after starting the database and running production queries for a short period of time (for example, after the first hour of the day):

```
col value for 999,999,999,999 heading "Shared Pool Size"
col bytes for 999,999,999,999 heading "Free Bytes"
select to_number(v$parameter.value) value, v$sgastat.bytes,
       (v$sgastat.bytes/v$parameter.value)*100 "Percent Free"
from    v$sgastat, v$parameter
where   v$sgastat.name = 'free memory'
and     v$parameter.name = 'shared_pool_size'
and     v$sgastat.pool = 'shared pool';

Shared Pool Size        Free Bytes Percent Free
--------------- ---------------- ------------
   1,073,741,824     581,983,848   54.2014696
```

If you have plenty of contiguous free memory (greater than 2M), after running most of the queries in your production system (you'll have to determine how long this takes), then you do not need to increase the SHARED_POOL_SIZE parameter. I have never seen this parameter go all the way to zero (Oracle saves a portion for emergency operations via the SHARED_POOL_RESERVED_SIZE parameter).

TIP
The V$SGASTAT view shows how fast the memory in the shared pool is being depleted. Remember it is only a rough estimate. It shows you any memory that has never been used combined with any piece of memory that has been reused. Free memory will go up and down as the day goes on, depending on how the pieces are fragmented.

Using the X$KSMSP Table to Get a Detailed Look at the Shared Pool

You can query the X$KSMSP table to get total breakdown for the shared pool. This table will show the amount of memory that is free, memory that is freeable, and memory that is retained for large statements that won't fit into the current shared pool. Consider the following query for a more accurate picture of the shared pool. Refer to Chapter 13 for an in-depth look at this query and how it is adjusted as Oracle is started and as the system begins to access shared pool memory.

```
select     sum(ksmchsiz) Bytes, ksmchcls Status
from       x$ksmsp
group by   ksmchcls;


          Bytes STATUS
--------------- --------
    238,032,888 freeabl
    128,346,176 recr
          3,456 R-freea
    124,551,032 perm
     29,387,280 R-free
     16,771,472 R-perm
     66,884,304 free

7 rows selected.
```

Oracle does not state anywhere what the values for status in the X$KSMSP table indicate (KSMSP stands for Kernel Service layer Memory management Sga heaP; I always remember it as Kernel Shared Memory Shared Pool instead). In the following table, I offer the following possible descriptions based on the behavior of these values as researched in Chapter 13. In Chapter 5, I also show how to graph these results in Enterprise Manager.

Status	Possible Meaning
Free	This is the amount of contiguous free memory available.
Freeabl	Freeable but not flushable shared memory currently in use.
Perm	I have read that this status is permanently allocated and non-freeable memory, but in testing it, I find that it behaves as free memory not yet moved to the free area for use.
Recr	Allocated memory that is flushable when the shared pool is low on memory.
R-free	This is SHARED_POOL_RESERVED_SIZE (default 5 percent of shared pool).
R-freea	This is probably reserved memory that is freeable but not flushable.
R-recr	Re-creatable chucks of memory in the reserved pool.
R-perm	Permanent chucks of memory in the reserved pool.

TIP
The general rule of thumb (exact sizing depends on your unique systems) is to make the SHARED_POOL_SIZE parameter around 50–150+ percent of the size of your DB_CACHE_SIZE. In a system that makes use of a large amount of stored procedures or Oracle supplied packages, but has limited physical memory, this parameter could make up as much as 150+ percent of the size of DB_CACHE_SIZE. In a system that uses no stored procedures, but has a large amount of physical memory to allocate to DB_CACHE_SIZE, this parameter may be 10–20 percent of the size of DB_CACHE_SIZE. I have worked on larger systems where the DB_CACHE_SIZE was set as high as 10s of Gigs. I'm sure that 100s of Gigs to Terabyte SGA's already exist (see examples at the end of this chapter). Petabyte databases are currently starting to make their entry. Note that in a shared server configuration (previously known as MTS), items from the PGA are allocated from the shared pool rather than the session process space.

Points to Remember About Cache Size

Here are some further notes about setting your cache and share pool sizes:

- If the dictionary cache hit ratio is low (less than 95 percent), then consider investigating and increasing SHARED_POOL_SIZE.

- If the library cache reload ratio is high (>1 percent), then consider investigating and increasing SHARED_POOL_SIZE.

- Size the data cache and shared pool appropriately for your systems in terms of workload requirements.

Waits Related to Initialization Parameters

Setting initialization parameters incorrectly often results in various types of performance issues that show up as general "waits" or "latch waits" in a STATSPACK report. In Chapter 14, I cover every type of wait and latch issue related to this. The following tables identify some waits and latch waits and their potential fixes.

Wait Problem	Potential Fix
Free buffer	Increase the DB_CACHE_SIZE; shorten the checkpoint; tune the code.
Buffer busy	Segment header: Add freelists or freelist groups or use ASSM.
Buffer busy	Data block: separate hot data; use reverse key indexes; small block sizes.
Buffer busy	Data block: increase initrans and/or maxtrans.
Buffer busy	UNDO header: use automatic undo management.
Buffer busy	UNDO block: commit more; use automatic undo management.
Latch free	Investigate the detail (listing in next table of this chapter for fixes).
Log buffer space	Increase the log buffer; use faster disks for the redo logs.
Scattered read	Indicates many full table scans: tune the code; cache small tables.
Sequential read	Indicates many index reads: tune the code (especially joins).
Write complete waits	Adds database writers; checkpoint more often; buffer cache too small.

Some latch problems have often been bug related in the past, so make sure you check Metalink for issues related to latches. Any of the latches that have a hit ratio less than 99 percent should be investigated.

Latch Problem	Potential Fix
Library cache	Use bind variables; adjust the SHARED_POOL_SIZE.
Shared pool	Use bind variables; adjust the SHARED_POOL_SIZE.
Row cache objects	Increase the shared pool. This is not a common problem.
Cache buffers chain	Shouldn't be a problem in 11*g*. If you get this latch wait, it means you need to reduce logical I/O rates by tuning and minimizing the I/O requirements of the SQL involved. High I/O rates could be a sign of a hot block (meaning a block highly accessed). Cache *buffer lru chain* latch contention can be resolved by increasing the size of the buffer cache and thereby reducing the rate at which new blocks are introduced into the buffer cache. Multiple buffer pools, if it's found they are needed, can help reduce contention. You can also create additional *cache buffer lru chain* latches by adjusting the configuration parameter DB_BLOCK_LRU_LATCHES. You may be able to reduce the load on the *cache buffer chain* latches by increasing the configuration parameter. _DB_BLOCK_HASH_BUCKETS may need to be increased or set to a prime number, but this should not be needed in 11*g*. Keep in mind there are now *in memory updates (IMU)* to consider as well.

Using Oracle Multiple Buffer Pools

There are pools for the allocation of memory. These pools relate to the DB_CACHE_SIZE and SHARED_POOL_SIZE. Each of these parameters, which were all-inclusive of the memory they allocate, now has additional options for memory allocation within each memory pool. I will cover the two separately.

Pools Related to DB_CACHE_SIZE
and Allocating Memory for Data

In this section, I will focus on the Oracle pools that are used to store the actual data in memory. The initialization parameters DB_CACHE_SIZE, DB_KEEP_CACHE_SIZE, and DB_RECYCLE_CACHE_SIZE are the determining factors for memory used to store data. DB_CACHE_SIZE refers to the total size in bytes of the main buffer cache (or memory for data) in the SGA. Two additional buffer pools are DB_KEEP_CACHE_SIZE and DB_RECYCLE_CACHE_SIZE. These additional two pools serve the same purpose as the main buffer cache (DB_CACHE_SIZE), with the exception that the algorithm to maintain the pool is different for all three available pools. Note that the BUFFER_POOL_KEEP, DB_BLOCK_BUFFERS, and BUFFER_POOL_RECYCLE parameters have been deprecated and should no longer be used. Unlike BUFFER_POOL_KEEP and BUFFER_POOL_RECYCLE, DB_KEEP_CACHE_SIZE and DB_RECYCLE_CACHE_SIZE are not subtracted from DB_CACHE_SIZE; they are allocated in addition to DB_CACHE_SIZE.

The *main buffer cache* (defined by *DB_CACHE_SIZE*) maintains the LRU (least recently used) list and flushes the oldest buffers in the list. While all three pools utilize the LRU replacement policy, the goal for the main buffer cache is to fit most data being used in memory.

The *keep pool* (defined by *DB_KEEP_CACHE_SIZE*) is hopefully never flushed; it is intended for buffers that you want to be "pinned" indefinitely (buffers that are very important and need to stay in memory). Use the keep pool for small tables (that fit in their entirety in this pool) that are frequently accessed and need to be in memory at all times.

The *recycle pool* (defined by *DB_RECYCLE_CACHE_SIZE*) is a pool from which you expect the data to be regularly flushed because too much data is being accessed to stay in memory. Use the recycle pool for large, less important data that is usually accessed only once in a long while (ad hoc user tables for inexperienced users are often put here).

The following examples give a quick look at how information is allocated to the various buffer pools. Remember, if no pool is specified, then the buffers in the main pool are used.

1. Create a table that will be stored in the keep pool upon being accessed:

```
Create table state_list (state_abbrev varchar2(2), state_desc
varchar2(25))
Storage (buffer_pool keep);
```

2. Alter the table to the recycle pool:

```
Alter table state_list storage (buffer_pool recycle);
```

3. Alter the table back to the keep pool:

```
Alter table state_list storage (buffer_pool keep);
```

4. Find the disk and memory reads in the keep pool:

```
select    physical_reads "Disk Reads",
          db_block_gets + consistent_gets "Memory Reads"
from      v$buffer_pool_statistics
where     name = 'KEEP';
```

Modifying the LRU Algorithm

In this section, I'm going to go over the deep edge for experts only. Skip this section if you've used Oracle for only a decade or less. There are five undocumented initialization parameters (defaults are in parentheses) that you can use to alter the LRU algorithm for greater efficiency when you really have studied and understand your system buffer usage well:

- **_DB_PERCENT_HOT_DEFAULT (50)** The percent of buffers in the hot region

- **_DB_AGING_TOUCH_TIME (3)** Seconds that must pass to increment touch count again

- **_DB_AGING_HOT_CRITERIA (2)** Threshold to move a buffer to the MRU end of LRU chain

- **_DB_AGING_STAY_COUNT (0)** Touch count reset to this when moved to MRU end

- **_DB_AGING_COOL_COUNT (1)** Touch count reset to this when moved to LRU end

By decreasing the value of the first of these parameters, you allow buffers to remain longer; increasing the values causes a flush sooner. Setting the second parameter lower gives higher value to buffers that are executed a lot in a short period of time. The third, fourth, and fifth parameters all relate to how quickly to move things from the hot end to the cold end and how long they stay on each end.

Pools Related to SHARED_POOL_SIZE and Allocating Memory for Statements

In this section, I focus on the pools that are used to store the actual statements in memory. Unlike the pools related to the data, the LARGE_POOL_SIZE is allocated outside the memory allocated for SHARED_POOL_SIZE, but it is still part of the SGA.

The LARGE_POOL_SIZE is a pool of memory used for the same operations as the shared pool. Oracle defines this as the size set aside for large allocations of the shared pool. You'll have to do your own testing to ensure where the allocations are coming from in your system and version of Oracle. The minimum setting is 300K, but the setting must also be as big as _LARGE_POOL_MIN_ALLOC, which is the minimum size of shared pool memory requested that will force an allocation in the LARGE_POOL_SIZE memory. Unlike the shared pool, the large pool does not have an LRU list. Oracle does not attempt to age memory out of the large pool.

You can view your pool settings by querying the V$PARAMETER view:

```
select     name, value, isdefault, isses_modifiable, issys_modifiable
from       v$parameter
where      name like '%pool%'
and        isdeprecated <> 'TRUE'
order by 1;


NAME                       VALUE        ISDEFAULT ISSES ISSYS_MOD
------------------------   -----------  --------- ----- ---------
java_pool_size             0            TRUE      FALSE IMMEDIATE
large_pool_size            0            TRUE      FALSE IMMEDIATE
olap_pool_size             0            TRUE      TRUE  DEFERRED
shared_pool_reserved_size  53687091     TRUE      FALSE FALSE
shared_pool_size           1073741824   FALSE     FALSE IMMEDIATE
streams_pool_size          0            TRUE      FALSE IMMEDIATE

6 rows selected.
```

TIP
The additional buffer pools (memory for data) available in Oracle are initially set to zero. You should not need to set them initially, but you may need to for your unique system.

Tuning the **PGA_AGGREGATE_TARGET** for Optimal Use of Memory

The PGA_AGGREGATE_TARGET, now included as part of MEMORY_TARGET, specifies the total amount of session PGA memory that Oracle will attempt to allocate across all sessions. Oracle will allocate what it feels is appropriate based on MEMORY_TARGET, but you should set a minimum value based on what you've seen in prior versions. Metalink note 223730.1 describes Automatic PGA_AGGREGATE_TARGET Management quite well. PGA_AGGREGATE_TARGET was introduced in Oracle 9i and should be used in place of the *_SIZE parameters such as SORT_AREA_SIZE, although a local session may still want to set a local SORT_AREA_SIZE for some local short-term operation. Also, since Oracle 9i, the PGA_AGGREGATE_TARGET parameter does not automatically configure ALL *_SIZE parameters. For example, both the LARGE_POOL_SIZE and JAVA_POOL_SIZE parameters are not affected by PGA_AGGREGATE_TARGET. The advantage of using PGA_AGGREGATE_TARGET is the ability to cap the total user session memory to minimize OS paging.

When PGA_AGGREGATE_TARGET is set, WORKAREA_SIZE_POLICY must be set to AUTO. Like the V$DB_CACHE_ADVICE view, the V$PGA_TARGET_ADVICE (Oracle 9.2 and later versions) and V$PGA_TARGET_ADVICE_HISTOGRAM views exist to assist in tuning the PGA_AGGREGATE_TARGET. Oracle Enterprise Manager provides graphical representations of these views.

The PGA_AGGREGATE_TARGET should be set to attempt to keep the ESTD_PGA_CACHE_HIT_PERCENTAGE greater than 95 percent. By setting this appropriately, more data will be sorted in memory that may have been sorted on disk.

The next query returns the minimum value for the PGA_AGGREGATE_TARGET that is projected to yield a 95 percent or greater cache hit ratio:

```
select min(pga_target_for_estimate)
from   v$pga_target_advice
where  estd_pga_cache_hit_percentage > 95;

MIN(PGA_TARGET_FOR_ESTIMATE)
----------------------------
                   299892736
```

Modifying the Size of Your SGA to Avoid Paging and Swapping

Before you increase the size of your SGA, you must understand the effects on the physical memory of your system. If you increase parameters that use more memory than what is available on your system, then serious performance degradation may occur. When your system processes jobs, if it doesn't have enough memory, it starts paging or swapping to complete the active task.

When *paging* occurs, information that is *not currently* being used is moved from memory to disk. This allows memory to be used by a process that *currently* needs it. If paging happens a lot, the system will experience decreases in performance, causing processes to take longer to run.

When *swapping* occurs, an *active* process is moved from memory to disk temporarily so that another *active* process that also desires memory can run. Swapping is based on system cycle time. If swapping happens a lot, your system is dead. Depending on the amount of memory available, an SGA that is too large can cause swapping.

Understanding the Oracle Optimizer

The Oracle optimizer was built to make your tuning life easier by choosing better paths for your poorly written queries. Rule-based optimization (now obsolete and unsupported) was built on a set of rules for how Oracle processes statements. Oracle 10*g* Release 2 only supported the use of the cost-based optimizer; the rule-based optimizer was no longer supported. Since Oracle 10*g* Release 2, Oracle has automatic statistics gathering turned on to aid the effectiveness of the cost-based optimizer. In Oracle, many features are only available when using cost-based optimization. The cost-based optimizer now has two modes of operation: normal mode and tuning mode. *Normal* mode should be used in production and test environments; *tuning* mode can be used in development environments to aid developers and DBAs in testing specific SQL code.

How Optimization Looks at the Data

Rule-based optimization is *Oracle-centric,* whereas cost-based optimization is *data-centric.* The optimizer mode under which the database operates is set via the initialization parameter OPTIMIZER_MODE. The possible optimizer modes are as follows:

- **ALL_ROWS**   Gets all rows faster (generally forces index suppression). This is good for untuned, high-volume batch systems. This is the default.

- **FIRST_ROWS**   Gets the first row faster (generally forces index use). This is good for untuned systems that process lots of single transactions.

- **FIRST_ROWS (1 | 10 | 100 | 1000)**   Gets the first *n* rows faster. This is good for applications that routinely display partial results to users such as paging data to a user in a web application.

- **CHOOSE**   Now obsolete and unsupported but still allowed. Uses cost-based optimization for all analyzed tables. This is a good mode for well-built and well-tuned systems (for advanced users). This option is not documented for 11*g*R2 but is still usable.

- **RULE**   Now obsolete and unsupported but still allowed. Always uses rule-based optimization. If you are still using this, you need to start using cost-based optimization, as rule-based optimization is no longer supported under Oracle 10*g* Release 2 and higher.

■ The default optimizer mode for Oracle 11*g* Release 2 is ALL_ROWS. Also, cost-based optimization is used even if the tables are not analyzed. Although RULE/CHOOSE are definitely desupported and obsolete and people are often scolded for even talking about it, I was able to set the mode to RULE in 11*g*R2. Consider the following error I received when I set OPTIMIZER_MODE to a mode that doesn't exist (SUPER_FAST):

```
SQL> alter system set optimizer_mode=super_fast

ERROR:
ORA-00096: invalid value SUPER_FAST for parameter optimizer_mode, must be

from among first_rows_1000, first_rows_100, first_rows_10, first_rows_1,

first_rows,all_rows, choose, rule
```

NOTE
The optimizer in Oracle 11g Release 2 uses cost-based optimization regardless of whether the tables have been analyzed or not.

TIP
There is no OPTIMIZER MODE called COST (a misconception). If you are using Oracle Database 9i Release 2 or an earlier version and are not sure what optimizer mode to use, then use CHOOSE or FIRST_ROWS and analyze all tables. As the data in a table changes, tables need to be reanalyzed at regular intervals. In Oracle 11g Release 2, the OPTIMIZER_MODES to use are ALL_ROWS and FIRST_ROWS.

Creating Enough Dispatchers

When using shared server, some of the things you need to watch for are high busy rates for the existing dispatcher processes and increases in wait times for response queues of existing dispatcher processes. If the wait time increases, as the application runs under normal use, you may wish to add more dispatcher processes, especially if the processes are busy more than 50 percent of the time.

Use the following statement to determine the busy rate:

```
select     Network,
           ((Sum(Busy) / (Sum(Busy) + Sum(Idle))) * 100) "% Busy Rate"
from       V$Dispatcher
group by   Network;

NETWORK         % Busy Rate
TCP1                      0
TCP2                      0
```

Use the following statement to check for responses to user processes that are waiting in a queue to be sent to the user:

```
select     Network Protocol,
           Decode (Sum(Totalq), 0, 'No Responses',
           Sum(Wait) / Sum(TotalQ) || ' hundredths of a second')
           "Average Wait Time Per Response"
from       V$Queue Q, V$Dispatcher D
where      Q.Type = 'DISPATCHER'
and        Q.Paddr = D.Paddr
group by   Network;


PROTOCOL         Average Wait Time Per Response
TCP1             0 hundredths of a second
TCP2             1 hundredths of a second
```

Use the following statement to check the requests from user processes that are waiting in a queue to be sent to the user:

```
select     Decode (Sum(Totalq), 0, 'Number of Requests',
           Sum(Wait) / Sum(TotalQ) || 'hundredths of a second')
           "Average Wait Time Per Request"
from       V$Queue
where      Type = 'COMMON';


Average Wait Time Per Request
12 hundredths of a second
```

Have Enough Open Cursors (OPEN_CURSORS)

If you don't have enough open cursors, then you will receive errors to that effect. The key is to stay ahead of your system by increasing the OPEN_CURSORS initialization parameter before you run out of open cursors.

Don't Let Your DDL Statements Fail (DDL Lock Timeout)

DDL statements (CREATE/ALTER/DROP) require exclusive locks and thus sometimes fail due to bad timing when they conflict with other statements that lock the table. The parameter DDL_LOCK_TIMEOUT specifies the amount of time (in seconds) the DDL statement will wait for the lock before timing out and failing. The default value is 0; the max value is 100,000 (27.77 hours). The following example shows setting the value to 1 hour or 3,600 seconds.

```
SQL> alter session set DDL_LOCK_TIMEOUT = 3600;
Session altered.
```

Two Important Exadata Initialization Parameters (EXADATA ONLY)

Oracle has two very important parameters to use to test major features of Exadata. The first is CELL_OFFLOAD_PROCESSING, which relates to Smart Scans (cell scans). The default value is TRUE, which means that Smart Scans are turned ON for Exadata (if you are using it). You can set this value to FALSE to turn off Smart Scans and check other features or compare speeds with and without this feature.

The second parameter is undocumented and should only be used with the consent of Oracle Support and also only for testing purposes. The second is _KCFIS_STORAGEIDX_DISABLED, which is used to disable storage indexes. This tells Oracle *not* to use storage index optimization on storage cells if set to TRUE. The default is FALSE. Another undocumented parameter (again check with Oracle Support) is also related to how the Smart Scan works and uses Bloom Filters. The parameter _BLOOM_FILTER_ENABLED is set to TRUE by default. With Exadata, bloom filters are used for join filtering with Smart Scans. _BLOOM_PRUNING_ENABLED also has a default of TRUE. Set these parameters to FALSE to disable them. See Chapter 11 for additional information.

25 Important Initialization Parameters to Consider

Top 25 Initialization Parameters

The following list is *my* list of the top 25 most important initialization parameters, in order of importance. Your top 25 may vary somewhat from my top 25 because everyone has a unique business, unique applications, and unique experiences.

1. **MEMORY_TARGET** This is the initialization parameter setting for all of the memory allocated to *both* the PGA and SGA combined (new in 11g). Setting MEMORY_TARGET enables Automatic Memory Management, so Oracle allocates memory for you based on system needs, but you can also set minimum values for key parameters. MEMORY_TARGET is used for everything that SGA_TARGET was used for but now additionally includes the PGA (especially important as MEMORY_TARGET now includes the important area PGA_AGGREGATE_TARGET). Important parameters such as DB_CACHE_SIZE, SHARED_POOL_SIZE, PGA_AGGREGATE_TARGET, LARGE_POOL_SIZE, and JAVA_POOL_SIZE are all set automatically when you set MEMORY_TARGET. Setting minimum values for important initialization parameters in your system is also a *very* good idea.

2. **MEMORY_MAX_TARGET** This is the maximum memory allocated for Oracle and the maximum value to which MEMORY_TARGET can be set.

3. **DB_CACHE_SIZE** Initial memory allocated to data cache or memory used for data itself. This parameter doesn't need to be set if you set MEMORY_TARGET or SGA_TARGET, but setting a value for this as a minimum setting is a good idea. Your goal should always be toward a memory resident database or at least toward getting all data that will be queried in memory.

4. **SHARED_POOL_SIZE** Memory allocated for data dictionary and for SQL and PL/SQL statements. The query itself is put in memory here. This parameter doesn't need to be set if you set MEMORY_TARGET, but setting a value for this as a minimum is a good idea. Note that SAP recommends setting this to 400M. Also note that the Result Cache gets its memory from the shared pool and is set with the RESULT_CACHE_SIZE and RESULT_CACHE_MODE (FORCE/AUTO/MANUAL) initialization parameters. Lastly, an important note for 11*g* is that this parameter now includes some SGA overhead (12M worth) that it previously did not (in 10*g*). In 11*g*, set this 12M higher than you did in 10*g*!

5. **SGA_TARGET** If you use Oracle's Automatic Shared Memory Management, this parameter is used to determine the size of your data cache, shared pool, large pool, and Java pool automatically (see Chapter 1 for more information). Setting this to 0 disables it. This parameter doesn't need to be set if you set MEMORY_TARGET, but you may want to set a value for this as a minimum setting for the SGA if you've calibrated it in previous versions. The SHARED_POOL_SIZE, LARGE_POOL_SIZE, JAVA_POOL_SIZE, and DB_CACHE_SIZE are all set automatically based on this parameter (or MEMORY_TARGET if used).

6. **PGA_AGGREGATE_TARGET** Soft memory cap for total of all users' PGAs. This parameter doesn't need to be set if you set MEMORY_TARGET, but setting a value as a minimum setting is a good idea. Note that SAP specifies to set this to 20 percent of available memory for OLTP and 40 percent for OLAP.

7. **SGA_MAX_SIZE** Maximum memory that SGA_TARGET can be set to. This parameter doesn't need to be set if you set MEMORY_TARGET, but you may want to set a value if you use SGA_TARGET.

8. **OPTIMIZER_MODE** FIRST_ROWS, FIRST_ROWS_*n,* or ALL_ROWS. Although RULE/CHOOSE are definitely desupported and obsolete and people are often scolded for even talking about it, I was able to set the mode to RULE in 11*g*R2. Consider the following error I received when I set OPTIMIZER_MODE to a mode that doesn't exist (SUPER_FAST):

```
SQL> alter system set optimizer_mode=super_fast

ERROR:
ORA-00096: invalid value SUPER_FAST for parameter optimizer_mode, must be from
among first_rows_1000, first_rows_100, first_rows_10, first_rows_1, first_rows,
all_rows, choose, rule
```

9. **SEC_CASE_SENSITIVE_LOGON** The default is TRUE, which makes passwords case sensitive (new in 11*g*). Set this to FALSE to disable this feature.

10. **SEC_MAX_FAILED_LOGIN_ATTEMPTS** This locks an account if the user fails to enter the correct password after this many tries (new in 11*g*). The default is 10 (consider lowering this value for *very* secure systems). The DBA must issue an "ALTER USER *username* ACCOUNT UNLOCK;" to unlock the account.

11. **CURSOR_SHARING** Converts literal SQL to SQL with bind variables, reducing parse overhead. The default is EXACT. Consider setting it to FORCE after research (see Chapter 4 for more information).

12. **OPTIMIZER_USE_INVISIBLE_INDEXES** The default is FALSE to ensure invisible indexes are *not* used by default (new in 11*g*). Set this parameter to TRUE to use *all* of the indexes and to check which ones might have been set incorrectly to be invisible; this could be a helpful tuning exercise, or it could also bring the system to halt so only use in development.

13. **OPTIMIZER_USE_PENDING_STATISTICS** The default is FALSE to ensure pending statistics are *not* used, whereas setting this to TRUE enables all pending statistics to be used (new in 11*g*).

14. **OPTIMIZER_INDEX_COST_ADJ** Coarse adjustment between the cost of an index scan and the cost of a full table scan. Set between 1 and 10 to force index use more frequently. Setting this parameter to a value between 1 and 10 pretty much guarantees index use, however, even when not appropriate, so be careful because it is highly dependent on the index design and implementation being correct. Please note that if you are using Applications 11*i*, setting OPTIMIZER_INDEX_COST_ADJ to any value other than the default (100) is not supported (see Metalink note 169935.1). I've seen a benchmark where this was set to 200. Also, see bug 4483286. SAP suggests that you *not* set it for OLAP, but set it to 20 for OLTP.

15. **DB_FILE_MULTIBLOCK_READ_COUNT** For full table scans to perform I/O more efficiently, this parameter reads the given number of blocks in a single I/O. The default value is 128 in 11*g*R2, but it is usually noted *not* to change this from the default.

16. **LOG_BUFFER** Buffer for uncommitted transactions in memory; it must be set in the PFILE if you want to change it. SAP says to use the default, whereas Oracle Applications sets it to 10M. I've seen benchmarks with it set over 100M.

17. **DB_KEEP_CACHE_SIZE** Memory allocated to keep pool or an additional data cache that you can set up outside the buffer cache for very important data that you don't want pushed out of the cache.

18. **DB_RECYCLE_CACHE_SIZE** Memory allocated to a recycle pool or an additional data cache that you can set up outside the buffer cache and in addition to the keep cache described in item 17. Usually, DBAs set this up for ad hoc user query data with poorly written queries.

19. **OPTIMIZER_USE_SQL_PLAN_BASELINES** The default is TRUE, which means Oracle uses these baselines if they exist (new in 11*g*). Note that Stored Outlines are deprecated (discouraged but they still work) in 11*g*, as they are replaced with SQL Plan Baselines.

20. **OPTIMIZER_CAPTURE_SQL_PLAN_BASELINES** The default is FALSE, which means that Oracle does not capture them by default, but if you create some, it will use them as stated in the previous parameter (new in 11*g*).

21. **LARGE_POOL_SIZE** Total blocks in the large pool allocation for large PL/SQL and a few other Oracle options less frequently used.

22. **STATISTICS_LEVEL** Used to enable advisory information and optionally keep additional OS statistics to refine optimizer decisions. TYPICAL is the default.

23. **JAVA_POOL_SIZE** Memory allocated to the JVM for JAVA stored procedures.

24. **JAVA_MAX_SESSIONSPACE_SIZE**   Upper limit on memory that is used to keep track of the user session state of JAVA classes.

25. **OPEN_CURSORS**   Specifies the size of the private area used to hold (open) user statements. If you get an "ORA-01000: maximum open cursors exceeded," you may need to increase this parameter, but make sure you are *closing* cursors that you no longer need. Prior to 9.2.0.5, these open cursors were also cached and, at times, caused issues (ORA-4031) if OPEN_CURSORS was set too high. As of 9.2.05, SESSION_CACHED_CURSORS now controls the setting of the PL/SQL cursor cache. Do *not* set the parameter SESSION_CACHED_CURSORS as high as you set OPEN_CURSORS, or you may experience ORA-4031 or ORA-7445 errors. SAP recommends setting this to 2000; Oracle Applications has OPEN_CURSORS at 600 and SESSION_CACHED_CURSORS at 500.

TIP
Setting certain initialization parameters correctly could be the difference between a report taking two seconds and two hours. Test changes on a test system thoroughly before implementing those changes in a production environment.

Initialization Parameters over the Years

Oracle has moved from a time where there were over four times as many documented parameters as undocumented in Oracle 6, to the undocumented parameters exceeding the documented in Oracle 8*i*, to four times as many undocumented as documented parameters in Oracle 10*g*, to six times more in 11*g*. Clearly, Oracle has migrated to a place where experts have more dials to set in 10*g* (undocumented), but the number of dials to set for the standard database setup (documented parameters) is not increasing anymore and is becoming standardized. The following table charts the changing numbers of documented and undocumented parameters:

Version	Documented	Undocumented	Total
6	111	19	130
7	117	68	185 (+42% vs. V6)
8.0	193	119	312
8.1	203	301	504 (+62% vs. V7)
9.0	251	436	687
9.2	257	540	797 (+58% vs. 8i)
10.2	257 (+0%)	1124 (+108%)	1381 (+73% vs. 9i)
11.2	341 (+33%%)	2053 (+83%)	2394 (+73% vs. 10g)

Finding Undocumented Initialization Parameters

Querying the table X$KSPPI shows you documented as well as undocumented initialization parameters. The query may only be done as user SYS, so be careful. See Chapter 13 for a complete look at the X$ tables. My top 13 undocumented initialization parameters are listed in Appendix A. Appendix C gives a complete listing as of the writing of this book of the X$ tables.

```
Col name for a15
Col value for a15
Col default1 for a15
Col desc1 for a30

select      a.ksppinm name, b.ksppstvl value, b.ksppstdf default1, a.ksppdesc desc1
from        x$ksppi a, x$ksppcv b
where       a.indx = b.indx
and         substr(ksppinm,1,1) = '_'
order       by ksppinm;
```

The following is a brief description of the columns in the X$KSPPI and X$KSPPCV tables:

- **KSPPINM** Parameter name
- **KSPPSTVL** Current value for the parameter
- **KSPPSTDF** Default value for the parameter

A partial output listing of the initialization parameters is shown here:

```
KSPPINM                         KSPPSTVL              KSPPSTDF
------------------------------- --------------------- ----------
...
_write_clones                   3                     TRUE
_yield_check_interval           100000                TRUE
active_instance_count                                 TRUE
aq_tm_processes                 1                     FALSE
archive_lag_target              0                     TRUE
...
```

TIP
Using undocumented initialization parameters can cause corruption. Never use these if you are not an expert and you are not directed by Oracle Support! Ensure that you work with Oracle Support before setting these parameters.

Understanding the Typical Server

There's nothing typical about most unique systems. The key to understanding Oracle is to understand its dynamic nature. Oracle continues to have many attributes of previous versions while also leading the way by implementing the future of distributed database and object-oriented programming. Experience from earlier versions of Oracle always benefits the DBA in future versions of Oracle. Here are some of the future changes to consider as you build your system:

- Oracle can be completely distributed and maintained at a single point. (Many databases and locations with one DBA managing the system looks like the corporate future.)

- Database maintenance is becoming completely visual (all point-and-click maintenance as in the Enterprise Manager). The V$ views are still your lowest-performance cost access method, but Enterprise Manager is easier to use for more complex inquiries that may require multiple V$ views to get the same result.

- Network throughput continues to be an issue that looks to be solved by technology.

- CPUs continue to get faster, eliminating the CPU as a system resource issue. (I/O, limitations on DRAM, and correct design will continue to be the issues.)

- Object-oriented and Agile development will be crucial to rapid system development.

- Current database design theory is being rewritten to focus more on denormalization.

- Graphics are causing the sizes of databases to become increasingly large. Also, the fact that disk space is getting less expensive has made businesses more willing to keep data around longer.

- While Oracle has excelled in the software market, no hardware maker has kept up over the past decade. With the advent of Exadata, Oracle may get us to Exabyte databases faster than anticipated.

Modeling a Typical Server

This section contains very rough estimates designed as setup guidelines. However, it is important to emphasize that these are only guidelines and that the reality is that every system is different and must be tuned to meet that system's demands. (CPU speed depends on the type of processor, e.g., RISC or SPARC vs. Intel.) The following table does not include guidelines for Oracle Applications. Oracle Applications tends to have unique issues that are addressed by Oracle in the application documentation and on Metalink.

Database Size	Up to 25G	100–200G	500–3,000G	10T-100T*
Number of users	100	200	500-2000	5000-20000
Number of CPU cores	4–8	8–16	16—64+	128—360
System memory	8G	16G	32–512G+	2T
SGA_MAX_SIZE*	2G	4G	8G–200G	500–700G
PGA_AGGREGATE_TARGET*	512M	1GB	2G–50G	50–100G
Total disk capacity	100G	500–1000G	1–3T	100T

Database Size	Up to 25G	100–200G	500–3,000G	10T-100T*
Percentage of query	75 percent	75 percent	75 percent	90 percent
Percentage of DML	25 percent	25 percent	25 percent	10 percent
Number of redo logs multiplexed	4–8 Yes	6–10 Yes	6–12 Yes	2–12 Yes
Number of control files	4	4	4	4
Percent batch	20 percent	20 percent	20 percent	50 percent
Percent online	80 percent	80 percent	80 percent	50 percent
Archiving used	Yes	Yes	Yes	Yes
Buffer hit ratio	95 percent +	95 percent +	95 percent +	98 percent +
Dictionary hit ratio	95 percent +	95 percent +	95 percent +	98 percent +
Library hit ratio	95 percent +	95 percent +	95 percent +	98 percent +
Other system software (other than Oracle)	Minimum	Minimum	Minimum	Minimum
Use parallel query?	Depends on queries	Depends on queries	Probably in many queries	Yes in many queries

*These are not typical. I've seen as high as almost 1T SGA with about 800G devoted to data caches (multiple). I've also seen an approximately 500G SGA, broken into about 400G of data cache in multiple data caches of different block sizes (none >300G) as well as keep/recycle caches (_KSMG_GRANULE_SIZE of larger caches are anywhere from 50–250M). I've seen a 100G shared pool and as high as 50G PGA_AGGREGATE_TARGET as well. Large SGAs present *many* considerations, including watching out for the dreaded "ORA-00064: Object is too large to allocate on this O/S." Larger corporate SGAs are currently in the low Gigs to 10s of Gigs (100G+ is still very rare at this time, 2012). Most very large systems have multiple caches and block sizes.

The following variables can be reason to deviate from the typical server configuration:

■ Heavy batch processing may require much larger ROLLBACK/UNDO, REDO, and TEMP tablespace sizes.

■ Heavy DML processing may require much larger ROLLBACK/UNDO, REDO, and TEMP tablespace sizes. Exadata best practice is a 32G logfile; you don't need as many at this size!

■ Heavy user access to large tables requires more CPU and memory and larger TEMP tablespace sizes.

- Poorly tuned systems require more CPU and memory and larger TEMP tablespace sizes.

- A greater number of disks, cache on disks, and controllers always increase performance by reducing I/O contention.

- An increase in the disk capacity can speed backup and recovery time by going to disk and not tape. Faster tape speeds lower backup and recovery times as well. Oracle's purchase of Sun also netted them StorageTek.

Sizing the Oracle Applications Database

The Oracle Applications Development Team wrote a note on Metalink (Note 216205.1 for 11*i* and 396009.1 for Release 12) that shows the initialization parameters that should be used (or not used) with various versions of Oracle Applications. I always review the settings that the Oracle Applications Development team recommends, as they often are dealing with large systems and they've learned some nice tricks. While I do feel a bit cautious in using SGA_TARGET and removing DB_CACHE_SIZE (without setting minimum values), the other things listed are very helpful in my opinion. SGA_TARGET has been around since 10*g*R1, and is also a 10*g*R2 and 11*g*R2 RAC Best Practice from Oracle. Oracle 10*g*R1 had some bugs, but 10*g*R2 and 11*g* seem to be solid. There are also some nice descriptions listed here. I am not sure why Applications does not use the new MEMORY_TARGET parameter (perhaps it's too new).

The common database parameters suggested are listed in Appendix A and 11*g*R2 specific parameters follow that listing (note that many comments were removed for brevity; see the actual note for full detail).

NOTE
MAX_COMMIT_PROPOGATION_DELAY is now an obsolete parameter in 11gR2 even though it is still listed in the note as a mandatory parameter for RAC (it's probable that you should not *use this parameter, but check with Oracle support).*

The following is abbreviated from Metalink Note ID 396009.1. Appendix A contains much more information on these parameter recommendations.

The following table should be used to size the relevant parameters (at the end of Note 396009.1):

Parameter Name	Development or Test Instance	11–100 Users	101–500 Users	501–1000 Users	1001–2000 Users
Processes	200	200	800	1200	2500
Sessions	400	400	1600	2400	5000
SGA_TARGET [Footnote 1]	1G	1G	2G	3G	14G

Parameter Name	Development or Test Instance	11–100 Users	101–500 Users	501–1000 Users	1001–2000 Users
SHARED_POOL_SIZE (csp)	N/A	N/A	N/A	1800M	3000M
SHARED_POOL_RESERVED_SIZE (csp)	N/A	N/A	N/A	180M	300M
SHARED_POOL_SIZE (no csp)	400M	600M	800M	1000M	2000M
SHARED_POOL_RESERVED_SIZE (no csp)	40M	60M	80M	100M	100M
PGA_AGGREGATE_TARGET	1G	2G	4G	10G	20G
Total Memory Required [Footnote 2]	~ 2GB	~ 3GB	~ 6GB	~ 13GB	~ 25GB

Specific Notes on Table

- **Footnote 1**   The parameter SGA_TARGET should be used for Oracle 10*g*- or 11*g*-based environments such as Release 12. This replaces the parameter DB_CACHE_SIZE, which was used in Oracle9*i*-based environments. Also, it is not necessary to set the parameter UNDO_RETENTION for 10*g*- or 11*g*-based systems because UNDO_RETENTION is set automatically as part of automatic undo tuning.

- **Footnote 2**   The total memory required refers to the amount of memory required for the database instance and associated memory, including the SGA and the PGA. You should ensure that your system has sufficient available memory in order to support the values provided above. The values provided above should be adjusted based on available memory so as to prevent paging and swapping.

The CSP and NOCSP options of the shared pool–related parameters refer to the use of CURSOR_SPACE_FOR_TIME, which is documented in the common database initialization parameters section. The use of CURSOR_SPACE_FOR_TIME results in much larger shared pool requirements.

The Development/Test instance refers to a small instance used for only development or testing in which no more than 10 users exist. The range of user counts provided in the table refers to active Applications users, not total or named users. For example, if you plan to support a maximum of 500 active Oracle Applications users, then you should use the sizing per the range 101–500 users. The parameter values provided in this document reflect a development/test instance configuration, and you should adjust the relevant parameters according to the Applications user counts (refer to the table).

Tips Review

- The key initialization parameters in Oracle are MEMORY_TARGET, MEMORY_MAX_TARGET, SGA_TARGET, SGA_MAX_SIZE, PGA_AGGREGATE_TARGET, DB_CACHE_SIZE, and SHARED_POOL_SIZE. If you use ASMM, then SGA_TARGET is the key initialization parameter.

- If you can't figure out why your system isn't using the value in your init.ora file, you probably have an SPFILE overriding it. And don't forget, you can also use a hint to override parameters at the query level in 11gR2.

- Changing initialization parameters dynamically is a powerful feature for both developers and DBAs. Consequently, a user with the ALTER SESSION privilege is capable of irresponsibly allocating 100M+ for the SORT_AREA_SIZE for a given session, if it is not restricted.

- In Oracle 11g Release 2, use the Enterprise Manager Grid Control to find problem queries.

- Physical memory is generally much faster than retrieving data from disk, so make sure the SGA is large enough to accommodate memory reads when it is effective to do so.

- Poor joins and poor indexing also yield very high hit ratios, so make sure your hit ratio isn't high for a reason other than a well-tuned system. An unusually high hit ratio may indicate the introduction of code that is poorly indexed or includes join issues.

- Hit ratios are useful to experienced DBAs but can be misleading to inexperienced DBAs. The best use of hit ratios is still to compare over time to help alert you to a substantial change to a system on a given day. Although some DBAs don't like using hit ratios, they are usually tool vendors who don't see the value of tracking hit ratios over time because their tools are point-in-time or reactive-based tuning solutions. Hit ratios should never be your only tool, but they should definitely be one of many proactive tools in your arsenal.

- In Oracle 11g Release 2, use the Top Activity monitor in Enterprise Manager to find problem queries.

- A low hit ratio for a query could be an indication of a missing, invisible, or suppressed index.

- Bad (slow) queries show in V$SQLAREA view with poor hit ratios the first time they are executed. Make sure you tune them at that time. The second time that they execute, they may not show a poor hit ratio.

- The database must be rebuilt if you change the DB_BLOCK_SIZE. Increasing the DB_FILE_MULTIBLOCK_READ_COUNT allows more block reads in a single I/O, giving a benefit similar to a larger block size. In 11g, the default is 128, so it may not need to be changed.

- SQL must be written *exactly* the same to be reused. Case differences and any other differences cause a reparse of the statement unless you use CURSOR_SHARING.

- Measure hit ratios for the data dictionary row cache of the shared pool with the V$ROWCACHE view. A hit ratio of over 95 percent should be achieved. However, when the database is initially started, hit ratios are around 85 percent.

- Measure hit ratios for the library cache of the shared pool with the V$LIBRARYCACHE view. A hit ratio of over 95 percent should be achieved. However, when the database is initially started, hit ratios will be around 85 percent.

■ The V$SGASTAT view shows how fast the memory in the shared pool is being depleted. Remember that it is only a rough estimate. It shows you any memory that has never been used combined with any piece of memory that has been reused. Free memory goes up and down as the day goes on according to how the pieces are fragmented.

■ The general rule of thumb (but more depends on your unique system) is to make the SHARED_POOL_SIZE parameter 50–150+ percent of the size of your DB_CACHE_SIZE.

■ The additional buffer pools (memory for data) available in Oracle are initially set to zero.

■ The optimizer in Oracle 11g Release 2 uses cost-based optimization regardless of whether the tables have been analyzed or not. CHOOSE and RULE are obsolete and unsupported settings for OPTIMIZER_MODE, yet they are still allowed; ALL_ROWS is the default.

■ Setting certain initialization parameters correctly could be the difference between a report taking two seconds and two hours. Test changes on a test system thoroughly before implementing those changes in a production environment.

■ Using undocumented initialization parameters can cause corruption. Never use these if you are not an expert and you are not directed by Oracle Support! Ensure that you work with Oracle Support before setting these parameters.

References

Rich Niemiec, *DBA Tuning: Now YOU Are the Expert* (TUSC).
Oracle Installation Guide, Oracle Corporation.
Oracle Metalink notes: 216205.1, 396009.1, 295626.1, 443746.1, 223730.1.
Performance Tuning Guide, Oracle Corporation.
Craig Shallahamer, *All about Oracle's Touch-Count Data Block Buffer Algorithm* (OraPub, excellent!).
Murali Vallath "Using Oracle Database 11g Release 2 Result Cache in an Oracle RAC Environment," http://www.oracle.com/technetwork/articles/datawarehouse/vallath-resultcache-rac-284280.html.

Thanks to Randy Swanson who did the update for this chapter in the 9i version of the book (where were you this time around?). Thanks to Lucas Niemiec for finding the scripts that show Oracle's installation settings. Thanks to Binu Joy who provided some great installation notes and SAP parameters for this chapter and Appendix A.

CHAPTER
5

Enterprise Manager
and Grid Control
(DBA and Developer)

Oracle Enterprise Manager Grid Control finally matches or exceeds the market's answer to monitoring and tuning the Oracle database. Oracle has usually been behind the market with an okay-to-good product over the years. No longer is this the case; Oracle has stepped up to the plate and delivered one of the best products ever (including support for Exadata). This chapter provides a quick tour of why Oracle's Enterprise Manager (EM) is now at the next level. The tour neither explores the entire product, nor teaches you how to use all of the features (that would take an entire book). Rather, this chapter exposes you to some of the tools and tuning features that you will find helpful in your tuning endeavors. With Oracle's focus on the grid since Oracle 10g and continuing into 11g, many screenshots show multiple instances so you can see either a single-instance or multi-instance cluster with the product. Oracle Enterprise Manager is an excellent tuning tool for all levels of DBAs and is especially valuable as you head into the decade of the grid. Oracle Database 11g offers two versions of EM. There is Grid Control (to manage RAC), which is a separate product, and Database Control (screenshots of both appear in this chapter), which is installed along with the database (unless you specify that you do not want to use it for monitoring your database). You can perform many RAC functions (see Chapter 11 for more information on RAC and Exadata) with Database Control (DB Control), but I highly recommend using Grid Control for many features when monitoring Oracle RAC databases.

One way to ensure great performance for your system is to monitor your system for potential performance issues before they become major problems. One vehicle that provides a graphical user interface (GUI) for tuning is the Oracle Enterprise Manager, along with related performance tuning add-on products. The Oracle Enterprise Manager product suite continues to change over time, but this particular version has taken a giant leap forward. With the statistics from the Automatic Workload Repository (AWR), this tool is now tremendously powerful. AWR snapshots are taken every hour by default, and once the AWR snapshot is taken, the Automatic Database Diagnostic Monitor (ADDM) analysis occurs immediately (STATISTICS_LEVEL must be set to TYPICAL or ALL) via the MMON background process. The results of ADDM are also stored in the AWR and accessible via EM.

In addition to monitoring, spectacular screens will show you where a problem is occurring, down to the "latch wait" or "global cache cr transfer wait." The tools for running the AWR Report (covered in detail in Chapter 14) are included, as are tools to change the `spfile.ora` or `init.ora` file. The tools for monitoring the grid are equally spectacular (yes, they are that good). Screens showing performance on every instance (each in a different color) allow you to click the graph to branch to an individual instance. You can delve into performance at the database, host, application server, network, or disk (ASM or non-ASM) level. Of all the Oracle products I have seen hit a home run over time, this one hit a grand slam with the Oracle Grid Control release.

Oracle's Enterprise Manager standard applications include a central management console and additional packs, and many products have an additional cost (please check with Oracle for any price implications for different modules). Accessing the AWR requires the Diagnostics Pack, and running SQL Tuning Sets requires the Tuning Pack. You can use ADDM (described in a previous paragraph) to see what Oracle advises after an hour of gathering statistics to AWR. You can use the SQL Tuning Advisor for tuning a specific SQL statement(s) (you can also run this from the Top Activity screen). Use the SQL Performance Analyzer to tune statements in a Guided Workflow, which shows the before and after tuning results for a set of SQL statements. You can compare an Oracle version's effect on SQL statements; for instance, you can compare a tuning set in 10g to 11g; you can even look at the before and after comparison of initialization parameter changes. Finally, you can even perform an Exadata simulation and run an AWR Report or active session history (ASH, or *mini-AWR*) report from EM.

The following tips are covered in this chapter:

- Enterprise Manager basics
- Policies and alerts
- Monitoring the database
- Tuning the Oracle Database using EM and ADDM
- The Database and Instance Server and Maintenance tabs
- Viewing the Oracle topology
- Monitoring and tuning the hosts
- Monitoring and tuning application servers
- Monitoring and tuning web applications
- Deployments and patching advisories
- Viewing and scheduling jobs
- Available reports, including the ASH and AWR Reports
- Monitoring and tuning ASM
- Real Application Testing (SQL Replay)
- Exadata Simulation

The Enterprise Manager (EM) Basics

Once EM is installed, the login screen (shown for EM Database Control in Figure 5-1) is displayed. Depending on how security is set up, you may need to enter the username, password, or database information at login screens, depending on which screens are accessed within the product.

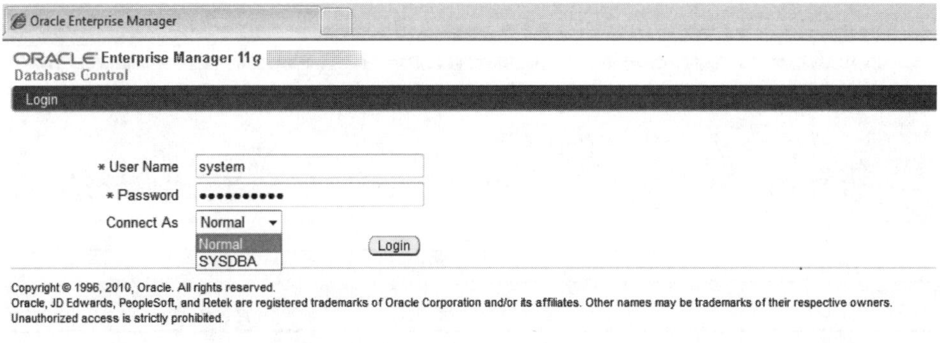

FIGURE 5-1.   *Oracle Enterprise Manager Login screen*

FIGURE 5-2. *Setup and Configuration screen*

Shortly after logging in to EM, check some of the Setup options that exist for customizing the product. In the upper-right corner of the screen, click the word "Setup" to display the Setup screen shown in Figure 5-2.

Some of the available setup options include Patching, Notification Methods, Blackout Periods, and access to various tools and other configuration items. For example, If you click Blackouts from the Setup screen, you'll see the screen shown in Figure 5-3. *Blackouts* are periods of time that allow the system to suspend monitoring for the performance of maintenance activities. This eliminates the skewing of the data during normal operating hours. Even though statistics gathering is suspended, the period is still recorded to ensure too many blackouts aren't scheduled by a DBA.

After familiarizing themselves with EM, DBAs should set up the preferences that are deemed best for the environment being monitored. At any time while using the product, you can click Preferences (located at the upper-right hand of the screen) to see all the preference options, as displayed in Figure 5-4. Several preferences should be set, including the e-mail addresses for sending various alerts or messages as well as notification rules. You can even change the tabs to

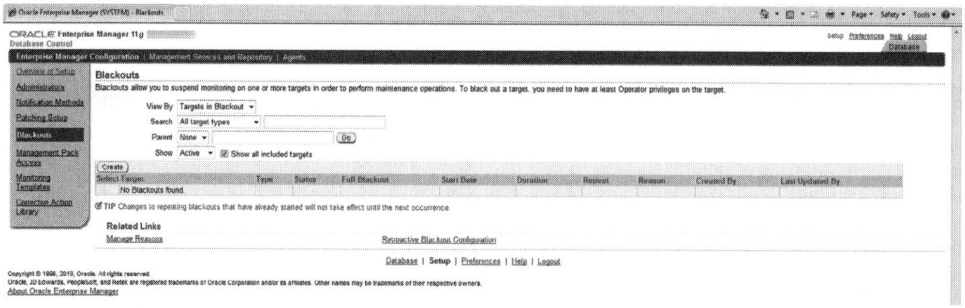

FIGURE 5-3. *Setup and Configuration for Blackouts*

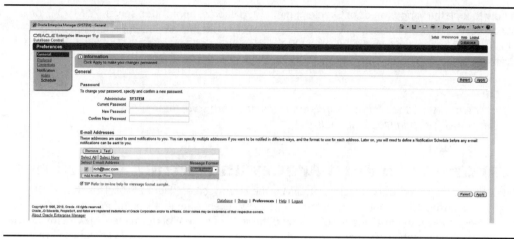

FIGURE 5-4. *Setting Preferences*

be exactly what seems most intuitive for the environment. It is best to stay within the Oracle standard, however, so another DBA can easily follow what's been done.

One of the best parts of EM is the great Help that is provided. No matter where you are, you will always see a Help tab or button that you can select to get specific help on any screen or item. The help can be for either a very general area like "monitoring database performance" or something very specific like the "setting e-mail address" (see Figure 5-5). Substantial help is included in the product

```
Oracle Enterprise Manager Online Help                          Contents  Search  View Topic

                                                         Locate in "Contents"  Printable Page

General page

You can specify one or more e-mail addresses and associated message formats for your Enterprise Manager account.

Specify the e-mail addresses and message formats you want associated with your Enterprise Manager account. All e-mail notifications you receive from Enterprise Manager will be sent to the e-mail
addresses you specify.

For example, user1@oracle.com, user2@oracle.com, user3@oracle.com

Specify the message format to be used with each e-mail address. You can choose either Long or Short formats:

Message Format Examples:

E-mail Subject (Long Format):

EM Alert: <severity> <target name> <message>;

E-mail Body (Long Format):

Subject: EM Alert: Critical: prod1.us.oracle.com - CPU Utilization is 90%

Date: Mon, 14 Oct 2004 12:56:46 +0000 (GMT)

From: "EMD Notifications" <admin1@oracle.com>

To: admin2@oracle.com

Name=prod1.us.oracle.com

Done                                      Internet | Protected Mode: Off           100%
```

FIGURE 5-5. *Online Help*

on how to tune the various areas of Oracle at the host, database, application server, ASM, O/S, or network levels. Also, an interesting feature is the 2 Day + books that are incorporated into the EM help. You can browse through the 2 Day + DBA book within EM, for example. The key is to take advantage of these resources and learn something every time you access EM.

TIP
In Oracle 11gR2, the Online Help is spectacular. Learn something every day by clicking the Help button.

Starting with All Targets and Other Groupings

The first thing displayed when logging into EM is the Home screen (Figure 5-6). This shows All Targets when using Grid Control (by default) and shows everything that's being monitored. You will immediately know if the instance is up or down, the state of system performance, how many active sessions are running (and how many are waiting), and many details of this given database instance or cluster database. This screen is the one that I want to see first thing in the morning so I know that the instance is up and running efficiently. It also shows if there are any Security Policy Violations, Patch Advisories (covered a bit later in this chapter), as well as many other links. New in 11gR2 is a High Availability section in the middle right-hand portion of the screen (Figure 5-6). With Grid Control, a nice feature is the ability to group common areas together. For instance, you can group all databases together into a group called PROD_DB so the group can be monitored together to see if they are all running. The same can be done for development databases (call them DEV_DB). A DBA usually configures things so the PROD_DB group is more proactive in sending alerts, pages, or e-mails than the DEV_DB group. Please note that you can view a RAC database using DB Control, and it will show all instances or the overall database. The main difference between DB

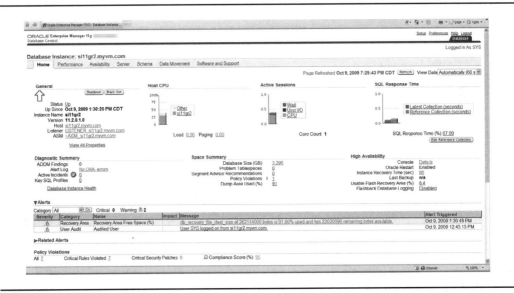

FIGURE 5-6.   *EM Home tab*

Control and Grid Control is that DB Control manages a *single* database, whereas Grid Control can manage multiple databases, hosts, and others. You can also see Chapter 8 of the 2 Day + RAC book— http://download.oracle.com/docs/cd/E11882_01/rac.112/e17264/racmon2.htm—for additional RAC DB Control screenshots.

For performance-related issues, you can go directly into the Top Activity screen (Figure 5-7) by clicking directly on the word CPU under the Active Sessions graph in the top middle-right portion of Figure 5-6. You can also go directly to Wait Activities by clicking the graph showing waits and then click Top Activity at the bottom of the Waits screen (the Top Activity screen option is listed at the bottom of most performance-related screens in EM). When systems have serious issues, I spend a lot of time on the Top Activity screen. Figure 5-7 shows a Top Activity screen with some performance spikes, especially around 2:27. You can move (click and drag) the shaded rectangle on the graph to the area that you would like to focus in on (you can look back in time to what happened before an issue occurred as well as after an issue happens). In the lower part of the screen you will see the associated Top SQL statements (on the lower left) and the associated Top Sessions (on the lower right). You can instantly see the cost of each SQL statement and how the statement adds up to the graph in the shaded rectangle area. You can instantly check the boxes next to all of the Top SQL statements that you would like the Tuning Advisor to tune for you (or at least make suggestions).

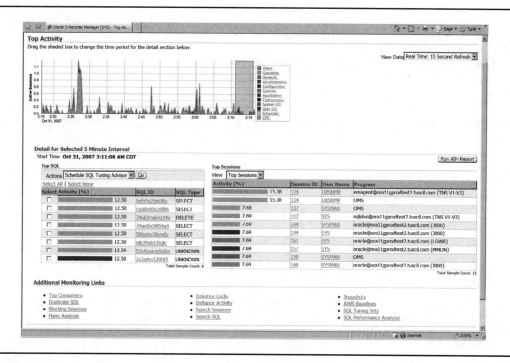

FIGURE 5-7. *Top Activity screen*

SQL Performance Analyzer (SPA)

The SQL Performance Analyzer gives a variety of options for tuning Oracle (Figure 5-8). You can use a Guided Workflow, compare 9*i* or 10.1 to 11*g*, or compare 10.2 to 11*g*. You can compare the effect of changing an initialization parameter, and you can even perform an Exadata simulation. Although I can't show all of the steps for each of these tasks, I'll try to show a few of the key screens here.

Clicking the Guided Workflow option brings up a step-by-step way to compare two different SQL Tuning Sets (Figure 5-9). This allows you to make changes to an environment, tune the SQL statements, or test another change.

After completing all of the Guided Workflow steps, Oracle shows the output comparing the SQL Tuning Sets before and after changes. Figure 5-10 shows the before and after elapsed times and the Tuning Advisor recommended changes for a given SQL Tuning Set. The graph on the left shows a sizable improvement in performance, yet the graph on the right reveals that the improvement was the result of only changing a single statement.

Instead of the Guided Workflow, this time let's choose to compare 10.2 to 11*g*. Figure 5-11 shows one of the screens that appear for this comparison (note the versions comparison in the middle of the screen).

Once I complete the steps to compare 10.2 and 11*g*, Oracle displays a detailed comparison (Figure 5-12). This screen is similar to the output from the Guided Workflow. You can see by the graph on the left that there was a nice improvement in performance, whereas the graph on the right shows that the improvement was the result of a little over half of the SQL statements.

New in 11*g*R2 is the ability to simulate Exadata. Clicking Exadata Simulation in SPA displays the Exadata Simulation screen (Figure 5-13).

Once I enter all of the information and run the associated jobs for the Exadata Simulation, Oracle displays a comparison of my current system to Exadata to see if it would be beneficial (Figure 5-14). For my test, I tried something easy to see if even the most simple queries would show I needed Exadata (when, in fact, I didn't). Fortunately, Oracle indeed showed that Exadata would *not* be beneficial as all statements were unchanged—to which I give them credit (I thought surely they would try to talk me into Exadata!).

FIGURE 5-8. *SQL Performance Analyzer screen*

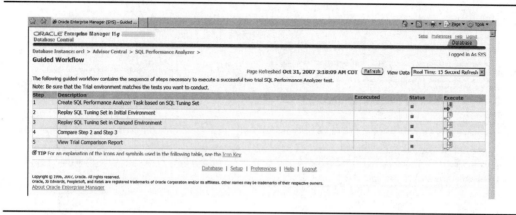

FIGURE 5-9.   *Guided Workflow screen*

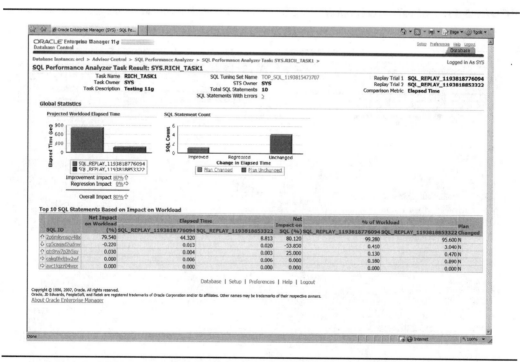

FIGURE 5-10.   *SQL Performance Analyzer (SPA) Task Result for a Guided Workflow*

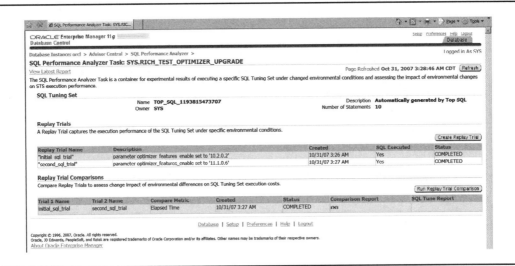

FIGURE 5-11. *SPA Task comparing 10.2 to 11g for a SQL Tuning Set*

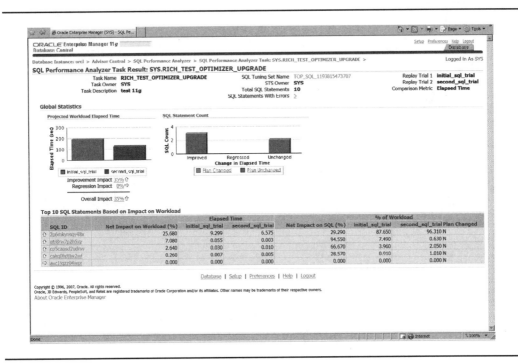

FIGURE 5-12. *SPA Task Result comparing 10.2 to 11g for a SQL Tuning Set*

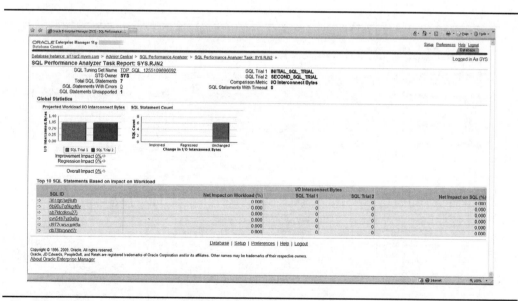

FIGURE 5-13. *Exadata Simulation*

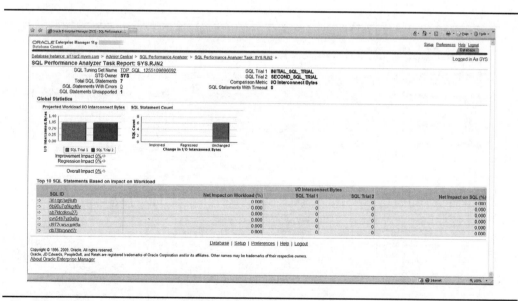

FIGURE 5-14. *SPA Task Report for an Exadata Simulation*

Automatic Database Diagnostic Monitor (ADDM)

As stated earlier, Oracle gathers stats every hour on the hour for AWR and runs an ADDM report directly after that. However, if a problem occurs after the hour (perhaps at 10:10 PM), the ADDM that ran at 10 PM doesn't reveal the problem and perhaps you really don't want to wait until 11 PM if the problem is severe. The answer is 11g's new ability to Run ADDM Now. After clicking the Performance tab from the main screen (Figure 5-6), the Average Active Sessions shows a major problem growing fast at 10:10 PM. You can click Run ADDM Now (Figure 5-15, middle right portion of the screen) to see what the issue is that is causing the spike.

Figure 5-16 shows eight ADDM findings related to SQL that are listed under "Impact %" to the system. The top issue is a hard parse issue followed by a PL/SQL execution issue.

You can also run an ADDM Report (`addmrpt.sql`) in SQL*Plus to see these findings (middle-right portion of the screen). In an effort to increase performance, ADDM analyzes a number of different database-related problems, including:

- Memory-related issues such as shared pool latch contention, log buffer issues, or database buffer cache–related problems

- CPU bottlenecks

- Disk I/O performance issues

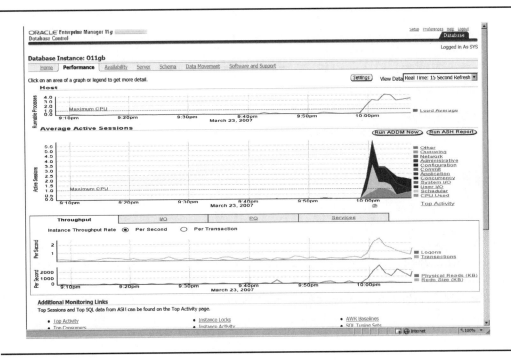

FIGURE 5-15. *Run ADDM Now option from the Performance tab*

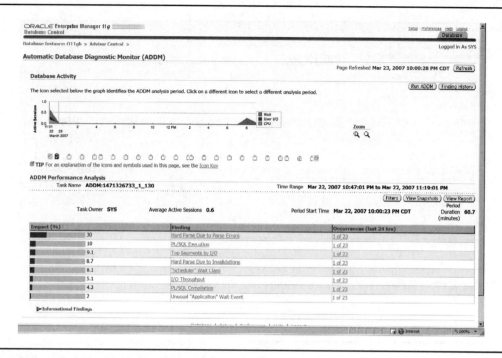

FIGURE 5-16. *ADDM screen*

- Database configuration problems

- Space-related issues, such as tablespaces running out of space

- Application and SQL tuning issues such as excessive parsing and excessive locking

- RAC-related issues such as global cache interconnect issues, lock manager issues, global resource contention issues, and any other *globally significant* issues

TIP
Use the SQL Tuning Advisor only to tune SQL statements, not conditions such as row locks.

By clicking one of the issues, the Performance Finding Details for ADDM screen is displayed. This screen displays the problem as well as offers solution(s) for fixing the problem or related SQL. In the example in Figure 5-17, the issues have to do with hard parsing SQL statements, latches in the shared pool, and concurrency issues.

The DBA can also schedule the Tuning Advisor (note that this is part of the SQL Tuning Pack) to investigate the SQL in greater detail and recommend changes in the SQL. By clicking the Schedule SQL Tuning Advisor button, Oracle's Tuning Advisor is employed to tune any SQL in question and offer suggestions. In Figure 5-18, the recommendations are displayed for the worst

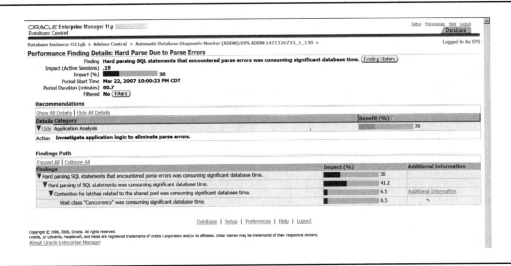

FIGURE 5-17. *ADDM Performance Finding Details for SQL*

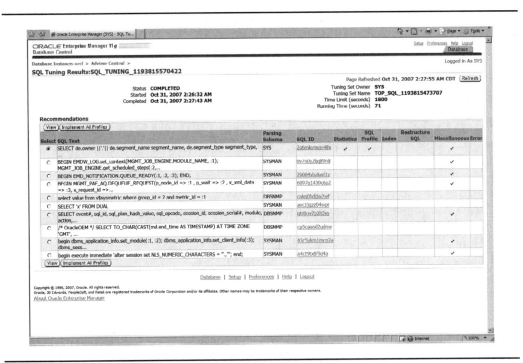

FIGURE 5-18. *SQL Tuning Advisor, SQL Tuning Results*

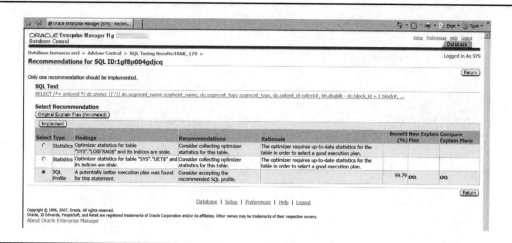

FIGURE 5-19. *SQL Tuning Advisor recommends a SQL Profile.*

SQL for a given SQL Tuning Set. The worst SQL seems like it will benefit from employing a SQL Profile and generating updated statistics.

By clicking the worst SQL, you can view the details of the recommendations (Figure 5-19). Employing the SQL Profile should help by 99.79 percent according to the recommendations. You can also click a link to compare the Explain Plans to see what is being changed and what the benefit will be.

The Explain Plans comparison shows that the order of table access has been changed as well as some of the joining methods. A HASH JOIN replaced a NESTED LOOPS JOIN, as seen in Figure 5-20.

TIP
Compare Explain Plans is a great SQL Tuning tool built into EM.

In Figure 5-21, you can check the SQL Statement statistics after the profile is employed. The system shows that the new SQL Profile substantially reduces the impact to the system that this particular SQL statement was having.

In Figure 5-22, it is evident from the Top Activity screen that the now-tuned SQL statement is no longer causing the negative impact (performance spike) that was previously felt. The entire system is now running much better, with fewer users waiting in the queue.

Database Instance Server Tab and Database Administration Tab

You'll find several tabs under the Database Instance Server or Cluster Database (depending on which one you select). Clicking the Server tab for EM Database Control or the Database Administration tab for Grid Control displays some very nice administration options. The scope of these options is well

Compare Explain Plans

Original Explain Plan (Annotated)
Indicates an adjustment from the original plan by the SQL Tuning Advisor
Plan Hash Value 2347322369

Expand All | Collapse All

Operation	Line ID	Object	Object Type	Order Rows	Bytes	Cost	Time	CPU Cost	I/O Cost
SELECT STATEMENT	0			121	0.270	983,655	11,804	12,350,714,281,984	168,630
SORT ORDER BY	1			120	0.270	983,655	11,804	12,350,714,281,984	168,630
NESTED LOOPS	2			119	0.270	983,654	11,804	12,350,698,553,344	168,630
HASH JOIN	3			7	1.708	1	1	8,647,788	0
NESTED LOOPS	4			5	0.176	1		710,600	0
VIEW	5			3	0.013	1		355,300	0
SORT AGGREGATE	6			2	0.059				
FIXED TABLE FULL	7	SYS.X$KSLLTR_CHILDREN	TABLE (FIXED)	1	120.000	1		355,300	0
FIXED TABLE FULL	8	SYS.X$KSLLTR_CHILDREN	TABLE (FIXED)	4	7.670	1		355,300	0
FIXED TABLE FULL	9	SYS.X$BH	TABLE (FIXED)	6	6.738	1		350,000	0
VIEW	10	SYS.DBA_EXTENTS	VIEW	118	0.114	89,423	1,074	1,122,790,014,976	15,330

New Explain Plan With SQL Profile
Plan Hash Value 2138758942

Expand All | Collapse All

Operation	Line ID	Object	Object Type	Order Rows	Bytes	Cost	Time	CPU Cost	I/O Cost
SELECT STATEMENT	0			124	0.262	1,972	24	702,635,712	1,926
SORT ORDER BY	1			123	0.262	1,972	24	702,635,712	1,926
HASH JOIN	2			122	0.262	1,971	24	687,481,920	1,926
HASH JOIN	3			7	1.568	1	1	8,647,788	0
NESTED LOOPS	4			5	0.176	0	1	710,600	0
VIEW	5			3	0.013	0	1	355,300	0
SORT AGGREGATE	6			2	0.059				
FIXED TABLE FULL	7	SYS.X$KSLLTR_CHILDREN	TABLE (FIXED)	1	120.000	0	1	355,300	0
FIXED TABLE FULL	8	SYS.X$KSLLTR_CHILDREN	TABLE (FIXED)	4	7.670	0	1	355,300	0
FIXED TABLE FULL	9	SYS.X$BH	TABLE (FIXED)	6	5.469	0	1	350,000	0
VIEW	10	SYS.DBA_EXTENTS	VIEW	121	18.229	1,970	24	671,240,320	1,926
UNION-ALL	11			120					
NESTED LOOPS	12			72	0.222	235	3	14,023,343	234

FIGURE 5-20. *Explain Plan comparison*

beyond this chapter, but you can get an idea from the screen in Figure 5-23 that some wonderful built-in tools are available to help the DBA work more effectively and efficiently. A couple of these frequently used options are displayed in this section of the chapter.

Under the Schema heading, you'll find information showing an individual schema (within a given instance) and the objects associated with that schema, including information about clusters, database links, functions, indexes, package bodies, packages, procedures, refresh groups (for snapshots), snapshots, synonyms, tables, triggers, and views. Multiple screens are associated with each choice. All of the columns for the given table can be displayed. All the storage information for the table (initial extent, next extent, pctincrease, minextents, maxextents, pctfree, and pctused) are also listed. The constraints, as well as options for adding or removing constraints, are available. There are options to allow for the enabling or disabling of constraints. Note that the number of rows and last analyzed date for all tables are displayed; this information shows up only if the table has been analyzed. The Show Object DDL option generates the create statement for a table or other object. Viewing the general information about an index such as the columns that are indexed and the index storage information is listed in this section.

TIP
The Schema information within the Oracle Enterprise Manager gives you a very quick way to look at tables and indexes when tuning the Oracle database.

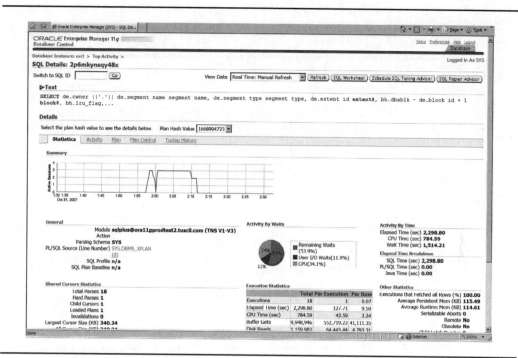

FIGURE 5-21.   *Top SQL Details—much better after tuning*

A new source of performance bottlenecks arrived with the advent of functions, packages, procedures, and triggers. At times, it is difficult to find the source code for a function, package, procedure, or trigger. With EM, the process is simplified by using the Schema links to select the code that is in question.

TIP
Use the Schema information to find code quickly to tune that is related to packages, procedures, and triggers for a given schema.

Database Instance Server Tab: Tablespaces

Clicking the Database Storage option Tablespaces while on the Administration tab will display the Tablespaces screen shown in Figure 5-24. This screen lists all of the tablespaces for this cluster database (or single instance if only a single instance is specified). Note the advancements in the product since Oracle 9*i*, including information on allocated and used space, the type of tablespace, extent management, and segment management. In 11*g*, you can move data to hot/cold portions of the disk (covered later in this chapter).

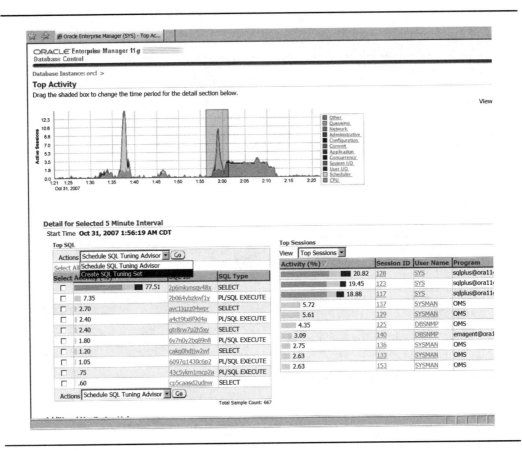

FIGURE 5-22. *Top Activity—better now!*

By clicking a specific tablespace (USERS in this example), the View Tablespace screen in Figure 5-25 is displayed. This screen includes additional information, including the actual datafile(s) underlying the tablespace. Also notice all the available pull-down Actions. Some of these are *very* powerful and huge time savers.

By choosing the Show Tablespace Contents from the pull-down menu, the screen in Figure 5-26 is displayed. This shows all of the segments that are contained in the given tablespace and is an excellent way to view objects that correspond to a heavily accessed tablespace.

Something more difficult to discover is the Extent Map. Clicking the Extent Map "+" sign (shown at the bottom of Figure 5-26) expands Show Tablespace Contents to display a *very cool* Extent Map, which is shown in Figure 5-27. This Extent Map provides a graphical view of all tablespaces, datafiles, segments, total data blocks, free data blocks, and percentage of free blocks available in the tablespace's current storage allocation. The tool gives you the option of displaying all segments for a tablespace or all segments for a datafile. The Extent Map also provides additional information for each segment, including average free space per block, chained rows, and the last date that the object was analyzed.

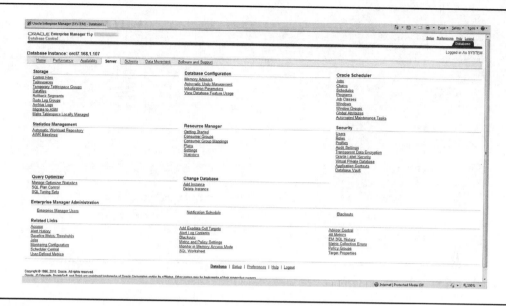

FIGURE 5-23.   *Database Instance Server Administration links*

TIP
The Extent Map, which displays the information in a tablespace block by block in a graphical manner, is a super-cool feature that's hard to find in EM.

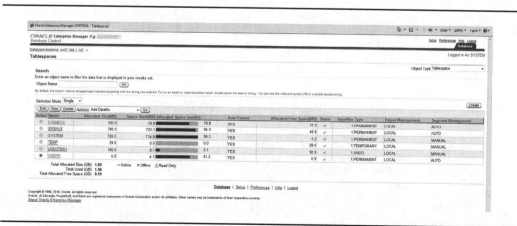

FIGURE 5-24.   *Database Instance Server links – Tablespaces*

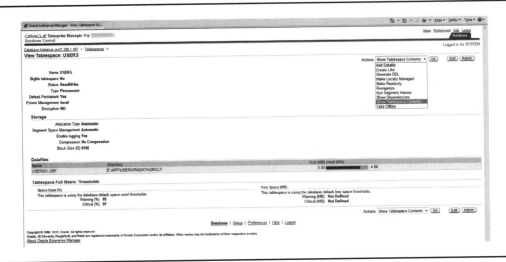

FIGURE 5-25. *Database Instance Server links for the USERS tablespace*

Database Instance Server Tab: Instance Level Focus

The Database Instance Server tab is useful for getting to many areas that are easier to change using EM instead of SQL (Figure 5-28). Items such as Manage Optimizer Statistics and Initialization Parameters are included at the cluster or instance level. But, at the instance level, there are also additional options, including the Automatic Workload Repository (AWR).

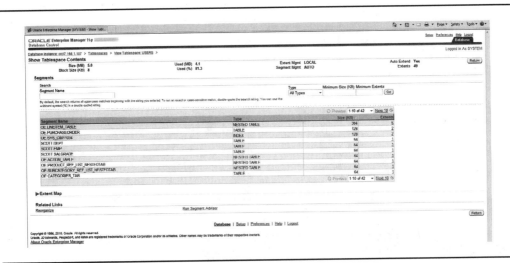

FIGURE 5-26. *Database Instance Server links – Show Tablespace Contents*

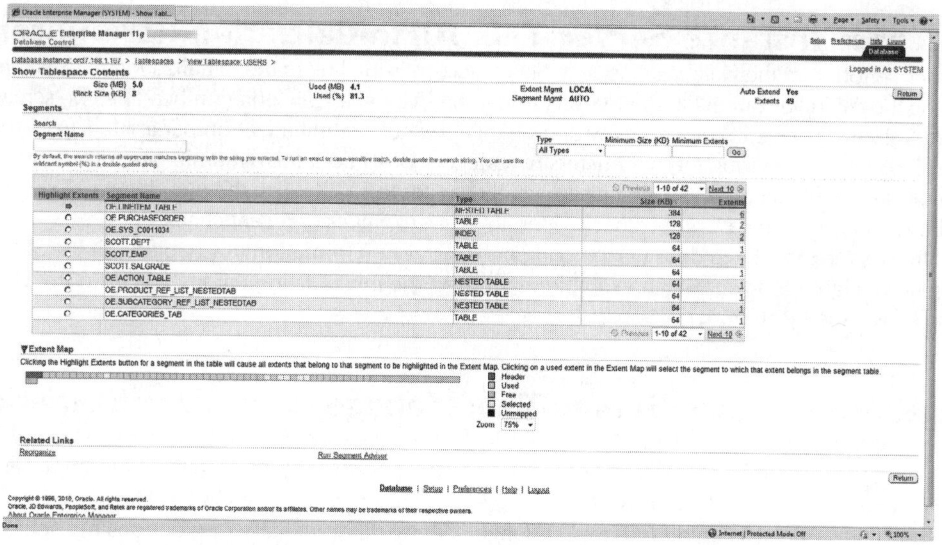

FIGURE 5-27. *Database Instance Server links – Extent Map*

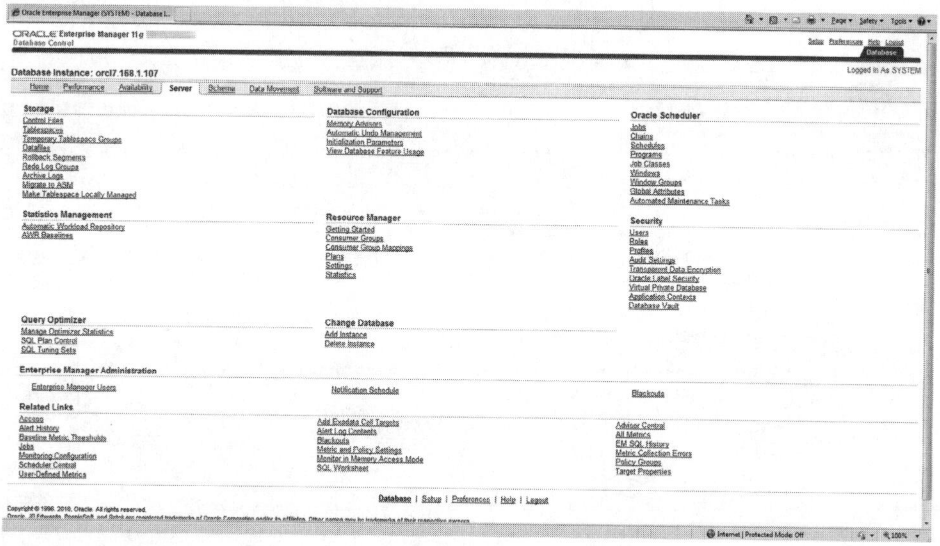

FIGURE 5-28. *Database Instance Server links*

Database Instance Server Tab: All Initialization Parameters

Another option from the Database Instance Server screen is the link to the Initialization parameters. By clicking the All Initialization Parameters link under the Database Configuration heading, the screen in Figure 5-29 is displayed. You can view and change the current initialization parameters from this screen. You can also group the parameters by category or sort out the dynamic parameters. In the example shown in Figure 5-29, the statistics level changes to TYPICAL in the pull-down menu. Other databases and/or instances can be checked for any current values or recent changes.

Clicking the SPFILE tab displays the contents (see more information in Chapter 4) if the SPFILE is being used. Figure 5-30 shows an example of viewing the initialization parameters from the SPFILE; it also shows the location.

Database Instance Server Tab: Manage Optimizer Statistics

Another option available from the Database Instance Server screen is the link to the Manage Optimizer Statistics Job screen (Figure 5-31). Keeping statistics up to date for dynamic tables can be a chore (worse if done for static tables too—don't do that). The Gather Statistics Job (GATHER_STATS_JOB) can help in this endeavor. Many different gathering options for optimizer statistics can be specified from this screen, as well as the scheduling and managing of specific jobs.

One option from the Database Instance Server screen, which exists only at the instance level (even with Database Administration in Grid Control), is the link to the Automatic Workload Repository (AWR). Once you click the AWR option from the Administration screen, the AWR General information is displayed. This screen includes information on all snapshots and collection levels.

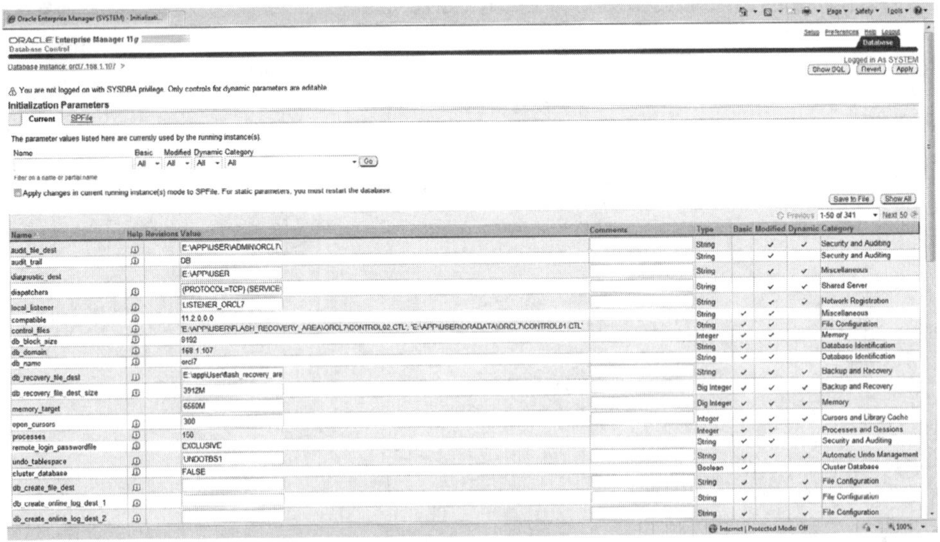

FIGURE 5-29. *Database Instance Server links – Current Initialization Parameters*

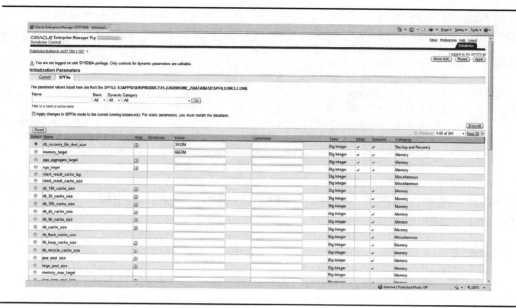

FIGURE 5-30. *Database Instance Server links – SPFILE Initialization Parameters*

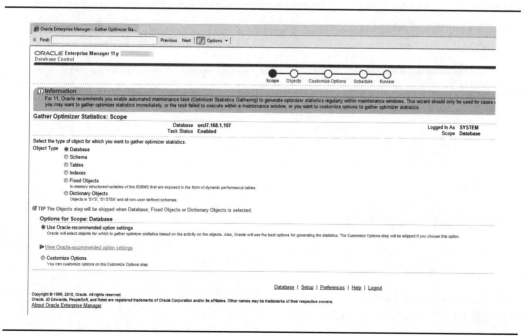

FIGURE 5-31. *Database Instance Server links – Manage Optimizer Statistics, Gather Optimizer Statistics*

See Chapter 14 for more on how snapshots work. In the example in Figure 5-32, there are 207 snapshots with a retention of 8 days and an interval of 60 minutes.

By clicking the Edit button (see Figure 5-32), you can change the interval or retention period. You can also edit the collection level.

Clicking the number of snapshots in the AWR General information screen (the number 207, as shown in Figure 5-33), displays the snapshots one at a time, as shown in Figure 5-34. The time that the snapshot was generated is listed along with the collection level.

Clicking any specific snapshot to begin and end with generates some basic snapshot details, as listed in Figure 5-35 (like a very mini-Statspack), or you can run and display an AWR report by clicking Report (covered in detail in Chapter 14—see that chapter for full display output).

Database Instance Server Tab: Resource Manager (Consumer Groups)

Another option available from the Administration screen is the link to the Consumer Groups under the Resource Management heading. Clicking this option displays a listing of Consumer Groups, as shown in Figure 5-36. A system that includes users in AR (Accounts Receivable), CRM (Customer Relationship Management), and BI (Business Intelligence) can be better visualized when services are set up for each of them (now it's easy to see who is using all of the resources). In Figure 5-36, you see a Batch Group as the second listing.

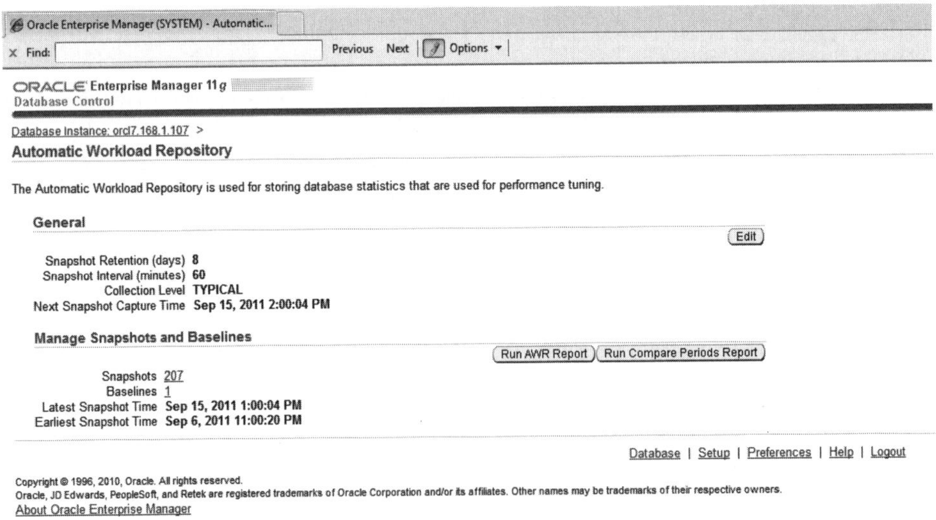

FIGURE 5-32. *Automatic Workload Repository (AWR)*

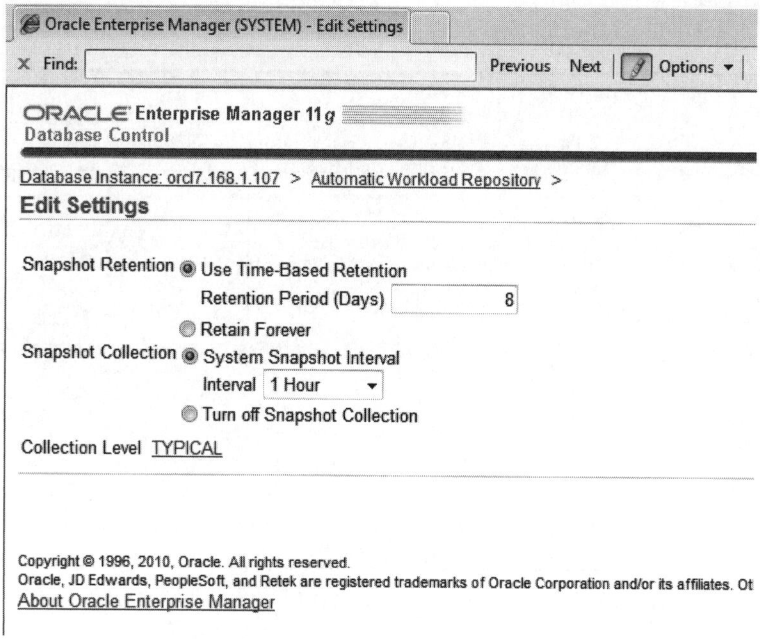

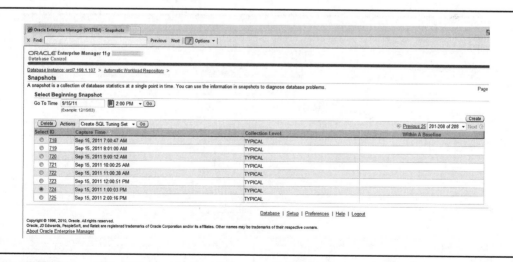

FIGURE 5-33. *Automatic Workload Repository (AWR) Edit settings*

FIGURE 5-34. *Automatic Workload Repository (AWR) Snapshot listing*

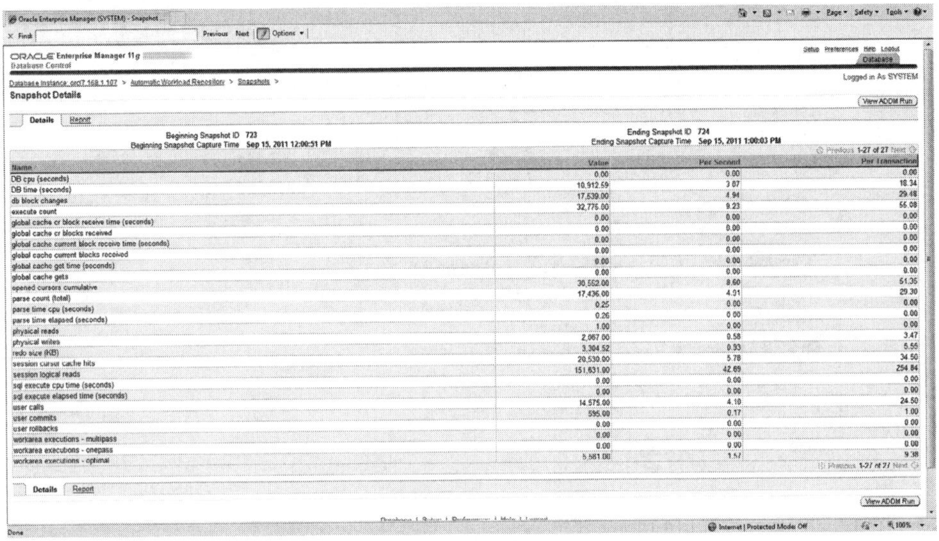

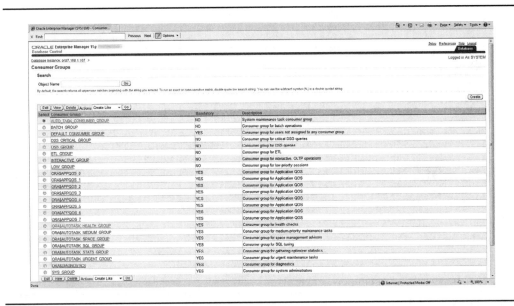

FIGURE 5-35. *Automatic Workload Repository (AWR) – Snapshot Details*

FIGURE 5-36. *Database Administration, Instance Level – Consumer Groups*

TIP
If you take the time to set up Services, you can use the Top Consumers screen to see quickly which business areas are consuming the most resources.

Database Maintenance Tab

The Maintenance tab also has several Administration links that are associated with maintenance, including Backup and Recovery, Data Guard, and Import/Export (see Figure 5-37). Once again, Oracle creates an excellent option to help make the DBA more productive. RAC and Exadata are covered in Chapter 11, but it's worth a quick look at a six-node cluster database that I have from 10gR2 to cover a few key points in the next few screens (note that you can use OEM 10gR2 Grid Control to manage an 11g database). Although the screenshots in this section are from 10gR2 (as well as in the "Monitoring the Application Server" and "Monitoring the Web Applications" sections), these are great examples that look at a many-node solution and the interconnect portion that are all worth investigating, as these are virtually the same in 11g.

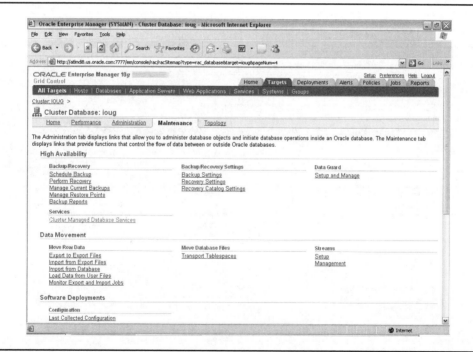

FIGURE 5-37. *Database Maintenance links*

Database Topology Tab

The Database Topology tab is something newer in the Oracle Grid Control product, but I've seen it in other software maintenance products. Figure 5-38 shows the topology for the six-node cluster that I'll work with in the Grid Control portion of this chapter. Notice that all tiers are shown for each of the nodes on the right part of the screen (Listener, ASM, Database, etc.) with detail information for the selected node on the left side of the screen. Something nice (not displayed) is information about the node, which pops up when the mouse rolls over one of the pictures in the right pane.

When, at the cluster level (note that Figure 5-38 is at the cluster database level), clicking the Interconnects tab shows information related to interconnect(s) between the nodes of a cluster (Figure 5-39). All six nodes and the corresponding interconnects are listed (complete with the subnet IP address). When there are interconnect performance issues, this screen is very helpful in identifying slow I/O transfer rates and/or errors.

Database Performance Tab

Click the Targets tab and then All Targets to select the ioug Cluster Database. Clicking the Performance tab displays the insightful graphs for this cluster and one of the main screens that can be used for tuning. The refresh rate can be set to 15 seconds (default), 1 minute, a manually

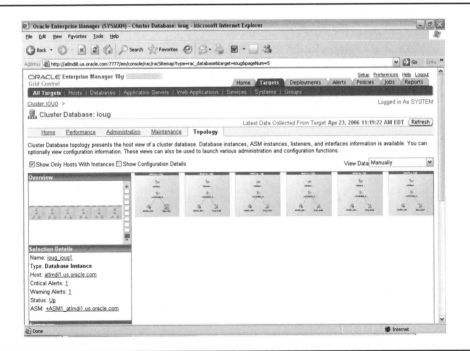

FIGURE 5-38. *Database Topology tab*

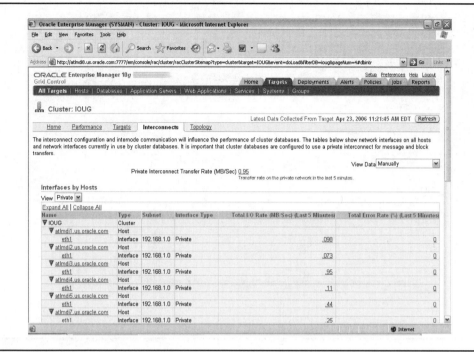

FIGURE 5-39.   *Cluster Interconnects detail*

specified time, or Historical (to see a week's worth of data—great stuff). This screen provides graphs for all major metrics related to tuning. Figure 5-40 shows the upper part of this screen. Clicking any individual graph displays a more detailed graph for the given performance metric. For example, Figure 5-42 displays the screen that results when the Cluster Host Load Average graph (first graph displayed in Figure 5-40) is selected. Note that in the Active Sessions, you can see a spike in Network Activity at about 11:10 A.M.

TIP
The Database or Cluster Performance Screen within EM is the quickest way to locate performance problems in your system.

Scrolling to the middle of the Cluster Database Performance screen, you'll see additional graphs and also many additional performance links (Figure 5-41). These include Database Locks, Top Sessions, Top Consumers, Cluster Cache Coherence, and Top Segments. Click each of these to drill into a specific problem. Below that, you'll see additional instance-level links, including Top Activity, Duplicate SQL, Blocking Sessions, Hang Analysis, Instance Activity, Search Sessions, Snapshots (quick link), and SQL Tuning Sets. Below those links are yet more links to the individual instances or directly to ASM. There are also links for each instance to Alerts, Policy Violations, and other Performance Statistics (I/O, CPU, etc.).

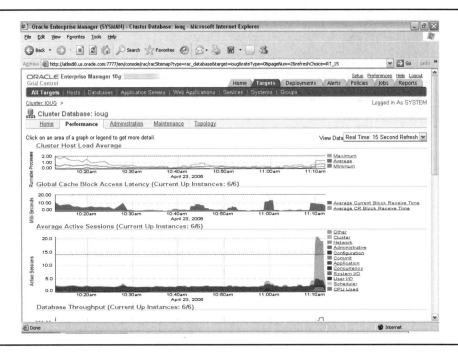

FIGURE 5-40. *Cluster Database Performance (top)*

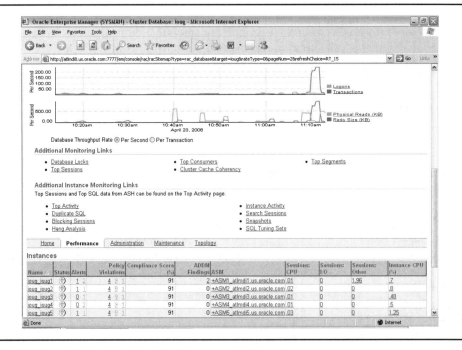

FIGURE 5-41. *Cluster Database Performance (mid-page)*

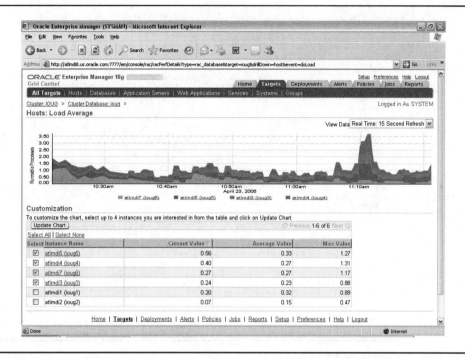

FIGURE 5-42.   *Cluster Database Performance – Load Average*

Clicking the Cluster Host Load Average graph in Figure 5-40 displays a larger version of that graph, which has a color for each of the nodes listed. In the example in Figure 5-42, there are four instances (on four physical nodes) in the ioug cluster that are displayed in the graph. Note that the instances are ioug3, ioug4, ioug5, and ioug6, and that the physical nodes that the instances reside on are atlmdi3, atlmdi4, atlmdi5, and atlmdi7. There could have been additional instances on these nodes from another database (but there was not in my test). The graph can show a maximum of four instances at one time, but you can choose which instances are displayed. The performance spike in this example at 11:10 A.M. occurred on two of the nodes.

Clicking the second graph in Figure 5-40 shows interconnect issues. The global cache block access latency and transfers have to do with sending blocks from one instance to another instance. Clicking the Cluster Cache Coherency link on the Cluster Database Performance screen (Figure 5-40) also displays this screen. In Figure 5-43, the number of block transfers increases greatly at about 11:10 A.M. Any block access latency over 20 ms should be cause to investigate further. Fixing this issue could involve tuning the query that is causing many blocks to be either read or transferred, getting a faster interconnect, eliminating any locking that is slowing the transfer (one instance hanging on to the block), or ensuring that you are using the private (not the public) interconnect.

The third graph shown in Figure 5-40, the Active Sessions graph, shows a large number of cluster waits. By clicking the Cluster link to the right of the graph, the detailed graph of all cluster waits is displayed (Figure 5-44). Here you can see many Global Cache (or gc)–type waits associated with this graph at a couple of times during the hour displayed. Below the graph, you

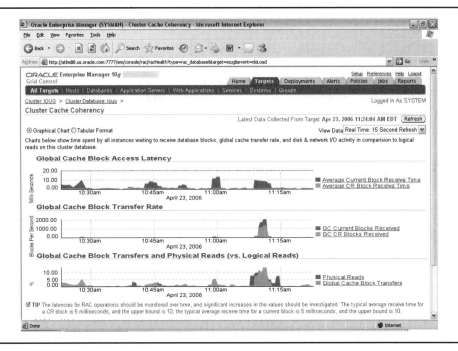

FIGURE 5-43. *Cluster Cache Coherency*

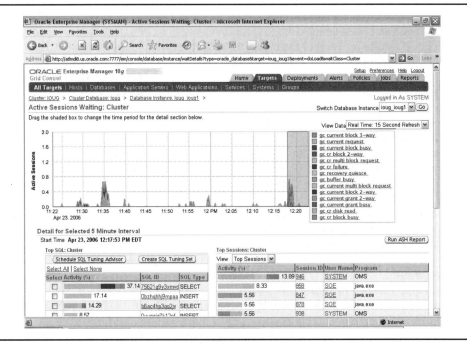

FIGURE 5-44. *Active Sessions Waiting – Cluster*

can see the actual Top SQL queries that are being run as well as the Top Sessions of the users who are running the queries. Note that this screen shows *only* the Top SQL and Top Sessions for Cluster waits. Once again, this very colorful screen shows each wait in a different color to make it very intuitive to use for tuning.

TIP
The Top SQL and Top Sessions section of the Database/Cluster Performance screen instantly tells you where the performance issues are and which users are consuming all of the resources.

By clicking the link to the right of the graph on "gc current block busy" wait, you are instantly transferred to the histogram for this wait to see if the waits are many short waits or fewer long waits. In this case, some of the waits are short (1–2 ms) and others are long (32 ms and longer) in the histogram shown in Figure 5-45. Later in this chapter, you will see a histogram for "db file sequential read" waits, where most of the waits are very short in duration, whereas a histogram of locking issues will reveal only long waits.

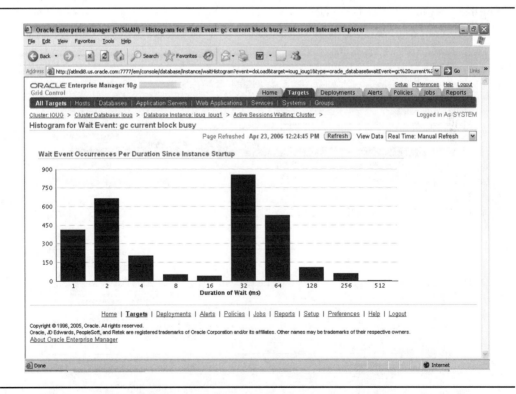

FIGURE 5-45. *Wait Events histogram for "gc current block busy" waits*

At the bottom of the Active Sessions Screen shown in Figure 5-44, the Top SQL statement (SQL ID = 75621g9y3xmvd) can be selected and the SQL statement for this query and the associated waits for it are displayed (Figure 5-46). We can see that this SQL statement is causing most of the global cache activity. The Top SQL section is a powerful tool to quickly find the most troublesome users and/or queries on a given system.

The second-worst SQL statement listed is also a potential problem. Figure 5-47 shows the second worst statement (SQL ID = 0bzhqhhj9mpaa) listed in the Top SQL section. Perhaps a look at the link to the "db file sequential read" to the right of the graph to see the histogram for these waits will provide some insight to the query.

TIP
Use the Top SQL section to find the sessions that are using the most resources on a system. By investigating a problem session in more detail, it is easy to free up resources for other processes.

Clicking the "db file sequential read" link displays the histogram in Figure 5-48. This shows that most of the waits are very fast. If these were slow, it would be worth checking the I/O or the size of the cache (to see if it can cache all needed blocks or if it is too small, causing additional I/O). Tuning the query that is causing the waits may limit the number of reads required (see Chapter 14 for details on how to fix different types of wait events).

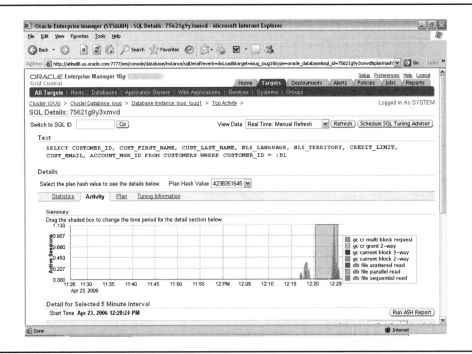

FIGURE 5-46. *Top SQL – SQL Details for worst SQL (SQL ID = 75621g9y3xmvd)*

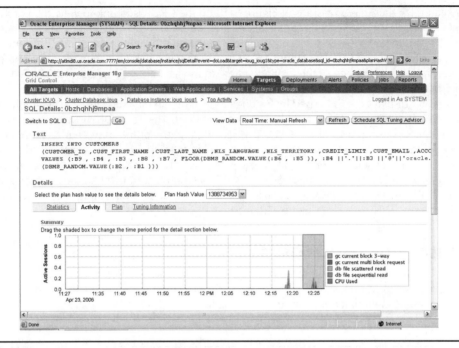

FIGURE 5-47. *Top SQL – SQL Details for second worst SQL (SQL ID = 0bzhqhhj9mpaa)*

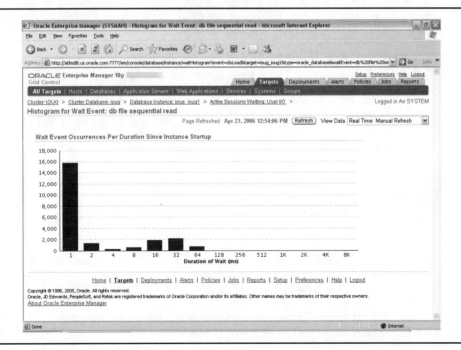

FIGURE 5-48. *Wait Event histogram for "db file sequential read" waits*

You can click the Active Sessions of Figure 5-40 on the CPU Used link to view the graph that displays CPU Used for each of the four instances that are up and running (Figure 5-49). Since a batch job is running on the worst instance, you decide to investigate the ioug_ioug2 instance to see what is driving up the CPU consumption on that instance. Clicking *either* the color of the graph that shows this instance *or* the instance name in the list below the graph will take you to an individual CPU graph for that given instance.

Figure 5-50 displays the CPU used by instance ioug_ioug2 in the ioug cluster. The graph shows that the amount of CPU has risen quickly over the past hour. The Top SQL shows clearly that a single statement is using most of the CPU. The rectangle in the graph may be placed/moved anywhere for the period (a slide bar may appear that allows you to move the rectangle—depending on the version you're using), in which case the Top SQL is only for that given five-minute interval.

By clicking the Top SQL statement (SQL ID = 07p193phmhx3z), you can see, as shown in Figure 5-51, that this is the PL/SQL that is using up all of the CPU. Your tuning efforts should focus directly on this statement to fix the CPU issue.

Monitoring the Hosts

While the Top SQL is usually the problem, digging into other areas of the infrastructure can quickly reveal issues. The Hosts tab under Targets displays all of the hosts out there. In this example, there are eight different hosts in the listing in Figure 5-52.

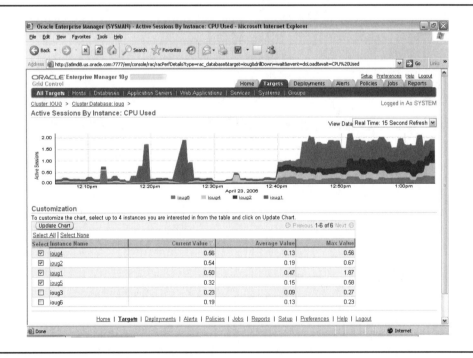

FIGURE 5-49. *Active Sessions By Instance – CPU Used*

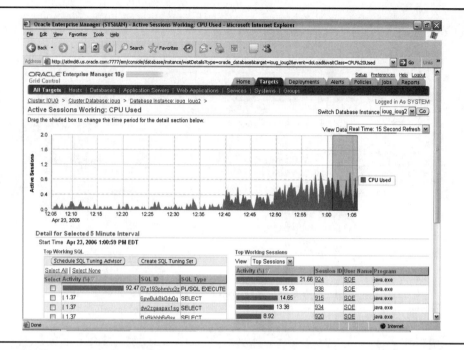

FIGURE 5-50. *Active Sessions by Instance – CPU Used on the ioug_ioug2 instance*

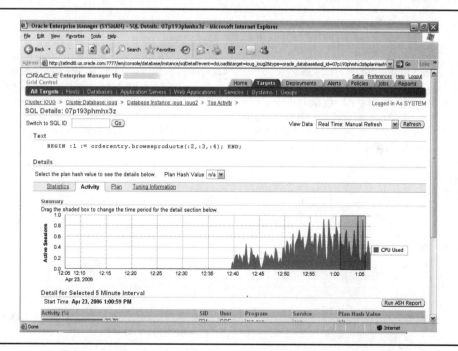

FIGURE 5-51. *Active Sessions by Instance – CPU Used for SQL ID = 07p193phmhx3z*

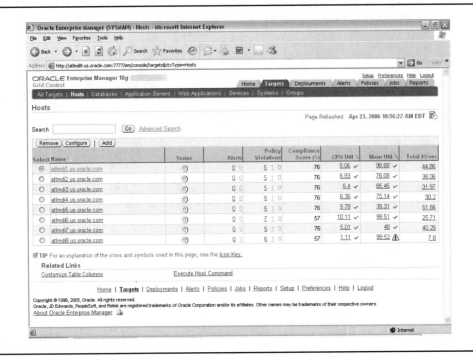

FIGURE 5-52. *The Hosts tab*

Clicking just one of the hosts (atlmdi1) displays all of the detailed information about that host. This includes the IP address, the OS (operating system), the number of CPUs, the amount of memory, the available disk space, how many users are logged on, and the availability of the system. It also shows any Alerts or Policy violations as it did at the database or instance level. Figure 5-53 shows that the host is currently UP.

By clicking the Availability link, the complete availability of this host is displayed over a period of time. In Figure 5-54, the host shown has been down over 27 percent of the time, yet the downtime occurred during the night (perhaps a maintenance window that requires a blackout to be set up).

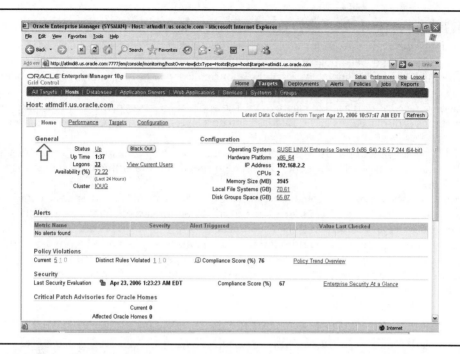

FIGURE 5-53.   *The Hosts tab—viewing information about a host*

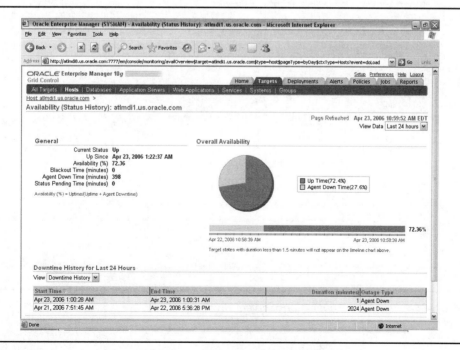

FIGURE 5-54.   *The Hosts tab—viewing information about host availability*

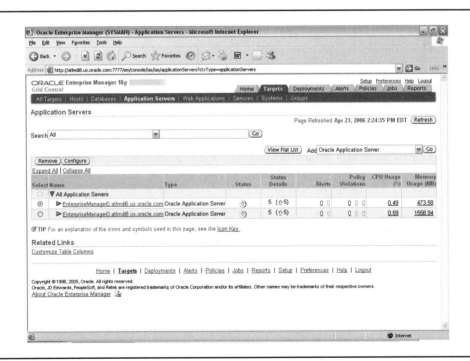

Monitoring the Application Servers

While database and host monitoring was crucial to the performance of client/server systems in the 1990s, the Internet and web applications have driven performance issues at the application-server level over the last decade. Finding issues at the application-server level (usually where the actual code is running) is critical to good performance. EM offers an Application Server tab to monitor all application servers, as displayed in Figure 5-55. The application server name as well as CPU and memory usage is displayed. As at the database and host levels, alerts and policy violations are also listed.

Clicking a specific application server (atlmdi6.us.oracle.com) displays the response time as well as component-level information in a screen specific to the application server chosen (Figure 5-56).

Perhaps the best information comes from clicking the Performance tab for a specific component. In Figure 5-57, the EM Application OC4J (Oracle Components for Java) performance is displayed showing Servlet and Java Server Pages (JSP) performance.

The Performance tab for the entire application server is displayed in Figure 5-58 and Figure 5-59. These screens are absolutely outstanding for getting a glimpse of CPU, memory, web cache, HTTP response, HTTP active connections, and servlet response time.

FIGURE 5-55. *Targets – Applications Servers*

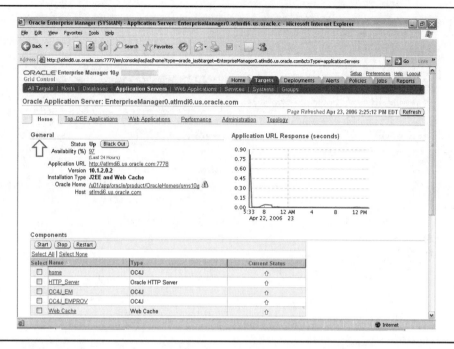

FIGURE 5-56.   *Targets – Applications Servers – specific server information*

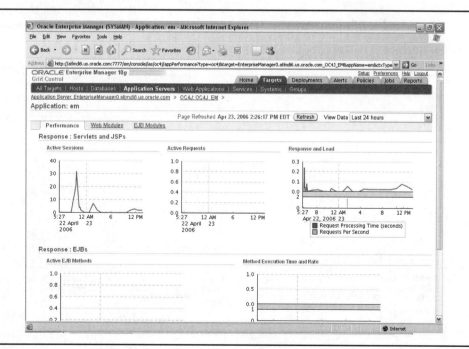

FIGURE 5-57.   *Targets – Applications Servers – OC4J performance*

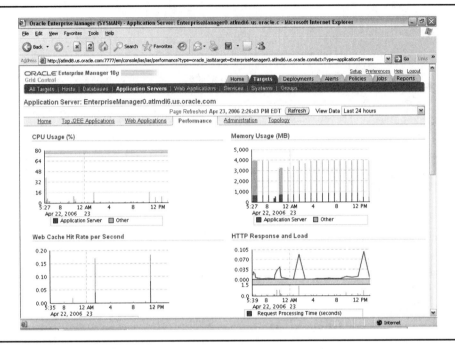

FIGURE 5-58. *Targets – specific application server performance*

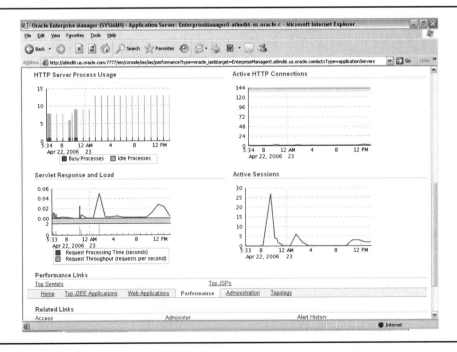

FIGURE 5-59. *Targets – specific application server performance (lower page)*

TIP
The application server is where performance problems now hide.
EM has many tools to view application server and web application
performance.

The Administration tab for the application server displays a plethora of options for configuration as well as maintenance (Figure 5-60). A Topology tab can be selected to display a topology diagram similar to that shown in the "Database Topology Tab" section.

Figure 5-61 shows a potential problem on the application server; the amount of memory usage has risen exponentially over the past hour. This could be due to an increasing number of connections or just one bad user eating up a lot of memory.

FIGURE 5-60.   *Targets – specific application server Administration tab*

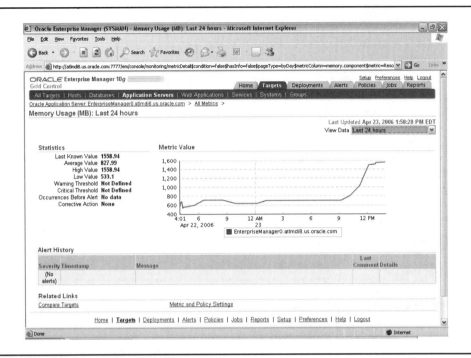

FIGURE 5-61. *Specific application server "All Metrics" Memory Usage*

Monitoring the Web Applications

One of the nicest aspects of EM is that you can monitor a piece of the infrastructure or investigate a specific program that is causing performance issues. In this section, viewing the web application itself will be discussed. By clicking the Targets tab and then the Web Applications tab, all of the information about a given web application is displayed. EM shows whether the application is up or down, how long it's been up, its availability, related topology, alerts, and a variety of performance information, as displayed in Figure 5-62.

EM also tests the performance of a given web application by allowing beacons to run at various times to measure its performance. These beacons are representative queries of what a user may be doing on a regular basis. Now the DBA knows when an application is slow because he or she will also be running a query that is similar to the user's query on a regular basis. Figure 5-63 shows the EM screen that displays the test performance of the beacon over a period of several hours. Not only can the performance of the application be measured, but also spikes in performance can be pinpointed for future evaluation.

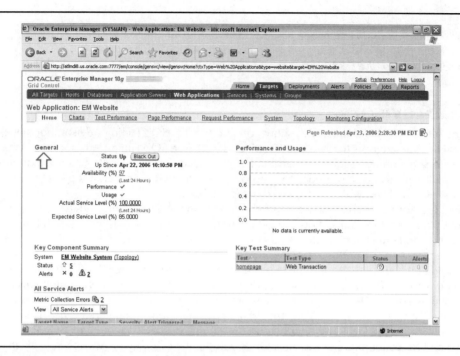

FIGURE 5-62. *Targets – specific web application*

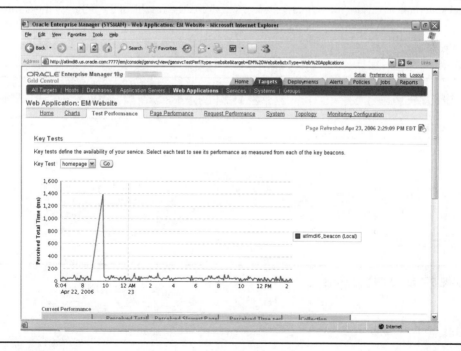

FIGURE 5-63. *Targets – specific web application test performance*

TIP
When a user finds that he or she has executed a problem query and needs the DBA to end it, a kill session screen is available and an excellent tool for the DBA to use (or you can still use SQL*Plus).

SQL Advisors

In many sections of this chapter, I've shown output from the SQL Tuning Advisor, but there are a couple of other advisors that are worth noting as well. The SQL Tuning Advisor (and also the Automatic SQL Tuning Results for high-load SQL) is used to tune a single statement or groups of statements and give recommendations as shown throughout the chapter. It is part of the SQL Advisors section of EM, which is displayed in Figure 5-64.

The SQL Access Advisor is used less frequently than the SQL Tuning Advisor but is more helpful than most DBAs think. You can get great recommendations on Indexes, Materialized Views, and Partitioning, and it offers a great way to investigate structural issues. Figure 5-65 shows the SQL Access Advisor main screen.

Wouldn't it be nice to get an Oracle patch immediately when an ORA-600 is encountered? You bet it would! Now, you have a way to do it. The SQL Repair Advisor will *potentially* allow you to bypass errors by having Oracle take a different route through compilation and execution, trying to find an error free path. While the original problem you encountered is not fixed (you should still log it into My Oracle Support and log a bug if needed), a temporary SQL Patch can be used and stored for future executions. Once you run the SQL Repair Advisor for a given error, if a solution is found, Oracle returns it in the SQL Repair Results (Figure 5-66). You can then choose to apply the SQL patch (prior to applying it, Oracle shows you the performance differential with the original statement to ensure it is still an efficient solution). The results of the SQL are the same; what differs is the way Oracle performs the query internally.

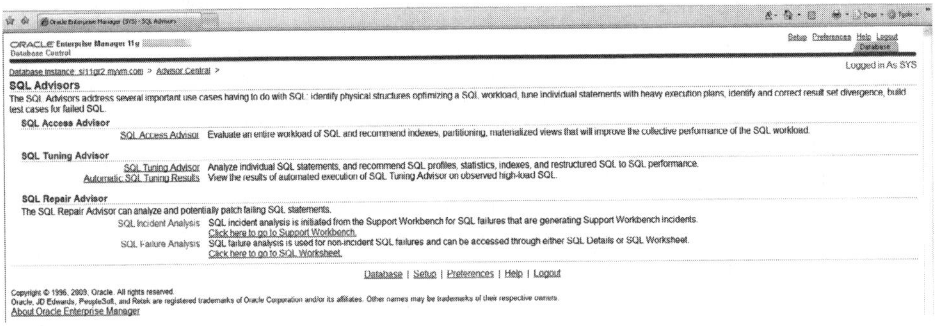

FIGURE 5-64. *SQL Advisors*

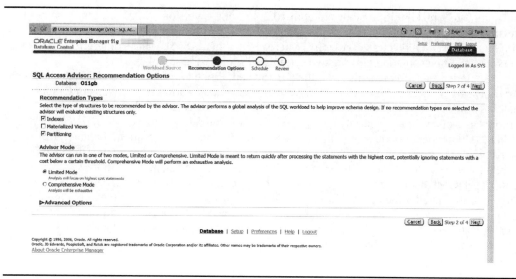

FIGURE 5-65.   *SQL Access Advisor*

Deployments Tab (Patching Options)

I've often received e-mails from DBAs who say they have a machine that runs an application well, but when they move it to a machine that is set up *exactly* the same, performance changes and they don't know why. Of course, the answer is that something is different on one of the systems. So I end up doing a line-by-line comparison of the two environments to find out what actually differs. Despite their claim that things are exactly the same, I usually discover many things are different (so many that I am often amazed that anyone claimed they were the same). Now a wonderful EM screen is available under the Deployments tab where you can compare two Oracle deployments to find out how they measure up against each other. The screen shows what's different in the hardware (all the way down to the chipset), the OS version, and the Oracle database version, as well as any other software such as one of the Agents or Clusterware versions.

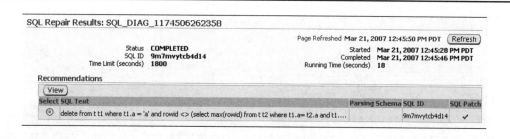

FIGURE 5-66.   *SQL Repair Results—a SQL patch is available!*

260 Oracle Database 11g Release 2 Performance Tuning Tips & Techniques

In Figure 5-67, the Oracle versions are both 10.2, but one is version 10.2.0.1.0 and the other is version 10.2.0.2.0. One machine is using dual x86_64 CPUs, whereas the other is using a single i686 CPU. One is Red Hat Linux, whereas the other is SuSE. These differences are not uncommon when someone tells me two systems are exactly the same!

Also under the Deployments tab is the Deployment Procedure Manager and with it the Patch Advisory section of EM. Depending on how you set this up, it allows notifications of Oracle patches as they become available for a specific environment. This includes patch upgrades to the product as well as Oracle Security Patches, which are often referred to as *critical patch updates (CPUs),* which come out quarterly on a prespecified day. One cool feature in the Patch Advisory is that you can set up a connection to My Oracle Support and scan for all patches that can be applied to your system. Then you can download the patches and stage them in the ORACLE_HOME directory for EM automatically. The entire Deployment Procedure Manager (Figure 5-68) includes the Patch Prerequisite Checker, Rolling Patch for Clusterware, One Click Extend Cluster Database, Patch RAC all nodes, Scale down RAC, Patch RAC Rolling, and Patch Oracle Database. There are stipulations for each of these, so please refer to the appropriate documentation if you plan to use one of these.

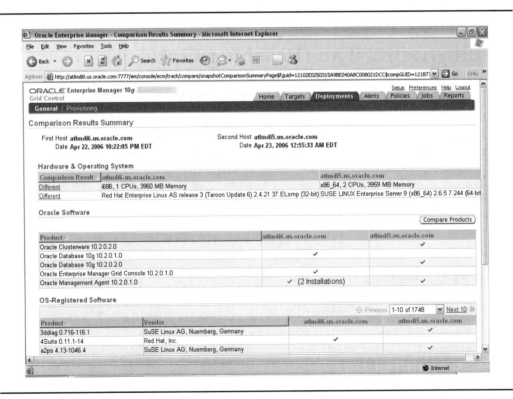

FIGURE 5-67. *Deployments—comparing two hosts*

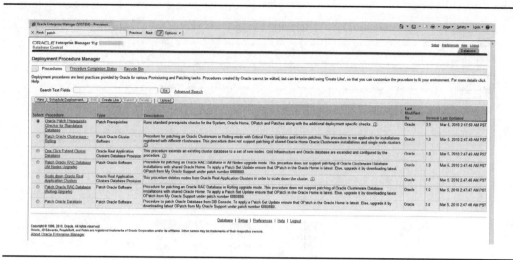

FIGURE 5-68. *Deployment Procedure Manager and critical patch advisories*

Scheduler Central and the Jobs Tab

Scheduler Central contains all scheduled tasks. It also includes links for the Oracle Scheduler, Jobs, and Automated Maintenance tasks (Figure 5-69). By clicking the Jobs tab, the job activity and all jobs are listed. It will show the time that each job will execute, as well as the target system on which the job will execute.

Clicking the Automatic SQL Tuning Scheduled task displays a spectacular screen (Figure 5-70) that shows the tuning result summary of everything that can be tuned and how you can improve

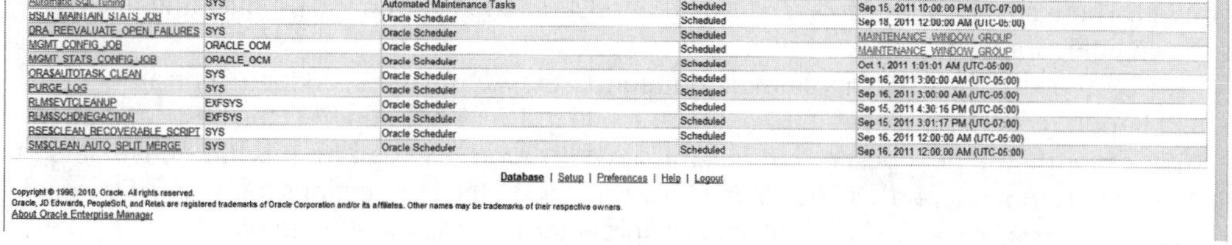

FIGURE 5-69. *Scheduler Central*

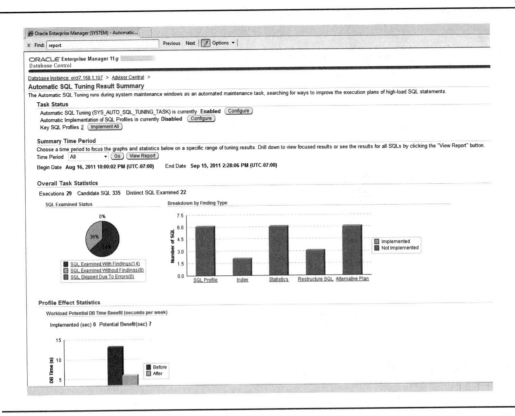

FIGURE 5-70. *Automatic SQL Tuning Result Summary*

performance. My Automatic SQL Tuning task ran every night from 10 PM to 2 AM and produced these results.

Reports Tab

The last part of EM to see is perhaps the best section of all, and that is the Reports section of EM. Many DBAs spend a lot of time writing reports when Oracle has already written almost all of the reports you need. On the Reports tab, you will find reports for pretty much anything ever required. There are about five to six pages of reports included within the product (the first page is shown in Figure 5-71).

The best report IMHO (in my humble opinion) is the Automatic Workload Repository (AWR) Report, covered in detail in Chapter 14 for 11g. The AWR Report is the best-generation Statspack report. The next best report is a mini-AWR report (as I call it). It is the Active Session History Report (ASH Report). It shows in a very quick way the key sections found in a Statspack or AWR report. Figure 5-72 shows the main choices for running the ASH Report.

Once the ASH Report has been generated clicking the Generate Report button, the ASH Report is displayed on the screen (Figure 5-73). The output looks very similar to the AWR Report, but it's a much smaller report.

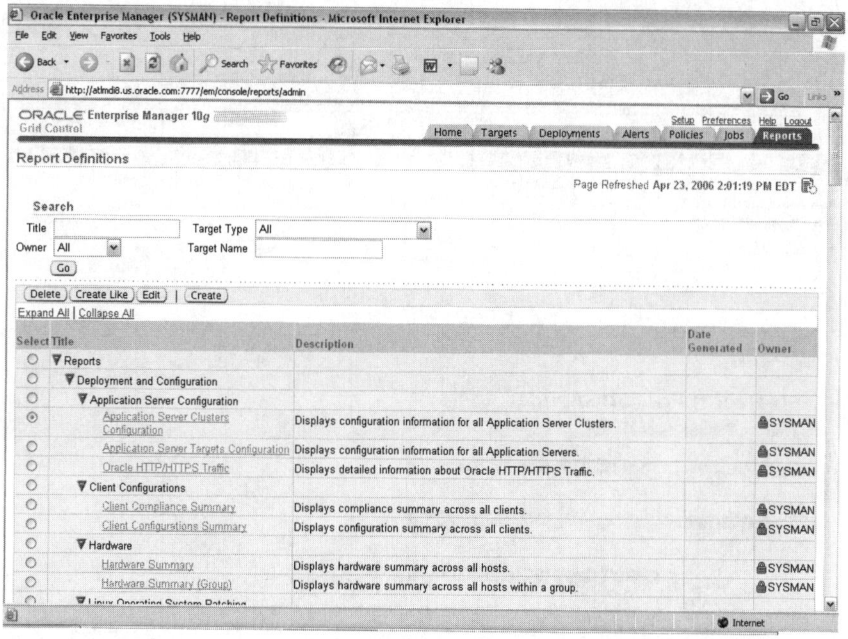

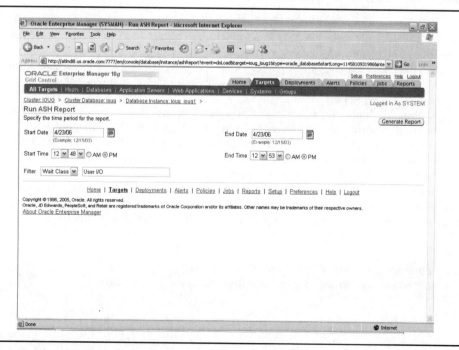

FIGURE 5-71. *The Reports tab*

FIGURE 5-72. *Running the ASH (Active Session History) Report*

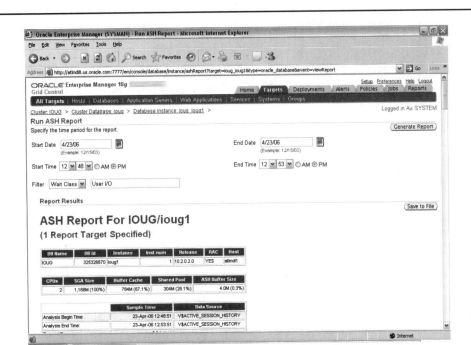

FIGURE 5-73. *The ASH Report output*

Some of the information in the ASH Report includes various Top Events and Load Profile (Figure 5-74), as in a Statspack or AWR Report. While the details of this report are beyond the scope of this chapter, please refer to Chapter 14 for tuning wait events and detailed information on the AWR Report, which includes much of the same information that will help in understanding the ASH Report.

Also, within the Tuning Pack, you will find a product called SQL Access Advisor (SAA). SAA can be used for tuning the entire workload (not just high-load SQL statements). SAA gives recommendations on how to improve performance of a workload through indexes (bitmap, b-Tree, functional, and concatenated), materialized views/logs, and a combination of these. SAA considers the cost of DML in terms of index maintenance and storage when it recommends additional access structure. SAA can also be used during the development phase to figure out what access structures are required before production deployment. You can use SQL Tuning Sets as input to SAA. Please check the Oracle documentation for additional information.

TIP
The Active Session History (ASH) report is a new and simple report that can be used to find and diagnose performance problems quickly.

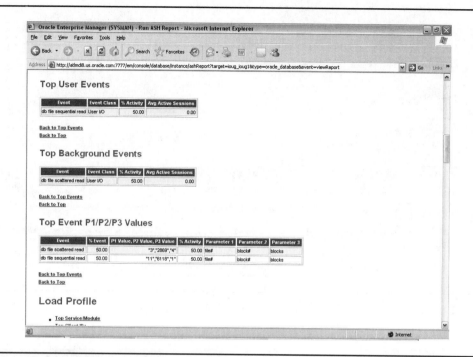

FIGURE 5-74. *The ASH Report output farther down the page*

Automatic Storage Management Performance

With the advent of Oracle's Automatic Storage Management (ASM), Oracle added many EM screens to assist in managing this new feature. ASM is covered in detail in Chapter 3, but here I show a couple of the screens for ASM as they are certainly helpful. In Figure 5-75, the main ASM home for a node shows that this instance of ASM is servicing the si11gr2.myvm.com (virtual machine) instance. The ASM instance is UP.

By clicking a specific disk group (DATA in this case), detailed information on disk usage is displayed, as well as information for all disks (DATA01_1, DATA01_2) in the disk group (Figure 5-76).

A new option allows you to move data to a hot or cold region of the physical disk. Simply check the box you desire (Figure 5-77 in the upper-right portion of the screen) to choose hot or cold based on the data access pattern.

TIP
The quickest and easiest way to monitor ASM is through EM.

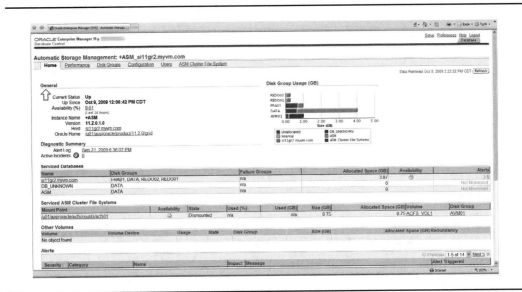

FIGURE 5-75. *Automatic Storage Management (ASM) home page*

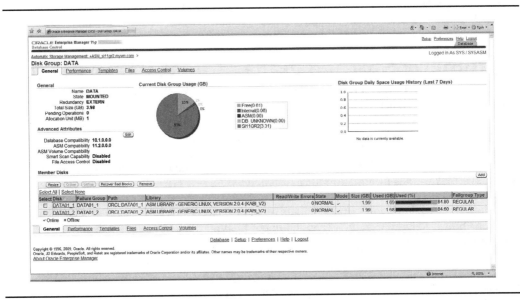

FIGURE 5-76. *The ASM Disk Group home page*

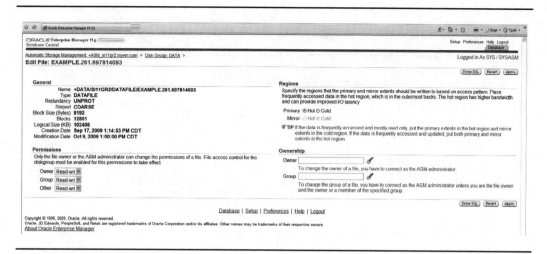

FIGURE 5-77. *Data disk group details, hot and cold regions*

Real Application Testing (Database Replay)

Oracle now has an incredible new option: Real Application Testing, which captures the *database workload* on one system (usually your current system) and replays it later on a different system (your future system). The Database Replay option is part of the Software and Support tab (Figure 5-78).

This is a great tool for testing upgrades to 11*g*—capture 10*g*R2 and then test against 11*g*. I recommend taking a full Oracle class on this to understand it fully.

Here are the steps in brief:

1. Capture workload on a database from 10*g* or 9.2.0.8 (Figure 5-79)

2. Restore the database on a test system to the SCN when capture begins.

3. Perform upgrade and make changes to the test system as needed.

4. Preprocess the captured workload if it is not preprocessed.

5. Configure the test system for replay (consider outside systems accessed/users … etc.).

6. Replay workload on the restored database.

7. Compare your results (Figure 5-80).

You can compare your results using a few different options. You can run a Synchronized Replay that replays everything with exact concurrency and commits with minimal data divergence. You can also perform an Unsynchronized Replay, which replays without the same concurrency or commits. Also, tdata divergence can be large depending on the load test performed. A report is created based on Data Divergence, Error Divergence, and Performance Divergence. A section of the report comparing the elapsed time is shown in Figure 5-80.

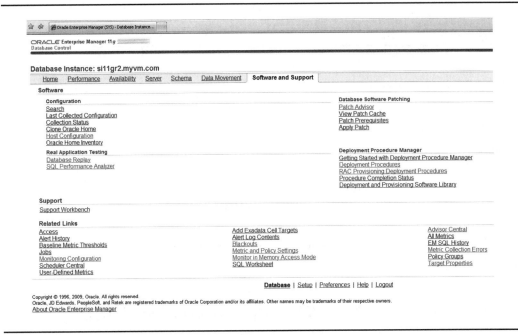

FIGURE 5-78. *Database Replay on the Software and Support tab*

TIP
A great way to test how your system will perform on new hardware or with a new version of Oracle is to use Oracle's Real Application Testing (Database Replay).

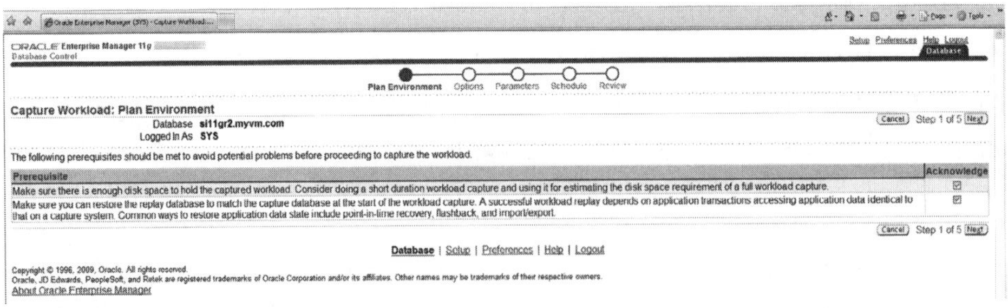

FIGURE 5-79. *Database Replay options – Capture Workload*

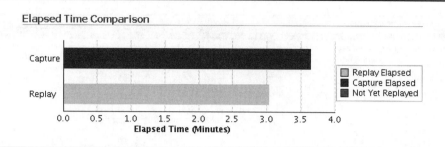

FIGURE 5-80. *Comparing elapsed time with Real Application Testing*

EM for Exadata

A new add-in for Exadata looks at performance related to Exadata. Keep in mind that an Exadata RAC Database Cluster is much the same as a RAC Database Cluster in Grid Control. You can also look at Exadata-specific hardware components, such as the Storage Server using the Exadata add-in for EM. In Figure 5-81, all three Exadata Storage Servers are currently UP.

You can also look at detailed information about a single Storage Server cell. Figure 5-82 shows the Cell Offload Efficiency (how much Exadata is helping; see Chapter 11 for detailed Exadata information), Cell Read/Write Throughput, and Cell Small Read Latency. Within EM,

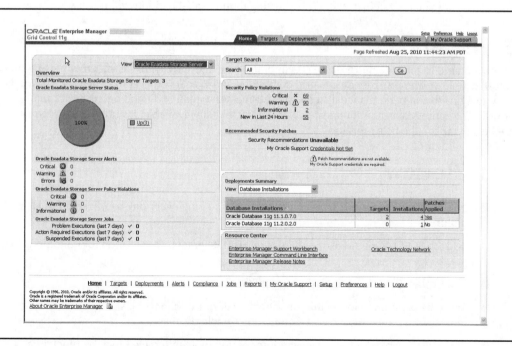

FIGURE 5-81. *Monitoring the Exadata Storage Server*

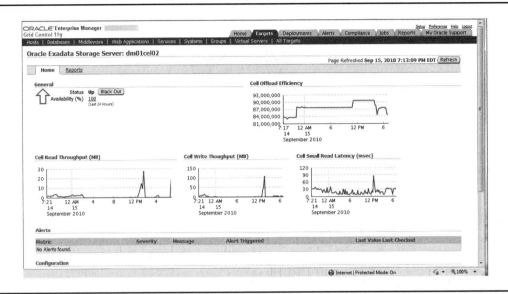

FIGURE 5-82. *Exadata Storage Server—monitoring an individual storage cell*

there are many Exadata screens that show detailed Exadata-specific information, for instance, Smart Scans. If you are familiar with EM, adjusting to the Exadata add-in will be easy.

Summary

DBAs are able to manage more databases and also manage systems more effectively using this versatile tool, which now extends into grid computing and Exadata. This comprehensive knowledge of system health and performance also enables businesses to plan and trend out usage for future growth. Enterprise Manager is the most powerful Oracle utility available. It's not just for beginners; the better you are, the better this tool is.

Tips Review

- In EM, the online help is spectacular. Learn something every day by clicking the Help button.

- Use the SQL Tuning Advisor only to tune SQL statements, not to monitor conditions like row locks.

- The Explain Plan Comparison is a great SQL Tuning tool built into EM.

- The schema information within the Oracle Enterprise Manager is a very quick way to look at tables and indexes when tuning the Oracle database.

- The Extent Map, which displays the information in a tablespace block by block in a graphical manner, is a super-cool feature that's hard to find in EM.

- If you take the time to set up Services, the Top Consumers screen can be used to see quickly which business areas are consuming the most resources.

- The Database or Cluster Performance screen within EM is the quickest way to locate performance problems in your system.

- The Top SQL and Top Sessions section of the Database/Cluster Performance screen instantly tells you where the performance issues are and which users are consuming all of the resources.

- The application server is the new hiding area for performance problems. EM has many tools for viewing application server and web application performance.

- The Active Session History (ASH) report is a new and simple report that you can use to find and diagnose performance problems quickly.

- The quickest and easiest way to monitor ASM is through EM.

- A great way to test how your system will perform on new hardware or with a new version of Oracle is to use Oracle's Real Application Testing (Database Replay).

References

Anil Khilani, *Oracle Troubleshooting Script.*
Rich Niemiec, *Tuning the Oracle Grid* (IOUG Collaborate 2011).
Rich Niemiec, *Tuning the Oracle Grid* (Oracle Open World 2010).
Rich Niemiec, *Exadata 101* (Oracle Open World 2010/2011).
Oracle Enterprise Manager Reference Manual (Oracle Corporation).
Tuning Pack 2.0 (Oracle White Paper).

Many thanks to Anil Khilani, Prabhaker Gongloor (GP), Valerie K. Kane, and David LeRoy of Oracle, who contributed a couple of the screen shots and a bit of the verbiage to this chapter. I want to also thank Ken Morse of Oracle, who contributed the majority of the screen shots and verbiage in the first tuning book on SQL Analyze, Oracle Expert, and Tuning Pack 2.0. Ken was a tremendous help in completing this chapter the first time around, while Valerie and David were instrumental the second time around.

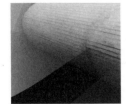

CHAPTER
6

Using EXPLAIN and SQL PLAN MANAGMENT (Developer and DBA)

TIPS & COVERED

F inding and fixing problem queries has a lot to do with using the tools that are available. Different tools need to be used for different situations. The tools covered in this chapter are Oracle's provided utilities: SQL TRACE (deprecated, but still works in 11g), TKPROF, EXPLAIN PLAN, and STORED OUTLINES (also known as PLAN STABILITY). With Oracle 10g, these tools were enhanced, including the addition of the DBMS_MONITOR and DBMS_SESSION packages and TRCSESS. The SQL tracing options have been centralized and extended using the DBMS_MONITOR package. Starting with Oracle 11g, SQL PLAN MANAGEMENT has been added and stored outlines are now called SQL Plan Baselines. Stored outlines still work but are deprecated (discouraged) and will probably be gone for good in a future release.

The tips covered in this chapter include the following:

- Simple steps for using SQL TRACE/TKPROF

- Sections of the SQL TRACE output

- Tracing a more complex query and what to look for to help performance

- Using DBMS_MONITOR

- Using TRCSESS

- Using EXPLAIN PLAN

- Reading EXPLAIN PLAN—top to bottom or bottom to top?

- Using DBMS_XPLAN

- Yet another EXPLAIN PLAN method—the parent/child tree structure method

- Tracing in developer tools

- Important columns in the PLAN_TABLE table

- Tracing for errors and the undocumented initialization parameters

- Building and using STORED OUTLINES

- Using STORED OUTLINES (PLAN STABILITY) to migrate SQL from the rule-based optimizer

- Using SQL PLAN MANAGEMENT (SPM), an *11g new feature*

- Converting from STORED OUTLINES to SQL PLAN MANAGMENT, an *11g new feature*

The Oracle SQL TRACE Utility

You use the Oracle SQL TRACE utility to measure timing statistics for a given query, a batch process, and an entire system. SQL TRACE is deprecated (discouraged and on the way out) in 11g, but it still works. It has been replaced with DBMS_MONITOR and DBMS_SESSION. I'm keeping this section as many people still use it, but please start using the newer packages. SQL TRACE is a thorough method for finding potential bottlenecks on the system. SQL TRACE has the following functionality:

■ SQL TRACE runs the query and generates statistics about an Oracle query (or series of queries) that is executed.

■ SQL TRACE helps developers analyze every section of a query.

Generally, the Oracle SQL TRACE utility records all database activity (particularly queries) in a *trace* file. The trace file is generated by Oracle SQL TRACE; however, it is very hard to read and should be changed into a readable format using the TKPROF utility.

Simple Steps for SQL TRACE with a Simple Query

The steps for setting up and running Oracle's SQL TRACE utility are listed here:

1. Set the following `init.ora` parameters (SPFILE users will need to use the ALTER SYSTEM command to change these parameters):

```
TIMED_STATISTICS = TRUE
MAX_DUMP_FILE_SIZE = unlimited (also see metalink article 108723.1)
```

The TIMED_STATISTICS parameter allows tracing to occur on the system. The MAX_DUMP_FILE_SIZE specifies the maximum file size in "minimum physical block size at device level" blocks. This is the largest size that the file will grow to; any further data to be recorded will be ignored, will not be written to the trace file, and might be missed. Both of these parameters may also be set via an ALTER SYSTEM command (for the entire system) and take effect when the next user logs in, but they will not affect those currently logged in to the system. You may also set the TIMED_STATISTICS and MAX_DUMP_FILE_SIZE parameters at the session level using the ALTER SESSION command (for an individual session). The output will be stored in the USER_DUMP_DEST (for Oracle 10.2 and earlier systems). After 11.1, the DIAGNOSTIC_DEST parameter is used instead, and its value is set automatically by Oracle. To determine the location of the files, run the following script:

```
SELECT value
FROM   v$diag_info
WHERE  name = 'Diag Trace';

The value returned is the path of the trace file.
```

2. Enable SQL TRACE for a SQL*Plus session (this starts tracing for an individual session):

```
alter session set SQL_TRACE true;
```

There are actually several different ways of starting and stopping trace sessions, which will be discussed later in this chapter.

3. Run the query to be traced:

```
Select table_name, owner, initial_extent, uniqueness
from    ind2
where   owner || '' = 'SCOTT' ; --Note: An index on "OWNER" is suppressed
```

4. Disable SQL TRACE for the SQL*Plus session:

```
alter session set SQL_TRACE false;
```

You do not actually have to stop the trace to examine the trace file, but it is a good idea.

After running SQL TRACE, your output filename will look something like the following (the SID is usually included in the trace filename):

```
orcl_ora_19554.trc
```

TIP
Setting TIMED_STATISTICS = TRUE in the initialization file enables the collection of time statistics. Also, as of 10g, the initialization parameter SQL_TRACE has been deprecated (see Appendix A for more information).

Finding the generated trace file may be the trickiest part of this whole process. The generated file should be named for the process ID of the trace session and includes that number in the filename. Looking for the date and time of the file makes it easy to find if you are the only one tracing something. In the previous example, 19554 is the process ID of the session being traced. The trace filenames may vary between ora% and ora_%, depending on the operating system on which the trace was performed, and the file should appear in the location specified by running the script listed in Step 1. Another way of finding the file is to put a marker inside the file output (such as issuing a query like SELECT 'Rich1' FROM DUAL;), and then use a file search utility like grep or Windows search to find the text and the file that contains it.

You can use the following query, running from the same session, to obtain the number included in the trace filename (assuming you can see the V$ views).

```
Select spid, s.sid,s.serial#, p.username, p.program
from    v$process p, v$session s
where   p.addr = s.paddr
and     s.sid = (select sid from v$mystat where rownum=1);
```

NOTE
Don't forget to grant select on V_$PROCESS, V_$SESSION, and V_$MYSTAT to the user if not already granted.

Run TKPROF at the operating system prompt to convert the TRACE file into a readable format. The following command creates the file `rich2.prf` in the current directory from the `ora_19554.trc` trace file and also logs in to the database as system/manager to get the EXPLAIN PLAN output:

```
tkprof orcl_ora_19554.trc rich2.prf explain=system/manager
```

The TKPROF utility translates the TRACE file generated by the SQL TRACE facility to a readable format. You can run TKPROF against a TRACE file that you have previously created, or you can run it while the program that is creating the TRACE file is still running. Table 6-1 lists options for TKPROF.

Variable	Definition
Tracefile	This is the name of the SQL TRACE file containing the statistics by SQL_TRACE.
Output_file	This is the name of the file where TKPROF writes its output.
print = number	This is the number of statements to include in the output. If this statement is not included, TKPROF lists all statements in the output.
Explain = username/password	Run the EXPLAIN PLAN on the user's SQL statements in the TRACE file. This option creates a PLAN_TABLE of its own, so the user needs to have privileges to create the table and space in which to create it. When TKPROF is finished, this table is dropped. Ensure that you use the username/password of the user who parsed the cursor (ran the query) to ensure the EXPLAIN PLAN output is for the correct user. See Metalink note 199081.1 for more information.
insert = filename	This option creates a script to create a table and store the TRACE file statistics for each SQL statement traced.
record = filename	This option produces a file of all the user's SQL statements.
Sys = yes|no	This option allows the user to request that the recursive SQL statements (issued by the SYS user) not be displayed in the output. The default is YES. Recursive SQL usually includes internal calls and any table maintenance, such as adding an extent to a table during an insert.
sort = parameters	A tremendous number of sorting options are available. My favorites are FCHCPU (CPU time of fetch), FCHDSK (disk reads for fetch), FCHCU and FCHQRY (memory reads for fetch), FCHROW (number of rows fetched), EXEDSK (disk reads during execute), EXECU and EXEQRY (memory reads during execute), EXEROW (rows processed during execute), EXECPU (execute CPU time), PRSCPU (parse CPU), and PRSCNT (times parsed).
waits = yes|no	Record summary for any wait events.
aggregate = yes|no	If no, then TKPROF does not combine multiple users of the same SQL text.
table = schema.table	The table in which TKPROF temporarily put execution plans before writing them to the output file.

TABLE 6-I.   *Command-Line Options for TKPROF*

The syntax for TKPROF is as follows:

```
tkprof tracefile output_file [sort = parameters] [print=number] [explain=username/password]
[waits=yes|no]

[aggregate=yes|no] [insert=filename] [sys=yes|no] [table=schema.table] [record=filename]
[width=number]
```

The following are some quick examples using the options described in Table 6-1.

Run TKPROF and list only the top five CPU (fetch + execute + parse) results:

```
tkprof orcl_ora_19554 rich3 explain=system/manager
sort=(FCHCPU,EXECPU,PRSCPU) print=5
```

Run TKPROF and omit all recursive statements:

```
tkprof orcl_ora_19554 rich4 explain=system/manager sys=no
```

Run TKPROF and create a file that will create a table and insert records from the trace:

```
tkprof orcl_ora_19554.trc rich5.prf explain=system/manager insert=insert1.ins
```

Run TKPROF and create a file that shows your TRACE session:

```
tkprof orcl_ora_19554.trc rich6.prf explain=system/manager record=record1.sql
```

TIP
*The TKPROF utility puts traced output into a readable format.
Without running TKPROF, reading the output of a TRACE would be
difficult. By specifying explain = username/password (as shown in the
accompanying examples), you are able to get the EXPLAIN execution
path, in addition to the execution statistics of the query.*

TIP
*To use multiple sort parameters, you can just repeat sort = parameter
on the command line, for example, TKPROF SOURCE_FILE
OUT_FILE SORT = PARM1 SORT = PARM2.*

TIP
*Run TKPROF from the command line without any parameter to get a
list of all the parameters.*

Now let's run a quick example and see the output:

```
alter session set sql_trace true ;
select table_name, owner, initial_extent, uniqueness
from   ind2
where  owner || '' = 'SCOTT' ;
alter session set sql_trace false ;
```

Here's the output:

```
select       TABLE_NAME, OWNER, INITIAL_EXTENT, UNIQUENESS
from         IND2
where        OWNER = 'SCOTT';
```

	count	cpu	elapsed	disk	query	current	rows
Parse:	1	1.00	2.00	0	0	0	
Execute:	1	0.00	0.00	0	0	2	0
Fetch:	2	69.00	113.00	142	430	0	36

Here is the execution plan (no index used):

```
TABLE ACCESS (FULL) OF 'IND2'
```

The preceding output shows 142 disk reads (physical reads) and 430 total reads (query + current). The number of memory reads is the total reads less the disk reads, or 288 memory reads (430 – 142). Having such a high number of disk reads compared to query reads is certainly a potential problem unless you are running a data warehouse or queries that often do require full table scans. The execution path shows a full table scan, confirming that you may have a potential problem.

TIP
A traced query with a large number of physical reads may indicate a missing index. The disk column indicates the physical reads (usually when an index is not used), and the query column added to the current column is the total number of block reads (the physical reads are included in this number). A query with a large number of query reads and a low number of disk reads may indicate the use of an index, but if the query reads are overly high, it could indicate a bad index or bad join order of tables. A query with a large number of current reads usually indicates a large DML (UPDATE, INSERT, DELETE) query.

The next listing shows what happens when you rerun the query (after restarting the system) to be traced, but now using an index on the OWNER column:

```
select    table_name, owner, initial_extent, uniqueness
from      ind2
where     owner = 'SCOTT' ;   (The index on "OWNER" is not suppressed)
```

The following listing shows the output of the file `rich2.prf`. Often you'll see zero (0) disk reads for queries that have frequently accessed data. The first time a query is run, there will always be disk reads.

```
select    table_name, owner, initial_extent, uniqueness
from      ind2
where     owner = 'SCOTT' ;
```

	count	cpu	elapsed	disk	query	current	rows
Parse:	2	0.00	0.00	0	0	0	0
Execute:	2	0.00	0.00	0	0	0	0
Fetch:	4	6.00	6.00	0	148	0	72

The following listing (abbreviated) shows the execution plan (index used):

```
TABLE ACCESS (BY ROWID) OF 'IND2'
   INDEX (RANGE SCAN) OF 'IND2_1' (NON-UNIQUE)
```

The Sections of a TRACE Output

The TRACE utility has multiple sections, including the SQL statements, statistics, information, and EXPLAIN PLAN. Each of these is discussed in the following text sections.

The SQL Statement

The first section of a TKPROF statement is the *SQL statement.* This statement will be exactly the same as the executed statement. If any hints or comments were in the statement, they are retained in this output. This can be helpful when you are reviewing the output from multiple sessions. If you find a statement that is causing problems, you can search for the exact statement. Remember, some of the statements from Oracle Forms are generated dynamically, so parts of the query (particularly WHERE clause predicates) may be displayed as bind variables (:1) and not actual text.

The Statistics Section

The *statistics* section contains all the statistics for this SQL statement and all the recursive SQL statements generated to satisfy this statement. This section has eight columns, the first being the type of call to the database. There are three types of calls: Parse, Execute, and Fetch. Each call type generates a separate line of statistics. The Parse is where the SQL statement itself is put into memory (library cache of the shared pool), or it can also reuse an exact cursor. The Execute is where the statement is actually executed, and the Fetch is where the data is retrieved. The other seven columns are the statistics for each type of call. Table 6-2 explains each column and its definition.

Information Section

The *information* section contains information about the number of library cache misses from parse and execute calls. If the number of misses is high, you may have a problem with the size of the shared pool. You should check the hit ratio and the reload rate of the library cache. This section also shows the username of the last user to parse this statement. You'll also find information about the current optimizer mode setting.

The Row Source Operation Section

The *row source operation* section lists the number of rows cross-referenced with the operation that used the rows.

Column	Definition
COUNT	The number of times this type of call was made.
CPU	The total CPU time for all of the calls of this type for this statement. If the TIMED_STATISTICS in the initialization parameter file is not set to TRUE, this statistic and the elapsed statistic will be 0.
ELAPSED	The total elapsed time for this call.
DISK	The total number of data blocks retrieved from disk to satisfy this call. This is the number of physical reads.
QUERY	The total number of data buffers retrieved from memory for this type of call. SELECT statements usually retrieve buffers in this mode. This is the number of consistent gets.
CURRENT	The total number of data buffers retrieved from memory for this type of call. UPDATE, INSERT, or DELETE usually accesses buffers in this mode, although SELECT statements may use a small number of buffers in this mode also. This is the number of db block gets.
ROWS	The total number of rows processed by this statement. The rows processed for SELECT statements appear in the row of Fetch statistics. INSERTs, UPDATEs, and DELETEs appear in the Execute row.

TABLE 6-2.   *Statistics for Each Type of Call*

TIP
The trace file is a point-in-time picture of what happened on the system at the time that the trace was run (includes the row source operation). In contrast, the EXPLAIN PLAN (detailed next) is generated when the TKPROF listing is created, which could be some time later. The row source operation listing is generated as part of the trace file and can be used to see if the database objects have changed since the trace was performed.

The EXPLAIN PLAN (Execution Plan)

I find this section of the TKPROF output to be the most useful. The first column of this section is the number of rows processed by each line of the execution plan. Here, you are able to see how slow a statement is. If the total number of rows in the Fetch statistics is low compared to the number of rows being processed by each line of the EXPLAIN PLAN, you may want to review the statement. This plan is generated when you use the explain option of the tkprof command and is the plan that would be generated if the SQL was executed at the time that the tkprof command was run. If you want the plan that was generated at the time that SQL was originally run, then use the row source operation plan command.

It is also possible that only one line of the execution plan is processing a large number of rows compared to the rest of the statement. This situation can be caused by full table scans or the use of a bad index.

Table 6-3 lists some of the problems to look for in the TKPROF output.

Digging into the TKPROF Output

When you compare the TKPROF output to the actual object's physical characteristics, you start to see how Oracle really works. Consider a CUSTOMER table with over 100,000 records contained in over 1,000 blocks. By querying DBA_TABLES and DBA_EXTENTS, you can see the blocks that are both allocated (1536) and being used (1382), as shown in the following listing:

```
select  sum(blocks)
from    dba_segments
where   segment_name = 'CUSTOMER';

SUM(BLOCKS)
-----------
       1536
```

Problem	Solution
The parsing numbers are high.	The SHARED_POOL_SIZE may need to be increased.
The disk reads are very high.	Indexes are not being used or may not exist.
The query and/or current (memory reads) are very high.	Indexes may be on columns with low cardinality (columns where an individual value generally makes up a large percentage of the table; like a YES|NO field). Removing/suppressing the index or using histograms or a bitmap index may increase performance. A poor join order of tables or bad order in a concatenated index may also cause this.
The parse elapse time is high.	There may be a problem with the number of open cursors.
The number of rows processed by a row in the EXPLAIN PLAN is high compared to the other rows.	This could be a sign of an index with a poor distribution of distinct keys (unique values for a column). This could also be a sign of a poorly written SQL statement.
The number of misses in the library cache during parse is greater than 1.	This indicates the statement had to be reloaded. You may need to increase the SHARED_POOL_SIZE in the `init.ora` file or do a better job of sharing SQL.

TABLE 6-3. *Problems to look for in the TKPROF output*

```
select blocks, empty_blocks
from   dba_tables
where  table_name = 'CUSTOMER';

    BLOCKS EMPTY_BLOCKS
---------- ------------
      1382          153
```

If you look at the TKPROF output of a query that counts all records in the CUSTOMER table (shown in the next listing), you see that it performs a full table scan because this is the first access after a startup. Also note that the number of blocks accessed (mostly physical disk access) is slightly higher than the total number of blocks in the physical table (seen in the previous queries). All but 4 of the 1387 query blocks read are disk reads. (Disk reads are a subset of the query, which is the sum of disk and memory reads in consistent mode.)

```
SELECT COUNT(*)
FROM CUSTOMER;
```

call	count	cpu	elapsed	disk	query	current	rows
Parse	1	3505.04	3700.00	0	0	0	0
Execute	1	0.00	0.00	0	0	0	0
Fetch	2	1101.59	18130.00	1383	1387	15	1
total	4	4606.63	21830.00	1383	1387	15	1

```
Misses in library cache during parse: 1
Optimizer goal: ALL_ROWS
Parsing user id (OE): 85
Number of plan statistics captured: 1
```

Rows	Execution Plan
0	SELECT STATEMENT MODE: ALL_ROWS
1	SORT (AGGREGATE)
114688	TABLE ACCESS MODE: ANALYZED (FULL) OF 'CUSTOMER' (TABLE)

If you run this query a second time (shown in the following listing), a big change occurs. Looking at the TKPROF output of a query that counts all records in the CUSTOMER table, this time you see that it still performs a full table scan, but now there are many fewer disk reads because most of the blocks needed are already cached in memory. Most of the 1387 query blocks read are memory reads. (Only 121 are disk reads.)

```
SELECT COUNT(*)
FROM CUSTOMER;
```

call	count	cpu	elapsed	disk	query	current	rows
Parse	1	0.00	0.00	0	0	0	0
Execute	1	0.00	0.00	0	0	0	0
Fetch	2	901.29	2710.00	121	1387	15	1
total	4	901.29	2710.00	121	1387	15	1

```
Misses in library cache during parse: 0
Optimizer goal: ALL_ROWS
Parsing user id (OE): 85
Number of plan statistics captured: 1
Rows            Execution Plan
0               SELECT STATEMENT     MODE: ALL_ROWS
1                 SORT (AGGREGATE)
114688            TABLE ACCESS       MODE: ANALYZED (FULL) OF 'CUSTOMER' (TABLE)
```

TIP
Full table scans are one of the first things Oracle pushes out of memory (becoming least recently used as soon as you run them) because they are so inefficient, generally using a lot of memory.

Using DBMS_MONITOR

In a multitier environment with connection pooling or a shared server, a session can span multiple processes and even multiple instances. DBMS_MONITOR is a built-in package introduced in Oracle 10g that allows any user's session to be traced from client machine to middle tier to the backend database. This makes it easier to identify the specific user who is creating a large workload. DBMS_MONITOR replaces trace tools such as DBMS_SUPPORT. The DBA role is required to use DBMS_MONITOR.

End-to-end application tracing can be based on the following:

- **Session**   Based on session ID (SID) and serial number.

- **Client Identifier**   Allows trace to be set across multiple sessions. Specifies the end user based on the logon ID. Set this using the DBMS_SESSION.SET_IDENTIFIER procedure.

- **Instance**   Specifies a given instance based on the instance name.

- **Service name**   Specifies a group of related applications. Set using the DBMS_SERVICE.CREATE_SERVICE procedure (which creates a DB service).

- **Module name**   Set by developers in their application code using procedure DBMS_APPLICATION_INFO.SET_MODULE. This name is used to represent the module or code being executed.

- **Action name**   Set by developers in their application code using procedure DBMS_APPLICATION_INFO.SET_ACTION. This name is used to represent the action being performed by the module.

End-to-end application tracing can generate the following details:

- **Waits**   If TRUE, then wait information is written to the trace file.

- **Binds**   If TRUE, then bind information is written to the trace file.

- **Instance name**   The name of the instance being traced if this parameter is set.
- **Plan stat** (new in 11*g*)   Frequency that row source statistics are written to trace file (possible values include NEVER, FIRST_EXECUTION (default), or ALL_EXECUTIONS).

Service name, module name, and action name are associated hierarchically; you can't specify an action name without specifying the module name and the service name, but you can specify only the service name, or only the service name and module name.

Oracle 11*g* has an important new parameter called *plan stat*. If you want to guarantee that a *row source plan* is present in the trace file for each SQL statement, then use a value of ALL_EXECUTIONS for the parameter.

TIP
In 11g, using a value of ALL_EXECUTIONS for the PLAN_STAT ensures that information regarding the execution plans is always contained in the trace file.

Setting Trace Based on Session ID and Serial Number

To set the trace based on session ID and serial number, first determine the SID and serial number of the session you want to trace:

```
Select sid,serial#,username
from   v$session;

    SID    SERIAL# USERNAME
---------- ---------- ------------------------------
    156       3588 SCOTT
    142       1054 SYS
```

To enable the trace using DBMS_MONITOR:

```
SQL> exec dbms_monitor.session_trace_enable(156,3588,TRUE,FALSE);
```

The third parameter is for waits (default is TRUE), and the fourth parameter is for bind variables (default is FALSE).

To turn off the trace:

```
SQL> exec dbms_monitor.session_trace_disable(156,3588);
```

To trace the current session, set the SID and SERIAL# to NULL:

```
SQL> exec dbms_monitor.session_trace_enable(null,null);
```

Setting Trace Based on Client Identifier

To set the trace based on a client identifier as the user, first set the identifier for the current session by running the following:

```
SQL> exec dbms_session.set_identifier('bryan id');
```

To verify the client identifier:

```
select  sid,serial#,username, client_identifier
from    v$session
where   client_identifier is not null;

       SID    SERIAL# USERNAME                           CLIENT_IDENTIFIER
---------- ---------- ------------------------------ ------------------
       156      3588 SCOTT                              bryan id
```

Now you can set the trace for this client identifier:

```
SQL> exec dbms_monitor.client_id_trace_enable('bryan id',true,false);
```

The second parameter is for waits (default is TRUE), and the third parameter is for bind variables (default is FALSE). The benefit of using CLIEND_ID traces is that tracing is enabled for all instances and is persistent across restarts. Whatever shared process or session ID the client with the identifier bryan id uses, this user's activities will be written to one more trace files. For a multitier environment, the connection between the end client and database is nonstatic; that is, the end client makes a request and can be routed to different database sessions from the middle tier. In 9i, you had no way to keep track of clients across many database sessions, whereas now, you can use end-to-end tracing to get the CLIENT_IDENTIFIER attribute. This column can also be found in V$SESSION.

To disable this client identifier trace:

```
SQL> exec dbms_monitor.client_id_trace_disable('bryan id');
```

Setting Trace for the Service Name/Module Name/Action Name

In order to use the action name, you must include the module name and the service name. In order to use the module name, the service name must be present. Tracing is enabled for a given combination of service name, module name, and action name globally for a database unless an instance name is specified for a procedure. The service name is determined by the connect string used to connect to a service.

An Oracle database is represented to clients as a service; that is, the database performs work on behalf of clients. A database can have one or more services associated with it. For example, you could have one database with two different services for web clients: book.us.acme.com for clients making book purchases and soft.us.acme.com for clients making software purchases. In this example, the database name is SALES.ACME.COM, so the name isn't even based on the database name. The service name is specified by the SERVICE_NAMES parameter in the initialization parameter file. A default service name is created automatically for the database with the same name as the global database name, a name comprising the database name (DB_NAME parameter) and the domain name (DB_DOMAIN parameter).

To enable tracing for a service name (assuming the service ebk2 has been created):

```
SQL> exec dbms_monitor.serv_mod_act_trace_enable(service_name=>'ebk2');
```

This traces all sessions that connect to the database using a service with the name of ebk2.

To enable tracing for a combination of service, module, and action:

```
SQL> exec dbms_monitor.serv_mod_act_trace_enable(service_name=>'ebk2', -module_name=>
'salary_update', action_name=>'insert_item');
```

To disable tracing in the preceding code, use the procedure
SERV_MOD_ACT_TRACE_DISABLE, as shown here:

```
SQL> exec dbms_monitor.serv_mod_act_trace_disable(service_name=>'ebk2', -module_name=>
'salary_update', action_name=>'insert_item');
```

To trace for the entire database or instance (not recommended):

```
SQL> execute DBMS_MONITOR.DATABASE_TRACE_ENABLE(waits => TRUE, binds => FALSE,
instance_name => 'ebk1');
```

TIP
When using DBMS_MONITOR, disable tracing when you are done;
otherwise, every session that meets the criteria specified will be
traced.

Enabled Tracing Views
DBA_ENABLED_TRACES and DBA_ENABLED_AGGREGATIONS are the views to look at to see
what enabled tracing and statistics gathering is in place. You can use these views to make sure all
the tracing options have been disabled. The following example shows the output from the
DBA_ENABLED_TRACES view:

```
select trace_type, primary_id, instance_name
from   dba_enabled_traces;

TRACE_TYPE  PRIMARY_ID INSTANCE_NAME
----------- ---------- -------------
SERVICE     ebk2
DATABASE               ebk1
```

TRCSESS Multiple Trace Files into One File
The TRCSESS utility allows trace data to be selectively extracted from multiple trace files and saved
into a single trace file based on criteria such as session ID or module name. This command-line
utility is especially useful in connection pooling and shared server configurations, where each user
request could end up in a separate trace file. TRCSESS lets you obtain consolidated trace
information pertaining to a single user session.

This consolidated trace file can be created according to several criteria:

- Session id
- Client id
- Service name

- Action name
- Module name

The command syntax for TRCSESS is as follows:

```
trcsess [output=] [session=] [clientid=] [service=] [action=] [module=]
[trace_file_names]

output= output destination default being standard output.
session= The SID and Serial# of the session to be traced, in the format SID.SERIAL#.
clientid= clientid to be traced.
service= service to be traced.
action= action to be traced.
module= module to be traced.

trace_file_names = list of trace file names, separated by spaces, which need to searched by the
trcsess command. If no files are listed, then all the files in the current directory will be
searched. The wild card character, *, may be used in the file names.
```

Example 1

This is from one of the examples in the earlier section "Using DBMS_MONITOR," where SERVICE_NAME = EBK2, MODULE= SALARY_UPDATE, and ACTION = INSERT_ITEM. Go to the DIAGNOSTIC_DEST directory or ADR_HOME, the location is *<DIAGNOSTIC_DEST dir>/rdbms/DB_NAME/SID/*trace, and run the following command:

```
trcsess output=combo.trc service="ebk2" module="salary_update" action="insert_item"
```

This searches all the trace files that meet the preceding criteria and creates a consolidated trace file named `combo.trc`.

Now TKPROF can be run against `combo.trc`:

```
tkprof combo.trc output=combo_report sort=fchela
```

Example 2
Set the client ID:

```
SQL> exec dbms_session.set_identifier('ebk3');
```

Enable tracing for the client ID:

```
SQL> EXECUTE DBMS_MONITOR.CLIENT_ID_TRACE_ENABLE('ebk3');
```

Trace by this client ID, and then issue this command (from the directory as before):

```
trcsess output=combo2.trc clientid=ebk3    *.trc
```

TRCSESS checks all the trace files for the specified client ID. Now TKPROF can be run against `combo2.trc` (the combined trace file).

Example 3

In the first case, all the trace files in the current directory are used as input, and a single trace file (`combo3.trc`) is created, with all session=17.1988 trace information. (Note that 17.1988 is the `<SID>.<Serial#>`.)

```
trcsess output=combo3.trc session=17.1988
trcsess output=combo4.trc session=17.1988 ebk2_ora_0607.trc ebk2_ora_0125.trc
```

In the second case, only the two trace files listed are used as input and a single trace file (`combo4.trc`) is created, with all session=17.1988 trace information from the two trace files listed.

Using EXPLAIN PLAN Alone

The EXPLAIN PLAN command allows developers to view the query execution plan that the Oracle optimizer uses to execute a SQL statement. This command is very helpful in improving the performance of SQL statements because it does not actually execute the SQL statement—it only outlines the plan and inserts this execution plan in an Oracle table. Prior to using the EXPLAIN PLAN command, a file called `utlxplan.sql` (located in the same directory as `catalog.sql`, typically `ORACLE_HOME/rdbms/admin`) must be executed under the Oracle account that will be executing the EXPLAIN PLAN command.

The script creates a table called PLAN_TABLE that the EXPLAIN PLAN command uses to insert the query execution plan in the form of records. This table can then be queried and viewed to determine if the SQL statement needs to be modified to force a different execution plan. Oracle supplies queries to use against the plan table, too: `utlxpls.sql` and `utlxplp.sql`. Either will work, but `utlxplp.sql` is geared toward parallel queries. An EXPLAIN PLAN example is shown next (executed in SQL*Plus).

Q. Why use EXPLAIN without TRACE?
A. The statement is *not* executed; it only shows what will happen if the statement is executed.

Q. When do you use EXPLAIN without TRACE?
A. When the query will take an exceptionally long time to run.

The procedures for running TRACE vs. EXPLAIN are demonstrated here:

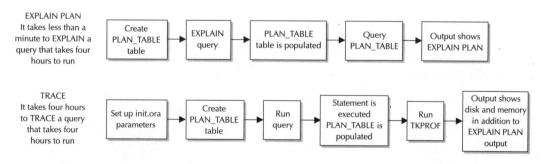

Q. How do I use EXPLAIN by itself?
A. Follow these steps:

1. Find the script; it is usually in the ORACLE_HOME/rdbms/admin directory:

   ```
   utlxplan.sql
   ```

2. Execute the script utlxplan.sql in SQLPLUS:

   ```
   @utlxplan (run this as the user who will be running the EXPLAIN plan)
   ```

   This script creates the PLAN_TABLE for the user executing the script. You can create your own PLAN_TABLE, but use Oracle's syntax—or else!

3. Run EXPLAIN PLAN for the query to be optimized (the SQL statement is placed after the FOR clause of the EXPLAIN PLAN statement):

   ```
   explain plan for
   select      CUSTOMER_NUMBER
   from        CUSTOMER
   where       CUSTOMER_NUMBER = 111;
   Explained.
   ```

4. Optionally, you can also run EXPLAIN PLAN for the query to be optimized using a tag for the statement:

   ```
   explain plan
   set statement_id = 'CUSTOMER' for
   select      CUSTOMER_NUMBER
   from        CUSTOMER
   where       CUSTOMER_NUMBER = 111;
   ```

TIP
Use the SET STATEMENT_ID = 'your_identifier' when the PLAN_TABLE will be populated by many different developers. I rarely use the SET STATEMENT_ID statement. Instead, I explain a query, look at the output, and then delete from the PLAN_TABLE table. I continue to do this (making changes to the query), until I see an execution plan that I think is favorable. I then run the query to see if performance has improved. If multiple developers/DBAs are using the same PLAN_TABLE, the SET STATEMENT_ID (case sensitive) is essential to identifying a statement.

5. Select the output from the PLAN_TABLE:

   ```
   select      operation, options, object_name, id, parent_id
   from        plan_table
   where       statement_id = 'CUSTOMER';
   ```

Operation	Options	Object Name	ID	Parent
select statement			0	
Table Access	By ROWID	Customer	1	
Index	Range Scan	CUST_IDX	2	1

TIP
Use EXPLAIN instead of TRACE so you don't have to wait for the query to run. EXPLAIN shows the path of a query without actually running the query. Use TRACE only for multiquery batch jobs to find out which of the many queries in the batch job are slow.

TIP
You can use the `utlxpls.sql` *and* `utlxplp.sql` *queries provided by Oracle to query the plan table without having to write your own query and without having to format the output.*

An Additional EXPLAIN Example for a Simple Query

This section walks you through a simple process of running a query and then checking the EXPLAIN PLAN for the information about how the query will be processed.

1. Run the query with the EXPLAIN syntax embedded prior to the query:

```
explain plan
set statement_id = 'query 1' for
select     customer_number, name
from       customer
where      customer_number = '111';
```

2. Retrieve the output of EXPLAIN by querying the PLAN_TABLE.

   To retrieve the information for viewing, you must execute a SQL statement. Two scripts provided in the Oracle documentation are displayed in Steps 2 and 3, along with the results of each based on the previous EXPLAIN PLAN command. Note that this example varies from the last example. The CUSTOMER_NUMBER column is an indexed number field, which, in the second example, is suppressed because of a datatype mismatch (111 is in quotes forcing a TO_CHAR operation). In the first example, I treated the CUSTOMER_NUMBER column correctly as a number field (111 is not in quotes). At times, the optimizer is smart enough *not* to do this to you, but when you use Pro*C or other similar coding, the optimizer may not be able to translate this for you.

```
select     operation, options, object_name, id, parent_id
from       plan_table
where      statement_id = 'query 1'
order by   id;
```

Operation	Options	Object Name	ID	Parent ID
select Statement			0	
Table Access	Full	Customer_Information	1	0

Alternatively, you could just run the `utlxpls.sql` script.

3. Retrieve more intuitive and easy-to-read output for EXPLAIN:

```
select      lpad(' ', 2*(level-1)) || operation || ' ' || options || ' ' ||
            object_name || ' ' || decode(id, 0, 'Cost = ' || position) "Query Plan"
from        plan_table
start       with id = 0
and         statement_id = 'query 1'
connect by prior id = parent_id
and         statement_id = 'query 1';
```

Here is the output:

```
Query Plan
select statement     Cost=220
     Table Access Full Customer
```

EXPLAIN PLAN—Read It Top to Bottom or Bottom to Top?

Whether you should read from top to bottom or bottom to top depends on how you write the query that retrieves the information from the PLAN_TABLE table. This is probably why many people disagree about which way to read the result. (All methods may be correct.) The following listing shows the order of execution based on the query that retrieves the information. In this example, the output is read top to bottom with one caveat: you must read it from the innermost to the outermost. This listing shows a method that should clear up any questions.

```
delete      from plan_table;
explain plan
set         statement_id = 'SQL1' for
select      to_char(sysdate, 'MM/DD/YY HH:MI AM'), to_char((trunc((sysdate -4 -1),
            'day') +1), 'DD-MON-YY')
from        bk, ee
where       bk_shift_date >= to_char((trunc(( sysdate - 4 - 1), 'day') + 1), 'DD-
            MON-YY')
and         bk_shift_date <= to_char((sysdate - 4), 'DD-MON-YY')
and         bk_empno = ee_empno(+)
and         substr(ee_hierarchy_code, 1, 3) in ('PNA', 'PNB', 'PNC', 'PND', 'PNE',
            'PNF')
order by    ee_job_group, bk_empno, bk_shift_date
/
select      LPad(' ', 2*(Level-1)) || Level || '.' || Nvl(Position,0)|| ' ' ||
            Operation || ' ' || Options || ' ' || Object_Name || ' ' || Object_Type
            || ' ' || Decode(id, 0, Statement_Id ||' Cost = ' || Position) || cost
            || ' ' || Object_Node "Query Plan"
from        plan_table
start       with id = 0 And statement_id = 'SQL1'
connect by prior id = parent_id
and         statement_id = 'SQL1'
/
Query Plan
1.0 SELECT STATEMENT    SQL1  Cost =
```

```
2.1 SORT ORDER BY (7ᵗʰ)
   3.1 FILTER (6th)
      4.1 NESTED LOOPS OUTER (5ᵗʰ)
         5.1 TABLE ACCESS BY ROWID BK (2ⁿᵈ)
            6.1 INDEX RANGE SCAN I_BK_06 NON-UNIQUE (1ˢᵗ)
         5.2 TABLE ACCESS BY ROWID EE (4ᵗʰ)
            6.2 INDEX UNIQUE SCAN I_EE_01 UNIQUE (3ʳᵈ)
```

Reading the EXPLAIN PLAN

Using the previous EXPLAIN PLAN, I will elucidate the steps. The numbers in the left column in Table 6-4 identify each step. They are listed in the order in which they are executed.

TIP

Whether the EXPLAIN PLAN is read from top to bottom or from bottom to top depends entirely on the query used to select information from the PLAN_TABLE. Both methods of reading the query may be correct, given that the query selecting the information is correctly structured.

Setting AUTOTRACE On

There is also an easier method available for generating an EXPLAIN PLAN and statistics about the performance of a query with SQL*Plus. The main difference between AUTOTRACE and EXPLAIN PLAN is that AUTOTRACE actually executes the query (in the way TRACE does) and automatically queries the plan table, whereas EXPLAIN PLAN does neither. The AUTOTRACE command generates similar information, as shown in the next listing. To use AUTOTRACE, the user must possess the PLUSTRACE role (by running `plustrce.sql`, which is usually located in the ORACLE_HOME/sqlplus/admin directory).

Step	Action
6.1	This is the index range scan of I_BK_06. This is the first step. This index is on the BK_SHIFT_DATE column. This step performs a scan of this index to produce a list of ROWIDs that fall between the two dates.
5.1	This retrieves the rows from the BK table.
6.2	This scans the I_EE_01 index. This index is on the EE_EMPNO column. Using the BK_EMPNO retrieved from the previous step, this index is scanned to retrieve the ROWIDs to produce a list of the EE_EMPNOs that match the BK_EMPNOs.
5.2	This retrieves the rows from the EE table.
4.1	This is a nested loop. The two lists are joined, producing one list.
3.1	This is a filter. The rest of the conditions of the WHERE clause are applied.
2.1	This is SORT_ORDER_BY. The remaining rows are sorted according to the ORDER BY clause.
1.0	This tells which type of statement it is.

TABLE 6-4. *Reading the EXPLAIN PLAN*

```
SET AUTOTRACE ON
select     count(last_name)
from       emp
where      name = 'branches';
```

The output is as follows:

```
COUNT(LAST_NAME)
----------------
               0
```

```
Execution Plan
-----------------------------------------------------------
Plan hash value: 141239332
-----------------------------------------------------------------------

| Id  | Operation          | Name        | Rows  | Bytes | Cost (%CPU)| Time|
-----------------------------------------------------------------------
|   0 | SELECT STATEMENT   |             |    1  |    8  |    1    (0)| 00:00:01|
|   1 |  SORT AGGREGATE    |             |    1  |    8  |            ||
|*  2 |   INDEX RANGE SCAN | EMP_NAME_IX |    1  |    8  |    1    (0)| 00:00:01|
-----------------------------------------------------------------------

Predicate Information (identified by operation id):
---------------------------------------------------
   2 - access("LAST_NAME"='BRANCHES')

Note:
- dynamic sampling used for this statement (level=2)
Statistics
-----------------------------------------------------------
9       recursive calls
0       db block gets
9       consistent gets
1       physical reads
0       redo size
529     bytes sent via SQL*Net to client
519     bytes received via SQL*Net from client
2       SQL*Net roundtrips to/from client
0       sorts (memory)
0       sorts (disk)
1       rows processed
```

The AUTOTRACE option provides an EXPLAIN PLAN and statistics for a query. AUTOTRACE provides many of the TRACE and TKPROF statistics such as disk reads (physical reads) and total reads (consistent reads + db block gets).

TIP
If the error "Unable to verify plan table format or existence" occurs when enabling AUTOTRACE, you must create a plan table using the `utlxplan.sql` *script.*

CAUTION

AUTOTRACE may fail when querying system views because the user may not have permission to view underlying objects.

Table 6-5 shows other AUTOTRACE options.

EXPLAIN PLAN When Using Partitions

Table partitions yield different outputs for their EXPLAIN PLANs (as shown in the following listing). Here, I've created a table with three partitions and a partitioned index. Broadly speaking, partitions are tables stored in multiple places in the database. For more information on partitioning tables, refer to Chapter 3.

```
create table dept1
     (deptno      number(2),
      dept_name      varchar2(30))
     partition by range(deptno)
     (partition d1 values    less than (10),
      partition d2 values    less than (20),
      partition d3 values    less than (maxvalue));

insert into dept1 values (1, 'DEPT 1');
insert into dept1 values (7, 'DEPT 7');
insert into dept1 values (10, 'DEPT 10');
insert into dept1 values (15, 'DEPT 15');
insert into dept1 values (22, 'DEPT 22');

create index dept_index
     on dept1 (deptno)
     local
     (partition d1,
      partition  d2 ,
      partition  d3 );
```

Option	Function
SET AUTOT ON	Turn on AUTOTRACE (short way)
SET AUTOT OFF	Turns off AUTOTRACE (short way)
SET AUTOT ON EXP	Shows only the EXPLAIN PLAN
SET AUTOTRACE ON STAT	Shows only the statistics
SET AUTOT TRACE	Does not show the output of the query

TABLE 6-5.   *AUTOTRACE Options*

I now generate an EXPLAIN PLAN that forces a full table scan to access the first two partitions:

```
explain plan for
select      dept_name
from        dept1
where       deptno  || '' = 1
or          deptno  || '' = 15;
```

When selecting from the plan table, you must select the additional columns PARTITION_START (starting partition) and PARTITION_STOP (ending partition). For a full table scan, all partitions will be accessed:

```
select      operation, options, id, object_name, partition_start,
            partition_stop
from        plan_table;
```

The output (for the full table scan) is shown here:

OPERATION	OPTIONS	ID	OBJECT NAME	PARTITION START	PARTITION STOP
SELECT STATEMENT					
PARTITION	CONCATENATED	0		1	3
RARTITION RANGE	FULL	1	DEPT1	1	3

The preceding example shows that a full table scan on the DEPT1 table is performed. All three partitions are scanned. The starting partition is 1, and the ending partition is 3.

Next, an EXPLAIN PLAN is generated in the following listing for an index range scan of partition 2 only (ensure that you delete from the plan table to clear it).

```
explain plan for select dept_name
from        dept1
where       deptno  = 15;
Explained.
```

Now I generate an EXPLAIN PLAN for an index range scan accessing only the second partition:

```
select      operation, options, id, object_name, partition_start,
            partition_stop
from        plan_table;
```

The output (for the index range scan) is shown here:

OPERATION	OPTIONS	ID	OBJECT NAME	PARTITION START	PARTITION STOP
SELECT STATEMENT		0			
PARTITION RANGE	SINGLE	1		2	2
TABLE ACCESS BY LOCAL INDEX ROWID		2	DEPT1	2	2
INDEX	RANGE SCAN	3	DEPT_INDEX	2	2

This output shows that the only partition of the table *or* index that is accessed is the second partition. This is because the value for DEPTNO = 15 is within the second partition of the DEPT1 table. The DEPTNO column is also indexed, and this value is also within the second partition of the index.

TIP
Partitions can also be viewed by the EXPLAIN PLAN by accessing the columns PARTITION_START and PARTITION_STOP in the PLAN_TABLE table.

Finding High Disk and/or Memory Reads Without Using TRACE

Is there another method for retrieving problem disk and memory read information without tracing everything? Yes! By using V$SQLAREA, you can find the problem queries on your system. This next listing shows how to find the problem queries. In this query, you are searching for queries where the disk reads are greater than 10,000 (missing or suppressed index potentials). If your system is much larger, you may need to set this number higher.

```
select      disk_reads, sql_text
from        v$sqlarea
where       disk_reads > 10000
order by    disk_reads desc;
```

DISK READS	SQL TEXT	
12987	select	order#,columns,types from orders
	where	substr(orderid,1,2)=:1
11131	select	custid, city from customer
	where	city = 'CHICAGO'

This output suggests that there are two problem queries causing heavy disk reads. The first has the index on ORDERID suppressed by the SUBSTR function; the second shows that there is a missing index on CITY.

In the query in the following listing, you are searching for queries where the memory reads are greater than 200,000 (over-indexed query potentials). If your system is much larger, you may need to set this number higher.

```
select      buffer_gets, sql_text
from        v$sqlarea
where       buffer_gets > 200000
order by    buffer_gets desc;
```

BUFFER GETS	SQL TEXT
300219	select order#,cust_no, from orders
	where division = '1'

The output suggests that one problem query is causing substantially heavy memory reads (300,219 blocks of data read into memory). The index on DIVISION appears to have a cardinality of 1 because this table has only a single division. What's happening here is that the entire index is being read and then the entire table is being read. The index should be suppressed for this statement to improve performance (and perhaps should be removed permanently if additional divisions will not be added).

Yet Another EXPLAIN PLAN Output Method: Building the Tree Structure

Although many people find the earlier EXPLAIN PLAN methods sufficient, others require a more theoretical approach that ties to the parent/child relationships of a query and the corresponding tree structure. For some people, this makes using EXPLAIN PLAN easier to visualize, and it is included here for that audience.

1. The following is the query to be explained:

```
explain plan
set statement_id = 'SQL2' for
select    cust_no ,cust_address ,cust_last_name, cust_first_name ,cust_mid_init
from      customer
where     cust_phone = '3035551234';
```

2. Here is the query used for this approach:

```
select    LPAD(' ',2*(LEVEL-1))||operation "OPERATION", options "OPTIONS",
          DECODE(TO_CHAR(id),'0','COST = ' || NVL(TO_CHAR(position),'n/a'),
          object_name) "OBJECT NAME", id ||'-'|| NVL(parent_id, 0)||'-'||
          NVL(position, 0) "ORDER", SUBSTR(optimizer,1,6) "OPT"
from   plan_table
start      with id = 0
and    statement_id = 'SQL2'
connect by prior id = parent_id
and        statement_id = 'SQL2';
```

3. Here is the output for this approach:

OPERATION	OPTIONS	OBJECT NAME	ORDER	OPT
SELECT STATEMENT		COST = 2	0-0-2	ALL_RO
TABLE ACCESS	BY INDEX ROWID	CUSTOMER	1-0-1	
INDEX	RANGE SCAN	IX_CUST_PHONE	2-1-1	ANALYZ

Note that two new columns are introduced:

- **ORDER**   This column contains the step ID, the parent ID, and the position of the step in the execution plan. The step ID identifies the step but does not imply the order of execution. The parent ID identifies the parent step of the step. The position indicates the order in which child steps are executed that have the same parent ID.

- **OPT**   This column contains the current mode of the optimizer.

4. The execution tree is constructed.
   Based on the execution plan in the illustration, an execution tree can be constructed to get a better feel for how Oracle is going to process the statement. To construct the tree, simply start with Step 1, find all other steps whose parent step is 1, and draw them in. Repeat this procedure until all the steps are accounted for. The execution tree for the execution plan for the query in this example is displayed here.

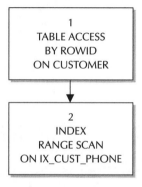

5. The execution plan is interpreted.

To understand how Oracle is going to process a statement, you must understand in what sequence Oracle is going to process the steps and what Oracle is doing in each step.

The sequence is determined by the parent/child relationship of the steps. Basically, the child step is always performed first, at least once, and feeds the parent steps from there. When a parent has multiple children, child steps are performed in the order of the step position, which is the third number displayed in the ORDER column of the execution plan. When the execution tree is constructed, if the lower-position children for a parent are arranged left to right, the execution tree reads left to right, bottom to top.

Another Example Using the Tree Approach

This section shows the simple process of using the tree approach and then viewing the information about how the query will be processed.

1. The following is the query to be explained:

```
select    a.cust_last_name, a.cust_first_name, a.cust_mid_init, b.order_desc,
          b.order_create_dt
```

```
from        order_hdr b, customer a
where       cust_phone = :host1
and         b.cust_no = a.cust_no
and         b.order_status = 'OPEN';
```

2. Here is the execution plan:

OPERATION	OPTIONS	OBJECT NAME	ORDER	OPT
SELECT STATEMENT		COST = n/a	0-0-0	ALL_RO
NESTED LOOPS			1-0-1	
TABLE ACCESS	BY ROWID	ORDER_HDR	2-1-1	
INDEX	RANGE SCAN	IX_ORDER_STATUS	3-2-1	
TABLE ACCESS	BY ROWID	CUSTOMER	4-1-2	
INDEX	UNIQUE SCAN	PK_CUSTOMER	5-4-1	

3. The following illustration shows the multitable execution tree.

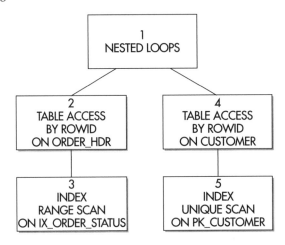

4. The execution plan sequence is determined for the query.
This statement has five steps. Child Step 3 is executed first. Because it is a range scan, it returns 0, 1, or many ROWIDs to Step 2. For each ROWID returned, Step 2 accesses the order table by ROWID, gets the requested data, and returns the data to Step 1. For each row of data received from Step 2, Step 1 sends the CUST_NO to Step 5. Step 5 uses the customer number to perform a unique scan to get the ROWID. The ROWID is then returned from Step 5 to Step 4. If no ROWID is found, Step 4 tells Step 1 to eliminate that particular row. If a ROWID is found, Step 4 accesses the table by ROWID and retrieves the data. Once it gets the data, if the phone number is correct, it returns the data to Step 1, where it is merged with the result from Steps 2 and 3 for that row and returned to the user. If the phone number is incorrect, Step 4 returns no row and Step 1 throws out the row.

5. The performance is reviewed.
Is this a good table access order? In most order-entry systems, where you have lots of customers and many open orders at a given time, why would you want to spin through all open orders first, get the data for each one, go to the CUSTOMER table for each of

those, and then throw out all but the one open order for the customer with the right phone number? To correct this situation, you want to go first to the customer table based on phone number because most of the rows will be filtered out in the first step, thus improving performance. How do you do this? Consider the changes made next.

6. Performance changes occur (the driving table is changed):

```
select      /*+ ORDERED */ a.cust_last_name, a.cust_first_name,
            a.cust_mid_init, b.order_desc, b.order_create_dt
from        customer a, order_hdr b
where       cust_phone = :host1
and         b.cust_no = a.cust_no
and         b.order_status = 'OPEN';
```

7. The *new* execution plan is determined:

OPERATION	OPTIONS	OBJECT NAME	ORDER	OPT
SELECT STATEMENT		COST = n/a	0-0-0	ALL_RO
NESTED LOOPS			1-0-1	
TABLE ACCESS	BY ROWID	CUSTOMER	2-1-1	
INDEX	RANGE SCAN	IX_CUST_PHONE	3-2-1	
TABLE ACCESS	BY ROWID	ORDER_HDR	4-1-2	
AND-EQUAL			5-4-1	
INDEX	RANGE SCAN	IX_ORDER_CUST	6-5-1	
INDEX	RANGE SCAN	IX_ORDER_STATUS	7-5-2	

8. The performance of the semituned query is reviewed.

Why did the table order change? Because you forced the table driving order with the ORDERED hint. Usually, the cost-based optimization will determine the best driving order based on table and index statistics. If not, the ORDERED hint can be used to force a driving order.

Is this a good table access order? The table order is good because the CUSTOMER half of the query is executed first and will probably return only one row to the ORDER half of the query. Is the AND-EQUAL optimal? In this case, no. Why churn through 1000 ROWIDs in the ORDER_STATUS index and all the ROWIDs in the CUST_NO index and keep only the ones that match? What you should do is either pick the most selective index of the two and use it, or create a composite index on CUST_NO and ORDER status. Changing the driving table was the right thing to do. Now, you must stop Oracle from using the ORDER_STATUS index to tune the query completely.

9. The *tuned* query is shown next (the index on ORDER_STATUS is suppressed):

```
select      /*+ ORDERED */ a.cust_last_name, a.cust_first_name,
            a.cust_mid_init, b.order_desc, b.order_create_dt
from        customer a, order_hdr b
where       cust_phone = :host1
and         b.cust_no = a.cust_no
and         b.order_status || '' = 'OPEN';
```

10. The *tuned* execution plan is shown next:

OPERATION	OPTIONS	OBJECT NAME	ORDER	OPT
SELECT STATEMENT		COST = n/a	0-0-0	ALL_RO
NESTED LOOPS			1-0-1	
TABLE ACCESS	BY ROWID	CUSTOMER	2-1-1	
INDEX	UNIQUE SCAN	PK_CUSTOMER	3-2-1	
TABLE ACCESS	BY ROWID	ORDER_HDR	4-1-2	
INDEX	RANGE SCAN	IX_ORDER_STATUS	5-4-1	

To determine how Oracle is going to process a SQL statement, you must generate and interpret an execution plan for the statement. With access to the tools that can generate execution plans for SQL, along with a rudimentary understanding of the information that is in an execution plan and the knowledge of how to construct an execution tree, a developer or DBA can begin exploring the vast variety of EXPLAIN PLANs that the diverse SQL code produces and learn fairly quickly how to tune and develop quality SQL.

Tracing/Explaining Problem Queries in Developer Products

Although you can issue the ALTER SESSION SET SQL_TRACE TRUE command on the SQL*Plus command line to TRACE SQL statements, doing this is tough when it comes to using developer products. One drawback to this option is that you are not able to trace a form or report; you need to cut the code out of the form or report and run it from SQL*Plus. This process can be very time-consuming if you do not know which statements you need to trace.

There is another way to create a trace of the execution of a form. If you are using Forms (versions 6*i*, 10*g*, and 11*g*), you can include `statistics = yes` on the command line. This way, you are able to trace individual forms. Later versions of Oracle Forms and Oracle Reports (all part of Fusion Middleware) allow tracing from inside a form or report. Please refer to the Forms and/or Reports (Fusion Middleware) documentation for an explanation of how to use these options. Oracle Applications often has a menu item to do this as well. You could also use DBMS_MONITOR to trace these products. Lastly, some methods for tracing PL/SQL programs are available: DBMS_PROFILER, DBMS_TRACE, and DBMS_HPROF.

TIP
You can also use TRACE within the Fusion Middleware (Developer) products. You simply need to set statistics = yes *on the command line for some products, or you may embed the tracing within an actual trigger to turn tracing on and off.*

Important Columns in the PLAN_TABLE Table

The descriptions for *some* of the more important columns available in the PLAN_TABLE table are as follows:

- **STATEMENT_ID** The value of the option STATEMENT_ID parameter specified in the EXPLAIN PLAN statement.

- **TIMESTAMP** The date and time when the EXPLAIN PLAN statement was issued.

■ **REMARKS**   Any comment (up to 80 bytes) you wish to associate with each step of the EXPLAIN PLAN. If you need to add or change a remark on any row of the PLAN_TABLE table, use the UPDATE statement to modify the rows of the PLAN_TABLE table.

■ **OPERATION**   The name of the internal operation performed in this step. In the first row generated for a statement, the column contains one of four values: DELETE, INSERT, SELECT, or UPDATE, depending on the type of statement.

■ **OPTIONS**   A variation on the operation described in the OPERATION column. See Appendix A of *Oracle Database 11g Performance Tuning Guide* for information on the contents of this column.

TIP
The OPERATION and OPTIONS columns of the PLAN_TABLE are the most important columns for tuning a query. The OPERATION column shows the actual operation performed (including type of join), and the OPTIONS column tells you when a full table scan is being performed (that may need an index).

■ **OBJECT_NODE**   The name of the database link used to reference the object (a table name or view name). For local queries using the parallel query option, this column describes the order in which output from operations is consumed.

■ **OBJECT_OWNER**   The name of the user who owns the schema containing the table or index.

■ **OBJECT_NAME**   The name of the table or index.

■ **OBJECT_INSTANCE**   A number corresponding to the ordinal position of the object as it appears in the original statement. The numbering proceeds from left to right, outer to inner, with respect to the original statement text. Note that view expansion results in unpredictable numbers.

■ **OBJECT_TYPE**   A modifier that provides descriptive information about the object, for example, NON-UNIQUE for indexes.

■ **OPTIMIZER**   The current optimizer mode.

■ **ID**   A number assigned to each step in the execution plan.

■ **PARENT_ID**   The ID of the next execution step that operates on the output of the ID step.

TIP
The PARENT_ID column is very important because it shows the dependencies of two steps in an EXPLAIN PLAN. If a step in the EXPLAIN PLAN has a PARENT_ID, it implies that this statement must run prior to the PARENT_ID that is specified.

■ **POSITION**   The order of processing for steps that all have the same PARENT_ID.

■ **OTHER**   Other information that is specific to the execution step that a user may find helpful.

■ **OTHER_TAG**   The contents of the OTHER column.

■ **COST**   The cost of the operation as *estimated* by the optimizer's cost-based approach. The value of this column does not have any particular unit of measurement; it is merely a weight value used to compare costs of execution plans.

■ **CARDINALITY**   The cost-based approach's *estimate* of the number of rows accessed by the operation.

■ **BYTES**   The cost-based approach's *estimate* of the number of bytes accessed by the operation.

■ **OTHER_XML**   This column can be queried to find out extra information that the optimizer used to determine the execution plan.

TIP
The BYTES column is extremely important when evaluating how to tune a query. When an index is used and the number of bytes is great, it implies that doing a full table scan would perhaps be more efficient (i.e., reading the index and data is more costly than just reading the data in a full table scan). Also, the number of bytes helps you determine which table should be accessed first in the query (driving table) because one table may limit the number of bytes needed from another. See Chapter 9 for tips on choosing the driving table.

TIP
Remember that both the COST and BYTES values in a query are estimates; it is quite possible for a version of a query with a higher estimated cost or bytes to run faster than another with a lower value.

Initialization Parameters for Undocumented TRACE

One area that the experts can investigate is the X$KSPPI table. A brief listing for undocumented TRACE parameters in `init.ora` is shown here (see Appendix A for additional information). Note that Oracle does not support use of undocumented features of the product.

```
select  ksppinm "Parameter Name", ksppstvl "Value",ksppstdf "Default"
from    x$ksppi x, x$ksppcv y
where   x.indx = y.indx
and     ksppinm like '/_%trace%' escape '/';
```

TIP
*The X$KSPPI table can be accessed only by the SYS user. See Chapter 13
for tips on accessing the X$ tables and using some of these parameters.
Do not use any undocumented parameters without consulting Oracle
Corporation. Also, the layout and column names of these views have
been known to change between Oracle releases.*

Tracing Errors Within Oracle for More Information

This section explains the use of one of the undocumented features of TRACE. Before using
undocumented `init.ora` parameters, please contact Oracle Corporation. To TRACE errors for a
session, you can alter and monitor the session (shown next), or set an event in the `init.ora` file (see
Chapter 13 for more information). You can also trace sessions for errors by running the query shown
next (used to TRACE a 4031 error). These queries build a TRACE file in your USER_DUMP_DEST that
will contain a dump of the full error text.

Use the following command to trace sessions for errors:

```
alter session set events='4031 trace name errorstack level 4';
```

TIP
*Tracing queries can help performance, but using the TRACE facility
built into the undocumented TRACE `init.ora` parameters (discussed
previously) can give you great insight into solving errors within
Oracle.*

Tracing by Enabling Events

Trace sessions can also be initiated by using this command:

```
SQL> Alter session set events '10046 trace name context forever, level 1';
Session altered.
```

The value of the level (1 in the previous command) can be 1 (*regular trace*), 4 (*trace bind
variables*), 8 (*trace wait states*), or 12 (*regular trace, plus bind variables and wait states*).
Information about bind variables and wait states can then appear in the trace file but will be
ignored by TKPROF when formatting the report. The trace file output for the previous command
looks like this:

```
SELECT SYSDATE   FROM DUAL  WHERE SYSDATE IN ( :b1  )
END OF STMT
PARSE #4:c=0,e=0,p=0,cr=0,cu=0,mis=0,r=0,dep=1,og=4,tim=0
BINDS #4:
 bind 0: dty=12 mxl=07(07) mal=00 scl=00 pre=00 oacflg=03 oacfl2=1 size=8 offset=0
   bfp=0ddcc774 bln=07 avl=07 flg=05
   value="11/19/2000 19:25:47"
WAIT #1: nam='SQL*Net message to client' ela= 0 p1=1413697536 p2=1 p3=0
```

To turn event tracing off, use the following command:

```
SQL> Alter session set events '10046 trace name context off';
Session altered.
```

Oracle 11*g* has a new syntax for setting events that makes it easier to trace processes without knowing the SID or SERIAL# (see My Oracle Support Note 813737.1 for additional information). You can now use the following command instead:

```
alter system set events 'sql_trace {process : ospid = 2345} level=12';
```

Using Stored Outlines

Oracle 8*i* introduced a facility called *STORED OUTLINES* that allows a query to use a predetermined execution plan every time that query is run, no matter where the query is run from. People sometimes speak of the STORED OUTLINES as storing an execution plan, but this is not really what happens. Instead, Oracle stores a series of *hints*—instructions to the database to execute a query in a precise way—to duplicate the execution plan as saved during a recording session.

Oracle can replicate execution plans for queries using stored outlines through a process similar to using the EXPLAIN PLAN functionality in SQL*PLUS. First, you set up the STORED OUTLINE session by telling Oracle to save outlines for queries you are about to run using the ALTER SESSION command. Next, you execute the query for which you want the outline stored. (You generally do this on a session-only basis so as not to affect other users.) Finally, if the execution plan is acceptable, you can save it to the database so it can be used by everyone everywhere. The following sections describe each of these steps in greater detail.

TIP
Oracle Corporation likes to refer to STORED OUTLINES as PLAN STABILITY. For further information on using STORED OUTLINES, see the Oracle documentation on PLAN STABILITY.

Setting Up STORED OUTLINES

Unfortunately, as with most of the spectacular new features that Oracle provides, the setup process for using STORED OUTLINES is complex. Many user *and* session privileges must be set up properly before outlines can be stored or stored ones can be used.

The following privileges are required to use STORED OUTLINES:

- CREATE ANY OUTLINE
- EXECUTE_CATALOG_ROLE (to use the DBMS_OUTLN package)
- PLUSTRACE (to use AUTOTRACE, if applicable)

Beyond permissions, STORED OUTLINES require the use of several specific session parameters (environment settings – ALTER SESSION SET):

- QUERY_REWRITE_ENABLED = TRUE
- STAR_TRANSFORMATION_ENABLED = TRUE

- OPTIMIZER_FEATURES_ENABLE = 11.2.0.1 (for example)

- USE_STORED_OUTLINES = TRUE (to use existing STORED OUTLINES)

- CREATE_STORED_OUTLINES = TRUE (to create or edit STORED OUTLINES)

- USE_PRIVATE_OUTLINES = TRUE (to use private outlines, current session only)

How OUTLINES Are Stored

As with most other features, Oracle stores OUTLINES in internal database tables whose contents are available through the usual distribution of system views (USER_*, ALL_*, and DBA_*). Of course, only the DBA privileged few can see the DBA views, whereas the ALL_* views display information about objects the user can see (but may not own), and the USER_* views show information about those objects the current user actually owns. For brevity, I'll focus on the USER_* views. STORED OUTLINES chiefly use these views:

- USER_OUTLINES

- USER_OUTLINE_HINTS

The contents of USER_OUTLINES look something like the following:

```
NAME                            CATEGORY                    USED    TIMESTAMP
VERSION
SQL_TEXT
SIGNATURE                       COMPATIBLE    ENABLED   FORMAT MIGRATED
SYS_OUTLINE_10011716022374501   DEFAULT                     UNUSED  17-JAN-10
11.2.0.1.0
select * from emp
E64F36A7F73BECFE2C61CBAA5781982F COMPATIBLE   ENABLED   NORMAL NOT-MIGRATED
```

A small listing from the USER_OUTLINE_HINTS table (multiple rows would probably be displayed) looks like this:

```
NAME                                NODE      STAGE   JOIN_POS
----------------------------------- --------- ------- ----------
HINT
----------------------------------------------------------------------------
SYS_OUTLINE_020213193254787          1         3         0
NO_EXPAND
SYS_OUTLINE_020213193254787          1         3         0
ORDERED
SYS_OUTLINE_020213193254787          1         3         0
NO_FACT(S_EMP)
```

Consider moving the OUTLINE tables to another tablespace (which is usually a good idea). The stored outlines are stored in the SYSTEM tablespace by default (which is almost always a mistake if you have a large number of them). You can use Data Pump to move them elsewhere. Initially, the OUTLN schema stores its data in the SYSTEM tablespace that is accessed via the USER_OUTLINES and USER_OUTLINE_HINTS views (which are based on OL$, OL$HINTS, and OL$NODES). The actual data is stored in global temporary tables that map to the OL$,

OL$HINTS, and OL$NODES synonyms. You can export OL$, OL$HINTS, and OL$NODES to a new tablespace that you create and then change the default tablespace for the OUTLN schema.

Creating and Using Stored Outlines

There are two kinds of stored outlines: *private,* which are session-specific, and *public,* which can affect the entire database. Which kind is being used is controlled by the USE_PRIVATE_OUTLINES session parameter setting. If this setting is TRUE, then private outlines are used. Generally, private outlines are best until an optimal execution plan is generated. Private outlines can be saved publicly using the CREATE OR REPLACE PRIVATE OUTLINE command; public outlines can be created from private ones using the CREATE OR REPLACE OUTLINE. . .FROM PRIVATE. . . command. This process is called *editing* and is used to copy an existing private outline to a public one. When the stored outlines are in place, Oracle uses them automatically and this process is invisible to the user executing the command.

TIP
Oracle applies STORED OUTLINES to query execution on a per-query basis. To be used on a given query, the query must match its stored equivalent perfectly. The slightest variation causes Oracle to decide that the queries are different and the outline should not be used. The rules are similar to those of cursor-sharing, which Oracle uses to parse queries with the shared pool.

Although outlines can be edited and updated using SQL*PLUS, this isn't really recommended because it's difficult. An easier and better way to update them is to use the outline editor provided with Oracle Enterprise Manager. For more information on Oracle Enterprise Manager, see Chapter 5.

Outlines can initially be created in a couple of different ways. Setting the CREATE STORED_OUTLINES session parameter to TRUE (if everything is set up correctly, of course) causes an outline (with a cryptic SYS-prefixed name for each generated outline) to be generated for *every* query executed, similar to using TRACE to monitor an entire session. A more precise (and controllable) way is to create an outline for a specific query using the CREATE OUTLINE command, as shown here:

```
create or replace outline pb_outline on
  select e.last_name, e.salary
  from   s_emp e
  where  userid = 'lngao';
```

In this example, PB_OUTLINE is the outline created. This method has the big advantage of giving you control over what's happening *and* the ability to give the outline a usable name.

Oracle provides some helpful packages that you can use to work with STORED OUTLINES. The DBMS_OUTLN and DBMS_OUTLN_EDIT (see the note following the paragraph) packages may offer additional possibilities when using stored outlines. Unlike most Oracle packages, these don't belong to the SYS user, however, and although they can be described in SQL*PLUS, their source code is not available from the USER_SOURCE view (unlike most packages, where at least the headers are visible). The tables underlying the views cannot be directly maintained either (they are system tables).

NOTE
*It is generally not recommended to use DBMS_OUTLN_EDIT in 10g
and 11g. It is now unpublished.*

Dropping Stored Outlines

How do you get rid of stored outlines when you don't want them anymore or when they impact
performance negatively? Use the DROP_UNUSED procedure in the DBMS_OUTLN package.

To drop all unused outlines:

```
execute dbms_outln.drop_unused
```

To remove outlines that *have* been used, first apply the DBMS_OUTLN.CLEAR_USED
procedure, which accepts an outline name (available from the USER_OUTLINES view) and can be
run against only one outline at a time. You could write a short PL/SQL program to clear outlines en
masse.

To determine whether an outline is actually being used, examine the USED column in
USER_OUTLINES. You can also query the OUTLINE_CATEGORY column in the V$SQL view
to see things that are still in the cache.

```
SELECT OUTLINE_CATEGORY, OUTLINE_SID
FROM    V$SQL
WHERE   SQL_TEXT = 'portion of query%'
```

Using SQL Plan Management (SPM) (11g New Feature)

In Oracle 11g, SQL Plan Management has been added to help preserve the performance of SQL
statements by only allowing execution plans that improve the performance of the statement being
executed. SPM is similar to, yet different from, stored outlines. Like stored outlines, SPM's goal is
to stabilize the execution plan of a SQL statement. Stored outlines freeze an execution plan for a
SQL statement, whereas SPM allows a new execution plan to be selected as long as it improves
the performance of the SQL statement. Some of the reasons that you would need SPM include:

- New version of Oracle (new optimizer version—use capture replay to test effect)
- Changes to optimizer statistics or data changes
- Schema, application, or metadata changes (use SQL Advisor to get suggestions)
- System settings changes (use SQL Replay to find what works)
- SQL Profile (statistics—data skews and correlated columns) creation

TIP
*Stored outlines freeze an execution plan whereas SPM allows a new
execution plan as long as the plan improves the performance of the
SQL statement. If both a stored outline and an SPM plan exist for a
SQL statement, the stored outline takes precedence.*

SPM terms

The following are terms related to the SMB hierarchy:

- **SQL Management Base (SMB)** SQL Plan History and SQL Plan Baseline are located within the SMB. The SMB is located in the SYSAUX tablespace and also contains SQL profiles.

- **SQL Plan History** A subset of SMB that includes both *accepted* and *not accepted* plans generated for a SQL statement.

- **SQL Plan Baseline** A subset of SQL Plan History that includes only the set of accepted plans generated for a SQL statement.

The following illustration shows a target chart of how this hierarchy looks.

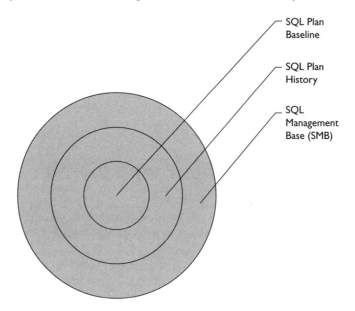

The following are terms related to the status of plans:

- **Accepted plan** A plan must be both ENABLED and ACCEPTED in order to be considered by the optimizer.

- **Enabled plan** The default value for an execution plan in Plan History or Plan Baseline is ENABLED. A plan must be both ENABLED and ACCEPTED to be considered by the optimizer.

- **Fixed plan** This execution plan gets priority over other plans for a SQL statement unless there are other fixed plans, in which case the fixed plan with the best performance is selected.

Some other terms include:

- **AUTOPURGE** A plan is automatically purged from Plan History if it has not been used for 53 weeks (based on the LAST_EXECUTED date in DBA_SQL_PLAN_BASELINES). This date can be modified using the DBMS_SPM.CONFIGURE package.

- **OPTIMIZER_USE_SQL_PLAN_BASELINES** The default is TRUE. The database parameter that determines if the Plan Baseline will be used if it is present for a SQL statement.

- **OPTIMIZER_CAPTURE_PLAN_BASELINES** The default is FALSE. Any SQL statements executed while this parameter is set to TRUE are added to the Plan Baseline (but not necessarily ACCEPTED).

- **DBA_SQL_PLAN_BASELINES** A view for gathering information about Plan Baselines that have been created.

TIP
A SQL Plan Baseline must be both ENABLED and ACCEPTED to be considered by the optimizer.

Using SPM

SPM is enabled and SQL statements are stored in the SQL Management Base using the following method:

1. Set the OPTIMIZER_CAPTURE_PLAN_BASELINES parameter to TRUE at the system or session level.

2. Use the SQL Tuning Set (see Chapter 15 of the *Oracle Database 11g Performance Tuning Guide* for details).

3. Extract the statement from the shared pool using the DBMS_SPM.LOAD_PLANS_ FROM_CURSOR_CACHE function (see the *Oracle Database 11g Performance Tuning Guide,* Chapter 15, for details).

Note that only repeatable SQL statements (that is, statements that have been parsed or executed more than once) are considered by SPM.

SPM is helpful for

- Database upgrades
- System and/or data changes
- Deployment of new application modules

SPM Example

Here is an example of how SPM works:

1. Turn capture on and run the SQL statement more than once so SPM can determine if the statement is repeatable and then turn capture off:

```
alter session set optimizer_capture_sql_plan_baselines=true;
select * /* ebk1 */ from emp where job='PRESIDENT';
select * /* ebk1 */ from emp where job='PRESIDENT';
alter session set optimizer_capture_sql_plan_baselines=false;
```

2. Query DBA_SQL_PLAN_BASELINES to determine the status of the SQL statement in SPM:

```
select  plan_name,  sql_handle,  enabled,  accepted,  fixed,
        module,  sql_text
from    dba_sql_plan_baselines;


PLAN_NAME                        SQL_HANDLE                     ENA ACC FIX MODULE
SQL_TEXT
--------------------------------------------------------------------------------
SQL_PLAN_1r9f32bakc2qmd8a279cc SQL_1ba5c312d5260ad3           YES YES NO  SQL*Plus
select * /* ebk1 */ from emp where job='PRESIDENT';
```

   Note that ENABLED is YES, ACCPTED is YES, and FIXED is NO. Also note the module that was used to add this plan (SQL*Plus).

3. Now make a change to the environment (index added) and run the SQL statement again:

```
create index ellen on emp(job);
alter session set optimizer_capture_sql_plan_baselines=true;
select * /* ebk1 */ from emp where job='PRESIDENT';
select * /* ebk1 */ from emp where job='PRESIDENT';
alter session set optimizer_capture_sql_plan_baselines=false;
```

4. Query DBA_SQL_PLAN_BASELINES to determine the status of the SQL statement in SPM:

```
PLAN_NAME                        SQL_HANDLE                     ENA ACC FIX MODULE
-------------------------------- ------------------------------ --- --- --- ----------
SQL_TEXT
--------------------------------------------------------------------------------
SQL_PLAN_1r9f32bakc2qmc581a482 SYS_SQL_1ba5c312d5260ad3       YES NO  NO  SQL*Plus
select * /* ebk1 */ from emp where job='PRESIDENT'

SQL_PLAN_1r9f32bakc2qmd8a279cc SYS_SQL_1ba5c312d5260ad3       YES YES NO  SQL*Plus
select * /* ebk1 */ from emp where job='PRESIDENT'
```

   Note that another PLAN NAME was added (with the same SQL_HANDLE) that has an ACCEPTED value of NO, which means the optimizer will not consider this plan.

   Now I'm going to set OPTIMIZER_USE_SQL_PLAN_BASELINE to false and allow the optimizer to choose a plan (not necessarily in the Plan Baseline). Then I will set the

OPTIMIZER_USE_SQL_PLAN_BASELINE to TRUE and force the optimizer to choose only an ACCEPTED plan in the Plan Baseline.

```
alter system set optimizer_use_sql_plan_baselines=false;

explain plan for
select * /* ebk1 */ from emp where job='PRESIDENT';

select * from table(dbms_xplan.display(null,null,'basic'));

PLAN_TABLE_OUTPUT
----------------------------------------------
| Id  | Operation                  | Name  |
----------------------------------------------
|   0 | SELECT STATEMENT           |       |
|   1 |  TABLE ACCESS BY INDEX ROWID| EMP   |
|   2 |   INDEX RANGE SCAN         | ELLEN |
----------------------------------------------


alter system set optimizer_use_sql_plan_baselines=true;

explain plan for
select * /* ebk1 */ from emp where job='PRESIDENT';

select * from table(dbms_xplan.display(null,null,'basic'));

PLAN_TABLE_OUTPUT
--------------------------------------------------------------------------------
Plan hash value: 3956160932


-----------------------------------
| Id  | Operation         | Name |
-----------------------------------
|   0 | SELECT STATEMENT  |      |
|   1 |  TABLE ACCESS FULL| EMP  |
-----------------------------------
```

Note that in the first case, the optimizer chooses a plan that makes use of the index, but, in the second case, it did not because that plan was not an ACCEPTED plan.

The next step is to evolve a SQL plan to allow a plan with an ACCEPTED status of NO to be changed to YES if the plan performs better than plans that already have an ACCEPTED value of YES:

```
set serveroutput on
set long 10000
DECLARE
  report clob;
BEGIN
  report := DBMS_SPM.EVOLVE_SQL_PLAN_BASELINE(
              sql_handle => 'SYS_SQL_1ba5c312d5260ad3');
  DBMS_OUTPUT.PUT_LINE(report);
END;
/
```

Here is the output:

```
                        Evolve SQL Plan Baseline
Report
------------------------------------------------------------------------

Inputs:
-------
  SQL_HANDLE = SQL_1ba5c312d5260ad3
  PLAN_NAME  =
TIME_LIMIT = DBMS_SPM.AUTO_LIMIT
  VERIFY     = YES
  COMMIT     = YES
Plan:
SQL_PLAN_1r9f32bakc2qmc581a482
------------------------------------
  Plan was verified: Time used .03 seconds.
  Plan passed performance criterion: 3.5 times better than baseline plan.
  Plan was changed to an accepted plan.

                             Baseline Plan    Test Plan    Stats Ratio
                             -------------    ---------    -----------
  Execution Status:            COMPLETE        COMPLETE
  Rows Processed:                 1               1
  Elapsed Time(ms):              .066            .052          1.27

CPU Time(ms):                    0               0
  Buffer Gets:                   7               2            3.5
  Physical Read Requests:        0               0
  Physical Write Requests:       0               0
  Physical Read
Bytes:                           0               0
  Physical Write Bytes:          0               0
  Executions:                    1               1


------------------------------------------------------------------------
                             Report Summary
------------------------------------------------------------------------
Number of plans verified: 1
Number of plans accepted: 1
PL/SQL procedure successfully completed.
```

Note that the plan, which was previously not ACCEPTED, is now ACCEPTED:

```
PLAN_NAME                        SQL_HANDLE                      ENA ACC FIX MODULE
------------------------------   -----------------------------   --- --- --- ----------
SQL_TEXT
------------------------------------------------------------------------
SQL_PLAN_1r9f32bakc2qmc581a482 SYS_SQL_1ba5c312d5260ad3          YES YES NO  SQL*Plus
select * /* ebk1 */ from emp where job='PRESIDENT'
```

```
SQL_PLAN_1r9f32bakc2qmd8a279cc SYS_SQL_1ba5c312d5260ad3       YES YES NO  SQL*Plus
select * /* ebk1 */ from emp where job='PRESIDENT'
```

Now when I run the SQL statement with OPTIMIZER_USE_SQL_PLAN_BASELINE set to
TRUE, this newly ACCEPTED plan is chosen because it performs better than other ACCEPTED
plans for this SQL statement:

```
alter system set optimizer_use_sql_plan_baselines=true;

explain plan for
select * /* ebk1 */ from emp where job='PRESIDENT';

select * from table(dbms_xplan.display(null,null,'basic'));

PLAN_TABLE_OUTPUT
--------------------------------------------------------------------------------
Plan hash value: 3484773650


---------------------------------------------
| Id  | Operation                   | Name  |
---------------------------------------------
|   0 | SELECT STATEMENT            |       |
|   1 |  TABLE ACCESS BY INDEX ROWID| EMP   |
|   2 |   INDEX RANGE SCAN          | ELLEN |
```

Using Fixed SQL Plan Baselines

Fixed plans (if present) are used instead of any other plans in the Plan Baseline for a SQL
statement. If more than one Fixed plan exists for a SQL statement, then the Fixed plan with the
best performance is used. Here is an example of how to set a plan to FIXED:

```
DECLARE
  l_plans_altered  PLS_INTEGER;
BEGIN
  l_plans_altered := DBMS_SPM.alter_sql_plan_baseline(
    sql_handle     => 'SYS_SQL_976227df3c76f615',
    plan_name      => NULL,
    attribute_name => 'fixed',
    attribute_value => 'YES');
END;
/

select plan_name, sql_handle, enabled, accepted, fixed, module, sql_text
from   dba_sql_plan_baselines;

PLAN_NAME                        SQL_HANDLE                      ENA ACC FIX MODULE
-------------------------------- ------------------------------- --- --- --- ----------
SQL_TEXT
--------------------------------------------------------------------------------
SQL_PLAN_9fsj7vwy7dxhpb59fb1c2 SYS_SQL_976227df3c76f615         YES NO  YES SQL*Plus
select * /* ebk20 */ from emp where job='PRESIDENT'

SQL_PLAN_9fsj7vwy7dxhpd8a279cc SYS_SQL_976227df3c76f615         YES YES YES SQL*Plus
select * /* ebk20 */ from emp where job='PRESIDENT'
```

Dropping a plan

Here is an example of how to drop a plan using the SQL_HANDLE:

```
set serveroutput on
declare
l_plan_dropped pls_integer; begin
l_plan_dropped := dbms_spm.drop_sql_plan_baseline
(sql_handle => 'SYS_SQL_976227df3c76f615', plan_name => NULL);end;
/
```

Converting from Stored Outlines to SQL Plan Management

Now I will walk you through an example of how to convert a SQL statement from using stored outlines to using SQL Plan Management.

To create a stored outline:

```
alter session set query_rewrite_enabled = true;
alter session set create_stored_outlines = true;
create or replace outline kev_outline on select * /* ebk2 */ from emp where job='PRESIDENT';
Session altered.
Session altered.
Outline created
```

To use the stored outline:

```
alter session set query_rewrite_enabled = true;
alter session set use_stored_outlines = true;
select * /* ebk2 */ from emp where job='PRESIDENT';
 Status of STORED OUTLINE:

select *
from  user_outlines;
```

NAME	CATEGORY		USED	TIMESTAMP
VERSION				
SQL_TEXT				
SIGNATURE	COMPATIBLE	ENABLED	FORMAT	MIGRATED
KEV_OUTLINE	DEFAULT		**USED**	31-JAN-10
11.2.0.1.0				
select * /* ebk2 */ from emp where job='PRESIDENT'				
A4D01876FBF006A2ECE8420DBA30780C	COMPATIBLE	ENABLED	NORMAL	**NOT-MIGRATED**

Note that MIGRATED status field shows it to be NOT-MIGRATED and the USED status field shows it to be USED.

To migrate this stored outline to a Plan Baseline:

```
set serveroutput on
DECLARE
  tst_outline clob;
BEGIN
  tst_outline := DBMS_SPM.MIGRATE_STORED_OUTLINE(attribute_name => 'OUTLINE_NAME',
attribute_value => 'KEV_OUTLINE');
END;
/
```

Here is the output:

```
PL/SQL procedure successfully completed.
```

To migrate all stored outlines:

```
DBMS_SPM.MIGRATE_STORED_OUTLINE(attribute_name => 'ALL')
```

To retrieve the status of the stored outline and the plan outline after the migration:

```
select *
from   user_outlines;

NAME                            CATEGORY                      USED   TIMESTAMP
------------------------------- ----------------------------- ------ ---------
VERSION
-----------------------------------------------------------------
SQL_TEXT
-------------------------------------------------------------------
SIGNATURE                       COMPATIBLE   ENABLED  FORMAT MIGRATED
------------------------------- ------------ -------- ------ ------------
KEV_OUTLINE                     DEFAULT                       USED   31-JAN-10
11.2.0.1.0
select * /* ebk2 */ from emp where job='PRESIDENT'
A4D01876FBF006A2ECE8420DBA30780C COMPATIBLE   ENABLED  NORMAL MIGRATED

select plan_name, sql_handle, enabled, accepted, fixed, module, origin, sql_text
from   dba_sql_plan_baselines;

PLAN_NAME                       SQL_HANDLE                    ENA ACC FIX MODULE
------------------------------- ----------------------------- --- --- --- ----------
ORIGIN
--------------
SQL_TEXT
--------------------------------------------------------------------------------
KEV_OUTLINE                     SYS_SQL_a698a39a23f57e6d       YES YES NO  DEFAULT
STORED-OUTLINE
select * /* ebk2 */ from emp where job='PRESIDENT'
```

Note that ACCEPTED is set to YES for the PLAN OUTLINE and MIGRATED is set to MIGRATED for STORED_OUTLINE. Because the status of the STORED OUTLINE is MIGRATED, the optimizer will not look at the STORED OUTLINE when determining which plan to use.

To drop the migrated stored outline:

```
DECLARE
  drp_outline PLS_INTEGER;
BEGIN
  drp_outline := DBMS_SPM.DROP_MIGRATED_STORED_OUTLINE();
END;
/
```

This drops all migrated stored outlines.

TIPS

&

REVIEW

Tips Review

- Setting TIMED_STATISTICS = TRUE in the init.ora will *enable the collection of time statistics*. Also, in 10*g*, the initialization parameter SQL_TRACE has been deprecated.

- The TKPROF utility converts traced output into a readable format. Without running TKPROF, reading the output of a TRACE would be difficult. By specifying explain = username/password, you can get the EXPLAIN execution path, in addition to the execution statistics for the query.

- To use multiple sort parameters, just repeat the sort = parameter on the command line, as TKPROF SOURCE_FILE OUT_FILE sort = parm1 sort = parm2.

- Run TKPROF from the command line without any parameter for a list of all the parameters.

- A traced query with a large number of physical reads usually indicates a missing index.

- A traced query output with only memory reads usually indicates that an index is being used.

- When using DBMS_MONITOR, be sure to disable tracing when you are done; otherwise, every session that meets the criteria specified is traced.

- The trace file is a point-in-time picture of what happened on the system at a given moment. In contrast, the EXPLAIN PLAN is generated when the TKPROF listing is analyzed, which could be some time later. The row source operation listing is generated as part of the trace file and can be used to see if the database objects have changed since the TRACE was performed.

- Using a value of ALL_EXECUTIONS for the PLAN_STAT ensures that information regarding the execution plan is always contained in the trace file.

- If multiple developers/DBAs are using the same PLAN_TABLE, SET STATEMENT_ID is essential to identifying a statement.

- Use EXPLAIN instead of TRACE so you don't have to wait for the query to run. EXPLAIN shows the path of a query without actually running the query. Use TRACE only for multiquery batch jobs to find out which of the many queries in the batch job is slow.

■ You can use the `utlxpls.sql` and `utlxplp.sql` queries provided by Oracle to query the PLAN_TABLE without having to write your own query and format the output.

■ Whether the EXPLAIN PLAN is read from top to bottom or from bottom to top depends entirely on the query used to select information from the PLAN_TABLE.

■ The AUTOTRACE option also provides an EXPLAIN PLAN for a query. AUTOTRACE also provides many TRACE and TKPROF statistics, such as disk reads (physical reads) and memory reads (consistent reads + db block gets).

■ If the error "Unable to verify plan table format or existence" occurs when enabling AUTOTRACE, you must create a PLAN_TABLE using `utlxplan.sql`.

■ AUTOTRACE may fail when querying system views because the user may not have permission to view underlying objects.

■ Partitions can also be viewed by the EXPLAIN PLAN by accessing the columns PARTITION_START and PARTITION_STOP in the PLAN_TABLE table.

■ Accessing the V$SQLAREA table can give YOU statistics that are often found when tracing a query.

■ You can also use TRACE within the Developer/2000 products. You simply need to set `statistics = yes` on the command line for Oracle Forms.

■ The OPERATION and OPTIONS columns of the PLAN_TABLE are the most important columns for tuning a query. The OPERATION column shows the actual operation performed (including type of join), and the OPTIONS column tells you when a full table scan IS being performed that may need an index.

■ The ID column of the PLAN_TABLE shows the order in which a statement is processed. One of the primary rules of tuning a SQL statement is to change the query SO that the ID of the order in which the steps in the query execute is changed. Changing the order in which steps execute in a query usually changes the performance of a query, either positively or negatively.

■ The PARENT_ID column of the PLAN_TABLE is very important because it shows the dependencies of two steps in an EXPLAIN PLAN. If a section of the EXPLAIN PLAN has a PARENT_ID, it implies that this statement *must* run prior to the PARENT_ID that is specified.

■ The BYTES column of the PLAN_TABLE is extremely important when evaluating how to tune a query. When an index is used and the number of BYTES is great, it implies that perhaps doing a full table scan would be more efficient (i.e., reading the index and data is more costly than just reading the data in a full table scan). Also, the number of bytes helps you determine which table should be accessed first in the query because one table may limit the number of bytes needed from another.

■ Both the COST and BYTES values in a query are estimates; it is quite possible for a version of a query with a higher estimated cost or bytes to actually run faster than another with a lower value.

■ The X$KSPPI table can be accessed only by the SYS user. See Chapter 13 for tips on accessing the X$ tables and using some of these parameters. Do not use *any* undocumented parameters without consulting Oracle Corporation. Note that the layout and column names of these views have been known to change between Oracle releases.

■ Tracing queries can improve performance, but using the TRACE facility built into the undocumented TRACE `init.ora` parameters can give great insight into (and better information for) solving errors within Oracle.

■ Oracle Corporation likes to refer to STORED OUTLINES as PLAN STABILITY.

■ Oracle applies STORED OUTLINES to query executions on a per-query basis. To be applied, a query must match its stored equivalent perfectly. The slightest variation could cause Oracle to decide that the queries are different and the outline should not be used. The rules are similar to those Oracle uses to parse queries when running them in the database.

■ Stored outlines are used to freeze an execution plan, whereas SQL Plan Management allows new execution plans as long as the plan improves the performance of the SQL statement. If both a stored outline and an SPM plan exist for a SQL statement, the stored outline takes precedence.

■ A Plan Baseline must be both ENABLED and ACCEPTED to be considered by the optimizer.

References

My Oracle Support Notes (Metalink): 293661.1, note 813737.1, 726802.1.
Oracle Database 11g Performance Tuning Guide, Oracle Corporation.
   Many thanks to Warren Bakker for upgrading this chapter to Oracle 11*g* and also 10*g*. Thanks to Mark Riedel for upgrading this chapter to Oracle 9*i,* and to Dave Hathway, Greg Pucka, and Roger Behm for their contributions to this chapter.

CHAPTER
7

Basic Hint Syntax
(Developer and DBA)

TIPS & COVERED

Although the cost-based optimizer is incredibly accurate in choosing the correct optimization path and use of indexes for thousands of queries on your system, it is not perfect. To this end, Oracle provides hints that you can specify for a given query to override the optimizer, hopefully achieving better performance for a given query. This chapter focuses on the basic syntax and use of hints. The chapters following this one (Chapters 8 and 9) have more complex examples, using various hints covered in this chapter.

Changes in 11g hints include the new hints RESULT_CACHE, MONITOR, and NO_MONITOR. Several formerly supported hints were removed from the SQL Reference (these were deprecated/discouraged in 10g): RULE, the anti-join hints (HASH_AJ, NL_AJ, MERGE_AJ), the semi-join hints (HASH_SJ, NL_SJ, MERGE_SJ), ROWID, and AND_EQUAL.

Because every system is diverse, the most useful hints for your system may not be the same ones that I have found to be best. Common to most systems is the use of the FULL, INDEX, and ORDERED hints. A system with the parallel option may use the PARALLEL hint most often. Tips covered in this chapter include the following:

- The top hints used, the available hints and groupings, and specifying multiple hints
- That when using an alias, you *must* use the alias, *not* the table name in the hint
- Using the FIRST_ROWS hint generally to force the use of indexes
- Using the ALL_ROWS hint generally to force a full table scan
- Using the FULL hint to perform a full table scan
- Using the INDEX hint to affect the use of an index
- Using the NO_INDEX hint to disallow a specified index from being used
- Using the INDEX_ASC hint to use an index ordered in ascending order
- Using the INDEX_DESC hint to use an index ordered in descending order
- Using the INDEX_JOIN hint to allow the merging of indexes on a single table
- Using the INDEX_COMBINE hint to access multiple bitmap indexes
- Performing fast full scans with the INDEX_FFS hint
- Using the ORDERED hint to specify the driving order of tables
- Using the LEADING hint to specify just the first driving table
- Using the NO_EXPAND hint to avoid OR expansion
- Using queries involving multiple locations and the DRIVING_SITE hint
- Using the USE_MERGE, USE_NL, and USE_HASH hints to change how tables are joined internally
- Processing subqueries earlier with PUSH_SUBQ
- Using the parallel query option and PARALLEL and NO_PARALLEL
- Using APPEND and NOAPPEND for faster data inserts

- Caching and pinning a table into memory with the CACHE hint in the buffer cache
- Using the NO_CACHE hint
- Caching table data with the RESULT_CACHE in the shared pool
- Overriding the CURSOR_SHARING setting with the CURSOR_SHARING_EXACT hint
- Miscellaneous Hints and Notes

Top Hints Used

I did an informal survey at TUSC to see which hints both DBAs and developers use in their day-to-day tuning. I asked them to give me only the top three that they used. The results were not surprising to me, but if you've never used hints, this is quite helpful in determining where to start. Here is the list of TUSC's top hints, in the order in which they are used:

1. INDEX
2. ORDERED
3. PARALLEL
4. FIRST_ROWS
5. FULL
6. LEADING
7. USE_NL
8. APPEND
9. USE_HASH
10. RESULT_CACHE

NOTE
The top three in this list are also the top three that I've used the most since hints were introduced. I've frequently used all of these in my tuning, so they are a great place to start.

Use Hints Sparingly

Hints fall into two primary categories: usage directives and compiler directives. *Usage directives* are those that can be set using initialization parameters in addition to the statement level (i.e., FIRST_ROWS, ALL_ROWS). If you have an OLTP database, setting the optimizer (at the instance level) from ALL_ROWS to FIRST_ROWS immediately focuses the optimizer on returning the first few rows faster (best response time for most OLTP applications). Setting the optimizer (at the instance level) to ALL_ROWS immediately focuses the optimizer on returning all rows faster (best throughput for all rows, which may be preferred for batch operations or data warehouses). The hints you give the optimizer influence its choices for join operations and the order of operations. In both database cases (OLTP and data warehouse), the goal is to solve performance issues system-wide instead of needing to tune individual queries.

When there are queries inside a data warehouse that behave more like OLTP queries or vice versa, you may need to use hints for those specific statements. As you begin to use hints, you may find yourself tuning the same type of problem over and over, an indication that you have improper instance-level settings or improper database structures (missing indexes or I/O contention, for example) that are impacting performance. Tuning the symptoms (using *compiler directives* in the short term) leads you to the pattern that can be fixed for the long term. Then you will hopefully be able to apply a usage directive to fix the problem system-wide. Try to use hints with this in mind and you'll use them only rarely.

Hints are best used sparingly. Hints are called "hints" and not "commands" for a reason: the cost-based optimizer may reject the instruction if it decides that the query will perform better without implementing the hint. Furthermore, hints can perform unpredictably when used with other hints, upgrading the database, applying patches, or changing database initialization/session parameters. Hints can provide valuable functionality but only use them when other ways of achieving the same goals do not work.

Fix the Design First

In a three-table join, depending on the column order of the index on the intersection table, the query usually accesses the tables in a particular order. By correctly indexing the intersection table and the joined columns of the other tables, you will eliminate many of your performance problems before they happen. If you are using an ORDERED or LEADING hint over and over for joins, review the indexes on the joined tables to help you change how the optimizer is looking at the problem. Rewriting SQL statements so they correctly use indexes will also solve many of your problems, eliminating the need for a hint. Putting a function on an indexed column may suppress the index and cause the tables to drive differently (be read in a different order). Use hints when you have exhausted the other avenues for tuning a query. If you find that you are using the same hint for the same problem over and over, you almost certainly have a problem that can be fixed system-wide instead. Always try to unlock the system problem inside each query level issue. This also helps you avoid the pain caused by hints working differently when you upgrade to a new version.

For example, consider a typical three-table join between STUDENT, CLASS, and STUDENT_CLASS tables. The STUDENT table contains one row for each student, the class table contains one row for each CLASS, and the STUDENT_CLASS table is the intersection table, as multiple students attend multiple classes. The primary keys for the tables may look like this:

STUDENT primary key STUDENT_ID

CLASS primary key CLASS_ID

STUDENT_CLASS concatenated primary key of (CLASS_ID, STUDENT_ID)

When the primary keys are defined in this manner, Oracle automatically creates indexes to support them. The intersection table, STUDENT_CLASS, has a concatenated index on two columns, CLASS_ID and STUDENT_ID, with CLASS_ID as the leading column. Is this the best column order for all of the application's queries? Unless you can forecast all of the queries that will join these tables, you should create a second index on the STUDENT_CLASS table's primary key columns:

STUDENT_CLASS secondary index on (STUDENT_ID, CLASS_ID)

When processing a join of these three tables, the optimizer can now choose to begin at either the STUDENT or CLASS table and will have an available index on STUDENT_CLASS that will support its needs. You may find that the secondary index is rarely used—but it is there when it is needed to support application users and their related business processes. By designing the indexing structures to support multiple access paths, you give the optimizer the tools it needs to choose the best execution path without resorting to a hint.

Available Hints and Groupings

The available hints vary according to the version of the database installed. While this chapter focuses on frequently used hints, many hints that are not covered in detail may give great performance gains for someone with a particular system. Hint functionality and syntax is listed in the Oracle documentation in the *SQL Reference Guide.*

Hints are separated into the different categories described in the following sections according to which type of operation is being modified by the hint. Each hint is discussed in detail, including syntax and examples, in the sections that follow. The view V$SQL_HINT lists the available hints, the version in which they became available, and the hint class (such as ACCESS, CACHE, etc.). A query of this view in my 11.2.0.2 database returned 269 rows.

Execution Path

Hints modify the execution path when an optimizer processes a particular statement. The instance-level parameter OPTIMIZER_MODE can be used to modify all statements in the database to follow a specific execution path, but a hint to a different execution path overrides anything that is specified in the instance parameter file. If a SQL statement has a hint specifying an optimization approach and goal, then the optimizer should use the specified approach regardless of the presence or absence of statistics, the value of the OPTIMIZER_MODE initialization parameter, and the OPTIMIZER_MODE parameter of the ALTER SESSION statement. Oracle also notes this in its documentation: If these statistics have not been gathered, or if the statistics are no longer representative of the data stored within the database, then the cost-based optimizer does not have sufficient information to generate the best plan.

Hints that change the execution path include the following:

■   ALL_ROWS

■   FIRST_ROWS(*n*)

Access Methods

The hints that are grouped into access methods allow the coder to vary the way the data is accessed. This group of hints is most frequently used, especially the INDEX hint. The INDEX hint provides direction as to whether and how indexes are used, and how the corresponding indexes will be merged to get the final answer.

The access method hints are listed here and described later in this chapter:

- FULL
- INDEX, INDEX_ASC, INDEX_DESC
- NO_INDEX, NO_INDEX_FFS, NO_INDEX_SS
- INDEX_COMBINE
- INDEX_JOIN
- INDEX_FFS
- INDEX_SS, INDEX_SS_ASC, INDEX_SS_DESC

Query Transformation Hints

Query transformation hints are especially helpful in a data warehouse if you are familiar with using fact and dimension tables. The FACT hint can designate a given table to be the FACT or driving table for a query. The NO_FACT hint does the opposite. The STAR_TRANSFORMATION hint is used to access the fact table efficiently when joining multiple tables. The NO_STAR_TRANSFORMATION hint instructs the optimizer *not* to perform a star query transformation when you may have a schema whose structures appear to be a data warehouse schema, but it's not actually a data warehouse. Persuading the cost-based optimizer to use star plans is assisted by using bitmap instead of b-tree indexes.

Some of the query transformations have nothing to do with star queries. Many transformations take place behind the scenes without using hints at all, but hints are available to help this process along. MERGE requests index values (not table values) as the primary data source; REWRITE rewrites a query to access a materialized view instead of source tables; and UNNEST works with subqueries to restructure the query to use a table join. Use NO_QUERY_TRANSFORMATION to avoid query transformations.

The query transformation hints are

- FACT, NO_FACT
- MERGE, NO_MERGE
- USE_CONCAT, NO_EXPAND
- NO_QUERY_TRANSFORMATION
- REWRITE, NO_REWRITE
- STAR_TRANSFORMATION, NO_STAR_TRANSFORMATION
- UNNEST, NO_UNNEST

Join Operations

The join operations group of hints controls how joined tables merge data together. A join operation may direct the optimizer to choose the best path for retrieving all rows for a query (*throughput*) or for retrieving the first row (*response time*).

Two hints are available to influence join order directly. LEADING specifies a table to start with for the join order to use, whereas ORDERED tells the optimizer to join the tables based on their order in the FROM clause, using the first table listed as the driving table (*accessed first*).

Hints available to direct the use of join operations include

- LEADING, ORDERED
- USE_HASH, NO_USE_HASH
- USE_MERGE, NO_USE_MERGE
- USE_NL, USE_NL_WITH_INDEX, NO_USE_NL

Parallel Execution

The parallel execution group of hints applies to databases using the parallel option (only available with Oracle Enterprise Edition). These hints override the table specification for the degree of parallelism.

The parallel execution hints are

- PARALLEL, NO_PARALLEL
- PARALLEL_INDEX, NO_PARALLEL_INDEX
- PQ_DISTRIBUTE

Other Hints

Other hints are not easily grouped into categories. The APPEND and NOAPPEND hints can be used without the parallel option, but they are frequently used with it. The cache grouping pertains to the hints that will put items as most recently used (CACHE) or least recently used (NOCACHE).

Like APPEND and CACHE, the following hints are available to influence the ways in which the optimizer processes the table accesses:

- APPEND, NOAPPEND
- CACHE, NOCACHE
- CURSOR_SHARING_EXACT
- DRIVING_SITE
- DYNAMIC_SAMPLING

- MODEL_MIN_ANALYSIS
- PUSH_PRED, NO_PUSH_PRED
- PUSH_SUBQ, NO_PUSH_SUBQ
- QB_NAME
- OPT_PARAM
- RESULT_CACHE, NO_RESULT_CACHE

Specifying a Hint

If you incorrectly specify a hint in any way, it becomes a comment and is ignored. No error is issued because the botched hint becomes a comment (unless the comment structure itself is incorrect). Be very careful to get the hint syntax *exactly* correct. The best way to ensure that a hint has been correctly specified is to run an EXPLAIN PLAN, or set AUTOTRACE to ON in SQL*Plus to see if the hint was used; check to see if the execution plan is producing the expected results if the hint should affect the plan. Some hints are overridden by the optimizer despite the fact that a hint is primarily for influencing decisions made by the Oracle optimizer. The basic hint syntax (in this example, it is for a FULL hint) is shown here. Note that the difference in these two formats is that the first uses multiline comment delimiters and the second uses inline comment delimiters. If you use the inline comment delimiter, then anything that comes after it (like column names) are ignored. You must continue the query on the next line.

```
select      /*+ FULL(table) */ column1,...
```

or

```
select      --+FULL(table)
            column1, ...
```

The (*TABLE*) in the preceding code snippet is the table name on which to perform a full table scan, or the alias for the table if you specified an alias in the FROM clause, as shown here:

```
select      /*+ FULL(employees) */ employee_id, last_name, department_id
from        employees
where       department_id = 1;
```

In this example, even if you have an index on the DEPARTMENT_ID column, a full table scan should be performed. The hint is not required to be uppercase. If using block comments with hints, be careful not to try to comment out the hinted text later with an enclosing block comment. The database ignores the second start block comment marker (it will be commented), uses the first closing block comment marker (from the hint) to close the initial block comments, and raises a syntax error when the second, unmatched block comment terminator is found.

```
select      /* FULL(employees) */ employee_id, last_name, department_id
from        employees
where       department_id = 1;
```

In this query, if there were an index on the DEPARTMENT_ID column, the index would be used because the hint is missing the plus sign (**+**) and becomes a comment.

When a hint accepts multiple arguments, spaces *or* commas may separate arguments:

```
select       /*+ index(employees emp_emp_id_pk emp_job_ix) */ …
```

or

```
select       /*+ index(employees,emp_emp_id_pk,emp_job_ix) */ …
```

TIP

Incorrect hint syntax leads to the hint being interpreted as a comment.
If an additional hint is specified correctly, it will be used.

By default, hints only affect the code block in which they appear. If you hint the access of the EMPLOYEES table in a query that is part of a UNION operation, the other queries within the UNION are not affected by your hint. If you want all of the unioned queries to use the same hint, you need to specify the hint in each of the queries. This also applies to views, subqueries, and subquery factoring (the WITH clause).

You can specify the query block name in hints to specify the query block to which the hint applies. Thus, in an outer query, you can specify a hint that applies to a subquery. The hint syntax for the *QUERY_BLOCK* argument is in the form

```
@query_block
```

where *QUERY_BLOCK* is a user-specified or system-generated identifier. Use the QB_NAME hint to specify the name for the query block. If you are using system-generated hints, you can view the query block names via the EXPLAIN PLAN for the query (an example is given later in this chapter).

Specifying Multiple Hints

You can use more than one hint at a time, although this may cause some or all of the hints to be ignored. Separate hints with spaces, as shown here:

```
select       /*+ FULL(table) CACHE(table)*/ column1,…
```

The (*TABLE*) in this code snippet is the table name to perform the full scan and cache on:

```
select       /*+ FULL(employees) CACHE(employees)*/
             employee_id, last_name, department_ID
from         employees
where        department_id = 1;
```

TIP

Multiple hints are separated with a space. Specifying multiple hints
that conflict with each other causes the query to use none *of the*
conflicting hints.

When Using an Alias, Hint the Alias, Not the Table

When you use aliases on a given table that you want to use in a hint, you must specify the alias and *not* the table name in the hint. If you specify the table name in the hint when an alias is used, the hint is *not* used.

```
select      /*+ FULL(table) */ column1,…
```

The (*TABLE*) in this code snippet has to be replaced with the alias that follows since the query uses an alias. If an alias is used, the alias *must* be used in the hint or the hint will *not* work:

```
select      /*+ FULL(A) */ employee_id, last_name, department_id
from        employees A
where       department_id = 1;
```

> **TIP**
> *If an alias is used, the alias* must *be used in the hint or the hint will*
> not *work.*

The Hints

The hints discussed here are available as of Oracle Database 11g Release 1 as well as being available in Oracle Database 11g Release 2. Consult the Oracle documentation for more information on these or other hints.

As of 11g, Oracle Database automatically maintains optimizer statistics if it is enabled. The database automatically collects optimizer statistics for tables with absent or stale statistics. If fresh statistics are required for a table, then the database collects them both for the table and associated indexes. The automatic optimizer statistics collection runs as part of AutoTask and is enabled by default to run in all predefined maintenance windows (which means, once daily). Automatic optimizer statistics collection relies on the modification monitoring feature. This monitoring is enabled by default when STATISTICS_LEVEL is set to TYPICAL or ALL. Monitoring tracks the approximate number of INSERTs, UPDATEs, and DELETEs for that table and whether the table has been truncated since the last time statistics were gathered. If a monitored table has been modified more than 10 percent, then these statistics are considered stale and gathered again. You use the DBMS_STATS package to manage the statistics manually.

The Oracle Demo Sample HR Schema

I used the sample Oracle demo HR schema to produce the examples that follow. In some cases, I created additional objects to facilitate working with some of the hints where they were not created with the sample schema.

```
create bitmap index employees_first_name_bmp on employees(first_name);
create bitmap index employees_commision_bmp on employees(commission_pct);
```

The FIRST_ROWS Hint

The FIRST_ROWS hint directs the optimizer to optimize a query on the basis of retrieving the first rows the fastest. This approach is especially helpful when users of the system are using online transaction processing systems to retrieve a single record on their screen. This approach would be a poor choice for a batch-intensive environment where a lot of rows are generally retrieved by a query. The FIRST_ROWS hint generally forces the use of indexes, which, under normal circumstances, may not have been used. The FIRST_ROWS or ALL_ROWS hint (the optimizer makes a best-guess effort to choose the better of the two) is used, even when statistics are not gathered for the optimizer.

The FIRST_ROWS hint is ignored in UPDATE and DELETE statements since all rows of the query must be updated or deleted. It is also ignored when any grouping statement is used (GROUP BY, DISTINCT, INTERSECT, MINUS, UNION) because all of the rows for the grouping have to be retrieved for the grouping to occur. The optimizer may also choose to avoid a sort when there is an ORDER BY in the statement if an index scan can do the actual sort. The optimizer may also choose NESTED LOOPS over a SORT MERGE when an index scan is available and the index is on the inner table. The inner table shortens the result set that is joined back to the outside table in the query, and specifying access paths overrides this hint.

You may also specify the number of rows (as in the second example that follows) that you want FIRST_ROWS to optimize getting (the default is one). Note that this is specified in powers of 10 up to 1000. Using FIRST_ROWS (n) is totally based on costs and is sensitive to the value of n. With small values of n, the optimizer tends to generate plans that consist of nested loops joins with index lookups. With large values of n, the optimizer tends to generate plans that consist of hash joins and full table scans (behaving more like ALL_ROWS).

Syntax

```
select     /*+ FIRST_ROWS(n) */ column1, …
```

Example

```
select     /*+ FIRST_ROWS */ employee_id, last_name, department_id
from       employees
where      department_id = 1;
```

Example

```
select     /*+ FIRST_ROWS(10) */ employee_id, last_name, department_id
from       employees
where      department_id = 1;
```

TIP
The FIRST_ROWS hint causes the optimizer to choose a path that retrieves the first row (or a specified number of rows) of a query fastest, at the cost of retrieving multiple rows slower. The FIRST_ROWS hint may be set as the default for the entire database by setting OPTIMIZER_MODE = FIRST_ROWS in the system parameter file; query-level hints will override the default setting for a given query. You can also set the optimizer to FIRST_ROWS_n (see Chapter 4 for additional information).

The ALL_ROWS Hint

The ALL_ROWS (*best throughput*) hint directs a query to optimize a query on the basis of retrieving all of the rows the fastest. This approach is especially helpful when users of the system are in a heavy batch report environment and running reports that retrieve a lot of rows. This would be a poor choice for a heavy transaction processing environment where users are trying to view a single record on a screen. The ALL_ROWS hint may suppress the use of indexes that under normal circumstances would have been used. Specifying access path hints overrides the use of this hint.

Syntax

```
select      /*+ ALL_ROWS */ column1, …
```

Example

```
select      /*+ ALL_ROWS */ employee_id, last_name, department_id
from        employees
where       department_id = 1;
```

TIP
The ALL_ROWS hint causes the optimizer to choose a path that retrieves all the rows of a query fastest, at the cost of retrieving one single row slower. The ALL_ROWS hint may be set as the default for the entire database by setting OPTIMIZER_MODE = ALL_ROWS in the system parameter file; query-level hints will override the default setting for a given query.

The FULL Hint

The FULL hint directs a query to override the optimizer and perform a full table scan on the specified table in the hint. The FULL hint has different functionality based on the query that you are tuning. You can use it to force a full table scan when a large portion of the table is being queried. The cost of retrieving the index *and* the rows may be greater than just retrieving the entire table. The full hint may also cause an unexpected result. Causing a full table scan may cause tables to be accessed in a different order, because a different driving table is used. This may lead to better performance, leading one to believe that the full table scan was the key benefit, when changing the order of the driving table was the real cause of the improved performance. The syntax for the FULL hint is as follows:

Syntax

```
select      /*+ FULL([query_block] table) */ column1,…
```

Here, (*TABLE*) is the table name to perform the full scan on. If an alias is used, the alias *must* be used in the hint or it will *not* work.

Note that you should only specify the table name in the hint, not the schema name.

Example

```
select      /*+ FULL(employees) */ employee_id, last_name, department_id
from        employees
where       department_id = 1;
```

The FULL hint in this example would be particularly helpful if the only department in the company was one (1). Going to an index on DEPARTMENT_ID and the EMPLOYEES table would be slower than simply performing a full table scan on the EMPLOYEES table.

The FULL hint is also a necessary part of using some of the other hints. The CACHE hint can cache a table in memory only when the full table is accessed. Some of the hints in the parallel grouping also necessitate the use of a full table scan. I cover each of these hints later in this chapter.

TIP
The FULL hint performs a full table scan on the table that is specified, not all tables in the query. The FULL hint may also lead to better performance, which is attributable to causing a change in the driving table of the query and not *to the actual full table scan.*

If multiple tables have the same name in the same query, assign aliases to them in the FROM clause and then reference the aliases in the hints.

The INDEX Hint

The INDEX hint is frequently used to request one or more indexes to be used for a given query. Oracle generally chooses the correct index or indexes with the optimizer, but when the optimizer chooses the wrong index or no index at all, this hint is excellent. You may also use multiple indexes with this hint, and Oracle will choose one or more of the indexes specified based on the best plan. If you only specify one index, the optimizer considers only the specified index.

Syntax

```
select      /*+ INDEX([query_block]table index1 [, index2...]) */ column1, ...
```

Example

```
select      /*+ INDEX (employees emp_emp_id_pk) */ employee_id, last_name
from        employees
where       employee_id = 7750;
```

In this example, the EMP_EMP_ID_PK index on the EMPLOYEES table is used.

Example

```
select      /*+ INDEX (employees emp_department_ix emp_emp_id_pk) */
            employee_id, last_name
from        employees
where       employee_id = 7750
and         department_id = 1;
```

In the second example, Oracle may use the EMP_DEPARTMENT_IX index or the EMP_EMP_ID_PK index or a merge of both of them. I've given these choices to the optimizer to decipher the best choice. It would have been best, however, to only specify the index on the EMPLOYEE_ID column (EMP_EMP_ID_PK) if this were the most restrictive statement (usually much more restrictive than the department).

TIP
The INDEX hint causes the optimizer to choose the index specified in the hint. Multiple indexes for a single table can be specified, but it is usually better to specify only the most restrictive index on a given query (and, that way, avoiding the merging of each index's result). If multiple indexes are specified, Oracle chooses which (one or more) to use, so be careful or your hint could potentially be overridden.

Example

```
select     /*+ INDEX */ employee_id, last_name
from       employees
where      employee_id = 7750
and        department_id = 1;
```

In this example, no index is specified. Oracle now weighs all of the possible indexes that are available and chooses one or more to be used. Since I have not specified a particular index, but I have specified the INDEX hint, the optimizer should *not* do a full table scan.

TIP
The INDEX hint, without a specified index, should not *consider a full table scan, even though no indexes have been specified. The optimizer will choose the best index or indexes for the query.*

As of Oracle Database 10g, you can specify column names as part of the INDEX hint. The columns can be prefixed with the table names (not table aliases). Each column listed in the hint must be a physical column in the table, not an expression or calculated column.

Syntax

```
select     /*+ INDEX ([@query_block][table.]column1 [[table2.]column2…]) */
           column1, …
```

Example

```
select     /*+ INDEX (employees.department_id) */ employee_id, last_name
from       employees
where      department_id = 1;
```

The NO_INDEX Hint

The NO_INDEX hint disallows the optimizer from using a specified index. This is a great hint for tuning queries with multiple indexes. Although you may not know which of multiple indexes to drive the query with, you might know which ones that you *don't* want the optimizer to use. You may also want to disallow an index for many queries prior to dropping an index or making an index invisible (11*g* only) that you don't think is necessary.

Syntax

```
select     /*+ NO_INDEX([@query_block] table index1 [,index2…]) */ column1, …
```

Example

```
select     /*+ NO_INDEX (employees emp_department_ix) */ employee_id, last_name
from       employees
where      employee_id = 7750
  and      department_id = 1;
```

In this example, the specified index on the employees table should *not* be used. If the NO_INDEX hint is used and no index is specified, a full table scan is performed. If the NO_INDEX and a conflicting hint (such as INDEX) are specified for the same index, then both hints are ignored (as in the example that follows).

Example

```
select     /*+ NO_INDEX(employees emp_department_ix)
               INDEX(employees emp_department_ix) */
           last_name, department_id
from       employees
where      department_id = 1
and        last_name = 'SMITH';
```

TIP
The NO_INDEX hint must be in the tuning expert's toolkit. It is used to remove an index from consideration by the optimizer, so you may evaluate the need for the index prior to dropping it or so you can evaluate other indexes. Be careful not to conflict with other index hints. The NO_INDEX is one of my personal favorites when I want to drop an index and check which index (if any) will be used instead of the one that I plan to drop.

The INDEX_JOIN Hint

The INDEX_JOIN hint merges separate indexes from a single table together so *only* the indexes need to be accessed. This approach saves a trip to back to the table.

Syntax

```
select      /*+ INDEX_JOIN([@query_block] table index1 [,index2…]) */ column1, …
```

Example

```
select      /*+ INDEX_JOIN(employees emp_emp_id_pk emp_department_ix) */
            employee_id, last_name
from        employees
where       employee_id = 7750
and         department_id = 1;
```

In this query, the optimizer should merge both specified indexes and *not* need to access the table. All information needed is contained in these two indexes when they are merged. For a more detailed example, see Chapter 8.

TIP
Not only does The INDEX_JOIN hint allow you to access only indexes on a table, which is a scan of fewer total blocks, but also it can be five times faster (in some of my tests) than using an index and scanning the table by ROWID.

The INDEX_COMBINE Hint

The INDEX_COMBINE hint is used to specify multiple bitmap indexes when you want the optimizer to use *all* indexes that you specify. You can also use the INDEX_COMBINE hint to specify single indexes (this is preferred over using the INDEX hint for bitmaps). For b-tree indexes, use the INDEX hint instead of this one. The INDEX_COMBINE hint is similar to the INDEX_JOIN hint but is used for bitmap indexes.

Syntax

```
select      /*+ INDEX_COMBINE([@query_block] table index1 [,index2…]) */ column1, …
```

Example

```
select      /*+ INDEX_COMBINE (employees employees_first_name_bmp,
            employees_commission_bmp) */
            employee_id, last_name
from        employees
where       first_name = 'MATT'
and         commission_pct = 5;
```

TIP
The INDEX_COMBINE hint causes the optimizer to merge multiple bitmap indexes for a single table instead of choosing which one is better (as with the INDEX hint).

The INDEX_ASC Hint

The INDEX_ASC hint currently does *exactly* the same thing as the INDEX hint. Since indexes are already scanned in ascending order, this does nothing more than the current INDEX hint. So what is it good for? Oracle does not guarantee that indexes will be scanned in ascending order in the future, but this hint does guarantee that an index will be scanned in ascending order.

Syntax

```
select     /*+ INDEX_ASC ([@query_block] table index1 [, index2…]) */ column1, …
```

Example

```
select     /*+ INDEX_ASC(employees emp_department_ix) */
           department_id, employee_id, last_name
from       employees
where      department_id <= 30;
```

In this example, the specified index should be used.

TIP
As of Oracle8i, the INDEX_ASC does exactly what the INDEX hint does because indexes are already scanned in ascending order. INDEX_ASC guarantees this to be true, however, as Oracle may change this default in the future. As of Oracle9i, descending indexes are actually sorted in descending order. Oracle treats descending indexes as function-based indexes. The columns marked DESC are sorted in descending order.

The INDEX_DESC Hint

The INDEX_DESC hint causes indexes to be scanned in descending order (of their indexed value or order), which is the opposite of the INDEX and INDEX_ASC hints. This hint is overridden when the query has multiple tables because the index needs to be used in the normal ascending order to be joined to the other table in the query. Some restrictions for this include that it does not work for bitmap indexes or for descending indexes (because it causes the index to be scanned in ascending order), and it does not work across partitioned index boundaries but performs a descending index scan of each partition. The execution plan should list "INDEX RANGE SCAN DESCENDING" for an operation when this hint is adopted, and the data *might* come back in reverse order (though the *only* way to be certain of sorting is to use an ORDER BY clause).

Syntax

```
select     /*+ INDEX_DESC ([@query_block] table index1 [,index2…]) */ column1, …
```

Example

```
select     /*+ INDEX_DESC(employees emp_department_ix) */
           department_id, employee_id, last_name
```

```
from        employees
where       department_id <= 30;
```

TIP
The INDEX_DESC processes an index in descending order of how it was built. This hint should not be used if more than one table exists in the query.

The INDEX_FFS Hint

The INDEX_FFS hint indicates a fast full scan of the index should be performed. That is, all values in the index will be read without sorting. INDEX_FFS accesses only the index and *not* the corresponding table. The fast full scan of the index is used only if all of the information that the query needs to retrieve is in the index. This hint can give great performance gains, especially when the table has a large number of columns.

Syntax

```
select      /*+ [@query_block] INDEX_FFS(table index) */ column1, …
```

Example

```
select      /*+ INDEX_FFS (employees emp_name_ix) */ first_name, last_name
from        employees
where       last_name = 'SMITH';
```

The INDEX_FFS hint is used only if the index contains all the columns in the SELECT list. The NO_INDEX_FFS has the same syntax, but this hint tells the optimizer *not* to perform fast full index scans of the specified indexes. You must specify both the table and index in both of these hints.

TIP
The INDEX_FFS processes only the index and does not take the result and access the table. All columns that are used and retrieved by the query must be contained in the index.

The ORDERED Hint

The ORDERED hint directs tables to be accessed in a particular order, based on the order of the tables in the FROM clause of the query, which is often referred to as the driving order for a query. Generally, the last table in the FROM clause is the driving table in queries (this is version dependent); however, using the ORDERED hint causes the first table in the FROM clause to be the driver. The ORDERED hint also guarantees the driving order. When the ORDERED hint is not used, Oracle may internally switch the driving table, when you compare how tables are listed in the FROM clause (EXPLAIN PLAN can show how tables are accessed). The complexity of possibilities when this hint is used is so great that much of the next chapter is focused on this subject (please see Chapter 8 for more information regarding tuning joins). This chapter briefly covers this hint, mainly for syntactical purposes.

Syntax

```
select    /*+ ORDERED */ column1, …
```

Example

```
select    /*+ ORDERED */ employee_id, last_name,
          d.department_id
from      employees e, departments d
where     e.department_id = d.department_id
and       d.department_id = 10
and       e.employee_id = 7747;
```

If both tables (EMPLOYEES and DEPARTMENTS) have been analyzed *and* there are *no* indexes on either table, the EMPLOYEES table should be accessed first and the DEPARTMENTS table is accessed second. There are many possible variations (covered in the next two chapters) that cause this to work differently.

Example

```
select    /*+ ORDERED */ employee_id, last_name,
          d.department_id, j.job_title
from      employees e, departments d, jobs j
where     e.department_id = d.department_id
and       d.department_id = 10
and       e.employee_id = 7747
and       e.job_id = j.job_id
/
```

In this example for a three-table join, EMPLOYEES should be joined first to DEPARTMENTS (second as listed in the FROM clause), and then the result set joined to JOBS. There are many possible join-order variations (covered in the next chapter) that could cause this to work differently, but generally, when the ORDERED hint is used, if accepted, the join order should be as specified.

TIP
The ORDERED hint is one of the most powerful hints available. It processes the tables of the query in the sequential order that they are listed in the FROM clause. There are many variations that cause this to work differently. The version of Oracle, the existence of indexes on the tables, and which tables have been analyzed can all cause this to work differently. However, when a multitable join is slow and you don't know what to do, this is one of the first hints you should try!

The LEADING Hint

As the complexity of queries becomes greater, figuring out the order of *all* of the tables using the ORDERED hint becomes more difficult. You can often figure out which table should be the accessed *first* (driving table), but you may not know which table to access after that one. The LEADING hint allows you to specify *one* table to drive the query; the optimizer figures out which table to use after that. If you specify more than one table with this hint, it is ignored. The ORDERED hint overrides the LEADING hint.

Syntax

```
select      /*+ LEADING([@query_block] table [table]…) */ column1, …
```

Example

```
select      /*+ LEADING(d) */ employee_id, last_name,
            d.department_id, j.job_title
from        departments d, employees e, jobs j
where       e.department_id = d.department_id
and         d.department_id = 10
and         e.employee_id = 7747
and         e.job_id = j.job_id;
```

As stated in the discussion of the ORDERED hint, the process by which a leading table is selected is complex. In this example, the EMPLOYEES table would probably be chosen as the driving table as it is the intersection table. The LEADING() hint allows you to specify another table (I chose DEPARTMENTS as the driving table) to be the first table accessed in the query. Be sure you have properly configured the indexes to support the join order you specify.

TIP
The LEADING hint works similar to the ORDERED hint. The LEADING hint is used to specify a single table to drive a query while allowing the optimizer to figure out the rest.

The NO_EXPAND Hint

The NO_EXPAND hint is used to keep the optimizer from "going off the deep end" when evaluating IN-lists that are combined with an OR. It disallows the optimizer from using "OR expansion." *OR expansion* refers to converting a query to apply OR conditions to execute as separate subqueries whose results are merged with UNION ALL instead of applying OR conditions as a filter. Without the NO_EXPAND hint, the optimizer may create a very long execution plan or use an INLIST INTERATOR access method. To use OR expansion, use the USE_CONCAT hint.

Syntax

```
select      /*+ NO_EXPAND [@query_block] */ column1, …
```

Example

```
select      /*+ NO_EXPAND */ department_id, employee_id, last_name
from        employees
where       manager_id = 200
or          manager_id = 210;
```

I have used the NO_EXPAND hint and was able to increase performance to almost 50 times faster than without the hint. For simple queries, there may not be much difference in the EXPLAIN PLAN with or without the hint. However, when using a query that joins the EMPLOYEES and

DEPARTMENTS tables and selects at least one column from each table, you can see a *big* difference in the EXPLAIN PLAN.

TIP
The NO_EXPAND hint prevents the optimizer from using OR expansion and is used when the query becomes substantially more complex as a result of the expansion.

The DRIVING_SITE Hint

The DRIVING_SITE hint is for processing distributed queries in the designated database. The table specified in the hint should determine the driving site that will be used to process the actual join.

Syntax

```
select     /*+ DRIVING_SITE ([@query_block] table) */ column1, …
```

Example

```
select     /*+ DRIVING_SITE (deptremote) */ employee_id, last_name
from       employees, departmentoratusc deptremote
where      employees.department_id = deptremote.deptno
and        deptremote.department_id = 10
and        employee_id = 7747;
```

Oracle normally retrieves the rows from the remote site and joins them at the local site if this hint is not specified. Because the EMPLOYEE_ID = 7747 limits the result set, I would rather pass the small number of rows from the EMPLOYEES table to the remote site instead of pulling an entire DEPARTMENTS table department back to my local site to process to minimize the overhead of data transfer.

A similar benefit may be achieved by limiting the rows that are retrieved from a remote site by creating a view locally for the remote table (if you can have a limiting WHERE clause in the view that still retrieves the desired data). The local view should include the WHERE clause that will be used, so the view will limit the rows returned from the remote database before they are sent back to the local database. I have personally tuned queries from hours to seconds using this method of creating a remote view versus using the DRIVING_SITE hint.

When using the DRIVING_SITE hint, the location specification is not specified in the hint (just the table name). However, if an alias is used, the alias has to be used instead of the table name in the hint.

TIP
The DRIVING_SITE hint is extremely powerful, as it will potentially limit the amount of information that will be processed over your network. The table specified with the DRIVING_SITE hint is the location where the join will be processed. Using views for remote tables can also lead to better performance by limiting the number of rows passed from the remote site before the records are sent to the local site.

The USE_MERGE Hint

The USE_MERGE hint is a hint that tells the optimizer to use a MERGE JOIN operation when performing a join. A MERGE JOIN operation may be useful when queries perform set operations on large numbers of rows, perhaps on non-equijoin conditions.

Assume you are joining two tables together. In a MERGE JOIN, the row set returned from each table is sorted and then merged to form the final result set. Because each result is sorted and then merged together, this action is most effective when retrieving all rows from a given query. If you want the first row faster instead, the USE_NL might be a better hint (to force a nested loops join).

In the following illustration, the EMPLOYEES and DEPARTMENTS tables are joined, and that result set is then joined to the JOBS table via a MERGE JOIN operation.

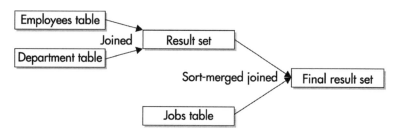

Syntax

```
select      /*+ USE_MERGE([@query_block] table [table]) */ column1, …
```

where the first table should be accessed by a merge join. The second table specification is optional, and, if unspecified, the optimizer decides what to join the first table to.

Example

```
select      /*+ use_merge(j) */ employee_id, last_name,
            d.department_id, j.job_title
from        departments d, employees e, jobs j
where       e.department_id = d.department_id
and         d.department_id = 10
and         e.employee_id = 7747
and         e.job_id = j.job_id;
```

The USE_MERGE hint in this query causes the jobs table to be joined in a *sort-merge join* to the returned row source resulting from the join of the EMPLOYEES and DEPARTMENTS tables. The rows are sorted and then merged together to find the final result. The NO_USE_MERGE hint uses the same syntax but instructs the optimizer to not use merge joins when selecting execution paths for a query. The optimizer will instead favor other join methods such as hash joins and nested loops joins. See Chapter 9 for a more detailed discussion of joins.

TIP
*In a join of three or more tables, the USE_MERGE hint causes the
table(s) specified in the hint to be sort-merge joined with the resulting
row set from a join of the other tables in the join.*

The USE_NL Hint

The USE_NL (*use nested loops*) hint is usually the fastest way to return a single row (in terms of
response time); it may be slower at returning all the rows. This hint causes a statement to be
processed using nested loops, which takes the first matching row from one table based on the
result from another table. This is the opposite of a merge join, which retrieves rows that match
the conditions from each table and then merges them together.

Syntax

```
select       /*+ USE_NL([@query_block] table1[,  table2]) … */ column1, …
```

where *table1* should be the first table read (usually the smaller of the two tables by blocks) and
table2 the inner or lookup table. Reversing the order of the tables *might* persuade the cost-based
optimizer to read the tables in the suggested order; if not, try the LEADING or ORDERED hints to
specify the order of the tables, which can affect performance. If only one table is specified in the
hint, use a nested loops access method with the optimizer, choosing the table listed in the hint to
be the inner or lookup table.

Example

```
select       /*+ ORDERED USE_NL(d e) */ e.employee_id, e.last_name,
             d.department_id, d.department_name
from         employees e, departments d
where        e.department_id = d.department_id
and          d.department_id = 110
and          e.employee_id = 206;
```

The USE_NL hint directs the optimizer to take the resulting rows returned from the EMPLOYEES
table and process them with the matching rows from the DEPARTMENTS table (the specified nested
loop table). The first row that matches from the DEPARTMENTS table can be returned to the user
immediately (as in a web-based application), as opposed to waiting until all matching rows are
found. The ORDERED hint specifies that the EMPLOYEES table should be processed first. Note that
there is a difference between using this query with or without the ORDERED hint as well.

TIP
*The USE_NL hint usually provides the best response time (first row
comes back faster) for smaller result sets, whereas the USE_MERGE
hint usually provides the best throughput when the USE_HASH hint
can't be used.*

The NO_USE_NL hint uses the same syntax but instructs the optimizer not to use nested
loops joins. A related hint, USE_NL_WITH_INDEX, takes two parameters—the name of the inner
or lookup table for the join along with the name of the index to use when performing the join.

The USE_HASH Hint

The USE_HASH (*use hash join*) hint is usually the fastest way to join many rows together from multiple tables *if you have adequate memory for this operation.* The USE_HASH <hint or method> is similar to the nested loops where one result of one table is looped through the result from the joined table. The difference is that the second table (the lookup table) is put into memory and should usually be the smaller table. You must have a large enough HASH_AREA_SIZE or PGA_AGGREGATE_TARGET (see Chapter 4) for this to work properly; otherwise, the operation will occur on disk (which slows things down).

> **NOTE**
> *Don't confuse USE_HASH with HASH, which is used with* hash clusters—*physical data structures that store master and detail rows together in the same databases as already joined.*

Syntax

```
select      /*+ USE_HASH ([@query_block]table1 [, table2,...]) */ column1, …
```

Example

```
select      /*+ use_hash(d) */ employee_id, last_name,
            d.department_id
from        employees e, departments d
where       e.department_id = d.department_id;
```

The USE_HASH hint directs the optimizer to take the rows returned from the EMPLOYEES table and process them with the matching rows from the DEPARTMENTS table (the specified hash table), which are hashed into memory. The first row that matches from the DEPARTMENTS table can be returned to the user immediately, as opposed to waiting until all matching rows are found. There are cases in which the optimizer overrides this hint, and environmental settings greatly affect the optimizer's decision to use hash joins. In the preceding query, if you added the condition "AND D.DEPARTMENT_ID=1", the optimizer would override the USE_HASH hint and do the more efficient nested loops join (since the DEPARTMENTS table has been narrowed down by this condition) or use a merge join.

The NO_USE_HASH hint has a similar syntax but instructs the optimizer to not use hash joins when selecting execution paths for a query. The optimizer should instead use other join methods such as nested loops or merge joins. You often need to add the ORDERED hint in addition to table join hints to drive things the way you want them.

> **TIP**
> *The USE_HASH hint usually provides the best response time for larger result sets.*

SWAP_JOIN_INPUTS is an undocumented hint (there are Metalink articles about it) used to persuade the cost-based optimizer to use the specified table as the lookup hash table. Even though it is undocumented, it is listed in the V$SQL_HINT view.

Syntax

```
Select        /*+ SWAP_JOIN_INPUTS(table1) */
```

The QB_NAME Hint

The QB_NAME hint is used to assign a name to a query block within a statement. You can then assign a hint elsewhere in the statement that references the query block. For example, if you have a query that contains a subquery, you can assign a query block name to the subquery and then provide the hint at the outermost query level. If two or more query blocks are given the same QB_NAME value, the optimizer ignores the hints. You can also use the query block names when looking at execution plans to decide to which part of the query a particular operation belongs.

If you have a complex query, with subqueries in the EXPLAIN PLAN, it appears that the optimizer generates a default name for these query blocks, such as emp@sel$4. By using the QB_NAME hint, you can specify the name instead (use a name that means something to you). This option is very helpful when trying to tune extremely complex queries that contain more than one subquery.

Syntax

```
Select        /*+ QB_NAME(query_block) */ column1…
```

Example

```
select        /*+ FULL(@deptblock departments) */ employee_id
from          employees
where         employees.department_id IN
                  (select /*+ QB_NAME(deptblock) */ department_id
                   from   departments
                   where location_id = 10);
```

Even though the FULL hint is specified in the outer query (main query), it should affect the subquery because you used the query block specified in the inner query (subquery).

The PUSH_SUBQ Hint

The PUSH_SUBQ hint can lead to dramatic performance gains (an increase of more than 100 times in terms of performance) when used in the appropriate situation. The best situation in which to use this hint is when the subquery returns a relatively small number of rows (quickly); those rows can then be used to substantially limit the rows in the outer query. PUSH_SUBQ causes the subquery to be evaluated at the earliest possible time. This hint cannot be used when the query uses a merge join and cannot be used with remote tables. Moving the subquery to be part of the main query (when possible) can lead to the same gains when the tables are driven in the correct order (accessing the former subquery table first).

Syntax

```
select        /*+ PUSH_SUBQ [(@query_block)] */ column1, …
```

Example

```
select      /*+ cardinality(e,1000000) push_subq  */
            e.department_id,
            e.employee_id,
            m.last_name   as manager_last_name,
            max(e.salary) as max_salary
from        employees e,
            employees m,
            departments d
where       e.employee_id in (
              select employee_id
              from   job_history jh)
and         to_char(e.hire_date,'Month') = 'June'
and         e.manager_id = m.employee_id (+)
and         e.department_id = d.department_id
group by    e.department_id, e.employee_id, m.last_name, e.salary;
```

This query processes the subquery to be used by the outer query at its earliest possible time. I used the undocumented CARDINALITY() hint to simulate a large dataset because is was impossible to get PUSH_SUBQ to do anything with the small amount of rows I had. CARDINALITY tells the optimizer to use the indicated number as the expected number of rows in a data source instead of data dictionary statistics or defaults.

TIP
The PUSH_SUBQ hint can improve performance greatly when the subquery returns only a few rows very fast, and those rows can be used to limit the rows returned in the outer query.

The PARALLEL Hint

The PARALLEL hint tells the optimizer to break a query into pieces (the *degree of parallelism*) and process each piece with a different process simultaneously. The degree of parallelism is applied to each parallelizable operation of a SQL statement. A query that requires a sort operation causes the number of processes used to be double the degree specified, as both the table accesses and the sorts are parallelized. A query coordinator process is also invoked to split and put the results together, so if you set the degree of parallelism for a query to four, it may use four processes for the query plus four *more* processes for the sorting, plus one *more* process for the breaking up and putting together of the four pieces, or nine (9) total processes.

PARALLEL can be applied to the INSERT, UPDATE, and DELETE portions of a statement (you have to commit immediately after if you use this) as well as to SELECT commands. You should create tables with the PARALLEL clause when you plan to use this option (which should make using the hint unnecessary, although the degree of parallelism can be changed with the hint). See Chapter 11 for a detailed look at all of the requirements and rules associated with this powerful option.

Syntax

```
/*+ PARALLEL ([@query_block]table, degree) */
```

The *degree* is the number of pieces (processes) into which the query is broken.

Example

```
select     /*+ PARALLEL (employees) */ employee_id, hire_date
from       employees
order by   hire_date;
```

This statement does not specify a degree of parallelism. The default degree of parallelism is dictated by the table definition when the table was created or the system default is used.

Example

```
select     /*+ PARALLEL (employees,4) */ employee_id, hire_date
from       employees
order by   hire_date;
```

This statement specifies a degree of parallelism of 4. Per previous discussion, as many as nine query servers may be allocated or created to satisfy this query. In 11gR2, this hint has been modified. In 11gR2, if you have multiple tables and you specify the PARALLEL hint with a numeric value, that is the degree of parallelism used for all the tables in the query, overriding the parallel setting at the table level. If you specify a table name (as in the previous example), then the PARALLEL hint applies to only that table; any other tables accessed by the query use the table's parallelism setting.

TIP
Using the PARALLEL hint enables the use of parallel operations. If the degree is not specified with the hint, the default degree specified during table creation is used.

The NO_PARALLEL Hint

If a table is created with a parallel degree set, the table should automatically be queried in parallel and should use that degree for all full table scan queries. You may, however, also "turn off" the use of parallel operations in any one given query on a table that has been specified to use parallel operations by using the NO_PARALLEL hint. The NO_PARALLEL hint results in a query with a degree of one (1).

NOTE
The NO_PARALLEL hint used to be NOPARALLEL before Oracle standardized the naming.

Syntax

```
select     /*+ NO_PARALLEL ([@query_block]table) */ ...
```

Example

```
select      /*+ NO_PARALLEL(employees) */ employee_id, hire_date
from        employees
order by    hire_date;
```

TIP
Using the NO_PARALLEL hint disables parallel operations in a statement that would otherwise use parallel processing due to a parallel object definition.

The PARALLEL_INDEX Hint

The PARALLEL_INDEX hint asks the optimizer to parallelize index scans (full, range, or fast full) for b-tree indexes. Oracle documentation suggests that PARALLEL_INDEX works with partitioned indexes, but I found that it worked with nonpartitioned indexes too. Essentially PARALLEL_INDEX is a PARALLEL hint for index reads and, like the PARALLEL hint, specifying the degree of parallelism is optional.

Syntax

```
/*+ PARALLEL_INDEX([@query_block] table index [degree]) */
```

Example

```
select      /*+ PARALLEL_INDEX(employees emp_emp_id_pk) */ count(*)
from        employees;
```

NO_PARALLEL_INDEX (formerly NOPARALLEL_INDEX) is used to avoid parallel index reads.

Syntax

```
/*+ NO_PARALLEL_INDEX([@query_block] table index) */
```

The PQ_DISTRIBUTE Hint

The PQ_DISTRIBUTE hint is used to specify how parallel queries are split. This hint allows you to specify how the work is distributed among the Parallel Query (PQ) servers and might help improve the performance of parallelized table joins.

Syntax

```
/*+ PQ_DISTRIBUTE ([@query_block] table outer_distr inner_distr) */
```

where the combination of OUTER_DISTR and INNER_DISTR is one of the following:

hash, hash	Map rows to parallel processes through a hashing algorithm. Oracle documentation recommends this for hash and sort-merge joins between tables of similar size.
broadcast, none	Server processes receive all rows of outer table but inner table rows are randomly assigned to processes. Oracle documentation recommends this when the outer table is small compared to the inner table.
none, broadcast	All rows of the inner table are sent to each server process but the outer table rows are randomly partitioned between server processes. Oracle documentation recommends this when the inner table is small compared to the outer table.
partition, none	Rows of the outer table are sent to the query server using the partitioning of the inner table; the inner table must be partitioned by the join keys. Oracle documentation recommends this when the number of inner table partitions is about equal to the number of server processes. The hint will be ignored if the inner query is not partitioned.
none, partition	Rows of the inner table are sent to the query server using the partitioning of the outer table; the outer table must be partitioned by the join keys. Oracle documentation recommends this when the number of outer table partitions is about equal to the number of server processes. The hint is ignored if the outer query is not partitioned.
none, none	Equipartitioned tables are matched up to query servers by partitions. Probably the best option when available. This hint is ignored if the tables are not equipartitioned on the join key.

Example

```
select     /*+ USE_HASH(departments,employees)
               PARALLEL(employees)
               PQ_DISTRIBUTE (employees none,none) */
           departments.department_id, employee_id, hire_date
from       employees, departments
where      employees.department_id = departments.department_id
order by   hire_date;
```

The PQ_DISTRIBUTE hint can be very temperamental. I had to force use of a hash join with USE_HASH before different settings would take effect.

The APPEND Hint

The APPEND hint can *drastically* improve the performance of INSERTs (at times dramatically), but with a potential cost in terms of physical database space. The APPEND hint does not check to see if there is space within currently used blocks for inserts but instead appends the data into new blocks. You might potentially waste space, but you will gain speed. If you never delete rows from a table, you should definitely consider the APPEND hint.

If an INSERT is parallelized using the PARALLEL hint, then APPEND is used by default. You can use the NOAPPEND hint (next section) to override this behavior. Also note that before you can use this example, you must first enable parallel DML.

Syntax

```
insert /*+ APPEND */ …
```

Example

```
insert /*+ APPEND */  into sales_hist
   select *
   from   sales
   where  cust_id = 8890;
```

There are a couple of things to consider when using the APPEND hint. First, remember that APPEND ignores existing free space, so you can waste a lot of disk space when using this option. Second, APPEND does not work with single-row inserts using a VALUES clause; it only works with INSERTS whose data comes from subqueries. Finally, a COMMIT should follow an INSERT using APPEND to avoid an error when querying back newly inserted data.

TIP
The APPEND hint inserts values into a table without checking the free space in the currently used blocks, instead appending the data into new blocks. Great performance is often the end result at the cost of physical disk space (and well worth it).

The NOAPPEND Hint

The NOAPPEND hint overrides the default for the PARALLEL inserts (the default, of course, is APPEND). The NOAPPEND hint turns off the direct-path insert option.

Syntax

```
insert     /*+ NOAPPEND */ …
```

Example

```
insert /*+ NOAPPEND */
into job_history (employee_id, start_date, end_date, job_id,department_id)
   select employee_id, hire_date, to_date('12/31/2099','mm/dd/yyyy'),
          job_id, department_id
   from   employees e
   where  not exists(
             select 0
             from   job_history jh
             where  jh.employee_id = e.employee_id);
```

TIP
The NOAPPEND hint overrides a PARALLEL hint, which normally uses the APPEND hint by default.

The CACHE Hint

The CACHE hint causes a full table scan to be cached (pinned) into memory (into the buffer cache), so future queries accessing the same table find it in memory instead of going to disk. This creates one potentially huge problem. If the table is very large, then it takes up an enormous amount of memory (data block buffer cache space in particular). For small lookup tables, however, this is an excellent option. Tables can be created with the CACHE option to be cached the first time they are accessed.

Syntax

```
select    /*+ CACHE([@query_block] table) */ column1, …
```

Example

```
select    /*+ FULL(departments) CACHE(departments) */ department_id, location_id
from      departments;
```

The entire DEPARTMENTS table is now cached in memory and is marked as a most recently used object (MRU).

TIP
The CACHE hint should be used with small lookup tables that are often accessed by users. This ensures the table remains in memory.

The NOCACHE Hint

The NOCACHE hint causes a table that is specified to be CACHED at the database level to *not* get cached when you access it and is usually used to override an existing table specification.

Syntax

```
select    /*+ NOCACHE(table) */ column1, …
```

Example

```
alter     table departments cache;

select    /*+ NOCACHE(departments) */ department_id, location_id
from      departments;
```

In this example, the table should not be cached despite the ALTER statement and is put on the Least Recently Used (LRU) list.

TIP
The NOCACHE hint should be used to prevent caching a table specified with the CACHE option—basically, when you want to access the table but you don't *want to cache it.*

The RESULT_CACHE Hint

Oracle 11g provides a new, separate shared memory pool to store query results. This Result Cache is allocated directly from the shared pool but is maintained separately. Queries executed often may experience better performance when using the new pool through the RESULT_CACHE hint. Setting the RESULT_CACHE_MODE initialization parameter to FORCE stores all results in the new cache for every query executed (this may not be desirable), but the NO_RESULT_CACHE hint can be used to override this behavior. The difference between RESULT_CACHE and CACHE is *where* the data is stored. NO_RESULT_CACHE requests that data not be cached in the shared pool (it still can be cached in the buffer cache).

The RESULT_CACHE hint should work with individual parts of a query (query blocks) as well as entire result sets. The RESULT_CACHE operation appears in an execution plan as RESULT_CACHE with a system-generated temporary table name when the hint is used or when the query results are retrieved from the Result Cache.

Syntax

```
select      /*+ RESULT_CACHE */ column1 …
```

Example

```
select      /*+ RESULT_CACHE */ employee_id, last_name
from        employees
where       department_id = 10;
```

TIP
The RESULT_CACHE hint caches query results in the shared pool; the NO_RESULT_CACHE hint is used when you don't want to cache data in the shared pool (it still can be cached in the buffer cache).

The CURSOR_SHARING_EXACT Hint

The CURSOR_SHARING_EXACT hint is used to ensure that literals in SQL statements are not replaced with bind variables. This hint can be used to correct any minor issues when you *don't* want to use cursor sharing; even though, the instance-level CURSOR_SHARING parameter is set to either FORCE or SIMILAR.

Syntax

```
select      /*+ CURSOR_SHARING_EXACT */ column1, …
```

Example

```
select      /*+ CURSOR_SHARING_EXACT */ employee_id, last_name
from        employees
where       employee_id = 123;
```

In this example, Oracle will not be able to reuse a current statement in the shared pool unless it is *exactly* like this one (including white space and the 123 literal). It should not create a bind variable. Additional examples related to cursor sharing are in Chapter 4.

TIP
The CURSOR_SHARING_EXACT hint overrides the system parameter file setting of CURSOR_SHARING to either FORCE or SIMILAR.

Some Miscellaneous Hints and Notes

In this section, I wanted to list "the best of the rest" of the hints that are available. Each hint is listed with a brief explanation. Please see the Oracle documentation if you want to use one of them.

- **DYNAMIC_SAMPLING**   The DYNAMIC_SAMPLING hint is set from 0 to 10. The higher number set, the more effort the compiler puts into dynamic sampling. It generates statistics at run time for use in a query.

- **INDEX_SS**   The INDEX_SS hint instructs the optimizer to use the skip-scan option for an index on the specified table. A skip-scan is when Oracle skips the first column of a concatenated index and uses the rest of the index. This hint works well with a two-part concatenated index, where you often use both parts but infrequently need only the second part (at times you don't have any condition for the first part). You need to specify both the table and the index.

- **INDEX_SS_ASC**   The INDEX_SS_ASC hint is the same as the INDEX_SS hint, but this could change in a future version of Oracle.

- **INDEX_SS_DESC**   The INDEX_SS_DESC hint uses the same syntax as the INDEX_SS hint but instructs the optimizer to scan the index skip-scan in descending order.

- **MODEL_MIN_ANALYSIS**   The MODEL_MIN_ANALYSIS hint instructs the optimizer to omit some compile-time optimizations of spreadsheet rules. This hint can reduce the compilation time required during spreadsheet analysis and is used with SQL modeling queries (queries using the MODEL clause).

- **MONITOR**   The MONITOR hint turns index monitoring on for short queries. For MONITOR to work, the initialization/session parameter CONTROL_MANAGEMENT_PACK_ACCESS must be set to "DIAGNOSTIC+TUNING". NO_MONITOR turns off index monitoring, even for long-running queries. *Monitoring* refers to entries logged in the V$SQL_MONITOR and V$SQL_PLAN_MONITOR tables during query execution.

- **NATIVE_FULL_OUTER_JOIN** When the full outer join condition between two tables is an equijoin, Oracle Database automatically uses a native execution method based on a hash join. This hint instructs the optimizer to consider using the hash full–outer join execution method, when it might not normally do so. If you specify NO_NATIVE_FULL_OUTER_JOIN, then the full outer join is executed as a union of left outer join and an antijoin.

- **NOLOGGING** There is *no* "NOLOGGING" *hint* to turn off archive logging for a DML statement although developers sometimes think there is. You can, however, ALTER TABLE EMP NOLOGGING and then do an INSERT /*+ APPEND */ into the EMP table to bypass the redo if the database is in ARCHIVELOG mode (careful as this has major recovery implications—back up after this). If the database is in NOARCHIVELOG mode (not recommended), any direct load operations, such as the INSERT /*+ APPEND */, are not recoverable. NOLOGGING works with many DDL commands, such as for creating tables, creating indexes, and rebuilding indexes (careful as this also has major recovery implications; back up after and don't leave tables and indexes in NOLOGGING mode).

- **OPT_PARAM** This hint allows you to modify the parameter setting in effect for the duration of the query. This only works with session parameters that can be changed! Remember to put parameter names in single quotes.

- **PUSH_PRED** This hint causes WHERE clause conditions to be pushed into a query view to exclude rows as soon as possible in the select process. NO_PUSH_PRED reverses this activity.

- **REWRITE_OR_ERROR** The REWRITE_OR_ERROR hint in a query produces the following error if the query did not rewrite for queries against materialized views (this happens when there are no suitable materialized views for query rewrite to use):

  ORA-30393: a query block in the statement did not rewrite

  Support Metalink note 1215173.1 discusses this hint.

- **USE_NL_WITH_INDEX** The USE_NL hint instructs the optimizer to use a nested loops join with the specified table as the nondriving table (or as the inner table that is *looped* through with the result of the driving table). The USE_NL_WITH_INDEX hint allows you to also specify the index that is used during access. However, the optimizer must be able to use that index with at least one join.

Undocumented Hints

The *Oracle SQL Reference* contains seldom-used hints that I have not mentioned. Other hints are mentioned in the Oracle documentation but not the SQL guide. These hints are generally found in sources such as the *Data Warehouse Guide* or performance tuning manuals but without a formal write-up of their syntax and functionality. Some hints exist but are not mentioned anywhere in the documentation (as mentioned previously, V$SQL_HINT gives you a complete list of all 269 hints). A few undocumented hints like SWAP_JOIN_INPUTS are included in Metalink articles describing their syntax and functionality, but most are a complete mystery. Distinguishing between undocumented hints and mere comments included in the hint comment structure can be difficult. What might appear to be an undocumented hint may actually be nothing more than a comment that uses the same comment delimiters (/* */) as hints, but without the "+" sign.

Generally, you should not use undocumented hints unless directed to by Oracle Support. Undocumented features tend to be unsupported.

The RULE hint is undocumented and is unsupported in 11gR2; even though, it was supported in previous versions of the database. The RULE optimizer mode was officially desupported in Oracle 10.1. My Oracle Support/Metalink (Doc ID 189702.1) has a good writeup on this change, and also contains links and tips for migrating to the cost-based optimizer. Even the *Performance Tuning Guide* for Oracle 10.1 release says, "The CHOOSE and RULE optimizer hints are no longer supported. The functionalities of those hints still exist but will be removed in a future release." I believe these hints are currently only retained to support upgrades from older systems (such as 9i). However, as Oracle9i moves into complete obsolescence, the RULE-related parameter settings and hints will most likely be removed from the software. Prepare now!

RULE invokes the *rule-based optimizer,* an older way of determining an execution path for a query based on a set of rules. The rule-based optimizer is generally less efficient than the cost-based optimizer but can be useful under some rare conditions, generally where no valid statistics for query objects exist:

- CAST conversions of collections to temporary tables

- TABLE() function temporary table conversions (pipelined functions)

- When joining views (including views of views and inline views)

- When joining many tables together (more than three, *very* rarely) and the cost-based optimizer becomes overwhelmed and chooses a suboptimal path

- Queries against system tables where the cost-based optimizer is not making optimal choices

It has been suggested that the undocumented CARDINALITY hint (which allows override of the cardinality statistic) can overcome some of these limitations, but CARDINALITY requires an estimate of the number of rows beforehand and table cardinality is only a part of what the cost-based optimizer uses to determine an execution path.

Because the RULE hint is unsupported (according to the 11g and 10g documentation), only use it with extreme caution, if at all. The RULE hint should probably only be used when migrating queries written for the rule-based optimizer to the cost-based optimizer.

Using Hints with Views

Although hints can be hard-coded into views, doing so is generally a bad idea because it is impossible to know how a view will be used (selected standalone, joined to other tables or views, or even used by other views). It is better to push a hint into a view when needed in a query rather than permanently embed a hint in a view through a *global hint.*

To use a global hint, use the view name followed by a period followed by the name of the affected table designation, as used inside the view (table name or alias).

Example

```
select /*+ USE_HASH(v.d) */ count(*)
from    emp_details_view v
where employee_id = 100;
```

When using global hints, you need to know the usage of tables and aliases in the target view. In this example, the EMP_DETAILS_VIEW uses the alias d for DEPARTMENTS, so that designator must be used in the global hint.

TIP
Use the global hint technique to push hints into views when needed rather than hard-coding hints into views.

Notes on Hints and Stored Outlines (or SQL Plan Baselines in 11g)

SQL Plan Baselines or stored outlines, which still work, but are deprecated/discouraged in 11g, are covered in Chapter 6, but a note here is relevant for the discussion on hints. Migrating from stored outlines to SQL Plan Baselines is also covered in Chapter 6. Stored outlines or baselines allow a query to use a predetermined execution plan every time that query is run, no matter where the query is run from. People sometimes speak of the STORED OUTLINES as storing an execution plan, but this is not really what happens. Instead, Oracle stores a series of hints to duplicate the execution plan as saved during a recording session. If you want to query the hints for a stored outline, you can use the following query to USER_OUTLINE_HINTS:

Example

```
select     hint
from       user_outline_hints
where      name = 'your_outline_name';
```

The very same considerations regarding using hints apply to stored outlines: unpredictable behavior when upgrading, applying patches, or changing initialization/session parameters. Also, if the query structure changes in any way, the stored outline may stop working.

Why Isn't My Hint Working?

Often a hint won't behave like you want it to. Sometimes the optimizer overrides the hint, but usually people have a problem related to one of the following:

- The hint syntax is incorrect.
- The table(s) is not analyzed or the statistics are not current.
- There is a conflict with another hint.
- The hint requires a system parameter to be set for it to work.
- The table name was aliased in the query, but you used the table name, not the alias, in the hint.
- The hint requires a different version of Oracle than you have.
- You don't understand the correct application for the hint.

- You haven't slept lately—for many of the reasons cited here.
- There is a software bug.

Hints at a Glance

The following table lists each hint discussed in this chapter (and a couple of others) and how the hint is used.

Hint	Use
FIRST_ROWS	Generally forces the use of indexes
ALL_ROWS	Generally forces a full table scan
FULL	Forces a full table scan
INDEX	Forces the use of an index
NO_INDEX	Disallows a specified index from being used
INDEX_JOIN	Allows the merging of indexes on a single table
INDEX_ASC	Uses an index ordered in ascending order
INDEX_DESC	Uses an index ordered in descending order
INDEX_COMBINE	Accesses multiple bitmap indexes
INDEX_FFS	Does a fast full index scan
ORDERED	Specifies the driving order of tables
LEADING	Specifies just the first driving table
NO_EXPAND	Helps eliminate OR expansion
STAR_TRANSFORMATION	Forces a star query transform
DRIVING_SITE	Processes data by driving it from a particular database
USE_MERGE	Changes how tables are joined internally to merge joining
USE_HASH	Changes how tables are joined internally to hash joining
USE_NL	Changes how tables are joined internally to nested loops
PUSH_SUBQ	Forces the subquery to process earlier
PARALLEL	Causes full table scan queries to split a query into pieces and process each piece with a different process
NO_PARALLEL	Turns off use of parallel operations for one given query
PARALLEL_INDEX	Performs an index scan in parallel
NO_PARALLEL_INDEX	Does not perform an index scan in parallel
PQ_DISTRIBUTE	Controls how parallel queries are divided up
APPEND	Appends data into new blocks
NOAPPEND	Checks for free space within current blocks before using new ones

Hint	Use
CACHE	Causes a full table scan to be pinned into memory
NOCACHE	Causes a table that is specified to be cached at the database level to not get cached when accessed
RESULT_CACHE	Caches data in the shared memory pool
NO_RESULT_CACHE	Causes data not to be cached in the shared memory pool
CURSOR_SHARING_EXACT	Overrides the CURSOR_SHARING setting
QB_NAME	Assigns a name to a query block

TIPS
&
REVIEW

Tips Review

- Incorrect hint syntax leads to the hint being interpreted as a comment.

- Multiple hints are separated with a space between them. At times, specifying multiple hints can cause the query to use *none* of the hints.

- If an alias is used, the alias *must* be used in the hint or it will *not* work.

- The FIRST_ROWS hint causes the optimizer to choose a path that retrieves the first row of a query fastest, at the cost of retrieving multiple rows slower.

- The ALL_ROWS hint causes the optimizer to choose a path that retrieves all rows of a query fastest, at the cost of retrieving one single row slower.

- The FULL hint performs a full table scan on the table that is specified (not all tables in the query).

- The INDEX hint tells the optimizer to choose the index specified in the hint.

- The NO_INDEX hint disallows the optimizer from using the specified index.

- The INDEX_JOIN hint allows you to access and merge together only indexes on a table, which is a scan of fewer total blocks and often faster than scanning the table by ROWID.

- The INDEX_COMBINE hint tells the optimizer to merge multiple *bitmap* indexes for a single table instead of choosing which one is better (as in the INDEX hint).

- The INDEX_ASC does exactly what the INDEX hint does, since indexes are already scanned in ascending order. It guarantees this, however, as Oracle may change this default in the future.

- The INDEX_DESC processes an index in the descending order of how it was built. This hint is not used if more than one table exists in the query.

- The INDEX_FFS processes *only* the index and does not take the result and access the table. All columns that are used and retrieved by the query *must* be contained in the index.

■   The ORDERED hint is one of the most powerful hints. It processes the tables of the query in the order that they are listed in the FROM clause (the *first* table in the FROM is processed first). There are, however, many variations that cause this hint to work differently.

■   The LEADING hint is used to specify a single table to drive a query with while allowing the optimizer to figure out the rest of the query. The ORDERED hint overrides LEADING.

■   The NO_EXPAND hint prevents the optimizer from using OR expansion.

■   The DRIVING_SITE hint is extremely powerful, as it potentially limits the amount of information to be processed over your network. The table specified with the DRIVING_SITE hint is the location where the join will be processed.

■   Using views for remote tables can also lead to better performance by limiting the number of rows passed from the remote site *before* the records are sent to the local site.

■   The USE_NL hint *usually* provides the best response time (first row comes back faster) for smaller result sets, whereas the USE_MERGE hint *usually* provides the best throughput when the USE_HASH hint can't be used.

■   The USE_HASH hint *usually* provides the best response time for larger result sets.

■   The PUSH_SUBQ hint can improve performance greatly when the subquery returns only a few rows very fast and those rows can be used to limit the rows returned in the outer query.

■   The PARALLEL hint enables the use of parallel operations. If the degree is not specified with the hint, the default degree specified during table creation is used.

■   In 11*g*R2, if you have multiple tables and you specify the PARALLEL hint with a numeric value, that is the degree of parallelism used for all the tables in the query, overriding the parallel setting at the table level. If you also specify a table name, then the PARALLEL hint applies to only that table; any other tables accessed by the query use the table's parallelism setting.

■   The NO_PARALLEL hint disables parallel operations in a statement that would otherwise use parallel processing due to a parallel object definition.

■   The APPEND hint inserts values into a table without checking the free space in the currently used blocks, but instead appending the data into new blocks.

■   The NOAPPEND hint overrides a PARALLEL hint, which normally uses the APPEND hint by default.

■   The CACHE hint should be used with small lookup tables that are often accessed by users. This ensures that the table remains in memory.

■   The NOCACHE hint prevents caching a table specified with the CACHE option—basically, when you want to access the table but you *don't* want to cache it.

■   The RESULT_CACHE hint caches query results in the shared pool; NO_RESULT_CACHE is used when you don't want to cache data in the shared pool (it still can be cached in the buffer cache).

- The CURSOR_SHARING_EXACT hint overrides the instance-level setting of CURSOR_SHARING to either FORCE or SIMILAR.

- Use the global hint technique to push hints into views when needed rather than hard-coding hints into views.

References

Metalink Document 453567.1: SQL Query Result Cache.
Rich Niemiec, *Tuning Tips: You Will Be Toast!,* TUSC.
Oracle11gR1 Performance Tuning Guide.
Oracle 11gR1 SQL Language Reference.

Many thanks to Mark Riedel for upgrading this chapter to Oracle 11g! Lucas Niemiec also did some research on a few of the hints and Metalink notes listed.

One final note from the "Oracle Database Sample Schemas 11g Release 1 (11.1) – Part No. B28328-03." During a complete installation of Oracle Database, the Sample Schemas can be installed automatically with the seed database. If, for some reason, the seed database is removed from your system (or not installed), you will need to reinstall the Sample Schemas before you can duplicate the examples you find in Oracle documentation and training materials. Using DBCA is by far the most intuitive and simple way to install the Sample Schemas. During Step 9 of the database creation process, the check box "Example Schemas" needs to be checked for any Sample Schema to be created. DBCA installs all five schemas (HR, OE, PM, IX, SH) in your database. You can also create Sample Schemas manually by running SQL scripts, rather than using DBCA. The scripts are included in the example disk but are archived in a .jar file. (Thanks to Janet Stern for this note.)

CHAPTER
8

Query Tuning: Developer
and Beginner DBA

TIPS & COVERED

This chapter focuses on specific queries that you may encounter and some general information for tuning those specific queries, but it has also been updated to include some basic information on Oracle's 11g Automatic SQL Tuning and some queries to access Oracle's 11g Automatic Workload Repository (AWR). Examples of query tuning are spread throughout this book as well as instructions on making them more effective in terms of your system's architecture. This chapter centers on some of the most common queries that can be tuned on *most* systems. A query can display several variations in behavior, depending on system architecture, the data distribution in the tables, what tool or application is accessing the database, the specific version of Oracle Database, and a variety of other exceptions to the rules. Your results will vary; use your own testing to come up with the most favorable performance. The goal in this chapter is to show you many of the issues to watch for and how to fix them.

This chapter uses strictly cost-based examples for timings (except where noted). No other queries were performed at the time of the tests performed for this chapter. Many hints are also used throughout this chapter. For a detailed look at hints and the syntax and structure of hints, please refer to Chapter 7. Multiple table and complex queries are the focus of the next chapter and are not covered here.

Please note that this is not an all-inclusive chapter. Many other queries are covered throughout the book, which need to be investigated when trying to increase performance for a given query. Some of the most dramatic include using the parallel features of Oracle Database (Chapter 11), using partitioned tables and indexes (Chapter 2), and using PL/SQL to improve performance (Chapter 10). Note the benefits of using EXPLAIN and TRACE for queries (Chapter 6). Oracle Database 11g provides the Automatic Workload Repository (AWR) and Automatic Database Diagnostic Monitor (ADDM). The Enterprise Manager views of these new features are shown in Chapter 5. Tips covered in this chapter include the following:

- What queries do I tune? Querying the V$SQLAREA and V$SQL views
- Some useful new 11g views for locating resource-intensive sessions and queries
- When should I use an index?
- What if I forget the index?
- Creating and checking an index
- What if I create a bad index?
- Exercising caution when dropping an index
- Using invisible indexes
- Function based indexes and virtual columns
- Increasing performance by indexing the SELECT and WHERE columns
- Using the Fast Full Scan feature to guarantee success
- Making queries "magically" faster
- Caching a table into memory
- Using the new 11g Result Cache

- Choosing between multiple indexes on a table (use the most selective)
- Indexes that can get suppressed
- Tuning OR Clauses
- Using the EXISTS clause and the nested subquery
- That table is a view!
- SQL and the Grand Unified Theory
- Automatic SQL Tuning and the SQL Tuning Advisor
- Using the SQL Performance Analyzer (SPA)

What Queries Do I Tune? Querying V$SQLAREA and V$SQL Views

V$SQLAREA and V$SQL are great views that you can query to find the worst-performing SQL statements that need to be optimized. The value in the DISK_READS column signifies the volume of disk reads that are being performed on the system. This, combined with the executions (DISK_READS/EXECUTIONS), return the SQL statements that have the most disk hits per statement execution. Any statement that makes the top of this list is most likely a problem query that needs to be tuned. The AWR Report or Statspack Report also lists the resource-intensive queries; see Chapter 14 for detailed information.

Selecting from the V$SQLAREA View to Find the Worst Queries

The following query can be used to find the worst queries in your database. This query alone is worth the price of this book if you've not heard of V$SQLAREA yet.

To find the worst queries:

```
select      b.username username, a.disk_reads reads,
              a.executions exec, a.disk_reads /decode
            (a.executions, 0, 1,a.executions) rds_exec_ratio,
            a.sql_text Statement
from        V$sqlarea a, dba_users b
where       a.parsing_user_id = b.user_id
and         a.disk_reads > 100000
order       by a.disk_reads desc;

USERNAME    READS   EXEC  RDS_EXEC_RATIO STATEMENT
--------    ------- ----- -------------- --------------------
---------------------------------------------------
ADHOC1      7281934    1      7281934    select custno, ordno
from cust, orders
```

```
ADHOC5    4230044    4         1057511  select ordno
from orders where trunc(ordno) = 721305

ADHOC1    801716     2          400858  select custno,
ordno from cust where substr(custno,1,6) = '314159'
```

The DISK_READS column in the preceding statement can be replaced with the BUFFER_GETS column to provide information on SQL statements requiring the largest amount of memory.

Now consider the output in a second example where there is a count of a billion-row table (EMP3) and a count of what was originally a 130M row table (EMP2), where all of the rows in EMP2, except the first 15 rows inserted, were deleted. Note that Oracle counts all the way up to the high water mark (HWM) of EMP2 (it read over 800,000, 8K blocks even though *all* of the data was only in 1 block). This listing would have told you something is wrong with the query on EMP2 that needs to be addressed, given that it only has 15 rows in it (analyzing the table will not improve this).

```
USERNAME    READS   EXEC  RDS_EXEC_RATIO STATEMENT
--------   -------  ----- --------------- ------------------------
SCOTT      5875532    1         5875532  select count(*)  from emp3
SCOTT       800065    1          800065  select count(*)  from emp2
```

For this issue, if the EMP2 table was *completely* empty, you could simply truncate the table to fix it. Since the table still has 15 rows, you have a few options; *which* option you choose depends on your unique situation. I can

- EXPORT/TRUNCATE/IMPORT; CREATE TABLE emp2b AS SELECT * FROM emp2 (CTAS) and then DROP and RENAME (I have to worry about indexes/related objects, etc.)

- Do an "ALTER TABLE *emp2* MOVE TABLESPACE *new1*" and rebuild the indexes.

- If it has a primary key, use DBMS_REDEFINITION.CAN_REDEF_TABLE to verify that the table can be redefined online.

Please check the Oracle documentation for syntax/advantages/disadvantages and stipulations (not all are listed here) for each of these options, so you can apply the best option to your situation (each of these options have major downsides, including users not being able to access the table and related objects getting dropped depending on which you use, so *be careful*). Once I reorganize the table, the next count(*) only reads 1 block instead of 800,065 blocks (it was well worth fixing the problem). Note in the query, I change "emp2" to emP2" so I can find that cursor in the cache.

```
alter table emp2 move;    -- You can specify a tablespace

select count(*)
from    emP2;

select      b.username username, a.disk_reads reads,
            a.executions exec, a.disk_reads /decode
            (a.executions, 0, 1,a.executions) rds_exec_ratio,
            a.sql_text Statement
```

```
from        V$sqlarea a, dba_users b
where       a.parsing_user_id = b.user_id
and         a.sql_text like '%emP2%'
order       by a.disk_reads desc;
```

```
USERNAME    READS   EXEC  RDS_EXEC_RATIO  STATEMENT
--------    -----   ----  --------------  --------------------
SCOTT           1      1               1  select count(*) from emP2
```

You can also shrink space in a table, index-organized table, index, partition, subpartition, materialized view, or materialized view log. You do this using ALTER TABLE, ALTER INDEX, ALTER MATERIALIZED VIEW, or ALTER MATERIALIZED VIEW LOG statement with the SHRINK SPACE clause. See the *Oracle Administrators Guide* for additional information. Lastly, if you want to use the "ALTER TABLE *table* MOVE TABLESPACE *tablespace_name*" command, consider using the same size tablespace (or smaller if appropriate) to move things "back and forth" so as not to waste space.

TIP
Query V$SQLAREA to find your problem queries that need to be tuned.

Selecting from the V$SQL View to Find the Worst Queries

Querying V$SQL allows you to see the shared SQL area statements individually versus grouped together (as V$SQLAREA does). Here is a faster query to get the top statements from V$SQL (this query can also access V$SQLAREA by only changing the view name):

```
select *
from    (select address,
            rank() over ( order by buffer_gets desc ) as rank_bufgets,
            to_char(100 * ratio_to_report(buffer_gets) over (), '999.99') pct_bufgets
from    v$sql )
where   rank_bufgets < 11;
```

```
ADDRESS    RANK_BUFGETS  PCT_BUF
--------   ------------  -------
131B7914              1    66.36
131ADA6C              2    24.57
131BC16C              3     1.97
13359B54              4      .98
1329ED20              5      .71
132C7374              5      .71
12E966B4              7      .52
131A3CDC              8      .48
131947C4              9      .48
1335BE14             10      .48
1335CE44             10      .48
```

You can alternatively select SQL_TEXT instead of ADDRESS if you want to see the SQL:

```
COL SQL_TEXT FOR A50
select *
from  (select sql_text,
          rank() over ( order by buffer_gets desc ) as rank_bufgets,
          to_char(100 * ratio_to_report(buffer_gets) over (), '999.99')
pct_bufgets
from  v$sql )
where  rank_bufgets < 11;
```

TIP
You can also query V$SQL to find your problem queries that need to be tuned.

Oracle 11g Views for Locating Resource-Intensive Sessions and Queries

Oracle 11g provides many new views, giving you access to a wealth of information from the OS (operating system) and the Automatic Workload Repository (AWR). The AWR provides metric-based information, which is useful for monitoring and diagnosing performance issues. Metrics are a set of statistics for certain system attributes as defined by Oracle. Essentially, they are context-defined statistics that are collated into historical information within the AWR.

Accessing the AWR and ADDM information via Enterprise Manager is covered in Chapter 5 as well as in the Oracle documentation. In this section, I am only looking at pulling some specific information out of these views using SQL to locate queries that may need tuning.

Selecting from V$SESSMETRIC to Find Current Resource-Intensive Sessions

This query shows the sessions that are heaviest in physical reads, CPU usage, or logical reads over a defined interval (15 seconds, by default). You may want to adjust the thresholds as appropriate for your environment.

To find resource-intensive sessions:

```
Select TO_CHAR(m.end_time,'DD-MON-YYYY HH24:MI:SS') e_dttm,   -- Interval End Time
          m.intsize_csec/100 ints,     -- Interval size in sec
          s.username usr,
          m.session_id sid,
          m.session_serial_num ssn,
          ROUND(m.cpu) cpu100,         -- CPU usage 100th sec
          m.physical_reads prds,       -- Number of physical reads
          m.logical_reads lrds,        -- Number of logical reads
          m.pga_memory pga,            -- PGA size at end of interval
          m.hard_parses hp,
          m.soft_parses sp,
```

```
        m.physical_read_pct prp,
        m.logical_read_pct lrp,
        s.sql_id
from    v$sessmetric m, v$session s
where (m.physical_reads > 100
or      m.cpu > 100
or      m.logical_reads > 100)
and     m.session_id = s.sid
and     m.session_serial_num = s.serial#
order by m.physical_reads DESC, m.cpu DESC, m.logical_reads DESC;


E_DTTM                    INTS USR SID SSN  CPU100  PRDS LRDS    PGA HP SP PRP
LRP         SQL_ID
-------------------- ---- --- --- ---- ------ ----- ---- ------ -- -- ---
---------- --------------
20-NOV-2010 00:11:07   15 RIC 146 1501   1758 41348    1 781908  0  0 100
.512820513 03ay719wdnqz1
```

Viewing Available AWR Snapshots

The next few queries access AWR snapshot information.

> *Query the DBA_HIST_SNAPSHOT view to find more information about specific AWR snapshots:*

```
select  snap_id,
        TO_CHAR(begin_interval_time,'DD-MON-YYYY HH24:MI:SS') b_dttm,
        TO_CHAR(end_interval_time,'DD-MON-YYYY HH24:MI:SS') e_dttm
from    dba_hist_snapshot
where   begin_interval_time > TRUNC(SYSDATE);


SNAP_ID  B_DTTM               E_DTTM
-------- -------------------- --------------------
    503 25-MAY-2011 00:00:35 25-MAY-2011 01:00:48
    504 25-MAY-2011 01:00:48 25-MAY-2011 02:00:00
    505 25-MAY-2011 02:00:00 25-MAY-2011 03:00:13
    506 25-MAY-2011 03:18:38 25-MAY-2011 04:00:54
    507 25-MAY-2011 04:00:54 25-MAY-2011 05:00:07
```

Selecting from the DBA_HIST_SQLSTAT
View to Find the Worst Queries

SQL statements that have exceeded predefined thresholds are kept in the AWR for a predefined time (seven days, by default). You can query the DBA_HIST_SQLSTAT view to find the worst queries. The following is the equivalent statement to the V$SQLAREA query earlier in this chapter.

To query DBA_HIST_SQLSTAT view to find the worst queries:

```
select snap_id, disk_reads_delta reads_delta,
       executions_delta exec_delta, disk_reads_delta /decode
    (executions_delta, 0, 1,executions_delta) rds_exec_ratio,
    sql_id
from   dba_hist_sqlstat
where  disk_reads_delta > 100000
order  by disk_reads_delta desc;
```

SNAP_ID	READS_DELTA	EXEC_DELTA	RDS_EXEC_RATIO	SQL_ID
38	9743276	0	9743276	03ay719wdnqz1
39	9566692	0	9566692	03ay719wdnqz1
37	7725091	1	7725091	03ay719wdnqz1

Note that in the output, the same SQL_ID appears in three different AWR snapshots. (In this case, it was executed during the first one and is still running). You could also choose to filter on other criteria, including cumulative or delta values for DISK_READS, BUFFER_GETS, ROWS_PROCESSED, CPU_TIME, ELAPSED_TIME, IOWAIT, CLWAIT (cluster wait), and so on. Run a DESC command of the view DBA_HIST_SQLSTAT to get a full list of its columns. This listing shows different SQL_IDs at the top of the list.

SNAP_ID	READS_DELTA	EXEC_DELTA	RDS_EXEC_RATIO	SQL_ID
513	5875532	1	5875532	f6c6qfq28rtkv
513	800065	1	800065	df28xa1n6rcur

Selecting Query Text from the DBA_HIST_SQLTEXT View

The query text for the offending queries shown in the previous two examples can be obtained from the DBA_HIST_SQLTEXT view with the following query:

To query DBA_HIST_SQLTEXT:

```
select command_type,sql_text
from   dba_hist_sqltext
where  sql_id='03ay719wdnqz1';
```

COMMAND_TYPE	SQL_TEXT
3	select count(1) from t2, t2

```
select command_type,sql_text
from   dba_hist_sqltext
where  sql_id='f6c6qfq28rtkv';
```

COMMAND_TYPE	SQL_TEXT
3	select count(*) from emp3

Selecting Query EXPLAIN PLAN
from the DBA_HIST_SQL_PLAN View

The EXPLAIN PLAN for the offending SQL is also captured. You may view information about the execution plan through the DBA_HIST_SQL_PLAN view. If you want to display the EXPLAIN PLAN, the simplest way is to use the DBMS_XPLAN package with a statement such as this one:

```
select *
from    table(DBMS_XPLAN.DISPLAY_AWR('03ay719wdnqz1'));

PLAN_TABLE_OUTPUT
--------------------------------------------------------------------------------
--------------------------------------------------------------------------------
SQL_ID 03ay719wdnqz1
--------------------
select count(1) from t2, t2

Plan hash value: 1163428054
-----------------------------------------------------------------------
| Id | Operation            | Name  | Rows  | Cost (%CPU)| Time        |
-----------------------------------------------------------------------
|  0 | SELECT STATEMENT     |       |       | 10G(100)   |             |
|  1 | SORT AGGREGATE       |       |   1   |            |             |
|  2 | MERGE JOIN CARTESIAN |       | 6810G | 10G  (2)   |999:59:59 |
|  3 | INDEX FAST FULL SCAN | T2_I1 | 2609K | 3996 (2)   | 00:00:48 |
|  4 | BUFFER SORT          |       | 2609K | 10G  (2)   |999:59:59 |
|  5 | INDEX FAST FULL SCAN | T2_I1 | 2609K | 3994 (2)   | 00:00:48 |
-----------------------------------------------------------------------
```

As you can see, this particular query is a Cartesian join, which is normally not a valid table join (certainly not a good idea as it joins *every* row of one table with *every* row of another table) and can lead to the massive resource consumption. This query was used to show how to take advantage of some of the new 11*g* functionality for identifying and collecting information about poorly performing SQL. Here is the output for the query that was used earlier that queries the EMP3 table, which is over 1 billion rows (still fast at 5 minutes, even though it's 1B rows):

```
select *
from    table(DBMS_XPLAN.DISPLAY_AWR('f6c6qfq28rtkv'));

PLAN_TABLE_OUTPUT
----------------------------------------------------------------
SQL_ID f6c6qfq28rtkv
--------------------
select count(*) from emp3

Plan hash value: 1396384608
```

```
--------------------------------------------------------------------
| Id  | Operation          | Name | Rows  | Cost (%CPU)| Time      |
--------------------------------------------------------------------
|  0  | SELECT STATEMENT   |      |       | 1605K(100)|            |
|  1  |  SORT AGGREGATE    |      |     1 |           |            |
|  2  | TABLE ACCESS FULL| EMP3 | 1006M| 1605K  (1)| 05:21:10  |
--------------------------------------------------------------------
```

When Should I Use an Index?

In Oracle version 5, many DBAs called the indexing rule the 80/20 Rule; you needed to use an index if less than 20 percent of the rows were being returned by a query. In version 7, this number was reduced to about 7 percent on average, and in versions 8i and 9i, the number was closer to 4 percent. In versions 10g and 11g, Oracle is better at retrieving the entire table, so the value continues to be in the 5 percent or less range, although it depends not only on the number of rows but also on how the blocks are distributed as well (see Chapter 2 for additional information). Figure 8-1 shows when an index should generally be used (in V5 and V6 for rule-based optimization and in V7, V8i, V9i, V10g, and V11g for cost-based optimization). However, based on the distribution of data, parallel queries or partitioning can be used and other factors need to be considered. In Chapter 9, you will see how to make this graph for your own queries. If the table has fewer than 1000 records (small tables), then the graph is also different. For small tables, Oracle's cost-based optimizer generally uses the index when only less than 1 percent of the table is queried. This graph shows you the progress in versions of Oracle. The lower the percentage of rows returned, the more likely you would use an index. This graph shows the speed of a full table scan becoming faster. Because of the many variables starting with Oracle 9i, the percentage could continue to decrease as the trend shows happening from V5 to V8i,

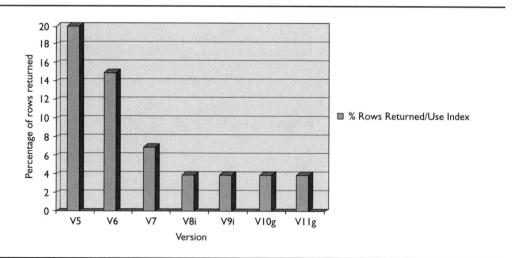

FIGURE 8-1. *When to generally use an index based on the percentage of rows returned by a query*

or it could increase slightly, depending on how you architect the database. In Oracle 9*i*, Oracle 10*g*, and Oracle11*g*, you create where the graph goes and Exadata and Exalogic enhancements can further alter this graph (where percentage could decrease to less than 1 percent); your choice may depend on how the data and indexes are architected, how the data is distributed within the blocks, and how it is accessed.

TIP
When a small number of rows ("small" is version and hardware dependent) are returned to meet a condition in a query, you generally want to use an index on that condition (column), given that the small number of rows also returns a small number of individual blocks (usually the case).

What If I Forget the Index?

Although it seems obvious that columns, which are generally restrictive, require indexes, this requirement is not always such common knowledge among users or managers. I once went to a consulting job where their database was suffering from incredibly poor performance. When I asked for a list of tables and indexes, they replied, "We have a list of tables, but we haven't figured out what indexes are yet and if we should use them or not—do you think you can help our performance?" My first thought was, "Wow, can I ever—my dream tuning job." My second thought was that I had been training experts too long and had forgotten that not everyone is as far along in their performance education. While basic index principles and structure are covered in Chapter 2, this section will focus on query-related issues surrounding indexes.

Even if you have built indexes correctly for most columns needing them, you may miss a crucial column here and there. If you forget to put an index on a restrictive column, then the speed of those queries will not be optimized. Consider the following example where the percent of rows returned by any given CUST_ID is less than 1 percent (there are about 25M rows on the SALES2 table and about 25K of them are CUST_ID=22340. Under these circumstances, an index on the CUST_ID column should normally be implemented. The next query does *not* have an index on CUST_ID:

```
select  count(*)
from    sales2
where   cust_id = 22340;

  COUNT(*)
----------
    25750


Elapsed: 00:00:08.47 (8.47 seconds)

Execution Plan
----------------------------------------------------------
Plan hash value: 2862189843
```

```
----------------------------------------------------------------
| Id  | Operation            | Name   | Rows | Cost (%CPU)| Time     |
----------------------------------------------------------------
|  0  | SELECT STATEMENT     |        |    1 | 32639   (1)| 00:06:32 |
|  1  |  SORT AGGREGATE      |        |    1 |            |          |
|  2  |   TABLE ACCESS FULL  | SALES2 |  24M | 32639   (1)| 00:06:32 |
----------------------------------------------------------------
119260 consistent gets (memory reads)
119258 physical reads (disk reads)
1,000 times more blocks read than using an index (we'll see this in a moment)
```

Not only is the query extremely slow, but it also uses a tremendous amount of memory and CPU to perform the query. This results in an impatient user and a frustrating wait for other users due to the lack of system resources. (Sound familiar?)

Creating an Index

To accelerate the query in the last example, I build an index on the CUST_ID column. The storage clause must be based on the size of the table and the column. The table is over 25 million rows (the space for the index is about 461M). Specifying automatic segment-space management for the underlying tablespace allows Oracle to manage segment space automatically for best performance. I could also perform an ALTER SESSION SET SORT_AREA_SIZE = 500000000 (if I had the necessary OS memory) and the index creation would be much faster.

```
create index sales2_idx1 on sales2(cust_id)
tablespace rich
storage (initial 400M next 10M pctincrease 0);

Index Created.
```

Invisible Index

Oracle 11g has a new feature called invisible indexes. An invisible index is invisible to the optimizer by default. Using this feature, you can test a new index without affecting the execution plans of the existing SQL statements or you can test the effect of dropping an index without actually dropping it (the index continues to be maintained even though it is not seen by the optimizer; this ensures if you make it visible again, it's up to date). Note that Chapter 2 has additional information and queries related to invisible indexes.

You can create an invisible index or you can alter an existing index to make it invisible. To enable the optimizer to use *all* invisible indexes (not a good idea usually), a new initialization parameter called OPTIMIZER_USE_INVISIBLE_INDEXES can be set to TRUE. This parameter is set to FALSE by default. You can run this CREATE instead of the one in the previous section:

```
create index sales2_idx1 on sales2(cust_id)
tablespace rich
storage (initial 400M next 10M pctincrease 0) invisible;

Index Created
```

Checking the Index on a Table

Before creating indexes, check for current indexes that exist on that table to ensure there are no conflicts.

Once you have created the index, verify that it exists by querying the DBA_IND_COLUMNS view:

```
select  table_name, index_name, column_name, column_position
from    dba_ind_columns
where   table_name = 'SALES2'
and     table_owner = 'SH'
order   by index_name, column_position;

TABLE_NAME INDEX_NAME  COLUMN_NAME COLUMN_POSITION
---------- ----------- ----------- ---------------
SALES2     SALES2_IDX1 CUST_ID                   1
```

The TABLE_NAME is the table that is being indexed; the INDEX_NAME is the name of the index; the COLUMN_NAME is the column being indexed; and the COLUMN_POSITION is the order of the columns in a multipart index. Because our index involves only one column, the COLUMN_POSITION is '1' (CUST_ID is the first and only column in the index). In the concatenated index section (later in this chapter), you will see how a multipart index appears.

Query USER_INDEXES to verify the visibility of the index:

```
select index_name, visibility
from   user_indexes
where index_name = 'SALES2_IDX1';

INDEX_NAME                VISIBILITY
------------------------- ----------
SALES2_IDX1               VISIBLE
```

Is the Column Properly Indexed?

Rerun the same query now that the CUST_ID column is properly indexed. The query is dramatically faster, and more important, it no longer "floods" the system with a tremendous amount of data to the SGA (it has a much lower number of block reads) and subsequently reduces the physical I/O as well. Originally, this query took around 120,000 physical reads. Now it only takes about 60 physical reads (1000× less) and over 800× faster. Even though the query itself runs in seconds, this time difference can be a big deal if the query runs many times.

```
select  count(*)
from    sales2
where   cust_id = 22340;

  COUNT(*)
----------
   25750
```

```
Elapsed: 00:00:00.01 (0.01 seconds - )

Execution Plan
-----------------------------------------------------------
Plan hash value: 3721387097
-------------------------------------------------------------------------------
| Id  | Operation          | Name        | Rows  | Bytes | Cost (%CPU)| Time     |
-------------------------------------------------------------------------------
|   0 | SELECT STATEMENT   |             |     1 |     4 |    10   (0)| 00:00:01 |
|   1 |  SORT AGGREGATE    |             |     1 |     4 |            |          |
|*  2 |   INDEX RANGE SCAN | SALES2_IDX  |  3514 | 14056 |    10   (0)| 00:00:01 |
-------------------------------------------------------------------------------

127 consistent gets (memory reads)
60 physical reads (disk reads)
```

TIP
The first tip concerning slow queries is that you'll have a lot of them if you don't index restrictive columns (return a small percentage of the table). Building indexes on restrictive columns is the first step toward better system performance.

What If I Create a Bad Index?

In the query to the PRODUCT table, I have a COMPANY_NO column. Since this company's expansion has not occurred, all rows in the table have a COMPANY_NO = 1. What if I am a beginner and I have heard that indexes are good and have decided to index the COMPANY_NO column? Consider the following example which selects only certain columns from the PLAN_TABLE after executing the query.

The cost-based optimizer will analyze the index as bad and suppress it. The table *must* be reanalyzed after the index is created for the cost-based optimizer to make an informed choice. The index created on COMPANY_NO is correctly suppressed by Oracle internally (since it would access the entire table and index):

```
select  product_id, qty
from    product
where   company_no = 1;

Elapsed time: 405 seconds (all records are retrieved via a full table scan)

OPERATION            OPTIONS           OBJECT NAME
------------------   ---------------   -----------
SELECT STATEMENT
TABLE ACCESS         FULL              PRODUCT

49,825 consistent gets (memory reads)
41,562 physical reads (disk reads)
```

You can force an originally suppressed index to be used (bad choice), as follows:

```
select   /*+ index(product company_idx1) */ product_id, qty
from     product
where    company_no = 1;
```

Elapsed time: 725 seconds   (all records retrieved using the index on company_no)

OPERATION	OPTIONS	OBJECT NAME
SELECT STATEMENT		
TABLE ACCESS	BY ROWID	PRODUCT
INDEX	RANGE SCAN	COMPANY_IDX1

4,626,725 consistent gets (memory reads)
80,513 physical reads (disk reads)

Indexes can also be suppressed when they cause poorer performance by using the FULL hint:

```
select   /*+ FULL(PRODUCT) */ product_id, qty
from     product
where    company_no = 1;
```

Elapsed time: 405 seconds (all records are retrieved via a full table scan)

OPERATION	OPTIONS	OBJECT NAME
SELECT STATEMENT		
TABLE ACCESS	FULL	PRODUCT

49,825 consistent gets (memory reads)
41,562 physical reads (disk reads)

Next, consider a similar example in an 11*g*R2 database on a faster server with a 25M row table where I am summing *all* rows together. Oracle *is* once again smart enough to do a full table scan since I am summing the *entire* table. A full table scan only scans the table, but if I force an index (as in the second example), it has to read many more blocks (almost 50 percent more), scanning both the table and the index (resulting in a query that is almost four times slower).

```
select sum(prod_id)
from    sales
where   cust_id=1;

SUM(PROD_ID)

------------
  1939646817

Elapsed: 00:00:08.58
```

```
Execution Plan
-------------------------------------------------------------------------
| Id  | Operation            | Name    | Rows  | Bytes | Cost (%CPU)| Time     |
|   0 | SELECT STATEMENT     |         |     1 |     7 | 33009   (2)| 00:06:37 |
|   1 |  SORT AGGREGATE      |         |     1 |     7 |            |          |
|*  2 |   TABLE ACCESS FULL| SALES3  |   24M|  165M| 33009   (2)| 00:06:37 |
-------------------------------------------------------------------------


Statistic
-------------------------------------------------------------
     119665   consistent gets
     119660   physical reads
```

Now let's try scanning the index and then go to the table (bad idea):

```
select /*+ index (sales3 sales3_idx) */ sum(prod_id)
from    sales

where   cust_id=1


SUM(PROD_ID)
-----------
 1939646817

Elapsed: 00:00:33.9

Execution Plan
----------------------------------------------------------------------------
| Id  | Operation                    | Name      | Rows  |Bytes| Cost (%CPU)|Time     |
|   0 | SELECT STATEMENT             |           |     1 |  7  | 213K (1)   |00:42:37 |
|   1 |  SORT AGGREGATE              |           |     1 |  7  |            |         |
|   2 |   TABLE ACCESS BY INDEX ROWID | SALES3    |   24M|165M| 213K (1)   |00:42:37 |
|*  3 |    INDEX RANGE SCAN          | SALES3_IDX|   24M|     |47976 (1)   |00:09:36 |
----------------------------------------------------------------------------


Statistic
-----------------------------------------------------------
     168022   consistent gets
     168022   physical reads
```

TIP
*Bad indexes (indexing the wrong columns) can cause as much trouble
as forgetting to use indexes on the correct columns. While Oracle's
cost-based optimizer generally suppresses poor indexes, problems
can still develop when a bad index is used at the same time as a good
index.*

Exercising Caution When Dropping an Index

Some people's first reaction when they find a query that is using a poor index is to drop the
index. Suppressing the index should be your first reaction, however, and investigating the impact
of the index on other queries should be the next action. Unless your query was the only one

being performed against the given table, changing/dropping an index might be a detrimental solution. The invisible index feature in 11*g* can be used to determine the effect of dropping an index without actually dropping it. Issue the following command against the index that needs to be dropped.

```
alter index sales2_idx1 invisible;
```

An invisible index is an index that continues to be maintained but is ignored by the optimizer unless you explicitly set it back to being visible or turn *all* invisible indexes on by setting the OPTIMIZER_USE_INVISIBLE_INDEXES to TRUE (careful). This way you can test the effect of dropping a particular index. If you want to reverse it, all you need to do is

```
alter index sales2_idx visible;
```

The next section investigates indexing columns that are both in the SELECT and WHERE clauses of the query.

Indexing the Columns Used in the SELECT and WHERE

The preceding section described how dropping an index can hurt performance for a query. Consider the following query where the index was created to help. I built a million-row EMPLOYEES table from the famous SCOTT.EMP table. This query does not have indexed columns:

```
select  ename
from    employees
where   deptno = 10;

Elapsed time: 55 seconds (a full table scan is performed)

OPERATION              OPTIONS          OBJECT NAME
-----------------      --------------   -----------
SELECT STATEMENT
TABLE ACCESS           FULL             EMPLOYEES
```

First, I place an index on the DEPTNO column to try to improve performance:

```
Create index dept_idx1 on employees (deptno)
Tablespace test1
Storage (initial 20M next 5M pctincrease 0);

select  ename
from    employees
where   deptno = 10;

Elapsed time: 70 seconds (the index on deptno is used but made things worse)
```

```
OPERATION             OPTIONS           OBJECT NAME
------------------    --------------    -----------
SELECT STATEMENT
TABLE ACCESS          BY INDEX ROWID    EMPLOYEES

INDEX                 RANGE SCAN        DEPT_IDX1
```

This situation is now worse. In this query, only the ENAME is selected. If this is a crucial query on the system, choose to index both the SELECT and the WHERE columns. By doing this, you create a concatenated index:

```
Drop index dept_idx1;

Create index emp_idx1 on employees (deptno, ename)
Tablespace test1
Storage (initial 20M next 5M pctincrease 0);
```

The query is now tremendously faster:

```
select    ename
from      employees
where     deptno = 10;

Elapsed time: Less than 1 second (the index on deptno AND ename is used)

OPERATION             OPTIONS        OBJECT NAME
------------------    ----------     -----------
SELECT STATEMENT
INDEX                 RANGE SCAN     EMP_IDX1
```

The table itself did not have to be accessed, which increases the speed of the query. Indexing both the column in the SELECT clause and the column in the WHERE clause allows the query to only access the index.

Consider the following 25M-row SALES3 table (created from SALES2). I have a two-part single index on the CUST_ID and PROD_ID columns. Oracle only needs to access the index (no table access), since all needed information is contained in the index (60K reads instead of the 160K you saw earlier).

```
select sum(prod_id)
from    sales3
where   cust_id=1;

SUM(PROD_ID)
------------
  1939646817

Elapsed: 00:00:05.4
```

```
Execution Plan
| Id | Operation           | Name            | Rows | Bytes |Cost (%CPU|Time      |
-----------------------------------------------------------------------------------
|  0 |SELECT STATEMENT     |                 |    1 |     7 |16690  (2)|00:03:21 |
|  1 |SORT AGGREGATE       |                 |    1 |     7 |          |         |
|* 2 |INDEX FAST FULL SCAN |SALES_IDX_MULTI|   24M|  165M|16690  (2)|00:03:21 |

Statistics:
----------------------------------
60574  consistent gets
60556  physical reads
```

TIP
For crucial queries on your system, consider concatenated indexes on the columns contained in both the SELECT and the WHERE clauses so only the index is accessed.

Using the Fast Full Scan

The preceding section demonstrated that if I index both the SELECT and the WHERE columns, the query is much faster. Oracle does not guarantee that only the index will be used under these circumstances. However, there is a hint that guarantees (under most circumstances) that only the index will be used. The INDEX_FFS hint is a fast full scan of the index. This hint accesses only the index and not the corresponding table. Consider a query from a table with 100M rows with the index on CUST_ID called SALES2_IDX.

First, you check the number of blocks read for a full table scan and then a full index scan:

```
select /*+ full(sales2) */ count(*)
from   sales2;

  COUNT(*)
----------
 100153887

Elapsed: 00:01:42.63

Execution Plan
----------------------------------------------------------
Plan hash value: 2862189843
----------------------------------------------------------------------
| Id | Operation            | Name   | Rows | Cost (%CPU)| Time     |
----------------------------------------------------------------------
|  0 | SELECT STATEMENT      |        |    1 | 32761   (1)| 01:06:32 |
|  1 |  SORT AGGREGATE       |        |    1 |            |          |
|  2 |   TABLE ACCESS FULL|  SALES2 |   24M| 32761   (1)| 01:06:32 |
----------------------------------------------------------------------
```

```
Statistics
----------------------------------------------------------
    820038  consistent gets
    481141  physical reads
```

Now let's try to select using a full index scan instead:

```
select /*+ index_ffs (sales2 sales2_idx) */ count(*)
from sales2;

  COUNT(*)
----------
 100153887

Elapsed: 00:24:06.07

Execution Plan
----------------------------------------------------------
Plan hash value: 3956822556

---------------------------------------------------------------------------
| Id  | Operation             | Name       | Rows  | Cost (%CPU)| Time     |
---------------------------------------------------------------------------
|   0 | SELECT STATEMENT      |            |     1 | 81419   (2)| 00:16:18 |
|   1 |  SORT AGGREGATE       |            |     1 |            |          |
|   2 |   INDEX FAST FULL SCAN| SALES2_IDX |   24M| 81419   (2)| 00:16:18 |
---------------------------------------------------------------------------

Statistics
----------------------------------------------------------
    298091  consistent gets
    210835  physical reads
```

The query with the INDEX_FFS hint now only accesses the index. Instead of scanning over 800K blocks (of which 400K were physical reads), you only scan around 300K blocks (of which 210K are physical reads). Also note, sometimes your queries scan the *entire* index (as this one did), which is often not as good as if you have a limiting condition, so be careful; using an index search is much better than a full index scan when possible. Oracle often scans the index versus scanning the table for a count(*), by default, in 11g. Running either of these queries a second time (see next section) does not get rid of the physical scans since the query retrieves enough data to fill half of the number of blocks as in the total buffer cache (it is pushed out of the cache quickly since it is not a short table; see Chapter 14 for additional details).

TIP
The INDEX_FFS (available since Oracle 8) processes only the index and does not access the table. All columns that are used and retrieved by the query must be contained in the index.

Making the Query "Magically" Faster

Consider the following query from the last example in which the user adds a hint called "RICHS_SECRET_HINT." The user overheard a conversation about this hint at a recent user group and believes this hint (buried deep in the X$ tables) is the hidden secret to tuning. First, the query is run and no index can be used (a large EMPLOYEES table with over 14M rows):

```
select   ename, job
from     employees
where    deptno = 10
and      ename = 'ADAMS';

Elapsed time: 45.8 seconds (one record is retrieved in this query)

OPERATION              OPTIONS       OBJECT NAME
-----------------      ----------    -----------
SELECT STATEMENT
TABLE ACCESS           FULL          EMPLOYEES
```

There is *no* index that can be used on this query. A full table scan is performed.

The user now adds Rich's secret hint to the query:

```
select   /*+ richs_secret_hint */ ename, job
from     employees
where    deptno = 10
and      ename = 'ADAMS';

Elapsed time: under 1 second (one record is retrieved in this query)

OPERATION              OPTIONS       OBJECT NAME
-----------------      ----------    -----------
SELECT STATEMENT
TABLE ACCESS           FULL          EMPLOYEES
```

The hint worked and the query is "magically" faster, although a full table scan was still performed in the second query. Actually, the data is now stored in memory and querying the data from memory is now much faster than going to disk for the data—so much for the magic! By effectively using the 11*g* Result Cache, you can *magically* make things faster as well. See the "Using the New 11*g* Result Cache" section later in this chapter (Chapters 1 and 4 also include additional information).

TIP
When running a query multiple times in succession, it becomes faster because you have now cached the data in memory (although full table scans are aged out of memory quicker than indexed scans). At times, people are tricked into believing that they have made a query faster, when in actuality they are accessing data stored in memory. Flushing the buffer cache or restarting the test system can help you get accurate tuning results for comparisons.

Caching a Table in Memory

While it is disappointing that there is no "secret hint" for tuning (ORDERED and LEADING are the hints closest to magic), you can use the last section to learn from, and then you can use this knowledge to your advantage. In the last section, the query ran faster the second time because it was cached in memory. What if the tables used most often were cached in memory all the time? Well, the first problem is that if you cannot cache every table in memory, you must focus on the smaller and more often used tables to be cached. You can also use multiple buffer pools as discussed in Chapter 4. The following query is run against an unindexed customer table to return one of the rows:

```
select prod_id, cust_id
from    sales
where   cust_id=999999999
and     prod_id is not null;

    PROD_ID    CUST_ID
---------- ----------
        13  999999999

Elapsed: 00:00:00.84

Execution Plan
-------------------------------------------------------------
Plan hash value: 781590677
---------------------------------------------------------------------------
| Id  | Operation          | Name  | Rows  | Bytes | Cost(%CPU)| Time     |
---------------------------------------------------------------------------
|   0 | SELECT STATEMENT   |       |    50 |  1300 |  1241   (2)| 00:00:15 |
|*  1 |  TABLE ACCESS FULL | SALES |    50 |  1300 |  1241   (2)| 00:00:15 |
---------------------------------------------------------------------------
```

The database is then stopped and restarted so as to not influence the timing statistics (you can also perform an "ALTER SYSTEM FLUSH BUFFER_CACHE" but only do this on a test system). The table is altered to cache the records:

```
alter table sales cache;

Table altered.
```

Query the unindexed, but now cached, SALES table and it still takes 0.84 seconds. The table has been altered to be cached, but the data is not in memory yet. Every subsequent query will now be faster (after the first one). I query the unindexed (but now cached) SALES table to return one of the rows in 0.04 seconds, or 21 times faster (this increase in speed could add up fast if this query is run thousands of times):

```
select prod_id, cust_id
from    sales
where   cust_id=999999999
and     prod_id is not null;
```

```
    PROD_ID    CUST_ID
---------- ----------
        13  999999999

Elapsed: 00:00:00.04

Execution Plan
----------------------------------------------------------------
Plan hash value: 781590677

--------------------------------------------------------------------------------
| Id  | Operation          | Name  | Rows  | Bytes | Cost(%CPU)| Time     |
--------------------------------------------------------------------------------
|   0 | SELECT STATEMENT   |       |    50 |  1300 |  1241   (2)| 00:00:15 |
|*  1 |  TABLE ACCESS FULL | SALES |    50 |  1300 |  1241   (2)| 00:00:15 |
--------------------------------------------------------------------------------
```

The query is faster because the table is now cached in memory; in fact, all queries to this table are now fast regardless of the condition used. A cached table is "pinned" into memory and placed at the "most recently used" end of the cache; it is pushed out of memory only after other full table scans to tables that are not cached are pushed out. Running a query multiple times places the data in memory so subsequent queries are faster—only caching a table ensures that the data is not later pushed out of memory. Oracle 11*g* caches frequently used data, by default, as you access things over and over.

TIP
Caching an often-used but relatively small table into memory ensures that the data is not pushed out of memory by other data. Be careful, however—cached tables can alter the execution path normally chosen by the optimizer, leading to an unexpected execution order for the query (for instance, affecting the driving table in nested loop joins).

Using the New 11g Result Cache

In Oracle 11*g*, a new feature called the Result Cache lets you cache SQL results in an area of the SGA to improve performance.

The following RESULT_CACHE hint caches the results on execution:

```
select /*+ result_cache */ SUM(sal)
from   scott.emp
where  deptno=20;
```

When a query with RESULT_CACHE hint is run, Oracle will see if the results of the query have already been executed, computed, and cached, and, if so, retrieve the data from the cache instead of querying the data blocks and computing the results again. Take the following important points into consideration before using this feature:

- The Result Cache feature is useful only for SQL queries that are executed over and over again frequently.

- The underlying data doesn't change very often. When the data changes, the result set is removed from the cache.

If you are executing the same queries over and over, using the RESULT_CACHE hint often makes subsequent queries run faster. Chapters 1 and 4 contain additional information on this.

TIP
If you are executing the same queries over and over (especially grouping or calculation functions), using the RESULT_CACHE hint often makes subsequent queries run faster.

Choosing Among Multiple Indexes (Use the Most Selective)

Having multiple indexes on a table can cause problems when you execute a query where the choices include using more than one of the indexes. The optimizer almost always chooses correctly. Consider the following example where the percent of rows returned by any given PRODUCT_ID is less than 1 percent where the data is equally distributed between the blocks. Under these circumstances, place an index on the PRODUCT_ID column. The following query has a single index on PRODUCT_ID:

```
select  product_id, qty
from    product
where   company_no = 1
and     product_id = 167;

Elapsed time: 1 second (one record is retrieved; the index on product_id is used)

OPERATION           OPTIONS       OBJECT NAME
------------------  ----------    -----------
SELECT STATEMENT
TABLE ACCESS        BY ROWID      PRODUCT
INDEX               RANGE SCAN    PROD_IDX1

107 consistent gets (memory reads)
1 physical reads (disk reads)
```

Now create an additional index on the COMPANY_NO column. In this example, all of the records have a COMPANY_NO = 1, an extremely poor index. Rerun the query with both indexes (one on PRODUCT_ID and one on COMPANY_NO) existing on the table:

```
select  product_id, qty
from    product
```

```
where   company_no = 1
and     product_id = 167;

Elapsed time: 725 seconds (one record is returned; a full table scan is performed)

OPERATION           OPTIONS      OBJECT NAME
-----------------   ----------   -----------
SELECT STATEMENT
TABLE ACCESS        FULL         PRODUCT

4,626,725 consistent gets (memory reads)
80,513 physical reads (disk reads)
```

Oracle has chosen not to use either of the two indexes (perhaps because of a multiblock initialization parameter or some other "exception to the rule"), and the query performed a full table scan. Depending on the statistical data stored and version of Oracle used, I have seen this same query use the right index, the wrong index, no index at all, or a merge of both indexes. The correct choice is to force the use of the correct index. The correct index is the most restrictive. Rewrite the query to force the use of the most restrictive index, as follows, or better yet, fix the real initialization parameter issue (the less hints that you use, the better—especially when you upgrade to the next version of Oracle).

To rewrite the query to force the use of the most restrictive index:

```
select /*+ index(product prod_idx1) */ product_id, qty
from    product
where   company_no = 1
and     product_id = 167;

Elapsed time: 1 second (one record is retrieved)

OPERATION           OPTIONS      OBJECT NAME
-----------------   ----------   -----------
SELECT STATEMENT
TABLE ACCESS        BY ROWID     PRODUCT
INDEX               RANGE SCAN   PROD_IDX1

107 consistent gets (memory reads)
1 physical reads (disk reads)
```

TIP
When multiple indexes on a single table can be used for a query, use the most restrictive index when you need to override an optimizer choice. While Oracle's cost-based optimizer generally forces the use of the most restrictive index, variations will occur, depending on the version of Oracle used, the structure of the query, and the initialization parameters that you may use. Fix the larger issue if you see this as a trend.

TIP
Bitmap indexes usually behave differently because they are usually much smaller. See Chapter 2 for more information on the differences between bitmap indexes and other indexes.

The Index Merge

Oracle's index merge feature allows you to merge two separate indexes and use the result of the indexes instead of going to the table from one of the indexes. Consider the following example (in 11g, if you use a rule-based hint, which Oracle does not support, Oracle includes a note *in the EXPLAIN PLAN* that specifically suggests you use the cost-based optimizer). Also note that OPTIMIZER_MODE set to CHOOSE is not supported either, so use either ALL_ROWS or FIRST_ROWS instead.

The following statistics are based on 1,000,000 records. The table is 210M.

```
create    index year_idx on test2 (year);
create    index state_idx on test2 (state);

select    /*+ rule index(test2) */ state, year
from      test2
where     year = '1972'
and       state = 'MA';

SELECT STATEMENT Optimizer=HINT: RULE
    TABLE ACCESS (BY INDEX ROWID) OF 'TEST2'
      INDEX (RANGE SCAN) OF 'STATE_IDX' (NON-UNIQUE)

Note
---------------------------------------------------
    - rule based optimizer used (consider using cbo)

Elapsed time: 23.50 seconds

select    /*+ index_join(test2 year_idx state_idx) */
state,    year
from      test2
where     year = '1972'
and       state = 'MA';

SELECT STATEMENT
    VIEW OF 'index$_join$_001'
        HASH JOIN
            INDEX (RANGE SCAN) OF 'YEAR_IDX' (NON-UNIQUE)
            INDEX (RANGE SCAN) OF 'STATE_IDX' (NON-UNIQUE)

Elapsed time: 4.76 seconds
```

In the first query, I test the speed of using just one of the indexes and then going back to the table (under certain scenarios, Oracle tunes this with an AND-EQUAL operation to access data from the indexes). I then use the INDEX_JOIN hint to force the merge of two separate indexes and use the result of the indexes instead of going back to the table. When the indexes are both small compared to the size of the table, this can lead to better performance. On a faster system, the second query takes only 0.06 seconds, so your mileage will vary.

Now, let's consider a query to the 25M row SALES3 table on a faster server with separate indexes on the CUST_ID and PROD_ID columns. Using an index merge of the two indexes yields a *very* slow response time and many blocks read (over 200K physical reads):

```
select /*+ index_join (sales3 sales3_idx sales3_idx2) */ sum(prod_id)
from    sales3
where   cust_id=1;

SUM(PROD_ID)
------------
  1939646817

Elapsed: 00:01:37.5

Execution Plan
-----------------------------------------------------------------------------
| Id  | Operation             | Name          |Rows| Bytes |Cost(%CPU)|Time    |
-----------------------------------------------------------------------------
|   0 |SELECT STATEMENT       |               | 1 |     7 |  158K (1)|00:31:47|
|   1 | SORT AGGREGATE        |               | 1 |     7 |          |         |
|*  2 |  VIEW                 | index$_join$_001| 24M|  165M| 158K (1)|00:31:47|
|*  3 |   HASH JOIN           |               |    |       |          |         |
|*  4 |    INDEX RANGE SCAN   | SALES3_IDX    | 24M| 165M |48211 (2) |00:09:39|
|   5 |    INDEX FAST FULL SCAN| SALES3_IDX2  | 24M| 165M |63038 (1) |00:12:37|
-----------------------------------------------------------------------------

Statistic
----------------------
8536   consistent gets
217514  physical reads
```

If I drop the two indexes on SALES3 and replace them with a two-part single index on the CUST_ID and PROD_ID columns, performance improves greatly—over ten times faster. Another benefit is the reduction of physical block reads from over 200K to only 60K.

```
select sum(prod_id)
from    sales3
where   cust_id=1;SUM(PROD_ID)
------------
  1939646817

Execution Plan
------------------------------
| Id  | Operation           | Name          |Rows | Bytes |Cost(%CPU)|Time     |
-----------------------------------------------------------------------------
|   0 |SELECT STATEMENT     |               | 1 |     7 |16690 (2) |00:03:21 |
|   1 |SORT AGGREGATE       |               | 1 |     7 |          |         |
|*  2 |INDEX FAST FULL SCAN|SALES_IDX_MULTI| 24M| 165M |16690(2)  |00:03:21 |
-----------------------------------------------------------------------------

Statistic
----------------------
60574   consistent gets
60556   physical reads
```

Indexes That *Can* Get Suppressed

Building the perfect system with all of the correctly indexed columns does not guarantee successful system performance. With the prevalence in business of bright-eyed ad-hoc query users comes a variety of tuning challenges. One of the most common is the suppression of perfectly good indexes. A modification of the column side of a WHERE clause often results in that index being suppressed (unless function-based indexes are utilized or the super-smart optimizer figures out a better path). Alternative methods for writing the same query do exist that do not modify the indexed column. A couple of those examples are listed next. Oracle *does* use the indexes in many cases, internally fixing the suppression (they continue to get better at this from version to version), especially when an index search or a full index scan can be run instead of a full table scan. If you use 3GL code or code within applications, the results vary, so I continue to show these areas that are a problem with certain tools or applications for you to consider when you run into that full table scan that you didn't expect.

A math function is performed on the column:

```
select   product_id, qty
from     product
where    product_id+12 = 166;

Elapsed time: 405 second

OPERATION          OPTIONS   OBJECT NAME
---------------    -------   -----------
SELECT STATEMENT
TABLE ACCESS       FULL      PRODUCT
```

The math function is performed on the other side of the clause (Oracle often fixes this internally):

```
select   product_id, qty
from     product
where    product_id = 154;

Elapsed time: 1 second

OPERATION          OPTIONS       OBJECT NAME
---------------    -------       --------------
SELECT STATEMENT
TABLE ACCESS       BY ROWID      PRODUCT
     INDEX         RANGE SCAN    PROD_IDX1
```

A function is performed on the column:

```
select   product_id, qty
from     product
where    substr(product_id,1,1) = 1;

Elapsed time: 405 second
```

```
OPERATION            OPTIONS   OBJECT NAME
----------------     -------   -----------
SELECT STATEMENT
TABLE ACCESS         FULL      PRODUCT
```

The function is rewritten so the column is not altered (a LIKE or function-based index would fix this):

```
select   product_id, qty
from     product
where    product_id like '1%';
```

```
Elapsed time: 1 second
```

```
OPERATION            OPTIONS      OBJECT NAME
----------------     ----------   -----------
SELECT STATEMENT
TABLE ACCESS         BY ROWID     PRODUCT
INDEX                RANGE SCAN   PROD_IDX1
```

As I stated previously, Oracle is often smart enough to figure out the issue and still use the index. The following query shows that the index is scanned with no table access despite the attempt to suppress the index (adding zero (0) or using an NVL gave the same result). In the following case, everything needed is in the index. Oracle figures out the substring function on the leading edge of the index but is still able to use *only* the index despite needing both columns from the index (versus using the index to access back to the table).

```
select sum(prod_id)
from    sales3
where   substr(cust_id,1)=1;
```

```
SUM(PROD_ID)
------------
  1939646817
```

```
Elapsed: 00:00:12.49
```

```
Execution Plan
```

Id	Operation	Name	Rows	Bytes	Cost(%CPU	Time
0	SELECT STATEMENT		1	7	17651(8)	00:03:32
1	SORT AGGREGATE		1	7		
* 2	INDEX FAST FULL SCAN	SALES_IDX_MULTI	248K	1695K	17651 (8)	00:03:32

TIP
At times, modifying the column side of the query can result in the index being suppressed unless a function-based index is used. Oracle may also fix this issue during parsing.

Function-Based Indexes

One of the largest problems with indexes, as seen in the previous section, is that indexes are often suppressed by developers and ad-hoc users. Developers using functions often suppress indexes. There is a way to combat this problem. Function-based indexes allow you to create an index based on a function or expression. The value of the function or expression is specified by the person creating the index and is stored in the index. Function-based indexes can involve multiple columns, arithmetic expressions, or maybe a PL/SQL function or C callout.

The following example shows how to create a function-based index:

```
CREATE INDEX emp_idx ON emp (UPPER(ename));
```

An index that uses the UPPER function has been created on the ENAME column. The following example queries the EMP table using the function-based index:

```
select  ename, job, deptno
from    emp
where   upper(ename) = 'ELLISON';
```

The function-based index (EMP_IDX) can be used for this query. For large tables where the condition retrieves a small amount of records, the query yields substantial performance gains over a full table scan. See Chapter 2 for additional details and examples.

The following initialization parameters must be set (subject to change with each version) to use function-based indexes (the optimization mode must be cost-based as well). When a function-based index is not working, this is often the problem.

```
query_rewrite_enabled = true
query_rewrite_integrity = trusted (or enforced)
```

TIP
Function-based indexes can lead to dramatic performance gains when used to create indexes on functions often used on selective columns in the WHERE clause.

To check the details for function-based indexes on a table, you may use a query similar to this:

```
select  table_name, index_name, column_expression
from    dba_ind_expressions
where   table_name = 'SALES2'
and     table_owner = 'SH'
order   by index_name, column_position;
```

Virtual Columns

Oracle 11g has introduced a new feature called the virtual column, a column that allows you to define a function on other column(s) in the same table. Here is an example of creating a table with a virtual column:

```
CREATE TABLE my_employees (
    empId          NUMBER,
```

```
firstName      VARCHAR2(30),
lastName       VARCHAR2(30),
salary         NUMBER(9,2),
bonus          NUMBER GENERATED ALWAYS AS (ROUND(salary*(5/100)/12))
               VIRTUAL,
CONSTRAINT myemp_pk PRIMARY KEY (empId));
```

An important point to remember is that indexes defined against virtual columns are equivalent to function-based indexes.

The "Curious" OR

The cost-based optimizer often has problems when the OR clause is used. The best way to think of the OR clause is as multiple queries that are then merged. Consider the following example where there is a single primary key on COL1, COL2, and COL3. Prior to Oracle 9*i*, the Oracle Database performed this query in the following way:

```
select  *
from    table_test
where   pk_col1 = 'A'
and     pk_col2 in ('B', 'C')
and     pk_col3 = 'D';

2       Table Access By Rowid TABLE_TEST
1       Index Range Scan TAB_PK
```

> **NOTE**
> *PK_COL2 and PK_COL3 were not used for index access.*

Since Oracle 9*i*, Oracle HAS improved how the optimizer handles this query (internally performing an OR-expansion). In Oracle 11*g*, the optimizer uses the full primary key and concatenates the results (as shown next), which is much faster than using only part of the primary key (as in the preceding access path). Even though the access path for the preceding query looks better because there are fewer lines, don't be tricked; fewer lines in the EXPLAIN PLAN doesn't mean a more efficient query.

```
5 Concatenation
2 Table Access By Rowid TAB
1 Index Unique Scan TAB_PK
4 Table Access By Rowid TAB
3 Index Unique Scan TAB_PK
```

To get this desired result prior to 9*i*, you would have needed to break up the query as shown here (I show this since often making a query longer can make it faster, as it's processed differently):

```
select  *
from    table_test
where   (pk_col1 = 'A'
```

```
and      pk_col2 = 'B'
and      pk_col3 = 'D')
or       (pk_col1 = 'A'
and      pk_col2 = 'C'
and      pk_col3 = 'D');

5   Concatenation
2   Table Access By Rowid TAB
1   Index Unique Scan TAB_PK
4   Table Access By Rowid TAB
3   Index Unique Scan TAB_PK
```

TIP
Oracle has improved the way that it performs the OR clause. The
NO_EXPAND hint can still be helpful, as it prevents the optimizer
from using OR expansion, as described in Chapter 7.

Using the EXISTS Function and the Nested Subquery

Another helpful tip to remember is to use the EXISTS function instead of the IN function in most
circumstances. The EXISTS function checks to find a single matching row to return the result in
a subquery. Because the IN function retrieves and checks all rows, it is slower. Oracle has also
improved the optimizer so it often performs this optimization for you as well. Consider the
following example, where the IN function leads to very poor performance. This query is faster
only if the ITEMS table is extremely small:

```
select    product_id, qty
from      product
where     product_id = 167
and       item_no in
(select   item_no
 from     items);

Elapsed time: 25 minutes (The items table is 10 million rows)
```

```
OPERATION              OPTIONS       OBJECT NAME
-----------------      ----------    -----------
SELECT STATEMENT
NESTED LOOPS SEMI
  TABLE ACCESS         BY ROWID      PRODUCT
    INDEX              RANGE SCAN    PROD_IDX1
    SORT
      TABLE ACCESS     FULL          ITEMS
```

In this query, the entire ITEMS table is retrieved.

This query is faster when the condition PRODUCT_ID = 167 substantially limits the outside query:

```
select      product_id, qty
from        product a
where       product_id = 167
and         exists
(select     'x'
 from       items b
 where      b.item_no = a.item_no);
```

```
Elapsed time: 2 seconds (The items table query search is limited to 3 rows)

OPERATION              OPTIONS       OBJECT NAME
-----------------      ----------    -----------
SELECT STATEMENT
NESTED LOOPS SEMI
   TABLE ACCESS        BY ROWID      PRODUCT
      INDEX            RANGE SCAN    PROD_IDX1
      INDEX            RANGE SCAN    ITEM_IDX1
```

In this query, only the records retrieved in the outer query (from the PRODUCT table) are checked against the ITEMS table. This query can be substantially faster than the first query if the ITEM_NO in the ITEMS table is indexed or if the ITEMS table is very large, yet the items are limited by the condition PRODUCT_ID = 167 in the outer query.

TIP
Using the nested subquery with an EXISTS clause may make queries dramatically faster, depending on the data being retrieved from each part of the query. Oracle11g often makes this translation internally, saving you time and giving you performance gains!

That Table Is Actually a View!

Views can hide the complexity of SQL but they can also add to the complexity of optimization. When looking at a SELECT statement, unless you have instituted some kind of naming convention for views, you cannot tell if an object is a table or a view from the SELECT statement alone. You must examine the object in the database to tell the difference. Views can join multiple tables. Be careful about joining views or using a view designed for one purpose for a different purpose, or you may pay a heavy performance price. Ensure that all tables involved in the view are actually required by your query. Also keep in mind that different types of triggers can also hide performance issues behind a simple query. Good developer documentation can save a lot of time in finding performance issues in complex code.

SQL and Grand Unified Theory

Many physicists have searched for a single theory that explains all aspects of how the universe works. Many theories postulated have worked well in certain circumstances and break down in others. This is fine for theoretical physics, but it can spell disaster in a database. When writing

SQL, one should not attempt to write the "Grand Unified SQL" statement that will do all tasks, depending on the arguments passed to it. This typically results in suboptimal performance for most tasks performed by the statement (or you feel the effect during the next upgrade). It is better to write separate, highly efficient statements for each task that needs to be performed.

Tuning Changes in Oracle Database 11g

The general SQL tuning principles remain the same in 11g, but some significant optimizer changes should be noted.

- The RULE (and CHOOSE) OPTIMIZER_MODE has been deprecated and desupported in 11g. (The only way to get rule-based behavior in 11g is by using the RULE hint in a query, which is *not* supported either). In general, using the RULE hint is not recommended, but for individual queries that need it, it is there. Consult with Oracle support before using the RULE hint in 11g.

- In 11g, the cost-based optimizer has two modes: NORMAL and TUNING.

    - In NORMAL mode, the cost-based optimizer considers a very small subset of possible execution plans to determine which one to choose. The number of plans considered is far smaller than in past versions of the database in order to keep the time to generate the execution plan within strict limits. SQL profiles (statistical information) can be used to influence which plans are considered.

    - The TUNING mode of the cost-based optimizer can be used to perform more detailed analysis of SQL statements and make recommendations for actions to be taken and for auxiliary statistics to be accepted into a SQL profile for later use when running under NORMAL mode. TUNING mode is also known as the *Automatic Tuning Optimizer mode,* and the optimizer can take several minutes for a single statement (good for testing). See the *Oracle Database Performance Tuning Guide Automatic SQL Tuning* (Chapter 17 in the 11.2 docs).

Oracle states that the NORMAL mode should provide an acceptable execution path for most SQL statements. SQL statements that do not perform well in NORMAL mode may be tuned in TUNING mode for later use in NORMAL mode. This should provide a better performance balance for queries that have defined SQL profiles, with the majority of the optimizer work for complex queries being performed in TUNING mode once, rather than repeatedly, each time the SQL statement is parsed.

Oracle 11g Automatic SQL Tuning

Oracle Database 10g introduced the SQL Tuning Advisor to help DBAs and developers improve the performance of SQL statements. The Automatic SQL Tuning Advisor includes statistics analysis, SQL profiling, access path analysis, and SQL structure analysis, and can be performed through the SQL Tuning Advisor. The SQL Tuning Advisor uses input from the ADDM, from resource-intensive SQL statements captured by the AWR, from the cursor cache, or from SQL Tuning Sets. Oracle 11g has extended the SQL Tuning Advisor by adding additional features such as SQL Replay, Automatic SQL Tuning, SQL Statistics Management, and SQL Plan Management.

Since this chapter is focused on query tuning, I'll describe how to pass specific SQL to the SQL Tuning Advisor in the form of a SQL Tuning Set, and then I'll cover 11*g*'s Automatic SQL Tuning Advisor and SQL Performance Analysis (SQL Replay).The Oracle recommended interface for the SQL Tuning Advisor is Oracle Enterprise Manager (see Chapter 5), but you can use the APIs via the command line in SQL*Plus. I cover the command-line session so you can better understand the analysis procedure for a single query. This section is only a small glance into the functionality of the SQL Tuning Advisor. You also have the capability to create SQL Tuning Sets and SQL profiles as well as the ability to transport SQL Tuning Sets from one database to another.

Ensuring the Tuning User Has Access to the API

Access to these privileges should be restricted to authorized users in a production environment. The privileges are granted by SYS. The "ADMINISTER SQL TUNING SET" privilege allows a user to access only his or her own tuning sets.

```
GRANT ADMINISTER SQL TUNING SET to &TUNING_USER;  -- or
GRANT ADMINISTER ANY SQL TUNING SET to &TUNING_USER;
GRANT ADVISOR TO &TUNING_USER
GRANT CREATE ANY SQL PROFILE TO &TUNING_USER;
GRANT ALTER ANY SQL PROFILE TO &TUNING_USER;
GRANT DROP ANY SQL PROFILE TO &TUNING_USER;
```

Creating the Tuning Task

If you want to tune a single SQL statement, for example,

```
select COUNT(*)
from    t2
where   UPPER(owner) = 'RIC';
```

you must first create a tuning task using the DBMS_SQLTUNE package:

```
DECLARE
  tuning_task_name VARCHAR2(30);
  tuning_sqltext  CLOB;
BEGIN
  tuning_sqltext :=    'SELECT COUNT(*) ' ||
                       'FROM t2 ' ||
                       'WHERE UPPER(owner) = :owner';
  tuning_task_name := DBMS_SQLTUNE.CREATE_TUNING_TASK(
             sql_text  => tuning_sqltext,
            bind_list  => sql_binds(anydata.ConvertVarchar2(100)),
            user_name  => 'RIC',
              scope    => 'COMPREHENSIVE',
         time_limit  => 60,
          task_name  => 'first_tuning_task13',
         description => 'Tune T2 count');
END;
/
```

Making Sure the Task Can Be Seen in the Advisor Log

To see the task, query the USER_ADVISOR log:

```
select task_name
from   user_advisor_log;

TASK_NAME
------------------
first_tuning_task13
```

Executing the SQL Tuning Task

To execute the tuning task, you use the DBMS_SQLTUNE package, as shown here:

```
BEGIN
DBMS_SQLTUNE.EXECUTE_TUNING_TASK( task_name => 'first_tuning_task13' );
END;
/
```

Checking Status of the Tuning Task

To see the specific tuning task, query the USER_ADVISOR log:

```
select status
from   user_advisor_tasks
where  task_name = 'first_tuning_task13';

STATUS
---------
COMPLETED
```

Displaying the SQL Tuning Advisor Report

To see the SQL Tuning Advisor Report, you also use the DBMS_SQLTUNE package:

```
SET LONG 8000
SET LONGCHUNKSIZE 8000
SET LINESIZE 100
SET PAGESIZE 100

select dbms_sqltune.report_tuning_task('first_tuning_task13')
from   dual;
```

Reviewing the Report Output

The report output shown next is lengthy, but it essentially recommends creating a function-based index on the owner column of table T2. Had the SQL Tuning Advisor recommended the use of a SQL profile, this could have been accepted by using the DBMS_SQLTUNE.ACCEPT_SQL_PROFILE package.

```
DBMS_SQLTUNE.REPORT_TUNING_TASK('FIRST_TUNING_TASK13')
-------------------------------------------------------------------------------
GENERAL INFORMATION SECTION
-------------------------------------------------------------------------------
Tuning Task Name              : first_tuning_task13
Tuning Task Owner             : RIC
Workload Type                 :  Single SQL Statement
Scope                         : COMPREHENSIVE
Time Limit(seconds)           : 60
Completion Status             : COMPLETED
Started at                          : 11/20/2010 20:49:56
Completed at                        : 11/20/2010 20:49:56
Number of Index Findings  : 1
Number of SQL Restructure Findings: 1


DBMS_SQLTUNE.REPORT_TUNING_TASK('FIRST_TUNING_TASK13')
-------------------------------------------------------------------------------


-------------------------------------------------------------------------------
Schema Name: RIC
SQL ID     : 8ubrqzjkkyj3g
SQL Text   : SELECT COUNT(*) FROM t2 WHERE UPPER(owner) = 'RIC'
-------------------------------------------------------------------------------
FINDINGS SECTION (2 findings)
-------------------------------------------------------------------------------

1- Index Finding (see explain plans section below)


DBMS_SQLTUNE.REPORT_TUNING_TASK('FIRST_TUNING_TASK13')
-------------------------------------------------------------------------------


-------------------------------------------------------------
The execution plan of this statement can be improved by creating one or more
indices.

Recommendation (estimated benefit: 100%)
-----------------------------------------
Consider running the Access Advisor to improve the physical schema design
or creating the recommended index.
create index RIC.IDX$$_00CF0001 on RIC.T2(UPPER('OWNER'));

Rationale

DBMS_SQLTUNE.REPORT_TUNING_TASK('FIRST_TUNING_TASK13')
-------------------------------------------------------------------------------
   Creating the recommended indexes significantly improves the execution plan
of this statement. However, it might be preferable to run "Access Advisor"
```

using a representative SQL workload as opposed to a single statement. This
will allow Oracle to get comprehensive index recommendations which takes into
account index maintenance overhead and additional space consumption.

2- Restructure SQL finding (see plan 1 in explain plans section)

The predicate UPPER("T2"."OWNER")='RIC' used at line ID 2 of the execution
plan contains an expression on indexed column "OWNER". This expression

DBMS_SQLTUNE.REPORT_TUNING_TASK('FIRST_TUNING_TASK13')
----
prevents the optimizer from selecting indices on table "RIC"."T2".

Recommendation

- Rewrite the predicate into an equivalent form to take advantage of
indices. Alternatively, create a function-based index on the expression.

Rationale

The optimizer is unable to use an index if the predicate is an inequality
condition or if there is an expression or an implicit data type conversion

DBMS_SQLTUNE.REPORT_TUNING_TASK('FIRST_TUNING_TASK13')
----
on the indexed column.

EXPLAIN PLANS SECTION

1- Original

Plan hash value: 1374435053

DBMS_SQLTUNE.REPORT_TUNING_TASK('FIRST_TUNING_TASK13')

| Id | Operation | Name | Rows | Bytes | Cost (%CPU) |Time |

0	SELECT STATEMENT		1	6	4049 (3)	00:00:49
1	SORT AGGREGATE		1	6		
* 2	INDEX FAST FULL SCAN	T2_I1	26097	152K	4049 (3)	00:00:49

Predicate Information (identified by operation id):
----
2 - filter(UPPER("OWNER")='RIC')

DBMS_SQLTUNE.REPORT_TUNING_TASK('FIRST_TUNING_TASK13')

2- Using New Indices

Plan hash value: 2206416184

| Id | Operation | Name | Rows | Bytes |Cost (%CPU)| Time |

0	SELECT STATEMENT		1	6	524 (2)	00:00:07
1	SORT AGGREGATE		1	6		
* 2	INDEX RANGE SCAN	IDX$$_00CF0001	237K	1390K	524 (2)	00:00:07

Tuning SQL Statements Automatically Using SQL Tuning Advisor

Now let's look at Oracle 11*g*'s Automatic SQL Tuning Advisor. Oracle 11*g*'s Automatic SQL Tuning Advisor analyzes Automatic Workload Repository data to find high-load SQL statements that have been executed repeatedly. It then uses SQL Tuning Advisor to tune those statements, creates SQL profiles, if needed, and tests them thoroughly. If it thinks implementing the SQL profile is beneficial, it automatically implements them. No intervention is needed. Automatic SQL Tuning Advisor runs during the normal maintenance window. The DBA can then run reports against those recommendations and validate those SQL profiles.

Enabling Automatic SQL Tuning Advisor

The following procedure is used to enable Automatic SQL Tuning Advisor:

```
BEGIN
DBMS_AUTO_TASK_ADMIN.ENABLE( client_name => 'sql tuning advisor',  operation =>
   NULL,  window_name => NULL);
END;
/
```

Configuring Automatic SQL Tuning Advisor
To query what is currently set, run the following query:

```
select  parameter_name, parameter_value
from    dba_advisor_parameters
where   task_name = 'SYS_AUTO_SQL_TUNING_TASK'
and     parameter_name IN ('ACCEPT_SQL_PROFILES',
                           'MAX_SQL_PROFILES_PER_EXEC',
                           'MAX_AUTO_SQL_PROFILES');
```

```
PARAMETER_NAME                      PARAMETER_VALUE
----------------------------------- -------------------------------
ACCEPT_SQL_PROFILES                 FALSE
MAX_SQL_PROFILES_PER_EXEC           20
MAX_AUTO_SQL_PROFILES               10000
```

Now change SQL_PROFILE parameters as follows:

```
SQL> CONNECT / AS SYSDBA

BEGIN
  DBMS_SQLTUNE.set_tuning_task_parameter(
  task_name => 'SYS_AUTO_SQL_TUNING_TASK',
  parameter => 'ACCEPT_SQL_PROFILES',
```

```
    value      => 'TRUE');
END;
/
```

The next step is to force the execution of the task so you see the results immediately:

```
exec dbms_sqltune.execute_tuning_task(task_name=>'SYS_AUTO_SQL_TUNING_TASK');
```

Viewing Automatic SQL Tuning Results
The following procedure reports the most recent run:

```
VARIABLE p_report CLOB;
BEGIN
  :p_report := DBMS_SQLTUNE.report_auto_tuning_task(
    begin_exec   => NULL,
    end_exec     => NULL,
    type         => DBMS_SQLTUNE.type_text,      -- 'TEXT'
    level        => DBMS_SQLTUNE.level_typical,  -- 'TYPICAL'
    section      => DBMS_SQLTUNE.section_all,    -- 'ALL'
    object_id    => NULL,
    result_limit => NULL);
END;
```

Print :p_report prints the report and recommendation:

```
Set long 1000000
PRINT :p_report

GENERAL INFORMATION SECTION
-------------------------------------------------------------------------------
Tuning Task Name              : SYS_AUTO_SQL_TUNING_TASK
Tuning Task Owner             : SYS
Workload Type                 : Automatic High-Load SQL Workload
Execution Count               : 14
Current Execution             : EXEC_1259
Execution Type                : TUNE SQL
Scope                         : COMPREHENSIVE
Global Time Limit(seconds)    : 3600
Per-SQL Time Limit(seconds)   : 1200
Completion Status             : COMPLETED
Started at                    : 02/03/2011 17:14:17
Completed at                  : 02/03/2011 17:14:27
Number of Candidate SQLs      : 3
Cumulative Elapsed Time of SQL (s)  : 50


-------------------------------------------------------------------------------
SUMMARY SECTION
-------------------------------------------------------------------------------
                    Global SQL Tuning Result Statistics
-------------------------------------------------------------------------------

Number of SQLs Analyzed              : 3
Number of SQLs in the Report         : 3
Number of SQLs with Findings         : 3
Number of SQLs with Statistic Findings  : 3
```

```
--------------------------------------------------------------------------------
     SQLs with Findings Ordered by Maximum (Profile/Index) Benefit, Object ID
--------------------------------------------------------------------------------
object ID  SQL ID   statistics profile(benefit) index(benefit) restructure
---------- -------------- ---------- ---------------- -------------- -----------
      42 4q8yn4bnqw19s     1
      43 fvzwdtr0ywagd     1
      44 5sp4ugqbs4ms6     1


--------------------------------------------------------------------------------
     Objects with Missing/Stale Statistics (ordered by schema, object, type)
--------------------------------------------------------------------------------
Schema Name            Object Name          Type        State Cascade
-------------------    -------------------- ----------- ------- -------
             SYS OBJECT_TAB                TABLE MISSING NO


--------------------------------------------------------------------------------
DETAILS SECTION
--------------------------------------------------------------------------------
 Statements with Results Ordered by Maximum (Profile/Index) Benefit, Object ID
--------------------------------------------------------------------------------
Object ID   : 42
Schema Name : SYS
SQL ID      : 4q8yn4bnqw19s
SQL Text    : insert into object_tab select * from object_tab


--------------------------------------------------------------------------------
FINDINGS SECTION (1 finding)

1- Statistics Finding
---------------------
  Table "SYS"."OBJECT_TAB" was not analyzed.
  Recommendation
  --------------
  - Consider collecting optimizer statistics for this table.
    execute dbms_stats.gather_table_stats(ownname => 'SYS', tabname =>
        'OBJECT_TAB', estimate_percent => DBMS_STATS.AUTO_SAMPLE_SIZE,
        method_opt => 'FOR ALL COLUMNS SIZE AUTO');

  Rationale
  ---------
    The optimizer requires up-to-date statistics for the table in order to
    select a good execution plan.


--------------------------------------------------------------------------------
EXPLAIN PLANS SECTION
--------------------------------------------------------------------------------
1- Original
-----------
Plan hash value: 622691728

| Id  | Operation              | Name        | Rows  | Bytes | Cost (%CPU)| Time     |
--------------------------------------------------------------------------------
|   0 | INSERT STATEMENT       |             | 4674K|  419M|  7687  (1)| 00:01:33 |
|   1 |  LOAD TABLE CONVENTIONAL | OBJECT_TAB |       |      |           |          |
|   2 |   TABLE ACCESS FULL    | OBJECT_TAB  | 4674K|  419M|  7687  (1)| 00:01:33 |
--------------------------------------------------------------------------------


--------------------------------------------------------------------------------
Object ID  : 43
Schema Name: SYS
SQL ID     : fvzwdtr0ywagd
```

```
SQL Text   : select count(*) from object_tab where UPPER(owner)='SYS'

-------------------------------------------------------------------------------
FINDINGS SECTION (1 finding)
-------------------------------------------------------------------------------

1- Statistics Finding
---------------------
  Table "SYS"."OBJECT_TAB" was not analyzed.

  Recommendation
  --------------
  - Consider collecting optimizer statistics for this table.
    execute dbms_stats.gather_table_stats(ownname => 'SYS', tabname =>
         'OBJECT_TAB', estimate_percent => DBMS_STATS.AUTO_SAMPLE_SIZE,
         method_opt => 'FOR ALL COLUMNS SIZE AUTO');

  Rationale
  ---------
    The optimizer requires up-to-date statistics for the table in order to
    select a good execution plan.

-------------------------------------------------------------------------------
EXPLAIN PLANS SECTION
-------------------------------------------------------------------------------


1- Original
-----------
Plan hash value: 2592930531
-------------------------------------------------------------------------------
-
| Id | Operation            | Name        | Rows  | Bytes | Cost (%CPU)| Time     |
-------------------------------------------------------------------------------
|  0 | SELECT STATEMENT     |             |     1 |    17 |  7703   (1)| 00:01:33 |
|  1 |  SORT AGGREGATE      |             |     1 |    17 |            |          |
|* 2 |   TABLE ACCESS FULL| OBJECT_TAB   | 2000K |   32M |  7703   (1)| 00:01:33 |
-------------------------------------------------------------------------------
Predicate Information (identified by operation id):
-------------------------------------------------
   2 - filter(UPPER("OWNER")='SYS')


-------------------------------------------------------------------------------
Object ID : 44
Schema Name: SYS
SQL ID    : 5sp4ugqbs4ms6
SQL Text   : select count(*) from object_tab where UPPER(owner)='SCOTT'

-------------------------------------------------------------------------------
FINDINGS SECTION (1 finding)
-------------------------------------------------------------------------------

1- Statistics Finding
---------------------
  Table "SYS"."OBJECT_TAB" was not analyzed.

  Recommendation
  --------------
  - Consider collecting optimizer statistics for this table.
    execute dbms_stats.gather_table_stats(ownname => 'SYS', tabname =>
         'OBJECT_TAB', estimate_percent => DBMS_STATS.AUTO_SAMPLE_SIZE,
         method_opt => 'FOR ALL COLUMNS SIZE AUTO');
  Rationale
```

```
---------
    The optimizer requires up-to-date statistics for the table in order to
    select a good execution plan.

-------------------------------------------------------------------------------
EXPLAIN PLANS SECTION
-------------------------------------------------------------------------------
1- Original
-----------
Plan hash value: 2592930531
-------------------------------------------------------------------------------
| Id  | Operation           | Name       | Rows  | Bytes | Cost (%CPU)| Time     |
-------------------------------------------------------------------------------
|   0 | SELECT STATEMENT    |            |    1  |   17  |  7703   (1)| 00:01:33 |
|   1 |  SORT AGGREGATE     |            |    1  |   17  |            |          |
|*  2 |   TABLE ACCESS FULL | OBJECT_TAB |  311  | 5287  |  7703   (1)| 00:01:33 |
-------------------------------------------------------------------------------

Predicate Information (identified by operation id):
---------------------------------------------------
   2 - filter(UPPER("OWNER")='SCOTT')
```

Check the recommendation section. Tuning Advisor has recommended that you collect statistics. Just by running the following statement, you would improve the performance of the problem SQL listed in the SQL Tuning Advisor report:

```
execute dbms_stats.gather_table_stats(ownname => 'SYS', tabname => -
          'OBJECT_TAB', estimate_percent => DBMS_STATS.AUTO_SAMPLE_SIZE,  -
          method_opt => 'FOR ALL COLUMNS SIZE AUTO');
```

Using SQL Performance Analyzer (SPA)

The concept of SQL Tuning Sets and the SQL Tuning Advisor were introduced in 10*g* as described in earlier sections of this chapter. Oracle 11*g* makes use of SQL Tuning Sets with the SQL Performance Analyzer, often referred to as SPA. The SPA compares the performance of specific SQL statements defined in a particular SQL Tuning Set, before and after a database change. The database change could be a major upgrade from 10*g* to 11*g*, an initialization parameter change, or simply an index or statistics collection change. Chapter 5 covers how to do this in Enterprise Manager. Because this chapter focuses on SQL Tuning, let's see what the SQL Performance Analyzer can do with queries before and after creating an index. In Chapter 9, I cover more uses for SPA, especially in database and application upgrades, as well as Real Application Testing and Database Replay. SPA is a part of Real Application Testing and is not available in the database by default. The use of SQL Performance Analyzer (SPA) and Database Replay requires the Oracle Real Application Testing licensing option (from Oracle's Real Application Manual).

Step 1: Set Up the Testing Environment

For this test, a table is created called OBJECT_TAB, and the table is populated to simulate a decent workload:

```
create table object_tab as
  select *
  from   dba_objects;
```

```
insert into object_tab
 select *
 from    object_tab;

commit;
```

The OBJECT_TAB table does not have any indexes; statistics are collected (as displayed here):

```
exec dbms_stats.gather_table_stats(USER,'OBJECT_TAB',cascade=>TRUE);
```

Next, the shared pool is flushed to clear out SQL statements in memory to get a new workload:

```
alter system flush shared_pool;
```

Step 2: Execute the Queries
Execute the following testing queries:

```
select count(*)
from    object_tab
where   object_id=100;

select  count(*)
from     object_tab
where    object_id<100;

select count(*)
from    object_tab
where   object_id=1000;

select count(*)
from    object_tab
where   object_id<=1000;
```

Later on you'll create an index for the OBJECT_ID column and compare the performance of the SQL statement before and after the index is created.

Step 3: Create SQL Tuning Set

```
exec DBMS_SQLTUNE.create_sqlset(sqlset_name=>'sql_replay_test');
```

Step 4: Load SQL Tuning Set
The following procedure loads the Tuning Set by obtaining SQL statements from the CURSOR_CACHE that query the OBJECT_TAB table.

```
DECLARE
   l_cursor DBMS_SQLTUNE.sqlset_cursor;
BEGIN
   OPEN l_cursor FOR
   SELECT VALUE(a)
   FROM TABLE(DBMS_SQLTUNE.select_cursor_cache(
```

```
        basic_filter => 'sql_text LIKE ''%object_tab%'' and parsing_schema_name =
  ''SYS''',
        attribute_list => 'ALL')
   ) a;
DBMS_SQLTUNE.load_sqlset(sqlset_name => 'sql_replay_test',populate_cursor=>
 l_cursor);
END;
/
```

Step 5: Query from the SQL Tuning Set

```
select sql_text
from    dba_sqlset_statements
where   sqlset_name = 'sql_replay_test';


SQL_TEXT
-------------------------------------------------------------
Select count(*) from object_tab where object_id=100;
Select count(*) from object_tab where object_id<100;
Select count(*) from object_tab where object_id=1000;
Select count(*) from object_tab where object_id<=1000;
```

Step 6: Print from the SQL Tuning Set

```
VARIABLE v_task VARCHAR2(64);
EXEC :v_task :=
DBMS_SQLPA.create_analysis_task(sqlset_name=>'sql_replay_test');
print :v_task
V_TASK
-----------------------
TASK_832
```

Don't forget to note this TASK ID (record it somewhere for later use).

Step 7: Execute Before Analysis Task
Execute the contents of the Tuning Set before the database change to gather performance
information:

```
BEGIN
    DBMS_SQLPA.execute_analysis_task(task_name => :v_task,execution_type => 'test
 execute',
        execution_name => 'before_change');
END;
/
```

Step 8: Make the Necessary Changes
Add an index that you already know you need to improve performance of the queries in the
Tuning Set (and regather statistics):

```
create index object_tab_indx_id on object_tab(object_id);
exec dbms_stats.gather_table_stats(USER,'OBJECT_TAB',cascade=>TRUE);
```

Step 9: Execute after Create Index Analysis Task

```
VARIABLE v_task VARCHAR2(64);
BEGIN
    DBMS_SQLPA.execute_analysis_task(task_name => 'TASK_832',execution_type =>
'test execute',
        execution_name => 'after_change');
END;
/
```

Step 10: Execute Compare Analysis Task

```
VARIABLE v_task VARCHAR2(64);
--EXEC :v_task := DBMS_SQLPA.create_analysis_task(sqlset_name =>
'sql_replay_test');
BEGIN
    DBMS_SQLPA.execute_analysis_task( task_name   => 'TASK_832', execution_type =>
'compare performance',
      execution_params => dbms_advisor.arglist(
                    'execution_name1',
                    'before_change',
                    'execution_name2',
                     'after_change'));
END;
/
```

Step 11: Print the Final Analysis

```
SET LONG 100000000
SET PAGESIZE 0
SET LINESIZE 200
SET LONGCHUNKSIZE 200
SET TRIMSPOOL ON
spool /tmp/report.txt

SELECT DBMS_SQLPA.report_analysis_task('TASK_832')
from    dual;

spool off
```

Report Output

```
General Information
-------------------------------------------------------------------------------
---------
 Task Information:                     Workload Information:
--------------------------------------- ---------------------------------------
-----
  Task Name    : TASK_832             SQL Tuning Set Name       :
sql_replay_test
  Task Owner   : SYS                  SQL Tuning Set Owner      : SYS
  Description  :                      Total SQL Statement Count : 7
```

```
Execution Information:
---------------------------------------------------------------------------------
-----
  Execution Name      : EXEC_847
  Started             : 02/04/2010 15:57:00
  Execution Type      : COMPARE PERFORMANCE
  Last Updated        : 02/04/2010 15:57:00
  Description         :
  Global Time Limit   : UNLIMITED
  Scope               : COMPREHENSIVE
  Per-SQL Time Limit  : UNUSED
  Status              : COMPLETED
  Number of Errors    : 0
  Number of Unsupported SQL  : 1

Analysis Information:
---------------------------------------------------------------------------------
---------
 Before Change Execution:                         After Change Execution:
 --------------------------------------------     ----------------------------------
---------
  Execution Name      : before_change              Execution Name      : after_change
  Execution Type      : TEST EXECUTE               Execution Type      : TEST EXECUTE
  Scope               : COMPREHENSIVE              Scope               : COMPREHENSIVE
  Status              : COMPLETED                  Status              : COMPLETED
  Started             : 02/04/2010 15:50:08        Started             : 02/04/2010 15:56:13
  Last Updated        : 02/04/2010 15:51:41        Last Updated        : 02/04/2010 15:56:15
  Global Time Limit   : UNLIMITED                  Global Time Limit   : UNLIMITED
  Per-SQL Time Limit  : UNUSED                     Per-SQL Time Limit  : UNUSED
  Number of Errors    : 0                          Number of Errors    : 0


  --------------------------------------------
  Comparison Metric: ELAPSED_TIME
  --------------------------------------------
  Workload Impact Threshold: 1%
  --------------------------------------------
  SQL Impact Threshold: 1%
  --------------------------------------------

Report Summary
---------------------------------------------------------------------------------
---------

Projected Workload Change Impact:
-------------------------------------------
  Overall Impact      :  99.59%
  Improvement Impact  :  99.59%
  Regression Impact   :  0%

SQL Statement Count
-------------------------------------------
  SQL Category   SQL Count  Plan Change Count
  Overall            7              4
  Improved           4              4
  Unchanged          2              0
  Unsupported        1              0

Top 6 SQL Sorted by Absolute Value of Change Impact on the Workload
---------------------------------------------------------------------------------
---------
  |          |         | Impact on | Execution | Metric   | Metric | Impact  | Plan  |
  | object_id | sql_id  | Workload  | Frequency | Before   | After  | on SQL  | Change|
```

```
-------------------------------------------------------------------------------
----------
|        19 | 2suq4bp0p1s9p |    27.56% |     1 | 11598790 |     34 |     100% | y      |
|        21 | 7j70yfnjfxy9p |    25.02% |     1 | 10532117 |   2778 |   99.97% | y      |
|        22 | c8g33h1hn04xh |    24.28% |     1 | 10219529 |    370 |     100% | y      |
|        23 | g09jahhhn7ft3 |    22.72% |     1 |  9564149 |   1123 |   99.99% | y      |
|        18 | 033g69gb60ajp |     -.04% |     2 |    42989 |  50359 |  -17.14% | n      |
|        24 | gz549qa95mvm0 |       0% |     2 |    41798 |  42682 |   -2.11% | n      |
-------------------------------------------------------------------------------
---------
Note: time statistics are displayed in microseconds
```

TIPS

REVIEW

Wow! Overall impact is a positive 99.59 percent! Having viewed the queries, this makes sense. The query accessed a 1.1-million row table, yet only 16 rows satisfied the OBJECT_ID = 100 condition. By adding an index on the OBJECT_ID column, performance is drastically improved!

Tips Review

- Query V$SQLAREA and V$SQL to find problem queries that need to be tuned.

- When a small number of rows ("small" is version dependent) are to be returned based on a condition in a query, you generally want to use an index on that condition (column), given that the rows are not skewed within the individual blocks.

- The first tip concerning slow queries is that you will have a lot of them if you are missing indexes on columns that are generally restrictive. Building indexes on restrictive columns is the first step toward better system performance.

- Bad indexes (indexing the wrong columns) can cause as much trouble as forgetting to use indexes on the correct columns. While Oracle's cost-based optimizer generally suppresses poor indexes, problems can still develop when a bad index is used at the same time as a good index.

- For crucial queries on your system, consider concatenated indexes on the columns contained in both the SELECT and the WHERE clauses.

- The INDEX_FFS processes *only* the index and will not take the result and access the table. All columns that are used and retrieved by the query *must* be contained in the index. This method is a much better way to guarantee the index will be used.

- When a query is run multiple times in succession, it becomes faster since you have now cached the data in memory. At times, people are tricked into believing that they have actually made a query faster when, in actuality, they are accessing data stored in memory.

- Caching an often-used but relatively small table into memory ensures that the data is not pushed out of memory by other data. Also, be careful—cached tables can alter the execution path normally chosen by the optimizer, leading to an unexpected execution order for the query (it can affect the driving table in nested loop joins).

- Oracle 11g provides a CACHE_RESULT feature, which you can use to cache the result of a query, allowing subsequent queries to access the result set directly instead finding the result through aggregating data stored in the database block buffers a subsequent time.

- When multiple indexes on a single table can be used for a query, use the most restrictive index. While Oracle's cost-based optimizer generally forces use of the most restrictive index, variations occur, depending on the Oracle version and the query structure.

- Any modification to the column side of the query results in the suppression of the index unless a function-based index is created. Function-based indexes can lead to dramatic performance gains when used to create indexes on functions often used on selective columns in the WHERE clause.

- Oracle's optimizer now performs OR-expansion, which improves the performance of certain queries that ran poorly in prior versions.

- Using the nested subquery with an EXISTS clause may make queries dramatically faster, depending on the data being retrieved from each part of the query. Oracle11g often makes this translation internally, saving you time and giving you performance gains!

References

Deb Dudek, *DBA Tips, or a Job Is a Terrible Thing to Waste* (TUSC).
Rich Niemiec, *DBA Tuning Tips: Now YOU Are the Expert* (TUSC).
Oracle® Database Performance Tuning Guide 11g *Release 2 (11.2).*
Query Optimization in Oracle 9*i*, An Oracle Whitepaper (Oracle).

Rama Balaji added several new sections and helped with the update for 11*g*. Thanks to Connor McDonald for his feedback on V$SQLAREA. Rob Christensen contributed the major portion of the previous update to this chapter.

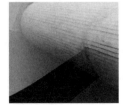

CHAPTER
9

Table Joins and
Other Advanced Tuning
(Advanced DBA and Developer)

With Oracle Database 11*g*, Oracle introduced a new option called Real Application Testing. Real Application Testing allows you to capture a complete database workload on one database and replay it on another database. You can replay the exact workload and you even have the option to synchronize workload timing. This tool is very valuable for load testing on a new application release, database patch, or database upgrade. If you need to tune a specific object or set of queries, 11*g* also offers the SQL Performance Analyzer (SPA). This tool provides the ability to examine a SQL workload on a database, record a portion of it based on what you want collected/tested, and then take that workload and examine it in another environment. The new environment can include any database changes (including initialization parameter changes), hardware changes, or environment changes. This tool not only offers a powerful new way to examine the potential impact of change with more predictable results, but also allows the targeting of a specific change while measuring its potential impact.

This chapter was originally the most painful to write due to the complexities of Oracle joins and block level tuning. I've included many examples from Oracle and other products over the years to show different possible tuning patterns and how to solve future patterns. This chapter includes a section that shows how to link tuning to mathematical equations as well as a detailed look at relational versus object relational performance, as well as a section that shows how to develop your own tuning theory and compare results for your unique system. This chapter is not *strictly* 11*g* related; rather, it is focused on advanced query tuning concepts, showing the evolution of the Oracle database. Oracle is growing much faster and is truly more of a platform than a database these days.

The driving table or the first table accessed in a query is an important aspect of superior performance. Using the Enterprise Manager Tuning Pack and Automatic Workload Repository (AWR) statistics, Oracle can do a lot to help you tune things (see Chapter 5 for more information). If the optimizer has designated the wrong table as the driving table in a query, the optimizer's choice can be the difference between hours and seconds. Usually, the cost-based optimizer chooses the correct table, but your indexing on tables affects how this works. If you need to change the driving table using a hint on the same table over and over, this symptom often indicates an indexing plan that still needs work. When you have to tune multiple tables using hints, tuning increasing numbers of tables gets progressively harder. With only two or three tables, it's easy enough to use an ORDERED hint (guaranteeing the order of the tables) and then to try variations of the table order until you achieve the fastest outcome. However, a ten-table join has 3,628,800 possible combinations, which makes trying all these combinations slightly time-consuming. Using a LEADING hint (you specify the first or leading table to drive the query with) simplifies this chore, but it is still far more daunting than building the correct indexing scheme in the first place.

One of the greatest challenges of this book was trying to put driving tables into a helpful format for readers, using the EXPLAIN PLAN, Autotrace, and TKPROF. The optimizer's complexity and all the potential paths for joining and optimizing a query can be mindboggling. Suppressing a single index in a query can affect the driving table, how Oracle joins tables in a query, and how Oracle uses or suppresses other indexes. This chapter focuses on helping you make better decisions when choosing a driving table. Although I have a good understanding of how Oracle performs these complexities, putting that understanding into words was the challenging task for the first half of this chapter. The challenge for the second half was relating performance tuning to mathematical equations and also comparing join performance of relational to object-relational queries.

The tips covered in this chapter include the following:

- Real Application Testing
- Database Replay
- SQL Performance Analyzer
- Join methods
- Table join initialization parameters
- A two-table join: equal-sized tables (cost-based)
- A two-table INDEXED join: equal-sized tables (cost-based)
- Forcing a specific join method
- Eliminating join records (candidate rows) in multitable joins
- A two-table join between a large table and a small table
- Three table joins: not as much fun (cost-based)
- Bitmap join indexes
- Third-party product tuning
- Tuning distributed queries
- When you have everything tuned
- Miscellaneous tuning snippets
- Tuning at the block level (advanced)
- Tuning using simple mathematical techniques
- Join tuning: relational vs. object-relational performance

Real Application Testing

Real Application Testing is used to capture a database workload on one system and replay it later on a different system and is very useful when comparing two different systems or different versions of Oracle. You can perform Real Application Testing in text mode (covered in this section) or through Oracle Enterprise Manager. It's a great way to test your upgrade to 11*g* (capture on your 10*g*R2 system and then test it against 11*g*).

To perform Real Application Testing, the basic steps are as follows:

1. Capture workload on a database, from 10*g* or even as far back as 9.2.0.8.

2. Restore the database on a test system to the SCN when capture begins.

3. Perform upgrade and make changes to the test system as needed.

4. Preprocess the captured workload if it is not preprocessed.

5. Configure the test system for replay.

6. Replay workload on the test system (can be synchronized or unsynchronized).

7. Create a report that shows Data, Error, and Performance divergences.

Database Replay

Database Replay is used to replay a workload in a manner that you would like to test. You can have a replay that executes exactly as it was captured or use other Oracle options to replay it in a different manner. Database Replay can be used in command line mode or through Enterprise Manager.

Set Up Source Database for Database Replay Capture

As stated earlier, you can utilize database releases prior to 11g for capturing a workload for replay on an 11g database. First, however, some setup is required. For database release 10.2.0.4, there are no required patches for the capture functionality; for releases prior to 10.2.0.4 (as well as other earlier releases), a patch is required.

Run the `wrrenbl.sql` script—only required for 10.2.0.4 and optional for releases prior to 11g. The script enables the PRE_11G_ENABLE_CAPTURE database initialization parameter:

```
cd $ORACLE_HOME/rdbms/admin
sqlplus / as sysdba
SQL> @wrrenbl.sql
```

Prepare to Capture Workload

You need to prepare the source database where you will be capturing the workload for replay.

To create a directory location where the workload capture file can be written:

```
c:\oracle>mkdir dbcapture
```

To create a directory within the source database where the workload will be captured:

```
SQL> create directory dbcapture as 'c:\oracle\dbcapture';
```

Capture the Workload

Prior to executing the workload, you need to initiate the capture.

1. Start the capture process.

    ```
    SQL> exec dbms_workload_capture.start_capture('NRML_ACTIVITY', 'DBCAPTURE');
    ```

2. Run the workload.

3. When complete, or when you have captured the desired workload, stop the capture process:

    ```
    SQL> exec dbms_workload_capture.finish_capture();
    ```

4. Execute a report on the capture:

    ```
    -- Capture Report
    DECLARE
      cap_id            NUMBER;
    ```

```
    cap_rpt              CLOB;
    buffer               VARCHAR2(32767);
    buffer_size          CONSTANT BINARY_INTEGER := 32767;
    amount               BINARY_INTEGER;
    offset               NUMBER(38);
    file_handle          UTL_FILE.FILE_TYPE;
    directory_name       CONSTANT VARCHAR2(80) := 'DBCAPTURE';
    v_filename           CONSTANT VARCHAR2(80) := 'Capture.html';

BEGIN
  cap_id  :=
DBMS_WORKLOAD_CAPTURE.GET_CAPTURE_INFO(dir=>directory_name);
  cap_rpt := DBMS_WORKLOAD_CAPTURE.REPORT(capture_id => cap_id,
                          format => DBMS_WORKLOAD_CAPTURE.TYPE_HTML);

  -- Write Report to file
  DBMS_OUTPUT.ENABLE(100000);

  -- --------------------------------
  -- OPEN NEW XML FILE IN WRITE MODE
  -- --------------------------------
  file_handle := UTL_FILE.FOPEN(location     => directory_name,
                                filename     => v_filename,
                                open_mode    => 'w',
                                max_linesize => buffer_size);

  amount := buffer_size;
  offset := 1;

  WHILE amount >= buffer_size
  LOOP
      DBMS_LOB.READ(lob_loc   => cap_rpt,
                    amount    => amount,
                    offset    => offset,
                    buffer    => buffer);

      offset := offset + amount;

      UTL_FILE.PUT(file     => file_handle,
                   buffer   => buffer);

      UTL_FILE.FFLUSH(file => file_handle);
  END LOOP;

  UTL_FILE.FCLOSE(file => file_handle);
END;
/
```

Prepare the Workload for Replay

Note that the database that processes the captured workload must be an 11.1.0.6 or above database as the packages to process the captured workload are not available in prior releases. The following steps show how to prepare the workload for replay:

1. Create a directory location for the captured workload to be placed in for processing and replay on both the processing database and the replay database if the processing and replay databases are different. Best practice is to process the workload on the same database that will execute the replay.

   ```
   c:\oracle> mkdir replay
   ```

2. Copy the captured workload files to another directory if on the same host as database where workload was captured or to destination system location to be processed.

   ```
   copy c:\oracle\dbcapture\* c:\oracle\Replay
   ```

3. Create directory in the Oracle database that will process the captured workload.

   ```
   SQL> create directory REPLAY as 'c:\oracle\replay';
   ```

Process the Workload for Replay

This process is resource-intensive. It should, therefore, be done on a nonproduction system. If you capture the workload on your production system, move the capture files to a test or development system to prepare them for replay.

Process the captured workload:

```
SQL> exec dbms_workload_replay.process_capture ('REPLAY');
```

The process creates the following files in the REPLAY directory (and a few others) during the processing of the captured workload (you may also have a subdirectory in 11gR2, for instance, pp11.2.0.2.0, which you would need to add to any of the directory locations):

```
wcr_login.pp
WCR_SCN_ORDER.EXTB
WCR_SEQ_DATA.EXTB
WCR_CONN_DATA.EXTB
wcr_process.wmd
```

Prepare to Replay the Workload

Next, you need to prepare the replay database. In the following steps, you prepare the replay database. Keep in mind this is version/system dependent, and there may be variations needed for your system.

1. Go to the database where the replay will be executed if different from the database that processed the workload. If the replay database is the same as the database that processed the workload, skip to Step 3; otherwise, proceed to Step 2.

2. If you have not done so already, go to the "Prepare the Workload for Replay" section, earlier in this chapter, and execute the steps on the database that will replay the workload.

3. Initialize the replay:

```
SQL> exec dbms_workload_replay.initialize_replay ('TEST_REPLAY','REPLAY');
```

4. Prepare for workload replay:

```
SQL> exec dbms_workload_replay.prepare_replay(synchronization=>TRUE);
```

5. Calibrate the workload to determine the number of workload replay clients. At the command line, change to the REPLAY directory and calibrate:

```
cd c:\oracle\replay
c:\oracle\replay> wrc mode=calibrate

Workload Replay Client: Release 11.1.0.6.0 - Production on Thu Jul 24 10:38:41 2008
Copyright (c) 1982, 2007, Oracle.  All rights reserved.
Report for Workload in: .
----------------------
Recommendation:
Consider using at least 1 clients divided among 1 CPU(s).

Workload Characteristics:
- max concurrency: 9 sessions
- total number of sessions: 46

Assumptions:
- 1 client process per 50 concurrent sessions
- 4 client process per CPU
- 256K OF memory cache per concurrent session
- think time scale = 100
- connect time scale = 100
- synchronization = TRUE
```

Execute the Workload Replay

Now that the workload has been captured and processed, the workload is ready to be replayed. Follow these steps to execute the workload on the new system:

1. Note the number of workload replay clients indicated in the previous section that you need to execute the processed workload.

2. Open up a window for each workload replay client that you will need as these will each be separate executions. As indicated in the previous step, you only need one client as indicated in the previous step.

3. From the command line, enter the `replay` command with the `wrc` utility for the number of replay clients needed, with one command in each window:

```
c:\oracle\proccapture>wrc system/xxxxx@orcl11g replaydir=c:\oracle\replay
```

4. Repeat for each of the replay clients needed.

```
c:\oracle\proccapture>wrc system/xxxxx@orcl11g replaydir=c:\oracle\replay
Workload Replay Client: Release 11.1.0.6.0 - Production on Thu Jul 24 15:09:15 2008
Copyright (c) 1982, 2007, Oracle.  All rights reserved.
```

```
Wait for the replay to start (15:09:15)
Replay started (15:09:40)
Replay finished (16:01:41)
```

5. AWR information will be available for the time period in which the workload replay was executed. Oracle recommends that the executed workload replay cover at least one complete snap period to provide the most useful data. You can take a snapshot prior to beginning and immediately after the workload execution (this is optional).

```
SQL> execute DBMS_WORKLOAD_REPOSITORY.CREATE_SNAPSHOT ();
```

6. From another window, log into the database where the workload replay will be executed and start the workload replay process. An indication that the workload has been started will appear:

```
SQL> exec dbms_workload_replay.start_replay ;

PL/SQL procedure successfully completed.
```

7. Monitor the workload replay until it is completed.

8. Once the workload replay is complete, take another AWR snapshot (optional).

```
SQL> execute DBMS_WORKLOAD_REPOSITORY.CREATE_SNAPSHOT ();
```

9. Execute workload replay report extraction, and evaluate the results from the report:

```
-- Replay Report
DECLARE
  cap_id            NUMBER;
  rep_id            NUMBER;
  rep_rpt           CLOB;
  buffer            VARCHAR2(32767);
  buffer_size       CONSTANT BINARY_INTEGER := 32767;
  amount            BINARY_INTEGER;
  offset            NUMBER(38);
  file_handle       UTL_FILE.FILE_TYPE;
  directory_name    CONSTANT VARCHAR2(80) := 'PROCCAPTURE';
  v_filename        CONSTANT VARCHAR2(80) := 'Replay.html';

BEGIN
    cap_id := DBMS_WORKLOAD_REPLAY.GET_REPLAY_INFO(dir => 'PROCCAPTURE');

    select max(id)
    into rep_id
    from dba_workload_replays
    where capture_id = cap_id ;

    rep_rpt := DBMS_WORKLOAD_REPLAY.REPORT(replay_id => rep_id,
                                    format => DBMS_WORKLOAD_REPLAY.TYPE_HTML);

    -- Write Report to file
DBMS_OUTPUT.ENABLE(100000);
```

```
--  -------------------------------
--  OPEN NEW XML FILE IN WRITE MODE
--  -------------------------------
file_handle := UTL_FILE.FOPEN(location     => directory_name,
                              filename      => v_filename,
                              open_mode     => 'w',
                              max_linesize  => buffer_size);


amount := buffer_size;
offset := 1;

  WHILE amount >= buffer_size
  LOOP
      DBMS_LOB.READ(lob_loc   => rep_rpt,
                    amount    => amount,
                    offset    => offset,
                    buffer    => buffer);

      offset := offset + amount;

      UTL_FILE.PUT(file      => file_handle,
                   buffer    => buffer);

      UTL_FILE.FFLUSH(file => file_handle);
  END LOOP;

    UTL_FILE.FCLOSE(file => file_handle);
END;
```

10. Go to the directory used in the script, `C:\oracle\replay`, and view the `Replay.html` file.

SQL Performance Analyzer

The SQL Performance Analyzer (SPA) is a great tool for measuring and reporting on performance before and after instituting a change. SPA uses the DBMS_SQLTUNE package to accomplish its analysis. In Chapter 8, you learned how to use SPA for a simple tuning issue in which SPA recommended an index that improved performance by over 99 percent. But SPA is much broader. This tool is one of the most powerful ways to answer some of the most common performance questions:

- What will be the impact of removing this index?
- What will be the impact of adding an index to this table?
- What will be the impact of changing an index from a b-tree to a bitmap?
- What will be the impact of reorganizing and ordering this table?
- What will be the impact of partitioning this table?

- What will be the impact of changing a table to an index-organized table?

- What will be the impact of regathering the cost-based optimizer stats?

- What will be the impact of updating the database patch level?

- What will be the impact of upgrading the database to the next version?

- What will be the impact of changing this database initialization parameter?

- What will happen if I change the database from using file systems to ASM?

Create a SQL Tuning Set

To make a comparison using SPA, the first step is to create a SQL Tuning Set. The first execution of the SQL Tuning Set is the one to use as a baseline; use the second to make the comparison. Create a SQL Tuning Set (as shown here) prior to making any changes, and then create a second Tuning Set after you've made the changes. You can also do this in Enterprise Manager (see Chapter 5 for additional information).

```
-------------------------------------------------------------------------
-- Script: spa_create_sts.sql
-- Setup a SQL Tuning Set to create a for the SQL Performance Analyzer.
-------------------------------------------------------------------------
set feedback on
-------------------------------------------------------------------------
-- Set up the SQL Set and what sql we want to make part of the sql tuning set
-------------------------------------------------------------------------
BEGIN
    -- Create the sql set
    DBMS_SQLTUNE.CREATE_SQLSET(sqlset_name => 'STS_SPA_1');
    -- Limit the sql in the set to Just on the ORDERS and ORDER_ITEMS
    -- The CAPTURE_CURSOR_CACHE_SQLSET will collect SQL statements
    -- over a period of time.  This helps build a more realistic
    -- set of SQL load from the system
    DBMS_SQLTUNE.CAPTURE_CURSOR_CACHE_SQLSET(
         sqlset_name => 'STS_SPA_1'
        ,basic_filter=> q'#UPPER(sql_text) LIKE '%ORDER%' #'
        ,time_limit  => 300
        ,repeat_interval => 2
    );
END;
/
```

Note that this procedure runs for five minutes, capturing SQL statements every two seconds.

Create an Analysis Task

After creating a SQL Tuning Set with the SQL workload execution, you create an analysis task.

```
dbms_sqlpa.create_analysis_task(sqlset_name => 'my_sts',
task_name => 'my_spa_task',
description => 'test index changes');
```

Execute Analysis Task

After creating the analysis task, you need to execute the task for a baseline tuning set. After executing the analysis task, you can make your changes for comparison against the baseline. This requires creating a second SQL Tuning Set, a second analysis task, and then executing that task. Then you can generate a comparison.

Pre-change:

```
dbms_sqlpa.execute_analysis_task(task_name => 'my_spa_task',
execution_type => 'test execute',
execution_name => 'before_index_change');
```

Post change:

```
dbms_sqlpa.execute_analysis_task(task_name => 'my_spa_task',
execution_type => 'test execute',
execution_name => 'after_index_change');
```

Now you have two SQL Tuning Sets and are ready to generate a comparison.

To generate comparison:

```
dbms_sqlpa.execute_analysis_task(
task_name => 'my_spa_task',
execution_type => 'compare performance',
execution_name => 'analysis_results',
execution_params => dbms_advisor.arglist('execution_name1','before_index_change',
'execution_name2', 'after_index_change',
'comparison_metric','buffer_gets'));

-------------------------------------------------------------------------
-- Script: spa_compare.sql
-- Executes a SQL Tuning Set Comparison and then outputs a report from SPA
-------------------------------------------------------------------------
spool SPA_COMPARE_REPORT.out

-- Get the whole report for the single statement case.
SELECT DBMS_SQLPA.REPORT_ANALYSIS_TASK('my_spa_task') from dual;

-- Show me the summary for the sts case.
SELECT DBMS_SQLPA.REPORT_ANALYSIS_TASK('my_spa_task', 'TEXT', 'TYPICAL', 'SUMMARY')
FROM   DUAL;
```

```
-- Show me the findings for the statement I'm interested in.
SELECT DBMS_SQLPA.REPORT_ANALYSIS_TASK('my_spa_task', 'TEXT', 'TYPICAL', 'FINDINGS', 5)
FROM   DUAL;

spool off
```

Query Performance Analyzer Advisor Tasks

You can show the Advisor tasks using the DBA_ADVISOR_TASKS or USER_ADVISOR_TASKS views:

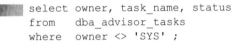

```
select owner, task_name, status
from   dba_advisor_tasks
where  owner <> 'SYS' ;
```

```
OWNER                             TASK_NAME                         STATUS
------------------------------    ------------------------------    ----------
SCOTT                             TASK_1949                         COMPLETED
SCOTT                             TASK_1950                         COMPLETED
SCOTT                             TASK_1948                         INITIAL
SCOTT                             TASK_1943                         INITIAL
SCOTT                             TASK_2700                         INITIAL
SCOTT                             TASK_1946                         INITIAL
SCOTT                             TASK_1923                         INITIAL
SCOTT                             TASK_1945                         INITIAL
SCOTT                             TASK_1944                         INITIAL
SCOTT                             TASK_1947                         INITIAL
```

Cancel an Executing SQL Performance Analyzer Analysis Task

If a SQL Performance Analyzer analysis task is in the process of executing, you can cancel it manually at any time. You may need to do this for tasks you wish to interrupt due to resource issues, database performance impact issues, and so on.

Syntax

```
DBMS_SQLPA.CANCEL_ANALYSIS_TASK ('my_spa_task') ;
```

Remove SQL Performance Analyzer Analysis Task

After you have utilized the information from the SQL Performance Analyzer analysis, you may no longer need the analysis task. To clear space and remove unused or unneeded analysis tasks, it is best to drop them. Oracle provides a procedure within the DBMS_SQLPA package to remove an analysis task.

Syntax

```
DBMS_SQLPA.DROP_ANALYSIS_TASK ('my_spa_task') ;
```

Example

```
SQL> exec DBMS_SQLPA.DROP_ANALYSIS_TASK ('TASK_1923') ;

PL/SQL procedure successfully completed
```

Determine Active SQL Tuning Sets

Before you can drop a SQL Tuning Set, you must remove all references to the SQL Tuning Set, including SPA analysis tasks as well as SQL Tuning Advisor tasks. You can determine references to SQL Tuning Sets via the DBA_SQLSET_REFERENCES view. Having the reference ID is critical to being able to inactivate a SQL set reference.

```
SQL> select id, sqlset_owner, sqlset_name, description from DBA_SQLSET_REFERENCES;

 ID SQLSET_OWNER SQLSET_NAME Description
--- ------------ ----------- ------------------------------------------------
  2 SCOTT        STS_SPA_1   created by: SQL Tuning Advisor - task: TASK_1926
  3 SCOTT        STS_SPA_1   created by: SQL Tuning Advisor - task: TASK_1927
  5 SCOTT        STS_SPA_1   created by: SQL Tuning Advisor - task: TASK_1929
  8 SCOTT        STS_SPA_1   created by: SQL Tuning Advisor - task: TASK_1932
  7 SCOTT        STS_SPA_1   created by: SQL Tuning Advisor - task: TASK_1931
  4 SCOTT        STS_SPA_1   created by: SQL Tuning Advisor - task: TASK_1928
  6 SCOTT        STS_SPA_1   created by: SQL Tuning Advisor - task: TASK_1930

7 rows selected.
```

Remove SQL Tuning Set

After you have finished the SQL Performance Analyzer analysis, to conserve space and remove unneeded results from SQL Performance Analyzer activities, you may want to remove SQL Tuning Sets. You can only remove inactive SQL Tuning Sets. To remove an active SQL Tuning Set, you have to first remove the SPA analysis tasks that reference the SQL Tuning Set. After removing all analysis tasks, you must remove the SQL Tuning Set references; otherwise, an ORA-13757 error will result indicating the SQL Tuning Set is still active.

Remove SQL Tuning Set Reference

Syntax

```
DBMS_SQLTUNE.REMOVE_SQLSET_REFERENCE ('<tuning set name>') ;
```

Example

```
SQL> exec DBMS_SQLTUNE.REMOVE_SQLSET_REFERENCE ('STS_SPA_1', 2) ;

PL/SQL procedure successfully completed.
```

Drop SQL Tuning Set

Ensure all references to the SQL Tuning Set being dropped have first been removed, and then you can drop the SQL Tuning Set itself.

Syntax

```
DBMS_SQLTUNE.DROP_SQLSET ('<tuning set name>') ;
```

Example (references have not been removed)

```
SQL> exec DBMS_SQLTUNE.DROP_SQLSET ('STS_SPA_1');

BEGIN DBMS_SQLTUNE.DROP_SQLSET ('STS_SPA_1') ; END;
*
ERROR at line 1:
ORA-13757: "SQL Tuning Set" "STS_SPA_1" owned by user "SCOTT" is active.
ORA-06512: at "SYS.DBMS_SQLTUNE_INTERNAL", line 8597
ORA-06512: at "SYS.DBMS_SQLTUNE", line 3015
ORA-06512: at line 1

Example (references have been removed):
SQL> exec DBMS_SQLTUNE.DROP_SQLSET ('STS_SPA_1');

PL/SQL procedure successfully completed.
```

Join Methods

Since the days of Oracle 6, the optimizer has used three primary ways to join row sources together: the nested loops join, the sort-merge join, and the cluster join. (There is also the favorite of the ad-hoc query user—the Cartesian join.) Oracle 7.3 introduced the hash join, and Oracle 8*i* introduced the index join, making for a total of five primary join methods. Each method has a unique set of features and limitations. Before you attack a potential join issue, you need to know the answers to the following questions:

- Which table will drive the query (first table accessed), and when will other tables be accessed given the path that is chosen for the query? What are the alternate driving paths?

- What are the Oracle join possibilities (described in this section)? Remember, each join possibility for Oracle can yield different results, depending on the join order, the selectivity of indexes, and the available memory for sorting and/or hashing.

- Which indexes are available, and what is the selectivity of the indexes? The selectivity of an index can not only cause the optimizer to use or suppress an index, but it can also change the way the query drives and may determine the use or suppression of other indexes in the query.

■ Which hints provide alternate paths, and which hints suppress or force an index to be used? These hints change the driving order of the tables, and they change how Oracle performs the join and which indexes it uses or suppresses.

■ Which version of Oracle are you using? Your choices vary, depending on the version and release of Oracle you are using. The optimizer also works differently, depending on the version.

Nested Loops Joins

Suppose somebody gave you a telephone book and a list of 20 names to look up, and then asked you to write down each person's name and corresponding telephone number. You would probably go down the list of names, looking up each one in the telephone book one at a time. This task would be pretty easy because the telephone book is alphabetized by name. Moreover, somebody looking over your shoulder could begin calling the first few numbers you write down while you are still looking up the rest. This scene describes a NESTED LOOPS join.

In a NESTED LOOPS join, Oracle reads the first row from the first row source and then checks the second row source for matches. All matches are then placed in the result set and Oracle goes on to the next row from the first row source. This continues until all rows in the first row source have been processed. The first row source is often called the outer or *driving* table, whereas the second row source is called the *inner* table. Using a NESTED LOOPS join is one of the fastest methods of receiving the first records back from a join.

NESTED LOOPS joins are ideal when the driving row source (the records you are looking for) is small and the joined columns of the inner row source are uniquely indexed or have a highly selective nonunique index. NESTED LOOPS joins have an advantage over other join methods in that they can quickly retrieve the first few rows of the result set without having to wait for the entire result set to be determined. This situation is ideal for query screens where an end user can read the first few records retrieved while the rest are being fetched. NESTED LOOPS joins are also flexible in that any two-row sources can always be joined by NESTED LOOPS—regardless of join condition and schema definition.

However, NESTED LOOPS joins can be very inefficient if the inner row source (second table accessed) does not have an index on the joined columns or if the index is not highly selective. If the driving row source (the records retrieved from the driving table) is quite large, other join methods may be more efficient.

Figure 9-1 illustrates the method of executing the query shown next where the DEPT table is accessed first and the result is then looped through the EMP table with a NESTED LOOPS join. The type of join performed can be forced with a hint and will vary due to different variables on your system.

```
select   /*+ ordered */ ename, dept.deptno
from     dept, emp
where    dept.deptno = emp.deptno;
```

SORT-MERGE Joins

Suppose two salespeople attend a conference and each collect over 100 business cards from potential new customers. They now each have a pile of cards in random order, and they want to

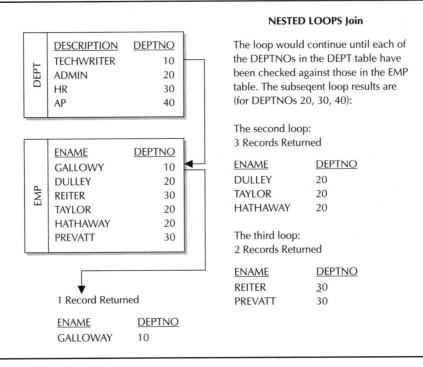

NESTED LOOPS Join

The loop would continue until each of the DEPTNOs in the DEPT table have been checked against those in the EMP table. The subseqent loop results are (for DEPTNOs 20, 30, 40):

The second loop:
3 Records Returned

ENAME	DEPTNO
DULLEY	20
TAYLOR	20
HATHAWAY	20

The third loop:
2 Records Returned

ENAME	DEPTNO
REITER	30
PREVATT	30

FIGURE 9-1. *NESTED LOOPS (DEPT is the driving table)*

see how many cards are duplicated in both piles. The salespeople alphabetize their piles, and then they call off names one at a time. Because both piles of cards have been sorted, it becomes much easier to find the names that appear in both piles. This example describes a SORT-MERGE join.

In a SORT-MERGE join, Oracle sorts the first row source by its join columns, sorts the second row source by its join columns, and then merges the sorted row sources together. As matches are found, they are put into the result set.

SORT-MERGE joins can be effective when lack of data selectivity or useful indexes render a NESTED LOOPS join inefficient, or when both of the row sources are quite large (greater than 5 percent of the blocks accessed). However, SORT-MERGE joins can be used only for equijoins (WHERE D.deptno = E.deptno, as opposed to WHERE D.deptno >= E.deptno). SORT-MERGE joins require temporary segments for sorting (if SORT_AREA_SIZE or the automatic memory parameters like MEMORY_TARGET are set too small). This can lead to extra memory utilization and/or extra disk I/O in the temporary tablespace.

Figure 9-2 illustrates the method of executing the query shown next when a SORT-MERGE join is performed.

```
select  /*+ ordered */ ename, dept.deptno
from    emp, dept
where   dept.deptno = emp.deptno;
```

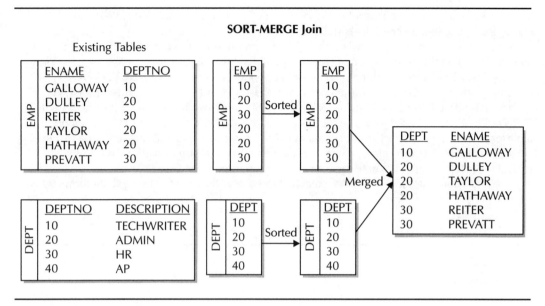

FIGURE 9-2.   *SORT-MERGE join*

CLUSTER Joins

A CLUSTER join is really just a special case of the NESTED LOOPS join that is not used very often. If the two row sources being joined are actually tables that are part of a cluster, and if the join is an equijoin between the cluster keys of the two tables, then Oracle can use a CLUSTER join. In this case, Oracle reads each row from the first row source and finds all matches in the second row source by using the CLUSTER index.

CLUSTER joins are extremely efficient because the joining rows in the two row sources will actually be located in the same physical data block. However, clusters carry certain caveats of their own, and you cannot have a CLUSTER join without a cluster. Therefore, CLUSTER joins are not very commonly used.

HASH Joins

HASH joins are the usual choice of the Oracle optimizer when the memory is set up to accommodate them. In a HASH join, Oracle accesses one table (usually the smaller of the joined results) and builds a hash table on the join key in memory. It then scans the other table in the join (usually the larger one) and probes the hash table for matches to it. Oracle uses a HASH join efficiently only if the parameter PGA_AGGREGATE_TARGET is set to a large enough value. If MEMORY_TARGET is used, the PGA_AGGREGATE_TARGET is included in the MEMORY_TARGET, but you may still want to set a minimum (see Chapter 4 for additional information). If you set the SGA_TARGET, you must set the PGA_AGGREGATE_TARGET as the SGA_TARGET does not include the PGA (unless you use MEMORY_TARGET as just described). The HASH join is similar to a NESTED LOOPS join in the sense that there is a nested loop that occurs—Oracle first builds a hash table to facilitate the operation and then loops through the hash table. When using an ORDERED hint, the first table in the FROM clause is the table used to build the hash table.

HASH joins can be effective when the lack of a useful index renders NESTED LOOPS joins inefficient. The HASH join might be faster than a SORT-MERGE join, in this case, because only one row source needs to be sorted, and it could possibly be faster than a NESTED LOOPS join because probing a hash table in memory can be faster than traversing a b-tree index. As with SORT-MERGE joins and CLUSTER joins, HASH joins work only on equijoins. As with SORT-MERGE joins, HASH joins use memory resources and can drive up I/O in the temporary tablespace if the sort memory is not sufficient (which can cause this join method to be extremely slow). Finally, HASH joins are available only when cost-based optimization is used (which should be 100 percent of the time for your application running on Oracle 11g).

Figure 9-3 illustrates the method of executing the query shown in the listing that follows when a HASH join is used.

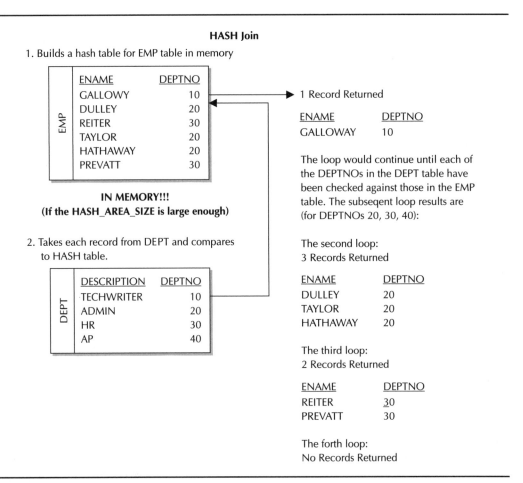

HASH Join

1. Builds a hash table for EMP table in memory

EMP

ENAME	DEPTNO
GALLOWY	10
DULLEY	20
REITER	30
TAYLOR	20
HATHAWAY	20
PREVATT	30

IN MEMORY!!!
(If the HASH_AREA_SIZE is large enough)

2. Takes each record from DEPT and compares to HASH table.

DEPT

DESCRIPTION	DEPTNO
TECHWRITER	10
ADMIN	20
HR	30
AP	40

1 Record Returned

ENAME	DEPTNO
GALLOWAY	10

The loop would continue until each of the DEPTNOs in the DEPT table have been checked against those in the EMP table. The subseqent loop results are (for DEPTNOs 20, 30, 40):

The second loop:
3 Records Returned

ENAME	DEPTNO
DULLEY	20
TAYLOR	20
HATHAWAY	20

The third loop:
2 Records Returned

ENAME	DEPTNO
REITER	30
PREVATT	30

The forth loop:
No Records Returned

FIGURE 9-3. *HASH join*

```
select  /*+ ordered */ ename, dept.deptno
from    emp, dept
where   dept.deptno = emp.deptno;
```

INDEX-MERGE Joins

Prior to Oracle 8*i*, you always had to access the table unless the index contained all of the information required. As of Oracle 8*i*, if a set of indexes exists that contains all of the information required by the query, then the optimizer can choose to generate a sequence of HASH joins between the indexes. Each of the indexes are accessed using a range scan or fast full scan, depending on the conditions available in the WHERE clause. This method is extremely efficient when a table has a large number of columns, but you want to access only a limited number of those columns. The more limiting the conditions in the WHERE clause, the faster the execution of the query. The optimizer evaluates this as an option when looking for the optimal path of execution.

You must create indexes on the appropriate columns (those that will satisfy the entire query) to ensure that the optimizer has the INDEX-MERGE join as an available choice. This task usually involves adding indexes on columns that may not be indexed or on columns that were not indexed together previously. The advantage of INDEX-MERGE joins over fast full scans is that fast full scans have a *single* index satisfying the entire query. INDEX-MERGE joins have multiple indexes satisfying the entire query.

Two indexes (one on ENAME and one on DEPTNO) have been created prior to the execution of the corresponding query in this next listing. The query does not need to access the table! Figure 9-4 shows this INDEX-MERGE join in graphical format.

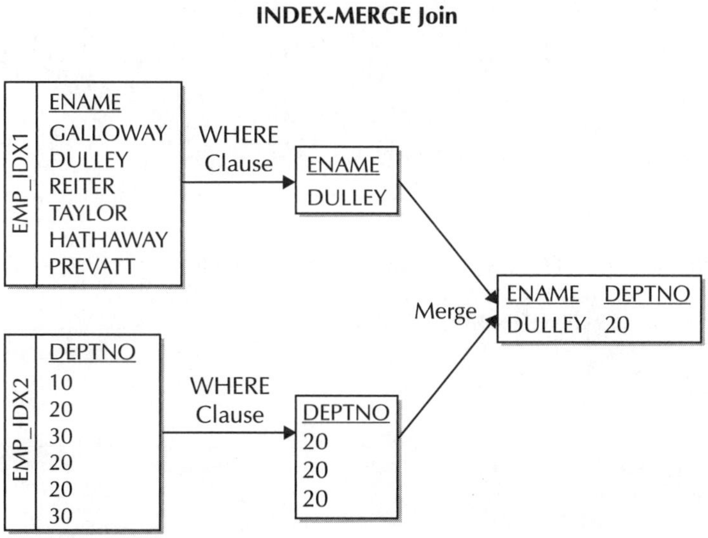

INDEX-MERGE Join

FIGURE 9-4. *An INDEX MERGE join of EMP_IDX1 and EMP_IDX2*

```
select   ENAME, DEPTNO
from     EMP
where    DEPTNO = 20
and      ENAME = 'DULLY';
```

To show the improved efficiency, consider this example that uses the TEST2 table. The TEST2 table has 1 million rows and is 210M in size. First, you create the indexes:

```
create   index doby on test2  ( doby );
create   index state on test2  ( state );
create   index dobmsy on test2  (state, doby );
```

Neither DOBY nor STATE are very limiting when queried individually; consequently, the first indication is to execute a full table scan, as shown in this listing:

```
select   /*+ FULL(test2) */  state, doby
from     test2
where    doby = 1972
and      state = 'MA';


SELECT STATEMENT
TABLE ACCESS (FULL) OF 'TEST2'

Elapse time: 12.6 seconds
```

Using a single index on DOBY is slower than the full table scan:

```
select   /*+ index(test2 doby) */ state, doby
from     test2
where    doby = 1972
and      state = 'MA';

SELECT STATEMENT
TABLE ACCESS (BY INDEX ROWID) OF 'TEST2'
INDEX (RANGE SCAN) OF 'DOBY' (NON-UNIQUE)

Elapsed time: 13:45 seconds
```

Using a single index on STATE is also slower than a full table scan:

```
select   /*+ index(test2 state) */ state, doby
from     test2
where    doby = 1972
and      state = 'MA';


SELECT STATEMENT
TABLE ACCESS (BY INDEX ROWID) OF 'TEST2'
INDEX (RANGE SCAN) OF 'STATE' (NON-UNIQUE)

Elapsed time: 23.50 seconds
```

However, using an INDEX-MERGE join of DOBY and STATE is quicker than a full table scan because the table does not need to be accessed, as in this listing:

```
select  /*+ index_join(test2 doby state) */ state, doby
from    test2
where   doby = 1972
and     state = 'MA';

SELECT STATEMENT
VIEW OF 'index$_join$_001'
HASH JOIN
INDEX (RANGE SCAN) OF 'DOBY' (NON-UNIQUE)
INDEX (RANGE SCAN) OF 'STATE' (NON-UNIQUE)

Elapsed time: 4.76 seconds
```

However, the INDEX_FFS (if a single index on all needed columns exists) is still the most efficient method, as shown here:

```
select  /*+ index_ffs(test2 dobmsy) */ state, doby
from    test2
where   doby = 1972
and     state = 'MA';

SELECT STATEMENT
INDEX (FAST FULL SCAN) OF 'DOBMSY' (NON-UNIQUE)

Elapsed time: 3.6 seconds
```

Although fast full scan is the most efficient option in this case, the INDEX join accommodates more situations. Also, an INDEX_FFS is *often* a problem as it scans through many index blocks and shows up as a severe amount of `'db file sequential read'` waits (so try to tune it by using a better index or having a more selective query so it doesn't need to scan the whole index). Your mileage will vary; this example is only to show how to tune. Which solution is best will be clearer on your unique system after detailed testing.

Table Join Initialization Parameters

Performance of SORT-MERGE joins and HASH joins is strongly impacted by certain initialization parameters. Join performance can be crippled if certain parameters are not set properly.

SORT-MERGE and HASH Join Parameters

The initialization parameter DB_FILE_MULTIBLOCK_READ_COUNT specifies how many blocks Oracle should read at a time from disk when performing a sequential read such as a full table scan. In 11g, my default was 128 (128 * 8192 = 1048576, or 1M; but this is platform dependent and 1M for most platforms), which should be more than sufficient. Because SORT-MERGE joins often involve full table scans, setting this parameter correctly reduces overhead when scanning large tables.

The initialization parameter PGA_AGGREGATE_TARGET (this can be part of the memory allocated with MEMORY_TARGET, if used, as described earlier) specifies how much memory can be used for sorting, which has a strong impact on performance of all sorts. Because SORT-MERGE joins require sorting of both row sources, the amount of memory allocated for sorting can greatly impact SORT-MERGE join performance. If an entire sort cannot be completed in the amount of memory specified, then a temporary segment in the temporary tablespace is allocated. In this case, the sort is performed in memory one part at a time, and partial results are stored on disk in the temporary segment. If memory allocated for sorting is set very small, then excessive disk I/O is required to perform even the smallest of sorts. If it is set too high, then the operating system may run out of physical memory and resort to swapping. The same is true for HASH joins. If the HASH table can't be built because of insufficient memory, a HASH join could be excessively slow using disk I/O instead.

Table 9-1 provides a quick view of the primary join types.

Category	NESTED LOOPS Join	SORT-MERGE Join	HASH Join
Optimizer hint	USE_NL	USE_MERGE	USE_HASH
When you can use it	Any join	Any join	Equijoins only
Resource concerns	CPU, disk I/O	Memory, temporary segments	Memory, temporary segments
Features	Efficient with highly selective indexes and restrictive searches. Used to return the first row of a result quickly.	Better than NESTED LOOPS when an index is missing or the search criteria are not very selective. Can work with limited memory.	Better than NESTED LOOPS when an index is missing or the search criteria are not very selective. It is usually faster than a SORT-MERGE.
Drawbacks	Very inefficient when indexes are missing or if the index criteria are not limiting.	Requires a sort on both tables. It is built for best optimal throughput and does not return the first row until all rows are found.	Can require a large amount of memory for the hash table to be built. Does not return the first rows quickly. Can be extremely slow if it must do the operation on disk.

TABLE 9-1. *Primary Join Methods*

A Two-Table Join: Equal-Sized Tables (Cost-Based)

Consider the following tables (they have been analyzed) that will be used for this example:

```
SMALL1  10000 rows  No Indexes
SMALL2  10000 rows  No Indexes
```

This section of examples is important as you learn more about how the cost-based optimizer works, with all conditions being equal in a join (same size tables/no indexes).

Example 1

Neither table has an index and there aren't any other noteworthy conditions on the tables. Oracle uses a HASH join if the initialization parameters have been set up to allow a HASH join; otherwise, it uses a SORT-MERGE join. In this example, both tables are equal, so the first one in the FROM clause is used and Oracle uses a HASH join:

```
select   small1.col1, small2.col1
from     small1, small2
where    small1.col1 = small2.col1;
```

Join Method: HASH Join (If Hash Initialization Parameters Are Set Up)   The SMALL1 table is accessed first and used to build a hash table. Oracle accesses the SMALL1 table and builds a hash table on the join key (COL1) in memory. It then scans SMALL2 and probes the hash table for matches to SMALL2.

```
---------------------------------------------------------------------------
| Id  | Operation            | Name   | Rows  | Bytes | Cost (%CPU)| Time     |
---------------------------------------------------------------------------
|   0 | SELECT STATEMENT     |        |     1 |     6 |    88  (55)| 00:00:02 |
|   1 |  SORT AGGREGATE      |        |     1 |     6 |            |          |
|*  2 |   HASH JOIN          |        | 6701K |   38M |    88  (55)| 00:00:02 |
|   3 |    TABLE ACCESS FULL | SMALL1 | 10000 | 30000 |    20   (0)| 00:00:01 |
|   4 |    TABLE ACCESS FULL | SMALL2 | 10000 | 30000 |    20   (0)| 00:00:01 |
---------------------------------------------------------------------------
```

Join Method: SORT-MERGE Join (If Hash Initialization Parameters Are Not Set Up)
Although SMALL1 would normally be the driving table (because it is first in the FROM clause and this example uses cost-based optimization), a SORT-MERGE join forces the sorting of each of the tables before they are merged together (because there are no indexes). A full table scan is needed on both tables, and the order in the FROM clause has no impact, but the SMALL1 table is *accessed* first for this operation (an EXPLAIN or AUTOTRACE shows this).

Now change the order of the tables in the FROM clause:

The SMALL2 table is listed first and is also accessed first as the driving table. A HASH join is performed. A full table scan is needed on both tables, and the order in the FROM clause has no impact on the driving table, as shown here:

```
select   small1.col1, small2.col1
from     small2, small1
where    small1.col1 = small2.col1;
```

Join Method: HASH Join (If Hash Initialization Parameters Are Set Up)   The SMALL2 table is accessed first and used to build a hash table. Oracle accesses the SMALL2 table and builds a hash table on the join key (COL1) in memory. It then scans SMALL1 and probes the hash table for matches to SMALL1.

```
-----------------------------------------------------------------------
| Id  | Operation          | Name   | Rows  | Bytes | Cost (%CPU)| Time     |
-----------------------------------------------------------------------
|   0 | SELECT STATEMENT   |        |     1 |     6 |    88  (55)| 00:00:02 |
|   1 |  SORT AGGREGATE    |        |     1 |     6 |            |          |
|*  2 |   HASH JOIN        |        | 6701K |   38M |    88  (55)| 00:00:02 |
|   3 |    TABLE ACCESS FULL| SMALL2 | 10000 | 30000 |    20   (0)| 00:00:01 |
|   4 |    TABLE ACCESS FULL| SMALL1 | 10000 | 30000 |    20   (0)| 00:00:01 |
-----------------------------------------------------------------------
```

Join Method: SORT-MERGE Join (If Hash Initialization Parameters Are Not Set Up)
Although SMALL2 would normally be the driving table (because it is first in the FROM clause and using cost-based optimization), a SORT-MERGE join forces the sorting of each of the tables before they are merged together (because there are no indexes). A full table scan is needed on both tables, and the order in the FROM clause has no impact, but the SMALL2 table is *accessed* first for this operation (an EXPLAIN or AUTOTRACE will show this).

Example I Outcomes

If you have set up the initialization parameters for hashing, Oracle builds a hash table from the join values of the *first* table (accessed first), and then it probes that table for values from the second table. Forcing a USE_MERGE hint *always* causes the first table to be accessed first in my testing regardless of the order in the FROM clause.

Finally, if neither table is analyzed in Example 1, Oracle accesses what it believes to be the smallest table first (very important point here). Before I ran the ANALYZE, it listed SMALL2 as slightly less than 10,000 rows, and it *always* accessed it first regardless of the order in the FROM clause. Once I ran an ANALYZE on both tables, they both were listed at 10,000 rows, and the *first table listed in the FROM clause was always accessed first as the driving table.*

Example 2

Neither table has an index, and you will use the ORDERED hint, as in this listing:

```
select   /*+ ORDERED */ small1.col1, small2.col1
from     small1, small2
where    small1.col1 = small2.col1;
```

Join Method: HASH Join (If Hash Initialization Parameters Are Set Up)   The SMALL1 table is accessed first and used to build a hash table. Oracle accesses the SMALL1 table and builds a hash table on the join key (COL1) in memory. It then scans SMALL2 and probes the hash table for matches to SMALL2.

```
---------------------------------------------------------------------------
| Id  | Operation            | Name   | Rows  | Bytes | Cost (%CPU)| Time     |
---------------------------------------------------------------------------
|   0 | SELECT STATEMENT     |        |     1 |     6 |    88  (55)| 00:00:02 |
|   1 |  SORT AGGREGATE      |        |     1 |     6 |            |          |
|*  2 |   HASH JOIN          |        | 6700K|   38M|    88  (55)| 00:00:02 |
|   3 |    TABLE ACCESS FULL| SMALL1 | 10000 | 30000 |    20   (0)| 00:00:01 |
|   4 |    TABLE ACCESS FULL| SMALL2 | 10000 | 30000 |    20   (0)| 00:00:01 |
---------------------------------------------------------------------------
```

Join Method: SORT-MERGE Join (If Hash Initialization Parameters Are Not Set Up)
Although SMALL1 would normally be the driving table (because it is first in the FROM clause and using cost-based optimization), a SORT-MERGE join forces the sorting of each of the tables before they are merged together (because there are no indexes). A full table scan is needed on both tables, and the order in the FROM clause has no impact, but the SMALL1 table is *accessed* first for this operation (an EXPLAIN or AUTOTRACE will show this).

> *Now change the order of the tables in the FROM clause:*

```
select  /*+ ORDERED */ small1.col1, small2.col1
from    small2, small1
where   small1.col1 = small2.col1;
```

Join Method: HASH Join (If Hash Initialization Parameters Are Set Up)   The SMALL2 table is accessed first and used to build a hash table. Oracle accesses the SMALL2 table and builds a hash table on the join key (COL1) in memory. It then scans SMALL1 and probes the hash table for matches to SMALL1.

```
---------------------------------------------------------------------------
| Id  | Operation            | Name   | Rows  | Bytes | Cost (%CPU)| Time     |
---------------------------------------------------------------------------
|   0 | SELECT STATEMENT     |        |     1 |     6 |    88  (55)| 00:00:02 |
|   1 |  SORT AGGREGATE      |        |     1 |     6 |            |          |
|*  2 |   HASH JOIN          |        | 6700K|   38M|    88  (55)| 00:00:02 |
|   3 |    TABLE ACCESS FULL| SMALL2 | 10000 | 30000 |    20   (0)| 00:00:01 |
|   4 |    TABLE ACCESS FULL| SMALL1 | 10000 | 30000 |    20   (0)| 00:00:01 |
---------------------------------------------------------------------------
```

Join Method: SORT-MERGE Join (If Hash Initialization Parameters Are Not Set Up)
Although SMALL2 would normally be the driving table (because it is first in the FROM clause and using cost-based optimization), a SORT-MERGE join forces the sorting of each of the tables before they are merged together (because there are no indexes). A full table scan is needed on both tables, and the order in the FROM clause has no impact, but the SMALL2 table is *accessed* first for this operation (an EXPLAIN or AUTOTRACE will show this).

Example 2 Outcomes

If hash initialization parameters are set up, Oracle builds a hash table from the join values of the *first* table listed and then probes that hash table for values from the *second* table listed. If hash initialization parameters are not set up, the *first* table in the FROM clause in cost-based optimization *is* accessed first and is the driving table when an ORDERED hint is used; but in a SORT-MERGE join, this has no impact because each table must be sorted and then all tables must be merged together.

TIP
Using cost-based optimization, the first table in the FROM clause is the driving table when the ORDERED hint is used. This overrides the optimizer from choosing the driving table. If a SORT-MERGE join is used, then the order of the tables has no impact because neither will drive the query (although the first listed table is accessed first for the operation and is the driving table). Knowing which table is generally the driving table when using an ORDERED hint in small joins can help you solve larger table join issues and also help you find indexing problems.

TIP
When hash initialization parameters are set up, the optimizer uses HASH joins in lieu of SORT-MERGE joins. With HASH joins, the first table is used to build a hash table (in memory if available), and the second table in the FROM clause then probes for corresponding hash table matches. The first table in the FROM clause (using the ORDERED hint) is the first table accessed in a HASH join.

A Two-Table INDEXED Join: Equal-Sized Tables (Cost-Based)

To get a better understanding of the driving table and how Oracle processes a query, an example where all conditions are equal in both tables is instructive. Although the queries in this section look strange because I am trying to keep all conditions equal, they are helpful in understanding the way joins work. Consider the following tables (they have been analyzed) that will be used for this example:

```
SMALL1   10000 rows   Index on COL1
SMALL2   10000 rows   Index on COL1
```

NOTE
This section of examples is important as you learn how the cost-based optimizer works using indexes. Although the query in this section wouldn't normally be written, it shows how the driving table works with a two-table join, all conditions being equal. In other words, it is only for instructional purposes.

Example 1

Both tables have an index on the COL1 column, as in this example:

```
select   small1.col1, small2.col1
from     small1, small2
where    small1.col1 = small2.col1
and      small1.col1 = 77
and      small2.col1 = 77;
```

Join Method: HASH Join (If Hash Initialization Parameters Are Set Up)   The SMALL1 index (since the SMALL1 table is the first table listed in the FROM clause) is the query's driving statement. The SMALL1 index is accessed first and used to build a hash table. Oracle accesses the SMALL1 index and builds a hash table on the join key (COL1) in memory. It then scans the SMALL2 index and probes the hash table for matches to SMALL2. Also note, switching the order of the predicates in the two AND clauses does *not* change anything.

```
----------------------------------------------------------------------
| Id | Operation         | Name      | Rows  | Bytes | Cost (%CPU)| Time     |
----------------------------------------------------------------------
|  0 | SELECT STATEMENT  |           |    1  |    6  |   5  (20)| 00:00:01 |
|  1 | SORT AGGREGATE    |           |    1  |    6  |          |          |
|* 2 |   HASH JOIN       |           | 29630 |  173K |   5  (20)| 00:00:01 |
|  3 |    INDEX RANGE SCAN|SMALL1 IDX|  667  | 2001  |   2   (0)| 00:00:01 |
|  4 |    INDEX RANGE SCAN|SMALL2 IDX|  667  | 2001  |   2   (0)| 00:00:01 |
----------------------------------------------------------------------
```

Join Method: NESTED LOOPS Join (If Hash Initialization Parameters Are Not Set Up)
The SMALL1 index (since the SMALL1 table is the first table listed in the FROM clause) is the query's driving statement. Oracle retrieves the records from the index on SMALL1 and then takes each record and checks for matches in the SMALL2 index. A NESTED LOOPS join is faster when the source rows from the SMALL1 table are a small set and there is a reasonably selective index on the SMALL2 joining column (brief EXPLAIN PLAN listed here).

```
SELECT STATEMENT
   NESTED LOOPS (Cost=2 Card=3 Bytes=90) (small1 result checks small2 matches)
      INDEX (RANGE SCAN) OF 'SMALL1_IDX'  (This is first/gets first row to check)
      INDEX (RANGE SCAN) OF 'SMALL2_IDX'  (This is second/checks for matches)
```

Now change the order of the tables in the FROM clause:

```
select   small1.col1, small2.col1
from     small2, small1
where    small1.col1 = small2.col1
and      small1.col1 = 77
and      small2.col1 = 77;
```

Join Method: HASH Join (If Hash Initialization Parameters Are Set Up)   The SMALL2 index (since the SMALL2 table is the first table listed in the FROM clause) is the query's driving statement. The SMALL2 index is accessed first and used to build a hash table. Oracle accesses the SMALL2 index and builds a hash table on the join key (COL1) in memory. It then scans the SMALL1 index and probes the hash table for matches to SMALL1. Also note, switching the order of the predicates in the two AND clauses does *not* change anything.

```
---------------------------------------------------------------------------
| Id | Operation            | Name       | Rows  | Bytes | Cost (%CPU)| Time     |
---------------------------------------------------------------------------
|  0 | SELECT STATEMENT     |            |     1 |     6 |    5  (20)| 00:00:01 |
|  1 |  SORT AGGREGATE      |            |     1 |     6 |           |          |
|* 2 |   HASH JOIN          |            | 29630 |  173K |    5  (20)| 00:00:01 |
|  3 |    INDEX RANGE SCAN|SMALL2 IDX|     667 |  2001 |    2   (0)| 00:00:01 |
|  4 |    INDEX RANGE SCAN|SMALL1 IDX|     667 |  2001 |    2   (0)| 00:00:01 |
---------------------------------------------------------------------------
```

Join Method: NESTED LOOPS Join (If Hash Initialization Parameters Are Not Set Up)
The SMALL2 index (since the SMALL2 table is the first table in the FROM clause) is the query's driving statement. Oracle retrieves the records from the index on SMALL2 and then takes each record and checks for matches in the SMALL1 index. A NESTED LOOPS join is faster when the source rows from the SMALL2 table are a small set and there is a reasonably selective index on the SMALL1 joining column (brief EXPLAIN PLAN listed here).

```
SELECT STATEMENT
    NESTED LOOPS (Cost=2 Card=3 Bytes=90)   (small2 result checks small1 matches)
        INDEX (RANGE SCAN) OF 'SMALL2_IDX'  (This is first/gets first row to check)
        INDEX (RANGE SCAN) OF 'SMALL1_IDX'  (This is second/checks for matches)
```

Example 1 Outcomes
All conditions being equal, the index from the first table is accessed first (the *first* table in the FROM clause) in cost-based optimization and is the driving table. The index is used on the join condition for the second table. In Example 1, Oracle uses a HASH join to join the queries, but a NESTED LOOPS join or SORT-MERGE join is also possible, depending on other factors in the table and index.

Example 2
Both tables have an index on the COL1 column, and I use the ORDERED hint, as shown here:

```
select  /*+ ORDERED */ small1.col1, small2.col1
from    small1, small2
where   small1.col1 = small2.col1
and     small1.col1 = 77
and     small2.col1 = 77;
```

Join Method: HASH Join (If Hash Initialization Parameters Are Set Up)   The SMALL1 index (since the SMALL1 table is the first table listed in the FROM clause) is the query's driving statement. The SMALL1 index is accessed first and used to build a hash table. Oracle accesses the SMALL1 index and builds a hash table on the join key (COL1) in memory. It then scans the SMALL2 index and probes the hash table for matches to SMALL2. Also note, switching the order of the predicates in the two AND clauses does *not* change anything.

```
-------------------------------------------------------------------------
| Id  | Operation             | Name        | Rows  | Bytes | Cost (%CPU)| Time     |
-------------------------------------------------------------------------
|  0  | SELECT STATEMENT      |             |    1  |    6  |    5  (20)| 00:00:01 |
|  1  |  SORT AGGREGATE       |             |    1  |    6  |           |          |
|* 2  |   HASH JOIN           |             | 29630 |  173K |    5  (20)| 00:00:01 |
|  3  |    INDEX RANGE SCAN|SMALL1 IDX|   667 |  2001 |    2   (0)| 00:00:01 |
|  4  |    INDEX RANGE SCAN|SMALL2 IDX|   667 |  2001 |    2   (0)| 00:00:01 |
-------------------------------------------------------------------------
```

Join Method: NESTED LOOPS Join (If Hash Initialization Parameters Are Not Set Up)
The SMALL1 index (since the SMALL1 table is the first table listed in the FROM clause) is the
query's driving statement. Oracle retrieves the records from the index on SMALL1 and then takes
each record and checks for matches in the SMALL2 index. A NESTED LOOPS join is faster when
the source rows from the SMALL1 table are a small set and there is a reasonably selective index
on the SMALL2 joining column (brief EXPLAIN PLAN listed next).

```
SELECT STATEMENT
    NESTED LOOPS (Cost=2 Card=3 Bytes=90) (small1 result checks small2 matches)
        INDEX (RANGE SCAN) OF 'SMALL1_IDX'  (This is first/gets first row to check)
        INDEX (RANGE SCAN) OF 'SMALL2_IDX'  (This is second/checks for matches)
```

Now change the order of the tables in the FROM clause:

```
select  /*+ ORDERED */ small1.col1, small2.col1
from    small2, small1
where   small1.col1 = small2.col1
and     small1.col1 = 77
and     small2.col1 = 77;
```

Join Method: HASH Join (If Hash Initialization Parameters Are Set Up)   The SMALL2
index (since the SMALL2 table is the first table listed in the FROM clause) is the query's driving
statement. The SMALL2 index is accessed first and used to build a hash table. Oracle accesses
the SMALL2 index and builds a hash table on the join key (COL1) in memory. It then scans the
SMALL1 index and probes the hash table for matches to SMALL1. Also note, switching the order
of the predicates in the two AND clauses does *not* change anything.

```
-------------------------------------------------------------------------
| Id  | Operation             | Name        | Rows  | Bytes | Cost (%CPU)| Time     |
-------------------------------------------------------------------------
|  0  | SELECT STATEMENT      |             |    1  |    6  |    5  (20)| 00:00:01 |
|  1  |  SORT AGGREGATE       |             |    1  |    6  |           |          |
|* 2  |   HASH JOIN           |             | 29630 |  173K |    5  (20)| 00:00:01 |
|  3  |    INDEX RANGE SCAN|SMALL2 IDX|   667 |  2001 |    2   (0)| 00:00:01 |
|  4  |    INDEX RANGE SCAN|SMALL1 IDX|   667 |  2001 |    2   (0)| 00:00:01 |
-------------------------------------------------------------------------
```

Join Method: NESTED LOOPS Join (If Hash Initialization Parameters Are Not Set Up)
The SMALL2 index (since the SMALL2 table is the first table in the FROM clause) is the query's
driving statement. Oracle retrieves the records from the index on SMALL2 and then takes each

record and checks for matches in the SMALL1 index. A NESTED LOOPS join is faster when the source rows from the SMALL2 table are a small set and there is a reasonably selective index on the SMALL1 joining column (brief EXPLAIN PLAN listed here).

```
SELECT STATEMENT
    NESTED LOOPS (Cost=2 Card=3 Bytes=90)    (small2 result checks small1 matches)
        INDEX (RANGE SCAN) OF 'SMALL2_IDX'   (This is first/gets first row to check)
        INDEX (RANGE SCAN) OF 'SMALL1_IDX'   (This is second/checks for matches)
```

Example 2 Outcomes
All conditions being equal, the index from the first table is accessed first (the *first* table listed in the FROM clause) in cost-based optimization using a HASH or NESTED LOOPS join and is the driving statement with or without the ORDERED hint. Only the ORDERED hint guarantees the order in which all the tables are accessed. The index is used on the join condition for the second table.

> **TIP**
> *Using cost-based optimization and a NESTED LOOPS join as the means of joining, the first table in the FROM clause is the driving table (all other conditions being equal), but only the ORDERED hint guarantees this. In NESTED LOOPS joins, choosing a driving table that is the smaller result set (not always the smaller table) makes fewer loops through the other result set (from the nondriving table) and usually results in the best performance.*

Forcing a Specific Join Method

When choosing an execution plan for a query involving joins, the Oracle optimizer considers all possible join methods and table orders. The optimizer does its best to evaluate the merits of each option and to choose the optimal execution plan, but sometimes the optimizer does not choose the best solution because of poor indexing strategies.

In these situations, you can use the USE_NL, USE_MERGE, and USE_HASH hints to request a specific join method, and you can use the ORDERED hint to request a specific join order for all tables (or use LEADING to use the first table in the FROM clause as the driving table and leave the order of remaining the tables for Oracle to figure out). The optimizer does its best to observe the wishes of these hints, but if you ask for something impossible (such as a SORT-MERGE join on an antijoin), the optimizer ignores the hint.

When tuning SQL that uses joins, you should run benchmark comparisons between different join methods and table execution order. For example, if a report joins two tables that form a master-detail relationship and the proper primary-key and foreign-key indexes are in place, the optimizer will probably choose to use a NESTED LOOPS join. However, if you know that this particular report joins all of the master records to all of the detail records, you might think it's faster to use a SORT-MERGE join or HASH join instead. Run a benchmark to ensure that you have the best solution.

In the following three listings, the first listing shows an example query and its TKPROF output, the second listing shows the same query with a USE_MERGE hint, and the third listing shows it with a USE_HASH hint. In this example, the indexes were built so that a full table scan must be executed on the PURCHASE_ORDER_LINES table. (Using an index would have been the better choice but not as instructive.) You can see that in this situation the HASH join reduced CPU time by almost 40 percent and logical I/Os by about 98 percent. The goal is not to demonstrate how to tune this type of query, but how to use different types of joining.

Forcing a NESTED LOOPS join

```
select       /*+ USE_NL (a b) */
             b.business_unit,b.po_number,b.vendor_type,a.line_number,
             a.line_amount,a.line_status,a.description
from         purchase_order_lines a, purchase_orders b
where        b.business_unit = a.business_unit
and          b.po_number = a.po_number
order by     b.business_unit,b.po_number,a.line_number;
```

```
Rows    Execution Plan
0       SELECT STATEMENT  GOAL: CHOOSE
73369    SORT (ORDER BY)
73369     NESTED LOOPS
73726      TABLE ACCESS  GOAL: ANALYZED (FULL) OF 'PURCHASE_ORDER_LINES'
73369      TABLE ACCESS  GOAL: ANALYZED (BY ROWID) OF 'PURCHASE_ORDERS'
73726       INDEX  GOAL: ANALYZED (UNIQUE SCAN) OF 'PURCHASE_ORDERS_PK' (UNIQUE)
```

The PURCHASE_ORDER_LINES table is the driving table. Each record (one at a time) is taken from the PURCHASE_ORDER_LINES table, and for each one, you loop through for matches in the PURCHASE_ORDERS table. This is slow because the driving table list is large. (PURCHASE_ORDER_LINES has a large number of rows.)

Forcing a SORT-MERGE Join

```
Select       /*+ USE_MERGE (a b) */
             a.business_unit,a.po_number,a.vendor_type,b.line_number,
             b.line_amount,b.line_status,b.description
from         purchase_orders a,purchase_order_lines b
where        b.business_unit = a.business_unit
and          b.po_number = a.po_number
order by     a.business_unit,a.po_number,b.line_number;
```

```
Rows    Execution Plan
0       SELECT STATEMENT  GOAL: CHOOSE
73369    SORT (ORDER BY)
73369    MERGE JOIN
886       SORT (JOIN)
886        TABLE ACCESS  GOAL: ANALYZED (FULL) OF 'PURCHASE_ORDERS'
73726     SORT (JOIN)
73726      TABLE ACCESS  GOAL: ANALYZED (FULL) OF 'PURCHASE_ORDER_LINES'
```

For the SORT-MERGE case, Oracle sorts both tables and then merges the result. This method is still not an efficient way to perform the query.

Forcing a HASH join

```
select      /*+ USE_HASH (a b) */
            a.business_unit,a.po_number,a.vendor_type,b.line_number,
            b.line_amount,b.line_status,b.description
from        purchase_orders a,purchase_order_lines b
where       b.business_unit = a.business_unit
and         b.po_number = a.po_number
order by    a.business_unit,a.po_number,b.line_number;


Rows        Execution Plan
0           SELECT STATEMENT   GOAL: CHOOSE
73369        SORT (ORDER BY)
137807        HASH JOIN
886            TABLE ACCESS   GOAL: ANALYZED (FULL) OF 'PURCHASE_ORDERS'
73726          TABLE ACCESS   GOAL: ANALYZED (FULL) OF  'PURCHASE_ORDER_LINES'
```

The HASH join has proven to be the most efficient because it puts the PURCHASE_ORDERS table into a hash table and then scans to retrieve the corresponding records from PURCHASE_ORDER_LINES. If you cannot get the correct access order, you can use the SWAP_JOIN_INPUTS hint as well.

Oracle chose to do a NESTED LOOPS join 10g and a HASH join in 11g. NESTED LOOPS is not the most efficient way of joining in this case, but if you don't set the memory parameters appropriately, Oracle might choose NESTED LOOPS over a HASH Join. For this query, by using the USE_HASH hint, you can cut CPU time by almost 40 percent and logical I/Os by about 98 percent. Although the CPU reduction is impressive, the reduction in logical I/Os (memory reads) is saving SGA memory for other users. Sometimes when you are retrieving a large amount of data, access using a full table scan is the most efficient method. In 11g, Oracle uses the HASH join method frequently, provided the initialization parameters related to it are set appropriately.

TIP
To change the method that Oracle uses to join multiple tables, use the USE_MERGE, USE_NL, and USE_HASH hints. Multiple tables may need to be specified for the hint to work, and the driving order is usually from first to last in the FROM clause.

Eliminating Join Records (Candidate Rows) in Multitable Joins

Suppose you have a list of 1000 residents of your town along with each resident's street address, and you are asked to prepare an *alphabetized* list of residents who have the newspaper delivered to their home. (Only 50 get the newspaper.) You could first alphabetize the list of 1000 names (all residents in the town) and then look up each street address in the list of 50 residents who get the newspaper. (Sort the 1000 and then find the 50.) A faster method would be to look up each street address of those who get the newspaper first, and then get the names of the residents at that street and do the alphabetization last. (Find the 50 who get the newspaper from the list of 1000 and then sort the 50 matches.) Either way, you need to look at the 1000 street addresses.

However, these lookups will eliminate many names from the list, and the sorting will be faster when you have a list of only 50 to sort.

You can apply the same concept when writing SQL table joins together. The Oracle optimizer is pretty smart about choosing the most efficient order in which to perform tasks, but how a query is written can constrain the options available to the optimizer.

The query in this next listing leaves the optimizer no choice but to read all of Acme's invoice lines (the large table/the intersection table), when, in fact, only the unpaid invoices (the small table) are of interest:

```
select      v.vendor_num, i.invoice_num, sum (l.amount)
from        vendors v, invoices i, invoice_lines l
where       v.vendor_name = 'ACME'
and         l.vendor_num = v.vendor_num
and         i.vendor_num = l.vendor_num
and         i.invoice_num = l.invoice_num
and         i.paid = 'N'
group by    v.vendor_num, i.invoice_num
order by    i.invoice_num;
```

You could rewrite this query, as shown here:

```
select      v.vendor_num, i.invoice_num, sum (l.amount)
from        vendors v, invoices i, invoice_lines l
where       v.vendor_name = 'ACME'
and         i.vendor_num = v.vendor_num
and         i.paid = 'N'
and         l.vendor_num = i.vendor_num
and         l.invoice_num = i.invoice_num
group by    v.vendor_num, i.invoice_num
order by    i.invoice_num;
```

In the rewritten query in this listing, the optimizer eliminates all of the paid invoices (the new intersection table) before joining to the INVOICE_LINES table. If most of the invoices in the database have already been paid, then the rewritten query is significantly faster. (The schema design in this example is dubious and is used only for illustrative purposes.)

TIP
In a three-table join, the driving table is the intersection table or the table that has a join condition to each of the other two tables in the join. Try to use the most limiting table as the driving table (or intersection table) so your result set from the join of the first two tables is small when you join it to the third table.

A Two-Table Join Between a Large and Small Table

Consider the following tables that will be used for this example:

```
PRODUCT   70 thousand rows   Index on PRODUCT_ID
PRODUCT_LINES   4 million rows   Index on PRODUCT_ID
```

This section uses only cost-based optimization. This section of examples is important because it looks at a situation often encountered. It involves a two-table join between a small (business small) table and a large table. The subsequent conditions (beyond the join itself) are on the column that you are joining. At times, the index on this column in the subsequent condition is suppressed. Unfortunately, this situation leads to seven possible situations, based on various conditions. This section covers three of the main situations, and the results are summarized at the end.

Example 1

Neither table can use an index (they are suppressed), and there are no other conditions, as shown in this example:

```
select   product.name, product_lines.qty
from     product, product_lines
where    product.product_id || '' = product_lines.product_id || '';
```

EXPLAIN PLAN Output

```
SELECT STATEMENT
   HASH JOIN
     TABLE ACCESS FULL OF 'PRODUCT'
     TABLE ACCESS FULL OF 'PRODUCT_LINES'
```

The order of the tables in the FROM clause can be reversed, as shown here:

```
select   product.name, product_lines.qty
from     product_lines, product
where    product.product_id || '' = product_lines.product_id || '' ;
```

EXPLAIN PLAN Output

```
SELECT STATEMENT
   HASH JOIN
     TABLE ACCESS FULL OF 'PRODUCT'
     TABLE ACCESS FULL OF 'PRODUCT_LINES'
```

Example 1 Outcome

All conditions being equal, the *first* table in the FROM clause in cost-based optimization is the driving table (first accessed). Because these tables are different sizes, however, Oracle chooses the *smaller table to be the driving table* regardless of the order in the FROM clause. The PRODUCT table is used to build a hash table on the join key (PRODUCT_ID), and then the PRODUCT_LINES table is scanned, probing the hash table for join key matches.

TIP
Using cost-based optimization, when a large table and a small table are joined, the smaller table is the driving table (accessed first), and the smaller table is used to build a hash table in memory on the join key. The larger table is scanned and then probes the hash table for matches to the join key. Also note that if there is not enough memory for the hash, the operation can become extremely slow because the hash table may be split into multiple partitions that could be paged to disk. If the ORDERED hint is specified, then the first table in the FROM clause is the driving table, and it will be the one used to build the hash table.

Example 2
A subsequent clause allows the large table to use the PRODUCT_ID index:

```
select    product.name, product_lines.qty
from      product, product_lines
where     product.product_id = product_lines.product_id
and       product_lines.product_id = 4488;
```

EXPLAIN PLAN Output

```
SELECT STATEMENT
   MERGE JOIN
      TABLE ACCESS BY INDEX ROWID PRODUCT
        INDEX RANGE SCAN PRODUCT_ID1
      BUFFER SORT
        TABLE ACCESS BY INDEX ROWID PRODUCT_LINES
           INDEX RANGE SCAN PRODUCT1
```

The order of the tables in the FROM clause can be reversed, as shown here:

```
select    product.name, product_lines.qty
from      product_lines, product
where     product.product_id = product_lines.product_id
and       product_lines.product_id = 4488;
```

EXPLAIN PLAN Output

```
SELECT STATEMENT
   MERGE JOIN
      TABLE ACCESS BY INDEX ROWID PRODUCT
        INDEX RANGE SCAN PRODUCT_ID1
      BUFFER SORT
        TABLE ACCESS BY INDEX ROWID PRODUCT_LINES
           INDEX RANGE SCAN PRODUCT1
```

Example 2 Outcomes

When a subsequent condition on PRODUCT_ID on the large table exists, the larger table is always the driving table regardless of the order in the FROM clause. The order of the tables in the FROM clause does not alter the order in which Oracle performs this join unless an ORDERED hint is used. In Example 2, a SORT-MERGE join is executed. For this example, a HASH join is also possible.

TIP
Using cost-based optimization, when a large and small table are joined, the larger table is the driving table if an index can be used on the large table. If the ORDERED hint is specified, then the first table in the FROM clause is the driving table.

Example 3

A subsequent clause, shown in the following listing, allows the small table to use the PRODUCT_ID index. The large table still drives the query after getting this condition (on PRODUCT_ID) passed to it by the join. Oracle is smart enough to figure out that PRODUCT_ID exists in both tables and it is more efficient to limit the PRODUCT_LINES table. In the upcoming section "Three-Table Joins: Not as Much Fun," Oracle's excellent internal processing to improve queries will become more evident.

```
select   product.name, product_lines.qty
from     product, product_lines
where    product.product_id = product_lines.product_id
and      product.product_id = 4488;
```

EXPLAIN PLAN Output

```
SELECT STATEMENT
   MERGE JOIN
      TABLE ACCESS BY INDEX ROWID PRODUCT
        INDEX RANGE SCAN PRODUCT_ID1
        BUFFER SORT
        TABLE ACCESS BY INDEX ROWID PRODUCT_LINES
           INDEX RANGE SCAN PRODUCT1
```

The order of the tables in the FROM clause can be reversed, as shown here:

```
select   product.name, product_lines.qty
from     product_lines, product
where    product.product_id = product_lines.product_id
and      product.product_id = 4488;
```

EXPLAIN PLAN Output

```
SELECT STATEMENT
   MERGE JOIN
      TABLE ACCESS BY INDEX ROWID PRODUCT
```

```
    INDEX RANGE SCAN PRODUCT_ID1
  BUFFER SORT
 TABLE ACCESS BY INDEX ROWID PRODUCT_LINES
  INDEX RANGE SCAN PRODUCT1
```

Example 3 Outcomes

When a subsequent condition on PRODUCT_ID on the small table exists, the larger table gets this condition passed to it via the join and is *still* the driving table. The order of the tables in the FROM clause does not alter the procedure unless an ORDERED hint is used. For this example, a HASH join is also possible.

Summary

The examples in this section demonstrate the value of some of the optimizer's behavior. The optimizer almost always chooses how to drive a query correctly, but sometimes it must be corrected for a given query. It chooses the right path in most situations.

Three-Table Joins: Not as Much Fun

In a three-table join, Oracle joins two of the tables and joins the result with the third table.

When the query in the following listing is executed, the EMP, DEPT, and ORDERS tables are joined together, as illustrated in Figure 9-5.

```
select   /*+ ORDERED */ ENAME, DEPT.DEPTNO, ITEMNO
from     EMP, DEPT, ORDERS
where    emp.deptno = dept.deptno
and      emp.empno = orders.empno;
```

Which table is the driving table in a query? People often give different answers, depending on the query that accesses the PLAN_TABLE. This query would drive with the EMP table accessed first, the DEPT table accessed second, and the ORDERS table accessed third (there are always exceptions to the rule).

Three-Table Join

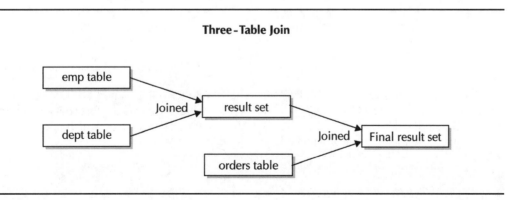

FIGURE 9-5. *A three-table join*

This next listing shows a query that has only one possible way to be accessed (the subqueries must be accessed first) and a query to the PLAN_TABLE that will be used for the remainder of this chapter. This listing is provided to ensure that you understand how to read the output effectively.

```
explain plan for
  select      cust_last_name, cust_first_name
  from        customers
  where       customer_id =
    (select   customer_id
     from     order_lines
     where    quantity = 1
     and      product_id =
       (select  p.product_id
        from      product_information p
        where     p.product_id = 807
        and       product_description = 'test'));
```

The following listing is a quick and simple EXPLAIN PLAN query (given the PLAN_TABLE is empty). Throughout this chapter, I show many of these, but I also show the output using Autotrace (SET AUTOTRACE ON) and timing (SET TIMING ON).

```
select      lpad(' ',2*level)||operation oper, options, object_name
from        plan_table
connect     by prior id = parent_id
start       with id = 1
order by    id;
```

EXPLAIN PLAN Output

Next, you can see abbreviated EXPLAIN PLAN output. (Additional EXPLAIN PLAN information can be found in Chapter 6.)

```
OPER                      OPTIONS                 OBJECT_NAME
------------------        --------------------    --------------
TABLE ACCESS              BY INDEX ROWID          CUSTOMERS
  INDEX                   RANGE SCAN              CUSTOMERS_IDX1
    TABLE ACCESS          BY INDEX ROWID          ORDER_LINES
      INDEX               RANGE SCAN              ORDER_LINES_IDX1
        TABLE ACCESS      BY INDEX ROWID          PRODUCT_INFORMATION
          INDEX           RANGE SCAN              PRODUCT_INFORMATION_IDX1
```

The order of access is PRODUCT_INFORMATION, ORDER_LINES, and CUSTOMERS. The innermost subquery (to the PRODUCT_INFORMATION table) must execute first so it can return the PRODUCT_ID to be used in the ORDER_LINES table (accessed second), which returns the CUSTOMER_ID that the CUSTOMERS table (accessed third) needs.

TIP
To ensure that you are reading your EXPLAIN PLAN correctly, run a query in which you are sure of the driving table (with nested subqueries).

One exception to the previous subquery is shown here:

```
explain plan for
select      cust_last_name, cust_first_name
 from       customers
 where      customer_id =
   (select  customer_id
    from     order_lines o
    where    o.product_id = 807
    and      quantity = 1
    and      o.product_id =
     (select  p.product_id
      from     product_information p
      where    p.product_id = 807
      and      product_description = 'test'));
```

EXPLAIN PLAN Output

OPER	OPTIONS	OBJECT_NAME
TABLE ACCESS	BY INDEX ROWID	CUSTOMERS
INDEX	RANGE SCAN	CUSTOMERS_IDX1
FILTER		
TABLE ACCESS	BY INDEX ROWID	ORDER_LINES
INDEX	RANGE SCAN	ORDER_LINES_IDX1
TABLE ACCESS	BY INDEX ROWID	PRODUCT_INFORMATION
INDEX	RANGE SCAN	PRODUCT_INFORMATION_IDX1

The expected order of table access is based on the order in the FROM clause: PRODUCT_INFORMATION, ORDER_LINES, and CUSTOMERS. The actual order of access is ORDER_LINES, PRODUCT_INFORMATION, and CUSTOMERS. The ORDER_LINES query takes the PRODUCT_ID from the subquery to the PRODUCT_INFORMATION table and executes first (Oracle is very efficient).

Bitmap Join Indexes

Oracle changes the boundaries of relational database design and implementation with the addition of new indexing features. The bitmap join index allows you to build a single index across the joined columns of two tables. The ROWIDs from one table are stored along with the matching values from the other table. This feature is an incredible performance gold mine, as was the case of the function-based index, and it is as powerful as the designer, developer, or DBA who implements it. This section focuses on the bitmap join index.

Bitmap Indexes

To fully appreciate where a bitmap join index is helpful, it is important to understand a bitmap index. Bitmap indexes are most helpful in a data warehouse environment because they are generally great (fast) when you are only selecting data. A bitmap index is smaller than a b-tree index because it stores only the ROWID and a series of bits. In a bitmap index, if a bit is set, it means that a row in the corresponding ROWID (also stored) contains a key value. For example, consider the EMP table with two new columns: gender and marital status:

EMPNO	GENDER (M/F)	Married (Y/N)
1001	F	Y
1002	F	Y
1003	F	N
1004	M	N
1005	M	Y

The bitmaps stored may be the following (the actual storage depends on the algorithm used internally, which is more complex than this example):

EMPNO=	GENDER=F	Married = Y
1001	1	1
1002	1	1
1003	1	0
1004	0	0
1005	0	1

As you can tell from the preceding example, finding all of the females by searching for the gender bit set to a '1' in the example would be easy. You can similarly find all of those who are married or even quickly find a combination of gender and marital status. Oracle stores ranges of rows for each bitmap as well, which is why bitmaps don't do well when you update the bitmap-indexed column (as you can lock an entire range of rows).

You should use b-tree indexes when columns are unique or near-unique; you should at least consider bitmap indexes in all other cases. Although you generally would *not* use a b-tree index when retrieving 40 percent of the rows in a table, using a bitmap index generally makes this task faster than doing a full table scan. Using an index in this situation is seemingly in violation of the 80/20 or 95/5 rules, which are generally to use an index when retrieving 5–20 percent or less of the data and to do a full table scan when retrieving more. Bitmap indexes are smaller and work differently than b-tree indexes, however. You can use bitmap indexes even when retrieving large percentages (20–80 percent) of a table. You can also use bitmaps to retrieve conditions based on NULLs (because NULLs are also indexed), and can be used for not-equal conditions for the same reason. The best way to find out is to test!

Bitmap Index Caveats
Bitmap indexes do not perform well in a heavy DML (UPDATE, INSERT, DELETE) environment and generally are not used in certain areas of an OLTP environment. There is a heavy cost if you are doing a lot of DML, so be very careful with this. Applying NOT NULL constraints and

fixed-length columns allows bitmaps to use less storage, so a good designer is once again worth his or her weight in gold. Use the INDEX_COMBINE hint instead of the INDEX or AND_EQUAL hints for bitmap indexes. Like b-tree indexes, bitmap indexes should be rebuilt (ALTER INDEX . . . REBUILD) if there is a lot of DML (UPDATE, INSERT, DELETE) activity. Bitmaps are very good for multicolumn read-only indexes that together make a reasonably selective value but separately do not. These columns when indexed together, if often used together in a WHERE clause, are a good choice for a bitmap.

Bitmap Join Index

In a typical business relational database, you are often joining the same two or three tables over and over. The bitmap join index can give you substantial gains when properly applied to many of these circumstances. In a bitmap join index, the ROWIDs from one table are stored along with the indexed column from the joined table. The bitmap join index in Oracle is a lot like building a single index across two tables. You must build a primary key or unique constraint on one of the tables. When you are looking for information from just the columns in the index or a count, then you will be able to access the single join index. Let's look at a very simple example to learn how to use it. Then I'll show you how to apply it to multiple columns and multiple tables.

Example I

Let's create two sample tables from our friendly EMP and DEPT tables, as shown in this listing:

```
create table emp1
as select * from scott.emp;

create table dept1
as select * from scott.dept;
```

You must then add a unique constraint (or have a primary key) to the DEPT1 table to use this type of index. You can then create the bitmap index on the EMP1 table that includes the columns of both tables.

```
alter table dept1
add constraint dept_constr1 unique (deptno);
Table altered.

create bitmap index empdept_idx
on emp1(dept1.deptno)
from emp1, dept1
where emp1.deptno = dept1.deptno;
Index created.
```

You are now storing the ROWID to the DEPT1 table in the bitmap index that maps to the DEPTNO column in the EMP1 table. To test how well this works, you can perform a simple count (*) of the intersection rows between the two tables (you would generally have additional limiting conditions), forcing the use of the bitmap index with an INDEX hint.

```
select /*+ index(emp1 empdept_idx) */ count(*)
from    emp1, dept1
where   emp1.deptno = dept1.deptno;
```

```
COUNT(*)
--------------
14

Elapsed: 00:00:00.01

Execution Plan (Explain plan)

------------------------------------------------------------
   0   SELECT STATEMENT
   1  0    SORT (AGGREGATE)
   2  1      BITMAP CONVERSION (COUNT)
   3  2        BITMAP INDEX (FULL SCAN) OF 'EMPDEPT_IDX'
```

You can see from the EXPLAIN PLAN output that the bitmap index was used (or you could use SET AUTOTRACE ON while in SQL*Plus; see below).

Execution Plan (Autotrace)
```
------------------------------------------------------------
Plan hash value: 1300569923
-------------------------------------------------------------------------------
| Id  | Operation                    | Name        |Rows|Bytes|Cost (%CPU|Time     |
-------------------------------------------------------------------------------
|  0  | SELECT STATEMENT             |             | 1  |  3  |  1   (0)|00:00:01|
|  1  |  SORT AGGREGATE              |             | 1  |  3  |         |         |
|  2  |   BITMAP CONVERSION COUNT    |             | 15 | 45  |  1   (0)|00:00:01|
|  3  |    BITMAP INDEX FULL SCAN    |EMPDEPT_IDX  |    |     |         |         |
-------------------------------------------------------------------------------
```

Although this simplistic example shows how to count an index (instead of the table) and applies some benefits of the bitmap join index, the next section explores better uses of the bitmap join index by manipulating columns outside the join in the index.

Best Uses for the Bitmap Join Index

Example 1 shows a basic use of the bitmap join index, focusing on just the joined columns. The next three sections show targeted areas where you may discover better uses for bitmap join indexes.

Bitmap Join Indexes on Columns Other Than the Join

Consider this example where the EMP1 and DEPT1 tables are once again joined on the DEPTNO column. In this example, you want to index the LOC column instead of the join column. This allows you to select the location column from the DEPT1 table by directly accessing only the index and the EMP1 table. Remember, the join condition must be on the primary key or unique column. The example in the following listing assumes that the unique constraint on DEPT1.DEPTNO from the example in the earlier listing (where I added a unique constraint to the DEPT1 table) exists.

```
Create bitmap index emp_dept_location
on      emp1 (dept1.loc)
from    emp1, dept1
where   emp1.deptno = dept1.deptno;
```

The query shown next can now use the bitmap join index appropriately:

```
select  emp1.empno, emp1.ename, dept1.loc
from    emp1, dept1
where   emp1.deptno = dept1.deptno;
```

Bitmap Join Indexes on Multiple Columns

Consider an example where you want an index on multiple columns. The syntax is still the same, but now you include multiple columns in the index. The next example assumes that the unique constraint on DEPT1.DEPTNO from the example in the earlier listing (where I added a unique constraint to the DEPT1 table) exists.

```
create bitmap index emp_dept_location_deptname
on      emp1 (dept1.loc, dept1.dname)
from    emp1, dept1
where   emp1.deptno = dept1.deptno;
```

The query in the following listing is able to use the bitmap join index appropriately:

```
select  emp1.empno, emp1.ename, dept1.loc, dept1.dname
from    emp1, dept1
where   emp1.deptno = dept1.deptno;
```

Bitmap Join Indexes on Multiple Tables

As you become more familiar with using the bitmap join index, you will be able to solve complex business problems that involve multiple tables. The following example shows how to apply the bitmap join index to multiple tables. The syntax is still the same, but it has now been expanded to include multiple columns in the index and multiple tables being joined for the index. The example shown next assumes that the unique constraint on DEPT1.DEPTNO from the example in the earlier listing (where I added a unique constraint to the DEPT1 table) exists and, additionally, that it exists on SALES1.EMPNO (creation not shown).

```
Create bitmap index emp_dept_location_ms
on      emp1 (dept1.loc, sales1.marital_status)
from    emp1, dept1, sales1
where   emp1.deptno = dept1.deptno
and     emp1.empno = sales1.empno;
```

The query in this next listing is now able to use the bitmap join index appropriately:

```
select  emp1.empno, emp1.ename, dept1.loc, sales1.marital_status
from    emp1, dept1, sales1
where   emp1.deptno = dept1.deptno
and     emp1.empno = sales1.empno;
```

Bitmap Join Index Caveats

Because the result of the join is stored, only one table can be updated concurrently by different transactions, and parallel DML is supported only on the fact table. Parallel DML on the dimension table marks the index as unusable. No table can appear twice in the join, and you can't create a bitmap join index on an index-organized table (IOT) or a temporary table.

Another Nice Use for the Bitmap Join Index

A nice tuning trick when you are counting rows is to try to count the index instead of the table. Consider the following large table example used for counting. These tables each contain roughly two million rows, so that you can see the possible impact on a larger scale. The new tables, EMP5 and EMP6, each have 2 million rows with EMPNO indexes on them.

To add the constraint and run a join without the bitmap index:

```
alter table emp5
add constraint emp5_constr unique (empno);

select count(*)
from emp5, emp6
where emp5.empno=emp6.empno;

COUNT(*)

------------------
2005007
Elapsed: 00:01:07.18

Execution Plan
-----------------------------------------------------------
   0    SELECT STATEMENT
   1  0    SORT (AGGREGATE)
   2  1      NESTED LOOPS
   3  2        TABLE ACCESS (FULL) OF 'EMP6'
   4  2        INDEX (RANGE SCAN) OF 'EMP5I_EMPNO' (NON-UNIQUE)

Statistics
-----------------------------------------------------------
6026820  consistent gets
7760  physical reads
```

There is an index on the EMP5 table, but there is no correlation or index back to the EMP6 table because the index on EMP6 contains only EMPNO as the second part of a concatenated index. The result is a relatively slow query.

If you make EMPNO the only part or the leading part of the concatenated index, you solve this problem. Use the new bitmap join index, as shown here:

```
create bitmap index emp5_j6
on emp6(emp5.empno)
from emp5,emp6
where emp5.empno=emp6.empno;

Index created.

Elapsed: 00:02:29.91

select /*+ index(emp6 emp5_j6) */ count(*)
```

```
from emp5, emp6
where emp5.empno=emp6.empno;

COUNT(*)
-------------------
2005007


Elapsed: 00:00:00.87

Execution Plan
-----------------------------------------------------------
0   SELECT STATEMENT
1   0    SORT (AGGREGATE)
2   1    BITMAP CONVERSION (COUNT)
3   2    BITMAP INDEX (FULL SCAN) OF 'EMP5_J6'

Statistics
-----------------------------------------------------------
970   consistent gets
967   physical reads
```

Performing a count of the bitmap join index makes this very fast. I chose this example for a reason. The real problem with the original slow query was not that it took a minute to execute, but that it performed over 6 million memory block reads and over 7000 disk block reads. You may not receive any wait events, but you have a poorly written query that will cause problems when you have volumes of users on the system. Take a step up to expert level by finding queries with large memory and disk reads and start doing proactive tuning now so you don't get to wait states and need to tune things reactively. Using a bitmap join index is one way to improve performance.

Third-Party Product Tuning

Sometimes, you are at the mercy of a third-party product. Although you cannot modify the code, you can often modify the use of indexes. The following three examples are from a financial third-party product.

Example I

This query took 22 minutes to run. By providing a hint (using SQL Plan Management) to use a more efficient index, I reduced the query execution time to 15 seconds.

This next listing shows the query before the hint was added:

```
update PS_COMBO_DATA_TBL
set      EFFDT_FROM = TO_DATE ('1990-01-01', 'YYYY-MM-DD'),
         EFFDT_TO = TO_DATE ('2099-01-01', 'YYYY-MM-DD')
where    SETID = 'RRD'
and      PROCESS_GROUP = 'GROUP1'
and      COMBINATION = 'ACCT/NOLOC'
and      VALID_CODE = 'V'
```

```
and     EFFDT_OPEN = 'Y'
and     EXISTS
 (select  'X'
  from      PS_JRNL_LN
  where     BUSINESS_UNIT = '00003'
  and       PROCESS_INSTANCE = 0000085176
  and       JRNL_LINE_STATUS = '3'
  and       ACCOUNT = PS_COMBO_DATA_TBL.ACCOUNT
  and       PRODUCT = PS_COMBO_DATA_TBL.PRODUCT );
```

Now, here's the query after the index hint was added:

```
update  PS_COMBO_DATA_TBL
set     EFFDT_FROM = TO_DATE ('1990-01-01', 'YYYY-MM-DD'),
        EFFDT_TO = TO_DATE ('2099-01-01', 'YYYY-MM-DD')
where   SETID = 'RRD'
and     PROCESS_GROUP = 'GROUP1'
and     COMBINATION = 'ACCT/NOLOC'
and     VALID_CODE = 'V'
and     EFFDT_OPEN = 'Y'
and     EXISTS
 (select  /*+ INDEX(PS_JRNL_LN PSGJRNL_LN) */ 'X'
  from      PS_JRNL_LN
  where     BUSINESS_UNIT = '00003'
  and       PROCESS_INSTANCE = 0000085176
  and       JRNL_LINE_STATUS = '3'
  and       ACCOUNT = PS_COMBO_DATA_TBL.ACCOUNT
  and       PRODUCT = PS_COMBO_DATA_TBL.PRODUCT );
```

Example 2

The query in the next listing was taking 33 minutes to run. By creating a concatenated index on the PS_GROUP_CONTROL table (columns: DEPOSIT_BU, DEPOSIT_ID, PAYMENT_SEQ_ NUM), I reduced the query execution time to 30 seconds, as shown here:

```
select   C.BUSINESS_UNIT, C.CUST_ID, C.ITEM,
         C.ENTRY_TYPE, C.ENTRY_REASON, C.ENTRY_AMT,
         C.ENTRY_CURRENCY, C.ENTRY_AMT_BASE,
         C.CURRENCY_CD, C.POSTED_FLAG, D.PAYMENT_SEQ_NUM
from     PS_PENDING_ITEM C,
         PS_GROUP_CONTROL D
where    D.DEPOSIT_BU = :1
and      D.DEPOSIT_ID = :2
and      D.PAYMENT_SEQ_NUM = :3
and      D.GROUP_BU = C.GROUP_BU
and      D.GROUP_ID = C.GROUP_ID
order by D.PAYMENT_SEQ_NUM;
```

Here is the EXPLAIN PLAN before the index was added:

Execution Plan
```
    SELECT STATEMENT
      SORT ORDER BY
        NESTED LOOPS
          ANALYZED TABLE ACCESS FULL PS_GROUP_CONTROL
            ANALYZED TABLE ACCESS BY ROWID PS_PENDING_ITEM
              ANALYZED INDEX RANGE SCAN PS_PENDING_ITEM
```

And here's the EXPLAIN PLAN after the index was added:

Execution Plan
```
SELECT STATEMENT
    SORT ORDER BY
      NESTED LOOPS
        ANALYZED TABLE ACCESS BY ROWID PS_GROUP_CONTROL
          INDEX RANGE SCAN PSAGROUP_CONTROL
            ANALYZED TABLE ACCESS BY ROWID PS_PENDING_ITEM
              ANALYZED INDEX RANGE SCAN PS_PENDING_ITEM
```

Example 3

The query shown next was taking 20 minutes to run and was reduced to 30 seconds. To achieve this, I created a concatenated unique index on the PS_CUST_OPTION table (columns: CUST_ID, EFFDT) instead of the current index, which is only on CUST_ID. This forces Oracle to use a concatenated unique index rather than a single-column index, as shown here:

```
INSERT INTO PS_PP_CUST_TMP  (PROCESS_INSTANCE,
  DEPOSIT_BU, DEPOSIT_ID, PAYMENT_SEQ_NUM, CUST_ID,
  PAYMENT_AMT, PAYMENT_DT, PP_METHOD, SETID,
  SUBCUST_QUAL1, SUBCUST_QUAL2, PP_HOLD, PP_MET_SW,
  PAYMENT_CURRENCY)
select    DISTINCT P.PROCESS_INSTANCE, P.DEPOSIT_BU,
          P.DEPOSIT_ID, P.PAYMENT_SEQ_NUM, C.CUST_ID,
          P.PAYMENT_AMT, P.PAYMENT_DT, O.PP_METHOD,
          O.SETID, C.SUBCUST_QUAL1, C.SUBCUST_QUAL2,
          O.PP_HOLD, 'N', P.PAYMENT_CURRENCY
from      PS_CUST_OPTION O, PS_CUSTOMER C, PS_ITEM I,
          PS_SET_CNTRL_REC S, PS_PAYMENT_ID_ITEM X,
          PS_PP_PAYMENT_TMP P
where     P.PROCESS_INSTANCE = 85298
and       S.SETCNTRLVALUE = I.BUSINESS_UNIT
and       I.CUST_ID = C.CUST_ID
and       I.ITEM_STATUS = 'O'
and       (X.REF_VALUE = I.DOCUMENT
or        SUBSTR (X.REF_VALUE, 3, 7)
          = SUBSTR (I.DOCUMENT, 4, 7))
and       S.RECNAME = 'CUSTOMER'
and       S.SETID = C.SETID
```

```
and       O.SETID = C.REMIT_FROM_SETID
and       O.CUST_ID = C.REMIT_FROM_CUST_ID
and       O.EFFDT =
      (select  MAX (X.EFFDT)
      from  PS_CUST_OPTION X
      where  X.SETID = O.SETID
      and  X.CUST_ID = O.CUST_ID
      and  X.EFF_STATUS = 'A'
      and  X.EFFDT <= P.PAYMENT_DT)
and       O.PP_METHOD <> ' '
and       P.DEPOSIT_BU = X.DEPOSIT_BU
and       P.DEPOSIT_ID = X.DEPOSIT_ID
and       P.PAYMENT_SEQ_NUM = X.PAYMENT_SEQ_NUM
and       X.REF_QUALIFIER_CODE = 'D';
```

Here's the EXPLAIN PLAN before the index was added:

```
Execution Plan
     INSERT STATEMENT
       SORT UNIQUE
         NESTED LOOPS
           NESTED LOOPS
             NESTED LOOPS
               NESTED LOOPS
                 NESTED LOOPS
                   ANALYZED TABLE ACCESS BY ROWID PS_PP_PAYMENT_TMP
                    ANALYZED INDEX RANGE SCAN PSAPP_PAYMENT_TMP
                    ANALYZED INDEX RANGE SCAN PSAPAYMENT_ID_ITEM
                     ANALYZED INDEX RANGE SCAN PSDSET_CNTRL_REC
                  ANALYZED INDEX RANGE SCAN PSEITEM
                 ANALYZED TABLE ACCESS BY ROWID PS_CUSTOMER
                 ANALYZED INDEX UNIQUE SCAN PS_CUSTOMER
               ANALYZED TABLE ACCESS BY ROWID PS_CUST_OPTION
              ANALYZED INDEX RANGE SCAN PSACUST_OPTION
  SORT AGGREGATE
           ANALYZED TABLE ACCESS BY ROWID PS_CUST_OPTION
           ANALYZED INDEX RANGE SCAN PSACUST_OPTION
```

Here's the EXPLAIN PLAN after the index was added:

```
Execution Plan
     INSERT STATEMENT
       SORT UNIQUE
         NESTED LOOPS
           NESTED LOOPS
             NESTED LOOPS
               NESTED LOOPS
                 NESTED LOOPS
                    ANALYZED TABLE ACCESS BY ROWID PS_PP_PAYMENT_TMP
                     ANALYZED INDEX RANGE SCAN PSAPP_PAYMENT_TMP
                    ANALYZED INDEX RANGE SCAN PSAPAYMENT_ID_ITEM
                   ANALYZED INDEX RANGE SCAN PSDSET_CNTRL_REC
```

```
            ANALYZED INDEX RANGE SCAN PSEITEM
        ANALYZED TABLE ACCESS BY ROWID PS_CUSTOMER
          ANALYZED INDEX UNIQUE SCAN PS_CUSTOMER
        ANALYZED TABLE ACCESS BY ROWID PS_CUST_OPTION
          ANALYZED INDEX RANGE SCAN PS_CUST_OPTION
      SORT AGGREGATE
        ANALYZED TABLE ACCESS BY ROWID PS_CUST_OPTION
          ANALYZED INDEX RANGE SCAN PS_CUST_OPTION
```

TIP
*You may not be able to modify actual code for some third-party
products, but you can often add, force, or suppress indexes (using
SQL Plan Management) to improve performance.*

Tuning Distributed Queries

When improperly written, distributed queries can sometimes be disastrous and lead to poor
performance. In particular, a NESTED LOOPS join between two row sources on separate nodes
of a distributed database can be very slow because Oracle moves all the data to the local machine
(depending on how the query is written). The following listing shows a simple distributed query
and its execution plan. This query is slow because, for each row retrieved from the CUSTOMERS
table, a separate query is dispatched to the remote node to retrieve records from the BOOKINGS
table. This results in many small network packets moving between the two database nodes, and the
network latency and overhead degrade performance.

```
select    customer_id, customer_name, class_code
from      customers cust
where     exists
(select   1
from      bookings@book bkg
where     bkg.customer_id = cust.customer_id
and       bkg.status = 'OPEN' )
order by  customer_name;
```

TKPROF output (note that TKPROF still works in 11g and is located in $ORACLE_HOME/bin):

Call	count	cpu	elapsed	disk	query	current	rows
Parse	1	0.00	0.01	0	0	0	0
Execute	1	0.00	0.00	0	0	0	0
Fetch	156	0.41	11.85	0	476	2	155
total	158	0.41	11.86	0	476	2	155

```
Rows   Execution Plan
0      SELECT STATEMENT   GOAL: CHOOSE
155      SORT (ORDER BY)
467        FILTER
467          TABLE ACCESS  GOAL: ANALYZED (FULL) OF 'CUSTOMERS'
0              REMOTE [BOOK.WORLD]
                 SELECT "CUSTOMER_ID","STATUS" FROM "BOOKINGS" BKG WHERE
                    "STATUS"='open' AND "CUSTOMER_ID"=:1
```

The query in the preceding listing can be rewritten in a form that causes less network traffic. In the next listing, one query is sent to the remote node to determine all customers with open bookings. The output is the same, but performance is greatly improved. Both versions of the query use roughly the same CPU time and logical I/Os on the local node, but the elapsed time is about 97 percent better here. This gain is attributable to reduced network overhead.

```
select     customer_id, customer_name, class_code
from       customers
where      customer_id in
(select    customer_id
from       bookings@book
where      status = 'OPEN' )
order by   customer_name;
```

TKPROF output:

Call	count	cpu	elapsed	disk	query	current	rows
Parse	1	0.00	0.01	0	0	0	0
Execute	1	0.00	0.00	0	0	0	0
Fetch	156	0.07	0.27	0	467	0	155
total	158	0.07	0.28	0	467	0	155

```
Rows   Execution Plan
0      SELECT STATEMENT   GOAL: CHOOSE
155      SORT (ORDER BY)
155        NESTED LOOPS
156          VIEW
1000           SORT (UNIQUE)
1000             REMOTE [BOOK.WORLD]
                   SELECT "CUSTOMER_ID","STATUS" FROM "BOOKINGS" BOOKINGS WHERE
                     "STATUS"='open'
155            TABLE ACCESS   GOAL: ANALYZED (BY ROWID) OF 'CUSTOMERS'
156            INDEX   GOAL: ANALYZED (UNIQUE SCAN) OF 'SYS_C002109'
                 (UNIQUE)
```

When distributed queries cannot be avoided, use IN clauses, set operators such as UNION and MINUS, and use everything else you can to reduce the network traffic between nodes of the database. Views that limit the records in a table can also improve performance by reducing what is sent from the remote client to the local client.

TIP
When distributed queries cannot be avoided, use IN clauses, set operators such as UNION and MINUS, and use everything else you can to reduce the network traffic between database nodes. Queries written in a manner that causes looping between distributed nodes (distributed databases) can be extremely slow.

When You Have Everything Tuned

If you have successfully tuned all of *your* queries, then you can start working on those that go to the data dictionary views. Is it possible to get tuning tips or techniques from looking at data dictionary queries and how they are structured? The answer is yes! You can see them in the SQL_TRACE output. The next example shows that even Oracle's own views have some highly complex joining schemes (note that this process has one less step than 10*g* required, and it still takes a fraction of a second and only 37 memory reads).

```
select   *
from     dba_ind_columns
where    table_name = 'PRODUCT_LINES';
```

Execution plan output:

```
| Id   | Operation                       | Name      |
--------------------------------------------------------
|    0 | SELECT STATEMENT                |           |
|    1 |  NESTED LOOPS OUTER             |           |
|    2 |   TABLE ACCESS BY INDEX ROWID   | COL$      |
|*   3 |    INDEX UNIQUE SCAN            | I_COL3    |
|*   4 |   TABLE ACCESS CLUSTER          | ATTRCOL$  |
|    5 |    NESTED LOOPS                 |           |
|    6 |     NESTED LOOPS                |           |
|    7 |      NESTED LOOPS OUTER         |           |
|    8 |       NESTED LOOPS              |           |
|    9 |        NESTED LOOPS             |           |
|   10 |         NESTED LOOPS            |           |
|   11 |          NESTED LOOPS           |           |
|*  12 |           INDEX SKIP SCAN       | I_OBJ2    |
|   13 |           TABLE ACCESS CLUSTER  | ICOL$     |
|*  14 |            INDEX UNIQUE SCAN    | I_OBJ#    |
|   15 |          TABLE ACCESS BY INDEX ROWID | OBJ$ |
|*  16 |           INDEX RANGE SCAN      | I_OBJ1    |
|*  17 |         TABLE ACCESS BY INDEX ROWID | IND$  |
|*  18 |          INDEX UNIQUE SCAN      | I_IND1    |
|*  19 |        TABLE ACCESS CLUSTER     | COL$      |
|*  20 |       TABLE ACCESS CLUSTER      | ATTRCOL$  |
|   21 |      TABLE ACCESS CLUSTER       | USER$     |
|*  22 |       INDEX UNIQUE SCAN         | I_USER#   |
|   23 |     TABLE ACCESS CLUSTER        | USER$     |
|*  24 |      INDEX UNIQUE SCAN          | I_USER#   |
```

Miscellaneous Tuning Snippets

The issues covered in this section will help the advanced DBA. I'll discuss external tables, consider the "Snapshot Too Old" issue along with how to set the event to dump every wait, and explore what's really going on by performing block dumps.

External Tables

External tables allow you to access data that is not inside the database. Relational databases took off in the 1980s because of the ability to access data through relational tables. This was the first move away from mainframes and legacy systems that stored information in flat files or some facsimile of that. Oracle 11g continues the next paradigm in relational database technology. External tables extend the relational model beyond the database. Now you have a means by which to access all of the legacy data. You have a way to access all of that information dumped into flat files (perhaps, via third-party products).

One of the most costly parts of the extract, transform, load (ETL) process used for data warehousing and business intelligence is loading data into temporary tables so it can be used with other tables already in the database. Although external tables were introduced primarily to assist in the ETL process, Pandora's box cannot be closed. I have seen a plethora of uses for external tables, and I believe it's just the beginning. If Java and XML were minor aspects integrated into the relational model, the use of external tables brings the entire machine into the database and forever changes the rules of engagement.

This simple example shows you exactly how to use external tables. First, you need a flat file of data to access for the examples. You do this by simply spooling some data from our familiar friend, the EMP table:

```
set head off
set verify off
set feedback off
set pages 0
spool  emp4.dat

select empno||','||ename ||','|| job||','||deptno||','
from    scott.emp;


spool off
set head on
set verify on
set feedback on
set pages 26
```

Partial output of the `emp4.dat` file:

```
7369,SMITH,CLERK,20,
7499,ALLEN,SALESMAN,30,
7521,WARD,SALESMAN,30,
7566,JONES,MANAGER,20,
7654,MARTIN,SALESMAN,30,
```

Then you need to create a directory from within SQL*Plus so Oracle knows where to find your external tables:

```
SQL> create directory rich_new as '/u01/home/oracle/rich';

Directory created.
```

You then create the actual table definition that will reference the flat file that resides externally. Note that even if you successfully create the table, access to the external table may not necessarily result in a successful query. If the data is not stored in a way that matches the column definition of your table, you will get an error when you select the actual data. An example of the create table command is shown here:

```
create table emp_external4
 (empno char(4), ename char(10), job char(9), deptno char(2))
organization external
 (type oracle_loader
  default directory rich_new
  access parameters
  (records delimited by newline
  fields terminated by ','
  (empno , ename, job, deptno ))
 location ('emp4.dat'))
reject limit unlimited;

SQL> desc emp_external4
Name                                         Null? Type
-------------------------------------------- -------- --------------
EMPNO                                                 CHAR(4)
ENAME                                                 CHAR(10)
JOB                                                   CHAR(9)
DEPTNO                                                CHAR(2)

select   *
from     emp_external4;

EMPNO     ENAME           JOB           DEPTNO
--------  --------------  ------------  --------------
7369      SMITH           CLERK         20
7499      ALLEN           SALESMAN      30
7521      WARD            SALESMAN      30
...
```

There is currently no support for DML (INSERT, UPDATE, DELETE) commands, but you can always do this outside the database because the data is in a flat file. By using shell scripting, as shown next, you can certainly replicate those commands. Although you can't create an index currently, external tables are pleasantly and surprisingly fast.

```
SQL> insert into emp_external4 ...;
              *
ERROR at line 1:
ORA-30657: operation not supported on external organized table

SQL> create index emp_ei on emp_external4(deptno);
                 *
ERROR at line 1:
ORA-30657: operation not supported on external organized table
```

To count records, you can either use the Unix command or do it within the database. Either way, you have a means to work with data in flat files that are not within the database. This next listing is the wc (word count) command with the −1 option, which indicates to count the lines. This is a simple Unix command for counting records in a flat file. I created a file with 200,020 rows for the next more intensive test.

```
$ wc -l emp4.dat
   200020  200020 4400400 emp4.dat
$ ls -l emp4.dat
-rwxr-xr-x  1 oracle  oinstall 4400400 Aug  9 06:31 emp4.dat
```

You can also count the records in the flat file using SQL, since you've now built an external table. The command shown next takes less than one second to return its result:

```
select count(*)
from  emp_external4;

   COUNT(*)
----------
    200020
Elapsed: 00:00:00.63
```

Once you know you can count records in less than one second, you press on to look for specific information. Can you count selective pieces of data that fast? Yes. The code in the next listing looks for specific employee numbers (EMPNO) from the flat file, which is now referenced via an external table. The result is returned once again in less than one second.

```
select count(*)
from   emp_external4
where  empno=7900;

   COUNT(*)
----------
        20
Elapsed: 00:00:00.82
```

Once you know you can scan through 200,000 records in less than one second (on a single-processor machine in my case), you want to see how fast you can scan through millions of records. The example shown next builds a second table and joins it with the first so you can test scanning through four million rows. The result is less than three seconds to scan through this massive amount of data using only modest hardware.

```
create table emp_external5
(empno char(4), ename char(10), job char(9), deptno  char(2))
organization external
   ...
location ('emp5.dat'));
```

Now you join the two 200,000-row tables to create a join that merges the 20 rows in the first result set with the 20 rows of the second table, as shown here. This results in a join accessing 4 million rows with a result set of 400 rows. The result is an answer in less than 3 seconds.

```
select a.empno, b.job, a.job
from   emp_external4 a, emp_external5 b
where  a.empno = b.empno
and    a.empno = 7900
and    b.empno = 7900;

400 rows selected.
Elapsed: 00:00:02.46
```

Here is the execution plan for the previous join:

```
Execution Plan
----------------------------------------------------------
   0    SELECT STATEMENT
   1  0    SORT AGGREGATE
   2  1      HASH JOIN
   3  2        EXTERNAL TABLE ACCESS (FULL) OF 'EMP_EXTERNAL5'
   4  3        EXTERNAL TABLE ACCESS (FULL) OF 'EMP_EXTERNAL4'
```

You can also use hints with external tables, and you can join external tables with regular tables. You can parallelize the operation, and you can even insert the data from the external table directly into the database at any time. The possibilities are endless. External tables are not simply a serious advantage of using Oracle; they are one of the greatest benefits to relational technology in the past decade. They give you the window into the data that is *not* in your database. They allow you to access those legacy systems that have data stored in a multitude of flat files. They provide you the path to consolidate those legacy systems by moving step-by-step into the future.

Consider the quick use for an external table to read the alert file shown in the following listing. The original script for this was written by Dave Moore and passed to me by Howard Horowitz. The following is an alteration of those scripts:

```
SQL> Create directory alert1 as 'c:\app\user\diag\rdbms\orcl\orcl\trace';
Directory created.
SQL> Create table alert_log (text varchar2(200))
Organization EXTERNAL
(Type oracle_loader
Default directory alert1
Access parameters
(Records delimited by newline
Badfile 'rich1.bad'
Logfile 'rich1.log')
Location ('alert_ora.log'))
Reject limit unlimited;
Table created.

select *
from   alert_log
```

```
where   rownum < 25;

TEXT
-----------------------------------------------------------------------------
Sun Mar 06 16:45:43 2011
Starting ORACLE instance (normal)
...
Oracle Database 11g Enterprise Edition Release 11.2.0.1.0 - 64bit Production
With the Partitioning, OLAP, Data Mining and Real Application Testing options.
Using parameter settings in client-side pfile

 C:\APP\USER\CFGTOOLLOGS\DBCA\ORCL\INITORCLTEMP.ORA on machine USER-PC
System parameters with non-default values:
  processes                = 150
  memory_target            = 6560M
(partial listing only of selected data)
```

CAUTION
External tables are one of the best Oracle inventions in many versions. Your innovative mind will drive you to new heights using external tables. But be careful: data residing outside the database is not subject to the same Oracle backups and security as data inside the database.

Snapshot Too Old: Developer Coding Issue

Oracle holds undo information in case you need to roll back a transaction and also to keep a read-consistent version of data. Long-running queries may need the read-consistent versions of the data in undo segments because they may not be at the same System Change Number (SCN) as the ones currently in memory. (They may have been changed since the start of the query.) If the undo segment holding the original data is overwritten, the user receives the dreaded Snapshot Too Old error. With advances in Oracle 11g, this error is, indeed, not rare (using automatic undo management), but there is another, more frequent occurrence of the error in the later versions of Oracle.

In their infinite wisdom, developers find wonderful ways to update information that they are querying within the same piece of code causing this problem. They are the ones both querying and updating and causing the Snapshot Too Old error to occur. One flawed developer method is known as the *Fetch Across Commit.* In this method, the developer first selects a large number of rows from a table into a cursor and then fetches the rows to use for an update to the table, committing after a select number (say, every 1000 records) based on a counter. What happens is that the cursor needs a read-consistent image of the table, yet the developer is committing 1000 records within the same code to the table. The result is a Snapshot Too Old error.

NOTE
See an excellent paper by Dave Wotton (listed in the references) on understanding Snapshot Too Old for a detailed explanation of this esoteric problem. This doesn't happen as much as it used to.

TIP
*In addition to the more typical reasons, when developers modify the
data as it is being selected, fetching across commits, the Snapshot Too
Old error can occur. To fix this problem, close and reopen the cursor
causing the issue.*

Set Event to Dump Every Wait

In Chapter 14, you will learn about two excellent tuning tools that Oracle offers: Statspack and
AWR. These are great tools for showing everything in a single report for you to analyze. But what
if you have a burning issue and you directly need to dump exactly what the system is doing so
you can see every wait on the system? If the compilation of all waits in the V$ views is not
enough to solve problems and you need to see the waits in real time, the answer is the very
dangerous "Set Event 10046 at the system level." You can also do this at the session level
(see Chapter 13 for additional settings beyond this section).

This event dumps every single wait that occurs so you can search through and see exactly
what's causing the problem. You should use this strategy *only* as a last resort, and you should
rarely use it. You need a lot of disk space to use it when you have a lot of waits.

When you're ready to dump the problem, here's how to turn it on:

```
Alter system set events '10046 trace name context forever, level 12';

System altered.
```

NOTE
*You are also often required to increase the max size of dump files to
get all the info you need within the single trace file.*

The following listing shows what you'll get (in your DIAGNOSTIC_DEST):

```
Trace file c:\app\user\diag\rdbms\orcl\orcl\trace\orcl_ora_1776.trc
Oracle Database 11g Enterprise Edition Release 11.2.0.1.0 - 64bit Production
With the Partitioning, OLAP, Data Mining and Real Application
======================
PARSING IN CURSOR #9 len=61 dep=0 uid=84 oct=3 lid=84 tim=95022706805 hv=2099451087
ad='2ffbfaf28' sqlid='8y7yrd1yk656g'
select count(*)
from small2 a, small1 b
where a.empno=b.empno
END OF STMT
PARSE #9:c=0,e=1414,p=0,cr=0,cu=0,mis=1,r=0,dep=0,og=1,plh=1041396182,tim=95022706804
EXEC #9:c=0,e=38,p=0,cr=0,cu=0,mis=0,r=0,dep=0,og=1,plh=1041396182,tim=95022706929
WAIT #9: nam='SQL*Net message to client' ela= 3 driver id=1111838976 #bytes=1 p3=0 obj#=76920
tim=95022706981
... (PARTIAL LISTING - SELECTED LINES ONLY)
```

Although this output shows some irrelevant waits that came up when you quickly turn this on
and off, when you have a real problem, the waits will be clear. You are looking for a section with
something like the following, which shows a latch free issue. (See Chapter 14 for steps on how to

resolve this issue.) When you don't know what you're waiting for, this gives you a slightly more "at the street" level understanding of exactly what's going on than the V$ views do:

```
WAIT #2: nam='latch free' ela= 0 p1=-2147423252 p2=105 p3=0
WAIT #2: nam='latch free' ela= 0 p1=-2147423252 p2=105 p3=1
WAIT #2: nam='latch free' ela= 0 p1=-1088472332 p2=106 p3=0
WAIT #2: nam='latch free' ela= 0 p1=-2147423252 p2=105 p3=0
WAIT #2: nam='latch free' ela= 0 p1=-2147423252 p2=105 p3=1
WAIT #2: nam='latch free' ela= 1 p1=-2147423252 p2=105 p3=2
WAIT #2: nam='latch free' ela= 0 p1=-2147423252 p2=105 p3=0
WAIT #2: nam='latch free' ela= 1 p1=-2147423252 p2=105 p3=1
WAIT #2: nam='latch free' ela= 0 p1=-2147423252 p2=105 p3=0
WAIT #2: nam='latch free' ela= 0 p1=-2147423252 p2=105 p3=1
```

When you have a nice dump of the problem, here's how you turn it off:

```
Alter system set events '10046 trace name context off';

System altered.
```

CAUTION
Using the event 10046 at the system level can give a real-time dump of waits. Be careful because you can quickly use a lot of space very quickly on a very busy system. Only an expert who has the help of Oracle Support should use this method.

14 Hours to 30 Seconds with the EXISTS Operator

Although the Oracle optimizer is very good at ensuring a query is efficient, you can change a multitable join into a query with a subquery using the EXISTS operator. You can only do this if the table to put into the subquery doesn't have anything being selected from it in the SELECT statement. In this example, the goal is to pull one row back to use for test data in a test system:

```
--query with table join
explain plan for
SELECT MEMBER_NO
    , CONTRACT
    , DEP
    , SBSB_CK
    , SBSB_ID
    , GRGR_ID
    , MEME_BIRTH_DT
    , x.MEME_CK
    , MEME_REL
    , MEME_SFX
    , MEME_LAST_NAME
    , MEME_FIRST_NAME
    , to_timestamp('06/01/2006','mm/dd/yyyy')
    , 'PHASE 3'
```

```
    , CREATE_WHO
    , CREATE_DT
    , UPDATE_WHO
    , UPDATE_DT FROM PROD_PH.XREF_MEME x
          , PROD.CMC_MEPE_PRCS_ELIG
WHERE x.meme_ck = e.meme_ck
    and rownum = 1;

--Star query plan with B-TREE indexes!
-----------------------------------------------------------------------
| Id | Operation              | Name             | Rows  | Bytes | Cost  |
-----------------------------------------------------------------------
|  0 | SELECT STATEMENT       |                  | 1272G | 123T  | 274M  |
|  1 |  MERGE JOIN CARTESIAN  |                  | 1272G | 123T  | 274M  |
|  2 |   TABLE ACCESS FULL    | XREF_MEME        | 638K  | 65M   | 757   |
|  3 |   BUFFER SORT          |                  | 1991K |       | 274M  |
|  4 |    INDEX FAST FULL SCAN| CMCX_MEPE_SECOND | 1991K |       | 429   |
-----------------------------------------------------------------------


-- exists subquery example
SELECT MEMBER_NO
    , CONTRACT
    , DEP
    , SBSB_CK
    , SBSB_ID
    , GRGR_ID
    , MEME_BIRTH_DT
    , x.MEME_CK
    , MEME_REL
    , MEME_SFX
    , MEME_LAST_NAME
    , MEME_FIRST_NAME
    , to_timestamp('06/01/2006','mm/dd/yyyy')
    , 'PHASE 3'
    , CREATE_WHO
    , CREATE_DT
    , UPDATE_WHO
    , UPDATE_DT
  FROM PROD_PH.XREF_MEME x
WHERE exists(
          select 0
            from prod.cmc_mepe_prcs_elig e
           where e.meme_ck = x.meme_ck
      )
    and rownum = 1;


----------------------------------------------------------------------------------
| Id | Operation              | Name             | Rows  | Bytes |TempSpc| Cost  |
----------------------------------------------------------------------------------
|  0 | SELECT STATEMENT       |                  | 1     | 112   |       | 5067  |
|* 1 |  COUNT STOPKEY         |                  |       |       |       |       |
|* 2 |   HASH JOIN SEMI       |                  | 635K  | 67M   | 72M   | 5067  |
|  3 |    TABLE ACCESS FULL   | XREF_MEME        | 638K  | 65M   |       | 757   |
|  4 |    INDEX FAST FULL SCAN| CMCX_MEPE_CLUSTER| 1991K | 9726K |       | 464   |
----------------------------------------------------------------------------------
```

You can see from this example that using EXISTS instead of joining the tables can be very beneficial. Thanks to Mark Riedel of TUSC for sending this, as he puts it, "the TUSC patented EXISTS statement." We first discovered this around 1990.

Tuning at the Block Level (Advanced)

Although block tuning is covered briefly in Chapter 14, here I cover it in a bit more depth. An internal table called the *buffer hash table* (X$BH) holds block headers. There is a hash chain to which blocks are linked that are protected by a *CBC latch* (*cache buffers chains latch*). This hash chain links to the actual address located in memory (the memory set up with DB_CACHE SIZE, which is the cache used for data). For a given block in Oracle, only one version of a block is CURRENT, and no more than six other CR versions of the block (as of 11g) exist. Thus, only seven versions of a given block (maximum) are in memory at a time (forming a hash chain of six), although different blocks can be hashed to the same chain (depending on the hashing algorithm). When you perform a data manipulation language (DML) transaction—INSERT, UPDATE, or DELETE—you always need the CURRENT version of a block. In some versions of Oracle 8, you had to set _DB_BLOCK_HASH_BUCKETS to a prime number to keep the dba blocks evenly balanced in the hash buckets (more information on this in Chapter 14) and to avoid a long hash chain arising from the way the hash was calculated. If you didn't set this to a prime number, you could get a very long hash chain (as many blocks were hashed to the same chain), and then get major CBC latch waits (CBC latches are used in both 10g and 11g, although not under all conditions). I am told that the hashing algorithm changed in certain versions of Oracle 10g and 11g and will not need to be prime in the future (so don't change it; the default for me was *not* prime in 11gR2).

Also note that since Oracle 10g and continuing into 11g, Oracle has something called *in-memory undo (IMU),* which can give you some hard-to-understand results when you are viewing information at the block level. If you are familiar with IMU, which was new in 10g, you will find that blocks don't show up as dirty when you query X$BH and they have been dirtied. This is because updates are made *inside the actual block,* as opposed to in the UNDO block, before images are taken. I discovered that this happens only for certain retention settings, though. There is a parameter, _IN_MEMORY_ UNDO=TRUE, in the initialization file that is set to FALSE for some TPC benchmarks. Other parameters include _IMU_POOLS and _DB_WRITER_FLUSH_IMU. If you access the block trying to update a different row in the block, the IMU is flushed to the UNDO block, and the block shows as dirty (in my tests anyway, although I was told this depends on what the UNDO retention is set to). IMU writes the UNDO and REDO to memory instead of to disk (which is what the _IMU_POOLS parameter is for). IMU transactions always have room reserved in the current log file for writing out their REDO. They also acquire an *interested transaction list* (ITL) in the block header and reserve space in the UNDO segment. Several sections of IMU statistics are displayed in the AWR Report or the Statspack Report.

When you are querying a block for the first time, you always use the CURRENT version. If the block is being used, you will build a *CLONE* of the block called a *CONSISTENT READ (CR)* version by applying any UNDO needed to the CURRENT version of the block to get it to a point in time that makes it useful to you (perhaps you need a version of the block before the DML was performed and not committed by another user). This complex and Oracle-patented process may include reading the ITL (which is populated when someone does a DML on a block), mapping the record to the UNDO HEADER, or directly to the UNDO BLOCK, and then applying the UNDO to get the correct CR version that you need. So let's take a look at how this happens:

- User 1 updates a record in block 777 (user1 has not committed).
- User 2 queries the same block and sees that the lock byte is set for a row being queried.
- User 2 goes to the ITL portion of the block and gets the transaction ID (XID).
- The XID maps to the UNDO block, which holds the information before the update was performed.
- A clone of the block is made (call it *block 778*).
- The UNDO information is applied to the block, rolling it back to where it used to be.
- Block 777 is a CURRENT block.
- Block 778 is a CONSISTENT READ block before the User 1 update occurred.
- If another user wants to do a query before the commit, that user can also read the CR version.

Also note that REDO goes forward; UNDO goes back. Yes, the UNDO (ROLLBACK) information is applied to the block, but this has the effect of undoing the most recent changes to the block, including setting the SCN for the block to a past time, not a future time. This is why they are called ROLLBACK segments.

Note *especially* the fact that the block is not *rolled back* to what it was, but it is *rolled forward* to what it used to be. While the result is the same, how Oracle performs this operation is *critical* to understanding how Oracle works. Oracle blocks are always moving forward in time (this is why the REDO works—it's always applying things forward sequentially). There are also links to all blocks for the least recently used (LRU) and least recently used-write (LRU-W) to help make buffer replacement and writing much faster. This information is also maintained in the buffer headers.

If nothing has been advanced enough for you so far, this section is worth the price of the book and should keep you busy for the next decade tuning your system to perfection (if you'd like). Oracle often has perplexing new features: either I can't seem to get them working or there's simply a bug in the program that I am unaware of. How do you find out if a problem is yours or Oracle's? Dump the blocks one at a time.

Consider the intense example in the listing that follows. Find the table/index block information that you want to dump, as shown here:

```
SELECT FILE_ID, BLOCK_ID, BLOCKS FROM DBA_EXTENTS
WHERE SEGMENT_NAME = 'EMP'
AND OWNER = 'SCOTT';


  FILE_ID        BLOCK_ID        BLOCKS
---------- --------------- ------------
        1           50465             3
```

Dump the table/index block information, as demonstrated here:

```
ALTER SYSTEM DUMP DATAFILE 5 BLOCK 50465;
ALTER SYSTEM DUMP DATAFILE 5 BLOCK 50466;
```

```
ALTER SYSTEM DUMP DATAFILE 5 BLOCK 50467;

-- You could also issue the following command to dump the range of blocks:

ALTER SYSTEM DUMP DATAFILE 5 BLOCK MIN 50465 BLOCK MAX 50467;
```

The ALTER SYSTEM command selects and then dumps the data blocks for the EMP table owned by SCOTT to a trace file for the current user session in the DIAGNOSTIC_DEST directory, much like TKPROF. The information that is dumped is very cryptic, but it can be helpful for tuning purposes.

The information in the listing that follows compares portions of the block dumps of two different bitmap join indexes. One is on the DEPTNO column, where the tables are also being joined by DEPTNO. The other is on the LOCATION column, where the table is being joined by DEPTNO. By comparing index information, you can see that the LOCATION column was included in the stored part of the index, even though the query was going back to the table to retrieve the location column in the query. The problem was an Oracle bug that you would discover only by performing this dump (partially shown in this next listing; only the first record is displayed for each).

```
DUMP OF BITMAP JOIN INDEX ON location JOINING deptno ON EMP1/DEPT1
row#0[3912] flag: -----, lock: 0
col 0; len 7; (7): 43 48 49 43 41 47 4f
col 1; len 6; (6): 00 40 f3 31 00 00
col 2; len 6; (6): 00 40 f3 31 00 0f
col 3; len 3; (3): c9 36 0a
...
----- end of leaf block dump -----End dump data blocks tsn: 0 file#:
DUMP OF BITMAP JOIN INDEX ON deptno JOINING deptno ON EMP1/dept1 TABLE ***
row#0[3917] flag: -----, lock: 0
col 0; len 2; (2): c1 0b
col 1; len 6; (6): 00 40 f3 31 00 00
col 2; len 6; (6): 00 40 f3 31 00 0f
col 3; len 3; (3): c9 40 21
...
----- end of leaf block dump -----End dump data blocks tsn: 0 file#:
```

The best use for dumping blocks is to see how Oracle really works (unless data encryption is enabled, making it unhelpful). Get ready for a long night if you plan to use this tip; I spent a weekend playing with this the first time I used it.

TIP

Dumping data blocks can be a valuable tool to understand how Oracle works and to investigate problem-tuning areas. Only a tuning expert should use block dumps, and even an expert should use the help of Oracle Support. Oracle does not publish the structure of block dumps, so they can change at any time.

Now let's look at an example to show you how to interpret some of the output that you get from a block dump as well as some other helpful queries that you can do when you do the deep dive into block dumps.

This query will give you the block number for *every* record of a table:

```
select rowid,empno,
       dbms_rowid.rowid_relative_fno(rowid) fileno,
       dbms_rowid.rowid_block_number(rowid) blockno,
       dbms_rowid.rowid_row_number(rowid)  rowno, rownum table_rownum,
       rpad(to_char(dbms_rowid.rowid_block_number(rowid), 'FM0xxxxxxx') || '.' ||
            to_char(dbms_rowid.rowid_row_number  (rowid), 'FM0xxx'  ) || '.' ||
            to_char(dbms_rowid.rowid_relative_fno(rowid), 'FM0xxx'  ), 18) myrowid
from   emp1;
```

ROWID	EMPNO	FILENO	BLOCKNO	ROWNO	TABLE_ROWNUM
MYROWID					
AAAMfcAABAAANOKAAA	7369	5	56586	0	1
0000dd0a.0000.0001					
AAAMfcAABAAANOKAAB	7499	5	56586	1	2
0000dd0a.0001.0001					
AAAMfcAABAAANOKAAC	7521	5	56586	2	3
0000dd0a.0002.0001					

(partial listing)

Most of the information found in block dumps can be found in the data dictionary or can be accessed using a built-in package such as DBMS_SPACE. In certain scenarios, however, knowing how to read a block dump might benefit you; for instance, it may help you determine exactly why a transaction is blocked. You will probably use other tools prior to dumping a block, `utllockt.sql`, for instance, or EM (Enterprise Manager), but if you want to see exactly what is holding a lock on a row in a block, and how many rows are blocked, the block dump output can be quite useful. You may also want to look at row chaining or to look at the space utilization in the block for each row or simply to look at the block because a block is corrupted and you want to take a closer look at it. Sometimes, looking at what is stored in a corrupted block can help you figure out where the corruption originated, for example, text that comes from a third-party tool or a block for which large chunks were changed to all zeros (disk repair utilities).

Key Sections of a Block Dump

Sections to note within the block dump include the block ITL, the flag section, and the block data section. Each section is discussed in the text that follows.

The Block ITL Section in a Block Dump

One of the key sections of a block dump is the *interested transaction list (ITL)*. The ITL section shown next appears in the early part of the dump. This one shows *two* ITL slots (two is the *minimum* number of ITL slots for both tables and indexes—if you don't believe what you read, you can dump it yourself to make sure). The XID is the transaction ID. The UBA is the Undo Block Address. I'll discuss the Flag in a moment. The lock shows the number of records locked (four records are locked in the first ITL slot because I deleted four rows for this example), and the SCN/FSC is either the SCN for committed information (Flag is a C) or FSC (Free Space Credit), which is the amount of bytes that will be recovered within the block if the transaction is committed. This number is a hexadecimal number. For this example, it is 9d, which is 157 bytes recovered if the transaction to delete four records is committed; the transaction could also be rolled back.

```
Itl               Xid              Uba            Flag Lck      Scn/Fsc
0x01  0x0004.010.00000fba  0x0080003d.08b5.10  ----  4  fsc 0x009d.00000000
0x02  0x0004.016.00000fae  0x008000cc.08af.34  C---  0  scn 0x0000.003deb5b
```

Here is another block dump example of an ITL section where three updates were being done on the EMP1 table, DEPTNO column: one user updating all records with DEPTNO=10 (6 records), one user updating all records with DEPTNO=20 (4 records), and a third user updating all records with DEPTNO=30 (5 records).

```
Itl               Xid              Uba            Flag Lck      Scn/Fsc
0x01  0x0002.010.00000b7c  0x00c536ec.03c8.2a  ----  6  fsc 0x0000.00000000
0x02  0x0004.007.00000b0d  0x00c00ccb.0407.28  ----  4  fsc 0x0000.00000000
0x03  0x0006.019.00000bf9  0x00c012ce.0420.3b  ----  5  fsc 0x0000.00000000
```

The Flag Section

The Flag section is a bit complex. It tells you what state the transaction is in (CBUT):

----	The transaction is active, or it is committed pending block cleanout.
C---	The transaction has been committed, and the row locks have been cleaned out.
-B--	The Undo Block Address contains UNDO for this block.
--U-	The transaction is committed (the SCN is the upper bound), but block cleanout has not occurred (a fast commit).
---T	This transaction was still active when the SCN for block cleanout was recorded.
C-U-	The block was cleaned by delayed block cleanout, and the undo segment information has been overwritten. The SCN will show the lowest SCN that could be re-created by the UNDO segment.

The Block Dump Data Section

The next block dump shows the data section. This is the first part (the header section) of the block dump data section.

```
tab 0, row 13, @0x1b0b
tl: 39 fb: --H-FL-- lb: 0x0  cc: 8
```

Following is the description of this header information:

```
tab = this data is for table 0
row 13 = 14th Row (0-13 total rows)
Offset: 1b0b (in Hex) - Offset from header
tl: Total bytes of row plus the header = 39
fb: --H-FL-- = flag byte; ( -KCHDFLPN)
H = Head of row piece, F = First data piece, L=Last piece
D = Deleted; P= First column continues from previous piece (chaining) ; N= Last
column continues in next piece; K = Cluster Key; C = Cluster table member
lb: lock byte is 1+ if this row is locked = 0 (unlocked)
cc: Column count = 8
```

The data part of the block dump data section starts with the line `col0`, as is shown in the block dump that follows:

```
col  0: [ 3]   c2 50 23
col  1: [ 6]   4d 49 4c 4c 45 52
col  2: [ 5]   43 4c 45 52 4b
col  3: [ 3]   c2 4e 53
col  4: [ 7]   77 b6 01 17 01 01 01
col  5: [ 2]   c2 0e
col  6: *NULL*
col  7: [ 2]   c1 0b...
```

The following example shows how to interpret the output from the block dump data section for the first column (`col0`), which is the EMPNO column:

```
col  0: [ 3]   c2 50 23
```

```
Hex to Decimal:   Col0 = EMPNO = 7934
50 (Hex) = 80 (Decimal) - 1 = 79
23 (Hex) = 35 (Decimal) - 1 = 34
c2: Number in the thousands (c2 is exponent)
```

The following example shows how to interpret the dump output from the block dump data section for the second column (`col1`), which is ENAME:

```
col  1: [ 6]   4d 49 4c 4c 45 52
```

```
Hex to Character:     Col1 = ENAME = MILLER
4d (Hex) = M (Character) [= 77 (decimal)]
49 (Hex) = I (Character)
4c (Hex) = L (Character)
4c (Hex) = L (Character)
45 (Hex) = E (Character)
52 (Hex) = R (Character)
```

Also note that the hex values correspond to the character mapping tables (which depend on the NLS settings for your database). For example, if you search "ASCII code character" on Google, you get a table of hex/decimal ASCII codes, in which 4d/77 corresponds to M.

This example from the dump output from the block dump data shows the HIREDATE column, which is a DATE field:

```
col  4: [ 7]   77 b6 01 17 01 01 01
```

```
Hex to Decimal: Col4 = HIREDATE = 23-JAN-82
77 (Hex) = 119 (Decimal) - 100 = 19 <century>
B6 (Hex) = 182 (Decimal) - 100 = 82 <year>
01(Hex) = 1 (Decimal) <month>
17 (Hex) = 23 (Decimal) <day>
01 01 01 (Hex) = This is the Hour, Minute, Second
(The Default time is 00:00:00)
```

You may want to select the hex data from the table. The following example uses SELECT dump() and gets the ENAME from the hex:

```
select   dump(ename,16), ename
from  emp1
where   dump(ename,16) like '%4d,49,4c,4c,45,52';
DUMP(ENAME,16)                                    ENAME
------------------------------------------------  --------------
Typ=1 Len=6: 4d,49,4c,4c,45,52                    MILLER
```

Let's query a new block (56650) from EMP1 and watch the EMP1 buffer header change (so far it's clean—the dirty bit is N—and consists of only one copy (or record), and it's the current version, with state=1):

```
select lrba_seq, state, dbarfil, dbablk, tch, flag, hscn_bas,cr_scn_bas,
       decode(bitand(flag,1),  0, 'N', 'Y') dirty,  /* Dirty bit */
       decode(bitand(flag,16), 0, 'N', 'Y') temp, /* temporary bit */
       decode(bitand(flag,1536),0,'N','Y') ping, /* ping (to shared or null) bit */
       decode(bitand(flag,16384), 0, 'N', 'Y') stale,  /* stale bit */
       decode(bitand(flag,65536), 0, 'N', 'Y') direct,  /* direct access bit */
       decode(bitand(flag,1048576), 0, 'N', 'Y') new  /* new bit */
from   x$bh
where dbablk = 56650
order by dbablk;

LRBA_SEQ         STATE    DBARFIL    DBABLK       TCH       FLAG     HSCN_BAS
---------- ---------- ---------- ---------- ---------- ---------- -----------
CR_SCN_BAS D T P S D N
---------- - - - - - -
         0          1          1      56650          0   35659776  4294967295
              0 N N N N N N
```

Watch the EMP1 buffer header when you delete a row:

```
delete from emp1
where comm = 0;

1 row deleted.
```

Let's query the block (56650) and watch the EMP1 buffer header. There are now two copies (or records): one copy is the current version (state=1), and one is a clone (CR, state=3):

```
select lrba_seq, state, dbarfil, dbablk, tch, flag, hscn_bas,cr_scn_bas,
       decode(bitand(flag,1), 0, 'N', 'Y') dirty,   /* Dirty bit */
       decode(bitand(flag,16), 0, 'N', 'Y') temp,   /* temporary bit */
       decode(bitand(flag,1536),0,'N','Y') ping, /* ping (to shared or null) bit */
       decode(bitand(flag,16384), 0, 'N', 'Y') stale,  /* stale bit */
       decode(bitand(flag,65536), 0, 'N', 'Y') direct,  /* direct access bit */
       decode(bitand(flag,1048576), 0, 'N', 'Y') new  /* new bit */
from   x$bh
where dbablk = 56650
order by dbablk;
```

LRBA_SEQ	STATE	DBARFIL	DBABLK	TCH	FLAG	HSCN_BAS
CR_SCN_BAS	D T P S D N					
0	1	1	56650	1	8200	4294967295
0	N N N N N N					
0	3	1	56650	2	524288	0
4347881	N N N N N N					

Note that V$TRANSACTION now has the record (created when transactions have UNDO):

```
SELECT  t.addr, t.xidusn USN, t.xidslot SLOT, t.xidsqn SQN, t.status,
        t.used_ublk UBLK, t.used_urec UREC, t.log_io LOG,
        t.phy_io PHY, t.cr_get, t.cr_change CR_CHA
FROM    v$transaction t, v$session s
WHERE   t.addr = s.taddr;
```

ADDR	USN	SLOT	SQN	STATUS	UBLK
UREC	LOG	PHY	CR_GET	CR_CHA	
69E50E5C	5	42	652 ACTIVE		1
1	3	0	3	0	

The column names in the output have these meanings:

- USN is the Undo Segment Number (rollback segment ID).

- SLOT is the slot number in the rollback segment's transaction table.

- SQN (Wrap) is the sequence number for the transaction.

- USN+SLOT+SQN are the three values that uniquely identify a transaction XID.

- UBLK is the block for the last UNDO entry (it tells you how many UNDO blocks there are).

- UREC is the record number of the block (it shows how many table and index entries the transaction has inserted, updated, or deleted).

If you are doing an INSERT or DELETE, then you will see that UREC is set to (*number of indexes for this table*) + (*how many rows you insert/delete*). If you UPDATE a column, then UREC will be set to (*number of indexes that his column belongs to*) * 2 + (*number of updated rows*). If the column belongs to no index, then the UREC is set to the number of rows that were updated. If UBLK and UREC decrease each time you query, then the transaction is rolling back. When UREC reaches zero, the rollback is finished.

If you dump the block at this time, you see the locked record in the first row of the ITL section:

```
Itl           Xid                  Uba           Flag  Lck     Scn/Fsc
0x01  0x0005.02a.0000028c  0x008000af.02b6.01   ----   1   fsc 0x0029.00000000
0x02  0x0004.016.00000fae  0x008000cc.08af.34   C---   0   scn 0x0000.003deb5b
```

Now let's do an INSERT in four other sessions to get X$BH up to six versions of the block. There are now six copies: one copy is the current version (state=1) and five are clones (CR, state=3):

LRBA_SEQ	STATE	DBARFIL	DBABLK	TCH	FLAG	HSCN_BAS

CR_SCN_BAS	D	T	P	S	D	N

LRBA_SEQ	STATE	DBARFIL	DBABLK	TCH	FLAG	HSCN_BAS
0	3	1	56650	1	524416	0
4350120 N N N N N						
0	3	1	56650	1	524416	0
4350105 N N N N N						
365	1	1	56650	7	33562633	4350121
0 Y N N N N						
0	3	1	56650	1	524416	0
4350103 N N N N N						
0	3	1	56650	1	524416	0
4350089 N N N N N						
0	3	1	56650	1	524288	0
4350087 N N N N N						

NOTE
The Least Redo Block Address (LRBA) is set only for the current block, and the current block is the one with the DIRTY flag set to 'Y'.

Can you get more than six versions of a block? Probably, but this is unsupported. In the following listing, I've selected the maximum-allowed CR buffers per data block address (dba).

```
select a.ksppinm, b.ksppstvl, b.ksppstdf, a.ksppdesc
from   x$ksppi a, x$ksppcv b
where  a.indx = b.indx
and    substr(ksppinm,1,1) = '_'
and    ksppinm like '%&1%'
order  by ksppinm;


KSPPINM              KSPPSTVL  KSPPSTDF KSPPDESC
-------------------- --------  -------- ---------------------------------------------
_db_block_max_cr_dba    6      TRUE     Maximum Allowed Number of CR buffers per dba
```

Now consider an example in 11g where I am updating/selecting multiple times in a block to get the maximum number of CR versions of a block:

```
select lrba_seq, state, dbarfil, dbablk, tch, flag, hscn_bas,cr_scn_bas,
       decode(bitand(flag,1), 0, 'N', 'Y') dirty,   /* Dirty bit */
       decode(bitand(flag,16), 0, 'N', 'Y') temp,  /* temporary bit */
       decode(bitand(flag,1536),0,'N','Y') ping, /* ping (to shared or null) bit */
       decode(bitand(flag,16384), 0, 'N', 'Y') stale,  /* stale bit */
       decode(bitand(flag,65536), 0, 'N', 'Y') direct,  /* direct access bit */
       decode(bitand(flag,1048576), 0, 'N', 'Y') new  /* new bit */
```

```
from  x$bh
where dbablk = 56650
order by dbablk;
```

LRBA_SEQ	STATE	DBARFIL	DBABLK	TCH	FLAG	HSCN_BAS
CR_SCN_BAS	D T P S D N					
0	3	10	1410707	1	524288	0
23105852	N N N N N N					
0	3	10	1410707	1	524288	0
23105815	N N N N N N					
0	3	10	1410707	1	524288	0
23105727	N N N N N N					
0	3	10	1410707	1	524288	0
23105710	N N N N N N					
0	3	10	1410707	1	524288	0
23105677	N N N N N N					
0	3	10	1410707	1	524288	0
23105674	N N N N N N					
4051	1	10	1410707	4	35651593	23105710
0	Y N N N N N					

```
7 rows selected.
```

Now I am going to run the 11*g* command to flush the buffer cache:

```
SQL> alter system flush buffer_cache;
System Altered.
```

Now I'll rerun all of my SELECTs/UPDATEs to refill the cache to see the result. The result is that I get five CR versions and one CURRENT version of the block, but the original seven buffered blocks that I had are now reset to mostly zeros. Oracle has populated all new records in X$BH and zeroed out the original ones after the buffer cache flush (5 CR and 1 CURRENT + 7 other zeroed out):

LRBA_SEQ	STATE	DBARFIL	DBABLK	TCH	FLAG	HSCN_BAS
CR_SCN_BAS	D T P S D N					
0	3	10	1410707	1	524288	0
23106121	N N N N N N					
0	3	10	1410707	1	524288	0
23106120	N N N N N N					
0	3	10	1410707	1	524288	0
23106118	N N N N N N					
0	3	10	1410707	1	524288	0
23106116	N N N N N N					
0	3	10	1410707	1	524288	0
23106115	N N N N N N					
4051	1	10	1410707	2	33554433	23106121
0	Y N N N N N					
0	0	10	1410707	0	0	0
0	N N N N N N					
0	0	10	1410707	0	0	0
0	N N N N N N					

```
0               0       10      1410707         0           0           0
  O N N N N N N
0               0       10      1410707         0           0           0
  O N N N N N N
0               0       10      1410707         0           0           0
  O N N N N N N
0               0       10      1410707         0           0           0
  O N N N N N N
0               0       10      1410707         0           0           0
  O N N N N N N
```

```
13 rows selected.
```

This listing still has room for one more active CR block. The listing gives a good feeling for how Oracle handles the buffer cache flush. Testing things at the block level can help you to understand new functionality but shouldn't be used every day. Block tuning should be primarily used in a test system for often-run code that needs detailed attention.

A deeper dive into block tuning is beyond the scope of this book. However, some of the queries I've presented in this section will allow you to investigate what is going on at the block level in the very rare case that you need to see it. The best reason to perform block dumps is to see what's going on inside of Oracle. In the next section, you get a brief look at the block level of bitmap indexes and a few other types.

A Brief Look at an Index Block Dump

Now let's take a quick look at some index block dumps. First let's look at a bitmap index. Each of the indexed rows consists of five lines:

row#0	**Row identification**
col 0	Indexed value length in hex.
col 1	ROWID for the first occurrence of the indexed value.
col 2	ROWID for the last occurrence of the indexed value.
col 3	Actual bitmap that has a value of 1, when the value occurred in the range between the first and last ROWID; otherwise, 0 in swap byte notification. First byte usually cx where x is (8,…,f). When all slots for cf are filled, a new segment starts.

Consider the following bitmap index block dump:

```
row#0[8010] flag: ---D-, lock: 2
col 0; len 1; (1):   31
col 1; len 6; (6):   02 40 2d 60 00 00
col 2; len 6; (6):   02 40 2d 60 00 07
col 3; len 1; (1):   00

row#1[7989] flag: ---D-, lock: 2
col 0; len 1; (1):   31
```

```
col 1; len 6; (6):  02 40 2d 60 00 00
col 2; len 6; (6):  02 40 2d 60 00 07
col 3; len 2; (2):  c8 03

row#2[7968] flag: -----, lock: 2
col 0; len 1; (1):  31
col 1; len 6; (6):  02 40 2d 60 00 00
col 2; len 6; (6):  02 40 2d 60 00 07
col 3; len 2; (2):  c8 07
```

If you insert 64 rows (0–63) and then take a block dump (note the 3f in col 2):

```
row#0[8008] flag: -----, lock: 0
col 0; len 1; (1):  31
col 1; len 6; (6):  02 40 2d 60 00 00
col 2; len 6; (6):  02 40 2d 60 00 3f
col 3; len 9; (9):  cf ff ff ff ff ff ff ff ff
```

then you insert one more row (0–64), you get the following (note the 40 in col 2):

```
row#0[8007] flag: -----, lock: 0
col 0; len 1; (1):  31
col 1; len 6; (6):  02 40 2d 60 00 00
col 2; len 6; (6):  02 40 2d 60 00 40
col 3; len 10; (10):  cf ff ff ff ff ff ff ff ff 00
```

An index value exists in a block with ROWID=02 40 2d 60 00 40 (40(hex) => 64 (decimal)). The previous end ROWID was 3f (3*16+15 = 63). When the index is updated, you must have enough space to accommodate growth; if you don't, a split occurs. Not just that, a lock is placed on the entry in the leaf index—but this entry can span over multiple blocks. As a side effect, for the duration of a lock, no other transaction can update the blocks in the affected block range. Bitmap indexes are used for a column with just a few different values, so on bigger tables each bitmap likely covers quite a few blocks. A lock placed on those blocks can have disastrous effects on other transactions, which is why bitmap indexes are almost always used for query-only data or mostly static data.

Now let's see how the block dump of a reverse key index looks. Note that a reverse key index will be marked with the value NORMAL/REV in dba_indexes (index_type). You can see here that the hex values in col 1 are reversed:

Regular index entry:

```
col 0; len 2; (2):  c1 02
col 1; len 7; (7):  78 69 0c 19 03 27 10
col 2; len 6; (6):  02 40 2e 70 00 00
```

Reverse key:

```
col 0; len 2; (2):  02 c1
col 1; len 7; (7):  10 27 03 19 0c 69 78
col 2; len 6; (6):  02 40 2e 70 00 00
```

Finally, let's take a quick look at how a regular index (ascending) differs from a descending index when you do an index block dump:

A regular index:

```
col 0; len 1; (1):    61
col 0; len 2; (2):    61 61
col 0; len 3; (3):    61 61 61
col 0; len 4; (4):    61 61 61 61
col 0; len 5; (5):    61 61 61 61 61
col 0; len 6; (6):    61 61 61 61 61 61
col 0; len 7; (7):    61 61 61 61 61 61 61
col 0; len 8; (8):    61 61 61 61 61 61 61 61
col 0; len 9; (9):    61 61 61 61 61 61 61 61 61
col 0; len 10; (10):  61 61 61 61 61 61 61 61 61 61
```

A descending index:

```
col 0; len 10; (10):  9e 9e 9e 9e 9e 9e 9e 9e 9e ff
col 0; len 9; (9):       9e 9e 9e 9e 9e 9e 9e 9e ff
col 0; len 8; (8):       9e 9e 9e 9e 9e 9e 9e ff
col 0; len 7; (7):       9e 9e 9e 9e 9e 9e ff
col 0; len 6; (6):       9e 9e 9e 9e 9e ff
col 0; len 5; (5):       9e 9e 9e 9e ff
col 0; len 4; (4):       9e 9e 9e ff
col 0; len 3; (3):       9e 9e ff
col 0; len 2; (2):       9e ff
```

You can see from all of these examples that the block dump can give you insight into new features as well as details about internal data structures and indexes in Oracle. Use the block dump sparingly and generally on a test system, however.

Tuning Using Simple Mathematical Techniques

This section discusses some simple but effective mathematical techniques you can use to significantly improve the performance of some Oracle SQL–based systems. These techniques can leverage the effectiveness of Oracle performance diagnostic tools and uncover hidden performance problems that can be overlooked by other methods. Using these techniques also helps you make performance predictions at higher loads.

NOTE
Joe A. Holmes provided the material for this section. I am extremely grateful for his contribution because I believe it ties all the chapters of this book together.

The methodology called *Simple Mathematical Techniques* involves isolating and testing the SQL process in question under ideal conditions, graphing the results of rows processed versus time, deriving equations using simple methods (without regression), predicting performance, and interpreting and applying performance patterns directly to tuning SQL code.

Traditional Mathematical Analysis

First of all, do not be intimidated by this section. You *will* be able to understand this, and the information provided will help you predict response times for your queries as the tables grow.

Traditional mathematical methods are very useful for analyzing performance. These may include graphing performance metrics on an *x-y* coordinate axis to obtain a picture of what a process is really doing and applying Least Squares Regression or Polynomial Interpolation to derive equations for predicting performance at higher loads. Computer science academics and specialists use these techniques extensively for performance analysis, which is laden with problems. First, textbook notation and explanations are often very complex and difficult to understand. Most math textbooks I have encountered that treat approximation and interpolation, for example, are steeped in theory rather than providing clear and practical examples.

Second, little or no information is available on how to apply this kind of analysis directly to tuning SQL code. This is probably because SQL analysis requires more specific interpretations to be useful rather than something broader or more general.

Seven-Step Methodology

The following are seven steps in the methodology. Note that deriving performance equations and interpreting patterns are discussed in more detail in the sections that follow.

1. Isolate the SQL code in question.

   The SQL code in question is isolated from surrounding system code and placed in a SQL*PLUS or PL/SQL script that can be run independently to duplicate the production process.

2. Run tests under ideal conditions.

   In this context, "ideal" is defined as one SQL process running on a dedicated machine with hardware-processing power fixed and executed under high-volume data.

3. Graph performance observations on an *x-y* coordinate axis.

   From tests, the number of rows processed (*x*) versus time (*y*) for each SQL statement within a process is graphed on an *x-y* coordinate axis. This is referred to as a *row-time metric.* Ideally, the optimizer is, for the most part, more mechanical and less random, creating a more clearly defined and predictable trendline. The basic line shape can provide clues to the cause of underlying performance problems.

4. Use simple equation determination.

   Once points are plotted on a graph, you assume that what appears straight is a linear function and what appears curved upward is a quadratic function. (Other shapes may appear, but they are beyond the scope of this section.) From these observations, you can use either a simple two-point linear or three-point quadratic method to determine the equations. You can perform both methods easily by hand or with a basic calculator. You can also use spreadsheets like Microsoft Excel with graphing and trendline (regression) capabilities. Each separate SQL statement is graphed and analyzed individually.

5. Predict performance.

   You can use derived equations to predict performance at much higher loads than are practical to test. Because the accuracy of the predictions may decrease as the predicted load increases, it is suggested that you make only ballpark predictions.

   It may be advantageous to calculate two performance lines: the first as a lower bound if the performance line is truly linear, and the second as an upper bound if the performance line might turn out to be a quadratic curve. The predicated value would, therefore, lie somewhere in between. Later, you may want to try a test to see how close your prediction was to the actual time. Also be aware that it is not as important whether a slow-running process is predicted to take 20 or 24 hours, but rather, whether it can be improved to, say, 1 hour.

6. Interpret performance patterns and experiment.

   The shape of the performance lines and the nature of the equations can provide clues about the cause of underlying performance problems and support (or sometimes contradict) the interpretations of diagnostic tools. You can conduct experiments on SQL code based on pattern clues and the correction applied to production code. You can graph tests of an improved process again and compare the results with the original process.

7. Keep a record of results to build expertise.

   To build up your expertise at using both these mathematical methods and your interpretation of Oracle diagnostic tools, keep a record of before and after performance graphs, the true cause of performance problems, and the effective solutions you found. Graphs provide hard evidence of performance problems that you can present in a clear visual form to management and end users.

Deriving Performance Equations

The following sections discuss two simple methods for equation determination based on simplified versions of Newton's Divided Difference Interpolating Polynomial. You can use these methods if you assume that what appears as a straight line is linear and what appears as upward sloping is quadratic.

Simple Linear Equation Determination

The following is a simple two-point method for determining a linear best-performance line equation:

$y = a_0 + a_1x$ (This is the final equation to use for linear queries.)

y = the number of rows in the table

x = the time to process the query

a_1 = the slope of the line (Calculate this with two query tests.)

a_0 = the y-intercept of the line (Calculate this with two query tests.)

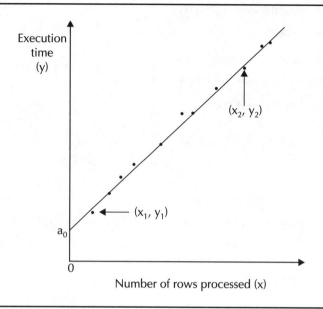

FIGURE 9-6. *Linear best-performance line*

Figure 9-6 shows points from an ideal test that appears linear. You visually select two points (x_1, y_1) and (x_2, y_2) that define a straight line of minimum slope, where slope: $a_1 = (y_2 - y_1)/(x_2 - x_1)$:

y-intercept: $a_0 = y_1 - a_1 x_1$

A Simple Example   These equations look great, but let's look at a real-life query (using a basic query to the EMP table). You must time the query on the basis of two different table sizes to get an equation for the line.

```
select  ename, deptno
from    emp
where   deptno = 10;
```

For a very small system, consider the response for two tests:

  1. When 1000 records were in the EMP table, this query took 2 seconds.

  2. When 2000 records were in the EMP table, this query took 3 seconds.

    Therefore, you know that

        $y_1 = 2$ (seconds)

        $x_1 = 1000$ (records)

        $y_2 = 3$ (seconds)

        $x_2 = 2000$ (records)

■ Step 1   Find the slope of the line.

$a_1 = (y_2 - y_1)/(x_2 - x_1)$

$a_1 = (3 - 2)/(2000 - 1000)$

$a_1 = 0.001$ (The slope of the line is 0.001.)

■ Step 2   Get the y-intercept.

$a_0 = y_1 - a_1 x_1$

$a_0 = 2 - (0.001)(1000)$

$a_0 = 2 - 1$

$a_0 = 1$ (The y-intercept is 1.)

■ Step 3   Now you can calculate response for any size EMP table.

You now have everything you need for this query, so you can figure out how long this query will take as the number of rows in the EMP table increases.

What will the response time be for 3,000 rows?

$y = a_0 + a_1 x$ (The response time is y, and x is the number of rows in the table.)

$y = 1 + (0.001)(3000)$

$y = 1 + 3$

$y = 4$ seconds (The response time for this query in a 3,000-row EMP table will be 4 seconds.)

What will the response time be for 100,000 rows?

$y = a_0 + a_1 x$

$y = 1 + (0.001)(100,000)$

$y = 101$ seconds (The response time for a 100,000-row EMP table will be 1 minute and 41 seconds.)

Simple Quadratic Equation Determination

Unfortunately, many queries don't behave linearly. Consequently, the preceding section doesn't always help you. But never fear—a simple method for curved lines is next. Once again, do not be intimidated by this section. You *will* be able to understand this, and with this information, you will be able to predict query scaling (predict any response time for an increased number of rows). The following is a simple three-point method for determining a quadratic best-performance equation. This is the equation you will use:

$y = a_0 + a_1 x + a_2 x^2$ (This is the final equation to use for nonlinear queries.)

y = response time for a query

x = number of rows

a_0, a_1, a_2 = constants derived from the curve the query creates

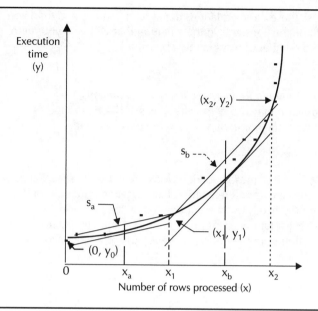

FIGURE 9-7. *Quadratic best-performance curve*

Figure 9-7 shows points from an ideal test.

You visually select three points, $(0, y_0)$, (x_1, y_1), and (x_2, y_2), that appear to be of minimum slope on a quadratic-like curve. The midpoint between 0 and x_1 is x_a, and the midpoint between x_1 and x_2 is x_b, such that

$x_a = (x_1 + 0)/2$ and $x_b = (x_2 + x_1)/2$

When joined, $(0, y_0)$ and (x_1, y_1) form a *secant* (a straight line that connects two points on a curve) with slope S_a, and (x_1, y_1) and (x_2, y_2) form a secant with slope S_b. The x midpoints (x_a, y_a) and (x_b, y_b) lie on the desired curve with tangents having slopes S_a and S_b, respectively. From the derivative of a quadratic equation, which gives the slope of the curve at the midpoints, you have

$S_a = (y_1 - y_0)/(x_1 - 0) = a_1 + 2a_2x_a$

S_a = slope of the lower part of the curve

$S_b = (y_2 - y_1)/(x_2 - x_1) = a_1 + 2a_2x_b$

S_b = slope of the upper part of the curve

Using Gauss elimination, you solve for the a_i coefficients, such that

$a_2 = (S_b - S_a)/[2(x_b - x_a)] = (S_b - S_a)/x_2$
$a_1 = S_a - 2a_2x_a = S_a - a_2x_1$
$a_0 = y_0$

You'll have to use these three equations to get a_0, a_1, and a_2 and then you can use the final equation. These will be the constants in the equation that will give you the response time of a query as you vary the number of rows in the table.

NOTE
This method will not work in all cases. If any a_i coefficients are negative, the equation may dip below the X axis and something else must be used. Often, the origin or $a_0 = y_0 = 0$ works best with this method.

A Simple Example   All of these equations look great, but let's look at a real-life query. You must time the query using two different table sizes to get an equation for the line. The ORDERS table has an index on ORDNO, but it is suppressed by the NVL function (causing the nonlinear response time). The real solution to this problem is to eliminate NULLs in the ORDERS table and remove the NVL function from the query. However, this example is for instructional purposes to generate a quadratic equation.

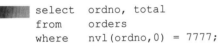

```
select   ordno, total
from     orders
where    nvl(ordno,0) = 7777;
```

For your system, consider the response of this query for two tests:

- When there were 100 records in the ORDERS table, this query took 5 seconds.

- When there were 2000 records in the ORDERS table, this query took 1000 seconds.

You want to know how long this query will take when you have 10,000 rows in the ORDERS table. Therefore, you know that

$y_1 = 5$ (seconds)

$x_1 = 100$ (records)

$y_2 = 1000$ (seconds)

$x_2 = 2000$ (records)

$y_0 = 1$ (second – estimate); this is the y-intercept

You could calculate y_0 by using two points near the lower part of the curve (near 100 rows using the linear equations from the preceding section), but because the lower part of the curve is small (5 seconds for 100 rows), you can guesstimate this to be 1 second. (You should calculate it.)

- **Step 1**   Calculate S_a and S_b.

    $S_a = (y_1 - y_0)/(x_1 - 0)$

    $S_a = (5 - 1)/(100 - 0)$

    $S_a = 0.04$ (The slope of the lower part of the curve is almost horizontal.)

$S_b = (y_2 - y_1)/(x_2 - x_1)$

$S_b = (1000 - 5)/(2000 - 100)$

$S_b = 0.52$ (The slope of the upper part of the curve is much higher than the lower part.)

■ **Step 2**   Calculate a_0, a_1, and a_2.

$a_2 = (S_b - S_a)/x_2$

$a_2 = (0.52 - 0.04)/2000$

$a_2 = 0.00024$

$a_1 = S_a - a_2x_1$

$a_1 = 0.04 - (0.00024)(100)$

$a_1 = 0.016$

$a_0 = y_0$

$a_0 = 1$ (The y-intercept is 1.)

■ **Step 3**   Create the equation to use as the table grows.

$y = a_0 + a_1x + a_2x_2$

$y = 1 + (0.016)x + (0.00024)x^2$ (This is your equation to calculate future responses.)

■ **Step 4**   Calculate the *expected* response for 10,000 rows.

$y = 1 + (0.016)x + (0.00024)x^2$

$y = 1 + (0.016)(10,000) + (0.00024)(10,000^2)$

$y = 24,161$ (The query will take 24,161 seconds, or just under seven hours; you have a problem.)

You'll have to fix the NVL problem soon so the users don't have to wait seven hours. But in reality, you have calculated only a couple of points, and this should be extended out further to get a better future estimate of performance.

TIP
Spreadsheets like Microsoft Excel are very useful tools for graphing performance metrics and automatically deriving trendline equations. For example, to create a graph using Excel, list the observed (x,y) data in cells. Highlight the cells, and select Chart Wizard | XY (Scatter) | Chart Sub-type. Select a Line subtype and click Next | Next | Finish to create the graph. To derive a trendline equation, click the graph line once, and select Chart | Add Trendline. On the Type tab, select Linear, Polynomial Order = 2 (for quadratic) or other model type. To show the trendline equation, on the Options tab, select Display Equation On Chart. Then click OK to complete the graph. The solution equation can be programmed back into the spreadsheet (depending on your spreadsheet version) and used to predict values at higher volumes.

Pattern Interpretation

Graphical performance patterns provide clues to underlying SQL problems and solutions, as seen in Figure 9-8. The ultimate goal in using these methods is to convert a steep linear or quadratic best-performance line to one that is both shallow and linear by optimizing the SQL process. This may involve experiments with indexes, temporary tables, optimizer hint commands, or other Oracle SQL performance tuning methods.

With pattern interpretation, performing your own application-specific SQL experiments to develop expertise at using these methods is important. Table 9-2 shows more specific interpretations—based on my personal experience—that provide a general idea of how you can apply what you observe directly to tuning SQL code. Assuming the scale is correct, pattern interpretation often provides a more accurate picture of what is actually happening to a process and may support or even contradict what a diagnostic tool tells you.

General Linear and Quadratic Interpretations

A shallow linear performance line usually indicates a relatively efficient process compared to something much steeper or curved. The slope a_1 indicates the rate y increases for a given x. Scale is important because a shallow line on one scale can look steep on another, and vice versa. A large a_0 coefficient always indicates an inefficient process.

An upward-sloping (concave) quadratic curve almost always indicates a problem with the process because as more rows are added, the time to process each additional row increases. Coefficient a_2 affects the bowing of the curve. If it is very small, the equation may be more linear. However, even a very slight bowing may be an indicator of something more insidious under much higher volumes.

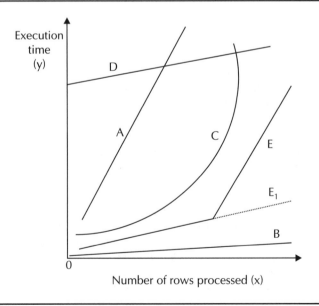

FIGURE 9-8. *Examples of performance patterns*

Pattern in Figure 9-8	Possible Problem	Possible Solution
A	Missing index on a query SELECTing values.	Create an index. Fix a suppressed index.
A	Over-indexed table suffering during DML statements.	Drop some of the indexes or index fewer columns (or smaller columns) for the current indexes.
B	No problem.	Don't touch it (perhaps you just installed Exadata)!
C	Missing index on a query SELECTing values.	Create an index. Fix a suppressed index.
C	Over-indexed table suffering during an INSERT.	Drop some of the indexes or index fewer columns (or smaller columns) for the current indexes.
D	Doing a full table scan or using the ALL_ROWS hint when you shouldn't be.	Try to do an indexed search. Try using the FIRST_ROWS hint to force the use of indexes.
E	The query was fine until some other limitation (such as disk I/O or memory) was encountered.	Find out which ceiling you hit caused this problem. Increasing the SGA may solve the problem, but this could be many things.
E_1	If the limitation in line E is corrected, processing should continue along a straight line.	Further tuning may improve the process to line B.

TABLE 9-2. *Graphical Representations of Various Tuning Situations*

In rare cases, a quadratic curve might appear downward sloping (convex), indicating a process where as more rows are added, the time to process each additional one decreases (i.e., economies of scale). This is desirable and may occur at a threshold, where a full table scan is more efficient than using an index.

Indexing

Missing indexes commonly cause poor SQL performance. In Figure 9-8, line A or C could result from a missing index, depending on code complexity and data volume. Proper indexing improves performance to line B. Over indexing can be as bad as missing indexes. Line A or C could be a process that is forced to use an index, whereas a full table scan would improve the process to B. Inserting into an indexed table is always slower than into an index-free table. Line A or C could be from an INSERT into a heavily indexed table versus line B with no indexing.

Indexing Example   This listing illustrates what can happen with indexing analysis. Suppose you have two tables, TABLE_A and TABLE_B, and there is a one-to-many relationship between them based on KEY_FIELD. There does not have to be a join between the two tables.

```
TABLE_A
KEY_FIELD   NUMBER
TOTAL       NUMBER

TABLE_B
KEY_FIELD   NUMBER
AMOUNT      NUMBER
```

You want to perform the following update within a KEY_FIELD:

```
table_a.total = table_a.total + sum(table_b.amount)
```

The SQL statement shown next will do this. Note that the EXISTS subquery must be used to prevent the NULLing out of any TABLE_A.TOTAL fields, where TABLE_A.KEY_FIELD does not match TOTAL_B.KEY_FIELD.

```
update  table_a ta  set ta.total =
(select    ta.total + sum(tb.amount)
from       table_b tb
where      tb.key_field = ta.key_field
group by   ta.total)
where  exists
(select    null
from       table_b tb2
where      tb2.key_field = ta.key_field);
```

If there is a unique index on the TABLE_A.KEY_FIELD and a nonunique index on TABLE_B.KEY_FIELD, then the performance will be similar to line *B* in Figure 9-8. However, if there is no index on TABLE_B.KEY_FIELD or the cost-based optimizer decides to shut it off, a line will be generated similar to *A* or *C*. The reason is that the EXISTS subquery heavily depends on indexing.

I have seen cases where the number of rows in TABLE_A was small (< 2000), but the cost-based optimizer shut off the index on TABLE_B and reported a small EXPLAIN PLAN cost. This was regardless of the number of rows in TABLE_B (which was up to 800,000 rows). Actual tests showed a steep performance line that contradicted the EXPLAIN PLAN cost. This is an example of uncovering a problem that may have been overlooked by a diagnostic tool.

When the optimizer (cost-based) finds a query to retrieve less than 5–6 percent (based on the average distribution) of the data in a table, the optimizer generally drives the query with an index if one exists. Figure 9-9 shows how Oracle has evolved through the past years prior to Oracle 9*i*. In Oracle 10*g*, the optimizer is very good at analyzing not only the number of rows, but also the distribution of data as well and also knows if the query has been run previously. The first time a query is executed is different from the second time even if this was weeks ago. While the response time still depends on the percentage of blocks (better than looking at the percentage of rows) retrieved by the query, what kind of disks, cache for the disks, cache for the operating system, and previous queries change the upper part of the graph greatly (where you retrieve most of the table). Everything starts depending more on your hardware and access patterns. In 11*g*, this continues to improve, and in Exadata, you have a whole new paradigm with even greater efficiencies. I have left the following graph in Figure 9-9 in this version of the book to show where Oracle has been in the past (Chapter 8 shows a graph of where we are currently with 11*g*).

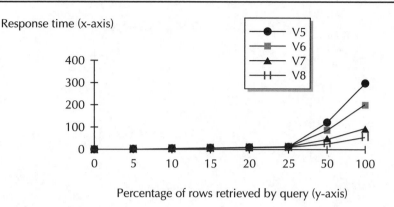

Response time (x-axis)

Percentage of rows retrieved by query (y-axis)

FIGURE 9-9. *Optimum percentage of rows for index for older versions of Oracle*

Optimizer Execution Plan

You can graph performance patterns to leverage available diagnostic tools. For example, you analyzed a slow and complex SQL statement that used views and ran high-volume data under the Oracle cost-based optimizer. Results showed a very high performance line identical to *D* in Figure 9-8. The Oracle EXPLAIN PLAN also showed an inefficient execution plan. Once an effective optimizer hint command was found (i.e., FIRST_ROWS) and added directly to the SQL statements that defined the views, performance improved dramatically to line *B*.

Multiple Table Joins

Complex *multiple-table join* statements often run poorly regardless of the conventional tuning used and may be similar to lines *A* or *C* in Figure 9-8. From past experience, rather than trying to tune only the statement with conventional techniques, a more effective solution is to decompose it into a series of simple SQL statements using temporary tables. The final result would be the same, but at much faster speed, represented by a composite line at *B*.

Jackknifing

Jackknifing is a pattern where a performance line starts off shallow but then veers steeply upward at a certain threshold point, similar to *E* in Figure 9-8. Two linear equations may define the behavior; its cause could be anything from disk I/O or memory limitations to a switch in the optimizer execution plan due to changing data volumes. Possible solutions are to increase the system's limitations, run fresh optimizer statistics, or break the statement into selection ranges. Proper tuning might either straighten out the line to E_1 or improve it further to line *B*.

Riding the Quadratic Curve

Often, a poorly performing SQL process is designed and tested on low-volume data, but in production under higher volumes, its true and degrading quadratic nature is revealed, as shown by curve *A* in Figure 9-10. In this example, a process was created and tested up to x_1. Performance was believed to be close to line *B*, but once in production and when the volume was increased to x_3, the line really turned out to be curve *A*.

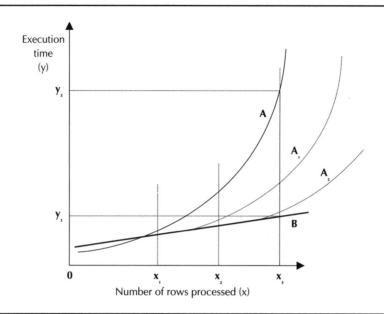

FIGURE 9-10.   *Example of riding the quadratic curve*

If you cannot find a proper tuning solution, you can still improve a quadratic process of unknown cause by breaking the original statement into lower-volume selection ranges and riding the shallow part of the quadratic curve. Suppose in Figure 9-10, you break the process into three selection ranges: from $[0$ to $x_0]$ that rides the lower part of curve A, from $[x_1$ to $x_2]$ that rides the lower part of curve A_1, and from $[x_2$ to $x_3]$, that rides the lower part of curve A_2. The overall result is something closer to line B from $[0$ to $x_3]$ with y_2' taking a lot less time than the original y_2. Although this technique may not be the best solution, it could still solve the problem.

Instead of running everything all at once, breaking up the process using a SQL loop and commit mechanism can sometimes buy better overall performance for processes like updates and deletes that use rollback segments.

Volatility Effects

Running under ideal conditions and graphing the results makes it much easier to analyze the effects of outside traffic and its resulting volatility. For example, line A in Figure 9-11 is from an inefficient linear process run under ideal conditions. Suppose a controlled amount of traffic from another process is then run at the same time. It could be a large query, insert, update, or backup, etc. This second test moves line A by 100 percent to A_1. In other words, the process with added traffic on the system is twice as slow.

Now suppose you optimize the original process. Under an ideal test of the new process, the best performance line shifts down to B. If you were to predict what would happen if you applied the same controlled traffic to the new process, you might predict a 100 percent shift to B_1.

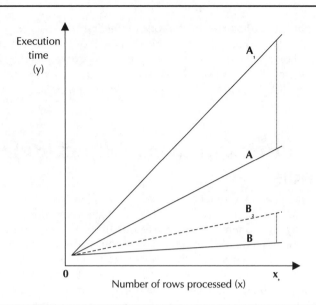

FIGURE 9-11.   *Example of volatility effects*

However, since the slopes between *A* and *B* differ (with *A* being much steeper than *B*), the 100 percent time increase from *B* to B_1 would be much less than from *A* to A_1. In fact, an actual traffic test on line *B* might prove to be much less than even the predicted 100 percent due to the overall efficiency of the line *B* process. In general, more efficient SQL processes are less susceptible to added traffic effects than less efficient processes.

Mathematical Techniques Conclusions

Simple Mathematical Techniques is an effective Oracle SQL performance analysis and tuning methodology that involves running tests under ideal conditions, graphing performance observations, and using simple linear and quadratic equation determination for predicting performance at higher loads. It also includes the interpretation of performance patterns that can be applied directly to tuning SQL code.

The methodology acts as a catalyst by combining the use of some traditional mathematical analysis with Oracle diagnostic tools to aid in their interpretation and to leverage their effectiveness. It can also help you identify hidden problems that may be overlooked by other diagnostic methods by providing a broad picture of performance. The technique can also help you overcome performance-tuning barriers such as inexperience with Oracle, lack of hard evidence, or difficulties with diagnostic tool interpretation that may prevent effective performance tuning. You can also analyze volatility effects from outside traffic. Graphs provide a visual picture of performance for presentation to management and end users. And you can use spreadsheets such as Microsoft Excel with these techniques for quick and easy performance analysis.

Tip
If you want an Oracle symphony as great as one of Beethoven's, you must learn and know how to apply mathematical techniques to your tuning efforts. You don't have to learn everything that you learned in college calculus; merely apply the simple equations in this chapter to tie everything in this book together. Thank you Joe Holmes for doing the math for us!

Join Tuning: Relational vs. Object-Relational Performance

Searching for query optimization to reduce response time or avoid excessive use of system resources has become an important direction over the past few years; this is especially true in light of cloud technology and pooling of database resources. In many queries, joins between tables are necessary to obtain required business information. This section demonstrates cases where it is better to use a particular join method for the relational and object-relational models supported by Oracle. In order to accomplish this, I will work with Oracle's TKPROF tool (see Chapter 6 for more information on TKPROF). In the listing that follows, you can see the result structure of the TKPROF tool and how the TKPROF output looks (without the data for each column). I will use some of the key columns to calculate metrics (note that since this testing was done with Euro numbering, you can replace the comma with a decimal for U.S.).

call	count	cpu	elapsed	disk	query	current	rows
Parse(a)	(d)	--	--	--	--	--	--
Execute(b)	(e)	--	--	--	--	--	--
Fetch(c)	(j)	--	--	--	--	--	(i)
Total	---	--	--	(k)	(f)	(g)	(h)

According to this listing, which shows a result of a typical file obtained through the TKPROF tool, I will analyze the following rates, which will serve as criteria for the optimization process:

- **Blocks read (*f+g*) to rows processed (*h*)**   This rate indicates the relative cost of the query. When more blocks have to be accessed in relation to the returned rows, the fetched row is more expensive. A similar relation can be deduced from the rate: read blocks over executions (*f+g*)/*e*. The procured value for this rate should be less than 10; however, values in the range of 10 to 20 are acceptable. Values greater than 20 could indicate some possibility for optimization in this field.

- **Parse count (*d*) over execute count (*e*)**   Ideally, the parsing count should be close to one. If this value is high in relation to the execution count, then the statement has been parsed several times. This indicates that there could be problems in the shared pool size (too small). Poor use of bind variables can be another reason for unnecessary parsing.

■ **Rows fetched (*i*) to fetches (*j*)**   This rate indicates the level in which the array fetch capability has been used. Array fetch is an Oracle feature that permits fetching more than one row for every fetch executed. A value close to 1 indicates that no array processing occurred, which signifies that there is a good possibility for optimization.

■ **Disk reads (*k*) to logical reads (*f+g*)**   This is (generally) a miss rate for data in the cache buffer. It shows the percentage of the times when the engine could not find the solicited rows in the buffer cache and, therefore, had to bring the data blocks from the disk. Generally, the values of this rate should represent less than 10 percent (ideally less than 5 percent, depending on the query mix).

The join methods analyzed in this section are HASH, SORT-MERGE, and NESTED LOOPS. To force the Oracle optimizer to execute a specific join, method hints are necessary. The hints to use include the following:

■ **USE_MERGE (*table_name*)**   Forces the optimizer to use the SORT-MERGE method.

■ **USE_HASH (*table_name*)**   Forces the optimizer to use the HASH method.

■ **USE_NL (*table_name*)**   Forces the optimizer to use the NESTED LOOPS method.

■ **INDEX (*table_name*)** Forces the optimizer to use a table index.

However, in some object-relational queries, especially when REFs are used, this *table_name* is not available; that's why in these queries, the internal table name (alias) provided by Oracle is used. This internal name can be obtained in this way (it only works with Oracle 10*g* and 11*g*):

I. Run an EXPLAIN PLAN for the specific query.

2. View the EXPLAIN PLAN utilizing DBMS_XPLAN.

```
SELECT plan_table_output
FROM TABLE(DBMS_XPLAN.DISPLAY ('PLAN_TABLE', NULL,'ALL'));
```

The DBMS_XPLAN.DISPLAY function accepts three parameters, in this order:

■ **Table_name**   The table name where the EXPLAIN PLAN data is saved. The default value is PLAN_TABLE.

■ **Statement_id**   The ID of the statement plan to be shown. The default value is NULL unless you set a value to identify this particular statement.

■ **Format**   Controls the detail level shown. The default value is TYPICAL. Other values include BASIC, ALL, and SERIAL.

The following query retrieves (in addition to a lot of other columns and data) the alias of the involved tables in the statements found in the execution plan table. In this case, the table is the PLAN_TABLE. For example, if you have tables whose aliases are B@SEL$1 and P000003$@SEL$1, and you want to join these tables through the SORT-MERGE method, here is the query to use:

```
SELECT /*+ USE_MERGE (B@SEL$1 P000003$SEL$1)*/ [columns]
FROM...
```

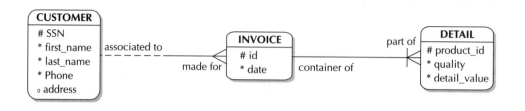

FIGURE 9-12. *Entity-relation model for the test*

If you need two or more joins in a query in order to achieve the possible combinations of these methods, you must use several hints.

Models Used

Here, the relational and object-relational models will be analyzed as they apply to a particular case of three tables, where CUSTOMER, INVOICE, and DETAIL data could be found, as shown in Figure 9-12.

In the object-relational model, DETAIL is a nested table located in INVOICE. See the code listing at the end of this section (preceding the Tips Review), which shows the creation of the tables in both models. For both models, tables with many and few rows are used. The smaller tables will be about 10 percent of the size of the larger tables. Table 9-3 shows the table sizes for both models.

Note the presence of indexes in the tables on the joining columns. Place special attention on the indexing of the NESTED_TABLE_ID pseudo-column in the nested table DETAIL.

Results

First, the results for the join between INVOICE and DETAIL tables are executed, and then the join between the three tables (CUSTOMER, INVOICE, and DETAIL) is executed.

Two-Table Join (INVOICE and DETAIL)

In the following test, you use queries with both large and small tables.

Tables	Many Rows	Few Rows
CUSTOMER	3375	343
INVOICE	12,000	1200
DETAIL	23,481	2363

TABLE 9-3. *Table Sizes*

For the relational model, the query is

```
SELECT  /*+ ORDERED USE_HASH(d) INDEX(i) INDEX(d)*/
        i.invoice_date, d.quantity, d.detail_value
FROM    invoice i, detail d
WHERE   i.id = d. invoice_id;
```

For the object-relational model, the query is

```
SELECT /*+ ORDERED USE_HASH(D@SEL$1) INDEX(I@SEL$1) INDEX(D@SEL$1)*/
        i.invoice_date, d.quantity, d.detail_value
FROM    invoice i, TABLE(i.detail) d;
```

In this case, the HASH join method is used; however, for the SORT-MERGE and NESTED LOOPS methods, the same syntax is applied.

Joins with Large Tables   In Figure 9-13, results are presented corresponding to the join of two tables with many rows using indexes in both.

In Figures 9-14 and 9-15, the EXPLAIN PLANs made with the HASH method are presented in a screen shot from JDeveloper. Note that the EXPLAIN PLANs for both models are the same, even though the object-relational model has a nested table, as it is internally treated as a typical relational table.

RATE	$(f + g) / h$	d / e	i / j	$k / (f + g)$	JOIN METHOD
NORMAL VALUE	Less than 10	1 (or close to 1)	The bigger the better	1 (or close to 1)	
RELATIONAL MODEL	1.063966611	1	14.98353148	0.00872593	**HASH**
	1.12976449	1	14.98353148	0	**MERGE**
	48.38222393	1	14.98353148	0	**NL**
OBJECT-RELATIONAL MODEL	0.160877053	1	14.98353148	0.0751958	**HASH**
	0.02801697	1	14.98353148	0	**MERGE**
	0.863527534	1	14.98353148	0	**NL**

FIGURE 9-13.   *Results for the test with many rows in both models*

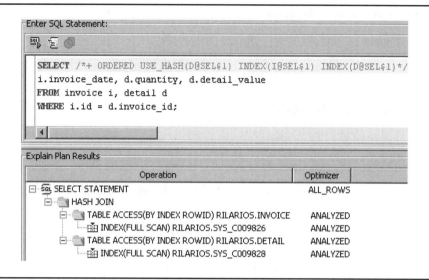

FIGURE 9-14. *Explain plan for the HASH method in the relational model*

Figures 9-16 and 9-17 show that in every join method, in terms of the ratio of blocks read (logical reads) to rows processed, the object-relational model behaves better than the relational model. The number of logical reads is *much* smaller for the object-relational model than for the relational model. The performance gets slightly better using the SORT-MERGE rather than the HASH method; worst by far is the performance of the NESTED LOOPS method.

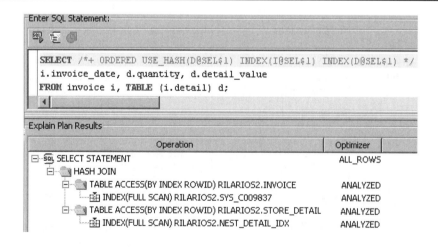

FIGURE 9-15. *Explain plan for the HASH method in the object-relational model (JDev)*

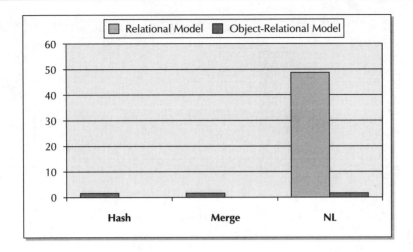

FIGURE 9-16. *Blocks read (f+g) to rows processed (h) for large tables*

In Figure 9-18, observe that, in general, all models behave well: the HASH method shows a bit worse performance in the object-relational model, but the difference is negligible compared with the HASH performance in the relational model.

Joins with Small Tables   Figure 9-19 shows results for the same queries tested as before, but now, it represents tests with small tables.

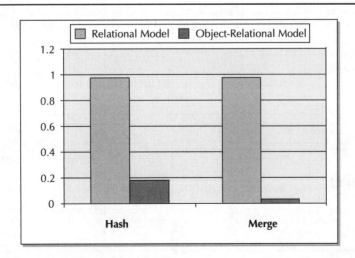

FIGURE 9-17. *Blocks read (f+g) to rows processed (h) without NL for large tables*

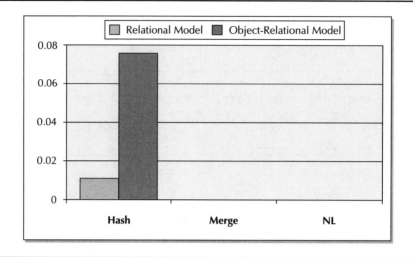

FIGURE 9-18. *Disk reads (k) to logical reads (f+g) for large tables*

RATE	(f + g) / h	d / e	i / j	k / (f + g)	JOIN METHOD
NORMAL VALUE	Less than 10	1 (or close to 1)	While bigger the better	Less than 10%	
RELATIONAL MODEL	0.977147694	1	14.8710692	0.01299263	**HASH**
	1.035548032	1	14.8710692	0	**MERGE**
	5.424883623	1	14.87106918	0	**NL**
OBJECT-RELATIONAL MODEL	0.171174979	1	14.87106918	0.07654321	**HASH**
	0.038038884	1	14.87106918	0	**MERGE**
	0.875739645	1	14.87106918	0	**NL**

FIGURE 9-19. *Results for test with small tables in both models*

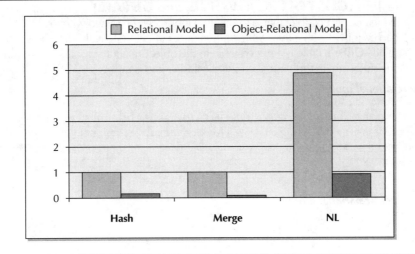

FIGURE 9-20. *Blocks read (f+g) to rows processed (h) for small tables*

Again, the object-relational model has an advantage over the relational model in the ratio of blocks read (logical reads) to rows processed, and you can observe that in every join method, especially in SORT-MERGE, performance is better (see Figure 9-20).

According to Figure 9-21, good results are obtained in both models. Though the HASH method in the object-relational model performs the worst, the difference is minor compared with the performance drawbacks of the relational model.

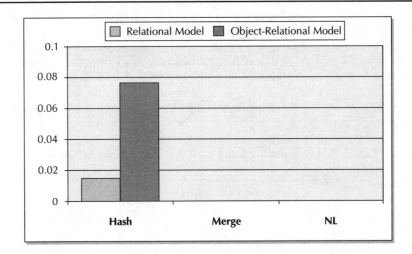

FIGURE 9-21. *Disk reads (k) to logical reads (f+g) for small tables*

Three-Table Join (CUSTOMER, INVOICE, and DETAIL)

Combining join methods is possible; that is to say, two tables can be joined with the HASH method, and the result can be joined with a third table through a SORT-MERGE method. It should be noted that, in this case, the DETAIL table is a nested table in the object-relational model. The queries to use for this part of the study are (in this case, the HASH-MERGE join is):

For the relational model:

```
SELECT /*+ ORDERED  USE_MERGE(i) USE_HASH(d) INDEX(c) INDEX(d) INDEX(i) */
       c.first_name, c.last_name, f.invoice_date, d.quantity, d.detail_value
FROM   customer c, invoice i, detail d
WHERE  c.ssn = i.sn_cust
AND    i.id = d.invoice_id;
```

For the object-relational model:

```
SELECT /*+ ORDERED USE_MERGE(P000004$@SEL$1 I@SEL$1) USE_HASH(D@SEL$1)
           INDEX(P000004$@SEL$1) INDEX(I@SEL$1) INDEX(D@SEL$1)  */
       i.ref_cust.first_name, i.ref_cust.last_name, i.invoice_date,
       d.quantity, d.valor_detalle
FROM   invoice i, TABLE(i.detail) d;
```

Note that the table names for the object-relational model (object alias) are obtained through the DBMS_XPLAN.DISPLAY function as explained previously. Also note that in the query for the object-relational model, the CUSTOMER table is not in the FROM clause, due to the use of pointers (REF) to that specific table. Those pointers are located in the INVOICE table.

Join with Large Tables   In Figure 9-22, results are presented corresponding to the three-table join using indexes (for the three) against the test tables with many rows.

In Figures 9-23 and 9-24, the EXPLAIN PLANs for the joins with the HASH-MERGE method are presented. As in Figures 9-14 and 9-15, the EXPLAIN PLANs in both models are the same, even when, in the object-relational model, a nested table is used (as before, it is treated as a typical relational table).

In Figures 9-25 and 9-26, observe again that the object-relational model performs better than the relational model (on the ratio of blocks read to rows processed), especially when the SORT-MERGE method is involved. In the disk reads (k) to logical reads ($f+g$) rate (Figure 9-27), you can observe that, in general, both models are efficient. Although the worst-performing join method is the one involving the HASH method in the object-relational model, the difference is not significant.

Join with Small Tables   In Figures 9-28 and 9-29, the performance advantage presented by the object-relational model over the relational model is again observed in the ratio of blocks read to rows processed.

RATE	(f + g) / h	d / e	i / j	k / (f + g)	JOIN METHOD
NORMAL VALUE	Less than 10	One	The bigger the better	Less than 10%	
RELATIONAL MODEL	1.131255057	1	14.98353148	0.01299263	HASH-HASH
	0.998552021	1	14.98353148	0	HASH-MERGE
	48.38371449	1	14.98353148	0	HASH-NL
	1.128060985	1	14.98353148	0	MERGE-HASH
	0.998552021	1	14.98353148	0	**MERGE-MERGE**
	48.84749372	1	14.98353148	0	MERGE-NL
	12.10297687	1	14.98353148	0	NL-HASH
	11.77539287	1	14.98353148	0	NL-MERGE
	59.82053575	1	14.98353148	0	NL-NL
OBJECT-RELATIONAL MODEL	0.1622632	1	14.98353148	0.01087237	HASH-HASH
	0.030327215	1	14.98353148	0	HASH-MERGE
	1.324106355	1	14.98353148	0	HASH-NL
	0.030327215	1	14.98353148	0	MERGE-HASH
	0.030327215	1	14.98353148	0	**MERGE-MERGE**
	1.195782753	1	14.98353148	0	MERGE-NL
	1.236107027	1	14.98353148	0.00078156	NL-HASH
	1.036711891	1	14.98353148	0	NL-MERGE
	1.938883522	1	14.98353148	0	NL-NL

FIGURE 9-22.   *Results for test with large tables in both models*

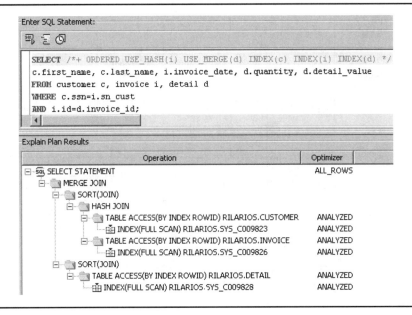

FIGURE 9-23. *EXPLAIN PLAN for the HASH-MERGE method in the relational model*

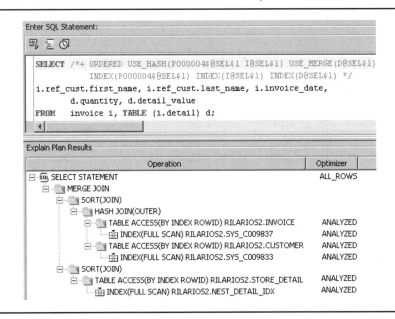

FIGURE 9-24. *EXPLAIN PLAN for the HASH-MERGE method in the object-relational model*

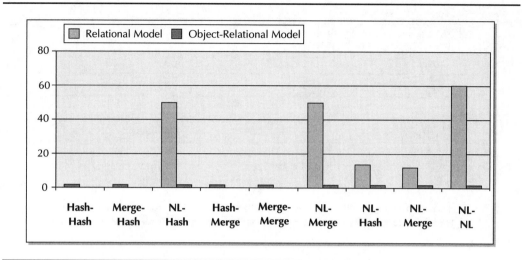

FIGURE 9-25. *Blocks read (f+g) to rows processed (h) for large tables*

The disk reads (*k*) to logical reads (*f+g*) ratio (Figure 9-30) are similar in both models, but as seen in previous tests, the joins that involve the HASH method in the object-relational model have the worst performance.

Results for the join with few rows can be seen in Figure 9-31.

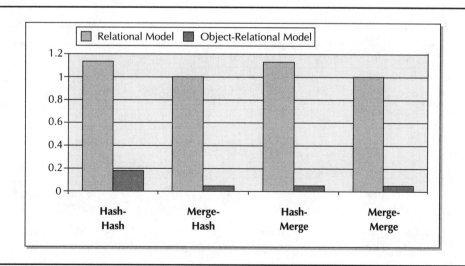

FIGURE 9-26. *Blocks read (f+g) to rows processed (h) without NL for large tables*

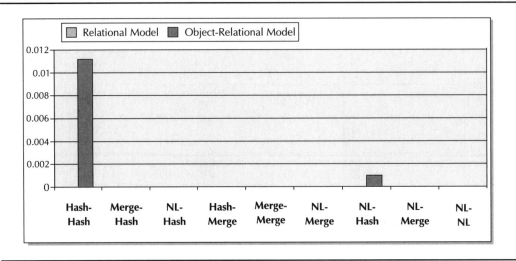

FIGURE 9-27. *Disk reads (k) to logical reads (f+g) for large tables*

Conclusion

Clearly, the object-relational model performs better than the relational model in all of these tests, especially when the ratio of the blocks read (logical reads) to rows processed is the measured value and when the SORT-MERGE join is involved. However, in terms of ratio of disk reads(k) to logical reads ($f+g$), the object-relational model turns out to be slightly more expensive, especially when

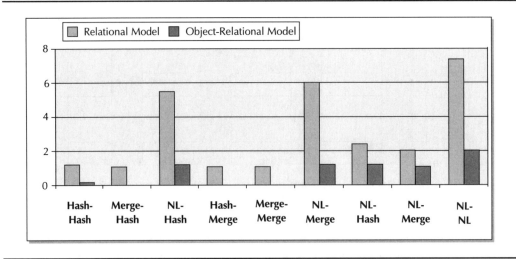

FIGURE 9-28. *Blocks read (f+g) to rows processed (h) for small tables*

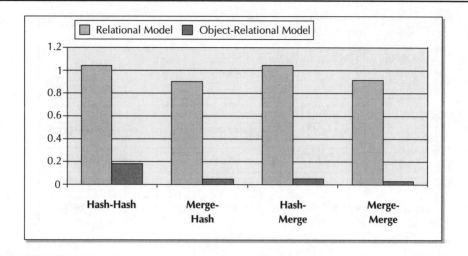

FIGURE 9-29.   *Blocks read (f+g) to rows processed (h) without NL for small tables*

the HASH join is involved. Such cost differences were reduced significantly when other join methods were used. In general, the object-relational model offers good performance, surpassing the relational model. Because a variety of variables can be encountered in an application, readers should do their own testing to validate any potential gains. However, the results suggest that the object-relational model offers great performance that, at a minimum, should be considered where needed. Listed next are the creation scripts for both the relational and object-relational objects used in this section.

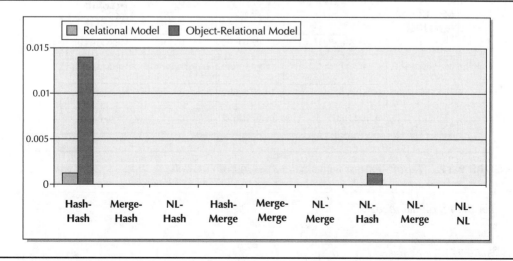

FIGURE 9-30.   *Disk reads (k) to logical reads (f+g) for small tables*

RATE	(f + g) / h	d / e	i / j	k / (f + g)	JOIN METHOD
NORMAL VALUE	Less than 10	One	The bigger the better	Less than 10%	
RELATIONAL MODEL	1.037663986	1	14.8710692	0.00163132	**HASH-HASH**
	0.904782057	1	14.8710692	0	**HASH-MERGE**
	5.426999577	1	14.8710692	0	**HASH-NL**
	1.035548032	1	14.8710692	0	**MERGE-HASH**
	0.904782057	1	14.8710692	0	**MERGE-MERGE**
	5.837917901	1	14.8710692	0	**MERGE-NL**
	2.392297926	1	14.8710692	0	**NL-HASH**
	2.063055438	1	14.8710692	0	**NL-MERGE**
	7.318662717	1	14.8710692	0	**NL-NL**
OBJECT-RELATIONAL MODEL	0.176669484	1	14.8710692	0.01196172	**HASH-HASH**
	0.045646661	1	14.8710692	0	**HASH-MERGE**
	1.307269653	1	14.8710692	0	**HASH-NL**
	0.045646661	1	14.8710692	0	**MERGE-HASH**
	0.026627219	1	14.8710692	0	**MERGE-MERGE**
	1.195266272	1	14.8710692	0	**MERGE-NL**
	1.256551141	1	14.8710692	0.00100908	**NL-HASH**
	1.058326289	1	14.8710692	0	**NL-MERGE**
	1.96238377	1	14.8710692	0	**NL-NL**

FIGURE 9-31. *Results for test with small tables in both models*

For the relational model:

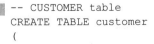

```
-- CUSTOMER table
CREATE TABLE customer
(
```

```
   ssn          NUMBER(8)     PRIMARY KEY,   --Social Security Number
   first_name   VARCHAR2(20) NOT NULL,
   last_name    VARCHAR2(30) NOT NULL,
   phone        NUMBER(7)    NOT NULL,
   address      VARCHAR2(40)
);

-- INVOICE table
CREATE TABLE invoice
(
id  NUMBER(8) PRIMARY KEY,                  -- Invoice Number
invoice_date  DATE NOT NULL,                -- Invoice Date
sn_cust       NUMBER(8) REFERENCES customer NOT NULL
);

-- Detail table
CREATE TABLE detail
(
quantity       NUMBER(3),                   -- Quantity of Product
detail_value   NUMBER(8),
product_id     VARCHAR2(20),
invoice_id     NUMBER(8) REFERENCES invoice,
PRIMARY KEY(invoice_id, product_id)
);
```

For the object-relational model:

```
-- Customer type and its respective table
CREATE TYPE customer_type AS OBJECT
(
   ssn          NUMBER(8),
   first_name   VARCHAR2(20),
   last_name    VARCHAR2(30),
   phone        NUMBER(7),
   address      VARCHAR2(40)
);
/
CREATE TABLE customer OF customer_type
(
  ssn          PRIMARY KEY,
  first_name   NOT NULL,
  last_Name    NOT NULL,
  phone        NOT NULL
);
/

--Detail type
CREATE TYPE detail_type AS OBJECT
(
  product_id     VARCHAR2(20),
  quantity       NUMBER(3),
```

```
   detail_value  NUMBER(8) --Valor del detalle.
);
/

--Nested table type based on detail type
CREATE TYPE nest_detail AS TABLE OF detail_type;
/

--Invoice type and its respective table
CREATE TYPE invoice_type AS OBJECT
(
   id            NUMBER(8),
   invoice_date  DATE,
   detail        nest_detail,  --Nested table of details
   ref_cust      REF customer_type
);
/

CREATE TABLE invoice OF invoice_type
(
   id            PRIMARY KEY,
   invoice_date  NOT NULL,
   ref_cust      NOT NULL,
   SCOPE FOR (ref_cust) IS customer
) NESTED TABLE detail STORE AS store_detail;
/

--Index on nested table.
CREATE INDEX nest_detail_idx on store_detail(nested_table_id);
```

TIPS & REVIEW

Tips Review

- The optimizer often uses HASH joins in lieu of SORT-MERGE joins if the correct initialization parameters are set. With HASH joins, the driving table is used as a hash table; on the join key, the other table is scanned and the result probes the hash table for matches. If there is not enough memory, the hash table can be split into multiple partitions and it may also be swapped to disk. Be careful, however; HASH joins can be slow when memory is low or the tables are poorly indexed.

- If the ORDERED hint is used, then the first table in the FROM clause is also the driving table. The LEADING hint is also helpful in tuning multitable joins. Oracle Enterprise Manager and the Tuning Pack are helpful as well and are covered in Chapter 5.

- Using cost-based optimization and NESTED LOOPS joins as the means of joining, the first table in the FROM clause is the driving table (all other conditions being equal), but only the ORDERED hint guarantees this. In NESTED LOOPS joins, choosing a driving table that is the smaller result set (not always the smaller table) means making fewer loops to the other result set (from the nondriving table) and usually results in the best performance.

- The columns that are retrieved can change which indexes Oracle uses and also change the way Oracle joins the tables in the query.

- To change the way Oracle joins multiple tables, use the USE_MERGE, USE_NL, and USE_HASH hints.

- In a three-table join, the driving table is the intersection table or the table that has a join condition to each of the other two tables in the join. Try to use the most limiting table as the driving table (or intersection table), so your result set from the join of the first two tables is small when you join it to the third table. Also, ensure that all join conditions on all tables are indexed!

- To ensure that you are reading your EXPLAIN PLAN correctly, run a query for which you are sure of the driving table (with nested subqueries).

- You may not be able to modify actual code for some third-party products, but you can often add, force, or suppress indexes to improve performance.

- When distributed queries cannot be avoided, use IN clauses, set operators such as UNION and MINUS, and do whatever else you can to reduce the network traffic between database nodes. Queries written in a manner that causes looping between distributed nodes (distributed databases) can be extremely slow.

- If you want an Oracle symphony as great as Beethoven's, you must learn how to tune at the block level and know how to apply mathematical techniques to your tuning efforts. You don't have to relearn everything you learned in college calculus; merely apply the simple equations in this chapter to tie everything in this book together.

- If you've read and understood this entire chapter, you're probably among the top-tuning professionals and you will see the heights and joys that I've seen with tuning Oracle.

References

E. Aronoff, K. Loney, and N. Sonawalla, *Advanced Oracle Tuning and Administration* (Oracle Press, Osborne McGraw-Hill, 1997).

Mike Ault, "Advantages of Oracle9*i* Real Application Clusters" (TUSC, 2002).

Janet Bacon, "Reading a Block Dump" (TUSC).

Block Level Reading Tool from Terlingua Software (www.tlingua.com).

Bradley Brown, *Oracle Web Development* (McGraw-Hill, 1999).

S. Chapra and R. Canale, *Numerical Methods for Engineers; with Programming and Software Applications, 3/e* (McGraw-Hill, 1998).

Kevin Gilpin, Mark Bobak, Jonathon Lewis, Metalink notes "EM Grid Control 10*g*" (otn.oracle.com, Oracle Corporation).

Guy Harrison, *Oracle SQL High-Performance Tuning 2/e* (Prentice Hall, 2000).

J. A. Holmes, "Leveraging Oracle Performance Tuning Tools Using Simple Mathematical Techniques," *SELECT Magazine,* Vol. 5, No. 4, July 1998, IOUG-A, pp. 36–42.

J. A. Holmes, "Seven Deadly SQL Traps and How to Avoid Them," *SELECT Magazine,* Vol. 6, No 4, July 1999, IOUG-A, pp. 22–26.

J. A. Holmes, "Amazing SQL*Plus Tricks," *SELECT Magazine,* Vol. 7, No. 4, July 2000, IOUG-A, pp. 26–33.

J. A. Holmes, "SQL Performance Analysis and Tuning Using Simple Mathematical Techniques," *The Carleton Journal of Computer Science,* No. 2, 1998, Carleton University Press Inc., Ottawa, ON, pp. 9–14.
R. Jain, *The Art of Computer Systems Performance Analysis: Techniques for Experimental Design, Measurement, Simulation and Modeling* (John Wiley & Sons, Inc., 1991).
Scott Marin, *The Machinations of Oracle* (Terlingua Software).
Dave Moore, *Oracle Professional,* February 2002, Managing Oracle9i Real Application.
James Morle, *Scaling Oracle8i* (Addison-Wesley, 1999).
Rich Niemiec, "Oracle10g New Features" (TUSC Presentation).
Oracle11g Documentation (Oracle Corporation).
Real Application Cluster Documentation Set(technet.oracle.com).
Jay Rossiter, "Oracle Enterprise Manager 10g: Making the Grid a Reality" (Oracle Corporation)
Oracle 10g and Oracle 9i documentation.
Craig Schallahamer, "All about Oracle's Touch Count Algorithm" (orapub.com).
Roger Schrag, "Tuning Joins" (Database Specialists).
Randy Swanson, "Oracle10g new features" (www.tusc.com).
Dave Wotton, "Understanding 'Snapshot Too Old'"
(http://home.clara.net/dwotton/dba/snapshot.htm).
"Clusters: An Oracle White Paper," March 2001.
"Oracle RAC—Cache Fusion delivers Scalability: An Oracle White Paper," May 2001.
"Building Highly Available Database Servers using RAC: An Oracle White Paper," May 2001.
The tips and techniques section of www.ioug.org.
Other websites: www.tusc.com, www.oracle.com, www.ixora.com, www.laoug.org, www.ioug.org, technet.oracle.com, and www.lookuptables.com.

Thanks to Mike Messina who added the Real Application Testing, Database Replay, and SQL Performance Analyzer sections. Special thanks to Francisco Javier Moreno, Guillermo L. Ospina Romero, and Rafael I. Larios Restrepo from the University Nacional in Medellín, Colombia (who contributed the excellent section "Join Tuning: Relational vs. Object-Relational Performance" in this chapter); Maurizio Bonomi of Italy (detailed join sections); Joe Holmes of Canada (for the Tuning Mathematical Techniques section); Veljko Lavrnic (VL), Scott Martin, and Tirth (tink) for help and insight with the block tuning section; and Roger Schrag (basic join sections). Thanks to Joe Trezzo, Andy Mendelsohn, Sean McGuire, Mike Broulette, Judy Corley, Greg Pucka, Randy Swanson, Bob Taylor, and Mark Greenhalgh for their contributions to this chapter.

CHAPTER
10

Using PL/SQL to
Enhance Performance
(Developer and DBA)

As with each release before it, Oracle 11g continues to elevate PL/SQL performance and functionality to new levels. This chapter focuses on helpful tips that are new with 11g (up to 11gR2) as well as tips that continue to be useful from older versions. Once you have great queries to monitor your system, you need to automate them. PL/SQL gives you the capability to do so while also providing some great packages and procedures that you can use for tuning. The PL/SQL engine processes all PL/SQL requests and passes the statements onto Oracle for execution. When PL/SQL is passed to Oracle, it is placed in Oracle's System Global Area (SGA), more particularly in the shared pool. In Oracle, PL/SQL source code can be stored in the database in the form of procedures, functions, packages, and triggers. Once these objects are stored in the database in compiled format, they can be executed from any Oracle tool by any user who has been granted EXECUTE privilege on that object. Upon execution, the p-code (executable code) is loaded into the shared pool and executed by Oracle. A PL/SQL object remains in the shared pool until the object is aged out with a Least Recently Used (LRU) algorithm. If any process calls the object, it does not have to be reloaded into the SGA shared pool as long as it has not been aged out. Therefore, Oracle looks in the shared pool (which is very efficient) for the object prior to going to disk (which is not as efficient) to load the object. How well the SQL within the PL/SQL is tuned is probably the biggest factor driving performance, yet I will cover other tuning considerations in this chapter. The last portion of this chapter is dedicated to understanding and being able to locate the PL/SQL. Here are the tips covered in this chapter:

- Leverage the PL/SQL Function Result Cache to improve performance (new in 11g).

- Reference sequences directly in PL/SQL expressions (new in 11g).

- Use named parameters in SQL function calls (new in 11g).

- Simplify loops with the CONTINUE statement (new in 11g).

- Leverage compile-time warnings to catch programming mistakes (improved in 11g).

- Using Table triggers (improved in 11g)

- Increase performance with native compilation (improved in 11g).

- Maximize performance with the optimizing compiler (improved in 11g).

- Use DBMS_APPLICATION_INFO for real-time monitoring.

- Use a custom replacement of DBMS_APPLICATION_INFO for real-time monitoring in a RAC environment.

- Log timing information in a database table.

- Reduce PL/SQL program unit iterations and iteration time.

- Use ROWID for iterative processing.

- Standardize on data types, IF statement order, and PLS_INTEGER.

- Reduce the calls to SYSDATE.

- Reduce the use of the MOD function.

- Improve shared pool use by pinning objects.

- Identify the PL/SQL that needs to be pinned.

- Use and modify DBMS_SHARED_POOL.SIZES.

- Get detailed object information from DBA_OBJECT_SIZE.

- Find invalid objects.

- Find disabled triggers.

- Use PL/SQL associative arrays for fast reference table lookups.

- Find and tune the SQL when objects are used.

- Consider the time component when working with Oracle's DATE data type.

- Use PL/SQL to tune PL/SQL.

- Understand the implications of PL/SQL location.

- Specify a rollback segment for a large cursor.

- Use temporary database tables for increased performance.

- Integrate a user-tracking mechanism to pinpoint execution location.

- Limit the use of dynamic SQL.

- Use pipelined table functions to build complex result sets.

- Suppress debugging commands with conditional compilation.

- Take advantage of the samples just for the beginners (beginners start here).

Leverage the PL/SQL Function Result Cache to Improve Performance (New in 11g)

Perhaps the best new developer feature in Oracle Database 11*g* is the PL/SQL Function Result Cache. This feature provides a quick way to build a cache of function results that will be used automatically when a subsequent call to a function is made with the same parameter values. It essentially eliminates the hand-coded caches that you've had to build in the past using PL\SQL array structures. More importantly, the new Function Result Cache works at the instance-level, not the session-level as is the case with hand-coded mechanisms.

Let's start the example with these tables:

```
Table Name   Rows         Column         Type        Length
-----------  -----------  -------------  ---------   ------
countries            65   country_id     number
                          country_name   varchar2       50
cities            1,111   city_id        number
                          country_id     number
                          city_name      varchar2       50
```

```
residents    1,000,000   resident_id    number
                         first_name     varchar2      50
                         last_name      varchar2      50
                         salary         number
                         city_id        number
```

```
Table Name   Constraint Name   Type  Column          Related Constraint
-----------  ---------------   ----  ------------    ------------------
countries    countries_pk      PK    country_id
countries    countries_uk1     UK    country_name
cities       cities_pk         PK    city_id
cities       cities_uk1        UK    country_id
                                     city_name
cities       cities_fk1        FK    country_id      countries_pk
residents    residents_pk      PK    resident_id
residents    residents_fk1     FK    city_id         cities_pk
```

There are a total of 398,124 USA residents with these totals in some key cities:

```
City Name         Count
--------------    -----
Anchorage         907
Baltimore         865
Chicago           869
Dallas            924
New York City     890
```

Next, you create a function that returns the average salary for a specified country:

```
CREATE OR REPLACE FUNCTION get_avg_sal(p_country_c in varchar2) return number is
  v_avg_n number;
BEGIN
  select trunc(avg(r.salary), 2)
    into v_avg_n
    from residents r,
         countries c,
         cities    t
   where r.city_id      = t.city_id
     and t.country_id   = c.country_id
     and c.country_name = p_country_c;
  return v_avg_n;
END get_avg_sal;
```

The baseline performance is obtained by executing the function several times to compute the average salary of residents in the USA:

```
select get_avg_sal('USA') from dual;

GET_AVG_SAL('USA')
------------------
        515368.02
```

```
Execution Times
---------------
0.421 seconds
0.359 seconds
0.358 seconds
0.359 seconds
0.374 seconds
```

The initial execution, which incurs the overhead of parsing the statement, is ignored to yield an average execution time of 0.3625 seconds. Not a bad showing overall considering the RESIDENTS table contains 1 million records. However, let's see how this seemingly fast performance can compound into poor performance when the function is utilized within a complex query. The task is to determine the number of Chicago residents who earn more than the average salary. Here are the results:

```
select count(*)
  from residents r,
       cities     c,
       countries cr
 where r.city_id        = c.city_id
   and c.country_id     = cr.country_id
   and cr.country_name  = 'USA'
   and c.city_name      = 'Chicago'
   and r.salary         > get_avg_sal(cr.country_name);


  COUNT(*)
----------
       434


Executed in 309.318 seconds
```

Clearly, the problem here is that the GET_AVG_SAL function is being executed 869 times, once for each resident who lives in Chicago. Realizing that the GET_AVG_SAL function can only return 65 different values (one for each country), one might be inclined to build a caching mechanism into the function call. With 11*g*, however, you can implement a cache in a matter of seconds by simply adding the RESULT_CACHE keyword to the function definition:

```
CREATE OR REPLACE FUNCTION get_avg_sal(p_country_c in varchar2) return number
result_cache is
 v_avg_n number;
BEGIN
  select trunc(avg(r.salary), 2)
    into v_avg_n
    from residents r,
         countries c,
         cities     t
   where r.city_id       = t.city_id
     and t.country_id    = c.country_id
     and c.country_name  = p_country_c;
  return v_avg_n;
END get_avg_sal;
```

With the Result Cache enabled, the average execution time of the function has dropped to 0.0155 seconds, as shown here:

```
select get_avg_sal('USA') from dual;

GET_AVG_SAL('USA')
-----------------
        515368.02

Execution Times
---------------
1.373 seconds
0.015 seconds
0.016 seconds
0.016 seconds
0.015 seconds
```

The complex Chicago query now completes in a blazing 0.749 seconds!

Let's take a closer look at what is happening within the function. First, the function is modified slightly to generate console output every time it executes:

```
CREATE OR REPLACE FUNCTION get_avg_sal(p_country_c in varchar2) return number result_cache is
  v_avg_n number;
BEGIN
  dbms_output.put_line('Executing Function Body');
  select trunc(avg(r.salary), 2)
    into v_avg_n
    from residents r,
         countries c,
         cities    t
   where r.city_id     = t.city_id
     and t.country_id  = c.country_id
     and c.country_name = p_country_c;
  return v_avg_n;
END get_avg_sal;
```

Now let's run the complex Chicago query:

```
select count(*)
  from residents r,
       cities     c,
       countries cr
 where r.city_id       = c.city_id
   and c.country_id    = cr.country_id
   and cr.country_name = 'USA'
   and c.city_name     = 'Chicago'
   and r.salary        > get_avg_sal(cr.country_name);

  COUNT(*)
----------
       434
```

```
Executing Function Body

Executed in 1.591 seconds
```

The single 'Executing Function Body' indicates that the function body was only executed a single time. When you reexecute the query,

```
/
    COUNT(*)
----------
       434


Executed in 0.749 seconds
```

The 'Executing Function Body' text does not appear because the results are coming from the result cache. As an added benefit, the Result Cache is automatically leveraged by any session of the instance. In comparison, a manually coded cache would be session-specific (each session would maintain its own copy of the cache array and values). To test this, start a new SQL session and run the complex Chicago query:

```
select count(*)
   from residents r,
        cities     c,
        countries cr
  where r.city_id        = c.city_id
    and c.country_id      = cr.country_id
    and cr.country_name = 'USA'
    and c.city_name       = 'Chicago'
    and r.salary          > get_avg_sal(cr.country_name);

    COUNT(*)
----------
       434


Executed in 0.811 seconds
```

Clearly, the new database session is utilizing the cache that was populated in the original session for the get_avg_sal('USA') function call. If you alter the query to report on Dublin, Ireland, you will see that the function must be executed again to fill the cache with data for Ireland.

```
select count(*)
   from residents r,
        cities     c,
        countries cr
  where r.city_id        = c.city_id
    and c.country_id      = cr.country_id
    and cr.country_name = 'Ireland'
    and c.city_name       = 'Dublin'
    and r.salary          > get_avg_sal(cr.country_name);
```

```
  COUNT(*)
----------
       431
```

Executing Function Body

Executed in 1.872 seconds

If you are wondering what happens to the cache when the underlying table data is changed, let's take a look using a few SQL commands (run in a relaunched database):

```
select get_avg_sal('USA') from dual;

GET_AVG_SAL('USA')
------------------
        515368.02
```

Executing Function Body

Executed in 2.278 seconds

```
update residents r
   set r.salary = r.salary + 100;

1000000 rows updated
```

Executed in 32.152 seconds

```
commit;

Commit complete
```

Executed in 0 seconds

```
select get_avg_sal('USA') from dual;

GET_AVG_SAL('USA')
------------------
        515368.02
```

Executed in 0.015 seconds

Clearly the cache is not aware of the underlying data manipulations and the result being returned is now incorrect. Oracle provides a utility package, DBMS_RESULT_CACHE, that you can leverage to force an immediate purging of the cache. Purging, of course, allows the cache to be repopulated with the proper values, taking into account the sweeping salary change that was made. Note that EXECUTE privileges for the DBMS_RESULT_CACHE package are not provided by default.

```
select get_avg_sal('USA') from dual;

GET_AVG_SAL('USA')
------------------
          515368.02

Executed in 0.016 seconds

exec dbms_result_cache.flush;
PL/SQL procedure successfully completed

Executed in 0.031 seconds

select get_avg_sal('USA') from dual;

GET_AVG_SAL('USA')
------------------
          515468.02

Executing Function Body

Executed in 1.186 seconds
```

The appropriate long-term solution is to alter the function definition to identify underlying dependencies that the cache needs to take into account. Do this with the RELIES_ON clause:

```
CREATE OR REPLACE FUNCTION get_avg_sal(p_country_c in varchar2)
return number result_cache relies_on(cities, residents) is
 v_avg_n number;
BEGIN
  dbms_output.put_line('Executing Function Body');
  select trunc(avg(r.salary), 2)
    into v_avg_n
    from residents r,
         countries c,
         cities     t
   where r.city_id      = t.city_id
     and t.country_id   = c.country_id
     and c.country_name = p_country_c;
  return v_avg_n;
END get_avg_sal;
```

The Result Cache now monitors changes to the CITIES and RESIDENTS tables and refreshes itself as needed. The CITIES table is listed as a dependency to track any reorganizations that may occur, such a new city being added to a country. Let's see how this change impacts the results:

```
select get_avg_sal('USA') from dual;

GET_AVG_SAL('USA')
------------------
         515468.02

Executing Function Body

Executed in 0.92 seconds

select get_avg_sal('USA') from dual;

GET_AVG_SAL('USA')
------------------
         515468.02

Executed in 0.015 seconds

update residents r
    set r.salary = r.salary + 100;
1000000 rows updated
Executed in 32.277 seconds
commit;
Commit complete
Executed in 0.031 seconds

select get_avg_sal('USA') from dual;

GET_AVG_SAL('USA')
------------------
         515568.02

Executing Function Body

Executed in 1.435 seconds
```

The cache now responds to changes in the underlying tables that the function relies on and refreshes itself as needed.

In addition to the DBMS_RESULT_CACHE package mentioned earlier, Oracle provides several performance views to monitor the result cache. They are V$RESULT_CACHE_STATISTICS, V$RESULT_CACHE_MEMORY, V$RESULT_CACHE_OBJECTS, and V$RESULT_CACHE_DEPENDENCY. From a developer perspective, the most useful of these views are V$RESULT_CACHE_STATISTICS and V$RESULT_CACHE_OBJECTS. The former provides a summary overview of the entire result cache, whereas the latter provides details for each object in the cache.

The V$RESULT_CACHE_STATISTICS view always returns ten records providing summary information about the entire Result Cache. Here's an example of the information returned by V$RESULT_CACHE_STATISTICS:

```
select * from sys.v_$result_cache_statistics;

    ID NAME                              VALUE
---------- ------------------------------ ----------
     1 Block Size (Bytes)                 1024
     2 Block Count Maximum                1056
     3 Block Count Current                  32
     4 Result Size Maximum (Blocks)         52
     5 Create Count Success                  2
     6 Create Count Failure                  0
     7 Find Count                         1739
     8 Invalidation Count                    0
     9 Delete Count Invalid                  0
    10 Delete Count Valid                    0

10 rows selected
```

These name-value pairs are defined as follows:

Name	Value
Block Size (Bytes)	Size of each memory block.
Block Count Maximum	Maximum number of memory blocks allowed.
Block Count Current	Number of memory blocks currently allocated.
Result Size Maximum (Blocks)	Maximum number of blocks allowed for a single result.
Create Count Success	Number of cache results successfully created.
Create Count Failure	Number of cache results that failed to create.
Find Count	Number of cached results that were successfully serviced by the cache (so the function body did not need to be executed).
Find Copy Count	Number of cached results that were copies.
Hash Chain Length	As more blocks are hashed to the same hash chain, the length increases. If this becomes too long, scanning the long hash chain could cause performance degradation.
Invalidation Count	Total number of invalidations. An invalidation occurs when the cached results are no longer valid due to a dependency. For example, when the salaries were changed in the previous example, the cache became invalid and would be refreshed on the next function call.
Delete Count Invalid	Number of invalid cached results deleted.
Delete Count Valid	Number of valid cached results deleted.

The STATUS column of V$RESULT_CACHE_STATISTICS indicates the viability of the data in the cache with values being limited to

- **New**   Result is still under construction.
- **Published**   Result is available for use.
- **Bypass**   Result will be bypassed for use.
- **Expired**   Result has exceeded expiration time.
- **Invalid**   Result is no longer available for use.

The rows in the V$RESULT_CACHE_OBJECTS view with the value 'Result' for the TYPE column are of most interest as they allow you to review information such as hit rates. The view contains a "Published Result" record (TYPE = 'Result' and STATUS = 'Published') for each unique combination of function name and input parameters that is still valid in the cache. The V$RESULT_CACHE_OBJECTS view also contains "Invalid" records (STATUS = 'Invalid') that result when cache entries are invalidated, such as when a change in a RELIES_UPON object causes the cache to be refreshed. Based on the SQL that has been issued during this discussion, you can expect the view to have two published result records: one for the numerous calls to `get_avg_sal('USA')` and one for the calls to `get_avg_sal('Ireland')`. Here is a portion of the record for the USA call:

```
ID                      6
TYPE                    Result
STATUS                  Published
BUCKET_NO               599
HASH                    1988862551
NAME                    "SCOTT"."GT_AVG_SAL"::8."GET_AVG_SAL"#8440831613f0f5d3 #1
NAMESPACE               PLSQL
CREATION_TIMESTAMP      1/23/2009 9:58:57 AM
CREATOR_UID             5512
DEPEND_COUNT            3
BLOCK_COUNT             1
SCN
COLUMN_COUNT            1
PIN_COUNT               0
SCAN_COUNT              4345
ROW_COUNT               1
ROW_SIZE_MAX            7
ROW_SIZE_MIN            7
ROW_SIZE_AVG            7
BUILD_TIME              146
LRU_NUMBER              0
INVALIDATIONS           NULL
OBJECT_NO               NULL
SPACE_OVERHEAD          274
SPACE_UNUSED            743
```

These columns are identified as follows:

Column Name	Description
ID	Identifier for the cache object (also the ID of the first block)
TYPE	Type of the cache object
STATUS	Status of the object
BUCKET_NO	Internal hash bucket for the object
HASH	Hash value for the object
NAME	Name (for example, SQL prefix or PL/SQL function name)
NAMESPACE	The type of cached result (SQL or PL/SQL)
CREATION_TIMESTAMP	Time when the object was created
CREATOR_UID	The ID of the user who created the result
DEPEND_COUNT	The number of dependencies for each result, or the number of dependents if the TYPE is a dependency
BLOCK_COUNT	Total number of blocks in the cached object
SCN	Either the build SCN for a result or the SCN at which a dependency was invalidated
COLUMN_COUNT	Number of columns in the cached result
PIN_COUNT	Number of active scans on this result
SCAN_COUNT	Total number of scans initiated on the cached result
ROW_COUNT	Total number of rows in the cached result
ROW_SIZE_MAX	Size of the largest row (in bytes)
ROW_SIZE_MIN	Size of the smallest row (in bytes)
ROW_SIZE_AVG	Average size of a row (in bytes)
BUILD_TIME	Amount of time (in hundredths of a second) it took to build the cached result
LRU_NUMBER	LRU list position (the smaller the value, the more recent the usage)
OBJECT_NO	The data dictionary object number for the dependency object
INVALIDATIONS	The number of times the dependency object has invalidated its dependent objects
SPACE_OVERHEAD	Overhead (in bytes) for the result
SPACE_UNUSED	Unused space (in bytes) for the result

In conclusion, the new PL/SQL Function Result Cache makes possible enormous performance gains for a minimum of development effort. It shouldn't be used as a crutch for poorly written/designed functions but as another tool for creating highly efficient routines.

Reference Sequences Directly in PL/SQL Expressions (New in 11g)

With 11*g*, you can now reference sequences directly in PL/SQL expressions without the archaic "select from dual" construct. The result is more streamlined code that is easier to read and maintain. Oracle also promises improved performance and scalability.

Let's start with a PL/SQL block written the "old fashioned" way with a "select from dual" construct being used to pull values from a sequence:

```
drop sequence my_seq;

create sequence my_seq
minvalue 1
start with 1
increment by 1
nocache;

DECLARE

  v_time_start_i integer;
  v_time_end_i   integer;
  v_value_i      integer;

BEGIN

  v_time_start_i := dbms_utility.get_time;

  for i in 1..100000 loop
    select my_seq.nextval
      into v_value_i
      from dual;
  end loop;

  v_time_end_i := dbms_utility.get_time;

  dbms_output.put_line('Execution Time: '||
                       (v_time_end_i - v_time_start_i)/100||
                       ' seconds');

END;
/
```

This block executes in 61.47 seconds (averaged across three executions).

With 11*g*, you can streamline the code by referencing the NEXTVAL and CURRVAL pseudocolumns directly within the PL/SQL code, as shown here:

```
drop sequence my_seq;

create sequence my_seq
minvalue 1
```

```
start with 1
increment by 1
nocache;

DECLARE

  v_time_start_i integer;
  v_time_end_i   integer;
  v_value_i      integer;

BEGIN

  v_time_start_i := dbms_utility.get_time;

  for i in 1..100000 loop
    v_value_i := my_seq.nextval;
  end loop;

  v_time_end_i := dbms_utility.get_time;

  dbms_output.put_line('Execution Time: '||
                       (v_time_end_i - v_time_start_i)/100||
                       ' seconds');

END;
/
```

The average execution time with this block is 61.90 seconds. While the ability to reference the sequence value directly in PL/SQL has simplified the code, a performance gain has not been realized. In fact, the performance has degraded slightly. To investigate further, the previous tests are repeated with sequences using various cache sizes. The results are summarized here.

Time (in Seconds) to Fetch 100,000 Values from a Sequence

	Calling Convention	
Cache Size	Select from Dual	Inline
None	61.47	61.90
20	6.76	6.72
500	3.94	3.89

So it would appear that the inline construct has a slight performance advantage, particularly when the sequences are defined with a cache. However, the advantage is so slight that I am reluctant to say definitively that the new construct is indeed faster. A second round of testing with the same parameters as before and the performance advantage now tips in favor of the "select from dual" construct.

Time (in Seconds) to Fetch 100,000 Values from a Sequence

Cache Size	Calling Convention	
	Select from Dual	Inline
None	61.36	62.37
20	6.80	6.96
500	3.96	3.99

As of this writing, the ability to reference a sequence generator directly in a PL/SQL expression can definitely streamline your code, but no performance benefits are realized at this time.

Use Named Parameters in SQL Function Calls (New in 11g)

When passing formal parameter values to PL/SQL subprograms, Oracle has always permitted position, named, and mixed notations. It is generally an accepted best practice to use the named notation, as it both increases code readability and offers a level of protection against changes to a subprogram's signature. Unfortunately, prior to 11g, the named notation was not available when PL/SQL functions were called from within a SQL command. This limitation left PL/SQL function calls that were embedded in SQL statements vulnerable to undesired effects if the subroutine signatures were not changed in a very careful manner.

Let's look at an example. First, I create a function that accepts a person's first and last names and formats them into a single string using the format *LastName, FirstName*:

```
CREATE OR REPLACE FUNCTION format_name(p_first_c in varchar2 default null,
                                       p_last_c  in varchar2 default null)
return varchar2 is
BEGIN
  return(p_last_c||', '||p_first_c);
END format_name;
```

I'll now use this function to format a couple of fictitious records from an EMPLOYEES table. I start out by using the positional notation that was mandatory prior to 11g:

```
select t.*,
       format_name(t.first_name, t.last_name) as name
  from emps t
 where emp_id in (1, 7);

    EMP_ID FIRST_NAME  MIDDLE_NAME  LAST_NAME    NAME
---------- ----------- ------------ ------------ -------------------------
         1 Richard     John         Irons        Irons, Richard
         7 Julianne    Amy          Perrineau    Perrineau, Julianne

2 rows selected
```

For comparison purposes, I'll employ the same data using a PL/SQL block, as that method has always offered the use of named notation:

```
DECLARE
  cursor v_emps_cur is
    select *
      from emps
     where emp_id in (1, 7);
BEGIN
  dbms_output.put_line(lpad('EMP ID',        10, ' ')||' '||
                       rpad('FIRST NAME',  11, ' ')||' '||
                       rpad('MIDDLE NAME', 11, ' ')||' '||
                       rpad('LAST NAME',   11, ' ')||' '||
                       rpad('NAME',        25, ' '));

  dbms_output.put_line(lpad('-', 10, '-')||' '||
                       rpad('-', 11, '-')||' '||
                       rpad('-', 11, '-')||' '||
                       rpad('-', 11, '-')||' '||
                       rpad('-', 25, '-'));

  for r in v_emps_cur loop
    dbms_output.put_line(lpad(r.emp_id,       10, ' ')||' '||
                         rpad(r.first_name,  11, ' ')||' '||
                         rpad(r.middle_name, 11, ' ')||' '||
                         rpad(r.last_name,   11, ' ')||' '||
                         format_name(p_first_c => r.first_name,
                                     p_last_c  => r.last_name));
  end loop;
END;
/

    EMP ID FIRST NAME  MIDDLE NAME LAST NAME   NAME
---------- ----------- ----------- ----------- -------------------------
         1 Richard     John        Irons       Irons, Richard
         7 Julianne    Amy         Perrineau   Perrineau, Julianne

PL/SQL procedure successfully completed
```

As expected, the results are identical to what was returned by the SQL statement. Now let's fast-forward to a future enhancement in which the FORMAT_NAME function supports the middle name as well:

```
CREATE OR REPLACE FUNCTION format_name(p_first_c  in varchar2 default null,
                                       p_middle_c in varchar2 default null,
                                       p_last_c   in varchar2 default null)
return varchar2 is
BEGIN
  return(p_last_c||', '||p_first_c||' '||p_middle_c);
END format_name;
```

Note that the developer interjected the new middle name parameter between the existing parameters. Reexecuting the SQL and PL/SQL extraction commands from before, you see that the former is returning incorrect results because of the positional notation:

```
    EMP_ID FIRST_NAME  MIDDLE_NAME LAST_NAME   NAME
---------- ----------- ----------- ----------- ------------------------
         1 Richard     John        Irons       , Richard Irons
         7 Julianne    Amy         Perrineau   , Julianne Perrineau

2 rows selected

    EMP_ID FIRST_NAME  MIDDLE_NAME LAST_NAME   NAME
---------- ----------- ----------- ----------- ------------------------
         1 Richard     John        Irons       Irons, Richard
         7 Julianne    Amy         Perrineau   Perrineau, Julianne

PL/SQL procedure successfully completed
```

With 11g, you can now utilize the named notation with SQL to limit the impact of function signature changes, as shown here:

```
select t.*,
       format_name(p_first_c => t.first_name,
                   p_last_c  => t.last_name) as name
  from emps t
 where emp_id in (1, 7);

    EMP_ID FIRST_NAME  MIDDLE_NAME LAST_NAME   NAME
---------- ----------- ----------- ----------- ------------------------
         1 Richard     John        Irons       Irons, Richard
         7 Julianne    Amy         Perrineau   Perrineau, Julianne

2 rows selected
```

TIP
Named notation continues to be the preferred method for passing parameters to subroutines. With 11g, you can now extend this best practice approach to SQL statements to yield consistency across the entire code base.

Simplify loops with the CONTINUE Statement (New in 11g)

The CONTINUE statement is used to cycle a loop (and skip the remaining statements) without requiring a branch to the end or raising an exception. The CONTINUE statement has two forms:

CONTINUE;

CONTNUE WHEN boolean expression;

The first form executes unconditionally and the second form executes only when the boolean expression is TRUE. The CONTINUE statement will not necessarily improve performance but it provides better structured coding techniques and helps to avoid the awkward GOTO statement.

The following example displays only numbers divisible by three from within a loop.

Without CONTINUE statement:

```
BEGIN
   for v_count_i in 1 .. 20 loop
     if mod(v_count_i, 3) != 0 then
       goto skip;
     end if;
     dbms_output.put_line('Value = ' || v_count_i);
     <<skip>>
     null;
   end loop;
END;

Results:
Value = 3
Value = 6
Value = 9
Value = 12
Value = 15
Value = 18
```

With CONTINUE statement:

```
BEGIN
   for v_count_i in 1 .. 20 loop
     if mod(v_count_i, 3) != 0 then
       continue;
     end if;
     dbms_output.put_line('Value = ' || v_count_i);
   end loop;
END;

Results:
Value = 3
Value = 6
Value = 9
Value = 12
Value = 15
Value = 18
```

With CONTINUE statement using WHEN clause:

```
BEGIN
   for v_count_i in 1 .. 20 loop
     continue when mod(v_count_i, 3) != 0;
     dbms_output.put_line('Value = ' || v_count_i);
```

```
   end loop;
END;

Results:
Value = 3
Value = 6
Value = 9
Value = 12
Value = 15
Value = 18
```

From a performance perspective, neither of these techniques has a distinctive advantage over each other. Consider the following modified versions of the samples executed over a much larger number of iterations:

```
DECLARE
   v_total_count_i binary_integer := 0;
   v_div3_count_i  binary_integer := 0;
BEGIN
   for v_count_i in 1 .. 10000000 loop
     v_total_count_i := v_total_count_i + 1;
     if mod(v_count_i, 3) != 0 then
       goto skip;
     end if;
     v_div3_count_i := v_div3_count_i + 1;
     <<skip>>
     null;
   end loop;
   dbms_output.put_line('Total Iterations: '||v_total_count_i);
   dbms_output.put_line('  Divisible by 3: '||v_div3_count_i);
END;
/

Total Iterations: 10000000
  Divisible by 3: 3333333
PL/SQL procedure successfully completed
Executed in 10.343 seconds

DECLARE
   v_total_count_i binary_integer := 0;
   v_div3_count_i  binary_integer := 0;
BEGIN
   for v_count_i in 1 .. 10000000 loop
     v_total_count_i := v_total_count_i + 1;
     if mod(v_count_i, 3) != 0 then
       continue;
     end if;
     v_div3_count_i := v_div3_count_i + 1;
   end loop;
   dbms_output.put_line('Total Iterations: '||v_total_count_i);
```

```
    dbms_output.put_line('  Divisible by 3: '||v_div3_count_i);
END;
/

Total Iterations: 10000000
  Divisible by 3: 3333333
PL/SQL procedure successfully completed
Executed in 10.358 seconds

DECLARE
  v_total_count_i binary_integer := 0;
  v_div3_count_i  binary_integer := 0;
BEGIN
  for v_count_i in 1 .. 10000000 loop
    v_total_count_i := v_total_count_i + 1;
    continue when mod(v_count_i, 3) != 0;
    v_div3_count_i := v_div3_count_i + 1;
  end loop;
  dbms_output.put_line('Total Iterations: '||v_total_count_i);
  dbms_output.put_line('  Divisible by 3: '||v_div3_count_i);
END;
/

Total Iterations: 10000000
  Divisible by 3: 3333333
PL/SQL procedure successfully completed
Executed in 10.374 seconds
```

In this particular execution, both uses of the new CONTINUE statement were outpaced by the original GOTO technique; however, the gap was very small and repeated executions show that the lead can easily tip in any direction.

TIP
The new CONTINUE statement creates loop constructs that are more streamlined, but there are no performance gains to be realized at this time.

Leverage Compile-Time Warnings to Catch Programming Mistakes (Improved in 11g)

Since 10g, the PL/SQL Compiler has had the capability to provide compile-time warnings regarding common programming mistakes. These warnings cover an assortment of issues that, if left unattended, may result in performance problems or logic errors.

Before moving into the examples, note that the PL/SQL Compiler does not issue compile-time warnings by default. This functionality is controlled by the Oracle Server parameter, PLSQL_WARNINGS. This parameter can be set specifically for a desired session by altering the session, as shown here:

```
alter session set plsql_warnings='ENABLE:ALL';
```

To ensure that compilation warnings are given consistently, however, it is recommended that the parameter be configured at the database level (consider setting this *only* for development or test systems, not for production systems).

Consider the following sample procedure in which the developer has created an if-then condition that is unreachable during execution. The PL/SQL Compiler issues a warning drawing the developer's attention to the problem.

```
create or replace procedure warning_proc is
BEGIN
  if 1 = 2 then
    dbms_output.put_line('Inside If Statement');
  end if;
  dbms_output.put_line('After If Statement');
END warning_proc;
/

SP2-0804: Procedure created with compilation warnings

SQL> show errors

Errors for PROCEDURE WARNING_PROC:

LINE/COL ERROR
-------- ---------------------------
4/5      PLW-06002: Unreachable code
```

In 11g, Oracle included additional deficiencies that the PL/SQL Compiler can detect. Easily the most notable of these is PLW-06009, which detects the inappropriate use of the WHEN OTHERS exception handler. Consider the following example:

```
create or replace procedure warning_proc is
  v_ctr_n number(2);
BEGIN
  for i in 1..100 loop
    v_ctr_n := i;
  end loop;
EXCEPTION
  when OTHERS then
    null;
END warning_proc;
/

SP2-0804: Procedure created with compilation warnings

SQL> show errors

Errors for PROCEDURE WARNING_PROC:
```

```
LINE/COL ERROR
-------- --------------------------------------------------------------------
8/8      PLW-06009: procedure "WARNING_PROC" OTHERS handler does not end
         in RAISE or RAISE_APPLICATION_ERROR
```

The developer has made a programming error that will cause the variable v_ctr_n to be overflowed on the last iteration of the loop. Normally, this error would not be a major concern because the overflow would trip a runtime exception that could be used to respond to and handle the overflow. However, the developer's inappropriate use of the WHEN OTHERS exception handler effectively suppresses any such runtime exception, so the system pretends as if nothing has gone wrong. Indeed, if the procedure is executed, it seems to complete successfully:

```
SQL> exec warning_proc;
PL/SQL procedure successfully completed.
```

While there are a few legitimate cases in which WHEN OTHERS NULL might be useful, in general, it is an extremely bad programming habit that developers should avoid. Runtime exceptions that should be ignored should be isolated with an exception handler specific to that exception. The WHEN OTHERS handler, when employed, should propagate the exception (or raise a new one) to identify the failure condition to the calling subroutine. Tweaking the previous code in this manner yields the desired runtime results, as shown here:

```
create or replace procedure warning_proc is
  v_ctr_n number(2);
BEGIN
  for i in 1..100 loop
    v_ctr_n := i;
  end loop;
EXCEPTION
  when OTHERS then
    raise;
END warning_proc;
/

SQL> exec warning_proc;
BEGIN warning_proc; END;
*
ERROR at line 1:
ORA-06502: PL/SQL: numeric or value error: number precision too large
ORA-06512: at "TUSC_11G_BOOK.WARNING_PROC", line 9
ORA-06512: at line 1
```

TIP
Experienced and novice developers alike should leverage the PL/SQL compile time warnings to catch obscured programming problems before code deployment.

Using Table Triggers (Improved in 11g)

Oracle 11g offers two major enhancements to table triggers. The first is the capability to control the execution order of triggers with the same triggering event. The second is a new compound trigger type that allows a single trigger to respond to both statement-level and row-level events.

Oracle has always provided the capability to create multiple triggers with the same triggering event on a table. The problem with doing so has always been that the execution order of those triggers was not controllable. Consider the following table with three triggers with the same triggering events:

```
create table trigger_table(col1 number not null);

create or replace trigger trigger_table_rbi_1
before insert on trigger_table
for each row
BEGIN
  dbms_output.put_line('Trigger #1');
END;
/

create or replace trigger trigger_table_rbi_2
before insert on trigger_table
for each row
BEGIN
  dbms_output.put_line('Trigger #2');
END;
/

create or replace trigger trigger_table_rbi_3
before insert on trigger_table
for each row
BEGIN
  dbms_output.put_line('Trigger #3');
END;
/
```

When data is inserted into the table, the triggers fire in a random order:

```
insert into trigger_table values (1);
Trigger #3
Trigger #2
Trigger #1
1 row inserted

insert into trigger_table values (2);
Trigger #3
Trigger #2
Trigger #1
1 row inserted
```

```
insert into trigger_table values (3);
Trigger #3
Trigger #2
Trigger #1
1 row inserted
```

Even though you may see a pattern (LIFO) in the execution order demonstrated in this example, don't be fooled. The execution order is not guaranteed by Oracle and any pattern that you may see is truly coincidental and should not be relied upon. With 11*g*, you can chain triggers together into an implicit execution order using the new FOLLOWS clause.

To get the triggers to fire in the desired order, you need to re-create the last two triggers to specify the FOLLOWS clause:

```
create or replace trigger trigger_table_rbi_2
before insert on trigger_table
for each row
follows trigger_table_rbi_1
BEGIN
  dbms_output.put_line('Trigger #2');
END;
/

create or replace trigger trigger_table_rbi_3
before insert on trigger_table
for each row
follows trigger_table_rbi_2
BEGIN
  dbms_output.put_line('Trigger #3');
END;
/
```

With the new triggers in place, the execution order is now predictable:

```
insert into trigger_table values(4);
Trigger #1
Trigger #2
Trigger #3
1 row inserted

insert into trigger_table values(5);
Trigger #1
Trigger #2
Trigger #3
1 row inserted

insert into trigger_table values(6);
Trigger #1
Trigger #2
Trigger #3
1 row inserted
```

For the discussion on the new compound triggers, let's start with a basic business problem: preventing the overbooking of developer resources. First I create a table and seed it with current engagement information:

```
create table engagements
(
 engmnt_key number       not null,
 developer  varchar2(10) not null,
 project    varchar2(10) not null,
 start_date date         not null,
 stop_date  date         not null,
 constraint engagements_pk primary key (engmnt_key)
);

insert into engagements values (1, 'Bob',   'ABC', '01-Jan-2009', '20-Jan-2009');
insert into engagements values (2, 'Dan',   'ABC', '01-Jan-2009', '20-Jan-2009');
insert into engagements values (3, 'Chris', 'ABC', '01-Jan-2009', '31-Jan-2009');
commit;
```

Next, I create a trigger that protects against the overbooking of resources:

```
create or replace trigger engagements_rbiu
before insert or update on engagements
for each row
DECLARE
  v_overlaps_i integer;
BEGIN
  select count(*)
    into v_overlaps_i
    from engagements
   where engmnt_key <> :new.engmnt_key
     and developer   = :new.developer
     and (
           start_date between :new.start_date and :new.stop_date
           or
           stop_date between :new.start_date and :new.stop_date
         );
  if (v_overlaps_i <> 0) then
     raise_application_error(-20000, 'You are overbooking '||:new.developer);
  end if;
END;
/
```

Now let's attempt to overbook a resource purposely to confirm that the trigger is working:

```
insert into engagements values (4, 'Bob', 'DEF', '15-Jan-2009',
'31-Jan-2009');
ORA-20000: You are overbooking Bob
ORA-06512: at "ENGAGEMENTS_RBIU", line 15
ORA-04088: error during execution of trigger 'ENGAGEMENTS_RBIU'
```

So far, so good. What if you want to assign multiple developers to a new project all at once, can you do so?

```
insert into engagements
select engmnt_key + 0.1,
       developer,
       'DEF',
       start_date + 30,
       stop_date  + 30
  from engagements;
ORA-04091: table ENGAGEMENTS is mutating, trigger/function may not see it
ORA-06512: at "ENGAGEMENTS_RBIU", line 4
ORA-04088: error during execution of trigger 'ENGAGEMENTS_RBIU'
```

A classic limitation of row-level triggers is that they are forbidden to read the table they are attached to if multiple records are being manipulated by a single statement. A workaround for this limitation is to delay the row-level trigger's reading of the table to the statement-level using a stored package and three independent triggers. The stored package contains an array that is used to accumulate the values of the individual records that are being changed by the statement. The package also contains a procedure that loops through the array to validate the individual records (the work currently being done in the previous trigger). Three triggers are then attached to the table to coordinate the validation via the stored package as outlined next:

Triggering Event	Work Performed
Statement level before INSERT/UPDATE	Call a procedure in the package to reset the array.
Row level before INSERT/UPDATE	Call a procedure in the package to add the pertinent data to the array for the current record.
Statement level after INSERT/UPDATE	Call a procedure in the package to validate the individual records using the data that was accumulated in the array.

With the new compound triggers, all of this can now be performed in a single trigger.

The basic structure for a compound trigger is shown here:

```
CREATE OR REPLACE TRIGGER <trigger-name>
for <dml-event> on <table-name>
compound trigger
  --Global declaration.
  BEFORE STATEMENT IS
    --Local declaration.
  BEGIN
    --Code.
  END BEFORE STATEMENT;
  BEFORE EACH ROW IS
    --Local declaration.
  BEGIN
    --Code.
```

```
   END BEFORE EACH ROW;
   AFTER EACH ROW IS
     --Local declaration.
   BEGIN
     --Code.
   END AFTER EACH ROW;
   AFTER STATEMENT IS
     --Local declaration.
   BEGIN
     --Code.
   END AFTER STATEMENT;
END <trigger-name>;
```

So you replace the original trigger with a new compound trigger that employs the appropriate logic to delay the row-level processing to the statement-level so the mutation errors are avoided:

```
drop trigger engagements_rbiu;

CREATE OR REPLACE TRIGGER engagements_ciu
for insert or update on engagements
compound trigger

   type pg_engmnt_rec is record(engmnt_key engagements.engmnt_key%type,
                                developer  engagements.developer%type,
                                start_date engagements.start_date%type,
                                stop_date  engagements.stop_date%type);
   type pg_engmnt_table is table of pg_engmnt_rec index by binary_integer;
   pg_engmnt_array pg_engmnt_table;

   BEFORE STATEMENT IS
   BEGIN
     --At the start of the statement we reset the tracking array.
     pg_engmnt_array.delete;
   END BEFORE STATEMENT;

   AFTER EACH ROW IS
     i binary_integer;
   BEGIN
     --As each row is processed we store the values needed
     --for validation in the array.
     i := pg_engmnt_array.count + 1;
     pg_engmnt_array(i).engmnt_key := :new.engmnt_key;
     pg_engmnt_array(i).developer  := :new.developer;
     pg_engmnt_array(i).start_date := :new.start_date;
     pg_engmnt_array(i).stop_date  := :new.stop_date;
   END AFTER EACH ROW;

   AFTER STATEMENT IS
     v_overlaps_i integer;
   BEGIN
     --At the conclusion of the statement we loop the array
     --to perform the overbooking protection logic.
```

```
       for i in 1..pg_engmnt_array.count loop
         select count(*)
           into v_overlaps_i
           from engagements
          where engmnt_key <> pg_engmnt_array(i).engmnt_key
            and developer   = pg_engmnt_array(i).developer
            and (
                  start_date between pg_engmnt_array(i).start_date
                                 and pg_engmnt_array(i).stop_date
                  or
                  stop_date between pg_engmnt_array(i).start_date
                                and pg_engmnt_array(i).stop_date
                );
         if (v_overlaps_i <> 0) then
           raise_application_error(-20000,
                 'You are overbooking '||pg_engmnt_array(i).developer);
         end if;
       end loop;
     END AFTER STATEMENT;

 END engagements_ciu;
```

The complex triggering logic—now implemented gracefully as a single trigger—provides resource-overbooking protection under all circumstances:

```
insert into engagements values (4, 'Bob', 'DEF', '15-Jan-2009',
'31-Jan-2009');
ORA-20000: You are overbooking Bob
ORA-06512: at "ENGAGEMENTS_CIU", line 47
ORA-04088: error during execution of trigger 'ENGAGEMENTS_CIU'

insert into engagements
select engmnt_key + 0.1,
       developer,
       'DEF',
       start_date + 30,
       stop_date  + 30
  from engagements;
ORA-20000: You are overbooking Chris
ORA-06512: at "ENGAGEMENTS_CIU", line 47
ORA-04088: error during execution of trigger 'ENGAGEMENTS_CIU'
```

TIP
The introduction of compound triggers in conjunction with execution order control are welcome enhancements.

Increase Performance with Native Compilation (Improved in 11g)

Native compilation is the process by which a stored PL/SQL program is compiled into native code that does not need to be interpreted at runtime. In comparison, code that is not natively compiled is stored in an intermediate form that must be interpreted at runtime.

The ability to compile PL/SQL code natively has been around since Oracle 9i; however, the implementation has changed significantly with 11g. In 9i and 10g, the compiled program units were stored and executed externally as C programs. The compilation required an external C-compiler and system configuration by a DBA. Starting with 11g, the database can handle the native compilation on its own and an external compiler is no longer needed. The natively compiled program units are stored within the databases in the system tablespace.

Because the natively compiled code does not need to be interpreted at runtime, the expectation is that it will execute faster. However, the native compilation only applies to the procedural code in a PL/SQL program unit, not any embedded SQL statements. As a result, the performance gains to be realized really depend upon how much procedural code exists in relation to SQL code. At a bare minimum, a natively compiled program unit that is SQL heavy should execute at least as fast as its non-natively compiled counterpart. As the volume of procedural code increases, the faster the natively compiled code should be.

To begin, let's start with four stored procedures utilizing various amounts of procedural and SQL code. The first procedure contains absolutely no SQL, whereas the rest contains increasing amounts of SQL intermixed with the PL/SQL.

```
create or replace function native_comp_1 return number as
  v_avg_n    number := 0;
  v_total_n number := 0;
BEGIN
  for i in 1..10000000 loop
    v_total_n := v_total_n + i;
    v_avg_n    := v_total_n/i;
  end loop;
  return(v_avg_n);
END;

create or replace function native_comp_2 return number as
  cursor c1 is
    select *
      from residents;
BEGIN
  for c1_rec in c1 loop
    null;
  end loop;
  return(null);
END;

create or replace function native_comp_3 return number as
  v_salary_n number := 0;
  cursor c1 is
```

```
    select salary
      from residents;
BEGIN
  for c1_rec in c1 loop
    v_salary_n := v_salary_n + c1_rec.salary;
  end loop;
  return(v_salary_n);
END;

create or replace function native_comp_4 return number as
  type v_csal_table is table of number
                        index by varchar2(50);
  v_csal_array v_csal_table;
  v_idx_c       varchar2(50);
  v_salary_n    number := 0;
  cursor c1 is
    select c.country_name,
           r.salary
      from countries c,
           cities     c2,
           residents r
     where c.country_id = c2.country_id
       and c2.city_id   = r.city_id;
BEGIN
  --Load array with salary totals by country.
  for c1_rec in c1 loop
    v_idx_c := c1_rec.country_name;
    if not v_csal_array.exists(v_idx_c) then
      v_csal_array(v_idx_c) := 0;
    end if;
    v_csal_array(v_idx_c) := v_csal_array(v_idx_c) +
                             c1_rec.salary;
  end loop;
  --Compute the total for countries that begin with "N".
  v_idx_c := v_csal_array.first;
  while (v_idx_c is not null) loop
    if (v_idx_c like 'N%') then
      v_salary_n := v_salary_n + v_csal_array(v_idx_c);
    end if;
    v_idx_c := v_csal_array.next(v_idx_c);
  end loop;
  return(v_salary_n);
END;
```

The default compilation mode (native or interpreted) can be set at the system level via the PLSQL_CODE_TYPE database initialization parameter. Alternatively, the mode can be changed at the session level using one of the following commands:

```
alter session set plsql_code_type=interpreted;
alter session set plsql_code_type=native;
```

The session/system needs to be altered prior to compiling a given program unit. Altering the compilation mode parameter does not impact program units that are already compiled in the database. To ascertain the compilation type from an existing program unit, query the PLSQL_CODE_TYPE column of the USER_PLSQL_OBJECT_SETTINGS dictionary table.

Here are the results when the test procedures are compiled in interpreted mode:

```
Procedure       Code Type    Iterations Fastest   Slowest    Average
--------------  -----------  ---------- ---------- ---------- ----------
native_comp_1   INTERPRETED  20               5.36 6.12       5.4465
native_comp_2   INTERPRETED  20               1.97 2.28       2.138
native_comp_3   INTERPRETED  20               1.17 1.48       1.3555
native_comp_4   INTERPRETED  20               2.81 3.21       2.8895
```

Here are the results when the test procedures are compiled natively:

```
Procedure       Code Type    Iterations Fastest   Slowest    Average
--------------  -----------  ---------- ---------- ---------- ----------
native_comp_1   NATIVE       20               4.79 5.14       4.846
native_comp_2   NATIVE       20               1.88 2.14       2.0515
native_comp_3   NATIVE       20                .98 1.36       1.2065
native_comp_4   NATIVE       20               2.49 2.68       2.582
```

Native compilation provided increased performance across the board, particularly with the program units that contained more procedural logic in relation to SQL commands, as detailed in the table:

Function	Interpreted	Native	% Increase
NATIVE_COMP_1	5.4465	4.846	11.02
NATIVE_COMP_2	2.138	2.0515	4.05
NATIVE_COMP_3	1.3555	1.2065	10.99
NATIVE_COMP_4	2.8895	2.582	10.64

With nothing to lose and everything to gain, setting the database default to native compilation would seem to make sense. Any performance degradation caused by it—and I have yet to come across any—should be handled on a one-off basis, shifting individual program units back to native interpretation as needed.

Maximize Performance with the Optimizing Compiler (Improved in 11g)

With each release of the database, Oracle tweaks the PL/SQL compiler to yield faster performance. You've already seen how natively compiled PL/SQL code can execute faster than code that is interpreted and compiled. Now let's take a look at what is possible when you give the compiler greater freedom to "tweak" your PL/SQL programs as it compiles them. Since 10g Oracle has given developers the ability to control the level of optimization that is applied via the PLSQL_OPTIMIZE_LEVEL parameter.

The valid values for the PLSQL_OPTIMIZE_LEVEL parameter are identified in the table:

Level	Description
0	A compatibility setting used to mimic the behaviors of Oracle 9*i* and earlier. Most PL/SQL performance gains and features available in 10*g* and higher (11*g*) are be available at this level.
1	Applies a variety of optimizations to PL/SQL programs, including the elimination of unnecessary computations and exceptions, but generally does not rearrange the original code.
2	This is the default setting. All the optimizations of Level 1, plus a variety of additional optimizations that may significantly reorganize the original code.
3	All the optimizations of Level 1 and 2, plus a variety of additional optimization techniques that—at lower levels—would need to be explicitly requested.

One of the specific optimizations triggered at Level 2 is subroutine inlining. Subroutine inlining is a new 11*g* optimization that replaces modularized subroutines with copies of the subroutine. The intent is to eliminate the inherent overhead when calling modularized program units. The effects should be most dramatic when the subprogram is called repeatedly as part of a large volume loop. The primary caveat is that subroutine inlining can only occur if the subroutine being called is within the same program unit as the caller.

When a stored program is installed/recompiled, the compiler optimization level defaults from the database configuration, which can be ascertained with the following query:

```
select value
  from v$parameter
 where name = 'plsql_optimize_level';
```

Alternatively, you can set a specific optimizer level by altering the current session:

```
alter session set plsql_optimize_level=X;
```

Remember, the optimizer level setting only comes into play at the next compilation. It does not impact compiled programs already in the database. Use the ALTER command to recompile any existing program units with the current optimizer setting.

So you can see what the various optimizer levels bring to the table, I will demonstrate using some stored functions that are compiled at each of the levels and then executed. Note I'm using native compilation throughout this test. First up is a simple function that uses a basic for-loop and a nested function to compute a running total of the numbers between 1 and 100 million. This procedure does not interact with any database tables.

```
CREATE OR REPLACE FUNCTION optcomp_1 return number is
   v_total_n number;
   PROCEDURE update_total(p_curr_tot_n in out number,
                          p_salary_n   in      number) is
   BEGIN
     p_curr_tot_n := p_curr_tot_n + p_salary_n;
   END update_total;
BEGIN
```

```
   v_total_n := 0;
   for i in 1..100000000 loop
     update_total(p_curr_tot_n => v_total_n,
                  p_salary_n   => i);
   end loop;
   return(v_total_n);
END optcomp_1;
```

Procedure	Level	Iterations	Fastest	Slowest	Average
optcomp_1	0	10	34.4	34.81	34.598
optcomp_1	1	10	27.14	27.52	27.333
optcomp_1	2	10	19.17	19.43	19.287
optcomp_1	3	10	11.53	11.67	11.614

Clearly, the performance increases with each optimizer level. Unfortunately, Oracle does not publish the exact optimizations that are being applied to the code at each level, but it is possible to get some insight, particularly with respect to subroutine inlining.

The technique calls for enabling all PL/SQL warnings prior to compilation:

```
alter session set plsql_code_type=native;
alter session set plsql_optimize_level=3;
alter session set plsql_warnings = 'enable:all';

alter function optcomp_1 compile;
SP2-0807: Function altered with compilation warnings

show errors;
Errors for FUNCTION TUSC_11G_BOOK.OPTCOMP_1:
LINE/COL ERROR
-------- ----------------------------------------------------------------
11/5     PLW-06005: inlining of call of procedure 'UPDATE_TOTAL' was done
3/3      PLW-06006: uncalled procedure "UPDATE_TOTAL" is removed.
```

The compilation warnings confirm that subroutine inlining was performed and the original subroutine removed. At Levels 2 and 3, the optimizer is free to rearrange the code to replace the function call (to UPDATE_TOTAL) with a copy of the subroutine, thereby eliminating the overhead. The overhead is small (remember, we are dealing with 100 million loop iterations in this example), but it does exist.

In the second example, the basic for-loop is replaced with a cursor to the RESIDENTS table that I have been experimenting with. Recall that this table contains 1 million records. The cursor fetches the salary of each resident and then passes that to a nested subroutine that updates a running total variable:

```
CREATE OR REPLACE FUNCTION optcomp_2 return number is
   v_total_n number;
   cursor c1 is
     select r.resident_id,
            r.salary
       from residents r;
   PROCEDURE update_total(p_curr_tot_n in out number,
```

```
                          p_salary_n    in      number) is
   BEGIN
     p_curr_tot_n := p_curr_tot_n + p_salary_n;
   END update_total;
BEGIN
  v_total_n := 0;
  for c1_rec in c1 loop
    update_total(p_curr_tot_n => v_total_n,
                 p_salary_n   => c1_rec.salary);
  end loop;
  return(v_total_n);
END optcomp_2;
```

These are the testing results:

Procedure	Level	Iterations	Fastest	Slowest	Average
optcomp_2	0	10	8.2	8.35	8.244
optcomp_2	1	10	7.86	7.92	7.878
optcomp_2	2	10	.88	1.33	.978
optcomp_2	3	10	.84	1.11	.952

As before, you can see that performance improves with each optimizer level, with a significant gain as you move beyond Level 1. Looking at the compiler warnings, you will see that the optimizer is inlining both the nested function call (UPDATE_TOTAL) as well as the cursor definition:

```
LINE/COL ERROR
-------- ------------------------------------------------------------------
15/5     PLW-06005: inlining of call of procedure 'UPDATE_TOTAL' was done
14/3     PLW-06005: inlining of call of procedure 'C1' was done
7/3      PLW-06006: uncalled procedure "UPDATE_TOTAL" is removed.
3/3      PLW-06006: uncalled procedure "C1" is removed.
```

Moving on, the program is revised to no longer fetch the salary in the cursor. The UPDATE_TOTAL nested procedure now has the additional task of fetching the salary for each resident based upon the resident identifier:

```
CREATE OR REPLACE FUNCTION optcomp_3 return number is
  v_total_n number;
  cursor c1 is
    select r.resident_id
      from residents r;
  PROCEDURE update_total(p_curr_tot_n in out number,
                         p_resident_n in number) is
    v_salary_n number;
  BEGIN
    select r.salary
      into v_salary_n
      from residents r
     where r.resident_id = p_resident_n;
    p_curr_tot_n := p_curr_tot_n + v_salary_n;
```

```
    END update_total;
BEGIN
  v_total_n := 0;
  for c1_rec in c1 loop
    update_total(p_curr_tot_n => v_total_n,
                 p_resident_n => c1_rec.resident_id);
  end loop;
  return(v_total_n);
END optcomp_3;
```

These are the testing results:

Procedure	Level	Iterations	Fastest	Slowest	Average
optcomp_3	0	10	34.7	38.18	35.068
optcomp_3	1	10	34.22	34.28	34.248
optcomp_3	2	10	24.84	24.89	24.872
optcomp_3	3	10	24.52	24.62	24.589

This less efficient design definitely takes longer to execute, but it still achieves a significant performance improvement once the optimizer reaches Level 2. You see almost no further improvement as you move to Level 3, however. The PL/SQL compilation warnings reveal that the cursor and the UPDATE_TOTAL procedure call are being inlined just as before. Optimizations or not, the limiting factor here is the 1 million individual queries being issued to perform piecemeal fetching of resident salaries.

The final iteration of the test program replaces the cursor loop with a basic for-loop spanning the range 0 to 1 million. This is possible because the resident IDs are densely packed in this range.

```
CREATE OR REPLACE FUNCTION optcomp_4 return number is
   v_total_n number;
   PROCEDURE update_total(p_curr_tot_n in out number,
                          p_resident_n in number) is
     v_salary_n number;
   BEGIN
     select r.salary
       into v_salary_n
       from residents r
      where r.resident_id = p_resident_n;
     p_curr_tot_n := p_curr_tot_n + v_salary_n;
   END update_total;
BEGIN
  v_total_n := 0;
  for i in 1..1000000 loop
    update_total(p_curr_tot_n => v_total_n,
                 p_resident_n => i);
  end loop;
  return(v_total_n);
END optcomp_4;
```

These are the testing results:

```
Procedure       Level Iterations Fastest    Slowest    Average
--------------- ----- ---------- ---------- ---------- ----------
optcomp_4       0     10         25.08      25.11      25.098
optcomp_4       1     10         24.97      25         24.986
optcomp_4       2     10         24.29      24.58      24.422
optcomp_4       3     10         23.61      23.69      23.636
```

This program shows the least amount of improvement as the optimization level increases. As in the previous example, the real limitation here is the high volume of one-off queries that are being issued to retrieve each resident's salary. Regardless, optimization Level 3 has once again turned in the best performance. The specific optimizations being reported by the compiler are shown here:

```
LINE/COL ERROR
-------- ----------------------------------------------------------------
16/5     PLW-06005: inlining of call of procedure 'UPDATE_TOTAL' was done
3/3      PLW-06006: uncalled procedure "UPDATE_TOTAL" is removed.
```

Let's investigate subprogram inlining a bit further. As noted earlier, inlining becomes possible at optimization Level 2. That doesn't mean that it will happen at Level 2, just that the optimizer will consider it. The optimizer could choose not to perform inlining based upon some analytical result. If inlining is going to be performed automatically by the optimizer, it would most likely occur at Level 3. Suppose automatic inlining were occurring and the impact was reduced performance? You could reduce the optimization level to prevent the inlining, but you may sacrifice other optimizations in the process. The preferred solution is to stop the inlining and nothing else. You can accomplish this with the INLINE pragma. The INLINE pragma provides a mechanism by which the developer can coerce or prevent inlining. In the case of coercion, it is nothing more than that—a suggestion that the optimizer perform inlining, but the optimizer has the final word. In the case of prevention, however, the optimizer must obey. To demonstrate, I slightly revised the OPTCOMP_1 function that I experimented with earlier to add an INLINE pragma to prevent the inlining of the UPDATE_TOTAL function:

```
CREATE OR REPLACE FUNCTION optcomp_5 return number is
   v_total_n number;
   PROCEDURE update_total(p_curr_tot_n in out number,
                          p_salary_n   in      number) is
   BEGIN
     p_curr_tot_n := p_curr_tot_n + p_salary_n;
   END update_total;
BEGIN
   v_total_n := 0;
   for i in 1..100000000 loop
     pragma inline(update_total, 'no');
     update_total(p_curr_tot_n => v_total_n,
               p_salary_n   => i);
   end loop;
   return(v_total_n);
END optcomp_5;
```

These are the testing results:

Procedure	Level	Iterations	Fastest	Slowest	Average
optcomp_5	0	10	34.2	34.22	34.211
optcomp_5	1	10	27.43	27.52	27.453
optcomp_5	2	10	19.26	19.3	19.282
optcomp_5	3	10	18.98	19	18.987

The results are nearly identical to what you saw before, with the sole exception being the results at Level 3. Unlike before, there is almost no improvement as the level changes from 2 to 3. Earlier, Level 3 yielded a performance increase of eight seconds over Level 2. Reviewing the PL/SQL warnings reveals that the inlining was blocked by the pragma directive:

```
LINE/COL ERROR
-------- ---------------------------------------------------------------
12/5     PLW-06008: call of procedure 'UPDATE_TOTAL' will not be inlined
```

Comparing these warnings to those from the analysis of OPTCOMP_1 reveals that the optimizer choose to perform inlining at Level 3 originally.

Clearly, the optimizer is capable of making notable improvements in PL/SQL performance. The test scenarios that I tried did not uncover any situations in which optimization Levels 2 or 3 failed to increase performance, although it is always a possibility. It is probably best to leave the optimizer at the Level 2, the default, but those wishing to squeeze out every last bit of performance may want to increase that to Level 3.

Use DBMS_APPLICATION_INFO for Real-Time Monitoring

The DBMS_APPLICATION_INFO package provides a powerful mechanism for communicating point-in-time information about execution in an environment. The following example illustrates this, as it enables a long-running PL/SQL program unit to provide information on the progress of the routine every 1000 records. The PL/SQL code segment updates the application information with the number of records processed and the elapsed time every 1000 records.

The following is an example illustrating the update of all employees' salaries:

```
DECLARE
    CURSOR cur_employee IS
      SELECT employee_id, salary, ROWID
      FROM   s_employee_test;
    lv_new_salary_num NUMBER;
    lv_count_num       PLS_INTEGER := 0;
    lv_start_time_num PLS_INTEGER;
BEGIN
    lv_start_time_num := DBMS_UTILITY.GET_TIME;
    FOR cur_employee_rec IN cur_employee LOOP
      lv_count_num := lv_count_num + 1;
      -- Determination of salary increase
      lv_new_salary_num := cur_employee_rec.salary;
```

```
      UPDATE s_employee_test
      SET    salary      = lv_new_salary_num
      WHERE  rowid = cur_employee_rec.ROWID;
      IF MOD(lv_count_num, 1000) = 0 THEN
         DBMS_APPLICATION_INFO.SET_MODULE('Records Processed: ' ||
            lv_count_num, 'Elapsed: ' || (DBMS_UTILITY.GET_TIME -
            lv_start_time_num)/100 || ' sec');
      END IF;
   END LOOP;
   COMMIT;
   DBMS_APPLICATION_INFO.SET_MODULE('Records Processed: ' ||
      lv_count_num, 'Elapsed: ' || (DBMS_UTILITY.GET_TIME -
      lv_start_time_num)/100 || ' sec');
END;
/
```

To monitor the progress, query the V$SESSION view, as shown in the following example:

```
SELECT username, sid, serial#, module, action
FROM   V$SESSION
WHERE  username = 'SCOTT';
```

Please note that this query needs to be run in a separate session from the one executing the PL/SQL block.

The following is the output from the V$SESSION view, when queried three different times. The last output is when the PL/SQL program unit was completed.

```
USERNAME    SID SERIAL# MODULE                   ACTION
---------- --- ------- ------------------------ -----------------
SCOTT        7       4 SQL*Plus
SCOTT       10      10 Records Processed: 1000   Elapsed: 0.71 sec

USERNAME    SID SERIAL# MODULE                   ACTION
---------- --- ------- ------------------------ -----------------
SCOTT        7       4 SQL*Plus
SCOTT       10      10 Records Processed: 10000  Elapsed: 4.19 sec

USERNAME    SID SERIAL# MODULE                   ACTION
---------- --- ------- ------------------------ -----------------
SCOTT        7       4 SQL*Plus
SCOTT       10      10 Records Processed: 25000  Elapsed: 9.89 sec
```

Your response time will depend on how fast your system is and how well it is architected. The reason for the two records being returned for each query in the preceding output is both the execution of the PL/SQL program unit to update employees' salary and the SQL statement to monitor the progress via the V$SESSION view are executed under the SCOTT schema in two different SQL*Plus sessions. The preceding example illustrates a valuable technique to deploy in an environment and provides a real-time monitoring mechanism. It becomes easier to determine accurately how long a program has been running and to estimate how long a program has to complete.

If DBAs do not want users' queries against the V$SESSION view to return information for all users, they can create a view based on the V$SESSION view that limits the retrieval to only the executing user's session information. This can be accomplished by executing the commands as the SYS user. The following syntax creates the new view (the new view is named SESSION_LOG, but any name can be used). Including "USER" in the query that follows returns the name of the session user (the user who logged on) with the data type VARCHAR2:

```
CREATE VIEW session_log AS
SELECT *
FROM    V$SESSION
WHERE   username = USER;
```

The following syntax creates a public synonym:

```
CREATE PUBLIC SYNONYM session_log FOR session_log;
```

The following syntax grants SELECT permission to all users:

```
GRANT SELECT ON session_log TO PUBLIC;
```

Once the SESSION_LOG view is set up, as shown in the preceding statements, the preceding V$SESSION view query can be changed to SELECT from the SESSION_LOG view, as in the following query, to limit the output to only the user executing the query:

```
SELECT username, sid, serial#, module, action
FROM    session_log;
```

TIP
Use the Oracle-supplied package DBMS_APPLICATION_INFO package to log point-in-time information to the V$SESSION view to enable monitoring of long-running processes.

Log Timing Information in a Database Table

Monitoring performance is an ongoing process. Many variables in an environment can change and affect performance over time; therefore, performance should be monitored continuously. Some of the variables include user growth, data growth, reporting growth, application modification/enhancement deployment, and additional load on the system from other applications. With this in mind, an Oracle system must be regularly monitored to ensure performance remains at, or above, an acceptable level (Oracle ADDM does this for you as well). One method for monitoring the system performance is to create a mechanism for logging timing statistics for certain aspects of an application. Batch programs are good candidates for this monitoring procedure. The monitoring procedure can be accomplished by inserting timing statistics into a database table. The following example provides the database table logging method by creating a database table and then integrating INSERT statements for the timing of the process into the table. Oracle's own SQL monitoring starts when a SQL statement runs parallel or when it has consumed at least five seconds of CPU or I/O time in a single execution. You can monitor the statistics for SQL statement execution using many

V$ views (especially V$SQL and V$SQL_MONITOR). See Chapter 12 for many great queries to the V$ views used for Oracle monitoring.

In this example, the important information to log in the database table is the program identifier (some unique method of identifying the program), the date and time the program is executed, and the elapsed time of the execution. One column has been added for this application, namely, the number of records updated. This additional column is important for this application to monitor the growth of employee records being processed. When creating a timing log table for your application, add columns to store additional important processing information that may affect your timing results. Create the following table to log the timing information:

```
CREATE TABLE process_timing_log
    (program_name       VARCHAR2(30),
     execution_date     DATE,
     records_processed NUMBER,
     elapsed_time_sec  NUMBER);
```

Once you have created the table, you can enhance PL/SQL program units to log the timing information into the PROCESS_TIMING_LOG table, as illustrated in the following program:

```
CREATE OR REPLACE PROCEDURE update_salary AS
    CURSOR cur_employee IS
        SELECT employee_id, salary, ROWID
        FROM   s_employee_test;
    lv_new_salary_num NUMBER;
    lv_count_num        PLS_INTEGER := 0;
    lv_start_time_num PLS_INTEGER;
    lv_total_time_num NUMBER;
BEGIN
    lv_start_time_num := DBMS_UTILITY.GET_TIME;
    FOR cur_employee_rec IN cur_employee LOOP
        lv_count_num := lv_count_num + 1;
        -- Determination of salary increase
        lv_new_salary_num := cur_employee_rec.salary;
        UPDATE s_employee_test
        SET    salary      = lv_new_salary_num
        WHERE  rowid = cur_employee_rec.ROWID;
    END LOOP;
    lv_total_time_num := (DBMS_UTILITY.GET_TIME -
        lv_start_time_num)/100;
    INSERT INTO process_timing_log
        (program_name, execution_date, records_processed,
         elapsed_time_sec)
    VALUES
        ('UPDATE_SALARY', SYSDATE, lv_count_num,
         lv_total_time_num);
    COMMIT;
END update_salary;
/
```

As shown in the preceding code segment, the timer is started at the beginning of the program unit and then stopped at the end of the program unit. The difference between the start and ending times is logged into the PROCESS_TIMING_LOG for each execution of the UPDATE_SALARY program. If the UPDATE_SALARY program unit is executed three times, as shown in the following syntax, then three timing records are inserted into the PROCESS_TIMING_LOG table:

```
EXECUTE update_salary
EXECUTE update_salary
EXECUTE update_salary
```

The following script retrieves the information from the PROCESS_TIMING_LOG table:

```
SELECT program_name,
       TO_CHAR(execution_date,'MM/DD/YYYY HH24:MI:SS') execution_time,
       records_processed, elapsed_time_sec
FROM   process_timing_log
ORDER BY 1,2;
```

PROGRAM_NAME	EXECUTION_TIME	RECORDS_PROCESSED	ELAPSED_TIME_SEC
UPDATE_SALARY	07/02/2002 19:43:57	25252	8.89
UPDATE_SALARY	07/02/2002 19:44:07	25252	9.11
UPDATE_SALARY	07/02/2002 19:44:15	25252	8.62

This output shows one possible result. There is a difference in the elapsed time for the same program execution. If the difference increases over time, this may indicate a need to analyze the program unit further or the application to determine what caused the execution time increase. With logging mechanisms in place, the elapsed time can be monitored at any point in time because the timing information is being logged to a database table.

In the preceding example, the time logged was per program unit. If the program is complex and executed for an extended period of time, you may want to change the logging of timing statistics in the program. The INSERT into the PROCESS_TIMING_LOG table could be performed after a certain number of iterations or to log timing for certain functionality in a program unit.

Another method is to use the DBMS_PROFILER package to get timing statistics per line of PL/SQL code. See Metalink (My Oracle Support) article 104377.1, "Performance of New PL/SQL Features" for more information.

TIP
Log (INSERT) execution timing information into a database table for long-running PL/SQL program units to integrate a proactive performance monitoring mechanism into your system. The database table can be reviewed at any point in time to determine if performance has decreased over time.

TIP
System load in terms of number of active sessions can have a large impact on the performance of program execution; therefore, modifying the database table logging method to include a column for the number of active sessions can be helpful. You can fill this column by adding one additional query to the program unit being executed to retrieve the count from the V$SESSION view.

Reduce PL/SQL Program Unit Iterations and Iteration Time

Any PL/SQL program unit involving looping logic is a strong candidate for performance improvements. Potential improvements for these types of programs can be accomplished in two ways. The first is to reduce the number of iterations by restructuring the logic to accomplish the same functional result. The second is to reduce the time per iteration. Either reduction often improves performance dramatically.

To bring this point into perspective, think of the following scenario: You need to process 9000 employee records in a PL/SQL routine, and to process each employee takes 2 seconds. This equates to 18,000 seconds, which equates to 5 hours. If the processing per employee is reduced to 1 second, the time to process the 9000 employees is reduced by 9000 seconds, or 2.5 hours . . . quite a difference!

The following example shows a minor restructuring of a PL/SQL program unit to illustrate reducing per-loop processing and overall processing. The program unit processes a loop 1,000,000 times. Each iteration adds to the incremental counter used to display a message each 100,000 iterations and adds to the total counter used to check for loop exiting. To view DBMS_OUTPUT, make sure you issue the SET SERVEROUTPUT ON command first.

```
CREATE OR REPLACE PACKAGE stop_watch AS
    pv_start_time_num       PLS_INTEGER;
    pv_stop_time_num        PLS_INTEGER;
    pv_last_stop_time_num   PLS_INTEGER;
-- This procedure creates a starting point for the timer routine and
-- is usually called once at the beginning of the PL/SQL program unit.
PROCEDURE start_timer;
--
This procedure retrieves a point in time and subtracts the current
-- time from the start time to determine the elapsed time. The
-- interval elapsed time is logged and displayed. This procedure is
-- usually called repetitively for each iteration or a specified
-- number of iterations.
PROCEDURE stop_timer;
END stop_watch;
/
```

The package has been created.

```
CREATE OR REPLACE PACKAGE BODY stop_watch AS
PROCEDURE start_timer AS
BEGIN
    pv_start_time_num      := DBMS_UTILITY.GET_TIME;
    pv_last_stop_time_num := pv_start_time_num;
END start_timer;
PROCEDURE stop_timer AS
BEGIN
    pv_stop_time_num := DBMS_UTILITY.GET_TIME;
    DBMS_OUTPUT.PUT_LINE('Total Time Elapsed: ' ||
        TO_CHAR((pv_stop_time_num - pv_start_time_num)/100,
```

```
            '999,999.99') || ' sec    Interval Time: ' ||
            TO_CHAR((pv_stop_time_num - pv_last_stop_time_num)/100,
            '99,999.99') || ' sec');
        pv_last_stop_time_num := pv_stop_time_num;
    END stop_timer;
END;
/
```

The package body has been created.

```
SET SERVEROUTPUT ON
DECLARE
    lv_counter_num       PLS_INTEGER := 0;
    lv_total_counter_num PLS_INTEGER := 0;
BEGIN
    stop_watch.start_timer;
    LOOP
        lv_counter_num       := lv_counter_num + 1;
        lv_total_counter_num := lv_total_counter_num + 1;
        IF lv_counter_num >= 100000 THEN
            DBMS_OUTPUT.PUT_LINE('Processed 100,000 Records. ' ||
                'Total Processed ' || lv_total_counter_num);
            lv_counter_num := 0;
            EXIT WHEN lv_total_counter_num >= 1000000;
        END IF;
    END LOOP;
    stop_watch.stop_timer;
END;
/
Processed 100,000 Records. Total Processed 100000
Processed 100,000 Records. Total Processed 200000
Processed 100,000 Records. Total Processed 300000
Processed 100,000 Records. Total Processed 400000
Processed 100,000 Records. Total Processed 500000
Processed 100,000 Records. Total Processed 600000
Processed 100,000 Records. Total Processed 700000
Processed 100,000 Records. Total Processed 800000
Processed 100,000 Records. Total Processed 900000
Processed 100,000 Records. Total Processed 1000000
Total Time Elapsed:       .71 sec    Interval Time:       .71 sec

PL/SQL procedure successfully completed.
```

By changing the program to only add to the LV_TOTAL_COUNTER_NUM variable each time the incremental counter reaches 100,000, overall execution time is reduced:

```
DECLARE
    lv_counter_num       PLS_INTEGER := 0;
    lv_total_counter_num PLS_INTEGER := 0;
BEGIN
    stop_watch.start_timer;
```

```
LOOP
    lv_counter_num          := lv_counter_num + 1;
    IF lv_counter_num >= 100000 THEN
        DBMS_OUTPUT.PUT_LINE('Processed 100,000 Records. Total ' ||
            'Processed ' || lv_total_counter_num);
        lv_total_counter_num := lv_total_counter_num +
            lv_counter_num;
        lv_counter_num := 0;
        EXIT WHEN lv_total_counter_num >= 1000000;
    END IF;
END LOOP;
stop_watch.stop_timer;
END;
/
```

The DBMS_OUTPUT.PUT_LINE output for each batch of processed records was not included in the following output:

```
Total Time Elapsed:          .47 sec     Interval Time:          .47 sec

PL/SQL procedure successfully completed.
```

The preceding example illustrates the performance difference achieved by changing the iteration logic to reduce the timing per iteration. The example is basic and shows a 34 percent increase on 1 million iterations. Based on the restructuring and the iterations, this improvement can make a huge difference.

TIP
When a PL/SQL program unit involves extensive looping or recursion, concentrate on reducing the execution time per iteration. The benefits add up fast, and it is easy to do the math to determine the overall improvement potential. Also review the looping or recursion for restructuring to reduce the number of iterations, while keeping the functionality. With the extreme flexibility of PL/SQL and SQL, a variety of ways typically exist to accomplish the same result. If a PL/SQL program unit is not performing optimally, sometimes you have to rewrite the logic another way.

Use ROWID for Iterative Processing

The ROWID variable can improve PL/SQL programs that retrieve records from the database, perform manipulation on the column values, and then complete with an UPDATE to the retrieved record. When retrieving each record, the ROWID can be added to the selected column list. When updating each record, the ROWID can be used in the predicate clause. The ROWID is the fastest access path to a record in a table, even faster than a unique index reference.

The performance improvement of using the ROWID is illustrated in the following example. The example retrieves each of the 25,000 employee records, calculates a new salary for each employee, and then updates the employees' salary. The actual salary calculation is not shown in this example. The first PL/SQL code segment shows the timing results with the UPDATE using the EMPLOYEE_ID column, which has a unique index on the column:

```
DECLARE
    CURSOR cur_employee IS
        SELECT employee_id, salary
        FROM    s_employee_test;
    lv_new_salary_num NUMBER;
BEGIN
    stop_watch.start_timer;
    FOR cur_employee_rec IN cur_employee LOOP
        -- Determination of salary increase
        lv_new_salary_num := cur_employee_rec.salary;
        UPDATE s_employee_test
        SET     salary      = lv_new_salary_num
        WHERE   employee_id = cur_employee_rec.employee_id;
    END LOOP;
    COMMIT;
    stop_watch.stop_timer;
END;
/
```

The following output shows the timing of two executions of the preceding code segment:

```
Total Time Elapsed:        1.71 sec    Interval Time:        1.71 sec
PL/SQL procedure successfully completed.

Total Time Elapsed:        1.59 sec    Interval Time:        1.59 sec
PL/SQL procedure successfully completed.
```

In the following procedure, the same functionality is maintained while changing the UPDATE to perform the UPDATE based on the ROWID. This involves adding the ROWID in the SELECT statement and changing the UPDATE predicate clause.

```
DECLARE
    CURSOR cur_employee IS
        SELECT employee_id, salary, ROWID
        FROM    s_employee_test;
    lv_new_salary_num NUMBER;
BEGIN
    stop_watch.start_timer;
    FOR cur_employee_rec IN cur_employee LOOP
        -- Determination of salary increase
        lv_new_salary_num := cur_employee_rec.salary;
        UPDATE s_employee_test
        SET     salary = lv_new_salary_num
        WHERE   rowid  = cur_employee_rec.ROWID;
    END LOOP;
    COMMIT;
    stop_watch.stop_timer;
END;
/
```

The following output shows the timing of two executions of the preceding code segment:

```
Total Time Elapsed:        1.45 sec    Interval Time:        1.45 sec
PL/SQL procedure successfully completed.

Total Time Elapsed:        1.48 sec    Interval Time:        1.48 sec
PL/SQL procedure successfully completed.
```

As evidenced from the timings, execution is faster using the ROWID. The first PL/SQL code segment UPDATE statement retrieves the result by using the index on EMPLOYEE_ID to get the ROWID and then goes to the table to search by ROWID. The second PL/SQL code segment UPDATE statement goes directly to the table to search by ROWID, thus eliminating the index search. The performance improvement increases when more records are involved and when the index used does not refer to a unique index.

TIP
Use the ROWID variable to enhance performance when SELECTing a record in a PL/SQL program unit and then manipulating the same record in the same PL/SQL program unit.

Standardize on Data Types, IF Statement Order, and PLS_INTEGER

Several minor programming modifications can be introduced into your standard PL/SQL development that can improve performance. Three of these techniques are outlined in this section:

- Ensure the same data types in comparison operations.

- Order IF conditions based on the frequency of the condition.

- Use the PLS_INTEGER PL/SQL data type for integer operations.

Ensure the Same Data Types in Comparison Operations

When variables or constant values are compared, they should have the same data type definition. If the comparison does not involve the same data types, then Oracle implicitly converts one of the values, thus introducing undesired overhead. Any time values are compared in a condition, the values should be the same data type. You should use this standard when developing PL/SQL program units as it is good programming style.

The following procedure illustrates the cost of comparing different data types, namely, a numeric data type to a character value in the IF statement:

```
CREATE OR REPLACE PROCEDURE test_if (p_condition_num NUMBER) AS
    lv_temp_num          NUMBER := 0;
    lv_temp_cond_num     NUMBER := p_condition_num;
```

```
BEGIN
   stop_watch.start_timer;
   FOR lv_count_num IN 1..100000 LOOP
      IF lv_temp_cond_num = '1' THEN
         lv_temp_num := lv_temp_num + 1;
      ELSIF lv_temp_cond_num = '2' THEN
         lv_temp_num := lv_temp_num + 1;
      ELSIF lv_temp_cond_num = '3' THEN
         lv_temp_num := lv_temp_num + 1;
      ELSIF lv_temp_cond_num = '4' THEN
         lv_temp_num := lv_temp_num + 1;
      ELSIF lv_temp_cond_num = '5' THEN
         lv_temp_num := lv_temp_num + 1;
      ELSIF lv_temp_cond_num = '6' THEN
         lv_temp_num := lv_temp_num + 1;
      ELSIF lv_temp_cond_num = '7' THEN
         lv_temp_num := lv_temp_num + 1;
      ELSE
         lv_temp_num := lv_temp_num + 1;
      END IF;
   END LOOP;
   stop_watch.stop_timer;
END;
/
```

The following illustrates the execution of the TEST_IF procedure:

```
EXECUTE test_if(8)
```

The following output is the execution result of the TEST_IF procedure:

```
Total Time Elapsed:         .26 sec   Interval Time:       .26 sec
PL/SQL procedure successfully completed.
```

Unnecessary overhead is introduced with the different data types. If the procedure is changed to the same data type comparisons, the following execution is much faster:

```
CREATE OR REPLACE PROCEDURE test_if (p_condition_num NUMBER) AS
   lv_temp_num        NUMBER := 0;
   lv_temp_cond_num   NUMBER := p_condition_num;
BEGIN
   stop_watch.start_timer;
   FOR lv_count_num IN 1..100000 LOOP
      IF lv_temp_cond_num = 1 THEN
         lv_temp_num := lv_temp_num + 1;
      ELSIF lv_temp_cond_num = 2 THEN
         lv_temp_num := lv_temp_num + 1;
      ELSIF lv_temp_cond_num = 3 THEN
         lv_temp_num := lv_temp_num + 1;
      ELSIF lv_temp_cond_num = 4 THEN
         lv_temp_num := lv_temp_num + 1;
```

```
      ELSIF lv_temp_cond_num = 5 THEN
          lv_temp_num := lv_temp_num + 1;
      ELSIF lv_temp_cond_num = 6 THEN
          lv_temp_num := lv_temp_num + 1;
      ELSIF lv_temp_cond_num = 7 THEN
          lv_temp_num := lv_temp_num + 1;
      ELSE
          lv_temp_num := lv_temp_num + 1;
      END IF;
   END LOOP;
   stop_watch.stop_timer;
END;
/
```

The following code listing illustrates the execution of the new TEST_IF procedure:

```
EXECUTE test_if(8)

Total Time Elapsed:          .17 sec    Interval Time:          .17 sec
PL/SQL procedure successfully completed.
```

As shown in the preceding examples, the execution is 23 percent faster. The improvement increases as the frequency of execution increases.

Therefore, in the final example, the comparison in the IF statement of LV_TEMP_COND_NUM to a 1,2,3, and so forth, is comparing a NUMBER to a PLS_INTEGER. Some internal Oracle conversion overhead is still taking place. To eliminate this overhead, the 1,2,3 . . . should be changed to 1.0, 2.0, 3.0 . . . . When I made this change to the final example, the timing was reduced to 0.16 seconds.

TIP
Ensure all conditional comparisons compare the same data types. Additionally, ensure the data types within the numeric family are comparing the same subtype.

Order IF Conditions Based on the Frequency of the Condition

The natural programming method when developing IF statements with multiple conditions is to order the conditional checks by some sequential order. This order is typically alphabetical or numerically sequenced to create a more readable segment of code, but it usually is not the most optimal order. Especially when using the ELSIF condition several times in an IF statement, the most frequently met condition should appear first, followed by the next most frequent match, and so forth.

In the preceding section, the execution of the procedure was always carried out by passing an 8, which meant every loop had to check all eight conditional operations of the IF logic to satisfy the condition. If you pass a 1, which is equivalent to saying the first condition satisfies all IF executions, you get a more optimized result, as shown in the following example:

```
EXECUTE test_if(1)

Total Time Elapsed:          .05 sec    Interval Time:          .05 sec
PL/SQL procedure successfully completed.
```

The preceding output illustrates a performance improvement from the preceding section with the correct ordering of IF conditions. Therefore, take the extra step of analyzing IF condition order before coding them.

TIP
Ensure the string of PL/SQL IF conditions appear in the order of most frequently satisfied, not a numerical or alphanumerical sequential order.

Use the PLS_INTEGER PL/SQL Data Type for Integer Operations

The typical standard for declaring a numeric data type is to use the NUMBER data type. In PL/SQL release 2.2, Oracle introduced the PLS_INTEGER data type. This data type can be used in place of any numeric family data type declaration, as long as the content of the variable is an integer and remains within the bounds of –2147483648 and +2147483647. Therefore, most counters and operations with integers can use this data type. The PLS_INTEGER involves fewer internal instructions to process, thus improving performance when using this numeric data type. The more references to this variable, the more improvement realized. Operations on NUMBER data types use library arithmetic, whereas operations on the data types PLS_INTEGER, BINARY_FLOAT, and BINARY_DOUBLE use *hardware arithmetic*. For local integer variables, use PLS_INTEGER. For variables that can never have the value NULL, do not need overflow checking, and are not used in performance-critical code, use SIMPLE_INTEGER (see the "PL/SQL Language Reference Guide" for more types and additional information). Note also that if you assign a PLS_INTEGER variable to a NUMBER variable, then PL/SQL converts the PLS_INTEGER value to a NUMBER value (because the internal representations of the values differ). However, whenever possible, you should avoid these implicit conversions.

This improvement for PLS_INTEGER is illustrated in the following PL/SQL code segment. The code segment is the same example as used in the previous two sections, with the data type declarations being changed to PLS_INTEGER from NUMBER.

```
CREATE OR REPLACE PROCEDURE test_if (p_condition_num PLS_INTEGER) AS
    lv_temp_num          PLS_INTEGER := 0;
    lv_temp_cond_num     PLS_INTEGER := p_condition_num;
BEGIN
    stop_watch.start_timer;
    FOR lv_count_num IN 1..100000 LOOP
       IF lv_temp_cond_num = 1 THEN
          lv_temp_num := lv_temp_num + 1;
       ELSIF lv_temp_cond_num = 2 THEN
          lv_temp_num := lv_temp_num + 1;
```

```
      ELSIF lv_temp_cond_num = 3 THEN
         lv_temp_num := lv_temp_num + 1;
      ELSIF lv_temp_cond_num = 4 THEN
         lv_temp_num := lv_temp_num + 1;
      ELSIF lv_temp_cond_num = 5 THEN
         lv_temp_num := lv_temp_num + 1;
      ELSIF lv_temp_cond_num = 6 THEN
         lv_temp_num := lv_temp_num + 1;
      ELSIF lv_temp_cond_num = 7 THEN
         lv_temp_num := lv_temp_num + 1;
      ELSE
         lv_temp_num := lv_temp_num + 1;
      END IF;
   END LOOP;
   stop_watch.stop_timer;
END;
/
```

The following illustrates the execution of the TEST_IF procedure:

```
EXECUTE test_if(1)
```

The following performance improvement is evident based on the execution results:

```
Total Time Elapsed:         .03 sec   Interval Time:         .03 sec
PL/SQL procedure successfully completed.
```

TIP
Use the PLS_INTEGER type when processing integers to improve performance.

TIP
If a number with precision is assigned to a PLS_INTEGER variable, the value will be rounded to a whole number as if the ROUND function had been performed on the number.

Reduce the Calls to SYSDATE

The SYSDATE variable is a convenient method of retrieving the current date and time. Calls to SYSDATE involve some overhead; therefore, if this variable is needed to log the date of certain processing, the call to this variable should be made once at the start of the program rather than at each iteration. This technique of calling SYSDATE once at the start of the program assumes the date logging is desired at the point in time the program started.

The reduction of SYSDATE calls is illustrated in the following example. The example loops through 10,000 iterations, calling SYSDATE (only the date portion of the variable because the TRUNC function is used to truncate the time portion) every iteration.

```
DECLARE
    lv_current_date     DATE;
BEGIN
    stop_watch.start_timer;
    FOR lv_count_num IN 1..10000 LOOP
        lv_current_date := TRUNC(SYSDATE);
    END LOOP;
    stop_watch.stop_timer;
END;
/
```

The following output shows the timing of two executions of the preceding code segment:

```
Total Time Elapsed:        .04 sec    Interval Time:       .04 sec
PL/SQL procedure successfully completed.

Total Time Elapsed:        .01 sec    Interval Time:       .01 sec
PL/SQL procedure successfully completed.
```

The following PL/SQL code segment has been modified to retrieve the SYSDATE only once, at the beginning of the program, and set to another variable each iteration.

```
DECLARE
    lv_current_date     DATE := TRUNC(SYSDATE);
    lv_final_date       DATE;
BEGIN
    stop_watch.start_timer;
    FOR lv_count_num IN 1..10000 LOOP
        lv_final_date := lv_current_date;
    END LOOP;
    stop_watch.stop_timer;
END;
/
```

The following output shows the timing of two executions of the preceding code segment:

```
Total Time Elapsed:        .00 sec    Interval Time:       .00 sec
PL/SQL procedure successfully completed.

Total Time Elapsed:        .01 sec    Interval Time:       .01 sec
PL/SQL procedure successfully completed.
```

As evident in the preceding example, overhead is associated with the SYSDATE call, and the number of calls to SYSDATE should be reduced, if possible.

TIP
Attempt to limit the calls to SYSDATE in iterative or recursive loops because overhead is associated with this variable. Set a PL/SQL DATE variable to SYSDATE in the declaration and reference the PL/SQL variable to eliminate the overhead.

Reduce the Use of the MOD Function

Certain PL/SQL functions are more costly to use than others. MOD is one function that has better overall performance when applied using additional PL/SQL logic. This is illustrated in the following example. MOD is a useful function, but if it is executed in an IF statement, as illustrated here, additional overhead is introduced.

```
BEGIN
    stop_watch.start_timer;
    FOR lv_count_num IN 1..10000 LOOP
        IF MOD(lv_count_num, 1000) = 0 THEN
            DBMS_OUTPUT.PUT_LINE('Hit 1000; Total: ' || lv_count_num);
        END IF;
    END LOOP;
    stop_watch.stop_timer;
END;
/
```

The following output shows the timing of two executions of the preceding code segment:

```
Hit 1000; Total: 1000
Hit 1000; Total: 2000
Hit 1000; Total: 3000
Hit 1000; Total: 4000
Hit 1000; Total: 5000
Hit 1000; Total: 6000
Hit 1000; Total: 7000
Hit 1000; Total: 8000
Hit 1000; Total: 9000
Hit 1000; Total: 10000
Total Time Elapsed:        .04 sec    Interval Time:        .04 sec
PL/SQL procedure successfully completed.

Total Time Elapsed:        .04 sec    Interval Time:        .04 sec
```

Here, I have modified the preceding PL/SQL code segment to eliminate use of the MOD function and perform the same check with additional PL/SQL logic, as illustrated in the following code segment:

```
DECLARE
    lv_count_inc_num PLS_INTEGER := 0;
BEGIN
    stop_watch.start_timer;
    FOR lv_count_num IN 1..10000 LOOP
```

```
        lv_count_inc_num := lv_count_inc_num + 1;
        IF lv_count_inc_num = 1000 THEN
            DBMS_OUTPUT.PUT_LINE('Hit 1000; Total: ' || lv_count_num);
            lv_count_inc_num := 0;
        END IF;
    END LOOP;
    stop_watch.stop_timer;
END;
/


Hit 1000; Total: 1000
Hit 1000; Total: 2000
Hit 1000; Total: 3000
Hit 1000; Total: 4000
Hit 1000; Total: 5000
Hit 1000; Total: 6000
Hit 1000; Total: 7000
Hit 1000; Total: 8000
Hit 1000; Total: 9000
Hit 1000; Total: 10000
Total Time Elapsed:         .01 sec    Interval Time:        .01 sec
PL/SQL procedure successfully completed.


Total Time Elapsed:         .00 sec    Interval Time:        .00 sec
```

As shown in the two preceding examples, the MOD function adds overhead. You can get better performance with PL/SQL IF statements.

Improve Shared Pool Use by Pinning PL/SQL Objects

The SHARED_POOL_SIZE parameter sets the amount of shared pool allocated in the SGA (see Chapter 4 and Appendix A for a detailed look at SHARED_POOL_SIZE and closely related shared pool parameters). The shared pool stores all SQL statements and PL/SQL blocks executed in the Oracle database. Given the method by which Oracle manages the shared pool, as far as aging, the shared pool can become fragmented. In addition, since Oracle will not age any objects that are currently being processed by a session, you may get an Oracle error indicating that the shared pool does not have enough memory for a new object. The exact error message is "ORA-4031: unable to allocate *XXX* bytes of shared memory" (where *XXX* is the number of bytes Oracle is attempting to allocate). If you receive this error, it means you should increase the size of your SGA shared pool as soon as possible. The method to do this prior to Oracle 9i was to modify the initialization parameter SHARED_POOL_SIZE and then shut down and start up the database. The quick, but costly, method of eliminating this error until the next database shutdown was to flush the SGA shared pool. You accomplished this with the following command (only allowed if ALTER SYSTEM privilege is assigned to a user).

> *To flush the SGA shared pool:*

```
alter system flush shared_pool;
```

In Oracle 9*i*, you could modify the SHARED_POOL_SIZE parameter without shutting down the database as long as you didn't exceed the SGA_MAX_SIZE. This eliminated the need to do things that you had to do in previous versions. You still had to pin the large objects into the shared pool when the database had started and make sure the shared pool was large enough for all of these statements to be cached. In both 10*g* and 11*g*, Oracle uses Automatic Memory Management (AMM). In 11*g*, you can set the MEMORY_TARGET (but you can also set a minimum for the SHARED_POOL_SIZE). Oracle internally manages the memory parameters for you and can be altered dynamically as long as you don't exceed the value of MEMORY_MAX_TARGET (see Chapter 4 on setting initialization parameters).

Pinning (Caching) PL/SQL Object Statements into Memory

In the event that you cannot maintain a sufficient SHARED_POOL_SIZE to keep all statements in memory, keeping the most important objects cached (pinned) in memory may become necessary. The following example shows how to pin PL/SQL object statements (the procedure PROCESS_DATE is pinned in the example that follows) in memory using the DBMS_SHARED_POOL.KEEP procedure:

To pin PL/SQL object statements:

```
begin
dbms_shared_pool.keep('process_date','p');
end;
/
```

or

```
execute sys.dbms_shared_pool.keep ('SYS.STANDARD');
```

By pinning an object in memory, the object will not be aged out or flushed until the next database shutdown. Also consider MetaLink note 61760.1: DBMS_SHARED_POOL should be created as user SYS. No other user should own this package. Any user requiring access to the package should be granted EXECUTE privileges by SYS. If you create the package in the SYS schema, and run the sample code in a different schema, you first need to

■ Grant the EXECUTE_CATALOG_ROLE role to the user running the example (i.e., TEST), and grant EXECUTE privilege on DBMS_SHARED_POOL to TEST

and then you need to

■ Fully qualify the package, as in SYS.DBMS_SHARED_POOL.KEEP, because the `dbmspool.sql` script does *not* create a public synonym for this package.

TIP
Use the DBMS_SHARED_POOL.KEEP procedure to pin PL/SQL objects into the shared pool.

NOTE
To use this procedure in earlier versions of Oracle, you had to first run the dbmspool.sql *script. The* prvtpool.plb *script is automatically executed after* dbmspool.sql *runs. In 11g, the* dbmspool.sql *script is called by* catpdbms.sql, *and* catpdbms.sql *is called by* catproc, *so the procedure is already created in 10g and 11g.*

Pinning All Packages

To pin all packages in the shared pool, execute the following as the SYS user (this code comes from My Oracle Support):

```
declare
own varchar2(100);
nam varchar2(100);
cursor pkgs is
    select      owner, object_name
    from        dba_objects
    where       object_type = 'PACKAGE';
begin
    open pkgs;
    loop
        fetch pkgs into own, nam;
        exit when pkgs%notfound;
        dbms_shared_pool.keep(own || '.' || nam, 'P');
    end loop;
end;
/
```

A more targeted approach, pinning only packages that need to be reloaded, would be better than pinning *all* packages, especially because most DBA interfaces since Oracle 9i involve PL/SQL packages. At the very least, you should check to make sure you are not trying to pin invalid packages as well. Common packages that are shipped with Oracle (that should be kept) include STANDARD, DBMS_STANDARD, and DIUTIL.

TIP
Use the DBMS_SHARED_POOL.KEEP procedure in PL/SQL to pin all packages when the database is started (if memory/shared pool permits) and to avoid errors involving loading packages in the future.

Identify PL/SQL Objects That Need to Be Pinned

Fragmentation causing several small pieces to be available in the shared pool, and not enough large contiguous pieces, is a common occurrence. The key to eliminating shared pool errors (as noted in the preceding section) is to understand which of the objects will be large enough to cause problems when you attempt to load them. Once you know the problem PL/SQL, you can then pin this code when the database has started (and the shared pool is completely contiguous). Doing this ensures that your large packages are already in the shared pool when they are called, instead of searching for a large contiguous piece of the shared pool (which may not be there later as the system is used). You can query the V$DB_OBJECT_CACHE view to determine PL/SQL that is both large and currently not marked "kept." These are objects that may cause problems (due to their size and need for a large amount of contiguous memory) if they need to be reloaded at a later time. This query only shows the current statements in the cache. The example that follows searches for those objects requiring greater than 100K:

```
select      name, sharable_mem
from        v$db_object_cache
where       sharable_mem > 100000
and         type in ('PACKAGE', 'PACKAGE BODY', 'FUNCTION',
            'PROCEDURE')
and         kept = 'NO';
```

TIP
Query the V$DB_OBJECT_CACHE table to find objects that are not pinned and are also large enough to cause problems potentially.

Use and Modify DBMS_SHARED_POOL.SIZES

An alternative and very precise indication of shared pool allocation can be viewed through the DBMS_SHARED_POOL.SIZES package procedure. This call accepts a MINIMUM SIZE parameter and displays all cursors and objects within the shared pool of a size greater than that provided. The following is the actual statement issued to retrieve this:

```
select      to_char(sharable_mem / 1000 ,'999999') sz, decode
            (kept_versions,0,' ',rpad('yes(' || to_char(kept_versions)
            || ')' ,6)) keeped, rawtohex(address) || ',' || to_char
            (hash_value)  name, substr(sql_text,1,354) extra, 1 iscursor
from        v$sqlarea
where       sharable_mem > &min_ksize * 1000
union
select      to_char(sharable_mem / 1000 ,'999999') sz, decode(kept,'yes',
            'yes   ','') keeped, owner || '.'  || name  || lpad(' ',29 -
            (length(owner) + length(name) ) )  || '(' || type || ')'
            name, null  extra, 0 iscursor
from        v$db_object_cache v
where       sharable_mem > &min_ksize * 1000
order by    1 desc;
```

The preceding query can be placed into a procedure package, of your own construction, to display a formatted view of cursors and objects within the shared pool.

Find Large Objects

You can use the DBMS_SHARED_POOL.SIZES package procedure (*DBMS_SHARED_POOL* is the package and *SIZES* is the procedure within the package) to view the objects using shareable memory higher than a threshold that you set.

> *Execute the DBMS_SHARED_POOL.SIZES package as displayed next for a threshold of 100K (the output follows):*

```
Set serveroutput on size 10000;
begin
sys.dbms_shared_pool.sizes(100);
end;
/
SIZE(K)  _ KEPT _ ___ NAME
118        YES        SYS.STANDARD          (PACKAGE)
109                   SELECT    DT.OWNER,DT.TABLE_NAME,DT.TABLESPACE_NAME,
                                DT.INITIAL_EXTTENT,DT.NEXT_EXTENT,DT.NUM_ROWS,
                                DT.AVG_ROW_LEN,
                                SUM(DE.BYTES) PHY_SIZE
                      FROM      DBA_TABLES DT,DBA_SEGMENTS DE
                      WHERE     DT.OWNER = DE.OWNER
                      AND       DT.TABLE_NAME = DE.SEGMENT_NAME
                      AND       DT.TABLESPACE_NAME = DE.TABLESPACE_NAME
                      GROUP BY  DT.OWNER,DT.TABLE_NAME,DT.TABLESPACE_NAME,
                                DT.INITIAL_EXTENT,DT.NEX
                                (0B14559C,3380846737)    (CURSOR)
22                    RDBA.RDBA_GENERATE_STATISTICS (PACKAGE)
PL/SQL procedure successfully completed.
```

Get Detailed Object Information from DBA_OBJECT_SIZE

Query the DBA_OBJECT_SIZE view to show the memory used by a particular object along with much more detailed information concerning the object:

```
Compute sum of source_size on report
Compute sum of parsed_size on report
Compute sum of code_size on report
Break on report
select    *
from      dba_object_size
where     name = 'RDBA_GENERATE_STATISTICS';
```

OWNER	NAME	TYPE	SOURCE SIZE	PARSED SIZE	CODE SIZE
RDBA	RDBA_GENERATE_STATISTICS	PACKAGE	5023	4309	3593
RDBA	RDBA_GENERATE_STATISTICS	PACKAGE BODY	85595	0	111755
SUM			90618	4309	115348

(partial display only...not all columns shown)

Get Contiguous Space Currently in the Shared Pool

Why does the shared pool return errors when an object is loaded? The answer is that a large enough piece of the shared pool is not available to fit the piece of code. In the last section you learned how to find the size of the code that you have. You also saw in a previous section how to pin pieces of code into the shared pool. Now, let's look at the query that will tell you which code, of the code that has made it into the shared pool, is either very large and should be pinned or should be investigated and shortened if possible.

The following query accesses an X$ table (see Chapter 13), and you must be the SYS user to access these tables:

```
select    ksmchsiz, ksmchcom
from      x$ksmsp
where     ksmchsiz > 10000
and       ksmchcom like '%PL/SQL%';
```

This query shows that the packages that have been accessed are very large and should be pinned at the time that the database has started. If the last line of this query is eliminated, it will also show the large pieces of free memory (KSMCHCOM = 'free memory' and KSMCHCOM = 'permanent memory') that are still available (unfragmented) for future large pieces of code to be loaded. See Chapter 13 for more details on the X$ tables and example output.

TIP
Query X$KSMSP to find all large pieces of PL/SQL that have appeared in the shared pool. These are candidates for pinning when the database has started.

Find Invalid Objects

Developers often change a small section of PL/SQL code that fails to compile upon execution, forcing an application failure. A simple query, reviewed daily, helps you spot these failures before the end user does:

```
col       "Owner" format a12
col       "Object" format a20
col       "OType" format a12
col       "Change DTE" format a20
select    substr(owner,1,12) "Owner", substr(object_name,1,20)
          "Object", object_type "OType", to_char(last_ddl_time,
          'DD-MON-YYYY HH24:MI:SS') "Change Date"
from      dba_objects
where     status <> 'VALID'
order by  1, 2;
```

The preceding example displays any objects that are INVALID, meaning they were never compiled successfully or changes in dependent objects have caused them to become INVALID.

If you have a procedure called PROCESS_DATE, for example, which was found to be INVALID, you could manually recompile this procedure with the following command:

```
alter procedure PROCESS_DATE compile;
```

Once this command is executed and PROCESS_DATE passes the recompile, Oracle would change the procedure automatically from INVALID to VALID. Another manual method that exists is to call the DBMS_UTILITY.COMPILE_SCHEMA package procedure as outlined next to recompile all stored procedures, functions, and packages for a given schema.

To call the DBMS_UTILITY.COMPILE_SCHEMA package procedure:

```
begin
dbms_utility.compile_schema('USERA');
end;
/
```

NOTE
You could also run the utlrp.sql script to recompile all the INVALID objects in the database. See the script for restrictions on running this script.

To find the state of all PL/SQL objects for your schema, execute the following:

```
column      object_name  format a20
column      last_ddl_time heading 'last ddl time'
select      object_type, object_name, status, created, last_ddl_time
from        user_objects
where       object_type in ('PROCEDURE', 'FUNCTION', 'PACKAGE',
            'PACKAGE BODY', 'TRIGGER');
```

OBJECT_TYPE	OBJECT_NAME	STATUS	CREATED	last ddl
PACKAGE	DBMS_REPCAT_AUTH	VALID	12-MAY-02	12-MAY-02
PACKAGE BODY	DBMS_REPCAT_AUTH	VALID	12-MAY-02	12-MAY-02
TRIGGER	DEF$_PROPAGATOR_TRIG	VALID	12-MAY-02	12-MAY-02
PROCEDURE	ORA$_SYS_REP_AUTH	VALID	12-MAY-02	12-MAY-02
TRIGGER	REPCATLOGTRIG	VALID	12-MAY-02	12-MAY-02

TIP
You can recompile an entire schema (either all or just the invalid objects) with DBMS_UTILITY.COMPILE_SCHEMA.

Find Disabled Triggers

In some respects, a disabled trigger is far more dangerous than an invalid object because it doesn't fail—*it just doesn't execute!* Disabled triggers can have severe consequences for applications, and consequently business processes, that depend on business logic stored within procedural code.

The following script identifies disabled triggers:

```
col        "Owner/Table" format a30
col        "Trigger Name" format a25
col        "Event" format a15
col        "Owner" format a10
select     substr(owner,12) "Owner", trigger_name "Trigger Name",
           trigger_type "Type", triggering_event "Event",
           table_owner||'.'||table_name "Owner/Table"
from       dba_triggers
where      status <> 'ENABLED'
order by   owner, trigger_name;
```

If you modify the preceding query to check only the SYS schema and certain columns, as shown next, you get a list of disabled triggers that are provided by Oracle:

```
select     trigger_name "Trigger Name",STATUS,
           trigger_type "Type", triggering_event "Event"
from       dba_triggers
where      status <> 'ENABLED'
and        owner = 'SYS'
order by   owner, trigger_name;
```

Trigger Name	STATUS	Type	Event
AURORA$SERVER$SHUTDOWN	DISABLED	BEFORE EVENT	SHUTDOWN
AURORA$SERVER$STARTUP	DISABLED	AFTER EVENT	STARTUP
NO_VM_CREATE	DISABLED	BEFORE EVENT	CREATE
NO_VM_DROP	DISABLED	BEFORE EVENT	DROP
SYS_LOGOFF	DISABLED	BEFORE EVENT	LOGOFF
SYS_LOGON	DISABLED	AFTER EVENT	LOGON

To find all triggers for your schema, execute the following code:

```
column     trigger_name      format a15
column     trigger_type      format a15
column     triggering_event  format a15
column     table_name        format a15
column     trigger_body      format a25
select     trigger_name, trigger_type, triggering_event,
           table_name, status, trigger_body
from       user_triggers;
```

TRIGGER NAME	TRIGGER TYPE	TRIGGERING EVENT	TABLE NAME	STATUS	TRIGGER BODY
UPDATE_TOTAL	AFTER STATEMENT	INSERT OR UPDATE OR DELETE	ORDER_MAIN	ENABLED	begin update total_orders set order_total =

```
10;
```

```
                                                                          end;
```

TIP
Query DBA_TRIGGERS (for system-wide objects) or USER_TRIGGERS (for your schema only) to find the state of triggers and avoid errors with disabled triggers. Disabled triggers can have fatal results for an application: they don't fail; they just don't execute.

Use PL/SQL Associative Arrays for Fast Reference Table Lookups

Programs that are designed to process data coming into a system usually incorporate numerous reference table lookups to validate and/or code the incoming data properly. When the reference tables are searched, using a unique key that is a numerical data type, the query performance against the reference tables can be drastically improved by loading the reference tables into PL/SQL *associative arrays* (formerly known as *index-by tables*). Consider an incoming dataset that contains a single numerical column that must be translated to a coded string using a reference table. Here is a program to handle this task using the classic approach of repeated searches against the reference table.

To load the reference tables:

```
DECLARE
  v_code_c ref_table.ref_string%type;
  cursor v_lookup_cur (p_code_n IN number) is
    select ref_string
      from ref_table
     where ref_num = p_code_n;
  cursor v_inbound_cur is
    select *
      from incoming_data;
BEGIN
  --Open a cursor to the incoming data.
  for inbound_rec in v_inbound_cur loop
    BEGIN
      --Calculate the reference string from the reference data.
      open v_lookup_cur(inbound_rec.coded_value);
      fetch v_lookup_cur into v_code_c;
      if v_lookup_cur%notfound then
        close v_lookup_cur;
        raise NO_DATA_FOUND;
      end if;
      close v_lookup_cur;
      dbms_output.put_line(v_code_c);
      --processing logic...
      --Commit each record as it is processed.
      commit;
    EXCEPTION
      when NO_DATA_FOUND then
        null;--Appropriate steps...
      when OTHERS then
        null;--Appropriate steps...
    END;
  end loop;
END;
/
```

Although this program may appear to be written efficiently, it is, in fact, hampered by the repeated queries against the reference table. Even though Oracle may have the entire reference table in memory, due to pinning or prior queries, a certain amount of overhead is still involved with processing the queries.

A more efficient technique is to load the entire reference table into a PL/SQL associative array. The numerical column (that the searches are performed against) is loaded as the array index. When a lookup against the reference data is required, the array is used instead of the actual reference table—the code in the incoming data that must be translated is used as the array index. The inherent nature of working with PL/SQL associative arrays is that if an INVALID array index is used (meaning the code in the incoming data does not match any value in the reference table), the NO_DATA_FOUND exception will be raised.

Here is the same processing program rewritten using an associative array to store the reference data:

```
DECLARE
   type v_ref_table is table of ref_table.ref_string%type index by binary_integer;
   v_ref_array v_ref_table;
   v_code_c ref_table.ref_string%type;
   cursor v_lookup_cur is
     select *
       from ref_table;
   cursor v_inbound_cur is
     select *
       from incoming_data;
BEGIN
  --First, load the reference array with data from the reference table.
  for lookup_rec in v_lookup_cur loop
    v_ref_array(lookup_rec.ref_num) := lookup_rec.ref_string;
  end loop;
  --Open a cursor to the incoming data.
  for inbound_rec in v_inbound_cur loop
    BEGIN
      --Calculate the reference string from the reference data.
      v_code_c := v_ref_array(inbound_rec.coded_value);
      dbms_output.put_line(v_code_c);
      --processing logic...
      --Commit each record as it is processed.
      commit;
    EXCEPTION
      when NO_DATA_FOUND then
        null;--Appropriate steps...
      when OTHERS then
        null;--Appropriate steps...
    END;
  end loop;
END;
/
```

The result should be a drastic increase in the processing speed due to the reduced overhead in working with the PL/SQL associative arrays in comparison to the actual database table.

Finally, quite some time ago, the requirement that an associative array be indexed by a numeric value was lifted. Thus, the index of an associative array can be a string value. This capability makes it possible to use the same solution when the coded values that need to be resolved are not necessarily of a numerical nature. Consider the traditional example that some inbound data is carrying a two-character representation of a state code that needs to be resolved and validated. A slight modification to the previous procedure, as shown next, makes this possible. The index type for the array must be a VARCHAR2 type.

```
DECLARE
   type v_ref_table is table of states_table.state_name%type
     index by states_table.state_code%type;
   v_ref_array v_ref_table;
   v_state_c states_table.state_name%type;
   cursor v_lookup_cur is
     select state_code,
            state_name
       from states_table;
   cursor v_inbound_cur is
     select *
       from incoming_data;
BEGIN
   --First, load the reference array with data from the reference table.
   for lookup_rec in v_lookup_cur loop
     v_ref_array(lookup_rec.state_code) := lookup_rec.state_name;
   end loop;
   --Open a cursor to the incoming data.
   for inbound_rec in v_inbound_cur loop
     BEGIN
       --Calculate the reference string from the reference data.
       v_state_c := v_ref_array(inbound_rec.coded_value);
       dbms_output.put_line(v_state_c);
       --processing logic...
       --Commit each record as it is processed.
       commit;
     EXCEPTION
       when NO_DATA_FOUND then
         null;--Appropriate steps...
       when OTHERS then
         null;--Appropriate steps...
     END;
   end loop;
END;
/
```

TIP
Load reference tables into PL/SQL associative arrays for faster lookups. This takes advantage of the performance of array indexes in PL/SQL.

Find and Tune the SQL
When Objects Are Used

At times, the hardest part of tuning stored objects is finding the actual code that is stored in the database. This section looks at queries that retrieve the SQL that can be tuned. In this section, I query views that retrieve information about the actual source code that exists behind the stored objects.

Retrieve the code for a procedure you created called PROCESS_DATE:

```
column     text   format a80
select     text
from       user_source
where      name = 'PROCESS_DATE'
order by   line;
```

This query works for procedures, triggers, or functions. For packages, change the last line in the query to

```
order by type, line;
```

```
TEXT
procedure process_date is
  test_num number;
 begin
 test_num := 10;
 if test_num = 10 then
  update order_main
  set        process_date = sysdate
  where   order_num = 12345;
 end if;
 end;
```

The following example retrieves the code for the familiar DBMS_RULE package:

```
column    text format a80
select    text
from      dba_source
where     name  = 'DBMS_RULE'
and       type  = 'PACKAGE'
order by  line;
```

```
TEXT
--------------------------------------------------------------------------------
PACKAGE dbms_rule AUTHID CURRENT_USER AS

   PROCEDURE evaluate(
         rule_set_name           IN      varchar2,
         evaluation_context      IN      varchar2,
         event_context           IN      sys.re$nv_list := NULL,
         table_values            IN      sys.re$table_value_list := NULL,
         column_values           IN      sys.re$column_value_list := NULL,
```

```
        variable_values         IN      sys.re$variable_value_list := NULL,
        attribute_values        IN      sys.re$attribute_value_list := NULL,
        stop_on_first_hit        IN      boolean := FALSE,
        simple_rules_only        IN      boolean := FALSE,
        true_rules               OUT     sys.re$rule_hit_list,
        maybe_rules              OUT     sys.re$rule_hit_list);

    PROCEDURE evaluate(
        rule_set_name            IN      varchar2,
        evaluation_context       IN      varchar2,
        event_context            IN      sys.re$nv_list := NULL,
        table_values             IN      sys.re$table_value_list := NULL,
        column_values            IN      sys.re$column_value_list,
        variable_values          IN      sys.re$variable_value_list := NULL,
        attribute_values         IN      sys.re$attribute_value_list := NULL,
        simple_rules_only        IN      boolean := FALSE,
        true_rules_iterator      OUT     binary_integer,
        maybe_rules_iterator     OUT     binary_integer);
    FUNCTION get_next_hit(
        iterator                 IN      binary_integer)
    RETURN sys.re$rule_hit;
    PROCEDURE close_iterator(
        iterator                 IN      binary_integer);
END dbms_rule;

35 rows selected.
```

The following example attempts to retrieve the package body for the DBMS_JOB package:

```
column      text    format a80
select      text
from        dba_source
where       name   = 'DBMS_JOB'
and         type   = 'PACKAGE BODY'
order by    line;


TEXT
PACKAGE BODY dbms_job wrapped
0
abcd
abcd
...
:2 a0 6b d a0 ac :3 a0 6b b2
ee :2 a0 7e b4 2e ac e5 d0
b2 e9 93 a0 7e 51 b4 2e
:2 a0 6b 7e 51 b4 2e 6e a5
57 b7 19 3c b0 46 :2 a0 6b
ac :2 a0 b2 ee ac e5 d0 b2
e9 :2 a0 6b :3 a0 6e :4 a0 :5 4d a5
57 :2 a0 a5 57 b7 :3 a0 7e 51
```

In this example, the package was wrapped (protected) using the WRAP command, and the output is unreadable. If you find yourself tuning the preceding code, you need sleep!

You can use the following query to retrieve the source code for a trigger:

```
column    trigger_name        format a15
column    trigger_type        format a15
column    triggering_event    format a15
column    table_name          format a15
column    trigger_body        format a25
select    trigger_name, trigger_type, triggering_event, table_name, trigger_body
from      user_triggers;
```

```
TRIGGER NAME  TRIGGER TYPE    TRIGGERING EVEN  TABLE NAME  TRIGGER BODY
UPDATE_TOTAL  AFTER STATEMENT INSERT OR UPDATE  ORDER_MAIN  begin
                              OR DELETE                       update order_main
                                                              set order_total = 10;
                                                            end;
```

The following example shows how to find the dependencies for PL/SQL objects:

```
column    name                format a20
column    referenced_owner    format a15 heading R_OWNER
column    referenced_name     format a15 heading R_NAME
column    referenced_type     format a12 heading R_TYPE
select    name, type, referenced_owner, referenced_name,referenced_type
from      user_dependencies
order by  type, name;
```

```
NAME            TYPE        R OWNER   R NAME      R TYPE
INSERT_RECORD   PROCEDURE   USERA     ORDER_MAIN  TABLE
INSERT_RECORD   PROCEDURE   SYS       STANDARD    PACKAGE
PROCESS_DATE    PROCEDURE   SYS       STANDARD    PACKAGE
PROCESS_DATE    PROCEDURE   USERA     ORDER_MAIN  TABLE
```

TIP
Finding the source code behind PL/SQL package procedures involves querying the USER_SOURCE and DBA_SOURCE views. Finding the source code behind a trigger involves querying the USER_TRIGGERS and DBA_TRIGGERS views. You can find dependencies among PL/SQL object by querying the USER_DEPENDENCIES and the DBA_DEPENDENCIES views.

Consider the Time Component When Working with DATE Data Types

When working with the Oracle DATE data type, think of it as a TIME data type, which is more accurate. This is because the DATE data type always stores a complete temporal value, down to the second. It is impossible to insert a date value only into either a PL/SQL variable or database column that is defined as a DATE. If you do not keep this behavior in mind during application design, the finished product may exhibit undesirable side effects. One of the most common side effects of improper date management within an application is when reports, which filter the data by a date value, return different results across multiple executions.

When a column or variable of this type (DATE) is initialized with a value, any missing component (if any) is automatically supplied by Oracle. If the initialization value contains only the date component, only then does Oracle supply the time component, and vice versa. This begs the question of how can you tell which component, if any, is missing during the initialization? Quite simply, both components are automatically present only when a date variable is initialized from another date variable. The system variable SYSDATE is one such date variable. Thus, whenever a column or variable is initialized from SYSDATE, it will contain a value representing the date and time when the initialization occurred.

If it is January 10, 1998, at 3:25:22 A.M., and you execute the following command

```
Date_Var_1 date := SYSDATE;
```

the value contained in the variable DATE_VAR_1 will be

```
10-JAN-1998 03:25:22.
```

You can also initialize a date variable using a text string. For example, if

```
Date_Var_2 date := '10-JAN-98';
```

the value contained in the variable DATE_VAR_1 will be

```
10-JAN-98 00:00:00
```

Here is a simple PL/SQL block that will allow you to see this for yourself:

```
DECLARE
   date_var_2 DATE;
BEGIN
   date_var_2 := '10-JAN-98';
   DBMS_OUTPUT.PUT_LINE('Selected date is '|| to_char(date_var_2, 'DD-MON-YYYY
HH24:MI:SS'));
END;
/

10-JAN-1998 00:00:00
```

TIP
A DATE data type always stores a complete temporal value, down to the second. It is impossible to insert a date value only into either a PL/SQL variable or database column that is defined as a DATE.

At this point, it should be clear that DATE_VAR_1 and DATE_VAR_2 are not equal. Even though they both contain a date component of 10-JAN-98, they are not equal because their time components differ by almost three and a half hours. Herein lies the problem with a program that does not anticipate the time component that is inherent with date values. Consider an application that uses the SYSDATE variable to initialize the accounting date of records inserted into a database table. If a PL/SQL processing program (or a simple SQL SELECT statement) does not take the time component of the records into account, then records will be missed during processing.

Given that the date values in a table *contain time values* other than 12:00 midnight, the following statements would miss records. The problem is the time is not the same and these statements all miss records:

```
select     *
from       table
where      date_column = SYSDATE;
select     *
from       table
where      date_column = trunc(SYSDATE);
select     *
from       table
where      date_column = '10-JAN-98';
select     *
from       table
where      date_column between '01-JAN-98' and '10-JAN-98';
```

The solution is to truncate the time on both sides of the WHERE clause.

One way to prevent this problem is to negate the difference in time components on both sides of the conditional test:

```
select     *
from       table
where      trunc(date_column) = trunc(SYSDATE);
select     *
from       table
where      trunc(date_column) = '10-JAN-98';
select     *
from       table
where      trunc(date_column) between '01-JAN-98' and '10-JAN-98';
```

One note on these examples: If you modify the NLS_DATE_FORMAT to a different value than the default, these examples might not work. I used "*dd-mon-yy hh:mi:ss*" as my format, and the modified queries returned no rows. When I logged out and back in to reset the NLS_DATE_FORMAT setting, the same queries then returned rows.

The tuned solution is where the time is truncated on the noncolumn side of the WHERE clause. This technique has the undesired effect of suppressing any indexes that might otherwise improve query performance—the TRUNC function on the COLUMN_NAME suppresses the index on the column. The desired technique is to adjust the filter conditions to include all possible times within a given date. Also note in the example that follows that .000011574 of one day is one second.

```
select     *
from       table
where      date_column between trunc(SYSDATE) and
           trunc(SYSDATE + 1) - .000011574;
```

```
select    *
from      table
where     date_column between to_date('10-JAN-98') and
          to_date('11-JAN-98') - .000011574;

select    *
from      table
where     date_column between to_date('01-JAN-98') and
          to_date('11-JAN-98') - .000011574;
```

TIP
*The Oracle DATE data type has both date and time included in it.
Avoid suppressing indexes when trying to match dates. The key
is never to modify the column side in the WHERE clause. Do all
modifications on the noncolumn side. As you saw in Chapter 2,
you can add a function-based index to overcome this issue.*

Use PL/SQL to Tune PL/SQL

You can also use PL/SQL to time your PL/SQL and ensure that it is performing to your standards.
Here is a simple example of how you can write a script that allows you to test and tune your
procedures (a procedure called GET_CUSTOMER in this example) directly from SQL*Plus
(or PL/SQL within SQL*Plus):

```
set serveroutput    on
declare
cust_name char(100);
begin
dbms_output.put_line('Start Time:
    '||to_char(sysdate,'hh24:mi:ss'));
    get_customer(11111,cust_name);
    dbms_output.put_line('Complete Time:
    '||to_char(sysdate,'hh24:mi:ss'));
    dbms_output.put_line(cust_name);
end;
/
```

TIP
*Use PL/SQL to display the start and end times for your PL/SQL.
Basically, don't forget to use PL/SQL to tune your PL/SQL. Use things
like the package DBMS_PROFILER (mentioned earlier in this chapter)
to get timing statistics per line of PL/SQL code.*

NOTE
You could also use DBMS_HPROF, which is new in 11g. The profiler reports the dynamic execution profile of a PL/SQL program organized by function calls, accounting for SQL and PL/SQL execution times separately. The plshprof *command-line utility is in the* $ORACLE_HOME/bin/ *directory and generates an HTML report from either one or two profiler output files.*

Understand the Implications of PL/SQL Object Location

At TUSC, we generally recommend storing the PL/SQL objects on the server side, for many of the obvious reasons. The server is usually much more powerful and objects are reused much more often (especially when pinned into the shared pool). The security methods employed are also more straightforward. Sending the PL/SQL to be processed on the client side can be dependent on the power of the client and can lessen the number of roundtrips from client to server. But, when written correctly, the calls may be limited back to the server (see the next section for an example). There is certainly a continuing debate on this one, but with the evolving thin client, the server is probably the only place to store the PL/SQL. Figure 10-1 diagrams how PL/SQL is executed when stored on the server side. Some additional reasons for storing code on the server are listed here:

- Performance is improved because the code is already compiled code (p-code).

- You can pin objects in the Oracle SGA.

- It enables transaction-level security at the database level.

- You have less redundant code and fewer version control issues.

- You can query the source code online because it is stored in the data dictionary.

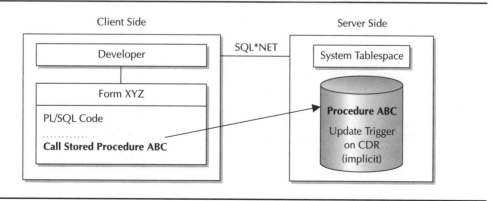

FIGURE 10-1.   *Executing an object on the server side*

- Performing impact analysis is easier since the code is stored in the data dictionary.

- It uses less memory because only one copy of the code is in memory.

- If packages are used, then the entire package is loaded upon initially being referenced.

TIP
Where to store the PL/SQL code is an ongoing debate. Generally, the server side is the preferred place to store the code, and it may become the only choice as thin clients become more prevalent.

Use Rollback Segments to Open Large Cursors

This section is intended for developers and DBAs not using Oracle's automatic undo management. Any skilled PL/SQL developer should be familiar with the need to size and use rollback segments properly when attempting large INSERTs/UPDATEs/DELETEs to the database. If a rollback segment of the appropriate size is not explicitly set prior to the performance of a large data manipulation operation, the operation may fail. The error code usually returned is "ORA-01562: failed to extend rollback segment." The reason for the failure is that transactions that do not explicitly set the rollback segment use one that is randomly assigned by Oracle. If this randomly assigned rollback segment is insufficiently sized to hold the entire transaction, the operation fails. You can eliminate errors of this type by anticipating the amount of data that will be changed, choosing an appropriately sized rollback segment (the DBA_ROLLBACK_SEGS view is helpful in this regard), and setting this rollback segment just prior to the DML statement. The following example demonstrates the proper set of statements:

```
commit;
set transaction use rollback segment rbs1;
update big_table
set column_1 = column_1 * 0.234;
commit;
```

You can also determine the current UNDO retention period by querying the TUNED_UNDORETENTION column of V$UNDOSTAT. In DBA_TABLESPACES, query the column RETENTION, which contains a value of GUARANTEE/NOGUARANTEE to get the retention guarantee setting for the UNDO tablespace. The NOT APPLY is used for tablespaces other than the UNDO tablespace.

It is a little known fact that Oracle uses rollback segments when cursors are employed, even if DML statements are not being issued from within the cursor loop. The rollback segments are used as a type of work area as a cursor loop is being executed. Thus, a cursor loop will quite possibly fail if a rollback segment of insufficient size is used to read the cursor. The failure does not occur immediately—only after numerous iterations of the cursor loop have been performed. Because the error message that is returned is the same as what would be returned when a single DML statement fails, many developers are fooled into thinking that the error lies elsewhere in their code. Valiant efforts are made to manage transaction sizes properly *within* the cursor loops, but to no avail. To successfully open a large cursor, it is imperative to set a large rollback segment just prior to the opening of the cursor:

```
commit;
set transaction use rollback segment rbs_big;
for C1_Rec in C1 loop
-- your processing logic goes here ...
end loop;
```

If large amounts of data are being manipulated within the cursor loop, the code should be setting rollback segments within the cursor loop as well. This prevents the DML statements from utilizing the same rollback segment that is being used to ensure that the large cursor can be read.

TIP

If you are not using automatic undo management (see Chapter 3 for more information), then you may need to specify a large enough rollback segment when opening a large cursor.

TIP

If you are using automatic undo management and Flashback together, you may need to increase the size of a fixed UNDO tablespace (and the UNDO retention period, or an autoextend UNDO tablespace with a MAXSIZE limit). "Snapshot too old" errors during a Flashback indicate that need to ensure sufficient UNDO data is retained to support these flashback operations.

Use Active Transaction Management to Process Large Quantities of Data

When coding procedures that will process large quantities of data, remember to take into account the size of the rollback segments. The rollback segments are the weak link in a program that performs mass data manipulation. A procedure that performs a single COMMIT statement at the end just won't do if it is processing millions of rows of data. It could be argued that a single transaction could be used to process mass quantities of data, provided the rollback segments were large enough. This logic has two flaws: 1) rarely is it feasible to devote gigabytes of valuable drive space to serve as undo space; and 2) should a hardware or software error occur, then the entire dataset would have to be reprocessed. Thus, active transaction management is always the desired technique when processing large quantities of data; it yields efficient utilization of drive space (devoted to UNDO segments) and provides for automatic recovery in the event of hardware/software failures. Also ensure that the UNDO tablespace has enough space to accommodate the UNDO_RETENTION setting.

Active transaction management is a coding technique that consists of three components: setting transactions for cursor and DML statements, performing intermittent database COMMITs, and utilizing a table column as a processing flag to indicate which records have been processed. Consider the following database procedure:

```
declare
  counter number;
  cursor C1 is
    select     rowid,column_1,column_2,column_3
    from       big_table
    where      process_time is NULL;
begin
  Counter := 0;
  commit;
  set transaction use rollback segment rbs_big;
  for C1_Rec in C1 loop
    -- Commit every 1000 records processed.
    if (Counter = 0) or (Counter >= 1000)
      then
        commit;
        set transaction use rollback segment rbs_medium;
        Counter := 0;
      else
        Counter := Counter + 1;
    end if;
    -- Processing logic...
    update big_table
    set process_time = sysdate
    where rowid = C1_Rec.rowid;
  end loop;
  commit;
end;
/
```

The SET TRANSACTION statements ensure that an appropriately sized rollback segment is used for both cursor reading and DML statements on systems that use rollback segments. The database COMMIT for every 1000 records processed does two things: prevents the DML statements from exceeding the capacity of the rollback segment (or UNDO segment) and divides the records being processed into discrete units in the event that there is a hardware/software failure. Finally, the PROCESS_TIME column serves as the processing flag that allows the procedure to identify records that have not yet been processed. With automatic undo management, the database manages UNDO segments in an UNDO tablespace. When you start a transaction, it is assigned automatically to an available UNDO segment. You cannot specify which UNDO segment should be used, and you do not need to do so.

TIP
Maintaining sufficient space for rollback or undo segments can be critical in transactional processing. Limiting the amount of data manipulated between COMMITs is key to avoiding "snapshot too old" errors.

Use Temporary Database Tables for Increased Performance

PL/SQL tables are great for specific cases, especially when repeated iterations are involved and the amount of data is relatively small. As outlined earlier in this chapter, the memory cost (per session) can add up fast if not used properly. When a temporary storage area is needed to house large volumes of records for a short period of time, the method of creating, indexing, and querying a temporary database table should be viewed as a viable and useful option. I have seen far too many developers abandon the common method of temporary database tables after the introduction and expansion of PL/SQL tables; remember, PL/SQL tables are not the preferred method in all cases.

Oracle writes UNDO data for temporary tables to facilitate transaction recovery, rollback to savepoints, read consistency, and reclaiming of space. Thus, transactions in temporary tables generate redos because you need to log the changes made to the rollback or undo segments. The redo generated should be less than the redo generated for DML on permanent tables.

Limit the Use of Dynamic SQL

Oracle provides the Oracle-supplied package DBMS_SQL and the native dynamic SQL command EXECUTE IMMEDIATE, both of which provide for or allow the creation of dynamic SQL and PL/SQL commands. These are extremely powerful features, but also dangerous if not used appropriately. When designing and developing Oracle applications, one of the hardest decisions that must be made is where to draw the line on building in dynamic capabilities and flexibility. Developing dynamic and flexible applications is extremely helpful from a functional perspective. However, the more dynamic and flexible an application, the more potential for performance degradation.

A completely accurate and functional application is considered a failure if it does not perform at acceptable levels. Users will reject an application if they have to wait to do their job. I am not advocating the elimination of dynamic or flexible applications, but a balance must exist. Build flexibility into applications when necessary, not just to make every application module more flexible for the future in case business rules may change. Only build flexibility into applications when you are sure the flexibility is needed and the performance impact will be negligible.

Both the DBMS_SQL package and the EXECUTE IMMEDIATE command provide the dynamic and flexible means in PL/SQL program units. Use these features when needed, but do not abuse them, unless you want to set yourself up for failure.

TIP
If you integrate the DBMS_SQL package into a PL/SQL program unit to create SQL statements dynamically for a production application, remember optimizing the generated SQL statements will be difficult.

TIP
Use bind variables with dynamic SQL to minimize resource contention and maximize performance.

Use Pipelined Table Functions to Build Complex Result Sets

Occasionally, I encounter situations in which a DML SELECT statement is incapable of providing the necessary information. Typically, this occurs when the data doesn't reside in database tables or the number of transformations necessary to get table data into a usable form exceeds the capabilities of SQL and inline functions. Historically, the solution to such a problem would have been the creation of a preprocessor that, when called, would accumulate the data in some type of intermediate table, perhaps a global temporary table, for subsequent extraction using a simple DML select. However, pipelined table functions not only allow you to combine these two steps but also allow you to eliminate the overhead associated with maintaining the data in an intermediate table.

Pipelined table functions are functions that produce a collection of rows (such as a nested table) that can be queried like a physical database table or assigned to a PL/SQL collection variable. You can use a table function in place of the name of a database table in the FROM clause of a query or in place of a column name in the SELECT list of a query.

To demonstrate, I will start with the assumption that this simple table is the only table in my schema:

```
create table states
(
state_code varchar2(2)    not null,
state_name varchar2(100) not null,
constraint states_pk  primary key (state_code),
constraint states_uk1 unique (state_name),
constraint states_chk1 check (state_code = upper(state_code))
);
```

The problem to be solved is that I need a way to create a SQL script to reproduce all of the custom constraints in my schema subject to the following requirements:

- The script is to be created on an application server, not the database server, by a Java Server Pages (JSP) approach.

- The script needs to ensure that dependencies between constraints are taken into account.

- The script should leave disabled constraints in a disabled state when they are reproduced.

- The script should protect against revalidation of existing data when enabled check and foreign key restraints are reproduced.

Now, it *might* be possible to solve this problem with a huge SQL query using multiple table joins and several UNION clauses and a healthy dose of DECODE statements, but the end result would most likely be a monstrosity that would be difficult to maintain. So I will opt for a more elegant solution that involves pipelined table functions that, as you will see, are founded in some very basic PL/SQL functionality. By using a pipelined table function, I simplify what the JSP needs to do to get the desired information from the database . . . issue a simple DML SELECT statement. The pipelined table function will return the DDL commands to the JSP in the proper format, adhering to all the requirements. From the JSP's perspective, the pipelined table function looks and behaves like a table, so it can simply issue the query and iterate over the returning result set, writing the commands to a file as they are fetched.

A pipelined table function is declared by specifying the PIPELINED keyword. The PIPELINED keyword indicates that the function returns rows iteratively. The return type of the pipelined table function must be a supported collection type, such as a nested table or a varray (it cannot be an associative array type). This collection type can be declared at the schema level or inside a package. Inside the function, you return individual elements of the collection type. Here is the package header for the solution to the problem. Note that the GET_CONSTRAINT_DDL function returns a collection type and uses the PIPELINED keyword.

```
CREATE OR REPLACE PACKAGE ddl_extract_pkg is

   --Record and array types to support pipelined tabled functions.
   type sg_constraint_ddl_rec is record (ddl_name varchar2(100),
                                         ddl_text varchar2(1000));
   type sg_constraint_ddl_array is table of sg_constraint_ddl_rec;

   --Public routines.
   FUNCTION get_constraint_ddl return sg_constraint_ddl_array pipelined;

END ddl_extract_pkg;
/
```

In PL/SQL, the PIPE ROW statement causes a pipelined table function to return a row and continue processing. The statement enables a PL/SQL table function to return rows as soon as they are produced. The PIPE ROW statement may be used only in the body of pipelined table functions; an error is raised if it is used anywhere else. The PIPE ROW statement can be omitted for a pipelined table function that returns no rows. A pipelined table function may have a RETURN statement that does not return a value. The RETURN statement transfers the control back to the consumer and ensures the next fetch gets a NO_DATA_FOUND exception.

Before looking at the package body, I will briefly discuss some of the key components of the solution:

- First, to avoid the tedious assembly of reconstructive DDL from various dictionary tables, the DBMS_METADATA package is utilized. The DBMS_METADATA package is a supplied package that does the work of building DDL from the dictionary. It requires some initial PL/SQL-based configuration calls that would have invalidated its use in the "do it in a monstrous SQL statement" approach. By using the DBMS_METADATA package, you ensure that you will capture all of the nuances of reconstructive DDL (such as storage parameters, tablespaces, and segment attributes) if desired.

- Once the base reconstructive DDL has been obtained from DBMS_METADATA, it will be processed using string commands to implement the specified functionality.

- The internal processing of the pipelined function is where the dependency order of the constraints must be taken into account. The order in which records are returned by the function (via the PIPE ROW statement) defines the order in which the calling DML SELECT statement receives them.

- It should also be noted (from the "PL/SQL Language Reference Guide"):

A pipelined table function always references the current state of the data. If the data in the collection changes after the cursor opens for the collection, then the cursor reflects the changes. PL/SQL variables are private to a session and are not transactional. Therefore, **read consistency,** well known for its applicability to table data, **does not apply to PL/SQL collection variables**.

```
CREATE OR REPLACE PACKAGE BODY ddl_extract_pkg is

  --scrub_raw_ddl function.
  --
  --Description: This function performs basic scrubbing routines on a
  --             DDL command returned by dbms_metadata.get_ddl.
  --
  --Syntax: scrub_raw_ddl(p_status_c, p_cons_type_c, p_ddl_c);
  --
  --Where: p_status_c    = The current status (Enabled/Disabled).
  --       p_cons_type_c = The constraint type (P, U, C, R).
  --       p_ddl_c       = The constraint reconstruction DDL.
  --
  FUNCTION scrub_raw_ddl (p_status_c     IN varchar2,
                          p_cons_type_c  IN varchar2,
                          p_ddl_c        IN varchar2) return varchar2 is
    v_new_ddl_c varchar2(1000);
  BEGIN
    --Capture the passed DDL.
    v_new_ddl_c := p_ddl_c;
    --Trim off any carriage returns.
    v_new_ddl_c := replace(v_new_ddl_c, chr(10), null);
    --Trim off any whitespace.
    v_new_ddl_c := trim(v_new_ddl_c);
    --For Check and Relational constraints, if the constraint is
    --currently disabled then we will leave it that way.
    --Otherwise, we will enable it but without the re-validation of existing data.
    if ( p_cons_type_c in ('C', 'R') ) then
      if ( ( p_status_c = 'ENABLED' ) ) then
        if ( instr(v_new_ddl_c, ' NOVALIDATE') = 0 ) then
          v_new_ddl_c := v_new_ddl_c||' NOVALIDATE';
        end if;
      end if;
    end if;
    --Properly terminate the command.
    v_new_ddl_c := v_new_ddl_c||';';
    --Return.
    return(v_new_ddl_c);
  END scrub_raw_ddl;

  --get_constraint_ddl function.
  --
  --Description: Pipelined table function returning proper DDL commands to
  --             reconstruct the custom constraints (PK, UK, CHK, FK) for all
  --             tables within the current schema.
  --
  FUNCTION get_constraint_ddl return sg_constraint_ddl_array pipelined is
```

```
    v_mdc_i      integer;
    v_raw_sql_c varchar2(1000);

    --The function returns a collection of records of type X.
    --So, in the code we will return single records of type X.
    v_out_record sg_constraint_ddl_rec;

    --Cursor to control the extraction order to prevent dependency errors.
    --Check constraints, then PK, then UK, then FK.
    --We do this to prevent dependencies errors.
    cursor v_extract_order_cur is
      select 1            as a_cons_order,
             'C'          as a_cons_type,
             'CONSTRAINT' as a_cons_group
        from dual
       union all
      select 2, 'P', 'CONSTRAINT'
        from dual
       union all
      select 3, 'U', 'CONSTRAINT'
        from dual
       union all
      select 4, 'R', 'REF_CONSTRAINT'
        from dual
       order by 1;

    --Cursor to access the custom constraints from the data dictionary.
    cursor v_constraints_cur (p_type_c   IN varchar2) is
      select owner,              table_name,
             constraint_name,    constraint_type,
             status,             validated
        from user_constraints
       where table_name       = 'STATES'
         and constraint_type  = p_type_c
         and generated        <> 'GENERATED NAME';

BEGIN

    --Configure the dbms_metadata package.
    v_mdc_i := dbms_metadata.session_transform;
    dbms_metadata.set_transform_param(v_mdc_i, 'PRETTY',             false);
    dbms_metadata.set_transform_param(v_mdc_i, 'SEGMENT_ATTRIBUTES', false);
    dbms_metadata.set_transform_param(v_mdc_i, 'STORAGE',            false);
    dbms_metadata.set_transform_param(v_mdc_i, 'TABLESPACE',         false);
    dbms_metadata.set_transform_param(v_mdc_i, 'CONSTRAINTS_AS_ALTER', true);
    dbms_metadata.set_transform_param(v_mdc_i, 'CONSTRAINTS',        true);
    dbms_metadata.set_transform_param(v_mdc_i, 'REF_CONSTRAINTS',    true);
    dbms_metadata.set_transform_param(v_mdc_i, 'SQLTERMINATOR',      false);

    --Open the cursor that controls the extraction order...
    for extract_order_rec in v_extract_order_cur loop
      --Open the cursor to access the constraints of the
      --current type (PK, UK, etc).
      for constraints_rec in v_constraints_cur(extract_order_rec.a_cons_type) loop
```

```
            --Initialize the next pipeline record to be returned.
            v_out_record.ddl_name := constraints_rec.constraint_name;
            v_out_record.ddl_text := null;
            --Get the raw DDL for the current constraint.
            v_raw_sql_c := dbms_metadata.get_ddl(extract_order_rec.a_cons_group,
                                        constraints_rec.constraint_name,
                                        constraints_rec.owner);
            --Scrub the raw DDL.
            --The cleaned DDL will be placed into the record
            --being returned to the pipeline.
            v_out_record.ddl_text := scrub_raw_ddl(constraints_rec.status,
                                        extract_order_rec.a_cons_type,
                                        v_raw_sql_c);
            --Return the constructed command to the pipeline.
            pipe row(v_out_record);
        end loop;
      end loop;
      return;
  END get_constraint_ddl;
END ddl_extract_pkg;
/
```

After the package is installed, executing it is as simple as issuing a DML SELECT statement . . . almost. There are a couple of minor nuances to remember when accessing a PIPELINED table function from SQL:

■ The SQL TABLE collection expression must be used to inform Oracle that the collection being returned from a pipelined table function should be treated as a table for purposes of query and DML operations.

■ The desired columns to be accessed from the collection must be explicitly enumerated. The column list wildcard (*) cannot be used.

```
select x.ddl_name,
       x.ddl_text
  from table(ddl_extract_pkg.get_constraint_ddl) x
 order by 1;

DDL_NAME       DDL_TEXT
-----------    ------------------------------------------------------
STATES_CHK1    ALTER TABLE "TRS3_PROC"."STATES" ADD CONSTRAINT "S
               TATES_CHK1" CHECK (state_code = upper(state_code))
                ENABLE NOVALIDATE;

STATES_PK      ALTER TABLE "TRS3_PROC"."STATES" ADD CONSTRAINT "S
               TATES_PK" PRIMARY KEY ("STATE_CODE") ENABLE;

STATES_UK1     ALTER TABLE "TRS3_PROC"."STATES" ADD CONSTRAINT "S
               TATES_UK1" UNIQUE ("STATE_NAME") ENABLE;
```

TIP
Avoid intermediate tables by using pipelined table functions to build complex result sets.

TIP
Use DBMS_METADATA to create reconstructive DDL from the data dictionary.

Leave Those Debugging Commands Alone!

During the development of nearly any PL/SQL module, it inevitably becomes littered with a plethora of debugging commands. More important than the debugging commands themselves is the strategic location chosen by the developer to maximize the benefit of the debugging. For complex algorithms, effective debugging often becomes artistic in nature, and only someone intimately familiar with the code knows the precise location of debug statements to yield maximum benefit. Unfortunately, prior to putting the code into production those strategically placed debugging statements must be either removed or disabled (commented out) because PL/SQL lacks the conditional compilation that is a given in many programming languages. Until now, that is! Oracle has given the PL/SQL developer the power to leave those debugging commands in place so that they can be reactivated on the fly should an issue arise.

With conditional compilation, you can enter an if-then control structure that is only evaluated at compile time. The intent is to use the if-then control structure to control which textual statements (from the THEN or ELSE clauses) are included in the program as it compiles. The conditional compilation control structure is identified by the conditional compilation trigger character ($), which is prepended to the keywords (IF, THEN, ELSE, ELSIF, END, and ERROR) of a standard if-then block (the exception being that the block terminator is END in lieu of END IF). The Oracle PL/SQL compiler performs a preliminary scan of the source code looking for the conditional compilation trigger character, $. If any valid trigger characters are found, then the compiler evaluates the compilation condition to determine which code text, if any, should be included in the actual compilation of the code.

Here is the basic structure of the conditional compilation block:

```
$if test_expression $then text_to_include
  [ $elsif test_expression $then text_to_include ]
  [ $else text_to_include ]
$end
```

Conditional compilation uses either a *selection directive* or an *inquiry directive* to determine which text is to be included in the compiling program. The selection directive allows a static expression to be evaluated at compile time.

Here is the simplest form of a conditional compilation command that uses the selection directive:

```
$if static_boolean_expression $then text_to_include; $end
```

At compile time, if STATIC_BOOLEAN_EXPRESSION evaluates to TRUE, then the TEXT_TO_INCLUDE is included in the compiling program; otherwise, the TEXT_TO_INCLUDE is skipped. To demonstrate, I'll start with a package specification that will be used exclusively to store conditional compilation constants for debugging purposes:

```
CREATE OR REPLACE PACKAGE debug_pkg IS
   debug constant boolean := true;
END debug_pkg;
/
```

Next, I create the package specification for some fictional component of a business application:

```
CREATE OR REPLACE PACKAGE worker_pkg as
   PROCEDURE run_prc;
END worker_pkg;
/
```

I follow that with the package body that includes a conditional compilation command referencing the static constant in the debugging package:

```
CREATE OR REPLACE PACKAGE BODY worker_pkg as
   PROCEDURE run_prc is
   BEGIN
     dbms_output.put_line('Processing started.');
     $if debug_pkg.debug $then dbms_output.put_line('Debugging is on.'); $end
     dbms_output.put_line('Processing completed.');
   END;
END worker_pkg;
/
```

Since the static constant was set to TRUE at the time I compiled this package body, the extra DBMS_OUTPUT command is included in the compiled program. This can be verified by executing the RUN_PRC procedure:

```
set serverout on;
exec worker_pkg.run_prc;

Processing started.
Debugging is on.
Processing completed.
PL/SQL procedure successfully completed
```

Changing the DEBUG_PKG package causes all dependent objects to recompile, and, as that occurs, the current value of the conditional compilation control constant is used to determine if the debugging statements are compiled into the recompiled code:

```
CREATE OR REPLACE PACKAGE debug_pkg IS
   debug constant boolean := false;
END debug_pkg;
/
```

This time around, because the static constant was set to FALSE, the extra DBMS_OUTPUT command is not be included in the compiled program as the WORKER_PKG package automatically recompiles. This can be verified by executing the RUN_PRC procedure again:

```
set serverout on;
exec worker_pkg.run_prc;

Processing started.
Processing completed.
PL/SQL procedure successfully completed
```

Let's pause for a moment and perform a traditional activity of querying the data dictionary to retrieve the source of a stored package.

```
select text
  from user_source
 where name = 'WORKER_PKG'
   and type = 'PACKAGE BODY'
 order by line;

TEXT
--------------------------------------------------------------------------------
PACKAGE BODY worker_pkg as
  PROCEDURE run_prc is
  BEGIN
    dbms_output.put_line('Processing started.');
    $if debug_pkg.debug $then dbms_output.put_line('Debugging is on.'); $end
    dbms_output.put_line('Processing completed.');
  END;
END worker_pkg;

8 rows selected
```

What I discovered is that the _SOURCE (such as USER_SOURCE, DBA_SOURCE) dictionary tables can no longer be relied upon to reveal the precise code that is executing within the database. The _SOURCE dictionary tables are, after all, just that . . . the source code. To ascertain the exact code that has been compiled, taking into account conditional compilation, Oracle now provides the DBMS_PREPROCESSOR package:

```
set serverout on

BEGIN
  dbms_preprocessor.print_post_processed_source('PACKAGE BODY',
                                                 USER,
                                                 'WORKER_PKG');
END;
/

PACKAGE BODY worker_pkg as
  PROCEDURE run_prc is
  BEGIN
    dbms_output.put_line('Processing started.');
```

```
      dbms_output.put_line('Processing completed.');
   END;
END worker_pkg;

PL/SQL procedure successfully completed
```

Now back to the debugging package. To have a bit more granularity over which procedures are debugged, I simply need to introduce some procedure-specific control constants:

```
CREATE OR REPLACE PACKAGE debug_pkg IS
   debug_run_prc constant boolean := true;
   debug_xxx_prc constant boolean := false;
   debug_yyy_prc constant boolean := false;
   debug_zzz_prc constant boolean := false;
END debug_pkg;
/
```

And then I update the worker package to utilize the new constants:

```
CREATE OR REPLACE PACKAGE BODY worker_pkg as
   PROCEDURE run_prc is
   BEGIN
     dbms_output.put_line('Processing started.');
     $if debug_pkg.debug_run_prc $then
       dbms_output.put_line('Debugging is on.');
     $end
     dbms_output.put_line('Processing completed.');
   END;
END worker_pkg;
/
```

Let's make sure that everything is still working as expected:

```
set serverout on;
exec worker_pkg.run_prc;

Processing started.
Debugging is on.
Processing completed.
PL/SQL procedure successfully completed
```

Keep in mind that a physical dependency exists between the package containing the static constants and the packages referencing them for conditional compilation. Thus, if you alter the DEBUG_PKG package to change the setting for a single constant, it is still going to cause a cascading recompilation of all procedures/functions that are dependent upon that package—regardless of whether or not the changed constant is referenced in the dependent package. In an application with a large population of stored code, this may be undesirable behavior. In such scenarios, you can disperse the static constants across more packages, or with Oracle Database 10g Release 2, you can switch to another method of controlling conditional compilation: *inquiry directives.*

First, I start by cleaning up a bit:

```
drop package debug_pkg;

Package dropped
```

The conditional compilation inquiry directive allows the test conditions to be tied to the compilation environment via the following predefined directive names:

- Any of the Oracle PL/SQL compilation initialization parameters, such as PLSQL_CCFLAGS, PLSQL_CODE_TYPE, or PLSQL_WARNINGS
- The module line number from PLSQL_LINE
- The current source unit name from PLSQL_UNIT. Note that this directive name returns NULL for anonymous blocks
- A custom name-value pair introduced via PLSQL_CCFLAGS

For this example, I will construct a custom name-value pair via the PLSQL_CCFLAGS initialization parameter:

```
alter session set PLSQL_CCFLAGS = 'MyDebugMode:TRUE';
```

Next I modify the test procedure to switch to an inquiry directive:

```
CREATE OR REPLACE PACKAGE BODY worker_pkg as
  PROCEDURE run_prc is
  BEGIN
    dbms_output.put_line('Processing started.');
    $if $$MyDebugMode $then
      dbms_output.put_line('Debugging is on.');
    $end
    dbms_output.put_line('Processing completed.');
  END;
END worker_pkg;
/
```

And a quick test reveals that everything is working per expectations:

```
set serverout on;
exec worker_pkg.run_prc;

Processing started.
Debugging is on.
Processing completed.

PL/SQL procedure successfully completed.
```

Unlike when I was using selection directives tied to a static constant, altering the value of my custom inquiry directive does not cause automatic recompilation of the package:

```
alter session set PLSQL_CCFLAGS = 'MyDebugMode:FALSE';

Session altered.
```

```
set serverout on;
exec worker_pkg.run_prc;

Processing started.
Debugging is on.
Processing completed.
PL/SQL procedure successfully completed.
```

Until another stimulus causes the package to recompile, the change in the custom inquiry directive will not be realized:

```
alter package worker_pkg compile;

Package altered.

set serverout on;
exec worker_pkg.run_prc;

Processing started.
Processing completed.
PL/SQL procedure successfully completed.
```

Optionally, to adjust the behavior of a specific package without altering the session, you can specify the PL/SQL persistent compiler parameters during a forced recompilation of the module:

```
alter package worker_pkg compile PLSQL_CCFLAGS = 'MyDebugMode:TRUE' reuse settings;

Package altered.

set serverout on;
exec worker_pkg.run_prc;

Processing started.
Debugging is on.
Processing completed.
PL/SQL procedure successfully completed.
```

The REUSE SETTINGS clause is used to bypass the normal compiler behavior of dropping and reloading (from the session) all the persistent compiler parameters. Thus, the only compiler parameter that is updated during the forced recompile is the one that was specified as part of the ALTER command.

The error directive provides a quick method for supplying debugging output within your procedures. For example, if you create a procedure that uses some PL/SQL functionality that was introduced in Oracle Database 11.2, but this procedure also has to run on an Oracle 10.2 database, then you could use the error directive to write an error message identifying the database release as not supported by the procedure. See Example 2-59 in the "PL/SQL Language Reference Guide" for 11.2.

TIP
Suppress debugging commands in PL/SQL code with conditional compilation.

TIP
Use the static constants defined in DBMS_DB_VERSION as selection directives to control conditional compilation. The DBMS_DB_VERSION package specifies the Oracle version numbers and other information, which is useful for simple conditional compilation selections based on Oracle versions.

The "Look and Feel": Just for the Beginners

Since many developers and DBAs who may read this book are beginners at PL/SQL, I am also including examples of a piece of PL/SQL code, a procedure, a function, a package, and a trigger. I feel it is important that you have a feel for what these objects look like and how they differ, especially if you haven't seen some of them before. This section is intentionally placed as the last section of this chapter as a short reference section only and to give you a feel for how each looks. The goal is not to teach you how to write PL/SQL (please refer to Joe Trezzo's *PL/SQL Tips and Techniques* [McGraw-Hill, 1999] for that).

Both procedures and functions can take parameters and can be called from PL/SQL. However, procedures typically perform an action. The parameters used in procedures can be in(put), out(put), or in(put)/out(put) parameters, whereas functions typically compute a value and the parameters can only be in(put) parameters. As a matter of fact, you can't even specify the "direction" of the parameters. Functions only permit the passing of one return value. Functions are "selectable," so you can create your own user-defined functions that return information (you can have multiple RETURN statements in a function, but each RETURN statement can only pass a single expression).

Functions can also be used when creating indexes so the index key is sorted in a fashion that matches your queries.

PL/SQL Example

Here is an example of a piece of PL/SQL code:

```
declare
    acct_balance        NUMBER(11,2);
    acct                CONSTANT NUMBER(4)  := 3;
    debit_amt           CONSTANT NUMBER(5,2)  := 500.00;
begin
  select  bal into acct_balance
  from    accounts
  where   account_id = acct
  for     update of bal;
    if acct_balance >= debit_amt THEN
    update       accounts
    set   bal = bal - debit_amt
    where        account_id = acct;
    else
    insert into temp values
        (acct, acct_balance, 'Insufficient funds');
            -- insert account, current balance, and message
```

```
      end if;
   commit;
end;
/
```

Create a Procedure Example

Here is an example of how to create a procedure. I have listed it here in case you have never witnessed one before:

```
create or replace procedure
      get_cust (in_cust_no in char, out_cust_name out char,
      out_cust_addr1 out char, out_cust_addr2 out char,
      out_cust_city out char, out_cust_st out char,
      out_cust_zip out char, out_cust_poc out char) IS
begin
   select  name, addr1, addr2, city, st, zip, poc
   into     out_cust_name, out_cust_addr1, out_cust_addr2,
            out_cust_city, out_cust_st, out_cust_zip,
            out_cust_poc
   from     customer cust, address addr
   where    cust.cust_no = addr.cust_no
   and      addr.primary_flag  = 'Y'
   and      cust.cust_no = in_cust_no;
end       get_cust;
/
```

Execute the Procedure from PL/SQL Example

Here is an example of how to execute a PL/SQL procedure from within a block of PL/SQL code. As before, I have listed it here in case you have never witnessed one before:

```
get_cust (12345, name, addr1, addr2, city, st, zip, poc);
```

Create a Function Example

Here is an example of how to create a function. Once again, I have listed it here in case you have never witnessed one before:

```
create or replace function  get_cust_name (in_cust_no number)
return char
IS
   out_cust_name cust.cust_last_name%type;
begin
   select  cust_last_name
   into     out_cust_name
   from     cust
   where    customer_id = in_cust_no;
   return   out_cust_name;
end get_cust_name;
```

Execute the GET_CUST_NAME Function from SQL Example

Here is an example of how to execute the GET_CUST_NAME function:

```
select    get_cust_name(12345)
from      dual;
```

Create a Package Example

Here is an example of how to create a package:

```
Create or replace package emp_actions IS   -- package specification
   procedure hire_employee
         (empno NUMBER, ename CHAR, ...);
   procedure retired_employee (emp_id NUMBER);
end emp_actions;
/
Create or replace package body emp_actions IS   -- package body
   procedure hire_employee
         (empno NUMBER, ename CHAR, ...)
is
   begin
      insert into emp VALUES (empno, ename, ...);
   end hire_employee;
   procedure fire_employee (emp_id NUMBER) IS
   begin
      delete from emp WHERE empno = emp_id;
   end fire_employee;
end emp_actions;
/
```

Database Trigger Example Using PL/SQL

Here is an example of how to create a trigger using PL/SQL:

```
create trigger audit_sal
   after update of sal ON emp
   for each row
begin
   insert into emp_audit VALUES( ...)
end;
```

Tips Review

- Named notation continues to be the preferred method for passing parameters to subroutines. With Oracle Database 11*g*, this best practice approach has been extended to SQL statements to yield consistency across the entire code base.

■ Experienced and novice developers alike should leverage the PL/SQL compile-time warnings to catch obscured programming problems before code deployment.

■ The new CONTINUE statement creates loop constructs that are more streamlined, but there are no performance gains to be realized at this time.

■ The introduction of compound triggers in conjunction with execution order control are welcome enhancements.

■ Use the Oracle-supplied package DBMS_APPLICATION_INFO package to log point-in-time information to the V$SESSION view to enable monitoring of long-running processes.

■ Log (INSERT) execution timing information into a database table for long-running PL/SQL program units to integrate a proactive performance-monitoring mechanism into your system. The database table can be reviewed at any point in time to determine if performance has decreased over time.

■ System load in terms of number of active sessions can have a large impact on the performance of program execution; therefore, it would be helpful to modify the database table logging method to include a column for the number of active sessions. This column can be filled by adding one additional query to the program unit being executed to retrieve the count from the V$SESSION view.

■ When a PL/SQL program unit involves extensive looping or recursion, concentrate on reducing the execution time per iteration. Execution time adds up fast, and it is easy to do the math to determine the overall improvement potential. The looping or recursion should also be reviewed for restructuring to reduce the number of iterations, while maintaining functionality. With the extreme flexibility of PL/SQL and SQL, typically a variety of ways exist to accomplish the same result. If a PL/SQL program unit is not performing optimally, sometimes you have to rewrite the logic another way.

■ Use the ROWID variable to enhance performance when SELECTing a record in a PL/SQL program unit and then manipulating the same record in the same PL/SQL program unit.

■ Ensure that all conditional comparisons compare the same data types. Additionally, ensure that the data types within the numeric family are comparing the same subtype.

■ Ensure the string of PL/SQL IF conditions appear in the order of most frequently satisfied, not a sequential order based numerically or alphanumerically.

■ Use the PLS_INTEGER type when processing integers to improve performance.

■ If a number with precision is assigned to a PLS_INTEGER variable, the value will be rounded to a whole number as if the ROUND function had been performed on the number.

■ Attempt to limit the calls to SYSDATE in iterative or recursive loops because overhead is associated with this variable. Set a PL/SQL DATE variable to SYSDATE in the declaration and reference the PL/SQL variable to eliminate the overhead.

■ Use the DBMS_SHARED_POOL.KEEP procedure to pin PL/SQL objects into the shared pool.

■ Query the V$DB_OBJECT_CACHE view to find objects that are not pinned and are also large enough to potentially cause problems.

■ Query X$KSMSP to find all large pieces of PL/SQL that have appeared in the shared pool. These are candidates to be pinned when the database has started.

■ You can recompile an entire schema (either all or just the invalid objects) with DBMS_UTILITY.COMPILE_SCHEMA.

■ Query DBA_TRIGGERS (for system-wide objects) *or* USER_TRIGGERS (for your schema only) to find the state of triggers and avoid errors with disabled triggers. Disabled triggers can have fatal results for an application: they don't *fail;* they just don't execute.

■ Load reference tables into PL/SQL associative arrays for faster lookups, taking advantage of the performance of array indexes in PL/SQL.

■ Finding the source code behind PL/SQL objects involves querying the USER_SOURCE, DBA_SOURCE, USER_TRIGGERS, and DBA_TRIGGERS views. Find dependencies by querying the USER_DEPENDENCIES and the DBA_DEPENDENCIES views.

■ A DATE data type always stores a complete temporal value, down to the second. It is impossible to insert a date value only into either a PL/SQL variable or database column that is defined as a DATE.

■ The Oracle DATE has both date and time included in it. Avoid suppressing indexes when trying to match dates. The key is to never modify the column side in the WHERE clause. Do all modifications on the noncolumn side.

■ Use PL/SQL to display the start and end times for your PL/SQL. Basically, don't forget to use PL/SQL to tune your PL/SQL. Use things like the package DBMS_PROFILER (mentioned earlier in this chapter) to get timing statistics per line of PL/SQL code. In Oracle 11g, you can also use DBMS_HPROF.

■ Generally, the server side is the preferred place to store the PL/SQL.

■ If you are using automatic undo management and Flashback together, you may need to increase the size of a fixed UNDO tablespace (and the UNDO retention period, or an autoextend UNDO tablespace with a MAXSIZE limit). "Snapshot too old" errors during a Flashback indicate that need to ensure sufficient UNDO data is retained to support these flashback operations.

■ Maintaining sufficient space for rollback or undo segments can be critical in transactional processing. Limiting the amount of data manipulated between COMMITs is key to avoiding "snapshot too old" errors.

■ Avoid intermediate tables by using pipelined table functions to build complex result sets.

■ If you integrate the DBMS_SQL package into a PL/SQL program unit to create SQL statements dynamically for a production application, remember that optimizing the generated SQL statements will be difficult.

■ Use bind variables with dynamic SQL to minimize resource contention and maximize performance.

- Use DBMS_METADATA to create reconstructive DDL from the data dictionary.

- Suppress debugging commands with conditional compilation.

- Use the static constants defined in DBMS_DB_VERSION as selection directives to control conditional compilation.

References

Advanced Application Developer's Guide (Oracle Corporation).

Bradley Brown, "OOPs-Objected Oriented PL/SQL," *SELECT Magazine,* April 1996.

Steven Feuerstein, *Oracle PL/SQL Programming, 4/e* (O'Reilly & Associates, 2005).

Steven Feuerstein, "Using SQL to Examine Stored Code," *Integrator,* February 1996.

Kevin Loney and Bob Bryla, *Oracle Database 10*g *DBA Handbook* (McGraw-Hill, 2005).

Frank Naude's underground Oracle web page (www.orafaq.com).

*Oracle Database PL/SQL User's Guide and Reference 11*g *Release 2* (Oracle Corporation).

SQL Language Reference Manual (Oracle Corporation).

Joe Trezzo, *PL/SQL Tips and Techniques* (Oracle Press, 1999).

Joe Trezzo, *Procedures, Functions, Packages, and Triggers* (TUSC, 1999).

Scott Urman and Tim Smith, *Oracle PL/SQL Programming* (Oracle Press, 1996).

Thanks to Bob Taylor, Joe Trezzo, and Dave Ventura of TUSC for contributions to this chapter. Bob Taylor did the outstanding Oracle 11*g* update to the chapter. Thanks, Bob!

CHAPTER
11

Exadata, Tuning RAC, and Using Parallel Features

With Oracle's acquisition of Sun, a paradigm shift is occurring in the database market, the hardware world, and the IT industry as a whole. Not unknown to Wall Street, this shift is called *industry consolidation.* It first happened after the industrial revolution; check your local antique store for the consolidated companies of that era. While this current shift is just beginning, early tremors are showing that a major shift is on its way. Oracle is widening its influence into the world of hardware and will challenge the Fortune 50 companies as one of the top performers. With Java, Oracle's influence could quickly move into the consumer world. Exadata is the beginning of their move into the hardware world. Oracle has quickly followed that up in less than two years with a second version of Exadata, Exalogic machines, Oracle Database Appliance, Exadata Storage Expansion Rack, and SuperCluster. Their slogan "Software and Hardware Engineered Together" is certainly an accurate description of how well Exadata is performing, but it also reveals a barrier to entry for other companies that might try to compete. Exadata is hardware that combines the power of the database, while leveraging features at the hardware level that other hardware providers will not be able to replicate easily (or at all). I've now worked on a quarter, half, and full rack of Exadata machines and every one of them performed with *client-gasping* performance. Every client I've talked to who is using Exadata is already considering adding more machines to other areas of their business. Exadata has quickly become the fastest selling product Oracle has ever had!

While Oracle has touched upon hardware in the past with the likes of ncube and the Network Computer (NC), with the acquisition of Sun, Oracle has gone into the water head first, introducing the Exadata box (prior to the acquisition of Sun, Oracle partnered with HP on Exadata V1). With the second and third versions of Exadata (V2 and V2-8), the Exadata Storage Expansion Rack, Exalogic, and the latest Oracle Unbreakable Linux Kernel, Oracle is becoming a serious contender, if not the leader, in taking the entire stack—software to hardware. In late September 2011, Oracle introduced the Oracle Database Appliance for small businesses and for departmental servers. On September 26, 2011, Oracle introduced their new SPARC SuperCluster T4-4, which includes 16 T4 processors with 8 cores each (each core has 8 threads). This Solaris-based machine has 1200 threads total on the entire SuperCluster when you add all cores on the machine (more on this later in the chapter). In early October 2011 at OpenWorld, Oracle introduced the Oracle Exalytics Business Intelligence Machine, which includes the TimesTen In-Memory Database computing OBIEE and Essbase Analytics in 1T of memory—can you say instant BI! They also introduced the Oracle Social Network and the Oracle Public Cloud. Other hardware of note includes the Big Data Appliance for unstructured data using Hadoop and NoSQL, Pillar Storage Systems for SAN data, ZFS for NAS, and StorageTek server expandable to 10 units that can store up to 1E of data with a 2:1 compression! I'll cover each of these new offerings briefly so you can see where they might fit in the future. Please see Oracle's site for the latest hardware offering; this chapter will serve as a base for what will surely change quickly over time.

In this chapter, I'll also cover the 11*g* Big Data Appliance, RAC, and parallel features in Oracle. Oracle first introduced their parallel server in Oracle 6.1 (beta) and Oracle 6.2 (limited customer release production) but only widely used it on VAX/VMS. Not until Oracle 9*i*, when they rewrote the code for the RAC product almost completely (95 percent) I am told, did Oracle truly have a clustering product. In Oracle 10*g*, RAC not only matured but had become the cornerstone for grid computing (entire grids of servers using the Oracle RAC or clustering architecture). In 11*g*, RAC has become Oracle's competitive advantage and the centerpiece of Exadata/Exalogic/SuperCluster hardware. In fact, Exadata became a quick way to have an eight-node RAC cluster instantly (Exadata X2-2, more on this shortly). In addition to using many servers to help increase availability and improve performance, Oracle has also improved the parallel query technology that was first introduced with Oracle release 7.1. In Oracle 11*g*, most operations can be parallelized, including queries (parallel SQL execution), DML, DDL operations, intrapartition parallelism, parallelism for data replication and recovery, and data loading; multiple parallel query server processes can even execute against the same partition.

The tips covered in this chapter include the following:

- Exadata terminology and the basics about Exadata X2-2 and X2-8

- About the Exadata Storage Expansion Rack (basics only)

- About the Exalogic X2-2 (basics only)

- Leveraging Smart Scans

- How fast is the Flash Cache

- Using Storage indexes

- Using Hybrid Columnar Compression (HCC)

- Using I/O Resource Management (IORM)

- Leveraging Exadata security, utilities, and best practices

- About the Oracle Database Appliance (basics only)

- About the SPARC SuperCluster T4-4 (basics only)

- About the Big Data Appliance, ZFS, Pillar, and StorageTek (brief notes)

- The Oracle Public Cloud and the Oracle Social Network is coming (brief notes)

- Real Application Clusters (RAC) overview and architecture

- Tuning the RAC interconnect

- Finding RAC wait events

- Tuning the RAC using Enterprise Manager Grid Control

- Basic concepts of parallel operations

- Parallel DDL and DML statements and operations

- Managing parallel server resources and parallel statement queuing

- Parallelism and partitions

- Inter- and intra-operation parallelization

- Creating table and index examples using parallel operations

- Parallel DML statements and examples

- Monitoring parallel operations via the V$ views

- Using EXPLAIN PLAN and AUTOTRACE on parallel operations

- Tuning parallel execution and initialization parameters

- Parallel loading
- Performance comparisons and monitoring parallel operations
- Optimizing Parallel Operations

Exadata Terminology and the Basics

When I think of Exadata (V2-2), I think of it as a "prebuilt eight-node RAC cluster with Super SAN." The eight servers have all the CPU power you need (96 CPU cores—the original version had 64), mega DRAM server memory (768G), a super-fast interconnect (40Gb/s), and 168 disks with a raw disk storage of either 100T of SAS disk (about 28T useable after mirroring, software, etc.) or 336T of SATA storage (about 100T useable after mirroring, software, etc.). The storage server includes an additional 168 CPU cores, a large amount of flash memory (5.376T), and 394G DRAM. The database could store *much* more database data after compression. The Exadata (X2-8) is a two-node server, similar to the (X2-2), but it has 128 CPU cores and 2T of DRAM on the servers. My take on it: if you need it and can afford it—you want it!

As I said, you can load a full rack with 336T of SATA storage. SATA is big and slow; I think of it like a 33 1/3 LP vinyl album (7200 RPM). SATA stands for *Serial Advanced Technology Attachment* (or basically, something plugged into your computer). You can also have 100T of SAS storage instead. SAS is smaller and faster; I think of it like the old 45 records (15K RPM). SAS stands for *Serial Attached SCSI* (Small Computer System Interface), or again, something plugged into your computer. As of July 2011, Oracle added an Exadata Storage Expansion Rack that allows you to grow the storage capacity of the X2-2 and X2-8 by connecting to it via InfiniBand. It has 18 additional storage servers with 216 CPU cores, 6.75T of Flash Cache (around 1.9M flash IOPS), 216 2T 7.2K RPM SAS drives (432T of raw disk space, which is roughly 194T of mirrored uncompressed usable capacity). Used for an on-disk backup, it has a speed of around 27T/hour.

How fast is it? In general, it's 5 to 100× faster than much of the data warehousing competition and 20× faster than most OLTP competition. It also includes hot-swappable redundant power. Each database server has a dual-port InfiniBand (40 Gb/s card), disk controller HBA (Host Bus Adapter) with a 512M battery backup cache, and 4×1GbE interfaces and Integrated Lights Out Management (ILOM) for remote power on, etc. It can also load data at a rate of 12T/hour and process 1.5M I/O's per second using all of the Flash Cache combined.

What makes it so fast? Fast hardware, many CPUs, Flash Cache, lots of DRAM (Parallel Query in DRAM in 11.2), compression (saves 10×–70×), partition pruning (saves 10×–100×), storage indexes (saves 5×–10×), Smart Scan (saves 4×–10×). You can turn a 1T search into a 500M search or even 50M when you leverage all these features. If anything, I think Oracle might be understating the true power of this hardware (Oracle calls it a "database machine").

Exadata Stats

At the time of writing, the following database machines were available and Oracle had already sold their 1000th Exadata machine in June 2011 (at the current rate, Oracle estimates they will quadruple this to 4000 by May 2012, which is their year-end). The Exadata machine now delivers 1.5M flash IOPS (I/Os per second). This figure is sure to change as you read this. Oracle is accelerating the hardware world as they did the software world. You can now build anything you can dream of!

The original Exadata was on HP hardware (V1) but quickly became an *all* Oracle/Sun solution after the Sun acquisition. The first version of V2 was V2-2. The next version, X2-8, was announced at Oracle OpenWorld in the fall of 2010. In 2011, Oracle enhanced both the X2-2 and the X2-8. They also added the Exadata Storage Expansion Rack (details on this in the next section) in 2011. As of the writing of this chapter, these are the details for each version:

A version 2 (X2-2) Exadata machine that is only manufactured by Oracle (Sun) includes:

- 8 compute servers (x4170 M2s):
    - 8 servers × 2 CPU sockets × 6 cores = 96 cores
    - 8 servers × 4 disks × 300G (10K RPM) each (9.6T SAS on server)
- 8 compute servers × 96G DRAM = 768G DRAM
- 3 InfiniBand switches (40 Gb/s) × 36 ports = 108 ports
- 14 storage servers with 168 CPU cores and Flash Cache:
    - 96G × 4 banks = 394G DRAM per storage server
    - 14 storage servers × 394G = 5.376T Flash Cache
    - 12 disks per storage server × 14 servers = 168 disks
    - 168 disks × 600G SAS = 101T SAS (15K RPM) or...
    - 168 disks × 2T SATA = 336T SATA (7.2K RPM)
- Data load rate = 12T/hour

A version 2 (X2-8) Exadata machine that is only manufactured by Oracle (Sun) includes:

- 2 compute servers (7560 CPU at 2.26 GHz and 5T SAS):
    - 2 servers (x4800's) × 8 CPU sockets × 8 cores = 128 cores
    - 2 servers × 8 disks × 300G (10K RPM) each (4.8T SAS on server)
- 2 compute servers × 1T DRAM = 2T DRAM
- 3 InfiniBand switches (40Gb/s) × 36 ports = 108 ports
- 14 storage servers with 168 CPU cores and Flash Cache:
    - 96G × 4 banks = 394G DRAM per storage server
    - 14 storage servers × 394G = 5.376T Flash Cache
    - 12 disks per storage server × 14 servers = 168 disks
    - 168 disks × 600G SAS = 101T SAS (15K RPM) or...
    - 168 disks × 2T SATA = 336T SAS (7.2K RPM)
- Data load rate = 12T/hour

Where did all my disk space go?

■ 100T SAS = 28T usable (your mileage will vary)

■ 336T SATA = 100T usable (your mileage will vary)

Apply some compression and get it back:

■ 28T usable × 10 = 280T SAS

■ 100T usable × 10 = 1P SATA

InfiniBand, 40G/s each way:

■ 3 InfiniBand switches × 36 ports = 108 ports

Full rack (X2-2) or ½ or ¼ rack to start (check with Oracle for latest configurations):

	Full	Half	Quarter
Compute servers/cores	8/96	4/48	2/24
Storage servers/disks*	14/168	7/84	3/36
Storage SAS	100T	50T	21.6T
Storage SAS (usable)*	45T	22.5T	9.25T
Storage SATA	336T	168T	72T
Storage SATA (usable)*	150T	75T	31.5T
Flash Cache	5.3T	2.6T	1.1T
Flash IOPs (maximum)	1,500,000	750,000	375,000
palphaDisk IOPs (maximum)	25,000	12,500	5,400
InfiniBand switches	3	3	2
Data load rates	5T/hr	2.5T/hr	1T/hr

* 600G SAS or 2T SATA; uncompressed storage

* For all storage 1T – 1024 × 1024 × 1024 × 1024 bytes (formatted capacity is less)

Exadata Storage Expansion Rack Briefly

As of July 2011, Oracle added an *Exadata Storage Expansion Rack* that allows you to grow storage capacity of the X2-2 and X2-8 by connecting to it via InfiniBand. This addition is great news for those who are looking to have Petabytes of information. It is also welcome news for those who would like to store more of their archived-to-tape data on disk. It has 18 additional storage servers with 216 CPU cores, 6.75T of Flash Cache (around 1.9M flash IOPs), 216 – 2T 7.2K RPM SAS, drives (432T of raw disk space, roughly 194T of mirrored uncompressed usable capacity). Used for an on-disk backup, Exadata Storage Expansion Rack has a speed of around 27T/hour.

Exadata Storage Server software uses the following features (covered in detail later in this chapter):

■ Smart Scan technology

■ Smart Flash Cache

- Storage indexes

- Hybrid columnar compression

- IORM/DBRM both available

- Smart Scans of data mining model scoring

- Automatic Storage Management (ASM)

- Backup with RMAN

- Restores using Flashback technologies

- Redundant power and InfiniBand switches

In July 2011, Oracle's e-mail system was on nine Exadata racks. Here's what's possible:

- 32 × X2-8s (64-node RAC cluster maximum at this time):

  - 4096 CPUs on the compute servers

  - 5376 CPUs on the storage servers

  - 32 X2-8's (10.7P on the compute servers)

- It would take 41,227 Storage Expansion Racks to get to the maximum 8E (Exabytes of mirrored uncompressed storage) 11*g* Database:

  - Compression gives you 80–500+ Exabytes. At 10× compression, you would only need 4,123 Storage Expansion Racks. At 70× compression, you would only need 589 Storage Expansion Racks to get to 8E.

  - About 109,777 years of YouTube storage (730T/year) with 10× compression.

  - Or greater than 1 million years with higher level of compression (current YouTube).

  - 64 bit allows 16E to be in memory (18,446,744,073,709,551,616).

Exalogic Briefly

Here are some stats on the current *Exalogic Elastic Cloud*, which is the machine geared to run applications (especially Java business applications) fast on the Web (think Amazon, Facebook, Google, Twitter, Yahoo!, Apple, Salesforce.com, eBay, and anyone else who wants to be an Internet commerce player all need one or two of these). As of October 2011, Exalogic initial sales were faster than Exadata when it was introduced. When you tie the Exalogic box to the Exadata box, you can get 2M database requests per second. The Exalogic machine looks the same except there are more servers and fewer disks (in a sense, it's close to the inverse of Exadata). The Exalogic machine also integrates much of Oracle's middle-tier acquisitions into the machine. Exalogic is beyond the scope of this book, but here are its current stats.

An Exalogic Elastic Cloud (X2-2) includes (serves 1M HTTP requests per second):

- **EL X2-2** 30 compute servers, 360 CPU cores, 2.8T DRAM, 4T SSD Read Cache, 40T SAS. Fusion apps will smoke!

- **1M HTTP/sec** I heard that you could fit Facebook on two of the X2-2s even though there are, as of this writing, more than 500M people on Facebook (rapidly rising to over 750M).

Smart Scans

Smart Scans are done internally by Oracle, and when they are used, you commonly realize a 10x savings in query time. Oracle filters data based on WHERE clause conditions (predicates), and it filters on row, column, and join conditions. Oracle also performs incremental backup filtering. Smart Scans work with uncommitted data, locked rows, chained rows, compressed data, and even encrypted data (only in 11.2). You can *see* and monitor the benefits with Grid Control (OEM).

Smart Scans leverage Bloom filters used for faster join filtering. Bloom filters are a quick way to search for matches. They save space and are transparent to the user. Bloom filters are basically hardware-level filters that test to see if the elements are in a set. Google BigTable uses Bloom filters to reduce disk lookups as well. Oracle's join filtering is a perfect application for Bloom filters. Following are some simple Smart Scan comparisons.

Without Smart Scan (push whole table via network):

- 5T table scan

- Network bandwidth (40 Gb/s)

- 40 Gb/s (gigabit/sec) = 5 G/s (gigabyte/sec) (If you have 14 storage cells, then each cell has a data transfer rate of 0.357 G/s.)

16 minutes, 40 seconds (5T at 5G/s)—*without smart scan*

With Smart Scan (limit first at hardware level):

- 5T Table Scan

- Limit result *before* it hits the network

- Effectively scan 21 G/s (1.5G/storage cell × 14 cells)

3 minutes, 58 seconds (5T at 21G/s)—*with smart scan*

Flash Cache

The Flash Cache is composed of solid-state disks (information stored on chips). It is between 20x–50x faster than disk (depending on the disks). The Flash Cache caches *hot* data (frequently used data). It does this as the *last* step (so it returns data to you *first* and then caches it for next time based on the settings you give it). It uses PCIe-based flash cards (PCIe or Peripheral Component Interconnect express). It knows which objects *not* to cache, such as full table scans, but *you* can also specify exactly which data you want to cache using the STORAGE clause or you can specify it at the table/partition level with CREATE/ALTER:

- **STORAGE** CELL_FLASH_CACHE KEEP
- **Table/partition level** CREATE or ALTER

Flash Cache also has a write-through cache that you can use to accelerate reads. With this feature, data written to disk *might* also be written to cache (again, stored in the cache *after* the user gets it written to disk) for future reads.

The Flash Cache caches:

- Hot data/index blocks
- Control file reads/writes
- File header reads/writes

The Flash Cache does not cache:

- Mirror copies, backups or Data Pump
- Tablespace formatting
- Table scans (or, at least, this is rare; for example, small tables are possibilities)

The Flash Cache LRU (least recently used) settings for caching include:

- **CELL_FLASH_CACHE storage clause**
  - **DEFAULT** Normal, large I/Os not cached.
  - **KEEP** Use Flash Cache more aggressively/it may not occupy > 80 percent of all cache.
  - **NONE** Flash Cache not used.
- **CACHE (NOCACHE) hint** I/O cached/not-cached in the Flash Cache
  - SELECT /*+ CACHE */ ...
- **EVICT hint** Data removed from the Flash Cache. ASM rebalance data is evicted from cache when done.

Large I/O (full table scans) on objects with CELL_FLASH_CACHE set to DEFAULT are not cached.

Setting the KEEP cache:

```
ALTER TABLE CUSTOMER
STORAGE (CELL_FLASH_CACHE KEEP);
Table Altered.
```

Query to see if a table is currently set to cache or not:

```
SELECT      TABLE_NAME, TABLESPACE_NAME,
            CELL_FLASH_CACHE
FROM        USER_TABLES
WHERE       TABLE_NAME = 'CUSTOMER';


TABLE_NAME    TABLESPACE_NAME      CELL_FL
-----------   ------------------   -------
CUSTOMER      R_TEST               KEEP
```

Here is how the Flash Cache works: A database request comes to CELLSRV (*cell storage server*). The CELLSRV (first time) gets data from disk and the data is cached based on settings, hints, and so on. The data that goes to WRITE may also be cached after being written if it is deemed that it may be needed again. The CELLSRV (next time) checks the Memory Hash Table that lists what is cached. If cached, the data goes to Flash Cache; if not cached, it may cache based on settings and so on. You can also query the hardware cells directly as listed here:

```
CELLCLI> list flashcache detail (allows you to monitor)
CELLCLI> list flachcachecontent where ObjectNumber=62340 detail
```

SQL*Plus Query—is it working?

```
SELECT      NAME, VALUE
FROM        V$SYSSTAT
WHERE       NAME IN ('physical read total IO requests',
            'physical read requests optimized');


Name                                         Value
------------------------------------------   --------
physical read total IO requests              36240
physical read requests optimized             23954
```

This second line times block size (*8192) is the bytes of Flash Cache used; it's working!

It is working ... 4G query:

```
SELECT      NAME, VALUE, VALUE*8192 VALUE2
FROM        V$SYSSTAT
WHERE       NAME IN ('physical read total IO requests',
            'physical read requests optimized');


NAME                              VALUE          VALUE2
------------------------------    ----------     --------------
physical read total IO requests   10,862,844     88,988,418,048
physical read requests optimized   2,805,003     22,978,584,576
```

run2...

```
physical read total IO requests   11,320,185     92,734,955,520
physical read requests optimized   3,203,224     26,240,811,008
```

run4...

```
physical read total IO requests  11,993,845      98,253,578,240
physical read requests optimized  3,793,000      31,072,256,000
```

It is working . . . V$SQL:

```
select     sql_text, optimized_phy_read_requests, physical_read_requests,
           io_cell_offload_eligible_bytes
from       v$sql
where      sql_text like '%FIND YOUR SQL%'

SQL_TEXT    OPTIMIZED_PHY_READ_REQUESTS PHYSICAL_READ_REQUESTS
----------- --------------------------- ----------------------
IO_CELL_OFFLOAD_ELIGIBLE_BYTES
------------------------------
SELECT....  567790                      688309
4.2501E+10
Run 2.....
SELECT…     762747                      906729
4.9069E+10
run 4 ....
SELECT...   1352166                     1566537
6.8772E+10
```

NOTE
The Exadata PCIe card Smart Flash Cache (that is, the stored Exadata hardware PCIe Card Cache) is not *the same as the 11gR2 Database Flash Cache (file stored) used with Oracle Enterprise Linux.*

Finally, keep in mind that Flash Cache wears out faster than disks (see the specifications for more information; Flash Cache wears out faster in higher elevations). Oracle does give you uncounted "extra" space to make up for this, however.

Storage Indexes

A storage index utilizes minimum and maximum values for certain columns to help queries run faster by eliminating rows (similar to partitioning). A performance gain of 10× is common with storage indexes (could be higher/lower depending on the minimum/maximum (min/max) and how many rows can be eliminated for a given query). These indexes primarily maintain summary information about the data *(like metadata in a way)*. The memory structure resides in the CELL LEVEL (storage). It groups data into min/max for various columns (based on usage patterns), and it eliminates I/Os where there is no match. A storage index is 100 percent transparent to the user. Indexing is performed at the hardware level, and one storage index is used for every 1M of disk. A storage index does *not* perform like a B-tree Index, but more like partition elimination—where you skip data *not* meeting the query conditions. Oracle builds 100 percent of the storage indexes based on query patterns and data use; no additional coding is required. Consider the following queries to see if storage indexing is working on a two-node RAC cluster.

Is it working for me?

```
SELECT      NAME, VALUE
FROM        V$SYSSTAT
WHERE NAME LIKE ('%storage%');


NAME                                              VALUE
---------------------------------------------   --------
cell physical IO bytes saved by storage index   25604736
```

This is the actual savings from an Exadata-built storage index; it's working on this node!

Check both servers...(only savings on one node during this test):

```
SELECT      NAME, VALUE
FROM        GV$SYSSTAT
WHERE       NAME LIKE ('%storage%');


NAME                                              VALUE
---------------------------------------------   -----------
cell physical IO bytes saved by storage index   19693854720
cell physical IO bytes saved by storage index             0
```

This is the actual savings from the Exadata-built storage index; it's working!

Hybrid Columnar Compression (11.2)

Hybrid Columnar Compression (HCC), also known as *Exadata Hybrid Columnar Compression (EHCC)*, is data that is organized by a hybrid of columns/rows and compressed versus data organized by basic row format. A performance gain anywhere from 10×to 30× is common. The tables are organized in compression units (CU), which contain around 1000 rows (more or less depending on the amount of data in the rows). CUs span many blocks. HCC is very good for bulk-loaded data, but is not built for OLTP or single block read operations. It is primarily built for data warehouses and queried data, not for frequently updated data.

Using the old OLTP compression algorithm, you could get 2–3× compression or so. Yet, with HCC, 10× compression in a typical data warehouse is common. In limited tests, I got anywhere from 4–11×. HCC also allows archive compression (used for cold data), which gives you anywhere from 15× to 70× compression (I got approximately 32× compression in limited tests). The nice thing about hybrid columnar compression is that operations are faster because the query runs without decompression. The compressed version is processed in the Flash Cache, which results in lower I/O. The compressed version is also sent over InfiniBand; it is cloned compressed; and it is even backed up compressed! As a result, it scans *much* less (compressed) data!

Note that you can still use standard table compression for OLTP, and a single block lookup is still generally *faster* than other columnar storage. The updated rows migrate to normal/lower-level compression. HCC fully supports:

- B-tree indexes
- Bitmap indexes

- Text indexes
- Materialized views
- Partitioning
- Parallel queries
- Data guard physical standby
- Logical standby and Streams (in a future release)
- Smart Scans of HCC tables!

Don't forget the many other types of Oracle compression that also give Oracle an advantage over the competition:

Data Pump compression	Compression = {ALL | DATA_ONLY | NONE}
RMAN Backup compression	Compression LOW/HIGH (new in 11.2)
Secure File compression (large objects/images)	LOW/MEDIUM/HIGH (2–3x compression) Deduplication and encryption
Normal OLTP table compression (since 9.2)	11g now supports INSERT/UPDATE FASTER algorithm
Data Guard Redo Transport compression	See My Oracle Support Doc ID 729551.1 for information using the initialization parameter _REDO_TRANSPORT_COMPRESS_ALL

I/O Resource Management (IORM)

Oracle's latest I/O Resource Management (IORM) tool can be used with Exadata to manage multiple workloads and set resources as you deem necessary. Although I don't cover this in detail here, please consider the following ways that you set up three instances with different resources. Instance A gets 50 percent, instance B gets 30 percent, and instance C gets 20 percent. You can further break down the 50 percent that instance A gets into the various user- and task-related percentages.

Set I/O resources for different instance:

- Instance A = 50%
- Instance B = 30%
- Instance C = 20%

Further set I/O based on users and tasks:

- Instance A Interactive = 50%
- Instance A Reporting = 20%
- Instance A Batch = 15%
- Instance A ETL = 15%

You can also continue to use Database Resource Manager (DBRM) as in the past. DBRM has been enhanced for Exadata. It allows management of inter- and intradatabase I/O. With interdatabase I/O, you manage using IORM and Exadata storage software. For intradatabase I/O, you manage using Consumer Groups. You can set limits for CPU, UNDO, degree of parallelism (DOP), active sessions, and much more. Please see the Oracle documentation for more details. This section is only a brief introduction so you can see what's possible.

Use *All* Oracle Security Advantages with Exadata

Oracle is known for its incredible security. Their first customer was the CIA (Central Intelligence Agency), so they've always been focused on security (for over 30+ years). Don't forget to investigate these security and recovery options that are available with Exadata:

- Audit Vault
- Total Recall/Flashback (recovery)
- Database Vault
- Label security
- Advanced security
- Secure encrypted backup (Please use!) (also available—incremental backup with change tracking file, which is much faster)
- Data masking
- Data Guard (recovery)
- Failure groups (automatic for storage cell failure)

Best Practices

There are many best practices that will help you get the most out of Exadata. I'll start with a list of *must haves* and *don't do's*. Note, however, that these can change at any time, so check Oracle's docs for the latest information.* Here is my list as of the writing of this chapter (late-2011):

- Must have Bundle Patch 5 (see MetaLink note 888828.1 for the latest).
- Must have ASM to use Exadata.
- Must have three floor tiles on a raised floor (must support 2219 lbs./964 kg) with holes (cooling) for a full rack (between 1560 CFM and 2200 CFM front to back – less for a half or quarter rack). You don't want to melt it! All of this is subject to change, so please check the latest specifications.
- Must have the correct power needs.
- Must use Oracle Linux 5.3 (x86_64) and Oracle DB 11.2 (currently).
- Must use RMAN for backups.

- Ensure InfiniBand is connected and MTU is set to 65520.

- Check disk group balance and notes on auto-extend.

- Capture performance baselines *early* in your implementation.

- Consider StorageTek SL500 tape backup (many positive reviews but it is pricey).

- Use an ASM allocation unit (AU) size of 4M (currently).

- Don't add any foreign hardware … or *no support!*

- Don't change BIOS/Firmware … or *no support!*

Next, I'd like to list some Oracle stated best practices. Note that these can change at any time, as well, so please check your Oracle docs for the latest. Best practices include:

- CREATE ALL celldisk and griddisks.

- Use DCLI to run on *all* storage servers at once (helpful and saves time).

- Use IORM for resource management.

- Decide fast recovery area (FRA) and MAA needs before you install.

- Ensure Database 11.2.0.1+ (11.2.1.3.1) and ASM 11.2.0.1+ (minimums currently).

- Compatible with 11.2.0.1+ (minimum currently).

- Set log file size at 32G (whoa!).

- To optimize fast scan rates, ensure database extent sizes are at least 4M (locally managed tablespaces (LMT) can have a uniform or auto-allocate extent policy).

- Move data with Data Pump (usually, but many other options are available).

* This is an abbreviated list. Please see My Oracle Support Doc ID 757552.1 for the full document. Note 1274475.1 is the subsection for performance-specific information.

Summary: Exadata = Paradigm Shift!

I've covered many topics in this section, including Exadata terminology and basics, Flash Cache, storage indexes, Smart Scans, Hybrid Columnar Compression (HCC), I/O Resource Manager, security, and best practices. What makes Exadata fast is fast hardware, many CPUs, fast Flash Cache, lots of DRAM on database servers and storage, compression (saves 10x–70x), partition pruning (saves 10x–100x), storage indexes (saves 5x–10x), Smart Scan (saves 4x–10x), and other features not covered (see Oracle Docs for more information). Exadata is the best way to turn a 1T search into a 500M search or even a 50M search. I believe that Exadata is *The Real Deal* and will drive future accelerated hardware innovation by all major hardware vendors.

Oracle Database Appliance

Exadata may be overkill for some customers. When Oracle introduced the Oracle Database Appliance, they were thinking about small- and medium-sized businesses (SMBs) and customers that needed departmental servers. As Oracle Database Appliance was just introduced in late

September 2011, I have only a few details. The goal, however, is to have a quickly implemented, mid-sized server. It includes:

- Oracle 11g with ASM and RAC running on Oracle Linux
- High availability fault tolerant—two nodes/dual server
- Cluster in a box (Oracle Clusterware comes installed)
- 2 cores to 24 cores (Xeon)—2 core minimum/4 core for RAC
- 96G RAM × 2 servers = 192G RAM
- 12T of raw SAS storage (easily load up to a 4T data warehouse with 3× mirroring)
- Oracle Appliance Manager (for quick patching and system management)
- Auto memory management, auto tuning, auto disk backup
- It also includes a ready to go in a *couple of hours* (software and RAC preloaded)

The Oracle Database Appliance can be ready to go in a *couple of hours* (software and RAC is preloaded). It even has a phone-home capability; it calls for service and has one-button patching. Introducing the Oracle Database Appliance is just another way that Oracle is leveraging its Sun acquisition to create a full line of hardware that benefits its customers. While the hardware itself is inexpensive (50K USD was the current hardware price), the software license cost can certainly add up if you use the maximum CPU configuration, but it's still much lower priced than a quarter rack at the current time (a quarter rack is over 2x faster though). I'm confident that this will evolve over time, so please check with Oracle for the latest configuration and pricing.

SPARC SuperCluster

On September 26, 2011, Oracle announced the new SPARC SuperCluster T4-4. SPARC SuperCluster runs the Solaris operating system (Solaris 11 or Solaris 10 8/11) with hardware using the new T4 multithreaded SPARC processor. Each T4 has eight cores, and there are eight threads per core. A SuperCluster has four T4-4 servers, which are servers with four T4s each in them. So a SuperCluster has 16 total T4s with 8 cores each or 128 cores. Because each core has 8 threads, there are up to 1024 threads, not including the storage cores/threads (a SuperCluster has 1200 when you include everything). SPARC SuperCluster also has 198T of disk, 8.66T of Flash Cache, and 4T of DRAM. Here are some other details:

- Includes the new SPARC T4 microprocessor (5× faster than T3)
  - L1 and L2 cache (16K each) specific to a core
  - L3 shared by all eight cores—4M (new on T4)
  - Prefetching of instructions and data (new on T4)
  - Out of order execution (new on T4)
  - Out of order execution (new on T4)

- Out of order execution (new on T4)
- Dual instruction use (new on T4)
- Memory management unit page size = 2G
- Dynamically threaded
- You can have up to eight SuperCluster racks without adding any InfiniBand changes
- ZFS Storage Appliance (7320) implemented
- Solaris 11 or 10 operating system
- Oracle VM (virtual machine) also available

A SPARC SuperCluster T4-4, which is only manufactured by Oracle (Sun), includes:

- 4 compute servers (T4 CPU at 3 GHz and 4.8T SAS)
  - 4 servers (×T4-4) × 4 CPU sockets × 8 cores = 128 cores × 8 threads per core = 1024 CPU threads on the servers alone (1200 threads on a SuperCluster)
  - 4 servers × 8 disks × 300G (10K RPM) each (9.6T SAS on server OR 19.2T (600G disks)
- 4 compute servers ×1T DRAM = 4T DRAM
- 3 InfiniBand switches ×36 ports = 108 ports
- 896 Gb/s InfiniBand interconnect (almost Tb/sec InfiniBand!)
- 40 GB/s storage bandwidth
- 8 storage servers with additional CPU cores and Flash Cache (also includes ZFS 7320 controllers; two actual servers are included, *each* with two 4-core CPUs and 8 disks)
  - 8 storage servers with 8.66T Flash Cache
  - 8 × 2 = 16 disks × 300G (in ZFS) + 8 × 4 = 32 disks × 300G (in servers) = 14.4G
  - 12 disks per storage server × 8 servers = 96 additional disks (4 disks are 18G)
  - 72 disks × 600G SAS + 20 disks ×2T = 83.2T mix (**97T total** including 14.4G)

    or…
  - 92 disks × 2T SATA = 184T SATA (**198T total** including 14.4G)

Oracle is primarily targeting their SPARC Solaris install base to migrate to SPARC SuperCluster. Oracle's goal is not only to make migrating easy for this install base, but also to give them the speed of Exadata and Exalogic in a single SPARC-based machine. When you review the last few sections, you can see that Oracle is leveraging its Sun acquisition with the fastest hardware on earth for parallel database processing (rack(s) of Exadata), fastest middleware server or Internet eBusiness application server machine(s) (rack(s) of Exalogic), large company migration from Solaris to mix of Exadata/Exalogic speed systems (rack(s) of SuperCluster), small business or department server (Oracle Database Appliance(s)), and infinite storage (rack(s) of Exadata Storage Expansion Racks). I'm sure Oracle has already exceeded all of this, even as amazing as it sounded at the time I wrote this. My advice: Teach your kids Oracle!

Oracle Exalytics Business Intelligence Machine

Oracle leverages their TimesTen acquisition with the introduction of Exalytics. With the TimesTen In-Memory Database for Exalytics leveraging 1T of DRAM and 40 cores of processing power, all your hot BI data is processed in memory. The server includes Oracle Business Intelligence Enterprise Edition (OBIEE) and Essbase (Oracle is leveraging its Hyperion acquisition here) in what Oracle calls their "speed of thought" server. Exalytics also includes 3.6T of internal storage, redundant power supplies, two 40 Gb/s InfiniBand connections, 2×10 Gb/s Ethernet connections, and 4×1 Gb/s Ethernet connections. Exalytics currently shows a relational dashboard performance of 20× and modeling performance of 79× compared to off-the-shelf hardware. As Larry Ellison put it in one presentation: "The response time is so fast that ... there is no response time; it's already done."

Other Oracle Hardware to Consider

In this section, I cover some of the other hardware that you should at least consider as you implement your business solutions. All of these come from recent Oracle acquisitions.

The Oracle Big Data Appliance

The Oracle Big Data Appliance is used to acquire, organize, analyze, and make sense of all the unstructured data in your company or on the Web. Big data is all the data on weblogs, social media, e-mail, sensors, photographs, videos, and all the other big data that is coming. The Oracle Big Data Appliance is an engineered system that includes an open source version of Apache Hadoop, Oracle NoSQL Database (think of it as version 2 of Oracle, a highly scalable key-value database), Oracle Data Integrator Application Adapter for Hadoop (simplifies data integration in Hadoop), and an open source version of R (Oracle R Enterprise integrates with the open source statistical environment R to deliver advanced analytics). You can also integrate the Oracle Big Data Appliance with the Oracle Database, Exadata, or Exalytics.

ZFS Storage Servers

The Sun ZFS Storage 7420 has 1P (1 Petabyte or 1000T) of raw storage capacity. This is a high-performance Network Attached Storage (NAS) system with SAN storage capabilities. It supports an active-active cluster option, supports Oracle Database HCC (Hybrid Columnar Compression), and has data compression and in-line deduplication. The ZFS 7320 has 192T of raw storage capacity (and can be configured with 4T of read optimized cache), and the ZFS 7120 has 120T of raw storage capacity. The ZFS 7320 is used inside the Oracle SPARC SuperCluster.

Pillar Storage System

The Pillar Axiom 600 is your high-performance SAN storage system. It has a patented quality of service (QoS) architecture that is dynamic, depending on the various service level agreements that you might have for your business applications. It can support multiple applications with different priority levels using its QoS storage profiles. It scales to 8 storage controllers and up to 128 RAID controllers. It has a modular storage system with policy controllers, storage controllers, and storage enclosures as the building blocks. Pillar Axiom 600 also supports Oracle Database HCC, includes dual power, dual fans, and redundant storage controllers. It is used for Oracle databases,

Microsoft Exchange, and storage consolidation or virtualization projects. It is also a very energy efficient storage system.

StorageTek Modular Library System

One of the biggest companies I know of recently had to recover from tape. Most companies have online fast recovery areas (FRA) for quick recoveries, as well as online backups located on slower 2T SATA disks. But there is still a place for an offsite tape backup, and StorageTek makes it fast and easy. Looking inside one of these machines is like watching a production assembly line where tapes are moved around as needed automatically. Another benefit of the Sun acquisition was getting this incredible company called StorageTek. It is no surprise that Oracle now archives more data than anyone else in the world.

The StorageTek SL8500, with a maximum configuration of 10 libraries (there are many models/sizes to choose from if you need something smaller), includes the ability to back up 500P (500 Petabytes) native or 1E (1 Exabyte) with a 2:1 compression (at a speed of 553T/hour). To put this in perspective, a few years ago (around 2005), a business magazine estimated that the average Fortune 1000 company had an average size of 1P for *all* of their databases. That means all Fortune 1000 databases could have been backed up with this device (maximum 10 library configuration) with a 2:1 compression in 2005. After reading these last few sections, you should start to see the future of Oracle accelerating at the speed of thought!

The Oracle Public Cloud and the Oracle Social Network

As of the writing of this chapter, Oracle had introduced the Oracle Public Cloud and Oracle Social Network at OpenWorld in October 2011. While little information is available at this time, I did want to mark this as yet another acceleration point for Oracle and provide what information is currently available. I do believe that each of these has the possibility of radically changing the way you do business today!

The *Oracle Public Cloud* is standards-based (you can move things from the Oracle cloud to the Amazon cloud) and consists of your choice of Oracle offerings, including Oracle Fusion CRM Cloud Service, Oracle Fusion HCM Cloud Service, Oracle Social Network Cloud Service, Oracle Java Cloud Service, Oracle Database Cloud Service—all running on Oracle Exadata and Exalogic servers to offer elastic capacity on demand. Charges are on a monthly subscription basis. I certainly see more cloud services arriving by the time you read this.

The *Oracle Social Network* is an extremely advanced social networking collaboration application that is truly revolutionary. The capability to run your business while integrating people or processes is accelerated using the Oracle Social Network. You can quickly put together teams, pass documents or contracts among team members with appropriate security controls, connect with partners, and get/share real-time information. With instant connections and full security to the Oracle Social Network, you can quickly accelerate deals, change teams, or get instant access to critical business information. Oracle has leveraged what MySpace and Facebook did into the world of Oracle business applications so that instant collaboration and access to information enhances all areas of business processes. It may take a decade for companies to fully leverage the ways in which this could significantly enhance business processes.

Parallel Databases

A *parallel clustered database* is a complex application that provides access to the same database (group of data tables, indexes, and other objects) from any server in the cluster concurrently without compromising data integrity. Parallel databases typically contain multiple instances of a database (located on many nodes/servers) accessing the same physical storage or data concurrently. In terms of storage access type, parallel systems are implemented in two ways: a shared-nothing model or a shared-disk model.

In a *shared-nothing* model, also termed a *data-partitioning model,* each system owns a portion of the database and each partition can only be read or modified by the owning system. Data partitioning enables each system to locally cache its portion of the database in processor memory without requiring cross-system communication to provide data access concurrency and coherency controls. Both IBM's and Microsoft's databases can operate this way and have in the past. Perhaps Oracle's adoption of the shared-disk model is what gave them a huge lead in grid computing.

In a *shared-disk* model, all the disks containing data are accessible by all nodes of the cluster. Disk sharing architecture requires suitable lock management techniques to control the update concurrency. Each of the nodes in the cluster has direct access to all disks on which shared data is placed. Each node has a local database buffer cache. Oracle's RAC database operates this way.

With due emphasis on high availability and high performance, Oracle has provided Oracle Parallel Server (OPS) for a long time. With Oracle 9*i*, it drove into the next generation and rebuilt OPS as Real Application Clusters (RAC). RAC follows the shared-disk model and thus has access to all the shared disks as well as to an extensive mechanism to coordinate the resources across the nodes. Shared-disk technology has advanced rapidly over the past few years, giving RAC added advantages. Storage area network (SAN) technology hides much of the complexity of hardware units, controllers, disk drives, and interconnects from the servers and provides just *storage volumes.* In the same way, a group of servers together in a cluster provide a single system image and computing resource. Oracle's acquisition of Sun only strengthens an already-compelling RAC story.

Real Application Clusters (RAC)

High performance and high availability of information systems constitute a key requirement for day-to-day business operations. As the dependence on stored information grew over the last couple of decades, large amounts of data are being accumulated and analyzed. There is an ever-increasing demand for high-performance databases, and at the same time, awareness of and requirements for keeping such databases online all the time has increased. Global operations and e-business growth depend very much on highly available stored data. With uneven and unpredictable loads on the database systems, it has become imperative for many business groups to search for high-performance systems and suitable parallel systems to support complex and large database systems. Scalability is another important feature. As the business grows, data accumulation and data interaction increase. More and more users and applications begin to use the database systems. The database systems should be able to support the increased demand for data without losing ground in performance and scope of availability.

Oracle 9*i* introduced Real Application Clusters (RAC) to solve these issues. In Oracle 10*g*, Oracle started to perfect Grid Control for managing clusters of databases. In 11*g*, Oracle introduces *Oracle RAC One Node.* RAC One Node represents an Oracle RAC database that runs only one active Oracle database instance and can be managed using Server Control Utility (SVRCTL) as any

Oracle RAC database. You can add nodes that can be used for failover, but you cannot add additional *instances* without first converting Oracle RAC One Node to Oracle RAC. You can convert from single instance to RAC One Node or RAC using Oracle's Database Configuration Assistant (DBCA) at any time. You can use Online Database Relocation with SVRCTL to perform a live migration of the database instance and connections to one of the failover nodes. This gives you the ability to move a database easily from an overworked server to a less utilized server in the same cluster. RAC One Node helps you to consolidate many databases into one cluster with minimal overhead while also providing the high-availability benefits of client failover, online rolling patch application, and rolling upgrades for the operating system and Oracle Clusterware. Please see the documentation for full details and use. Oracle also enhanced Grid Control to make adding or subtracting nodes as well as managing the cluster infrastructure easier. Oracle 11*g* also adds zero downtime patching and a 64-bit ASM cluster file system, eliminating the need for a third-party cluster file system. This section by no means covers all aspects of RAC functioning. It merely highlights some important concepts and some of RAC's inner workings. The scope of this book does not cover RAC specifically. You can switch from single instance Oracle DB to RAC One Node or RAC at any time (if you have the appropriate licenses!).

Oracle RAC Architecture

At a very high level, RAC is multiple Oracle instances (on separate nodes) accessing a single Oracle database. The database is a single physical database stored on a shared storage system. Each of the instances resides on a separate host (also called a node or server). All the nodes are clustered through a private interconnect, and all nodes have access to the shared storage. All the nodes concurrently execute transactions against the same database. The cluster manager software, usually supplied by the cluster vendor, provides a single system image, controls node membership, and monitors the node status. Broadly, the major components include:

- Nodes/servers
- High-speed private interconnect (connects the nodes together)
- Cluster Manager or OSD (operating system–dependent layer)
- Shared disk or storage
- Cluster file system or raw devices
- Volume manager
- Public network
- The database software

Cluster Interconnect

If a block of data has been changed in the cache memory on one node and the user asks for it on another node, Oracle uses cache fusion to pass one block through the interconnect (such as InfiniBand) to the cache on the other node. Parallel processing relies on passing messages among multiple processors. Processors running parallel programs call for data and instructions and then perform calculations. Each processor checks back periodically with the other nodes or a master node to plan its next move or to synchronize the delivery of results. These activities rely on message-passing software, such as the industry-standard Message Passing Interface (MPI).

In parallel databases, there is a great deal of message passing and data blocks, or pages, transferring to the local cache of another node. Much of the functionality and performance depends on the efficiency of the transport medium or methodology. The transport medium becomes very critical for the overall performance of the cluster and usage of the parallel application. Because parallel databases do not impose any constraints on the nodes to which users can connect and access, users have a choice to connect to any node in the cluster. Irrespective of the nature of the application, OLTP, or data warehousing databases, the movement of data blocks from one node to another using the interconnect is widely practiced. The role of the cluster interconnect to provide some kind of extended cache encompassing the cache from all the nodes is one of the most significant design features of the cluster. In general, the cluster interconnect is used for the following high-level functions:

- Health, status, and synchronization of messages
- Distributed lock manager (DLM) messages
- Accessing remote file systems
- Application-specific traffic
- Cluster alias routing

High performance, by distributing the computations across an array of nodes in the cluster, requires the cluster interconnect to provide a high data transfer rate and low latency communication between nodes. Also, the interconnect needs to be capable of detecting and isolating faults, and using alternative paths. Some of the essential requirements for the interconnect are

- Low latency for short messages
- High speed and sustained data rates for large messages
- Low host-CPU utilization per message
- Flow control, error control, and heartbeat continuity monitoring
- Host interfaces that execute control programs to interact directly with host processes (OS bypass)
- Switch networks that scale well

Many of the cluster vendors have designed very competitive technology. Many of the interconnect products come close to the latency levels of a SMP (symmetric multiprocessing) bus.

Internal Workings of the Oracle RAC System

Oracle 11g uses Global Cache Services to coordinate activity. A lock is treated as a held resource. RAC is a multi-instance database. Multiple instances access the same database concurrently. In terms of structure, the difference between a RAC instance and a stand-alone Oracle instance is miniscule. Besides all the usual Oracle background processes, many special processes are spawned to coordinate interinstance communication and to facilitate resource sharing among nodes in a cluster. The Oracle documentation goes through all of the processes if you are interested in knowing more. Here is a brief description of some of the main ones:

- **ACMS**   The Atomic Controlfile to Memory Service (ACMS) is an agent on a per-instance basis that helps to ensure a distributed SGA memory update is globally committed on success and globally aborted on failure.

- **LMON**   The Global Enqueue Service Monitor (LMON) monitors the entire cluster to manage global enqueues and resources. LMON manages instance and process expirations and the associated recovery for the Global Cache Service.

- **LMD**   The Global Enqueue Service Daemon (LMD) is the lock agent process that manages enqueue manager service requests for Global Cache Service enqueues to control access to global enqueues and resources. The LMD process also handles deadlock detection and remote enqueue requests.

- **LMSn**   These Global Cache Service processes (LMSn) are processes for the Global Cache Service (GCS). RAC software provides for up to ten Global Cache Service processes. The number of LMSn processes varies depending on the amount of messaging traffic among nodes in the cluster. The LMSn processes do these things:

    - Handle blocking interrupts from the remote instance for Global Cache Service resources.

    - Manage resource requests and cross-instance call operations for shared resources.

    - Build a list of invalid lock elements and validate lock elements during recovery.

    - Handle global lock deadlock detection and monitor lock conversion timeouts.

- **LCK0 process**   The Instance Enqueue Process manages global enqueue requests and cross-instance broadcast. Manages non-cache fusion and library/row cache requests.

- **RMSn**   RAC management processes include tasks like the creation of resources as nodes are added.

- **RSMN**   Remote Slave Monitor (RSMN) performs remote instance tasks for a coordinating process.

- **GTX0-j**   The Global Transaction Process supports global XA transactions.

Global Cache Service (GCS) and Global Enqueue Service (GES)

GCS and GES (which are basically RAC processes) play the key role in implementing Cache Fusion. GCS ensures a single system image of the data even though the data is accessed by multiple instances. The GCS and GES are integrated components of Real Application Clusters that coordinate simultaneous access to the shared database and to shared resources within the database and database cache. GES and GCS together maintain a Global Resource Directory (GRD) to record information about resources and enqueues. GRD remains in memory and is stored on all the instances. Each instance manages a portion of the directory. This distributed nature is a key point for fault tolerance of the RAC.

The coordination of concurrent tasks within a shared cache server is called *synchronization*. Synchronization uses the private interconnect and heavy message transfers. The following types of resources require synchronization: data blocks and enqueues. GCS maintains the modes for blocks in the global role and is responsible for block transfers between instances. LMS processes handle the GCS messages and do the bulk of the GCS processing.

An *enqueue* is a shared memory structure that serializes access to database resources. It can be local or global. Oracle uses enqueues in three modes: null (N) mode, share (S) mode, and exclusive (X) mode. Blocks are the primary structures for reading and writing into and out of buffers. An enqueue is often the most requested resource.

GES maintains or handles the synchronization of the dictionary cache, library cache, transaction locks, and DDL locks. In other words, GES manages enqueues other than data blocks. To synchronize access to the data dictionary cache, latches are used in exclusive (X) mode and in single-node cluster databases. Global enqueues are used in cluster database mode.

Cache Fusion and Resource Coordination

Because each node in a Real Application Cluster has its own memory (cache) that is not shared with other nodes, RAC must coordinate the buffer caches of different nodes while minimizing additional disk I/O that could reduce performance. Cache Fusion is the technology that uses high-speed interconnects to provide cache-to-cache transfers of data blocks between instances in a cluster. Cache Fusion functionality allows direct memory writes of dirty blocks to alleviate the need to force a disk write and reread (or ping) of the committed blocks. This is not to say that disk writes do not occur; disk writes are still required for cache replacement and when a checkpoint occurs. Cache Fusion addresses the issues involved in concurrency between instances: concurrent reads on multiple nodes, concurrent reads and writes on different nodes, and concurrent writes on different nodes.

Oracle only reads data blocks from disk if they are not already present in the buffer caches of any instance. Because data block writes are deferred, they often contain modifications from multiple transactions. The modified data blocks are written to disk only when a checkpoint occurs. Before I go further, you need to be familiar with a couple of concepts introduced in Oracle 9i RAC: resource modes and resource roles. Because the same data blocks can concurrently exist in multiple instances, there are two identifiers that help to coordinate these blocks:

- **Resource mode** The modes are null, shared, and exclusive. The block can be held in different modes, depending on whether a resource holder intends to modify data or merely read it.

- **Resource role** The roles are locally managed and globally managed.

Global Resource Directory (GRD) is *not* a database. It is a collection of internal structures and is used to find the current status of the data blocks. Whenever a block is transferred out of a local cache to another instance's cache, the GRD is updated. The following information about a resource is available in GRD:

- Data Block Identifiers (DBA)

- Location of most current versions

- Data blocks modes (N, S, X)

- Data block roles (local or global)

Past Image

To maintain data integrity, a new concept of past image was introduced in the 9*i* version of RAC. A *past image (PI)* of a block is kept in memory before the block is sent and serves as an indication of whether it is a dirty block. In the event of failure, GCS can reconstruct the current version of the block by reading PIs. This PI is different from a CR block, which is needed to reconstruct read-consistent images. The CR version of a block represents a consistent snapshot of the data at a point in time.

For example, Transaction-A of Instance-A has updated row-2 on block-5, and later another Transaction-B of Instance-B has updated row-6 on the same block-5. Block-5 has been transferred from Instance-A to B. At this time, the past image (PI) for block-5 is created on Instance-A.

SCN Processing

System change numbers (SCNs) uniquely identify a committed transaction and the changes it makes. An SCN is a logical timestamp that defines a committed version of a database at one point in time. Oracle assigns every committed transaction a unique SCN.

Within RAC, since you have multiple instances that perform commits, the SCN changes need to be maintained within an instance, but at the same time, they must also be synchronized across all instances with a cluster. Therefore, SCN is handled by the Global Cache Service using the Lamport SCN generation scheme, or by using a hardware clock or dedicated SCN server. SCNs are recorded in the redo log so recovery operations can be synchronized in Real Application Clusters.

Is RAC Unbreakable?

Can RAC be brought down? Sure it can. Any bad design or choice will bring it down. Besides the database itself, many components are involved in providing database service. RAC may be up and running, but clients cannot reach it. The intermediate network components involved between client machines and database servers may fail. Natural outages that destroy all of the hardware—fire, flood, and earthquake—will make the cluster and database inoperable.

Assuming that failures are localized or contained, however, RAC provides maximum protection and provides continuous database service. Even with the loss of many of the components, a RAC cluster can still function. But it calls for redundant design in terms of all the components involved. Design is the key word. Just setting up two or more nodes is not enough; dual interconnects, dual paths to storage units, dual storage units, dual power supplies, dual public network interfaces, and so on, will create a robust Real Application Cluster. For example, this table shows the effects of individual component failures:

Component	Effect of Failure	Result
CPU panic/crash	Node failed, other node still active.	Okay
Memory crash	Node failed, other node still active.	Okay
Interconnect	With dual interconnects, okay	Okay
OS failure/freeze	Node failed, other node still active.	Okay
Cluster Manager s/w	Custer freezes, all nodes go down.	Down
DB instance crash	Instance running on other node provides database service.	Okay

Component	Effect of Failure	Result
Control file (corrupt/lost)	Multiplexed control file used.	Okay
Redo log file	Multiplexed REDO file.	Okay
Lost data file	Requires media recovery.	Down
Human error	Depends on type of mistake; Flashback can get you back up and running quickly!	Down
Dropped object	DB is available, but applications stall; Flashback can get you back up and running quickly!	Down
DB software bug	DB may stall on all instances. Rolling patches can keep systems up while fixing this.	Down

As long as one of the Oracle instances is available in the cluster, client applications have data access and can execute their applications without any problems. Oracle Exadata makes many of these events of the past non-issues because Exadata Machines are already designed for dual components and high availability.

Summary

This section by no means covers all aspects of RAC internal functioning. It merely highlights some important concepts and some of the inner workings of RAC (subject to change, of course). Understanding special RAC requirements and implementation of the global shared cache helps you properly plan RAC implementation and its usage. An entire book is needed to cover RAC fully, but the next few sections should help you with tuning RAC.

RAC Performance Tuning Overview

Performance issues related to a RAC implementation should focus on the following areas *in the order listed:*

- Traditional database tuning and monitoring (most of this book)

- RAC cluster interconnect performance (this chapter and Chapter 5)

- Monitoring workload performance (most of this book, especially Chapter 5)

- Monitoring contention uniquely associated with RAC (this chapter)

- Prior to tuning RAC specific operations, each instance should be tuned separately:

    - APPLICATION tuning

    - DATABASE tuning

    - OS tuning

- Then, begin tuning RAC. Normal or traditional database monitoring is covered in other areas of this book (especially Chapter 5). Aspects of database performance related to RAC are covered in this chapter. After tuning each instance individually, then focus on the processes that communicate through the cluster interconnect.

RAC Cluster Interconnect Performance

The most complex aspect of RAC tuning involves monitoring and the subsequent tuning of processes associated with the Global Services Directory (GSD). The group of processes associated with the GSD is the Global Enqueue Service (GES) and the Global Cache Service (GCS). The GSD processes communicate through the cluster interconnects. If the cluster interconnects are not configured to process data packets efficiently, then the entire RAC implementation performs poorly. This is true regardless of performance-related tuning and configuration efforts in other areas.

Finding RAC Wait Events—Sessions Waiting

You can monitor sessions that wait on nonidle wait events that impact interconnect traffic with a query that lists GCS waits using the global dynamic performance view GV$SESSION_WAIT. You may also see these waits in a Statspack or AWR Report. The following are the major waits being monitored:

Wait	Wait Description
global cache busy	A wait event that occurs whenever a session has to wait for an ongoing operation on the resource to complete.
gc buffer busy	A wait event that is signaled when a process has to wait for a block to become available because another process is obtaining a resource for this block.
buffer busy global CR	A wait on a consistent read (block needed for reading) via the global cache.

To identify the sessions experiencing waits on the system, perform the following tasks:

- Query GV$SESSION_WAIT to determine whether any sessions are experiencing RAC-related waits (at the current time).
- Identify the objects that are causing contention for these sessions.
- Try to modify the object or query to reduce contention.

For example, query GV$SESSION_WAIT to determine whether any sessions are experiencing RAC cache–related waits. Note that the GV$ views are used much more to show statistics for the entire cluster, whereas the V$ views still show statistics from a single node. If you plan to use RAC, you must extend the V$ views and queries to the GV$ views for multiple nodes. This section is only an initial guide to help you see all of the components. The scope of this book does not cover RAC specifically, but some things that will help you tune RAC.

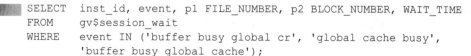

```
SELECT   inst_id, event, p1 FILE_NUMBER, p2 BLOCK_NUMBER, WAIT_TIME
FROM     gv$session_wait
WHERE    event IN ('buffer busy global cr', 'global cache busy',
         'buffer busy global cache');
```

The output from this query should look something like this:

```
INST_ID EVENT                                      FILE_NUMBER BLOCK_NUMBER WAIT_TIME
------- ------------------------------------------ ----------- ------------ ----------
      1 global cache busy                                    9          150         15
      2 global cache busy                                    9          150         10
```

Run this query to identify objects that are causing contention for these sessions and the object that corresponds to the file and block for each FILE_NUMBER/BLOCK_NUMBER combination returned (this query is a bit slower):

```
SELECT owner, segment_name, segment_type
FROM   dba_extents
WHERE  file_id = 9
AND    150 BETWEEN block_id AND block_id+blocks-1;
```

The output is similar to

```
OWNER        SEGMENT_NAME                        SEGMENT_TYPE
----------   ----------------------------------  ----------------
SYSTEM       MOD_TEST_IND                        INDEX
```

Modify the object to reduce the chances for application contention by doing the following:

- Reduce the number of rows per block.
- Adjust the block size to a smaller block size.
- Modify INITRANS and FREELISTS.

RAC Wait Events and Interconnect Statistics

The RAC events are listed next in the Statspack or AWR Report if you are running RAC (multiple instances). As stated earlier, you need to run Statspack or AWR Report for *each* instance that you have. For Statspack, you run the `statspack.snap` procedure and the `spreport.sql` script on each node you want to monitor to compare to other instances. One of the best methods for seeing if a node is operating efficiently is to compare the report from that node to one from another node that accesses the same database. I cover Grid Control tuning in Chapter 5. Remember that single-instance tuning should be performed before attempting to tune the processes that communicate via the cluster interconnect—this is very important! In other words, tune the system in single instance before you move it to RAC.

Some of the top wait events that you may encounter are listed briefly next; wait events are covered in more detail in Chapter 14. The top global cache (gc) waits to look out for include:

- **gc current block busy**   Happens when an instance requests a CURR (current version of a block) data block (wants to do some DML) and the block to be transferred is in use. A block cannot be shipped if Oracle hasn't written the REDO for the block changes to the log file.

- **gc buffer busy**   A wait event that occurs whenever a session has to wait for an ongoing operation on the resource to complete because the block is in use. The process has to wait for a block to become available because another process is obtaining a resource for this block.

- **gc cr request/gc cr block busy**   This happens when one instance is waiting for blocks from another instance's cache (sent via the interconnect). This wait says that the current instance can't find a consistent read (CR) version of a block in the local cache. If the block is not in the remote cache, then a db file sequential read wait will also follow this one. Tune the SQL that is causing large amounts of reads that get moved from node to node. Try to put users who are using the same blocks on the same instance so blocks are not moved from instance to instance. Some non-Oracle application servers move the same process from node to node looking for the fastest node (unaware that they are moving the same blocks from node to node). Pin these long processes to the same node. Potentially increase the size of the local cache if slow I/O combined with a small cache is the problem. Monitor V$CR_BLOCK_SERVER to see if an issue like reading UNDO segments is occurring. Correlated to the waits, the values for P1,P2,P3 are file, block, lenum, respectively. For the value for P3, lenum, look in V$LOCK_ELEMENT for the row where LOCK_ELEMENT_ADDR has the same value as lenum. This happens when an instance requests a CR data block and the block to be transferred hasn't arrived at the requesting instance. This wait is the one I see the most, and it's usually because the SQL is poorly tuned and *many* index blocks are being moved back and forth between instances.

Figure 11-1 shows the AWR Report RAC Section. You can see that there are six instances (nodes) in this cluster. You can also see things like the number of blocks sent and received as well as how many of the blocks are being accessed in the local cache (93.1 percent) versus the disk or another instance. As you would guess, accessing blocks in the local cache is faster, but accessing one of the remote caches on one of the other nodes is almost always faster (given a fast enough interconnect and no saturation of the interconnect) than going to disk.

The following is another valuable query to derive session wait information. The INSTANCE_ID lists the instance where the waiting session resides. The SID is the unique identifier for the waiting session (GV$SESSION). The P1, P2, and P3 columns list event-specific information that may be useful for debugging. LAST_SQL lists the last SQL executed by the waiting session.

```
SET NUMWIDTH 10
COLUMN STATE FORMAT a7 tru
COLUMN EVENT FORMAT a25 tru
COLUMN LAST_SQL FORMAT a40 tru
SELECT  sw.inst_id INSTANCE_ID, sw.sid SID, sw.state STATE, sw.event EVENT,
        sw.seconds_in_wait SECONDS_WAITING, sw.p1, sw.p2, sw.p3,
        sa.sql_text LAST_SQL
FROM    gv$session_wait sw, gv$session s, gv$sqlarea sa
WHERE   sw.event NOT IN ('rdbms ipc message','smon timer','pmon timer',
         'SQL*Net message from client','lock manager wait for remote message',
         'ges remote message', 'gcs remote message', 'gcs for action',
         'client message', 'pipe get', 'null event', 'PX Idle Wait',
         'single-task message', 'PX Deq: Execution Msg',
```

```
          'KXFQ: kxfqdeq - normal deqeue', 'listen endpoint status',
          'slave wait','wakeup time manager')
AND       sw.wait_time_micro > 0
AND       (sw.inst_id = s.inst_id and sw.sid = s.sid)
AND       (s.inst_id = sa.inst_id and s.sql_address = sa.address)
ORDER BY seconds_waiting DESC;
```

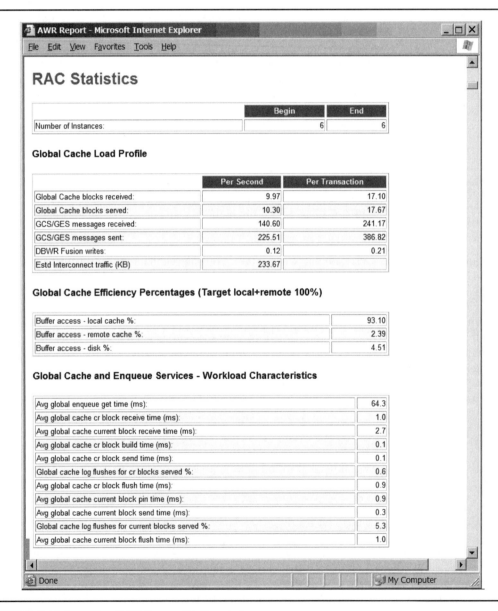

FIGURE 11-1. *The AWR Report RAC statistics*

Here is a query that gives a description of the parameter names of the events seen in the last section.

```
COLUMN EVENT   FORMAT a30 tru
COLUMN p1text FORMAT a25 tru
COLUMN p2text FORMAT a25 tru
COLUMN p3text FORMAT a25 tru
SELECT DISTINCT event EVENT, p1text, p2text, p3text
FROM    gv$session_wait sw
WHERE sw.event NOT IN ('rdbms ipc message','smon timer','pmon timer',
       'SQL*Net message from client','lock manager wait for remote message',
       'ges remote message', 'gcs remote message', 'gcs for action',
       'client message','pipe get', 'null event', 'PX Idle Wait',
       'single-task message', 'PX Deq: Execution Msg',
       'KXFQ: kxfqdeq - normal deqeue','listen endpoint status',
       'slave wait','wakeup time manager')
AND    wait_time_micro > 0
ORDER BY event;
```

Contents of the GV$SESSION_WAIT view are as follows:

Column	Data Type	Description
INST_ID	NUMBER	Number of the instance in the RAC configuration.
SID	NUMBER	Session identifier.
SEQ#	NUMBER	Sequence number that uniquely identifies this wait, incremented for each wait.
EVENT	VARCHAR2(64)	Resource or event for which the session is waiting.
P1TEXT	VARCHAR2(64)	Description of the first additional parameter.
P1	NUMBER	First additional parameter.
P1RAW	RAW(4)	First additional parameter.
P2TEXT	VARCHAR2(64)	Description of the second additional parameter.
P2	NUMBER	Second additional parameter.
P2RAW	RAW(4)	Second additional parameter.
P3TEXT	VARCHAR2(64)	Description of the third additional parameter.
P3	NUMBER	Third additional parameter.
P3RAW	RAW(4)	Third additional parameter.
WAIT_CLASS_ID	NUMBER	Identifier of the wait class.
WAIT_CLASS#	NUMBER	Number of the wait class.
WAIT_CLASS	VARCHAR2(64)	Name of the wait class.

Column	Data Type	Description
WAIT_TIME	NUMBER	A nonzero value is the session's last wait time in hundredths of seconds. A zero value means the session is currently waiting; a negative 1 means it was less than a hundredth of a second (see WAIT_TIME_MICRO); a negative 2 means TIME_STATISTICS=FALSE.
SECONDS_IN_WAIT	NUMBER	If WAIT_TIME = 0, then SECONDS_IN_WAIT is the seconds spent in the current wait condition. If WAIT_TIME > 0, then SECONDS_IN_WAIT is the seconds since the start of the last wait, and SECONDS_IN_WAIT – WAIT_TIME/100 is the active seconds since the last wait ended. This column is being deprecated in favor of WAIT_TIME_MICRO.
STATE	VARCHAR2(19)	State.
WAIT_TIME_MICRO	NUMBER	Amount of time (microseconds) in current wait if waiting, and amount of time since the start of the last wait if not currently waiting. This column is replacing the SECONDS_IN_WAIT column, which is being deprecated.
TIME_REMAINING_MICRO	NUMBER	If NULL, session is not waiting. If > 0, it's the time remaining to wait for current wait to end. If = 0, process timed out. If negative 1, session may wait indefinitely.
TIME_SINCE_LAST_WAIT_TIME_MICRO	NUMBER	The value is 0 if session is currently waiting; otherwise, it's the time in microseconds since the last wait.

New with 11g are the WAIT_TIME_MICRO, TIME_REMAINING_MICRO, and TIME_SINCE_LAST_WAIT_TIME_MICRO columns. The SECONDS_IN_WAIT column is being deprecated in favor of the WAIT_TIME_MICRO column, which has a more precise measurement (microseconds). True proof of how much faster the database is in recent releases is evident with the move from waits being measured in seconds to waits being measured in microseconds.

TIP
Use V$SESSION_WAIT or GV$SESSION_WAIT, Statspack, or the AWR Report to find RAC wait events.

GES Lock Blockers and Waiters
Sessions that are holding global locks that persistently block others can be problematic to a RAC implementation and are, in many instances, associated with application design. Sessions waiting on a lock to release cannot proceed (hang) and are required to poll the blocked object to determine

status. Large numbers of sessions holding global locks will create substantial interconnect traffic and inhibit performance. The following queries will help you find blocking sessions:

```
-- GES LOCK BLOCKERS:
--INSTANCE_ID   The instance on which a blocking session resides
--SID           Unique identifier for the session
--GRANT_LEVEL   Lists how GES lock is granted to user associated w/ blocking session
--REQUEST_LEVEL Lists the status the session is attempting to obtain
--LOCK_STATE    Lists current status the lock has obtained
--SEC           Lists how long this session has waited

SET numwidth 10
COLUMN LOCK_STATE FORMAT a16 tru;
COLUMN EVENT FORMAT a30 tru;

SELECT dl.inst_id INSTANCE_ID, s.sid SID ,p.spid SPID,
    dl.resource_name1 RESOURCE_NAME,
    decode(substr(dl.grant_level,1,8),'KJUSERNL','Null','KJUSERCR','Row-S (SS)',
    'KJUSERCW','Row-X (SX)','KJUSERPR','Share','KJUSERPW','S/Row-X (SSX)',
    'KJUSEREX','Exclusive',request_level) AS GRANT_LEVEL,
    decode(substr(dl.request_level,1,8),'KJUSERNL','Null','KJUSERCR','Row-S (SS)',
    'KJUSERCW','Row-X (SX)','KJUSERPR','Share','KJUSERPW','S/Row-X (SSX)',
    'KJUSEREX','Exclusive',request_level) AS REQUEST_LEVEL,
    decode(substr(dl.state,1,8),'KJUSERGR','Granted','KJUSEROP','Opening',
    'KJUSERCA','Canceling','KJUSERCV','Converting') AS LOCK_STATE,
    s.sid, sw.event EVENT, sw.wait_time_micro SEC
FROM    gv$ges_enqueue dl, gv$process p, gv$session s, gv$session_wait sw
WHERE   blocker = 1
AND     (dl.inst_id = p.inst_id and dl.pid = p.spid)
AND     (p.inst_id = s.inst_id and p.addr = s.paddr)
AND     (s.inst_id = sw.inst_id and s.sid = sw.sid)
ORDER BY sw.wait_time_micro DESC;


GES LOCK WAITERS:
--INSTANCE_ID   The instance on which a blocking session resides
--SID           Unique identifier for the session
--GRANT_LEVEL   Lists how GES lock is granted to user associated w/ blocking session
--REQUEST_LEVEL Lists the status the session is attempting to obtain
--LOCK_STATE    Lists current status the lock has obtained
--SEC           Lists how long this session has waited

SET numwidth 10
COLUMN LOCK_STATE FORMAT a16 tru;
COLUMN EVENT FORMAT a30 tru;

SELECT dl.inst_id INSTANCE_ID, s.sid SID, p.spid SPID,
    dl.resource_name1 RESOURCE_NAME,
    decode(substr(dl.grant_level,1,8),'KJUSERNL','Null','KJUSERCR','Row-S (SS)',
    'KJUSERCW','Row-X (SX)','KJUSERPR','Share','KJUSERPW','S/Row-X (SSX)',
    'KJUSEREX','Exclusive',request_level) AS GRANT_LEVEL,
    decode(substr(dl.request_level,1,8),'KJUSERNL','Null','KJUSERCR','Row-S (SS)',
    'KJUSERCW','Row-X (SX)','KJUSERPR','Share','KJUSERPW','S/Row-X (SSX)',
    'KJUSEREX','Exclusive',request_level) AS REQUEST_LEVEL,
    decode(substr(dl.state,1,8),'KJUSERGR','Granted','KJUSEROP','Opening',
    'KJUSERCA','Canceling','KJUSERCV','Converting') AS LOCK_STATE,
    s.sid,sw.event EVENT, sw.wait_time_micro SEC
```

```
FROM    gv$ges_enqueue dl, gv$process p,gv$session s,gv$session_wait sw
WHERE   blocked = 1
AND     (dl.inst_id = p.inst_id and dl.pid = p.spid)
AND     (p.inst_id = s.inst_id and p.addr = s.paddr)
AND     (s.inst_id = sw.inst_id and s.sid = sw.sid)
ORDER BY sw.wait_time_micro DESC;
```

Cache Fusion Reads and Writes

Cache Fusion reads occur when a user on one system queries a block and then a user on another system queries the same block. The block is passed over the high speed interconnect (versus being read from disk). *Cache fusion writes* occur when a block previously changed by another instance needs to be written to disk in response to a checkpoint or cache aging. When this occurs, Oracle sends a message to notify the other instance that a fusion write will be performed to move the data block to disk. Fusion writes do not require an additional write to disk and are a subset of all physical writes incurred by an instance. The ratio DBWR fusion writes to physical writes shows the proportion of writes that Oracle manages with fusion writes.

> *Here is a query to determine ratio of cache fusion writes:*

```
SELECT A.inst_id "Instance",
       A.VALUE/B.VALUE "Cache Fusion Writes Ratio"
FROM    GV$SYSSTAT A, GV$SYSSTAT B
WHERE   A.name='DBWR fusion writes'
AND     B.name='physical writes'
AND     B.inst_id=a.inst_id
ORDER   BY A.INST_ID;
```

Here is some sample output:

```
Instance Cache Fusion Writes Ratio
--------- ------------------------
        1               .216290958
        2               .131862042
```

A larger than usual value for cache fusion writes ratio may indicate:

- Insufficiently large caches
- Insufficient checkpoints
- Large numbers of buffers written due to cache replacement or checkpointing

Cluster Interconnect Tuning—Hardware Tier

Cluster interconnect tuning is a very important piece of the clustered configuration. Oracle depends on the cluster interconnect for movement of data between the instances. Using a dedicated private network for the interconnect is extremely important.

The following query helps determine if the instances have the correct network address registered:

```
SQL> SELECT * FROM GV$CLUSTER_INTERCONNECTS;

INST_ID NAME   IP_ADDRESS       IS_ SOURCE
---------- ------ ---------------- --- -------------------------------
      1 eth1   10.16.0.168      NO  Oracle Cluster Repository
      2 eth1   10.16.0.170      NO  Oracle Cluster Repository
```

The column SOURCE indicates that the interconnect is registered with the OCR (Oracle Cluster Repository). The possible values for this column are as follows:

- **Oracle Cluster Repository**   The interconnect information is configured using the OCR.

- **Cluster Interconnect**   The interconnect information is configured using `oifcfg`; you can override this information using the parameter CLUSTER_INTERCONNECTS (which is usually not a good idea).

- **Operating system dependent**   A third-party cluster manager is configured, and Oracle Clusterware is only a bridge between Oracle RDBMS and the third-party cluster manager.

The important test on the cluster interconnect should start with a test of the hardware configuration. Tests to determine the transfer rate versus the actual implemented packet size should be undertaken to ensure the installation has been completed per specification. Starting with Oracle Database 10*g* Release 2, using a crossover cable when configuring interconnects between two nodes is *not* supported. Hence, a switch is required to act as a bridge between the nodes participating in the cluster. Now as you determine the performance of the system, you have to determine the speed of the switch independent of the speed of the interconnect to determine the true latency of the switch and the interconnect.

The speed of the cluster interconnect solely depends on the hardware vendor and the layered operating system. Oracle, in its current version, depends on the operating system and the hardware for sending packets of information across the cluster interconnect. For example, one type of cluster interconnect supported between SUN 4800s is the User Datagram Protocol (UDP). However, Solaris on this specific version of the interconnect protocol, has an OS limitation of a 64K packet size used for data transfer. To transfer 256K worth of data across this interconnect protocol would take this configuration over four round trips. On a high-transaction system where you have a large amount of interconnect traffic, this could cause a serious performance issue.

After the initial hardware and operating system level tests to confirm the packet size across the interconnect, perform subsequent tests from the Oracle database to ensure that there is not any significant added latency using cache-to-cache data transfer or the cache fusion technology. The query that follows provides the average latency of a consistent block request on the system. The data in these views are a cumulative figure since the last time the Oracle instance was bounced. The data from these views do not reflect the true performance of the interconnect or give a true picture of the latency in transferring data. To get a more realistic picture of performance, bounce all the Oracle instances and test again. To obtain good performance, the latency across the cluster interconnect must be as low as possible. Latencies on the cluster interconnect could be caused by

- Large number of processes in the run queues waiting for CPU or scheduling delays
- Platform-specific OS parameter settings that affect IPC buffering or process scheduling
- Slow, busy, or faulty interconnects

Oracle recommends that the average latency of a consistent block request typically should not exceed 15 milliseconds, depending on the system configuration and volume. When you are sending many blocks across the interconnect, this figure is really too high (especially since going to disk is usually this fast). For a high-volume system, latency should be in the single-digit millisecond-to-microsecond range. The average latency of a consistent block request is the average latency of a consistent read request roundtrip from the requesting instance to the holding instance and back to the requesting instance.

```
set numwidth 20
column "AVG CR BLOCK RECEIVE TIME (ms)" format 9999999.9
select b1.inst_id, b2.value "GCS CR BLOCKS RECEIVED",
       b1.value "GCS CR BLOCK RECEIVE TIME",
       ((b1.value / b2.value) * 10) "AVG CR BLOCK RECEIVE TIME (ms)"
from   gv$sysstat b1, gv$sysstat b2
where  b1.name = 'gc cr block receive time'
and    b2.name = 'gc cr blocks received'
and    b1.inst_id = b2.inst_id
and    b2.value <> 0;

INST_ID GCS CR BLOCKS RECEIVED GCS CR BLOCK RECEIVE TIME  AVG CR BLOCK RECIVE TIME (ms)
------- ---------------------- -------------------------  -----------------------------
      1                   2758                    112394                         443.78
      2                   1346                      1457                           10.8

2 rows selected.
```

In the preceding output, notice that the AVG CR BLOCK RECEIVE TIME is 443.78 (ms); this is significantly high when the expected average latency, as recommended by Oracle, should not exceed 15 (ms). A high value is possible if the CPU has limited idle time and the system typically processes long-running queries. However, an average latency of less than one millisecond with user-mode IPC is possible. Latency can also be influenced by a high value for the DB_MULTI_BLOCK_READ_COUNT parameter. This is because a requesting process can issue more than one request for a block, depending on the setting of this parameter. Correspondingly, the requesting process may have to wait longer. This kind of high latency requires further investigation of the cluster interconnect configuration and that tests be performed at the operating system level. When such high latencies are experienced over the interconnect, another good test is to perform a test at the operating system level by checking the actual ping time. Checking the ping time helps to determine if there are any issues at the OS level. After all, the performance issue may not be from data transfers within the RAC environment.

Apart from the basic packet transfer tests that you can perform at the OS level, you can undertake other checks and tests to ensure that the cluster interconnect has been configured correctly. There are redundant private high-speed interconnects between the nodes participating in the cluster. Implementing network interface card (NIC) bonding or pairing helps interconnect load balancing and failover when one of the interconnects fails. The user network connection does not interfere with the cluster interconnect traffic. That is, they are isolated from each other. At the operating system level, the `netstat` and `ifconfig` commands display network-related data structures. In 11.2.0.2, Oracle introduced Redundant Interconnect Usage. Oracle Grid Infrastructure and Oracle RAC can now make use of redundant network interconnects, without using other network technology, to enhance optimal communication in the cluster. Redundant Interconnect Usage enables load-balancing and high availability across multiple (up to four) private networks (also known as *interconnects*). The output that follows, from `netstat-i`, indicates that four network adapters are configured and NIC pairing is implemented:

```
[oracleoradb3 oracle]$ netstat -i
Kernel Interface table
Iface     MTU Met    RX-OK RX-ERR RX-DRP RX-OVR    TX-OK TX-ERR TX-DRP TX-OVR Flg
bond0    1500   0     3209      0      0      0     4028      0      0      0 BMmRU
bond0:1  1500   0     4390      0      0      0     6437      0      0      0 BMmRU
bond1    1500   0     7880      0      0      0    10874      0      0      0 BMmRU
eth0     1500   0     1662      0      0      0     2006      0      0      0 BMsRU
eth1     1500   0     1547      0      0      0     2022      0      0      0 BMsRU
eth2     1500   0     4390      0      0      0     6437      0      0      0 BMRU
eth3     1500   0     3490      0      0      0     4437      0      0      0 BMRU
lo      16436   0     7491      0      0      0     7491      0      0      0 LRU
```

The values in the IFACE column are defined as follows:

■ **bond0**   The public interconnect created using the bonding functionality (bonds Eth0 and Eth1).

■ **bond0:1**   The Virtual IP (VIP) assigned to bond0.

■ **bond1**   A private interconnect alias created using bonding functionality (bonds ETH2 and ETH3).

■ **ETH0 and ETH1**   The physical public interfaces that are bonded/paired together (bond0).

■ **ETH2 and ETH3**   The physical private interfaces that are bonded/paired together (bond1).

■ **lo**   This is the loopback; that is, the output also indicates that a loopback option is configured. Verify whether Oracle is using the loopback option using the `ORADEBUG` command, which is discussed later in this section. The use of the loopback IP depends on the integrity of the routing table defined on each of the nodes. Modifying the routing table can result in the inoperability of the interconnect.

Also found in the preceding `netstat` output is the maximum transmission unit (MTU), which is set at 1500 bytes (this is a standard setting for UDP). MTU definitions do not include the data-link header. However, packet-size computations include data-link headers. The maximum packet size displayed by the various tools is MTU plus the data-link header length. To get the maximum benefit from the interconnect, MTU should be configured to the highest possible value supported. For example, a setting as high as 9K using jumbo frames would improve interconnect bandwidth and data transmission.

Apart from the basic packet transfer tests that you could perform at the OS level, you can undertake other checks and tests to ensure that the cluster interconnect has been configured correctly. Perform checks from the Oracle instance to ensure proper configuration of the interconnect protocol. If the following commands are executed as user 'SYS', a trace file is generated in the user dump destination directory that contains certain diagnostic information pertaining to the UDP/IPC configurations. (See Chapter 13 for more on the DEBUG functionality.) Please do not use this until you read the Oracle documentation on it.

```
SQL> ORADEBUG SETMYPID
        ORADEBUG IPC
```

The following is the extract from the trace file pertaining to the interconnect protocol. The output confirms that the cluster interconnect is being used for instance-to-instance message transfer:

```
SSKGXPT 0x3671e28 flags SSKGXPT_READPENDING     info for network 0
socket no 9     IP 172.16.193.1         UDP 59084
sflags SSKGXPT_WRITESSKGXPT_UP
        info for network 1
        socket no 0     IP 0.0.0.0      UDP 0
        sflags SSKGXPT_DOWN
context timestamp 0x4402d
        no ports
```

The preceding output is from a Sun 4800 and indicates the IP address and that the protocol used is UDP. On certain operating systems such as Tru64 the trace output does not reveal the cluster interconnect information. The following NDD Unix command at the operating system–level confirms the actual UDP size definition. The following output is from a SUN environment:

```
oradb1:RAC1:oracle # ndd -get /dev/udp
name to get/set ? udp_xmit_hiwat
value ?
length ?
8192
name to get/set ? udp_recv_hiwat
value ?
length ?
8192
```

This output reveals that the UDP has been configured for an 8K packet size. Applying this finding to the data gathered from Oracle's views indicates that it would take 14050 trips for all the blocks to be transferred across the cluster interconnect (112394/8 =14050). If this were set to be 64K, then the number of roundtrips would be significantly reduced (112394/64 = 1756 trips).

Another parameter that affects the interconnect traffic is the DB_FILE_MULTIBLOCK_READ_COUNT. This parameter helps read a certain number of blocks at a time from disk. When data needs to be transferred across the cluster interconnect, this parameter determines the size of the block that each instance would request from the other during read transfers. Sizing this parameter should be based on the interconnect latency and the packet sizes as defined by the hardware vendor and after considering operating system limitations (for example, the SUN UDP max setting is only 64K). The following kernel parameters define the UDP parameter settings:

- UDP_RECV_HIWAT
- UDP_XMIT_HIWAT

Setting these parameters to 65536 each increases the UDP buffer size to 64K.

Another parameter, CLUSTER_INTERCONNECTS, provides Oracle information on the availability of additional cluster interconnects that you could use for cache fusion activity across the cluster interconnect. The parameter overrides the default interconnect settings at the operating system level with a preferred cluster traffic network. While this parameter does provide certain advantages on systems where high interconnect latency is noticed by helping reduce such latency, configuring this parameter could affect the interconnect high-availability feature. In other words, an interconnect failure that is normally unnoticeable could instead cause an Oracle cluster failure as Oracle still attempts to access the network interface. The parameter also overrides the network classifications stored by oifcfg in the OCR.

Resource Availability

Resources available on any machine or node or to an Oracle instance are limited, meaning they are not available in abundance, and if a process on the system needs them, they may not be immediately available. A physical limit is imposed on the amount of resources available on any system. For example, the processor resources are limited by the number of CPUs available on the system, and the amount of memory or cache area is limited by the amount of physical memory available on the system. Now, for an Oracle process, this is further limited by the actual amount of memory allocated to the SGA. Within the SGA, the shared pool, the buffer cache, and so on, are again preallocated from the shared pool area. These memory allocations are used by a regular single-instance configuration.

In a RAC environment, there are no parameters to allocate any global specific resources, for example, global cache size or global shared pool area. Oracle allocates a certain portion of the available resources from the SGA for global activity. The availability of global resources can be monitored using the view GV$RESOURCE_LIMIT. For example, the following query displays the current number of resources available for global activity. In the output that follows, the availability of resources is limited by the column "LIMIT_VALUE," and when these resources are low, the method to increase the limit is to increase the SHARED_POOL_SIZE.

The following query generates the output containing the current utilization of resources:

```
SELECT RESOURCE_NAME, CURRENT_UTILIZATION CU, MAX_UTILIZATION MU,
       INITIAL_ALLOCATION IA, LIMIT_VALUE LV
FROM   GV$RESOURCE_LIMIT
WHERE  MAX_UTILIZATION > 0
ORDER BY INST_ID, RESOURCE_NAME;


RESOURCE_NAME                       CU         MU IA          LV
------------------------- ----------- ----------- ---------- ----------
cmtcallbk                           0           1        187  UNLIMITED
dml_locks                           2          59        748  UNLIMITED
enqueue_locks                      19          27       2261       2261
```

```
enqueue_resources          22        45        968    UNLIMITED
gcs_shadows              2259      2579      18245        18245
ges_big_msgs               27        28        964    UNLIMITED
ges_cache_ress            338      1240          0    UNLIMITED
ges_procs                  35        36        320          320
ges_reg_msgs               44        81       1050    UNLIMITED
max_rollback_segments      11        11        187        65535
max_shared_servers          1         1  UNLIMITED    UNLIMITED
processes                  31        34        150          150
sessions                   37        40        170          170
sort_segment_locks          0         1  UNLIMITED    UNLIMITED
transactions                2         4        187    UNLIMITED
(truncated output)
```

When the SHARED_POOL_SIZE is increased by 10M, the global resource allocation also changes to the following new values.

```
gcs_resources            2553      2553      19351        19351
gcs_shadows              1279      1279      19351        19351
```

The rule should be: when the MAX_UTILIZATION (MU) gets close to the LIMIT_VALUE (LV) and remains constant at this value for a considerable amount of time, consider increasing the SGA.

Oracle also maintains several global areas within its memory that are specifically related to Oracle. Although allocation sizes are constant for these areas, they are also included in the SHARED_POOL_SIZE parameter; for example, the following query lists memory areas maintained specially for a RAC environment:

```
SELECT  *
FROM    v$sgastat
where   name like 'g%';
```

```
POOL          NAME                           BYTES
-----------   --------------------------   ----------
shared pool   ges enqueue cur. usage pe          16
shared pool   ges deadlock xid hash tab       11036
shared pool   ges recovery domain table         108
shared pool   ges process hash table           9504
shared pool   gcs res hash bucket             65536
shared pool   gcs close obj                    4104
shared pool   ges lmd process descripto        2684
shared pool   gcs scan queue array              216
shared pool   ges process array              281600
shared pool   gcs resources                 7379392
...
41 rows selected.
```

Tuning RAC Using Enterprise Manager Grid Control

The Oracle Enterprise Manager Grid Control, the AWR Report, and the Statspack report are all good sources of information to determine the interconnect latency. The best RAC tuning tool is Oracle Enterprise Manager Grid Control. Although this is covered in detail in Chapter 5 with many 11*g* examples, a quick look at a six-node cluster database that I have from 10*g*R2 is helpful for covering a few key points (note that you can use OEM 10*g*R2 Grid Control to manage an 11*g* database). While the screen shots in this section are from 10*g*R2, this example, which looks at a many-node solution and the interconnect portion, is worth investigating here as well; these solutions are virtually the same in 11*g*. To look at a clustered database (or RAC/Grid database), you must go to the Targets/All Targets screen and click the cluster database to view it. In this example, click the "ioug" cluster database to display the monitored information for this cluster database (see Figure 11-2). This screen shows that six instances are all up at this time. Some CPU is being used (around 25 percent), and there are just under 20 active sessions.

A *very* important section of this page is the Diagnostic Summary section, which, in this example, shows that there are four interconnect findings.

TIP
Find Interconnect issues using Enterprise Manager Grid Control.

At the bottom of the same screen, you find some of the most useful links and information for a cluster database (see Figure 11-3). These links include all of the instances associated with the cluster database. The six instances (ioug_ioug1 through ioug_ioug6) are also displayed here, making it very easy to see information for an individual instance by clicking through to that instance.

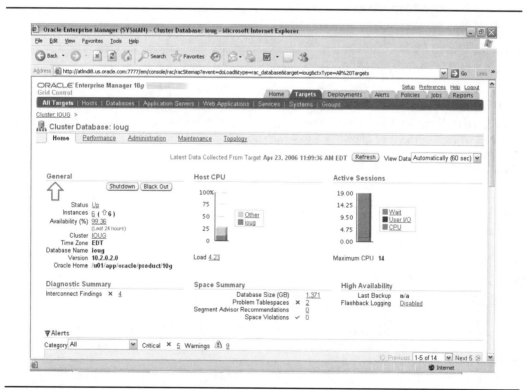

FIGURE 11-2. *Diagnostics Summary Section to monitor issues for RAC databases*

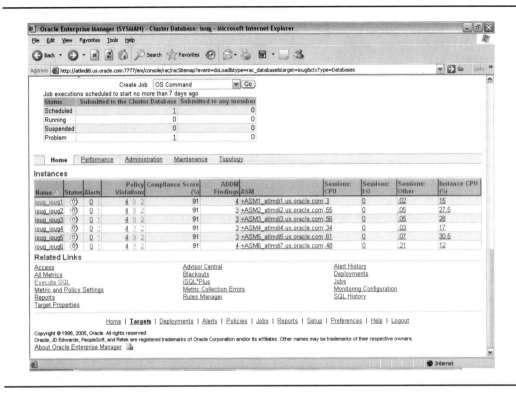

FIGURE 11-3. *Monitoring all six instances of a clustered database*

By clicking one of the instances (ioug_ioug1 in this example), the main informational screen for an instance is displayed (Figure 11-4). You'll also see a pull-down menu, as shown in Figure 11-4, in the upper-right corner that allows you to switch quickly to another database instance.

Database Performance Tab

Clicking the Performance tab displays the insightful graphs for this cluster and one of the main screens that can be used for tuning the interconnect. Figure 11-5 shows the upper part of this screen. Clicking any individual graph displays a more detailed graph for the given performance metric. Moving to the middle of this screen displays additional graphs.

TIP
The Database or Cluster Performance screen within OEM is the quickest way to locate performance problems in your system.

Figure 11-6 shows many additional performance links. These include Database Locks, Top Sessions, Top Consumers, Cluster Cache Coherence, and Top Segments. Each of these is used to drill into a specific problem.

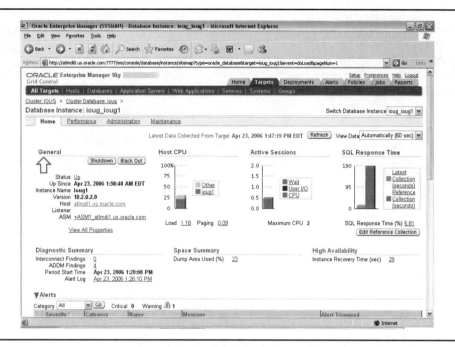

FIGURE 11-4. *Monitoring an individual instance of a RAC database*

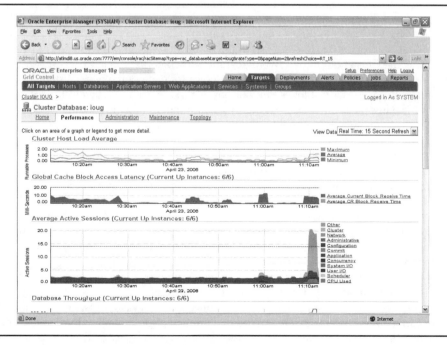

FIGURE 11-5. *Monitoring cluster database performance*

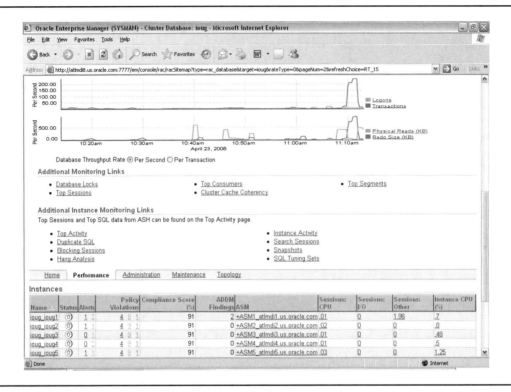

FIGURE 11-6. *Cluster database additional performance links*

By clicking the Cluster Host Load Average graph shown earlier in Figure 11-5, you can display a larger version of that graph, which has a color for each of the nodes listed. In the example in Figure 11-7, four instances (on four physical nodes) in the ioug cluster are displayed in the graph. The instances are ioug3, ioug4, ioug5, and ioug6, and the physical nodes that the instances reside on are atlmdi3, atlmdi4, atlmdi5, and atlmdi7.

Clicking the second graph in Figure 11-5 shows interconnect issues. The global cache block access latency and transfers have to do with sending blocks from one instance to another instance. Clicking the Cluster Cache Coherency link on the Cluster Database Performance screen (Figure 11-8) also displays this screen. In Figure 11-8, the number of block transfers increases greatly at about 11:10 A.M. Any block access latency over 20 ms should be investigated further. Fixing this issue could involve tuning the query that is causing many blocks to be either read or transferred, getting a faster interconnect, eliminating any locking that is slowing the transfer (one instance hanging on to the block), or using the public (instead of private) interconnect.

The third graph in Figure 11-5, the Active Sessions graph, shows a large number of cluster waits. By clicking the "Cluster" link to the right of the graph (but at the instance level), you display the detailed graph of all cluster waits (Figure 11-9). You can see many global cache (or gc) waits associated with this graph at a couple of times during the hour displayed. Below the graph, you can see the actual Top SQL queries that are being run as well as the Top Sessions of the users who are running the queries. This screen shows *only* the Top SQL and Top Sessions for

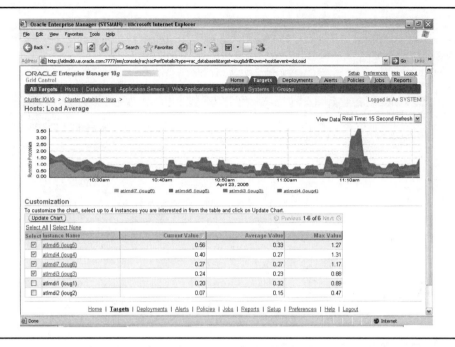

FIGURE 11-7.   *Cluster database performance load average*

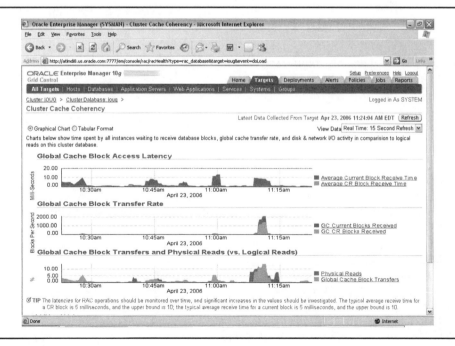

FIGURE 11-8.   *Cluster cache coherency*

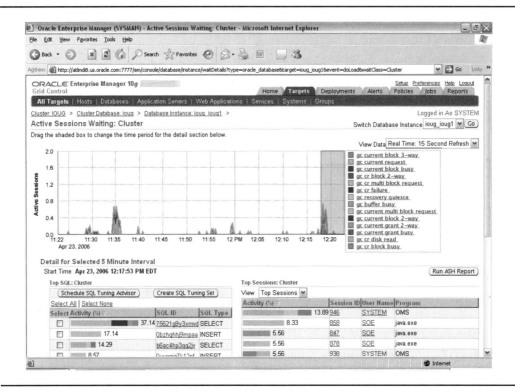

FIGURE 11-9. *Active sessions waiting—cluster*

cluster waits. Once again, this colorful screen shows each wait in a different color, making it very intuitive to use for tuning.

TIP
You can investigate specific global cache wait events in Enterprise Manager.

By clicking the link to the right of the graph—"gc current block busy" wait—you are instantly transferred to the histogram for this wait to see if the waits are many short waits or fewer long waits. In this case, some of the waits are short (1–2 ms) and others are long (32 ms and longer), as the histogram in Figure 11-10 shows.

NOTE
Chapter 5 provides a more detailed look at how to use Enterprise Manager Grid Control as well as many more screen shots than those shown here. Chapter 5 also tells you how to find specific SQL statements that are causing problems and how to tune them with the Enterprise Manager Grid Control tuning features.

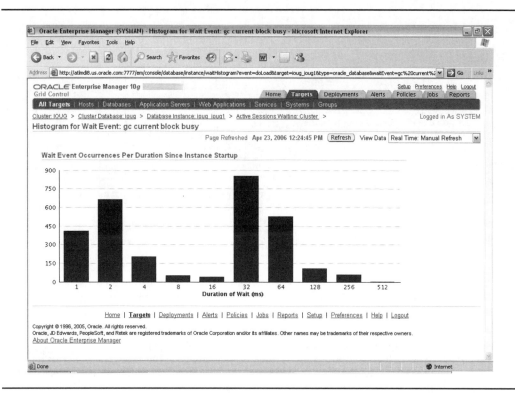

FIGURE 11-10.   *Wait events histogram for "gc current block busy" waits*

Basic Concepts of Parallel Operations

Using parallel operations enables multiple processes (and potentially processors) to work together simultaneously to resolve a single SQL statement. This feature improves data-intensive operations, is dynamic (the execution path is determined at run time), and (when wisely implemented) makes use of all of your processors and disk drives. There are some overhead costs and administrative requirements, but using parallel operations can improve the performance of many queries.

Consider a full table scan. Rather than have a single process execute the table scan, Oracle can create multiple processes to scan the table in parallel. The number of processes used to perform the scan is called the *degree of parallelism (DOP)*. The degree can be set in a hint at the time of table creation or as a hint in the query. Figure 11-11 shows a full table scan of the EMP table broken into four separate parallel query server processes. (The degree of parallelism is four.) A fifth process, the query coordinator, is created to coordinate the four parallel query server processes.

TIP
Parallel processes commonly involve disk accesses. If the data is not distributed across multiple disks, using the Parallel Execution Option (PEO) may lead to an I/O bottleneck.

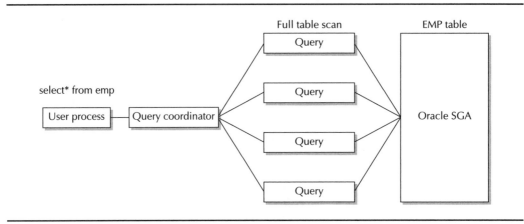

FIGURE 11-11. *A simple full table scan with parallel execution (disk access not shown)*

If the rows returned by the full table scan shown in Figure 11-11 also need to be sorted, the resulting operation will look like Figure 11-12 instead. Now Oracle may use one process to coordinate the query, four processes to run the query, and four processes to sort the query. The total is now nine processes, although the degree of parallelism is still 4. If you have nine processors (CPUs), your machine can use all nine processors for the operation (depending on your system setup and other operations that are being performed at the same time). If you have fewer than nine processors available, you may encounter some CPU bottleneck issues as Oracle manages the query.

Because the query coordination parts of the operation take resources, fast-running queries are not usually enhanced (and may be degraded) with the use of parallel operations.

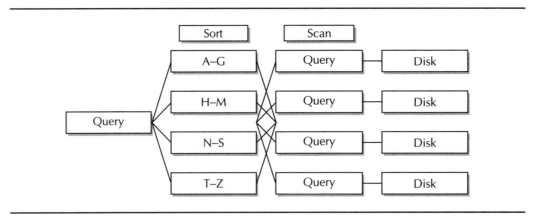

FIGURE 11-12. *A simple full table scan requiring a sort with parallel execution (SGA not shown)*

TIP
Using parallel operations on very small tables or very fast queries can also degrade performance because the query coordination may also cost performance resources. You should evaluate whether the parallel cost exceeds the nonparallelized cost.

Both queries in Figure 11-11 and Figure 11-12 require access to the physical disks to retrieve data, which is then brought into the SGA. Balancing data on those disks based on how the query is "broken up" makes a large I/O difference.

TIP
When the parallel degree is set to N, it is possible to use (2*N) + 1 total processes for the parallel operation. Although parallel operations deal with processes and not processors, when a large number of processors are available, Oracle generally uses the additional processors to run parallel queries, often enhancing the performance of the query.

Parallel DML and DDL Statements and Operations

Oracle supports parallelization of both DDL and DML operations. Oracle can parallelize the following operations on tables and indexes:

- SELECT
- UPDATE, INSERT, DELETE
- MERGE
- CREATE TABLE AS
- CREATE INDEX
- REBUILD INDEX
- MOVE/SPLIT/COALESCE PARTITION
- ENABLE CONSTRAINT

The following operations can also be parallelized within a statement:

- SELECT DISTINCT
- GROUP BY
- ORDER BY
- NOT IN
- UNION and UNION ALL
- CUBE and ROLLUP

- Aggregate functions such as SUM and MAX
- NESTED LOOPS joins
- SORT-MERGE joins
- Star transformations

TIP
As of Oracle 8i, parallel DML statements are allowed. This functionality applies to partitioned tables and indexes.

Oracle uses the cost-based optimizer to determine whether to parallelize a statement and to determine the degree of parallelism applied.

Parallel DML Statements and Operations

Most operations can be parallelized, including queries, DML, and DDL operations. Intrapartition parallelism is also supported; multiple parallel query server processes can execute against the same partition.

The degree of parallelism may be limited by a number of factors. Although the partitioning strategy does not play as significant a role for parallelism, you should still be aware of other limiting factors:

- The number of processors available on the server
- That you still need to have the partition option enabled, and UPDATE, DELETE, and MERGE are parallelized only for partitioned tables
- The number of parallel query server processes allowed for the instance, set via the PARALLEL_MAX_SERVERS initialization parameter
- The parallel degree limit supported for your user profile if you use the Database Resource Manager
- The number of parallel query server processes used by other users in the instance
- The setting for the PARALLEL_ADAPTIVE_MULTI_USER parameter, which may limit your parallelism in order to support other users

Monitoring your parallel operations in multiuser environments to guarantee they are allocated the resources that you planned for them to use is important. The Database Resource Manager can help allocate resources.

Managing Parallel Server Resources and Parallel Statement Queuing

If you use the Database Resource Manager to manage parallel server resources, and a consumer group uses up all its assigned resources, Oracle might be forced to downgrade the parallelism of the parallel statements issued by users assigned to that consumer group. You configure the allocation of parallel server resources for a consumer group with the PARALLEL_TARGET_PERCENTAGE directive. This directive specifies the maximum percentage of the parallel server pool that a particular consumer group can use.

In 11.2.0.2, Oracle introduced parallel statement queuing, which offers the following features:

- When no more parallel servers are available, the parallel statement is queued. The parallel statement is dequeued and processed as parallel servers are freed up.

- A resource plan can be used to control the order of the parallel statement queue. When parallel servers are freed up, the resource plan is used to select a consumer group. The parallel query at the head of its queue is run.

- Parallel servers can be reserved for critical consumer groups.

This feature adds stability to the execution of SQL statements in parallel, but can introduce an additional wait time for parallel statements if the database server is running at full capacity. For a parallel statement to be queued, the following conditions must be met:

- The PARALLEL_DEGREE_POLICY initialization parameter is set to AUTO.

- The number of active parallel servers across all consumer groups exceeds the value of the PARALLEL_SERVERS_TARGET initialization parameter.

- The sum of the number of active parallel servers for the consumer group and the degree of parallelism of the parallel statement exceeds the target number of active parallel servers. In other words, (V$RSRC_CONSUMER_GROUP.CURRENT_PQ_SERVERS_ACTIVE + DOP of statement) > (PARALLEL_TARGET_PERCENTAGE/100 * PARALLEL_SERVERS_TARGET).

You can also use the NO_STATEMENT_QUEUING and STATEMENT_QUEUING hints in SQL statements to manage parallel statement queuing.

Parallelism and Partitions

Oracle's partitioning feature can have a significant impact on parallel operations. *Partitions* are logical divisions of table data and indexes, and partitions of the same table or index can reside in multiple tablespaces. Given this architecture, the following important distinctions exist with parallel operations on partitions:

- Operations are performed in parallel on partitioned objects *only* when more than one partition is accessed.

- If a table is partitioned into 12 logical divisions and a query executed against the table accesses only 6 of those partitions (because the dimension of the data dictates the partition in which the data is stored), a maximum of 6 parallel server processes can be allocated to satisfy the query. In 11*g*, when partition granules are used to access a table or index, the maximum allowable DOP is the number of partitions (*block range granules* are the basic unit of *most* parallel operations, even on partitioned tables; *partition granules* are the basic unit of parallel index range scans, joins between two equipartitioned tables, parallel operations that modify multiple partitions of a partitioned object, and partitioned table/index creation).

Inter- and Intra-operation Parallelization

Due to the distribution of data, the processor allocated to each parallel server process, and the speed of devices servicing the parallel server data request, each parallel query server process may complete at a different time. As each server process completes, it passes its result set to the next lower operation in the statement hierarchy. Any single parallel server process may handle or service statement operation requests from any other parallel execution server at the next higher level in the statement hierarchy.

> **TIP**
> *Any server process allocated for a statement may handle any request from a process within the same statement. Therefore, if some processes are faster than others, the ones that are faster can process the rows produced by the child set of parallel execution processes as soon as they are available instead of waiting for the ones that are slower (but only at the next higher statement hierarchy level).*

The optimizer evaluates a statement and determines how many parallel query server processes to use during its execution. This intra-operation parallelization is different from interoperation parallelization. *Intra-operation parallelization* is dividing a single task within a SQL statement, such as reading a table, among parallel execution servers. When multiple parts of a SQL statement are performed in parallel, the results from one set of parallel execution servers are passed to another set of parallel execution servers. This is known as *interoperation parallelization.*

The degree of parallelism is applied to each operation of a SQL statement that can be parallelized, including the sort operation of data required by an ORDER BY clause. As shown earlier in Figure 11-12, a query with a degree of parallelism of 4 may acquire up to nine processes.

Examples of Using Inter- and Intra-operations (PARALLEL and NOPARALLEL Hints)

You can parallelize SQL statements via a SQL hint or with the object-level options declared for the table or index. The following listing illustrates a statement hint:

```
select      /*+ parallel (ORDER_LINE_ITEMS) */
            Invoice_Number, Invoice_Date
from        ORDER_LINE_ITEMS
order by    Invoice_Date;
```

The preceding statement does *not* specify a degree of parallelism. The default degree of parallelism dictated by the table definition or the initialization parameters will be used. When you create a table, you can specify the degree of parallelism to use for the table, as shown here:

```
create table ORDER_LINE_ITEMS
            (Invoice_Number  NUMBER(12) not null,
             Invoice_Date    DATE not null)
parallel 4;
```

When you execute queries against the ORDER_LINE_ITEMS table without specifying a degree of parallelism for the query, Oracle uses 4 as the default degree. To override the default, specify the new value within the PARALLEL hint, as shown in this next listing. Also shown in the listing is the PARALLEL_INDEX hint, whose only difference from the PARALLEL hint is that the index name is also specified.

```
select      /*+ parallel (ORDER_LINE_ITEMS, 6) */
            Invoice_Number, Invoice_Date
from        ORDER_LINE_ITEMS
order by    Invoice_Date;
select      /*+ parallel_index (ORDER_LINE_ITEMS, invoice_number_idx, 6) */
            Invoice_Number, Invoice_Date
from        ORDER_LINE_ITEMS
where       Invoice_Number = 777
order by    Invoice_Date;
```

This listing specifies a degree of parallelism of 6. As many as 13 parallel execution servers may be allocated or created to satisfy this query.

To simplify the hint syntax, use table aliases, as shown in the following listing. If you assign an alias to a table, you must use the alias, not the table name, in the hint.

```
select      /*+ parallel (oli, 4) */
            Invoice_Number, Invoice_Date
from        ORDER_LINE_ITEMS oli
order by    Invoice_Date;
```

TIP
Using the PARALLEL hint enables the use of parallel operations. If you use the PARALLEL hint but do not specify the degree of parallelism with the hint or set it at the table level, the query still executes in parallel, but the DOP is calculated from the initialization parameters CPU_COUNT and PARALLEL_THREADS_PER_CPU.

You can also "turn off" the use of parallel operations in a given query on a table that has been specified to use parallel operations. The ORDER_LINE_ITEMS table has a default degree of parallelism of 4, but the query shown here overrides that setting via the NOPARALLEL hint:

```
select      /*+ noparallel (oli) */
            Invoice_Number, Invoice_Date
from        ORDER_LINE_ITEMS oli
order by    Invoice_Date;
```

TIP
The use of the NOPARALLEL hint disables parallel operations in a statement that would otherwise use parallel processing due to a parallel object definition.

To change the default degree of parallelism for a table, use the PARALLEL clause of the ALTER TABLE command:

```
alter table order_line_items
parallel (degree 4);
```

To disable parallel operations for a table, use the NOPARALLEL clause of the ALTER TABLE command:

```
alter table order_line_items
noparallel;
```

The coordinator process evaluates the following in determining whether to parallelize the statement:

- Hints contained in the SQL statement
- Session values set via the ALTER SESSION FORCE PARALLEL command
- Tables/indexes defined as parallel as well as table/index statistics

You are advised to specify an explicit degree of parallelism either in the SQL statement itself or in the table definition. You can rely on default degrees of parallelism for many operations, but for performance management of time-sensitive operations, you should specify the degree of parallelism using a hint.

TIP
Specify the degree of parallelism using a hint instead of relying on the table definition to ensure that all operations are tuned for the given query.

Creating Table and Index Examples Using Parallel Operations

To further illustrate the application of parallel operations in SQL statements, consider the implementations of parallel operations for table and index creation shown in the following listings.

Using parallel operations for table creation

```
create table ORDER_LINE_ITEMS
tablespace tbsp1
storage (initial 75m next 75m pctincrease 0)
parallel (degree 4)
as
select    /*+ parallel (OLD_ORDER_LINE_ITEMS,4) */ *
from      OLD_ORDER_LINE_ITEMS;
```

Using parallel operations for index creation

```
create index ORDER_KEY on ORDER_LINE_ITEMS (Order_Id, Item_Id)
tablespace idx1
storage (initial 10m next 1m pctincrease 0)
parallel (degree 5) NOLOGGING;
```

The CREATE INDEX statement creates the ORDER_KEY index using parallel sort operations. The CREATE TABLE statement creates a new table ORDER_LINE_ITEMS with a degree of parallelism of four by selecting from an existing OLD_ORDER_LINE_ITEMS table using a parallel operation. In the preceding table creation listing, two separate operations within the CREATE TABLE command are taking advantage of parallelism: the query of the OLD_ORDER_LINE_ITEMS table is parallelized, and the insert into ORDER_LINE_ITEMS is parallelized.

NOTE
Although parallel queries increase the performance of operations that modify data, the redo log entries are written serially and could cause a bottleneck. By using the NOLOGGING option, you can avoid this bottleneck during table and index creation.

Because the writes to the redo log files are serial, redo log writes may effectively eliminate the parallelism you have defined for your statements. Using NOLOGGING forces the bulk operations to avoid logging, but individual INSERT commands are still written to the redo log files. If you use the NOLOGGING option, you must have a way to recover your data other than via the archived redo log files.

TIP
Use NOLOGGING to remove the I/O bottleneck caused by serial writes to the redo logs.

Up to this point, I have ignored the physical location of the data queried in the example SELECT statements. If a full-scanned table's data is all contained on a single disk, you may succeed only in creating a huge I/O bottleneck on the disk. An underlying principle of the performance gains that you can achieve using parallel operations is that the data is stored on different devices, all capable of being addressed independently of one another.

Not only that, but using the PEO may make your system perform *worse*. If your system has processing power to spare but has an I/O bottleneck, using PEO will generate more I/O requests faster, creating a larger queue for the I/O system to manage. If you already have an I/O bottleneck, creating more processes against that same bottleneck will not improve your performance. You need to redesign your data distribution across your available I/O devices.

TIP
Make sure your data is properly distributed or the parallel query server processes may add to existing I/O bottleneck problems.

Returning to the CREATE INDEX statement shown earlier in the "Using parallel operations for index creation" listing, consider the following tips:

- Index creation uses temporary tablespace if there is not enough memory available to perform the sort in memory (SORT_AREA_SIZE). Construct the temporary tablespace in such a way that the physical data files are striped across at least as many disks as the degree of parallelism of the CREATE INDEX statement.

- When adding/enabling a primary or unique key for a table, you cannot create the associated index in parallel. Instead, create the index in parallel first and then use ALTER TABLE to add/enable the constraint and specify the USING INDEX clause. For this to work, the index must have the same name and columns as the constraint.

Real-World Example of Distributing Data for Effective Parallel Operations

Returning to the CREATE TABLE statement example, the following conditions/sequence of events might be pursued if this were an initial data load of a small but growing data warehouse:

1. A tablespace (TBSP1) is created comprising four data files, each 100MB in size, on separate disks.

2. The CREATE TABLE statement is then executed specifying MINEXTENTS 4, creating four extent allocations of 75M each (and thus on four separate disks/devices) because extents cannot span datafiles.

3. The table storage definition is subsequently changed to a NEXT allocation of 25M for subsequent, smaller data loads/population.

4. The temporary tablespace definition in this instance uses at least four data files to compose the tablespace physically.

This method illustrates that careful planning and management of table and temporary tablespace construction can provide the underlying physical data distribution necessary to extract the most performance from parallel DDL operations. But all this is not necessary if you use ASM.

TIP
Effective parallel operations depend greatly on how the data is physically located. Avoid introducing I/O bottlenecks into your database.

You can use the Oracle Managed File (OMF) feature to create datafiles for your tablespaces. If you use this feature, all of the OMF datafiles created are placed in the directory specified via the DB_CREATE_FILE_DEST initialization parameter. To avoid creating I/O conflicts, you should point that parameter to a logical volume spanning multiple disks. You can move OMF datafiles after they have been created, following the standard procedures for moving datafiles and renaming them internally via the ALTER DATABASE or ALTER TABLESPACE command.

Parallel DML Statements and Examples

The Oracle 8 RDBMS introduced the capability to perform DML operations in parallel. Parallel DML support must be enabled within a SQL session to perform a parallelized DML statement operation. The following conditions apply to parallel DML:

- You cannot enable a parallel DML session without first completing your transaction. You must first perform a commit or rollback.

- The session must be enabled via the ALTER SESSION ENABLE PARALLEL DML command.

- You cannot access a table modified by parallel DML until the parallel transaction has ended (via commit or rollback).

NOTE
Parallel DML mode does not affect parallel DDL or parallel queries.

The following statements prevent parallel DML:

- SELECT for UPDATE
- LOCK TABLE
- EXPLAIN PLAN

NOTE
Statement failure does not disable parallel DML within your session.

Parallel DML Restrictions

Consider the following restrictions when using parallel DML. These restrictions apply to parallel DML (including direct-path INSERT) and come from the Oracle documentation, "Oracle Database VLDB and Partitioning Guide" (11.2). This is only a subsection, so please refer to this document for more information:

- Intrapartition parallelism for UPDATE, MERGE, and DELETE operations require that the COMPATIBLE initialization parameter be set to 9.2 or greater.

- The INSERT VALUES statement is never executed in parallel.

- A transaction can contain multiple parallel DML statements that modify different tables, but after a parallel DML statement modifies a table, no subsequent serial or parallel statement (DML or query) can access the same table again in that transaction.

- This restriction also exists after a serial direct-path INSERT statement: no subsequent SQL statement (DML or query) can access the modified table during that transaction.

- Queries that access the same table are allowed before a parallel DML or direct-path INSERT statement, but not after.

- Any serial or parallel statements attempting to access a table that has been modified by a parallel UPDATE, DELETE, or MERGE, or a direct-path INSERT during the same transaction are rejected with an error message.

- Parallel DML operations cannot be done on tables with triggers.

- Replication functionality is not supported for parallel DML.

- Parallel DML cannot occur in the presence of certain constraints: self-referential integrity, delete cascade, and deferred integrity. In addition, direct-path INSERT offers no support for any referential integrity.

- Parallel DML can be done on tables with object columns provided the object columns are not accessed.

- Parallel DML can be done on tables with LOB columns provided the table is partitioned. However, intrapartition parallelism is not supported.

- A transaction involved in a parallel DML operation cannot be or become a distributed transaction.

- Clustered tables are not supported.

- Parallel UPDATE, DELETE, and MERGE operations are not supported for temporary tables.

Violations of these restrictions could cause the statement to execute serially without warnings or error messages in most cases.

TIP
Parallel DML does not work for all types of tables, and sometimes only works for certain columns within them. You must manage your tables to enable parallel DML operations properly.

Parallel DML Statement Examples

The next two listings illustrate the use of parallel DML statements. In the first listing, a new transaction is created for the session and parallel DML is enabled:

```
commit;
alter session enable parallel dml;
```

In the second listing, shown next, a table named COSTS (a partitioned table from the Oracle sample schema SH) is updated, with a degree of parallelism of 4, and the table is then queried:

```
update      /*+ PARALLEL (costs, 4) */ COSTS
set         Unit_Price = Unit_Price * 1.15
where       Prod_Id > 148;
38421 rows updated.

select      COUNT(*)
from        COSTS;
```

```
select COUNT(*) from COSTS
*
ERROR at line 1:
ORA-12838: cannot read/modify an object after modifying it in parallelcommit;
Commit complete.
```

The query fails because the parallel transaction has not been committed on this table. But if you do the same SELECT, but for a different table, you will not get this error.

TIP
You must issue a commit or rollback after using parallel DML statements. Otherwise, you will receive an error doing a SELECT statement on the same table that follows a parallel DML statement on that table.

The next listing shows a parallel DDL statement. Note that, in this example, two different sections are parallelized: the query, with a degree of 6, and the population of the table, with a degree of 4.

```
create table COST_SUMMARY
parallel 4
as    select /*+ PARALLEL (COSTS, 6) */
      Prod_Id, Time_Id, SUM(Unit_Cost) Cost
from  COSTS
group by Prod_Id, Time_Id;
```

Instead of using the CREATE TABLE AS SELECT syntax, you could have created the table first and then parallelized an INSERT, as shown here. The APPEND hint fills only new blocks and is used here only for the purpose of showing you the syntax for it:

```
insert    /*+ APPEND PARALLEL (COST_SUMMARY,4) */
into      COST_SUMMARY (Prod_Id, Time_Id, Cost)
select    /*+ PARALLEL (COSTS, 6) */
          Prod_Id, Time_Id, SUM(Unit_Cost) Cost
from      COSTS
group by Prod_Id, Time_Id;
36189 rows created.
```

TIP
You can use the PARALLEL hint in multiple sections of an INSERT AS SELECT.

NOTE
Rollback segment resources should not be a problem if you are using automatic undo management.

Monitoring Parallel Operations via the V$ Views

The V$ dynamic performance views are always a great place for instance monitoring and evaluating the current performance of the database; parallel operations are no exception. The key performance views for monitoring parallel execution at a system level are V$PQ_TQSTAT and V$PQ_SYSSTAT. In general, V$ views beginning with *V$PQ* views give statistics and DBA information (mostly tuning information) whereas the *V$PX* views give details at the process level about parallel sessions and operations (mostly the mechanics). In the following sections, you will see examples of the most commonly used V$ views for monitoring parallel operations.

V$PQ_TQSTAT

Detailed statistics on all parallel server processes and the producer/consumer relationship between them are presented in the V$PQ_TQSTAT view. Additional information is presented on the number of rows and bytes addressed by each server process. V$PQ_TQSTAT is best used by the DBA tuning long-running queries that require very specific tuning and evaluation of data distribution between server processes. The following listing shows an example of the data available from V$PQ_TQSTAT. This view is good for locating uneven distribution of work between parallel execution servers.

```
select     DFO_Number, TQ_ID, Server_Type,
           Num_Rows, Bytes, Waits, Process
from       V$PQ_TQSTAT;

DFO_NUMBER TQ_ID SERVER_TYPE NUM_ROWS    BYTES WAITS TIMEOUTS PROCE
---------- ----- ----------- -------- ------- ----- -------- -----
         1     0 Consumer       14315  123660    14        0 P000
         2     0 Producer       23657  232290     7        0 P003
         2     0 Producer       12323   90923     7        0 P002
         2     0 Producer       12321   92300     7        0 P001
         2     0 Consumer      190535 2234322    48        2 QC
```

In this example, you can see the results for two parallel operations. The first parallel operation involves only one parallel execution server. The second parallel operation involves three parallel execution servers (P001, P002, and P003) and a coordinator process (QC). For the second parallel operation (DFO_Number = 2), you can see that process P003 did more work than any other process. More testing is required to determine if a problem exists. Also note that the last record in the output is for a query coordinator process. It has a higher-than-average number of waits because it needs to communicate with all the other query server processes.

V$PQ_SYSSTAT

V$PQ_SYSSTAT provides parallel statistics for all parallelized statement operations within the instance. V$PQ_SYSSTAT is ideal for evaluating the number of servers executing currently high-water mark levels and the frequency of startup and shutdown of parallel servers, as shown here:

```
select     Statistic, Value
from       V$PQ_SYSSTAT;
```

```
STATISTIC                  VALUE
--------------------      -------
Servers Busy                  12
Servers Idle                   0
Servers Highwater             12
Server Sessions               39
Servers Started               13
Servers Shutdown               7
Servers Cleaned Up             0
Queries Queued                 0
Queries Initiated              5
Queries Initiated (IPQ)        0
DML Initiated                  3
DML Initiated (IPQ)            0
DDL Initiated                  0
DDL Initiated (IPQ)            0
DFO Trees                      5
Sessions Active                3
Local Msgs Sent            91261
Distr Msgs Sent                0
Local Msgs Recv'd          91259
Distr Msgs Recv'd              0
```

TIP
To determine easily if parallel DML is being used, query the DML-initiated statistic before and after executing a parallel DML statement.

This next listing illustrates the statistics found on a freshly started instance. These statistics show parallel servers executing during the UPDATE statement in the section "Parallel DML Statements and Examples" earlier in this chapter, where there was a degree of parallelism of 4.

```
select     Statistic, Value
from       V$PQ_SYSSTAT;

STATISTIC                  VALUE
--------------------      -------
Servers Busy                   4
Servers Idle                   0
Servers Highwater              4
Server Sessions                4
Servers Started                0
Servers Shutdown               0
Servers Cleaned Up             0
Queries Queued                 0
Queries Initiated              0
Queries Initiated (IPQ)        0
DML Initiated                  1
DML Initiated (IPQ)            0
DDL Initiated                  0
```

```
DDL Initiated (IPQ)          0
DFO Trees                    1
Sessions Active              1
Local Msgs Sent              8
Distr Msgs Sent              0
Local Msgs Recv'd           12
Distr Msgs Recv'd            0
```

As you can see, four parallel execution servers were used and no new processes were started. Next, query V$PQ_SYSSTAT after an INSERT operation, specifying a parallel degree of 4. The subsequent execution of the INSERT statement produces the statistics from the V$PQ_SYSSTAT view.

```
STATISTIC                 VALUE
--------------------      -------
Servers Busy                 4
Servers Idle                 0
Servers Highwater            8
Server Sessions             16
Servers Started              4
Servers Shutdown             4
Servers Cleaned Up           0
Queries Queued               0
Queries Initiated            0
Queries Initiated (IPQ)      0
DML Initiated                2
DML Initiated (IPQ)          0
DDL Initiated                0
DDL Initiated (IPQ)          0
DFO Trees                    3
Sessions Active              2
Local Msgs Sent            108
Distr Msgs Sent              0
Local Msgs Recv'd          122
Distr Msgs Recv'd            0
```

Query V$PQ_SYSSTAT after a SELECT on a table defined with a hint specifying a parallel degree of 5. The following listing illustrates V$PQ_SYSSTAT output following the query. Note the values for Servers Busy and Servers Highwater.

```
select      Statistic, Value
from        V$PQ_SYSSTAT;

STATISTIC                 VALUE
--------------------      -------
Servers Busy                 5
Servers Idle                 0
Servers Highwater            8
Server Sessions             20
Servers Started              5
Servers Shutdown             4
Servers Cleaned Up           0
```

```
Queries Queued            0
Queries Initiated         1
Queries Initiated (IPQ)   0
DML Initiated             2
DML Initiated (IPQ)       0
DDL Initiated             0
DDL Initiated (IPQ)       0
DFO Trees                 4
Sessions Active           2
Local Msgs Sent         117
Distr Msgs Sent           0
Local Msgs Recv'd       136
Distr Msgs Recv'd         0
```

In this case, the hint has overridden the default degree of parallelism defined for the table, using five parallel query server processes.

TIP
If the number of servers started consistently increases, consider increasing the PARALLEL_MIN_SERVERS initialization parameter. However, if a parallel execution server is started through the PARALLEL_MIN_SERVERS parameter, it will not exit until the database shuts down, the parallel process aborts, or the process is killed. This can lead to process memory fragmentation, so increase this number only when you are sure it is needed.

TIP
A PARALLEL hint overrides the degree of parallelism defined for a table when determining the degree of parallelism for an operation.

V$PQ_SESSTAT

To provide the current session statistics, query the V$PQ_SESSTAT view. Use this view to see the number of queries executed within the current session, as well as the number of DML operations parallelized. Here's a sample output of a simple query from this view:

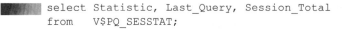

```
select Statistic, Last_Query, Session_Total
from    V$PQ_SESSTAT;

STATISTIC                  LAST_QUERY   SESSION_TOTAL
----------------------     ----------   -------------
Queries Parallelized            0             1
DML Parallelized                1             2
DDL Parallelized                0             0
DFO Trees                       1             3
Server Threads                  6             0
Allocation Height               6             0
Allocation Width                0             0
```

```
Local Msgs Sent                    27               171
Distr Msgs Sent                     0                 0
Local Msgs Recv'd                  27               167
Distr Msgs Recv'd                   0                 0
```

The output shown in V$PQ_SESSTAT refers only to the current session, so it is most useful when performing diagnostics during testing or problem resolution processes. Note that V$PX_SESSTAT has a similar name but a completely different set of columns. V$PX_SESSTAT joins session information from V$PX_SESSION with the V$SESSTAT table. V$PX_SESSION can also give information on the process requested degree (REQ_DEGREE) as compared to the actual degree (DEGREE) that ends up being used. A listing of V$ views related to parallel operations is given in the section "Other Parallel Notes" at the end of this chapter.

The next listing shows a simple example of querying V$PX_SESSTAT. In this example, if you tried to execute a parallel query where the specified degree of parallelism (12) is greater than PARALLEL_MAX_SERVERS (10), you might see the following:

```
Select      DISTINCT Req_Degree, Degree
from        V$PX_SESSTAT;

     REQ_DEGREE          DEGREE
------------------  ------------------
             12               10
```

The V$PX_SESSTAT view is populated only while a parallel operation is executing; as soon as the parallel operation finishes, the contents of this view are cleared.

Using EXPLAIN PLAN and AUTOTRACE on Parallel Operations

You can use the EXPLAIN PLAN command to see tuned parallel statements. When you create a PLAN_TABLE for your database (via the `utlxplan.sql` script in the `/rdbms/admin` subdirectory under the Oracle software home directory), Oracle includes columns that allow you to see how parallelism affects the query's execution path. The information about the parallelization of the query is found in the OBJECT_NODE, OTHER_TAG, and OTHER columns in PLAN_TABLE.

TIP
New columns may be added to the PLAN_TABLE with each new release of Oracle. You should drop and re-create your PLAN_TABLE following each upgrade of the Oracle kernel. If you upgrade an existing database to a new version of Oracle, you should drop your old PLAN_TABLE and re-execute the utlxplan.sql script to see all of the new PLAN_TABLE columns. You can also view the plan using Oracle Enterprise Manager in the SQL Details page.

The OBJECT_NODE column is the name of the database link used to reference the object. The OTHER column provides information about the query server processes involved. The OTHER_TAG column describes the function of the OTHER column's entries. The OTHER column contains a derived SQL statement—either for a remote query or for parallel query operations.

Value	Description
PARALLEL_COMBINED_WITH_CHILD	The parent of this operation performs the parent and child operations together; OTHER is NULL.
PARALLEL_COMBINED_WITH_PARENT	The child of this operation performs the parent and child operations together; OTHER is NULL.
PARALLEL_TO_PARALLEL	The SQL in the OTHER column is executed in parallel, and results are returned to a second set of query server processes.
PARALLEL_TO_SERIAL	The SQL in the OTHER column is executed in parallel, and the results are returned to a serial process (usually the query coordinator).
PARALLEL_FROM_SERIAL	The SQL operation consumes data from a serial operation and outputs it in parallel; OTHER is NULL.
SERIAL	The SQL statement is executed serially (the default); the OTHER column is NULL.
SERIAL_FROM_REMOTE	The SQL in the OTHER column is executed at a remote site.

TABLE 11-1. *Possible Values for PLAN_TABLE.OTHER_TAG for Parallel Operations*

Table 11-1 shows the possible values for OTHER_TAG and their associated OTHER values.

When an operation is parallelized, it may be partitioned to multiple query server processes based on ranges of ROWID values; the ranges are based on contiguous blocks of data in the table. You can use the OTHER_TAG column to verify the parallelism within different query operations, and you can see the parallelized query in the OTHER column. For example, the query in this next listing forces a MERGE JOIN to occur between the CUSTOMERS and SALES tables; because a MERGE JOIN involves full table scans and sorts, multiple operations can be parallelized. You can use the OTHER_TAG column to show the relationships between the parallel operations.

```
Alter table sales parallel (degree 4);
Alter table customers parallel (degree 4);
select /*+ FULL(customers) FULL(sales) USE_MERGE(customers sales)*/
      customers.cust_last_Name, sales.amount_sold
  from customers, sales
 where customers.cust_ID = sales.cust_ID
   and sales.time_ID = to_date('18-AUG-01', 'DD-MON-YY');
```

Next, you can see the partial EXPLAIN PLAN for the MERGE JOIN query:

```
MERGE JOIN
    SORT JOIN
       PARTITION RANGE SINGLE
          TABLE ACCESS FULL SALES
     SORT JOIN
      TABLE ACCESS FULL CUSTOMERS
```

As shown in the plan, Oracle performs a full table scan (TABLE ACCESS FULL) on each table, sorts the results (using the SORT JOIN operations), and merges the result sets. The query of PLAN_TABLE in the next listing shows the OTHER_TAG for each operation. The query shown in the listing following the OTHER_TAG for each operation generates the EXPLAIN PLAN listings.

```
select
   LPAD(' ',2*Level)||Operation||' '||Options
                ||' '||Object_Name   Q_Plan, Other_Tag
from PLAN_TABLE
where Statement_ID = 'TEST'
connect by prior ID = Parent_ID and Statement_ID = 'TEST'
start with ID=1;
```

The result of the query for the MERGE JOIN example is shown here:

```
Q_PLAN                                      OTHER_TAG
------------------------------------------  ----------------------------------------
  PX COORDINATOR
    PX SEND QC (RANDOM) :TQ10001            PARALLEL_TO_SERIAL
      MERGE JOIN                            PARALLEL_COMBINED_WITH_PARENT
        SORT JOIN                           PARALLEL_COMBINED_WITH_PARENT
          PX RECEIVE                        PARALLEL_COMBINED_WITH_PARENT
            PX SEND BROADCAST :TQ10000      PARALLEL_TO_PARALLEL
              PX BLOCK ITERATOR             PARALLEL_COMBINED_WITH_CHILD
                TABLE ACCESS FULL SALES     PARALLEL_COMBINED_WITH_PARENT
        SORT JOIN                           PARALLEL_COMBINED_WITH_PARENT
          PX BLOCK ITERATOR                 PARALLEL_COMBINED_WITH_CHILD
            TABLE ACCESS FULL CUSTOMERS     PARALLEL_COMBINED_WITH_PARENT
```

You can see (by their OTHER_TAG values) that each of the TABLE ACCESS FULL operations is parallelized and provides data to a parallel sorting operation. The SORT JOIN operations are PARALLEL_COMBINED_WITH_PARENT (their "parent" operation is the MERGE JOIN). The MERGE JOIN operation is PARALLEL_TO_SERIAL (the merge is performed in parallel; output is provided to the serial query coordinator process).

The OBJECT_NODE column values display information about the query server processes involved in performing an operation. The following listing shows the OBJECT_NODE column for the TABLE ACCESS FULL of CUSTOMERS operation performed for the MERGE JOIN query.

```
set long 1000
select Object_Node
  from PLAN_TABLE
 where Operation||' '||Options = 'TABLE ACCESS FULL'
   and Object_Name = 'CUSTOMERS';

OBJECT_NODE
-----------
:Q15000
```

As shown in this listing, the OBJECT_NODE column references a parallel query server process. (Q15000 is an internal identifier Oracle assigned to the process for this example.)

TIP
When using the EXPLAIN PLAN command for a parallelized query, you cannot rely on querying just the operations-related columns to see the parallelized operations within the EXPLAIN PLAN. At a minimum, you should query the OTHER_TAG column to see which operations are performed in parallel. If an operation is not performed in parallel and you think it should be, you may need to add hints to the query, set a degree of parallelism for the tables, or check the size of the query server pool to make sure query server processes are available for the query's use. Also, Consumer Group limitations and settings are in place for PARALLEL_ADAPTIVE_MULTI_USER and PARALLEL_MIN_PERCENT. These could also prevent parallelism from occurring.

Oracle provides a second script, `utlxplp.sql`, also located in the `/rdbms/admin` subdirectory under the Oracle software home directory. The `utlxplp.sql` script queries the PLAN_TABLE, with emphasis on the parallel query data within the table. You must create the PLAN_TABLE (via the `utlxplan.sql` script) and populate it (via the EXPLAIN PLAN command) prior to running the `utlxplp.sql` script.

TIP
When using EXPLAIN PLAN for parallel operations, use the utlxplp.sql script to view the PLAN_TABLE.

Using the set autotrace on Command
You can have the EXPLAIN PLAN automatically generated for every transaction you execute within SQL*Plus. The `set autotrace on` command causes each query, after being executed, to display both its execution path and high-level trace information about the processing involved in resolving the query.

To use the `set autotrace on` command, you must have first created the PLAN_TABLE table within your account. When using the `set autotrace on` command, you do not set a STATEMENT_ID, and you do not have to manage the records within the PLAN_TABLE. To disable the AUTOTRACE feature, use the `set autotrace off` command.

If you use the `set autotrace on` command, you will not see the EXPLAIN PLAN for your queries until *after* they complete—unless you specify TRACEONLY. The EXPLAIN PLAN command shows the execution paths without running the queries first. Therefore, if the performance of a query is unknown, use the EXPLAIN PLAN command before running it. If you are fairly certain that the performance of a query is acceptable, use `set autotrace on` to verify its execution path.

The next listing shows the effect of the `set autotrace on` command. When a MERGE JOIN query is executed, the data is returned from the query followed by the EXPLAIN PLAN. The EXPLAIN PLAN is in two parts: the first part shows the operations involved, and the second part shows the parallel-related actions. Here, you can see the first part of the AUTOTRACE output.

```
set autotrace on
select     /*+ parallel (ORDER_ITEMS) */
           order_id
from       order_items
order by   quantity;
```

```
         ORDER_ID
--------------------
               2454 (Partial listing…)
777 rows selected.

Execution Plan
----------------------------------------------------------
Plan hash value: 701983788

--------------------------------------------------------------------------------------
--------------------
| Id  | Operation            | Name       | Rows  | Bytes | Cost (%CPU)| Time     |   TQ
|IN-OUT| PQ Distrib |
--------------------------------------------------------------------------------------
--------------------
|   0 | SELECT STATEMENT     |            |   777 |  5320 |    3  (34)| 00:00:01 |
|     |            |
|   1 |  PX COORDINATOR      |            |       |       |           |          |
|     |            |
|   2 |   PX SEND QC (ORDER) | :TQ10001   |   777 |  5320 |    3  (34)| 00:00:01 | Q1,01
| P->S | QC (ORDER) |
|   3 |    SORT ORDER BY     |            |   777 |  5320 |    3  (34)| 00:00:01 | Q1,01
| PCWP |            |
|   4 |     PX RECEIVE       |            |   777 |  5320 |    2   (0)| 00:00:01 | Q1,01
| PCWP |            |
|   5 |      PX SEND RANGE   | :TQ10000   |   777 |  5320 |    2   (0)| 00:00:01 | Q1,00
| P->P | RANGE      |
|   6 |       PX BLOCK ITERATOR |         |   777 |  5320 |    2   (0)| 00:00:01 | Q1,00
| PCWC |            |
|   7 |        TABLE ACCESS FULL| ORDER_ITEMS |   777 |  5320 |    2   (0)| 00:00:01 | Q1,00
| PCWP |            |
--------------------------------------------------------------------------------------
--------------------
```

The AUTOTRACE output shows the operations and the objects on which they act. The information near the far right (*Q1* and so on) identifies the parallel query servers used during the query. The AUTOTRACE also shows the step ID values to describe the parallelism of the execution path's operations, as shown here (this one you can read from bottom to top).

Tuning Parallel Execution and the Initialization Parameters

Parameters related to physical memory are generally set much higher in a database that uses parallel operations than in a nonparallel environment. If you are using MEMORY_TARGET (sets memory for PGA/SGA), you should set it higher for a system using parallel operations. Many of the related parameters (detailed here) are set automatically, but you may want to set minimums. See Chapter 4 for information on setting MEMORY_TARGET and other initialization parameters. The settings shown in Table 11-2 are general parameter settings, but your settings must be based on your unique business environment. Also note that OPTIMIZER_PERCENT_PARALLEL and ENQUEUE_RESOURCES (deprecated in 10.2 and removed in 11g) are obsolete and thus not shown in this table.

NOTE
Table 11-2 is a limited list; PARALLEL_DEGREE_POLICY, PARALLEL_MIN_TIME_THRESHOLD, PARALLEL_DEGREE_LIMIT, and PARALLEL_FORCE_LOCAL should also be considered.

Initialization Parameter	Meaning	Suggested Values
COMPATIBLE	Setting this parameter to the release level of the instance allows you to take advantage of all of the functionality built into the RDBMS engine. Oracle recommends backing up the database *before* changing this parameter!	Generally set to the default value for the database version (11.2.0.0). Standby databases must use a consistent setting for both the primary and standby.
DB_BLOCK_SIZE*	Sets the database block size for the database.	In general, use the largest supported size for data warehousing (32K for 64-bit only, otherwise 16K) and smaller sizes for OLTP (8K). In Oracle, you can create caches and tablespaces with differing database block sizes.
DB_CACHE_SIZE* (Usually set automatically when you set MEMORY_TARGET, but you may still want to set a minimum – See Chapter 4)	To support a larger number of processes performing parallel queries and DML operations, increase the memory available.	Increase to support parallel operations.
DB_FILE_MULTIBLOCK_READ_COUNT*	Determines how many blocks are read at once during a full table scan. Improves the performance of parallel operations using table scans.	OS-dependent. On Windows and Linux this is 128.
DISK_ASYNCH_IO*	Supports asynchronous writes to the operating system, reducing a potential I/O bottleneck.	Whether DISK_ASYNCH_IO should be set to TRUE depends on whether the OS supports asynchronous I/O and how stable it is on that platform.
DML_LOCKS*	Sets the maximum number of DML locks acquired for the database. The default value assumes an average of four tables referenced per transaction.	Default value is 4*TRANSACTIONS. Increase to support parallel DML.
LARGE_POOL	The large pool allocation heap is used by parallel execution for message buffers. In 10*g*, parallel execution allocates buffers out of the large pool only when SGA_TARGET is set.	Default value should be okay, but if you increase the value of PARALLEL_EXECUTION_MESSAGE_SIZE, you should set this parameter to a higher value.

TABLE 11-2.   *Oracle 11g Parallel Initialization Parameters* *

Initialization Parameter	Meaning	Suggested Values
LOG_BUFFER*	Increase to support the transaction volume generated by parallel DML.	Default value is 16M, set to 512K minimum. Increase if parallel DML is used extensively.
PARALLEL_ADAPTIVE_MULTI_USER	Reduces the degree of parallelism based on number of active parallel users.	Set this to FALSE and control parallel resources with the Database Resource Manager instead if needed.
PARALLEL_EXECUTION_MESSAGE_SIZE	Specifies the size of messages for all parallel operations. Larger values than the default requires a larger shared pool size.	Operating system-dependent; values range from 2148 to 65535. Setting this parameter to a larger value than the default leads to better throughput for parallel operations but uses more memory, which may cause performance problems for nonparallel operations or applications.
PARALLEL_MAX_SERVERS	Maximum number of parallel query server processes allowed to exist simultaneously.	Default value is derived from the values of [CPU_COUNT × PARALLEL_THREADS_PER_CPU × 2 (if PGA_AGGREGATE_TARGET > 0)] × 5.
PARALLEL_FORCE_LOCAL	Whether a parallel operation is restricted to a single instance in a RAC environment.	Default value is FALSE and recommended value is FALSE. Performance degradation could occur if this is set to TRUE at times, so be careful.
PARALLEL_MIN_PERCENT	If this percentage of the degree of parallelism (number of servers) required by the query is not available, statement terminates with an error (ORA-12827). This is effective when a serial execution of the statement is undesired.	Default value is 0, range of values is 0–100. If 0, parallel operations always execute in parallel. If 100, operations execute in parallel only if all servers can be acquired.
PARALLEL_MIN_SERVERS	Minimum number of servers created when instance originates. As servers idle out or terminate, the number of servers never falls below this number.	0–OS limit. Realistically, start with 10–24. Consider changing if V$ views show heavy use of parallel queries. *Set this parameter!*

TABLE 11-2. *Oracle 11g Parallel Initialization Parameters* (Continued)

Initialization Parameter	Meaning	Suggested Values
PARALLEL_THREADS_PER_CPU	Specifies the default degree of parallelism for the instance, based on the number of parallel execution processes a CPU can support during parallel operations.	Any nonzero number; default is OS-dependent. This "number times CPUs" is the number of threads used in parallel operations.
PGA_AGGREGATE_TARGET	Enables the automatic sizing of SQL working areas used by memory-intensive SQL operators such as a sort and hash join.	A useful parameter to help control paging because you set the PGA target to the total memory on your system that is available to the Oracle instance and subtract the SGA. It is used for sorting operations as well as others, as discussed in Chapter 4. (Usually set automatically when you set MEMORY_TARGET, but you may still want to set a minimum. See Chapter 4.)
RECOVERY_PARALLELISM	Number of recovery processes that will be devoted to instance or media recovery.	A value between 2 and PARALLEL_MAX_SERVERS. A value of 0 or 1 indicates that serial recovery will be performed.
SHARED_POOL_SIZE*	Size of Oracle shared pool. Portion of shared pool is used for query server communication.	Increase existing parameter value by 5–10 percent for heavy, concurrent PQ use. This parameter does not need to be set if SGA_TARGET is used and set properly. (Usually set automatically when you set MEMORY_TARGET, but you may still want to set a minimum. See Chapter 4.)
TAPE_ASYNCH_IO*	Supports asynchronous writes to the operating system, reducing a potential I/O bottleneck.	This parameter affects writes only to serial devices. This is useful for parallel backup operations or for use with RMAN, but not important for parallel query or DML. The default is TRUE.
TRANSACTIONS*	Specifies the number of concurrent transactions, which increases if parallel DML is extensively used.	Default value is derived from SESSIONS setting. Increase to support parallel DML.

* Has an indirect effect on parallel options.

TABLE 11-2. *Oracle 11g Parallel Initialization Parameters* (Continued)

TIP
Be sure your environment is properly configured to support the increase in processes and transactions generated by parallel operations.

The parameters in the initialization file define and shape the environment used by parallel operations. You enable parallel operations for your commands by using a PARALLEL hint on a SQL statement or using the PARALLEL clause during a CREATE/ALTER table command. When you are considering adjusting any initialization parameter (or removing deprecated parameters), fully investigate the "Oracle 11g Database Administrator's Guide," the "Database Upgrade Guide," or the appropriate server installation guide for your system *prior* to experimenting with an Oracle database.

Parallel Loading

To use parallel data loading, start multiple SQL*Loader sessions using the PARALLEL keyword. Each session is an independent session requiring its own control file. This listing shows three separate direct path loads, all using the PARALLEL=TRUE parameter on the command line:

```
sqlldr USERID=SCOTT/PASS CONTROL=P1.CTL DIRECT=TRUE PARALLEL=TRUE
sqlldr USERID=SCOTT/PASS CONTROL=P2.CTL DIRECT=TRUE PARALLEL=TRUE
sqlldr USERID=SCOTT/PASS CONTROL=P3.CTL DIRECT=TRUE PARALLEL=TRUE
```

Each session creates its own log, bad, and discard files (p1.log, p1.bad, etc.) by default. You can have multiple sessions loading data into different tables, but the APPEND option is still required. APPEND is very fast because it fills only unused blocks. The SQL*Loader REPLACE, TRUNCATE, and INSERT options are not allowed for parallel data loading. If you need to delete the data using SQL commands, you must manually delete the data.

TIP
*If you use parallel data loading, indexes are not maintained by the SQL*Loader session unless you are loading a single table partition. Before starting a parallel loading process, you must drop all indexes on the table and disable all of its PRIMARY KEY and UNIQUE constraints. After the parallel loads completely, you need to re-create or rebuild the table's indexes. Inserting data using APPEND and UNRECOVERABLE is the fastest way to insert data into a table without an index. External tables may provide faster extract, transform, and load (ETL) operations.*

In parallel data loading, each load process creates temporary segments for loading the data; the temporary segments are later merged with the table. If a parallel data load process fails before the load completes, the temporary segments will not have been merged with the table. If the temporary segments have not been merged with the table being loaded, no data from the load will have been committed to the table.

You can use the SQL*Loader FILE parameter to direct each data loading session to a different datafile. By directing each loading session to its own database datafile, you can balance the I/O load of the loading processes. Data loading is very I/O-intensive and must be distributed across multiple disks for parallel loading to achieve significant performance improvements over serial loading.

TIP
Use the FILE parameter to direct the writes generated by parallel data loads.

After a parallel data load, each session may attempt to re-enable the table's constraints. As long as at least one load session is still under way, attempting to re-enable the constraints will fail. The final loading session to complete should attempt to re-enable the constraints, and it should succeed. You should check the status of your constraints after the load completes. If the table being loaded has PRIMARY KEY and UNIQUE constraints, you should first re-create or rebuild the associated indexes in parallel and then manually enable the constraints.

TIP
The PARALLEL option for data loading improves performance of loads, but it can also waste space when not properly used.

Performance Comparisons and Monitoring Parallel Operations

To show the performance difference between a nonparallel operation and a parallel operation, I performed the following tests:

- Started the database with 12 parallel server processes and checked the background processes that were created
- Ran a query without PARALLEL and checked the speed
- Ran a query with PARALLEL that required sorting with a degree of 6
- Checked the output of V$PQ_SYSSTAT and V$PQ_SESSTAT

The next listing shows the `ps -ef` output (`ps -ef` is a Unix or Linux OS command) for 12 running parallel servers. I started the database with the parameter PARALLEL_MIN_SERVERS = 12. The name of the database is FDR1.

```
#ps -ef
oracle   2764      1  0 17:08:30     ?    0:00 ora_pmon_fdr1
oracle   2766      1  0 17:08:34     ?    0:00 ora_lgwr_fdr1
oracle   2768      1  0 17:08:38     ?    0:00 ora_reco_fdr1
oracle   2770      1  0 17:08:42     ?    0:00 ora_d000_fdr1
oracle   2769      1  0 17:08:40     ?    0:00 ora_s000_fdr1
```

```
oracle  2767     1  0 17:08:36   ?  0:00 ora_smon_fdrl
oracle  2771     1  4 17:08:44   ?  0:33 ora_p000_fdrl
oracle  2772     1  5 17:08:46   ?  0:42 ora_p001_fdrl
oracle  2773     1  4 17:08:48   ?  0:33 ora_p002_fdrl
oracle  2774     1  4 17:08:50   ?  0:32 ora_p003_fdrl
oracle  2775     1  5 17:08:52   ?  0:40 ora_p004_fdrl
oracle  2776     1 14 17:08:54   ?  1:26 ora_p005_fdrl
oracle  2819  2802 13 17:12:39   ?  1:44 ora_p006_fdrl
oracle  2820  2802  1 17:12:41   ?  0:05 ora_p007_fdrl
oracle  2821  2802  0 17:12:43   ?  0:01 ora_p008_fdrl
oracle  2822  2802  0 17:12:45   ?  0:01 ora_p009_fdrl
oracle  2825  2802  2 17:12:47   ?  0:11 ora_p010_fdrl
oracle  2826  2802 10 17:12:49   ?  1:18 ora_p011_fdrl
```

Next, run the query *without* using parallel execution servers. A partial result set is shown here. You can time this in a variety of ways, as shown in Chapter 6, or by just SELECT SYSDATE FROM DUAL.

```
select     Job_Sub_Code job, SUM(Amount_Cost), SUM(Amount_Credit),
           SUM(Amount_Debit)
from       JOB_ORDER_LINE_ITEMS
group by   Job_Sub_Code;

JOB SUM(AMOUNT_COST) SUM(AMOUNT_CREDIT) SUM(AMOUNT_DEBIT)
--- ---------------- ------------------ -----------------
02       9834013.62         20611471.9                  0
04       38670782.7         43440986.1                  0
05       1252599.77         7139753.85                  0
07          8899.66                  0                  0
12       1689729.94         3355174.16                  0
14        103089.64         3287384.45                  0
```

For this test, the elapsed time was 2 minutes, 30 seconds.
    Next, run the query using PARALLEL:

```
select     /*+ PARALLEL (JOB_ORDER_LINE_ITEMS,6) */
           Job_Sub_Code, SUM(Amount_Cost), SUM(Amount_Credit),
           SUM(Amount_Debit)
from       JOB_ORDER_LINE_ITEMS
group by   Job_Sub_Code;
```

For this test, the elapsed time was just over one minute. The query runs more than twice as fast, with a degree of 6.

TIP
Increasing the degree of a parallel operation does not always decrease the execution time. It depends on your complete system setup. The degree specifies only the number of parallel execution servers that should be used for the operation. The number of parallel execution servers used depends on the parameter settings and the Database Resource Manager settings.

The following listing shows the V$ view data when executing the preceding query using PARALLEL with a degree of 12:

```
select      Statistic, Value
from        V$PQ_SYSSTAT;

STATISTIC                 VALUE
---------------------     -----
Servers Busy                 12
Servers Idle                  0
Servers Highwater            12
Server Sessions              39
Servers Started              13
Servers Shutdown              7
Servers Cleaned Up            0
Queries Queued                0
Queries Initiated             5
Queries Initiated (IPQ)       0
DML Initiated                 0
DML Initiated (IPQ)           0
DDL Initiated                 0
DDL Initiated (IPQ)           0
DFO Trees                     5
Local Msgs Sent           91261
Distr Msgs Sent               0
Local Msgs Recv'd         91259
Distr Msgs Recv'd             0


select      *
from        V$PQ_SESSTAT;

STATISTIC                LAST_QUERY  SESSION_TOTAL
-----------------------  ----------  -------------
Queries Parallelized              1              4
DML Parallelized                  0              0
DDL Parallelized                  0              0
DFO Trees                         1              4
Server Threads                   12              0
Allocation Height                 6              0
Allocation Width                  1              0
Local Msgs Sent               20934          83722
Distr Msgs Sent                   0              0
Local Msgs Recv'd             20934          83722
Distr Msgs Recv'd                 0              0
```

Optimizing Parallel Operations in RAC

The benefits of using parallel operations with an Oracle database have been well established, with the feature first being offered in version 7.1. Parallel execution of SQL statements on traditional Unix-based symmetric multiprocessor (SMP) architectures greatly increases utilization of the server and the speed of large resource-intensive operations. In a Real Application Clusters (RAC) architecture, the equivalent of a parallel SMP deployment is placed into effect and utilizes all the available servers (nodes) in the cluster. Use of parallel operations with RAC greatly enhances the scale-out cluster architecture.

Objectives of Parallel Operations

The objective of a parallel implementation is to use all available resources of the database platform architecture to increase overall processing potential. Resources included in this type of deployment are memory, processor, and I/O. Parallel operations that can be performed in any scale-up or single-system SMP image environment can also be performed in the scale-out RAC cluster environment. Operations that are included are as follows:

- Queries (based on full table scan)
- Create Table As
- Index builds/rebuilds
- DML operations (INSERT, UPDATE, DELETE) on partitioned tables
- Data loads

You can perform the first four operations referenced in this list with the use of SQL hints or by setting the degree of parallelism at the object level. Configure node groups to restrict parallel operations to specific nodes. Therefore, when implementing a large RAC architecture (more than two servers), allocate named servers to named groups to restrict or enable parallel operations.

RAC Parallel Usage Models

Several usage models are available for parallel execution with RAC. Because splitting a query across multiple nodes can degrade performance as well, take care when using the PARALLEL query with RAC! The models included are as follows:

- **Standard** Use of parallel query for large datasets. In this deployment, the degree of parallelism is usually defined to utilize all of the available resources in the cluster.
- **Restricted** This deployment restricts processing to specific nodes in the cluster. The referenced nodes can be logically grouped for specific types of operations.
- **Parallel index builds/rebuilds** In cases where large index builds are required, parallelism can be utilized to maximize the use of cluster node resources.

INIT.ORA Parameters

Several standard parameters can be set to implement parallel processes at the server level as discussed earlier in the chapter. The two general parallel parameters to consider are as follows:

Parameter Name	Type	Description
PARALLEL_MAX_SERVERS	Integer	Maximum number of parallel processes per instance
PARALLEL_MIN_SERVERS	Integer	Minimum number of server processes per instance

The RAC-specific parameter is as follows:

Parameter Name	Type	Description
INSTANCE_GROUPS	Integer	Defines the logical groups for enabling processing of specific servers

V$ Views for Viewing Parallel Statistics

Several database views are used to obtain parallel operation statistics. The view names referenced here are prefaced with the GV$ identifier, which depicts the RAC-level statistics:

View Name	Description
GV$PQ_SYSSTAT	All parallel-related statistics for the entire RAC configuration
GV$PQ_SESSTAT	Session-specific parallel statistics by session ID

Parallel Configuration and Associated Baseline Test

The INIT.ORA parameters set in a test environment are listed next. For the examples outlined in this section, I utilized a two-node RAC architecture running under Red Hat Advanced Server 2.1 (I could have also used version 3 or 4). The "*" identifies these as global across all of the RAC instances.

> *.PARALLEL_MAX_SERVERS=5
>
> *.PARALLEL_MIN_SERVERS=2

The listing that follows indicates that the TEST1 and TEST2 instances each initiated two parallel background processes at database startup:

```
UID       PID      PPID   C STIME TTY       TIME CMD
oracle    39414    1      0 11:18 ?         00:00:00 ora_p000_TEST1
oracle    39418    1      0 11:18 ?         00:00:00 ora_p001_TEST1
oracle    520      1      0 11:19 ?         00:00:00 ora_p000_TEST2
oracle    523      1      0 11:19 ?         00:00:00 ora_p001_TEST2
```

A query of the GV$PQ_SYSSTAT table shows the base status of the parallel processes within the Oracle kernel:

```
SELECT inst_id,statistic,value
FROM   gv$pq_sysstat
WHERE  value > 0
order by 1, 2;

INST_ID    STATISTIC                           VALUE
--------   --------------------------------    ---------
      1    Servers Busy                            1
           Servers Idle                            1
           Servers Highwater                       1
           Server Sessions                         1
      2    Servers Busy                            1
           Servers Idle                            1
           Servers Highwater                       1
           Server Sessions                         1
```

Parallel Query Test Examples

In this section, I examine the use of the parallel query with the two-node RAC architecture referenced in the preceding section. The two tests I performed are

■ Unbounded test where the query is executed using both RAC nodes

■ Bound test where the query is restricted to a single RAC node

Test 1: Unbounded Test

In the unbounded test, I ran a simple query utilizing standard SQL with parallel hints. As with any query, to utilize parallel operations, a full table scan must be part of the statement.

```
select /*+ full(c_test) parallel(c_test,6) */ sum(s_test_quantity) testcnt
from   q_test;
```

When executing the query using a parallel hint that requests six parallel workers, three processes are initiated on each of the server nodes:

```
UID       PID     PPID  C STIME TTY     TIME CMD
oracle    15888    1    0 11:13 ?       00:00:03 ora_p000_TEST1
oracle    15879    1    0 11:13 ?       00:00:03 ora_p001_TEST1
oracle    15956    1    1 11:23 ?       00:00:02 ora_p002_TEST1
oracle    17811    1    0 11:23 ?       00:00:01 ora_p000_TEST2
oracle    17620    1    0 11:22 ?       00:00:01 ora_p001_TEST2
oracle    17621    1    3 11:24 ?       00:00:01 ora_p002_TEST2
```

Statistics obtained from the GV$PQ_SYSSTAT view demonstrate that each of the instances started additional servers:

```
INST_ID    STATISTIC                        VALUE
---------- ------------------------------ ----------
1          DFO Trees                           7
           Distr Msgs Recv'd                  80
           Distr Msgs Sent                    80
           Local Msgs Recv'd                 204
           Local Msgs Sent                   116
           Queries Initiated                   6
           Server Sessions                    10
           Servers Busy                        1
           Servers Highwater                   3
           Servers Idle                        1
           Servers Shutdown                    1
           Servers Started                     1
           Sessions Active                     1

2          Distr Msgs Recv'd                  12
           Distr Msgs Sent                     6
           Server Sessions                     6
           Servers Busy                        1
           Servers Highwater                   3
           Servers Idle                        1
           Servers Shutdown                    1
           Servers Started                     1
```

Test 2: Bounded Test

To restrict parallel processing to specific cluster nodes, I employed instance groups to create logical server groupings. Control is via the INIT.ORA with the parameter INSTANCE_GROUPS. INSTANCE_GROUPS is a RAC-related parameter that is specified only in parallel mode. Used in conjunction with the runtime parameter PARALLEL_INSTANCE_GROUP, INSTANCE_GROUPS allows for the restriction of parallel query operations to a limited number of instances. For the tests in this section, I used the INSTANCE_GROUPS identified here:

```
# Init.ora Parameter Setting for Parallel Options
SALES1.INSTANCE_GROUPS='test1'
SALES2.INSTANCE_GROUPS='test2'
```

The session that follows is altered prior to the execution of the query to be assigned to the FINANCE group. Even though the query is initiated on the test1 node, based on the INSTANCE_GROUP setting, all of the processing is executed on TEST2.

```
alter session set parallel_instance_group = 'test2';

select /*+ full(q_amount) parallel(q_stock,6) */ sum(q_quant) ocnt
from   q_stock;
```

Note in the process listing that all of the parallel workers requested are indeed run only on the TEST2 node, as no CPU time is being utilized by the processes on TEST1.

```
UID      PID     PPID   C STIME TTY     TIME CMD
oracle   29994   1      0 14:13 ?       00:00:00 ora_p000_TEST1
oracle   29996   1      0 14:13 ?       00:00:00 ora_p001_TEST1
oracle   2631    1      0 14:51 ?       00:00:01 ora_p000_TEST2
oracle   2633    1      0 14:51 ?       00:00:01 ora_p001_TEST2
oracle   2676    1      4 14:57 ?       00:00:01 ora_p002_TEST2
oracle   2678    1      3 14:57 ?       00:00:01 ora_p003_TEST2
oracle   2680    1      4 14:57 ?       00:00:01 ora_p004_TEST2
```

A query of the GV$PQ_SYSSTAT table also shows that an additional three servers were started on the second TEST2 instance. Why only three servers and not four? Remember the setting of the INIT.ORA parameter PARALLEL_MAX_SERVERS. The value of the parameter is five, thus only an additional three are added to the initial two (although the high-water mark did hit six).

```
INST_ID    STATISTIC                        VALUE
---------- ------------------------------ ----------
1          DFO Trees                           3
           Distr Msgs Recv'd                  74
           Distr Msgs Sent                    74
           Local Msgs Recv'd                   2
           Local Msgs Sent                     1
           Queries Initiated                   3
           Server Sessions                     1
           Servers Busy                        1
           Servers Highwater                   1
           Servers Idle                        1
           Sessions Active                     2

2          Distr Msgs Recv'd                  22
           Distr Msgs Sent                    11
           Server Sessions                    11
           Servers Busy                        6
           Servers Highwater                   6
           Servers Started                     3
```

In the preceding example, the query was restricted to the test node by using the TEST_10 instance group. The INIT.ORA example that follows allows for the TEST_10 instance group to now run across both the TEST1 and TEST2 nodes. Note that the INIT.ORA parameter INSTANCE_GROUPS must be entered explicitly for each of the groups.

```
# Init.ora Parameter Setting for Parallel Options
TEST1.instance_groups='TEST_20'
TEST1.instance_groups='TEST_10'
TEST2.instance_groups='TEST_10'
```

Create Table As

Using the Create Table As (CTAS) feature within Oracle can be extremely useful for making copies of table objects. For large tables, the operation can be performed in parallel in the same manner as with the parallel query examples in the prior section. The SQL statement that follows is an example of using CTAS with the parallel option. Instance groups can also be used to restrict processing to specific nodes. Thus, based on the INSTANCE_GROUPS parameter, the query is executed only on the TEST1 node.

```
alter session set parallel_instance_group = 'TEST_20';

create table c_district_backup parallel (degree 3)
as
select *
from   c_district;
```

Index Builds

Performing index creates or rebuilds for large tables is another resource-intensive operation where performance can be greatly improved with parallel operations. The INDEX CREATE statement requests a parallel degree of 6 for the operation. Similar to the previous examples, this operation can also utilize the INSTANCE_GROUPS parameter to restrict the operation to specific nodes.

```
alter session set parallel_instance_group = 'TEST_20';

create unique index C_STOCK_I1 on C_STOCK (s_i_id, s_w_id)
tablespace stock_indx
parallel (degree 6);
```

Performance Considerations and Summary

The downside of parallel operations is the exhaustion of server resources. The easiest server resource to monitor is CPU utilization. If normal CPU utilization were relatively high, deploying a large number of parallel processes would not be advisable. Exceeding the total number of CPUs would cause performance degradation as well. Data layout is another immediate consideration. If I/O bottlenecks currently exist, use of parallel operations may exacerbate this condition. Ensure that data files for parallel target objects are spread across a reasonable number of disk spindles.

The use of parallel operations within a RAC deployment provides for the flexibility to utilize all server hardware included in the cluster architecture. Utilizing instance groups, database administrators can further control the allocation of these resources based on application requirements or service level agreements.

Other Parallel Notes

Planning (or reengineering) the physical location of data files is key to successful parallel data access. Determine an appropriate degree of parallelism for each parallelized SQL statement and parallelize the creation of your physical design. Don't let the initialization parameters dictate how the degree of parallelism is determined. Remember, you're usually trying to optimize a small number of slow queries, not every table access. Experiment with conservative parameters; use parallel operations for table or index creations and hint the degree of parallelism you identify as optimal. Use proper syntax for the parallel hints or they will be ignored. Other V$ views that may be helpful to you include V$PX_SESSION (session performing parallel operations), V$PX_SESSTAT (statistics for sessions performing parallel operations), V$PX_PROCESS (parallel processes), V$PX_PROCESS_SYSSTAT (statistics for parallel execution servers), V$SESSTAT (user session statistics), V$FILESTAT (file I/O statistics), V$PARAMETER (init.ora parameters), and V$PQ_TQSTAT (workload statistics for parallel execution servers).

The parallel features offered in Oracle are incredibly powerful tools when used in a targeted fashion—most databases can be tuned to place indexes in the right quantity and location to deliver acceptable performance. Use parallel operations for those statements that cannot be written any other way but to scan an entire table or address a partitioned large table/index. Parallelized operations are powerful tools for managing data warehouses or performing periodic maintenance activities. Configure the database environment to take full advantage of the benefits parallelism offers.

Oracle Documentation Is Online

Don't forget that all of the Oracle documentation (multiple Oracle versions) for all of the products is online at http://tahiti.oracle.com.

For the complete archives of all Oracle documentation (back to Oracle 9i; however, versions 8.1.7 and 7.3.4 are listed under Previously Released Oracle Documentation), please visit www.oracle.com/technology/documentation/index.html.

Tips Review

- Exadata is the next generation of relational database architecture. Get ready for it!

- What makes Exadata fast is fast hardware, many CPUs, fast Flash Cache, lots of DRAM on database servers and storage, compression (save 10x–70x), partition running (save 10x–100x), storage indexes (save 5x–10x), Smart Scan (save 4x–10x), and other features not covered (see Oracle Docs for more information). Exadata is the best way to turn a 1T search into a 500M search or even 50M search.

- Use V$SESSION_WAIT, Statspack, or the AWR Report to find RAC wait events.

- Find interconnect issues using Enterprise Manager Grid Control.

- The Database or Cluster Performance screen within OEM is the quickest way to locate performance problems in your system.

- You can investigate specific global cache wait events in Enterprise Manager.

- Parallel processes commonly involve disk accesses. If the data is not distributed across multiple disks, using parallel operations may lead to an I/O bottleneck.

- When the parallel degree is set to *N*, it is possible to use $(2*N) + 1$ total processes for the parallel operation. Although parallel operations deal with processes and *not* processors, when a large number of processors are available, Oracle generally uses the additional processors to run parallel queries, often enhancing query performance.

- Using parallel operations on very small tables or very fast queries can degrade performance because the query coordination also uses performance resources. You should evaluate whether the parallel cost exceeds the nonparallelized cost.

- As of Oracle 8*i*, parallel DML statements are allowed. This functionality applies to partitioned tables and indexes.

- Using the PARALLEL hint enables the use of parallel operations. If the degree is not specified with the hint, the default degree during table creation is used, or the degree of parallelism (DOP) is calculated from the initialization parameters CPU_COUNT and PARALLEL_THREADS_PER_CPU.

- The use of the NOPARALLEL hint disables parallel operations in a statement that would otherwise use parallel processing due to a parallel object definition.

- Specify the degree of parallelism using a hint instead of relying on the table definition to ensure that all operations are tuned for the given query.

- Make sure your data is properly distributed, or the parallel query server processes may add to existing I/O bottleneck problems.

- Use NOLOGGING to remove the I/O bottleneck caused by serial writes to the redo logs.

- Parallel DML does not work for all types of tables, and sometimes only works for certain columns within them. You must manage your tables to enable parallel DML operations properly.

- You *must* issue a commit or rollback after using parallel DML statements. Otherwise, you receive an error doing a SELECT statement on the same table that follows a parallel DML statement on that table.

- The PARALLEL hint may be used in multiple sections of an INSERT . . . AS SELECT.

- To easily determine if parallel DML is being used, query the DML initiated statistic before and after executing a parallel DML statement.

- If the number of servers started consistently increases, consider increasing the PARALLEL_MIN_SERVERS initialization parameter. However, if a parallel execution server is started through the PARALLEL_MIN_SERVERS parameter, it does not exit until the database shuts down, the parallel process aborts, or the process is killed. This can lead to process memory fragmentation, so increase the number of servers only when you are sure it is needed.

- A PARALLEL hint overrides the degree of parallelism defined for a table when determining the degree of parallelism for an operation.

- New columns may be added to the PLAN_TABLE with each new release of Oracle. You should drop and re-create your PLAN_TABLE following each upgrade of the Oracle kernel. If you upgrade an existing database to a new version of Oracle, you should drop your old PLAN_TABLE and re-execute the `utlxplan.sql` script to see all of the new PLAN_TABLE columns. You can also view the plan using Oracle Enterprise Manager on the SQL Details page.

- When using the EXPLAIN PLAN command for a parallelized query, you cannot rely on querying just the operations-related columns to see the parallelized operations within the EXPLAIN PLAN. At a minimum, you should query the OTHER_TAG column to see which operations are performed in parallel. If an operation is not performed in parallel and you think it should be, you may need to add hints to the query, set a degree of parallelism for the tables, or check the size of the query server pool to make sure query server processes are available for the query to use. Also, Consumer Group limitations and settings are in place for PARALLEL_ADAPTIVE_MULTI_USER and PARALLEL_MIN_PERCENT. These could also prevent parallelism from occurring.

- When using EXPLAIN PLAN for parallel operations, use the `utlxplp.sql` script to view the PLAN_TABLE.

- Be sure your environment is properly configured to support the increase in processes and transactions generated by parallel operations.

- If you use parallel data loading, indexes are not maintained by the SQL*Loader session, unless you are loading a single table partition. Before starting a parallel loading process, you must drop all indexes on the table and disable all of its PRIMARY KEY and UNIQUE constraints. After the parallel loads complete, you need to re-create or rebuild the table's indexes. Inserting data using APPEND and UNRECOVERABLE is the fastest way to insert data into a table without an index. External tables may provide faster extract, transform, and load (ETL) operations.

- Use the FILE parameter to direct the writes generated by parallel data loads.

- The PARALLEL option for data loading improves performance of loads, but can also waste space when not properly used.

- Increasing the degree of a parallel operation does not always decrease the execution time. It depends on your complete system setup. The degree specifies only the number of parallel execution servers that *should* be used for the operation. The number of parallel execution servers used depends on the parameter settings and the Database Resource Manager settings.

- Go to http://tahiti.oracle.com on the Internet for a quick connection to Oracle documentation.

- Exadata, Exalogic, Exadata Storage Expansion Rack, Oracle Database Appliance, SPARC SuperCluster, Exalytics BI Machine, ZFS, Pillar Storage, and the latest StorageTek combines probably more hardware speed than the entire hardware industry put out prior to Oracle buying Sun. Hardware speeds *were* doubling every 18 months; enter Oracle and hardware speed is now accelerating exponentially with Oracle at the wheel (in the last two years Oracle has probably accelerated hardware/software performance 2,000–20,000 times if you know how to use it). The Terabytes database will soon be the Exabytes database. Teach your kids Oracle!

References

"Advanced Compression with Oracle Database 11*g* R2," Oracle Corporation, Steven Lu.

Exadata V2, Sun Oracle Database Machine, Oracle.

Rich Niemiec, "Oracle RAC Tuning" (Collaborate and Oracle World Conference Paper).

Rich Niemiec, "Oracle 11*g* R1/R2 Best Features."

Oracle Data Warehousing Guide (Oracle Corporation).

Oracle Database Appliance, Oracle, October 2011.

"Oracle Enterprise Manager Deployment and High Availability Best Practices," Jim Viscusi. (Oracle Corporation), Jim Bulloch (Oracle Corporation), Steve Colebrook-Taylor (Barclays Global Investors).

Oracle Exadata Database Machine X2-2 and X2-8, Oracle, October 2011.

Oracle Exadata Implementation Workshop, Oracle Corporation, McLean, Virginia.

Oracle Exadata Storage Expansion Rack X2-2, Oracle, October 2011.

"Oracle Exalogic Elastic Cloud," an Oracle White Paper, September 2011.

Oracle Learning Library, multiple sessions/topics. (This resource is *very* good!!)

Oracle Server Concepts (Oracle Corporation).

Oracle Server Reference (Oracle Corporation).

Oracle Server Tuning (Oracle Corporation).

Pillar Axiom 600, Oracle, October 2011.

SPARC SuperCluster T4-4, Oracle, October 2011.

StorageTek SL8500 Modular Library System, Oracle, October 2011.

Sun Storage F5100 Flash Array, Oracle, October 2011.

Sun ZFS Storage Appliance, Oracle, October 2011.

Jake Van der Vort, *Oracle Parallel Query* (TUSC).

Websites:

http://download.oracle.com/docs/cd/E11882_01/server.112/e16541/parallel003.htm#VLDBG1455, www.tusc.com, www.oracle.com, and www.ioug.org.

Special thanks go to Madhu Tumma of Credit Suisse First Boston for writing the original section "Real Application Clusters" for this chapter. Jake Van der Vort did a major portion of the original parallel query chapter. Kevin Loney did the update to Oracle 9*i* for the original parallel query chapter. Brad Nash did most of the Oracle 10*g* update and added the RAC information. Special thanks to Murali Vallath for many contributions to this chapter and his great book on RAC.

CHAPTER
12

The V$ Views
(Developer and DBA)

Senior DBAs often tell junior DBAs that back in version 6 they used to know every V$ view by heart. Version 6 had only 23 V$ views, so the DBAs from the old days had it pretty easy. Oracle 9i had 259 V$ views and almost 400 X$ tables. Oracle 10gR2 (10.2.0.1.0) had 340 V$ views and 530 X$ tables. Oracle 11gR2 has 525 V$ views and 945 X$ tables (this number also depends on the version, OS, and options that you use as well).

Almost every great tuning or DBA product has one aspect in common. Most of them access the V$ views to get the insightful information that is retrieved about the database, individual queries, or an individual user. Accessing the V$ views has become quite prevalent due to the numerous presentations by Joe Trezzo and other V$ gurus. If you currently don't look at the V$ views, you don't know what you're missing. The V$ views look into the heart of the Oracle database. They are the link to moving from the average to the expert DBA.

Chapter 13 more extensively explores the X$ tables, which are the underlying part of the V$ views. Appendixes B and C provide information about the V$ views and also the creation scripts from the X$ tables. Unfortunately, I can't show every great V$ script due to space limitations, and I'll try not to duplicate things that are covered in depth in other chapters. Please check our web site (www.tusc.com) for the latest V$ scripts available.

Topics covered in this chapter include the following:

- Creating V$ views and granting access to them

- Getting a listing of all V$ views

- Getting a listing of the X$ scripts that make up the V$ views

- Examining the underlying objects that make up the DBA_ views

- Querying V$DATABASE to get database creation time and archiving information

- Learning about the Automatic Workload Repository (AWR)

- Querying V$LICENSE to view licensing limits and warning settings

- Accessing V$OPTION to view all options that have been installed

- Querying V$SGA and using MEMORY_TARGET to allocate basic memory for Oracle

- Querying V$SGASTAT to allocate detailed memory for Oracle

- Finding `init.ora` settings in V$PARAMETER

- Determining hit ratio for data (V$SYSSTAT and V$SYSMETRIC)

- Determining hit ratio for the data dictionary (V$ROWCACHE and V$SYSMETRIC)

- Determining hit ratio for shared SQL and PL/SQL (V$LIBRARYCACHE and V$SYSMETRIC)

- Using the Result Cache

- Deciding which objects need to be pinned and whether there is contiguous free memory (V$DB_OBJECT_CACHE)

- Finding the problem queries by accessing V$SESSION_LONGOPS, V$SQLAREA, V$SQLTEXT, V$SESSION, and V$SESS_IO

- Finding out what users are doing and which resources they are using

■ Identifying locking problems and killing the corresponding session

■ Finding users with multiple sessions

■ Balancing I/O using the views V$DATAFILE, V$FILESTAT, and DBA_DATA_FILES

■ Determining whether freelists are sufficient

■ Checking privileges and roles

■ Finding Waits with V$SESSION, V$SESSION_WAIT, V$SESSION_EVENT, V$SESSION_WAIT_CLASS, V$SESSION_WAIT_HISTORY, V$SYSTEM_EVENT, and V$SYSTEM_WAIT_CLASS

■ Using a table grouping the V$ views by category to match the TUSC poster

Creating and Granting Access to V$ Views

The V$ views are created by the `catalog.sql` script. As of Oracle 11gR2, there are approximately 525 V$ views. The actual number varies by version and platform. Here is the number of views from Oracle 6 to Oracle 11gR2:

Version	V$ Views	X$ Tables
6	23	(?)
7.1	72 (+213% vs. V6)	126
8.0	132	200
8.1	185 (+157% vs. V7)	271 (+115% vs. V7)
9.0	227	352
9.2	259 (+29% vs. 8*i*)	394 (+45% vs. 8*i*)
10.1	340	543
10.2	372 (+44% vs. 9*i*)	613 (+56% vs. 9*i*)
11.1	484	798
11.2	525 (+41% vs. 10*g*)	945 (+54% vs. 10*g*)

The views are all created with the prefix *V_$* and *GV_$*. Two of the views are created by the `catldr.sql` script, which is used for SQL*Loader direct load statistical information. The underlying view definitions (technically, these views are never created; their definitions are hard-coded into the binary) for each V$ and GV$ view can be seen in the V$ view named V$FIXED_VIEW_DEFINITION. The V$ views are created by selecting instance specific-information from GV$ views. For almost every V$ view, there is a corresponding GV$ view. GV$, or global V$, views contain the same information as the V$ views, but across all instances of a RAC database (each instance is identified by its instance ID). The GV$ views are created by selecting from one or more X$ tables. A view is created for each *V_$* and *GV_$* view to allow users to access the view. Users cannot access the actual V$ views (they actually access the V_$ views; the V$ objects are only visible to SYS). In other words, this method provides access to these views via a view on a view. The view name changes the prefix of each view to *V$*. Lastly, a public synonym is created for each view because the SYS user owns the tables.

The following listing shows an example of a V$ and GV$ view creation in the `cdfixed.sql` script called by the `catalog.sql` script.

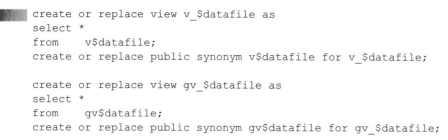

```
create or replace view v_$datafile as
select *
from    v$datafile;
create or replace public synonym v$datafile for v_$datafile;

create or replace view gv_$datafile as
select *
from    gv$datafile;
create or replace public synonym gv$datafile for gv_$datafile;
```

The complete sequence of events is detailed in the following steps.

1. The GV$ view definitions are created from the X$ tables when the database is created:

   ```
   create  or replace view gv$fixed_table as
   select  inst_id,kqftanam, kqftaobj, 'TABLE', indx
   from    x$kqfta
   union all
   select  inst_id,kqfvinam, kqfviobj, 'VIEW', 65537
   from    x$kqfvi
   union all
   select  inst_id,kqfdtnam, kqfdtobj, 'TABLE', 65537
   from    x$kqfdt;
   ```

2. The version-specific catalog script is executed as the following:

   ```
   SQL> @catalog (this is in the $ORACLE_HOME/rdbms/admin directory)
   ```

3. A V_$ view is created from the V$ view when the CREATE database script executes the following:

   ```
   create or replace view v_$fixed_table
   as
   select *
   from    v$fixed_table;
   ```

4. A new V$ synonym is created on the V_$ view:

   ```
   create or replace public synonym v$fixed_table for v_$fixed_table;
   ```

5. A new GV$ synonym is created on the GV_$ view:

   ```
   create or replace public synonym gv$fixed_table for gv_$fixed_table;
   ```

TIP
The V$ views that are accessed by SYSTEM are actually synonyms that point to the V_$ views that are views of the original V$ views based on the X$ tables. (Better read that one again!)

The only operation that you can perform on these views is a SELECT. To provide access to the V$ views, you must grant access to the underlying V_$ view.

You cannot grant access to the V$ views (even as the SYS user), however:

```
connect sys/change_on_install as sysdba

Grant select on v$fixed_table to Richie;
ORA-02030: can only select from fixed tables/views.
```

Although the error message (following the preceding code) for attempting to grant access to V$FIXED_TABLE is erroneous, the GRANT is not allowed. You may, however, grant access to the underlying V_$ view that is behind the V$ view.

To connect to the SYS superuser, use the following:

```
Connect sys/change_on_install as sysdba
Connected.
```

To grant access to an underlying view to the desired user, use the following:

```
grant select on v_$fixed_table to Richie;
Grant succeeded.
```

To connect as the desired user, use this:

```
conn    Richie/Rich
Connected.
```

Access the V$FIXED_TABLE view via the synonym V$FIXED_TABLE, which is created for V_$FIXED_TABLE with the following:

```
select count(*)
from    v$fixed_table;

COUNT(*)
--------
    1968
```

You still *can't* access the V_$FIXED_TABLE even though that grant was made (SYS can access it, however):

```
select count(*)
from    v_$fixed_table;
ORA-00942: table or view does not exist.
```

You *can* access the V_$FIXED_VIEW if you preface it with SYS:

```
conn    Richie/Rich
select count(*)
from    SYS.v_$fixed_table;

COUNT(*)
--------
    1968
```

To avoid confusion, give access to the V_$ views and notify the DBA that he or she has access to the V$ views. Using this method, you may give access to the V$ view information without giving out the password for the SYS or SYSTEM accounts. The key is granting SELECT access to the original SYS owned V_$ view.

TIP
When other DBAs need access to the V$ view information, but not the SYS or SYSTEM passwords, grant the user access to the V_$ views. The user may then access the V$ views that have public synonyms to the V_$ views. However, scripts could always be written to query the SYS. V_$ views directly, to avoid the performance cost of dereferencing the public synonym, but this savings is small.

CAUTION
You should grant non-DBA users privileges to the V$ views only as needed, and use caution. Remember, performance costs come with querying the V$ views, and the larger your environment, the greater those costs.

Obtaining a Count and Listing of All V$ Views

To get a count of all V$ views for a given version of Oracle, query the V$FIXED_TABLE view. The number of V$ views continues to change even within the same version. The examples that follow display the V$ view queries for Oracle 11g. The frontier in the world of the V$ views continues to expand with each version of Oracle.

To get a count of V$ views, query as shown here:

```
select  count(*)
from    v$fixed_table
where   name like 'V%';

COUNT(*)
--------
     525
```

Many of the V$ views continue to be undocumented. The methods of exploring information continue to expand in Oracle because the number of views continues to expand. In Oracle 8 (now desupported), the GV$ views were introduced. The GV$ (global V$) views are the same as the V$ views with an additional column for the instance ID.

To get a list of GV$ views, query as shown here (this is partial listing; you'll find a complete list in Appendix B):

```
select  name
from    v$fixed_table
where   name like 'GV%'
order by name;
```

```
NAME
---------------------------------
GV$ACCESS
GV$ACTIVE_INSTANCES
GV$ACTIVE_SERVICES
GV$ACTIVE_SESS_POOL_MTH
GV$ACTIVE_SESSION_HISTORY
GV$ADVISOR_PROGRESS
GV$ALERT_TYPES
GV$AQ
GV$ARCHIVE
GV$ARCHIVE_DEST
GV$ARCHIVE_DEST_STATUS
GV$ARCHIVE_GAP
GV$ARCHIVE_PROCESSES
GV$ARCHIVED_LOG
...
```

TIP
Query V$FIXED_TABLE to obtain a listing of all GV$ and V$ views in the database. The GV$ views are the exact same as the V$ views, except the instance ID contains an identifier, and the GV$ views contain data for all instances of an Oracle RAC database.

Getting a Listing for the X$ Scripts That Make Up the V$ Views

To understand where the V$ view information comes from, query the underlying X$ tables (see Chapter 13 for X$ table information). At times, querying the underlying X$ tables may be advantageous because the V$ views are often the join of several X$ tables. The X$ tables are very cryptic because they are similar to the underlying table constructs of the Oracle data dictionary. Oracle creates V$ views in the SGA to allow users to examine the information stored in the X$ tables in a more readable format. In fact, when SELECTs are performed against the V$ views, the SELECTs are actually retrieving information out of the SGA—and more specifically, out of the X$ tables, which are truly memory constructs that interface the software code constructs (which is why they are so cryptic).

With the knowledge of the V$ view underlying a given SELECT statement, you have the capability to create customized views; simply copy the existing V$ view underlying the SELECT statement and modify it or create a new customized SELECT on the X$ tables. This technique allows more selective and more optimized queries. The next listing is used to access the underlying query to the X$ tables. To get a listing of the X$ tables that make up the V$ views, you must access the V$FIXED_TABLE_DEFINITION view (output formatted for readability).

```
select    *
from      v$fixed_view_definition
where     view_name = 'GV$FIXED_TABLE';
```

Output

```
VIEW_NAME        VIEW_DEFINITION
--------------   -----------------------------------------------------------
GV$FIXED_TABLE   select  inst_id, kqftanam, kqftaobj, 'TABLE', indx
                 from    x$kqfta
                 union all
                 select  inst_id, kqfvinam, kqfviobj, 'VIEW', 65537
                 from    x$kqfvi
                 union all
                 select  inst_id, kqfdtnam, kqfdtobj, 'TABLE', 65537
                 from    x$kqfdt
```

TIP
*Access the V$FIXED_VIEW_DEFINITION view to get all information
about the underlying X$ tables that make up a V$ view.*

Also note that, as of Oracle 8, there are indexes on the underlying X$ tables to provide faster execution of queries performed on the V$ views (amazing that it took Oracle until version 8 to use indexes!). You can view the index information on the underlying X$ tables through the V$INDEXED_FIXED_COLUMN view (see Chapter 13 for more information).

Examining the Underlying Objects That Make Up the DBA_ Views

Some people think the DBA_ views also come from the X$ tables and/or the V$ views. They actually come from Oracle's underlying database tables (although some access the X$ tables as well). To look at the objects that make up the DBA_ views, access DBA_VIEWS, as shown in this listing:

NOTE
You may need to set long 2000000 to see all of this output.

```
select text
from   dba_views
where  view_name='DBA_IND_PARTITIONS';

TEXT
--------------------------------------------------------------------------------
select u.name, io.name, 'NO', io.subname, 0, ip.hiboundval, ip.hiboundlen

SQL> set long 2000000
(RUN IT AGAIN)

select text
from   dba_views
where  view_name='DBA_IND_PARTITIONS';
```

```
TEXT
--------------------------------------------------------------------------------
select u.name, io.name, 'NO', io.subname, 0,
       ip.hiboundval, ip.hiboundlen, ip.part#,
       decode(bitand(ip.flags, 1), 1, 'UNUSABLE', 'USABLE'), ts.name,
       ip.pctfree$,ip.initrans, ip.maxtrans,
       decode(bitand(ip.flags, 65536), 65536,
              ds.initial_stg * ts.blocksize, s.iniexts * ts.blocksize),
       decode(bitand(ip.flags, 65536), 65536,
              ds.next_stg * ts.blocksize, s.extsize * ts.blocksize),
       decode(bitand(ip.flags, 65536), 65536, ds.minext_stg, s.minexts),
       deode(bitand(ip.flags, 65536), 65536, ds.maxext_stg, s.maxexts),
       decode(bitand(ip.flags, 65536), 65536,
              ds.maxsiz_stg * ts.blocksize,
              decode(bitand(s.spare1, 4194304), 4194304, bitmapranges, NULL)),
       decode(bitand(ts.flags, 3), 1, to_number(NULL),
              decode(bitand(ip.flags, 65536), 65536, ds.pctinc_stg, s.extpct)),
       decode(bitand(ts.flags, 32), 32, to_number(NULL),
              decode(bitand(ip.flags, 65536), 65536,
                     ds.frlins_stg, decode(s.lists, 0, 1, s.lists))),
       decode(bitand(ts.flags, 32), 32, to_number(NULL),
              decode(bitand(ip.flags, 65536), 65536,
                     ds.maxins_stg, decode(s.groups, 0, 1, s.groups))),
       decode(mod(trunc(ip.flags / 4), 2), 0, 'YES', 'NO'),
       decode(bitand(ip.flags, 1024), 0, 'DISABLED', 1024, 'ENABLED', null),
       ip.blevel, ip.leafcnt, ip.distkey, ip.lblkkey, ip.dblkkey,
       ip.clufac, ip.rowcnt, ip.samplesize, ip.analyzetime,
       decode(bitand(decode(bitand(ip.flags, 65536), 65536, ds.bfp_stg, s.cacheh
int), 3),
              1, 'KEEP', 2, 'RECYCLE', 'DEFAULT'),
       decode(bitand(decode(bitand(ip.flags, 65536), 65536, ds.bfp_stg, s.cacheh
int), 12)/4,
              1, 'KEEP', 2, 'NONE', 'DEFAULT'),
       decode(bitand(decode(bitand(ip.flags, 65536), 65536, ds.bfp_stg, s.cacheh
int), 48)/16,
              1, 'KEEP', 2, 'NONE', 'DEFAULT'),
       decode(bitand(ip.flags, 8), 0, 'NO', 'YES'), ip.pctthres$,
       decode(bitand(ip.flags, 16), 0, 'NO', 'YES'),'','',
       decode(bitand(ip.flags, 32768), 32768, 'YES', 'NO'),
       decode(bitand(ip.flags, 65536), 65536, 'NO', 'YES')
from   obj$ io, indpartv$ ip, ts$ ts, sys.seg$ s, user$ u, ind$ i, tab$ t,
       sys.deferred_stg$ ds
where  io.obj# = ip.obj# and ts.ts# = ip.ts# and ip.file#=s.file#(+) and
       ip.block#=s.block#(+) and ip.ts#=s.ts#(+) and io.owner# = u.user# and
       i.obj# = ip.bo# and i.bo# = t.obj# and ip.obj# = ds.obj#(+) and
       i.type# != 9 and
       bitand(t.trigflag, 1073741824) != 1073741824
       and io.namespace = 4 and io.remoteowner IS NULL and io.linkname IS NULL
       union all
select u.name, io.name, 'YES', io.subname, icp.subpartcnt,
       icp.hiboundval, icp.hiboundlen, icp.part#, 'N/A', ts.name,
       icp.defpctfree, icp.definitrans, icp.defmaxtrans,
       icp.definiexts, icp.defextsize, icp.defminexts, icp.defmaxexts,
       icp.defmaxsize, icp.defextpct, icp.deflists, icp.defgroups,
```

```
            decode(icp.deflogging, 0, 'NONE', 1, 'YES', 2, 'NO', 'UNKNOWN'),
            decode(bitand(icp.flags, 1024), 0, 'DISABLED', 1024, 'ENABLED', null),
            icp.blevel, icp.leafcnt, icp.distkey, icp.lblkkey, icp.dblkkey,
            icp.clufac, icp.rowcnt, icp.samplesize, icp.analyzetime,
            decode(bitand(icp.defbufpool, 3), 1, 'KEEP', 2, 'RECYCLE', 'DEFAULT'),
            decode(bitand(icp.defbufpool, 12)/4, 1, 'KEEP', 2, 'NONE', 'DEFAULT'),
            decode(bitand(icp.defbufpool, 48)/16, 1, 'KEEP', 2, 'NONE', 'DEFAULT'),
            decode(bitand(icp.flags, 8), 0, 'NO', 'YES'), TO_NUMBER(NULL),
            decode(bitand(icp.flags, 16), 0, 'NO', 'YES'),'','',
            decode(bitand(icp.flags, 32768), 32768, 'YES', 'NO'), 'N/A'
from        obj$ io, indcompartv$ icp, ts$ ts, user$ u, ind$ i, tab$ t
where       io.obj# = icp.obj# and icp.defts# = ts.ts# (+) and
            u.user# = io.owner# and i.obj# = icp.bo# and i.bo# = t.obj# and
            i.type# != 9 and
            bitand(t.trigflag, 1073741824) != 1073741824
            and io.namespace = 4 and io.remoteowner IS NULL and io.linkname IS NULL
      union all
select u.name, io.name, 'NO', io.subname, 0,
            ip.hiboundval, ip.hiboundlen, ip.part#,
            decode(bitand(ip.flags, 1), 1, 'UNUSABLE',
                    decode(bitand(ip.flags, 4096), 4096, 'INPROGRS', 'USABLE')),
            null, ip.pctfree$, ip.initrans, ip.maxtrans,
            0, 0, 0, 0, 0, 0, 0, 0,
            decode(mod(trunc(ip.flags / 4), 2), 0, 'YES', 'NO'),
            decode(bitand(ip.flags, 1024), 0, 'DISABLED', 1024, 'ENABLED', null),
            ip.blevel, ip.leafcnt, ip.distkey, ip.lblkkey, ip.dblkkey,
            ip.clufac, ip.rowcnt, ip.samplesize, ip.analyzetime,
            'DEFAULT', 'DEFAULT', 'DEFAULT',
            decode(bitand(ip.flags, 8), 0, 'NO', 'YES'), ip.pctthres$,
            decode(bitand(ip.flags, 16), 0, 'NO', 'YES'),
            decode(i.type#,
                    9, decode(bitand(ip.flags, 8192), 8192, 'FAILED', 'VALID'),
                    ''),
            ipp.parameters,
            decode(bitand(ip.flags, 32768), 32768, 'YES', 'NO'),
            decode(bitand(ip.flags, 65536), 65536, 'NO', 'YES')
from        obj$ io, indpartv$ ip,  user$ u, ind$ i, indpart_param$ ipp, tab$ t
where       io.obj# = ip.obj# and io.owner# = u.user# and
            ip.bo# = i.obj# and ip.obj# = ipp.obj# and i.bo# = t.obj# and
            bitand(t.trigflag, 1073741824) != 1073741824
            and io.namespace = 4 and io.remoteowner IS NULL and io.linkname IS NULL
```

Never modify the underlying objects; many DBAs have corrupted their database in this manner. Do *not* do the following here, but note that it is possible:

```
Connect sys/change_on_install as sysdba
Connected.

DELETE FROM OBJAUTH$;  -- Don't do this! If you commit this, your database is
over!
34065 rows deleted.

Rollback;
Rollback complete
```

TIP
*The DBA_ views are not derived from the X$ tables or V$ views. The
fact that you can delete rows from OBJ$ is a great reason to never be
the SYS superuser.*

Using Helpful V$ Scripts

The rest of this chapter is dedicated to scripts that are helpful in analyzing different areas of the
Oracle database. Many of these scripts are dynamic and provide valuable insight into areas of the
database that you may need to analyze to determine resource contention at a point in time.
Typically, the result is that the DBA performs some operation to eliminate the contention
immediately by tuning a query or increasing an `init.ora` parameter to reduce the resource
contention in the future. Revoking access to a given ad-hoc query user, or restricting his or her
system resource use with profiles, could be an emergency option as well. The next four sections
include scripts that retrieve the following:

- Basic database information

- Information about the Automatic Workload Repository (AWR)

- Basic licensing information

- Database options installed in your database

Basic Database Information

Getting the basic information about your instance is usually as easy as logging in to SQL*Plus
because all of the information shows in the banner at that time. If you would like to see the full
banner header, you can access the V$VERSION view to display the banner. The following listing
shows a quick way to see the version you are using as well as other information:

Version Information:

```
select *
from   v$version;
```

Output from 11.1 Testing:

```
BANNER
---------------------------------------------------------------------------
Oracle Database 11g Enterprise Edition Release 11.1.0.6.0 - Production
PL/SQL Release 11.1.0.6.0 - Production
CORE    11.1.0.6.0      Production
TNS for 32-bit Windows: Version 11.1.0.6.0 - Production
NLSRTL Version 11.1.0.6.0 - Production
```

Output from 11.2 Testing:

```
BANNER
--------------------------------------------------------------------------------
Oracle Database 11g Enterprise Edition Release 11.2.0.1.0 - 64bit Production
PL/SQL Release 11.2.0.1.0 - Production
CORE   11.2.0.1.0  Production
TNS for 64-bit Windows: Version 11.2.0.1.0 - Production
NLSRTL Version 11.2.0.1.0 - Production
```

Database Information:

```
select name, created, log_mode
from   v$database;

NAME     CREATED    LOG_MODE
-------- ---------- ------------
ORCL     10-JAN-11  ARCHIVELOG
```

Accessing V$DATABASE gives you basic information concerning the database. The most important information in the output is to ensure that you are in the desired ARCHIVELOG mode. The output also gives you the exact date when the database was created, as you can see in the preceding listing.

Another way to view the archive log status for the database is to simply use the ARCHIVE LOG LIST command as the SYS user in SQL*Plus:

```
SQL> archive log list

Database log mode              Archive Mode
Automatic archival             Enabled
Archive destination            USE_DB_RECOVERY_FILE_DEST
Oldest online log sequence     41
Current log sequence           43
```

TIP
Query V$VERSION and V$DATABASE to view basic database information such as the version, to find out when your database was created, and to find out basic archiving information.

Basic Automatic Workload Repository (AWR) Information
With the advent of the Automatic Workload Repository (AWR), you now have many areas to watch. By default, the repository is populated every hour with a retention period of seven days. Here are some queries that are worth knowing for the AWR (the MMON background process is used to flush AWR data from memory to disk). See Chapter 5 for detailed information on AWR, licensing related to the V$ views based on the AWR, and using information from the AWR for tuning purposes.

How much space is the AWR using?

```
select occupant_name, occupant_desc, space_usage_kbytes
from   v$sysaux_occupants
where  occupant_name like '%AWR%';

OCCUPANT_NAME OCCUPANT_DESC                                             SPACE_USAGE_KBYTES
------------- --------------------------------------------------------- ------------------
SM/AWR        Server Manageability - Automatic Workload Repository                  108992
```

What's the oldest AWR information on the system?

```
select dbms_stats.get_stats_history_availability
from   dual;

GET_STATS_HISTORY_AVAILABILITY
-------------------------------------------------------------------------------
02-APR-11 09.30.34.291000000 AM -06:00
```

What's the retention period for AWR information?

```
select dbms_stats.get_stats_history_retention
from   dual;

GET_STATS_HISTORY_RETENTION
---------------------------
                         31
```

To change the retention period for AWR information to 15 days:

```
EXEC dbms_stats.alter_stats_history_retention(15);


select dbms_stats.get_stats_history_retention
from   dual;

GET_STATS_HISTORY_RETENTION
---------------------------
                         15
```

TIP
*Query V$SYSAUX_OCCUPANTS to ensure that the Automatic
Workload Repository (AWR) isn't taking up too much space. Use
DBMS_STATS to check history and retention.*

Basic Licensing Information

The V$LICENSE view allows a DBA to monitor system activity in terms of overall database
licensing, warnings, and current use at any time. It provides a DBA with a log of the maximum
number of concurrent sessions at any time, which allows a company to ensure it is licensed

properly. The current number of sessions is displayed along with the session warning level and session maximum level. A session warning level of 0 indicates that the `init.ora` session warning parameter was not set; therefore, no warning message displays. A session maximum level of 0 indicates that the `init.ora` session maximum parameter was not set; therefore, there is no limit on the number of sessions. As of 10.2, Oracle no longer offers per-session licensing, only per user and per CPU. So LICENSE_MAX_SESSIONS and LICENSE_SESSIONS_WARNING are now deprecated. You can still use them to prevent heavy login events, however.

As a DBA, execute the script periodically to find out the actual number of sessions on the system throughout the day. Setting the `init.ora` parameter LICENSE_MAX_SESSIONS = 110 limits the sessions to 110. Setting the `init.ora` parameter LICENSE_SESSIONS_WARNING = 100 gives every user past the 100th a warning message so they will (hopefully) notify the DBA that the system is closing in on a problem. The LICENSE_MAX_USERS `init.ora` parameter sets the number of named users who can be created in the database. In this next listing, there is no limit on the number of users and the value is set to 0.

```
select *
from   v$license;
```

SESS_MAX	SESS_WARNING	SESS_CURRENT	SESS_HIGHWATER	USERS_MAX
110	100	44	105	0

(selected columns listed above)

Database Options Installed in Your Database

The script shown next describes what options are installed on your database and are available for use. If you have purchased a product that does not show up in this list, you may have incorrectly installed it. Query the V$OPTION view to check for installed products or log on to SQL*Plus to see the products that are installed (does your open source database do all this?).

```
select *
from   v$option;
```

To get the following output, you need to order by PARAMETER:

Output

PARAMETER	VALUE
Active Data Guard	TRUE
Advanced Compression	TRUE
Advanced replication	TRUE
Application Role	TRUE
Automatic Storage Management	FALSE
Backup Encryption	TRUE
Basic Compression	TRUE
Bit-mapped indexes	TRUE
Block Change Tracking	TRUE
Block Media Recovery	TRUE

Change Data Capture	TRUE
Coalesce Index	TRUE
Connection multiplexing	TRUE
Connection pooling	TRUE
DICOM	TRUE
Data Mining	TRUE
Database queuing	TRUE
Database resource manager	TRUE
Deferred Segment Creation	TRUE
Duplexed backups	TRUE
Enterprise User Security	TRUE
Export transportable tablespaces	TRUE
Fast-Start Fault Recovery	TRUE
File Mapping	TRUE
Fine-grained Auditing	TRUE
Fine-grained access control	TRUE
Flashback Data Archive	TRUE
Flashback Database	TRUE
Flashback Table	TRUE
Incremental backup and recovery	TRUE
Instead-of triggers	TRUE
Java	TRUE
Join index	TRUE
Managed Standby	TRUE
Materialized view rewrite	TRUE
Materialized view warehouse refresh	TRUE
OLAP	TRUE
OLAP Window Functions	TRUE
Objects	TRUE
Online Index Build	TRUE
Online Redefinition	TRUE
Oracle Data Guard	TRUE
Oracle Database Vault	FALSE
Oracle Label Security	FALSE
Parallel backup and recovery	TRUE
Parallel execution	TRUE
Parallel load	TRUE
Partitioning	TRUE
Plan Stability	TRUE
Point-in-time tablespace recovery	TRUE
Proxy authentication/authorization	TRUE
Real Application Clusters	FALSE
Real Application Testing	TRUE
Result Cache	TRUE
SQL Plan Management	TRUE
Sample Scan	TRUE
SecureFiles Encryption	TRUE
Server Flash Cache	TRUE
Spatial	TRUE
Streams Capture	TRUE
Transparent Application Failover	TRUE

```
Transparent Data Encryption          TRUE
Trial Recovery                       TRUE
Unused Block Compression             TRUE
XStream                              TRUE

67 rows selected
```

The previous listing shows that the database has the PARTITIONING option installed (TRUE), but it does not have Real Application Clusters (RAC) installed (FALSE). Also note that Automatic Storage Management (ASM) is FALSE because this is a test environment; however, ASM would almost always be used on most production systems.

TIP
Query the V$OPTION view to retrieve the Oracle options you have installed. The V$VERSION view gives you the versions of the installed base options.

Summary of Memory Allocated (V$SGA)

V$SGA gives the summary information for the System Global Area (SGA) memory structures of your system, as shown in this next listing. The "Database Buffers" is the number of bytes allocated to memory for data. It comes from the `init.ora` parameter DB_CACHE_SIZE, if set. The "Redo Buffers" comes primarily from the value of the `init.ora` parameter LOG_BUFFER, which is used to buffer changed records and flushed to the REDO logs whenever a COMMIT is issued.

Consider this smaller SGA output listed using the SHO SGA command:

```
SQL> SHO SGA

Total System Global Area   535662592 bytes
Fixed Size                   1334380 bytes
Variable Size              201327508 bytes
Database Buffers           327155712 bytes
Redo Buffers                 5844992 bytes
```

Automatic Memory Management (AMM) and MEMORY_TARGET

Oracle 9i simplified PGA memory management by introducing a PGA_AGGREGATE_TARGET parameter. Oracle10g simplified SGA memory management by providing Automatic Shared Memory Management (ASMM) and by providing the SGA_TARGET parameter. Oracle 11g offers Automatic Memory Management (AMM) that unifies both PGA memory and SGA memory in a single parameter setting, the MEMORY_TARGET parameter (see Chapter 4 for more information on this). As a result,

Oracle 11*g* provides a data dictionary table called V$MEMORY_DYNAMIC_COMPONENTS. Here is a query that shows the dynamic components using AMM parameters:

```
select  component,current_size,min_size,max_size
from    v$memory_dynamic_components
where   current_size !=0;
```

```
COMPONENT                          CURRENT_SIZE   MIN_SIZE   MAX_SIZE
---------------------------------  ------------   --------   --------

shared pool                         184549376    184549376  184549376
large pool                            4194304      4194304    4194304
java pool                            12582912     12582912   12582912
SGA Target                          536870912    536870912  536870912
DEFAULT buffer cache                327155712    327155712  327155712
PGA Target                          318767104    318767104  318767104
```

6 rows selected.

The V$MEMORY_TARGET_ADVICE view provides tuning advice for setting the MEMORY_TARGET parameter.

Issue the following query to obtain advice on the effects of increasing or shrinking the MEMORY_TARGET parameter:

```
select   *
from     v$memory_target_advice
order by memory_size;
```

MEMORY_SIZE	MEMORY_SIZE_FACTOR	ESTD_DB_TIME	ESTD_DB_TIME_FACTOR	VERSION
204	.25	382	1	0
408	.5	382	1	0
612	.75	382	1	0
816	1	382	1	0
1020	1.25	382	1	0
1224	1.5	382	1	0
1428	1.75	382	1	0
1632	2	382	1	0

8 rows selected.

When MEMORY_TARGET is set, SGA_TARGET and PGA_AGGREGATE_TARGET initially have zero values (automatically set) unless you set minimum values. To use Automatic Shared Memory Management (ASMM), set SGA_TARGET to a nonzero value.

Consider a larger SGA in this example and a different way to show it:

```
COLUMN value FORMAT 999,999,999,999

select *
from   v$sga;
```

```
NAME                          VALUE
-------------------- ----------------
Fixed Size                  2,188,768
Variable Size           4,513,073,696
Database Buffers        2,315,255,808
Redo Buffers               17,420,288
```

If SGA_TARGET is used, it dynamically resizes internally:

```
select (
    (select sum(value) from v$sga) -
    (select current_size from v$sga_dynamic_free_memory)
    ) "SGA_TARGET"
from dual;


SGA_TARGET
----------
4448796672
```

This output indicates a relatively large SGA (over 4.5G) with a buffer cache that includes DB_CACHE_SIZE, DB_KEEP_CACHE_SIZE, and DB_RECYCLE_CACHE_SIZE of over 2.5G. As discussed in Chapters 1 and 4, I could have just set the SGA_TARGET to something like 4.5G and set the other parameters to enforce minimum sizes only. The predominant part of the Variable Size category is the buffer cache and shared pool. (The shared pool for this SGA is 1G.) This SGA is over 4.5G of the actual physical system memory in the preceding listing. This information is also given in the AWR or Statspack Report (still available in 11gR2; see Chapter 14) and can also be displayed by issuing an SHOW SGA command as the SYS superuser.

TIP
Access the V$SGA view to get a baseline idea of the system's physical memory allocated for data, shared pool, large pool, java pool, and log buffering of Oracle.

Detailed Memory Allocated (V$SGASTAT)

A more detailed V$ view query to retrieve information about memory allocation for the SGA is in the V$SGASTAT view. This view provides dynamic information about SGA and memory resources. (It changes as the database is accessed.) This statement describes the SGA sizes at a detailed level. The records FIXED_SGA, BUFFER_CACHE, and LOG_BUFFER are the same values for both V$SGA and V$SGASTAT. The remaining records in V$SGASTAT make up the only other V$SGA record (the Variable Size or Shared Pool record).

Fixed Size (V$SGA)	= FIXED_SGA (V$SGASTAT)
Database Buffers (V$SGA)	= BUFFER_CACHE (V$SGASTAT)
Redo Buffers (V$SGA)	= LOG_BUFFER (V$SGASTAT)
Variable Size (V$SGA)	= 872 other records (V$SGASTAT)

In Oracle 9.2, V$SGASTAT had only 43 total records; in 10*g*, it had 602; and in 11*g*, it has 875, as shown here (partial listing only):

```
select  *
from    v$sgastat;

POOL           NAME                                BYTES
-----------    -------------------------    ----------
               fixed_sga                       2188768
               buffer_cache                 2315255808
               log_buffer                     17420288
               shared_io_pool                973078528
shared pool    hot latch diagnostics               160
shared pool    transaction                      681560
shared pool    vproblem_bucket                     848
shared pool    vnot_exist_incident                3200
shared pool    KCB buffer wait statistic          3352
shared pool    KCB tablespace encryption          1088
shared pool    invalid low rba queue              4096
shared pool    bt_qentry                         28512
shared pool    ksunfy: system-global sta          4840
shared pool    v_ipsprbcnt                         664
shared pool    vproblem_int                       2448
shared pool    PLDIA                           7175064
shared pool    PRTDS                             80680
shared pool    execution ID memory                3352
shared pool    DISPATCHERS INFO                   2496
shared pool    CCUR                           49301552
shared pool    SQLA                          242679584
shared pool    trace buf hdr xtend                 208
etc...
875 rows selected
```

This information is also given in the AWR or Statspack Report (see Chapter 14), along with the starting and ending values over the duration of the Statspack Report.

TIP
Accessing V$SGASTAT gives you a detailed breakdown for the Oracle SGA and breaks down all buckets for the shared pool allocation.

Finding spfile.ora/init.ora Settings in V$PARAMETER

The script in the next listing displays the init.ora parameters for your system. It also provides information on each parameter that identifies whether the current value was the default value (ISDEFAULT=TRUE). It further shows whether the parameter is modifiable with the ALTER SESSION command and with the ALTER SYSTEM command (ISSYS_MODIFIABLE=IMMEDIATE). You can modify these with the ALTER SESSION and ALTER SYSTEM commands instead of modifying the init.ora file and shutting down and restarting the instance. The example in this listing displays some of the init.ora parameters that you can modify with one of the ALTER commands. (IMMEDIATE means it can be modified and it will take effect immediately.) Note that you can use an ALTER command, but for some parameters, such as O7_DICTIONARY_ACCESSIBILITY, you can only use an ALTER SYSTEM . . . SCOPE=SPFILE command to modify it, and *then* you have to bounce the database for it to take effect. The query here shows the parameter values in effect for the instance (not what is necessarily in the parameter file):

```
select     name, value, isdefault, isses_modifiable,
           issys_modifiable
from       v$parameter
order by   name;
```

Query of V$PARAMETER

NAME	VALUE	ISDEFAULT	ISSES	ISSYS_MOD
O7_DICTIONARY_ACCESSIBILITY	FALSE	TRUE	FALSE	FALSE
active_instance_count		TRUE	FALSE	FALSE
aq_tm_processes	0	TRUE	FALSE	IMMEDIATE
archive_lag_target	0	TRUE	FALSE	IMMEDIATE
asm_diskgroups		TRUE	FALSE	IMMEDIATE
asm_diskstring		TRUE	FALSE	IMMEDIATE
asm_power_limit	1	TRUE	TRUE	IMMEDIATE
...partial output listing)				

Version-dependent columns are also available.

TIP
Query V$PARAMETER to get the current values for the init.ora parameters. V$PARAMETER also shows which init.ora parameters have been changed from their original defaults: ISDEFAULT=FALSE. It also shows which parameters may be changed only for a given session if ISSES_MODIFIABLE=TRUE. Lastly, it shows which parameters may be changed without shutting down and restarting the database for ISSYS_MODIFIABLE=IMMEDIATE as well as ISSYS_MODIFIABLE= DEFERRED for a parameter that is enforced for all new logins but not currently logged-on sessions. If the parameter ISSYS_MODIFIABLE= FALSE, then the instance must be shut down and restarted for the parameter to take effect. See Chapter 4 for more information on the initialization parameters.

Determining Hit Ratio for Data (V$SYSSTAT & V$SYSMETRIC)

Query V$SYSSTAT (as shown in the next listing) to see how often your data is being read from memory. V$SYSSTAT gives the hit ratio for the setting of the database block buffers. This information can help you identify when your system needs more data buffers (DB_CACHE_SIZE) or when a system is not tuned very well. (Both lead to low hit ratios.) Generally, you should ensure the read hit ratio is greater than 95 percent. Increasing the hit ratio on your system from 98 percent to 99 percent could mean performance that is 100+ percent faster (depending on what is causing the disk reads).

```
select 1-(sum(decode(name, 'physical reads', value,0))/
          (sum(decode(name, 'db block gets', value,0)) +
          (sum(decode(name, 'consistent gets', value,0)))))
          "Read Hit Ratio"
from      v$sysstat;


Read Hit Ratio
--------------
    .996558641
```

In *10g and 11g, you can also go directly to AWR information in V$SYSMETRIC:*

The V$SYSMETRIC view displays the system metric values captured for the most current time interval. It does this for a 60-second interval (INTSIZE_CSEC DOLUMN = 6017) and another for a 15-second duration (INTSIZE_CSEC DOLUMN = 1504); both are displayed in hundredths of a second. The following query displays the two rows:

```
select metric_name, to_char(begin_time,'DD-MON-YY HH24MISS') BEGIN_TIME,
       to_char(end_time, 'DD-MON-YY HH24MISS') END_TIME, value
from    v$sysmetric
where   metric_name like 'Buffer Cache Hit Ratio';
```

METRIC_NAME	BEGIN_TIME	END_TIME	VALUE
Buffer Cache Hit Ratio	18-NOV-08 165342	18-NOV-08 165442	99.85
Buffer Cache Hit Ratio	18-NOV-08 165512	18-NOV-08 165527	100.00

In addition to the V$SYSMETRIC view, V$SYSMETRIC_SUMMARY displays a summary of system metric values for the long-duration system metrics (the 60-second ones) along with minimum, maximum, and average values over a 60-second duration. V$SYSMETRIC_HISTORY displays the last 90 minutes of 60-second duration metric values.

The hit ratio in this listing is very good, but that does not mean the system is perfectly tuned. A high hit ratio could mean that overly indexed queries are being used. If this hit ratio is well below 95 percent, you may need to increase the instance parameter, DB_CACHE_SIZE, or tune some of the queries that are causing disk reads (if possible and efficient to do so). One exception to this (many others are covered in Chapter 4) is when the distribution of data within the individual blocks is greatly skewed. Despite this possibility, hit ratios less than 90 percent almost always involve systems that are poorly tuned—other than those that are built in a Petri dish by someone who has built an extremely rare balance of data within each block (see Chapter 4 for additional information on data hit ratios).

You can also use the new V$DB_CACHE_ADVICE view to help you resize the data cache if you feel it is necessary. The next listing creates a list of values that shows you the effects of larger and smaller data caches and the resulting effect on physical reads:

```
column buffers_for_estimate format 999,999,999 heading 'Buffers'
column estd_physical_read_factor format 999.90 heading 'Estd Phys|Read Fact'
column estd_physical_reads format 999,999,999 heading 'Estd Phys| Reads'
```

```
SELECT   size_for_estimate, buffers_for_estimate,
         estd_physical_read_factor, estd_physical_reads
FROM     V$DB_CACHE_ADVICE
WHERE    name = 'DEFAULT'
AND      block_size =
              (SELECT value
               FROM   V$PARAMETER
               WHERE  name = 'db_block_size')
AND      advice_status = 'ON';
```

SIZE_FOR_ESTIMATE	Buffers	Estd Phys Read Fact	Estd Phys Reads
4	501	63.59	243,243,371
8	1,002	45.65	174,614,755
12	1,503	2.61	9,965,760
16	2,004	1.00	3,824,900
20	2,505	.76	2,909,026
24	3,006	.57	2,165,817
28	3,507	.41	1,555,860
32	4,008	.33	1,253,696

Determining Hit Ratio for the Data Dictionary (V$ROWCACHE)

You use the V$ROWCACHE view (as in this next listing) to find how often the data dictionary calls are effectively hitting the memory cache allocated by the SHARED_POOL_SIZE instance parameter. Chapter 4 discusses this in detail. The only goal here is to review the V$ view access. If the dictionary hit ratio is not adequate, the overall system performance suffers greatly.

```
select   sum(gets), sum(getmisses),(1 - (sum(getmisses) / (sum(gets)
         + sum(getmisses)))) * 100 HitRate
from     v$rowcache;
```

SUM(GETS)	SUM(GETMISSES)	HITRATE
110673	670	99.9982558

In 10g and 11g, you can also go directly to AWR information in V$SYSMETRIC:

```
select metric_name, value
from   v$sysmetric
where  metric_name = 'Row Cache Hit Ratio';
```

METRIC_NAME	VALUE
Row Cache Hit Ratio	99.99

The recommended hit ratio is 95 percent or greater. If the hit ratio falls below this percentage, it indicates that the SHARED_POOL_SIZE parameter may need to be increased. But remember, you saw in the V$SGASTAT view that the shared pool is made up of many pieces, of which this is only one.

NOTE
Environments that make heavy use of public synonyms may struggle to get their dictionary cache hit rate higher than 75 percent even if the shared pool is huge. This is because Oracle must often check for the existence of nonexistent objects.

Determining Hit Ratio for the Shared SQL and PL/SQL (V$LIBRARYCACHE)

Accessing the V$LIBRARYCACHE view shows how well the actual statements (SQL and PL/SQL) are accessing memory. If the SHARED_POOL_SIZE parameter is too small, enough room may not be available to store all of the statements into memory. If the shared pool becomes extremely fragmented, large PL/SQL routines may not fit into the shared pool. If statements are not reused effectively, an enlarged shared pool may cause more harm than good (see Chapter 4 for additional details).

There is an execution ratio (pinhitratio) and a reload hit ratio. The recommended hit ratio for pin hits is 95+ percent, and the reload hit ratio should be 99+ percent (less than 1 percent reloads). Reloads occur when a statement has been parsed previously, but the shared pool is usually not large enough to keep in memory as other statements are parsed. The body of the statement is pushed out of memory (the head is still there); when the statement is again needed, a reload is recorded to reload the body. A reload could also occur if the execution plan for the statement changes. If either of the hit ratios falls below these percentages, it indicates that you should investigate the shared pool in greater detail. The following listing shows how to query for all of the information discussed:

Query V$LIBRARYCACHE to see if SQL is being reused:

```
select    sum(pins) "Executions", sum(pinhits) "Hits",
          ((sum(pinhits) / sum(pins)) * 100) "PinHitRatio",
          sum(reloads) "Misses", ((sum(pins) / (sum(pins)
          + sum(reloads))) * 100)  "RelHitRatio"
from      v$librarycache;

Executions      Hits PinHitRatio    Misses RelHitRatio
---------- ---------- ----------- ---------- -----------
   7002504   6996247  99.9106462       327  99.9953305
```

The V$SYSMETRIC view also displays the Library Cache system metric values captured for the most current time interval for 60-second and 15-second durations. The following query displays two rows, one for the last 60-second and one for the last 15-second intervals:

```
select metric_name, to_char(begin_time,'DD-MON-YY HH24MISS') BEGIN_TIME,
       to_char(end_time, 'DD-MON-YY HH24MISS') END_TIME, value
```

```
from    v$sysmetric
where   metric_name like 'Library Cache Hit Ratio';

METRIC_NAME            BEGIN_TIME         _END_TIME          VALUE
---------------------- ----------------  ----------------  ----------
Library Cache Hit Ratio 04-MAY-11 140251  04-MAY-11 140351     99.07
Library Cache Hit Ratio 04-MAY-11 140351  04-MAY-11 140406     99.82
```

Query V$SQL_BIND_CAPTURE to see if binds per SQL statement are greater than 20 (issue):

```
select sql_id, count(*) bind_count
from    v$sql_bind_capture
where   child_number = 0
group  by sql_id
having count(*) > 20
order  by count(*);

SQL_ID        BIND_COUNT
------------- ----------
9qgtwh66xg6nz        21
```

Find the problem SQL to fix:

```
select sql_text, users_executing, executions, users_opening, buffer_gets
from    v$sqlarea
where   sql_id =  '9qgtwh66xg6nz'
order  by buffer_gets;

SQL_TEXT
--------------------------------------------------------------------------------
USERS_EXECUTING EXECUTIONS USERS_OPENING BUFFER_GETS
--------------- ---------- ------------- -----------
update seg$ set type#=:4,blocks=:5,extents=:6,minexts=:7,maxexts=:8,extsize=:9,e
xtpct=:10,user#=:11,iniexts=:12,lists=decode(:13, 65535, NULL, :13),groups=decod
e(:14, 65535, NULL, :14), cachehint=:15, hwmincr=:16, spare1=DECODE(:17,0,NULL,:
17),scanhint=:18 where ts#=:1 and file#=:2 and block#=:3
              0         90             0         690
```

Query V$SQL_BIND_CAPTURE to see if average binds are greater than 15 (issue):

```
select avg(bind_count) AVG_NUM_BINDS from
       (select sql_id, count(*) bind_count
        from    v$sql_bind_capture
        where   child_number = 0
        group  by sql_id);

AVG_NUM_BINDS
-------------
   3.35471698
```

Using the Result Cache

Up to version 10*g*, the SHARED_POOL_SIZE consisted of the Library Cache and Dictionary Cache. You can obtain hit ratios for these caches by querying V$ROWCACHE and V$LIBRARYCACHE data dictionary views. Oracle 11*g* provides an additional area of memory called *Result Cache Memory* (set with the RESULT_CACHE_MAX_SIZE parameter). This memory (also part of the shared pool) stores the results of SQL and PL/SQL functions in memory. The RESULT_CACHE_MODE initialization parameter controls the behavior of this memory. When RESULT_CACHE_MODE is set to MANUAL, queries need to employ a RESULT_CACHE hint to use this memory. When RESULT_CACHE_MODE is set to FORCE, all queries use this memory, if possible. The following shows an example of a query using the RESULT_CACHE hint, resulting in the use of the Result Cache Memory:

```
select      /*+ result_cache */ deptno, avg(sal)
from        emp
group by    deptno;
```

The following query displays the objects that are cached along with other attributes:

```
column cache_id format A20

select   type,status,name,cache_id,cache_key
from     v$result_cache_objects;
```

Type	Status	Cache Name	CACHE_ID	CACHE_KEY
Dependency	Published	SCOTT.EMP	SCOTT.EMP	SCOTT.EMP
Result	Published	select /*+ result_ca che */ deptno, avg(s al) from scott.emp g roup by deptno	1bhc1ku3h4yxm07dd0z1 pv4zzu	21ny1f0hxsxck0k982493x1x28

```
2 Rows selected.
```

The following query displays all the memory blocks and corresponding statistics:

```
col chunk          for 9999999   HEADING        'Chunk#'
col offset         for 9999999   HEADING        'Offset#'
col free           for A5        HEADING        'Free?'
col position       for 9999999   HEADING        'Position'

select  chunk, offset, free, position
from    v$result_cache_memory;
```

Chunk#	Offset#	Free?	Position
0	0	NO	0
0	1	NO	0
0	2	NO	0
0	3	YES	0
0	4	YES	0
0	5	YES	0

```
0        6 YES       0
0        7 YES       0
0        8 YES       0
0        9 YES       0
..........................
```

The following query monitors Result Cache Memory usage. For a system that makes good use of Result Cache Memory, you should see a low value for Create Count Failures and a high value for Find Count.

To query Result Cache Memory usage:

```
column name format a20
select name, value from v$result_cache_statistics;

Cache Name                VALUE
-------------------- ----------
Block Size (Bytes)         1024
Block Count Maximum        3072
Block Count Current          32
Result Size Maximum          30
Create Count Success          1
Create Count Failure          0
Find Count                    0
Invalidation Count            0
Delete Count Invalid          0
Delete Count Valid            0

10 rows selected.
```

TIP
Query V$LIBRARYCACHE to see how often your SQL and PL/SQL are being read from memory. The pinhitratio should generally be 95 percent or greater, and the number of reloads should not be greater than 1 percent. Query V$SQL_BIND_CAPTURE to see if binds per SQL are too high and CURSOR_SHARING is needed. Use the Result Cache to force results from a query to remain in the Result Cache Memory portion of the shared pool.

Identifying PL/SQL Objects That Need to Be Kept (Pinned)

Fragmentation resulting in several small pieces being available in the shared pool and not enough large contiguous pieces is a common occurrence in the shared pool. The key to eliminating shared pool errors (see Chapters 4 and 13 for more information) is to understand which objects can cause problems. Once you know the potential problem PL/SQL objects, you can then pin this code when the database is started (and the shared pool is completely contiguous). You can query the V$DB_OBJECT_CACHE view to determine PL/SQL that is both large and currently not marked *kept*.

This query shows only the current statements in the cache. The example in this listing searches for those objects requiring greater than 100K.

```
select  name, sharable_mem
from    v$db_object_cache
where   sharable_mem > 100000
and     type in ('PACKAGE', 'PACKAGE BODY',
        'FUNCTION', 'PROCEDURE')
and     kept = 'NO';

NAME                                SHARABLE_MEM
----------------------------------- ------------
MGMT_JOB_ENGINE                           238590
DBMS_STATS_INTERNAL                       220939
STANDARD                                  435820
DBMS_RCVMAN                               354875
WK_CRW                                    183688
DBMS_BACKUP_RESTORE                       258495
DBMS_STATS                                446886
...
```

TIP
Query the V$DB_OBJECT_CACHE view to find objects that are not pinned and are also potentially large enough to cause fragmentation problems in the shared pool.

Finding Problem Queries by Monitoring V$SESSION_LONGOPS

If you want to track long running SQL queries, Oracle provides a data dictionary table called V$SESSION_LONGOPS (available since 9*i*). Run the following query to get the SID, serial number, and message for long running queries:

```
select sid, serial#, message
from   v$session_longops;

       SID    SERIAL# MESSAGE
---------- ---------- ---------------------------------------------
       292       3211 Table Scan:   SYSTEM.STATS$USER_LOG: 2477
                      7 out of 24777 Blocks done
       375      64234 Table Scan:   SYSTEM.STATS$USER_LOG: 2477
                      7 out of 24777 Blocks done
        68      29783 Table Scan:   SYSTEM.STATS$USER_LOG: 2477
                      7 out of 24777 Blocks done
......... ..
```

Starting with 11*g*, you can monitor the performance of SQL statements while they are being executed. Oracle provides two data dictionary views to monitor the performance of long-running statements: V$SQL_MONITOR and V$SQL_PLAN_MONITOR.

```
select     key, sql_id, sql_exec_id,
           to_char(max(sql_exec_start) ,'DD/MM/YYYY HH24:Mi:SS')
           sql_exec_start,
           sql_child_address child_address
from       v$sql_monitor
group by   key, sql_id, sql_exec_id, sql_child_address
order by   sql_exec_start;

       KEY SQL_ID        SQL_EXEC_ID SQL_EXEC_START      CHILD_AD
---------- ------------- ----------- ------------------- --------
3.6078E+11 ahvccymgw92jw   16777217 20/11/2008 12:59:08 28172AC0
3.3930E+11 ahvccymgw92jw   16777220 20/11/2008 12:59:11 28172AC0
1.6321E+11 ahvccymgw92jw   16777221 20/11/2008 12:59:12 28172AC0
2.7917E+11 ahvccymgw92jw   16777224 20/11/2008 12:59:14 28172AC0
2.3193E+11 ahvccymgw92jw   16777223 20/11/2008 12:59:14 28172AC0
..........

col id format 999
col operation format a25
col object format a6
set colsep '|'
set lines 100

select     p.id,
           rpad(' ',p.depth*2, ' ')||p.operation operation,
           p.object_name object,
           p.cardinality card,
           p.cost cost,
           substr(m.status,1,4) status,
           m.output_rows
from       v$sql_plan p, v$sql_plan_monitor m
where      p.sql_id=m.sql_id
and        p.child_address=m.sql_child_address
and        p.plan_hash_value=m.sql_plan_hash_value
and        p.id=m.plan_line_id
and        m.sql_id=' ahvccymgw92jw'
and        m.sql_exec_id=16777217
and        m.sql_exec_start=to_date('20/11/2008 12:59:08 ','DD/MM/YYYY HH24:MI:SS')
order by p.id;
```

ID	OPERATION	OBJECT	CARD	COST	STAT	OUTPUT_ROWS
0	SELECT STATEMENT			4941855	DONE	0
1	RESULT CACHE	2k8xzg			DONE	0
		unm7z5				
		0c8ssc				
		mhy1t6				
		ph				
2	SORT		1		DONE	1

```
    3|        NESTED LOOPS       |       |  289220332|   4941855|DONE|  616317649
    4|          TABLE ACCESS     |EMP    |      74130|        69|DONE|     150000
    5|          TABLE ACCESS     |EMP    |       3902|        67|DONE|  616317649
```

6 rows selected.

The STAT column displays EXEC when the query is still running. This status shows which step is being executed at a point in time. In the V$SESSION_LONGOPS view, you can query TIME_REMAINING and SOFAR columns, but using these to estimate how long something will take is tough. Oracle considers operations to be linearly running, so later operations may take longer than earlier ones (and vice versa). Lastly, not every long-running query shows up in this view. The following criteria must be met (note that it is not the scans that must meet the minimum block threshold, but the objects being scanned):

■ Must be running over 6 seconds of actual time AND

■ Be a full table scan of a table that occupies over 10,000 blocks OR

■ Be a full index scan of an index that occupies over 1,000 blocks OR

■ Be a hash join (as few as 20 blocks reported to show up)

This changes from version to version; do your own testing to make sure.

Finding Problem Queries by Querying V$SQLAREA

V$SQLAREA provides a means of identifying the *potential* problem SQL statements or SQL statements that need to be optimized to improve overall database optimization by reducing disk access. The DISK_READS column displays the volume of disk reads that are being performed on the system. This, combined with the EXECUTIONS column (DISK_READS/EXECUTIONS), returns the SQL statements that have the most disk hits per statement execution. The DISK_READS value is set to 100000, but it could be set much higher or lower on production systems (depending on the database) to reveal only the top problem statements on your system. Once identified, review and optimize the top statements to improve overall performance. Typically, a statement with very large disk reads is not using an index or the execution path is forcing the statement to not use the proper indexes.

One potentially misleading part of the query in the following listing is the RDS_EXEC_RATIO column. RDS_EXEC_RATIO contains the number of disk reads divided by the executions. In reality, a statement may be read once using 100 disk reads and then forced out of memory (if memory is insufficient). If it is read again, then it will read 100 disk reads again and the RDS_EXEC_RATIO will be 100 (or 100 + 100 reads divided by 2 executions). But if the statement happens to be in memory the second time (memory is sufficient), the disk reads will be 0 (the second time) and the RDS_EXEC_RATIO will be only 50 (or 100 + 0 divided by 2 executions). Any statement that makes the top of this list is a problem and needs to be tuned—period!

NOTE

The following code was formatted for ease of reading.

```
select      b.username username, a.disk_reads reads,
            a.executions exec, a.disk_reads /decode
            (a.executions, 0, 1,a.executions) rds_exec_ratio,
            a.sql_text Statement
from        v$sqlarea a, dba_users b
where       a.parsing_user_id = b.user_id
and         a.disk_reads       > 100000
order by    a.disk_reads desc;
```

```
USERNAME   READS     EXEC   RDS_EXEC_RATIO   STATEMENT
--------   -------   ----   --------------   --------------------------------
ADHOC1     7281934     1         7281934     select   custno, ordno
                                             from     cust, orders
ADHOC5     4230044     4         1057511     select   ordno
                                             from     orders
                                             where    trunc(ordno) = 721305
ADHOC1      801715     2          499858     select   custno, ordno
                                             from     cust
                                             where    decode(custno,1,6) = 314159
```

The DISK_READS column in the preceding statement can be replaced with the BUFFER_GETS column to provide information on SQL statements that may not possess the large disk hits (although they usually do) but possess a large number of memory hits (higher than normally desired). These statements are using a large amount of memory that is allocated for the data (DB_CACHE_SIZE). The problem is not that the statement is being executed in memory (which is good), but that the statement is hogging a lot of the memory. Many times, this problem is attributable to a SQL statement using an index when it should be doing a full table scan or a join. These types of SQL statements can also involve a join operation that is forcing the path to use a different index than desired, or using multiple indexes and forcing index merging or volumes of data merging. Remember, the bulk of system performance problems are attributable to poorly written SQL and PL/SQL statements.

TIP

Query the V$SQLAREA to find problem queries (and users).

Finding Out What Users Are Doing and Which Resources They Are Using

Joining V$SESSION and V$SQLTEXT displays the SQL statement that is currently being executed by each session, as shown here. This query is extremely useful when a DBA is trying to determine what is happening in the system at a given point in time.

```
select      a.sid, a.username, s.sql_text
from        v$session a, v$sqltext s
where       a.sql_address      = s.address
```

```
and        a.sql_hash_value = s.hash_value
order by a.username, a.sid, s.piece;


SID   USERNAME     SQL_TEXT
---   ----------   ------------------------------------
 11   PLSQL_USER   update s_employee set salary = 10000
  9   SYS          select a.sid, a.username, s.sql_text
  9   SYS          from v$session a, v$sqltext
  9   SYS          where a.sql_address  = s.address
  9   SYS          and a.sql_hash_value  = s.hash_value
  9   SYS          order by a.username, a.sid, s.piece
(...partial output listing)
```

The SQL_TEXT column displays the entire SQL statement, but the statement is stored in the V$SQLTEXT view as a VARCHAR2(64) data type and, therefore, spans multiple records. The PIECE column is used to order the statement. To view the resources being used by each of the users, simply use the query in the next listing. The goal of this statement is to highlight the physical disk and memory hits for each session. Recognizing users who are performing a large number of physical disk or memory reads is very easy.

```
select    a.username, b.block_gets, b.consistent_gets,
          b.physical_reads, b.block_changes, b.consistent_changes
from      v$session a, v$sess_io b
where     a.sid = b.sid
order by  a.username;
```

USERNAME	BLOCK_GETS	CONSISTENT_GETS	PHYSICAL_READS	BLOCK_ CHANGES	CONSISTENT_CHANGES
PLSQL_USER	39	72	11	53	1
SCOTT	11	53	12	0	0
SYS	14	409	26	0	0
SYSTEM	8340	10197	291	2558	419

TIP
Query V$SESSION, V$SQLTEXT, and V$SESS_IO to find the problem users and what they are executing at a given point in time.

Finding Out Which Objects a User Is Accessing

Querying V$ACCESS can point you to potential problem objects (potentially missing indexes) once you have found the problem user or query on your system. It can also be helpful when you want to modify a particular object and need to know who is using it at a given point in time, as shown here:

```
select a.sid, a.username, b.owner, b.object, b.type
from   v$session a, v$access b
where  a.sid = b.sid;
```

```
SID  USERNAME   OWNER   OBJECT                  TYPE
---  --------   -----   --------------------    -------
  8  SCOTT      SYS     DBMS_APPLICATION_INFO   PACKAGE
  9  SYS        SYS     DBMS_APPLICATION_INFO   PACKAGE
  9  SYS        SYS     X$BH                    TABLE
 10  SYSTEM     PUBLIC  V$ACCESS                SYNONYM
 10  SYSTEM     PUBLIC  V$SESSION               SYNONYM
 10  SYSTEM     SYS     DBMS_APPLICATION_INFO   PACKAGE
 10  SYSTEM     SYS     V$ACCESS                VIEW
 10  SYSTEM     SYS     V$SESSION               VIEW
 10  SYSTEM     SYS     V_$ACCESS               VIEW
```

This script displays all objects being accessed, including synonyms, views, and stored source code.

TIP
Query V$ACCESS to find all objects that are being accessed by a user at a given time. This can help to pinpoint problem objects, while also being helpful when modifying a particular object (find out who is accessing it). However, this operation would be very expensive on a system with a large shared pool and hundreds of users.

Getting Detailed User Information

A method for analyzing user statistics is extremely valuable when testing a new or updated application module to determine overhead. This method also provides a window to a user who is having performance problems because it provides statistics on a variety of areas for each user. In addition, it can serve as a guideline for setting profiles to limit a particular user. The script in this next listing limits the statistics only to areas that have a value (b.value != 0). Note the IMUs (*in memory undo*) that are listed only exist in 10g and 11g.

```
select    a.username, c.name, sum(b.value) value
from      v$session a, v$sesstat b, v$statname c
where     a.sid        = b.sid
and       b.statistic# = c.statistic#
and       b.value      != 0
group by  name, username;
```

USERNAME	NAME	VALUE
SYS	DB time	3690
	redo size	2143640
SYS	redo size	98008
	user calls	28
SYS	user calls	337
	IMU Flushes	1
SYS	IMU Flushes	2
	IMU commits	19

```
SYS                        IMU commits                                    1
                           redo writes                                 4443
                           redo entries                                8728
...etc.
```

Using Indexes

Oracle 9*i* introduced the ability to monitor the use of indexes. This view indicates whether the index is used but not how often it is used. You need to turn monitoring ON and OFF individually for indexes that you want to monitor. You initiate monitoring with the ALTER INDEX command, and index use is then tracked by querying the V$OBJECT_USAGE view. Here is a description of the V$OBJECT_USAGE view:

```
SQL> desc v$object_usage

Name                      Null?     Type
------------------------- --------- -----------------------------
INDEX_NAME                NOT NULL  VARCHAR2(30)
TABLE_NAME                NOT NULL  VARCHAR2(30)
MONITORING                          VARCHAR2(3)
USED                                VARCHAR2(3)
START_MONITORING                    VARCHAR2(19)
END_MONITORING                      VARCHAR2(19)
```

Before any index is monitored, the view has no records:

```
select   *
from     v$object_usage;

no rows selected
```

You start monitoring on four indexes (connect to user schema-owning indexes):

```
alter index HRDT_INDEX1 monitoring usage;
alter index HRDT_INDEX2 monitoring usage;
alter index HRDT_INDEX3 monitoring usage;
alter index HRDT_INDEX4 monitoring usage;
```

The view now shows the four indexes with a start time but no use yet:

```
select index_name, table_name, monitoring, used,
       start_monitoring, end_monitoring
from   v$object_usage;

INDEX_NAME   TABLE_NAME  MON USE START_MONITORING     END_MONITORING
-----------  ----------- --- --- -------------------- ------------------
HRDT_INDEX1  HRS_DETAIL  YES NO  10/13/2011 03:11:34
HRDT_INDEX2  HRS_DETAIL  YES NO  10/13/2011 03:11:38
HRDT_INDEX3  HRS_DETAIL  YES NO  10/13/2011 03:11:46
HRDT_INDEX4  HRS_DETAIL  YES NO  10/13/2011 03:11:52
```

If you query using HRDT_INDEX1, the view now shows that this index has been used:

```
select index_name, table_name, monitoring, used,
       start_monitoring, end_monitoring
from   v$object_usage;

INDEX_NAME  TABLE_NAME MON USE START_MONITORING    END_MONITORING
----------- ---------- --- --- ------------------- -------------------
HRDT_INDEX1 HRS_DETAIL YES YES 10/13/2011 03:11:34
HRDT_INDEX2 HRS_DETAIL YES NO  10/13/2011 03:11:38
HRDT_INDEX3 HRS_DETAIL YES NO  10/13/2011 03:11:46
HRDT_INDEX4 HRS_DETAIL YES NO  10/13/2011 03:11:52
```

You end the monitoring on HRDT_INDEX4, and the view now shows an end monitoring time:

```
alter index HRDT_INDEX4 nomonitoring usage;
select index_name, table_name, monitoring, used,
       start_monitoring, end_monitoring
from   v$object_usage;

INDEX_NAME  TABLE_NAME MON USE START_MONITORING    END_MONITORING
----------- ---------- --- --- ------------------- -------------------
HRDT_INDEX1 HRS_DETAIL YES YES 10/13/2011 03:11:34
HRDT_INDEX2 HRS_DETAIL YES NO  10/13/2011 03:11:38
HRDT_INDEX3 HRS_DETAIL YES NO  10/13/2011 03:11:46
HRDT_INDEX4 HRS_DETAIL NO  NO  10/13/2011 03:11:52 10/13/2011 03:16:01
```

TIP
Use the V$OBJECT_USAGE view to find out if indexes are being used. Perhaps some indexes are not needed.

Identifying Locking Issues

Identifying locking issues is instrumental in locating the user who is waiting for someone or something else. You can use this strategy to identify users who are currently being locked in the system and to determine whether an Oracle-related process is truly locked or just running slowly. You can also identify the current statement that the locked user is currently executing. The next listing provides an example of identifying locking issues.

NOTE
These statements were not tuned in the early version of the book. (Now that's embarrassing!)

```
select    /*+ ordered */ b.username, b.serial#, d.id1, a.sql_text
from      v$lock d, v$session b, v$sqltext a
where     b.lockwait  = d.kaddr
and       a.address   = b.sql_address
and       a.hash_value = b.sql_hash_value;
```

```
USERNAME        SERIAL#          ID1   SQL_TEXT
--------      ----------    ----------  ----------------------------
AUTHUSER           53         393242   update emp set salary = 5000
```

You also need to identify the user in the system *who* is causing the problem of locking the previous user, as shown in this listing. (Usually this is the user/developer who presses CTRL-ALT-DEL as you approach his or her desk.)

```
select    /*+ ordered */ a.serial#, a.sid, a.username, b.id1, c.sql_text
from      v$lock b, v$session a, v$sqltext c
where     b.id1 in
          (select    /*+ ordered */ distinct e.id1
           from      v$lock e, v$session d
           where     d.lockwait   = e.kaddr)
and       a.sid        = b.sid
and       c.hash_value = a.sql_hash_value
and       b.request    = 0;


SERIAL#   SID   USERNAME      ID1    SQL_TEXT
-------   ---   --------    ------   -------------------------------------
     18    11   JOHNSON     393242   update authuser.emp set salary=90000
```

JOHNSON will make everyone happy by forgetting a crucial WHERE clause. Unfortunately, JOHNSON has locked the authorized user of this table.

You can also look at locking in more detail to see exactly what's running and blocking. In Chapter 9, I discuss block-level tuning; there I describe some of these columns and also how to perform queries to V$TRANSACTION (which shows all DML [UPDATE/INSERT/DELETE] transactions currently running). In the following listing, you can see four transactions all running at the same time to the same block of information. There is no blocking because the initrans is set to handle (at least set to 4 ITL slots) all four changes within the same block at the same time. If there was a problem, the LMODE would have been 0 and the REQUEST would have been 6 (TX6), as in the third query that follows.

Four users are updating different rows in the same block:

```
select /*+ ordered */ username, v$lock.sid, trunc(id1/power(2,16)) rbs,
       bitand(id1,to_number('ffff','xxxx'))+0 slot,
       id2 seq, lmode, request
from   v$lock, v$session
where  v$lock.type = 'TX'
and    v$lock.sid = v$session.sid;
```

USERNAME	SID	RBS	SLOT	SEQ	LMODE	REQUEST
SCOTT	146	6	32	85	6	0
SCOTT	150	4	39	21557	6	0
SCOTT	151	5	34	1510	6	0
SCOTT	161	7	24	44	6	0

```
select xid, xidusn, xidslot, xidsqn, status, start_scn
from   v$transaction
order by start_scn;
```

XID	XIDUSN	XIDSLOT	XIDSQN	STATUS	START_SCN
0600200055000000	6	32	85	ACTIVE	16573480
0400270035540000	4	39	21557	ACTIVE	16573506
05002200E6050000	5	34	1510	ACTIVE	16573545
070018002C000000	7	24	44	ACTIVE	16574420

Here three users are trying to update the exact same row:

```
select /*+ ordered */ username, v$lock.sid, trunc(id1/power(2,16)) rbs,
       bitand(id1,to_number('ffff','xxxx'))+0 slot,
       id2 seq, lmode, request
from   v$lock, v$session
where  v$lock.type = 'TX'
and    v$lock.sid = v$session.sid;
```

USERNAME	SID	RBS	SLOT	SEQ	LMODE	REQUEST
SCOTT	146	4	47	21557	0	6
SCOTT	150	4	47	21557	6	0
SCOTT	161	4	47	21557	0	6

```
select xid, xidusn, xidslot, xidsqn, status, start_scn
from   v$transaction
order by start_scn;
```

XID	XIDUSN	XIDSLOT	XIDSQN	STATUS	START_SCN
04002F0035540000	4	47	21557	ACTIVE	16575501

Here two users are blocked:

```
SELECT sid, blocking_session, username, blocking_session_status
FROM   v$session
WHERE  username='SCOTT'
ORDER BY blocking_session;
```

SID	BLOCKING_SESSION	USERNAME	BLOCKING_SESSION_STATUS
146	150	SCOTT	VALID
161	150	SCOTT	VALID
150		SCOTT	NO HOLDER

Killing the Problem Session

A user may have run something that he or she really didn't want to run, or a problem query may need to be eliminated during business hours and rerun at night. If the operation in the preceding section needs to be aborted, you could execute the statements in the next listing (to find and then kill the session):

```
select username, sid, serial#, program, terminal
from    v$session;
```

You can also do this in a single statement using:

```
select /*+ ordered */ username, v$lock.sid, trunc(id1/power(2,16)) rbs,
       bitand(id1,to_number('ffff','xxxx'))+0 slot,
       id2 seq, lmode, request
from    v$lock, v$session
where   v$lock.type = 'TX'
and     v$lock.sid = v$session.sid;

alter system kill session '11,18';
```

You can't kill your own session though:

```
alter system kill session '10,4';
*
ERROR at line 1:
ORA-00027: cannot kill current session
```

The order of the parameters is SID and then SERIAL#. Make sure you describe V$SESSION (DESC V$SESSION) because many of its columns are helpful. In previous versions of Oracle, you could kill the current user session. Thankfully, you can no longer kill your own session accidentally, as just shown in the preceding listing.

TIP
Identify users who are locking others and kill their session (if necessary).

Finding Users with Multiple Sessions

At times, users enjoy opening multiple sessions to accomplish several tasks at once, and this can be a problem. The problem may also be a developer who has built a poor application that begins spawning multiple processes. Either of these could degrade the system's overall performance. In the following output, the usernames that are NULL are background processes. The query to the V$SESSION view in this listing displays these types of issues:

```
select    username, count(*)
from      v$session
group by  username;
```

```
USERNAME      COUNT(*)
-----------   --------
PLSQL_USER           1
SCOTT                1
JOHNSON              9
DBSNMP               3
SYS                  4
SYSTEM               1
                    14
```

On certain OS platforms, if a user starts a session and reboots his or her PC, oftentimes the process continues in the background on the server as the user starts another session. If the user is running multiple reports on multiple terminals or PCs, this could also affect the system's overall performance.

NOTE
The rows in V$SESSION that have NULL values for username are the Oracle background processes.

TIP
Identify users who are running multiple sessions and determine whether the problem is administrative (the user is using multiple terminals) or system related (sessions are not being cleaned or are spawning runaway processes).

Querying for Current Profiles
Profiles are limits on a given schema (user). To view the profiles for your system, execute the query shown here:

```
select    substr(profile,1,10) Profile,
          substr(resource_name,1,30) "Resource Name",
          substr(limit,1,10) Limit
from      dba_profiles
group by  substr(profile,1,10), substr(resource_name,1,30),
          substr(limit,1,10);
```

PROFILE	Resource Name	LIMIT
DEFAULT	CONNECT_TIME	UNLIMITED
DEFAULT	CPU_PER_CALL	UNLIMITED
DEFAULT	COMPOSITE_LIMIT	UNLIMITED
DEFAULT	CPU_PER_SESSION	UNLIMITED
DEFAULT	FAILED_LOGIN_ATTEMPTS	10
DEFAULT	IDLE_TIME	UNLIMITED
DEFAULT	LOGICAL_READS_PER_CALL	UNLIMITED
DEFAULT	LOGICAL_READS_PER_SESSION	UNLIMITED
DEFAULT	PASSWORD_LIFE_TIME	180
DEFAULT	PASSWORD_LOCK_TIME	1

```
DEFAULT      PASSWORD_REUSE_MAX              UNLIMITED
DEFAULT      PASSWORD_GRACE_TIME             7
DEFAULT      PASSWORD_REUSE_TIME             UNLIMITED
DEFAULT      PASSWORD_VERIFY_FUNCTION        NULL
DEFAULT      PRIVATE_SGA                     UNLIMITED
DEFAULT      SESSIONS_PER_USER               UNLIMITED
MONITORING   IDLE_TIME                       DEFAULT
MONITORING   PRIVATE_SGA                     DEFAULT
MONITORING   CONNECT_TIME                    DEFAULT
MONITORING   CPU_PER_CALL                    DEFAULT
MONITORING   COMPOSITE_LIMIT                 DEFAULT
MONITORING   CPU_PER_SESSION                 DEFAULT
MONITORING   FAILED_LOGIN_ATTEMPTS           DEFAULT
MONITORING   LOGICAL_READS_PER_CALL          DEFAULT
MONITORING   LOGICAL_READS_PER_SESSION       DEFAULT
MONITORING   PASSWORD_LIFE_TIME              DEFAULT
MONITORING   PASSWORD_LOCK_TIME              DEFAULT
MONITORING   PASSWORD_REUSE_MAX              DEFAULT
MONITORING   PASSWORD_GRACE_TIME             DEFAULT
MONITORING   PASSWORD_REUSE_TIME             DEFAULT
MONITORING   PASSWORD_VERIFY_FUNCTION        DEFAULT
MONITORING   SESSIONS_PER_USER               DEFAULT

32 rows selected.
```

Finding Disk I/O Issues

The views V$DATAFILE, V$FILESTAT, and DBA_DATA_FILES provide file I/O activity across all database datafiles and disks. Ideally, the physical reads and writes should be distributed equally. If the system is not configured properly, overall performance suffers. The script in this next listing identifies the actual distribution and makes identifying where an imbalance exists easy. Chapter 3 looks at this topic in great detail; this section just shows the quick-hit query to get a baseline.

```
select    a.file#, a.name, a.status, a.bytes,
          b.phyrds, b.phywrts
from      v$datafile a, v$filestat b
where     a.file# = b.file#;
```

The queries in the following listings provide an improved formatted report for file and data distribution issues. The first listing gets the datafile I/O, and the second listing gets the disk I/O:

```
Set TrimSpool On
Set Line      142
Set Pages      57
Set NewPage     0
Set FeedBack Off
Set Verify    Off
Set Term      On
TTitle        Off
BTitle        Off
Clear Breaks
Break On Tablespace_Name
```

```
Column TableSpace_Name For A12      Head "Tablespace"
Column Name       For A45          Head "File Name"
Column Total      For 999,999,990  Head "Total"
Column Phyrds     For 999,999,990  Head "Physical|Reads  "
Column Phywrts    For 999,999,990  Head "Physical| Writes "
Column Phyblkrd   For 999,999,990  Head "Physical  |Block Reads"
Column Phyblkwrt  For 999,999,990  Head "Physical  |Block Writes"
Column Avg_Rd_Time  For 90.9999999 Head "Average |Read Time|Per Block"
Column Avg_Wrt_Time For 90.9999999 Head "Average |Write Time|Per Block"
Column Instance            New_Value _Instance  NoPrint
Column Today               New_Value _Date      NoPrint
select   Global_Name Instance, To_Char(SysDate, 'FXDay, Month DD, YYYY HH:MI') Today
from     Global_Name;
TTitle On
TTitle Left 'Date Run: ' _Date Skip 1-
Center 'Data File I/O' Skip 1 -
      Center 'Instance Name: ' _Instance Skip 1
select   C.TableSpace_Name, B.Name, A.Phyblkrd +
         A.Phyblkwrt Total, A.Phyrds, A.Phywrts,
         A.Phyblkrd, A.Phyblkwrt
from     V$FileStat A, V$DataFile B, Sys.DBA_Data_Files C
where    B.File# = A.File#
and      B.File# = C.File_Id
order by TableSpace_Name, A.File#
/

select object_name, statistic_name, value
from v$segment_statistics
where value > 100000
order by value;


OBJECT_NAME  STATISTIC_NAME     VALUE
-----------  ----------------   ------
ORDERS       space allocated    96551
ORDERS       space allocated    134181
ORDERS       logical reads      140976
ORDER_LINES  db block changes   183600
```

This second listing gets the disk I/O:

```
Column TableSpace_Name For A12      Head "Tablespace"
Column Total      For 9,999,999,990 Head "Total"
Column Phyrds     For 9,999,999,990 Head "Physical|Reads  "
Column Phywrts    For 9,999,999,990 Head "Physical| Writes "
Column Phyblkrd   For 9,999,999,990 Head "Physical  |Block Reads"
Column Phyblkwrt  For 9,999,999,990 Head "Physical  |Block Writes"
Column Avg_Rd_Time   For 9,999,990.9999 Head "Average |Read Time|Per Block"
Column Avg_Wrt_Time  For 9,999,990.9999 Head "Average |Write Time|Per Block"
Clear Breaks
Break on Disk Skip 1
Compute Sum Of Total On Disk
Compute Sum Of Phyrds On Disk
Compute Sum Of Phywrts On Disk
Compute Sum Of Phyblkrd On Disk
Compute Sum Of Phyblkwrt On Disk
TTitle Left 'Date Run: ' _Date Skip 1-
      Center 'Disk I/O' Skip 1 -
      Center 'Instance Name: ' _Instance Skip 2
```

```
select      SubStr(B.Name, 1, 13) Disk, C.TableSpace_Name,
            A.Phyblkrd + A.Phyblkwrt Total, A.Phyrds, A.Phywrts,
            A.Phyblkrd, A.Phyblkwrt, ((A.ReadTim /
            Decode(A.Phyrds,0,1,A.Phyblkrd))/100) Avg_Rd_Time,
            ((A.WriteTim / Decode(A.PhyWrts,0,1,A.PhyblkWrt)) /
            100) Avg_Wrt_Time
from        V$FileStat A, V$DataFile B, Sys.DBA_Data_Files C
where       B.File# = A.File#
and         B.File# = C.File_Id
order by    Disk,C.Tablespace_Name, A.File#
/
Set FeedBack On
Set Verify    On
Set Term      On
Ttitle        Off
Btitle        Off
```

TIP
The views V$DATAFILE, V$FILESTAT, and DBA_DATA_FILES provide
file I/O activity across all database datafiles and disks. Ensure that
both datafiles and disks are properly balanced for optimal
performance.

Finding Rollback Segment Contention

This helpful query shows the actual waits on an UNDO or rollback segment. You can display
rollback information (including automatic UNDO). You can also query shrinks and wraps from
the views shown here.

NOTE
Automatic or system-managed UNDO is used in this database.

```
select    a.name, b.extents, b.rssize, b.xacts,
          b.waits, b.gets, optsize, status
from      v$rollname a, v$rollstat b
where     a.usn = b.usn;
```

File Name	EXTENTS	RSSIZE	XACTS	WAITS	GETS	OPTSIZE	STATUS
SYSTEM	6	385024	0	0	164		ONLINE
_SYSSMU1$	6	4317184	0	0	3947		ONLINE
_SYSSMU2$	6	3334144	0	0	2985		ONLINE
_SYSSMU3$	7	450560	1	0	204		ONLINE
_SYSSMU4$	4	253952	0	0	244		ONLINE
_SYSSMU5$	17	2088960	0	1	5426		ONLINE
_SYSSMU6$	7	450560	0	0	1070		ONLINE
_SYSSMU7$	3	188416	0	0	275		ONLINE
_SYSSMU8$	2	122880	0	0	182		ONLINE
_SYSSMU9$	2	122880	0	0	182		ONLINE
_SYSSMU10$	2	122880	0	0	182		ONLINE

TIP
*Querying V$ROLLNAME, V$ROLLSTAT, and V$TRANSACTION
provides information on how users are using rollback segments if you
use an RBS tablespace. Generally, more than five users should not be
accessing a rollback segment at one time. If using Automatic Undo
Management (and you should), the previous query is really not
needed.*

The query in this listing shows the waits on the entire system as a whole:

```
Set TrimSpool On
Set NewPage    0
Set Pages     57
Set Line      132
Set FeedBack  Off
Set Verify    Off
Set Term      On
TTitle        Off
BTitle        Off
Clear Breaks
Column Event        For A40 Heading "Wait Event"
Column Total_Waits For 999,999,990 Head "Total Number| Of Waits   "
Column Total_Timeouts For 999,999,990 Head "Total Number|Of TimeOuts"
Column Tot_Time     For 999,999,990 Head "Total Time|Waited  "
Column Avg_Time     For  99,990.999 Head "Average Time|Per Wait   "
Column Instance New_Value _Instance      NoPrint
Column Today    New_Value _Date          NoPrint

select    Global_Name Instance, To_Char(SysDate,
          'FXDay DD, YYYY HH:MI') Today
from      Global_Name;

TTitle On
TTitle Left 'Date Run: ' _Date Skip 1-
      Center 'System Wide Wait Events' Skip 1 -
      Center 'Instance Name: ' _Instance Skip 2

select    event, total_waits, total_timeouts,
          (time_waited / 100)  tot_time, (average_wait / 100)
          Avg_time
from      v$system_event
order by  total_waits desc
/
```

```
Date Run: Friday    01, 2006 09:24
                                            System Wide Wait Events
                                             Instance Name: ORCL
```

Wait Event	Total Number Of Waits	Total Number Of TimeOuts	Total Time Waited	Average Time Per Wait
db file sequential read	2,376,513	0	30,776	0.010
db file scattered read	136,602	0	6,069	0.040
rdbms ipc message	103,301	99,481	276,659	2.680
latch: redo writing	57,488	0	0	0.000
...etc...				

Determining Whether Freelists Are Sufficient

If you have multiple processes doing large inserts, using the default value of 1 for freelists (list of free database blocks) may not be enough. If you are not using Automatic Space Segment Management (ASSM), you may need to increase freelists and/or freelist groups (see Chapter 14 for additional information). To check if the freelist groups storage parameter is sufficient, run the report shown in this listing:

```
Set TrimSpool On
Set Line 132
Set Pages 57
Set NewPage    0
Set FeedBack Off
Set Verify Off
Set Term Off
TTitle Off
BTitle Off

Column Pct Format 990.99 Heading "% Of      |Free List Waits"
Column Instance New_Value _Instance NoPrint
Column Today    New_Value _Date NoPrint

select    Global_Name Instance, To_Char
          (SysDate, 'FXDay DD, YYYY HH:MI') Today
from      Global_Name;

TTitle On
TTitle Left 'Date Run: ' _Date Skip 1-
       Center 'Free list Contention' Skip 1 -
       Center 'If Percentage is Greater than 1%' Skip 1 -
       Center 'Consider increasing the number of free lists' Skip 1 -
       Center 'Instance Name: ' _Instance

select    ((A.Count / (B.Value + C.Value)) * 100) Pct
from      V$WaitStat A, V$SysStat B, V$SysStat C
where     A.Class = 'free list'
and       B.Statistic# =  (select   Statistic#
                           from     V$StatName
                           where    Name = 'db block gets')
and       C.Statistic# =  (select   Statistic#
                           from     V$StatName
                           where    Name = 'consistent gets')
/

Date Run: Friday    01, 2006 09:26
                                    Free list Contention
                             If Percentage is Greater than 1%
                       Consider increasing the number of free lists
                                    Instance Name: ORCL

     % Of
Free List Waits
---------------
          0.00
(of course... I'm using ASSM)
```

If the activity rate is greater than 1 percent, then you need to increase the number of freelist groups.

TIP
Ensure that freelists and freelist groups are sufficient when using multiple processes to do inserts. The default storage value for freelists is only 1. If you use ASSM, Oracle manages this for you, but a high-transaction environment should be well tested prior to employing ASSM. Nonetheless, using ASSM is generally a good practice.

Checking for Privileges and Roles

This section contains several V$ scripts that show various security privileges. The title of each script in the following listings gives you a quick idea of what it retrieves for you. The output can be *very large,* depending on your system, so run with caution.

Object-level privileges that have been granted by username

```
select b.owner || '.' || b.table_name obj,
       b.privilege what_granted, b.grantable,
       a.username
from   sys.dba_users a, sys.dba_tab_privs b
where  a.username = b.grantee
order by 1,2,3;
```

Object-level privileges that have been granted by grantee

```
Select   owner || '.' || table_name obj,
         privilege what_granted, grantable, grantee
from     sys.dba_tab_privs
where    not exists
         (select  'x'
         from sys.dba_users
         where   username = grantee)
order by 1,2,3;
```

System-level grants by username

```
select    b.privilege what_granted,
          b.admin_option, a.username
from      sys.dba_users a, sys.dba_sys_privs b
where     a.username = b.grantee
order by  1,2;
```

System-level grants by grantee

```
select    privilege what_granted,
          admin_option, grantee
from      sys.dba_sys_privs
```

```
where     not exists
          (select  'x' from sys.dba_users
           where username = grantee)
order by 1,2;
```

Roles granted by username

```
select    b.granted_role ||
          decode(admin_option, 'YES',
      ' (With Admin Option)',
          null) what_granted, a.username
from      sys.dba_users a, sys.dba_role_privs b
where     a.username = b.grantee
order by  1;
```

Roles granted by grantee

```
select    granted_role  ||
          decode(admin_option, 'YES',
      ' (With Admin Option)', null) what_granted,
          grantee
from      sys.dba_role_privs
where     not exists
          (select 'x'
           from sys.dba_users
           where username = grantee)
order by 1;
```

Usernames with corresponding granted privileges

```
select a.username,
 b.granted_role || decode(admin_option,'YES',
    ' (With Admin Option)',null) what_granted
from    sys.dba_users a, sys.dba_role_privs b
where   a.username = b.grantee
UNION
select a.username,
b.privilege || decode(admin_option,'YES',
    ' (With Admin Option)', null) what_granted
from    sys.dba_users a, sys.dba_sys_privs b
where   a.username = b.grantee
UNION
select   a.username,
         b.table_name || ' - ' || b.privilege
         || decode(grantable,'YES',
     ' (With Grant Option)',null) what_granted
from     sys.dba_users a, sys.dba_tab_privs b
where    a.username = b.grantee
order by 1;
```

TIP
*Document the privileges that you have for your system so you are
ready for any type of security situation.*

Usernames with corresponding profile, default tablespace, and temporary tablespace

```
Select    username, profile, default_tablespace,
          temporary_tablespace, created
from      sys.dba_users
order by username;
```

Wait Events V$ Views

This section contains several V$ scripts that show wait events. Personally, I prefer using the
Statspack Report, the AWR Report, or Enterprise Manager to find wait events. That said, here are
some nice views to look at wait events. Several new views have been added for Oracle 11gR2,
but the *best* thing is that everything you found in V$SESSION_WAIT is now in V$SESSION.

Who is waiting right now: Query V$SESSION_WAIT / V$SESSION

```
select event, sum(decode(wait_time,0,1,0)) "Waiting Now",
       sum(decode(wait_time,0,0,1)) "Previous Waits",
       count(*) "Total"
from v$session_wait
group by event
order by count(*);

WAIT_TIME = 0 means that it's waiting
WAIT_TIME > 0 means that it previously waited this many ms
```

EVENT	Waiting Now	Previous Waits	Total
db file sequential read	0	1	1
db file scattered read	2	0	2
latch free	0	1	1
enqueue	2	0	2
SQL*Net message from client	0	254	480
...			

```
select event, sum(decode(wait_time,0,1,0)) "Waiting Now",
       sum(decode(wait_time,0,0,1)) "Previous Waits",
       count(*) "Total"
from v$session
group by event
order by count(*);
```

EVENT	Waiting Now	Previous Waits	Total
db file sequential read	0	1	1
db file scattered read	2	0	2

```
latch free                     0                    1                    1
enqueue                        2                    0                    2
SQL*Net message from client 0                    254                  480
...
```

Who is waiting right now: SPECIFIC waits, query V$SESSION_WAIT

```
SELECT /*+ ordered */ sid, event, owner, segment_name, segment_type,p1,p2,p3
FROM    v$session_wait sw, dba_extents de
WHERE   de.file_id = sw.p1
AND     sw.p2 between de.block_id and de.block_id+de.blocks - 1
AND     (event = 'buffer busy waits' OR event = 'write complete waits')
AND     p1 IS NOT null
ORDER BY event,sid;
```

Who is waiting: Last 10 Waits, query V$SESSION_WAIT_HISTORY

```
SELECT /*+ ordered */ sid, event, owner, segment_name, segment_type,p1,p2,p3
FROM    v$session_wait_history sw, dba_extents de
WHERE   de.file_id = sw.p1
AND     sw.p2 between de.block_id and de.block_id+de.blocks - 1
AND     (event = 'buffer busy waits' OR event = 'write complete waits')
AND     p1 IS NOT null
ORDER BY event,sid;
```

Finding what P1, P2, P3 stand for: Query V$EVENT_NAME

```
col name for a20
col p1 for a10
col p2 for a10
col p3 for a10
select event#,name,parameter1 p1,parameter2 p2,parameter3 p3
from    v$event_name
where   name in ('buffer busy waits', 'write complete waits');


EVENT#        NAME                 P1          P2          P3
------------- -------------------- ----------  ----------  ----------
          143 write complete waits file#       block#
          145 buffer busy waits    file#       block#      id
```

All waits since the session started: Query V$SESSION_EVENT

```
select sid, event, total_waits, time_waited
from    v$session_event
where   time_waited > 0
order   by time_waited;

SID        EVENT                                TOTAL_WAITS TIME_WAITED
---------- ------------------------------------ ----------- -----------
       159 process startup                                2           1
```

```
167 latch: redo allocation          4          1
168 log buffer space                2          3
166 control file single write       5          4
```
. . .

All SESSION waits by class: Query V$SESSION_WAIT_CLASS

```
select sid, wait_class, total_waits
from   v$session_wait_class;

    SID WAIT_CLASS           TOTAL_WAITS
---------- -------------------- -----------
    168 Other                          2
    168 Concurrency                    1
    168 Idle                       12825
    168 User I/O                      12
    168 System I/O                  4448
    169 Other                          1
    169 Idle                       12812
    170 Idle                       13527
```

ALL waits since the system started: Query V$SYSTEM_EVENT

```
select event, total_waits, time_waited, event_id
from   v$system_event
where  time_waited > 0
order  by time_waited;

EVENT                               TOTAL_WAITS TIME_WAITED    EVENT_ID
---------------------------------- ----------- ----------- ----------
enq: TX - row lock contention             1196      366837  310662678
enq: TM - contention                       170       52074  668627480
db file sequential read                  17387       31630 2652584166
control file parallel write              12961       23117 4078387448
db file scattered read                    4706       15762  506183215
class slave wait                            20       10246 1055154682
```

SYSTEM waits by class: Query V$SYSTEM_WAIT_CLASS

```
select wait_class, total_waits
from   v$system_wait_class
order  by total_waits desc;

WAIT_CLASS           TOTAL_WAITS
-------------------- -----------
Idle                      161896
Other                      65308
System I/O                 24339
User I/O                   22227
Application                 1404
Commit                       524
Network                      522
```

```
Concurrency                 221
Configuration                55
...
```

SYSTEM waits by class: Query V$ACTIVE_SESSION_HISTORY

```
-- In the query below, the highest count session is leader in non-idle wait events.
select session_id,count(1)
from    v$active_session_history
group  by session_id
order by 2;

-- In the query below, find the SQL for the leader in non-idle wait events.

select c.sql_id, a.sql_text
from v$sql a, (select sql_id,count(1)
                      from v$active_session_history b where sql_id is not null
                      group by sql_id
                      order by 2 desc) c
where rownum <= 5
order by rownum;
```

TIP
In 11g, all wait event columns that are in V$SESSION_WAIT are now in V$SESSION. So make sure you query V$SESSION for wait information since it's a faster view. V$ACTIVE_SESSION_HISTORY (ASH) rolls many of the great statistics into one view as well as one report (ASH Report).

Some of the Major V$ View Categories

The views in this section are categorized according to their primary function. Not all are listed (please see Appendix B for a complete listing of the V$ views complete with X$ table queries). You will often need to join one category to another category to retrieve the desired information. The V$ views can be queried the same as any other Oracle view, but keep in mind that the information in these tables changes rapidly. You can insert the information from the V$ views into a pre-created table to allow for the compilation of data over a period of time—data to be analyzed later or to build statistical reports and alerts based on different conditions in your database.

Most DBA monitoring tools on the market today use the V$ view (and X$ table) information. Querying this database information without a DBA monitoring tool requires that you have an in-depth understanding of the information stored in each view and how to query the view properly. Table 12-1 contains a list of V$ views categorized according to their primary function. The views are listed in categories related to the operation that they monitor. This list is not exhaustive. It contains only the most commonly used views. Some views have changed from version to version of Oracle. This information is contained on the TUSC V$ Poster.

Category	Description and Associated V$ Views
Advisors	Information related to cache advisors **V$ views:** V$ADVISOR_PROGRESS, V$DB_CACHE_ADVICE, V$JAVA_POOL_ADVICE, V$MEMORY_TARGET_ADVICE, VPGA_TARGET_ADVICE, VPGA_TARGET_ADVICE_HISTOGRAM, VPX_BUFFER_ADVICE, VSHARED_POOL_ADVICE, V$SGA_TARGET_ADVICE, and V$STREAMS_POOL_ADVICE
ASM	VASM_ALIAS, VASM_ATTRIBUTE, VASM_CLIENT, VASM_DISK, VASM_DISK_IOSTAT, VASM_DISK_STAT, V$ASM_DISKGROUP, V$ASM_DISKGROUP_STAT, VASM_FILE, VASM_OPERATION, V$ASM_TEMPLATE, V$ASM_USER, VASM_USER_GROUP, VASM_USERGROUP_MEMBER
Backup/recovery	Information related to database backups and recovery, including last backup, archive logs, state of files for backup, and recovery **V$ views:** V$ARCHIVE, V$ARCHIVED_LOG, V$ARCHIVE_DEST, V$ARCHIVE_DEST_STATUS, V$ARCHIVE_GAP, V$ARCHIVE_PROCESSES, V$BACKUP, V$BACKUP_ASYNC_IO, V$BACKUP_CORRUPTION, V$BACKUP_DATAFILE, V$BACKUP_DEVICE, V$BACKUP_PIECE, V$BACKUP_REDOLOG, V$BACKUP_SET, V$BACKUP_SYNC_IO, V$BLOCK_CHANGE_TRACKING, V$COPY_CORRUPTION, V$DATABASE_BLOCK_CORRUPTION, V$DATABASE_INCARNATION, V$DATAFILE_COPY, V$DELETED_OBJECT, V$FAST_START_SERVERS, V$FAST_START_TRANSACTIONS, V$INSTANCE_RECOVERY, V$MTTR_TARGET_ADVICE, V$PROXY_ARCHIVEDLOG, V$PROXY_DATAFILE, V$RMAN_CONFIGURATION, V$RECOVERY_FILE_STATUS, V$RECOVERY_LOG, V$RECOVERY_PROGRESS, V$RECOVERY_STATUS, V$RECOVER_FILE, V$BACKUP_ARCHIVELOG_DETAILS, V$BACKUP_ARCHIVELOG_SUMMARY, V$BACKUP_CONTROLFILE_DETAILS, V$BACKUP_CONTROLFILE_SUMMARY, V$BACKUP_COPY_DETAILS, V$BACKUP_COPY_SUMMARY, V$BACKUP_DATAFILE_DETAILS, V$BACKUP_DATAFILE_SUMMARY. V$BACKUP_FILES, V$BACKUP_PIECE_DETAILS, V$BACKUP_SET_DETAILS, V$BACKUP_SET_SUMMARY, V$BACKUP_SPFILE, V$BACKUP_SPFILE_DETAILS, V$BACKUP_SPFILE_SUMMARY, V$DATABASE, V$DATAFILE, V$DATAFILE_HEADER, V$FLASHBACK_DATABASE_LOG, V$FLASHBACK_DATABASE_LOGFILE, V$FLASHBACK_DATABASE_STAT, V$FLASHBACK_TXN_GRAPH, V$FLASHBACK_TXN_MODS, VHM_CHECK, VINSTANCE, V$OBSOLETE_BACKUP_FILES, V$OFFLINE_RANGE, V$PROXY_ARCHIVELOG_DETAILS, V$PROXY_ARCHIVELOG_SUMMARY, V$PROXY_COPY_DETAILS, V$PROXY_COPY_SUMMARY, V$RECOVERY_AREA_USAGE, V$RECOVERY_FILE_DEST(10,1), V$RESTORE_POINT, V$RMAN_BACKUP_JOB_DETAILS, V$RMAN_BACKUP_SUBJOB_DETAILS, V$RMAN_BACKUP_TYPE, V$RMAN_COMPRESSION_ALGORITHM, V$RMAN_ENCRYPTION_ALGORITHMS, V$RMAN_OUTPUT, V$RMAN_STATUS, and V$UNUSABLE_BACKUPFILE_DETAILS
Caches	Information related to the various caches, including objects, library, cursors, and the dictionary **V$ views:** V$ACCESS, V$BUFFER_POOL, V$BUFFER_POOL_STATISTICS, V$CPOOL_CC_INFO, V$CPOOL_CC_STATS, V$CPOOL_CONN_INFO, V$CPOOL_STATS, VDB_CACHE_ADVICE, VDB_OBJECT_CACHE, V$JAVA_POOL_ADVICE, V$LIBRARYCACHE, V$LIBRARY_CACHE_MEMORY, V$PGASTAT, V$MEMORY_CURRENT_RESIZE_OPS, V$MEMORY_DYNAMIC_COMPONENTS, V$MEMORY_RESIZE_OPS, V$PGA_TARGET_ADVICE, V$PGA_TARGET_ADVICE_HISTOGRAM, V$RESULT_CACHE_DEPENDENCY, V$RESULT_CACHE_MEMORY, V$RESULT_CACHE_OBJECTS, V$RESULT_CACHE_STATISTICS, V$ROWCACHE, V$ROWCACHE_PARENT, V$ROWCACHE_SUBORDINATE, V$SESSION_CURSOR_CACHE, V$SESSION_OBJECT_CACHE, V$SGA, V$SGASTAT, V$SGA_CURRENT_RESIZE_OPS, V$SGA_DYNAMIC_COMPONENTS, V$SGA_DYNAMIC_FREE_MEMORY, VSGA_RESIZE_OPS, VSGAINFO, V$SHARED_POOL_ADVICE, V$SHARED_POOL_RESERVED, VSQL, VSQLAREA, V$SYSTEM_CURSOR_CACHE, V$SUBCACHE, V$JAVA_LIBRARY_CACHE_MEMORY, V$PROCESS_MEMORY, and V$SGA_TARGET_ADVICE

TABLE 12-1. *V$ Views Categories*

Category	Description and Associated V$ Views
Cache fusion/RAC	V$ACTIVE_INSTANCES, V$BH, V$CACHE, V$CACHE_TRANSFER, V$CLUSTER_INTERCONNECTS, V$CONFIGURED_INTERCONNECTS, VCR_BLOCK_SERVER, VCURRENT_BLOCK_SERVER, V$DYANMIC_REMASTER_STATS, V$GC_ELEMENT, V$GC_ELEMENTS_WITH_COLLISIONS, V$GCSHVMASTER_INFO, V$GCSPFMASTER_INFO, V$GES_BLOCKING_ENQUEUE, V$GES_ENQUEUE, V$HVMASTER_INFO, V$INSTANCE_CACHE_TRANSFER, V$LIBRARYCACHE, V$PX_INSTANCE_GROUP, and V$RESOURCE_LIMIT
Control files	Information related to instance control files **V$ views:** V$CONTROLFILE, V$CONTROLFILE_RECORD_SECTION, and V$DATABASE
Cursors/SQL statements	Information related to cursors and SQL statements, including the open cursors, statistics, and actual SQL text **V$ views:** V$OPEN_CURSOR, V$SQL, V$SQLAREA, V$SQLFN_ARG_METADATA, V$SQLFN_METADATA, V$SQLTEXT, V$SQLTEXT_WITH_NEWLINES, V$SQL_BIND_DATA, V$SQL_BIND_METADATA, V$SQL_CS_HISTOGRAM, V$SQL_CS_SELECTIVITY, V$SQL_CS_STATISTICS, VSQL_CURSOR, VSQL_OPTIMIZER_ENV, VSQL_PLAN, VSQL_PLAN_MONITOR, V$SQL_PLAN_STATISTICS, V$SQL_PLAN_STATISTICS_ALL, V$SQL_REDIRECTION, V$SESSION_CURSOR_CACHE, VSQL_SHARED_CURSOR, VSQL_SHARED_MEMORY, V$SQL_MONITOR, V$SQLCOMMAND, V$SQLSTATS_PLAN_HASH, V$SQL_WORKAREA, V$SQL_WORKAREA_ACTIVE, V$SQL_WORKAREA_HISTOGRAM, V$SYS_OPTIMIZER_ENV, V$SYSTEM_CURSOR_CACHE, V$MUTEX_SLEEP, V$MUTEX_SLEEP_HISTORY (for those dubious shared latches), V$SQL_BIND_CAPTURE, V$SQL_JOIN_FILTER, V$SQL_AREA_PLAN_HASH, V$SQLSTATS, V$SYS_OPTIMIZER_ENV, and V$VPD_POLICY
Database instances	Information related to the actual database instance **V$ views:** V$ACTIVE_INSTANCES, V$ARCHIVER_PROCESSES, V$BGPROCESS, V$DATABASE, V$INSTANCE, V$PROCESS, VSGA, VSGASTAT, V$BLOCKING_QUIESCE, and V$CLIENT_STATS **RAC views:** V$BH and V$ACTIVE_INSTANCES
Direct Path operations	Information related to the SQL*Loader (and the Direct Path API) direct load option **V$ views:** V$LOADISTAT and V$LOADPSTAT
Distributed/ heterogeneous services	**V$ views:** V$DBLINK, V$GLOBAL_TRANSACTION, V$GLOBAL_BLOCKED_LOCKS, V$HS_AGENT, V$HS_PARAMETER, V$HS_SESSION, and V$IOSTAT_NETWORK
File mapping interface	Information related to file mapping **V$ Views:** VMAP_COMP_LIST, VMAP_ELEMENT, V$MAP_EXT_ELEMENT, V$MAP_FILE, VMAP_FILE_EXTENT, VMAP_FILE_IO_STACK, V$MAP_LIBRARY, and V$MAP_SUBELEMENT
Fixed view	Information related to the V$ tables themselves **V$ views:** V$FIXED_TABLE, V$FIXED_VIEW_DEFINITION, and V$INDEXED_FIXED_COLUMN
General	General information related to various pieces of system information **V$ views:** VDB_PIPES, VCONTEXT, V$GLOBALCONTEXT, V$LICENSE, V$OPTION, V$RESERVED_WORDS, V$SQLCOMMAND, V$TEMPORARY_LOBS, V$THRESHOLD_TYPES, V$TIMER, V$TIMEZONE_NAMES, V$TOPLEVELCALL, V$TYPE_SIZE, V$_SEQUENCES, and V$VERSION. V$DB_TRANSPORTABLE_PLATFORM, V$TRANSPORTABLE_PLATFORM, and V$SCHEDULER_RUNNING_JOBS

TABLE 12-1. *V$ Views Categories (Continued)*

Category	Description and Associated V$ Views
I/O	Information related to I/O, including files and statistics **V$ views:** V$DATAFILE, V$DATAFILE_HEADER, V$DBFILE, V$DNFS_CHANNELS, V$DNFS_FILES, V$DNFS_SERVERS, V$DNFS_STATS, V$FILESPACE_USAGE, V$FILESTAT, V$WAITSTAT, V$TEMPSTAT, V$FILE_HISTOGRAM, V$FILEMETRIC, V$FILEMETRIC_HISTORY, V$IOFUNCMETRIC, V$IOFUNCMETRIC_HISTORY, V$IO_CALIBRATION_STATUS, V$IOSTAT_CONSUMER_GROUP, V$IOSTAT_FILE, V$IOSTAT_FUNCTION, V$IOSTAT_FUNCTION_DETAIL, V$IOSTAT_NETWORK, V$NFS_CLIENTS, VNFS_LOCKS, VNFS_OPEN_FILES, V$SECUREFILE_TIMER, V$SEGMENT_STATISTICS, V$SYSAUX_OCCUPANTS. V$TABLESPACE, V$TEMP_SPACE_HEADER, V$TEMPFILE, and V$TEMPSEG_USAGE
Latches/locks	Information related to latches and locks **V$ views:** V$ACCESS, V$ENQUEUE_LOCK, V$ENQUEUE_STAT, V$EVENT_NAME, V$GLOBAL_BLOCKED_LOCKS, V$LATCH, V$LATCHHOLDER, V$LATCHNAME, V$LATCH_CHILDREN, V$LATCH_MISSES, V$LATCH_PARENT, V$LIBCACHE_LOCKS, V$LOCK, V$LOCK_TYPE, V$LOCKED_OBJECT, V$RESOURCE, V$RESOURCE_LIMIT, V$TRANSACTION_ENQUEUE, V$_LOCK, V$_LOCK1, V$ENQUEUE_STATISTICS. **RAC views:** VCR_BLOCK_SERVER, VGCSHVMASTER_INFO, V$GCSPFMASTER_INFO, V$GC_ELEMENT, V$GES_BLOCKING_ENQUEUE, V$GES_ENQUEUE, V$HVMASTER_INFO, V$NFS_LOCKS, V$GES_RESOURCES, and V$PROCESS
Log Miner	Information related to Log Miner **V$ views:** V$LOGMNR_CALLBACK, V$LOGMNR_CONTENTS, V$LOGMNR_DICTIONARY, V$LOGMNR_LATCH, V$LOGMNR_LOGS, V$LOGMNR_PARAMETERS, V$LOGMNR_PROCESS, V$LOGMNR_REGION, V$LOGMNR_SESSION, V$LOGMNR_STATS, V$LOGMNR_TRANSACTION, and V$LOGMNR_DICTIONARY_LOAD
Metrics	Information related to metrics **V$ views:** V$METRICNAME, V$SERVICEMETRIC, V$EVENTMETRIC, V$FILEMETRIC, V$FILEMETRIC_HISTORY, V$IOFUNCMETRIC, V$METRIC, V$METRIC_HISTORY, V$RSRCMGRMETRIC, V$RSRCMGRMETRIC_HISTORY, V$SERVICEMETRIC_HISTORY, V$SESSMETRIC, V$SYSMETRIC, V$SYSMETRIC_HISTORY, V$SYSMETRIC_SUMMARY, V$THRESHOLD_TYPES, V$WAITCLASSMETRIC, and V$WAITCLASSMETRIC_HISTORY
Multithreaded/ shared servers	Information related to multithreaded and parallel servers, including connections, queues, dispatchers, and shared servers **V$ views:** V$CIRCUIT, V$DISPATCHER, V$DISPATCHER_RATE, V$QUEUE, V$QUEUEING_MTH, V$REQDIST, V$SHARED_SERVER, V$SHARED_SERVER_MONITOR, and V$DISPATCHER_CONFIG
Object usage	Information related to object use and dependencies **V$ views:** V$OBJECT_DEPENDENCY, V$OBJECT_PRIVILEGE, and V$OBJECT_USAGE
Overall system	Information related to the overall system performance **V$ tables:** V$ALERT_TYPES, V$EMON, V$EVENTMETRIC, V$EVENT_HISTOGRAM, V$EVENT_NAME, V$GLOBAL_TRANSACTION, VHM_CHECK, VMEMORY_CURRENT_RESIZE_OPS, V$OSSTAT, V$RESUMABLE, V$SEGMENT_STATISTICS, V$SHARED_POOL_RESERVED, VSGA, VSORT_SEGMENT, V$STATNAME, V$SYS_OPTIMIZER_ENV, VSYS_TIME_MODEL, VSYSSTAT, V$SYSTEM_CURSOR_CACHE, V$SYSTEM_EVENT, V$SYSTEM_FIX_CONTROL, V$TEMPFILE, V$TEMPORARY_LOBS, V$TEMPSEG_USAGE, V$TEMP_EXTENT_MAP, V$TEMP_EXTENT_POOL, V$TEMP_SPACE_HEADER, V$TRANSACTION, V$SYSTEM_WAIT_CLASS, V$TEMP_HISTOGRAM, V$WAITSTAT, and V$XML_AUDIT_TRAIL
Parallel query and parallel execution	Information related to the Parallel Query option **V$ views:** V$EXECUTION, V$PARALLEL_DEGREE_LIMIT_MTH, V$PQ_SESSTAT, V$PQ_SLAVE, V$PQ_SYSSTAT, V$PQ_TQSTAT, V$PX_INSTANCE_GROUP, V$PX_PROCESS, V$PX_PROCESS_SYSSTAT, V$PX_SESSION, and V$PX_SESSTAT

TABLE 12-1.   *V$ Views Categories (Continued)*

Category	Description and Associated V$ Views
Parameters	Information related to various Oracle parameters, including initialization and NLS per session **V$ views:** V$NLS_PARAMETERS, V$NLS_VALID_VALUES, V$OBSOLETE_PARAMETER, V$PARAMETER, V$PARAMETER2, V$SPPARAMETER, V$SYSTEM_PARAMETER, V$SYSTEM_PARAMETER2, and V$PARAMETER_VALID_VALUES
Redo logs	Information related to redo logs, including statistics and history **V$ views:** V$INSTANCE, V$LOG, V$LOGFILE, V$LOGHIST, V$LOG_HISTORY, V$REDO_DEST_RESP_HISTOGRAM, and V$THREAD (RAC related)
Replication and materialized views	Information related to replication and materialized views **V$ views:** V$MVREFRESH, V$REPLPROP, and V$REPLQUEUE
Resource Manager	Information related to resource management **V$ Views:** V$ACTIVE_SESSION_POOL_MTH, V$ACTIVE_SESSION_ HISTORY, V$IO_CALIBRATION_STATUS, V$IOSTAT_CONSUMER_GROUP, V$RSRC_CONS_GROUP_HISTORY, V$RSRC_CONSUMER_GROUP, V$RSRC_CONSUMER_GROUP_CPU_MTH, V$RSRC_PLAN, V$RSRC_PLAN_CPU_MTH, V$RSRC_PLAN_HISTORY, V$RSRC_SESSION_INFO, V$RSRCMGRMETRIC, and V$RSRCMETRIC_HISTORY.
Rollback segments and UNDO	Information on rollback segments, including statistics and transactions **V$ views:** V$ROLLNAME, V$ROLLSTAT, V$TRANSACTION, and V$UNDOSTAT
Security/privileges	Information related to security **V$ views:** V$ENABLEDPRIVS, V$OBJECT_PRIVILEGE, V$PWFILE_USERS, V$VPD_POLICY, V$WALLET, and V$XML_AUDIT_TRAIL
Sessions (includes some replication information and heterogeneous services)	Information related to a session, including object access, cursors, processes, and statistics **V$ views:** V$ACTIVE_SESSION_HISTORY, V$ARCHIVE_PROCESSES, V$BGPROCESS, V$CONTEXT, V$MYSTAT, V$PROCESS, V$SESS_TIME_MODEL, V$SESSION, V$SESSION_BLOCKERS,V$SESSION_CONNECT_INFO, V$SESSION_CURSOR_CACHE, V$EMON, V$SESSION_EVENT, V$SESSION_FIX_CONTROL, V$SESSION_LONGOPS, V$SESSION_OBJECT_CACHE, V$SESSION_WAIT, V$SESSION_WAIT_CLASS, V$SESSION_WAIT_HISTORY, V$SESSTAT, V$SESS_IO, V$SES_OPTIMIZER_ENV, V$SESSMETRIC, and V$CLIENT_STATS, V$TSM_SESSIONS, and V$WAIT_CHAINS
Services (all new for 10.1)	V$ACTIVE_SERVICES, V$SERV_MOD_ACT_STATS, V$SERVICE_EVENT, V$SERVICEMETRIC, V$SERVICEMETRIC_HISTORY, V$SERVICE_STATS, V$SERVICE_WAIT_CLASS, and V$SERVICES
Sorting	Information related to sorting **V$ views:** V$SORT_SEGMENT, V$TEMPSEG_USAGE, V$TEMP_EXTENT_MAP, V$TEMP_EXTENT_POOL, V$TEMP_SPACE_HEADER, V$TEMPFILE, V$TEMPSTAT
Standby databases (Data Guard)	Information related to standby databases **V$ views:** V$ARCHIVE_DEST, V$ARCHIVE_DEST_STATUS, V$ARCHIVE_GAP, V$ARCHIVED_LOG, V$DATABASE, V$DATAGUARD_STATUS, V$INSTANCE, V$FOREIGN_ARCHIVED_LOG, V$FS_FAILOVER_STATS, V$LOGSTDBY_STATS, V$MANAGED_STANDBY, V$STANDBY_LOG, V$DATAGUARD_CONFIG, V$DATAGUARD_STATS, V$LOGSTDBY_PROCESS, V$LOGSTDBY_PROGRESS, V$LOGSTDBY_STATE, V$LOGSTDBY_TRANSACTION, and V$STANDBY_EVENT_HISTOGRAM

TABLE 12-1. *V$ Views Categories* (Continued)

Category	Description and Associated V$ Views
Streams/AQ	Information related to streams and Advanced Queuing **V$ Views:** VAQ, VARCHIVE_DEST_STATUS, V$ARCHIVED_LOG, V$DATABASE, V$BUFFERED_PUBLISHERS, V$BUFFERED_QUEUES, V$BUFFERED_SUBSCRIBERS, V$METRICGROUP, V$PERSISTENT_PUBLISHERS, V$PERSISTENT_QMN_CACHE, V$PERSISTENT_QUEUES, V$PERSISTENT_SUBSCRIBERS, V$PROPAGATION_RECEIVER, V$PROPAGATION_SENDER, V$QMON_COORDINATOR_STATS, V$QMON_SERVER_STATS, V$QMON_TASK_STATS, V$QMON_TASKS, V$RULE, V$RULE_SET, V$RULE_SET_AGGREGATE_STATS, V$STREAMS_APPLY_COORDINATOR, V$STREAMS_APPLY_READER, V$STREAMS_APPLY_SERVER, V$STREAMS_CAPTURE, V$STREAMS_MESSAGE_TRACKING, V$STREAMS_POOL_ADVICE, V$STREAMS_POOL_STATISTICS, V$STREAMS_TRANSACTION, V$XSTREAM_CAPTURE, V$XSTREAM_MESSAGE_TRACKING, V$XSTREAM_OUTBOUND_SERVER, V$XSTREAM_TRANSACTION.
Statistics	Information related to statistics in general **V$ Views:** V$SEGMENT_STATISTICS, V$SEGSTAT, V$SEGSTAT_NAME, V$SESSSTAT, V$SGASTAT, V$SQLSTATS, V$SQLSTATS_PLAN_HASH, V$STATISTICS_LEVEL, V$STATNAME, V$TEMPSTAT, V$UNDOSTAT, V$WAITSTAT
Transactions	Information related to transactions in general **V$ Views:** V$CORRUPT_XID_LIST, V$GLOBAL_TRANSACTION, V$LOCKED_OBJECT, V$LOGSTDBY_TRANSACTION, V$RESUMABLE, V$STREAMS_TRANSACTION, V$TRANSACTION, V$TRANSACTION_ENQUEUE, V$UNDOSTAT, and V$XSTREAM_TRANSACTION
Views new to 11.1	V$ASM_ATTRIBUTE, V$ASM_DISK_IOSTAT, V$CALLTAG, V$CLIENT_RESULT_CACHE_STATS, V$CORRUPT_XID_LIST, V$CPOOL_CC_INFO, V$CPOOL_CC_STATS, V$CPOOL_STATS, V$DETACHED_SESSION, V$DIAG_INFO, V$DNFS_CHANNELS, V$DNFS_FILES, V$DNFS_SERVERS, V$DNFS_STATS, V$DYNAMIC_REMASTER_STATS, V$ENCRYPTED_TABLESPACES, V$ENCRYPTION_WALLET, V$FLASHBACK_TXN_GRAPH, V$FLASHBACK_TXN_MODS, V$FOREIGN_ARCHIVED_LOG, V$FS_FAILOVER_HISTOGRAM, V$FS_FAILOVER_STATS, V$HM_CHECK, VHM_CHECK_PARAM, VHM_FINDING, VHM_INFO, VHM_RECOMMENDATION, VHM_RUN, VINCMETER_CONFIG, V$INCMETER_INFO, V$INCMETER_SUMMARY, V$IOFUNCMETRIC, V$IOFUNCMETRIC_HISTORY, V$IOSTAT_CONSUMER_GROUP, V$IOSTAT_FILE, V$IOSTAT_FUNCTION, V$IOSTAT_NETWORK, V$IO_CALIBRATION_STATUS, V$IR_FAILURE, V$IR_FAILURE_SET, V$IR_MANUAL_CHECKLIST, VIR_REPAIR, VLOBSTAT, V$MEMORY_CURRENT_RESIZE_OPS, V$MEMORY_DYNAMIC_COMPONENTS, V$MEMORY_RESIZE_OPS, V$MEMORY_TARGET_ADVICE, V$NFS_CLIENTS, V$NFS_LOCKS, VNFS_OPEN_FILES, VOBJECT_PRIVILEGE, V$PERSISTENT_PUBLISHERS, V$PERSISTENT_QUEUES, V$PERSISTENT_SUBSCRIBERS, V$PROCESS_GROUP, V$PX_INSTANCE_GROUP, V$REDO_DEST_RESP_HISTOGRAM, V$RESULT_CACHE_DEPENDENCY, V$RESULT_CACHE_MEMORY, V$RESULT_CACHE_OBJECTS, V$RESULT_CACHE_STATISTICS, V$RMAN_COMPRESSION_ALGORITHM, V$RMAN_ENCRYPTION_ALGORITHMS, V$RSRCMGRMETRIC, V$RSRCMGRMETRIC_HISTORY, V$SECUREFILE_TIMER, V$SESSION_FIX_CONTROL, V$SQL_CS_HISTOGRAM, V$SQL_CS_SELECTIVITY, V$SQL_CS_STATISTICS, V$SQL_FEATURE, V$SQL_FEATURE_DEPENDENCY, V$SQL_FEATURE_HIERARCHY, V$SQL_HINT, V$SQL_MONITOR, V$SQL_PLAN_MONITOR, V$SQLFN_ARG_METADATA, V$SQLFN_METADATA, V$SSCR_SESSIONS, V$STREAMS_MESSAGE_TRACKING, V$SUBSCR_REGISTRATION_STATS, V$SYSTEM_FIX_CONTROL, V$WAIT_CHAINS, V$WORKLOAD_REPLAY_THREAD, V$XS_SESSION, V$XS_SESSION_ATTRIBUTE, and V$XS_SESSION_ROLE.

TABLE 12-1. *V$ Views Categories* (Continued)

Category	Description and Associated V$ Views
Views new to 11.2	V$ASM_ACFSSNAPSHOTS, V$ASM_ACFSVOLUMES, V$ASM_FILESYSTEM, V$ASM_USER, V$ASM_USERGROUP, V$ASM_USERGROUP_MEMBER, VASM_VOLUME, VASM_VOLUME_STAT, V$CPOOL_CONN_INFO, V$EMON, V$IOSTAT_FUNCTION_DETAIL, V$LIBCACHE_LOCKS, V$PERSISTENT_QMN_CACHE, V$QMON_COORDINATOR_STATS, V$QMON_SERVER_STATS, V$QMON_TASK_STATS, V$QMON_TASKS, V$SQLCOMMAND, V$STANDBY_EVENT_HISTOGRAM, V$STREAMS_POOL_STATISTICS, and V$TOPLEVELCALL

TABLE 12-1. *V$ Views Categories* (Continued)

NOTE
The V$ROLLNAME view is created slightly differently than the other V$ views. The V$ROLLNAME is a join of an X$ table and the UNDO$ table. Some of the V$ timing fields are dependent on the TIMED_STATISTICS init.ora parameter being set to TRUE; otherwise, there will be no timing data in these fields.

Tips Review

- The V$ views that are accessed by SYSTEM are actually synonyms that point to the V_$ views that are views of the original V$ views based on the X$ tables. (Better read that one again.)

- When other DBAs need access to the V$ view information, but *not* the SYS or SYSTEM passwords, grant the user access to the V_$ views. The user may then access the V$ views that have public synonyms to the V_$ views.

- In Oracle 11*g*, query V$FIXED_TABLE to get a listing of all GV$ and V$ views in the database. The GV$ views are exactly the same as the V$ views, except the instance ID contains an identifier. For almost every V$ view, there is a corresponding GV$ view. GV$, or global V$, views contain the same information as the V$ views, but across all instances of a RAC database (each instance is identified by its instance ID).

- Query V$FIXED_VIEW_DEFINITION to retrieve the query that creates the V$ and GV$ views from the X$ tables.

- The DBA_ views are *not* derived from the X$ tables or V$ views. The fact that you can delete rows from OBJ$ is a great reason to *never* be the SYS superuser.

- Query the V$DATABASE view to find out when your database was created and also to determine basic archiving information.

- Query V$SYSAUX_OCCUPANTS to ensure that the Automatic Workload Repository (AWR) isn't taking up too much space. Use DBMS_STATS to check history and retention.

- Query the V$LICENSE view to see the maximum sessions you are allowed. You can also set warnings when you get close to the maximum.

- Query the V$OPTION view to retrieve the Oracle options you have installed. The V$VERSION view gives you the actual versions of products installed.

- Access the V$SGA view to get a baseline idea of the system's physical memory that is allocated for data, shared pool, and log buffering in Oracle.

- Access V$SGASTAT to get a detailed breakdown for the Oracle SGA and all buckets for the shared pool allocation.

- Query V$PARAMETER and find out the current values for the init.ora parameters. It also shows which init.ora parameters have been changed from their original defaults (ISDEFAULT = FALSE) and which parameters may be changed without shutting down and restarting the database.

- Query V$LIBRARYCACHE to see how often your SQL and PL/SQL are being read from memory. The pinhitratio should optimally be at 95 percent or greater, and the number of reloads should not be greater than 1 percent.

- The Result Cache Memory area is now part of the shared pool, if used. Use the RESULT_CACHE_MAX_SIZE initialization parameter to allocate memory to the Result Cache and RESULT_CACHE_MODE to set it. Use the RESULT_CACHE hint to put results (of long-running functions or calculations) into the Result Cache for future use and faster queries.

- Query V$SQL_BIND_CAPTURE to see if binds per SQL are too high and CURSOR_SHARING is needed.

- Query the V$DB_OBJECT_CACHE view to find objects that are not pinned and are also large enough to cause potential problems.

- Query the V$SESSION_LONGOPS view to find long-running queries. In 11g, the status column shows EXEC for the step being executed.

- Query the V$SQLAREA to find problem queries (and users).

- Query V$SESSION, V$SQLTEXT, and V$SESS_IO to find the problem users and what they are executing at a given point in time.

- Query V$ACCESS to find all objects that are being accessed by a user at a given time. This can help to pinpoint problem objects, while also being helpful when modifying a particular object (find out who is accessing it).

- Identify users who are locking others and kill their session (if necessary).

- Identify users who are holding multiple sessions and determine whether the problem is administrative (the user is using multiple terminals) or system related (sessions are not being cleaned or they are spawning runaway processes).

- The views V$DATAFILE, V$FILESTAT, and DBA_DATA_FILES provide file I/O activity across all database datafiles and disks.

- Querying V$ROLLNAME, V$ROLLSTAT, and V$TRANSACTION provides information on how users are using rollback segments. V$UNDOSTAT gives you UNDO information. (Rollback segments are quickly becoming passé.)

■ Ensure that the freelists value is sufficient when using multiple processes to do inserts. The default storage value is 1.

■ Document the privileges that you have for your system so you can be ready for any type of security situation.

References

Ask Tom Oracle, asktom.oracle.com.

My Oracle Support (MetaLink) notes: 276103.1, 296765.1, 287679.1, 1019592.6 (Script Library), 243132.1, and 245055.1.

Oracle 11g Server: SQL Language Reference Manual (Oracle Corporation).

Oracle11g Server: Application Developer's Guide (Oracle Corporation).

Rich Niemiec and Kevin Loney, *How I Broke into Your Database* (COUG, 2001).

Gints Plivna, *Long Running Operations in Oracle,* 2011.

Joe Trezzo, "The V$ Arsenal: Key V$ Scripts Every DBA Should Use Regularly" (TUSC, 1997).

Joe Trezzo, "The V$ Views—A DBA's Best Friend" *IOUG-A Proceedings* (TUSC, 1997).

Many thanks to Rama Balaji who did much of the update for this chapter; Joe Trezzo wrote most of this chapter for the original book. Also, thanks to Kevin Gilpin who supplied a lot of material for this update, and to Robert Freeman, Bob Yingst, and Greg Pucka who contributed to this chapter in some way. To obtain a poster that contains the V$ view definitions grouped by category, call Rolta TUSC at (630) 960-2909 and request one (while supplies last).

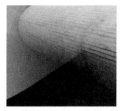

CHAPTER
13

The X$ Tables
(Advanced DBA)

W hy do people climb mountains? Because they are there! Why do people open the hood of their car and look at what's inside? Because they can! Why do DBAs look at the X$ tables? Because they are there and they can!

Oracle now has 945 X$ tables, and they are the last frontier for the expert DBA to explore and analyze the deepest cavern of the Oracle database. Querying the X$ tables can give secrets to undocumented features and parameters, information about future Oracle versions, and shorter or faster routes to database information. The X$ tables are rarely mentioned in the Oracle documentation or the Oracle user community. Therefore, I am including them in this book as one of the only references available. The queries in this chapter were tested accessing version 11.2 of the database.

The tips covered in this chapter include:

- Introducing the X$ tables

- Creating V$ views and X$ tables

- Obtaining a list of X$ tables that make up the V$ views

- Obtaining a list of all the X$ tables

- Obtaining a list of all the X$ indexes

- Using hints with X$ tables and indexes

- Monitoring space allocations in the shared pool

- Creating queries to monitor the shared pool

- Obtaining information about redo log files

- Setting initialization parameters

- Buffer cache/data block details

- Obtaining database- and instance-specific information

- Effective X$ table use and strategy

- Related Oracle internals topics

- Some common X$ table groups

- Some common X$ table and non-V$ fixed view associations

- Common X$ table joins

- X$ table naming conventions

Introducing the X$ Tables

The X$ tables are intriguing to mischievously curious DBAs. There are 945 X$ tables in 11gR2 (11.2.0.1) compared to only 613 in Oracle 10gR2 (10.2.0.1) and just 394 in Oracle 9i Release 2 (9.2.0.1.0). There are also 628 indexes on the X$ tables. Appendix C lists all of these. The Oracle dynamic tables are designed just as many robust Oracle application data models are. A set of tables is available to users (DBAs) via a set of synonyms on a set of views based on these tables. The synonym names start with *V$* and are the object names published in the reference manual of the Oracle documentation set. These synonyms on the V$ views are used as the primary method of querying data from these tables. Interested DBAs, however, keep and use a toolkit of practical X$ table queries that supplement their V$ view queries.

The X$ tables contain instance-specific information spanning a variety of areas. They contain information about the current configuration of the instance, information about the sessions connected to the instance, and a gold mine of performance information. The X$ tables are platform-specific. The documented column definitions of the V$ views may be consistent from platform to platform, but the underlying SQL statements referencing the X$ tables may differ. The Oracle kernel consists of layers. The X$ table names contain an abbreviation for the particular kernel layer to which they pertain.

The X$ tables are not permanent or even temporary tables that reside in database datafiles. The X$ tables reside only in memory. When you start up your instance, they are created. They exist even before you create your control file. When you shut down your instance, they are destroyed. All 945 X$ tables are defined right after the instance is started (before mount). They are defined, but they cannot all be queried. Many of them require at least a mounted, if not open, database. To observe this, query the X$KQFTA and X$KQFDT table after starting your instance with the nomount option.

The X$ tables are owned by the SYS database user and are read-only, which is why they are referred to as *fixed tables* and the V$ views are referred to as *fixed views.* This statement might be a juicy invitation for you to try to verify this read-only property. Any attempt to alter these tables with a DDL or DML statement is met with an ORA-02030 error.

Oracle has extensively used the decode function in the underlying SQL statements of the data dictionary views. If you compare the V$ view underlying SQL statements from version to version, you will likely find differences in the implementation of some V$ views. The columns of the V$ views may stay more constant in terms of their name and meaning, which allows Oracle RDBMS engineers to change the X$ tables from version to version while not disrupting too much of the Oracle user community's use of the V$ views. The fact that the V$ views are accessed through synonyms gives Oracle engineers another level of flexibility to alter the underlying structures, also with little or no impact on the user community's use of the V$ views. Oracle's extensive use of the decode function in the underlying V$ view SQL statements also facilitates the platform-specific implementation of a query, returning the generic data that a user of a particular V$ view expects from platform to platform. Consequently, running the correct scripts when upgrading a database is important to ensure the dictionary views are created in a way that matches the underlying X$ tables.

NOTE
Application designers and developers may save themselves some development and maintenance pain by adopting a similar strategy. They can employ views and synonyms for application software access to an application's underlying tables and stored programmatic objects (Java and PL/SQL). DBAs should investigate whether designers and developers can benefit from using this strategy. In some cases, the costs are higher than the benefits.

Although this section is by no means a complete treatment of useful X$ table queries, it introduces some of the commonly used X$ table queries, grouped by the major tuning areas to which they pertain. Because X$ table queries are a supplement to queries of fixed views rather than a replacement for them, this section includes queries of both X$ tables and related fixed views.

Misconceptions about the X$ Tables

Do not use the X$ tables if you have a heart condition or are an inexperienced DBA—or you may ruin the entire database. (At least this is what some people will tell you. Sounds pretty scary.)

The most common misconception about the X$ tables is that the DBA can drop one or update one, thus ruining the database. However, X$ tables cannot be ruined. The only user who can select from these tables is the SYS user. A SELECT statement is the only command available to be performed on these X$ tables. An error occurs if you attempt to grant SELECT access to a user. Consider the following attempts to drop or alter an X$ table in the following listings. In the first listing, you cannot drop any of the X$ tables (even as the SYS user):

```
connect sys/change_on_install as sysdba
drop table x$ksppi;
ORA-02030: can only select from fixed tables/views
```

In this next listing, you are not able to update, insert, or delete any data in the X$ tables (even as the SYS user):

```
update  x$ksppi
set     ksppidf = 'FALSE'
where   ksppidf = 'TRUE';
ORA-02030: can only select from fixed tables/views
```

NOTE
When you mention the X$ tables, most people say, "Oh, pretty scary. I would never touch those tables." The fact is DML commands (UPDATE, INSERT, DELETE) are not allowed on the X$ tables, even as the SYS superuser.

TIP
Only the SYS superuser can select from the X$ tables. An error occurs if an attempt is made to grant SELECT access to a user. But the X$ tables are not completely harmless. Because they are not documented, they could lead to data being misinterpreted. For example, if a V$ view definition is modified to use a brand-new X$ table, but the DBA has created his or her own view on the X$ tables, he or she might not have accurate information following an upgrade.

Granting Access to View the X$ Tables

You cannot grant access to the X$ tables even if you are the SYS user. If you try to make grants to the X$ tables, you get the error in the following listing:

```
connect sys/change_on_install as sysdba
grant select on X$ksppi to richn;
ORA-02030: can only select fixed from fixed tables/views
```

Although the error message for attempting to grant access to X$KSPPI in the previous code is a little cryptic at first, it clarifies that you can perform only a SELECT and that the grant is not allowed. However, you may build your own X$ views from the original X$ tables and then grant access to those views. Consider the examples in the following six listings, which give access to the X$KSPPI table via a view called X$_KSPPI and a synonym called X$KSPPI.

Connecting to the SYS superuser

```
Connect sys/change_on_install as sysdba
Connected.
```

Creating a view mirroring the X$KSPPI table

```
create view rich$_ksppi as
select      *
from        x$ksppi;

View created.
```

Creating a synonym for the newly created view

```
create public synonym x$_ksppi for rich$_ksppi;
Synonym created.
```

Granting the desired user access to the newly created view

```
grant select on x$_ksppi to richn;
Grant succeeded.
```

Connecting as the desired user

```
conn richn/tusc
Connected.
```

Accessing the X$_KSPPI view via the synonym created for X$_KSPPI

```
select      count(*)
from        x$_ksppi;

COUNT(*)
2399
```

You can now give access to the X$ table information without giving the password to the SYS account. The key is creating a view that references the original SYS-owned X$ tables.

TIP
A DBA may need access to the X$ table information, but not the SYS password. Create a view under a different name that mirrors the desired tables. Name these tables according to the appropriate synonyms of the original tables.

Creating V$ Views and X$ Tables

The X$ tables are virtual or fixed tables, which are created in memory at database startup and maintained real-time in memory. These tables store up-to-date information on the current activity of the database at the current point in time or since the last database startup. In the SGA, V$ views are created (see Chapter 12) on these X$ tables to allow users to view this information in a more readable format. The X$ tables are fixed tables, and because they have been created in memory, access to these tables is very limited.

The V$ views are known as the virtual tables, fixed tables, V$ tables, dynamic performance tables, and by a half-dozen other names. The first hurdle to understanding the X$ tables is to become familiar with their creation, security, content, and relationship to the V$ views.

In addition, these X$ tables are very cryptic in nature. They are similar to the underlying table construction of the Oracle data dictionary. Therefore, Oracle creates V$ views that are more readable and practical. In addition, Oracle has built other views (USER, DBA, ALL) within the scripts called by `catalog.sql` script for easier use. Oracle has also created a public synonym on V_$ views in the `cdfixed.sql` file that changes the name back to a view with a prefix of V$. An example of a V_$ view and the creation of a V$ public synonym in `cdfixed.sql` is shown here:

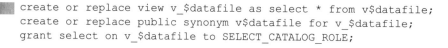

```
create or replace view v_$datafile as select * from v$datafile;
create or replace public synonym v$datafile for v_$datafile;
grant select on v_$datafile to SELECT_CATALOG_ROLE;
```

TIP
See Chapter 12 and Appendix B for detailed V$ view information and Appendix C for detailed X$ information.

Once the `catalog.sql` file has been executed, the V$ views are available only to users with the SELECT_CATALOG_ROLE privilege. At this point, you can grant access to V$ views by granting SELECT on the V$ view. Therefore, all SELECTs performed against the V$ views are actually retrieving information out of the SGA, more specifically out of the X$ tables. DBAs cannot modify X$ tables in any manner, and they cannot create indexes on these tables. Oracle began providing indexes on the X$ tables in version 8. In addition, the V$ views are the underlying views that are used for Oracle monitoring tools. Here you can see how to get a listing of all V$ views:

```
select     kqfvinam name
from       x$kqfvi
order by   kqfvinam;
```

Here is the partial output:

```
NAME
GO$SQL_BIND_CAPTURE
GV$ACCESS
GV$ACTIVE_INSTANCES
GV$ACTIVE_SERVICES
GV$ACTIVE_SESSION_HISTORY
GV$ACTIVE_SESS_POOL_MTH
GV$ADVISOR_PROGRESS
GV$ALERT_TYPES
...
V$WLM_PC_STATS
V$WORKLOAD_REPLAY_THREAD
V$XML_AUDIT_TRAIL
V$_LOCK
V$_LOCK1
V$_SEQUENCES

1023 rows selected.
```

Note that the GV$ views are the same as the V$ tables except that you can see multiple instances with Oracle Real Application Clusters (RAC). The only difference between the GV$ and V$ tables is a column that shows the instance ID.

Obtaining a List of the X$ Tables That Make Up the V$ Views

To obtain a list of the X$ tables that comprise the V$ views, you must access the V$FIXED_VIEW_DEFINITION view. This view shows how the V$ views were created. By knowing which X$ tables comprise a V$ view, you may be able to build a faster query that goes directly to the X$ tables, as shown here:

```
select    *
from      v$fixed_view_definition
where     view_name = 'GV$FIXED_TABLE';
```

Here is the output:

```
VIEW NAME          VIEW DEFINITION
GV$FIXED_TABLE     select inst_id,kqftanam, kqftaobj, 'TABLE', indx
                     from x$kqfta
                     union all
                     select inst_id,kqfvinam, kqfviobj, 'VIEW', 65537
                     from x$kqfvi
                     union all
                     select inst_id,kqfdtnam, kqfdtobj, 'TABLE', 65537
                     from x$kqfdt
```

TIP
Access the X$KQFVI table for a listing of all V$ and GV$ views.
Access the V$FIXED_VIEW_DEFINITION view to get all of the
information regarding the underlying X$ tables that comprise
a V$ view.

Obtaining a List of All the X$ Tables

The names of the X$ tables are in the X$KQFTA table (which contains 913 of the X$ tables), the
X$KQFDT table (which contains another 32 of the X$ tables), and the X$KQFVI table, which
contains the V$/GV$ as described in the previous section. The V$FIXED_TABLE view combines
all three of these tables so you can obtain a listing of any desired grouping. The query in this next
listing shows how to obtain a listing of the X$ tables:

```
select      name
from        v$fixed_table
where       name like 'X%'
order by    name;
```

Following is the partial output (for a complete listing, see Appendix C):

```
NAME
---------------------
X$ABSTRACT_LOB
X$ACTIVECKPT
X$ASH
X$BH
X$BUFFER
X$BUFFER2
X$BUFFERED_PUBLISHERS
X$BUFFERED_QUEUES
X$BUFFERED_SUBSCRIBERS
X$CELL_NAME
... (there are 945 in Oracle 11gR2)
```

The following query shows output from X$KQFDT, which is a partial listing of the X$ tables:

```
select      kqfdtnam, kqfdtequ
from        x$kqfdt;
```

```
KQFDTNAM                            KQFDTEQU
------------------------------      ---------
X$KSLLTR_CHILDREN                   X$KSLLTR
X$KSLLTR_PARENT                     X$KSLLTR
X$KCVFHONL                          X$KCVFH
X$KCVFHMRR                          X$KCVFH
X$KCVFHALL                          X$KCVFH
X$KGLTABLE                          X$KGLOB
X$KGLBODY                           X$KGLOB
```

```
X$KGLTRIGGER                    X$KGLOB
X$KGLINDEX                      X$KGLOB
X$KGLCLUSTER                    X$KGLOB
X$KGLCURSOR                     X$KGLOB
... (there are 32 in Oracle 11gR2)
```

TIP
*Query V$FIXED_TABLE for the names of the X$ tables, or you can
also access the two X$ tables X$KQFTA and X$KQFDT for partial
listings that when combined make up the full list.*

Obtaining a List of All the X$ Indexes

If you often query the V$ views or X$ tables for information, you will find it helpful to understand
which indexes are being used, as shown here:

```
select    table_name, index_number, column_name
from      v$indexed_fixed_column
order by  table_name, index_number, column_name, column_position;
```

Here is the partial output (full listing in Appendix C):

```
TABLE_NAME                          INDEX_NUMBER COLUMN_NAME
-------------------------------     ------------ -----------
X$ASH                                          1 NEED_AWR_SAMPLE
X$ASH                                          1 SAMPLE_ADDR
X$ASH                                          1 SAMPLE_ID
X$BUFFER                                       1 OBJNO
X$BUFFER2                                      1 OBJNO
X$DIAG_ADR_CONTROL                             3 COLA
X$DIAG_ADR_INVALIDATION                        3 ADR_PATH_IDX
X$DIAG_ALERT_EXT                               3 ADR_PATH_IDX
X$DIAG_AMS_XACTION                             3 ADR_PATH_IDX
X$DIAG_DDE_USER_ACTION                         3 ADR_PATH_IDX
X$DIAG_DDE_USER_ACTION_DEF                     3 ADR_PATH_IDX
X$DIAG_DDE_USR_ACT_PARAM                       3 ADR_PATH_IDX
```

```
... (there are 628 X$ indexes in Oracle 11gR2)
```

Only five X$ tables have multicolumn indexes, as shown in this listing:

```
SELECT    DISTINCT a.table_name, a.index_number,
          a.column_name,a.column_position
FROM      v$indexed_fixed_column a, v$indexed_fixed_column b
WHERE     a.table_name = b.table_name
AND       a.index_number = b.index_number
AND       a.column_name != b.column_name
ORDER BY a.table_name,a.index_number, a.column_position;
```

TABLE_NAME	INDEX_NUMBER	COLUMN_NAME	COLUMN_POSITION
X$ASH	1	SAMPLE_ADDR	0
X$ASH	1	SAMPLE_ID	1
X$ASH	1	NEED_AWR_SAMPLE	2
X$KESWXMON	2	SQLID_KESWXMON	0
X$KESWXMON	2	EXECID_KESWXMON	1
X$KESWXMON	2	EXECSTART_KESWXMON	2
X$KESWXMON_PLAN	2	SQLID_KESWXMONP	0
X$KESWXMON_PLAN	2	EXECID_KESWXMONP	1
X$KESWXMON_PLAN	2	EXECSTART_KESWXMONP	2
X$KTFBUE	1	KTFBUESEGTSN	0
X$KTFBUE	1	KTFBUESEGFNO	1
X$KTFBUE	1	KTFBUESEGBNO	2
X$KTSLCHUNK	1	KTSLCHUNKTSN	0
X$KTSLCHUNK	1	KTSLCHUNKSEGFNO	1
X$KTSLCHUNK	1	KTSLCHUNKSEGBLKNO	2

To see the data about the X$ tables from which the information is retrieved, perform this query to the V$FIXED_VIEW definition table:

```
select      *
from        v$fixed_view_definition
where       view_name = 'GV$INDEXED_FIXED_COLUMN';
```

Here is the output:

VIEW_NAME	VIEW DEFINITION
V$INDEXED_FIXED_COLUMN	select c.inst_id, kqftanam, kqfcoidx, kqfconam, kqfcoipo from x$kqfco c, x$kqfta t where t.indx = c.kqfcotab and kqfcoidx != 0

TIP
Access the V$INDEXED_FIXED_COLUMN view for a listing of all X$TABLE indexes.

Using Hints with X$ Tables and Indexes

As with other tables, you can also use hints with the X$ tables to achieve greater performance. The queries in the next two listings show the EXPLAIN PLAN and statistics while changing the driving table using an ORDERED hint. Note that I am using aliases for the tables and would need to hint the alias (and not the table) if I used a hint requiring the table (such as the index hint). The ORDERED hint does not require the table name but accesses tables in the order listed in the FROM clause.

Forcing the X$KSBDP table as the driving table

```
select    /*+ ordered */ p.ksbdppro, p.ksbdpnam,
          d.ksbdddsc,p.ksbdperr
from      x$ksbdd d, x$ksbdp p
where     p.indx = d.indx;
```

```
Execution Plan
------------------------------------------------------------------------------
| Id  | Operation              | Name           |Rows|Bytes|Cost (%CPU)|Time    |
|  0  | SELECT STATEMENT       |                | 100|8300 |   0    (0)|00:00:01|
|  1  |  NESTED LOOPS          |                | 100|8300 |   0    (0)|00:00:01|
|  2  |   FIXED TABLE FULL      | X$KSBDD       | 100|4700 |   0    (0)|00:00:01|
|* 3  |   FIXED TABLE FIXED INDEX| X$KSBDP (ind:1)|  1|  36 |   0    (0)|00:00:01|
```

Using the ordered hint to force the driving table to be X$KSBDP

```
select    /*+ ordered */ p.ksbdppro, p.ksbdpnam,
          d.ksbdddsc,p.ksbdperr
from      X$ksbdp p, X$ksbdd d
where     p.indx = d.indx;
```

```
Execution Plan
------------------------------------------------------------------------------
| Id  | Operation              | Name           |Rows|Bytes|Cost (%CPU)|Time    |
|  0  | SELECT STATEMENT       |                | 100| 8300|   0    (0)|00:00:01|
|  1  |  NESTED LOOPS          |                | 100| 8300|   0    (0)|00:00:01|
|  2  |   FIXED TABLE FULL      |X$KSBDP         | 100| 3600|   0    (0)|00:00:01|
|* 3  |   FIXED TABLE FIXED INDEX|X$KSBDD (ind:2)|  1|  47|   0    (0)|00:00:01|
```

TIP
*Oracle generally uses the indexes as needed, but from time to time,
you may use hints to achieve a desired result.*

Monitoring Space Allocations in the Shared Pool

You can use the X$KSMLRU table to monitor space allocations in the shared pool that may be causing space allocation contention. The *relevant* columns in this table are as follows:

Column	Definition
ADDR	Address of this row in the array of fixed tables
INDX	Index number of this row in the array of fixed tables
INST_ID	Oracle instance number
KSMLRCOM	Description of allocation type
KSMLRSIZ	Size in bytes of the allocated chunk
KSMLRNUM	Number of items flushed from the shared pool to allocate space
KSMLRHON	Name of the object being loaded
KSMLROHV	Hash value of the object being loaded
KSMLRSES	Session performing the allocation, joins to V$SESSION.SADDR

You can use the X$KSMSP table to examine the current contents of the shared pool. Each row represents a chunk of memory in the shared pool. The *relevant* columns in this table are as follows:

Column	Definition
ADDR	Address of this row in the array of fixed tables
INDX	Index number of this row in the array of fixed tables
INST_ID	Oracle instance number
KSMCHCOM	Description of the allocated chunk of memory
KSMCHPTR	Physical address of this chunk of memory
KSMCHSIZ	The size of this chunk of allocated shared memory
KSMCHCLS	The class of this chunk of allocated shared memory, which has the following possible values: **recr** An allocated chunk of shared memory that is flushable if the shared pool is low on memory **freeabl** A freeable, but not flushable, chunk of shared memory that is currently in use **free** A free chunk of shared memory **perm** A permanently allocated, nonfreeable chunk of shared memory **R-free** Free memory in the reserved pool **R-freea** A freeable chunk in the reserved pool **R-recr** A re-creatable chunk in the reserved pool **R-perm** A permanent chunk in the reserved pool

Creating Queries to Monitor the Shared Pool

The shared pool is often a key area impacted by performance. This section focuses on queries that help you investigate the shared pool.

ORA-04031 Errors

V$SHARED_POOL_RESERVED.REQUEST_FAILURES [or SUM(X$KGHLU.KGHLUNFU)] gives the number of ORA-04031 errors that have occurred since the instance was started. If any ORA-04031 errors are occurring, then SHARED_POOL_SIZE and/or JAVA_POOL_SIZE are too small, the shared pool is fragmented, or application code may not be being shared optimally. The query in this listing checks the ORA-04031 errors that have occurred since the instance was started. Also, see Chapter 4 for setting parameters related to automating memory management, including MEMORY_TARGET, MEMORY_MAX_TARGET, and/or SGA_TARGET.

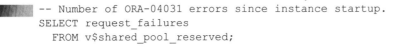

```
-- Number of ORA-04031 errors since instance startup.
SELECT request_failures
  FROM v$shared_pool_reserved;
```

If any ORA-04031 errors have occurred, then some SHARED_POOL_SIZE, JAVA_POOL_SIZE, and/or application tuning is in order. Consider one or more of the following:

- Pin large, high-use [high values for X$KSMLRU.KSMLRSIZ, COUNT(X$KSMLRU.KSMLRHON), and/or X$KSMLRU.KSMLRNUM] PL/SQL packages in memory with DBMS_SHARED_POOL.KEEP:

  ```
  EXECUTE dbms_shared_pool.keep('PACKAGENAME');
  ```

- Pin large, high-use Java classes with DBMS_SHARED_POOL.KEEP. You can pin a Java class by enclosing it in double quotes:

  ```
  EXECUTE dbms_shared_pool.keep('"FullJavaClassName"', 'JC');
  ```

TIP
Enclose the class in double quotes if it contains a slash (/); otherwise, you will get an ORA-00995 error.

- Increase the size of the shared pool by increasing the SHARED_POOL_SIZE initialization parameter if the percentage of SHARED_POOL free memory is low *and* there is contention for Library Cache space allocation *and/or* more than zero occurrences of the ORA-04031 error. The earlier section "Shared Pool" notes that increasing the shared pool is *not* always recommended if a low amount of shared pool memory is observed. If you are increasing the size of the shared pool, you might also need to raise the value of the parameter MEMORY_TARGET, MEMORY_MAX_TARGET, and/or SGA_TARGET (see Chapter 4 for additional information).

- Increase the size of the shared pool reserved area by increasing the SHARED_POOL_RESERVED_SIZE initialization parameter (the default is 5 percent of SHARED_POOL_SIZE).

- Promote the sharing of SQL, PL/SQL, and Java code by application developers.

Large Allocations Causing Contention

The object being loaded (X$KSMLRU.KSMLRHON) is a *keep* candidate (consider keeping it with DBMS_SHARED_POOL.KEEP) if the X$KSMLRU.KSMLRCOM value is MPCODE or PLSQL%.

If you use features such as Shared Servers (previously called MTS), Recovery Manager, or Parallel Query, you should configure a larger shared pool and also configure a large pool that is bigger than the default. These features will create large allocations in the shared pool and use the large pool instead if it is large enough.

```
          -- Amount of each type of shared pool allocation causing contention.

SELECT    ksmlrcom, SUM(ksmlrsiz)
FROM      x$ksmlru
GROUP BY  ksmlrcom;
```

```
KSMLRCOM              SUM(KSMLRSIZ)
-------------------   -------------
                                  0
qkxr.c.kgght                   4156
idndef : qcuAllocId            4096
```

TIP
*If X$KSMLRU.KSMLRCOM is similar to Fixed UGA, then a high
amount of session-specific allocation is occurring, which suggests that
OPEN_CURSORS may be set too high. This is relevant only in cases
where Shared Servers are being used.*

Shared Pool Fragmentation

This section takes a closer look at the shared pool using a plethora of queries to help you conduct detailed investigations when needed. (The shared pool is also discussed in detail in Chapter 4.) The shared pool may be fragmented if you observe a large number of entries in X$KSMLRU, particularly a large number of them with small KSMLRSIZ values, or if you observe many chunks of type "free" in X$KSMSP. Contrast this with a large number of entries in X$KSMLRU with medium to high values of KSMLRSIZ, which is not likely to be a symptom of a fragmented shared pool; rather, it indicates that large PL/SQL packages and/or Java classes need to be kept in the shared pool and possibly also that the shared pool itself is too small, and perhaps that application code is not being effectively shared (or some combination thereof). In identifying the problem, take the time to monitor the application code use over time to find out which code the user sessions are attempting to load. Network with application users, developers, designers, and application vendors. The queries in the following listings will help you find contention and fragmentation issues.

Finding contention and fragmentation issues

```
    -- Names of and sessions for shared pool allocations causing contention.
  SELECT ksmlrhon, ksmlrsiz, ksmlrses
    FROM x$ksmlru
   WHERE ksmlrsiz > 1000
ORDER BY ksmlrsiz;

Shared Pool Memory Allocated
    -- Shared pool memory allocated.
SELECT sum(ksmchsiz)||' bytes' "TotSharPoolMem"
  FROM x$ksmsp;

TotSharPoolMem
-----------------------------------------------
58719640 bytes
```

Fragmentation of shared pool

```
    -- Fragmentation of Shared Pool.
  SET VERIFY off
```

```
    COLUMN PctTotSPMem for a11
    SELECT ksmchcls        "ChnkClass",
           SUM(ksmchsiz) "SumChunkTypeMem",
           MAX(ksmchsiz) "LargstChkofThisTyp",
           COUNT(1)       "NumOfChksThisTyp",
           ROUND((SUM(ksmchsiz)/tot_sp_mem.TotSPMem),2)*100||'%' "PctTotSPMem"
      FROM x$ksmsp,
           (select sum(ksmchsiz) TotSPMem from x$ksmsp) tot_sp_mem
GROUP BY ksmchcls, tot_sp_mem.TotSPMem
ORDER BY SUM(ksmchsiz);
```

ChnkClas	SumChunkTypeMem	LargstChkofThisTyp	NumOfChksThisTyp	PctTotSPMem
R-freea	59000	21984	173	0%
R-recr	3977156	3977156	1	1%
R-perm	16553296	4193168	5	5%
R-free	21397980	2097032	85	6%
free	31038572	2396208	8893	9%
perm	51740844	3981312	29	15%
recr	86619156	44908	40129	24%
freeabl	145125076	334348	46223	41%

```
8 rows selected.
```

Information about SHARED_POOL_RESERVED_SIZE

```
    -- Information regarding shared_pool_reserved_size.
SELECT free_space,free_count,max_free_size,max_used_size,
       request_misses,max_miss_size
  FROM v$shared_pool_reserved;
```

FREE_SPACE	FREE_COUNT	MAX_FREE_SIZE	MAX_USED_SIZE	REQUEST_MISSES	MAX_MISS_SIZE
2980600	14	212900	0	0	0

Low Free Memory in Shared and Java Pools

If a low percentage of the shared or Java pools' memory is free, then the shared and/or Java pools may have crossed the fine line between an optimal amount of free memory and not enough free memory. To determine this, consider how many free chunks exist, the size of the largest chunk, whether there are a high number of reloads, and whether there have been any ORA-04031 errors. The two queries shown here will help.

Amount of shared pool free memory

```
    -- Amount of shared pool free memory.
SELECT *
  FROM v$sgastat
 WHERE name = 'free memory'
   AND pool = 'shared pool';
```

```
POOL          NAME                            BYTES
-----------   -------------------------   ----------
shared pool   free memory                    3819124
```

Amount of Java pool free memory

```
    -- Amount of java pool free memory.
SELECT *
  FROM v$sgastat
 WHERE name = 'free memory'
   AND pool = 'java pool';
```

```
POOL          NAME                            BYTES
-----------   -------------------------   ----------
java pool     free memory                   44626368
```

Library Cache Hit Ratio

A low library cache hit ratio is a symptom of one of several problems. The shared and/or Java pools may be too small; the SHARED_POOL_RESERVED_SIZE may be too small; CURSOR_SHARING may need to be set to FORCE; there may be inefficient sharing of SQL, PL/SQL, or Java code; or there may be insufficient use of bind variables. Investigate which application code is being used over time and how efficiently it is used (code sharing). Monitor the shared and Java pool freespace over time. If the amount of free memory in the shared and Java pools is relatively high, no ORA-04031 errors are occurring, and the library cache hit ratio is low, then poor code sharing is probably occurring. The queries in the following listings help you investigate this area. I include some V$ view queries here because of the applicable nature to this subject.

Library cache hit ratio

```
    -- Library cache hit ratio.
  SELECT ROUND(SUM(pinhits)/SUM(pins),2)*100||'%' "Library Cache Hit Ratio"
    FROM v$librarycache
ORDER BY namespace;

Library Cache Hit Ratio
-----------------------
90%
```

Library cache reload ratio

```
    -- Library cache reload ratio.
SELECT namespace,
       ROUND(DECODE(pins,0,0,reloads/pins),2)*100||'%' "Reload Ratio"
  FROM v$librarycache;
```

```
NAMESPACE              Reload Ratio
------------------     -----------------------------------------
SQL AREA               0%
TABLE/PROCEDURE        1%
BODY                   0%
TRIGGER                0%
INDEX                  12%
CLUSTER                0%
DIRECTORY              0%
QUEUE                  11%
APP CONTEXT            0%
RULESET                0%
SUBSCRIPTION           0%
RULE                   11%
TEMPORARY TABLE        99%
TEMPORARY INDEX        95%
EDITION                0%
DBLINK                 0%
OBJECT ID              0%
SCHEMA                 0%
DBINSTANCE             0%
```

Library cache high-use objects (make this a top 10 list by adding "WHERE ROWNUM<11")

```
    -- Library cache high-use objects (You may want to limit listing).
SELECT name,type
  FROM v$db_object_cache
ORDER BY executions;
```

Library cache object sizes

```
    -- Library cache object sizes (you may want to limit listing).
SELECT *
  FROM v$db_object_cache
ORDER BY sharable_mem;
```

Shared pool object sharing efficiency (you may want to limit these)

```
Column name format a40
Column type format a15

    -- Execute counts for currently cached objects.
SELECT name, type, COUNT(executions) ExecCount
  FROM v$db_object_cache
GROUP BY name, type
ORDER BY ExecCount;

    -- Currently cached objects that have execute counts of just 1.
    -- Consider converting these objects to use bind variables.
SELECT distinct name, type
  FROM v$db_object_cache
```

```
GROUP BY name, type
  HAVING COUNT(executions) = 1;


        -- Currently unkept, cached objects that have execute counts > 1.
        -- Consider pinning these objects.
    SELECT distinct name, type, COUNT(executions)
      FROM v$db_object_cache
     WHERE kept = 'NO'
  GROUP BY name, type
    HAVING COUNT(executions) > 1
  ORDER BY COUNT(executions);


-- Currently unkept, cached objects that are similar. Each of these
-- statements has at least 10 versions currently cached, but has only
-- been executed less than 5 times each. Consider converting these
-- objects to use bind variables and possibly also pinning them.
    SELECT SUBSTR(sql_text,1,40) "SQL", COUNT(1) , SUM(executions) "TotExecs"
      FROM  v$sqlarea
     WHERE executions < 5
       AND kept_versions = 0
  GROUP BY SUBSTR(sql_text,1,40)
    HAVING COUNT(1) > 10
  ORDER BY COUNT(1) ;
Clear columns
```

A high percentage of reloads indicates that the shared and/or Java pools are too small, code sharing is insufficient, and possibly also large code objects are repeatedly being used. Monitor the application code used over time. If particular large code objects are identified as frequently used, consider pinning them and/or increasing the size of the SHARED_POOL_RESERVED_SIZE. If features such as Shared Servers, Recovery Manager, or Parallel Query are used, consider a larger SHARED_POOL_SIZE and/or larger LARGE_POOL_SIZE (if setting parameters like MEMORY_TARGET and/or SGA_TARGET, please refer to Chapter 4 and ensure you *always* set a minimum for the SHARED_POOL_SIZE even if you use these other parameters).

High Number of Hard Parses

You should review similar queries with low numbers of executions to uncover opportunities to combine them into statements using bind variables. A high ratio of hard parses may mean that the shared pool itself is too small or perhaps a SQL statement is repeatedly nudging other code out of the precious shared pool or Java pool cache space. Identify these statements and consider pinning. Consider also setting the parameter CURSOR_SHARING = FORCE. The next listing shows various queries to view parse activity:

```
    -- Overall Parse Activity.
SELECT name, value
  FROM v$sysstat
 WHERE name = 'parse count (total)'
    OR name = 'parse count (hard)';
```

```
NAME                                                              VALUE
---------------------------------------------------------------- ----------
parse count (total)                                               11357
parse count (hard)                                                 924


    -- Ratio of hard parses to total parses.
SELECT ROUND((b.value/a.value),2)*100||'%' HardParseRatio
  FROM v$sysstat a, v$sysstat b
 WHERE a.name = 'parse count (total)'
   AND b.name = 'parse count (hard)';


HARDPARSERATIO
---------------
8%


    -- SQL Statements experiencing a high amount of parse activity.
SELECT sql_text, parse_calls, executions
  FROM v$sqlarea
 WHERE parse_calls > 100
   AND kept_versions = 0
   AND executions < 2*parse_calls;


SQL_TEXT
-------------------------------------------------------------------------------
PARSE_CALLS EXECUTIONS
----------- ----------
lock table sys.mon_mods$ in exclusive mode nowait
        126        126
lock table sys.col_usage$ in exclusive mode nowait
        269        269
(...partial listing only)
```

Mutex/Latch Waits and/or Sleeps

If mutex (see Chapter 14 for detail on mutexes) or latch waits are high but shared and Java pool freespace is also high, consider reducing the size of the shared and/or Java pools. When this happens, it could indicate that sessions are spending time scanning the unnecessarily large list of free shared pool chunks (be very careful before you do this—the goal is to get everything *in* memory—so ensure that you have enough allocated). Monitor the amount of shared and Java pool freespace over time. If ample freespace is available in these pools and no ORA-04031 errors are occurring, consider reducing the sizes of these pools. Investigate when the miss ratio and sleeps are high for any of the mutex/latches in the following list:

- Row cache objects
- Library Cache
- Shared pool
- Shared Java pool

If freespace in the shared and Java pools is low, then you should consider the other tuning areas, such as increasing the shared and/or Java pools, pinning objects, and combining similar SQL statements to use bind variables. The query in this next listing helps you acquire some of these metrics. A mutex (which replaced many types of Library Cache latches other than the library load lock latch) is used to eliminate the possibility of two processes simultaneously using a common resource (while one or both are trying to change it); when one session is changing it, the second can't view it or change it, and when one session is viewing it, the second can't change it.

Oracle moved from latches to mutexes (mutual exclusion) in some areas of the Library Cache because mutexes are lighter weight and provide more granular concurrency than latches. Mutexes require less memory space and fewer instructions. Oracle uses mutexes instead of Library Cache latches and Library Cache pin latches to protect objects in the Library Cache. With a mutex, if I have the resource and I can't get it after trying a specified number of times asking (spins), you sleep and try again a very short time later. Use the V$MUTEX_SLEEP view (covered in Chapter 12) in addition to the V$LATCH query listed next to query mutex/latch information:

```
Column name for a20
    -- Shared pool latch efficiency.
SELECT name,
       ROUND(misses/decode(gets,0,1,gets),2)*100||'%' as "WillToWaitMissRatio",
       ROUND(immediate_misses/decode(immediate_gets,0,1,
       immediate_gets),2)*100 ||'%' "ImmMissRatio",
       sleeps
  FROM v$latch
 WHERE name in ('row cache objects', 'shared pool');
Clear columns

NAME                 WillToWaitMissRatio
-------------------- ----------------------------------------
ImmMissRatio                                           SLEEPS
----------------------------------------------- ----------
row cache objects    0%
0%                                                          0
shared pool          0%
0%                                                          3
```

No issues occur in the output above (minimal sleeps). Remember that before increasing the SHARED_POOL_SIZE, you should consider whether there are any shared pool or library latch/mutex waits. Depending on what you observe, it may actually be more appropriate to reduce the size of the shared pool, for instance, if you have a sufficient amount of free shared pool memory available, a low number of reloads, and a high number of shared pool latch waits. The reason to consider reducing the shared pool in this case is that with an oversized shared pool, sessions will hold the shared pool latch slightly longer than is needed otherwise because the shared pool needs to scan a larger amount of space to determine exactly where to allocate the space it is requesting. Fixing the issues causing a shared pool issue and then ensuring it is large enough to fit all statements in memory is a key to good performance. Fix the problem and then make sure the shared pool is large enough (too many people make it way too small and problems occur)!

Miscellaneous

After exhausting previously discussed shared and Java pool tuning options, you could consider some undocumented parameters. The number of the Library Cache hash table bucket count can be increased by setting _KGL_BUCKET_COUNT (see Appendix A for more information on the undocumented initialization parameters); note that 9 (the default) puts this at ((2 to the 9th power)*256)–1 = 131071) which should be more than enough for most systems. Oracle 11*g* still has an _KGL_LATCH_COUNT parameter. Remember that you should never set the underscore parameters without direction from Oracle Support. In 11*g*, *each* Library Cache bucket (131,071) is protected by a mutex! Also, in 11*g*, the _KGL_LATCH_COUNT is set at 0 and probably doesn't need to be set, but consult with Oracle Support before setting this.

Adjusting this parameter is, as with all undocumented parameters, unsupported by Oracle. Implement such changes only under the direction of Oracle Support and after thoroughly testing under direct simulation of production conditions.

Note that any particular database may experience conditions that are a combination of two or more of the previous conditions. Frequently, you must evaluate multiple conditions and decide on two or more potential corrective measures.

Also note that after each query on X$KSMLRU, the values in this table are reset back to zero. To effectively monitor the table, consider capturing the contents of it to a permanent table with an INSERT INTO . . . AS SELECT . . . statement or by simply spooling the output to a file. Furthermore, whenever you query X$KSMLRU, you might always want to select all of the columns instead of just one or the few you might be interested in at a particular moment; otherwise, you may miss some information that you later decide you want to see.

CAUTION
When "resetting" the X$KSMLRU table, note rows may still be in this table after each query. Do not interpret the remaining rows appearing after each query as entries pertaining to contention-causing code, but rather to preallocated entries in this table. If no problem statements are in X$KSMLRU, then the KSMLRHON and KSMLRSIZ values are NULL and zero, respectively. If they are non-NULL, then these rows pertain to contention-causing code. Make sure multiple DBAs do not simultaneously query X$KSMLRU because each of them may observe misleading results.

Remember that when you decide to alter initialization parameters to remedy performance problems, you can now alter many of them by using an `alter system` command. Despite the ease of doing this, you should first test such changes on a test system. For example, if you attempt to make the SHARED_POOL_SIZE too small, the SQL*Plus session may hang and/or consume a large amount of memory and CPU resources during the execution of the `alter system` command. Or, prior to Oracle 9i, if you set the _KGL_LATCH_COUNT parameter too high, you get an ORA-600 [17038] error when you next try to start the database. The point here is to *be careful* and know what you're doing before changing any of these parameters.

Obtaining Information about Redo Log Files

The X$KCCCP table contains information about the current redo log file. The X$KCCLE table contains information about all redo log files, as shown here:

```
    -- Percentage full of the current redo log file.
SELECT ROUND((cpodr_bno/lesiz),2)*100||'%' PctCurLogFull
  FROM x$kcccp a, x$kccle b
 WHERE a.cpodr_seq = leseq;


PCTCURLOGFULL
---------------
35%
```

If you observe in V$LOG_HISTORY or in the "log file space waits" statistic that log switches are occurring more frequently than is appropriate for your database, you may decide to alter the redo log file configuration. You can perform this task while the database is open to users and all tablespaces are online. If you want to minimize the impact on database performance while this or other similar maintenance is performed that involves a DBA-induced log switch with the `alter system switch log file` command, you can use the query in the preceding listing to measure how much redo log information has to be copied to complete the archive of the current log file. This is particularly relevant in cases of databases with large redo log files (500M or larger).

You can also use this query as a tuning aid to measure how much redo activity is created by a particular transaction or process, if it is possible to isolate a particular database to one session that is guaranteed as the only creator of redo records, other than Oracle itself. Capturing before and after results of this query when testing such a transaction may be useful.

Setting Initialization Parameters

Oracle 9*i* introduced the concept of the server parameter file, or SPFILE. This file allows DBAs to make persistent initialization parameter changes with the `alter system` command without having to incorporate these changes manually into a traditional parameter file, or PFILE, to implement the persistence of the parameter change. SPFILES also allow the DBA to save the current instance configuration instantaneously to a file for archival or backup purposes. This flexibility introduces a bit of initialization parameter management complexity in that the Oracle instance can be started with either a PFILE or an SPFILE. This complexity raises a few questions for the DBA when managing initialization parameters. The DBA must know what Oracle will use as an initialization parameter file at instance startup time, where the initialization parameters will be saved when an `alter system . . . scope=spfile` or `alter system . . . scope=both` command is issued, and whether a currently running Oracle instance was started using a PFILE, an SPFILE, or both.

If the SPFILE in the platform-specific default location with the platform-specific default name exists, then Oracle uses it to start the instance. To get Oracle to use an SPFILE other than the one residing in the default location with the default filename, you must first rename, relocate, or delete this default SPFILE, and then relocate and/or rename the desired SPFILE from the nondefault location to the default location and name. Alternatively, you can specify this nondefault SPFILE in the SPFILE initialization parameter in a PFILE that is used to start the instance.

Note that the concept of the platform-specific default name and location for the PFILE still exists; this concept is used if no SPFILE is in the SPFILE default location and name. As in pre–Oracle 9*i* versions, you can use a nondefault PFILE to start an instance with the PFILE option of the `startup` command. These are the only ways that Oracle will use a nondefault parameter file to start the instance. There is no startup SPFILE command. SPFILES and PFILES are not interchangeable. SPFILES are (mostly) binary files that can be altered only with `alter system` commands and can be created only with `create spfile` commands.

As in pre–Oracle 9*i* versions, PFILES are simply text files that may be created and altered with a text editor. An attempt to use an SPFILE in the `startup pfile` command will result in an ORA-01078 error. If an instance was started with an SPFILE, then any changes made using the `alter system . . . scope=spfile` or `alter system . . . scope=both` commands are saved to the SPFILE that was used to start the instance, even if the default SPFILE exists and was not used to start the instance. If both a PFILE and an SPFILE are used to start an Oracle instance, Oracle overrides any parameters specified in the PFILE with those specified in the SPFILE, if any conflicts occur.

The question of which file was used to start an Oracle instance has five possible answers:

- On startup, the database first looks for `spfile<SID>.ora` in the default location, and then looks for `spfile.ora` in the default location. An SPFILE in the default location was used with the default name and no PFILE was used.

- A PFILE in the default location with the default name was used and a nondefault SPFILE was used.

- A nondefault PFILE was used and a nondefault SPFILE was used.

- A PFILE in the default location with the default name was used and no SPFILE was used.

- A nondefault PFILE was used and no SPFILE was used.

NOTE
Both an SPFILE and a PFILE may have been used to start an instance, however. Check the following queries in the order listed to answer the question of which files may have been used for the initialization parameters to start the instance.

Case 1

Run the query in this listing to check for SPFILE-specified initialization parameters:

```
    -- Check for spfile-specified initialization parameters.
SELECT count(1)
  FROM v$spparameter
 WHERE isspecified = 'TRUE';

  COUNT(1)
----------
        29
```

Or simply use the SQL*Plus command SHOW PARAMETER SPFILE. This tells you exactly which SPFILE was used to start the database (gets set automatically when the database is started without specifying a PFILE or SPFILE). If you start the database with the PFILE option, then this parameter is NULL. The following is the equivalent to the query in the preceding listing but involves less typing:

```
SQL> SHOW PARAMETER SPFILE
```

Case 2

Run this query to determine which SPFILE was used to start the instance:

```
     -- Determine which spfile was used to start the instance.
SELECT value
  FROM v$parameter
 WHERE name = 'spfile';
```

Look for a PFILE in the default location. If the SPFILE parameter value from the query in the preceding listing (to V$PARAMETER) is non-NULL and the value is not the default value for the SPFILE, then a PFILE was used, and it specified an alternate SPFILE in the SPFILE parameter. If this is the case and if the default PFILE exists, then it was used to start the instance.

Case 3

If the SPFILE parameter value from the query in the Case 2 listing (to V$PARAMETER) is non-NULL and the value is not the default value for the SPFILE, then a PFILE was used, and it specified an alternate SPFILE in the SPFILE parameter. If this is the case and if the default PFILE does not exist, then you must determine the location of the nondefault PFILE. See Case 5.

Case 4

If the SPFILE parameter value from the query in the listing in Case 2 (to V$PARAMETER) is NULL, then a PFILE was used and no SPFILE was used. If this is the case and if the default PFILE exists, then it was used to start the instance.

Case 5

If it is determined from Cases 1 through 3 that no SPFILE was used at all, and that the default PFILE was not used, then the remaining possibility is that a nondefault PFILE was used and no SPFILE was used. Many site-specific possibilities exist for a nondefault PFILE. A database startup, shutdown, or backup script, a third-party backup or database management software package, or a site-specific Oracle software directory structure may give a clue to what this file is. If there is uncertainty about this file, you can save the existing configuration initialization parameters by querying some of the Oracle X$ tables pertinent to initialization parameters. There is also the possibility that OEM, which can store a local copy of the parameter file, started the database.

Several X$ tables are relevant to initialization parameters: X$KSPSPFILE, X$KSPPSV, X$KSPPSV2, X$KSPPCV, X$KSPPCV2, X$KSPPI, and X$KSPPO. The X$KSPSPFILE table lists the contents of the SPFILE. The V$SPPARAMETER view, which is based on the X$KSPSPFILE table, excludes parameter names that start with an underscore, unless such "underscore" or "undocumented" parameters were explicitly specified in an SPFILE, in a PFILE, or with an `alter system` command and/or Oracle had to modify the DBA-specified value to fit a functional requirement of the parameter, such as a requirement that a particular parameter value be a prime number or a multiple of another DBA-specified parameter value, for example. To see all the parameter names, including those that the V$SPPARAMETER view excludes, query the X$KSPSPFILE table.

Note that if an SPFILE was not used to start an instance, then all of the values in the KSPSPFFTCTXSPVALUE column of X$KSPSPFILE are NULL and all of the values in the KSPSPFFTCTXISSPECIFIED column are FALSE. Conversely, if an SPFILE was used to start an instance, the values in the KSPSPFFTCTXISSPECIFIED column for which the particular parameter was specified in the SPFILE are TRUE and the value in the KSPSPFFTCTXSPVALUE column for such parameters is a non-NULL value.

The X$KSPPSV table lists the parameter names and values that are currently in effect for the instance. The V$SYSTEM_PARAMETER view, which is based on the X$KSPPSV table, excludes parameters that start with an underscore and have not been modified from their default value.

The X$KSPPSV2 table is very similar to the X$KSPPSV table. The difference is in how parameter values are stored that consist of lists of values. This table, like the X$KSPPSV table, lists parameters and parameter values that are currently in effect for this Oracle instance. A new session inherits parameter values from the system values. Each list parameter value appears as a separate row in the table. Presenting the list parameter values in this format enables you to quickly determine the values for a list parameter. For example, if a parameter value is "a,b" looking at X$KSPPSV does not tell you whether the parameter has two values ("a" and "b") or one value ("a,b"). X$KSPPSV2 makes the distinction between the list parameter values clear. Correspondingly, the V$SYSTEM_PARAMETER2 view is based on the X$KSPPSV2 table.

The X$KSPPCV and X$KSPPCV2 tables are similar to the X$KSPPSV and X$KSPPSV2 tables, except that the X$KSPPCV and X$KSPPCV2 tables apply to the current session, not necessarily the whole instance. If a parameter is changed with an `alter session` command, the change is reflected in the X$KSPPCV and X$KSPPCV2 tables. The V$PARAMETER and V$PARAMETER2 fixed views are based on the X$KSPPCV and X$KSPPCV2 tables, respectively.

The X$KSPPI table lists the initialization parameter names, types, and statuses. The V$PARAMETER, V$PARAMETER2, V$SYSTEM_PARAMETER, and V$SYSTEM_PARAMETER2 fixed views are based on the X$KSPPCV, X$KSPPCV2, X$KSPPSV, and X$KSPPSV2 tables; each of these X$ tables is joined with the X$KSPPI table in these fixed views to get the associated parameter names and other information. The query in this next listing is the query on which V$SYSTEM_PARAMETER is based, excluding the line in V$SYSTEM_PARAMETER that excludes parameter names that start with an underscore. The underlying SQL statements of the V$PARAMETER, V$PARAMETER2, and V$SYSTEM_PARAMETER2 fixed views have the same structure as the query in the listing in Case 2 described previously.

```
      -- All initialization parameter settings in effect for the instance.
   SELECT x.indx+1 InstanceNum,
          ksppinm ParamName,
          ksppity ParamType,
          ksppstvl ParamValue,
          ksppstdf IsDefaultVal,
```

```
       DECODE(bitand(ksppiflg/256,1),
              1,'TRUE',
                'FALSE') IsSessModifiable,
       DECODE (bitand(ksppiflg/65536,3),
              1,'IMMEDIATE',
              2,'DEFERRED',
                'FALSE') IsSysModifiable,
       DECODE (bitand(ksppstvf,7),
              1,'MODIFIED',
                'FALSE') IsModified,
       DECODE (bitand(ksppstvf,2),
                2,'TRUE',
                  'FALSE') IsAdjusted,
       ksppdesc Description,
       ksppstcmnt UpdateComment
    FROM x$ksppi x, x$ksppsv y
   WHERE (x.indx = y.indx)
ORDER BY ParamName;
```

The V$OBSOLETE_PARAMETER fixed view, which is based on the X$KSPPO table, lists obsolete initialization parameters. For some of these, such as SPIN_COUNT, you may note that they are now undocumented parameters.

Buffer Cache/Data Block Details

Four key performance-related buffer cache topics are the current buffer statuses, the identification of segments that are occupying the block buffers, the detection of hot (popular or high contention) data blocks, and the cause of buffer-cache-related latch contention and wait events. These topics are relevant to buffer cache tuning in all Oracle versions, but there are additional considerations in Oracle 8, 8*i,* and 9*i.* Oracle 8 introduced the concept of multiple buffer pools. Oracle 9*i* introduced the concept of multiple data block sizes and, therefore, the need for multiple buffer cache buffer sizes.

The X$ tables are used in the buffer-cache-related queries that follow:

X$ Table	Definition
X$BH	Status and number of pings for every buffer in the SGA
X$KCBWDS	Statistics on all buffer pools available to the instance
X$KCBWBPD	Statistics on all buffer pools available to the instance, including buffer pool names
X$KCBWAIT	Number of and time spent in waits for buffer pool classes
X$KCBFWAIT	Buffer cache wait count and time by file

The queries in the follow sections are relevant to these topics.

Buffer Statuses

A low number of buffers with a status of "Free" in X$BH does not necessarily mean that the buffer cache is undersized. It may, in fact, mean that the buffer cache is optimally sized such that Oracle will not have to perform frequent organization and maintenance on a superfluous number of buffers. Unfortunately, this same thought process leads many DBAs to undersize the buffer cache and leave memory sitting idle on their system. Similarly, if a large percentage of buffers are consistently free, then perhaps the buffer cache is oversized. See the subsequent sections discussing buffer cache contents, latches, and wait events for a better indication of the proper sizing and configuration of the buffer cache as it relates to the segments that are being used. Tuning and looking at Oracle at the block level is covered in detail in Chapter 9. The query in this listing shows how to see the state of the buffers in the buffer cache:

```
      -- Buffer cache buffer statuses.
  SET VERIFY off
  COLUMN PctTotBCMem for a11
  SELECT /*+ ordered */
          tot_bc_mem.TotBCMem,
          decode(state,
                    0,'Free',
                    1,'Exclusive',
                    2,'SharedCurrent' ,
                    3,'ConsistentRead',
                    4,'BeingRead',
                    5,'InMediaRecoveryMode',
                    6,'InInstanceRecoveryMode',
                    7,'BeingWritten',
                    8,'Pinned',
                    9,'Memory',
                   10,'mrite',
                   11,'Donated') "BlockState",
          SUM(blsiz) "SumStateTypeMem",
          COUNT(1)   "NumOfBlksThisTyp",
          ROUND(SUM(blsiz)/tot_bc_mem.TotBCMem,2)*100||'%' "PctTotBCMem"
     FROM (SELECT sum(blsiz) TotBCMem
           FROM x$bh) tot_bc_mem,
               x$bh
  GROUP BY tot_bc_mem.TotBCMem,
             decode(state,
                    0,'Free',
                    1,'Exclusive',
                    2,'SharedCurrent' ,
                    3,'ConsistentRead',
                    4,'BeingRead',
                    5,'InMediaRecoveryMode',
                    6,'InInstanceRecoveryMode',
                    7,'BeingWritten',
                    8,'Pinned',
                    9,'Memory',
                   10,'mrite',
                   11,'Donated')
  ORDER BY SUM(blsiz);
  CLEAR COLUMNS


   TOTBCMEM BlockState                    SumStateTypeMem NumOfBlksThisTyp PctTotBCMem
  ---------- -------------------------    --------------- ---------------- -----------
  209739776 Free                                12828672             1566 6%
  209739776 ConsistentRead                      43368448             5294 21%
  209739776 Exclusive                          153542656            18743 73%
```

Here is a quick reference listing the buffer states in X$BH:

Buffer State	Meaning
0	Free
1	Exclusive/Current (CURR)
2	Shared Current
3	Consistent Read (CR)
4	Being Read
5	In Media Recovery Mode
6	In Instance Recovery Mode
7	Being Written
8	Pinned
9	Memory
10	Mwrite
11	Donated

Segments Occupying Block Buffers

Noting the distribution of segment owners, types, and names among the occupied buffers is useful. Note, in particular, which objects occupy the most buffers. Observe the indexes currently in the cache. Question whether these indexes are appropriate. If they are nonselective indexes being used by selective queries (or vice versa), these indexes could be occupying precious buffers that could be used more effectively by the corresponding table blocks or by the blocks of other segments experiencing "buffer busy waits" wait events. Query V$SQLTEXT to observe the SQL statements currently using the segments occupying the highest percentages of the buffers and determine whether index usage in these statements is appropriate. The two queries in the following listings show the segments occupying block buffers and also the percentage of buffers occupied by segments in the buffer cache.

All segments occupying block buffers

```
    -- Segments Occupying Block Buffers (long listing / for testing usually).
SELECT o.*, d_o.owner, d_o.object_name, object_type, o.buffers, o.avg_touches
FROM (    SELECT obj object, count(1) buffers, AVG(tch) avg_touches
                   FROM x$bh
          GROUP BY obj) o,
dba_objects d_o
WHERE o.object = d_o.data_object_id
ORDER BY owner, object_name;
```

Percentage of buffers occupied by segments in the buffer cache

```
    -- Percentage of Buffers Occupied by Segments in the Buffer Cache.
    -- Note that this percentage is the percentage of the number of
```

```
      -- occupied buffers, not the percentage of the number of allocated
      -- buffers.
SELECT tot_occ_bufs.TotOccBufs,o.*,d_o.owner, d_o.object_name, object_type,
        ROUND((o.buffers/tot_occ_bufs.TotOccBufs)*100,2) || '%' PctOccBufs
FROM    (SELECT obj object, count(1) buffers, AVG(tch) avg_touches
            FROM x$bh
        GROUP BY obj) o,
          (SELECT COUNT(1) TotOccBufs
            FROM x$bh
          WHERE  state != 0) tot_occ_bufs,
        dba_objects d_o
  WHERE o.object = d_o.data_object_id
ORDER BY round((o.buffers/tot_occ_bufs.TotOccBufs)*100,2),owner, object_name;
```

Note also that only segments that are of the same block size as the block size of the default pool (the default block size) may be assigned to the keep or recycle pools. As of the first release of Oracle 9*i*, the keep and recycle pools are not available for use by segments that are not the default block size. This defeats some of the strategy involved with tuning segments that are either high or low access and are not the default block size. However, other tuning options are available for such segments, such as partitioning.

Pool-specific buffer cache buffer occupation

```
      -- Pool Specific Buffer Cache Buffer Occupation
SELECT DECODE(wbpd.bp_id,1,'Keep',
                          2,'Recycle',
                          3,'Default',
                          4,'2K Pool',
                          5,'4K Pool',
                          6,'8K Pool',
                          7,'16K Pool',
                          8,'32K Pool',
                            'UNKNOWN') Pool,
        bh.owner,
        bh.object_name object_name,
        count(1) NumOfBuffers
   FROM x$kcbwds wds, x$kcbwbpd wbpd,
        (SELECT set_ds,x.addr,o.name object_name,
                u.name owner
           FROM sys.obj$ o,
                sys.user$ u,
                x$bh x
          WHERE o.owner# = u.user#
            AND o.dataobj# = x.obj
            AND x.state !=0
            AND o.owner# !=0 ) bh
  WHERE wds.set_id >= wbpd.bp_lo_sid
    AND wds.set_id <= wbpd.bp_hi_sid
    AND wbpd.bp_size != 0
    AND wds.addr=bh.set_ds
  GROUP BY
```

```
DECODE(wbpd.bp_id,1,'Keep',
                  2,'Recycle',
                  3,'Default',
                  4,'2K Pool',
                  5,'4K Pool',
                  6,'8K Pool',
                  7,'16K Pool',
                  8,'32K Pool',
                    'UNKNOWN'),
       bh.owner,
       bh.object_name
ORDER BY 1,4,3,2;
```

Hot Data Blocks and the Causes of Latch Contention and Wait Events

The segment blocks returned by the query in the next listing are ones that are being accessed frequently, particularly if the value of the TCH (count) column changes (higher *and* lower) between consecutive executions of this query. The TCH column value is incremented every time a particular buffer is "touched" or "visited" by a transaction. This value can fluctuate as a buffer is moved up and down the LRU list. The reason for the fluctuation is that Oracle internally adjusts the TCH value according to its position in the LRU list and other factors, such as how long it has been since the buffer was last touched. In some scenarios of this algorithm, Oracle internally resets the TCH value back to 1.

```
-- Segments Occupying Hot Buffers (could be slow for a large cache / test).
-- This query defines a "hot" buffer as a buffer that has
-- a touch count greater than 10.
COL NAME FOR A35
SELECT /*+ ordered */ u.username ||'.'|| o.name  name,
       so.object_type type, bh.dbablk, bh.tch touches
FROM   x$bh  bh, dba_users u, sys.obj$ o, sys.sys_objects so
WHERE  bh.obj = o.obj#
and    bh.obj = so.object_id
and    o.owner# = u.user_id
AND    bh.tch  > 10
ORDER  BY bh.tch desc;
```

NAME	TYPE	DBABLK	TOUCHES
SYS.FILE$	TABLE	114	807
SYS.I_FILE#_BLOCK#	INDEX	82	804
SYS.C_USER#	CLUSTER	92	746
SYS.C_USER#	CLUSTER	90	737
SYS.I_FILE#_BLOCK#	INDEX	88	612
SYS.JOB$	TABLE	1473	506
SYS.JOB$	TABLE	1474	505
SYS.I_JOB_NEXT	INDEX	1490	485
SYS.I_FILE#_BLOCK#	INDEX	85	396
SYS.C_USER#	CLUSTER	91	344

```
SYS.I_OBJ1                        INDEX                 54721        340
(Output truncated...)

    -- Segments Occupying Hot Buffers (could be slow for a large cache / test).
    -- This query defines a "hot" buffer as a buffer that has
    -- a touch count greater than 10 and groups by OBJECT.
COL NAME FOR A35
SELECT /*+ ordered */ u.username ||'.'|| o.name  name,
       so.object_type type, count(bh.dbablk) blocks, sum(bh.tch) touches
FROM   X$bh  bh, dba_users u, sys.obj$ o, sys.sys_objects so
WHERE  bh.obj = o.obj#
and    bh.obj = so.object_id
and    o.owner# = u.user_id
AND    bh.tch  > 10
group  by u.username ||'.'|| o.name, so.object_type
ORDER  BY touches desc;


NAME                               TYPE                    BLOCKS    TOUCHES
---------------------------------- ------------------- ---------- ----------
SYS.C_FILE#_BLOCK#                 CLUSTER                    131      20263
SYS.OBJ$                           TABLE                       75      10407
SYS.I_FILE#_BLOCK#                 INDEX                       20       6063
SYS.I_OBJ1                         INDEX                       28       5453
SYS.C_USER#                        CLUSTER                      4       1984
SYS.JOB$                           TABLE                        2       1017
SYS.FILE$                          TABLE                        1        811
SYS.I_JOB_NEXT                     INDEX                        1        488
(Output truncated...)
```

Capture the SQL statements involving these segments by querying V$SQLTEXT for SQL_TEXT lines that contain these segment names, and analyze their execution plans with the EXPLAIN PLAN as described in Chapter 6. Consider the number of sessions accessing these blocks using the queries in this section and whether these blocks are tables or appropriate indexes. Table blocks appearing in this list that are being accessed by multiple sessions are candidates for the keep pool. Table segments in this list that incur frequent full table scans are candidates for being re-created in tablespaces that are configured for large block sizes (16K or larger). Conversely, table segments that incur single-row accesses are candidates for being re-created in tablespaces that are configured for smaller block sizes (2K, 4K, or 8K).

Note that you should balance rebuilding such single-row access tables in small block tablespaces with data locality considerations. If such a single-row access table is accessed *frequently* for similar data that is likely to be stored consecutively, then you should consider storing such segments in large block tablespaces instead of a small block tablespace. As a result, a lower number of physical block reads occurs because of the increased chance that the block containing the desired rows already resides in a buffer cache buffer from other recent queries.

Deciding how to size such objects depends on the default block size of the database and the amount of physical memory and SGA space available for creating a keep pool. Segments in buffers with a consistently low touch count are candidates for the recycle pool, depending on the block size of the particular table versus the default block size. You should review the application SQL code, particularly the indexing strategy, to reconsider the logic of accessing such blocks frequently, in an effort to reduce contention on them. The following queries will help. (Note that since 10gR2, the cache buffers chain latch can be shared—but not all the time. Also, in-memory

UNDO [IMU] lessens issues with the buffer cache especially in 11g.) Although Oracle does in-memory updates *all* the time, this updating happens in the buffer cache. IMU is new because UNDO and REDO in Oracle 9i had to be written out to disk quickly to protect the data.

Segments experiencing waits on the cache buffers' chains latch

```
        -- Segments Experiencing Waits on the Cache Buffers Chains Latch (slow - test)
    SELECT  /*+ ordered */
            de.owner ||'.'|| de.segment_name  segment_name,
            de.segment_type  segment_type,
            de.extent_id  extent#,
            bh.dbablk - de.block_id + 1  block#,
            bh.lru_flag,
            bh.tch,
            lc.child#
    FROM    (SELECT MAX(sleeps) MaxSleeps
             FROM   v$latch_children
             WHERE  name='cache buffers chains') max_sleeps,
             v$latch_children  lc,
             X$bh  bh,
             dba_extents  de
    WHERE   lc.name    = 'cache buffers chains'
      AND   lc.sleeps  > (0.8 * MaxSleeps)
      AND   bh.hladdr  = lc.addr
      AND   de.file_id = bh.file#
      AND   bh.dbablk between de.block_id and de.block_id + de.blocks - 1
    ORDER BY bh.tch;
```

Segments experiencing waits on the cache buffers' LRU chain latch

```
        -- Segments Experiencing Waits on Cache Buffers LRU Chain Latch (slow - test)
    SELECT  /*+ ordered */
            de.owner ||'.'|| de.segment_name  segment_name,
            de.segment_type  segment_type,
            de.extent_id  extent#,
            bh.dbablk - de.block_id + 1  block#,
            bh.lru_flag,
            bh.tch,
            lc.child#
    FROM    (SELECT MAX(sleeps) MaxSleeps
             FROM v$latch_children
             WHERE name='cache buffers lru chain') max_sleeps,
             v$latch_children  lc,
             X$bh  bh,
             dba_extents  de
    WHERE   lc.name    = 'cache buffers lru chain'
      AND   lc.sleeps  > (0.8 * MaxSleeps)
      AND   bh.hladdr  = lc.addr
      AND   de.file_id = bh.file#
      AND   bh.dbablk between de.block_id and de.block_id + de.blocks - 1
    ORDER BY bh.tch;
```

Sessions experiencing waits on the buffer busy waits or write complete waits events

```
        -- Sessions Experiencing Waits on the Buffer Busy Waits or Write
        -- Complete Waits Events. Note that the values returned by the p1, p2,
        -- and p3 parameters disclose the file, block, and reason for the wait.
        -- The cause disclosed by the p3 parameter is not externally published.
        -- The p3 parameter is a number that translates to one of several
        -- causes, among which are the buffer being read or written by
        -- another session.
  SELECT /*+ ordered */
         sid,event,owner,segment_name,segment_type,p1,p2,p3
    FROM v$session_wait sw, dba_extents de
   WHERE de.file_id = sw.p1
     AND sw.p2 between de.block_id and de.block_id + de.blocks - 1
     AND (event = 'buffer busy waits' OR event = 'write complete waits')
     AND p1 IS NOT null
ORDER BY event,sid;
```

Problem segments returned by queries in this section are likely to be the same as those returned by the query returning hot buffers earlier in this section. If they're not, a possible explanation may be that such a segment is accessed frequently by one session, as shown by the hot buffer query, but there may be no contention for it by other sessions, as may be shown by the absence of that segment from the result set of the other queries in this section. Other than that scenario, the segments returned by a hot buffers query are likely to also be returned by the other queries in this section that show the problem segment. Each of these queries conveniently includes the blocks of the particular segments associated with the latches or waits in question.

For table segments, you can use the DBMS_ROWID PL/SQL package to map the file and block numbers returned by these queries to the corresponding table rows. If one or a set of segments consistently shows up in the result sets of the queries in this section, then these are highly used segments. Investigate the application to reconsider the use of these popular segments. Ask questions such as the following:

- Is the indexing scheme appropriate?

- Are PL/SQL (or Java) loop exit conditions included where they should be?

- Are superfluous tables included in join queries?

- Can any SQL code be reengineered to alter a join strategy, either with reengineered subqueries, inline views, or similar alternatives?

- Should some hints, like ORDERED, USE_HASH, etc., be used?

- Are statistics up to date?

- Do any of the involved tables have a high watermark that is well beyond the actual blocks that contain rows?

- Could a table or index make advantageous use of partitioning or histograms?

- Should you use a keep pool?

If a variety of different segments are repeatedly showing up in the result of the buffer-busy query, the buffer cache is probably undersized or the disk subsystem is not writing changed (dirty) buffers out to the datafiles fast enough for them to be reused (or both). If there does not seem to be contention on particular segments, but rather on a varying set of segments, this problem indicates that Oracle is having trouble in general satisfying requests to load blocks into free buffers.

You should also review the storage parameter configuration of the problem segments returned by the queries in this section. Consider whether sufficient freelists are available for the tables and indexes that can be classified as high concurrent update (multiple sessions updating them concurrently). You should probably set freelists to two or higher for these segments, but do not set freelists higher than the number of CPUs in the database server. Another solution is to use Automatic Segment Space Management (ASSM). You should review the data block size and PCT_FREE because different conditions call for blocks of a table or index to contain more rows or fewer rows. In situations in which a particular segment block is popular, you may want to reconstruct the segment with a higher PCT_FREE; thus, the interblock contention for rows that were previously stored in the same block is reduced because the chance of those rows being stored in the same block has been reduced by simply reducing the number of rows that can be inserted into a block.

Obviously, more buffer cache buffers are required to accommodate a table reconstructed to have a larger PCT_FREE and, therefore, consist of more row-containing blocks. The trade-off is that this can reduce the performance of full table scan operations on such tables because more blocks must be visited to complete a full table scan. In general, you must consider the overall use of these tables and indexes to judge whether having more or fewer rows in the blocks of the particular table or index is more advantageous. These points can be summarized as follows:

- **Condition**   Higher PCT_FREE and, therefore, fewer rows per block:
    - **Advantage**   Less contention on updates of popular blocks.
    - **Disadvantage**   The segment consists of more blocks and, therefore, reduces full table scan performance.
- **Condition**   Lower PCT_FREE and, therefore, more rows per block:
    - **Advantage**   There is a better chance that the block containing a requested row is already in a buffer cache buffer from a recent query. Full tablescans will need to visit fewer blocks.
    - **Disadvantage**   Blocks being updated may contain more contention. If a block contains a row to be updated, all the other rows (more of them) in that block are now in a copy of the block that is incompatible with other sessions requesting a read of other rows in that block; thus, another read-consistent copy of the block must be read into another buffer cache buffer.

Obtaining Database- and Instance-Specific Information

You can obtain some database- and instance-specific information from the X$KCCDI table. Consider the following queries, which you can use to find overall instance- and database-specific information:

MAXLOGMEMBERS setting for a database

```
-- MAXLOGMEMBERS setting for a database.
SELECT dimlm
  FROM x$kccdi;
```

Datafile creation times

```
-- Datafile creation times.
SELECT indx file_id,
       fecrc_tim creation_date,
       file_name,
       tablespace_name
  FROM x$kccfe int,
       dba_data_files dba
 WHERE dba.file_id = int.indx + 1
ORDER BY file_name;
```

Background process names and process IDs

```
-- Background process names and process ids.
SELECT ksbdpnam ProcessName, ksbdppro OSPid
  FROM x$ksbdp
 WHERE  ksbdppro != '00' ;
```

```
PROCE OSPID
----- --------
PMON  437B9F3C
VKTM  437BAA14
GEN0  437BB4EC
DIAG  437BBFC4
DBRM  437BCA9C
VKRM  437CAE54
PSP0  437BD574
DIA0  437BE04C
MMAN  437BEB24
DBW0  437BF5FC
ARC0  437C626C
ARC1  437C6D44
ARC2  437C781C
ARC3  437C82F4
LGWR  437C00D4
CKPT  437C0BAC
SMON  437C1684
```

```
SMCO   437C5794
RECO   437C215C
CJQ0   437CA37C
QMNC   437C8DCC
MMON   437C2C34
MMNL   437C370C
```

```
23 rows selected.
```

Various instance resources

```
-- Various instance resources (very cool).
SELECT kviival ResourceValue, kviidsc ResourceName
    FROM x$kvii;
```

Note that the last query has different values returned for the resource values on different platforms.

Effective X$ Table Use and Strategy

Consider creating a separate X$ query user who has his or her own X$ views on the SYS X$ tables, as described earlier in the chapter. This user could manually or, with DBMS_JOB, perform periodic queries to capture X$ table data into some other tables so the contents of the X$ tables can be examined over time. If you do this, keep in mind that the data in the X$ tables is highly transient. Some scripts or jobs written to capture such information will likely miss a lot of it. On the other hand, you do not want to query these tables so frequently that the queries themselves and their associated activity information are a non-negligible percentage of the data in the tables.

In monitoring the X$KSMLRU table (and perhaps X$KSMSP and others), you may find it prudent to capture the contents of the table to a permanent table for analysis and comparison over time.

Related Oracle Internals Topics

Alas, more toys for the mischievously curious DBAs. Except for traces, you should not use the utilities described in the following sections in production without the guidance of Oracle Support. You can take them and run with them in a sandbox database to learn what useful information they provide.

Traces

Database sessions can be traced to collect session information about the work performed in the session and to diagnose problems. Traces can be turned on by a variety of methods:

- Set SQL_TRACE = TRUE with an `alter session` command.

- Set SQL_TRACE = TRUE in the initialization parameter file.

- Execute the DBMS_SYSTEM.SET_SQL_TRACE_IN_SESSION( ) PL/SQL procedure for another session.

- Create traces with the $ORACLE_HOME/rdbms/admin/dbmssupp.sql script.
- Execute the DBMS_SYSTEM.SET_EV( ) PL/SQL procedure to set tracing events in another session.
- Use the ORADEBUG command.

CAUTION
If you set SQL_TRACE = TRUE in the parameter file, it generates traces for every process connected to the database, including the background processes.

The simplest method to invoke a trace of a session is for the session itself to enable tracing with the following command:

```
SQL> alter session set sql_trace=true;

Session altered.
```

Developers may do this themselves from SQL*Plus and may also include it in PL/SQL code using the execute immediate facility. The DBA may optionally decide to make the trace files in the user dump destination readable by all (Unix and OpenVMS) by setting the hidden parameter _TRACE_FILES_PUBLIC to TRUE on instance startup.

Having users generate traces for themselves is simple but not always practical. Third-party applications usually do not permit the code to be modified for the insertion of `trace-start` commands, and there is usually no SQL prompt from where the trace can be started. You could use system logon triggers to identify the user connecting and optionally start a trace, but there are easier methods at your disposal.

In these situations, you need to be able to invoke a trace for another session. As the DBA, you have a number of methods to do this. In each case, however, you need to know the SID and the SERIAL# of the session you want to trace. You can find this information in the V$SESSION view, as shown here:

```
select sid, serial#
from   v$session where username = 'NICOLA';

       SID    SERIAL#
---------- ----------
       540         11
```

Once you have this information, you can use the SET_SQL_TRACE_IN_SESSION procedure of the DBMS_SYSTEM package to invoke the trace. The procedure takes three arguments: SID, SERIAL#, and a Boolean argument to start or stop the tracing. It is invoked as follows:

```
SQL> exec dbms_system.set_sql_trace_in_session(540,11,TRUE);
PL/SQL procedure successfully completed.
```

When sufficient tracing information has been collected, disable the trace as follows:

```
SQL> exec dbms_system.set_sql_trace_in_session(540,11,FALSE);
PL/SQL procedure successfully completed.
```

Alternatively, you can use the DBMS_SUPPORT package to start the trace. The DBMS_SUPPORT package is an option that can be loaded into the database from the rdbms/admin directory. To load the package, you must be connected to the database as a SYSDBA privileged user and then run the dbmssupp.sql script.

The DBMS_SUPPORT package offers much of the same functionality for tracing as the DBMS_SYSTEM package but with these additional features:

- It allows bind variables and session wait information to be optionally included in the trace file.

- It verifies the SID and SERIAL# specified for tracing, rejecting invalid combinations. This can be useful in critical situations. It can be very frustrating to have spent an hour believing you have collected useful trace information only to find that you mistyped something and the user dump destination directory is empty.

Use the START_TRACE_IN_SESSION procedure of the DBMS_SUPPORT to start the trace. The procedure takes four arguments: SID, SERIAL#, a Boolean specifying if wait information is recorded (default TRUE), and a Boolean specifying if bind variables are recorded (default FALSE). Invoke it as follows:

```
SQL> exec dbms_support.START_TRACE_IN_SESSION(540,13,TRUE,TRUE);
PL/SQL procedure successfully completed.
```

To stop tracing, use the STOP_TRACE_IN_SESSION procedure:

```
SQL> exec dbms_support.stop_trace_in_session(540,13);
```

Another method to invoke tracing for another session is to use the DBMS_SYSTEM.SET_EV method to set a tracing event for a session. This procedure allows database events to be set in any session in the database. By setting the 10046 event, you can gather complete tracing information about any session. As before, you need the SID and SERIAL# of the session you want to monitor. You can then set the event as follows:

```
SQL> exec dbms_system.set_ev(537,21,10046,12,'');
PL/SQL procedure successfully completed.
```

The first two arguments are the SID and SERIAL# of the session. The next argument is the event you want to set, which, in this case, is event 10046 to trace the session. The fourth argument sets the level of the event. Here the level is set to 12 to gather all wait and bind variable information in addition to the basic trace. The available levels are as follows:

Level	Information Gathered
0	All tracing disabled.
1	Standard tracing enabled.
2	Same as level 1.
4	Standard trace plus bind variable information.
8	Standard trace plus wait information. Very helpful for spotting latch waits.
12	Standard trace plus bind and wait information.
16	Generates STAT line dumps for each execution (see note below).

NOTE
STAT dumping has been amended in 11g so they are not aggregated across all executions but are dumped after execution. This change addresses cases where the cursor is not closed and the STAT information is, therefore, not dumped. Now Oracle guarantees to capture the STAT information following the execution.

To stop tracing, you need to set the event level to zero as follows:

```
SQL> exec dbms_system.set_ev(537,21,10046,0,'');
PL/SQL procedure successfully completed.
```

Finally, you could use the ORADEBUG facility to invoke the required trace. This will be explored further later in this chapter.

Once a trace file has been generated, you can use the standard TKPROF utility to interpret the contents of the trace. (The TKPROF tool is covered in detail in Chapter 6.) Oracle also offers the more advanced Trace Analyzer tool, which can be downloaded from MetaLink (see Note 224270.1). The more adventurous DBA may wish to examine the raw trace file, which can sometimes yield information not shown by TKPROF. The Trace Analyzer takes the trace files generated by the methods described previously and produces a series of formatted reports. The reports are typically written to the user dump destination directory The reports are very detailed and can take an extended period of time to produce, especially if your server is running poorly to begin with. To generate the report, you need to know the name of the trace file generated, and then you can invoke the analyzer as follows:

```
SQL> start /home/oracle/tusc/trca/run/trcanlzr.sql DEMOUC2_ora_16319.trc

Parameter 1:
Trace Filename or control_file.txt (required)

Value passed to trcanlzr.sql:
~~~~~~~~~~~~~~~~~~~~~~~~~~~~~
TRACE_FILENAME: DEMOUC2_ora_16319.trc

Analyzing DEMOUC2_ora_16319.trc
```

```
To monitor progress, login as TRCANLZR into another session and execute:
SQL> SELECT * FROM trca$_log_v;

... analyzing trace(s) ...


Trace Analyzer completed.
Review first trcanlzr_error.log file for possible fatal errors.
Review next trca_e44266.log for parsing messages and totals.

Copying now generated files into local directory

TKPROF: Release 11.2.0.1.0 - Development on Wed May 18 11:50:05 2011
Copyright (c) 1982, 2009, Oracle and/or its affiliates.  All rights reserved.

  adding: trca_e44266.html (deflated 89%)
  adding: trca_e44266.log (deflated 84%)
  adding: trca_e44266.tkprof (deflated 84%)
  adding: trca_e44266.txt (deflated 85%)
  adding: trcanlzr_error.log (deflated 81%)
test of trca_e44266.zip OK
deleting: trcanlzr_error.log
Archive:  trca_e44266.zip

  Length    Date    Time    Name
 --------   ----    ----    ----
   140676  05-18-11 11:50    trca_e44266.html
    15534  05-18-11 11:50    trca_e44266.log
    17065  05-18-11 11:50    trca_e44266.tkprof
    69535  05-18-11 11:50    trca_e44266.txt
 --------                   -------
   242810                   4 files

File trca_e44266.zip has been created

TRCANLZR completed.
```

The finished HTML report summarizes the trace file (see Figure 13-1). The report includes all of the details found on TKPROF, plus additional information normally requested and used for a transaction performance analysis.

DBMS_TRACE Package

The DBMS_TRACE package is another method of tracing, but unlike the preceding examples, it is designed specifically to trace PL/SQL rather than individual sessions. It can be extremely useful when trying to debug PL/SQL programs. To use the DBMS_TRACE package, the DBA must first load the following scripts from the rdbms/admin directory as a SYSDBA user:

```
TRACETAB.SQL
DBMSPBT.SQL
PRVTPBT.PLB
```

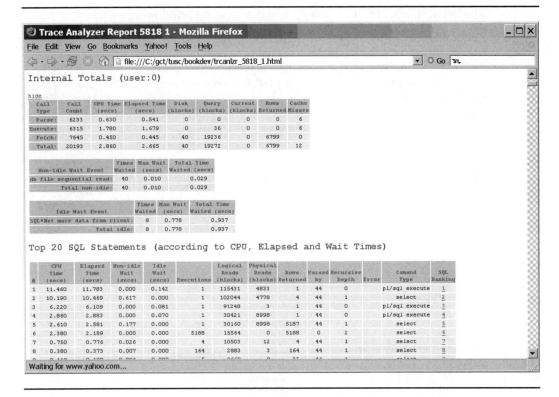

FIGURE 13-1. *Sample Trace Analyzer report*

Once the packages are loaded, PL/SQL can be traced using two methods:

```
SQL> alter session set plsql_debug=true;
```

All PL/SQL code created by the session after this point will have the additional hooks to allow it to be traced, including anonymous PL/SQL blocks. However, code created before this point cannot be traced with the DBMS_TRACE package. Alternatively, any existing PL/SQL package, procedure, or function can be recompiled using the following command:

```
SQL> alter [PROCEDURE | FUNCTION | PACKAGE BODY] <procedure name> compile debug;
```

TIP
Anonymous PL/SQL blocks cannot be traced using the "compile debug" method. PL/SQL tracing for the entire session must be enabled with the `alter session set plsql_debug=true` *command.*

Now to trace the PL/SQL code execution, you can start with the following command:

```
SQL> execute dbms_trace.set_plsql_trace(dbms_trace.trace_all_lines);
```

The argument here specifies which lines of PL/SQL to trace. The options are TRACE_ALL_LINES to trace every line executed, TRACE_ENABLED_LINES to trace only PL/SQL that was explicitly compiled with the debug option, TRACE_ALL_EXCEPTIONS to trace only exceptions, and TRACE_ENABLED_EXCEPTIONS to trace only exceptions of PL/SQL that was explicitly compiled with the debug option. When the tracing is complete, disable it with the following command:

```
SQL> execute dbms_trace.clear_plsql_trace();
```

The results of the trace can be seen in the PLSQL_TRACE_EVENTS table owned by the SYS schema. as shown here:

```
select event_seq as seq, stack_depth, event_kind as kind,
       event_unit as unit, event_line as line, event_comment
from   sys.plsql_trace_events;

   SEQ STACK_DEPTH  KIND UNIT                  LINE EVENT_COMMENT
------- -----------  ----- -------------------- ----- -----------------------------
 270001           7    51 RDBA_MONITOR_C         108 New line executed
 270002           7    51 RDBA_MONITOR_C         110 New line executed
 270003           8    51 RDBA_UTILITY           174 New line executed
 270004           8    51 RDBA_UTILITY           183 New line executed
 270005           8    51 RDBA_UTILITY           192 New line executed
 270006           8    51 RDBA_UTILITY           195 New line executed
 270007           9    51 DBMS_SQL                 9 New line executed
 270008          10    51 DBMS_SYS_SQL           882 New line executed
 270009          10    51 DBMS_SYS_SQL           883 New line executed
 270010           9    51 DBMS_SQL                 9 New line executed
 270011           9    51 DBMS_SQL                10 New line executed
 270012           8    51 RDBA_UTILITY           195 New line executed
 270013           8    51 RDBA_UTILITY           196 New line executed
```

Events

An *event* is similar to a system trigger in an Oracle instance. A trigger can capture pertinent information about the instance and individual database sessions to trace files. If an event is set in an initialization parameter file or with an `alter system` or `alter session` setting, then Oracle captures information to a trace file based on the conditions set in the event. Several events can be set. These can be described with the `oerr` command-line facility. Try the following command (in Unix only):

```
oerr ora 10046
```

A particularly useful tuning tool is event 10046 (described in Chapter 9 in detail). This event can be enabled in the initialization parameter file with the following line (although this is not something that you generally want to set at the database level):

```
event = '10046 trace name context forever, level 8'
```

Or it is more likely to be used at the session level with an `alter session` command:

```
alter session set events '10046 trace name context forever,level 12';
```

The trace information is captured to a file in the USER_DUMP_DEST directory derived from the DIAGNOSTIC_DEST parameter in the initialization parameter file. This event is equivalent to setting SQL_TRACE = TRUE in the initialization parameter file. At level 12, this event setting includes the values of bind variables and the occurrences of wait events. Other events are useful in troubleshooting database and performance issues. Do not set events in production databases without first consulting with Oracle Support and testing them in a test database.

You can use the `oradebug` command (covered later in this chapter in the "ORADEBUG" section) or DBMS_SUPPORT PL/SQL package to set events in sessions other than the current session. Also, to UNSET this event, you use

```
alter session set events '10046 trace name context off';
```

Dumps

Several structures in an Oracle instance or database can be dumped to a trace file for low-level analysis, such as these:

- Control files
- Datafile headers
- Redo log file headers
- Instance state
- Process state
- Library Cache
- Data blocks (covered in detail in Chapter 9)
- Redo blocks

Create these dumps with these commands:

```
alter session set events 'immediate trace name CONTROLF level 10';
alter session set events 'immediate trace name FILE_HDRS level 10';
alter session set events 'immediate trace name REDOHDR level 10';
alter session set events 'immediate trace name SYSTEMSTATE level 10';
alter session set events 'immediate trace name PROCESSSTATE level 10';
alter session set events 'immediate trace name library_cache level 10';
alter system dump datafile 10 block 2057;
alter system dump logfile '<logfilename>';
```

The trace files containing this dump information are in the USER_DUMP_DEST directory.

ORADEBUG

You use the `oradebug` command for troubleshooting the instance or sessions. The `oradebug` command can capture current instance state information, set events in sessions, and perform other low-level diagnostics. Type **oradebug help** from SQL*Plus to get the usage list shown next.

> **NOTE**
> You must be connected to AS SYSDBA to be able to access oradebug (version dependent listing—run this for your own version).

```
SQL> oradebug help
HELP            [command]                    Describe one or all commands
SETMYPID                                     Debug current process
SETOSPID        <ospid>                      Set OS pid of process to debug
SETORAPID       <orapid> ['force']           Set Oracle pid of process to debug
SETORAPNAME     <orapname>                   Set Oracle process name to debug
SHORT_STACK                                  Get abridged OS stack
CURRENT_SQL                                  Get current SQL
DUMP            <dump_name> <lvl> [addr]     Invoke named dump
DUMPSGA         [bytes]                      Dump fixed SGA
DUMPLIST                                     Print a list of available dumps
EVENT           <text>                       Set trace event in process
SESSION_EVENT   <text>                       Set trace event in session
DUMPVAR         <p|s|uga> <name> [level]     Print/dump a fixed PGA/SGA/UGA variable
DUMPTYPE        <address> <type> <count>     Print/dump an address with type info
SETVAR          <p|s|uga> <name> <value>     Modify a fixed PGA/SGA/UGA variable
PEEK            <addr> <len> [level]         Print/Dump memory
POKE            <addr> <len> <value>         Modify memory
WAKEUP          <orapid>                     Wake up Oracle process
SUSPEND                                      Suspend execution
RESUME                                       Resume execution
FLUSH                                        Flush pending writes to trace file
CLOSE_TRACE                                  Close trace file
TRACEFILE_NAME                               Get name of trace file
LKDEBUG                                      Invoke global enqueue service debugger
NSDBX                                        Invoke CGS name-service debugger
-G              <Inst-List | def | all>      Parallel oradebug command prefix
-R              <Inst-List | def | all>      Parallel oradebug prefix (return output
SETINST         <instance# .. | all>         Set instance list in double quotes
SGATOFILE       <SGA dump dir>               Dump SGA to file; dirname in double quotes
DMPCOWSGA       <SGA dump dir> Dump & map SGA as COW; dirname in double quotes
MAPCOWSGA       <SGA dump dir>               Map SGA as COW; dirname in double quotes
HANGANALYZE     [level] [syslevel]           Analyze system hang
FFBEGIN                                      Flash Freeze the Instance
FFDEREGISTER                                 FF deregister instance from cluster
FFTERMINST                                   Call exit and terminate instance
FFRESUMEINST                                 Resume the flash frozen instance
FFSTATUS                                     Flash freeze status of instance
SKDSTTPCS       <ifname>  <ofname>           Helps translate PCs to names
WATCH           <address> <len> <self|exist|all|target>  Watch a region of memory
DELETE          <local|global|target> watchpoint <id>    Delete a watchpoint
```

```
SHOW          <local|global|target> watchpoints        Show  watchpoints
DIRECT_ACCESS <set/enable/disable command | select query> Fixed table access
CORE                                        Dump core without crashing process
IPC                                         Dump ipc information
UNLIMIT                                     Unlimit the size of the trace file
PROCSTAT                                    Dump process statistics
CALL          [-t count] <func> [arg1]...[argn]  Invoke function with arguments
```

The following example shows using the `oradebug` command to invoke a trace of another session. Let's say a user complains of slow performance on a database, or you have identified the process ID from the operation system. To get the SPID, use the following query:

```
select spid
from   v$process
where  addr = (select paddr from v$session where username = 'NICOLA');
```

Then you use the `setospid` command to attach to the process and invoke the trace:

```
select spid
from   v$process
where  addr = (select paddr from v$session where username = 'NICOLA');
SQL> oradebug setospid 6943

Oracle pid: 28, Unix process pid: 18575, image: oracle@dc-umail10.myinunison.com (TNS V1-V3)
```

Now that you are attached, you can invoke the trace by setting the 10046 event. Here, I select a level 12 to force all bind variables and wait information to be written to the trace file:

```
SQL> oradebug event 10046 trace name context forever, level 12
Statement processed.
```

The session is now tracing. If you want to see the name of the trace file being generated, use the TRACEFILE_NAME option as follows:

```
SQL> oradebug tracefile_name

/home/oracle/app/oracle/diag/rdbms/demouc2/DEMOUC2/trace/DEMOUC2_ora_18575.trc
```

This shows you the name and location of the trace file. This file can then be processed with the TKPROF analysis tool to obtain detailed information about the operations of the monitored process.

If your Oracle database has trace file-size limitations specified in the SPFILE or `init.ora` file, you can override this from `oradebug` using the following command:

```
SQL> oradebug unlimit
Statement processed.
```

The DBA should remember, however, that Oracle buffers its writes to the trace file, and so the information contained in the file might not be completely, up to date. Fortunately, the `oradebug` command gives you the ability to flush the trace file write buffer as follows:

```
SQL> oradebug flush
Statement processed.
```

The `oradebug` command can also be used to suspend the execution of a process. For example, you might have a long-running database job that is about to fail due to space, or an intensive update job that you want to disable during a backup. The `oradebug` command allows specific sessions to be suspended as follows:

```
SQL> oradebug setospid 6943
Oracle pid: 11, Unix process pid: 6943, image: oraclelwdb@dc-mvndb3

SQL> oradebug suspend
Statement processed.
```

The Oracle operating system process 6943 is now suspended and will remain that way until you issue the `oradebug resume` command.

TIP
Do not use `oradebug suspend` on the Microsoft Windows platform. Due to the thread-based processing model of Windows, the whole database will be suspended, not just the process you are attached to.

When you want to disable tracing for the specified session, you can use the following `oradebug` command:

```
SQL> oradebug event 10046 trace name context off
Statement processed.
```

trcsess Utility
With the 10g (and continuing into the 11g) release of the database, Oracle provided users with another tracing utility: *trcsess*. This utility can be found in the `bin` directory under Oracle Home. The tool is designed to read database trace files and extract information the DBA is interested in. Trace information can be located based on session identifier (SID and serial number), client identifier, service name, action name, or module name. The tool is primarily designed for use in shared server or connection pooling environments where multiple processes may have to be traced to capture all relevant information. The tool does not interpret the trace information; it simply aggregates multiple trace files into a single one based on the criteria provided. The result is a combined trace file that can be analyzed using TKPROF, TRCANLZR, or another tool. For additional information on this tool, see MetaLink note: 280543.1.

Reading the Trace File

The preceding section showed several methods that can be used to generate a trace of a session. Once the session being traced has completed, the DBA needs to locate, read, and interpret the trace file. The trace file is written to the directory pointed to by the user dump destination parameter. You can see it from SQL*Plus with the following command:

```
SQL> show parameter user_dump_dest

NAME              TYPE      VALUE
----------------- --------- -----------------------------------------------------
user_dump_dest    string    /home/oracle/app/oracle/diag/rdbms/demouc2/DEMOUC2/trace
```

The trace file has the filename format `<sid>_ora_<process id>.trc`. The process ID can be found in the V$PROCESS view as follows:

```
select  spid
from    gv$process vp, gv$session vs
where   vs.sid = userenv('SID')
and     vs.paddr = vp.addr
and     vs.inst_id = vp.inst_id;

SPID
------------
4508
```

So, in this example, my trace file name is

```
/home/oracle/app/oracle/diag/rdbms/demouc2/DEMOUC2/trace/DEMOUC2_ora_4508.trc
```

Once located, I can read the trace file with the TKPROF tool (see Chapter 6) or the Trace Analyzer tool, shown earlier in this chapter. However, the curious DBA might be interested to see the contents of the trace file for himself or herself. Because the raw trace file is written in ANSI format, reading it can be accomplished with any standard file browser or editor. The trace file shows the traced session as a series of blocks. Each block represents a database call and is separated by a single line. At the top of the trace file is the standard trace file header that many DBAs are already familiar with:

```
Trace file
/home/oracle/app/oracle/diag/rdbms/demouc2/DEMOUC2/trace/DEMOUC2_ora_16319.trc
Oracle Database 11g Release 11.2.0.1.0 - Production
ORACLE_HOME = /home/oracle/app/oracle/product/11.2.0/dbhome_1
System name:    Linux
Node name:      dc-umail10.myinunison.com
Release: 2.6.18-164.el5
Version: 1 SMP Tue Aug 18 15:51:54 EDT 2009
Machine: i686
Instance name: DEMOUC2
Redo thread mounted by this instance: 1
Oracle process number: 28
Unix process pid: 16319, image: oracle@dc-umail10.myinunison.com (TNS V1-V3)
```

The trace file then shows each database call that was executed in the traced session in sequential order. The following example shows a simple SELECT statement:

```
PARSING IN CURSOR #7 len=57 dep=0 uid=86 oct=3 lid=86 tim=1305924518518576 hv=4215611583
ad='3b6289dc' sqlid='g12xs57xna85z'
select birthdate from user_detail where firstname = :"SYS_B_0"
END OF STMT
PARSE #7:c=2000,e=1202,p=0,cr=0,cu=0,mis=1,r=0,dep=0,og=1,plh=0,tim=1305924518518568
BINDS #7:
 Bind#0
  oacdty=01 mxl=32(06) mxlc=00 mal=00 scl=00 pre=00
  oacflg=10 fl2=0300 frm=01 csi=178 siz=32 off=0
  kxsbbbfp=009e47a0  bln=32  avl=06  flg=09
  value="Stacey"
EXEC #7:c=6999,e=51312,p=0,cr=84,cu=0,mis=1,r=0,dep=0,og=1,plh=1354678500,tim=1305924518569996
WAIT #7: nam='SQL*Net message to client' ela= 5 driver id=1650815232 #bytes=1 p3=0 obj#=91901
tim=1305924518570098
FETCH #7:c=0,e=142,p=0,cr=13,cu=0,mis=0,r=1,dep=0,og=1,plh=1354678500,tim=1305924518570284
WAIT #7: nam='SQL*Net message from client' ela= 193 driver id=1650815232 #bytes=1 p3=0
obj#=91901 tim=1305924518570621
WAIT #7: nam='SQL*Net message to client' ela= 7 driver id=1650815232 #bytes=1 p3=0 obj#=91901
tim=1305924518571472
FETCH
#7:c=1000,e=1096,p=0,cr=145,cu=0,mis=0,r=15,dep=0,og=1,plh=1354678500,tim=1305924518571755
WAIT #7: nam='SQL*Net message from client' ela= 282 driver id=1650815232 #bytes=1 p3=0
obj#=91901 tim=1305924518572099
WAIT #7: nam='SQL*Net message to client' ela= 2 driver id=1650815232 #bytes=1 p3=0 obj#=91901
tim=1305924518572192
FETCH #7:c=0,e=83,p=0,cr=6,cu=0,mis=0,r=15,dep=0,og=1,plh=1354678500,tim=1305924518572254
WAIT #7: nam='SQL*Net message from client' ela= 207 driver id=1650815232 #bytes=1 p3=0
obj#=91901 tim=1305924518572498
WAIT #7: nam='SQL*Net message to client' ela= 3 driver id=1650815232 #bytes=1 p3=0 obj#=91901
tim=1305924518572574
FETCH #7:c=0,e=101,p=0,cr=8,cu=0,mis=0,r=15,dep=0,og=1,plh=1354678500,tim=1305924518572659
WAIT #7: nam='SQL*Net message from client' ela= 218 driver id=1650815232 #bytes=1 p3=0
obj#=91901 tim=1305924518572912
WAIT #7: nam='SQL*Net message to client' ela= 1 driver id=1650815232 #bytes=1 p3=0 obj#=91901
tim=1305924518572970
FETCH
#7:c=1000,e=1035,p=0,cr=140,cu=0,mis=0,r=15,dep=0,og=1,plh=1354678500,tim=1305924518573993
WAIT #7: nam='SQL*Net message from client' ela= 212 driver id=1650815232 #bytes=1 p3=0
obj#=91901 tim=1305924518574308
WAIT #7: nam='SQL*Net message to client' ela= 2 driver id=1650815232 #bytes=1 p3=0 obj#=91901
tim=1305924518574474
FETCH #7:c=2999,e=2460,p=0,cr=354,cu=0,mis=0,r=9,dep=0,og=1,plh=1354678500,tim=1305924518576842
STAT #7 id=1 cnt=70 pid=0 pos=1 obj=91901 op='TABLE ACCESS FULL ARIJAK (cr=666 pr=0 pw=0 time=0
us cost=193 size=231 card=11)'
```

The first line shows information about the statement being executed. The tags can be interpreted as follows:

Tag	Meaning
Len	Length of SQL statement.
Dep	Recursive depth of the cursor. Blocks where dep is not zero are recursive calls made by the database on the user's behalf. Time spent here contributes to the "recursive CPU" usage recorded in V$SYSSTAT.
Uid	Schema user ID of parsing user—see USER_ID in DBA_USERS.
Oct	Oracle command type.
Lid	Privilege user ID—may not be the same as parsing user if executing another user's PL/SQL code.
Tim	Timestamp—the value is the value in V$TIMER when the line was written. Pre–Oracle 9*i*, the times recorded by Oracle are centiseconds (10 mS). As of Oracle 9*i*, some times are microseconds (1/1,000,000ths of a second).
Hv	SQL hash—maps to SQL_HASH in V$SQLAREA.
Ad	SQL address—maps to SQL_ADDRESS in V$SQLAREA.
Sqlid	SQL ID—the SQLID of the statement.

The trace file then shows the text of the SQL statement being executed. In this case, I am selecting the BIRTHDATE from the USER_DETAIL table. You can also see from the trace file that this statement has been assigned cursor number 7.

TIP

Cursors may be reassigned if the cursor is closed and released. Therefore, when reading a long trace file, remember that a cursor number referenced at one part of the trace file may not represent the same SQL statement as it does elsewhere in the trace file.

The trace file now shows the operations Oracle performs to actually satisfy the query. This basically amounts to a series of executions (EXEC) and fetches (FETCH). Both the EXEC and FETCH trace lines report the following tracing information:

Tag	Meaning
C	CPU time (100ths of a second)
toE	Elapsed time (100ths of a second in Oracle 7, 8, microseconds in Oracle 9 upward)
P	Number of physical reads
Cr	Number of buffers retrieved for CR reads
Cu	Number of buffers retrieved in current mode
Mis	Cursor missed in the cache
R	Number of rows processed
Dep	Recursive call depth (0 – user SQL, >0 – recursive)
Og	Optimizer goal: 1 – all rows, 2 – first rows, 3 – rule, 4 – choose
Tim	Timestamp (large number in 100ths of a second)

Applying this knowledge to the EXEC line from mytrace, I can determine the following:

```
EXEC #7:c=6999,e=51312,p=0,cr=84,cu=0,mis=1,r=0,dep=0,og=1,plh=1354678500,tim=1305924518569996
```

- A total of 6999 ms of CPU was used for this EXEC.

- Total elapsed time was 51312 ms.

- Physical reads were zero.

- Buffers retrieved in CR (consistent read) mode were 84.

- Buffers retrieved in current mode were zero.

- Library Cache misses were 1 (this statement was not found in the cache).

- Rows processed were zero.

- Recursive call depth was 0 (this was a user call).

- Optimizer goal was choosen.

Wait Information and Response Time

The trace file also includes wait (WAIT) information. This shows time Oracle spent waiting for certain items between parsing, executing, and fetching data. In this trace file, you can see this wait event:

```
WAIT #7: nam='SQL*Net message to client' ela= 5 driver id=1650815232 #bytes=1 p3=0 obj#=91901
tim=1305924518570098
```

The NAM field shows the event that was waited on. The ELA field shows the time waited. The meaning of the P1, P2, and P3 fields depends on the event. The information shown can also be observed by inspecting the GV$SESSION_WAIT view during statement execution. In this example, you can also see that Oracle waited on a "SQL*Net message to client" event for 5 ms. The wait is followed by this:

```
FETCH #7:c=0,e=142,p=0,cr=13,cu=0,mis=0,r=1,dep=0,og=1,plh=1354678500,tim=1305924518570284
```

The FETCH step takes 142 ms, reads 13 buffers in CR mode, and processes 1 row. The 142 ms includes the 5 ms from the WAIT step. Elapsed times for all WAIT events immediately preceding an EXEC or FETCH operation are incorporated in the total elapsed time shown for that event:

```
WAIT #7: nam='SQL*Net message from client' ela= 193 driver id=1650815232 #bytes=1 p3=0
obj#=91901 tim=1305924518570621
WAIT #7: nam='SQL*Net message to client' ela= 7 driver id=1650815232 #bytes=1 p3=0 obj#=91901
tim=1305924518571472
FETCH
#7:c=1000,e=1096,p=0,cr=145,cu=0,mis=0,r=15,dep=0,og=1,plh=1354678500,tim=1305924518571755
```

In the preceding example, the elapsed time for the FETCH operation shown on line 3 includes the elapsed times from lines 1 and 2.

Recursive Calls

The trace file identifies recursive calls by showing the call depth of each call. In the following extract, you see a user call (cursor #50) being serviced by a recursive call (cursor #54), which itself is serviced by two recursive calls (cursor #35).

```
EXEC #35:c=0,e=71,p=0,cr=0,cu=0,mis=0,r=0,dep=2,og=4,tim=4232475308506
FETCH #35:c=0,e=48,p=0,cr=3,cu=0,mis=0,r=1,dep=2,og=4,tim=4232475308664
EXEC #54:c=0,e=4986,p=0,cr=9,cu=0,mis=0,r=1,dep=1,og=4,tim=4232475309925
EXEC #50:c=30000,e=31087,p=0,cr=9,cu=0,mis=0,r=0,dep=0,og=4,tim=4232475335361
```

The CPU time, elapsed time, OS block reads, and CR and current block reads for all recursive calls are added to the totals for the originating call. In the preceding example, the total elapsed time for cursor #50 of 31,087 ms includes the 4,986 ms elapsed time for cursor #54, which itself includes the 71 ms spent executing in cursor #35 and the 48 ms spent fetching.

Module Info

The raw trace file includes module information recorded by calls to the DBMS_APPLICATION_INFO package.

```
APPNAME mod='SES' mh=3264509754 act='Job ID: 3407193' ah=1464295440
```

The entry includes the following tags:

Tag	Meaning
Mod	Module
Mh	Module hash value (see V$SESSION)
Act	Action
Ah	Action hash (see V$SESSION)

Commit

Commit operations are shown in the trace file as XCTEND (Transaction END) calls.

```
XCTEND rlbk=0, rd_only=0
```

The rlbk tag has a value of 1 if a rollback is performed or zero if it is committed. The rd_only tag has a value of 1 if the transaction was read-only or zero if blocks were changed.

Unmap

The unmap operation records when temporary tables are cleaned up.

```
UNMAP #1:c=0,e=0,p=0,cr=0,cu=0,mis=0,r=0,dep=0,og=4,tim=2559434286
```

The flag records the same information as for EXEC and FETCH operations.

Bind Variables

One of the most powerful features of the 10046 trace with a level of 8 or 12 is that bind variable information is captured in the trace. You can see this in the raw trace file as a series of BIND operations. The following example is taken from a 11g database with cursor sharing set to FORCE.

```
PARSING IN CURSOR #7 len=57 dep=0 uid=86 oct=3 lid=86 tim=1305924518518576
hv=4215611583 ad='3b6289dc' sqlid='g12xs57xna85z'
select birthdate from arijak where firstname = :"SYS_B_0"
END OF STMT
PARSE
#7:c=2000,e=1202,p=0,cr=0,cu=0,mis=1,r=0,dep=0,og=1,plh=0,tim=1305924518518568
Bind#0
  oacdty=01 mxl=32(06) mxlc=00 mal=00 scl=00 pre=00
  oacflg=10 fl2=0001 frm=01 csi=178 siz=32 off=0
  kxsbbbfp=009efbd4  bln=32  avl=06  flg=05
  value="Alex"
```

In the preceding example, the SQL statement is shown as you see it in the V$SQLTEXT, with the bind variable represented as SYS_B_0. However, the BIND operation listed shows that the bind variable zero of cursor #1 is being bound to the value "Alex". Note that you must be careful when interpreting the BIND information. Oracle replaces all static values with dynamically generated variable names such as SYS_B_*n*. However, named variables are *not* replaced. The BIND statements are listed in strict sequential order, with each value being bound to the next variable in the statement. Consider the following statement:

```
select *
from    SPROGS
where   name != 'Nicola'
and     birthday > ( to_date(:BIRTHDAY,'DDMONYY'));
```

If CURSOR_SHARING is set to FORCE, the value 'Nicola' is replaced with the variable SYS_B_0 and the value 'DDMONYY' is replaced with SYS_B_1. For the purposes of binding, however, SYS_B_0 is treated as a variable 0, BIRTHDAY is treated as variable 1, and SYS_B_1 is treated as variable 2:

```
PARSE #10:c=0,e=1397,p=0,cr=0,cu=0,mis=1,r=0,dep=0,og=4,tim=4646278930704
BINDS #10:
 bind 0: dty=1 mxl=32(06) mal=00 scl=00 pre=00 oacflg=10 oacfl2=0100 size=32 offset=0
   bfp=ffffffff7b957de8 bln=32 avl=06 flg=09
   value="Nicola"
 bind 1: dty=1 mxl=2000(200) mal=00 scl=00 pre=00 oacflg=03 oacfl2=0010 size=2000 offset=0
   bfp=ffffffff7ba79980 bln=2000 avl=07 flg=05
   value="03APR73"
 bind 2: dty=1 mxl=32(07) mal=00 scl=00 pre=00 oacflg=10 oacfl2=0100 size=32 offset=0
   bfp=ffffffff7b957d98 bln=32 avl=07 flg=09
   value="DDMONYY"
```

When tracing larger, more complex queries, remember that SYS_B_*n* does not necessarily bind to variable *n*.

Errors

The raw trace file will include errors that occur during the period of the trace. Two types of errors are recorded: execution errors and parsing errors. *Parsing errors* occur when the SQL statement cannot be parsed due to problems such as syntax or object permissions.

```
PARSE ERROR #7:len=50 dep=0 uid=44 oct=3 lid=44 tim=1515543106413 err=936
select date from birthday where name = :"SYS_B_0"
```

The preceding trace line shows error ORA-936 when parsing cursor #7. The information includes all of the same information as a successful parse operation, except for the SQL hash and address, as the failed statement is not stored in the Library Cache.

Execution errors simply list the error code and the time of the error.

```
ERROR #76:err=1555 tim=54406123
```

The preceding trace line shows that error ORA-1555 was raised during the execution of cursor #76.

Some Common X$ Table Groups

Some of the X$ tables can be logically grouped as shown in Tables 13-1 through 13-44. This is by no means a complete list. The descriptions for these tables are updated to the best of my knowledge (listed here are only a small and limited number of X$ tables even within a group). I am unsure of the value where the description or other field is missing or blank. Oracle Corporation does not provide a full description list. In the final section of the chapter, I include a *very nice* definition tree structure that was provided for an earlier version of the X$ tables. You can certainly use this with most versions to help you understand the naming conventions much better.

X$ Tables	Description *(being deprecated)
X$KCKCE	Features in use by the database instance that may prevent downgrading to a previous release*
X$KCKFM	Some sort of information about the version of database or database parts*
X$KCKTY	Features in use by the database instance that may prevent downgrading to a previous release*
X$KSULL	Information about license limits
X$OPTION	Installed options
X$VERSION	Oracle RDBMS software version

TABLE 13-1. *Version/Installation*

X$ Tables	Description
X$KSUSGSTA	Instance statistics
X$KCCDI	Main source of information for V$DATABASE
X$KSMSD	SGA component sizes (SHOW SGA)
X$KSMSS	Detailed SGA statistics
X$KSPPCV	Parameters and values that are in effect for the session
X$KSPPCV2	Parameters and values that are in effect for the session. List parameter values appear as separate rows
X$KSPPI	Parameter names and descriptions
X$KSPPO	Obsolete parameters
X$KSPPSV	Parameters and values that are in effect for the instance
X$KSPPSV2	Parameters and values that are in effect for the instance. List parameter values appear as separate rows
X$KSPVLD_VALUES	Valid values for parameters that accept ordinal values (also called list parameters).
X$KSPSPFILE	Parameter names specified with an SPFILE
X$KSQDN	Database name
X$OPTION	Installed options
X$KVII	Instance limits and other instance metadata (includes miscellaneous information)
X$KVIT	State of various buffer cache conditions
X$KSUXSINST	Main source of information for V$INSTANCE
X$QUIESCE	Quiescent state of the instance

TABLE 13-2.   *Instance/Database*

X$ Tables	Description
X$KSULV	Valid values of NLS parameters
X$NLS_PARAMETERS	Current values of NLS parameters

TABLE 13-3.   *NSL (National Language Support)*

X$ Table	Description
X$TIMEZONE_NAMES	Time zone names
X$TIMEZONE_FILE	Time zone file and version used by the database

TABLE 13-4. *Time Zones*

X$ Tables	Description
X$KCCAL	Information about archive log files from the control file
X$KCRRARCH	Information about the ARCH processes for the current instance
X$KCRRDSTAT	Archive destination status

TABLE 13-5. *Archive Log Files/Destinations/Processes*

X$ Tables	Description
X$KCCFE	File creation and other metadata
X$KCCTF	Temp file I/O information
X$KCVFH	Information source of V$DATAFILE and V$DATAFILE_HEADER
X$KCFIO	File I/O information
X$KCFTIO	Temp file I/O information
X$KCVFHALL	Datafile information similar to information in V$DATAFILE
X$KTFBFE	Free extents in files (ktfb free extents)
X$KTFBHC	Datafile information (similar to DBA_DATA_FILES)

TABLE 13-6. *Data Files*

X$ Tables	Description
X$KCCCF	Control file information
X$KCCOR	Datafile offline information from the control file
X$KCCRS	Information about the control file record sections
X$KCCRT	Log file information from the control files

TABLE 13-7. *Control Files*

X$ Tables	Description
X$KCCCP	Redo log block information
X$KCCFN	Information about file numbers, info for all file types
X$KCCLE	Information about redo log files in need of archiving

TABLE 13-8. *Redo Log Files*

X$ Table	Description
X$KCCTS	Tablespace information

TABLE 13-9. *Tablespaces*

X$ Tables	Description
X$KCBTEK	Encrypted tablespaces
X$KEWXOCF	SYSAUX tablespace occupants
X$KTFTHC	Space usage in each temp tablespace
X$KTFTME	Status of each unit of all temp tablespaces (i.e., temp map extents/blocks)
X$KTSSO	Sort segment activity by session
X$KTSTFC	Temp segment usage: blocks used, cached, etc.
X$KTSTSSD	System temporary sort segment data
X$KTTETS	Tablespace usage metrics

TABLE 13-10. *Sort/Temp Segments*

X$ Tables	Description
X$KTFBUE	Rollback/undo segment block/extent usage
X$KTTVS	Rollback/undo segment stats
X$KTUGD	Global rollback/undo data
X$KTURD	Rollback/undo segment stats
X$KTUSMST	Rollback/undo segment stats
X$KTUXE	Rollback/undo segment activity: wraps, etc.

TABLE 13-11. *Rollback/Undo Segments*

X$ Tables	Description
X$KCVFHTMP	Tempfile information
X$KDLT	Temporary LOB information

TABLE 13-12. *Temporary Objects*

X$ Table	Description
X$UGANCO	Database link information

TABLE 13-13. *Database Links*

X$ Table	Description
X$KNSTMVR	Materialized view and refresh information

TABLE 13-14. *Materialized Views*

X$ Tables	Description
X$KNSTRPP	Current parallel propagation information for replication
X$KNSTRQU	Replication deferred transaction queue statistics

TABLE 13-15. *Replication*

X$ Tables	Description
X$KCCBF	Information from the control file about data file and control file backups (RMAN)
X$KCCBL	Information from the control file about redo and archived log backups (RMAN)
X$KCCBP	Backup piece information from the control file (RMAN)

TABLE 13-16. *Backup*

X$ Tables	Description
X$KCCBS	Backup set information from the control file (RMAN)
X$KCCCC	Datafile copy corruptions from the control file (RMAN)
X$KCCDC	Datafile copy information from the control file (RMAN)
X$KCCFC	Corruption in datafile backups (RMAN)
X$KCVFHONL	Backup status of all online datafiles
X$KSFQDVNT	Supported backup devices (RMAN)
X$KSFQP	Performance information about ongoing or recently completed backups
X$KSFVQST	Backup information
X$KSFVSL	Backup information
X$KSFVSTA	Backup information

TABLE 13-16. *Backup* (continued)

X$ Tables	Description
X$KCRFX	Statistics about the current recovery process
X$KCRMF	Statistics and status of files involved in recovery
X$KCRMX	Statistics and status of files involved in recovery
X$KCVFHMRR	Displays status of files during media recovery
X$KRVSLV	Recovery slave status
X$KRVSLVS	Recovery slave statistics
X$KTPRXRS	Information about fast start servers performing parallel recovery
X$KTPRXRT	Information about transactions Oracle is currently recovering
X$ESTIMATED_MTTR	Estimates on the I/O work required if an instance recovery is needed right now
X$TARGETRBA	Target recovery block accesses or target redo block accesses

TABLE 13-17. *Recovery*

X$ Tables	Description
X$KCCDL	Information about deleted objects. Recovery catalog resync operation uses this to speed its optimize operation
X$KCCPA	Descriptions of archive log backups taken with proxy copy
X$KCCPD	Descriptions of datafile and control file backups taken with proxy copy
X$KCCRM	RMAN configuration
X$KCCRSR	RMAN status

TABLE 13-18. *RMAN*

X$ Table	Description
X$KCCSL	Standby database log files
X$KNSTACR	Standby database information: logical standby process stats
X$KNSTASL	Standby database information: logical standby apply process

TABLE 13-19. *Standby Databases*

X$LOGMNR_CALLBACK

X$LOGMNR_COL$

X$LOGMNR_COLTYPE$

X$LOGMNR_CONTENTS

X$LOGMNR_DICTIONARY

X$LOGMNR_ENCRYPTED_OBJ$

X$LOGMNR_ENCRYPTION_PROFILE$

X$LOGMNR_IND$

X$LOGMNR_INDPART$

X$LOGMNR_LOGFILE

X$LOGMNR_LOGS

X$LOGMNR_PARAMETERS

X$LOGMNR_PROCESS

X$LOGMNR_OBJ$

X$LOGMNR_REGION

TABLE 13-20. *LogMiner*

X$LOGMNR_SESSION
X$LOGMNR_TAB$
X$LOGMNR_TABCOMPART$
X$LOGMNR_TABSUBPART$
X$LOGMNR_TS$
X$LOGMNR_TYPE$
X$LOGMNR_TABPART$
X$LOGMNR_TABSUBPART$
X$LOGMNR_USER$

TABLE 13-20.   *LogMiner* (continued)

X$ Tables	Description
X$KGSCC	Session cursor cache
X$KMPCSO	Session client result cache info
X$KSUPR	Process info
X$KSUSE	Session info
X$MESSAGES	Messages that each background process processes
X$QESMMSGA	PGA memory limits, uses, estimates, etc.
X$QKSBGSES	Session optimizer fix control

TABLE 13-21.   *Sessions/Processes*

X$ Tables	Description
X$KOCST	Object cache statistics for the current session
X$KSLES	Waits on event by sessions
X$KSQRS	Session resource usage
X$KSUSIO	I/O statistics for each session
X$KSULOP	Session information about long-running operations
X$KSUMYSTA	Statistics for the current session
X$KSUPL	Session information

TABLE 13-22.   *Session Performance*

X$ Tables	Description
X$KSUPR	Main source of information for V$PROCESS
X$KSUSE	Information in V$SESSION
X$KSUSECON	Information about how each session connected and authenticated
X$KSUSECST	Session waits, including wait parameters
X$KSUSESTA	Session performance statistics

TABLE 13-22. *Session Performance* (continued)

X$ Table	Description
X$KTCXB	Transaction information, including locks requested and held, rollback segments used by the transaction, and the type of transaction
X$KTFTBTXNGRAPH	Flashback transaction graph
X$KTFTBTXNMODS	Flashback transaction modifications
X$KTUQQRY	Flashback transaction query
X$KTUXE	Transaction entry table

TABLE 13-23. *Transactions*

X$ Tables	Description
X$K2GTE	Information on the currently active global transactions
X$K2GTE2	Information on the currently active global transactions

TABLE 13-24. *Global Transactions*

X$ Tables	Description
X$KGSKASP	All available active session pool resource allocation methods
X$KGSKCFT	Data related to currently active resource consumer groups
X$KGSKCP	All resource allocation methods defined for resource consumer groups
X$KGSKDOPP	Available parallel degree limit resource allocation methods

TABLE 13-25. *Advanced Queuing (AQ) / Resource Management*

X$ Tables	Description
X$KGSKPFT	Names of all currently active resource plans
X$KGSKQUEP	Available queue resource allocation methods
X$KSRMSGDES	Queue messages
X$KSRMSGO	Queue publisher/subscriber information
X$KWQSI	Read/write statistics on queues

TABLE 13-25.   *Advanced Queuing (AQ) / Resource Management* (continued)

X$ Tables	Description
X$KCLCRST	Information about block server background processes used in cache fusion
X$KJBL	RAC DLM information
X$KJBLFX	RAC information
X$KJBR	RAC DLM resource statistics
X$KJDRHV	RAC instance information (the current and previous master instances and the number of remasterings of Global Enqueue Service resources)
X$KJDRPCMHV	RAC instance information (the current master instances and the number of remasterings of Global Cache Service resources except those belonging to files mapped to a particular master)
X$KJDRPCMPF	RAC instance information (the previous master instances and the number of remasterings of Global Cache Service resources except those belonging to files mapped to a particular master)
X$KJICVT	RAC DLM information (statistics for local and remote GES enqueue operations)
X$KJILKFT	RAC DLM information
X$KJIRFT	RAC DLM information (information about all resources currently known to the DLM)
X$KJISFT	RAC DLM information (miscellaneous Oracle RAC statistics)
X$KJITRFT	RAC DLM information (information about the message ticket usage)
X$KJMDDP	RAC information
X$KJMSDP	RAC information
X$KJXM	RAC information
X$KSIMAT	RAC information instance attributes
X$KSIMAV	RAC information attribute values for all instances
X$KSIMSI	Map of instance names to instance numbers for all instances mounting a particular database

TABLE 13-26.   *Real Application Clusters*

X$ Tables	Description
X$KGLCLUSTER	Likely currently loaded or recently referenced clusters
X$KGLCURSOR	Statistics on shared SQL area without the GROUP BY clause and contains one row for each child of the original SQL text entered
X$KGLINDEX	Object names with currently held locks and other information about these locks
X$KGLNA	Text of SQL statements belonging to shared SQL cursors
X$KGLNA1	Text of SQL statements belonging to shared SQL cursors: newlines and tabs not replaced with spaces
X$KGLOB	Database objects that are cached in the Library Cache. Objects include tables, indexes, clusters, synonym definitions, PL/SQL procedures and packages, and triggers
X$KGLST	Library Cache performance and activity information
X$KKSBV	Bind variable data (depending on setting of CURSOR_SHARING) for cursors owned by the current session
X$KKSCS	Information about why nonshared child cursors are nonshared
X$KKSSRD	Redirected SQL statements
X$KQFVI	SQL statements of all the fixed views
X$KQLFXPL	Execution plan for each child cursor loaded in the Library Cache
X$KQLSET	Information about subordinate caches currently loaded in the Library Cache
X$KSLEI	Wait statistics (totals) for each event
X$KXSBD	SQL or session bind data
X$KXSCC	Shared cursor cache. V$SQL_CURSOR debugging information for each cursor associated with the session querying this view. Memory use by each cursor of a session SQL cursor cache
X$QESMMIWT	Shared memory management is working. Join to X$QKSMMWDS
X$QKSMMWDS	Shared memory management working data size. Library Cache memory use by child cursors

TABLE 13-27. *Library Cache*

X$ Tables	Description
X$KGHLU	Shared pool reserved list performance information
X$KGICS	Systemwide cursor usage statistics: opens, hits, count, etc.
X$KSMFSV	Shared memory information

TABLE 13-28. *Shared Memory*

X$ Tables	Description
X$KSMHP	Shared memory information
X$KSMLRU	Shared memory: specific, loaded objects and their sizes, pin candidates
X$KSMFS	SGA sizes: fixed SGA, DB_BLOCK_BUFFERS, LOG_BUFFER
X$KSMSS	SGA size: shared pool (also listed in the "Instance/Database" section)
X$KSMJS	SGA size: Java pool
X$KSMLS	SGA size: large pool
X$KSMPP	Very similar to X$KSMSP, without DUR and IDX columns varying numbers on Linux, Solaris, and NT
X$KSMSP	Shared pool section sizes/values, etc.
X$KSMSPR	Shared pool reserved memory statistics/sizes
X$KSMSP_DSNEW	Shared memory information
X$KSMSP_NWEX	Shared memory information
X$KSMUP	Instance and memory structure sizes/statistics

TABLE 13-28. *Shared Memory* (continued)

X$ Tables	Description
X$ACTIVECKPT	Checkpoint statistics information
X$BH	Status and number of pings for every buffer in the SGA
X$KCBBHS	DBWR histogram statistics
X$KCBFWAIT	Buffer cache wait count and time by file
X$KCBKPFS	Buffer cache block prefetch statistics
X$KCBLSC	Buffer cache read/write/wait performance statistics
X$KCBSC	Buffer cache set read performance statistics
X$KCBWAIT	Number of and time spent in waits for buffer pool classes
X$KCBWBPD	Statistics on all buffer pools available to the instance, including buffer pool names
X$KCBWDS	Statistics on all buffer pools available to the instance

TABLE 13-29. *Buffer Cache*

X$ Tables	Description
X$KQRFP	Information about parent objects in the data dictionary
X$KQRFS	Information about subordinate objects in the data dictionary
X$KQRPD	Rowcache information: parent/child definition
X$KQRSD	Rowcache information: subordinate cache definition
X$KQRST	Rowcache performance statistics

TABLE 13-30. *Rowcache*

X$ Tables	Description
X$KGLLK	DDL locks currently held and requested
X$KSQEQ	Locks held by sessions
X$KSQST	Enqueue type, number of requests, number of waits, wait time, etc.
X$KTADM	DML lock info requested and held by sessions

TABLE 13-31. *Locks/Enqueues*

X$ Tables	Description
X$KSLLD	Latch names and levels
X$KSLLW	Statistics on latch waits, plus latch names
X$KSLPO	Latch posting
X$KSLWSC	Statistics on latch wait sleeps, plus latch names
X$KSUPRLAT	Information about current latch holders
X$MUTEX_SLEEP	Mutex sleep information
X$MUTEX_SLEEP_HISTORY	Mutex sleep history information

TABLE 13-32. *Latches*

X$ Tables	Description
X$KDXHS	Index histogram information
X$KDXST	Index statistics from the last analyze index validate structure command

TABLE 13-33. *Optimizer*

X$ Tables	Description
X$KMCQS	Multithread message queue information
X$KMCVC	Virtual circuit connection message transport statistical information
X$KMMDI	MTS dispatcher performance information
X$KMMDP	MTS dispatcher performance information
X$KMMRD	MTS dispatcher information
X$KMMSG	Shared servers process performance information
X$KMMSI	Shared servers process information

TABLE 13-34. *MTS*

X$ Tables	Description
X$KXFPCDS	PQ coordinator dequeue statistics
X$KXFPCMS	PQ coordinator message statistics
X$KXFPCST	PQ coordinator query statistics
X$KXFPDP	Metadata about current PQ sessions, such as number of degree of parallelism, etc.
X$KXFPPFT	Parallel query information
X$KXFPSDS	PQ slave dequeue statistics
X$KXFPSMS	PQ slave message statistics
X$KXFPSST	PQ slave query statistics
X$KXFPYS	Parallel query system statistics
X$KXFPNS	Performance statistics for sessions running parallel execution
X$KXFQSROW	Statistics on parallel execution operations, query statistics row

TABLE 13-35. *Parallel Query*

X$ Tables	Description
X$KZDOS	Operation system role-related security
X$KZRTPD	Fine-grained security policies and predicates associated with the cursors currently in the Library Cache
X$KZSPR	Privileges enabled for a session
X$KZSRO	Roles enabled for a session
X$KZSRT	List of users who have been granted SYSDBA and SYSOPER privileges (remote password file table entries)

TABLE 13-36. *Security-Granted Privileges and Roles, Fine-Grained Security Policies*

X$ Tables	Description
X$KGSKPP	Available CPU resource allocation methods defined for resource plans
X$KGSKQUEP	Available queuing resource allocation methods
X$KGSKTE	Possibly `rcg` names
X$KGSKTO	Possibly `rcg` types and attributes

TABLE 13-37.   *Resource/Consumer Groups*

X$ Tables	Description
X$CONTEXT	Context information
X$GLOBALCONTEXT	Context information

TABLE 13-38.   *Contexts*

NOTE
"Contexts" has nothing to do with Oracle Text, which used to be called "Context."

X$ Tables	Description
X$HOFP	Init parameters in use by the hs server and agent
X$HS_SESSION	Information about the hs agents currently running on a given host

TABLE 13-39.   *Heterogeneous Services*

X$ Table	Description
X$KWDDEF	PL/SQL reserved words

TABLE 13-40.   *PL/SQL*

X$ Tables	Description
X$KLCIE	Errors that occurred when updating indexes on a table during a load using the direct path API
X$KLPT	Statistics about the number of rows loaded into a partition, or subpartition, during a load using the direct path API

TABLE 13-41. *Loader/Direct Path API*

X$ Tables	Description
X$JOXFC	Compile, resolve, reference information: Java classes
X$JOXFD	Compile, resolve, reference information
X$JOXFR	Compile, resolve, reference information: Java resources
X$JOXFS	Source name and/or code
X$JOXFT	Reference names, resolve information, compile information, class name information

TABLE 13-42. *Java Source*

X$ Tables	Description
X$DUAL	Everybody loves the permanent table DUAL, including Oracle. When the database is in a nomount or mount state, the permanent table DUAL is not available. For some operations, such as recovery, which Oracle needs to do when the database is in a nomount or mount state, Oracle queries X$DUAL
X$KQFCO	Indexed columns of dynamic performance tables
X$KQFDT	Fixed dynamic or derived tables
X$KQFP	Fixed procedural object names
X$KQFSZ	Sizes of various database component types
X$KQFTA	Names of all the fixed tables
X$KQFVI	Names of all the fixed views
X$KSBDD	Descriptions of the background processes
X$KSBDP	Background process names
X$KSLED	Wait event names
X$KSURLMT	System resource limits
X$KSUSD	Statistics descriptions
X$TIMER	Lists the elapsed time in hundredths of seconds since the beginning of the epoch

TABLE 13-43. *Miscellaneous Tables*

Table Name	Probable Use
X$VINST	Unknown
X$RFMTE	Unknown
X$RFMP	Unknown
X$KTSPSTAT	Undo/rollback information
X$KSXRSG	Unknown
X$KSRREPQ	Unknown
X$KSXRMSG	Unknown
X$KSXRCONQ	Unknown
X$KSXRCH	Unknown
X$KSXAFA	Node affinity
X$KSUSEX	Session information
X$KSURU	Resource usage by session
X$KSUPGS	Unknown
X$KSUPGP	Process group info
X$KSUCF	Resource limits for Resource Manager
X$KSRMPCTX	Unknown
X$KSRCHDL	Unknown
X$KSRCDES	Unknown
X$KSRCCTX	Unknown
X$KSMNS	Shared memory information
X$KSMNIM	Shared memory information
X$KSMMEM	Shared memory information
X$KSMJCH	Shared memory information
X$KSMDD	Shared memory information
X$KRBAFF	Unknown
X$KQDPG	PGA row cache cursor stats
X$KKSAI	Cursor allocation info
X$KGLXS	Library Cache information
X$KGLTRIGGER	Triggers in Library Cache
X$KGLTR	Library Cache information
X$KGLTABLE	Tables in Library Cache
X$KGLSN	Unknown

TABLE 13-44.   *Other X$ Tables*

Table Name	Probable Use
X$KGLAU	Object authorizations
X$KGLRD	Unknown
X$KDNSSF	Lock information
X$KCRMT	Cache fusion information
X$KCLQN	Cache fusion information
X$KCLLS	Cache fusion information
X$KCLFX	Cache fusion information
X$KCLCURST	Cache fusion information
X$KCBWH	Information about functions pertaining to the buffer cache
X$KCBSW	Buffer cache information
X$KCBSH	Buffer cache information
X$KCBSDS	Buffer cache information
X$KCBLDRHIST	Buffer cache information
X$KCBKWRL	Buffer cache write list
X$KCBBF	Unknown
X$KCBBES	Unknown
X$CKPTBUF	Checkpoint information

TABLE 13-44.   *Other X$ Tables* (continued)

Some Common X$ Table and Non-V$ Fixed View Associations

Table 13-45 lists non-V$ fixed views (V$ views are listed in Appendixes B and C) that are based on at least one X$ table. Many of the fixed views are based on one or more X$ tables, plus other fixed views. You can use this list with the Oracle Reference manual and the $ORACLE_HOME/rdbms/admin/sql.bsq and $ORACLE_HOME/rdbms/admin/migrate.bsq as an aid in deciphering the meaning of X$ table and column contents and in constructing queries that join X$ tables to other X$ tables or to fixed views.

Fixed View	Base X$ Tables and/or Fixed Views
COLUMN_PRIVILEGES	OBJAUTH$, COL$, OBJ$, USER$, X$KZSRO
DBA_BLOCKERS	V$SESSION_WAIT, X$KSQRS, V$_LOCK, X$KSUSE
DBA_DATA_FILES	FILE$, TS$, V$DBFILE, X$KTFBHC
DBA_DDL_LOCKS	V$SESSION, X$KGLOB, X$KGLLK
DBA_DML_LOCKS	V$_LOCK, X$KSUSE, X$KSQRS
DBA_EXTENTS	UET$, SYS_DBA_SEGS, FILE$, X$KTFBUE, FILE$
DBA_FREE_SPACE	TS$, FET$, FILE$, X$KTFBFE
DBA_FREE_SPACE_COALESCED	X$KTFBFE
DBA_KGLLOCK	X$KGLLK, X$KGLPN
DBA_LMT_FREE_SPACE	X$KTFBFE
DBA_LMT_USED_EXTENTS	X$KTFBUE
DBA_LOCK_INTERNAL	V$LOCK, V$PROCESS, V$SESSION, V$LATCHHOLDER, X$KGLOB, DBA_KGLLOCK
DBA_SOURCE	OBJ$, SOURCE$, USER$, X$JOXFS
DBA_TEMP_FILES	X$KCCFN, X$KTFTHC, TS$
DBA_UNDO_EXTENTS	UNDO$, TS$, X$KTFBUE, FILE$
DBA_WAITERS	V$SESSION_WAIT, X$KSQRS, V$_LOCK, X$KSUSE
DICTIONARY	V$ENABLEDPRIVS, OBJ$, COM$, SYN$, OBJAUTH$, X$KZSRO
DISK_AND_FIXED_OBJECTS	OBJ$, X$KQFP, X$KQFTA, X$KQFVI
EXU8FUL	X$KZSRO, USER$
EXU9FIL	FILE$, V$DBFILE, X$KTFBHC, TS$, X$KCCFN, X$KTFTHC
EXU9TNEB	X$KTFBUE
IMP9TVOID	OBJ$, USER$, TYPE$, SESSION_ROLES, OBJAUTH$, X$KZSRO
INDEX_HISTOGRAM	X$KDXST, X$KDXHS
INDEX_STATS	OBJ$, IND$, SEG$, X$KDXST, INDPART$, INDSUBPART$
LOADER_DIR_OBJS	OBJ$, DIR$, V$ENABLEDPRIVS, X$KZSRO
LOADER_TAB_INFO	OBJ$, V$ENABLEDPRIVS, X$KZSRO, TAB$, USER$, OBJAUTH$
LOADER_TRIGGER_INFO	OBJ$, USER$, TRIGGER$, OBJAUTH$, V$ENABLEDPRIVS, X$KZSRO
ORA_KGLR7_DEPENDENCIES	OBJ$, DEPENDENCY$, USER$, X$KZSRO, V$FIXED_TABLE, OBJAUTH$

TABLE 13-45. *X$ Table and Non-V$ Fixed View Associations*

Fixed View	Base X$ Tables and/or Fixed Views
ORA_KGLR7_IDL_CHAR	ORA_KGLR7_OBJECTS, IDL_CHAR$, OBJAUTH$, X$KZSRO
ORA_KGLR7_IDL_SB4	ORA_KGLR7_OBJECTS, IDL_SB4$, OBJAUTH$, X$KZSRO, SYSAUTH$
ORA_KGLR7_IDL_UB1	ORA_KGLR7_OBJECTS, IDL_UB1$, OBJAUTH$, X$KZSRO, SYSAUTH$
ORA_KGLR7_IDL_UB2	ORA_KGLR7_OBJECTS, IDL_UB2$, OBJAUTH$, X$KZSRO, SYSAUTH$
QUEUE_PRIVILEGES	OBJAUTH$, OBJ$, USER$, X$KZSRO
ROLE_SYS_PRIVS	USER$, SYSTEM_PRIVILEGE_MAP, SYSAUTH$, X$KZDOS
ROLE_ROLE_PRIVS	USER$, SYSAUTH$, X$KZDOS
ROLE_TAB_PRIVS	USER$, TABLE_PRIVILEGE_MAP, OBJAUTH$, OBJ$, COL$, X$KZDOS, SYSAUTH$
SESSION_ROLES	X$KZSRO
TABLE_PRIVILEGES	OBJAUTH$, OBJ$, USER$, X$KZSRO

TABLE 13-45. *X$ Table and Non-V$ Fixed View Associations* (continued)

Common X$ Table Joins

Table 13-46 lists the X$ table column joins used in fixed views.

X$ Table and Column	Associated X$ Table and Column
X$BH.LE_ADDR	X$LE.LE_ADDR
X$KCCFN.FNFNO	X$KTFTHC.KTFTHCTFNO
X$HS_SESSION.FDS_INST_ID	X$HOFP.FDS_INST_ID
X$KCBSC.BPID	X$KCBWBPD.BP_ID
X$KCBSC.INST_ID	X$KCBWBPD.INST_ID
X$KCBWDS.SET_ID	X$KCBWBPD.BP_LO_SID
X$KCBWDS.SET_ID	X$KCBWBPD.BP_HI_SID
X$KCCFE.FEFNH	X$KCCFN.FNNUM
X$KCCFE.FENUM	X$KCCFN.FNFNO

TABLE 13-46. *Common Table Joins*

X$ Table and Column	Associated X$ Table and Column
X$KCCFE.FENUM	X$KCCFN.FNFNO
X$KCCFE.FEPAX	X$KCCFN.FNNUM
X$KCCFN.FNFNO	X$KCVFHTMP.HTMPXFIL
X$KCCFN.FNFNO	X$KCVFH.HCFIL
X$KCCFN.FNFNO	X$KTFTHC.KTFTHCTFNO
X$KCCLE.INST_ID	X$KCCRT.INST_ID
X$KCCLE.LETHR	X$KCCRT.RTNUM
X$KCCTF.TFFNH	X$KCCFN.FNNUM
X$KCCTF.TFNUM	X$KCCFN.FNFNO
X$KCFTIO.KCFTIOFNO	X$KCCTF.TFNUM
X$KCRMF.FNO	X$KCCFN.FNFNO
X$KCRMF.FNO	X$KCCFN.FNFNO
X$KCRMX.THR	X$KCRFX.THR
X$KGLCRSOR.KGLHDADR	X$KZRTPD.KZRTPDAD
X$KGLCRSOR.KGLHDPAR	X$KZRTPD.KZRTPDPA
X$KGLCURSOR.KGLHDPAR	X$KZRTPD.KZRTPDPA, X$KKSSRD.PARADDR
X$KGLCURSOR.KGLOBHD6	X$KSMHP.KSMCHDS
X$KGLLK.KGLLKHDL	X$KGLDP.KGLHDADR
X$KGLLK.KGLLKUSE	X$KSUSE.ADDR
X$KGLLK.KGLNAHSH	X$KGLDP.KGLNAHSH
X$KGLOB.KGLHDADR	X$KGLDP.KGLRFHDL
X$KGLOB.KGLHDADR	X$KGLLK.KGLLKHDL
X$KGLOB.KGLNAHSH	X$KGLDP.KGLRFHSH
X$KQFVI.INDX	X$KQFVT.INDX
X$KSBDP.INDX	X$KSBDD.INDX
X$KSLEI.INDX	X$KSLED.INDX
X$KSLES.KSLESENM	X$KSLED.INDX
X$KSLLW.INDX	X$KSLWSC.INDX
X$KSPPI.INDX	X$KSPPSV.INDX
X$KSPPI.INDX	X$KSPPCV.INDX
X$KSPPI.INDX	X$KSPPCV2.INDX
X$KSPPI.INDX	X$KSPPSV2.KSPFTCTXPN
X$KSQEQ.KSQLKRES	X$KSQRS.ADDR

TABLE 13-46. *Common Table Joins* (continued)

X$ Table and Column	Associated X$ Table and Column
X$KSQEQ.KSQLKSES	X$KSUSE.ADDR
X$KSUSE.KSUSEPRO	X$KXFPDP.KXFPDPPRO
X$KSUSECST.KSUSSOPC	X$KSLED.INDX
X$KSUXSINST	Joined with X$KVIT and X$QUIESCE to create V$INSTANCE, but with no specific column joins
X$KTCXB.KSQLKRES	X$KSQRS.ADDR
X$KTCXB.KSQLKSES	X$KSUSE.ADDR
X$KTCXB.KSQLKSES	X$KSUSE.ADDR
X$KTCXB.KTCXBSES	X$KSUSE.ADDR
X$KTCXB.KTCXBXBA	X$KTADM.KSSOBOWN
X$TARGETRBA.INST_ID	X$ESTIMATED_MTTR.INST_ID

TABLE 13-46. *Common Table Joins* (continued)

NOTE
See Appendixes B and C for detailed listings of all V$ views and X$ tables. There are 945 X$ tables in Oracle 11.2. Appendix C lists all X$ tables along with all indexes. There is also a cross-listing of many X$ to V$ tables.

X$ Table Naming Conventions

This summary lists X$ table definitions. The last revision was in Oracle 7.3.2, and the main purpose of this section is to show the naming conventions (these are great to get to know some of the Oracle acronyms; I've included these despite the fact that many are now outdated, but it is still nice to see where some of these names came from originally).

```
[K]ernel Layer
   [2]-Phase Commit
      [G]lobal [T]ransaction [E]ntry
         X$K2GTE  - Current 2PC tx
         X$K2GTE2 - Current 2PC tx

   [C]ache Layer
      [B]uffer Management
         Buffer [H]ash
            X$BH - Hash Table

         Buffer LRU Statistics
            X$KCBCBH - [C]urrent [B]uffers (buckets) - lru_statistics
            X$KCBRBH - [R]ecent [B]uffers (buckets) - lru_extended
```

```
Buffer [WAIT]s
  X$KCBWAIT  - Waits by block class
  X$KCBFWAIT - Waits by File

[W]orking Sets - 7.3 or higher
  X$KCBWDS - Set [D]escriptors

[C]ontrol File Management
  [C]ontrol [F]ile List - 7.0.16 or higher
    X$KCCCF - Control File Names & status

  [D]atabase [I]nformation
    X$KCCDI - Database Information

  Data [F]iles
    X$KCCFE - File [E]ntries ( from control file )
    X$KCCFN - [F]ile [N]ames

  [L]og Files
    X$KCCLE - Log File [E]ntries
    X$KCCLH - Log [H]istory ( archive entries )

  Thread Information
    X$KCCRT - [R]edo [T]hread Information

[F]ile Management
  X$KCFIO - File [IO] Statistics

[L]ock Manager Component ( LCK )
  [H]ash and Bucket Tables - 7.0.15 to 7.1.1, and 7.2.0 or higher
    X$KCLFH - File [H]ash Table
    X$KCLFI - File Bucket Table

  X$LE - Lock [E]lements
  X$LE_STAT - Lock Conversion [STAT]istics
  X$KCLFX - Lock Element [F]ree list statistics - 7.3 or higher
  X$KCLLS - Per LCK free list statistics - 7.3 or higher
  X$KCLQN - [N]ame (hash) table statistics - 7.3 or higher

[R]edo Component
  [M]edia recovery  - kcra.h - 7.3 or higher
    X$KCRMF - [F]ile context
    X$KCRMT - [T]hread context
    X$KCRMX - Recovery Conte[X]t

  [F]ile read
    X$KCRFX - File Read Conte[X]t -  7.3 or higher

Reco[V]ery Component
  [F]ile [H]eaders
    X$KCVFH - All file headers
    X$KCVFHMRR - Files with [M]edia [R]ecovery [R]equired
    X$KCVFHONL - [ONL]ine File headers
```

```
    [K]ompatibility Management - 7.1.1 or higher
      X$KCKCE - [C]ompatibility Segment [E]ntries
      X$KCKTY - Compatibility [TY]pes
      X$KCKFM - Compatibility [F]or[M]ats ( index into X$KCKCE )

  [D]ata Layer
    Sequence [N]umber Component
       X$KDNCE - Sequence [C]ache [E]ntries - 7.2 or lower

      [S]equence Enqueues - common area for enqueue objects
        X$KDNSSC - [C]ache Enqueue Objects - 7.2 or lower
        X$KDNSSF - [F]lush Enqueue Objects - 7.2 or lower
      X$KDNST - Cache [ST]atistics - 7.2 or lower

    Inde[X] Block Component
      X$KDXHS - Index [H]i[S]togram
      X$KDXST - Index [ST]atistics

  [G]eneric Layer
    [H]eap Manager
      X$KGHLU - State (summary) of [L]R[U] heap(s) - defined in ksmh.h

    [I]nstantiation Manager
      [C]ursor [C]ache
        X$KGICC - Session statistics - defined in kqlf.h
        X$KGICS - System wide statistics - defined in kqlf.h

    [L]ibrary Cache Manager  ( defined and mapped from kqlf )
      Bind Variables
        X$KKSBV - Library Object [B]ind [V]ariables

      Object Cache
        X$KGLOB - All [OB]jects
        X$KGLTABLE   - Filter for [TABLE]s
        X$KGLBODY    - Filter for [BODY] ( packages )
        X$KGLTRIGGER - Filter for [TRIGGER]s
        X$KGLINDEX   - Filter for [INDEX]es
        X$KGLCLUSTER - Filter for [CLUSTER]s
        X$KGLCURSOR  - Filter for [CURSOR]s

      Cache Dependency
        X$KGLDP - Object [D]e[P]endency table
        X$KGLRD - [R]ead only [D]ependency table - 7.3 or higher

      Object Locks
        X$KGLLK - Object [L]oc[K]s

      Object Names
        X$KGLNA - Object [NA]mes (sql text)
        X$KGLNA1 - Object [NA]mes (sql text) with newlines - 7.2.0 or higher

      Object Pins
        X$KGLPN - Object [P]i[N]s
```

```
    Cache Statistics
       X$KGLST - Library cache [ST]atistics

    Translation Table
       X$KGLTR - Address [TR]anslation

    Access Table
       X$KGLXS - Object Access Table

    Authorization Table - 7.1.5 or higher
       X$KGLAU - Object Authorization table

    Latch Cleanup - 7.0.15 or higher
       X$KGLLC - [L]atch [C]leanup for Cache/Pin Latches

[K]ompile Layer
  [S]hared Objects
    X$KKSAI - Cursor [A]llocation [I]nformation - 7.3.2 or higher

[L]oader
  [L]ibrary
    X$KLLCNT - [C]o[NT]rol Statistics
    X$KLLTAB - [TAB]le Statistics

[M]ulti-Threaded Layer
  [C]ircuit component
    X$KMCQS - Current [Q]ueue [S]tate
    X$KMCVC - [V]irtual [C]ircuit state

  [M]onitor Server/dispatcher
    [D]ispatcher
       X$KMMDI - [D]ispatcher [I]nfo (status)
       X$KMMDP - [D]ispatcher Config ( [P]rotocol info )

    [S]erver
    X$KMMSI - [S]erver [I]nfo ( status )
    X$KMMSG - [SG]a info ( global statistics)
    X$KMMRD - [R]equest timing [D]istributions

s[Q]l Version and Option Layer
  Kernel [V]ersions
    X$VERSION - Library versions

  Kernel [O]ptions - 7.1.3 or higher
    X$OPTION - Server Options

[Q]uery Layer
  [D]ictionary Cache Management
    X$KQDPG - [PG]a row cache cursor statistics

  [F]ixed Tables/views Management
    X$KQFCO - Table [CO]lumn definitions
    X$KQFDT - [D]erived [T]ables
    X$KQFSZ - Kernel Data structure type [S]i[Z]es
```

```
    X$KQFTA - Fixed [TA]bles
    X$KQFVI - Fixed [VI]ews
    X$KQFVT - [V]iew [T]ext definition - 7.2.0 or higher

  [R]ow Cache Management
    X$KQRST - Cache [ST]atistics
    X$KQRPD - [P]arent Cache [D]efinition - 7.1.5 or higher
    X$KQRSD - [S]ubordinate Cache [D]efinition - 7.1.5 or higher

[S]ervice Layer
  [B]ackground Management
    [D]etached Process
      X$KSBDD - Detached Process [D]efinition (info)
      X$KSBDP - Detached [P]rocess Descriptor (name)
      X$MESSAGES - Background Message table

  [I]nstance [M]anagement - 7.3 or higher
    X$KSIMAT - Instance [AT]tributes
    X$KSIMAV - [A]ttribute [V]alues for all instances
    X$KSIMSI - [S]erial and [I]nstance numbers

  [L]ock Management
    [E]vent Waits
      X$KSLED - Event [D]escriptors
      X$KSLEI - [I]nstance wide statistics since startup
      X$KSLES - Current [S]ession statistics

    [L]atches
      X$KSLLD - Latch [D]escriptor (name)
      X$KSLLT - Latch statistics [ + Child latches @ 7.3 or higher ]
      X$KSLLW - Latch context ( [W]here ) descriptors - 7.3+
      X$KSLPO - Latch [PO]st statistics - 7.3 or higher
      X$KSLWSC- No[W]ait and [S]leep [C]ount stats by Context -7.3+

  [M]emory Management
    [C]ontext areas
      X$KSMCX - E[X]tended statistics on usage - 7.3.1 or lower

    Heap Areas
      X$KSMSP - SGA Hea[P]
      X$KSMPP - [P]GA Hea[P] - 7.3.2 and above
      X$KSMUP - [U]GA Hea[P] - 7.3.2 and above
      X$KSMHP - Any [H]ea[P] - 7.3.2 and above
      X$KSMSPR- [S]hared [P]ool [R]eserved List - 7.1.5 or higher

    [L]east recently used shared pool chunks
      X$KSMLRU - LR[U] flushes from the shared pool

    [S]GA Objects
      X$KSMSD - Size [D]efinition for Fixed/Variable summary
      X$KSMSS - Statistics (lengths) of SGA objects
```

```
   SGA [MEM]ory
     X$KSMMEM - map of the entire SGA - 7.2.0 or higher
     X$KSMFSV - Addresses of [F]ixed [S]GA [V]ariables - 7.2.1+

[P]arameter Component
     X$KSPPI  - [P]arameter [I]nfo ( Names )
     X$KSPPCV - [C]urrent Session [V]alues - 7.3.2 or above
     X$KSPPSV - [S]ystem [V]alues - 7.3.2 or above

En[Q]ueue Management
   X$KSQDN - Global [D]atabase [N]ame
   X$KSQEQ - [E]n[Q]ueue Object
   X$KSQRS - Enqueue [R]e[S]ource
   X$KSQST - Enqueue [S]tatistics by [T]ype

[U]ser Management
   [C]ost
     X$KSUCF - Cost [F]unction (resource limit)

   [L]icense
      X$KSULL - License [L]imits

   [L]anguage Manager
     X$NLS_PARAMETERS - NLS parameters
     X$KSULV - NLS [V]alid Values - 7.1.2 or higher

   [MY] [ST]atistics
     X$KSUMYSTA - [MY] [ST]atisics (current session)

   [P]rocess Info
     X$KSUPL - Process (resource) [L]imits
     X$KSUPRLAT - [LAT]ch Holder
     X$KSUPR - Process object

   [R]esource
     X$KSURU - Resource [U]sage

   [S]tatistics
     X$KSUSD - [D]escriptors (statistic names)
     X$KSUSGSTA - [G]lobal [ST]atistics

   [SE]ssions
     X$KSUSECST - Session status for events
     X$KSUSESTA - Session [STA]tistics
     X$KSUSECON - [CON]nection Authentication - 7.2.1 or higher
     X$KSUSE - [SE]ssion Info
     X$KSUSIO - [S]ystem [IO] statistics per session

   [T]imer
     X$KSUTM - Ti[M]e in 1/100th seconds

   Instance [X]
     X$KSUXSINST - [INST]ance state
```

```
    [T]race management
       X$TRACE - Current traced events
       X$TRACES - All possible traces
       X$KSTEX - Code [EX]ecution - 7.2.1 or higher

  E[X]ecution Management
     Device/Node [A]ffinity - 7.3.2 and above
       X$KSXAFA - Current File/Node Affinity

[T]ransaction Layer
  Table [A]ccess [D]efinition
     X$KTADM - D[M]L lock

  [C]ontrol Component
     X$KTCXB - Transaction O[B]ject

  [S]or[T] Segments - 7.3 or higher
     X$KTSTSSD - [S]ort [S]egment [D]escriptor - per tablespace stats

  [T]ablespace
     X$KTTVS - [V]alid [S]aveundo

  [U]ndo
     X$KTURD - Inuse [D]escriptors
     X$KTUXE - Transaction [E]ntry (table) - 7.3.2 or above

Performance Layer [V] - 7.0.16 or higher
   [I]nformation tables
     X$KVII - [I]nitialisation Instance parameters
     X$KVIS - [S]izes of structure elements
     X$KVIT - [T]ransitory Instance parameters

Security Layer [Z]
  [D]ictionary Component
     X$KZDOS - [OS] roles

  [S]ecurity State
     X$KZSPR - Enabled [PR]ivileges
     X$KZSRO - Enabled [RO]les

  [R]emote Logins - 7.1.1 or higher
     X$KZSRT - [R]emote Password File [T]able entries

E[X]ecution Layer
  Parallel Query (Execute [F]ast) - 7.1.1 or higher
     [P]rocess and Queue Manager
        Statistics - 7.1.3 or higher
          X$KXFPYS - S[YS]tem Statistics
          X$KXFPDP - [D]etached [P]rocess (slave) statistics
          X$KXFQSROW - Table [Q]ueue Statistics - 7.3.2 or higher

        [C]oordinator Component
          X$KXFPCST - Query [ST]atistics
          X$KXFPCMS - [M]essage [S]tatistics
          X$KXFPCDS - [D]equeue [S]tatistics
```

```
        [S]lave Component
          X$KXFPSST - Query [ST]atistics
          X$KXFPSMS - [M]essage [S]tatistics
          X$KXFPCDS - [D]equeue [S]tatistics

      [S]hared Cursor
        X$KXSBD - [B]ind [D]ata - 7.3.2 and above
        X$KXSCC - SQL [C]ursor [C]ache Data - 7.3.2 and above

 [N]etwork Layer - 7.0.15 or higher
    Network [CO]nnections
      X$UGANCO - Current [N]etwork [CO]nnections
```

Future Version Impact

As noted several times in this chapter, the V$ views and X$ tables are constantly being enhanced as more and more features are added to Oracle. Performance of SELECTs on V$ views and X$ tables has improved as Oracle has added indexes (in V8) on the underlying X$ tables. More changes will certainly come in the future (did you see Exadata/Exalogic coming?)!

Why do I climb mountains? I don't have the time—I'm a DBA!

Why do I open the hood of my car and look at what's inside? To impress my wife!

Why do I look at the X$ tables? Because I don't spend a lot of time climbing mountains, and I don't know what's *really* under the hood of my car, but I do know how to use these to my advantage! Now you do, too!

Tips Review

- When you mention the X$ tables, most people say, "Ooh, pretty scary, I would never touch those tables." The fact is that DML commands (UPDATE, INSERT, DELETE) are not allowed on the X$ tables, even as the SYS superuser.

- Only the SYS superuser can SELECT from the X$ tables. An error occurs if an attempt is made to grant SELECT access to a user. A DBA may need access to the X$ table information, but *not* the SYS password. Create a view under a different name that mirrors the desired tables. Name these tables according to the appropriate synonyms of the original tables.

- Access the X$KQFVI table for a listing of all V$ and GV$ views.

- Access the V$FIXED_VIEW_DEFINITION view to obtain all of the information about the underlying X$ tables that make up a V$ view.

- Query V$FIXED_TABLE for the names of the X$ tables, or you may also access the two X$ tables X$KQFTA and X$KQFDT for partial listings, which when combined, make up the full list.

- Access the V$INDEXED_FIXED_COLUMN view for a listing of all X$ table indexes.

■ Oracle generally uses the indexes and uses the correct driving table as needed for accessing the X$ tables, but from time to time, you may use hints to achieve a desired result.

■ Anonymous PL/SQL blocks cannot be traced using the "compile debug" method. PL/SQL tracing for the entire session must be enabled with the `alter session set plsql_debug=true` command.

■ Do not use `oradebug suspend` on the Microsoft Windows platform. Due to Windows' thread-based processing model, the whole database will be suspended, not just the process you are attached to.

■ Cursors may be reassigned if the cursor is closed and released. Therefore, when reading a long trace file, remember that a cursor number referenced at one part of the trace file may not represent the same SQL statement as it does elsewhere in the trace file.

References

Steve Adams, *Oracle8i Internal Services for Waits, Latches, Locks, and Memory* (O'Reilly, 1999).
Eyal Aronoff and Noorali Sonawalla, *Monitoring Oracle Database: The Challenge* (IOUG, 1994).
Tony Jambu, *Select Magazine* column.
Frank Naude's underground Oracle web page (www.orafaq.com).
Miladin Modrakovic, "ORADEBUG—Undocumented Oracle Utility" (www.evdbt.com/Oradebug_Modrakovic.pdf).
Rich Niemiec, *Oracle Database 10g Performance Tuning Tips & Techniques* (McGraw-Hill, 2007).
Oracle dump information (www.ixora.com.au).
Oracle FAQs, www.orafaq.com.
Oracle Server: SQL Language Reference Manual (Oracle Corporation).
Oracle Server: Application Developer's Guide (Oracle Corporation).
Tanel Poder, "Memory Management and Latching Improvements in Oracle9i and 10g" (http://integrid.info/).
Tip of the Week, Wolfgang Genser (for an idea on making touch counts faster), www.oracle.com.
Joseph Trezzo, Journey to the Center of the X$ Tables (TUSC).
Joseph Trezzo, *Get the Most out of Your Money: Utilize the v$ Tables* (IOUG, 1994).

Metalink Notes
186859.995, 1066346.6, 153334.995, 258597.999, 235412.999, 135223.1, 221860.999, 104933.1, 83222.996, 43600.1, 129813.999, 10630.996, 86661.999, 4256.997, 2497.997, 102925.1, 95420.1, 14848.997, 235412.999, 62172.1, 135223.1, 221860.999, 83222.996, 163424.1, 104397.1, 33883.1, 346576.999, 96845.1, 73582.1, 221860.999, 212629.995, 162866.1, 138119.1, 137483.1, 186859.995, 1066346.6, 153334.995, 258597.999, 235412.999, 135223.1, 221860.999, 104933.1, 83222.996, 43600.1, 129813.999, 10630.996, 86661.999, 4256.997, 2497.997, 102925.1, 210375.995, 39366.1, 62294.1, 187913.1, 171647.1, 39817.1, 224270.1, 62294.1, 39817.1, 104239.1, 280543.1, 175982.1

Graham Thornton updated the 11g version of the chapter. Graham Thornton and Kevin Gilpin helped with the incredible job of updating this chapter in 10g. (Please read it quietly and with an English accent.)

CHAPTER
14

Using Statspack and the AWR Report to Tune Waits, Latches, and Mutexes

I f you could choose just two Oracle utilities to monitor and find performance problems on your system, those two utilities would be Enterprise Manager (Chapter 5) and the AWR (Automatic Workload Repository) Report and/or Statspack (both covered in this chapter). In Oracle 11gR2, the AWR Report has everything that is in Statspack—and a whole lot more! Statspack remains in 11gR2 but has *few* improvements. The Statspack utility has been available since Oracle 8.1.6 to monitor database performance. Statspack originally replaced the UTLBSTAT/UTLESTAT scripts available with earlier versions of Oracle. The AWR Report leverages the Automatic Workload Repository statistics and can be executed within Enterprise Manager Grid Control, if desired; it will probably replace Statspack for good in the future. Although the AWR Report has some very nice things in it that Statspack doesn't have, you must license the Oracle Diagnostics Pack to access the AWR dictionary views necessary for the AWR Report. Statspack is still a free utility. Although you are not supposed to modify the Statspack code, you can modify it. If you modify the code, however, Statspack is not supported.

In this chapter, you learn how to install the AWR Report and Statspack, how to manage them, and how to run and interpret the reports generated. Statspack includes data for both proactive and reactive tuning and is probably the best way to query most of the relevant V$ views and X$ tables and view the results in a single report. The AWR Report is a great way to mine the AWR for aggregate performance data in a report similar to, but better than, the Statspack Report.

Tips covered in this chapter include the following:

- What's new in 11gR2 for Statspack and AWR

- Creating a tablespace to hold the Statspack data apart from your application and SYSTEM objects

- Finding the files needed to create, manage, and drop the Statspack objects

- Changing the PERFSTAT password and locking the account when it is no longer in use

- Selecting the proper level for your reporting

- Times to avoid running Statspack Reports

- Running the AWR Report and Statspack together: cautionary notes

- Using Grid Control to run the AWR Report

- Tuning the top wait events, including Oracle Database 11g mutex wait events

- Using the Segment Statistics sections of the reports to find issues

- Tuning latches and mutexes

- Tuning at the block level to find hot blocks and ITL problems

- The top ten things to look for in the AWR Report and Statspack output

- Managing the Statspack data and analyzing and purging it as needed

- Monitoring Statspack space usage

- Including Statspack data in your backup and upgrade plans

- Using the ADDM Report (text) as a stand-alone tool

What's New in 11gR2 (11.2) Statspack and the AWR Report

Oracle Database 11*g* has a few new details in the report. I have listed the ones here that I see as important and helpful. Please see the Oracle document listed in "References" at the end of the chapter for a complete Statspack reference. New features in 11*g*R2 include the following:

- Still running SQL is now included! The SQL Statement section now includes SQL statements that have not yet completed; execution count shows as 0. These are usually the SQL statements that you want to know about.

- MEMORY_TARGET is a new initialization parameter for sizing all memory for Oracle (see Chapter 4). This version of the AWR Report and Statspack has a section for Memory Target Advice (from V$MEMORY_TARGET_ADVICE), information about the last resize operation, as well as any operations since the last Begin/End snapshots.

- The number of CPUs, cores, and sockets is now displayed in a few places.

NOTE
I had two CPUs, in two sockets with four cores each. This showed up as eight CPUs, eight cores, and two sockets. The CPU/core entries both seem to show the number of cores. The number of sockets shows the number of sockets and CPUs.

- The number of sorts has been replaced with W/A (workarea) MB processed. This new value is used because it now includes both the sorts *and* things like hash joins (basically items that are put in the PGA_AGGREGATE_TARGET area).

- There are many more operating system (O/S) statistics (from V$OSSTAT) that show detailed information on the operating system load, particularly in the AWR Report.

- I/O Statistics by Function shows which function or client (direct IO, RMAN, RECO, etc.) is using the I/O. Both a summary and detail section are included. The detail section breaks requests into small/large.

- Sections on Foreground Processes, Background Processes, and a combination of both are now included in the report. The Foreground Processes section is new.

- The initialization parameters at the end now show the entire parameter value and are not truncated in this version.

- DB Time has been added in many sections.

- Physical Memory is now displayed in G (Gigabytes) vs. M (Megabytes).

- You use `spup102.sql` to upgrade to 11 Statspack.

- Unfortunately, Statspack still stores the old hash value instead of the SQL_ID that is stored in most tables (SQL_ID is displayed in the AWR Report—nice!). Both HASH_VALUE and SQL_ID are in V$SQL and V$SQLAREA.

Installing Statspack

Statspack must be installed in every database to be monitored. If you are using the AWR Report, you do not need to run Statspack. Prior to installing Statspack, you should create a tablespace to hold the Statspack data. If you don't specify a tablespace, the SYSAUX tablespace is used. During the installation process, you are prompted for the name of the tablespace to hold the Statspack database objects. You should also designate a temporary tablespace that will be large enough to support the large inserts and deletes Statspack may perform.

The installation script, named `spcreate.sql`, is found in the `/rdbms/admin` subdirectory under the Oracle software home directory. The `spcreate.sql` script creates a user named PERFSTAT and creates a number of objects under that schema.

TIP
Allocate at least 120M for the initial creation of the PERFSTAT schema's objects. Oracle 11g requires about the same space as Oracle 10g, which is about 20M more space than Oracle 9i.

To start the `spcreate.sql` script, change your directory to the `ORACLE_HOME/rdbms/admin` directory and log in to SQL*Plus using an account with SYSDBA privileges:

```
SQL> connect system/manager as SYSDBA
SQL> @spcreate
```

During the installation process, you are prompted for the PERSTAT user password (for security purposes, a default password is no longer included); then you are prompted for a default tablespace for the PERFSTAT user (a list of available tablespaces are displayed along with this prompt). You are also asked to specify a temporary tablespace for the user. Once you have provided default and temporary tablespaces for the PERFSTAT account, the account is created and the installation script logs in as PERFSTAT and continues to create the required objects. If there is not sufficient space to create the PERFSTAT objects in the specified default tablespace, the script returns an error.

The `spcreate.sql` script calls three scripts: `spcusr.sql` to create the user, `spctab.sql` to create the underlying tables, and `spcpkg.sql` to create the packages. When run, each of these scripts generates a listing file (`spcusr.lis`, etc.). Although you start the installation script while logged in as a SYSDBA-privileged user, the conclusion of the installation script leaves you logged in as the PERFSTAT user. If you want to drop the PERFSTAT user at a later date, you can run the `spdrop.sql` script (which calls `spdusr.sql` and `spdtab.sql`) located in the `ORACLE_HOME/rdbms/admin directory`.

Security of the PERFSTAT Account

The `spcusr.sql` script creates the PERFSTAT account and asks you to supply a password (the default was PERFSTAT in previous versions). The Statspack utility does not need to use the PERFSTAT default password; change the password after the installation process completes.

Also, remember that in 11*g*, passwords are case sensitive. Consider if my username/password was perfstat/perfstat (which it shouldn't be because it would be too easy to hack):

```
SQL> connect perfstat/perfstat
Connected.

SQL> connect PERFSTAT/perfstat
Connected.

SQL> connect perfstat/PERFSTAT
ERROR:
ORA-01017: Invalid username/password; logon denied.

Warning: You are no longer connected to ORACLE.
```

The PERFSTAT user is granted the SELECT_CATALOG_ROLE. The PERFSTAT user is also granted several system privileges (CREATE/ALTER SESSION, CREATE TABLE, CREATE VIEW, CREATE/DROP PUBLIC SYNONYM, CREATE SEQUENCE, and CREATE PROCEDURE). Any user who can access your PERFSTAT account can select from all of the dictionary views. For example, such a user could query all of the database account usernames from DBA_USERS, all the segment owners from DBA_SEGMENTS, and the currently logged in sessions from V$SESSION. The PERFSTAT account, if left unprotected, provides a security hole that allows intruders to browse through your data dictionary and select targets for further intrusion.

In addition to the privileges it receives during the installation process, the PERFSTAT account also has any privileges that have been granted to PUBLIC. If you use PUBLIC grants instead of roles for application privileges, you must secure the PERFSTAT account. You can lock and unlock database accounts as needed. To lock the PERFSTAT account when you are not using Statspack, use the `alter user` command, as shown in the following listing:

```
alter user PERFSTAT account lock;
```

When you need to gather statistics or access the Statspack data, you can unlock the account:

```
alter user PERFSTAT account unlock;
```

Post-Installation

Once the installation process is complete, the PERFSTAT account owns 72 tables and 72 indexes (In 10.2, it owned 67 tables and 68 indexes), 75 public synonyms (Public actually owns all public synonyms), a sequence, a view, and a package (with body). In 9*i*, PERFSTAT owned only 36 tables, 37 indexes, a sequence, and a package. Oracle 8i ESTAT/BSTAT had only 27 tables.

You use the package, named Statspack, to manage the statistics collection process and the data in the tables. The collection tables, whose names all begin with "STATS$," use column definitions based on the V$ view definitions. For example, the columns in STATS$WAITSTAT are the columns found in V$WAITSTAT, with three identification columns added at the top:

```
desc stats$waitstat

Name                          Null?    Type
---------------------------   -------- -----------
SNAP_ID                       NOT NULL NUMBER(6)
DBID                          NOT NULL NUMBER
INSTANCE_NUMBER               NOT NULL NUMBER
CLASS                         NOT NULL VARCHAR2(18)
WAIT_COUNT                             NUMBER
TIME                                   NUMBER
```

The CLASS, WAIT_COUNT, and TIME columns are based on the CLASS, COUNT, and TIME columns from V$WAITSTAT. Statspack has added these identification columns:

Columns	Description
SNAP_ID	An identification number for the collection. Each collection is called a *snapshot* and is assigned an integer value.
DBID	A numeric identifier for the database.
INSTANCE_NUMBER	A numeric identifier for the instance for Real Application Cluster installations.

TIP
Do not use both Statspack and UTLBSTAT/UTLESTAT in the same database. The UTLBSTAT/UTLESTAT scripts are not built to be used in 11g, even though they are still provided. They are for reference only and do not appear to have been updated for several versions.

Each collection you perform is given a new SNAP_ID value that is consistent across the collection tables. You need to know the SNAP_ID values when executing the statistics report provided with Statspack.

Gathering Statistics

Each collection of statistics is called a *snapshot*. Snapshots of statistics have no relation to snapshots or materialized views used in replication. Rather, they are a point-in-time collection of the statistics available via the V$ views and are given a SNAP_ID value to identify the snapshot. You can generate reports on the changes in the statistics between any two snapshots. With Statspack, you can collect as many snapshots as you need and then generate reports against any combination of them. As with the UTLBSTAT/UTLESTAT reports, the Statspack Report is only valid if the database is *not* shut down and restarted between the evaluated snapshots.

TIP
*Be sure the TIMED_STATISTICS database initialization parameter is
set to TRUE prior to gathering statistics.*

To generate a snapshot of the statistics, execute the SNAP procedure of the Statspack package,
as shown in the following listing. You must be logged in as the PERFSTAT user to execute this
procedure.

```
execute STATSPACK.SNAP;
PL/SQL procedure successfully completed.
```

When you execute the SNAP procedure, Oracle populates your STATS$ tables with the current
statistics. You can then query those tables directly, or you can use the standard Statspack Report
(to see the change in statistics between snapshots).

Snapshots should be taken in one of two ways:

- To evaluate performance during specific tests of the system. For these tests, you can
  execute the SNAP procedure manually, as shown in the prior example.

- To evaluate performance changes over a long period of time. To establish a baseline of
  system performance, you may generate statistics snapshots on a scheduled basis. For
  these snapshots, you should schedule the SNAP procedure execution via the Oracle
  Scheduler or via an operating system scheduler.

For the snapshots related to specific tests, you may wish to increase the collection level, which
lets you gather more statistics. As noted in the section "Managing the Statspack Data" later in this
chapter, each snapshot has a cost in terms of space usage and query performance. For example,
since the V$SYSSTAT view has 588 rows in Oracle 11.2 on Windows (628 on Linux), every
snapshot generates 588 rows in STATS$SYSSTAT. In 10.2, there were only 347 rows, and in 9.2,
there were only 232 rows in V$SYSSTAT. Avoid generating thousands of rows of statistical data
with each snapshot unless you plan to use them.

To support differing collection levels, Statspack provides the I_SNAP_LEVEL parameter. By
default, the level value is set to 5. Prior to changing the level value, generate several snapshots and
evaluate the reports generated. The default level value is adequate for most reports. Alternative
level values are listed in the following table:

Level	Description
0–4	General performance statistics on all memory areas, locks, latches, pools, cluster DB statistics, events, and segment statistics, such as rollback/UNDO segments.
5	Same statistics from the lower levels, plus the most resource-intensive SQL statements above set thresholds. At level 5 and greater, the snapshot takes longer for a larger shared pool size.
6	Introduced in Oracle 9.0.1, level 6 includes the level 5 results plus SQL execution plans and plan usage data for high-resource usage SQL. The SQL must be in the shared pool at the time of the snapshot to be captured.

Level	Description
7–9	Introduced in Oracle 10g, level 7 includes level 6 results plus detailed Segment Level statistics, including logical reads, physical reads/writes, global cache cr/current served and buffer busy, ITL, and row lock waits.
10 and greater	Same statistics from level 6 plus parent/child latch data. This level can take a long time to complete and should be used only when directed by Oracle Support.

The greater the collection level, the longer the snapshot will take. The default value (5) offers a significant degree of flexibility during the queries for the most resource-intensive SQL statements. The parameters used for the resource-intensive SQL portion of the snapshot are stored in a table named STATS$STATSPACK_PARAMETER. You can query STATS$STATSPACK_PARAMETER to see the settings for the different thresholds during SQL statement gathering. Its columns include SNAP_LEVEL (the snapshot level), EXECUTIONS_TH (threshold value for the number of executions), DISK_READS_TH (threshold value for the number of disk reads), and BUFFER_GETS_TH (threshold value for the number of disk reads).

For a level 5 snapshot using the default thresholds, SQL statements are stored if they meet any of the following criteria:

■ The SQL statement has been executed at least 100 times.

■ The number of disk reads performed by the SQL statement exceeds 1,000.

■ The number of parse calls performed by the SQL statement exceeds 1,000.

■ The number of buffer gets performed by the SQL statement exceeds 10,000.

■ The sharable memory used by the SQL statement exceeds 1M.

■ The version count for the SQL statement exceeds 20.

When evaluating the snapshot's data and the performance report, keep in mind the SQL threshold parameter values are cumulative. A very efficient query, if executed enough times, will exceed 10,000 buffer gets. Compare the number of buffer gets and disk reads to the number of executions to determine the activity each time the query is executed.

To modify the default settings for the thresholds, use the MODIFY_STATSPACK_PARAMETER procedure in the STATSPACK package. Specify the snapshot level via the I_SNAP_LEVEL parameter, along with the parameters to change. Table 14-1 lists the available parameters for the MODIFY_STATSPACK_PARAMETER procedure.

To increase the BUFFER_GETS threshold for a level 5 snapshot to 100,000, issue the following command (note that the "-" mean the command continues on next line):

```
EXECUTE STATSPACK.MODIFY_STATSPACK_PARAMETER -
    (i_snap_level=>5, i_buffer_gets_th=>100000, -
    i_modify_parameter=>'true');
```

If you plan to run the SNAP procedure on a scheduled basis, you should pin the Statspack package following database startup. The following listing shows a trigger that is executed each time the database is started. The KEEP procedure of the DBMS_SHARED_POOL package pins

Parameter Name	Range of Values	Default	Description
I_SNAP_LEVEL	0, 5, 6, 7, 10	5	Snapshot level
I_UCOMMENT	Any text	Blank	Comment for the snapshot
I_EXECUTIONS_TH	Integer >= 0	100	Threshold for the cumulative number of executions
I_DISK_READS_TH	Integer >= 0	1000	Threshold for the cumulative number of disk reads (physical reads)
I_PARSE_CALLS_TH	Integer >= 0	1000	Threshold for the cumulative number of parse calls
I_BUFFER_GETS_TH	Integer >= 0	10000	Threshold for the cumulative number of buffer gets (logical reads)
I_SHARABLE_MEM_TH	Integer >= 0	1048576	Threshold for the amount of sharable memory allocated
I_VERSION_COUNT_TH	Integer >= 0	20	Threshold for the number of versions of the SQL statement
I_SEG_BUFF_BUSY_TH	Integer >= 0	100	Threshold for the number of buffer busy waits on a SEGMENT
I_SEG_ROWLOCK_W_TH	Integer >= 0	100	Threshold for the number of row lock waits on a SEGMENT
I_SEG_ITL_WAITS_TH	Integer >= 0	100	Threshold for the number of ITL waits on a SEGMENT
I_SEG_CR_BKS_SD_TH	Integer >= 0	1000	Threshold for the number of Consistent Read (CR) blocks served for a SEGMENT
I_SEG_CU_BKS_SD_TH	Integer >= 0	1000	Threshold for the number of Current (CU) blocks served for a SEGMENT
I_SEG_PHY_READS_TH	Integer >= 0	1000	Threshold for the number of physical reads on a SEGMENT
I_SEG_LOG_READS_TH	Integer >= 0	10000	Threshold for the number of logical reads on a SEGMENT
I_SESSION_ID	Valid SID from V$SESSION	0	Session ID of an Oracle session, if you wish to gather session-level statistics
I_MODIFY_PARAMETER	True or False	False	Set to True if you wish to save your changes for future snapshots

TABLE 14-1. *Modification Parameters*

the Statspack package in the shared pool. As an alternative to pinning, you can use the SHARED_POOL_RESERVED_SIZE initialization parameter to reserve shared pool area for large packages.

```
create or replace trigger PIN_ON_STARTUP
after startup on database
begin
    DBMS_SHARED_POOL.KEEP ('PERFSTAT.STATSPACK', 'P');
end;
/
```

TIP
Pin the Statspack package following database startup if you plan to run the SNAP procedure on a scheduled basis.

Running the Statistics Report

If you have generated more than one snapshot, you can report on the statistics for the period between the two snapshots. The database must not have been shut down between the times the two snapshots were taken. When you execute the report, you need to know the SNAP_ID values for the snapshots. If you run the report interactively, Oracle provides a list of the available snapshots and the times they were created.

To execute the report, go to the /rdbms/admin directory under the Oracle software home directory. Log in to SQL*Plus as the PERFSTAT user and run the spreport.sql file found there:

```
SQL> @$ORACLE_HOME/rdbms/admin/spreport
```

Oracle displays the database and instance identification information from V$INSTANCE and V$DATABASE and then calls a second SQL file, sprepins.sql.

The sprepins.sql script generates the report of the changes in the statistics during the snapshot time interval. The available snapshots are listed, and you will be prompted to enter beginning and ending snapshot IDs. Unless you specify otherwise, the output is written to a file named sp_*beginning_ending*.lst (for example, sp_1_2.lst for a report between SNAP_ID values of 1 and 2).

TIP
A second report, sprepsql.sql, can be used for additional research into the problem SQL statements identified via the spreport.sql report.

The Automatic Workload Repository (AWR) and the AWR Report

The AWR Report reports on the AWR stored data and is definitely the next generation of the Statspack Report. It does require additional licensing, so ensure that you are licensed to use it. AWR collects database statistics every 60 minutes (on the hour) out of the box (this is configurable), and this data is maintained for a week and then purged. The statistics collected by AWR are stored in the database. The AWR Report accesses the AWR to report statistical performance information similar to how Statspack has always done. Because the AWR schema was originally based on the Statspack schema, you will find much of what is included in Statspack in the AWR Report. Learning the AWR Report if you are familiar with Statspack is easy, *but* you will not find everything in Statspack that you find in the AWR Report. There are some newer/cooler parts of the AWR Report that Statspack users will definitely value.

The AWR data is stored separately from the Statspack data, so running both is a bit superfluous. If you choose to run *both,* ensure that you stagger AWR data collection from the Statspack collection —by at least 30 minutes—to avoid a performance hit as well as conflicts. You could also run both as you switch from one reporting tool to the other for overlap to ensure that you have coverage that shows comparison reports.

The Oracle database uses AWR for problem detection and analysis as well as for self-tuning. A number of different statistics are collected by the AWR, including wait events, time model statistics, active session history statistics, various system- and session-level statistics, object usage statistics, and information on the most resource-intensive SQL statements. To properly collect database statistics, set the initialization parameter STATISTICS_LEVEL to TYPICAL (the default) or ALL. Other Oracle Database 11*g* features use the AWR, such as Automatic Database Diagnostic Monitor (ADDM) and other Enterprise Manager Grid Control features as discussed in Chapter 5.

If you want to explore the AWR, feel free to do so. The AWR consists of a number of tables owned by the SYS schema and typically stored in the SYSAUX tablespace (currently no method exists that I know of to move these objects to another tablespace). All AWR table names start with the identifier "WR." AWR tables come with three different type designations:

- Metadata (WRM$)
- Historical/convertible data (WRH$, WRR$, and WRI$)
- AWR tables related to advisor functions (WRI$)

Most of the AWR table names are pretty self-explanatory, such as WRM$_SNAPSHOT or WRH$_ACTIVE_SESSION_HISTORY (a very valuable view to check out). Also Oracle Database 11*g* offers several DBA views that allow you to query the AWR repository. The views start with DBA_HIST and are followed by a name that describes the view. These include views such as DBA_HIST_FILESTATS, DBA_HIST_DATAFILE, or DBA_HIST_SNAPSHOT.

TIP
If you choose to run both *Statspack and AWR, ensure that you stagger the AWR data collection from Statspack collection by at least 30 minutes to avoid a performance hit as well as conflicts. If you are running the AWR Report, you should not also need to run Statspack.*

Manually Managing the AWR

Although AWR is meant to be automatic, provisions for manual operations impacting the AWR are available. You can manually modify the snapshot collection interval and retention criteria, create snapshots, and remove snapshots from the AWR. I will describe this process in more detail in the next few sections, but please refer to the Oracle documentation for full coverage of the AWR.

You can modify the snapshot collection interval using the DBMS_WORKLOAD_REPOSITORY package. The procedure DBMS_WORKLOAD_REPOSITORY.MODIFY_SNAPSHOT_SETTINGS is used in this example to modify the snapshot collection so it occurs every 15 minutes and retention of snapshot data is fixed at 20160 minutes (exactly 14 days):

```
-- This causes the repository to refresh every 15 minutes
-- and retain all data for 2 weeks.
exec dbms_workload_repository.modify_snapshot_settings -
(retention=>20160, interval=> 15);
```

Setting the interval parameter to 0 disables all statistics collection.

To view the current retention and interval settings for the AWR, use the DBA_HIST_WR_CONTROL view. Here is an example of how to use this view:

```
select *
from   dba_hist_wr_control;

     DBID SNAP_INTERVAL        RETENTION            TOPNSQL
---------- -------------------- -------------------- -------
1272868336 +00000 01:00:00.0    +00008 00:00:00.0   DEFAULT
```

In the preceding example, you see that the snapshot interval is every hour (the default), and the retention is set for eight days.

You can use the DBMS_WORKLOAD_REPOSITORY package to create or remove snapshots. The DBMS_WORKLOAD_REPOSITORY.CREATE_SNAPSHOT procedure creates a manual snapshot in the AWR, as seen in this example:

```
exec dbms_workload_repository.create_snapshot;
```

You can see what snapshots are currently in the AWR by using the DBA_HIST_SNAPSHOT view, as seen in this example:

```
select snap_id, begin_interval_time, end_interval_time
from   dba_hist_snapshot
order  by 1;

   SNAP_ID BEGIN_INTERVAL_TIME        END_INTERVAL_TIME
---------- -------------------------- --------------------------
       375 11-MAY-11 11.00.37.796 PM  13-MAY-11 01.16.48.897 PM
       376 13-MAY-11 01.16.48.897 PM  13-MAY-11 02.00.29.909 PM
       377 13-MAY-11 02.00.29.909 PM  13-MAY-11 03.00.42.797 PM
       378 13-MAY-11 03.00.42.797 PM  13-MAY-11 04.00.55.608 PM
```

Each snapshot is assigned a unique snapshot ID that is reflected in the SNAP_ID column. If you have two snapshots, the earlier snapshot always has a smaller SNAP_ID than the later snapshot. The END_INTERVAL_TIME column displays the time that the actual snapshot was taken.

Sometimes you might want to drop snapshots manually. The DBMS_WORKLOAD_REPOSITORY .DROP_SNAPSHOT_RANGE procedure can be used to remove a range of snapshots from the AWR. This procedure takes two parameters, LOW_SNAP_ID and HIGH_SNAP_ID, as seen in this example:

```
exec dbms_workload_repository.drop_snapshot_range -
(low_snap_id=>1107, high_snap_id=>1108);
```

AWR Automated Snapshots

Oracle Database 11g uses a scheduled job, GATHER_STATS_JOB, to collect AWR statistics. This job is created and enabled automatically when you create a new Oracle database under Oracle Database 11g. To see this job, use the DBA_SCHEDULER_JOBS view as seen in this example:

```
select  a.job_name, a.enabled, c.window_name,
        c.repeat_interval
from    dba_scheduler_jobs a, dba_scheduler_wingroup_members b,
        dba_scheduler_windows c
where   job_name='GATHER_STATS_JOB'
and     a.schedule_name=b.window_group_name
and     b.window_name=c.window_name;

(you can also add c.schedule_name, c.start_date to the Select if desired):
JOB_NAME                            ENABL WINDOW_NAME
--------------------------------    ----- --------------------------------

REPEAT_INTERVAL
-----------------------------------------------------------------------------
GATHER_STATS_JOB                    TRUE  WEEKEND_WINDOW
freq=daily;byday=SAT;byhour=0;byminute=0;bysecond=0

GATHER_STATS_JOB                    TRUE  WEEKNIGHT_WINDOW
freq=daily;byday=MON,TUE,WED,THU,FRI;byhour=22;byminute=0; bysecond=0
```

You can disable this job using the DBMS_SCHEDULER.DISABLE procedure, as seen in this example:

```
exec dbms_scheduler.disable('GATHER_STATS_JOB');
```

And you can enable the job using the DBMS_SCHEDULER.ENABLE procedure, as seen in this example:

```
exec dbms_scheduler.enable('GATHER_STATS_JOB');
```

AWR Snapshot Reports

Oracle provides reports that you can run to analyze the data in the AWR. These reports are much like the Statspack Reports prior to Oracle Database 10g. AWR has two reports: awrrpt.sql, which is the main AWR Report, and awrrpti.sql. Both reports are available in the $ORACLE_HOME/rdbms/admin directory. The output of these reports (run from SQL*Plus) is essentially the same, except that awrrpti.sql script allows you to define a specific instance to report on. The reports are much like the Statspack Reports of old, in that you define beginning and ending snapshot IDs, along with the report's output filename. Additionally, you can opt to produce the report in either text format or HTML format. As you will see when you run `awrrpt.sql`, the following simple example shows how similar this is to Statspack, other than the text itself (Statspack-looking output), or HTML (the screen shots in this chapter are the HTML) output:

```
SQL> @C:\oracle\product\11.2.0\Db_1\RDBMS\ADMIN\awrrpt

Current Instance
~~~~~~~~~~~~~~~~

    DB Id     DB Name      Inst Num Instance
  ----------- ------------ -------- ------------
  1071709215 ORCL              1 orcl

Specify the Report Type
~~~~~~~~~~~~~~~~~~~~~~~~
Would you like an HTML report, or a plain text report?
Enter 'html' for an HTML report, or 'text' for plain text
Defaults to 'html'
Enter value for report_type: html
```

TIP
With the new AWR Report, you can choose to get text (similar to Statspack output) or the new HTML format when you run `awrrpt.sql`. The HTML format is much better, as you can click various links within the report to navigate among sections easily. You can also run the AWR Report within Enterprise Manager.

As when using Statspack, creating a baseline in the AWR is a good idea. A *baseline* is defined as a range of snapshots that you can use to compare with other pairs of snapshots. The Oracle database server will exempt the snapshots assigned to a specific baseline from the automated purge routine. The main purpose of a baseline is, therefore, to preserve typical runtime statistics in the AWR repository, allowing you to run the AWR snapshot reports on the preserved baseline snapshots at any time and compare them to recent snapshots contained in the AWR. This way you can compare current performance (and configuration) to established baseline performance, which can help you determine database performance problems.

You can use the CREATE_BASELINE procedure contained in the DBMS_WORKLOAD_REPOSITORY stored PL/SQL package to create a baseline, as seen in this example (you could also create a snapshot when nobody is on the system as a comparison):

```
exec dbms_workload_repository.create_baseline -
(start_snap_id=>1109, end_snap_id=>1111, -
baseline_name=>'EOM Baseline');
```

Baselines can be seen using the DBA_HIST_BASELINE view, as seen in the following example:

```
select baseline_id, baseline_name, start_snap_id, end_snap_id
from   dba_hist_baseline;
```

```
BASELINE_ID BASELINE_NAME    START_SNAP_ID END_SNAP_ID
----------- ---------------  ------------- -----------
          1 EOM Baseline              1109        1111
```

In this case, the column BASELINE_ID identifies each individual baseline that has been defined. The name assigned to the baseline is listed, as are the beginning and ending snapshot IDs.

You can remove a baseline using the DBMS_WORKLOAD_REPOSITORY.DROP_BASELINE procedure, as seen in this example, which drops the EOM Baseline that I just created:

```
EXEC dbms_workload_repository.drop_baseline -
(baseline_name=>'EOM Baseline', Cascade=>FALSE);
```

NOTE
The cascade parameter causes all associated snapshots to be removed if it is set to TRUE; otherwise, the snapshots are cleaned up automatically by the AWR automated processes.

Run the AWR Report in Oracle Enterprise Manager Grid Control

Although, as I have demonstrated, you can use the DBMS_WORKLOAD_REPOSITORY package to manage the AWR repository, you can also manage AWR from the Oracle Enterprise Manager. Enterprise Manager is covered in detail in Chapter 5, but some of the AWR Report screens are covered in this chapter. Enterprise Manager provides a nice interface into the management of AWR (under the Workload section) and also provides an easy method for creating the AWR Report (under the Statistics Management section). Navigate to the database you wish to report on and then go to the Server page, as seen in the screen displayed in Figure 14-1. You can then click Automatic Workload Repository under the Statistics Management section.

The next AWR screen (Figure 14-2) provides a summary of the current AWR settings and gives you an option to modify them. You can also review details about the snapshots in the AWR and create baseline AWR snapshots (called *preserved snapshot sets* in Enterprise Manager). Some of the important things you'll see on the settings page include snapshot retention, how often snapshots are collected (or if collection is turned off), and the collection level.

If you click the link next to snapshots, the Snapshots page (Figure 14-3) displays the last several snapshots in the AWR and allows you to review older snapshots if you wish. You can click a specific snapshot number if you want detailed information on that snapshot or if you want a printable report based on the snapshot you selected. You can also get snapshot details by clicking the snapshots link on the AWR page, which takes you directly to this same snapshots page seen in Figure 14-3.

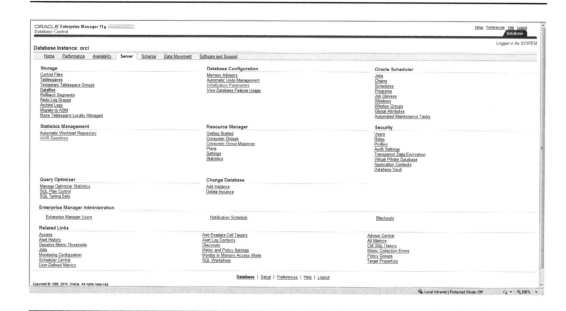

FIGURE 14-1. *Statistics Management and the Automatic Workload Repository*

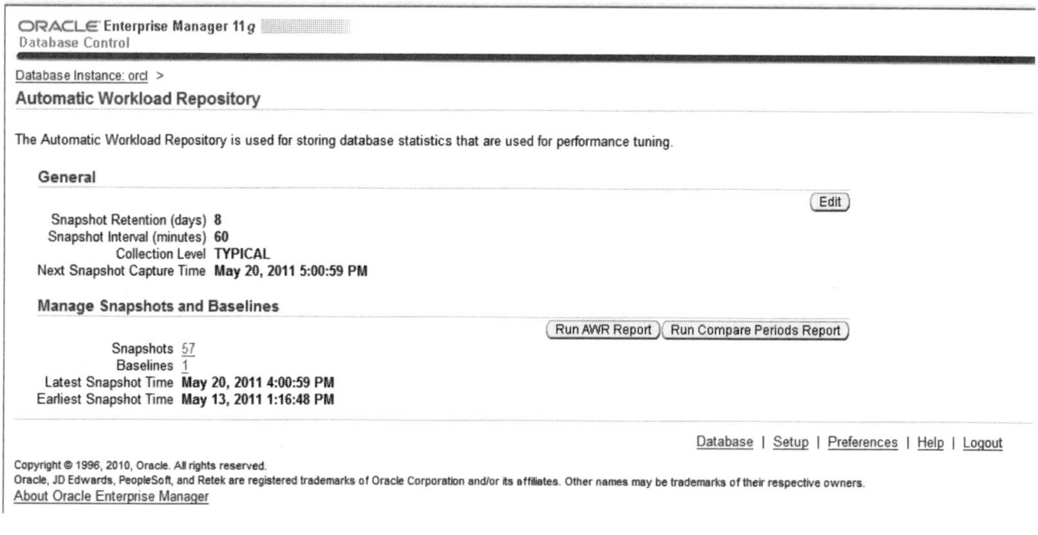

FIGURE 14-2. *AWR collection settings and snapshots*

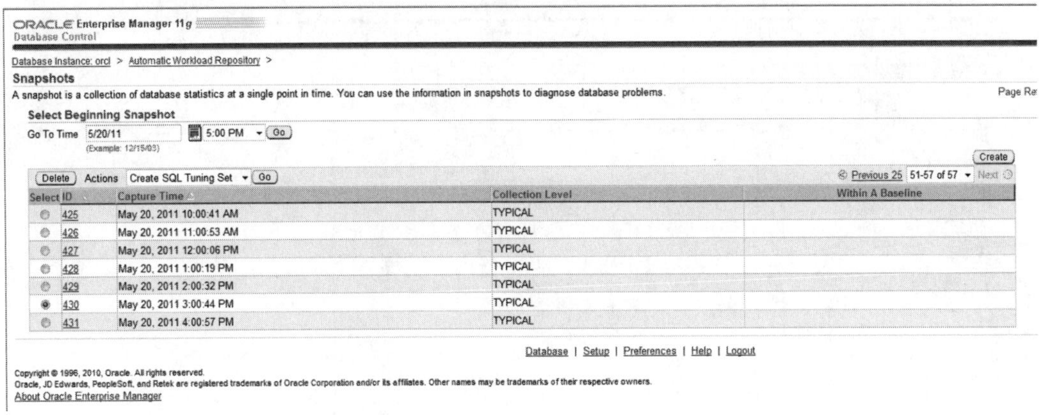

FIGURE 14-3. *Viewing the snapshots collected in AWR*

On this screen (Figure 14-3), you see the snapshot ID, which you can then use for starting and ending snapshots for running your AWR Report. You also see the capture date and time for each of these snapshots. As long as the snapshots exist, you can run a report starting with any snapshot and ending with any snapshot. If you take snapshots every hour, you can either run a report for an hour or you can run a report spanning 24 hours (as long as the instance is not shut down at any time between snapshots). If you are running Real Application Clusters (RAC), you must run the report for each instance individually. You can also click Create Preserved Snapshot from the Action list, and then click Go. Oracle then prompts you for the beginning and ending snapshots to assign to the preserved snapshot set. Once you have created snapshots, you can use the Actions pull-down box to perform many actions; for instance, you can create SQL tuning sets, create reports much like Statspack Reports from earlier versions of Oracle, and create an ADDM task that analyzes the snapshot set and produces an analysis report. You can also use the pull-down box to delete preserved snapshot sets, and you can compare two sets of snapshot pairs. Comparing snapshots allows you to determine if differences exist between a baseline snapshot and a recent set of snapshots. Using the report generated from this action, you can determine if the current system performance is diverging from the baseline performance in some way. Also, AWR and ADDM support RAC in 11.2. You might investigate the following Oracle scripts for more information: `awrginp.sql`, `awrgrpt.sql`, and `awrgrpti.sql`.

ORACLE Enterprise Manager 11g
Database Control

Database Instance: orcl > Automatic Workload Repository > Snapshots >
Snapshot Details

Setup Preferences Help Logout

Database

Logged in As SYSTEM

View ADDM Run

Details | Report

Beginning Snapshot ID 425
Beginning Snapshot Capture Time May 20, 2011 10:00:41 AM

Ending Snapshot ID 431
Ending Snapshot Capture Time May 20, 2011 4:00:57 PM

Previous 1-27 of 27 Next

Name	Value	Per Second	Per Transaction
DB cpu (seconds)	0.00	0.00	0.00
DB time (seconds)	67,656.06	3.13	16.96
db block changes	145,572.00	6.73	36.48
execute count	173,004.00	8.00	43.36
global cache cr block receive time (seconds)	0.00	0.00	0.00
global cache cr blocks received	0.00	0.00	0.00
global cache current block receive time (seconds)	0.00	0.00	0.00
global cache current blocks received	0.00	0.00	0.00
global cache get time (seconds)	0.00	0.00	0.00
global cache gets	0.00	0.00	0.00
opened cursors cumulative	156,207.00	7.23	39.15
parse count (total)	75,048.00	3.47	18.81
parse time cpu (seconds)	0.82	0.00	0.00
parse time elapsed (seconds)	0.98	0.00	0.00
physical reads	11,790.00	0.55	2.95
physical writes	12,701.00	0.59	3.18
redo size (KB)	26,180.36	1.21	6.56
session cursor cache hits	125,885.00	5.82	31.55
session logical reads	761,643.00	35.24	190.89
sql execute cpu time (seconds)	0.00	0.00	0.00
sql execute elapsed time (seconds)	0.00	0.00	0.00
user calls	56,605.00	2.62	14.19
user commits	3,986.00	0.18	1.00
user rollbacks	5.00	0.00	0.00
workarea executions - multipass	0.00	0.00	0.00
workarea executions - onepass	0.00	0.00	0.00
workarea executions - optimal	27,639.00	1.28	6.93

Previous 1-27 of 27 Next

Details | Report

View ADDM Run

Database | Setup | Preferences | Help | Logout

Done

Local intranet | Protected Mode: Off   100%

FIGURE 14-4.   *The Snapshot Details tab*

To run the AWR Report, you now need to choose beginning and ending snapshot IDs and run the report as discussed in the preceding section. You see the snapshot details for this particular period (ID 425 to ID 431) in Figure 14-4. Note that much of the statistical information contained in the AWR Report (and Statspack) is shown in this particular screen.

TIP
If you use Enterprise Manager, you can run the AWR Report directly from Grid Control.

Next, you click the Report tab to run the AWR Report. When you click this, you will probably see a little clock (this screen is not displayed here), which tells you that the report is being generated. Then you will see the actual report (shown in Figure 14-5) as it is displayed in Enterprise Manager. You can also generate the report (`awr_report_425_431.html` in my case) in a file that can be viewed at any time by clicking Save To File. Many of the AWR Report screenshots in this chapter come from this report, but I also show a higher-volume example at times. You can see from Figure 14-5 that the beginning of the AWR report looks exactly like the beginning of the Statspack Report.

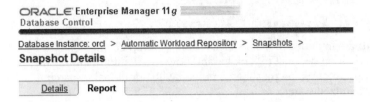

WORKLOAD REPOSITORY report for

DB Name	DB Id	Instance	Inst num	Startup Time	Release	RAC
ORCL	1272868336	orcl	1	11-May-11 03:05	11.2.0.1.0	NO

Host Name	Platform	CPUs	Cores	Sockets	Memory (GB)
USER-PC	Microsoft Windows x86 64-bit	8	8	2	16.00

	Snap Id	Snap Time	Sessions	Cursors/Session
Begin Snap:	425	20-May-11 10:00:41	41	2.8
End Snap:	431	20-May-11 16:00:57	35	3.8
Elapsed:		360.28 (mins)		
DB Time:		1.84 (mins)		

Report Summary

Cache Sizes

	Begin	End		
Buffer Cache:	2,208M	2,208M	Std Block Size:	8K
Shared Pool Size:	1,024M	1,024M	Log Buffer:	17,012K

Load Profile

	Per Second	Per Transaction	Per Exec	Per Call
DB Time(s):	0.0	0.0	0.00	0.00
DB CPU(s):	0.0	0.0	0.00	0.00
Redo size:	1,240.2	6,718.9		
Logical reads:	35.2	190.9		
Block changes:	6.7	36.5		
Physical reads:	0.6	3.0		
Physical writes:	0.6	3.2		

Done

FIGURE 14-5.   *The actual AWR Report is browsable or savable to a file.*

Interpreting the Statspack and AWR Report Output

Several sections are included in a Statspack output report. I cover each of the main sections, along with information on what to look for and how to use information that appears to be problematic. Most information must be combined with additional research to solve an issue, leading to an optimized system.

The Header Information

The first section of the report contains information about the database itself, including information on the database name, ID, release number, and host. Following this information is information on when the snapshot was started and ended and how many sessions were active. Always check to ensure the snapshot interval is what you were trying to measure, and make sure that it's a long enough interval to make it representative. If your interval is five minutes, that is almost always not long enough unless you are measuring something very short in duration. If your interval is five days, then you will have all kinds of peaks and valleys that average out, so it may be too long. But having one-day, one-hour (at peak), and one-hour (at non-peak) Statspack Reports handy is great to compare to a problem Statspack Report for any given day when an anomaly occurs on your system.

Generally, a Statspack Report should cover at least an hour of time and should be strategically timed to measure problematic periods of time. You may also want to look at an entire day so you can compare days over a period of time. The Cache Sizes section shows the values of the Buffer Cache (DB_CACHE_SIZE), Shared Pool Size (SHARED_POOL_SIZE), Std Block Size (DB_BLOCK_SIZE), and the Log Buffer (LOG_BUFFER). An example of the header information is displayed next. The equivalent information for the AWR Report is displayed in Figure 14-6.

```
Statspack report for

Database    DB Id      Instance     Inst Num  Startup Time     Release      RAC
~~~~~~~~ ----------- ------------ -------- ---------------- ----------- ---
         1272868336 orcl                1 28-Apr-11 03:19 11.2.0.1.0  NO

Host Name               Platform                   CPUs Cores Sockets   Memory (G)
~~~~ --------------- --------------------- ----- ----- ------- ------------
     USER-PC            Microsoft Windows x86      8     8       2        16.0

Snapshot       Snap Id    Snap Time        Sessions Curs/Sess Comment
~~~~~~~~ ---------- ------------------ -------- --------- ------------------
Begin Snap:          1 06-May-11 13:34:39     40      4.1
  End Snap:          2 06-May-11 13:48:13     41      3.5
  Elapsed:       13.57 (mins) Av Act Sess:      0.1
  DB time:        0.82 (mins)     DB CPU:       0.51 (mins)

Cache Sizes          Begin                                End
~~~~~~~~~~~ ----------                          ----------
   Buffer Cache:     2,208M        Std Block Size:            8K
   Shared Pool:     1,024M           Log Buffer:        16,392K
```

WORKLOAD REPOSITORY report for

DB Name	DB Id	Instance	Inst num	Startup Time	Release	RAC
ORCL	1272868336	orcl	1	28-Apr-11 03:04	11.2.0.1.0	NO

Host Name	Platform	CPUs	Cores	Sockets	Memory (GB)
USER-PC	Microsoft Windows x86 64-bit	8	8	2	16.00

	Snap Id	Snap Time	Sessions	Cursors/Session
Begin Snap:	333	06-May-11 13:25:59	39	2.4
End Snap:	334	06-May-11 13:51:50	39	3.9
Elapsed:		25.85 (mins)		
DB Time:		1.41 (mins)		

Report Summary

Cache Sizes

	Begin	End		
Buffer Cache:	2,208M	2,208M	Std Block Size:	8K
Shared Pool Size:	1,024M	1,024M	Log Buffer:	17,012K

FIGURE 14-6. *The AWR Report header information*

The Load Profile

The next portion of the report output, following the basic information, provides per-second and per-transaction statistics for the Load Profile. This section is excellent for monitoring throughput and load variations on your system. As the load on the system increases, you will see larger numbers per second. As you tune the system for maximum efficiency, you will usually see lower numbers for the per-transaction statistic. The following listing shows sample output for the Statspack Load Profile section:

```
Load Profile              Per Second      Per Transaction     Per Exec      Per Call
~~~~~~~~~~~~              -----------      ---------------     --------      --------
      DB time(s):              0.1                  0.3          0.00          0.00
       DB CPU(s):              0.0                  0.2          0.00          0.00
       Redo size:         69,439.8            334,461.3
   Logical reads:          1,158.7              5,580.7
   Block changes:             78.3                377.2
   Physical reads:           108.0                520.4
  Physical writes:            25.3                121.8
       User calls:            14.8                 71.2
```

Parses:	8.0	38.5
Hard parses:	0.2	1.0
W/A MB processed:	0.2	1.1
Logons:	0.1	0.4
Executes:	15.3	73.8
Rollbacks:	0.0	0.0
Transactions:	0.2	

The Load Profile helps to identify both the load and type of activity being performed. In this example, the activity recorded includes a large amount of both logical and physical activity, but especially redo activity (I performed a lot of inserts during this snapshot range).

Things to look for include the following:

- A large increase in Logical reads or Physical reads compared to a normal load for this period.

- An increase in Redo size, Block changes, and % Blocks changed per Read, all of which indicate increased DML (INSERT/UPDATE/DELETE) activity.

- A hard parse occurs when a SQL statement is executed and is *not* currently in the shared pool. A hard parse rate greater than 100/second could indicate that bind variables are not being used effectively; the CURSOR_SHARING initialization parameter should be used; or you have a shared pool–sizing problem. (See Chapter 4 on sizing the shared pool and a detailed discussion related to this.)

- A soft parse occurs when a SQL statement is executed and it *is* currently in the shared pool. A soft parse rate greater than 300/second could indicate program inefficiencies where statements are being parsed over and over again instead of the program efficiently parsing the statement only once per session.

Figure 14-7 shows the equivalent AWR Report information for a heavily used system (especially heavy DML).

TIP
Get to know your system by reviewing and understanding your system's regular Load Profile. Significant changes to the Load Profile during what should be similar workloads or common times during the day may warrant further investigation.

Instance Efficiency

The Instance Efficiency section shows information for many of the common hit ratios. DBAs generally measure these so they can be alerted to significant changes in system behavior when compared historically. Hit ratios (when managed regularly) are a great alert mechanism for general potential problems or specific potential problems, such as bad SQL, that has been introduced recently into the system. This can give you the opportunity to find the issue and address it before it has a serious/noticeable effect on the system. Waits (covered in depth later in this chapter) are another excellent way to find major problems, but waits usually show up after the problem becomes a large issue. Unfortunately, by that time, the business users will often raise it as a problem.

Load Profile

	Per Second	Per Transaction	Per Exec	Per Call
DB Time(s):	0.1	0.2	0.00	0.00
DB CPU(s):	0.0	0.1	0.00	0.00
Redo size:	44,342.7	122,373.4		
Logical reads:	1,369.0	3,777.9		
Block changes:	248.1	684.6		
Physical reads:	57.7	159.1		
Physical writes:	14.1	38.9		
User calls:	12.3	34.0		
Parses:	14.9	41.2		
Hard parses:	1.5	4.1		
W/A MB processed:	0.5	1.3		
Logons:	0.1	0.3		
Executes:	29.3	81.0		
Rollbacks:	0.0	0.0		
Transactions:	0.4			

FIGURE 14-7.   *The AWR Report load profile*

Monitoring hit ratios is just one piece among the thousands of pieces of your tuning arsenal. The reason that so many tuning tips are provided in this book is that in writing about tuning, I am writing about all of the turns that the optimizer will make and how to compensate for any issues. Although I don't believe you could capture everything in a book (you'd be *un*-writing the hardest part of Oracle—the optimizer), I do believe this compilation helps solve many of them. Some DBAs (usually those trying to sell you a tuning product) minimize the importance of hit ratios (*proactive tuning*) and focus completely on waits (*reactive tuning*), since focusing on waits is a great way to solve the current burning problems quickly. By monitoring the Instance Efficiency section (and using all of Statspack and Enterprise Manager), the DBA combines reactive and proactive tuning and will discover some problems before the users scream or wait events hit the top 5 list. Hit ratios are one important piece of the puzzle (so are waits). The listing that follows shows how well this Statspack section shows you all of the common hit ratios at once.

```
Instance Efficiency Indicators
~~~~~~~~~~~~~~~~~~~~~~~~~~~~~~~~~~
            Buffer Nowait %:   100.00       Redo NoWait %:    99.99
            Buffer   Hit  %:    99.30  Optimal W/A Exec %:   100.00
            Library Hit   %:    98.02       Soft Parse %:     97.48
         Execute to Parse %:    47.86       Latch Hit %:      99.97
    Parse CPU to Parse Elapsd %: 91.07    % Non-Parse CPU:    98.40
```

Things to look for include the following:

- A Buffer NoWait % of less than 99 percent. This value is the ratio of hits on a request for a specific buffer where the buffer was immediately available in memory. If the ratio is low, then there are (hot) blocks being contended for that should be found in the Buffer Wait section.

- A Buffer Hit % of less than 95 percent. This value is the ratio of hits on a request for a specific buffer when the buffer was in memory and no physical I/O was needed. While originally one of the few methods of measuring memory efficiency, it still is an excellent method for showing how often you need to do a physical I/O, which merits further investigation as to the cause. Unfortunately, if you have unselective indexes that are frequently accessed, that will drive your hit ratio higher, which can be a misleading indication of good performance to some DBAs. When you effectively tune your SQL and have effective indexes on your entire system, this issue is not encountered as frequently and the hit ratio is a better performance indicator. A high hit ratio is not a measure of good performance, but a low hit ratio is often a sign of performance that can be improved or should at least be looked into.

  - A hit ratio that is steadily at 95 percent and then one day goes to 99 percent should be checked for bad SQL or a bad index that is causing a surge of logical reads (check the load profile and top buffer gets SQL).

  - A hit ratio that is steadily at 95 percent and then drops to 45 percent should be checked for bad SQL (check the top physical reads SQL) causing a surge in physical reads that are not using an index or an index that has been dropped (I've seen this more often than you can imagine).

- A Library Hit % of less than 95 percent. A lower library hit ratio usually indicates that SQL is being pushed out of the shared pool early (could be due to a shared pool that is too small). A lower ratio could also indicate that bind variables are not used or some other issue is causing SQL not to be reused (in which case, a smaller shared pool may only be a bandage that potentially fixes a resulting library latch problem). Despite the rants about lowering your shared pool all the time to fix library cache and shared pool latching issues, most multiterabyte systems I've seen with heavy usage have shared pools in the gigabytes without any issues because they've fixed the SQL issues. You must fix the problem (use bind variables or CURSOR_SHARING) and then appropriately size the shared pool. I'll discuss this further when I get to latch issues.

- In-Memory Sort % of less than 95 percent in OLTP. In an OLTP system, you really don't want to do disk sorts. Setting the MEMORY_TARGET or PGA_AGGREGATE_TARGET (or SORT_AREA_SIZE in previous versions) initialization parameter effectively eliminates this problem.

- Soft Parse % of less than 95 percent. As covered in the Load Profile section (last section), a soft parse ratio that is less than 80 percent indicates that SQL is not being reused and needs to be investigated.

- A Latch Hit % of less than 99 percent is usually a big problem. Finding the specific latch will lead you to solving this issue. I cover this in detail in the "Latch Free" section of the chapter.

Instance Efficiency Percentages (Target 100%)

Buffer Nowait %:	100.00	Redo NoWait %:	100.00
Buffer Hit %:	99.66	In-memory Sort %:	100.00
Library Hit %:	94.84	Soft Parse %:	90.03
Execute to Parse %:	49.06	Latch Hit %:	100.02
Parse CPU to Parse Elapsd %:	94.43	% Non-Parse CPU:	95.15

FIGURE 14-8.   *The AWR Report Instance Efficiency Percentages*

Figure 14-8 shows how the Instance Efficiency section looks in the AWR Report (essentially the same as Statspack).

If you regularly run the AWR Report or Statspack, comparing hit ratios from one day to another can be a great barometer as to whether something drastic has changed. If an index was dropped on a frequently accessed column, the buffer hit ratio could drop greatly, giving you something to investigate. If an index was added to a table, it could cause the buffer hit ratio to soar if it causes a table join to occur in the wrong order, causing massive numbers of buffers to be read. A library hit ratio that rises or falls greatly from one day to the next indicates changing SQL patterns. Latch hit ratio changes can indicate contention issues that you need to investigate more.

Hit ratios can be a very proactive tool for a DBA who regularly monitors and understands a given production system, whereas many of the other tuning tools are reactive to problems that have already occurred.

TIP
Hit ratios are a great barometer of the health of your system. A large increase or drop from day to day is an indicator of a major change that needs to be investigated. Investigating waits is like investigating an accident that has already occurred, whereas investigating a change in hit ratios is like looking into the intersection with a changing traffic pattern that may cause an accident in the future if something is not adjusted. Generally, buffer and library cache hit ratios should be greater than 95 percent for OLTP, but they could be less for a data warehouse that performs many full table scans.

Remember also that a system with very high ratios in this section of the report may still have performance problems. As described previously, a poorly written query can cause volumes of index searches to join to other indexes, causing a high hit ratio (with lots of buffer gets), which is not good in this case. The database is doing most of its work in memory, but it shouldn't be doing so much work. Good hit ratios don't show the whole picture either. There are always cases where the database is working very efficiently, but performance is still bad; this report only shows the database operations, not the application operations, server actions, or networking issues that also impact the performance of the application.

The Shared Pool statistics that follow the Instance Efficiency section (both in the AWR Report and Statspack) show the percentage of the shared pool in use and the percentage of SQL statements that have been executed multiple times (as desired). Combining this data with the library, parse, and latch data helps you to size the shared pool. The following listing shows sample shared pool statistics from the Statspack Report:

```
Shared Pool Statistics          Begin    End
                                ------   -----
              Memory Usage %:    76.33    76.74
    % SQL with executions>1:     61.03    61.89
    % Memory for SQL w/exec>1:   75.89    76.57
```

As shown by the data in the preceding listing, at the time of the second snapshot, 76.74 percent of the shared pool's memory was in use. Of the statements in the shared pool, only 61.89 percent had been executed more than once, indicating a potential need to improve cursor sharing in the application. Adjusting the shared pool settings is covered in detail in Chapter 4.

Top Wait Events

The Top Wait Events section of Statspack is probably the most revealing section in the entire report when you are trying to eliminate bottlenecks quickly on your system. This section of the report shows the Top 5 Wait Events, the full list of Wait Events, and the Background Wait Events. Identifying major wait events helps to target your tuning efforts to the most burning issues on your system. If TIMED_STATISTICS is true, then the events are ordered in time waited; if false, then the events are ordered by the number of waits (in testing Microsoft Windows this still was ordered by wait time).

For example, the following listing shows the Top 5 Timed wait events for a report interval:

```
Top 5 Timed Events
~~~~~~~~~~~~~~~~~~~                                        % Total
Event                            Waits      Time (s)  Ela Time
-------------------------    ------------  ----------  --------
db file sequential read      399,394,399   2,562,115     52.26
CPU time                                     960,825     19.60
buffer busy waits            122,302,412     540,757     11.03
PL/SQL lock timer                  4,077     243,056      4.96
log file switch                  188,701     187,648      3.83
(checkpoint incomplete)
```

In the preceding example, the db file sequential read waits show an incredible number of waits (almost 400,000,000 which, assuming a 8K block size, is 3.2T of data read) and an incredible amount of time spent waiting on db file sequential reads. For this report, this wait event was due to a badly written SQL statement using too many indexes and reading many more blocks than it should have. Slow disk access contributed to the slow performance because of the large number of blocks needing to be read, but the real issue was the SQL itself (as usual). After tuning the code for only a single day, well over five terabytes of reads were eliminated (over 3T just in the SQL statement causing these reads alone) in a 24-hour period.

Here is another example. Consider the following Top 5 Wait Events for a system:

```
Top 5 Wait Events
~~~~~~~~~~~~~~~~~                                      Wait      % Total
Event                                       Waits  Time (cs)   Wt Time
------------------------------------  -----------  ---------  --------
db file sequential read                18,977,104  22,379,571    82.29
latch free                              4,016,773   2,598,496     9.55
log file sync                           1,057,224     733,490     2.70
log file parallel write                 1,054,006     503,695     1.85
db file parallel write                  1,221,755     404,230     1.49
```

In the preceding listing, you see a large number of waits related to reading a single block (db file sequential reads) and also waits for latches (latch free). You also see some pretty high waits for some of the writing to both datafiles and log files, as well as other potential issues with log file contention. To solve these issues (and to identify which ones are truly major issues), you must narrow them down by investigating the granular reports within other sections of Statspack or AWR.

In the listing that follows, you see a 10g (to compare to 11g) sample listing of waits on this very intense system (not as bad as the preceding one, though). Note that all waits were in one section.

```
                                                             Avg
                                            Total Wait      wait   Waits
Event                     Waits   Timeouts  Time (cs)       (ms)    /txn
------------------------  -----------  ----------  -----------  ------  ------
db file sequential read   18,977,104          0   22,379,571      12    17.4
latch free                 4,016,773  2,454,622    2,598,496       6     3.7
log file sync              1,057,224         10      733,490       7     1.0
enqueue                       90,140      1,723       67,611       8     0.1
library cache pin              3,062          0       29,272      96     0.0
db file scattered read        21,110          0       26,313      12     0.0
buffer busy waits             29,640          2       22,739       8     0.0
log file sequential read      31,061          0       18,372       6     0.0
row cache lock                22,402          0        3,250       1     0.0
LGWR wait for redo copy        4,436         45          183       0     0.0
SQL*Net more data to client   15,937          0          156       0     0.0
file identify                    125          0           12       1     0.0
wait for inquiry response         76          0           10       1     0.0
SQL*Net message to client  35,427,781          0        6,599       0    32.5
```

Oracle 11gR2 Statspack has a section on Foreground Wait Events, Background Wait Events, and Wait Events (fg and bg). A partial listing of these three sections is displayed next. Although only a partial listing, I've tried to include many of the most common problems. After the listing, I will discuss some of the common events that cause problems.

```
Foreground Wait Events  DB/Inst: ORCL/orcl  Snaps: 1-2
-> Only events with Total Wait Time (s) >= .001 are shown
-> ordered by Total Wait Time desc, Waits desc (idle events last)
```

Event	Waits	%Tim out	Total Wait Time (s)	Avg wait (ms)	Waits /txn	%Total Call Time
direct path read	648	0	6	9	3.8	8.9
enq: KO - fast object checkp	1	0	4	4108	0.0	6.0
direct path write	243	0	4	16	1.4	5.5
db file scattered read	62	0	3	45	0.4	4.0
control file sequential read	2,608	0	0	0	15.4	.4
log file switch completion	2	0	0	127	0.0	.4
log file sync	65	0	0	3	0.4	.2
db file sequential read	6	0	0	9	0.0	.1

Background Wait Events DB/Inst: ORCL/orcl Snaps: 1-2
-> Only events with Total Wait Time (s) >= .001 are shown
-> ordered by Total Wait Time desc, Waits desc (idle events last)

Event	Waits	%Tim out	Total Wait Time (s)	Avg wait (ms)	Waits /txn	%Total Call Time
db file parallel write	686	0	13	18	4.1	18.4
log file parallel write	910	0	4	4	5.4	5.6
control file parallel write	359	0	2	5	2.1	2.6
control file sequential read	934	0	1	1	5.5	.8
os thread startup	35	0	0	7	0.2	.4
direct path read	4	0	0	21	0.0	.1

Wait Events (fg and bg) DB/Inst: ORCL/orcl Snaps: 1-2
-> s - second, cs - centisecond, ms - millisecond, us - microsecond
-> %Timeouts: value of 0 indicates value was < .5%. Value of null is truly 0
-> Only events with Total Wait Time (s) >= .001 are shown
-> ordered by Total Wait Time desc, Waits desc (idle events last)

Event	Waits	%Tim out	Total Wait Time (s)	Avg wait (ms)	Waits /txn	%Total Call Time
db file parallel write	686	0	13	18	4.1	18.4
direct path read	652	0	6	10	3.9	9.0
enq: KO - fast object checkp	1	0	4	4108	0.0	6.0
log file parallel write	910	0	4	4	5.4	5.6
direct path write	246	0	4	15	1.5	5.5
db file scattered read	62	0	3	45	0.4	4.0
control file parallel write	359	0	2	5	2.1	2.6
control file sequential read	3,542	0	1	0	21.0	1.2
log file switch completion	2	0	0	127	0.0	.4
os thread startup	35	0	0	7	0.2	.4
log file sync	65	0	0	3	0.4	.2
db file sequential read	6	0	0	9	0.0	.1

Next are some of the most common problems; explanations and potential solutions are given as well. These sections are very important and worth their weight in gold!

DB File Scattered Read

The db file scattered read wait event generally indicates waits related to full table scans or fast full index scans. With the speed of disks and added flash cache, less indexing is certainly a wave of the future (especially on Exadata and Exalogic), but not yet. As full table scans are pulled into memory, they are scattered throughout the buffer cache since it is generally unlikely that they fall into contiguous buffers. A large number of db file scattered read waits indicate that there may be missing or suppressed indexes. This could also be preferred because performing a full table scan may be more efficient than an index scan. Check to ensure full table scans are necessary when you see these waits. Try to cache small tables to avoid reading them into memory over and over again. Locate the data on disk systems that have either more disk caching or are buffered by the OS file system cache. DB_FILE_MULTIBLOCK_READ_COUNT (default is 128 in 11gR2 for Windows or Linux) can make full scans faster (but it could also influence Oracle to do more of them). You can also partition tables and indexes so only a portion of the entire table or index is scanned. Slow file I/O (slow disks) can cause these waits. Correlated to each of the waits are the values for P1,P2,P3=file, block, blocks.

DB File Sequential Read

The db file sequential read event generally indicates a single block read (an index read, for example). A large number of db file sequential reads can indicate poor table joining orders or unselective indexing. This number will certainly be large (normally) for a high-transaction, well-tuned system. You should correlate this wait with other known issues within the Statspack or AWR Report such as inefficient SQL. Check to ensure index scans are necessary and check join orders for multiple table joins. The DB_CACHE_SIZE parameter also determines how often these waits show up; hash-area joins causing problems should show up in the PGA memory but similarly are memory hogs that can cause high wait numbers for sequential reads or can also show up as direct path read/write waits. Range scans can read a lot of blocks if the data is spread over many different blocks (density within blocks could cause issues with range scans, and reverse key indexes could be problematic with range scans). Loading data in a sorted manner can help range scans and reduce the number of blocks read. Partitioning can help, as it can eliminate some blocks. Look for unselective indexes that are causing a lot of db file sequential reads. Locate the data on disk systems that either have more disk caching and/or are buffered by OS file system cache. Correlated to the waits are the values for P1,P2,P3=file, block, blocks.

Buffer Busy Waits IDs and Meanings

A buffer busy wait is a wait for a buffer that is being used in an unsharable way or is being read into the buffer cache. Buffer busy waits should not be greater than 1 percent. Check the buffer wait statistics section (or V$WAITSTAT) to find out where the wait is. Follow the solution in this section for buffer busy waits associated with Segment Header, Undo Header, Undo Block, Data Block, and Index Block. Correlated to the waits are the values for P1,P2,P3=file, block, id (see the list in the following table from My Oracle Support). Some people argue that buffer busy waits can be helped by adding more ITL slots (*initrans*), but the information shown in the table should make it evident that initrans can help in the appropriate situation (based on the correlated TX enqueue wait).

Reason Code (ID)
(Block Class for 10g+)

<=8.0.6	8.1.6–9.2	>=10.1	Reason
0	0	n/a	A block is being read,
1003	100	n/a	You want to NEW the block, but the block is currently being read by another session (most likely for undo).
1007	200	n/a	You want to NEW the block, but someone else is using the current copy so you have to wait for them to finish.
1010	230	n/a	Trying to get a buffer in CR/CRX mode, but a modification has started on the buffer that has not yet been completed.
1012	–	n/a	A modification is happening on a SCUR or XCUR buffer, but has not yet completed
1012 (dup.)	231	n/a	CR/CRX scan found the CURRENT block, but a modification has started on the buffer that has not yet been completed.
1013	130	n/a	Block is being read by another session and no other suitable block image was found, e.g., CR version, so you have to wait until the read is completed. This wait may also occur after a buffer cache assumed deadlock. The kernel can't get a buffer in a certain amount of time and assumes a deadlock. Therefore, it reads the CR version of the block. This should not have a negative impact on performance, and basically replaces a read from disk with a wait for another process to read it from disk, as the block needs to be read one way or another.
1014	110	n/a	You want the CURRENT block either shared or exclusive but the block is being read into cache by another session, so you have to wait until its read() is completed.

Reason Code (ID) (Block Class for 10g+)			
<=8.0.6	**8.1.6–9.2**	**>=10.1**	**Reason**
1014 (duplicate)	120	n/a	You want to get the block in current mode, but someone else is currently reading it into the cache. Wait for them to complete the read. This occurs during buffer lookup.
1016	210	n/a	The session wants the block in SCUR or XCUR mode. If this is a buffer exchange or the session is in discrete TX mode, the session waits for the first time and the second time escalates the block as a deadlock and so does not show up as waiting very long. In this case, the statistic "exchange deadlocks" is incremented, and you yield the CPU for the "buffer deadlock" wait event.
1016 (duplicate)	220	n/a	During buffer lookup for a CURRENT copy of a buffer, you have found the buffer but someone holds it in an incompatible mode so you have to wait.

Buffer Busy/Segment Header

If the wait is on a segment header, you can increase the freelists or freelist groups (this can even help single instances) or increase the PCTUSED-to-PCTFREE gap. Use Automatic Segment Space Management (ASSM). If you are using ASSM, Oracle does this for you by using bitmap freelists. ASSM also removes the need to set PCTUSED.

Buffer Busy/UNDO Header

If the wait is on an undo header, you can address this by adding rollback segments or increasing the size of the UNDO area.

Buffer Busy/Undo Block

If the wait is on an UNDO block, you should try to commit more often (but not too often, or you'll get "log file sync" waits) or use larger rollback segments or UNDO areas. You may need to reduce the data density on the table driving this consistent read or increase the DB_CACHE_SIZE. Sizing initialization parameters is covered in Chapter 4.

Buffer Busy/Data Block

If the wait is on a data block, you can move "hot" data to another block to avoid this hot block or use smaller blocks (to reduce the number of rows per block, making it less "hot"). Check for scanning unselective data, and fix queries that are causing this or partition the table to eliminate unnecessary data scans. You can also increase initrans for a hot block (where users are simultaneously accessing the same block). Don't set initrans too high, as this takes 24 bytes per ITL slot, and you only need enough for the number of users accessing the *exact* same block for DML at the same time (usually something like 6 is more than enough). When a DML (INSERT/UPDATE/DELETE) occurs on a block, the lock byte is set in the block and any user accessing the record(s) being changed must check the ITL for information related to building the before image of the block. The Oracle Database writes information into the block, including all users who are "interested" in the state of the block, in the Interested Transaction List (ITL). To decrease waits in this area, you increase the initrans, which creates the space in the block to allow multiple ITL slots (for multiple DML user access). The default is two ITL slots per index or data block. You can also increase the PCTFREE value on the table where this block exists (Oracle uses space in PCTFREE to add ITL slots up to the number specified by MAXTRANS when there are not enough slots pre-built with the specified initrans). In 9*i*, maxtrans is not set; in 11g and 10g, maxtrans defaults to 255. Check for correlated TX4 enqueue waits as well. Each ITL slot takes about 24 bytes of space, so don't just set initrans to 255, or you may unnecessarily waste space.

Buffer Busy/Index Block
Use reverse key indexes and/or smaller blocks (to reduce the number of rows per block). Note that reverse key indexes can slow down range scans where you want the data to be sequentially located in the same block. Check for scanning unselective indexes (bad code/bad indexes). You may want to rebuild the index or partition the index to decrease the number of accesses to it. Increase initrans for a hot block (not too high, as this takes 24 bytes per slot) where multiple users are accessing the same block for DML (see "Tuning and Viewing at the Block Level" for more information on ITL). Check for correlated TX4 enqueue waits as well.

Latch Free
Latches are low-level queuing mechanisms (they're accurately referred to as *mutually exclusive mechanisms*) used to protect shared memory structures in the System Global Area (SGA). Latches are like locks on memory that are very quickly obtained and released. Latches are used to prevent concurrent access to a shared memory structure. If the latch is not available, a latch free miss is recorded. Most latch problems (waits, misses, and sleeps) are related to the failure to use bind variables (library cache mutex and shared pool latch), REDO generation issues (redo allocation latch), buffer cache contention issues (cache buffers lru chain), and hot blocks in the buffer cache (cache buffers chains). In 11g, the library cache pin (protects cursors/SQL) and library cache latch (protects the Library Cache) are both replaced by *mutexes* (program objects that negotiate mutual exclusion among threads). There are also latch and mutex waits related to bugs; check My Oracle Support (MetaLink) for bug reports if you suspect this is the case (oracle.com/support). When latch miss ratios are greater than 0.5 percent, you should investigate the issue. If the latch miss ratio is greater than 2% and there are a large number of them, you may have a serious problem.

TIP
In 11g, the library cache pin (protects cursors/SQL) and library cache latch (protects the Library Cache) are both replaced by mutexes (program objects that negotiate mutual exclusion among threads).

Cursor: pin S
In 11g, the library cache pin (protects cursors/SQL) is replaced with a library cache mutex. The cursor: pin S wait event happens because one session is waiting on another to increment (or decrement) the *reference count* (an exclusive atomic update to the mutex structure itself) to keep track of its use. SQL with high executions counts can cause this. You can modify a statement and

insert a comment into it so several statements do the same thing but are slightly different (this is the reverse of using bind variables where you're trying to use only one statement). Also, see "Oracle Bugs" for bugs related to this wait event. No blockers exist for this type of wait event. Correlated to each of the waits are the values for P1,P2,P3=idn, value, where. From value, you can get the session ID holding the mutex along with the reference count, and from where, you can locate where in the code the mutex was requested from; this value is helpful to Oracle support.

Cursor: pin S wait on X

This wait event is more likely to occur than the cursor: pin S wait. If you are not reusing SQL, you may see many cursor: pin S wait on X waits. A session wants a mutex in S (share mode) on a cursor (SQL statement), but another session is holding that mutex in X (exclusive) mode. The session in S mode is usually waiting on a hard parse of a cursor by the other session, which is holding the mutex in exclusive X mode. You'll also see the reverse of this: cursor: pin X wait on S. Consider setting CURSOR_SHARING as described in Chapter 4. This may also occur if the shared pool is under a heavy load or undersized. Correlated to each of the waits are the values for P1,P2,P3=idn, value, where. From value, you can get the session ID holding the mutex along with the reference count, and from where, you can locate where in the code the mutex was requested from; this value is helpful to Oracle support.

Library cache: mutex X

In 11*g*, the library cache latches are replaced by mutexes. Because there are *many* more of these structures now, the wait events become much more specific. The library cache mutex is generally used when you are pinning or unpinning code into the Library Cache. Limiting this behavior is key; this often includes using CURSOR_SHARING and appropriately sizing the shared pool. Under heavy loads, this wait event can exacerbate an already overloaded CPU. Correlated to each of the waits are the values for P1,P2,P3=idn, value, where. From value, you can get the session ID holding the mutex, and from where, you can locate where in the code the mutex was requested from; this value is helpful to Oracle support.

Enqueue

An *enqueue* is a lock that protects a shared resource. Locks protect shared resources such as data in a record to prevent two people from updating the same data at the same time. Locks include a queuing mechanism, which is FIFO (first in, first out). Note that Oracle's latching mechanism is not FIFO. Enqueue waits usually point to the *ST* enqueue, the *HW* enqueue, and the *TX4* enqueue. The ST enqueue is used for space management and allocation for dictionary-managed tablespaces. Use locally managed tablespaces (LMTs), or try to preallocate extents or at least make the next extent larger for problematic dictionary-managed tablespaces. HW enqueues are used with the high-water mark of a segment; manually allocating the extents can circumvent this wait. TX4 is one of the most common enqueue waits. TX4 enqueue waits are usually the result of one of three issues. The first issue involves duplicates in a unique index; you need to roll back to free the enqueue. The second concerns multiple updates to the same bitmap index fragment. Because a single bitmap fragment may contain multiple ROWIDs, you need to issue a commit or a rollback to free the enqueue when multiple users are trying to update the same fragment. The third and most likely issue arises when multiple users are updating the same block. If there are no free ITL slots when multiple users want to perform DML on a different row of the same block, a block-level lock could occur. You can easily avoid this scenario by increasing the initrans to create multiple ITL slots and/or by increasing the PCTFREE on the table (so Oracle can create the

ITL slots as needed). You could also use a smaller block size so there are fewer rows in the block and thus greater concurrency on the data is allowed. Two other TX4 waits are also less prevalent: waiting for a prepared statement and inserting a row into an index where another transaction is splitting the index block. When users want to change the exact same record in a block, a TX6 lock results. Lastly, while you no longer get TM locks, which are table locks when you don't index foreign keys, be sure to index foreign keys to avoid performance issues. Correlated to the transaction waits are the values for P1,P2,P3=lock type and mode, lockid1, lockid2 (a p2raw and a p3raw will also appear as p2/p3 in hex).

Log File Switch

If you see the logfile switch wait event, then all commit requests are waiting for 'logfile switch (archiving needed)' or 'logfile switch (chkpt.Incomplete)'. Ensure that the archive disk is not full or slow. DBWR may be too slow due to I/O. You may need to add more or larger REDO logs, and you may also need to add database writers if the DBWR is the problem.

Log Buffer Space

When a change is made, the changed block is copied to the log buffer. If the log buffer doesn't get written fast enough to the redo logs, it can cause log buffer space issues (things get backed up). Space issues can also be a problem when you commit a very large amount of data at once (make the log buffer larger for these types of transactions). This wait usually occurs because you are writing to the log buffer faster than LGWR can write the buffer contents out to the redo logs, or because log switches are too slow, but *usually* not because the log buffer is too small (although this is also the case at times). To address this problem, increase the size of the log files, or get faster disks to write to, but, as a last resort, increase the size of the log buffer (in very large systems, it is not uncommon to see a log buffer in the tens of megabytes). You might even consider using solid-state disks or flash disks for their high speed for redo logs.

Log File Sync

When a user changes data in a record, the block the record is contained in is copied to the log buffer (many records/rows are contained in a block). When a commit or rollback is issued, the log buffer is flushed (copied) to the redo logs by the LGWR (Log Writer). The process of writing the changed data from the log buffer to the redo log and getting a confirmation that the write successfully occurred is called a *log file sync*. To reduce log file sync waits, try to commit more records at once (try to commit a batch of 50 instead of one at a time if possible). If you commit 50 records one at a time, 50 log file syncs need to occur. Put redo logs on a faster disk or alternate redo logs on different physical disk arrays to reduce the archiving effect on the LGWR (or use solid-state disks or flash disks). Don't use RAID 5 because it is very slow for applications that write a lot; potentially consider using filesystem direct I/O or raw devices, which are very fast at writing information. Correlated to the waits are the values for P1,P2,P3=buffer#, unused, unused.

Global Cache CR Request

When using multiple instances (RAC/Grid), a global cache cr request wait occurs when one instance is waiting for blocks from another instance's cache (sent via the interconnect). This wait says that the current instance can't find a consistent read (cr) version of a block in the local cache. If the block is not in the remote cache, then a db file sequential read wait will also follow this one. Tune the SQL that is causing large amounts of reads that get moved from node to node.

Try to put users who are using the same blocks on the same instance so the blocks are not moved from instance to instance. Some non-Oracle application servers move the same process from node to node looking for the fastest node (unaware they are moving the same blocks from node to node). Pin these long processes to the same node. Potentially increase the size of the local cache if slow I/O combined with a small cache is the problem. Monitor V$CR_BLOCK_SERVER to see if an issue like reading UNDO segments has occurred. Correlated to the waits are the values for P1,P2,P3=file, block, lenum (look in V$LOCK_ELEMENT for the row where LOCK_ELEMENT_ADDR has the same value as lenum).

Log File Parallel Write
Put redo logs on fast disks (or use solid-state disks or flash disks) and don't use RAID 5. Separate redo logs from other data that might slow them down and ensure tablespaces are not left in hot backup mode. Correlated to the waits are the values for P1,P2,P3=files written to, blocks, requests.

DB File Parallel Write
Fix or speed up the operating system I/O and file system I/O by doing the database writing to database files. Correlated to the waits are the values for P1,P2,P3=files, blocks, requests/timeouts.

Direct Path Read
Oracle usually does direct path reads to read blocks directly into the PGA. Direct path reads are used for things such as sorting, parallel querying, and read aheads. The time here does not always reflect the true wait time. This is usually an issue with the file I/O (see if any disks are I/O bound using OS utilities, as described in Chapter 16). Check for sorting on disk instead of in memory (located in the Instance Statistics section of the report). Using async I/O could reduce the elapsed time, although it may not reduce the wait time. Correlated to the waits are the values for P1,P2,P3=file, start block, number of blocks.

Direct Path Write
Direct path writes are used for such things as direct load operations, parallel DML, and writes to uncached LOBs (Large Objects). The time here does not always reflect the true wait time. This wait usually reflects an issue with the file I/O (see if any disks are I/O bound using OS utilities, as described in Chapter 16). Check for sorting on disk (located in the Instance Statistics section of the report). Using async I/O could reduce the elapsed time, although it may not reduce the wait time. Correlated to the waits are the values for P1,P2,P3=file, start block, number of blocks.

Async Disk I/O
Oracle is waiting for the completion of an async write or for an async slave to write. The problem could arise from I/O issues with the DBWR (Database Writer), the LGWR (Log Writer), the ARCH (Archiver), and the CKPT (checkpoint process), but is usually some file I/O issue.

Idle Events
Several idle wait events are listed after the output that can be ignored. Idle events are generally listed at the bottom of each section and include things like SQL*Net messages to or from the client and other background-related timings. Idle events are listed in the STATS$IDLE_EVENT table.

Some of the most common wait problems and potential solutions are outlined here:

Wait Problem	Potential Fix
Sequential read	Indicates many index reads—tune the code (especially joins).
Scattered read	Indicates many full table scans—tune the code; cache small tables; get more Flash Cache.
Free buffer	Increase the DB_CACHE_SIZE; shorten the checkpoint; tune the code.
Buffer busy	Segment header—add freelists or freelist groups.
Buffer busy	Data block—separate "hot" data; use reverse key indexes; use smaller blocks; increase initrans (debatable); reduce block popularity; make I/O faster.
Buffer busy	UNDO header—add rollback segments or UNDO areas or simply use Automatic Undo Management.
Buffer busy	UNDO block—commit more; use larger rollback segments or undo areas or simply use Automatic Undo Management.
Latch/mutex wait	Investigate the detail (a listing later in this chapter includes fixes).
Enqueue—ST	Use LMTs or preallocate large extents.
Enqueue—HW	Preallocate extents above the high-water mark.
rightEnqueue—TX4	Increase initrans or use a smaller block size on the table or index.
Enqueue—TX6	Fix the code that is making the block unsharable (use V$LOCK to find).
Enqueue—TM	Index foreign keys; check application locking of tables.
Log buffer space	Increase the log buffer; use faster disks for the redo logs.
Log file switch	Archive destination slow or full; add more or larger redo logs.
Log file sync	Commit more records at a time; use faster redo log disks; use raw devices.
Write complete waits	Add database writers; checkpoint more often; buffer cache too small.
Idle event	Ignore it.

Following are some common idle events (by type of idle event):

- Dispatcher timer (shared server idle event)

- Lock manager wait for remote message (RAC idle event)

- Pipe get (user process idle event)

- Pmon timer (background process idle event)

- PX idle wait (parallel query idle event)

- PX deq credit: need buffer (parallel query idle event)

- PX deq: execution msg (parallel query idle event)

- Rdbms ipc message (background process idle event)

- Smon timer (background process idle event)

- SQL*Net message from client (user process idle event)

- Virtual circuit status (shared server idle event)

Oracle 11*g* also has a Wait Event Histogram that shows how many of the waits fall into various buckets (0–1 ms, 1–4 ms, 4–8 ms, 8–16 ms, and 32+ ms). This type of histogram is also provided for file I/O by tablespace to show if you are waiting on mostly short waits with a few very long waits or many medium length waits. A partial listing for this is below:

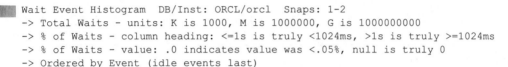

```
Wait Event Histogram  DB/Inst: ORCL/orcl  Snaps: 1-2
-> Total Waits - units: K is 1000, M is 1000000, G is 1000000000
-> % of Waits - column heading: <=1s is truly <1024ms, >1s is truly >=1024ms
-> % of Waits - value: .0 indicates value was <.05%, null is truly 0
-> Ordered by Event (idle events last)
```

Event	Total Waits	<1ms	<2ms	<4ms	<8ms	<16ms	<32ms	<=1s	>1s
ADR block file read	6	66.7					33.3		
Disk file operations I/O	60	100.0							
LGWR wait for redo copy	13	100.0							
SQL*Net break/reset to cli	364	100.0							
asynch descriptor resize	350	100.0							
control file parallel writ	359	89.7	.8	3.1	2.8	.8	1.7	1.1	
control file sequential re	3542	99.3	.1		.1	.2	.1	.1	
db file parallel write	686	29.6	5.7	6.7	7.6	8.3	32.4	9.8	
db file scattered read	62	11.3	4.8			14.5	14.5	54.8	
db file sequential read	6			16.7	33.3	50.0			
direct path read	652	3.8	3.1	.8	65.3	18.6	7.7	.8	
direct path write	246	22.4	14.6	6.1	4.9	18.7	18.7	14.6	

In 11*g*, the enqueue section actually spells out the type of enqueue. For instance, if it is a TX Enqueue, it will now say TX Transaction. If that isn't good enough, it goes one step further and even tells you the type of TX. For instance, for a TX4, the sections shows that it is a TX Transaction (row lock contention) and then it gives the Requests, Gets, Waits, and a few other bits of helpful information. See Figure 14-9 for a look at this section in the AWR Report. Note that in Figure 14-9, JS is spelled out as the Job Scheduler Enqueue.

TIP
Tuning by wait events is one of the best possible reactive tuning methods.

TIP
The Top 5 Wait events reveal to you the most important issues on your system at the macro level. Rarely do they point you to a specific problem. Other parts of the AWR Report or Statspack Report tell you why you are receiving the top 5 waits.

Enqueue Activity

- only enqueues with waits are shown
- Enqueue stats gathered prior to 10g should not be compared with 10g data
- ordered by Wait Time desc, Waits desc

Enqueue Type (Request Reason)	Requests	Succ Gets	Failed Gets	Waits
KO-Multiple Object Checkpoint (fast object checkpoint)	9	9	0	1
JS-Job Scheduler (queue lock)	5,651	5,651	0	1

Back to Wait Statistics

FIGURE 14-9. *The AWR Report enqueue activity*

Oracle Bugs

There are also Oracle bugs (Oracle used to call bugs *undocumented features*) to watch for that can cause a large number of wait events. In 11g, several bugs are related to the new mutex wait events. The first diagnostic step to resolve these issues is to apply the latest patchset available in your platform. Most of the buffer cache issues related to bugs can be avoided by applying these patchsets listed in the appropriate bug note. The following table summarizes the most common bugs related to Library Cache problems, possible workarounds, and the patchset that fixes the problem (it will be listed in the Bug Note when you go to it). Some notes below are related to the next version of the database (12.1.0.0). They are listed to show that the bug is *already* fixed; even though, the next version of the database isn't in beta yet (thanks My Oracle Support for these listings).

The following are "cursor: Pin S" waits that are related to bugs and fixed in Oracle 10g, 11, and 12 (future version):

NB	Bug	Fixed	Description
	9499302	11.1.0.7.7, 11.2.0.2, 12.1.0.0	Improve concurrent mutex request handling.
	9591812	11.2.0.2.2, 12.1.0.0	Wrong wait events in 11.2 ("cursor: mutex S" instead of "cursor: mutex X").
	6904068	11.2.0.2	High CPU usage when there are "cursor: pin S" waits (Windows, fixed 11.2.0.2).
	7441165	10.2.0.5/11.2.0.2	Prevent preemption while holding a mutex (fix only works on Solaris).
	88575526	10.2.0.4, 11.1.0.7	Session spins/OERI after "kksfbc child completion" wait (Windows only).

The following are "library cache: mutex X"–related bugs and fixed in Oracle 10g, 11g, and 12 (future version):

NB	Bug	Fixed	Description
	8860198	11.2.0.2, 12.1.0.0	"library cache: mutex X" waits using XMLType.
	10417716	12.1.0.0, 11.2.0.2 Exadata	Mutex X waits in 11g on an instance with heavy JAVA usage.
	11818335	11.2.0.2.2, 12.1.0.0	Additional support for bug 10411618 to allow dynamic mutex wait scheme changes.
	10204505	12.1.0.0	SGA autotune can cause row cache misses, Library Cache reloads, and parsing.
	10632113	12.1.0.0	OLS calls cause mutex contention even with low number of concurrent users.
	8981059	11.1.0.7.4, 11.2.0.1.2, 11.2.0.2, 12.1.0.0	High version count (due to USER_BIND_PEEK_MISMATCH) with bind peeking.
	9530750	12.1.0.0	High waits for "library cache: mutex X" for cursor build lock.
	10086843	12.1.0.0	Recursive SQL cursors not reused; PMON crashes instance with ORA-600 [kglLockOwnersListDelete].
	7352775	11.2.0.2, 12.1.0.0	Many child cursors when PARALLEL_INSTANCE_GROUP set incorrectly.
	9239863	11.2.0.2, 12.1.0.0	Excessive "library cache: mutex X" contention on hot objects.
	8793492	11.2.0.2	Mutex waits with Resource Manager.
	9140262	11.2.0.2	ORA-600 [ksliwat5] followed by CPU spike/"library cache: mutex X" waits.
	9282521	11.2.0.2	Excessive "library cache: mutex X" contention on hot objects.
	9003145	11.2.0.2	Dump (kglIsOwnerVersionable)/"library cache: mutex X" waits.
	9398685	11.2.0.2	High "library cache: mutex X" when using Application Context.
	10145558	11.1.0.7.7, 11.2.0.2	Selects on Library Cache V$/X$ views cause "library cache: mutex X" waits.
	7502237	11.1.0.7.7, 11.2.0.1	Unnecessary "library cache: mutex X" waits using stored Java.
	7307972	11.1.0.7.2, 11.2.0.1	Excessive waits on "library cache: mutex X".
	8431767	11.1.7.0, 11.2.0.2	High "library cache: mutex X" when using Application Context.
	7648406	10.2.0.5, 11.1.0.7.4, 11.2.0.1	Child cursors not shared for "table_..." cursors (that show as "SQL Text Not Available") when NLS_LENGTH_SEMANTICS = CHAR.

NB	Bug	Fixed	Description
	9312879	11.1.0.7.7, 11.2.0.1	"library cache: mutex X" waits after killing sessions/PMON slow to clean up.
	7155860	11.2.0.1	Spin on kgllkde causes "library cache: mutex X".
	8499043	11.1.0.7.2	SET_CONTEXT incurs unnecessary DLM overhead in RAC.
	5928271	11.1.0.7	Excessive waits on "library cache: mutex X".
	7317117	11.2.0.1	Unnecessary "library cache: mutex X" waits on LOB operations.

The following are "cursor: pin S wait on X"–related bugs and fixed in Oracle 10g, 11g, and 12 (future version):

NB	Bug	Fixed	Description
	5650841		Hang/deadlock from ANALYZE of cluster index.
	9944129	11.2.0.2, 12.1.0.0	SQL not shared due to INST_DRTLD_MISMATCH with global transaction.
	9694101	11.2.0.2, 12.1.0.0	Hang/deadlock between "cursor: pin S wait on X" and "library cache lock" involving dictionary objects.
	10171273	12.1.0.0, 11.2.0.2 Exadata	Long parse time with non-equi subpartitioning under interval partitioning.
	9472669	11.2.0.1 (patch 1 Windows), 11.2.0.2, 12.1.0.0	"cursor: pin S wait on X" waits for invalid SQL over DB link.
	10213073	11.2.0.1 (patch 1 Windows), 11.2.0.3, 12.1.0.0	CREATE SYNONYM and CREATE PACKAGE may incorrectly invalidate objects.
	11855965	10.2.0.4, 11.2.0.3, 12.1.0.0	Truncate partition takes a long time performing recursive delete on MLOG$.
	9935787	10.2.0.4, 10.2.0.5, 11.2.0.1, 11.2.0.3, 12.1.0.0	Long parse time for large inlists; can cause "cursor: pin S wait on X" waits.
	8508078	11.2.0.2, 12.1.0.0	Contention from many concurrent bad SQLs.
	9499302	11.1.0.7.7, 11.2.0.2, 12.1.0.0	Improve concurrent mutex request handling.
	8441239	11.2.0.1	"library cache lock" waits if long running TRUNCATE in progress.
	7234778	11.2.0.1	Unnecessary "cursor: pin S wait on X" waits.

NB	Bug	Fixed	Description
	8348464	11.1.0.7.2, 11.2.0.1	CREATE SYNONYM and CREATE PACKAGE may incorrectly invalidate objects.
	5485914	10.2.0.4	Mutex self-deadlock on EXPLAIN/TRACE of remote-mapped SQL.
	6011045	10.2.0.4 (patch 43 – Windows)	DBMS_STATS causes deadlock between "cursor: pin S wait on X" and "library cache lock" waits.
	6143420	10.2.0.5, 11.1.0.6	Deadlock involving "row cache lock" on DC_USERS and "cursor: pin S wait on X".
	7462072	10.2.0.4.3, 10.2.0.5	Unnecessary "cursor: pin S wait on X" waits.
	5983020	10.2.0.4	MMON deadlock with user session executing ALTER USER.
	7226463	10.2.0.5	EXECUTE IMMEDIATE no releasing mutex or library cache pin.
+	5907779	10.2.0.4	Self-deadlock hang on "cursor: pin S wait on X" (typically from DBMS_STATS).

The Life of an Oracle Shadow Process

Here is a breakdown of the life of an Oracle shadow process and where it might be waiting as it lives. This table is adapted from Oracle Doc ID 61998.1 and shows what's happening in less than one second within Oracle.

State	Notes
IDLE	Waits for "SQL*Net message from client" (waiting for the user). Receives the SQL*Net packet requesting PARSE/EXECUTE of a statement.
ON CPU	Decodes the SQL*Net packet.
WAITING	Waits for "latch free" to obtain the library cache mutex. Gets the library cache mutex.
ON CPU	Scans the shared pool for the SQL statement, finds match, frees mutex (if the statement, cursor, is already in memory, it does—"cursor: pin S"), sets up links to the shared cursor, etc., and begins to execute.
WAITING	Waits for "db file sequential read"; you need a block not in the cache (waits for I/O).
ON CPU	Block read from disk complete. Execution continues. Construct SQL*Net packet with first row of data to send to client and sends.
WAITING	Waits on "SQL*Net message from client" for acknowledgment packet received.
IDLE	Waits for next SQL*Net message from client.

RAC Wait Events and Interconnect Statistics

The RAC events are listed next in the report if you are running RAC (multiple instances). As stated earlier, you need to run Statspack or the AWR Report for *each* instance that you have. For Statspack, you run `statspack.snap` procedure and `spreport.sql` script on each node you want to monitor to compare to other instances. The greatest comparison report is one from another node that accesses the same database. I cover more on tuning RAC in Chapter 11 and will not repeat that information here. It's very important to remember that single-instance tuning should be performed before attempting to tune the processes that communicate via the cluster interconnect. In other words, tune the system as a single instance before you move it to RAC. For AWR on RAC, you can run `awrgdrpt.sql` to get a global report. However, according to `spdoc.txt`, section 4.2, for Statspack, it works only for a single database instance.

Some of the top wait events that you may encounter are listed briefly next and covered in more detail in Chapter 11. The top global cache (gc) waits to look for include the following:

- **gc (global cache) current block busy**   Happens when an instance requests a CURR data block (wants to do some DML) and the block to be transferred is in use.

- **gc (global cache) buffer busy**   A wait event that occurs whenever a session has to wait for an ongoing operation on the resource to complete because the block is in use.

- **gc (global cache) cr request**   Happens when an instance requests a CR data block and the block to be transferred hasn't arrived at the requesting instance. This is the one I see the most, and it's usually because the SQL is poorly tuned and *many* index blocks are being moved back and forth between instances.

Figure 14-10 shows the AWR Report RAC section. You can see that there are six instances (nodes) in this cluster. You can also see things like the number of blocks sent/received as well as how many of the blocks are being accessed in the local cache (93.1 percent) as opposed to on the disk or in another instance. As you would guess, accessing blocks in the local cache is faster, but accessing one of the remote caches on one of the other nodes is almost always faster (given a fast enough interconnect and no saturation of the interconnect) than going to disk (more on this in Chapter 11).

Top SQL Statements

The most resource-intensive SQL statements in the database are listed next, in descending order of CPU, Elapsed Time, Buffer Gets (or Gets), Disk Reads (or Reads), Executions, Parse Calls, Sharable Memory, and Version Count. Depending on where the problem is, you have plenty of places to investigate. If you saw many buffer gets as the top wait event (db file sequential reads), then you would investigate the statements in the descending order of buffer gets (focusing on the worst ones that are at the top of the list). Because the buffer gets statistic is cumulative, the query with the most buffer gets may not be the worst-performing query in the database; it may just have been executed enough times to earn the highest ranking. Compare the cumulative number of buffer gets to the cumulative number of disk reads for the queries; if the numbers are close, then you should evaluate the EXPLAIN PLAN for the query to find out why it is performing so many disk reads. If the disk reads are not high but the buffer gets are high and the executions are low,

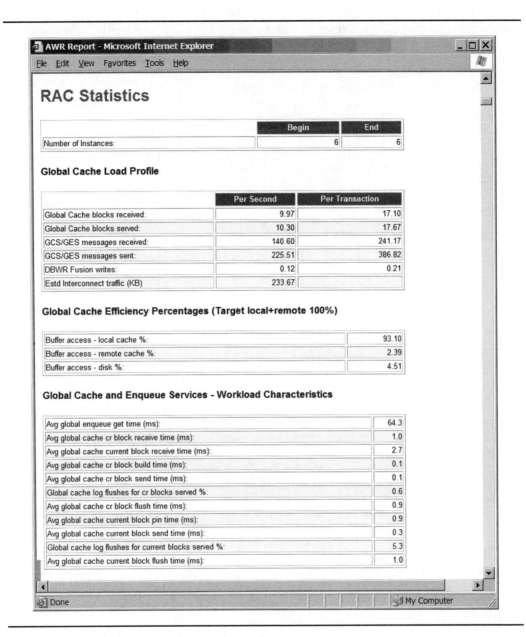

FIGURE 14-10. *The AWR Report RAC statistics*

then the query is either using a bad index or performing a join in the wrong order. This is also a system problem, as you are using a lot of your memory unnecessarily. Here is an example of this listing:

```
SQL ordered by Gets   DB/Inst: ORCL/orcl   Snaps: 1-2
-> End Buffer Gets Threshold:    10000 Total Buffer Gets:       943,141
-> Captured SQL accounts for  130.0% of Total Buffer Gets
-> SQL reported below exceeded  1.0% of Total Buffer Gets

                                                 CPU     Elapsed     Old
  Buffer Gets    Executions   Gets per Exec  %Total Time (s)  Time (s) Hash Value
---------------  -----------  -------------- ------ --------  --------- ----------
      494,112        12          41,176.0    58.2   18.17      18.17  3274221811
Module: sqlplus.exe
select occupant_name, occupant_desc, space_usage_kbytes from    v
$sysaux_occupants where  occupant_name like :"SYS_B_0"

      220,446        11          20,040.5    26.0    0.97       0.92  4106292964
select owner, segment_name, blocks from dba_segments where table
space_name = :tsname

      173,588        11          15,780.7    20.4    0.62       0.60   427474970
SELECT count(*), sum(blocks) FROM dba_segments where     OWNER =
'XDB' and TABLESPACE_NAME = 'SYSAUX'

       82,044         1          82,044.0     9.7    0.48      10.70   496629248
Module: SQL*Plus
select count(*) from emp4
```

You may also see the internal Oracle data dictionary operations listed as part of these sections. Your application commands commonly account for the great majority of the buffer gets and disk reads performed by the database. If the shared pool is flushed between the execution times of the two snapshots, the SQL portion of the output report will not necessarily contain the most resource-intensive SQL executed during the period. In 11g, V$SQL now shows SQL for multiple users with the same statement, and it shows child cursors; V$SQL_PLAN_STATISTICS shows the execution stats for each cached cursor; and V$SQL_PLAN_STATISTICS_ALL shows the joins plan and stats and many other performance-related statistics.

The AWR Report has many Top SQL sections. In 11gR2, Oracle now shows how many of the Physical Reads (or Reads) need to be optimized (see the Physical Reads UnOptimized section). An example of the SQL Statistics section is shown in Figure 14-11. They include the following sections:

- SQL ordered by Elapsed Time
- SQL ordered by CPU Time
- SQL ordered by User I/O Wait Time
- SQL ordered by Gets
- SQL ordered by Reads
- SQL ordered by Physical Reads (UnOptimized)

SQL Statistics

Back to Top

SQL ordered by Elapsed Time

- Resources reported for PL/SQL code includes the resources used by all SQL statements called by the code.
- % Total DB Time is the Elapsed Time of the SQL statement divided into the Total Database Time multiplied by 100
- %Total - Elapsed Time as a percentage of Total DB time
- %CPU - CPU Time as a percentage of Elapsed Time
- %IO - User I/O Time as a percentage of Elapsed Time
- Captured SQL account for 97.1% of Total DB Time (s): 85
- Captured PL/SQL account for 10.5% of Total DB Time (s): 85

Elapsed Time (s)	Executions	Elapsed Time per Exec (s)	%Total	%CPU	%IO	SQL Id	SQL Module	SQL Text
18.17	12	1.51	21.44	100.01	0.00	c1w244tcbckrh	sqlplus.exe	select occupant_name, occupant...
15.07	12	1.26	17.78	100.18	0.00	7xa8wfych4mad		SELECT SUM(blocks) FROM x$kewx...

FIGURE 14-11.   *The AWR Report SQL Statistics*

 SQL ordered by Executions

 SQL ordered by Parse Calls

 SQL ordered by Sharable Memory

 SQL ordered by Version Count

 SQL ordered by Cluster Wait Time (RAC)

 Complete List of SQL Text

TIP
Tuning the top 25 buffer get and top 25 physical get queries can yield system performance gains of anywhere from 5 percent to 5000+ percent. The SQL section of the Statspack Report tells you which queries to consider tuning first. The top 10 SQL statements should not be substantially more than 10 percent of all of your buffer gets or disk reads.

Instance Activity Statistics
Following the SQL statement listing, you will see the list of changes to statistics from V$SYSSTAT. Entitled "Instance Activity Stats," the V$SYSSTAT statistics are useful for identifying performance issues not shown in the prior sections. Here is a partial listing with some of the key sections listed.

Note the excellent IMU (In Memory Update) statistics; IMUs are covered in "Tuning and Viewing at the Block Level," later in this chapter:

```
Instance Activity Stats  DB/Inst: ORCL/orcl  Snaps: 1-2
```

Statistic	Total	per Second	per Trans
Batched IO (bound) vector count	0	0.0	0.0
Batched IO (full) vector count	0	0.0	0.0
Block Cleanout Optim referenced	3	0.0	0.0
CCursor + sql area evicted	13	0.0	0.1
CPU used by this session	3,183	3.9	18.8
CPU used when call started	3,141	3.9	18.6
CR blocks created	100	0.1	0.6
consistent gets	366,674,801	10,476.4	336.5
db block changes	19,788,834	565.4	18.2
db block gets	41,812,892	1,194.7	38.4
dirty buffers inspected	1,204,544	34.4	1.1
enqueue waits	87,613	2.5	0.1
free buffer requested	20,053,136	573.0	18.4
IMU CR rollbacks	100	0.1	0.6
IMU Flushes	249	0.3	1.5
IMU Redo allocation size	196,696	241.6	1,163.9
IMU commits	147	0.2	0.9
IMU contention	3	0.0	0.0
IMU ktichg flush	3	0.0	0.0
IMU pool not allocated	3	0.0	0.0
IMU recursive-transaction flush	0	0.0	0.0
IMU undo allocation size	873,968	1,073.7	5,171.4
IMU- failed to get a private stra	3	0.0	0.0
index fast full scans (full)	28,686	0.8	0.0
leaf node splits	21,066	0.6	0.0
logons cumulative	186	0.0	0.0
parse count (hard)	54,681	1.6	0.1
parse count (total)	1,978,732	56.5	1.8
physical reads	19,320,574	552.0	17.7
physical writes non checkpoint	2,027,920	57.9	1.9
recursive calls	5,020,246	143.4	4.6
sorts (disk)	2	0.0	0.0
sorts (memory)	1,333,831	38.1	1.2
sorts (rows)	14,794,401	422.7	13.6

These statistics can also be found in the AWR Report. In Figure 14-12, you can see a shortened version of these statistics from a 11gR2 database instance.

Things to Look for in the Instance Statistics Section

Compare the number of sorts performed on disk to the number performed in memory; increase the MEMORY_TARGET (if used and if needed to be increased) and the minimum PGA_AGGREGATE_TARGET (or SORT_AREA_SIZE for earlier versions) to reduce disk sorts (see Chapter 4 for more information). If physical reads are high, you are probably performing full table scans. If there are a significant number of full table scans of large tables, evaluate the most-used queries and try to reduce this inefficiency by using indexes. A large number

Instance Activity Statistics

- Instance Activity Stats
- Instance Activity Stats - Absolute Values
- Instance Activity Stats - Thread Activity

Back to Top

Instance Activity Stats

- Ordered by statistic name

Statistic	Total	per Second	per Trans
Batched IO (bound) vector count	5	0.00	0.01
Batched IO (full) vector count	0	0.00	0.00
Batched IO block miss count	16	0.01	0.03
Batched IO double miss count	1	0.00	0.00
Batched IO same unit count	10	0.01	0.02
Batched IO single block count	6	0.00	0.01
Batched IO slow jump count	0	0.00	0.00
Batched IO vector block count	0	0.00	0.00
Batched IO vector read count	0	0.00	0.00
Block Cleanout Optim referenced	10	0.01	0.02
CCursor + sql area evicted	15	0.01	0.03
CPU used by this session	6,339	4.09	11.28

FIGURE 14-12. *The AWR Report instance activity stats*

for consistent gets signals potentially over-indexed or nonselective index use. If dirty buffers inspected is high (over 5 percent) relative to free buffers requested, the memory parameters for the SGA may be too small (see Chapter 4 for additional use of these parameters and settings), or you may not be checkpointing often enough. If leaf node splits are high, consider rebuilding indexes that have grown and become fragmented if they are causing a performance degradation. The following sections look at a few of these scenarios.

The following listing shows the applicable rows from this section of the report:

```
Statistic                              Total      per Second    per Trans
-------------------------------   --------------   ------------  ----------
sorts (disk)                                  2          0.0          0.0
sorts (memory)                            3,062          3.8         18.1
sorts (rows)                            134,855        165.7        798.0
table scan rows gotten               30,089,991     36,965.6    178,047.3
table scans (direct read)                     1          0.0          0.0
table scans (long tables)                     5          0.0          0.0
table scans (short tables)                1,285          1.6          7.6
```

In the preceding example, the database performed almost all sorts in memory during the reporting interval. Of the table scans performed, most were of very small tables. The table scans (short tables) are tables that are smaller than 2 percent of the buffer cache in Oracle 11g (in V7, the value was 5 blocks; in V8, it was 20 blocks; and in 9i/10g, it was also 2 percent).

TIP
If many sorts are being performed to disk (greater than 1–5 percent of the total number of rows being sorted), you may need to increase the initialization parameters associated with sorting. See Chapter 4 for more information on these.

Key Areas to Consider

A few key areas to consider are explained in this section:

- **Consistent gets**   The number of blocks read from the buffer cache for queries without the SELECT FOR UPDATE clause. The value for this statistic plus the value of the "db block gets" statistic constitute what is referred to as *logical reads* (all reads cached in memory). These are usually the CURRENT version of the block, but can also be a Consistent Read (CR) version.

- **DB block gets**   The number of blocks read in the buffer cache that were accessed for INSERT, UPDATE, DELETE, or SELECT FOR UPDATE statements. These are CURRENT versions of the block. When these are changed, they are reflected in the 'db block changes' value.

- **Physical reads**   The number of data blocks that were not read from the buffer cache. This could be reads from disks, O/S cache, or disk cache to satisfy a SELECT, SELECT FOR UPDATE, INSERT, UPDATE, or DELETE statement.

By adding the "consistent gets" and "db block gets," you get the number of logical reads (memory reads). Using the following equation, you can calculate the buffer (data) cache hit ratio:

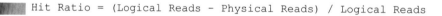

```
Hit Ratio = (Logical Reads - Physical Reads) / Logical Reads
```

TIP
The buffer cache hit ratio should be greater than 95 percent. If it is less than 95 percent, you should consider increasing the size of the data cache by increasing the MEMORY_TARGET (if used) or increasing the minimum setting for the DB_CACHE_SIZE initialization parameter (given that physical memory is available to do this).

- **Dirty buffers inspected**   This is the number of dirty (modified) data buffers that were aged out on the LRU list. A value here indicates that the DBWR is not keeping up. You may benefit by adding more DBWRs.

TIP
If the dirty buffers inspected is greater than 1–2 percent of free buffers requested, consider increasing the database writers as detailed in Chapter 3.

- **Enqueue waits (timeouts)**   The number of times that an enqueue (lock) was requested and the specific one that was requested was not available. If this statistic is greater than 0, investigate the locking issues.

- **Free buffer inspected**   "Free buffers inspected" includes buffers that were skipped because they were dirty, pinned, or busy. If you subtract those values ("dirty buffers inspected" and "buffer is pinned count") from this statistic, it leaves the buffers that could not be reused due to latch contention. A large number would be a good indicator of a too-small buffer cache. There is also a "free buffer requested" section that you can compare to this.

- **Parse count**   The number of times a SQL statement was parsed (total count). You can also check the version count of the SQL section to correlate with this one.

- **Recursive calls**   The number of recursive calls to the database. This type of call occurs for a few reasons—misses in the Dictionary Cache, dynamic storage extension, and when PL/SQL statements are executed. Generally, if the number of recursive calls is more than four per process, you should check the Dictionary Cache hit ratio, and see if there are tables or indexes with a large number of extents. Unless you have PL/SQL, the ratio of recursive calls to user calls should be 10 percent or less.

- **REDO size**   The size in bytes of the amount of REDO information that was written to the redo logs. This information can be used to help size the redo logs. Additional information on REDO sizing is in Chapter 3.

- **Sorts (disk)**   The number of sorts that were unable to be performed in memory and, therefore, required the creation of a TEMP segment in the temporary tablespace. This statistic divided by the sorts (memory) should not be greater than 5 percent. If it is, you should increase the SORT_AREA_SIZE (if used) or PGA_AGGREGATE_TARGET (note that you may need to increase MEMORY_TARGET if you don't set a minimum value for PGA_AGGREGATE_TARGET or you may need to increase MEMORY_TARGET if you increase the PGA_AGGREGATE_TARGET) parameter in the `init.ora` file.

- **Sorts (memory)**   The number of sorts that were performed in memory.

- **Sorts (rows)**   The total number of rows that were sorted.

TIP
The "sorts (disk)" statistic divided by the "sorts (memory)" statistic should not be greater than 1–5 percent. If it is, you should increase the PGA_AGGREGATE_TARGET (or SORT_AREA_SIZE and/or MEMORY_TARGET) parameter in the initialization file (if physical memory is available to do this). Remember that the memory allocated for SORT_AREA_SIZE is a per-user value and PGA_AGGREGATE_TARGET is across all sessions. See Chapter 4 for more information.

- **Table fetch by rowid** Indicates the number of rows that were accessed by using a ROWID. This ROWID came from either an index or a "WHERE ROWID = ..." statement. A high number *usually* indicates a well-tuned application as far as fetching the data goes.

- **Table fetch continued row** The number of rows that were fetched that were chained or migrated.

TIP

If chained rows are indicated, the problem needs to be fixed as soon as possible if performance degradation is evident. Chained rows can cause severe degradation of performance if a large number of rows are chained. See Chapter 3 for tips on eliminating chaining.

- **Table scans (long tables)** A long table is one that is larger than _SMALL_TABLE_THRESHOLD (which is a hidden/undocumented parameter) with no CACHE clause. The default value of _SMALL_TABLE_THRESHOLD is 2 percent of the buffer cache in Oracle 11g and Oracle 10g/9i. _SMALL_TABLE_THRESHOLD is a dangerous parameter to modify without careful benchmarking of the effects. As this affects all tables accessing it, increasing this parameter significantly, if at all, is unwise, as it can cause blocks to age more quickly and reduce your hit ratio. In Oracle, this parameter is the number of db blocks up to which the table is considered small. This threshold is used to determine the cutover point for direct-read operations. Any object that is smaller than the value of _SMALL_TABLE_THRESHOLD will not be worth performing direct reads for and thus will be read through the buffer cache. If the number of table scans per transaction is greater than 0, you may wish to review the application SQL statements and try to increase the use of indexes. Oracle does not want a large table to overrun the buffer cache; that's the reason this parameter ensures that every table larger than 2 percent of the buffer cache is considered a long table.

NOTE

Oracle's way of identifying table scans (long tables) and the related parameter has a different meaning in Oracle 11g (more than 2 percent of the buffer cache), Oracle 10g/9i (also more than 2 percent of the buffer cache), Oracle 8i (more than 20 blocks), and Oracle 7 (more than 5 blocks).

TIP

If full table scans are being performed, serious performance issues may result and data hit ratios will be distorted. These tables need to be identified so the appropriate indexes are created or used. See Chapters 8 and 9 on query tuning for more information.

- **Table scans (short tables)** A short table is one that is less than 2 percent of the buffer cache in 11g. Full table scans on short tables are preferred by Oracle.

Tablespace and File I/O Statistics

The next section of the report provides the I/O statistics. Prior to the Tablespace I/O and File I/O section, there is a section that shows the I/O Stats grouped by function, including the types of reads that are occurring (see the listing):

```
IO Stat by Function - summary  DB/Inst: ORCL/orcl  Snaps: 1-2
->Data Volume values suffixed with   M,G,T,P are in multiples of 1024,
   other values suffixed with       K,M,G,T,P are in multiples of 1000
->ordered by Data Volume (Read+Write) desc
```

| Function | ---------- Read --------- | | | --------- Write -------- | | | --- Wait ---- | |
	Data Volume	Requests /sec	Data Vol/sec	Data Volume	Requests /sec	Data Vol/sec	Count	Avg Tm(ms)
Direct Reads	641M	.8	.8M		.0			0.0
Others	55M	4.4	.1M	72M	1.1	.1M	3888	0.0
LGWR		.1		57M	1.3	.1M	65	0.0
Buffer Cache Re	46M	.1	.1M				68	0.0

If the I/O activity is not properly distributed among your files, you may encounter performance bottlenecks during periods of high activity. As a rule of thumb, you don't want more than 100 I/Os per second per 10,000 RPM disk (even with a RAID array). If the 'Av Rd(ms)' column (Average Reads per millisecond) is higher than 14 ms (given a fair amount of reading is being done), you may want to investigate, since most disks should provide at least this much performance. If this column shows 1,000 ms or more in the 'Av Rd(ms)' column (Average Reads per millisecond) or in the 'Av Buf Wt (ms)' column (Average Buffer Writes per millisecond), you probably have some type of I/O problem, and if it shows ###### (meaning it couldn't fit the value in the size of the field), then you have a serious I/O problem of some kind (this can also be a formatting problem, but anything greater than 1,000 is a problem when a fair number of reads are being done). I have seen I/O issues that are related to other problems, yet show up as an I/O problem. For disks with a lot of memory cached on the disk, the I/O time is often less than 1 ms for a disk where heavy reading is being done. You should use this section of the report to identify such bottlenecks and to measure how effectively you have resolved those problems. If you have the choice between 15K RPM 600G SAS drives and 7.2K RPM 2T SATA disks—*always* choose the SAS drives unless it's for archived information that will almost never be accessed.

Set the DB_FILE_MULTIBLOCK_READ_COUNT parameter in the initialization file (SPFILE or init.ora) to help improve the read time. This parameter controls the number of blocks that can be read in one I/O when a full table scan is being performed. In 11*g*, the default is set to 128, so it should be sufficient. Setting it can reduce the number of I/Os needed to scan a table, thus improving the performance of the full table scan. Unfortunately, the optimizer might do more full table scans as a result of setting DB_FILE_MULTIBLOCK_READ_COUNT (you don't want this behavior), so you may also need to set the OPTIMIZER_INDEX_COST_ADJ to a number, such as 10, to eliminate this problem and drive the use of indexes (be careful with this parameter and see Chapter 4 and Appendix A before setting it). Here is an example listing from this section of the report:

```
Tablespace IO Stats for DB: ORA10  Instance: ora10  Snaps: 1 -2
->ordered by IO's (Reads + Writes) desc
```

```
Tablespace
-----------------------------
                 Av       Av      Av                        Av      Buffer  Av Buf
          Reads  Reads/s  Rd(ms)  Blks/Rd       Writes  Writes/s  Waits  Wt(ms)
-------------- -------  ------  -------  ------------  --------  ----------  ------
TS_ORDERS
       1,108,981     32    12.1      1.0     1,006,453        29     6,445     4.9
TS_ORDER_SUM
         967,108     28    12.5      1.0       675,647        19        51     7.6
TS_ORDER_LINES
       1,389,292     40    10.1      1.0        22,930         1     1,753     3.9
```

Here are descriptions of some of the columns appearing in this output:

Column	Description
TABLESPACE	The name of the tablespace.
READS	The number of physical reads that were performed on the datafile to retrieve data.
AV BLKS/RD	The number of blocks per read that were read from the datafile to satisfy an average read.
WRITES	The number of writes to the data file.

Following the Tablespace I/O section, you'll see a File I/O section, as you can see here:

```
File IO Stats  DB/Inst: ORCL/orcl  Snaps: 1-2
->Mx Rd Bkt: Max bucket time for single block read
->ordered by Tablespace, File

Tablespace                   Filename
----------------------       ------------------------------------------------------
                     Av  Mx                                             Av
              Av     Rd  Rd    Av                        Av    Buffer  BufWt
       Reads  Reads/s (ms) Bkt Blks/Rd       Writes  Writes/s  Waits   (ms)
-------------- -------  ----- --- -------  ------------  --------  ----------  ------
EXAMPLE                      C:\APP\USER\ORADATA\ORCL\EXAMPLE01.DBF
           1       0    0.0        1.0            1         0        0

FLOW_1046531734508653        C:\APP\USER\ORADATA\ORCL\FLOW_1046531734508653.DBF
           1       0    0.0        1.0            1         0        0

FLOW_1064429114609071        C:\APP\USER\ORADATA\ORCL\FLOW_1064429114609071.DBF
           1       0    0.0        1.0            1         0        0

SYSAUX                       C:\APP\USER\ORADATA\ORCL\SYSAUX01.DBF
           3       0    6.7  16    1.0          110         0        0

SYSTEM                       C:\APP\USER\ORADATA\ORCL\SYSTEM01.DBF
           5       0    6.0  16    1.0          219         0        0
```

```
UNDOTBS1                     C:\APP\USER\ORADATA\ORCL\UNDOTBS01.DBF
            1        0   0.0        1.0            84          0          0

USERS                        C:\APP\USER\ORADATA\ORCL\USERS01.DBF
           79        0  10.3      107.0             5          0          0
                             C:\APP\USER\ORADATA\ORCL\USERS02.DBF
           32        0  32.2       82.3             1          0          0
                             C:\APP\USER\ORADATA\ORCL\USERS03.DBF
           79        0  11.6      120.9            11          0          0
                             C:\APP\USER\ORADATA\ORCL\USERS04
          529        1   0.0      127.2         4,935          6          0

 -----------------------------------------------------------------
```

An example of the AWR Report IO Stats is displayed in Figure 14-13. You can also see from this figure that Oracle gives tablespace I/O and file I/O information as well in this section.

Following the tablespace I/O statistics is a file I/O section breakdown—a very granular look at how the I/O is being distributed across the datafiles. If one of the datafiles is getting a majority of the reads and writes, you may be able to improve performance by creating multiple datafiles on separate disks or by striping the datafile across multiple disks. Also, stay away from RAID 5 (Chapter 3 has more on this) or you'll get slower write times. In 11*g*, Oracle allows you to move "hotter" data to the fastest portion of the disk. I show you how to do this in Chapter 5 on Enterprise Manager.

IO Stats

- IOStat by Function summary
- IOStat by Filetype summary
- IOStat by Function/Filetype summary
- Tablespace IO Stats
- File IO Stats

Back to Top

IOStat by Function summary

- 'Data' columns suffixed with M,G,T,P are in multiples of 1024 other columns suffixed with K,M,G,T,P are in multiples of 1000
- ordered by (Data Read + Write) desc

Function Name	Reads: Data	Reqs per sec	Data per sec	Writes: Data	Reqs per sec	Data per sec	Waits: Count	Avg Tm(ms)
Direct Reads	645M	0.78	.415870	0M	0.00	0M	0	
Others	88M	3.64	.056738	81M	0.97	.052225	6276	0.38
DBWR	0M	0.00	0M	79M	3.64	.050936	0	
LGWR	0M	0.03	0M	68M	1.37	.043843	65	3.83
Buffer Cache Reads	53M	0.61	.034172	0M	0.00	0M	943	4.49
Direct Writes	0M	0.00	0M	31M	0.09	.019987	0	
TOTAL:	786M	5.06	.506782	259M	6.06	.166993	7284	0.94

FIGURE 14-13. *The AWR Report—tablespace and file I/O stats*

TIP
*If the number of physical reads is heavier on one physical disk,
balancing the data properly will probably improve performance. See
Chapter 3 for tips on fixing I/O problems with either datafiles or
tablespaces.*

Segment Statistics

One of the new data dictionary views that Oracle provided in Oracle 9i was V$SEGMENT_STATISTICS.
This view quickly became a DBA favorite. Now Oracle 11g takes this approach to the next level
(even beyond what 10g did) with Segment Statistics reports for everything you could ever need.
Here are the sections that the AWR Report now shows in Oracle 11gR2:

- Segments by Logical Reads
- Segments by Physical Reads
- Segments by Physical Read Requests
- Segments by UnOptimized Reads
- Segments by Optimized Reads
- Segments by Direct Physical Reads
- Segments by Physical Writes
- Segments by Physical Write Requests
- Segments by Direct Physical Writes
- Segments by Table Scans
- Segments by DB Block Changes
- Segments by Row Lock Waits
- Segments by ITL Waits
- Segments by Buffer Busy Waits
- Segments by Global Cache Buffer Busy (RAC)
- Segments by CR Blocks Received (RAC)
- Segments by Current Blocks Received (RAC)

Figure 14-14 shows the section of the AWR Report dedicated to Segment Statistics. This is
particularly useful for finding what specific INDEX or DATA segment is causing a bottleneck of
some kind. Finding specific interested transaction list (ITL) waits was also very difficult prior to
Oracle providing this additional detail. Now, in the Segment Statistics section, you can see the
exact number of ITL waits by owner, tablespace name, object name, and subobject name (such
as an index partition subobject name).

Segment Statistics

- Segments by Logical Reads
- Segments by Physical Reads
- Segments by Physical Read Requests
- Segments by UnOptimized Reads
- Segments by Optimized Reads
- Segments by Direct Physical Reads
- Segments by Physical Writes
- Segments by Physical Write Requests
- Segments by Direct Physical Writes
- Segments by Table Scans
- Segments by DB Blocks Changes
- Segments by Row Lock Waits
- Segments by ITL Waits
- Segments by Buffer Busy Waits

Back to Top

Segments by Logical Reads

- Total Logical Reads: 2,123,183
- Captured Segments account for 92.2% of Total

Owner	Tablespace Name	Object Name	Subobject Name	Obj. Type	Logical Reads	%Total
SYS	TEMP	SYS_TEMP_0FD9D6626_B2FCBD		TABLE	908,928	42.81
SYS	SYSTEM	SEG$		TABLE	299,936	14.13

FIGURE 14-14. *The AWR Report Segment Statistics*

TIP
Segment statistics are a great way to pinpoint performance problems to a given table, index, or partition. Oracle 11gR2 contains many segment-level statistics in both the AWR Report and Statspack.

Additional Memory Statistics

Following the I/O statistics, the report lists many memory sections, including a section for sizing the MEMORY_TARGET, a section on all of the dynamic components related to the MEMORY_TARGET, a buffer pool advisory (for sizing the DB_CACHE_SIZE), buffer cache statistics by pool (default, keep, and recycle), instance recovery statistics (the number of REDO blocks), shared pool sizing advisory, and the PGA memory statistics and advisory. I won't be able to cover all of them here (initialization parameter sizing is in Chapter 4), but I show a sample listing of several of these sections next. The MEMORY_TARGET advisor (first listing) shows that by setting this above the current setting (Size Factor = 1; MEMORY_TARGET = 6.56G), I will not get additional benefits given the current load at this time. If the load changes, these values will change as well.

```
Memory Target Advice  DB/Inst: ORCL/orcl  Snaps: 1-2
-> Advice Reset: if this is null, the data shown has been diffed between
   the Begin and End snapshots.  If this is 'Y', the advisor has been
   reset during this interval due to memory resize operations, and
   the data shown is since the reset operation.


                  Memory Size    Est.       Advice
Memory Size (M)   Factor  DB time (s)  Reset
---------------   -----------  ------------  ------
        3,280           .5            64
        4,920           .8            48
        5,740           .9            64
        6,560          1.0            48
        7,380          1.1            48
        8,200          1.3            48
        9,020          1.4            48
        9,840          1.5            48
       10,660          1.6            48
       11,480          1.8            48
       12,300          1.9            48
       13,120          2.0            48
        -------------------------------------------------------------
```

You can easily see, under Memory Dynamic Components (shown next), *exactly* where memory is currently being allocated. Here, you see the SGA_TARGET is 4.272G, the DB_CACHE_SIZE is 2.208G, the PGA_AGGREGATE_TARGET is 2.288G, and the shared pool is just under 1G.

```
Memory Dynamic Components  DB/Inst: ORCL/orcl  Snaps: 1-2
-> Op - memory resize Operation
-> Cache:    D: Default,  K: Keep,  R:  Recycle
->  Mode:  DEF: DEFerred mode,   IMM: IMMediate mode


                    Begin Snap End Snap   Op    Last Op
Cache               Size (M) Size (M)  Count  Type/Mode   Last Op Time
-------------------- ---------- -------- ------- ---------- ---------------
D:buffer cache         2,208                  0 INITIAL
PGA Target             2,288                  0 STATIC
SGA Target             4,272                  0 STATIC
Shared IO Pool           928                  0 STATIC
java pool                 16                  0 STATIC
large pool                32                  0 STATIC
shared pool            1,024                  0 STATIC
streams pool              16                  0 STATIC
        -------------------------------------------------------------
```

The next section is the Buffer Pool Advisor. While much of this information is shown in other sections, the buffer pool statistics section is very detailed in this part of the report. It shows individual buffer pools for the keep and recycle pools, if they are used (Chapter 4 includes more information on using these buffer pools). This section also shows information for the different block sizes if you use multiple block sizes. As with MEMORY_TARGET, I also have an advisor (see the listing) that shows my current setting for the DB_CACHE_SIZE or memory allocated for data buffers (Size Factor = 1; DB_CACHE_SIZE = 2.208G). From this, you can see that I will not get many additional benefits, given the current load at this time, by increasing this value. If the load changes, these values will change as well. The hit ratio (99 percent) is shown in this listing.

```
Buffer Pool Advisory  DB/Inst: ORCL/orcl  End Snap: 2
-> Only rows with estimated physical reads >0 are displayed
-> ordered by Pool, Block Size, Buffers For Estimate


                                  Est
                                  Phys      Estimated                     Est
         Size for  Size   Buffers Read      Phys Reads   Est Phys % dbtime
  P      Est (M)  Factr (thousands) Factr   (thousands)  Read Time  for Rds
  ---    --------  ----- ----------- ------  ------------- ---------- --------
  D         208     .1        26     1.0       17,025        5,091      3.1
  D         416     .2        51     1.0       16,918        4,936      3.0
  D         624     .3        77     1.0       16,893        4,899      3.0
  D         832     .4       102     1.0       16,881        4,882      3.0
  D       1,040     .5       128     1.0       16,861        4,853      3.0
  D       1,248     .6       154     1.0       16,801        4,766      2.9
  D       1,456     .7       179     1.0       16,800        4,764      2.9
  D       1,664     .8       205     1.0       16,798        4,761      2.9
  D       1,872     .8       230     1.0       16,795        4,758      2.9
  D       2,080     .9       256     1.0       16,794        4,755      2.9
  D       2,208    1.0       272     1.0       16,792        4,753      2.9
  D       2,288    1.0       282     1.0       16,791        4,751      2.9
  D       2,496    1.1       307     1.0       16,790        4,750      2.9
  D       2,704    1.2       333     1.0       16,789        4,748      2.9
  D       2,912    1.3       359     1.0       16,788        4,746      2.9
  D       3,120    1.4       384     1.0       16,786        4,743      2.9
  D       3,328    1.5       410     1.0       16,785        4,743      2.9
  D       3,536    1.6       435     1.0       16,784        4,740      2.9
  D       3,744    1.7       461     1.0       16,781        4,737      2.9
  D       3,952    1.8       487     1.0       16,780        4,736      2.9
  D       4,160    1.9       512     1.0       16,777        4,731      2.9
         ------------------------------------------------------------------

Buffer Pool Statistics  DB/Inst: ORCL/orcl  Snaps: 1-2
-> Standard block size Pools  D: default,  K: keep,  R: recycle
-> Default Pools for other block sizes: 2k, 4k, 8k, 16k, 32k
-> Buffers: the number of buffers.  Units of K, M, G are divided by 1000


                                                    Free Writ    Buffer
                Pool     Buffer   Physical  Physical Buffer Comp    Busy
  P   Buffers  Hit%       Gets      Reads    Writes  Waits Wait   Waits
  --- -------  ----  ------------- ---------- --------- ------- ---- ----------
  D     271K    99     850,912      5,920     8,860      0    0         0
         ------------------------------------------------------------------
```

The next couple of sections (not all displayed here) relate to the memory needed for PGA and sorting or the PGA_AGGREGATE_TARGET parameter. There are also sections with shared pool statistics. The PGA_AGGREGATE_TARGET section is listed here (this value is sufficient with 100 percent of the hits being done in memory):

```
PGA Aggr Target Stats  DB/Inst: ORCL/orcl  Snaps: 1-2
-> B: Begin snap   E: End snap (rows identified with B or E contain data
   which is absolute i.e. not diffed over the interval)
-> PGA cache hit % - percentage of W/A (WorkArea) data processed only in-memory
-> Auto PGA Target - actual workarea memory target
-> W/A PGA Used    - amount of memory used for all WorkAreas (manual + auto)
-> %PGA W/A Mem    - percentage of PGA memory allocated to WorkAreas
-> %Auto W/A Mem   - percentage of WorkArea memory controlled by Auto Mem Mgmt
-> %Man W/A Mem    - percentage of WorkArea memory under Manual control


PGA Cache Hit % W/A MB Processed Extra W/A MB Read/Written
--------------- ---------------- -------------------------
          100.0              178                         0
```

The instance recovery section is the same in 11g as it was in 10g:

```
Instance Recovery Stats for DB: ORA10  Instance: ora10  Snaps: 1 -2
-> B: Begin snapshot, E: End snapshot
    Targt Estd                                Log File  Log Ckpt  Log Ckpt
    MTTR  MTTR  Recovery   Actual    Target      Size   Timeout   Interval
    (s)   (s)   Estd IO's  Redo Blks Redo Blks Redo Blks Redo Blks Redo Blks
  - ----- ----- ---------- --------- --------- --------- --------- ---------
  B    33    18      5898       706     13546    184320     13546 ##########
  E    33    24      5898       717     14524    184320     14524 ##########
       --------------------------------------------------------------
```

The Shared Pool Advisory as well as the SGA_TARGET Advisory follow the Latch section (I've moved them here to be with the other SGA components). Both of these are set sufficiently at the current load (a size factor greater than 1.0 yields no additional savings: SHARED_POOL_SIZE = 1G and SGA_TARGET = 4.272G). You may even consider decreasing them if this load is representative of your system during normal loads.

```
Shared Pool Advisory  DB/Inst: ORCL/orcl  End Snap: 2
-> SP: Shared Pool    Est LC: Estimated Library Cache   Factr: Factor
-> Note there is often a 1:Many correlation between a single logical object
   in the Library Cache, and the physical number of memory objects associated
   with it.  Therefore comparing the number of Lib Cache objects (e.g. in
   v$librarycache), with the number of Lib Cache Memory Objects is invalid

                                          Est LC Est LC  Est LC Est LC
     Shared     SP  Est LC                  Time   Time    Load   Load        Est LC
       Pool   Size    Size         Est LC  Saved  Saved    Time   Time          Mem
   Size (M) Factr     (M)         Mem Obj    (s)  Factr     (s)  Factr     Obj Hits
   --------- ----- -------- ------------- ------- ------ ------- ------ -----------
         352    .3       77         5,659 23,719    1.0     627    1.8   2,624,925
         464    .5      189        10,616 23,841    1.0     505    1.4   3,846,832
         576    .6      301        14,711 23,957    1.0     389    1.1   3,861,511
```

```
     688    .7    413    19,546  23,989   1.0    357   1.0   3,866,586
     800    .8    526    24,236  23,994   1.0    352   1.0   3,867,329
     912    .9    625    27,428  23,995   1.0    351   1.0   3,867,486
   1,024   1.0    654    28,240  23,995   1.0    351   1.0   3,867,530
   1,136   1.1    654    28,240  23,995   1.0    351   1.0   3,867,530
   1,248   1.2    654    28,240  23,995   1.0    351   1.0   3,867,530
   1,360   1.3    654    28,240  23,995   1.0    351   1.0   3,867,530
   1,472   1.4    654    28,240  23,995   1.0    351   1.0   3,867,530
   1,584   1.5    654    28,240  23,995   1.0    351   1.0   3,867,530
   1,696   1.7    654    28,240  23,995   1.0    351   1.0   3,867,530
   1,808   1.8    654    28,240  23,995   1.0    351   1.0   3,867,530
   1,920   1.9    654    28,240  23,995   1.0    351   1.0   3,867,530
   2,032   2.0    654    28,240  23,995   1.0    351   1.0   3,867,530
   2,144   2.1    654    28,240  23,995   1.0    351   1.0   3,867,530
          -------------------------------------------------------------

SGA Target Advisory  DB/Inst: ORCL/orcl  End Snap: 2

SGA Target SGA Size   Est DB      Est DB     Est Physical
  Size (M)  Factor  Time (s) Time Factor         Reads
---------- -------- -------- ----------- --------------
   1,602      .4  162,913        1.0      17,025,770
   2,136      .5  162,491        1.0      16,919,978
   2,670      .6  162,426        1.0      16,883,035
   3,204      .8  162,312        1.0      16,802,431
   3,738      .9  162,296        1.0      16,797,394
   4,272     1.0  162,296        1.0      16,792,356
   4,806     1.1  162,296        1.0      16,788,998
   5,340     1.3  162,280        1.0      16,785,639
   5,874     1.4  162,280        1.0      16,778,922
   6,408     1.5  162,280        1.0      16,778,922
   6,942     1.6  162,280        1.0      16,778,922
   7,476     1.8  162,280        1.0      16,778,922
   8,010     1.9  162,280        1.0      16,778,922
   8,544     2.0  162,280        1.0      16,778,922
          -------------------------------------------------------------
```

The next section is a great breakdown of the SGA areas that you are using during this snapshot interval. You can also see this real time by executing a "SHO SGA" command in SQL*Plus as a DBA or SYSDBA user.

```
SGA Memory Summary  DB/Inst: ORCL/orcl  Snaps: 1-2

                                                   End Size (Bytes)
SGA regions                     Begin Size (Bytes)   (if different)
----------------------------- -------------------- --------------------
Database Buffers                     2,315,255,808
Fixed Size                               2,188,768
Redo Buffers                            17,420,288
Variable Size                        4,513,073,696
                              -------------------- --------------------
sum                                  6,847,938,560
                              -------------------------------------------------------------
```

Advisory Statistics

- Instance Recovery Stats
- MTTR Advisory
- Buffer Pool Advisory
- PGA Aggr Summary
- PGA Aggr Target Stats
- PGA Aggr Target Histogram
- PGA Memory Advisory
- Shared Pool Advisory
- SGA Target Advisory
- Streams Pool Advisory
- Java Pool Advisory

Back to Top

Instance Recovery Stats

- B: Begin Snapshot, E: End Snapshot

	Targt MTTR (s)	Estd MTTR (s)	Recovery Estd IOs	Actual RedoBlks	Target RedoBlks	Log Sz RedoBlks	Log Ckpt Timeout RedoBlks	Log Ckpt Interval RedoBlks	Opt Log Sz(M)	Estd RAC Avail Time
B	0	12	339	1656	18569	165888	18569			
E	0	16	956	105516	140358	165888	140358			

Back to Advisory Statistics

FIGURE 14-15. *The AWR Report SGA Target Advisory*

The AWR Report shows statistics on the following advisories (see the SGA Target Advisory in Figure 14-15):

- Instance Recovery Stats
- MTTR Advisory
- Buffer Pool Advisory
- PGA Aggr Summary
- PGA Aggr Target Stats
- PGA Aggr Target Histogram
- PGA Memory Advisory
- Shared Pool Advisory
- SGA Target Advisory
- Streams Pool Advisory
- Java Pool Advisory

TIP
In Oracle 11g, multiple data block sizes are allowed. The AWR Report and/or Statspack shows statistics for each of these block sizes individually. Many advisories are available to help you size the SGA that both the AWR Report (see Figure 14-15) and Enterprise Manager (graphically, see Chapter 5) suggest. These suggestions should be tested first, however, and are not always the best choice. As Robert Freeman would say, "Your mileage may vary."

UNDO Statistics

The next section provides UNDO segment statistics. The first part of this section shows the UNDO tablespace and the number of transactions and UNDO blocks for the entire tablespace. Next, it gives information about how many UNDO blocks are utilized and the number of transactions that have occurred for a given segment (UNDOSTAT ROW). The AWR Report in Oracle 11g provides a summary and UNDO segment stats that were not available in previous versions. This new output is shown in Figure 14-16.

While I have eliminated the ROLLSTAT information from this version of the book (since most people now use AUTO UNDO), this information can still be reported in Statspack. By using the configuration file, `sprepcon.sql`, you can modify the DISPLAY_ROLLSTAT parameter.

Latch and Mutex Statistics

Latches are low-level queuing mechanisms (the accurate term is *mutual exclusion mechanisms*) used to protect shared memory structures in the SGA (memory). Latches are like locks on memory that are very quickly gotten and released, consuming roughly 32 bytes. Latches are used

Undo Statistics

- Undo Segment Summary
- Undo Segment Stats

Back to Top

Undo Segment Summary

- Min/Max TR (mins) - Min and Max Tuned Retention (minutes)
- STO - Snapshot Too Old count, OOS - Out of Space count
- Undo segment block stats:
- uS - unexpired Stolen, uR - unexpired Released, uU - unexpired reUsed
- eS - expired Stolen, eR - expired Released, eU - expired reUsed

Undo TS#	Num Undo Blocks (K)	Number of Transactions	Max Qry Len (s)	Max Tx Concurcy	Min/Max TR (mins)	STO/ OOS	uS/uR/uU/ eS/eR/eU
2	1.25	3,037	1,216	4	15/34.3	0/0	0/0/0/0/0/0

Back to Undo Statistics
Back to Top

Undo Segment Stats

- Most recent 35 Undostat rows, ordered by Time desc

End Time	Num Undo Blocks	Number of Transactions	Max Qry Len (s)	Max Tx Concy	Tun Ret (mins)	STO/ OOS	uS/uR/uU/ eS/eR/eU
06-May 13:49	508	847	1,216	3	34	0/0	0/0/0/0/0/0
06-May 13:39	544	1,753	608	4	24	0/0	0/0/0/0/0/0

FIGURE 14-16. *The AWR Report Undo Statistics*

to prevent concurrent access to a shared memory structure. If the latch is not available, then a latch free miss is recorded. In 11*g*, the *library cache pin* (protects cursors/SQL) and *library cache latch* (protects the Library Cache) are both replaced by *mutexes* (program objects that negotiate mutual exclusion among threads). Most latch and mutex problems are related to *not* using bind variables (library cache mutex waits and shared pool latch waits), redo generation issues (redo allocation latch waits), buffer cache contention issues (cache buffers lru chain waits), and hot blocks in the buffer cache (cache buffers chain waits). There are also latch waits related to bugs, so check My Oracle Support (MetaLink) as well. When latch miss ratios are greater than 0.5 percent, you should investigate the issue. In Oracle 11gR2, the Cache Buffers Chains (CBC) latch can be shared and is still heavily used.

Two types of latches are available: *willing to wait* latches (one example is a shared pool latch) and *not willing to wait* latches (an example is a redo copy latch). A process that is willing to wait will try to acquire a latch. If none are available, it spins and then requests the latch again. It continues to do this up to the _SPIN_COUNT initialization parameter (note that spinning costs CPU). If it can't get a latch after spinning up to the _SPIN_COUNT, it goes to sleep, to not do anything for a while, and then wakes up after one centisecond (one hundredth of a second). It does this twice. The process then starts this whole process again, spinning up to the _SPIN_COUNT and then sleeping for twice as long (two centiseconds). After doing this again, it doubles again. So the pattern is 1, 1, 2, 2, 4, 4, and so on. It repeats this until it gets the latch. Every time the latch sleeps, the process creates a latch sleep wait.

Some latches are "not willing to wait." A latch of this type does not wait for the latch to become available. It immediately times out and tries to obtain the latch again. A redo copy latch wait is an example of a "not willing to wait" latch. A "not willing to wait" latch generates information for the IMMEDIATE_GETS and the IMMEDIATE_MISSES columns of the V$LATCH view and also in the Statspack Report. The hit ratio for these latches should approach 99 percent, and the misses should never fall below 1 percent.

By viewing the Latch Activity section of Statspack or querying the V$LATCH view, you can see how many processes had to wait (a latch miss) or sleep (a latch sleep) and the number of times they had to sleep. If you see ##### in any field, it usually means bad news, as the value exceeds the length of the field. V$LATCHHOLDER, V$LATCHNAME, and V$LATCH_CHILDREN are also helpful in investigating latch issues. Here is a partial listing of the latch activity section; there are seven sections related to latches (latch activity, latch sleep, latch miss, mutex sleep summary, parent latch statistics, and child latch statistics) for the AWR Report and Statspack Report (this Statspack Report has no major problems as I am not missing more than 1 percent—partial display latches only):

```
Latch Activity  DB/Inst: ORCL/orcl  Snaps: I-2
->"Get Requests", "Pct Get Miss" and "Avg Slps/Miss" are statistics for
   willing-to-wait latch get requests
->"NoWait Requests", "Pct NoWait Miss" are for no-wait latch get requests
->"Pct Misses" for both should be very close to 0.0


                                   Pct   Avg   Wait                    Pct
                             Get   Get   Slps  Time    NoWait NoWait
Latch                    Requests  Miss  /Miss  (s)    Requests  Miss
----------------------- ---------- ----- ----- ------ --------- ------
AQ deq hash table latch          1  0.0            0          0
AQ dequeue txn counter l       706  0.0            0          0
ASM db client latch            543  0.0            0          0
```

ASM map operation hash t	1	0.0		0	0	
cache buffer handles	968,992	0.0	0.0		0	
cache buffers chains	761,708,539	0.0	0.4	21,519,841		0.0
cache buffers lru chain	8,111,269	0.1	0.8	19,834,466		0.1
enqueue hash chains	25,152	0.0		0	1	0.0
enqueues	16,151	0.0		0	0	
lob segment dispenser la	1	0.0		0	0	
lob segment hash table l	5	0.0		0	0	
lob segment query latch	1	0.0		0	0	
redo allocation	12,446,986	0.2	0.0		0	
redo copy	320	0.0		10,335,430		0.1
shared pool	22,339	0.1	0.0	0	0	
shared pool sim alloc	8	0.0		0	0	
shared pool simulator	888	0.0		0	0	

```
Latch Miss Sources for DB:
-> only latches with sleeps are shown
-> ordered by name, sleeps desc
```

Latch Name	Where	NoWait Misses	Sleeps	Waiter Sleeps
cache buffers chains	kcbgtcr: kslbegin	0	63,446	47,535
cache buffers chains	kcbgcur: kslbegin	0	9,820	7,603
cache buffers lru chain	kcbzgb: multiple sets nowa	0	4,859	0
enqueues	ksqdel	0	106,769	12,576
redo allocation	kcrfwr: redo allocation	0	942	1,032
redo allocation	kcrfwi: before write	0	191	53
redo allocation	kcrfwi: more space	0	2	39

Figures 14-17 and 14-18 show similar statistics from the AWR Report, including the new Mutex Sleep Summary in Figure 14-18.

A mutex (which replaces many types of library cache latches) is used to eliminate the possibility of two processes simultaneously using a common resource (while one or both are trying to change it); when one session is changing the resource, the second can't view it or change it, and when one session is viewing the resource, the second can't change it.

Oracle moved from latches to mutexes because a mutex is lighter weight and provides more granular concurrency than latches. A mutex requires less memory space and fewer instructions. Mutexes take advantage of CPU architecture that has "compare and swap" instructions (and similar types of benefits). Without going into a lot of detail, Oracle uses mutexes (*mutual exclusion*) instead of library cache latches and library cache pin latches to protect objects. With a mutex, if I have the resource and you can't get it after trying a specified number of times (spins), you sleep and try again a very short time later. In 10g, Oracle also used mutexes for pins, but you could use the undocumented parameter _KKS_USE_MUTEX_PIN=FALSE to override it (this parameter is no longer available in 11g). Figure 14-18 shows how the AWR Report displays a summary of the mutex sleeps that are occurring.

When you receive wait events on *cursor: Pin S wait on X,* you are probably waiting on a hard parse; the session needs a mutex in share mode on a resource and someone has it in exclusive mode. A *pin* is when a session wants to reexecute a statement that's in the Library Cache. Waits for pins generally happen with high rates of SQL execution, whereas waiting for a resource held in exclusive mode (X) usually is related to hard parsing. When a session wants a mutex in S (share mode) on a cursor (SQL statement), but another session is holding that

Latch Activity

- "Get Requests", "Pct Get Miss" and "Avg Slps/Miss" are statistics for willing-to-wait latch get requests
- "NoWait Requests", "Pct NoWait Miss" are for no-wait latch get requests
- "Pct Misses" for both should be very close to 0.0

Latch Name	Get Requests	Pct Get Miss	Avg Slps /Miss	Wait Time (s)	NoWait Requests	Pct NoWait Miss
AQ deq hash table latch	30	0.00		0	0	
AQ deq log cmt cbk chunk latch	54	0.00		0	0	
AQ deq log statistics latch	1	0.00		0	0	
AQ dequeue txn counter latch	1,395	0.00		0	0	
AQ ht cmt cbk chunk latch	2	0.00		0	0	
ASM db client latch	1,039	0.00		0	0	
ASM map operation hash table	3	0.00		0	0	
ASM network state latch	27	0.00		0	0	
AWR Alerted Metric Element list	11,306	0.00		0	0	
Change Notification Hash table latch	519	0.00		0	0	
Consistent RBA	2,061	0.00		0	0	

FIGURE 14-17. *The AWR Report latch activity*

mutex in X (exclusive) mode, the session waiting for the mutex in S mode will sleep. After asking enough times and not getting the latch, the session sleeps for a short time and then it begins trying again to get the mutex. A mutex is also not FIFO (First In, First Out); order is not guaranteed. All of this is for efficiency.

Library cache latches have also been replaced with mutexes. In fact, all library cache latches are replaced with mutexes other than the library cache load lock. The following queries help you find information related to mutex wait events when you get them. [This is an example of a cursor: pin S wait on X WAITEVENT; check My Oracle Support (MetaLink) for your exact wait and related values. Specific wait events are covered later in this section.]

Mutex Sleep Summary

- ordered by number of sleeps desc

Mutex Type	Location	Sleeps	Wait Time (ms)
Library Cache	kglget2 2	141	2
Cursor Pin	kkslce [KKSCHLPIN2]	7	-2
Library Cache	kgllkdl1 85	2	1

Back to Latch Statistics

FIGURE 14-18. *The AWR Report Mutex Sleep Summary*

P1 is the idn, which is the HASH_VALUE of the SQL statement I am waiting on. I can query V$SQL or V$SQLAREA to get the actual SQL_TEXT:

```
select  sql_text
from    v$sqlarea
where   hash_value=&&P1;
```

P2 is the mutex value, which is the session id (higher bits) and reference count (which is 0 if I am sleeping/waiting for an X mode holder):

```
select  decode(trunc(&&P2/4294967296), 0, trunc(&&P2/65536),
        trunc(&&P2/4294967296)) SID_HOLDING_THE_MUTEX
from    dual;
```

In 11*g*, I can also go to V$SESSION to see the blocker:

```
select  action, blocking_session, blocking_session_status, sql_id
from    v$session
where   sid = &SID_HOLDING_THE_MUTEX;     (get this from query above)
```

P3 is the location in the code where the wait is occurring. Knowing this location can be very helpful when Oracle Support is helping you with an issue. The library cache: mutex X WAITEVENT has the same values for P1, P2, and P3 according to Oracle's documentation. You can also investigate the V$MUTEX_SLEEP and V$MUTEX_SLEEP_HISTORY views for more information. You will generally find that the mutex type is almost always a library cache mutex or cursor pin mutex when querying these views. Cursor parent and cursor stat mutexes also show up in these views. See the following sample queries showing mutex sleeps.

```
select  mutex_type, count(*), sum(sleeps)
from    v$mutex_sleep
group   by mutex_type;
```

MUTEX_TYPE	COUNT(*)	SUM(SLEEPS)
Library Cache	8	3891
Cursor Pin	1	122

```
select  mutex_type, count(*), sum(sleeps)
from    v$mutex_sleep_history
group   by mutex_type;
```

MUTEX_TYPE	COUNT(*)	SUM(SLEEPS)
Library Cache	18	3891
Cursor Pin	25	117

One thing to remember about sleeping processes: These processes may also be holding other latches/mutexes that will not be released until the process is finished with them. This can cause even more processes to sleep while waiting for those latches. So you can see how important it is to reduce contention as much as possible. The following table explains the columns in this part of the report:

Column	Description
LATCH NAME	The name of the latch.
GETS	The number of times a "willing to wait" request for a latch was requested and it was available.
MISSES	The number of times a "willing to wait" request for a latch was initially requested but was not available.
SLEEPS	The number of times a "willing to wait request" for a latch failed until the spin count was exceeded and the process went to sleep. The number of sleeps may be greater than the misses. Processes may sleep multiple times before obtaining the latch.
NOWAIT MISSES	The number of times an immediate (not willing to wait) request for a latch was unsuccessful.

The following are some latches and mutexes to look for and remember:

Latch Free   When *latch free* is high in the wait events section of the report, then problems need to be investigated in the latch section of the report. This section helps you look for which latches are problematic. The problem could be a sleeping latch (couldn't get the latch and sleeping until the next try) or a spinning latch (waiting and retrying based on spin count).

Library Cache Mutex, Cursor Pin Mutex, and Shared Pool Latch   The Library Cache is a hash table you access through an array of hash buckets (similar to the buffer cache). The memory for the Library Cache comes from the shared pool (the Dictionary Cache used for Oracle internal objects is also part of the shared pool). The *library cache mutex* serializes access to objects in the Library Cache. Every time a SQL or PL/SQL procedure, package, function, or trigger is executed, this library cache mutex is used to search the shared pool for the exact statement so it can be reused. A single shared pool latch protected the allocation of memory in the Library Cache in Oracle 8*i*; as of Oracle 9*i*, seven child latches were available for this.

Contention for the shared pool latch, cursor pin mutex, or library cache mutex primarily occurs when the shared pool is too small or when statements are not reused. Statements are not generally reused when bind variables are not used. Common but not exact SQL can flood the shared pool with statements. Increasing the size of the shared pool, at times, only makes the problem worse. You can also set the value of the initialization parameter CURSOR_SHARING=FORCE (or CURSOR_SHARING=SIMILAR) to help fix this issue and to reduce problems when bind variables are not used. CURSOR_SHARING=FORCE (recommended) substitutes bind variables for literals. CURSOR_SHARING=SIMILAR (will be deprecated in the future) substitutes bind variables for literals if the execution plan is guaranteed to be the same. If you are not reusing SQL, you may see quite a few cursor: pin S wait on X wait events, in which waiting on a hard parse, a session wants a mutex in S (share) mode on a cursor (SQL statement), but another session is holding that mutex in X (exclusive) mode. You'll also see the reverse of this: cursor: pin X wait on S. The shared pool latch and library cache mutex issues also occur when space is needed in the Library Cache when the shared pool is too small for the number of SQL statements that need to be processed. A *hard* parse occurs when a new SQL statement is issued that does not exist in the shared pool currently because it has to be parsed. Oracle has to allocate memory for the statement from the shared pool, as well as check the statement syntactically and semantically. A hard parse is very expensive in terms of both CPU used and the number of mutexes that need to be used. A *soft* parse occurs when a session issues a SQL statement that is already in the shared pool, *and* it can use an existing version of that statement. As far as the application is concerned, it has asked to parse the statement. While space is being freed up to load a SQL or PL/SQL statement, the shared pool latch (held for allocate and free) is being held exclusively and other users must wait. You can help to reduce contention by increasing the shared pool or by pinning large SQL and PL/SQL statements in memory using the DBMS_SHARED_POOL.KEEP procedures to avoid reloads. Pinning helps reduce many of the mutex and latch waits and ORA-4031 issues as well.

You can increase the number of the Library Cache hash table bucket count by setting _KGL_BUCKET_COUNT (see Appendix A for more information on the undocumented initialization parameters); note that 9 (the default) puts this at ((2 to the 9th power)*256)–1 = 131071), which should be more than enough for most systems. The _KGL_LATCH_COUNT parameter (which is set to 0) is still in 11*g*. Remember that you should never set the underscore parameters without direction from Oracle Support. In 11*g*, *each* Library Cache bucket (131,071) is protected by a mutex!

Note that a count of X$KSMSP shows how many shared pool pieces there are; each row in the table represents a piece of memory in the shared pool. Columns to note are KSMCHCOM (describes the piece of memory), KSMCHPTR (the physical address of the piece of memory), KSMCHSIZ (piece size), and KSMCHCLS (the state/class of the piece of memory). Useful values of KSMCHCLS include the following:

- **recr**   A re-creatable piece currently in use that can be a candidate for flushing when the shared pool is low in available memory.

- **freeabl**   A freeable piece of memory that is currently in use and not a candidate for flushing but can be freed.

- **free**   A free unallocated piece of memory.

- **perm**   A permanently allocated piece of memory that can't be freed without deallocating the entire heap.

The shared pool architecture is similar to the buffer cache in that there are a fixed number of hash buckets (that grow to the next level as needed) protected by a fixed number of library cache mutexes (unless changed, as noted earlier). The number of buckets and latches are often (but not always) prime to avoid hashing anomalies. At startup, the database allocates 509 hash buckets and a library cache mutex for each bucket rounded up to the nearest prime number. As the number of objects in the Library Cache increases, Oracle increases the number of hash buckets in the following order: 509, 1021, 2039, 4093, 8191, 16381, 32749, 65521, 131071, and 4292967293. You can set the number of hash buckets by setting _KGL_BUCKET_COUNT as described earlier. When I installed 11*g*, the default value was 9, which gave me a Library Cache hash table bucket count of 131,071, and a library cache mutex count of 131,071 (many more than in the past; this should reduce a lot of contention). A single hash bucket can contain multiple SQL statements and potentially long hash chains, which explains why you can see long library cache mutex hold times even when no space allocation is needed and no LRU list search is involved.

Also note that a SQL hash value is not the only value used in determining which hash bucket is used; the initial tree starts with object handles, which include name, namespace (CURSOR is the main namespace; others include trigger and cluster), lock owner, lock waiter, pin owner, pin waiter, and other pre-SQL items. The object handle then points to the next level of the tree, the data heap itself (where the statement itself is for a cursor), which includes the type of heap, name (for example, SCOTT.EMP), flags (things like wrapped, valid), tables (for example, privilege, dependencies), and data blocks (everything else—the SQL text). This means that you can have hundreds of identical SQL statements all referenced by different users, and they will be distributed fairly evenly across the hash buckets with no super-long hash chains full of identical SQL, but you will need a larger shared pool. If the statement is *not* in the Library Cache, the library load lock latch (this is still a latch, even in 11g, and the only library cache latch that I saw still in 11g) is used to load it (the library cache mutex and shared pool latch are also needed in this process).

If the preceding paragraphs are complex or confusing, just focus on this paragraph. The main key to limiting latch and mutex issues on the library cache mutex or shared pool latch is to use bind variables, to use cursor sharing, to parse things once and execute them many times, to use SESSION_CACHED_CURSORS to move the cursors from the shared pool to the PGA, and, if you are sharing cursors and using bind variables, to increase the shared pool (although if you are not sharing statements, reducing it may help). Lastly, try not to do any DDL (ALTER, GRANT, REVOKE…) that would cause things to be invalidated and/or reloaded.

NOTE
I've seen more 5–10G+ shared pools in Oracle 11g than ever before.

Redo Copy Latch The *redo copy* latch is used to copy REDO records from the PGA into the redo log buffer. The number of redo copy latches has a default of 2*CPU_COUNT, but you can set this using the _LOG_SIMULTANEOUS_COPIES initialization parameter (the default was 16 copy latches on my system). Increasing this parameter may help to reduce contention for the redo copy latch.

Redo Allocation Latch The *redo allocation latch* allocates the space in the redo log buffer. You can reduce contention by increasing the size of the log buffer (LOG_BUFFER) or by using the NOLOGGING feature, which reduces the load on the redo log buffer. You should also try to avoid unnecessary commits.

Row Cache Objects The *row cache objects* latch contention usually means that contention is present in the data dictionary. This contention may also be a symptom of excessive parsing of SQL statements that depend on public synonyms. Increasing the shared pool usually solves this latch problem. You usually increase the shared pool for a library cache mutex problem well before this one is a problem. Also, according to My Oracle Support (MetaLink Note 166474.1), "Use Locally Managed tablespaces for your application objects, especially indexes. This will decrease Row Cache locks in a surprising fashion and consequently avoid common hanging problems."

Cache Buffers Chains (CBC) The *cache buffers chains (CBC)* latch is needed to scan the SGA buffer cache for database cache buffers. In Oracle 11g, the CBC can be shared, eliminating much of the contention. Tuning the code to use fewer buffers (and hence fewer CBCs) is the best solution to eliminating problems with this latch. Also, reducing the popularity of the block reduces the length of the hash chain (as discussed in the next item).

CBC latches are used when searching for, adding, or removing a buffer from the buffer cache. The buffer hash table, X$BH, holds headers (on a hash chain protected by a CBC latch) that point to DB_BLOCK_BUFFERS (data block buffers) in memory. Buffers are "hashed to a chain," and the _DB_BLOCK_HASH_BUCKETS parameter defines the number of chains (buckets) to which a buffer will hash. The more buckets (chains) present, the smaller the "chain" length will be with buffers hashed to the same chain (as long as the number is prime). The CBC latches are used to protect a buffer list in the buffer cache. If _DB_BLOCK_HASH_BUCKETS was not set to a prime number in the past, you probably had many buffers hashed to one chain and none hashed to others (causing hot blocks to tie up other blocks on the chain) because of hashing anomalies.

In 11*g*, my _DB_BLOCK_HASH_BUCKETS was set to a default of exactly 1M (1,048,576 = 1024×1024), which was about 4×the number of _DB_BLOCK_BUFFERS (set by Oracle behind the scenes based on the DB_CACHE_SIZE). Contention on this latch could indicate a "hot block" or bad setting for _DB_BLOCK_HASH_BUCKETS prior to 9*i*. Prior to version 8*i*, Oracle made this the prime number higher than DB_BLOCK_BUFFERS/4, which worked pretty well, although multiple blocks still got hashed to the same chain. In 8*i*, Oracle made this DB_BLOCK_BUFFERS*2, but they forgot to make it prime (which, because it is a hashed value, caused many blocks to be hashed to the same chain); *many* users experienced severe problems with this latch (you can set _DB_BLOCK_HASH_BUCKETS = next prime(DB_BLOCK_BUFFERS*2) to solve this issue in prior versions). In 9*i* and continuing through 10*g* and 11*g,* Oracle sets it to a value reducing this contention, and there are enough "hash latches," as people often call them. Your mileage may vary, so I continue to leave this section in the book. I also leave very important notes about other versions since most DBAs that I know still run multiple versions of the Oracle database. You will access *many* hash latches (latches used to scan the hash chain) because you need one every time you access a block, but you *should not* have a miss ratio of over 1–2 percent on this latch. In 11*g*, these hash latches (CBC latches) are shared, and the hash chain can be scanned in both directions.

CR Versions for a Given Block   Only one block is CURRENT, and no more than six other CR versions of the block are allowed (as of V9). All of them are located on the same doubly linked (can move both ways) hash chain. In 11*g*, you *can* see more than six versions of a block in memory for high volumes of SELECTs to a given block. They are in multiple states, but only six are in a state=3 (CR), and only one is state=1 (CURRENT). The number of CR blocks is limited to six as any DML activity clears or as more DML tries to be performed in a given block (more on IMUs later in "Tuning and Viewing at the Block Level"). For DML, you need the CURRENT version (of which there is only *one* current version of any given block), and for a read query, you can use the CURRENT version if it is not being used, and/or you can build a CONSISTENT READ (CR) version by applying any UNDO needed to the CURRENT version of a changed block after cloning it. This process of cloning a block to build a CR version may include: reading the ITL, mapping to the UNDO HEADER (the ITL also maps directly to the UNDO BLOCK), and applying the UNDO to get the correct CR version that you need, which happens when IMU is not used. When IMU is used, everything happens at the block level in memory until a commit or rollback. When you have multiple versions of a block (one CURRENT and a few CR versions), the hash chain gets longer, and the CBC latch gets held longer as it scans the hash chain. This is why Oracle now limits the number of clones (CR versions) of a block (limits the chain length). Although you can change this by setting _DB_BLOCK_MAX_CR_DBA, which is the maximum allowed number of CR buffers for a given DBA (data block address), it's a setting that performs well out of the box.

Hot Blocks   Blocks often accessed in the buffer cache cause "cache buffers chains" latch issues, or *hot blocks.* Hot blocks may also be a symptom of poorly tuned SQL statements. A hot record creates a hot block that can cause issues for other records inside that block as well as any block "hashed" to the same chain. To find the hot block, query V$LATCH_CHILDREN for the address and join it to V$BH to identify the blocks protected by this latch (doing this shows all blocks affected by the hot block). You can identify the object by querying the DBA_EXTENTS view according to the file# and DBABLK found in V$BH. Using a reverse-key index, if the hot block is on an index, moves sequential records to other blocks so they are not locked up by the hot block in the chain. If the hot block is the index root block, a reverse-key index won't help.

Cache Buffers LRU Chain   The *cache buffers lru chain* latch is used to scan the least recently used (LRU) chain containing all of the blocks in the buffer cache. A small buffer cache, excessive buffer cache throughput, many cache-based sorts, and the DBWR not keeping up with the workload are all culprits that can cause this issue. Try to fix the queries that are causing the excessive logical reads, and/or use multiple buffer pools.

Some of the most common latch problems and potential solutions are described in the following table:

Latch Problem	Potential Fix
Library Cache	Use bind variables; adjust the SHARED_POOL_SIZE.
IShared pool	Use bind variables; adjust the SHARED_POOL_SIZE.
REDO allocation	Minimize REDO generation and avoid unnecessary commits.
REDO copy	Increase the _LOG_SIMULTANEOUS_COPIES.
Row cache objects	Increase the shared pool size.
Cache buffers chain	Increase _DB_BLOCK_HASH_BUCKETS or make it prime.
Cache buffers lru chain	Use multiple buffer pools or fix queries causing excessive reads.

In Oracle9i (for people with multiple versions of Oracle to manage), you could configure LRU latches so each buffer pool has *n* CPUs worth of latches. For example, if the system has eight CPUs, you should set

```
buffer_pool_keep = buffers:XXXX, lru_latches=8
buffer_pool_recycle = buffers:YYYY, lru_latches=8
```

Here, *XXXX* and *YYYY* are the desired number of buffers in the keep and recycle pools, respectively. There is really no reason to have more LRU latches than the number of processes that may be concurrently executing.

In 11g, the parameters are now DB_KEEP_CACHE_SIZE and DB_RECYCLE_CACHE_SIZE, and both accept only the size in bytes (you cannot specify LRU_LATCHES):

```
db_keep_cache_size= 4G (you can also use K or M, and the default is 0)
db_recycle_cache_size=1G (you can also use K or M, and the default is 0)
```

Some latch problems have often been bug related in the past, so make sure you check My Oracle Support (MetaLink) for issues related to latches. Any of the latches that have a hit ratio less than 99 percent should be investigated. Some of the more common latches on the problem list were detailed in this chapter and include the cache buffers chains, REDO copy, library cache mutex, and the cache buffers lru chain.

TIP
Latches are like locks on pieces of memory (or memory buffers). If the latch hit ratio is less than 99 percent, you have a serious problem because not even the lock to get memory can be gotten.

Tuning and Viewing at the Block Level (Advanced)

Infrequently, when you have a hot block or some other block-level issue, you may need to find the exact location of the block for a given object and the number of versions (as was discussed in the preceding section). Here, I briefly discuss some of the block-level Oracle details.

CAUTION
This section should not be used by beginners.

An internal table called the buffer hash table (X$BH) holds block headers. Blocks are linked to a hash chain that is protected by a CBC latch (cache buffers chains latch). This links to the actual address located in memory (the memory set up with DB_CACHE_SIZE, SGA_TARGET, or MEMORY_TARGET, if used, which is the cache used for data). For a given block in Oracle, only one version of a block is CURRENT, and there are no more than five other CR versions of the block (as of V9). So only six versions of a given block (maximum) are in memory at a time. Later in this section, I tell you how to control this with an undocumented parameter. Oracle recommends that you not use the undocumented parameters unless you are directed by Oracle Support or your database may not be supported.

When you perform a DML (Data Manipulation Language) transaction, which is an INSERT, UPDATE, or DELETE, you always need the CURRENT version of a block. Oracle has something in Oracle 11g called *in-memory undo (IMU)*, which can give you some hard-to-understand results when you are viewing information at the block level (whether it's dirty or not). IMU was new as of 10g; what it means is that the UNDO records and REDO records for some transactions are stored in memory until the transaction commits. When a CR block is needed, the database first checks to see if the UNDO records are stored in the memory pool; if so, it applies the UNDO and REDO records from memory instead of retrieving them from the UNDO segments and redo logs/buffers (doing this in memory is much faster). When you are querying a block for the first time, you always use the CURRENT version of a block. If the block is being used, you build a CLONE of the block called a CONSISTENT READ (CR) version by applying any UNDO needed to the CURRENT version of the block to get it to a point in time that makes it useful to you (perhaps you need a version of the block before DML was performed and not committed by another user). This complex, Oracle-patented process may include reading the ITL (interested transaction list, which is populated when someone does a DML on a block) and mapping the record to the UNDO header, or else mapping it directly to the UNDO block and then applying the UNDO to get the correct CR version that you need. Let's take a look at how this happens:

1. User 1 updates a record in block 777 (user 1 has not committed).

2. User 2 queries the same block and sees that the lock byte is set for a row being queried.

3. User 2 goes to the ITL portion of the block and gets the XID (transaction ID).

4. The XID (transaction ID) maps to the UNDO block, which holds the information before the update was performed. If using IMU, then a check is done to see if the UNDO for this transaction is available in memory before going to the UNDO block.

5. A clone of the block is made (call it block 778).

6. The UNDO information is applied to the block, rolling it back to where it used to be (its contents go to a past state including the SCN).

7. Block 777 is a CURRENT block.

8. Block 778 is a CONSISTENT READ block before the user 1 update occurred.

9. If another user performs a query against the same block before the commit, that user can also read the CR version.

Note *especially* the fact that the block is not *rolled back* to what it was, but it is *rolled forward* (to what it used to be). While the result is the same, how Oracle performs this operation is *critical* to understanding how Oracle works. Oracle blocks are always moving forward in time (this is why the REDO works—it's always applying things forward sequentially). There are also links to all blocks for the LRU (least recently used) and LRU-W (least recently used—write) chains to help make buffer replacement and writing much faster. These links are also maintained in the buffer headers.

Here are some nice (rarely found) queries to get block-level information.

Finding the block number (56650) for a given object (EMP1)

```
select rowid,empno,
       dbms_rowid.rowid_relative_fno(rowid) fileno,
       dbms_rowid.rowid_block_number(rowid) blockno,
       dbms_rowid.rowid_row_number(rowid)   rowno, rownum,
       rpad(to_char(dbms_rowid.rowid_block_number(rowid), 'FM0xxxxxxx') || '.' ||
       to_char(dbms_rowid.rowid_row_number   (rowid), 'FM0xxx'  ) || '.' ||
       to_char(dbms_rowid.rowid_relative_fno(rowid), 'FM0xxx'  ), 18) myrid
from   emp1;

ROWID                  EMPNO    FILENO    BLOCKNO     ROWNO     ROWNUM              MYRID
------------------ ---------- ---------- ---------- ---------- ---------- ------------------

AAAM4cAABAAAN1KAAA      7369         1      56650          0          1 0000dd4a.0000.0001
AAAM4cAABAAAN1KAAB      7499         1      56650          1          2 0000dd4a.0001.0001
… (output truncated)
AAAM4cAABAAAN1KAAN      7934         1      56650         13         14 0000dd4a.000d.0001

14 rows selected.
```

Finding the versions (1 CURRENT and 5 CR versions) of a block for a given block number (56650)

```
select lrba_seq, state, dbarfil, dbablk, tch, flag, hscn_bas,cr_scn_bas,
       decode(bitand(flag,1),  0,  'N', 'Y') dirty,    /* Dirty bit */
       decode(bitand(flag,16), 0,  'N', 'Y') temp,    /* temporary bit */
       decode(bitand(flag,1536),0,'N','Y') ping,   /* ping (shared or null) bit */
       decode(bitand(flag,16384), 0, 'N', 'Y') stale, /* stale bit */
       decode(bitand(flag,65536), 0, 'N', 'Y') direct, /* direct access bit */
       decode(bitand(flag,1048576), 0, 'N', 'Y') new /* new bit */
from   x$bh
where dbablk = 56650
order by dbablk;


LRBA_SEQ        STATE    DBARFIL      DBABLK        TCH        FLAG     HSCN_BAS
---------- ---------- ---------- ---------- ---------- ---------- ----------
CR_SCN_BAS D T P S D N
---------- - - - - - -
         0            3          1       56650          1      524416            0
   4350120 N N N N N N
         0            3          1       56650          1      524416            0
   4350105 N N N N N N
       365            1          1       56650          7    33562633      4350121
         0 Y N N N N N
         0            3          1       56650          1      524416            0
   4350103 N N N N N N
         0            3          1       56650          1      524416            0
   4350089 N N N N N N
         0            3          1       56650          1      524288            0
   4350087 N N N N N N
```

NOTE
In the preceding listing, state=1 is CURRENT and state=3 is CR; only the CURRENT block is (can be) dirty.

Finding the setting for the maximum CR (consistent read) versions of a block

```
select a.ksppinm, b.ksppstvl, b.ksppstdf, a.ksppdesc
from   x$ksppi a, x$ksppcv b
where  a.indx = b.indx
and    substr(ksppinm,1,1) = '_'
and    ksppinm like '%&1%'
order  by ksppinm;


Enter a value for 1: db_block_max_cr_dba

KSPPINM        KSPPSTVL KSPPSTDF KSPPDESC
-------------------- -------- -=------ -------------------------------------------
_db_block_max_cr_dba        6 TRUE    Maximum Allowed Number of CR buffers per dba
```

Dumping what's inside the block for EMP1

```
SQL> select header_file, header_block, blocks from dba_segments
  2  where segment_name = 'EMP'
  3  and owner = 'SCOTT';

HEADER_FILE HEADER_BLOCK    BLOCKS
----------- ------------ ----------
          4           27          8


ALTER SYSTEM DUMP DATAFILE 4 BLOCK 28;
System Altered.
```

TIP
Never go to the block level unless you absolutely have to go there.
The block level is a great place to find hot block and ITL issues, but it
takes a lot of time and energy on the part of an advanced DBA to
pinpoint problems at this level.

Dictionary and Library Cache Statistics

The next two sections contain the Dictionary and Library Cache information. Listed first is all of the data dictionary information. This data pertains to all of the objects in the database. This information is accessed for every SQL statement that gets parsed and again when the statement is executed. The activity in this area can be very heavy. Maintaining a good hit ratio is very important to prevent recursive calls back to the database to verify privileges. You can also evaluate the efficiency of the Dictionary Cache by querying the V$ROWCACHE view. The query that follows shows the information that the Statspack Report lists for this section of the report:

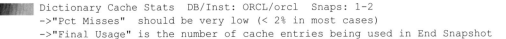

```
Dictionary Cache Stats  DB/Inst: ORCL/orcl  Snaps: 1-2
->"Pct Misses"  should be very low (< 2% in most cases)
->"Final Usage" is the number of cache entries being used in End Snapshot
```

Cache	Get Requests	Pct Miss	Scan Reqs	Pct Miss	Mod Reqs	Final Usage
dc_awr_control	13	0.0	0		0	1
dc_files	20	0.0	0		0	10
dc_global_oids	1,006	0.0	0		0	142
dc_histogram_data	4,176	0.0	0		0	18,600
dc_histogram_defs	9,618	3.9	0		0	8,856
dc_object_grants	259	0.0	0		0	195
dc_objects	6,643	0.0	0		0	5,719
dc_profiles	30	0.0	0		0	2
dc_rollback_segments	195	0.0	0		0	22
dc_segments	976	7.0	0		191	1,722
dc_sequences	1	0.0	0		1	22
dc_tablespace_quotas	416	0.0	0		0	2
dc_tablespaces	24,510	0.0	0		0	9

```
dc_users                        29,713      0.0       0                 0        460
global database name               581      0.0       0                 0          1
outstanding_alerts                  12      0.0       0                 0          7
        ------------------------------------------------------------------------
```

The second part of this section of the report deals with the performance of the Library Cache. These statistics are generated from the V$LIBRARYCACHE view. The Library Cache contains the shared SQL and PL/SQL areas. These areas are represented by the BODY, SQL AREA, TABLE/PROCEDURE, and TRIGGER values (these are values in the NAMESPACE column). They contain all of the SQL and PL/SQL statements that are cached in memory. The other names are areas that Oracle uses. If your "PCT MISS" value is high in this section of the report, you may need to improve cursor sharing in your application or increase the size of the shared pool (as discussed in the "Top Wait Events" section of this chapter). The following listing shows sample data for this section:

```
Library Cache Activity  DB/Inst: ORCL/orcl  Snaps: 1-2
->"Pct Misses"  should be very low


                          Get   Pct        Pin      Pct                 Invali-
Namespace             Requests  Miss    Requests    Miss     Reloads    dations
---------------       --------  ------  ----------  ------   ----------  --------
SQL AREA                 1,513   9.2       17,896    2.6          90         53
TABLE/PROCEDURE          3,500   0.0        7,423    1.3          43          0
BODY                       274   0.0        1,768    0.0           0          0
TRIGGER                    352   0.0          372    0.0           0          0
INDEX                       37   0.0           37  100.0           0          0
CLUSTER                    298   0.0           30    0.0           0          0
QUEUE                    2,114   0.0        2,514    0.0           0          0
APP CONTEXT                 63   0.0           63    0.0           0          0
SUBSCRIPTION                 2   0.0            2    0.0           0          0
EDITION                     27   0.0           50    0.0           0          0
DBLINK                      15   0.0            0                  0          0
SCHEMA                      34   0.0            0                  0          0
        ---------------------------------------------------------------------
```

Here is what the columns mean in this part of the report:

Column	Description
NAMESPACE	The name of the library namespace.
GET REQUESTS	The number of times the system requested a handle to an object in this namespace.
PCT MISS (Get Miss Ratio)	The number of *gethits* divided by the number of *gets* is the *get hit ratio*. The gethits are the number of times a request was made for an object and the object was already in the cache. The hit ratio should be as close to 0.99 as possible. The PCT MISS should be less than 1 percent.
PIN REQUESTS	The number of times an item in the cache was executed. A high number is what you are after.

Column	Description
PCT MISS (Pin Miss Ratio)	The number of *pinhits* divided by the number of *pins* shows the *pin hit ratio*. Pinhits are the number of times that objects the system is pinning are already in the cache. This ratio should be as close to 1 as possible. The miss ratio should be less than 1 percent.
RELOADS	The number of Library Cache misses on an execution step. The number of reloads divided by the number of pins should be around 0 percent. If the ratio between this is greater than 1 percent, you should probably increase the size of the shared pool.
INVALIDATIONS	The total number of times objects in this namespace were marked invalid because a dependent object was modified.

TIP
If the pin hit ratio is less than 0.95 when the report is run for an extended period of time, the SHARED_POOL_SIZE is probably too small for your best system performance. If the reloads are greater than 1 percent, this also points to a SHARED_POOL_SIZE that is too small.

SGA Memory Statistics

Following an SGA memory summary (from V$SGA) and a listing of the memory changes during the snapshot interval, the report lists the database initialization parameters in use at the beginning and end of the report.

Taken as a whole, the report generates a significant amount of data, allowing you to develop a profile of the database and its usage. By drawing on the initialization, file I/O, and SGA data, you can develop an understanding of the major components in the database configuration. Here is a sample listing of this section of the report:

```
SGA Memory Summary   DB/Inst: ORCL/orcl   Snaps: 1-2


                                                       End Size (Bytes)
SGA regions                   Begin Size (Bytes)         (if different)
---------------------------   --------------------   --------------------
Database Buffers                     2,315,255,808
Fixed Size                               2,188,768
Redo Buffers                            17,420,288
Variable Size                        4,513,073,696
                              --------------------   --------------------
sum                                  6,847,938,560
                              -----------------------------------------------

SGA breakdown difference   DB/Inst: ORCL/orcl   Snaps: 1-2
-> Top 35 rows by size, ordered by Pool, Name (note rows with null values for
   Pool column, or Names showing free memory are always shown)
-> Null value for Begin MB or End MB indicates the size of that Pool/Name was
   insignificant, or zero in that snapshot
```

```
Pool   Name                                  Begin MB       End MB    % Diff
------ ----------------------------------- -------------- -------------- --------
java p free memory                                16.0         16.0      0.00
large  PX msg pool                                 7.8          7.8      0.00
large  free memory                                24.2         24.2      0.00
shared ASH buffers                                15.5         15.5      0.00
shared CCUR                                       77.1         77.6      0.64
shared FileOpenBlock                              10.5         10.5      0.00
shared KGLH0                                      17.4         17.4      0.07
shared KGLHD                                      21.5         21.6      0.31
shared KGLS                                       28.8         29.0      0.64
shared PCUR                                       40.7         41.1      0.82
shared PLDIA                                      12.8         12.8      0.00
shared PLMCD                                      15.1         15.1      0.00
shared SQLA                                      393.6        396.4      0.70
shared db_block_hash_buckets                      22.3         22.3      0.00
shared free memory                               242.4        238.1     -1.75
stream free memory                                16.0         16.0      0.00
       buffer_cache                            2,208.0      2,208.0      0.00
       fixed_sga                                   2.1          2.1      0.00
       log_buffer                                 16.6         16.6      0.00
       shared_io_pool                            928.0        928.0      0.00
       -------------------------------------------------------------
```

```
SQL Memory Statistics  DB/Inst: ORCL/orcl  Snaps: 1-2

                               Begin            End          % Diff
                         -------------- -------------- --------------
      Avg Cursor Size (KB):     36.81          36.79           -.05
  Cursor to Parent ratio:       1.78           1.78            .16
          Total Cursors:      12,334         12,395            .49
          Total Parents:       6,928          6,951            .33
          -------------------------------------------------------------
```

Nondefault Initialization Parameters

This last section shows the parameters in the initialization file that are set to a value other than the default (see Figure 14-19). The list is generated by querying the V$PARAMETER view where the default column is equal to FALSE. This list can be used as a reference. While you are tuning the database, these parameters can provide a record of how the database performed with certain values. The output that follows shows this section of the Statspack Report:

```
init.ora Parameters  DB/Inst: ORCL/orcl  Snaps: 1-2

                                                            End value
Parameter Name                 Begin value                 (if different)
---------------------------- --------------------------------- --------------
audit_file_dest              C:\APP\USER\ADMIN\ORCL\ADUMP
audit_trail                  DB
compatible                   11.2.0.0.0
```

```
control_files                  C:\APP\USER\ORADATA\ORCL\CONTROL0
                               1.CTL, C:\APP\USER\FLASH_RECOVERY
                               _AREA\ORCL\CONTROL02.CTL
cursor_sharing                 FORCE
db_block_size                  8192
db_domain
db_name                        orcl
db_recovery_file_dest          C:\app\User\flash_recovery_area
db_recovery_file_dest_size     4102029312
diagnostic_dest                C:\APP\USER
dispatchers                    (PROTOCOL=TCP) (SERVICE=orclXDB)
memory_target                  6878658560
open_cursors                   300
optimizer_mode                 ALL_ROWS
processes                      150
remote_login_passwordfile      EXCLUSIVE
shared_pool_size               1073741824
undo_tablespace                UNDOTBS1
            -------------------------------------------------------------

End of Report ( c:\users\sp_1_2.lst )
```

init.ora Parameters

- if IP/Public/Source at End snap is different a '*' is displayed

Parameter Name	Begin value	End value (if different)
audit_file_dest	C:\APP\USER\ADMIN\ORCL\ADUMP	
audit_trail	DB	
compatible	11.2.0.0.0	
control_files	C:\APP\USER\ORADATA\ORCL\CONTROL01.CTL, C:\APP\USER\FLASH_RECOVERY_AREA\ORCL\CONTROL02.CTL	
cursor_sharing	FORCE	
db_block_size	8192	
db_domain		
db_name	orcl	
db_recovery_file_dest	C:\app\User\flash_recovery_area	
db_recovery_file_dest_size	4102029312	
diagnostic_dest	C:\APP\USER	
dispatchers	(PROTOCOL=TCP) (SERVICE=orclXDB)	
memory_target	6878658560	
open_cursors	300	
optimizer_mode	ALL_ROWS	
processes	150	
remote_login_passwordfile	EXCLUSIVE	
shared_pool_size	1073741824	
undo_tablespace	UNDOTBS1	

FIGURE 14-19. *The AWR Report initialization parameters*

Top 10 Things to Look for in AWR Report and Statspack Output

Many DBAs already know how to use Statspack but are not always sure what to check regularly. Remember to separate OLTP and batch activity when you run Statspack because they usually generate different types of waits. The SQL script `spauto.sql` can be used to run Statspack every hour on the hour. See the script in `$ORACLE_HOME/rdbms/admin/spauto.sql` for more information (note that JOB_QUEUE_PROCESSES must be greater than 0). Since every system is different, this is only a general list of things you should *regularly* check in your Statspack or AWR output:

- Top 5 wait events (timed events)
- Load profile
- Instance efficiency hit ratios
- Wait events
- Latch waits/Mutex sleeps
- Top SQL
- Instance activity
- File I/O and segment statistics
- Memory allocation
- Buffer waits

A final note on the top 5 wait events is to look for bugs when you have a *high* number of wait events that are normally not so high. You can only do this if you are regularly monitoring your reports or if you captured baselines for comparisons. Take a look at the following bug in Figure 14-20 from My Oracle Support (MetaLink) that shows the behavior of a high number of "Library Cache: Mutex X" (on Koka Cursors (LOBs) Non-Shared) that *dominates* the top 5 wait events. This is a clue you may have be a *bug* to search for or a *real bad* SQL statement. See the appropriate section of this chapter for how to fix major problems depending on the wait event.

Managing the Statspack Data

You should manage the data generated by Statspack to guarantee that the space usage and performance of the Statspack application meets your requirements as the application data grows. Managing Statspack data includes the following steps:

1. Regularly analyze the Statspack data. At a minimum, you should analyze the Statspack schema prior to running the `spreport.sql` script:

```
execute DBMS_UTILITY.ANALYZE_SCHEMA('PERFSTAT','COMPUTE');
```

```
☆ Problem : " Library Cache: Mutex X " On Koka Cursors (LOBs) Non-Shared :                                          ▣ Comments (0

    AWR:  Library cache: mutex X and Concurrency Wait Class dominates the Top 5 Wait Events


                                      Avg
                             %Time  Total  Wait
    Wait Class             Waits -outs  Time(s) (ms)  %DB time
    ----------------------------------------------------------- -------- ----
    library cache: mutex X 370,798,153       336,901    1   32.1 Concurrency
    DB CPU                    264,148                        25.1
    ksdxexeotherwait            1,548         1,275  824    .1 Other
    cursor: mutex S           751,745           627    1    .1 Concurrency
    latch: shared pool         34,948           386   11    .0 Concurrency
    ...
```

```
    Further AWR statistics will include High Concurrency Foreground Wait Events


                                       Avg
                             %Time  Total  Wait  wait  Waits%DB
    Event                  Waits -outs  Time  (s)  (ms)  /txn time
    -------------------------------------------------------------
    library cache: mutex X 370,798,153 100 336,901    1  1.4E+05   32.
    ksdxexeotherwait            1,548    0   1,275  824    0.6     .1
    cursor: mutex S           751,745  100     627    1  277.2     .1
    latch: shared pool         34,948    0     386   11   12.9     .0
    cursor: pin S           2,837,512  100     375    0 1,046.3    .0
    cursor: pin S wait on X     7,486   92     154   21    2.8     .0
    wait list latch free          808    0      63   78    0.3     .0
    latch free                    17     0       5  270    0.0     .0
    cursor: mutex X           18,935  100       2    0    7.0     .0
    ...
    ...
```

FIGURE 14-20. *Listing for a "Library Cache: Mutex X" heavy wait events bug*

2. Purge old data. Because you cannot generate valid interval reports across database shutdown/startup actions, data prior to the last database startup may not be as useful as the most current data. When the data is no longer needed, purge it from the tables. Oracle provides a script, `sppurge.sql`, to facilitate purges. The `sppurge.sql` script, located in the `/rdbms/admin` directory under the Oracle software home directory, lists the currently stored snapshots and prompts you for two input parameters: the beginning and ending snapshot numbers for the purge. The related records in the STATS$ tables are then deleted. Due to the size of the transactions involved, databases using rollback segments should force the session to use a large rollback segment during the deletes:

```
SQL> commit;
SQL> set transaction use rollback segment roll_large;
SQL> @sppurge
```

The `sppurge` script prompts you to back up your old statistics before purging them. You can back up the data by exporting the PERFSTAT schema.

3. Truncate the Statspack tables when the data is not needed. Old statistical data may no longer be relevant, or you may have imported the old statistics during database migrations or creations. To truncate the old tables, execute the `sptrunc.sql` SQL*Plus script from within the PERFSTAT account. The script is located in the `/rdbms/admin` directory under the Oracle software home directory.

4. Include the Statspack tables in your backup scheme. If you are using Export, Oracle provides a parameter file named `spuexp.par` to assist you.

5. Include the Statspack tables in your space monitoring procedures.

Upgrading Statspack

To upgrade old Statspack data to a new version of the database, execute the scripts provided by Oracle. Oracle does not support upgrading Statspack directly from 8.1.6 to 9.0.1 or 9.2 to 10.2 or 11; you must go through multiple steps. The scripts only upgrade your current schema to the next release level, for example 9.0.1 to 9.2, so you might have to run multiple scripts to complete the upgrade:

1. Upgrade from the 8.1.6 Statspack objects to 8.1.7 by executing the `spup816.sql` script.

2. Upgrade from the 8.1.7 Statspack objects to 9.0 by executing the `spup817.sql` script.

3. Upgrade from the 9.0 Statspack objects to 9.2 by executing the `spup90.sql` script.

4. Upgrade from the 9.2 Statspack objects to 10.1 by executing the `spup92.sql` script.

5. Upgrade from the 10.1 Statspack objects to 10.2 by executing the `spup10.sql` script.

6. Upgrade from the 10.2 Statspack objects to 11 by executing the `spup102.sql` script.

Deinstalling Statspack

Since Statspack includes public synonyms as well as private objects, you should remove the application via a SYSDBA-privileged account. Oracle provides a script, `spdrop.sql`, to automate the deinstallation process. From within the `/rdbms/admin` directory under the Oracle software home directory, log in to SQL*Plus and execute the script as shown in the following listing:

```
SQL> connect system/manager as SYSDBA
SQL> @spdrop
```

The `spdrop.sql` script calls scripts (`spdtab.sql`, `spdusr.sql`) that will drop the tables, the package, the public synonyms, and the PERFSTAT user. To reinstall Statspack, execute the `spcreate.sql` script, as shown earlier in this chapter.

Quick Notes on the New ADDM Report

You can also use the Automatic Database Diagnostics Monitor (ADDM) Report, called `addmrpt.sql`, to analyze a snapshot range. Run the `addmrpt.sql` script from SQL*Plus (the script is located in the `$ORACLE_HOME/rdbms/admin` directory). The script provides you with a list of snapshots from which you can generate the report (like Statspack or the AWR Report from SQL*Plus). You select a begin snapshot and an end snapshot, and finally, you define the name of the report that you want `addmrpt.sql` to create. The `addmrpt.sql` script then runs the ADDM analysis on the snapshot pair you entered and provides the output analysis report. Using ADDM through Enterprise Manager Grid Control (covered in Chapter 5) is much more detailed and is recommended. The resulting report contains a header and then detailed finding information. The command to run it is listed here, and following that command is the header; yours should look much like this example:

```
SQL> @C:\app\User\product\11.2.0\dbhome_2\RDBMS\ADMIN\addmrpt

Current Instance
~~~~~~~~~~~~~~~~

   DB Id     DB Name      Inst Num Instance
----------- ------------- -------- ------------
 1272868336 ORCL                 1 orcl

Instances in this Workload Repository schema
~~~~~~~~~~~~~~~~~~~~~~~~~~~~~~~~~~~~~~~~~~~~~~

   DB Id     Inst Num DB Name      Instance     Host
----------- -------- ------------- ------------ ------------
* 1272868336        1 ORCL          orcl         USER-PC

Using 1272868336 for database Id
Using             1 for instance number

Specify the number of days of snapshots to choose from
~~~~~~~~~~~~~~~~~~~~~~~~~~~~~~~~~~~~~~~~~~~~~~~~~~~~~~~~~
Entering the number of days (n) will result in the most recent
(n) days of snapshots being listed.  Pressing <return> without
specifying a number lists all completed snapshots.

Listing the last 3 days of Completed Snapshots

                                                      Snap
Instance     DB Name      Snap Id   Snap Started      Level
------------ ------------- --------- ----------------- -----
orcl         ORCL              342 09 May 2011 15:38     1
… (partial listing only)
                               358 11 May 2011 04:00     1
                               359 11 May 2011 05:00     1
                               360 11 May 2011 06:00     1
                               361 11 May 2011 07:00     1
                               362 11 May 2011 08:00     1
                               363 11 May 2011 11:44     1

Specify the Begin and End Snapshot Ids
~~~~~~~~~~~~~~~~~~~~~~~~~~~~~~~~~~~~~~~~
Enter value for begin_snap: 358
Begin Snapshot Id specified: 358

Enter value for end_snap: 363
End    Snapshot Id specified: 363
```

```
Specify the Report Name
~~~~~~~~~~~~~~~~~~~~~~~~
The default report file name is addmrpt_1_358_363.txt.  To use this name,
press <return> to continue, otherwise enter an alternative.

Enter value for report_name: awr_rep1
Using the report name awr_rep1

Running the ADDM analysis on the specified pair of snapshots ...
Generating the ADDM report for this analysis ...
```

Now look at the report output:

```
          ADDM Report for Task 'TASK_488'
          -------------------------------


Analysis Period
---------------
AWR snapshot range from 358 to 363.
Time period starts at 11-MAY-11 04.00.49 AM
Time period ends at 11-MAY-11 11.44.42 AM

Analysis Target
---------------
Database 'ORCL' with DB ID 1272868336.
Database version 11.2.0.1.0.
ADDM performed an analysis of instance orcl, numbered 1 and hosted at USER-PC.

Activity During the Analysis Period
-----------------------------------
Total database time was 12314 seconds.
The average number of active sessions was .44.
```

A summary information section is related to the ADDM analysis. Following the header and individual findings, the summary is listed. An example of such a finding is seen here:

```
Summary of Findings
-------------------
    Description              Active Sessions       Recommendations
                             Percent of Activity
    -------------------      -------------------   ---------------
1   Virtual Memory Paging    .44 | 100             3
... (partial listing only)

          Findings and Recommendations
          ----------------------------


Finding 1: Virtual Memory Paging
Impact is .44 active sessions, 100% of total activity.
---------------------------------------------------------
Significant virtual memory paging was detected on the host operating system.
```

```
Recommendation 1: Host Configuration
Estimated benefit is .44 active sessions, 100% of total .activity.
-----------------------------------------------------------------
Action
   Host operating system was experiencing significant paging but no
   particular root cause could be detected. Investigate processes that do
   not belong to this instance running on the host that are consuming
   significant amount of virtual memory. Also consider adding more physical
   memory to the host.

Recommendation 2: Database Configuration
Estimated benefit is .44 active sessions, 100% of total activity.
-----------------------------------------------------------------
Action
   Consider enabling Automatic Shared Memory Management by setting the
   parameter "sga_target" to control the amount of SGA consumed by this
   instance.

Recommendation 3: Database Configuration
Estimated benefit is .44 active sessions, 100% of total activity.
-----------------------------------------------------------------
Action
   Consider enabling Automatic PGA Memory Management by setting the
   parameter "pga_aggregate_target" to control the amount of PGA consumed
   by this instance.
```

If SQL issues are discovered, the finding looks like the one shown here, suggesting that I run the Tuning Advisor to tune the statement:

```
FINDING 1: 51% impact (309 seconds)
-----------------------------------
SQL statements consuming significant database time were found.
      ACTION: Run SQL Tuning Advisor on the SQL statement with SQL_ID
         "db78fxqxwxt7r".
         RELEVANT OBJECT: SQL statement with SQL_ID db78fxqxwxt7r and
         PLAN_HASH 3879501264
         SELECT a.emp, b.dname
         FROM EMP a, DEPT b
         WHERE a.deptno=b.deptno;
```

A few interesting things appear in this report. First, the finding indicates that the problem identified had a 51 percent overall impact in the DB time. In other words, the ADDM report is sorting its findings according to those processes that are consuming the most database time. I see, looking at this finding further, that it is a SQL statement that is causing problems (usually the source of most issues), and ADDM suggests that I tune the statement. Oracle gives me the SQL address and hash value so I can find the SQL statement in the SQL area. Note that the ACTION suggests that I run the SQL Tuning Advisor to generate some suggested tuning actions on the SQL statement in question. In Chapter 5 and Chapter 8, I discuss the SQL Tuning Advisor and show you just how it can help you tune SQL statements in Oracle Database 11g.

If not enough work has been done on the instance or if not enough work is being done currently, instead of giving you suggestions, it displays the following:

```
~~~~~~~~~~~~~~~~~~~~~~~~~~~~~~~~~~~~~~~~~~~~~~~~~~~~~~~~~~~~~~~~~~~~~~~~~~~~~~
THERE WAS NOT ENOUGH INSTANCE SERVICE TIME FOR ADDM ANALYSIS.
~~~~~~~~~~~~~~~~~~~~~~~~~~~~~~~~~~~~~~~~~~~~~~~~~~~~~~~~~~~~~~~~~~~~~~~~~~~~~~
```

The ADDM report is a good start for getting tips for tuning. As with any new utility, there is room for improvement and growth in future releases of Oracle, and it is best used from the Enterprise Manager interface if possible. I have not been able to address other aspects related to ADDM in this section, such as user-defined alerts and the SQL Tuning Advisor, which I discussed in Chapter 5 and Chapter 8.

TIP
The ADDM Report can be a helpful tuning utility, but ADDM is better used through Oracle's Enterprise Manager for maximum benefits.

Scripts in 11gR2

Here is a listing of scripts that you will find in 11gR2. Please refer to the documentation for a complete description of each of these.

Script	Description	Calls	Run As	Environment
spcreate.sql	Creates the Statspack environment.	spcpkg.sql spctab.sql spcpkg.sql	SYSDBA	Any instance
spdrop.sql	Drops the entire Statspack environment.	spdtab.sql and spdusr.sql	SYSDBA	Any instance
spreport.sql	The main script to generate the Statspack Report.	sprepins.sql	PERFSTAT user	Any instance
sprepins.sql	Generates a Statspack Instance Report for the database and instance specified.		PERFSTAT	Oracle RAC and Data Guard systems
sprepsql.sql	Generates a Statspack SQL Report for a given SQL hash value.	sprsqinsl.sql	PERFSTAT	Any instance
sprsqins.sql	Generates a Statspack SQL Report for the SQL hash value specified for the database and instance specified.	sprepcon.sql	PERFSTAT	Oracle RAC and Data Guard systems

Script	Description	Calls	Run As	Environment
spauto.sql	Automates Statspack statistics collection (snap) using DBMS_JOB.		PERFSTAT	Any instance with JOB_QUEUE_PROCESSES > 0
sprepcon.sql	Configures SQL*Plus variable to set things like thresholds. Called automatically as part of the Statspack instance report.		PERFSTAT	Instances where you want to show or hide sections of the report
sppurge.sql	Purges a range of snapshot IDs for a given database instance (does not purge baseline snapshots).		PERFSTAT	Use Statspack package procedure instead.
sptrunc.sql	Truncates all performance data in Statspack tables (CAREFUL!).		PERFSTAT	Any instance
spuexp.par	Exports parameter file for exporting the entire PERFSTAT user.		PERFSTAT	Taking export backups of the PERFSTAT schema.
spup816.sql	To upgrade from 8.1.6 to 8.1.7.		SYSDBA	DB with 8.1.6 version of Statspack schema and a valid backup
spup817.sql	To upgrade from 8.1.7 to 9.0.		SYSDBA	DB with 8.1.7 version of Statspack schema and a valid backup
spup90.sql	To upgrade from 9.0 to 9.2.		SYSDBA	DB with 9i version of Statspack schema and a valid backup

Script	Description	Calls	Run As	Environment
spup92.sql	To upgrade from 9.2 to 10.1.		PERFSTAT	DB with 9iR2 version of Statspack schema and a valid backup
spup10.sql	To upgrade from 10.1 to 10.2.		SYSDBA	DB with 10gR1 version of Statspack schema and a valid backup
spup102.sql	To upgrade from 10.2 to 11.1.		SYSDBA	DB with 10gR2 version of Statspack schema and a valid backup

NOTE
You must use the specific version of Statspack with that version of the database (for instance, you must use the 11.2 Statspack schema with the 11.2 database). Also note that spdoc.txt *is the complete instruction and documentation file for Statspack.*

Tips Review

- Allocate at least 120M for the initial creation of the PERFSTAT schema's objects. Oracle 11*g* requires approximately the same space as Oracle 10*g*, which is about 20M more space than Oracle 9*i*.

- Be sure the TIMED_STATISTICS database initialization parameter is set to TRUE prior to gathering statistics.

- Pin the Statspack package following database startup if you plan to run the SNAP procedure on a scheduled basis.

- A second report, sprepsql.sql, can be used for additional research into the problem SQL statements identified via the spreport.sql report.

- If you choose to run *both* Statspack and AWR, ensure that you stagger the data collection of AWR from the collection for Statspack (by at least 30 minutes) to avoid a performance hit as well as conflicts. If you are running the AWR Report, you should not need to also run Statspack.

- With the new AWR Report, you can choose to get text (like Statspack output) or the new HTML format when you run awrrpt.sql. The HTML format is *much* better, as you can click various links within the report to navigate among sections easily. You can also run the AWR Report within Enterprise Manager.

■ If you use Enterprise Manager, you can run the AWR Report directly from Grid Control.

■ Get to know your system by reviewing and knowing your system's regular Load Profile. Significant changes to the Load Profile during what should be similar workloads or common times during the day may warrant further investigation.

■ Hit ratios are a great barometer of the health of your system. A large increase or drop from day to day is an indicator of a major change that needs to be investigated. Investigating waits is like investigating an accident that has already occurred, while investigating a change in hit ratios is like looking into the intersection with a changing traffic pattern that may cause an accident in the future if something is not adjusted. Generally, buffer and library cache hit ratios should be greater than 95 percent for OLTP, but they could be lower for a data warehouse that may perform many full table scans.

■ Tuning by wait events is one of the best possible reactive tuning methods.

■ In 11g, the library cache pin (protects cursors/SQL) and library cache latch (protects the Library Cache) are both replaced by mutexes (program objects that negotiate mutual exclusion among threads).

■ The top 5 wait events reveal to you the largest issues on your system at the macro level. Rarely do they point you to a specific problem. Other parts of the AWR Report or Statspack Report will tell you why you are receiving the top 5 waits.

■ Tuning the top 25 buffer get and top 25 physical get queries can yield system performance gains of anywhere from 5 percent to 5000+ percent. The SQL section of the Statspack Report tells you which queries to consider tuning first. The top 10 SQL statements should not be substantially more than 10 percent of *all* of your buffer gets or disk reads.

■ If many sorts are being performed to disk (greater than 1–5 percent of the total number of rows being sorted), you may need to increase the initialization parameters associated with sorting. See Chapter 4 for more information on these.

■ The buffer hit ratio should be greater than 95 percent. If it is less than 95 percent, you should consider increasing the size of the data cache by increasing the MEMORY_TARGET (if used) or increasing the minimum setting for DB_CACHE_SIZE initialization parameter (given that physical memory is available to do this).

■ If full table scans are being performed, serious performance issues may result and data hit ratios will be distorted. These tables need to be identified so the appropriate indexes are created or used. See Chapters 8 and 9 on query tuning for more information.

■ If the number of physical reads is heavier on one physical disk, proper balancing of data will probably increase performance. See Chapter 3 for tips on fixing I/O problems with either data files or tablespaces.

■ Latches are like locks on pieces of memory (or memory buffers). If the latch hit ratio is less than 99 percent, you have a serious problem because not even the lock to get memory can be retrieved.

■ Never go to the block level unless you absolutely have to go there. The block level is a great place to find hot block and ITL issues, but it takes a lot of time and energy on the part of an advanced DBA to pinpoint problems at this level.

References

Steve Adams, *Oracle8i Internal Services for Waits, Latches, Locks, and Memory* (older, but excellent), (O'Reilly, 1999).

Robert Freeman, *Oracle 11g New Features* (Oracle Press).

Connie Dialeris and Graham Wood, "Performance Tuning with STATSPACK" (White Paper, 2000).

Connie Dialeris Green, Cecilia Gervasio, Graham Wood (guru), Russell Green, Patrick Tearle, Harald Eri, Stefan Pommerenk, and Vladimir Barriere, *Oracle 10g Server, Release 10.2,* (Production, Oracle Corporation).

Library Cache Latches Gone in Oracle 11*g*, (Tanel Poder blog, August 2008, January 2011).

Mutual Exclusion Events, Wikipedia.

Rich Niemiec, "IOUG Masters Tuning Class" (2002).

Rich Niemiec, *Tuning Oracle11g Using Statspack and AWR Report* (IOUG 2009).

Rich Niemiec, *Tuning the Oracle Grid* (IOUG 2011).

Oracle *Database Performance Tuning Guide* – 11*g* (Oracle Corporation).

Oracle Forums on http://www.oracle.com.

Notes from Richard Powell, Cecilia Gervasio, Russell Green, and Patrick Tearle.

Randy Swanson and Bob Yingst, "STATSPACK Checklist" (2002).

Wiki.oracle.com, Mutex (2011).

My Oracle Support (MetaLink) Notes: 135223.1, 135223.1, 148511.1, 148511.1, 155971.1, 181306.1, 22908.1, 29787.1, 33567.1, 39017.1, 61998.1, 62172.1, 62160.1, 34405.1, 727400.1, 1298015.1, 1268724.1, 1310764.1, and 62354.1.

Special thanks to Robert Freeman, who contributed much of the AWR information. Thanks to Kevin Loney for the entire installation portion of this chapter written for the last version and some added notes. Tuning is an iterative process; as Hollyann always says: "If at first you don't succeed, skydiving is not for you; try tuning instead!" Thanks to Greg Pucka for the original chapter on estat/bstat. Rich Niemiec upgraded this chapter (painful as usual!).

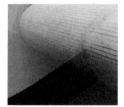

CHAPTER
15

Performing a Quick
System Review (DBA)

Oracle 11*g* introduced many new features that can be leveraged for automatic tuning. While some DBAs are great at planning and implementing a new version, fewer are good at evaluating and effectively implementing the new features that will help their system. With the introduction of Enterprise Manager combined with the Automatic Workload Repository (AWR) and the AWR Report (see Chapter 14 for a comparison to Statspack), you can monitor and tune your system in different and more productive ways. And with the advent of SQL Performance Analyzer (SPA), the SQL Tuning Advisor, Real Application Testing, Exadata Simulation, and the Result Cache comes different ways to fix your system more productively. One of the keys to a good system review is checking to see if you've implemented the features that fit your needs and have a good return on the license cost of the feature as well as the time it takes to implement it. Although nobody seems to like tests or evaluations, *simple* evaluations can help to point out future performance problems and/or current issues.

One of the key approaches to achieving a focus on improving and maintaining excellent system performance is to perform a system review on at least an annual basis. This review could be an internal or external review of your system performance. Many companies have developed methods for measuring system performance and overall system speed that are tailored directly for their system. This chapter does not describe the six-month process that many of the more detailed evaluations propose; instead, it serves as a very simple barometer of how your system rates compared to others in the industry. Variations in your business processes may cause your score to be higher or lower using this simple review. You will need to adjust these scales and/or some of the criteria to fit your unique system. Tips covered in this chapter include the following:

- The Total Performance Index (TPI) and reasons you might want to use it

- How to evaluate your Education Performance Index (EPI)

- How to evaluate your System Performance Index (SPI)

- How to evaluate your Memory Performance Index (MPI)

- How to evaluate your Disk Performance Index (DPI)

- How to evaluate your Total Performance Index (TPI)

- An overall system review example

- The immediate action items list

- The system information list

- Rating the DBA with the help of an impartial expert

Total Performance Index (TPI)

I created the Total Performance Index (TPI) as a basic tool for Oracle DBAs to measure their system and compare it to other systems, using a quick and simple scoring method as shown in the following table. This index is only meant to be a barometer to see if improvements might be beneficial. Many system categories differ based on your business case and system use, but this system tells you how close or far your system is to or from others in the industry. Four categories are included: Education, System, Memory, and Disk. This chapter shows how you can measure your TPI using several simple queries. For detailed information on a particular category, please refer to the chapter in this book related to that issue. To help identify how your system is progressing, use your TPI to compare future growth in the number of users or changes in hardware and software. You can also customize the index to conform to tools you use most often, such as Oracle Enterprise Manager (EM) or Automatic Database Diagnostics Monitor (ADDM). The following table gives you the overall breakdown by index:

Category Index	Maximum Score
Education Performance Index (EPI)	250
IparSystem Performance Index (SPI)	250
Memory Performance Index (MPI)	250
Disk Performance Index (DPI)	250
Total Performance Index (TPI)	**1000**

Education Performance Index (EPI)

This section measures the knowledge and education of your technical staff members. The following table illustrates how to receive a perfect EPI score. This rating system is not meant to be an all-encompassing benchmark of knowledge and education, but rather a barometer to see how your staff might benefit from educational improvements.

Category	Level Required	Maximum Score
DBAs required to tune database	Yes	30
Developers required to tune code written	Yes	30
DBAs last trained in tuning	Less than 1 year	30
Developers last trained in tuning	Less than 1 year	30
DBAs proficient in Enterprise Manager	Yes	30
DBAs proficient in using the V$ views	Yes	20
DBAs trained on 11g New Features	Yes	20
Developers trained on 11g New Features	Yes	20
DBAs trained to use EXPLAIN PLAN	Yes	10
Developers trained to use EXPLAIN PLAN	Yes	10
DBAs trained to use SQL Tuning Advisor	Yes	10
Developers trained to use SQL Tuning Advisor	Yes	10
Education Performance Index (EPI)	**Section Total**	**250**

Rate Your System

Are DBAs *required* to tune the database?	Yes	30 points
	No	0 points
	Score	30

Are developers *required* to tune the code that they write?	Yes	30 points
	No	0 points
	Score	0
When is the last time that your DBAs attended a training course that included tuning?	< 1 year	30 points
	1–2 years	20 points
	> 2 years	0 points
	Score	20
When is the last time that your developers attended a training course that included tuning?	< 1 year	30 points
	1–2 years	20 points
	> 2 years	0 points
	Score	20
Are DBAs proficient in using Enterprise Manager as a performance tuning tool?	Yes	30 points
	No	0 points
	Score	30
Are DBAs proficient in using the V$ views to find or fix deeper performance issues?	Yes	20 points
	No	0 points
	Score	20
Have DBAs been trained on 11g New Features?	Yes	20 points
	No	0 points
	Score	20
Have developers been trained on 11g New Features that are applicable?	Yes	20 points
	No	0 points
	Score	0
Have DBAs been trained on how to use EXPLAIN PLAN? (See Chapter 6 on EXPLAIN PLAN)	Yes	10 points
	No	0 points
	Score	10
Have developers been trained on how to use EXPLAIN PLAN?	Yes	10 points
	No	0 points
	Score	0

Have DBAs been trained on how to use SQL Performance Analyzer (SPA) and the SQL Tuning Advisor?	Yes No Score	10 points 0 points _____10_____
Have developers been trained on how to use SQL Performance Analyzer (SPA) and the SQL Tuning Advisor?	Yes No Score	10 points 0 points _____0_____
Example Education Performance Index (EPI)	**Total Score**	**_____160___(Grade: B)**

Grade Your System

EPI Grade	Comments	Score
A+	Top 10 percent of most systems	250
A	Top 20 percent of most systems	210–249
B	Top 40 percent of most systems	150–209
C	Top 70 percent of most systems	90–149
Needs help now	Bottom 30 percent of most systems	< 90

TIP
Measuring your EPI (Education Performance Index) can be helpful in identifying educational improvements that might be beneficial.

System Performance Index (SPI)

This section measures overall system issues. The following table illustrates how to receive a perfect SPI score. This rating system is not meant to be an all-encompassing benchmark of overall system issues; rather, it is a barometer to see if your system might benefit from improvements.

Category	Level Required	Maximum Score
Inside party database review performed	< 1 year	30
IT goals aligned with business goals	< 1 year	30
Ran AWR or Statspack last	< 1 month	30
Asked users about performance issues	< 2 months	30
Backup tested for recovery speed/success	Yes	30
Outside party database review performed	< 1 year	30
Outside party operating system review	< 1 year	20
Statistics/AWR frequency	AUTO	10
Good use/investigation of partitioning	Yes	10

Category	Level Required	Maximum Score
Good use/investigation of compression	Yes	10
Good application of 11*g* New Features	Yes	10
Parallel Query used or tested for gains	Yes	10
System Performance Index (SPI)	**Section Total**	**250**

Rate Your System

When is the last time your database was reviewed by a business user?	< 1 year 1–2 years > 2 years Score	30 points 20 points 0 points 30
Are IT goals regularly aligned with objectives of the business to ensure IT is delivering business ROI on IT investments?	< 1 year 1–2 years > 2 years Score	30 points 20 points 0 points 30
When is the last time you ran *and* reviewed the results of AWR Report or Statspack? Are you regularly reviewing Oracle Performance Advisors? (See Chapter 14)	< 1 month 1–3 months 4–6 months > 6 months Score	30 points 20 points 10 points 0 points 20
When is the last time users of your system were asked about system performance or where things could be improved? Are thresholds set appropriately?	< 2 months 3–6 months 7–12 months > 1 year Score	30 points 20 points 10 points 0 points 20
Has your backup plan been tested to determine if it would work and the time that it would take to recover?	Yes No Score	30 points 0 points 30
When is the last time your database was reviewed by an outside party?	< 1 year 1–2 years > 2 years Score	30 points 20 points 0 points 20

When is the last time that your operating system and storage layout was reviewed by an outside party?	< 1 year	20 points
	1–2 years	10 points
	> 2 years	0 points
	Score	_____20_____

How frequently do you collect statistics?	AUTO	10 points
	Monthly	5 points
	Unsure	0 points
	Score	_____10_____

Has partitioning been evaluated or implemented, and is it in use where advantageous?	Yes	10 points
	Not needed	10 points
	Not tested	0 points
	Score	_____10_____

Has compression been evaluated or implemented, and is it in use where advantageous?	Yes	10 points
	Not needed	10 points
	Not tested	0 points
	Score	_____10_____

Have 11*g* New Features been evaluated or implemented, and is it in use where advantageous?	Yes	10 points
	Not needed	10 points
	Not tested	0 points
	Score	_____10_____

Has Parallel Query been evaluated, and is it in use where advantageous?	Yes	10 points
	Not needed	10 points
	Not tested	0 points
	Score	_____10_____

Example System Performance Index (SPI)	**Total Score**	_____220_____ (A+)

Grade Your System

SPI Grade	Comments	Score
A+	Top 10 percent of most systems	> 210
A	Top 20 percent of most systems	180–210
B	Top 40 percent of most systems	140–179

SPI Grade	Comments	Score
C	Top 70 percent of most systems	80–139
Needs help now	Bottom 30 percent of most systems	< 80

TIP
Measuring your SPI (System Performance Index) can be helpful in identifying overall system improvements that might benefit your system.

Memory Performance Index (MPI)

This section measures memory use and allocation. The following table illustrates how to receive a perfect MPI score. This rating system is not meant to be an all-encompassing benchmark of memory use and allocation; rather, it is a barometer to see if your system might benefit from memory use and allocation improvements.

Category	Level Required	Maximum Score
Top 25 (worst memory) statements tuned	Yes	60
Top 10 statements memory use*	< 5 percent	30
Buffer cache hit ratio*	> 98 percent	30
Dictionary Cache hit ratio*	> 98 percent	30
Library Cache hit ratio*	> 98 percent	30
PGA sorts in memory	> 98 percent	30
Buffers in X$BH at state=0*	10–25 percent	20
Using Result Cache effectively	Yes	10
Pin/cache frequently used objects	Yes	10
Memory Performance Index (MPI)	**Section Total**	**250**

Adjust value only where needed based on knowledge of system.

Top 25 "Memory Abusers" Statements Tuned

I have found that the top 25 statements accessed on most systems, when left untuned, make up over 75 percent of all memory and disk reads of the entire system. The code that follows lists and illustrates how to find the greatest 25 memory abusers.

Query to get the 25 worst memory abusers

```
set serverout on size 1000000
declare
  top25 number;
```

```
 text1 varchar2(4000);
 x number;
 len1 number;
cursor c1 is
  select buffer_gets, substr(sql_text,1,4000)
  from v$sqlarea
  order by buffer_gets desc;
begin
 dbms_output.put_line('Gets'||'    '||'Text');
 dbms_output.put_line('----------'||' '||'---------------------');
 open c1;
 for i in 1..25 loop
   fetch c1 into top25, text1;
   dbms_output.put_line(rpad(to_char(top25),9)||' '||substr(text1,1,66));
   len1:=length(text1);
   x:=66;
   while len1 > x-1 loop
     dbms_output.put_line('"            '||substr(text1,x,66));
   x:=x+66;
   end loop;
 end loop;
end;
/
```

Sample partial output

```
Gets      Text
16409       select f.file#, f.block#, f.ts#, f.length from fet$ f, ts$ t where
"           e t.ts#=f.ts# and t.dflextpct!=0
6868        select job from sys.job$  where next_date < sysdate  order by next
"           t_date, job
6487        SELECT BUFFER_GETS,SUBSTR(SQL_TEXT,1,3500)    FROM V$SQLAREA ORDER
"            BY BUFFER_GETS DESC
3450        SELECT BUFFER_GETS,SUBSTR(SQL_TEXT,1,4000)    FROM V$SQLAREA ORDER
"            BY BUFFER_GETS DESC
(...Simplistic Partial Listing Displayed)
```

Rate Your System

How many of your top 25 memory statements in the V$SQLAREA view have you attempted to tune?		
	0	0 points
	1–5	20 points
	6–15	40 points
	16–25	60 points
	Score	___60___

Top 10 "Memory Abusers" as a Percent of All Statements

I have found that the top 10 statements accessed on most systems, when left untuned, can make up over 50 percent of all memory reads of the entire system. This section measures how severe the most harmful memory using statements are, as a percentage of the entire system.

Script to retrieve this percentage

```
set serverout on
DECLARE
 CURSOR c1 is
  select    buffer_gets
  from      v$sqlarea
  order by buffer_gets DESC;
 CURSOR c2 is
  select    sum(buffer_gets)
  from      v$sqlarea;
 sumof10 NUMBER:=0;
 mybg NUMBER;
 mytotbg NUMBER;
BEGIN
 dbms_output.put_line('Percent');
 dbms_output.put_line('-------');
 OPEN c1;
 FOR i IN 1..10 LOOP
  FETCH c1 INTO mybg;
  sumof10 := sumof10 + mybg;
 END
 LOOP;
 CLOSE c1;
 OPEN c2;
 FETCH c2 INTO mytotbg;
 CLOSE c2;
 dbms_output.put_line(sumof10/mytotbg*100);
END;
/
```

Sample output

```
Percent
-------
44.0708

PL/SQL procedure successfully completed.
```

Alternative SQL, which is faster (Oracle 9i,10g, and 11g only)

```
select sum(pct_bufgets) "Percent"
from    (select rank() over ( order by buffer_gets desc ) as rank_bufgets,
```

```
        to_char(100 * ratio_to_report(buffer_gets) over (), '999.99') pct_bufgets
      from    v$sqlarea )
where   rank_bufgets < 11;
```

```
   Percent
----------
     44.03
```

Rate Your System

Take your top 10 memory read statements in the V$SQLAREA view. What percentage are they of all memory reads?	> 25%	0 points
	20–25%	10 points
	5–19%	20 points
	< 5%	30 points
	Score	___30___

Buffer Cache Hit Ratio

The buffer cache hit ratio represents how often frequently requested blocks of data have been found in the memory structure without requiring disk access. Hit ratios are used more in third-party tuning products than ever before, and they are also being used more by Oracle than ever before, primarily because they are a great barometer. But hit ratios can be misleading and should always be used as a barometer and indicator that you may want to look deeper. Nobody ever uses hit ratios as the sole way to tune a system as some people claim (I've asked this in very large sessions and nobody ever does). People who say you shouldn't use them at all don't generally understand their value or how to use them. The DBAs who don't look at them can miss a *major* issue that could have been potentially fixed at a very low cost. Hit ratios are very rarely the indicator of good performance but often can be an indicator of bad performance. Their best use is as a barometer or an indicator of changing performance. Hit ratios can be easily calculated by using the dynamic performance view V$SYSSTAT (see Chapter 12 for additional examples). See Chapter 4 for initialization parameters used for memory allocation within Oracle.

Query for buffer cache hit ratio

```
select      (1 - (sum(decode(name, 'physical reads',value,0)) /
            (sum(decode(name, 'db block gets',value,0)) +
            sum(decode(name, 'consistent gets',value,0)))))) * 100 "Hit Ratio"
from        v$sysstat;
```

Sample output

```
 Hit Ratio
----------
98.8249067
```

Rate Your OLTP System

What is your buffer cache hit ratio?		
	< 90%	0 points
	90–94%	10 points
	95–98%	20 points
	> 98%	30 points
	Score	___30___

You can also expand the preceding query to include the actual ratings in your result. The query that follows shows how this is accomplished using the DECODE function. You can also apply this to the remainder of the queries in this chapter if you would like to include the score in your results. At TUSC, we use a PL/SQL procedure to accomplish the results (we also display them graphically).

Query for hit ratio with rating

```
select (1 - (sum(decode(name, 'physical reads',value,0)) /
(sum(decode(name, 'db block gets',value,0)) +
sum(decode(name, 'consistent gets',value,0))))) * 100 "Hit Ratio",
decode(sign((1-(sum(decode(name, 'physical reads',value,0)) /
(sum(decode(name, 'db block gets',value,0)) +
sum(decode(name, 'consistent gets',value,0))))) * 100 - 98),1,30,
decode(sign((1-(sum(decode(name, 'physical reads',value,0)) /
(sum(decode(name, 'db block gets',value,0)) +
sum(decode(name, 'consistent gets',value,0))))) * 100 - 95),1,20,
decode(sign((1-(sum(decode(name, 'physical reads',value,0)) /
(sum(decode(name, 'db block gets',value,0)) +
sum(decode(name, 'consistent gets',value,0))))) * 100 - 90),1,10,0)))
"Score"
from v$sysstat
/
```

Sample output

```
  Hit Ratio      Score
---------- ----------
99.8805856         30
```

The data in V$SYSSTAT reflects the statistics for logical and physical reads for all buffer pools. To derive the hit ratio for the buffer pools individually, query the V$BUFFER_POOL_STATISTICS dynamic performance view.

The buffer cache hit ratio can be used to validate physical I/O simulated in the dynamic performance view V$DB_CACHE_ADVICE. This dynamic performance view provides information that assists in sizing the cache by providing information that predicts the number of physical reads for each possible cache size. Included in the data is a physical read factor, which predicts the number of physical reads that are estimated to change if the buffer cache is resized to a given value. To use V$DB_CACHE_ADVICE, set the parameter DB_CACHE_ADVICE to ON and allow a representative workload to stabilize prior to querying the view. Following is the query to validate physical I/O simulated by the buffer cache advisory.

Query to validate physical I/O

```
COLUMN size_for_estimate FORMAT 999,999,999,999 heading 'Cache Size in MB'
COLUMN buffers_for_estimate      FORMAT 999,999,999 heading 'Buffers'
COLUMN estd_physical_read_factor FORMAT 999.99 heading 'Estd Phys Read Fctr'
COLUMN estd_physical_reads       FORMAT 999,999,999 heading 'Estd Phys Reads'
SELECT size_for_estimate,
       buffers_for_estimate,
       estd_physical_read_factor,
       estd_physical_reads
FROM V$DB_CACHE_ADVICE
WHERE name = 'DEFAULT'
  AND block_size = (SELECT value FROM V$PARAMETER
                    WHERE  name = 'db_block_size')
  AND advice_status = 'ON'
/
```

Sample output

```
Cache Size in MB      Buffers Estd Phys Read Fctr Estd Phys Reads
---------------- ------------ -------------------- ---------------
               4          501                 1.36          11,130
               8        1,002                 1.27          10,427
              12        1,503                 1.19           9,743
              16        2,004                 1.00           8,205
              20        2,505                  .96           7,901
              24        3,006                  .84           6,856
              28        3,507                  .81           6,629
              32        4,008                  .76           6,249
(...Simplistic Listing Displayed)
```

Dictionary Cache Hit Ratio

The Dictionary Cache hit ratio displays the percentage of memory reads for the data dictionary and other objects.

Query for Dictionary Cache hit ratio

```
select     (1-(sum(getmisses)/sum(gets))) * 100 "Hit Ratio"
from       v$rowcache;
```

Sample output

```
Hit Ratio
----------
95.4630137
```

Rate Your System

What is your dictionary cache hit ratio?

< 85%	0 points
86–92%	10 points
92–98%	20 points
> 98%	30 points
Score	_____ 20 _____

Library Cache Hit Ratio

The Library Cache hit ratio reveals the percentage of memory reads for actual statements and PL/SQL objects. Note that a high hit ratio is not *always* good; see Chapter 4 for a detailed explanation.

Query for Library Cache hit ratio

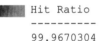
```
select    Sum(Pins) / (Sum(Pins) + Sum(Reloads)) * 100   "Hit Ratio"
from      v$LibraryCache;
```

Sample output

```
Hit Ratio
----------
99.9670304
```

The hit percentage is 99.97 percent, which means that only 0.03 percent of executions resulted in reparsing.

Rate Your System

What is your Library Cache hit ratio?

< 90%	0 points
90–95%	10 points
95–98%	20 points
> 98%	30 points
Score	_____ 30 _____

PGA Memory Sort Ratio

Automatic PGA Memory Management simplifies the way PGA memory is allocated. By default, PGA Memory Management is enabled. When running in this mode, Oracle adjusts, dynamically, the size of the portion of the PGA memory dedicated to work areas, which is based on 20 percent of the SGA memory size. When running in Automatic PGA Memory Management mode, sizing of work areas for all sessions is automatic. In 10g, the total amount of PGA memory available to active work areas in the instance is automatically derived from the SORT_AREA_SIZE or the PGA_AGGREGATE_TARGET (preferred) initialization parameter. In 11*g*, if you use the MEMORY_TARGET parameter, Oracle manages both the SGA and PGA. See Chapter 4 for initialization parameters used for memory allocation within Oracle and a discussion of the new parameters in 11*g* and Automatic Memory Management (AMM).

The objective is to have sort operations in the PGA performed in memory versus in the I/O subsystem (on disk) when possible. Statistics related to PGA memory sorts can be derived by the query in the next section or from the AWR Report, which reflects overall values for sorts in memory and disk, as well as the percentage of those in memory. The values reflect activity since the start of the instance. Values for a PGA Memory Sort Ratio greater than 98 percent are desired. Depending on the value of the memory currently allocated to the PGA by AMM (or set with PGA_AGGREGATE_TARGET), user sorts may fit into memory or be performed on disk in a specified temporary tablespace if this initialization parameter is not high enough to hold the sort.

Query for PGA Memory Sort Ratio

You can receive specific sorting statistics (memory, disk, and rows) by running the following queries or go to the AWR Report or Statspack output file (`report.txt`) to get these statistics (see Chapter 14 for more information on Statspack and AWR Report).

Query to get PGA memory sort ratio

```
select     a.value "Disk Sorts", b.value "Memory Sorts",
           round((100*b.value)/decode((a.value+b.value),0,1,(a.value+b.value)),2)
           "Pct Memory Sorts"
from       v$sysstat a, v$sysstat b
where      a.name = 'sorts (disk)'
and        b.name = 'sorts (memory)';
```

Sample output

```
Disk Sorts Memory Sorts    Pct Memory Sorts
---------- ------------ --------------------
        16        66977                99.98
```

Rate Your System

What percentage of sorts are performed in memory?		
	< 90%	0 points
	90–94%	10 points
	95–98%	20 points
	> 98%	30 points
	Score	_____30_____

Percentage of Data Buffers Still Free

When you start the Oracle database, users start using memory for their queries. Although this memory is reusable when the user's query is complete, when the following query runs on a system after two hours of processing, it is a good indication of how quickly the buffers are being used up (high-volume systems may need to vary the time frame to be much shorter). The number of free buffers divided by the total number of records in X$BH (which is the total data block buffers allocated—one record in the table for each buffer) is the percentage. Also note that you have to run this query as SYS. Remember that having many free buffers is not necessarily the best situation. See Chapter 13 on queries to this table for more information.

Query for free data buffers

```
SET VERIFY off
COLUMN PctTotBCMem for all
SELECT /*+ ordered */
       tot_bc_mem.TotBCMem,
       decode(state,
                 0,'Free',
                 1,'Exclusive',
                 2,'SharedCurrent' ,
                 3,'ConsistentRead',
                 4,'BeingRead',
                 5,'InMediaRecoveryMode',
                 6,'InInstanceRecoveryMode',
                 7,'BeingWritten',
                 8,'Pinned',
                 9,'Memory',
                10,'mrite',
                11,'Donated') "BlockState",
       SUM(blsiz) "SumStateTypeMem",
       COUNT(1)   "NumOfBlksThisTyp",
       ROUND(SUM(blsiz)/tot_bc_mem.TotBCMem,2)*100||'%' "PctTotBCMem"
    FROM (SELECT sum(blsiz) TotBCMem
          FROM X$bh) tot_bc_mem,
             X$bh
GROUP BY tot_bc_mem.TotBCMem,
           decode(state,
                 0,'Free',
                 1,'Exclusive',
                 2,'SharedCurrent' ,
                 3,'ConsistentRead',
                 4,'BeingRead',
                 5,'InMediaRecoveryMode',
                 6,'InInstanceRecoveryMode',
                 7,'BeingWritten',
                 8,'Pinned',
                 9,'Memory',
                10,'mrite',
                11,'Donated')
ORDER BY SUM(blsiz);
CLEAR COLUMNS
```

TOTBCMEM	BlockState	SumStateTypeMem	NumOfBlksThisTyp	PctTotBCMem
209739776	Free	12828672	1566	6%
209739776	ConsistentRead	43368448	5294	21%
209739776	Exclusive	153542656	18743	73%

Rate Your System

What percentage of buffers in X$BH are at a state=0 (free) after two hours of running in production (you may vary this to an appropriate level for your unique system)?	< 5%	0 points
	5–10%	30 points
	10–25%	20 points
	> 25%	0 points
	Score	____30____

Note that the reason you get 0 points for greater than 25 percent free is because the data buffers are probably oversized and potentially wasting memory. The scoring should be tailored to your individual system use. Remember this rating is only a general guideline and one that definitely needs to be tailored to your system.

Using the Result Cache Effectively

Oracle 11*g* provides a new, separate shared memory pool to store query results. This Result Cache is allocated directly from the shared pool upon database startup but is maintained separately. The Result Cache allows a query's result (for instance, a sum of all salaries after being calculated) to be cached in memory, allowing for large performance improvements for future queries executed multiple times that require the same results. By default, the Result Cache is set to 0.25 percent of the value of MEMORY_TARGET (if set), 0.50 percent of the value of SGA_TARGET (if set), or 1 percent of the SHARED_POOL_SIZE parameter (if set). You can also set it directly by using the RESULT_CACHE_MAX_SIZE = *amount* and the RESULT_CACHE_MODE=force parameters (set to force to use it automatically). Setting RESULT_CACHE_MAX_SIZE to 0 disables the Result Cache feature. You can use DBMS_RESULT_CACHE.FLUSH to clear it. Note results are *not* passed between RAC/Grid nodes. Please see Chapters 1 and 4 for more information. Also, check the documentation for other restrictions and rules.

Are you using the Result Cache effectively	Yes/no need	10 points
	No	0 points
	Score	____10____

Pinning/Caching Objects

Objects can be pinned into memory using DBMS_SHARED_POOL.KEEP if they are often-used objects, as shown in Chapter 10. Tables can also be pinned into memory by caching the table when it is created, or by using the ALTER command to cache a table. See Chapter 7 for more information on caching tables.

Some of the recommended packages to *consider* for pinning are the following:

DBMS_ALERT	DBMS_DESCRIBE
DBMS_DDL	DBMS_LOCK
DBMS_OUTPUT	DBMS_PIPE
DBMS_SESSION	DBMS_SHARED_POOL
DBMS_STANDARD	DBMS_UTILITY
STANDARD	

Rate Your System

Do you pin PL/SQL objects or cache tables when needed?	Yes/no need	10 points
	No	0 points
	Score	___10___
	Score	___230___ (A)
Example Memory Performance Index (MPI)	**Total Score**	___240___ (A+)

Grade Your System

MPI Grade	Comments	Score
A+	Top 10 percent of most systems	> 230
A	Top 20 percent of most systems	200–230
B	Top 40 percent of most systems	160–199
C	Top 70 percent of most systems	100–159
Needs help now	Bottom 30 percent of most systems	< 100

TIP
Measuring your MPI (Memory Performance Index) can be helpful in identifying potential memory allocation and usage improvements that could benefit your system.

Disk Performance Index (DPI)

This section measures disk use. The following table illustrates how to receive a perfect DPI score. This rating system is not meant to be an all-encompassing benchmark of disk use; rather, it is a barometer to see if disk use improvements might be beneficial. With the advent of SANs and other disk and disk-caching technology, you may need to alter the rating system to be more appropriate for your system. Strongly consider using Oracle features such as Automatic Storage Management (ASM), Locally Managed Tablespaces (LMTs) and Automatic Segment Space Management (ASSM). (See Chapter 4 for more information on these features.)

Category	Level Required	Maximum Score
Top 25 (worst disk) statements tuned	Yes	60
Top 10 statements disk use	< 5 percent	40
Tables/indexes collocated	No	30
Mission-critical table in LMTs w/ ASSM	Yes	30
redo logs/UNDO/data separated	Yes	30
Automatic UNDO Management	Yes	30
Disks used for temporary tablespaces	> 2	30
Disk Performance Index (DPI)	**Section Total**	**250**

Top 25 "Disk-Read Abuser" Statements Tuned

I have found that the top 25 statements with the most disk reads accessed on most systems, when left untuned, can make up over 75 percent of all disk and/or memory reads of the entire system. This section lists the most intense 25 disk reading statements for the entire system. The example that follows shows a pretty well-tuned system where only data dictionary queries show up (you would usually not tune these).

Query to get the 25 worst disk-read abusers

```
set serverout on size 1000000
declare
 top25 number;
 text1 varchar2(4000);
 x number;
 len1 number;
cursor c1 is
  select disk_reads, substr(sql_text,1,4000)
  from v$sqlarea
  order by disk_reads desc;
begin
 dbms_output.put_line('Reads'||'   '||'Text');
 dbms_output.put_line('----------'||'  '||'----------------------');
 open c1;
 for i in 1..25 loop
  fetch c1 into top25, text1;
  dbms_output.put_line(rpad(to_char(top25),9)||' '||substr(text1,1,66));
  len1:=length(text1);
  x:=66;
  while len1 > x-1 loop
   dbms_output.put_line('"              '||substr(text1,x,66));
  x:=x+66;
  end loop;
 end loop;
end;
/
```

Sample partial output

```
Reads    Text
1156       select file#, block#, ts# from seg$ where type# = 3
122        select distinct d.p_obj#,d.p_timestamp from sys.dependency$ d, obj
"          j$ o where d.p_obj#>=:1 and d.d_obj#=o.obj# and o.status!=5
111        BEGIN sys.dbms_ijob.remove(:job); END;
(...Simplistic Partial Listing Displayed)
```

Rate Your System

How many of your top 25 disk read statements in the V$SQLAREA view have you attempted to tune?		
	0	0 points
	1–5	20 points
	6–15	40 points
	16–25	60 points
	Score	60

Top 10 Disk-Read Abusers as Percentage of All Statements

This section measures the effect of the top 10 heaviest disk reading statements as a percentage of the entire system.

Script to retrieve this percentage

```
Set serverout on;
DECLARE
 CURSOR c1 is
  select    disk_reads
  from      v$sqlarea
  order by  disk_reads DESC;
 CURSOR c2 is
  select    sum(disk_reads)
  from      v$sqlarea;
 Sumof10 NUMBER:=0;
 mydr NUMBER;
 mytotdr NUMBER;
BEGIN
 dbms_output.put_line('Percent');
 dbms_output.put_line('-------');
 OPEN c1;
 FOR i IN 1..10 LOOP
  FETCH c1 INTO mydr;
  sumof10 := sumof10 + mydr;
 END LOOP;
 CLOSE c1;
 OPEN c2;
```

```
FETCH c2 INTO mytotdr;
CLOSE c2;
dbms_output.put_line(sumof10/mytotdr*100);
END;
/
```

Sample output

```
Percent
5.5183036
```

Alternative—simple and fast SQL

```
select sum(pct_bufgets)
from ( select rank() over ( order by disk_reads desc ) as rank_bufgets,
       to_char(100 * ratio_to_report(disk_reads) over (), '999.99')
pct_bufgets
       from   v$sqlarea )
where rank_bufgets < 11;

SUM(PCT_BUFGETS)
----------------
          68.59
```

Rate Your System

Take your top 10 disk-read statements in the V$SQLAREA view. What percentage are they of all disk reads?		
	> 25%	0 points
	20–25%	20 points
	5–19%	30 points
	< 5%	40 points
	Score	___40___

Tables/Indexes Separated

Tables and their corresponding indexes should be located on separate physical disks to decrease file I/O for a given disk. This is, of course, becoming harder to do, as DBAs are often unaware of where things are because of how a SAN may be managed. In Enterprise Manager, Oracle gives you a way to see and move *hot* (frequently used) and *cold* (not frequently used) data. Moving data to a hotter or colder region of the disk is now very easy. *Information Lifecycle Management (ILM),* or the management of data throughout its lifetime, is becoming more and more important. Older data can now be kept longer on physical, but slower, disks. Newer data can be cached to ensure speed when accessing it. Chapter 3 covers physical data and I/O in great detail and provides queries to assist in this matter. Note that if you use ASM (also covered in Chapters 1 and 3), you should ensure that when you add new disks you follow the tips on rebalancing that are listed in Chapter 3. Chapter 1 highlights many new rebalancing enhancements that have been made in 11*g*. For instance, ASM has a new feature in 11*g* called *intelligent data placement* that enables you to specify hot/cold disk regions in ASM to ensure that frequently accessed data is placed on the fast/outermost (hot) tracks.

Rate Your System

Are tables and their corresponding indexes located on the same physical disk or array?	Yes	0 points
	Disk array / ASM	20 points
	No	30 points
	Score	___30___

Mission-Critical Table Management

TUSC generally recommends managing mission-critical tables by storing them in locally managed tablespaces (LMTs) with automatic segment-space management (ASSM) utilized. Also, row chaining (usually when tables are stored in dictionary-managed tablespaces) may require rebuilding some objects. Row-chaining is also common when the database block size is too small.

Tablespaces implemented using automatic segment-space management are sometimes referred to as locally managed tablespaces with bitmap segment-space management, or bitmap tablespaces. To use automatic segment-space management, create locally managed tablespaces, with the segment space management clause set to AUTO. Automatic segment-space management in locally managed tablespaces eliminates the need to specify the PCTUSED, FREELISTS, and FREELIST GROUPS storage attributes for the tablespace. If possible, switch from manual space management to automatic segment-space management.

When a table is updated and the updated record block does not have enough room to fit the changes, a record is "chained" to another block. In this situation, a record spans more than one block and, in most instances, creates additional I/O. By analyzing a table for chained rows and querying the CHAINED_ROWS table, identifying tables that have chained records is possible. The CHAINED_ROWS table is created using the script utlchain.sql or utlchn1.sql, which resides in a file under the $ORACLE_HOME/rdbms/admin directory, where Oracle software is located (note that the exact name and location may vary depending on your platform). You may also consider the ALTER TABLE SHRINK SPACE COMPACT command, but please investigate the use/restrictions of this command in the Oracle documentation beforehand. To populate the CHAINED_ROWS table, use the ANALYZE command. The ANALYZE command has an option to determine chained rows in a table as follows:

```
ANALYZE table TABLE_NAME list chained rows into chained_rows;

Table analyzed.
```

The command places the output into a table called CHAINED_ROWS. The following query selects the most informative columns of the CHAINED_ROWS table:

```
SELECT OWNER_NAME,      /*owner of object*/
       TABLE_NAME,      /*Name of table*/
       CLUSTER_NAME,    /*Name of cluster if applicable*/
```

```
        HEAD_ROWID,         /*ID of the first part of the row*/
        ANALYZE_TIMESTAMP /*Timestamp associated with last analyze*/
FROM    CHAINED_ROWS;
```

Rate Your System

Are mission-critical tables stored in LMTs with ASSM,	No	0 points
and do you address chaining issues?	Yes	30 points
	Score	30

Key Oracle Files Separated

Separating often-accessed Oracle datafiles from each other can help eliminate I/O bottlenecks as well as eliminate potential saturation of the disk's memory cache. Separating heavily written files (especially redo logs) generally improves performance.

Rate Your System

Are redo logs on different disks than database datafiles?	Yes	30 points
	Disk array	20 points
	No	0 points
	Score	20

Automatic UNDO Management

TUSC recommends using Automatic UNDO Management (AUM) where possible. When configured in this manner, the database automatically determines how long UNDO data should be kept on the basis of the time queries take to run. UNDO data preserved within this window of time is said to be in the unexpired state. After this time, the state of the UNDO data changes to expired. UNDO data is a good candidate for overwriting only when it is in the expired state. The length of time that Oracle keeps UNDO data in the unexpired state depends on tablespace configuration. When creating a database with the Database Configuration Assistant (DBCA), the UNDO tablespace is set, by default, to extend itself automatically to maintain unexpired UNDO for the longest-running query. You can also specify a minimum UNDO retention period (in seconds) by setting the UNDO_RETENTION initialization parameter. This is only used with AUTOEXTEND tablespaces. Oracle extends the UNDO tablespace up to the size of MAXSIZE. Only when it is not possible to expand anymore is unexpired UNDO data overwritten.

When using a fixed-sized UNDO tablespace, Oracle automatically keeps the UNDO data in the unexpired state for the longest possible time for the tablespace of the specified size. If the UNDO tablespace does not have adequate free or expired space to store active UNDO data generated by current transactions, then Oracle might be forced to overwrite the unexpired UNDO data. This situation might cause long-running queries to fail with an error and an alert.

In the event that AUTOEXTEND is disabled (by default it is enabled) for Automatic UNDO Management, autoextending the UNDO tablespace will require adjusting the size of the tablespace manually. In this case, ensure that the tablespace is large enough to meet the read-consistency requirements for the longest-running query. Also, if using Flashback features, then make certain the tablespace is large enough to accommodate Flashback operations. The queries listed next estimate the number of bytes required when sizing the UNDO tablespace under different conditions. With Automatic UNDO Management, you do not have to create individual UNDO segments (Oracle does it for you). If you use AUM, you do not have to specify rollback segments.

The following information is appropriate for UNDO query A, B, and C. Sizing an UNDO tablespace requires three pieces of information:

- **(UR)** UNDO_RETENTION in seconds
- **(UPS)** Number of UNDO data blocks generated per second
- **(DBS)** Overhead varies based on extent and file size (DB_BLOCK_SIZE)

  UndoSpace = (UR * (UPS * DBS) + DBS)

Or, when the guesstimate equates to 0, then add a multiplier (24) to the overhead (DBS) to derive more appropriate results:

  UndoSpace = [UR * (UPS * DBS)] + (DBS * 24)

Two pieces of information can be obtained from the initialization file: UNDO_RETENTION and DB_BLOCK_SIZE. The third piece of the formula requires a query against the database. The number of UNDO blocks generated per second can be acquired from V$UNDOSTAT as follows:

```
SELECT (SUM(undoblks))/ SUM ((end_time - begin_time) * 86400)
FROM    v$undostat;
```

To convert days to seconds, you multiply by 86400, the number of seconds in a day. The result of the query returns the number of UNDO blocks per second. This value needs to be multiplied by the size of an UNDO block, which is the same size as the database block defined in DB_BLOCK_SIZE.

The query that follows represents a point-in-time estimate based on the UNDO blocks per second at the time of execution. The query can be utilized when UNDO space has not been allocated. If this time frame is during high activity or a worst-case scenario for UNDO, then the results derived provide a good estimate.

UNDO query A

```
SELECT (UR * (UPS * DBS) + DBS) AS "Bytes"
FROM    (SELECT value AS UR
         FROM    v$parameter
         WHERE   name = 'undo_retention'),
        (SELECT (SUM(undoblks) / SUM( ((end_time - begin_time) * 86400))) AS UPS
         FROM    v$undostat),
        (SELECT value AS DBS
         FROM    v$parameter
WHERE   name = 'db_block_size');
```

```
      Bytes
----------
126630.554
```

If the results derived from UNDO query A are low because of activity during the specified time frame, then UNDO query B can be utilized to derive results as follows:

UNDO query B

```
SELECT (UR * (UPS * DBS)) + (DBS * 24) AS "Bytes"
FROM    (SELECT value AS UR
          FROM    v$parameter
          WHERE   name = 'undo_retention'),
         (SELECT (SUM(undoblks)/SUM(((end_time - begin_time)*86400))) AS UPS
          FROM    v$undostat),
         (SELECT value AS DBS
          FROM    v$parameter
WHERE   name = 'db_block_size');
```

```
      Bytes
----------
335717.434
```

The following query is valid when UNDO space has already been allocated and the database has been running for some period of time.

UNDO query C

```
SELECT /*+ ordered */ d.file_name, v.status,
        TO_CHAR((d.bytes / 1024 /1024); '99999990.000'),
        NVL(TO_CHAR(((d.bytes - s.bytes) / 1024 /1024), '99999990.000'),
        TO_CHAR((d.bytes / 1024 / 1024), '99999990.000')), d.file_id,
        d.autoextensible, d.increment_by, d.maxblocks
FROM    sys.dba_data_files d, v$datafile v,
        (SELECT file_id, SUM(bytes) bytes
         FROM   sys.dba_free_space
         WHERE  tablespace_name ='NAME_OF_UNDO_TABLESPACE'
         GROUP  BY file_id) s
WHERE   (s.file_id (+)= d.file_id)
AND     (d.tablespace_name = 'NAME_OF_UNDO_TABLESPACE')
AND     (d.file_name = v.name);
```

If you are capturing the peak for UNDO query A, then UNDO query C might be the same at that point (where the two will come together). You can also use the UNDO Advisor.

Segment/File Query

```
col file_name for a40

select    segment_name, file_name
from      dba_data_files, dba_rollback_segs
where     dba_data_files.file_id = dba_rollback_segs.file_id;
```

Sample output (*Old* rollback segment way)

```
SEGMENT_NAME     FILE_NAME

------------     ----------------------
RBS1             /disk1/oracle/rbs1.dbf
RBS2             /disk2/oracle/rbs2.dbf
RBS3             /disk3/oracle/rbs3.dbf
RBS4             /disk4/oracle/rbs4.dbf
RBS5             /disk1/oracle/rbs1.dbf
RBS6             /disk2/oracle/rbs2.dbf
RBS7             /disk3/oracle/rbs3.dbf
RBS8             /disk4/oracle/rbs4.dbf
```

Sample output (*New* UNDO tablespace way)

```
SEGMENT_NAME                    FILE_NAME
----------------------------    -----------------------------------------
SYSTEM                          E:\APP\RICH\ORADATA\ORCL\SYSTEM01.DBF
SYSSMU1_3086899707$             E:\APP\RICH\ORADATA\ORCL\UNDOTBS01.DBF
SYSSMU2_1531987058$             E:\APP\RICH\ORADATA\ORCL\UNDOTBS01.DBF
SYSSMU3_478608968$              E:\APP\RICH\ORADATA\ORCL\UNDOTBS01.DBF
SYSSMU4_1451910634$             E:\APP\RICH\ORADATA\ORCL\UNDOTBS01.DBF
SYSSMU5_2520346804$             E:\APP\RICH\ORADATA\ORCL\UNDOTBS01.DBF
SYSSMU6_1439239625$             E:\APP\RICH\ORADATA\ORCL\UNDOTBS01.DBF
SYSSMU7_1101470402$             E:\APP\RICH\ORADATA\ORCL\UNDOTBS01.DBF
SYSSMU8_1682283174$             E:\APP\RICH\ORADATA\ORCL\UNDOTBS01.DBF
SYSSMU9_3186340089$             E:\APP\RICH\ORADATA\ORCL\UNDOTBS01.DBF
YSSMU10_378818850$              E:\APP\RICH\ORADATA\ORCL\UNDOTBS01.DBF
```

Rate Your System

Are you utilizing Automatic UNDO Management?	No	0 points
	Yes	30 points
	Score	___30___

Temporary Segment Balance

When the values specified in the initialization parameter file for MEMORY_TARGET (if used), PGA_AGGREGATE_TARGET, or SORT_AREA_SIZE (if used) (see Chapter 4 for detailed information) are not sufficient for sorting, users sort in their predefined temporary tablespace. If a large amount of sorting on disk is prevalent, you need to ensure that users are sorting efficiently. If you use TEMPFILES, then you must query DBA_TEMP_FILES instead of DBA_DATA_FILES to get this output. In 10g and

11*g*, you should be using TEMPFILES, which is another name for Locally Managed temporary tablespaces. A few of the advantages of TEMPFILES include:

- No need to check the data dictionary for freespace for a temporary tablespace because TEMPFILES use Locally Managed Tablespaces (LMT).

- Locally managed extents are faster with TEMPFILES and automatically track adjacent free space so coalescing is not necessary.

- TEMPFILES are always set to NOLOGGING; you cannot rename a TEMPFILE; you can not make a TEMPFILE *read only;* and you cannot create a TEMPFILE with the `alter database` command. If not using a TEMPFILE, you can use this next query.

Query (replace DBA_DATA_FILES to DBA_TEMP_FILES if using a TEMPFILE)

```
select    username, file_name
from      dba_data_files, dba_users
where     dba_data_files.tablespace_name = dba_users.temporary_tablespace;
```

Sample output

```
USERNAME    FILE_NAME

--------    --------------------------
SYS         /disk1/oracle/sys1orcl.dbf
TEDP        /disk1/oracle/tmp1orcl.dbf
SANDRA      /disk1/oracle/tmp1orcl.dbf
TEDR        /disk1/oracle/tmp2orcl.dbf
ROB         /disk1/oracle/tmp2orcl.dbf
DIANNE      /disk1/oracle/tmp2orcl.dbf
RICH        /disk1/oracle/tmp2orcl.dbf
DONNA       /disk1/oracle/tmp3orcl.dbf
DAVE        /disk1/oracle/tmp3orcl.dbf
ANDREA      /disk1/oracle/tmp3orcl.dbf
MIKE        /disk1/oracle/tmp3ora.dbf
```

Rate Your System

You can set up system users to utilize different disks for sorting. How many disks do you allocate for this?		
	All in system	0 points
	1	10 points
	2	20 points
	> 2	30 points
	Score	10
Example Disk Performance Index (DPI)	**Total Score**	**220** (A)

Grade Your System

DPI Grade	Comments	Score
A+	Top 10 percent of most systems	> 235
A	Top 20 percent of most systems	205–235
B	Top 40 percent of most systems	170–204
C	Top 70 percent of most systems	110–169
Needs help now	Bottom 30 percent of most systems	< 110

TIP
Measuring your DPI (Disk Performance Index) can be helpful in identifying potential disk improvements that might benefit your system.

Total Performance Index (TPI)

The Total Performance Index is the composite score of the Education, System, Memory, and Disk indices, as shown here:

Category Index	Maximum Score
Education Performance Index (EPI)	250
System Performance Index (SPI)	250
Memory Performance Index (MPI)	250
Disk Performance Index (DPI)	250
Total Performance Index (TPI)	**1000**

Example Education Performance Index (EPI)	Total Score	160	(B)
Example System Performance Index (SPI)	Total Score	220	(A+)
Example Memory Performance Index (MPI)	Total Score	240	(A+)
Example Disk Performance Index (DPI)	Total Score	220	(A)
Example Total Performance Index (TPI)	**Total Score**	**840**	**(A)**

Grade Your System

TPI Grade	Comments	Score
A+	Top 10 percent of most systems	> 925
A	Top 20 percent of most systems	795–924
B	Top 40 percent of most systems	620–794
C	Top 70 percent of most systems	380–619
Needs help now	Bottom 30 percent of most systems	< 380

TIP
Measuring your TPI (Total Performance Index) can be helpful in identifying bottlenecks; it is a simple barometer of your overall system performance and may help you find areas needing improvement.

Overall System Review Example

The following is an example rating scale. You can use the rating results to generate a yearly review for your system. Some of the items (such as backup and recovery ratings) are not covered in depth. The objective of this section is to give you ideas of some of the areas you might consider reviewing. This is not an actual client system review but a slightly modified version of several reviews to help generate discussion items for your review template. The goal is to give you a "feel" for a review.

Rating System

Here is an example rating report that you may use as a guideline as you detail an overall review and its ratings. Having a review that includes a rating for items that desperately need improvement or attention (where appropriate) is important in generating manager support. In many cases, DBAs needs managerial support to be allowed the time to address major issues with their system. At times, if the system is up and running, upper management may not realize that a change is needed. This review can be a catalyst for needed change as issues are identified.

Grade	Ranking	Comments
A+	Top 5 percent of systems	Excellent
A	Top 10 percent	Very good to excellent
A−	Top 15 percent	Very good
B, B+, B−	Top 25 percent	Good/could be improved
C, C+, C−	Top 50 percent	Requires improvement
D, D+, D−	Bottom 50 percent	Desperately requires improvement
F	Bottom 10 percent	Immediately needs to be corrected

TIP
Have your system reviewed on an annual basis by an outside party or, at the minimum, by someone inside your company.

Example System Review Rating Categories

The following table summarizes the results of the system review. Although some TPI categories are discussed, this section is an addition to the TPI that goes into greater depth. An overview of the recommended changes should follow this section, and the TPI rating could precede or follow this section. This section is more subjective, so an experienced person who you respect should make these evaluations. The ratings should include more detailed comments than those given here as an example. The recommended changes should be detailed with supporting documentation.

NOTE
This is an example, not an actual review.

Category	Grade	Comments
Overall review	C–	The system is running very poorly due to an insufficient amount of memory allocated for the data processing. Several areas need to be corrected immediately for substantially improved system performance, especially as additional users are added. Oracle 11g New Features are not implemented, Enterprise Manager features, such as SPA and the AWR Report, to help with tuning are not being used on a regular basis. An Exadata Simulation might be worth running to evaluate new hardware. You might also use Real Application Testing to test the new system.
Architecture	B	The overall architecture is good, but a review of the SAN and cache should be investigated to improve I/O distribution across available controllers. Compression should be investigated to save space and improve performance.
Hardware sizing	A–	The hardware is well sized for the business activity, but future growth may dictate a future hardware evaluation in the near future. The system is not tuned to take full advantage of the current hardware.
Security	F	Passwords are never changed, even when employees leave the company. Several unprotected files have hard-coded passwords. The default accounts are not locked when unused. This is unacceptable! The security information that Oracle provides at www.oracle.com/security has not been reviewed.
Memory allocation	B+	Of the 2G of memory, MEMORY_TARGET is set effectively, but more of the memory can be allocated to data by setting a (larger) minimum for the DB_CACHE_SIZE. Consider more Flash Cache (of some brand) to improve performance. Start investigating where you can utilize the Result Cache for better performance.
Database tuning	D–	The top 25 queries make up 98 percent of all resource usage. No effort has been made to tune these queries.
Disk configuration	B	Disk I/O is reasonably balanced but could be improved by partitioning a few of the hardest-hit tables and indexes.
Redo logs	B+	Redo logs are sized well, but you may want to add a few more of them for batch processing when they switch much faster.

Category	Grade	Comments
Archived log files	A+	File systems containing the archive log files are independent of other Oracle filesystems. Archived log files are archived to tape but also kept on disk for fast recoveries. New 11*g* DataGuard features are being used.
Rollback segments	A+	Automatic UNDO Management has been implemented and tuned.
Control files	A–	Multiple control files are located on different physical disks, but a backup of control files to TRACE does not exist.
Initialization parameters	A+	The system has 2GB of SGA. Obsolete initialization parameters have been removed.
Table design	C–	There is no database-level referential integrity.
Tables	C–	Tables are not partitioned to the degree that they could be, and Parallel should be set on some of the larger tables. Some of the smaller tables need to be altered so they will be cached in memory.
Indexes	C–	Indexes should be partitioned more. Bitmap indexes are not being employed for the low-cardinality (few unique rows) columns of query-only tables.
Tablespaces	C+	Tablespaces are severely undersized for future growth.

Items Requiring Immediate Action

Once you have reviewed your system, you need to make a comprehensive list of items that you need to address immediately. The following list is a summary (partial list only) of some of the issues that could warrant immediate action after a review:

■ Lock the default accounts when unused! Let's do it now.

■ SYSTEM and SYS passwords in production should be different in development.

■ All other default passwords should be changed. Change all user passwords, as security is currently compromised.

■ MEMORY_TARGET has been set, but minimums have not been set correctly for key initialization parameters. The minimum setting for DB_CACHE_SIZE needs to be increased immediately (MEMORY_TARGET is set correctly though)! You can do this with the system running in Oracle 11*g* if the MEMORY_TARGET is large enough. You can also use SGA_TARGET, so the DB_CACHE_SIZE is used only as a minimum for the SGA (see Chapters 1 and 4 for more information).

■ The top 25 queries causing disk and memory reads need to be tuned.

TIP
A system review should always include immediate action items. This ensures that the time needed for improvements will be allocated.

Other Items Requiring Action

The second list that you should make includes items needing attention, *after* the most pressing issues have been addressed. A summary example list is shown here. Your list should include more detail on how the action will be corrected:

- Monitor the items detailed in this document at least once per quarter with the current growth rate of the system.

- Resize the database objects that are currently oversized and undersized.

- Change all passwords at least once per quarter.

- Fix file protection so users are unable to delete Oracle software.

- Remove hard-coded passwords from scripts and backup jobs.

- Consider adding additional indexes for the top 25 worst disk read queries to improve query performance.

If you're making initialization parameter changes, compile a list with both the current and suggested values. Refer to Appendix A for a complete list of initialization parameters with descriptions. Lastly, make sure you repeat the review after you have made the changes to ensure everything has been implemented correctly.

System Information List

This section describes some of the system information that you should gather and keep with the review. As you look back on a review, you need to know what the system parameters were at the time of the review. Any ratings of specific items (such as backup and recovery) could be placed in this section. I also have included a sample DBA review that illustrates some of the areas that may be reviewed. Have someone else rate your DBA skills so you can continue to improve. This section has been greatly simplified for the book. It is a quick list designed to give a "picture" of the system as whole.

Memory-Related Values

The following are memory-related questions and answers about the system:

- What is the current memory for the hardware? **40G.**

- What is the current number of users? **500 total/50 concurrent.**

- What will be the future number of users? **100–150 concurrent in the next three months.**

- What other software is used on the system? **None that has a major influence.**

- Is the system client/server or browser/server? **Browser/server.**

- What response times are required? **Subsecond—OLTP transactions make up main mix.**

- How large is the database? **Currently 20T, with 500G currently free in the database.**

- How large are often-accessed tables? **One million rows is the average/100 million for the largest table.**

- What future software will affect memory? **None.**

- Are you implementing any other features/options? **Oracle Golden Gate in three months, SecureFiles in three months, Violin Memory Flash Memory in the next three months, and investigating Exadata over the next year.**

Disk-Related Values

The following are disk-related questions and answers:

- What is the maximum SAN capacity for the hardware? **20× current capacity.**

- What disk sizes are available? **Unknown.**

- What size will the database be in one year? **10 percent larger than current.**

- Is there a RAID (striping) level for database files/OS? **Yes; RAID 1+0.**

- Will you have multiplexed redo logs? **Yes.**

- What software will be installed in the future? **No additions in near future.**

- What system utilities will be installed? **Enterprise Manager.**

- What transfers happen nightly? **Bulk order transfers.**

- Any earlier notes on implementation? **Violin Memory Flash Memory in the next three months, and investigating Exadata over the next year also applies.**

CPU-Related Values

The following are CPU-related questions and answers:

- What is the maximum number of processors for the hardware? **6 dual currently/12 quad maximum.**

- Is there a future upgrade path? **Yes; path to 64 quad core processors.**

- What is the transaction processing load? **60 percent CPU average/90 percent sustained maximum.**

- What is the batch load? **Some heavy at night/okay during the day.**

- Are hot backups employed? **RMAN backups are employed with archiving.**

- Are batch processes running during the day? **None affect performance.**

- Will Parallel Query be used in the future? **Currently being used on some processes.**

- Will there be a future distributed setup? **Yes, with Oracle Golden Gate.**

Backup- and Recovery-Related Information

The following are backup- and recovery-related questions and answers:

- Does the system require 7×24 use? **No, it is 6×24.**

- How fast will recovery need to be (on-disk backup)? **12-hour maximum.**

- Are there "standby" disks in case of failure? **No, four-hour turnaround from HP.**

- How much data is "backed up"; is it being "tape-striped" with parity? **Unknown.**

- Has the UPS been established? **Yes.**

- Are export files also taken? **No.**

- Are cold backup procedures in place? **Not applicable.**

- Are export procedures in place? **Needs improvement/Implement Data Pump compatibility for export/import control files (new in 11g).**

- Are hot backup procedures in place? **Excellent.**

- Is the fast recovery area (FRA) sized properly? **Yes.**

- Are disaster recovery procedures in place? **Needs improvement (Data Guard suggested).**

The following is an example of some of the areas you may evaluate in a backup and recovery rating. Most Oracle DBA books evaluate features like these in greater depth. The layout should be identical to your system review.

Category	Grade	Comments
11g New Features used	A	Very good
Backup and recovery overall	A	Excellent. Recovery was tested in a simulated database failure.
Backup procedures	A	Excellent
Archiving procedures	A	Excellent
Recovery procedures	A–	Should have scripts ready to go for a recovery
Enterprise Manager set up	A+	Excellent
Hardware/ASM setup /tuned	B	Good
Backup knowledge	A	Very good
Recovery knowledge	A	Very good

Category	Grade	Comments
Disaster backup	A+	Excellent
Disaster recovery	A	Very good, rolling forward still being worked on

Naming Conventions and/or Standards and Security Information Questions

The following are naming convention, standards-related, or security-related questions and answers:

- Have you reviewed naming conventions being used? **Excellent**

- Have you checked file protections on key Oracle files? **Poor**

- Have you checked database security procedures? **Poor**

- Have you checked password procedures? **Poor**

- Have you reviewed security information at www.oracle.com/security and the security checklist at http://www.oracle.com/technetwork/topics/security/articles/index.html? **Not complete**

DBA Knowledge Rating

Having all DBAs reviewed by an impartial expert is paramount to identifying and improving their skills. Often, the primary DBA is too busy to attend training sessions or improve their skills on new versions of Oracle. Assessing DBAs helps identify their strengths and weaknesses. This process will fail if this review is used against a person. It *must* be used with the goal of identifying and improving skills.

Category	Rating
DBA knowledge overall	A
Oracle 11g New Features	A
Oracle Enterprise Manager	A+
Oracle architecture	A–
Oracle objects	B+
Oracle internals	B+
Oracle initialization parameters	B+
Oracle query tuning	A
Oracle database tuning	A
Oracle backup	A
Oracle recovery	A
Oracle ASM/Hardware	B–

Category	Rating
Oracle utilities	A
Operating system	B+

TIP

Reviewing a DBA's ability should be done only if the review is used as a means of improving the DBA's skills. Reviewing a person is a very sensitive issue and must be done by someone who has the goal of improvement in mind first and foremost.

Other Items to Consider in Your TPI and System Review

As I stated earlier, my goal in this chapter is to give the most basic barometer as a starting guide. There are many things here that may or may not be important to your specific system. Following are some items that I also think may be important to consider in the system review that you develop and the TPI that you customize for your system:

- Are all of the Oracle tools' schema objects in the SYSAUX tablespace?

- Are you effectively using ASM in your storage architecture?

- Are you effectively using transportable tablespaces if you often move a lot of data?

- Do you have appropriate Flashback technology implemented as a means of accelerated recovery and high availability? No query is slower than the one accessing a system that is down!

- Are statistics being collected often enough? Are they being collected too often on tables that are generally static? Is everything automated correctly?

- Have you used AWR and ADDM (see Chapters 1, 5, 14 for more information) to diagnose and fix potential problems?

- Has using Enterprise Manager Grid Control made you faster at deploying new nodes and diagnosing RAC issues?

- Do you have a sufficient test and development system to ensure proper testing before moving code to production?

- Have you set initialization parameters effectively that need minimum settings such as DB_CACHE_SIZE, SHARED_POOL_SIZE, PGA_AGGREGATE_TARGET, and JAVA_POOL_SIZE? Have you investigated the use of MEMORY_TARGET?

- Do you have an encrypted backup, or could your system potentially face downtime, causing severe delays in production performance? Once again, no query is slower than the one accessing a system that is down!

- Are you ready for the next hardware upgrade? Have you used Real Application Testing? Have you investigated future hardware Return on Investment (ROI), such as Violin Memory Flash Memory Arrays, Oracle Exadata, Exalogic, or Exadata Storage Expansion Rack?

Tips Review

- Measuring your Education Performance Index (EPI) helps you identify educational improvements that could be beneficial.

- Measuring your System Performance Index (SPI) helps you identify overall system improvements that could be beneficial.

- Measuring your Memory Performance Index (MPI) helps you identify potential memory allocation and usage improvements that could be beneficial.

- Measuring your Disk Performance Index (DPI) helps you identify potential disk improvements that could be beneficial.

- Measuring your Total Performance Index (TPI) helps you identify bottlenecks and is a simple barometer rating your overall system performance as it compares to others in the industry.

- Have your system reviewed on an annual basis by an outside party or, at a minimum, by someone inside your company.

- A system review should always include immediate action items. This ensures that the time needed for improvements will be allocated.

- Reviewing a DBA's ability should be done only if the review will be used as a means of improving the DBA's skills. Reviewing a person is a very sensitive issue and must be done by someone who has the goal of improvement first and foremost in mind.

- If you can't effectively monitor your own system, then contract someone who can. The cost of maintaining a database is usually far less than the cost of downtime when problems occur.

- Include new 11*g* items (covered throughout this book) in *your* items to review as needed.

References

Maurice Aelion, Dr. Oleg Zhooravlev, and Arie Yuster, *Tuning Secrets from the Dark Room of the DBA.*
Memory Performance Index, Disk Performance Index, Education Performance Index, Total Performance Index, MPI, DPI, EPI, SPI and TPI (Copyright TUSC/RJN 1998–2007).
Oracle 11g New Features Guide (Oracle Corporation).
Oracle11g SQL Language Reference Manual Versions (Oracle Corporation).

Many thanks to Brad Nash for updating the previous version of this chapter. Thanks to Lucas Niemiec for testing the queries in this chapter. Thanks to Randy Swanson, Judy Corley, Sean McGuire, and Greg Pucka of TUSC for contributions to this chapter.

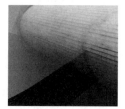

CHAPTER
16

Monitor the System
Using Unix Utilities
(DBA)

Part of being able to solve performance problems includes being able to use operating system utilities effectively. Using the correct utilities to find CPU, memory, and disk I/O issues is crucial to identifying where performance problems exist. Today's DBAs and system managers increasingly include performance management as part of their duties.

Basically, two main categories of activities are needed for system management. The first, accounting and monitoring, consists of tools such as accounting logs, software monitors, hardware monitors, or manual logs to monitor system usage, workload, performance, availability, and reliability. Accounting and monitoring help system administrators perform load balancing and control resource usage. The second, performance analysis, consists of using the monitored data to determine what system tuning is required and, by predicting future workload, when upgrading is required. In a broad sense, *system performance* refers to how well the computer resources accomplish the work they are supposed to do. This chapter gives you the utilities you need to accomplish both of these objectives.

Because the system utilities are part of Unix and vary from vendor to vendor, this chapter draws its details from one vendor and makes brief mention of other vendors. Including the details from Solaris, Linux, HPUX, and AIX would take up too much space. Oracle is dedicated to Linux, most recently with Oracle Linux with Unbreakable Enterprise Linux Kernel. Oracle also is dedicated to Solaris with the acquisition of Sun Microsystems and has announced that Exadata and Exalogic will run on both Oracle Linux and Solaris. In 2011, SAP certified a version of Oracle Linux and SAP also decided to certify SAP on Exadata in June 2011.

Unix/Linux Utilities

This chapter focuses on tips related to Unix and Linux utilities and shell scripts that can be used to find problems as well as gather statistics for monitoring. Tips covered in this chapter include:

- Using the `sar` command to monitor CPU usage
- Using `sar` and `vmstat` to monitor paging/swapping
- Using the `sar` command to monitor disk I/O problems
- Finding the worst user on the system using the `top` command
- Using the `uptime` command to monitor the CPU load
- Using the `mpstat` command to identify CPU bottlenecks
- Combining `ps` with selected V$ views
- Using `iostat` to identify disk I/O bottlenecks
- Determining shared memory usage using `ipcs`
- Monitoring system load using `vmstat`
- Monitoring disk free space
- Monitoring network performance

Using the sar Command to Monitor CPU Usage

The sar command has many different switches that you can set to display different pieces of performance information. With the −u switch, sar can be used to monitor CPU utilization. The sar utility is an effective way to see a quick snapshot of how much the CPU is "bogged down" or utilized (100 percent is not a good thing). Run this utility on a regular basis to get a baseline for your system, enabling you to identify when your system is running poorly. The sar command has the following benefits:

- Provides great information that you can use for performance tuning and monitoring
- Logs to a disk file (but does not provide per process information)
- Requires low overhead to run
- Is found on most Unix and Linux platforms

sar −u (Check for CPU Bogged Down)

With the −u switch, you can use sar to monitor CPU utilization. Of the two numbers following the switch for sar (in the following example the switch is −u), the first displays the number of seconds between sar readings, and the second is the number of times you want sar to run. Here is a sample report showing CPU utilization (the default):

Column	Description
%usr	Percent of CPU running in user mode
%sys	Percent of CPU running in system mode
%wio	Percent of CPU running idle with a process waiting for block I/O
%idle	Percent of CPU that is idle

 # sar -u 10 8

```
HP-UX sch1p197 B.11.11 E 9000/893    10/30/08

            %usr      %sys      %wio      %idle
11:55:53     80        14         3         3
11:56:03     70        14        12         4
11:56:13     72        13        21         4
11:56:23     76        14         6         3
11:56:33     73        10        13         4
11:56:43     71         8        17         4
11:56:53     67         9        20         4
11:57:03     69        10        17         4

Average      73        11        13         4
```

A low %IDLE time could point to which processes are using the most CPU or an underpowered CPU. Use the ps or `top` command (later in this chapter) to find a CPU-intensive job. A poorly written query requiring a large amount of disk access can also cause a large amount of CPU usage as well.

In the following sar output, the cause for concern is the large values being returned for %wio (waiting for block I/O) vs. actual heavy CPU usage:

```
# sar -u 5 4

             %usr     %sys      %wio      %idle
14:29:58       20       20        60          0
14:30:03       17       23        60          0
14:30:08       19       14        67          0
14:30:13       22       11        67          0
Average        21       16        64          0
```

This list shows a high %wio, waiting for I/O, time, pointing toward a disk contention problem. The iostat command (discussed later in this chapter) can be used to pinpoint disk contention.

TIP
Use the sar -u *command to see a quick snapshot of how much work the CPU is doing and whether the CPU is overwhelmed. Run* sar *on a regular basis to get a baseline for your system so you can identify when your system is running poorly. However, at times low CPU idle time can also be an I/O issue, not a CPU issue.*

Here are some things to look for in sar's output:

- Low CPU idle times.

- High percentage of time spent waiting on I/O or %wio > 10.

- Bottlenecks with %sys > 15, which could indicate that swapping, paging, or backups are causing a bottleneck.

- Abnormally high %usr, which could be due to applications not being tuned properly or CPU overutilization.

The sar –d Command (Find I/O Problems)

The sar -d command reports the activity of block devices on the system for each disk or tape drive. This command helps identify heavily accessed disks and unbalanced disk I/O. Disk-striping software frequently can help in cases where the majority of disk access goes to a handful of disks. When a large amount of data is making heavy demands on one disk or one controller, striping distributes the data across multiple disks and controllers. When the data is striped across multiple disks, accesses to it are averaged over all the I/O controllers and disks, thus optimizing overall disk throughput. Some disk-striping software also provides support for Redundant Array of

Inexpensive Disks (RAID) and the ability to keep one disk in reserve as a *hot standby* (that is, a disk that can be automatically rebuilt and used when one of the production disks fails). When thought of in this manner, RAID can be a very useful feature in terms of performance because a system that has been crippled by hard drive failure will be viewed by your user community as having pretty bad performance.

This information may seem obvious, but it is important to overall system performance. Frequently, the answer to disk performance simply rests on matching the disk architecture to system use. On Linux, the sar -d command does not return as much information, so you might want to use the iostat command instead. Here are some examples using sar -d to find disk I/O issues:

```
# sar -d
```

	device	%busy	avque	r+w/s	blks/s	avwait	avserv
09:34:54							
09:34:59	c0t6d0	0.60	0.50	1	6	3.84	5.38
	c3t6d0	0.20	0.50	1	6	3.85	3.76
	c7t0d0	0.20	0.50	4	50	2.60	0.89
	c7t0d2	8.78	21.61	270	4315	10.39	1.77
	c7t0d3	8.78	21.82	267	4273	10.77	1.80
	c7t0d4	23.15	0.50	252	13019	5.06	1.51
	c7t0d5	0.60	0.50	1	19	6.15	6.48
09:35:04	c0t6d0	2.60	0.50	16	140	5.04	1.69
	c3t6d0	0.40	0.50	1	7	1.12	9.02
	c7t0d0	1.60	1.23	10	152	6.01	5.30
	c7t0d1	2.40	1.07	10	155	5.45	6.31
	c7t0d2	0.80	19.38	15	234	10.02	1.71
	c7t0d3	0.40	21.89	12	198	10.89	1.85
	c7t0d4	24.60	0.50	274	10357	5.04	1.22

Things to watch for in the sar -d output include the following:

- %busy on a device that is greater than 50 percent
- If avwait is greater than avserv
- Unbalanced disk I/O load

Here's an example using sar-d that shows a disk I/O bottleneck. A high %BUSY and high AVQUE indicates a disk I/O bottleneck. Consider the following output, where disk sd17 is a big problem (it is 100 percent busy). If this condition persisted, an analysis of disk sd17 should lead to a reorganization of information from sd17 to a less-used disk. The sar command allows two significant numerical inputs (as shown next): the first is the number of seconds between running sar, and the second is how many times to run it (less than 5 indicates a five-second interval and 2 indicates two repetitions).

```
# sar -d 5 2
```

	device	%busy	avque	r+w/s	blks/s	avwait	avserv
13:37:11	fd0	0	0.0	0	0	0.0	0.0
	sd1	0	0.0	0	0	0.0	0.0

	sd3	0	0.0	0	0	0.0	0.0
	sd6	0	0.0	0	0	0.0	0.0
	sd15	0	0.0	0	0	0.0	0.0
	sd16	13	0.1	5	537	0.0	26.4
	sd17	100	6.1	84	1951	0.0	72.4
	sd18	0	0.0	0	0	0.0	0.0
13:37:16	fd0	0	0.0	0	0	0.0	0.0
	sd1	0	0.0	0	0	0.0	0.0
	sd3	1	0.0	1	16	0.0	32.7
	sd6	0	0.0	0	0	0.0	0.0
	sd15	3	0.1	1	22	0.0	92.3
	sd17	100	6.1	85	1955	0.0	71.5
	sd18	0	0.0	0	0	0.0	0.0
Average	fd0	0	0.0	0	0	0.0	0.0
	sd1	0	0.0	0	0	0.0	0.0
	sd3	0	0.0	0	3	0.0	32.7
	sd6	0	0.0	0	0	0.0	0.0
	sd15	1	0.0	0	4	0.0	92.3
	sd16	13	0.1	5	570	0.0	25.3
	sd17	100	6.1	85	1962	0.0	71.2
	sd18	0	0.0	0	0	0.0	0.0

Tuning Disk-Bound Systems

Conceptually, upgrading disk systems is fairly easy. Get faster disks, get faster controllers, and get more disks. The problem is predicting how much of an improvement you can expect from a given upgrade. If the system is truly spindle bound, and the load is parallelizable such that adding more disks is practical, this route is almost always the best way to go. When a straightforward upgrade path exists, no more likely or predictable way to improve a system's I/O exists than to increase the number of disks. The problem is that a straightforward path for this sort of upgrade isn't always obvious.

For example, assume you have one state-of-the-art disk on its own controller storing sendmail's message queue, and the system has recently started to slow down. There are two ways to add a second disk effectively to a sendmail system. First, you could add the disk as its own filesystem and use multiple queues to divide the load between the disks. This upgrade will work, but it will become more difficult to maintain and potentially unreliable if it is repeated too many times. Second, you could perform a more hardware-centric solution, upgrading to either create a hardware RAID system, install a software RAID system to stripe the two disks together, or add NVRAM (*nonvolatile RAM*—retains its contents even when power is lost) to accelerate the disk's performance. With any of these solutions, upgrading the filesystem might also become necessary. None of these steps is a trivial task, and there's no way to be nearly as certain about the ultimate effect on performance with the addition of so many variables.

Obviously, you can't add disks without considering the potential effect on the I/O controller. Some systems have limits that restrict the number of controllers that can be made available to the operating system. Although I rarely push the limits of controller throughput with a small number of disks because e-mail operations are so small and random, adding so many disks on a system that you run out of chassis space in which to install controller cards is possible.

Any time a system has I/O problems, do not make the mistake of quickly dismissing the potential benefits of running a high-performance filesystem. This solution is usually inexpensive and effective, and where available, it can offer the best bang for the buck in terms of speed improvement. If I am asked to specify the hardware for an e-mail server, in situations where I have complete latitude in terms of hardware vendors, I know I can get fast disks, controllers, RAID systems, and processors for any operating system. The deciding factor for the platform then usually amounts to which high-performance file systems are supported. This consideration is that important.

If a RAID system is already in use, performance might potentially be improved by rethinking its setup. If the storage system is running out of steam using RAID 5 but has plenty of disk space, perhaps going to RAID 0+1 will improve performance and increase the box's hardware life. If the system is having problems with write bandwidth, lowering the number of disks per RAID group and, therefore, having a greater percentage of the disk space devoted to parity may help. Using some of your unused space is certainly preferable to buying a new storage system. Changing the configuration of the storage system is especially worth considering if it wasn't set up by someone who really understands performance tuning.

If a RAID system has been set up suboptimally, you may be able to improve its performance by upgrading. Vendors often provide upgrade solutions to their RAID systems that can improve their throughput, both in terms of hardware components and the software that manages the system.

Lastly, to save money, the system might have originally included insufficient NVRAM or read cache. Performance might improve dramatically if you increase the NVRAM. See Chapter 3 for much more information on the topics in this section.

You can also use `tunefs/tune2fs` to help with disk issues. On AIX, see `chfs`. The `tunefs/tune2fs` command lists the current characteristics of a file system (careful—some commands cannot be run on an active system—check your documentation for more information before running these):

```
tunefs -v …/rdsk/c0txdx
```

To set *minfree* (the percentage of reserved filesystem blocks) to 5 percent (be careful, however; setting this could increase the overhead for file writes and reduce the file system's ability to avoid fragmentation):

```
tunesfs -m 5 /dev/dsk/c2d5s0
```

To change rotational delay from 1 to 0 (generally the default set with newfs and mkfs is 0, which should make tuning this with `tunefs` unnecessary):

```
tunefs -d 0 /dev/rdsk/c0txd0
```

Refer to Chapter 3 for additional information on tuning disk I/O at the database level.

The sar –b Command (Check the Buffer Cache)

The `sar -b` command reports on the system's buffer cache activities (*not* the Oracle buffer cache). It gives you the number of transfers per second between system buffers and block devices. The main parameters to look for are as follows:

- Read cache: %rcache > 90%, indicating the potential for bad disk I/O
- Write cache: %wcache < 70%, likewise indicating the potential for bad disk I/O

`sar -b`

9:48:44	bread/s	lread/s	%rcache	bwrit/s	lwrit/s	%wcache	pread/s	pwrit/s
09:48:49	437	422	0	404	413	2	0	0
09:48:54	604	858	30	617	630	2	0	0
09:48:59	359	451	20	431	479	10	0	0
09:49:04	678	750	10	671	633	0	0	0
09:49:09	369	577	36	473	511	7	0	0
Average	490	612	20	519	533	3	0	0

To look deeper into the buffer cache operation, consider a typical HP processor module. It consists of a CPU, a cache, a transaction look-aside buffer (TLB), and a coprocessor. These components are connected together with buses, and the processor module itself is connected to the system bus. The cache is a very high-speed memory unit. Typical access times are 10–20 nanoseconds (ns), compared to RAM, which is typically 80–90 ns. The cache can be accessed in one CPU cycle. Its contents and instructions and data that was recently or is anticipated to be used by the CPU are stored here. The TLB is used to translate virtual addresses into physical addresses. It's a high-speed cache whose entries consist of pairs of recently used virtual addresses and their associated physical addresses. The coprocessor is a specialized piece of hardware that does complex mathematical numerical instructions. For memory management in Unix, *vhand* is the paging daemon. The buffer cache, as you can see from the HP example, is a pool of memory designed to decrease file access time. Here are some other noteworthy buffer cache characteristics:

- The buffer cache can have a fixed state.

- The default system uses dynamic size allocation.

- The buffer cache can increase performance of disk reads and writes.

- Data is flushed from the buffer cache by the Sync process.

The sar –q Command (Check the Run Queue and Swap Queue Lengths)

The `sar -q` command reports on the system's run queue lengths and swap queue lengths. On Linux, it also gives the average load numbers. The –q switch gives the length of the run queue (runq-sz), the percentage of time the run queue was occupied (%runocc), the length of the swap queue (swpq-sz), and the percentage of time the swap queue was occupied (%swpocc); the smaller these numbers, the better. You need to compare `sar -q` to `sar -w` data to see if the runq-sz is greater than 4 or the %swpocc is greater than 5, which signals a potential issue.

`sar -q`

10:00:18	runq-sz	%runocc	swpq-sz	%swpocc
10:00:23	0.0	0	0.0	0
10:00:28	0.0	0	0.0	0
10:00:33	0.0	0	0.0	0

```
10:00:38      0.0        0      0.0         0
10:00:43      1.0        5      0.0         0

Average       1.0        1      0.0         0
```

Using the sar and vmstat Commands to Monitor Paging/Swapping

A quick way to determine if any swapping activity has occurred since the system started is to issue the command `vmstat -s`. Having a non-zero value in the swp/in and swp/out columns is a good indicator of a possible problem. You can delve into more detail using the `sar` command, which you can also use to check for system paging and swapping. Depending on the system, any paging and swapping could be a sign of trouble. In a virtual memory system, paging is when users who *are not* currently active are moved from memory to disk (a small issue). Swapping is when users who *are* currently active are moved to disk due to insufficient memory (very large issue). Swapping and paging could easily take an entire book due to the depth of the subject. Simple and fast commands to get a general picture of the state of your system are covered in this chapter.

Using sar –p to Report Paging Activities

The following table describes the fields displayed with the `sar -p` command. On Linux, use `sar -B`. On AIX, use `sar -r`.

Field	Description
atch/s	Page faults per second that are satisfied by reclaiming a page currently in memory (per second)
pgin/s	Page-in requests per second
ppgin/s	Pages paged in per second
pflt/s	Page faults from protection errors per second (illegal access to page) or "copy-on-writes"
vflt/s	Address translation page faults per second (valid page not in memory)
slock/s	Faults per second caused by software lock requests requiring physical I/O

`#sar -p 5 4`

```
           atch/s   pgin/s   ppgin/s   pflt/s   vflt/s   slock/s
14:37:41    13.15    20.12    179.08    11.16     2.19     58.57
14:37:46    34.33    20.56    186.23     4.19     1.40     57.49
14:37:51    22.36    19.56    151.30     2.20     0.00     60.88
14:37:56    24.75    22.36    147.90     1.80     0.00     60.28
Average     27.37    20.11    161.81     7.58     8.14     60.85
```

The key statistic to look for is an inordinate number of page faults of any kind. A high value usually indicates a high degree of paging. Remember that paging is not nearly as bad as swapping, but as paging increases, swapping will soon follow. You can review the daily reports over a period of time to see if paging is steadily increasing during a specific time frame. The command `sar -p` without any time intervals shows you the paging statistics from the entire day if you have enabled periodic automatic monitoring.

Using sar –w to Report Swapping and Switching Activities

The `sar` command with the `-w` switch shows swapping activity. On Linux, use the `-w` switch. On AIX, you have only paging, not swapping. The `sar-w` command displays the swpin/s, swpot/s, bswin/s, and bswot/s fields, which are the number of transfers and number of 512-byte units transferred for swapins and swapouts (including initial loading of some programs). The field PSWCH/S shows context switches that occur per second. PSWCH/S should be less than 50. Examine swapping activity closely if SWPOT/S rises above 0.

```
#sar -w 5 4

SunOS hrdev 5.10 Generic sun4m     08/05/08

            swpin/s   bswin/s   swpot/s   bswot/s   pswch/s
14:45:22     0.00      0.0      0.00      0.0        294
14:45:27     0.00      0.0      0.00      0.0        312
14:45:32     0.00      0.0      0.00      0.0        322
14:45:37     0.00      0.0      0.00      0.0        327
Average      0.00      0.0      0.00      0.0        315
```

A high count for process switching points toward a memory deficiency because actual process memory is being paged. Swapping is not a problem in the preceding example.

Using sar –r to Report Free Memory and Free Swap

The following command line and output illustrate the `sar` command with the `-r` switch:

```
# sar -r 5 4

            freemem   freeswap
14:45:21     517      1645911
14:45:26     294      1645907
14:45:36     378      1645919
14:45:41     299      1642633
Average      367      1644597
```

When freemem (*free memory*—listed here in 512-byte blocks) falls below a certain level, the system starts to page. If it continues to fall, the system then starts to swap out processes—a sign of a rapidly degrading system. Look for processes taking an extreme amount of memory, or else an excessive number of processes. On Linux and HPUX, use `vmstat`.

Using sar –g to Report Paging Activities

The following table describes the fields displayed with the `-g` switch. On Linux, use `sar -B`. On AIX, use `sar -r`.

Field	Description
pgout/s	Page-out requests per second.
ppgout/s	Pages paged out per second.
pgfree/s	Pages per second placed on the freelist by the page-stealing daemon.
pgscan/s	Pages per second scanned by the page-stealing daemon.
%ufs_ipf	The percentage of UFS inodes taken off the freelist by *iget* (a routine called to locate a file's inode entry) that had reusable pages associated with them. These pages are flushed and cannot be reclaimed by processes. This is the percentage of igets with page flushes.

```
#sar -g

           pgout/s  ppgout/s   pgfree/s   pgscan/s   %ufs ipf
14:58:34    2.40     74.40      132.80     466.40      0.00
14:58:39    1.80     55.69       90.62     263.87      0.00
14:58:44    2.20     62.32       98.00     298.00      0.00
14:58:49    4.59    142.32      186.43     465.07      0.00
14:58:54    0.80     24.75       24.15       0.00      0.00
```

A high ppgout value (pages being moved out of memory) points toward a memory deficiency.

Using sar –wpgr to Report on Memory Resources

More information about the system's utilization of memory resources can be obtained by using `sar -wpgr` (this combines the previously listed switches):

```
% sar -wpgr 5 5

07:42:30 swpin/s pswin/s swpot/s bswot/s pswch/s
         atch/s  pgin/s ppgin/s  pflt/s  vflt/s slock/s
         pgout/s ppgout/s pgfree/s pgscan/s %s5ipf
         freemem freeswp
07:42:35   0.00     0.0    0.00     0.0     504
           0.00    0.00    0.00    0.00    6.20    11.78
           0.00    0.00    0.00    0.00    0.00
          33139  183023
...
Average    0.00     0.0    0.00     0.0     515
Average    0.00    0.32    0.40    2.54    5.56    16.83
Average    0.00    0.00    0.00    0.00    0.00
Average   32926  183015
```

Check for page-outs (pgout/s means page-out requests per second; ppgout/s means page-out pages per second), and watch for their consistent occurrence. Look for a high incidence of address translation faults (vflt/s). Check for swap-outs (swpot/s). Occasional swap-outs may not be a cause for concern, as some number of them is normal (for example, inactive jobs). However, consistent swap-outs are usually bad news, indicating that the system is very low on memory and is probably sacrificing active jobs. If you find evidence of memory shortages in any of these, you can use ps to look for memory-intensive jobs.

TIP
Utilize the sar command to monitor and evaluate memory use and the potential need for additional memory. Paging is generally the movement of inactive processes from memory to disk. A high degree of paging is generally the predecessor to swapping. Swapping is the movement of active processes from memory to disk. If swapping starts to escalate, your system begins the downward "death spiral." Fixing memory hogs or adding memory is the correct solution.

What's a Good Idle Percentage for the CPU?

The optimum idle percentage depends on the system size and variation in time accessed. For instance, a system that is accessed with heavy CPU usage for short periods of time may have an 80 percent average CPU idle time. In contrast, a system with very small jobs, but many of them, may have the same 80 percent average CPU idle time. The idle percentage is not as important as what is available when you run a job that must complete immediately (and is very important to the business). A 50-percent idle CPU may be a problem for the company with a large CPU-bound job that must complete quickly, whereas a 10-percent idle CPU may be more than enough for a company that has a very small job (requiring little CPU) that must complete quickly. Oracle generally attempts to use the entire available CPU to complete a job.

I have found it helpful to run sar at regularly scheduled intervals throughout the day. The overhead of running sar is minimal, and it can be a great help in determining what was happening on your system last week when the problem actually started occurring. You have the ability to keep information in report format for 30 days by default. The following entries in crontab produce a snapshot of the system state every 20 minutes during working hours:

```
20,40 8-17 * * 1-5 /usr/lib/sa/sa1
```

The next entry produces a report of important activities throughout the workday:

```
5 18 * * 1-5 /usr/lib/sa/sa2 -s 8:00 -e 18:01 -i 1200 -A
```

To access the report at any time, simply type **sar** with the appropriate switches and you will see output for each sampling period. For further information, see your man pages for "sar," "sa1," and "sa2."

CPU Scheduler and Context Switching

The goal in tuning is to keep the CPU as busy as possible so it uses all available resources allotted to get things done faster. The five major process states are as follows:

- **SRUN**   The process is running or runnable.

- **SSLEEP**   The process is waiting for an event in memory or on the swap device.

- **SZOMB**   The process has released all system resources except for the process table. This is the final process state.

- **SIDL**   The process is being set up via fork and/or exec.

- **SSTOP**   The process has been stopped by job control or by process tracing and is waiting to continue.

The CPU scheduler handles context switches and interrupts. In multiprocessing environments, a *context switch* is when one process is suspended from execution on the CPU, its current state is recorded, and another process starts its execution. Obviously, in computer processing environments, the goal is good CPU and computer system component design in order to reduce context switch management overhead, or to have a processing load that works more efficiently and does not require too many context switches. Context switching occurs when any of the following occur:

- A time slice expires.

- A process exits.

- A process puts itself to sleep.

- A process puts itself in a stopped state.

- A process returns from user mode from a system call but is no longer the most eligible process to run.

- A real-time priority process becomes ready to run.

Checking Oracle CPU Utilization Within Oracle

This section explains how to examine the processes running in Oracle. V$SYSSTAT shows Oracle CPU usage for all sessions. The statistic "CPU used by this session" actually shows the aggregate CPU used by all sessions. V$SESSTAT shows Oracle CPU usage per session. You can use this view to see which particular session is using the most CPU.

For example, if you have eight CPUs, then, for any given minute in real time, you have eight minutes of CPU time available. On Windows and Unix-based systems, this can be either user time or system mode time ("privileged" mode, in Windows). If your process is not running, it is waiting. CPU utilized by all systems may, therefore, be greater than one minute per interval.

At any given moment, you know how much time Oracle has utilized *on* the system. So if eight minutes are available and Oracle uses four minutes of that time, then you know that 50 percent of all CPU time is used by Oracle. If your process is not consuming that time, then some other process is. Return to the system to discover what process is using up the CPU. Identify the process, determine why it is using so much CPU, and see if you can tune it. If the CPU_COUNT initialization parameter is manually set to 4 for an instance running on an eight-CPU system, that could also explain why it was only using up to 50 percent of the CPU resources. By default, an instance has CPU_COUNT set to the number of physical CPUs (or cores) on the server, but this parameter can be changed.

The major areas to check for Oracle CPU utilization are

- Reparsing SQL statements
- Inefficient SQL statements
- Read consistency
- Scalability limitations within the application
- Latch contention

Finding the Worst User on the System Using the top Command

The `top` command shows a continuous display of the most active processes. DBAs and operations experts often run this (or similar utilities) at the first sign of system performance issues. This display automatically updates itself on the screen every few seconds. The first lines give general system information, while the rest of the display is arranged in order of decreasing current CPU usage (the worst user is on "top"). If your system does not have "top" installed, it is commonly available from sunfreeware.com or various other sources on the Web. Simply do a web search for **"top program download"** and you should be rewarded with multiple locations from which to download the program. On AIX, the command is `topas`. On Solaris, both `prstat` and `top` are available.

```
# top

Cpu states:  0.0% idle, 81.0% user, 17.7% kernel,  0.8% wait,  0.5% swap
Memory: 765M real, 12M free, 318M swap, 1586M free swap

  PID     USERNAME  PRI  NICE   SIZE    RES  STATE  TIME   WCPU     CPU  COMMAND
23626     psoft     -25     2   208M  4980K  cpu    1:20  22.47%  99.63%  oracle
15819     root      -15     4  2372K   716K  sleep 22:19   0.61%   3.81%  pmon
20434     oracle     33     0   207M  2340K  sleep  2:47   0.23%   1.14%  oracle
20404     oracle     33     0    93M  2300K  sleep  2:28   0.23%   1.14%  oracle
23650     root       33     0  2052K  1584K  cpu    0:00   0.23%   0.95%  top
23625     psoft      27     2  5080K  3420K  sleep  0:17   1.59%   0.38%  sqr
23554     root       27     2  2288K  1500K  sleep  0:01   0.06%   0.38%  br2.1.adm
15818     root       21     4  6160K  2416K  sleep  2:05   0.04%   0.19%  proctool
  897     root       34     0  8140K  1620K  sleep 55:46   0.00%   0.00%  Xsun
20830     psoft      -9     2  7856K  2748K  sleep  7:14   0.67%   0.00%  PSRUN
20854     psoft      -8     2   208M  4664K  sleep  4:21   0.52%   0.00%  oracle
  737     oracle     23     0  3844K  1756K  sleep  2:56   0.00%   0.00%  tnslsnr
 2749     root       28     0  1512K   736K  sleep  1:03   0.00%   0.00%  lpNet
18529     root       14    10  2232K  1136K  sleep  0:56   0.00%   0.00%  xlock
    1     root       33     0   412K   100K  sleep  0:55   0.00%   0.00%  init
```

The preceding display shows the top user to be psoft with a PID (Process ID) of 23626 (this output may be slightly different on your system). This user is using 99.63 percent of one CPU.

If this output persisted for any length of time, finding out *who* this is and *what* he or she is doing would be imperative! I will show how to link this back to an Oracle user employing the ps command and querying the V$ views later in this chapter.

TIP
Use the top command to find the worst user on the system at a given point in time (the kill command usually follows for many DBAs). If the worst query only lasts a short period of time, it may not be a problem; but if it persists, additional investigation may be necessary.

Monitoring Tools

- There are GUI monitoring tools available on most platforms that either come bundled with the software or are available on the Internet. The Task Manager and "perfmon" are available on Windows; sdtprocess and Management Console are available for later versions of Solaris (once again www.sunfreeware.com has a plethora of free tools); nmon (within topas command) is available for AIX; and tools like Superdome Support Management Station (SMS), glance, and HP Servicecontrol Manager are available for HP. When using any tools remember to manage system performance with the following guidelines: Measure performance continuously.

- Assess systems and applications.

- Select the tool to use.

- Monitor.

- Troubleshoot issues that arise.

- Remove bottlenecks.

- Optimize applications.

- Plan for future workloads.

You will also find it worthwhile to remember to always use basic tuning guidelines:

- Do not tune at random except to solve an emergency.

- Measure before and after you tune.

- Tune one area at a time, and only change one thing at a time.

- Always use at least two tools when possible to evaluate tuning decisions.

- Know when to say stop.

Using the uptime Command to Monitor CPU Load

The `uptime` command is an excellent utility for quickly viewing the CPU load averages for the past 1, 5, and 15 minutes. The `uptime` command also displays how long the system has been running (the *uptime*) and the number of users on the system. You want to look at the load average. This is the *number of jobs* in the CPU run queue for the last 1, 5, and 15 minutes. Note that this is not the percentage of CPU being used.

```
# uptime
  3:10pm  up 5 day(s), 19:04,  2 users,  load average: 2.10, 2.50, 2.20
```

I have found that a system with an average run queue of 2–3 is acceptable. If you add the following script to your cron table to run every hour, your average system load will be emailed to you every two hours:

```
{uptime; sleep 120; uptime; sleep 120; uptime;} | mailx -s uptime
you@company.com
```

TIP
Use `cron` and `uptime` to have your system load emailed to you on a regular basis. See your Unix manual for any specific syntax when using these commands.

Using the mpstat Command to Identify CPU Bottlenecks

The `mpstat` command is a tool on Solaris, Linux, and AIX that reports per-processor statistics in tabular form. When using the `mpstat` command, you set the time interval between reports and the number of times `mpstat` should repeat. Each row of the table represents the activity of one processor. The first table shows the summary of activity since boot time. Pay close attention to the SMTX measurement. SMTX measures the number of times the CPU failed to obtain a mutex (mutual exclusion lock). Mutex stalls waste CPU time and degrade multiprocessor scaling. In the example that follows, there are four processors numbered 0–3, and a system that is heading toward disaster is displayed (this output is specific to Solaris).

```
# mpstat 10 5
```

CPU	minf	mjf	xcal	intr	ithr	csw	icsw	migr	smtx	srw	syscl	usr	sys	wt	idl
0	1	0	0	110	9	75	2	2	9	0	302	4	4	11	81
1	1	0	0	111	109	72	2	2	11	0	247	3	4	11	82
2	1	0	0	65	63	73	2	2	9	0	317	4	5	10	81
3	1	0	0	2	0	78	2	2	9	0	337	4	5	10	81
CPU	minf	mjf	xcal	intr	ithr	csw	icsw	migr	smtx	srw	syscl	usr	sys	wt	idl
0	2	8	0	198	12	236	113	35	203	60	1004	74	26	0	0
1	1	17	0	371	286	225	107	39	194	48	1087	60	40	0	0

2	0	22	0	194	82	267	127	38	227	49	1197	63	37	0	0
3	0	14	0	103	0	218	107	35	188	46	1075	71	29	0	0
CPU	minf	mjf	xcal	intr	ithr	csw	icsw	migr	smtx	srw	syscl	usr	sys	wt	idl
0	17	22	0	247	12	353	170	26	199	21	1263	54	46	0	0
1	8	14	0	406	265	361	165	27	200	25	1242	53	47	0	0
2	6	15	0	408	280	306	151	23	199	24	1229	56	44	0	0
3	10	19	0	156	0	379	174	28	163	27	1104	63	37	0	0
CPU	minf	mjf	xcal	intr	ithr	csw	icsw	migr	smtx	srw	syscl	usr	sys	wt	idl
0	0	19	0	256	12	385	180	24	446	19	1167	48	52	0	0
1	0	13	0	416	279	341	161	24	424	20	1376	45	55	0	0
2	0	13	0	411	290	293	144	22	354	15	931	54	46	0	0
3	0	14	0	140	0	320	159	22	362	14	1312	58	42	0	0
CPU	minf	mjf	xcal	intr	ithr	csw	icsw	migr	smtx	srw	syscl	usr	sys	wt	idl
0	23	15	0	264	12	416	194	31	365	25	1146	52	48	0	0
1	20	10	0	353	197	402	184	29	341	25	1157	41	59	0	0
2	24	5	0	616	486	360	170	30	376	20	1363	41	59	0	0
3	20	9	0	145	0	352	165	27	412	26	1359	50	50	0	0

TIP
If the SMTX column for the mpstat *output is greater than 200, you are heading toward CPU bottleneck problems.*

Combining ps with Selected V$ Views

Which process is using the most CPU? The following ps Unix command lists the top nine CPU users (much like the top command in "Finding the Worst User on the System Using the top Command," earlier in this chapter).

```
ps -e -o pcpu,pid,user,args | sort -k 3 -r | tail
```

%CPU	PID	USER	COMMAND
0.3	1337	oracle	oraclePRD
0.3	4888	oracle	oraclePRD (LOCAL=NO)
0.4	3	root	fsflush
0.4	1333	psoft	PSRUN PTPUPRCS
0.4	3532	root	./pmon
0.4	4932	oracle	oraclePRD (LOCAL=NO)
0.4	4941	oracle	oraclePRD (LOCAL=NO)
2.6	4943	oracle	oraclePRD (LOCAL=NO)
16.3	4699	oracle	oraclePRD

This command lists the %CPU used, the process ID (PID), the Unix username, and the command that was executed. If the top user was an Oracle user, you could then get the information on the process from Oracle using the queries listed next. You do this by passing the system PID obtained from the ps command into the following queries:

```
-- ps_view.sql
col username format a15
col osuser    format a10
```

```
col program   format a20
set verify off
select    a.username, a.osuser, a.program, spid, sid, a.serial#
from      v$session a, v$process b
where     a.paddr  =  b.addr
and       spid     = '&spid';

-- ps_sql.sql
set verify off
column username format a15
column sql_text   format a60
undefine sid
undefine serial#
accept sid prompt 'sid: '
accept serial prompt 'serial#: '
select    'SQL Currently Executing: '
from      dual;

select    b.username, a.sql_text
from      v$sql a, v$session b
where     b.sql_address      = a.address
and       b.sql_hash_value = a.hash_value
and       b.sid        = &sid
and       b.serial# = '&serial';

select    'Open Cursors:'
from      dual;

select    b.username, a.sql_text
from      v$open_cursor a, v$session b
where     b.sql_address      = a.address
and       b.sql_hash_value = a.hash_value
and       b.sid        = &sid
and       b.serial# = '&serial';
```

The following output shows an example that identifies the top CPU user utilizing the previously described commands and scripts:

```
$ ps -e -o pcpu,pid,user,args | sort -k 3 -r | tail

%CPU   PID    USER     COMMAND
0.4    650    nobody   /opt/SUNWsymon/sbin/sm_logscand
0.4    3242   oracle   ora_dbwr_DM6
0.4    3264   oracle   ora_dbwr_DMO
0.4    3316   oracle   ora_dbwr_CNV
0.4    4383   oracle   ora_dbwr_QAT
0.5    3      root     fsflush
0.8    654    root     /opt/SUNWsymon/sbin/sm_krd -i 10
1.7    652    root     /opt/SUNWsymon/sbin/sm_configd -i 10
3.6    4602   oracle   oracleCNV (LOCAL=NO)
```

```
$ sqlplus system/manager
SQL> @ps_view
Enter value for pid: 4602
```

Note that I use 4602 as the input, as it is the PID for the worst CPU from the `ps` command:

```
old   4:          and spid='&pid'
new   4:          and spid='4602'


USERNAME    OSUSER    PROGRAM                SPID    SID    SERIAL#
DBAENT      mag       sqlplus@hrtest         4602    10         105

SQL> @ps_sql
sid: 10
serial#: 105
```

Note that I use 10 as the SID and 105 as the serial#, as they were the values retrieved in the preceding query (PS_VIEW.SQL):

```
'SQLCURRENTLYEXECUTING:'
-----------------------
SQL Currently Executing:
old   5: and b.sid=&sid
new   5: and b.sid=10
old   6: and b.serial#='&serial'
new   6: and b.serial#='105'


USERNAME    SQL TEXT
DBAENT      select sum(bytes),sum(blocks) from dba_segments

'OPENCURSORS:'
Open Cursors:
old   5: and b.sid=&sid
new   5: and b.sid=10
old   6: and b.serial#='&serial'
new   6: and b.serial#='105'


USERNAME    SQL TEXT
DBAENT      select sum(bytes),sum(blocks) from dba_segments
```

Putting it all together (setting headings off), you get

```
DBAENT      mag       sqlplus@hrtest         4602     10         105
SQL Currently Executing:
DBAENT      select sum(bytes),sum(blocks) from dba_segments
Open Cursors:
DBAENT      select sum(bytes),sum(blocks) from dba_segments
```

If you had a problem with users executing ad-hoc queries and received problem queries that showed up in this result on a regular basis, you could add an automated `kill` command at the end to automate your job completely.

TIP
Combine operating system utilities with Oracle utilities to find problematic users quickly and effectively.

CPU/Memory Monitoring Tool on Windows XP

Task Manager can be used to monitor CPU and memory use under Windows XP. You can also select the columns to display in Task Manager, one of which is the process ID. However, because Oracle uses threaded processes, I did not find this feature useful in mapping to Oracle session IDs. The next screen shows a two-processor system under Windows XP:

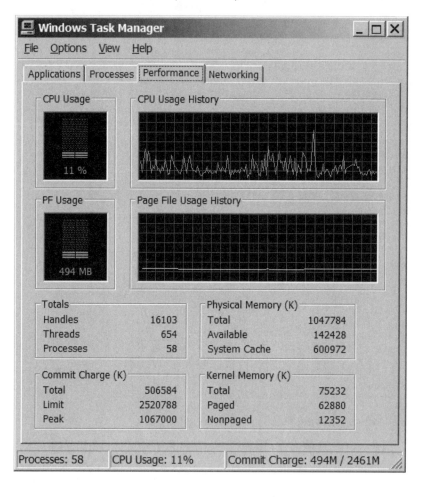

Using the iostat Command to Identify Disk I/O Bottlenecks

You can also use the `iostat` command to identify a disk bottleneck. The `iostat` command reports terminal and disk I/O activity, as well as CPU utilization. The first line of the output is for everything since booting the system, whereas each subsequent line shows only the prior interval specified.

Depending on the flavor of Unix, this command has several options (*switches*). The most useful switches are usually −d (transfers per second by disk), −x (extended statistics), −D (reads and writes per second by disk), −t (terminal or tty), and −c (CPU load).

Format: `iostat [option] [disk] [interval] [count]`

Using the −d switch, you can list the number of kilobytes transferred per second for specific disks, the number of transfers per second, and the average service time in milliseconds. This displays I/O only; it doesn't distinguish between read and writes.

Using iostat −d for Disk Drives sd15, sd16, sd17, and sd18

The output that follows shows that sd17 is severely overloaded compared to the other drives. Moving information from sd17 to one of the other drives would be a good idea if this information is representative of disk I/O on a consistent basis.

`# iostat -d sd15 sd16 sd17 sd18 5 5`

	sd15			sd16			sd17			sd18	
Kps	tps	serv	Kps	tps	serv	Kps	tps	serv	Kps	tps	serv
1	0	53	57	5	145	19	1	89	0	0	14
140	14	16	0	0	0	785	31	21	0	0	0
8	1	15	0	0	0	814	36	18	0	0	0
11	1	82	0	0	26	818	36	19	0	0	0
0	0	0	1	0	22	856	37	20	0	0	0

Using iostat −D

The −D switch reports the reads per second, writes per second, and percentage disk utilization:

`# iostat -D sd15 sd16 sd17 sd18 5 5`

	sd15			sd16			sd17			sd18	
rps	wps	util	rps	wps	util	rps	wps	util	rps	wps	util
0	0	0.3	4	0	6.2	1	1	1.8	0	0	0.0
0	0	0.0	0	35	90.6	237	0	97.8	0	0	0.0
0	0	0.0	0	34	84.7	218	0	98.2	0	0	0.0
0	0	0.0	0	34	88.3	230	0	98.2	0	0	0.0
0	2	4.4	0	37	91.3	225	0	97.7	0	0	0.0

This shows that the activity on sd17 is entirely read activity, whereas the activity on sd16 is strictly write activity. Both drives are at a peak level of utilization, and I may also have I/O problems. These statistics were gathered during a backup of sd17 to sd16. Your system should never look this bad!

Using iostat –x

Using the –x switch reports extended disk statistics for all disks. This combines many of the switches mentioned previously.

```
extended disk statistics
disk    r/s    w/s    Kr/s    Kw/s    wait    actv    svc_t    %w    %b
fd0     0.0    0.0    0.0     0.0     0.0     0.0     0.0      0     0
sd1     0.0    0.2    0.0     23.2    0.0     0.0     37.4     0     1
sd3     0.0    1.2    0.0     8.4     0.0     0.0     31.3     0     1
sd6     0.0    0.0    0.0     0.0     0.0     0.0     0.0      0     0
sd15    0.0    1.6    0.0     12.8    0.0     0.1     93.3     0     3
sd16    0.0    5.8    0.0     315.2   0.0     0.1     25.0     0     15
sd17    73.0   2.8    941.1   117.2   0.0     6.9     90.8     0     100
sd18    0.0    0.0    0.0     0.0     0.0     0.0     0.0      0     0

extended disk statistics
disk    r/s    w/s    Kr/s    Kw/s    wait    actv    svc_t    %w    %b
fd0     0.0    0.0    0.0     0.0     0.0     0.0     0.0      0     0
sd1     0.0    0.0    0.0     0.0     0.0     0.0     0.0      0     0
sd3     0.0    0.0    0.0     0.0     0.0     0.0     0.0      0     0
sd6     0.0    0.0    0.0     0.0     0.0     0.0     0.0      0     0
sd15    0.0    0.0    0.0     0.0     0.0     0.0     0.0      0     0
sd16    0.0    4.6    0.0     257.6   0.0     0.1     26.4     0     12
sd17    69.0   3.2    993.6   179.2   0.0     7.6     105.3    0     100
sd18    0.0    0.0    0.0     0.0     0.0     0.0     0.0      0     0
```

Once again, disks sd16 and sd17 are problems that I need to investigate and monitor further.

Combining iostat –x with Logic in a Shell Script

The script in this section takes the `iostat -x` output, sorts it by the busy field (%B), and prints out the ten busiest disks for the listed interval. Some options for this script are listed here, followed by the script example and output:

- This is the diskbusy script built on 1/1/2009:

    - The shell is running in `!/bin/ksh`.

    - This script gets an `iostat -x` listing and sorts it by %busy field.

    - Change print $10 to sort by a different field.

- Change to `iostat -x 5 5` to get a different interval and count (5 seconds/5 times).

    - Change `tail` to `tail -20` to get the top 20 busiest disks only.

```
iostat -x | awk '/^disk/'
iostat -x 5 5|grep -v '^  '  |grep -v '^disk'| awk '{
        print $10 ", " $0
        }' $* |
sort -n |
awk -F, '{
        print $2
        }' |
tail
```

Running the preceding shell script, I receive this output:

```
# ./diskbusy
```

disk	r/s	w/s	Kr/s	Kw/s	wait	actv	svc t	%w	%b
sd6	0.0	0.0	0.0	0.0	0.0	0.0	0.0	0	0
sd3	0.2	0.6	0.2	2.0	0.0	0.0	8.1	0	1
sd6	0.1	0.0	2.0	0.0	0.0	0.0	176.3	0	1
sd1	3.0	0.1	11.9	10.4	6.0	1.9	2555.3	3	3
sd17	3.4	0.7	37.4	17.2	0.0	0.2	54.6	0	4
sd16	4.1	0.8	38.6	26.0	0.0	0.6	129.5	0	6
sd17	99.0	14.2	790.8	795.2	0.0	3.6	31.4	0	99
sd17	100.0	14.0	798.8	784.0	0.0	3.5	30.8	0	100
sd17	95.0	14.2	760.0	772.8	0.0	3.6	32.7	0	100
sd17	95.5	14.0	764.3	762.7	0.0	3.5	31.6	0	100

In the preceding example, I run `iostat` five times and the top ten busiest disks are displayed over all five runs. The disk sd17 is listed five times because it hits the combined top ten all five times that `iostat` is run.

TIP
You can use the `sar` and `iostat` commands to find potential disk I/O problem areas. Utilizing the capabilities of shell scripting with these commands embedded can further enhance these commands.

Using the ipcs Command to Determine Shared Memory

Another helpful memory command that you can use to monitor the Oracle SGA is the `ipcs` command. The `ipcs` command displays the size of each shared memory segment for the SGA. If there is not enough memory for the entire SGA to fit in a contiguous piece of memory, the SGA will be built in noncontiguous memory segments. In the event of an instant crash, the memory might not be released. If this happen to you, note that the `ipcrm` command removes the segments (`ipcrm -m` for memory segments and `ipcrm -s` for semaphore segments). Use `ipcs -b` on Solaris and `ipcs -a` on Linux, HPUX, and AIX.

```
# ipcs -b

Shared Memory:
m    204 0x171053d8 --rw-r-----   oracle    dba     65536
m    205 0x1f1053d8 --rw-r-----   oracle    dba 100659200
m    206 0x271053d8 --rw-r-----   oracle    dba   1740800
Semaphores:
s 393218 00000000    --ra-r-----   oracle    dba     300
```

In the preceding example, the SGA is built in three noncontiguous segments (making up the 100M+ SGA). The instance is then shut down and started with a smaller SGA (so the SGA is made up of contiguous pieces of memory). After the SGA has been lowered to 70M, I again issue the `ipcs` command:

```
# ipcs -b

Shared Memory:
m   4403 0x0f1053d8 --rw-r-----   oracle    dba 71118848
Semaphores:
s 393218 00000000    --ra-r-----   oracle    dba     300
```

Fitting the entire SGA into a single shared memory segment is generally preferable because of the overhead that can be required to track more than one segment and the time required to switch back and forth between those segments. You can increase the maximum size of a single shared memory segment by increasing the SHMMAX setting in the `/etc/system` file (or `/etc/sysctl.conf` depending on version). See the Oracle install documentation for more specific information for your platform. On Solaris 10, the setting of the shared memory parameters moved to resource control, so if you modify the `/etc/system` file, any changes you make are ignored. Lastly, if you configure Hugepages, then the memory is pulled from a pool, and semaphores are not used. AMM requires the use of semaphores, so if you set MEMORY_TARGET (see Chapter 4 for setting the initialization parameters), you cannot use Hugepages.

TIP
Use the `ipcs` command to see if your SGA is built using multiple noncontiguous pieces of memory. A database crash can cause this to be problematic by not releasing the memory. Use the `ipcrm` command (only if the SGA pieces are not released after a database crash) to then remove the SGA pieces from memory. Do not issue the `ipcrm` command with a running database.

Using the vmstat Command to Monitor System Load

The `vmstat` command is a conglomeration of many of the other commands listed in this chapter. The advantage of `vmstat` is you get to see everything at once. The problem with `vmstat` is that you get to see everything at once and must evaluate it.

The vmstat command shows you these sets of processes:

r   Processes that are currently running

b   Processes that are able to run but are waiting on a resource

w   Processes that are able to run but have been swapped out

It additionally offers this information about CPU usage:

us   Percentage of user time for normal and priority processes

sy   Percentage of system time

id   Percentage of idle time

```
#vmstat 5 3

procs         memory              page               disk          faults        cpu
 r  b  w    swap    free   re   mf  pi po fr de sr  s0 s1 s6 s9   in    sy     cs  us sy id
19  5  0 1372992  26296    0    2  363  0  0  0  0  70 31  0  0  703  4846   662  64 36  0
23  3  0 1372952  27024    0   42  287  0  0  0  0  68 22  0  0  778  4619   780  63 37  0
16  4  0 1381236  36276    0   43  290  0  0  0  0  59 23  0  0 1149  4560  1393  56 44  0
```

Having any process in the b or w column is usually a sign of a problem system (the preceding system has a problem if this continues). If processes are blocked from running, the CPU is likely to be overwhelmed or a device is hung. The CPU idle time that is displayed in the preceding example is 0. Clearly the system is overwhelmed, as processes are blocked and people are waiting to get CPU time. On the reverse side, if the idle time is high, you may not be using your system to its full capacity (not balancing activities efficiently) or the system may be oversized for the task. I like to see an idle time of 5–20 percent for a static (not adding new users) system.

Be aware that as the amount of time the system is waiting on I/O requests increases, the amount of idle time on the CPU decreases. This is because system resources have to be expended to track those waiting I/O requests. I mention this to make sure that you take a look at the whole picture before making a decision. Eliminating an I/O bottleneck may free up significant amounts of CPU time. Time spent tracking I/O is reflected as 'sy' or system time in the vmstat output.

In the CPU columns of the report, the vmstat command summarizes the performance of multiprocessor systems. If you have a two-processor system and the CPU load is reflected as 50 percent, that doesn't necessarily mean that both processors are equally busy. Rather, depending on the multiprocessor implementation, it may indicate that one processor is almost completely busy and the next is almost idle. The first column of vmstat output also has implications for multiprocessor systems. If the number of runnable processes is not consistently greater than the number of processors, it is less likely that you can get significant performance increases by adding more CPUs to your system.

You can also use the vmstat command to view system paging and swapping. The PO (page-out) and PI (page-in) values indicate the amount of paging that is occurring on your system. A small amount of paging is acceptable during a heavy usage cycle but should not occur for a prolonged period of time. On most systems, paging will occur during Oracle startup.

TIP
Use the vmstat *command to find blocked processes (users waiting for CPU time) and also for paging or swapping problems. The* vmstat *command is a great way to see many of the* sar *options in one screen.*

Monitoring Disk Free Space

Often DBAs, especially those without in-house system administrators, need to monitor disk free space closely. For example, if the filesystem containing your archived redo logs fills, all activity on your database can instantly come to a halt! What follows is a script that allows you to monitor disk free space easily; it emails you a message if there is an issue. I would schedule this script to run about every 15 minutes. Scheduling a program to run at specified intervals is usually done through the cron process. You add or remove entries with the command crontab -e. This command should open your crontab file in a vi editor. Here's an example that checks disk free space every 15 minutes:

```
0,15,30,45 * * * * /usr/local/bin/diskfreespace.sh
```

This script runs the diskfreespace.sh program every 15 minutes, every day. For further information about scheduling programs via cron, refer to your systems man pages on "crontab." The command to view the man page (help page) for crontab is man crontab from the Unix prompt.

Finally, here is an example script to check file system free space on your host; it then emails you if there is less than 5 percent free space. You can edit this script for more or less free space by changing $PERC -gt 95 to, for example, $PERC -gt 90. This alerts you when the system has less than 10 percent free space. Note that this script is designed for Linux and will run unmodified on Solaris. To run it on HP, change the command df -kl to df -kP.

```
#!/bin/sh
# script name: diskfreespace.sh
#
#
df -kl | grep -iv filesystem | awk '{ print $6" "$5}' | while read LINE; do
        PERC=`echo $LINE | awk '{ print $2 }'`
        if [[ $PERC > 95 ]]; then
          echo "`date` - ${LINE} space used on `hostname` " | mailx -s "${LINE} on
`hostname` at ${CLIENT} is almost full" rich@tusc.com
        fi
        done
```

The df Command

One of the biggest and most frequent problems that systems have is running out of disk space, particularly in /tmp or /usr. There is no magic answer to the question, "How much space should be allocated to these directories?" but a good rule of thumb is between 1500K and 3000K for /tmp and roughly twice that for /usr (with larger systems these values need to be larger yet, especially for /tmp). Other filesystems should have about 5 or 10 percent of the system's available capacity. The df command shows the free disk space on each disk that is mounted. The -k option displays the information about each filesystem in columns, with the allocations in KB. On HPUX, use bdf.

```
% df -k

Filesystem             kbytes    used    avail capacity  Mounted on
/dev/dsk/c0t0d0s0       38111   21173    13128    62%    /
/dev/dsk/c0t0d0s6      246167  171869    49688    78%    /usr
/proc                       0       0        0     0%    /proc
fd                          0       0        0     0%    /dev/fd
swap                   860848     632   860216     0%    /tmp
/dev/dsk/c0t0d0s7      188247   90189    79238    53%    /home
/dev/dsk/c0t0d0s5      492351  179384   263737    40%    /opt
gs:/home/prog/met       77863   47127    22956    67%    /home/met
```

From this display, you can see the following information (all entries are in KB):

Column	Description
kbytes	Total size of usable space in file system (size is adjusted by allotted head room)
used	Space used
avail	Space available for use
capacity	Percentage of total capacity used
Mounted on	Mount point

The usable space has been adjusted to take into account a 10-percent reserve head room adjustment and thus reflects only 90 percent of actual capacity. The percentage shown under capacity is, therefore, used space divided by the adjusted usable space.

Monitoring Network Performance

Occasionally, you might notice a performance drop that can only be attributed to network performance. You know this because you have tuned every other aspect of the system, and network problems are all that are left. I say this because network tuning can be very difficult with many variables. I usually consider it "tuning of last resort." That's not to say that the network settings "out of the box" cannot be improved upon for your environment—they can. But you usually see a much larger percentage improvement by tuning your SQL statements than by tuning your TCP stack.

The settings that I describe here are Solaris specific, but analogs are available in Linux, HP, and AIX. Any Unix-based system that communicates using the TCP protocol uses some or all of the settings in some way. Making any of these changes requires that you are the superuser, or "root." You can view them if you are not, but you cannot make any changes. Here's a simple Perl script to list /dev/tcp parameters and their current values:

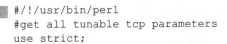

```
#/!/usr/bin/perl
#get all tunable tcp parameters
use strict;
```

```
#get all of the possible parameters
my tcp= `ndd /dev/tcp \?`;
foreach (@tcp)
{
(my $parameter, my $junk)= split(/\(/, $_);
(my $parameter, my $junk2)= split(/ /, $parameter);
chomp ($junk);
chomp ($parameter);
#now disregard parameters that we cannot change
if ( $junk ne "read only)" && $junk ne "write only)" && parameter ne   \
"tcp_host_param" && $parameter ne "?")
{
(my $type, my $junk)=split(/_/, $parameter);
my $result = `ndd /dev/tcp $parameter`;
chomp ($result);
print "$parameter\t";
print "$result\n";
}
}
```

Now that you have a listing of your TCP settings, you can take a look at tuning some of them. First, you have to determine if anything actually needs to be tuned! The `netstat -s` output helps you determine where your possible problems are located. The normal output has been truncated to allow you to focus on certain areas.

TCP

tcpRtoMax	= 60000	tcpMaxConn	= -1
tcpActiveOpens	=138398	tcpPassiveOpens	=157734
tcpCurrEstab	= 96	tcpOutSegs	=761862710
tcpOutDataSegs	=737025936	tcpOutDataBytes	=974079802
tcpRetransSegs	= 56784	tcpRetransBytes	=16421938
tcpOutAck	=24835587	tcpOutAckDelayed	=3487354
tcpInInorderSegs	=95997710	tcpInInorderBytes	=3154946802
tcpInUnorderSegs	= 54135	tcpInUnorderBytes	=3265601
tcpListenDrop	= 11	tcpListenDropQ0	= 0
tcpHalfOpenDrop	= 0	tcpOutSackRetrans	= 319

Here, you see a relatively high number of tcpActiveOpens and tcpPassiveOpens. I know that this number is high because I know the system has only been up for 25 hours. Incoming calls are "'passive opens" and outgoing calls are "active opens." These values seem to indicate that a high amount of network traffic on this box. This supposition is further reinforced by the size of tcpOutdataBytes. To determine if you are possibly reaching the maximum throughput on your network interface, the calculation is simple:

TcpRetransBytes/tcpOutDataBytes = retransmission %.

If this number is greater than 10 percent, then you most likely have a serious throughput problem. You should almost definitely add more bandwidth or reduce the amount of traffic coming and going to the box. Remember that only a certain amount of traffic can go through a network card and only a certain number of users can be connected or establishing connections at one time. You can determine if you are having a problem with user connections by looking at tcpListenDrop. If the value is greater than 0, connections are being dropped and you need to increase the size of the listen queue. You do that by increasing the Solaris operating system parameter TCP_CONN_REQ_MAX_Q0. The default on Solaris is 1024. I usually recommend changing this to 10000 instead. Here's the command to make the change on a running system:

```
'ndd -set /dev/tcp /tcp_conn_req_max_q0 10000'
```

A simple way to drastically improve the efficiency of managing *active* TCP connections is to increase the Solaris operating system parameter TCP_CONNECTION_HASH_SIZE. Increasing this improves the efficiency of hash table lookups on your system quite a bit. Additional memory is required to manage the increased size of the hash table, but if you are expecting many connections, it is well worth the cost. To make this point clearer, the system defaults to 512, and Sun engineers set this to 262144 when they are benchmarking their systems at times! The benefit must be extreme if they change the default so drastically (but such a change should still be tested for your system)! Because this is a read-only parameter, you must set it in the /etc/system file. A system reboot is required.

Another interesting phenomenon is the "slow start" bug. This intentional bug was intended to avoid congestion on the network by using a "delayed ACK." By using a delayed ACK, the application can piggyback its response onto the first response back to the server. It seems like a great idea, until . . . a sender request can't fit into a single packet. TCP then breaks up the packet before sending an ACK and sends a partial packet. The receiver is waiting for the complete packet before sending any more data, which it will not do until it receives a full packet. But the "slow start" phase only allows *one* packet. The sender needs to send *more* than one packet. This deadlock eventually times out, and the receiver sends the ACK that is needed to establish the connection. This problem doesn't normally show up, unless you have many short-lived connections that are experiencing this issue. For example, a web server may have serious performance problems due to this issue. On Solaris, as of 2.6, the TCP_SLOW_START_INITIAL parameter was added to bypass this problem. It defaults to 1, which is the normal behavior mentioned previously. I recommend that you consider changing this to either 2 or 4. Note that as of Solaris 8, this changes to 4 for the default, so no action should be needed.

```
ndd -set /dev/tcp tcp_slow_start_initial 4
```

Several timers can be set to improve performance as well. The most important one, in my opinion, is the TCP_KEEPALIVE_INTERVAL. This parameter sets how long the system will wait to verify that a connection is still valid. On a web server, which can have many short-lived connections, this setting can be critical. The setting defaults to 7200000 (which is 2 hours). On a busy web server, you want to clean up dead connections much faster, however.

```
ndd -set /dev/tcp tcp_keepalive_interval 10000
```

Sometimes the `netstat` output shows many connections that are in "FIN_WAIT_2." This connection is, essentially, "waiting to die." If an application does not close a connection actively or a browser crashes (that never happens!), a connection ends up in FIN_WAIT_2, using up resources that should be allocated to new connections. The default TCP_FIN_WAIT_2_FLUSH_INTERVAL is 675000 milliseconds. Ten percent of that seems to be a much more reasonable amount of time to wait before cleaning up the connections.

```
ndd -set /dev/tcp tcp_fin_wait_2_flush_interval 67500
```

TIP
Use the ndd *and* netstat *commands to tune network performance issues.*

Monitoring Using the spray Command

The spray command is a Unix command used to deliver a burst of data packets to another machine and report how many of the packets made the trip successfully and how long it took. Similar in scope to its little brother ping, spray can be used more effectively to monitor performance than ping because it can send more data. The results of the command, shown next, let you know whether the other machine was able to receive successfully all of the packets you sent. In the example shown here, a burst of data packets is being sent from the source machine (pacland) to the destination machine (galaxian). Usually sprayd must be registered as a service and started on the destination machine. Keep in mind, however, that at times spray is not always useful as a networking benchmark because drops can be caused by spray sending packets faster than they can be locally buffered (consult the docs and use with caution).

```
pacland % spray galaxian
sending 1162 packets of lnth 86 to galaxian ...
        no packets dropped by galaxian
5917 packets/sec, 508943 bytes/sec
```

In the preceding example, the destination machine (galaxian) successfully returned all of the data sent to it by the source machine (pacland). If galaxian were under heavy load, caused by either network traffic or other intense activity, some of the data packets would not have been returned by galaxian. The spray command defaults to sending 1162 86-byte packets. The spray command supports several command-line parameters that you can use to modify the count of packets sent, the length of each packet, and the number of buffers to use on the source machine. These parameters can be helpful in running more realistic tests. The listing that follows shows the spray command used with the -c option, which delivers 1000 packets, and the -l option, which sets each packet to 4096 bytes:

```
pacland % spray -c 1000 -d 20 -l 4096 galaxian

sending 1000 packets of lnth 4096 to galaxian ...
        no packets dropped by galaxian
95 packets/sec, 392342 bytes/sec
```

Simulating network data transmissions with spray can be made more realistic by increasing the number of packets and the length of each packet. The -c option lets you increase the total count of packets sent, and the -l option lets you set the length of each packet. Setting these can be helpful in mimicking certain transmission protocols. The -d option is used to set the delay between each packet transmission. This can be useful so you do not overrun the network buffers on the source machine. The listing that follows shows what a problem might look like. In this case, the source machine (pacland) overwhelms the destination machine (millipede) with data. This does not immediately indicate that a networking problem exists, but that the destination machine (millipede) might not have enough available processing power to handle the network requests.

```
pacland % spray -l 4096 millipede

sending 1162 packets of lnth 4096 to millipede ...
        415 packets (35.714%) dropped by millipede
73 packets/sec, 6312 bytes/sec
```

In the event that your tests with `spray` result in packet loss, your next step is to take a closer look at the destination machine you have been testing. First, look for a heavy process load, memory shortage, or other CPU problems. Anything on that system that might be bogging it down can cause degraded network performance. In the event that you cannot find anything wrong with your test system that might be causing a delayed network response, sending a similar test back to your initial test machine might indicate a larger network problem. At that point, it is time to start checking your routing hardware and your infrastructure with the analysis hardware. Here is an example of how to use `netstat` to monitor individual packet and error rates for each network interface:

```
pacland % netstat -i

Name Mtu   Network    Address      Ipkts       Ierrs   Opkts      Oerrs   Coll
ec3  1500  207.221.40 pacland       45223252   0        953351793  0       21402113
lo0  8304  loopback   localhost 2065169 0 2065169 0 0
```

The table that follows shows the values of the output from the `netstat` command.

Column	Description
Name	The name of the network interface (naming conventions vary among Unix versions)
MTU	The interface's maximum packet size
Network	The network that the interface connects to
Address	The interface's resolved Internet name
Ipkts	The number of incoming packets since the last time the system was rebooted
Ierrs	The number of incoming packet errors since the last time the system was rebooted
Opkts	The number of outgoing packets since the last time the system was rebooted
Oerrs	The number of outgoing packet errors since the last time the system was rebooted
Coll	The number of detected collisions

Monitoring Network Performance with nfsstat –c

Systems running NFS can skip `spray` and instead use `nfsstat -c`. The `-c` option specifies the client statistics, and `-s` can be used for server statistics. As the name implies, client statistics summarize this system's use of another machine as a server. The NFS service uses synchronous procedures called remote procedure calls (RPCs). This means the client waits for the server to complete the file activity before it proceeds. If the server fails to respond, the client retransmits the request. Just as with collisions, the worse the condition of the communication, the more traffic generated. The more traffic generated, the slower the network and the greater the possibility of collisions. So if the retransmission rate is large, you should look for servers that are under heavy loads, high collision rates that are delaying the packets en route, or Ethernet interfaces that are dropping packets.

```
% nfsstat -c

Client rpc:
calls     badcalls retrans badxid    timeout  wait    newcred  timers
74107     0        72      0         72       0       0        82

Client nfs:
calls     badcalls nclget   nclcreate
73690     0        73690    0
null      getattr  setattr  root      lookup   readlink  read
0  0%     4881  7% 1  0%    0  0%     130  0%  0   0%    465  1%
wrcache   write    create   remove    rename   link      symlink
0  0%     68161 92% 16  0%  1  0%     0  0%    0   0%    0  0%
mkdir     rmdir    readdir  statfs
0  0%     0  0%    32  0%   3  0%
```

The following fields are shown here:

Field	Description
calls	The number of calls sent
badcalls	The number of calls rejected by the RPC
retrans	The number of retransmissions
badxid	The number of duplicated acknowledgments received
timeout	The number of time-outs
wait	The number of times no available client handles caused waiting
newcred	The number of refreshed authentications
timers	The number of times the time-out value is reached or exceeded
readlink	The number of reads made to a symbolic link

If the time-out ratio is high, the problem may be unresponsive NFS servers or slow networks that are impeding the timely delivery and response of the packets. In this example, there are relatively few time-outs compared to the number of calls (72/74107 or about 1/10 of 1 percent) that retransmit. As the percentage increases toward 5 percent, system administrators should start to take a closer look. If badxid is roughly the same as retrans, the problem is probably an NFS server that is falling behind in servicing NFS requests, since duplicate acknowledgments are being received for NFS requests in roughly the same numbers as the retransmissions that are required. The same thing is true if badxid is roughly the same as timeout. However, if badxid is a much smaller number than retrans and timeout, then it follows that the problem is most likely the network.

Monitoring Network Performance with netstat

One way to check for network loading is to use `netstat` without any parameters:

```
% netstat

TCP
    Local Address         Remote Address       Swind Send-Q Rwind Recv-Q  State
    ------------------    -------------------- ----- ------ ----- ------ -------
AAA1.1023             bbb2.login            8760      0  8760      0 ESTABLISHED
AAA1.listen           Cccc.32980            8760      0  8760      0 ESTABLISHED
AAA1.login            Dddd.1019             8760      0  8760      0 ESTABLISHED
AAA1.32782            AAA1.32774           16384      0 16384      0 ESTABLISHED
...
```

In the report, the important field is the send-q field, which indicates the depth of the send queue for packets. If the numbers in send-q are large and increasing across several of the connections, the network is probably bogged down.

Corrective Network Actions

If you suspect that there are problems with the integrity of the network itself, you must try to determine where the faulty piece of equipment is. If the problem is that the network is extremely busy, thus increasing collisions, time-outs, retransmissions, and so on, you may need to redistribute the workload more appropriately. By partitioning and segmenting the network nodes into subnetworks that more clearly reflect the underlying workloads, you can maximize overall network performance. Installing additional network interfaces in your gateway and adjusting the addressing on the gateway to reflect the new subnetworks accomplishes this. Altering your cabling and implementing some of the more advanced intelligent hubs may be needed as well. By reorganizing your network, you maximize the amount of bandwidth that is available for access to the local subnetwork. Make sure systems that regularly perform NFS mounts of each other are on the same subnetwork.

If you have an older network and are having to rework your network topology, consider replacing the older coax-based networks with the more modern twisted-pair types, which are generally more reliable and flexible. Make sure the workload is on the appropriate machine(s). Use the machine with the best network performance to do its proper share of network file service tasks. Check your network for diskless workstations. These require large amounts of network resources to boot up, swap, page, etc. With the cost of local storage decreasing constantly, it is getting harder to believe that diskless workstations are still cost-effective when compared to regular workstations. Consider upgrading the workstations so they support users locally, or at least minimize their use of the network.

If your network server has been acquiring more clients, check its memory and its kernel buffer allocations for proper sizing. If the problem is that I/O-intensive programs are being run over the network, work with the users to determine what can be done to make that requirement a local, rather than a network, one. Educate your users to make sure they understand when they are using the network appropriately and when they are being wasteful with this valuable resource.

Displaying Current Values of Tunable Parameters

To display a list of the current values assigned to the tunable kernel parameters, you can use the `sysdef -i` command on Solaris. Linux, HPUX, and AIX have equivalent kernel tuning tools.

```
% sysdef -i

... (portions of display are deleted for brevity)
*
* System Configuration
*
swapfile             dev  swaplo blocks    free
/dev/dsk/c0t3d0s1    32,25     8 547112   96936
*
* Tunable Parameters
*
 5316608   maximum memory allowed in buffer cache (bufhwm)
    4058   maximum number of processes (v.v_proc)
      99   maximum global priority in sys class (MAXCLSYSPRI)
    4053   maximum processes per user id (v.v_maxup)
      30   auto update time limit in seconds (NAUTOUP)
      25   page stealing low water mark (GPGSLO)
       5   fsflush run rate (FSFLUSHR)
      25   minimum resident memory for avoiding deadlock (MINARMEM)
      25   minimum swapable memory for avoiding deadlock (MINASMEM)
*
* Utsname Tunables
*
     5.3   release (REL)
    DDDD   node name (NODE)
   SunOS   system name (SYS)
Generic_101318-31  version (VER)
*
* Process Resource Limit Tunables (Current:Maximum)
*
Infinity:Infinity   cpu time
Infinity:Infinity   file size
7ffff000:7ffff000   heap size
  800000:7ffff000   stack size
Infinity:Infinity   core file size
      40:     400   file descriptors
Infinity:Infinity   mapped memory
*
* Streams Tunables
*
       9   maximum number of pushes allowed (NSTRPUSH)
   65536   maximum stream message size (STRMSGSZ)
    1024   max size of ctl part of message (STRCTLSZ)
```

```
*
* IPC Messages
*
   200     entries in msg map (MSGMAP)
  2048     max message size (MSGMAX)
 65535     max bytes on queue (MSGMNB)
    25     message queue identifiers (MSGMNI)
   128     message segment size (MSGSSZ)
   400     system message headers (MSGTQL)
  1024     message segments (MSGSEG)
   SYS     system class name (SYS_NAME)
```

As stated earlier, over the years many enhancements have been tried to minimize the complexity of the kernel configuration process. As a result, many of the tables that were once allocated in a fixed manner are now allocated dynamically, or else linked to the value of the MAXUSERS field. The next step in understanding the nature of kernel tables is to look at the MAXUSERS parameter and its impact on Unix system configuration.

Modifying the Configuration Information File

Solaris uses the /etc/system file for modification of kernel-tunable variables. The basic format is this:

```
set parameter = value
```

It can also have this format:

```
set [module:]variablename = value
```

The /etc/system file can also be used for other purposes (for example, to force modules to be loaded at boot time, to specify a root device, and so on). The /etc/system file is used for permanent changes to the operating system values. Temporary changes can be made using adb kernel debugging tools. The system must be rebooted for the changes to become active using /etc/system. Once you have made your changes to this file, you can recompile to make a new Unix kernel. The command is mkkernel -s system. This new kernel, called vmunix.test, is placed in the /stand/build directory. Next, you move the present stand/system file to /stand/system.prev; then you can move the modified file /stand/build/system to /stand/system. Then you move the currently running kernel /stand/vmunix to /stand/vmunix.prev, and then move the new kernel, /stand/build/vmunix.test, into place in /stand/vmunix (i.e., mv /stand/build/vmunix.test /stand/vmunix). The final step is to reboot the machine to make your changes take effect.

Other Factors That Affect Performance

Good performance is difficult to define. Two common, but different and not necessarily equivalent, measures are used for performance. *Response time* is the time between the instant the user presses the ENTER key and the time the system provides a response. *Throughput* is the number of transactions accomplished in a fixed period of time. Of the two measures throughput is the better measure of how much work is actually getting accomplished. Response time is more visible and, therefore, used more frequently; it is a better measurement for meeting the system's business objectives. Some people don't look at everything when tuning. Remember to check all of these:

- **All hardware** Are the CPUs fast enough and are there enough of them? How much memory is there; is it enough?

- **Operating system and application software** Is the system configured correctly for the current environment?

- **People** Are people trained sufficiently on the system and applications to optimize their productivity?

- **Changes** What changes in workload and user requirements can be expected to occur?

A resource is a bottleneck if the size of a request exceeds the available resource. A *bottleneck* is a limitation of system performance due to the inadequacy of the hardware or software component or the system's organization.

Tuning a CPU System

- Upgrade to faster or more processors.

- Upgrade the system with a larger data/instruction cache.

- Spread applications across multiple systems and disks.

- Run long batch jobs during off-peak hours whenever possible.

- nice (a command that changes the priority of a process) unimportant applications.

- Lock frequently used processes in memory.

- Turn off system accounting.

- Optimize the applications.

Tuning Memory-Bound Systems

- Add physical memory.

- Use diskless workstations rather than X-terms.

- Reduce MAXDSIZ.

- Reduce the use of memory locking.

- Identify programs with memory leaks.

- Tune the applications.

- Reduce the size of the kernel drivers and subsystems.

- Reduce the size of the buffer cache.

Disk Tuning

- Add disk drives.
- Add disk channels.
- Use faster disks.
- Use striping.
- Use mirroring.
- Balance I/O across multiple spindles.
- Dedicate a disk section to an application.
- Use raw disk I/O.
- Increase the system buffer cache.
- Increase the kernel table sizes.
- Use the `tunefs` and `tune NFS commands`.

Volume Manager Factors That Can Affect Performance

- File system parameters
- Fragmentation
- Mirroring
- Scheduling
- Spindles
- Strictness
- Striping
- Workload
- Work type

Other Sources to Improve Performance

Another tool worth investigating is the Oracle Cluster Health Monitor (CHM). You can use it to track operating system resources on each node. CHM tracks every process and device level continuously. You can set thresholds, which when they are hit, set off an alert. Historical information can also be replayed. For more information see http://www.oracle.com/technetwork/database/enterprise-edition/ipd-overview-130032.pdf.

Oracle's ORION workload tool is another tool that you can use to create a representative workload that stresses a storage array in the same manner as your production application. Orion issues I/Os against raw disks using the same libraries an Oracle database would issue. It can also help you fine-tune the storage array for a production application. For more information see http://www.jameskoopmann.com/docs/MeasuringDiskIOOraclesORIONTool.htm.

Lastly, please see My Oracle Support (MetaLink) Note: 224176.1 for additional information on using O/S commands to diagnose Oracle Performance issues.

TIPS & REVIEW

Tips Review

- Use the `sar -u` command to see a quick snapshot of how the much the CPU is "bogged down."

- Use the `top` command to find the worst user on the system at a given point in time.

- Use `cron` and `uptime` to have your system load emailed to you on a regular basis.

- If the SMTX column for the `mpstat` output is greater than 200, you are heading toward CPU bottleneck problems.

- Combine operating system utilities with Oracle V$ views.

- Use the `sar` and `iostat` commands to find potential disk I/O problem areas. These commands are further enhanced by utilizing the capabilities of shell scripting.

- Paging is generally the movement of inactive processes from memory to disk. A high degree of paging is usually the predecessor to swapping. Swapping is the movement of active processes from memory to disk. If swapping starts to escalate, your system begins the downward "death spiral." Fixing memory hogs or adding memory is the correct solution.

- Use the `ipcs` command to see if your SGA is built using multiple noncontiguous pieces of memory. A database crash can cause this to be a problem by not releasing memory.

- Use the `ipcrm` command (only if the SGA pieces are not released after a database crash) to then remove the SGA pieces from memory. Do *not* issue the `ipcrm` command with a running database.

- Use the `vmstat` command to find blocked processes (users waiting for CPU time) and also for paging or swapping problems. The `vmstat` command is a great way to see many of the `sar` options in one screen.

- Use the `ndd` and `netstat` commands to tune network performance issues. Use `spray` to simulate network traffic.

References

Adrian Cockcroft, *Sun Performance and Tuning* (Sun Microsystems Press, 1998).
Mark Gurry and Peter Corrigan, *Oracle Performance Tuning* (O'Reilly, 2001).
Andy Johnston and Robin Anderson, *UNIX Unleashed, System Administrator's Edition* (Sams, 2001).
Performance and Tuning (Hewlett-Packard).
Solaris Internals™: Solaris 10 and OpenSolaris Kernel Architecture, 2006.
Websites: www.gsp.com, www.speedware.com, www.oracle.com/technetwork, www.jameskoopmann.com.

Many thanks to Doug Freyburger, who updated this version of the chapter. Thanks also to Mike Gallagher, Judy Corley, and Jon Vincenzo, who updated previous versions that we built upon.

APPENDIX
A

Key Initialization
Parameters (DBA)

O racle 11g Release 2 (11gR2) has 341 different documented and 2053 different undocumented initialization (init.ora/spfile.ora) parameters. This means you have a total of 2394 initialization parameters to play with; you can do a count(*) of X$KSPPI for the total number of parameters both documented and undocumented (you need to be SYS to access the X$ tables). A count of V$PARAMETER gives you a count of only the documented parameters. When I refer to the undocumented parameters, I am referring to parameters that start with an underscore (_), although some of them are actually even documented. There are also several parameters that I call documented (no "_" in front of them, but they are not really documented, only externalized or available for use, usually for backward compatibility). Even these numbers vary slightly on different versions of Oracle and platforms. The initialization parameters vary (in both name and number) according to the database version and release used. Run the queries listed at the end of this appendix (accessing the V$PARAMETER view and the X$KSPPI table) on your version of the database to get the number of parameters and details for your specific version. Tips covered in this chapter:

- Desupported and deprecated initialization parameters

- Top 25 documented initialization parameters with descriptions and suggested settings

- Top 10 documented initialization parameters that you better not forget (option dependent)

- Top 13 undocumented initialization parameters (Shhh!)

- Bonus 11 undocumented initialization parameters (mostly 11gR2 and Exadata)

- Complete listing of documented initialization parameters (there are 341 in 11gR2)

- Query for undocumented initialization parameters (there are 2053 in 11gR2)

Since every system is set up differently, my top 25 may not be the same as your top 25 (so feel free to write in this book as if it were yours). Hopefully, this appendix will give you a place to start until someone writes the 1000-page book on *all* of the initialization parameters. Please refer to Chapter 4 for a detailed look at the most important initialization parameters.

Obsoleted/Desupported Initialization Parameters

The following are *some* of the Oracle 11g obsoleted/desupported initialization parameters (query V$OBSOLETE_PARAMETER for the full list of 112 nonhidden obsolete parameters). Obsolete means these parameters are gone, although they sometimes become undocumented parameters, which means that they have an underscore (_) in front of them (none of them did in this version though).

- DDL_WAIT_FOR_LOCKS (11.1)

- DRS_START (11.2)

- GC_FILES_TO_LOCKS (11.2)

- LOGMNR_MAX_PERSISTENT_SESSIONS (11.1)

- MAX_COMMIT_PROPAGATION_DELAY (11.2)

- PLSQL_COMPILER_FLAGS (11.1)
- PLSQL_NATIVE_LIBRARY_DIR (11.2)
- PLSQL_NATIVE_LIBRARY_SUBDIR_COUNT (11.2)
- SQL_VERSION (11.2)

Deprecated Initialization Parameters

The following are Oracle 11gR2 deprecated initialization parameters. You can use these for backward compatibility, but they are probably going away in the future. To list the deprecated parameters for a given version, run the following SQL statement (note that 25 records were returned for this query in 11gR2, although some of these were deprecated in the past as noted in the list):

```
select name
from   v$parameter
where  isdeprecated = 'TRUE';
```

- ACTIVE_INSTANCE_COUNT (11.2)
- BACKGROUND_DUMP_DEST (11.1) (replaced by DIAGNOSTIC_DEST)
- BUFFER_POOL_KEEP (11.2, replaced in 9i with DB_KEEP_CACHE_SIZE)
- BUFFER_POOL_RECYCLE (11.2, replaced in 9i with DB_RECYCLE_CACHE_SIZE)
- COMMIT_WRITE (11.1, use COMMIT_LOGGING and COMMIT_WAIT)
- CURSOR_SPACE_FOR_TIME (11.1)
- FAST_START_IO_TARGET (11.2, replaced in 9i with FAST_START_MTTR_TARGET)
- GLOBAL_CONTEXT_POOL_SIZE (11.2, since 10.1)
- INSTANCE_GROUPS (11.1)
- LOCK_NAME_SPACE (11.2, since 10.1)
- LOG_ARCHIVE_LOCAL_FIRST (11.1)
- LOG_ARCHIVE_START (11.2)
- MAX_ENABLED_ROLES (11.2, since 10.1)
- PARALLEL_AUTOMATIC_TUNING (11.2, since 10.1)
- PARALLEL_IO_CAP_ENABLED (11.2)
- PARALLEL_SERVER (11.2, replaced since 9i with CLUSTER_DATABASE)
- PARALLEL_SERVER_INSTANCES (11.2, replaced since 9i with CLUSTER_DATABASE)
- PLSQL_DEBUG (11.1) (replaced by PLSQL_OPTIMIZE_LEVEL)
- PLSQL_V2_COMPATIBILITY (11.1)
- REMOTE_OS_AUTHENT (11.1)

- RESOURCE_MANAGER_CPU_ALLOCATION (11.1)

- SERIAL_REUSE (11.2, since 10.2)

- SQL_TRACE (11.2, since 10.2)

- STANDBY_ARCHIVE_DEST (11.1)

- TRANSACTION_LAG (11.1) *attribute* (of the CQ_NOTIFICATION$_REG_INFO)

- USER_DUMP_DEST (11.1) (replaced by DIAGNOSTIC_DEST)

Top 25 Initialization Parameters

The following list is *my* list of the top 25 most important initialization parameters, in order of importance. Your top 25 may vary somewhat from my top 25 because everyone's business, applications, and experiences are unique.

1. **MEMORY_TARGET**   This parameter sets all of the memory allocated to *both* the PGA and SGA combined (new in 11*g*). Setting this enables Automatic Memory Management, which is where Oracle allocates memory for you based on system needs, but you can also set minimum values for key parameters. MEMORY_TARGET is used for everything that SGA_TARGET is used for, but also includes the PGA (especially important as it now includes the important area PGA_AGGREGATE_TARGET). Important parameters such as DB_CACHE_SIZE, SHARED_POOL_SIZE, PGA_AGGREGATE_TARGET, LARGE_POOL_SIZE, and JAVA_POOL_SIZE are all set automatically when MEMORY_TARGET is set. Setting minimum values for important initialization parameters in your system is also a *very* good idea.

2. **MEMORY_MAX_TARGET**   This parameter sets the maximum memory allocated for Oracle and the maximum value that MEMORY_TARGET can be set to.

3. **DB_CACHE_SIZE**   Initial memory allocated to data cache or memory used for data itself. This parameter doesn't need to be set if you set MEMORY_TARGET or SGA_TARGET, but setting a value for this as a minimum setting is a good idea. Your goal should always be toward creating a memory resident database, or at least getting all data that will be queried in memory.

4. **SHARED_POOL_SIZE**   Memory allocated for data dictionary and for SQL and PL/SQL statements. The query itself is put in memory here. This parameter doesn't need to be set if you set MEMORY_TARGET, but setting a value for this as a minimum setting is a good idea. Note that SAP specifies setting this to 400M. Also note that the Result Cache gets its memory from the shared pool and is set with the RESULT_CACHE_SIZE and RESULT_CACHE_MODE (force/auto/manual) initialization parameters. Lastly, an important note for 11*g* is that this parameter now includes some SGA overhead (12M worth), which it previously did not have (in 10*g*). In 11*g*, set this 12Ms higher than you did in 10*g*!

5. **SGA_TARGET**   If you use Oracle's Automatic Shared Memory Management, this parameter is used to determine the size of your data cache, shared pool, large pool, and Java pool automatically (see Chapter 1 for more information). Setting this parameter to 0 disables it. This parameter doesn't need to be set if you set MEMORY_TARGET, but you may want to

set a value for this as a minimum setting for the SGA if you've calibrated it in previous versions. The SHARED_POOL_SIZE, LARGE_POOL_SIZE, JAVA_POOL_SIZE, and DB_CACHE_SIZE are all set automatically based on this parameter (or MEMORY_TARGET if used).

6. **PGA_AGGREGATE_TARGET**   Soft memory cap for total of all users' PGAs. This parameter doesn't need to be set if you set MEMORY_TARGET, but setting a value for this as a minimum setting is a good idea. Note that SAP specifies setting this to 20 percent of available memory for OLTP and 40 percent for OLAP.

7. **SGA_MAX_SIZE**   Maximum memory that SGA_TARGET can be set to. This parameter doesn't need to be set if you set MEMORY_TARGET, but you may want to set a value if you use SGA_TARGET.

8. **OPTIMIZER_MODE**   FIRST_ROWS, FIRST_ROWS_*n,* or ALL_ROWS. Although RULE and CHOOSE are definitely desupported and obsolete and people are often scolded for even talking about it, I was able to set the mode to RULE in 11*g*R2. Consider the following error that I received when I set OPTIMIZER_MODE to a mode that doesn't exist (SUPER_FAST):

```
SQL> alter system set optimizer_mode=super_fast

ERROR:
ORA-00096: invalid value SUPER_FAST for parameter optimizer_mode, must be from
among first_rows_1000, first_rows_100, first_rows_10, first_rows_1, first_rows,
all_rows, choose, rule
```

9. **SEC_CASE_SENSITIVE_LOGON**   The default is TRUE, which makes passwords case sensitive (new in 11*g*). Set this to FALSE to disable this feature.

10. **SEC_MAX_FAILED_LOGIN_ATTEMPTS**   This locks an account if the user fails entering the correct password after this many tries (new in 11*g*). The default is 10 (consider lowering this for *very* secure systems). The DBA must issue an "ALTER USER *username* ACCOUNT UNLOCK;" to unlock the account.

11. **CURSOR_SHARING**   Converts literal SQL to SQL with bind variables, reducing parse overhead. The default is EXACT. Consider setting this parameter to FORCE after research (see Chapter 4 for more information).

12. **OPTIMIZER_USE_INVISIBLE_INDEXES**   The default is FALSE to ensure invisible indexes are *not* used by default (new in 11*g*). Here's a helpful tuning exercise: set this to TRUE to use *all* of the indexes and check which ones might have been set incorrectly to be invisible (this test could also bring the system to halt, so only use in development).

13. **OPTIMIZER_USE_PENDING_STATISTICS**   The default is FALSE to ensure pending statistics are *not* used, whereas setting this to TRUE would enable all pending statistics to be used (new in 11*g*).

14. **OPTIMIZER_INDEX_COST_ADJ**   Coarse adjustment between the cost of an index scan and the cost of a full table scan. Set between 1 and 10 to force index use more frequently. Setting this parameter to a value between 1 and 10 would pretty much guarantee index use, even when not appropriate, so be careful, since it is highly dependent on the index design and implementation being correct. Please note that if you are using Applications 11*i,*

setting OPTIMIZER_INDEX_COST_ADJ to any value other than the default (100) is not supported (see MetaLink Note 169935.1). Also, see bug 4483286. SAP suggests that you *not* set it for OLAP, but set it to 20 for OLTP.

15. **DB_FILE_MULTIBLOCK_READ_COUNT** For full table scans to perform I/O more efficiently, this reads the given number of blocks in a single I/O. The default value is 128 in 11gR2, but the usual recommendation is *not* to change this from the default.

16. **LOG_BUFFER** Buffer for uncommitted transactions in memory; it must be set in the PFILE if you want to change it. SAP says to use the default, whereas Oracle Applications sets it to 10M.

17. **DB_KEEP_CACHE_SIZE** Memory allocated to keep pool or an additional data cache that you can set up outside the buffer cache for important data that you don't want pushed out of the cache.

18. **DB_RECYCLE_CACHE_SIZE** Memory allocated to the recycle pool or an additional data cache that you can set up outside the buffer cache and in addition to keeping the cache described in Item 15. Usually, DBAs set this up for ad-hoc user query data with poorly written queries.

19. **OPTIMIZER_USE_SQL_PLAN_BASELINES** The default is TRUE, which means Oracle uses them if they exist (new in 11g). Note that Stored Outlines are deprecated (discouraged but they still work) in 11g as they are replaced with SQL Plan Baselines.

20. **OPTIMIZER_CAPTURE_SQL_PLAN_BASELINES** The default is FALSE, which means that Oracle does not capture them by default, but if you create some, Oracle uses them as stated in Item 17 (new in 11g).

21. **LARGE_POOL_SIZE** Total blocks in the large pool allocation for large PL/SQL and a few other Oracle options less frequently used. This parameter doesn't need to be set if you set MEMORY_TARGET, but setting a value for this as a minimum setting is a good idea.

22. **STATISTICS_LEVEL** Used to enable advisory information and optionally keep additional O/S statistics to refine optimizer decisions. TYPICAL is the default.

23. **JAVA_POOL_SIZE** Memory allocated to the JVM for JAVA stored procedures; this parameter doesn't need to be set if you set MEMORY_TARGET, but setting a value for this as a minimum setting is a good idea.

24. **JAVA_MAX_SESSIONSPACE_SIZE** Upper limit on memory that is used to keep track of user session state for JAVA classes.

25. **OPEN_CURSORS** Specifies the size of the private area used to hold (open) user statements. If you get "ORA-01000: maximum open cursors exceeded," you may need to increase this parameter, but make sure you are *closing* cursors that you no longer need. Prior to 9.2.0.5, these open cursors were also cached and, at times, caused issues (ORA-4031) if OPEN_CURSORS was set too high. As of 9.2.05, SESSION_CACHED_CURSORS now controls the setting of the PL/SQL cursor cache. Do *not* set the parameter

SESSION_CACHED_CURSORS as high as you set OPEN_CURSORS, or you may experience ORA-4031 or ORA-7445 errors. SAP recommends setting this to 2000; Oracle Applications has OPEN_CURSORS at 600 and SESSION_CACHED_CURSORS at 500.

TIP
Setting certain initialization parameters correctly could be the difference between a report taking two seconds and two hours. Test changes on a test system thoroughly before implementing those changes in a production environment.

Top 20 Initialization Parameters Not to Forget

This section details some other important initialization parameters. However, these parameters may be important only in certain cases or only if you are using a certain feature or version of Oracle:

1. **CONTROL_FILES**   The location of your control files. You should have at least three copies.

2. **COMPATIBLE**   Set this to the correct version, or you'll miss things in the new version. Set to at least 11.2.0 for 11*g*R2.

3. **OPTIMIZER_FEATURES_ENABLE**   If this is not set, you are missing out on new features.

4. **AUDIT_TRAIL**   The default is set to DB in 11*g*R2. This parameter enables auditing for many major commands, including CREATE, ALTER, GRANT, and AUDIT.

5. **DIAGNOSTIC_DEST**   Trace, Alert, and Core Dump files are now in a new location. The DIAGNOSTIC_DEST specifies the root directory where these files are located. A basic example on how this works is to set the DIAGNOSTIC_DEST to a location (C:\APP\USER), for example. The corresponding locations for the dump files become *DIAGNOSTIC_DEST*\DIAG\RDBMS*dbname**instname**trace*:

   - background_dump_dest = C:\APP\USER\DIAG\RDBMS\ORCL\ORCL\TRACE

   - user_dump_dest = C:\APP\USER\DIAG\RDBMSORCL\ORCL\TRACE

   - core_dump_dest = C:\APP\USER\DIAG\RDBMSORCL\ORCL\CDUMP

   - Alert files go to C:\APP\USER\DIAG\RDBMS\ORCL\ORCL\ALERT

6. **UNDO_MANAGEMENT**   Set this to AUTO (default) for automatic UNDO management.

7. **UNDO_TABLESPACE**   Set this to the tablespace to use for UNDO management.

8. **UNDO_RETENTION**   The UNDO retention time in seconds.

9. **SPFILE**   This gives the location of the binary SPFILE used for startup. You can create a readable PFILE with the command `CREATE PFILE='path_and_name' from SPFILE='path and name';"` and you can create an SPFILE from a PFILE or from MEMORY. You can also do a *startup* (using the SPFILE) or do a `startup pfile=...` to use a given PFILE (`initSID.ora` or any name you specify). The SPFILE is in `ORACLE_HOME\database` directory.

10. **DB_BLOCK_SIZE**   Default block size for the database. A smaller block size reduces contention by adjacent rows, but a larger block size lowers the number of I/Os needed to pull back more records. A larger block size also helps in range scans where the blocks desired are sequentially stored. An 8K block size is used for most applications.

11. **CLUSTER_DATABASE**   You must set this to FALSE for single instance.

12. **JOB_QUEUE_PROCESSES**   If you want to use DBMS_JOB in 10g or earlier, you must set this parameter. Note that DBMS_JOB has been replaced by the Scheduler as of Oracle 10g, but it uses the same parameter. The default for this parameter went from 0 in 10g to 1000 in 11g. This parameter no longer *must* be set, but if it is set, it will cap the number of slave processes at this value.

13. **UTL_FILE_DIR**   Set to use the UTL_FILE package. Note that in 11g, the UTL_FILE package no longer opens a file if it is a symbolic link (created to close a known security hole).

14. **LOG_CHECKPOINT_INTERVAL**   Checkpoint frequency (in OS blocks—most OS blocks are 512 bytes) at which Oracle performs a database write of all dirty (modified) blocks to the datafiles in the database. Oracle also performs a checkpoint if more than one-quarter of the data buffers are dirty in the db cache and also on any log switch. The LGWR (log writer) also updates the SCN in the control files and datafiles with the SCN of the checkpoint.

15. **FAST_START_MTTR_TARGET**   Bounds time to complete a crash recovery. This is the time (in seconds) that the database takes to perform crash recovery of a single instance. If you set this parameter, LOG_CHECKPOINT_INTERVAL should *not* be set to 0. If you don't set this parameter, you can still see your estimated MTTR (mean time to recovery) by querying V$INSTANCE_RECOVERY for ESTIMATED_MTTR.

16. **RECOVERY_PARALLELISM**   Recover using the Parallel Query option for a faster recovery.

17. **MAX_SHARED_SERVERS**   Upper limit on shared servers when using shared servers.

18. **LICENSE_MAX_SESSIONS and LICENSE_MAX_USERS**   These limit concurrent and named users.

19. **LICENSE_SESSIONS_WARNING**   Here, you specify at which session+1 you get a license warning.

20. **CELL_OFFLOAD_PROCESSING**   The default of this is TRUE, which means that Smart Scans are set to be ON for Exadata (if you are using it). (*Exadata only.*)

TIP
Oracle includes some excellent options. Unfortunately, some of them do not work unless you have the initialization parameter set correctly.

Top 13 Undocumented Initialization Parameters (As I See It)

The following list is *my* list of the top 13 undocumented initialization parameters in order of importance. Your top 13 may vary somewhat, depending on your need for one of these parameters. Although the following warning describes well the risks associated with using these parameters, I note that the fastest RAC TPC (Transaction Processing Council) benchmark uses 17 undocumented parameters, as do many of the TPC benchmarks that I've seen.

CAUTION
These 13 parameters are neither supported by Oracle, nor do I recommend them on a production system. Use them only if directed by Oracle Support and if you have thoroughly tested them on your crash-and-burn system (and your closest friend has been using them for years). Undocumented initialization parameters can lead to database corruption (although some of them can get your database back up when it becomes corrupted).

1. **_ALLOW_RESETLOGS_CORRUPTION** This parameter saves you when you have corrupted redo logs. It allows the database to open with the datafiles at different SCN synchronization levels. This means some datafiles may contain changes that other datafiles do not (like the RBS or UNDO tablespace). This parameter may allow you to get to your data, but there is no easy way to determine if the data that is available after using this parameter is logically consistent. Regardless of data consistency, the DBA has to rebuild the database afterward. Failure to do so results in multiple ORA-600s occurring within the database at a later time.

2. **_CORRUPTED_ROLLBACK_SEGMENTS** Setting this parameter can be a means of last resort when you have corrupted rollback segments, which you can list with this parameter to be skip. The _CORRUPTED_ROLLBACK_SEGMENTS parameter can force the database open after a failed recovery, but at a very high cost. _CORRUPTED_ROLLBACK_SEGMENTS allows the database to open by assuming every transaction in the rollback segments is a complete, committed transaction. This leads to logical corruption throughout the database and can easily corrupt the data dictionary. An example would be where you transfer money from one bank to another. The transaction would only be complete if you can verify that all parts of it are complete. In Oracle, when creating a table, think of all the individual dictionary objects that are updated: fet$, uet$, tab$, ind$, col$, etc. By setting this parameter, you allow table creation to succeed, even if only fet$ was updated, but not uet$, or even if tab$ was updated, but not col$. Use it when you have no other means of recovery and export/import/rebuild soon after.

CAUTION
These first two parameters do not always work or may corrupt the database so badly that you cannot perform once the database is open. If they are used and do not work, then Oracle Support cannot do anything to salvage the database if the DBA breaks down and calls Support, but the DBA can do several things before using these parameters that will allow other recovery methods to be used afterward. So if you must use these parameters, please ensure that you use them with the help of Oracle Support. One good reason to use Oracle Support in this effort is the fact that the _ALLOW_RESETLOGS_CORRUPTION parameter is problematic, often requiring an event to be set as well, to get the database open.

3. **_HASH_JOIN_ENABLED**   Enables/disables hash joining if you have the memory needed. The default value is TRUE.

4. **_IN_MEMORY_UNDO**   Make in-memory undo for top-level transactions (Oracle's IMU really messed up my block-level tuning presentation as blocks in memory became more complex). The default is TRUE. Some applications have you set this to FALSE, so please check your application carefully for this parameter. This is one of the things that makes Oracle fast, so be careful changing this parameter!

5. **_TRACE_FILES_PUBLIC**   This parameter allows users to see the trace output without giving them major privileges elsewhere. The default is FALSE; both Oracle/SAP set this to TRUE.

6. **_FAST_FULL_SCAN_ENABLED**   This allows fast full index scans if only the index is needed. The default is TRUE, but Applications often recommends this be set to FALSE.

7. **_KSMG_GRANULE_SIZE**   This is the granule size multiple for SGA granule pieces of memory such as SHARED_POOL_SIZE and DB_CACHE_SIZE.

8. **_HASH_MULTIBLOCK_IO_COUNT**   Number of blocks that a hash join will read/write at once.

9. **_INDEX_JOIN_ENABLED**   Used to enable/disable the use of index joins. Default is TRUE.

10. **_OPTIMIZER_ADJUST_FOR_NULLS**   Adjust selectivity for null values. Default is TRUE.

11. **_TRACE_POOL_SIZE**   Trace pool size in bytes.

12. **_B_TREE_BITMAP_PLANS**   Enable the use of bitmap plans for tables with only b-tree indexes. The default is TRUE, but many applications recommend setting this to FALSE.

13. **_UNNEST_SUBQUERY**   Enables the unnesting of correlated or complex subqueries. The default is TRUE.

TIP
Undocumented initialization parameters can corrupt your database! Some of them can help you salvage a corrupted database. Try to use these only when all other choices have failed and with the help of Oracle Support.

Here are five additional initialization parameters that you can use for latch contention:

1. **_KGL_LATCH_COUNT**   Number of library cache latches (set this to the next prime number higher than 2*CPU). Setting this parameter too high (>66) causes ORA-600 errors (Bug 1381824). KGL stands for Kernel Generic Library or the Library Cache portion of the shared pool (there is also a Dictionary Cache portion). Many *KGL* undocumented parameters are available for debugging and improving shared pool performance.

2. **_LOG_SIMULTANEOUS_COPIES**   The number of redo copy latches (or simultaneous copies allowed into the redo log buffer). Redo records are written to the redo log buffer requiring the redo copy latch when changes are made. Use this parameter to reduce the contention on multi-CPU systems.

3. **_DB_BLOCK_HASH_BUCKETS**   Must be prime (set to next prime number higher than 2 * Cache buffers) in version 9*i* and 10*g* (there is an algorithm change in 11*g*). This parameter should not be a problem or need to be set as of 10*g*. On my system, this value was set to a default of 1048576 when there were only 332930 db block buffers (certainly eliminating hash chain issues). A _DB_BLOCK_HASH_LATCHES parameter (set to 32768, by default, in my system) is also available. My system is just under 7G MEMORY_TARGET.

4. **_DB_BLOCK_MAX_CR_DBA**   The maximum number of consistent read (CR) blocks for a given database block address (DBA). The default is 6 (six copies maximum of a CR block). Before this parameter was set, large use applications updating many rows within the same block caused so many CR versions that there were incredible issues with latches on the hash chain looking for the correct version of a given block (see the previous parameter for related information).

5. **_SPIN_COUNT**   Determines how often the processor takes a new request (reduces CPU time-outs). Also determines how many times a process tries to get a latch until it goes to sleep (when it is a willing-to-wait latch). Many processes spinning to get a latch can cost a lot of CPU, so be careful if you increase this value. In Oracle 7, this parameter was called the _LATCH_SPIN_COUNT.

Bonus 11 Undocumented Initialization Parameters

Here are 11 more (since this is version 11) undocumented parameters that are mostly new to Oracle 11*g*R2 that I think are worth looking into, but that I've not personally tested too much (other than the INIT_SQL_FILE parameter, which I've added to the bottom of the list; it is well worth reading through).

1. **_KCFIS_STORAGEIDX_DISABLED**   Don't use storage index optimization on storage cells if this is set to TRUE. The default is FALSE. (*Exadata only.*)

2. **_BLOOM_FILTER_ENABLED**   Set to TRUE by default. With Exadata, bloom filters are used for join filtering with smart scans. _BLOOM_PRUNING_ENABLED also has a default of TRUE. Set these to FALSE to disable. (*Exadata only.*)

3. **_COLUMN_COMPRESSION_FACTOR**   Set to 0 by default.

4. **_IMU_POOLS**   Located in the memory UNDO pools. The default is 3.

5. **_NESTED_LOOP_FUDGE**   The default is 100 (probably means 100 percent, similar to OPTIMIZER_INDEX_COST_ADJ, but I've not tested it).

6. **_OPTIMIZER_MAX_PERMUTATIONS**   The default is 2000 (seems high to me, but I've not tested it). This parameter determines the optimizer's maximum permutations per query block. (Note that 103 hidden parameters starting with _OPTIMIZER% are available.)

7. **_PGA_MAX_SIZE**   The maximum size of PGA for *one* process. Must be prime (set to next prime number greater than 2 * Cache buffers) in version 9*i* and 10*g* (there is an algorithm change in 11*g*). This parameter should not be a problem or need to be set as of 10*g*.

8. **_OPTIMIZER_IGNORE_HINTS**   The default is FALSE. Could be a way to check if you really need all of those hints you've put in over the years.

9. **_ALLOW_READ_ONLY_CORRUPTION**   The default is FALSE. This allows read-only open even if the database is corrupt. Careful with this parameter; consult Oracle support.

10. **_OPTIM_PEEK_USER_BINDS**   The default is TRUE, which allows Oracle to peek at the user's bind variable. Setting this FALSE when peeking is not favorable and can lead to *huge* performance gains since Oracle peeks and uses the *same* plan that is *not* optimized for the next bind. Related to this is OPTIMIZER_ADAPTIVE_CURSOR_SHARING, which has a default of TRUE but is also often set to FALSE.

11. **_INIT_SQL_FILE**   This SQL file (and its location) is executed upon database creation (usually sql.bsq, very interesting to read if you have a long night available). It is in the ORACLE_HOME\RDBMS\ADMIN directory by default.

The hidden parameters are used mainly by the Oracle development group. The implementation of hidden parameters can change from release to release, even when you only applied a patch to your database. Because they are not documented and *not supported*, they may not work as you expect, or as is described here. For a query that gives you a complete listing of all undocumented parameters, their default values, and descriptions, see the section "Listing of Undocumented Initialization Parameters (X$KSPPI/X$KSPPCV)," later in this chapter.

Listing of Documented Initialization Parameters (V$PARAMETER)

The following query retrieves the listing that follows on 11gR2 (341 rows returned on Windows). This particular query was run on 11.2.0.1.0.

```
Col name format a33
Col value for a10
Col ismodified for a5
Col description for a28 word_wrapped
```

```
select     name, value, ismodified, description
from       v$parameter
order by   name;
```

The following listing contains the output for this query and includes the parameter names, values, whether the parameter can be modified, and a brief description.

```
NAME                             VALUE      ISMOD DESCRIPTION
-------------------------------- ---------- ----- ----------------------------
O7_DICTIONARY_ACCESSIBILITY      FALSE      FALSE Version 7 Dictionary
                                                  Accessibility Support

active_instance_count                       FALSE number of active instances
                                                  in the cluster database

aq_tm_processes                  0          FALSE number of AQ Time Managers
                                                  to start

archive_lag_target               0          FALSE Maximum number of seconds of
                                                  redos the standby could lose

asm_diskgroups                              FALSE disk groups to mount
                                                  automatically

asm_diskstring                              FALSE disk set locations for
                                                  discovery

asm_power_limit                  1          FALSE number of processes for disk
                                                  rebalancing

asm_preferred_read_failure_groups           FALSE preferred read failure
                                                  groups

audit_file_dest                  C:\APP\USE FALSE Directory in which auditing
                                 R\ADMIN\OR       files are to reside
                                 CL\ADUMP

audit_sys_operations             FALSE      FALSE enable sys auditing

audit_trail                      DB         FALSE enable system auditing

background_core_dump             partial    FALSE Core Size for Background
                                                  Processes

background_dump_dest             c:\app\use FALSE Detached process dump
                                 r\diag\rdb       directory
                                 ms\orcl\or
                                 cl\trace

backup_tape_io_slaves            FALSE      FALSE BACKUP Tape I/O slaves

bitmap_merge_area_size           1048576    FALSE maximum memory allow for
                                                  BITMAP MERGE

blank_trimming                   FALSE      FALSE blank trimming semantics
                                                  parameter

buffer_pool_keep                            FALSE Number of database
                                                  blocks/latches in keep
                                                  buffer pool
```

```
NAME                               VALUE      ISMOD DESCRIPTION
---------------------------------- ---------- ----- ---------------------------
buffer_pool_recycle                           FALSE Number of database
                                                    blocks/latches in recycle
                                                    buffer pool

cell_offload_compaction            ADAPTIVE   FALSE Cell packet compaction
                                                    strategy

cell_offload_decryption            TRUE       FALSE enable SQL processing
                                                    offload of encrypted data to
                                                    cells

cell_offload_parameters                       FALSE Additional cell offload
                                                    parameters

cell_offload_plan_display          AUTO       FALSE Cell offload explain plan
                                                    display

cell_offload_processing            TRUE       FALSE enable SQL processing
                                                    offload to cells

cell_partition_large_extents       DEFAULT    FALSE Enables large extent
                                                    allocation for partitioned
                                                    tables

circuits                                      FALSE max number of circuits
client_result_cache_lag            3000       FALSE client result cache maximum
                                                    lag in milliseconds

client_result_cache_size           0          FALSE client result cache max size
                                                    in bytes

cluster_database                   FALSE      FALSE if TRUE startup in cluster
                                                    database mode

cluster_database_instances         1          FALSE number of instances to use
                                                    for sizing cluster db SGA
                                                    structures

cluster_interconnects                         FALSE interconnects for RAC use

commit_logging                                FALSE transaction commit log write
                                                    behavior

commit_point_strength              1          FALSE Bias this node has toward
                                                    not preparing in a two-phase
                                                    commit

commit_wait                                   FALSE transaction commit log wait
                                                    behavior

commit_write                                  FALSE transaction commit log write
                                                    behavior

compatible                         11.2.0.0.0 FALSE Database will be completely
                                                    compatible with this
                                                    software version
```

NAME	VALUE	ISMOD	DESCRIPTION
control_file_record_keep_time	7	FALSE	control file record keep time in days
control_files	C:\APP\USER\ORADATA\ORCL\CONTROL01.CTL, C:\APP\USER\FLASH_RECOVERY_AREA\ORCL\CONTROL02.CTL	FALSE	control file names list
control_management_pack_access	DIAGNOSTIC+TUNING	FALSE	declares which manageability packs are enabled
core_dump_dest	c:\app\user\diag\rdbms\orcl\orcl\cdump	FALSE	Core dump directory
cpu_count	8	FALSE	number of CPUs for this instance
create_bitmap_area_size	8388608	FALSE	size of create bitmap buffer for bitmap index
create_stored_outlines		FALSE	create stored outlines for DML statements
cursor_sharing	EXACT	FALSE	cursor sharing mode
cursor_space_for_time	FALSE	FALSE	use more memory in order to get faster execution
db_16k_cache_size	0	FALSE	Size of cache for 16K buffers
db_2k_cache_size	0	FALSE	Size of cache for 2K buffers
db_32k_cache_size	0	FALSE	Size of cache for 32K buffers
db_4k_cache_size	0	FALSE	Size of cache for 4K buffers
db_8k_cache_size	0	FALSE	Size of cache for 8K buffers
db_block_buffers	0	FALSE	Number of database blocks cached in memory
db_block_checking	FALSE	FALSE	header checking and data and index block checking
db_block_checksum	TYPICAL	FALSE	store checksum in db blocks and check during reads
db_block_size	8192	FALSE	Size of database block in bytes

NAME	VALUE	ISMOD	DESCRIPTION
db_cache_advice	ON	FALSE	Buffer cache sizing advisory
db_cache_size	0	FALSE	Size of DEFAULT buffer pool for standard block size buffers
db_create_file_dest		FALSE	default database location
db_create_online_log_dest_1		FALSE	online log/controlfile destination #1
db_create_online_log_dest_2		FALSE	online log/controlfile destination #2
db_create_online_log_dest_3		FALSE	online log/controlfile destination #3
db_create_online_log_dest_4		FALSE	online log/controlfile destination #4
db_create_online_log_dest_5		FALSE	online log/controlfile destination #5
db_domain		FALSE	directory part of global database name stored with CREATE DATABASE
db_file_multiblock_read_count	128	FALSE	db block to be read each IO
db_file_name_convert		FALSE	datafile name convert patterns and strings for standby/clone db
db_files	200	FALSE	max allowable # db files
db_flash_cache_file		FALSE	flash cache file for default block size
db_flash_cache_size	0	FALSE	flash cache size for db_flash_cache_file
db_flashback_retention_target	1440	FALSE	Maximum Flashback Database log retention time in minutes.
db_keep_cache_size	0	FALSE	Size of KEEP buffer pool for standard block size buffers
db_lost_write_protect	NONE	FALSE	enable lost write detection
db_name	orcl	FALSE	database name specified in CREATE DATABASE
db_recovery_file_dest	C:\app\User\flash_recovery_area	FALSE	default database recovery file location
db_recovery_file_dest_size	4102029312	FALSE	database recovery files size limit

NAME	VALUE	ISMOD	DESCRIPTION
db_recycle_cache_size	0	FALSE	Size of RECYCLE buffer pool for standard block size buffers
db_securefile	PERMITTED	FALSE	permit securefile storage during lob creation
db_ultra_safe	OFF	FALSE	Sets defaults for other parameters that control protection levels
db_unique_name	orcl	FALSE	Database Unique Name
db_writer_processes	1	FALSE	number of background database writer processes to start
dbwr_io_slaves	0	FALSE	DBWR I/O slaves
ddl_lock_timeout	0	FALSE	timeout to restrict the time that ddls wait for dml lock
deferred_segment_creation	TRUE	FALSE	defer segment creation to first insert
dg_broker_config_file1	C:\APP\USER\PRODUCT\11.2.0\DBHOME_2\DATABASE\DR1ORCL.DAT	FALSE	data guard broker configuration file #1
dg_broker_config_file2	C:\APP\USER\PRODUCT\11.2.0\DBHOME_2\DATABASE\DR2ORCL.DAT	FALSE	data guard broker configuration file #2
dg_broker_start	FALSE	FALSE	start Data Guard broker (DMON process)
diagnostic_dest	C:\APP\USER	FALSE	diagnostic base directory
disk_asynch_io	TRUE	FALSE	Use asynch I/O for random access devices
dispatchers	(PROTOCOL=TCP) (SERVICE=orclXDB)	FALSE	specifications of dispatchers
distributed_lock_timeout	60	FALSE	number of seconds a distributed transaction waits for a lock

NAME	VALUE	ISMOD	DESCRIPTION
dml_locks	1088	FALSE	dml locks - one for each table modified in a transaction
dst_upgrade_insert_conv	TRUE	FALSE	Enables/Disables internal conversions during DST upgrade
enable_ddl_logging	FALSE	FALSE	enable ddl logging
event		FALSE	debug event control - default null string
fal_client		FALSE	FAL client
fal_server		FALSE	FAL server list
fast_start_io_target	0	FALSE	Upper bound on recovery reads
fast_start_mttr_target	0	FALSE	MTTR target in seconds
fast_start_parallel_rollback	LOW	FALSE	max number of parallel recovery slaves that may be used
file_mapping	FALSE	FALSE	enable file mapping
fileio_network_adapters		FALSE	Network Adapters for File I/O
filesystemio_options		FALSE	IO operations on filesystem files
fixed_date		FALSE	fixed SYSDATE value
gcs_server_processes	0	FALSE	number of background gcs server processes to start
global_context_pool_size		FALSE	Global Application Context Pool Size in Bytes
global_names	FALSE	FALSE	enforce that database links have same name as remote database
global_txn_processes	1	FALSE	number of background global transaction processes to start
hash_area_size	131072	FALSE	size of in-memory hash work area
hi_shared_memory_address	0	FALSE	SGA starting address (high order 32-bits on 64-bit platforms)
hs_autoregister	TRUE	FALSE	enable automatic server DD updates in HS agent self-registration

NAME	VALUE	ISMOD	DESCRIPTION
ifile		FALSE	include file in init.ora
instance_groups		FALSE	list of instance group names
instance_name	orcl	FALSE	instance name supported by the instance
instance_number	0	FALSE	instance number
instance_type	RDBMS	FALSE	type of instance to be executed
java_jit_enabled	TRUE	FALSE	Java VM JIT enabled
java_max_sessionspace_size	0	FALSE	max allowed size in bytes of a Java sessionspace
java_pool_size	0	FALSE	size in bytes of java pool
java_soft_sessionspace_limit	0	FALSE	warning limit on size in bytes of a Java sessionspace
job_queue_processes	1000	FALSE	maximum number of job queue slave processes
large_pool_size	0	FALSE	size in bytes of large pool
ldap_directory_access	NONE	FALSE	RDBMS's LDAP access option
ldap_directory_sysauth	no	FALSE	OID usage parameter
license_max_sessions	0	FALSE	maximum number of non-system user sessions allowed
license_max_users	0	FALSE	maximum number of named users that can be created in the database
license_sessions_warning	0	FALSE	warning level for number of non-system user sessions
listener_networks		FALSE	listener registration networks
local_listener		FALSE	local listener
lock_name_space		FALSE	lock name space used for generating lock names for standby/clone database
lock_sga	FALSE	FALSE	Lock entire SGA in physical memory
log_archive_config		FALSE	log archive config parameter
log_archive_dest		FALSE	archival destination text string
log_archive_dest_1		FALSE	archival destination #1 text string

```
NAME                             VALUE       ISMOD DESCRIPTION
-------------------------------- ----------  ----- ----------------------------
log_archive_dest_10                          FALSE archival destination #10
                                                   text string

log_archive_dest_11                          FALSE archival destination #11
                                                   text string

log_archive_dest_12                          FALSE archival destination #12
                                                   text string

log_archive_dest_13                          FALSE archival destination #13
                                                   text string

log_archive_dest_14                          FALSE archival destination #14
                                                   text string

log_archive_dest_15                          FALSE archival destination #15
                                                   text string

log_archive_dest_16                          FALSE archival destination #16
                                                   text string

log_archive_dest_17                          FALSE archival destination #17
                                                   text string

log_archive_dest_18                          FALSE archival destination #18
                                                   text string

log_archive_dest_19                          FALSE archival destination #19
                                                   text string

log_archive_dest_2                           FALSE archival destination #2 text
                                                   string

log_archive_dest_20                          FALSE archival destination #20
                                                   text string

log_archive_dest_21                          FALSE archival destination #21
                                                   text string

log_archive_dest_22                          FALSE archival destination #22
                                                   text string

log_archive_dest_23                          FALSE archival destination #23
                                                   text string

log_archive_dest_24                          FALSE archival destination #24
                                                   text string

log_archive_dest_25                          FALSE archival destination #25
                                                   text string

log_archive_dest_26                          FALSE archival destination #26
                                                   text string

log_archive_dest_27                          FALSE archival destination #27
                                                   text string

log_archive_dest_28                          FALSE archival destination #28
                                                   text string
```

```
NAME                                VALUE       ISMOD DESCRIPTION
----------------------------------- ----------- ----- ----------------------------
log_archive_dest_29                             FALSE archival destination #29
                                                      text string

log_archive_dest_3                              FALSE archival destination #3 text
                                                      string

log_archive_dest_30                             FALSE archival destination #30
                                                      text string

log_archive_dest_31                             FALSE archival destination #31
                                                      text string

log_archive_dest_4                              FALSE archival destination #4 text
                                                      string

log_archive_dest_5                              FALSE archival destination #5 text
                                                      string

log_archive_dest_6                              FALSE archival destination #6 text
                                                      string

log_archive_dest_7                              FALSE archival destination #7 text
                                                      string

log_archive_dest_8                              FALSE archival destination #8 text
                                                      string

log_archive_dest_9                              FALSE archival destination #9 text
                                                    . string

log_archive_dest_state_1            enable      FALSE archival destination #1
                                                      state text string

log_archive_dest_state_10           enable      FALSE archival destination #10
                                                      state text string

log_archive_dest_state_11           enable      FALSE archival destination #11
                                                      state text string

log_archive_dest_state_12           enable      FALSE archival destination #12
                                                      state text string

log_archive_dest_state_13           enable      FALSE archival destination #13
                                                      state text string

log_archive_dest_state_14           enable      FALSE archival destination #14
                                                      state text string

log_archive_dest_state_15           enable      FALSE archival destination #15
                                                      state text string

log_archive_dest_state_16           enable      FALSE archival destination #16
                                                      state text string

log_archive_dest_state_17           enable      FALSE archival destination #17
                                                      state text string

log_archive_dest_state_18           enable      FALSE archival destination #18
                                                      state text string
```

```
NAME                                VALUE      ISMOD DESCRIPTION
----------------------------------- ---------- ----- ----------------------------
log_archive_dest_state_19           enable     FALSE archival destination #19
                                                     state text string

log_archive_dest_state_2            enable     FALSE archival destination #2
                                                     state text string

log_archive_dest_state_20           enable     FALSE archival destination #20
                                                     state text string

log_archive_dest_state_21           enable     FALSE archival destination #21
                                                     state text string

log_archive_dest_state_22           enable     FALSE archival destination #22
                                                     state text string

log_archive_dest_state_23           enable     FALSE archival destination #23
                                                     state text string

log_archive_dest_state_24           enable     FALSE archival destination #24
                                                     state text string

log_archive_dest_state_25           enable     FALSE archival destination #25
                                                     state text string

log_archive_dest_state_26           enable     FALSE archival destination #26
                                                     state text string

log_archive_dest_state_27           enable     FALSE archival destination #27
                                                     state text string

log_archive_dest_state_28           enable     FALSE archival destination #28
                                                     state text string

log_archive_dest_state_29           enable     FALSE archival destination #29
                                                     state text string

log_archive_dest_state_3            enable     FALSE archival destination #3
                                                     state text string

log_archive_dest_state_30           enable     FALSE archival destination #30
                                                     state text string

log_archive_dest_state_31           enable     FALSE archival destination #31
                                                     state text string

log_archive_dest_state_4            enable     FALSE archival destination #4
                                                     state text string

log_archive_dest_state_5            enable     FALSE archival destination #5
                                                     state text string

log_archive_dest_state_6            enable     FALSE archival destination #6
                                                     state text string

log_archive_dest_state_7            enable     FALSE archival destination #7
                                                     state text string

log_archive_dest_state_8            enable     FALSE archival destination #8
                                                     state text string
```

NAME	VALUE	ISMOD	DESCRIPTION
log_archive_dest_state_9	enable	FALSE	archival destination #9 state text string
log_archive_duplex_dest		FALSE	duplex archival destination text string
log_archive_format	ARC%S_%R.%T	FALSE	archival destination format
log_archive_local_first	TRUE	FALSE	Establish EXPEDITE attribute default value
log_archive_max_processes	4	FALSE	maximum number of active ARCH processes
log_archive_min_succeed_dest	1	FALSE	minimum number of archive destinations that must succeed
log_archive_start	FALSE	FALSE	start archival process on SGA initialization
log_archive_trace	0	FALSE	Establish archivelog operation tracing level
log_buffer	16785408	FALSE	redo circular buffer size
log_checkpoint_interval	0	FALSE	# redo blocks checkpoint threshold
log_checkpoint_timeout	1800	FALSE	Maximum time interval between checkpoints in seconds
log_checkpoints_to_alert	FALSE	FALSE	log checkpoint begin/end to alert file
log_file_name_convert		FALSE	logfile name convert patterns and strings for standby/clone db
max_dispatchers		FALSE	max number of dispatchers
max_dump_file_size	unlimited	FALSE	Maximum size (in bytes) of dump file
max_enabled_roles	150	FALSE	max number of roles a user can have enabled
max_shared_servers		FALSE	max number of shared servers
memory_max_target	6878658560	FALSE	Max size for Memory Target
memory_target	6878658560	FALSE	Target size of Oracle SGA and PGA memory
nls_calendar		FALSE	NLS calendar system name
nls_comp	BINARY	FALSE	NLS comparison

```
NAME                            VALUE      ISMOD DESCRIPTION
------------------------------- ---------- ----- ----------------------------
nls_currency                               FALSE NLS local currency symbol

nls_date_format                            FALSE NLS Oracle date format

nls_date_language                          FALSE NLS date language name

nls_dual_currency                          FALSE Dual currency symbol

nls_iso_currency                           FALSE NLS ISO currency territory
                                                 name

nls_language                    AMERICAN   FALSE NLS language name

nls_length_semantics            BYTE       FALSE create columns using byte or
                                                 char semantics by default

nls_nchar_conv_excp             FALSE      FALSE NLS raise an exception
                                                 instead of allowing implicit
                                                 conversion

nls_numeric_characters                     FALSE NLS numeric characters

nls_sort                                   FALSE NLS linguistic definition
                                                 name

nls_territory                   AMERICA    FALSE NLS territory name

nls_time_format                            FALSE time format

nls_time_tz_format                         FALSE time with timezone format

nls_timestamp_format                       FALSE time stamp format

nls_timestamp_tz_format                    FALSE timestampe with timezone
                                                 format

object_cache_max_size_percent   10         FALSE percentage of maximum size
                                                 over optimal of the user
                                                 session's object cache

object_cache_optimal_size       102400     FALSE optimal size of the user
                                                 session's object cache in
                                                 bytes

olap_page_pool_size             0          FALSE size of the olap page pool
                                                 in bytes

open_cursors                    300        FALSE max # cursors per session

open_links                      4          FALSE max # open links per session

open_links_per_instance         4          FALSE max # open links per
                                                 instance

optimizer_capture_sql_plan_     FALSE      FALSE automatic capture of SQL
baselines                                              plan baselines for
                                                 repeatable statements

optimizer_dynamic_sampling      2          FALSE optimizer dynamic sampling
```

NAME	VALUE	ISMOD	DESCRIPTION
optimizer_features_enable	11.2.0.1	FALSE	optimizer plan compatibility parameter
optimizer_index_caching	0	FALSE	optimizer percent index caching
optimizer_index_cost_adj	100	FALSE	optimizer index cost adjustment
optimizer_mode	ALL_ROWS	FALSE	optimizer mode
optimizer_secure_view_merging	TRUE	FALSE	optimizer secure view merging and predicate pushdown/movearound
optimizer_use_invisible_indexes	FALSE	FALSE	Usage of invisible indexes (TRUE/FALSE)
optimizer_use_pending_statistics	FALSE	FALSE	Control whether to use optimizer pending statistics
optimizer_use_sql_plan_baselines	TRUE	FALSE	use of SQL plan baselines for captured sql statements
os_authent_prefix	OPS$	FALSE	prefix for auto-logon accounts
os_roles	FALSE	FALSE	retrieve roles from the operating system
parallel_adaptive_multi_user	TRUE	FALSE	enable adaptive setting of degree for multiple user streams
parallel_automatic_tuning	FALSE	FALSE	enable intelligent defaults for parallel execution parameters
parallel_degree_limit	CPU	FALSE	limit placed on degree of parallelism
parallel_degree_policy	MANUAL	FALSE	policy used to compute the degree of parallelism (MANUAL/LIMITED/AUTO)
parallel_execution_message_size	16384	FALSE	message buffer size for parallel execution
parallel_force_local	FALSE	FALSE	force single instance execution
parallel_instance_group		FALSE	instance group to use for all parallel operations
parallel_io_cap_enabled	FALSE	FALSE	enable capping DOP by IO bandwidth
parallel_max_servers	80	FALSE	maximum parallel query servers per instance

NAME	VALUE	ISMOD	DESCRIPTION
parallel_min_percent	0	FALSE	minimum percent of threads required for parallel query
parallel_min_servers	0	FALSE	minimum parallel query servers per instance
parallel_min_time_threshold	AUTO	FALSE	threshold above which a plan is a candidate for parallelization (in seconds)
parallel_server	FALSE	FALSE	if TRUE startup in parallel server mode
parallel_server_instances	1	FALSE	number of instances to use for sizing OPS SGA structures
parallel_servers_target	32	FALSE	instance target in terms of number of parallel servers
parallel_threads_per_cpu	2	FALSE	number of parallel execution threads per CPU
permit_92_wrap_format	TRUE	FALSE	allow 9.2 or older wrap format in PL/SQL
pga_aggregate_target	0	FALSE	Target size for the aggregate PGA memory consumed by the instance
plscope_settings	IDENTIFIER S:NONE	FALSE	plscope_settings controls the compile time collection, cross reference, and storage of PL/SQL source code identifier data
plsql_ccflags		FALSE	PL/SQL ccflags
plsql_code_type	INTERPRETED	FALSE	PL/SQL code-type
plsql_debug	FALSE	FALSE	PL/SQL debug
plsql_optimize_level	2	FALSE	PL/SQL optimize level
plsql_v2_compatibility	FALSE	FALSE	PL/SQL version 2.x compatibility flag
plsql_warnings	DISABLE:ALL	FALSE	PL/SQL compiler warnings settings
pre_page_sga	FALSE	FALSE	pre-page sga for process
processes	150	FALSE	user processes
query_rewrite_enabled	TRUE	FALSE	allow rewrite of queries using materialized views if enabled

NAME	VALUE	ISMOD	DESCRIPTION
query_rewrite_integrity	enforced	FALSE	perform rewrite using materialized views with desired integrity
rdbms_server_dn		FALSE	RDBMS's Distinguished Name
read_only_open_delayed	FALSE	FALSE	if TRUE delay opening of read only files until first access
recovery_parallelism	0	FALSE	number of server processes to use for parallel recovery
recyclebin	on	FALSE	recyclebin processing
redo_transport_user		FALSE	Data Guard transport user when using password file
remote_dependencies_mode	TIMESTAMP	FALSE	remote-procedure-call dependencies mode parameter
remote_listener		FALSE	remote listener
remote_login_passwordfile	EXCLUSIVE	FALSE	password file usage parameter
remote_os_authent	FALSE	FALSE	allow non-secure remote clients to use auto-logon accounts
remote_os_roles	FALSE	FALSE	allow non-secure remote clients to use os roles
replication_dependency_tracking	TRUE	FALSE	tracking dependency for Replication parallel propagation
resource_limit	FALSE	FALSE	master switch for resource limit
resource_manager_cpu_allocation	8	FALSE	Resource Manager CPU allocation
resource_manager_plan		FALSE	resource mgr top plan
result_cache_max_result	5	FALSE	maximum result size as percent of cache size
result_cache_max_size	17203200	FALSE	maximum amount of memory to be used by the cache
result_cache_mode	MANUAL	FALSE	result cache operator usage mode
result_cache_remote_expiration	0	FALSE	maximum life time (min) for any result using a remote object
resumable_timeout	0	FALSE	set resumable_timeout

NAME	VALUE	ISMOD	DESCRIPTION
rollback_segments		FALSE	undo segment list
sec_case_sensitive_logon	TRUE	FALSE	case sensitive password enabled for logon
sec_max_failed_login_attempts	10	FALSE	maximum number of failed login attempts on a connection
sec_protocol_error_further_action	CONTINUE	FALSE	TTC protocol error continue action
sec_protocol_error_trace_action	TRACE	FALSE	TTC protocol error action
sec_return_server_release_banner	FALSE	FALSE	whether the server retruns the complete version information
serial_reuse	disable	FALSE	reuse the frame segments
service_names	orcl	FALSE	service names supported by the instance
session_cached_cursors	50	FALSE	Number of cursors to cache in a session.
session_max_open_files	10	FALSE	maximum number of open files allowed per session
sessions	248	FALSE	user and system sessions
sga_max_size	6878658560	FALSE	max total SGA size
sga_target	0	FALSE	Target size of SGA
shadow_core_dump	none	FALSE	Core Size for Shadow Processes
shared_memory_address	0	FALSE	SGA starting address (low order 32-bits on 64-bit platforms)
shared_pool_reserved_size	27682406	FALSE	size in bytes of reserved area of shared pool
shared_pool_size	0	FALSE	size in bytes of shared pool
shared_server_sessions		FALSE	max number of shared server sessions
shared_servers	1	FALSE	number of shared servers to start up
skip_unusable_indexes	TRUE	FALSE	skip unusable indexes if set to TRUE
smtp_out_server		FALSE	utl_smtp server and port configuration parameter
sort_area_retained_size	0	FALSE	size of in-memory sort work area retained between fetch calls

NAME	VALUE	ISMOD	DESCRIPTION
sort_area_size	65536	FALSE	size of in-memory sort work area
spfile	C:\APP\USER\PRODUCT\11.2.0\DBHOME_2\DATABASE\SPFILEORCL.ORA	FALSE	server parameter file
sql92_security	FALSE	FALSE	require select privilege for searched update/delete
sql_trace	FALSE	FALSE	enable SQL trace
sqltune_category	DEFAULT	FALSE	Category qualifier for applying hintsets
standby_archive_dest	%ORACLE_HOME%\RDBMS	FALSE	standby database archivelog destination text string
standby_file_management	MANUAL	FALSE	if auto then files are created/dropped automatically on standby
star_transformation_enabled	FALSE	FALSE	enable the use of star transformation
statistics_level	TYPICAL	FALSE	statistics level
streams_pool_size	0	FALSE	size in bytes of the streams pool
tape_asynch_io	TRUE	FALSE	Use asynch I/O requests for tape devices
thread	0	FALSE	Redo thread to mount
timed_os_statistics	0	FALSE	internal os statistic gathering interval in seconds
timed_statistics	TRUE	FALSE	maintain internal timing statistics
trace_enabled	TRUE	FALSE	enable in memory tracing
tracefile_identifier		FALSE	trace file custom identifier
transactions	272	FALSE	max. number of concurrent active transactions
transactions_per_rollback_segment	5	FALSE	number of active transactions per rollback segment
undo_management	AUTO	FALSE	instance runs in SMU mode if TRUE, else in RBU mode

```
NAME                              VALUE       ISMOD DESCRIPTION
-------------------------------   ----------  ----- ----------------------------
undo_retention                    900         FALSE undo retention in seconds

undo_tablespace                   UNDOTBS1    FALSE use/switch undo tablespace

use_indirect_data_buffers         FALSE       FALSE Enable indirect data buffers
                                                    (very large SGA on 32-bit
                                                    platforms)

user_dump_dest                    c:\app\use FALSE User process dump directory
                                  r\diag\rdb
                                  ms\orcl\or
                                  cl\trace

utl_file_dir                                  FALSE utl_file accessible
                                                    directories list

workarea_size_policy              AUTO        FALSE policy used to size SQL
                                                    working areas (MANUAL/AUTO)

xml_db_events                     enable      FALSE are XML DB events enabled

341 rows selected.
```

Listing of Undocumented Initialization Parameters (X$KSPPI/X$KSPPCV)

Using these parameters is neither supported by Oracle, nor do I recommend them on a production system. Use them only if you are directed to use them by Oracle Support *and* have thoroughly tested them on your crash-and-burn system. Undocumented initialization parameters can lead to database corruption (although a few of them can get your database back up when it becomes corrupted). Use at your own risk. The following query retrieves the undocumented parameters. No output is displayed due to space considerations:

```
Col name for a15
Col value for a15
Col value for a15
Col default1 for a15
Col desc1 for a30
select     a.ksppinm name, b.ksppstvl value, b.ksppstdf default1, a.ksppdesc desc1
from       x$ksppi a, x$ksppcv b
where      a.indx = b.indx
and        substr(ksppinm,1,1) = '_'
order      by ksppinm;
```

TIP
Undocumented initialization parameters often show a glimpse of things coming in the next version of Oracle (or things going away from the last version). However, some of them don't work or cause severe problems.

Oracle Applications Release 12 Recommendations (Note: 396009.1)

The Oracle Applications Development Team wrote a note on My Oracle Support (MetaLink Note: 216205.1 for 11*i* & 396009.1 for Release 12) that shows the initialization parameters that should be used (or not used) with various versions of Oracle Applications. I always review the settings that the Oracle Applications Development team recommends, as they often are dealing with large systems and they've learned some nice tricks. Although I do feel a bit cautious in using SGA_TARGET and removing DB_CACHE_SIZE (without setting minimum values), the other things listed are very helpful in my opinion. SGA_TARGET has been around since 10*g*R1 and is also a 10*g*R2 RAC Best Practice from Oracle. Oracle10*g*R1 had some bugs, but 10*g*R2 and 11*g* seem to be solid. There are also some nice descriptions listed here. Oracle Applications does not use the new MEMORY_TARGET parameter (I am told that E-Business Suite R12 requires 10.2.0.2 as a minimum release and MEMORY_TARGET did not exist in 10*g*R2). The common database parameters suggested are listed here and 11*g*R2 specific parameters follow this listing (note that many comments were removed for brevity; see the actual note for full details).

NOTE
MAX_COMMIT_PROPAGATION_DELAY is now an obsolete parameter in 11gR2 even though it is still listed here as a mandatory parameter for RAC in this note (it's here since it's not obsoleted until 10.2, but it is probable that you should not use this parameter with the 11gR2 database. As always, check with Oracle support).

The following is abbreviated from Note ID 396009.1:

```
###############################################################################
#
# Oracle E-Business Suite Release 12
# Common Database Initialization Parameters
#
# The following represents the common database initialization
# parameters file for Oracle E-Business Suite Release 12.
# Release-specific parameters are included in the respective release
# section. The release-specific parameters should be appended to the
# common database initialization parameter file.
#
# Mandatory parameters are denoted with the (MP) symbol as a
# comment. This includes parameters such as NLS and optimizer
# related parameters… (text deleted from this section)
#
###############################################################################

db_name = prodr12
control_files = ('/disk1/prodr12_DB/cntrlprodr12_1.dbf',
'/disk2/prodr12_DB/cntrlprodr12_2.dbf',
'/disk3/prodr12_DB/cntrlprodr12_3.dbf')

#########
#
# Database block size parameter
# The required block size for E-Business Suite is 8K. No other value may be used.
#
```

```
#########

db_block_size = 8192 (#MP)


#########
#
# _system_trig_enabled
#
# The _system_trig_enabled parameter must be set to TRUE.
# If _system_trig_enabled parameter is set to FALSE it will
# prevent system triggers from being executed.
#
#########

_system_trig_enabled = true (#MP)

o7_dictionary_accessibility = FALSE (#MP)


#########
#
# NLS and character set parameters
#
# Some NLS parameter values are marked as being mandatory settings.
# These are the only supported settings for these parameters for
# Oracle E-Business Suite Release 12. They must not be changed to other values.
# Other NLS parameters have been given default values, which can
# be changed as required.
#
#########

nls_language = american
nls_territory = america
nls_date_format = DD-MON-RR (#MP)
nls_numeric_characters = ".,"
nls_sort = binary (#MP)
nls_comp = binary (#MP)
nls_length_semantics = BYTE (#MP)

#audit_trail = true # Uncomment if you want to enable audit_trail.

user_dump_dest = /ebiz/prodr12/udump
background_dump_dest = /ebiz/prodr12/bdump
core_dump_dest = /ebiz/prodr12/cdump
max_dump_file_size = 20480 #Limit default trace file size to 10 MB.


########
# Timed statistics is required for use of SQL Trace and Statspack.
#
########

timed_statistics = true
_trace_files_public = TRUE

processes = 200 # Max. no. of users.
sessions = 400 # 2 x no. of processes.
db_files = 512 # Max. no. of database files.
dml_locks = 10000 # Database locks.
```

```
cursor_sharing = EXACT (#MP)
open_cursors = 600
session_cached_cursors = 500


########
#
# Cache parameters
#
# For Oracle 10g and 11g, the automatic SGA tuning option (sga_target)
# is required. This avoids the need for individual tuning of the different
# caches, such as the buffer cache, shared pool, and large pool. Use
# of the automatic SGA tuning option also improves manageability and
# overall performance.
#
# sga_target refers to the total size of the SGA. This includes
# all the sub-caches, such as the buffer cache, log buffer,
# shared pool, and large pool. The sizing table in the
# section Database Initialization Parameter Sizing contains
# sizing recommendations for sga_target.
#
# When the automatic SGA tuning option is used to dynamically size
# the individual caches, it is recommended to use a Server Parameter
# file (SPFILE) to store the initialization parameter values.
# Using an SPFILE allows the dynamically-adjusted values to persist
# across restarts. Refer to the Oracle Database Administrator's
# Guide for information on how to create and maintain an SPFILE.

sga_target = 2G
db_block_checking = FALSE
db_block_checksum = TRUE


########
#
# Log Writer parameters
#
# The log writer parameters control the size of the log buffer
# within the SGA, and how frequently the redo logs are checkpointed
# (when all dirty buffers written to disk and a new recovery point
# is created).
#
# A size of 10MB for the log buffer is a reasonable value for
# Oracle E-Business Suite. This represents a balance between
# concurrent programs and online users. The value of log_buffer
# must be a multiple of redo block size (normally 512 bytes).
#
# The checkpoint interval and timeout control the frequency of
# checkpoints.
#
########

log_checkpoint_timeout = 1200 # Checkpoint at least every 20 mins.
log_checkpoint_interval = 100000
log_buffer = 10485760
log_checkpoints_to_alert = TRUE


#########
#
# Shared pool parameters
#
# The shared pool should be tuned to minimize contention for SQL
```

```
# and PL/SQL objects. For Release 12, a reasonable starting point
# is a size of 600M and a 60M reserved area (10%).
#
########

shared_pool_size = 600M
shared_pool_reserved_size = 60M
_shared_pool_reserved_min_alloc = 4100

# cursor_space_for_time = FALSE # Disabled by default.

utl_file_dir = /ebiz/prodr12/utl_file_dir

aq_tm_processes = 1
job_queue_processes = 2
# log_archive_start = true # Uncomment if you want automatic archiving.
parallel_max_servers = 8 # Max. value should be 2 x no. of CPUs.
parallel_min_servers = 0


########
#
# Events parameters
#
# Events should only be set when explicitly by Oracle Support or Development.
# Refer to the appropriate release-specific section for events that may be set.
#
########

#########
#
# Optimizer parameters
#
# The following optimizer parameters must be set as below, and may
# not be changed. No other values are supported.
#
# Refer also to the release-specific section for any additional
# optimizer parameters which must be set.
#
#########

_sort_elimination_cost_ratio =5 (#MP)
_like_with_bind_as_equality = TRUE (#MP)
_fast_full_scan_enabled = FALSE (#MP)
_b_tree_bitmap_plans = FALSE (#MP)
optimizer_secure_view_merging = FALSE (#MP)
_sqlexec_progression_cost = 2147483647 (#MP)


#########
#
# Oracle Real Application Clusters (Oracle RAC) parameters
#
# The following Oracle RAC related parameters should be set when running
# E-Business Suite in an Oracle RAC environment.
#
# (Rich Niemiec note: please check on max_commit_propagation_delay before setting.)
#########

max_commit_propagation_delay = 0 (#MP)
cluster_database = TRUE (#MP)
```

```
#########
#
Private memory area parameters
#
# The automatic memory manager is used to manage the PGA memory. This
# avoids the need to manually tune the settings of sort_area_size and
# hash_area_size.
# The automatic memory manager also improves performance and scalability,
# as memory is released back to the operating system.
#
#########

pga_aggregate_target = 1G
workarea_size_policy = AUTO (#MP)
olap_page_pool_size = 4194304


###############################################################################
#
# End of Common Database Initialization Parameters Section
#
###############################################################################
```

Note
The dump file parameters listed are deprecated in 11gR2;
CURSOR_SPACE_FOR_TIME is deprecated in 11gR1; and
LOG_ARCHIVE_START was obsoleted in 10.1.

The following are specific to 11gR2 and are in addition to those above:

```
####################################################################
#
# Oracle E-Business Suite Release 12
# Release-Specific Database Initialization Parameters for 11gR2
#
####################################################################

#########
#
# Compatible
#
# Compatibility should be set to the current release.
#
#########

compatible = 11.2.0


#######
#
# Diagnostic Parameters
#
# As of Oracle Database 11g Release 1, the diagnostics for each database
# instance are located in a dedicated directory that can be specified
# via the DIAGNOSTIC_DEST initialization parameter. The format of
# the directory specified by DIAGNOSTIC_DEST is as follows:
```

```
#
# <diagnostic_dest><diagnostic_dest>/diag/rdbms/<dbname>/<instname>
#
# Diagnostic files are located in their own subdirectories of the
# DIAGNOSTIC_DEST directory, according to type:
#
# Trace files - <diagnostic_dest>/diag/rdbms/<dbname>/<instname>/trace
# Alert logs - <diagnostic_dest>/diag/rdbms/<dbname>/<instname>/alert
# Core files - <diagnostic_dest>/diag/rdbms/<dbname>/<instname>/cdumd
# Incident dump files -
#<diagnostic_dest>/diag/rdbms/<dbname>/<instname>/incident/<incdir#>

diagnostic_dest = ?/prod12

undo_management=AUTO (#MP)
undo_tablespace=APPS_UNDOTS1

#plsql_code_type = NATIVE #Uncomment if you want to use NATIVE compilation.


#########
#
# Optimizer Parameters
#
# Release 12 uses cost based optimization. The following optimizer
# parameters must be set as shown, and should not be changed.
#
#########

_optimizer_autostats_job=false (#MP) Turn off automatic statistics.

#########
#
# Database Password Case Sensitivity
#
# Oracle E-Business Suite does not currently integrate with this feature,
# so the parameter must be set to FALSE.
#
#########

sec_case_sensitive_logon = FALSE (#MP)

###############################################################################
#
# End of Release-Specific Database Initialization Parameters Section for 11gR2
#
###############################################################################
```

Here is the parameter removal list for Oracle Database 11g Release 2 for 12g applications:

If they exist, you should remove the following parameters from your database initialization parameters file for Oracle Database 11g Release 2 (11.2.X); this is part of MetaLink note listed above. (My personal feeling is that some of these *should* be used to enhance performance, but many are not set because DEFAULT is the correct setting ... please test carefully!)

```
_always_anti_join
_always_semi_join
_complex_view_merging
_index_join_enabled
_kks_use_mutex_pin
_new_initial_join_orders
_optimizer_cost_based_transformation
_optimizer_cost_model
_optimizer_mode_force
_optimizer_undo_changes
_or_expand_nvl_predicate
_ordered_nested_loop
_push_join_predicate
_push_join_union_view
_shared_pool_reserved_min_alloc
_sortmerge_inequality_join_off
_sqlexec_progression_cost
_table_scan_cost_plus_one
_unnest_subquery
_use_column_stats_for_function
always_anti_join
always_semi_join
background_dump_dest
core_dump_dest
db_block_buffers
db_cache_size
db_file_multiblock_read_count
DRS_START
enqueue_resources
event="10932 trace name context level 32768"
event="10933 trace name context level 512"
event="10943 trace name context forever, level 2"
event="10943 trace name context level 16384"
event="38004 trace name context forever, level 1"
hash_area_size
java_pool_size
job_queue_interval
large_pool_size
max_enabled_roles
nls_language
optimizer_dynamic_sampling
optimizer_features_enable
optimizer_index_caching
optimizer_index_cost_adj
optimizer_max_permutations
optimizer_mode
optimizer_percent_parallel
plsql_compiler_flags
plsql_native_library_dir
plsql_native_library_subdir_count
plsql_optimize_level
query_rewrite_enabled
rollback_segments
row_locking
```

```
sort_area_size
sql_trace
SQL_VERSION
timed_statistics
undo_retention
undo_suppress_errors
user_dump_dest
```

Database Initialization Parameter Sizing

This material is also part of Note 396009.1, and I think it is an excellent guideline!

This section provides sizing recommendations based on the active Oracle E-Business Suite user counts. The following table should be used to size the relevant parameters:

Parameter Name	Development or Test Instance	11–100 Users	101–500 Users	501–1000 Users	1001–2000 Users
PROCESSES	200	200	800	1200	2500
SESSIONS	400	400	1600	2400	5000
SGA_TARGET [Footnote 1]	1G	1G	2G	3G	14G
SHARED_POOL_SIZE (csp)	N/A	N/A	N/A	1800M	3000M
SHARED_POOL_RESERVED_SIZE (csp)	N/A	N/A	N/A	180M	300M
SHARED_POOL_SIZE (no csp)	400M	600M	800M	1000M	2000M
SHARED_POOL_RESERVED_SIZE (no csp)	40M	60M	80M	100M	100M
PGA_AGGREGATE_TARGET	1G	2G	4G	10G	20G
Total Memory Required [Footnote 2]	~ 2 GB	~ 3 GB	~ 6 GB	~ 13 GB	~ 25 GB

Specific Notes on Table

■ **Footnote 1** The parameter SGA_TARGET should be used for Oracle 10g- or 11g-based environments such as Release 12. This replaces the parameter DB_CACHE_SIZE, which was used in Oracle i-based environments. Also, it is not necessary to set the parameter UNDO_RETENTION for 10g or 11g-based systems since UNDO retention is set automatically as part of automatic UNDO tuning.

■ **Footnote 2** The total memory required refers to the amount of memory required for the database instance and associated memory, including the SGA and the PGA. You should ensure that your system has sufficient available memory in order to support the values provided here. The values provided should be adjusted based on available memory so as to prevent paging and swapping.

Top 10 Reasons *Not* to Write a Book

1. You like sleep and caffeine-enhanced water clogs your coffee maker.

2. You have enough trouble getting the time to read books, let alone write one.

3. You enjoy getting together with your family from time to time.

4. You're tired of being the first one in the office (actually, you've been there all night).

5. You hobby is golf and you never play.

6. You enjoy noticing the world around you rather than feeling a "purple haze all through your mind."

7. Kevin Loney will write on that subject eventually . . . you'll wait for his book.

8. You don't want to "show off" how much you know . . . you're far to humble.

9. Your PC is out of disk space already, although you've just loaded Windows 99.1415926.

10. You just got your *life* back after the last Oracle upgrade—no way!

TIP
Retirement is a good time to write a book, not *during one of the fastest tech growth cycles in history (not as fast as pre-2000 yet) followed by the Great Recession. Perhaps when the 2000-year bull market ends somewhere between 2018 and 2020 (good time to get out of the market in my opinion) that might be a better time.*

Tips Review

■ Setting certain initialization parameters correctly can be the difference between a report taking two seconds and two hours. Try changes out on a test system thoroughly *before* implementing those changes in a production environment!

■ Oracle has some excellent options. Unfortunately, some of them do *not* work unless the initialization parameter is set correctly.

■ Undocumented initialization parameters can corrupt your database! Some of them can also salvage a corrupted database. Try to use these only when all other choices have failed and use them only with the help and approval of Oracle Support.

■ Undocumented initialization parameters often show a glimpse of things coming in the next version of Oracle, but some of them don't work at all.

■ Retirement is a good time to write a book. Writing a book during the largest growth period in history followed by the most painful economic conditions since 1929 is *not.*

■ Technology and the rise of using the full 16 Exabytes of addressable memory in 64-bit should create a world in the future that you'll barely recognize. Oracle Exadata and the acceleration of hardware in addition to software may just be the boost we need to get us there!

References

Kevin Loney, *Oracle Database 10g DBA Handbook* (McGraw-Hill, 2005).
Metalink Notes: 22908.1, 216205.1, 316889.1, 396009.1.
Oracle Server Tuning (Oracle Corporation).
Oracle9i, Oracle10g, Oracle 11g Performance Tuning (Oracle Corporation).

Thanks to Lucas Niemiec for testing the queries and providing the new listings for 11gR2. Thanks also to Brad Brown, Joe Trezzo, Randy Swanson, Sean McGuire, Greg Pucka, Mike Broullette, and Kevin Loney for their contributions to this chapter.

APPENDIX
B

The V$ Views (DBA and Developer)

T he V$ views are very helpful in analyzing database issues. This appendix lists all views and creation scripts used to actually build the V$ and GV$ views. The V$ views vary in structure and number, depending on the database version and release used. Run the queries on your version of the database to get the number of views and structure for your specific version. The topics covered in this appendix include the following:

- Creation of V$ and GV$ views and x$ tables

- A list of all Oracle 11gR2 GV$ and V$ views

- Oracle 11g script listing of the X$ tables used in the creation of the V$ views

NOTE
V$ to X$ and X$ to V$ cross-references can be found in Appendix C.

Creation of V$ and GV$ Views and X$ Tables

To understand the creation of X$ tables, knowing the V$ and data dictionary views can be crucial. And both are critical to comprehending fully the intricacies of Oracle. While knowledge of the views and tables is critical to your career, their creation has, however, remained somewhat of a vexing mystery. Figure B-1 illustrates the creation of the underlying tables and the data dictionary views, whereas Figure B-2 illustrates the creation of the X$ tables and the V$ views.

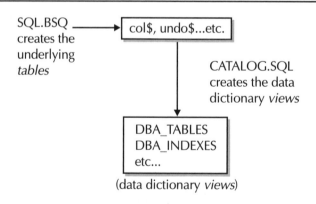

FIGURE B-1. *Creation of the data dictionary views*

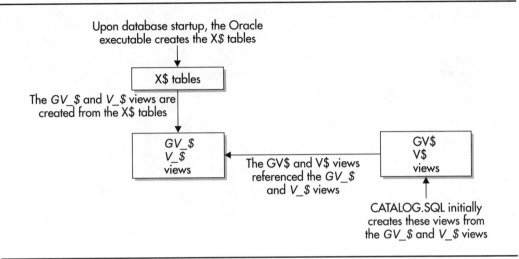

Upon database startup, the Oracle
executable creates the X$ tables

X$ tables

The *GV_$* and *V_$* views are
created from the X$ tables

GV_$
V_$
views

The GV$ and V$ views
referenced the GV_$
and V_$ views

GV$
V$
views

CATALOG.SQL initially
creates these views from
the *GV_$* and *V_$* views

FIGURE B-2.   *Creation of the X$ tables and the V$ views*

A List of Oracle 11g (11.2.0.1.0) GV$ Views

NOTE
*The Oracle 11g V$ views are about the same as the GV$ views,
minus the instance ID.*

Here is the Oracle 11*g* query to obtain this listing of all the GV$ views (496 views):

```
set pagesize 1000

select    name
from      v$fixed_table
where     name like 'GV%'
order by  name;
```

The listing itself follows:

```
NAME
-----------------------------------------------------------------------------
GV$ACCESS                        GV$ARCHIVE_GAP
GV$ACTIVE_INSTANCES              GV$ARCHIVE_PROCESSES
GV$ACTIVE_SERVICES               GV$ASH_INFO
GV$ACTIVE_SESSION_HISTORY        GV$ASM_ACFSSNAPSHOTS
GV$ACTIVE_SESS_POOL_MTH          GV$ASM_ACFSVOLUMES
GV$ADVISOR_PROGRESS              GV$ASM_ALIAS
GV$ALERT_TYPES                   GV$ASM_ATTRIBUTE
GV$AQ1                           GV$ASM_CLIENT
GV$ARCHIVE                       GV$ASM_DISK
GV$ARCHIVED_LOG                  GV$ASM_DISKGROUP
GV$ARCHIVE_DEST                  GV$ASM_DISKGROUP_STAT
GV$ARCHIVE_DEST_STATUS           GV$ASM_DISK_IOSTAT
```

```
NAME
--------------------------------------------------------------------------------
GV$ASM_DISK_STAT                     GV$DATABASE_INCARNATION
GV$ASM_FILE                          GV$DATAFILE
GV$ASM_FILESYSTEM                    GV$DATAFILE_COPY
GV$ASM_OPERATION                     GV$DATAFILE_HEADER
GV$ASM_TEMPLATE                      GV$DATAGUARD_CONFIG
GV$ASM_USER                          GV$DATAGUARD_STATS
GV$ASM_USERGROUP                     GV$DATAGUARD_STATUS
GV$ASM_USERGROUP_MEMBER              GV$DATAPUMP_JOB
GV$ASM_VOLUME                        GV$DATAPUMP_SESSION
GV$ASM_VOLUME_STAT                   GV$DBFILE
GV$AW_AGGREGATE_OP                   GV$DBLINK
GV$AW_ALLOCATE_OP                    GV$DB_CACHE_ADVICE
GV$AW_CALC                           GV$DB_OBJECT_CACHE
GV$AW_LONGOPS                        GV$DB_PIPES
GV$AW_OLAP                           GV$DB_TRANSPORTABLE_PLATFORM
GV$AW_SESSION_INFO                   GV$DELETED_OBJECT
GV$BACKUP                            GV$DETACHED_SESSION
GV$BACKUP_ASYNC_IO                   GV$DIAG_INFO
GV$BACKUP_CORRUPTION                 GV$DISPATCHER
GV$BACKUP_DATAFILE                   GV$DISPATCHER_CONFIG
GV$BACKUP_DEVICE                     GV$DISPATCHER_RATE
GV$BACKUP_PIECE                      GV$DLM_ALL_LOCKS
GV$BACKUP_REDOLOG                    GV$DLM_CONVERT_LOCAL
GV$BACKUP_SET                        GV$DLM_CONVERT_REMOTE
GV$BACKUP_SPFILE                     GV$DLM_LATCH
GV$BACKUP_SYNC_IO                    GV$DLM_LOCKS
GV$BGPROCESS                         GV$DLM_MISC
GV$BH                                GV$DLM_RESS
GV$BLOCKING_QUIESCE                  GV$DLM_TRAFFIC_CONTROLLER
GV$BSP                               GV$DNFS_CHANNELS
GV$BUFFERED_PUBLISHERS               GV$DNFS_FILES
GV$BUFFERED_QUEUES                   GV$DNFS_SERVERS
GV$BUFFERED_SUBSCRIBERS              GV$DNFS_STATS
GV$BUFFER_POOL                       GV$DYNAMIC_REMASTER_STATS
GV$BUFFER_POOL_STATISTICS            GV$EMON
GV$CALLTAG                           GV$ENABLEDPRIVS
GV$CELL                              GV$ENCRYPTED_TABLESPACES
GV$CELL_CONFIG                       GV$ENCRYPTION_WALLET
GV$CELL_REQUEST_TOTALS               GV$ENQUEUE_LOCK
GV$CELL_STATE                        GV$ENQUEUE_STAT
GV$CELL_THREAD_HISTORY               GV$ENQUEUE_STATISTICS
GV$CIRCUIT                           GV$EVENTMETRIC
GV$CLASS_CACHE_TRANSFER              GV$EVENT_HISTOGRAM
GV$CLASS_PING                        GV$EVENT_NAME
GV$CLIENT_RESULT_CACHE_STATS         GV$EXECUTION
GV$CLIENT_STATS                      GV$FAST_START_SERVERS
GV$CLUSTER_INTERCONNECTS             GV$FAST_START_TRANSACTIONS
GV$CONFIGURED_INTERCONNECTS          GV$FILEMETRIC
GV$CONTEXT                           GV$FILEMETRIC_HISTORY
GV$CONTROLFILE                       GV$FILESPACE_USAGE
GV$CONTROLFILE_RECORD_SECTION        GV$FILESTAT
GV$COPY_CORRUPTION                   GV$FILE_CACHE_TRANSFER
GV$CORRUPT_XID_LIST                  GV$FILE_HISTOGRAM
GV$CPOOL_CC_INFO                     GV$FILE_OPTIMIZED_HISTOGRAM
GV$CPOOL_CC_STATS                    GV$FILE_PING
GV$CPOOL_CONN_INFO                   GV$FIXED_TABLE
GV$CPOOL_STATS                       GV$FIXED_VIEW_DEFINITION
GV$CR_BLOCK_SERVER                   GV$FLASHBACK_DATABASE_LOG
GV$CURRENT_BLOCK_SERVER              GV$FLASHBACK_DATABASE_LOGFILE
GV$DATABASE                          GV$FLASHBACK_DATABASE_STAT
GV$DATABASE_BLOCK_CORRUPTION         GV$FOREIGN_ARCHIVED_LOG
```

NAME

GV$FS_FAILOVER_HISTOGRAM	GV$LOCKED_OBJECT
GV$FS_FAILOVER_STATS	GV$LOCKS_WITH_COLLISIONS
GV$GCSHVMASTER_INFO	GV$LOCK_ACTIVITY
GV$GCSPFMASTER_INFO	GV$LOCK_ELEMENT
GV$GC_ELEMENT	GV$LOCK_TYPE
GV$GC_ELEMENTS_WITH_COLLISIONS	GV$LOG
GV$GES_BLOCKING_ENQUEUE	GV$LOGFILE
GV$GES_ENQUEUE	GV$LOGHIST
GV$GLOBALCONTEXT	GV$LOGMNR_CALLBACK
GV$GLOBAL_BLOCKED_LOCKS	GV$LOGMNR_CONTENTS
GV$GLOBAL_TRANSACTION	GV$LOGMNR_DBA_OBJECTS
GV$HM_CHECK	GV$LOGMNR_DICTIONARY
GV$HM_CHECK_PARAM	GV$LOGMNR_DICTIONARY_LOAD
GV$HM_FINDING	GV$LOGMNR_EXTENTS
GV$HM_INFO	GV$LOGMNR_LATCH
GV$HM_RECOMMENDATION	GV$LOGMNR_LOGFILE
GV$HM_RUN	GV$LOGMNR_LOGS
GV$HS_AGENT	GV$LOGMNR_OBJECT_SEGMENTS
GV$HS_PARAMETER	GV$LOGMNR_PARAMETERS
GV$HS_SESSION	GV$LOGMNR_PROCESS
GV$HVMASTER_INFO	GV$LOGMNR_REGION
GV$INCMETER_CONFIG	GV$LOGMNR_SESSION
GV$INCMETER_INFO	GV$LOGMNR_STATS
GV$INCMETER_SUMMARY	GV$LOGMNR_SYS_DBA_SEGS
GV$INDEXED_FIXED_COLUMN	GV$LOGMNR_SYS_OBJECTS
GV$INSTANCE	GV$LOGMNR_TRANSACTION
GV$INSTANCE_CACHE_TRANSFER	GV$LOGSTDBY
GV$INSTANCE_LOG_GROUP	GV$LOGSTDBY_PROCESS
GV$INSTANCE_RECOVERY	GV$LOGSTDBY_PROGRESS
GV$IOFUNCMETRIC	GV$LOGSTDBY_STATE
GV$IOFUNCMETRIC_HISTORY	GV$LOGSTDBY_STATS
GV$IOSTAT_CONSUMER_GROUP	GV$LOGSTDBY_TRANSACTION
GV$IOSTAT_FILE	GV$LOG_HISTORY
GV$IOSTAT_FUNCTION	GV$MANAGED_STANDBY
GV$IOSTAT_FUNCTION_DETAIL	GV$MAP_COMP_LIST
GV$IOSTAT_NETWORK	GV$MAP_ELEMENT
GV$IO_CALIBRATION_STATUS	GV$MAP_EXT_ELEMENT
GV$IR_FAILURE	GV$MAP_FILE
GV$IR_FAILURE_SET	GV$MAP_FILE_EXTENT
GV$IR_MANUAL_CHECKLIST	GV$MAP_FILE_IO_STACK
GV$IR_REPAIR	GV$MAP_LIBRARY
GV$JAVAPOOL	GV$MAP_SUBELEMENT
GV$JAVA_LIBRARY_CACHE_MEMORY	GV$MAX_ACTIVE_SESS_TARGET_MTH
GV$JAVA_POOL_ADVICE	GV$MEMORY_CURRENT_RESIZE_OPS
GV$LATCH	GV$MEMORY_DYNAMIC_COMPONENTS
GV$LATCHHOLDER	GV$MEMORY_RESIZE_OPS
GV$LATCHNAME	GV$MEMORY_TARGET_ADVICE
GV$LATCH_CHILDREN	GV$METRIC
GV$LATCH_MISSES	GV$METRICGROUP
GV$LATCH_PARENT	GV$METRICNAME
GV$LIBCACHE_LOCKS	GV$METRIC_HISTORY
GV$LIBRARYCACHE	GV$MTTR_TARGET_ADVICE
GV$LIBRARY_CACHE_MEMORY	GV$MUTEX_SLEEP
GV$LICENSE	GV$MUTEX_SLEEP_HISTORY
GV$LISTENER_NETWORK	GV$MVREFRESH
GV$LOADISTAT	GV$MYSTAT
GV$LOADPSTAT	GV$NFS_CLIENTS
GV$LOBSTAT	GV$NFS_LOCKS
GV$LOCK	GV$NFS_OPEN_FILES

```
NAME
-------------------------------------------------------------------------------------
GV$NLS_PARAMETERS                    GV$RESULT_CACHE_DR
GV$NLS_VALID_VALUES                  GV$RESULT_CACHE_MEMORY
GV$OBJECT_DEPENDENCY                 GV$RESULT_CACHE_OBJECTS
GV$OBSOLETE_PARAMETER                GV$RESULT_CACHE_RD
GV$OFFLINE_RANGE                     GV$RESULT_CACHE_RR
GV$OPEN_CURSOR                       GV$RESULT_CACHE_STATISTICS
GV$OPTION                            GV$RESUMABLE
GV$OSSTAT                            GV$RFS_THREAD
GV$PARALLEL_DEGREE_LIMIT_MTH         GV$RMAN_COMPRESSION_ALGORITHM
GV$PARAMETER                         GV$RMAN_CONFIGURATION
GV$PARAMETER2                        GV$RMAN_ENCRYPTION_ALGORITHMS
GV$PARAMETER_VALID_VALUES            GV$RMAN_OUTPUT
GV$PERSISTENT_PUBLISHERS             GV$RMAN_STATUS_CURRENT
GV$PERSISTENT_QMN_CACHE              GV$ROLLSTAT
GV$PERSISTENT_QUEUES                 GV$ROWCACHE
GV$PERSISTENT_SUBSCRIBERS            GV$ROWCACHE_PARENT
GV$PGASTAT                           GV$ROWCACHE_SUBORDINATE
GV$PGA_TARGET_ADVICE                 GV$RSRCMGRMETRIC
GV$PGA_TARGET_ADVICE_HISTOGRAM       GV$RSRCMGRMETRIC_HISTORY
GV$POLICY_HISTORY                    GV$RSRC_CONSUMER_GROUP
GV$PQ_SESSTAT                        GV$RSRC_CONSUMER_GROUP_CPU_MTH
GV$PQ_SLAVE                          GV$RSRC_CONS_GROUP_HISTORY
GV$PQ_SYSSTAT                        GV$RSRC_PLAN
GV$PQ_TQSTAT                         GV$RSRC_PLAN_CPU_MTH
GV$PROCESS                           GV$RSRC_PLAN_HISTORY
GV$PROCESS_GROUP                     GV$RSRC_SESSION_INFO
GV$PROCESS_MEMORY                    GV$RULE
GV$PROCESS_MEMORY_DETAIL             GV$RULE_SET
GV$PROCESS_MEMORY_DETAIL_PROG        GV$RULE_SET_AGGREGATE_STATS
GV$PROPAGATION_RECEIVER              GV$SCHEDULER_RUNNING_JOBS
GV$PROPAGATION_SENDER                GV$SECUREFILE_TIMER
GV$PROXY_ARCHIVEDLOG                 GV$SEGMENT_STATISTICS
GV$PROXY_DATAFILE                    GV$SEGSTAT
GV$PWFILE_USERS                      GV$SEGSTAT_NAME
GV$PX_BUFFER_ADVICE                  GV$SERVICEMETRIC
GV$PX_INSTANCE_GROUP                 GV$SERVICEMETRIC_HISTORY
GV$PX_PROCESS                        GV$SERVICES
GV$PX_PROCESS_SYSSTAT                GV$SERVICE_EVENT
GV$PX_SESSION                        GV$SERVICE_STATS
GV$PX_SESSTAT                        GV$SERVICE_WAIT_CLASS
GV$QMON_COORDINATOR_STATS            GV$SERV_MOD_ACT_STATS
GV$QMON_SERVER_STATS                 GV$SESSION
GV$QMON_TASKS                        GV$SESSION_BLOCKERS
GV$QMON_TASK_STATS                   GV$SESSION_CLIENT_RESULT_CACHE
GV$QUEUE                             GV$SESSION_CONNECT_INFO
GV$QUEUEING_MTH                      GV$SESSION_CURSOR_CACHE
GV$RECOVERY_FILE_STATUS              GV$SESSION_EVENT
GV$RECOVERY_LOG                      GV$SESSION_FIX_CONTROL
GV$RECOVERY_PROGRESS                 GV$SESSION_LONGOPS
GV$RECOVERY_STATUS                   GV$SESSION_OBJECT_CACHE
GV$RECOVER_FILE                      GV$SESSION_WAIT
GV$REDO_DEST_RESP_HISTOGRAM          GV$SESSION_WAIT_CLASS
GV$REPLPROP                          GV$SESSION_WAIT_HISTORY
GV$REPLQUEUE                         GV$SESSMETRIC
GV$REQDIST                           GV$SESSTAT
GV$RESERVED_WORDS                    GV$SESS_IO
GV$RESOURCE                          GV$SESS_TIME_MODEL
GV$RESOURCE_LIMIT                    GV$SES_OPTIMIZER_ENV
GV$RESTORE_POINT                     GV$SGA
GV$RESULT_CACHE_DEPENDENCY           GV$SGAINFO
```

```
NAME
-----------------------------------------------------------------------------------------
GV$SGASTAT                              GV$STREAMS_POOL_STATISTICS
GV$SGA_CURRENT_RESIZE_OPS               GV$STREAMS_TRANSACTION
GV$SGA_DYNAMIC_COMPONENTS               GV$SUBCACHE
GV$SGA_DYNAMIC_FREE_MEMORY              GV$SUBSCR_REGISTRATION_STATS
GV$SGA_RESIZE_OPS                       GV$SYSAUX_OCCUPANTS
GV$SGA_TARGET_ADVICE                    GV$SYSMETRIC
GV$SHARED_POOL_ADVICE                   GV$SYSMETRIC_HISTORY
GV$SHARED_POOL_RESERVED                 GV$SYSMETRIC_SUMMARY
GV$SHARED_SERVER                        GV$SYSSTAT
GV$SHARED_SERVER_MONITOR                GV$SYSTEM_CURSOR_CACHE
GV$SORT_SEGMENT                         GV$SYSTEM_EVENT
GV$SORT_USAGE                           GV$SYSTEM_FIX_CONTROL
GV$SPPARAMETER                          GV$SYSTEM_PARAMETER
GV$SQL                                  GV$SYSTEM_PARAMETER2
GV$SQLAREA                              GV$SYSTEM_PARAMETER3
GV$SQLAREA_PLAN_HASH                    GV$SYSTEM_PARAMETER4
GV$SQLCOMMAND                           GV$SYSTEM_WAIT_CLASS
GV$SQLFN_ARG_METADATA                   GV$SYS_OPTIMIZER_ENV
GV$SQLFN_METADATA                       GV$SYS_TIME_MODEL
GV$SQLPA_METRIC                         GV$TABLESPACE
GV$SQLSTATS                             GV$TEMPFILE
GV$SQLSTATS_PLAN_HASH                   GV$TEMPORARY_LOBS
GV$SQLTEXT                              GV$TEMPSTAT
GV$SQLTEXT_WITH_NEWLINES                GV$TEMP_CACHE_TRANSFER
GV$SQL_BIND_DATA                        GV$TEMP_EXTENT_MAP
GV$SQL_BIND_METADATA                    GV$TEMP_EXTENT_POOL
GV$SQL_CS_HISTOGRAM                     GV$TEMP_PING
GV$SQL_CS_SELECTIVITY                   GV$TEMP_SPACE_HEADER
GV$SQL_CS_STATISTICS                    GV$THREAD
GV$SQL_CURSOR                           GV$THRESHOLD_TYPES
GV$SQL_FEATURE                          GV$TIMER
GV$SQL_FEATURE_DEPENDENCY               GV$TIMEZONE_FILE
GV$SQL_FEATURE_HIERARCHY                GV$TIMEZONE_NAMES
GV$SQL_HINT                             GV$TOPLEVELCALL
GV$SQL_JOIN_FILTER                      GV$TRANSACTION
GV$SQL_MONITOR                          GV$TRANSACTION_ENQUEUE
GV$SQL_OPTIMIZER_ENV                    GV$TRANSPORTABLE_PLATFORM
GV$SQL_PLAN                             GV$TSM_SESSIONS
GV$SQL_PLAN_MONITOR                     GV$TYPE_SIZE
GV$SQL_PLAN_STATISTICS                  GV$UNDOSTAT
GV$SQL_PLAN_STATISTICS_ALL              GV$VERSION
GV$SQL_REDIRECTION                      GV$VPD_POLICY
GV$SQL_SHARED_CURSOR                    GV$WAITCLASSMETRIC
GV$SQL_SHARED_MEMORY                    GV$WAITCLASSMETRIC_HISTORY
GV$SQL_WORKAREA                         GV$WAITSTAT
GV$SQL_WORKAREA_ACTIVE                  GV$WALLET
GV$SQL_WORKAREA_HISTOGRAM               GV$WLM_PCMETRIC
GV$SSCR_SESSIONS                        GV$WLM_PCMETRIC_HISTORY
GV$STANDBY_LOG                          GV$WLM_PC_STATS
GV$STATISTICS_LEVEL                     GV$WORKLOAD_REPLAY_THREAD
GV$STATNAME                             GV$XML_AUDIT_TRAIL
GV$STREAMS_APPLY_COORDINATOR            GV$_LOCK
GV$STREAMS_APPLY_READER                 GV$_LOCK1
GV$STREAMS_APPLY_SERVER                 GV$_RESUMABLE2
GV$STREAMS_CAPTURE                      GV$_SEQUENCES
GV$STREAMS_MESSAGE_TRACKING
GV$STREAMS_POOL_ADVICE                  496 rows selected.
```

A List of Oracle 11g (11.2.0.1.0) V$ Views

Here is the Oracle 11g query to get this listing (525 views):

```
set pagesize 1000

select    name
from      v$fixed_table
where     name like 'V%'
order by  name;
```

The listing itself follows:

```
NAME
--------------------------------------------------------------------------------
V$ACCESS                          V$BACKUP_CONTROLFILE_SUMMARY
V$ACTIVE_INSTANCES                V$BACKUP_COPY_DETAILS
V$ACTIVE_SERVICES                 V$BACKUP_COPY_SUMMARY
V$ACTIVE_SESSION_HISTORY          V$BACKUP_CORRUPTION
V$ACTIVE_SESS_POOL_MTH            V$BACKUP_DATAFILE
V$ADVISOR_PROGRESS                V$BACKUP_DATAFILE_DETAILS
V$ALERT_TYPES                     V$BACKUP_DATAFILE_SUMMARY
V$AQ1                             V$BACKUP_DEVICE
V$ARCHIVE                         V$BACKUP_PIECE
V$ARCHIVED_LOG                    V$BACKUP_PIECE_DETAILS
V$ARCHIVE_DEST                    V$BACKUP_REDOLOG
V$ARCHIVE_DEST_STATUS             V$BACKUP_SET
V$ARCHIVE_GAP                     V$BACKUP_SET_DETAILS
V$ARCHIVE_PROCESSES               V$BACKUP_SET_SUMMARY
V$ASH_INFO                        V$BACKUP_SPFILE
V$ASM_ACFSSNAPSHOTS               V$BACKUP_SPFILE_DETAILS
V$ASM_ACFSVOLUMES                 V$BACKUP_SPFILE_SUMMARY
V$ASM_ALIAS                       V$BACKUP_SYNC_IO
V$ASM_ATTRIBUTE                   V$BGPROCESS
V$ASM_CLIENT                      V$BH
V$ASM_DISK                        V$BLOCKING_QUIESCE
V$ASM_DISKGROUP                   V$BLOCK_CHANGE_TRACKING
V$ASM_DISKGROUP_STAT              V$BSP
V$ASM_DISK_IOSTAT                 V$BUFFERED_PUBLISHERS
V$ASM_DISK_STAT                   V$BUFFERED_QUEUES
V$ASM_FILE                        V$BUFFERED_SUBSCRIBERS
V$ASM_FILESYSTEM                  V$BUFFER_POOL
V$ASM_OPERATION                   V$BUFFER_POOL_STATISTICS
V$ASM_TEMPLATE                    V$CALLTAG
V$ASM_USER                        V$CELL
V$ASM_USERGROUP                   V$CELL_CONFIG
V$ASM_USERGROUP_MEMBER            V$CELL_REQUEST_TOTALS
V$ASM_VOLUME                      V$CELL_STATE
V$ASM_VOLUME_STAT                 V$CELL_THREAD_HISTORY
V$AW_AGGREGATE_OP                 V$CIRCUIT
V$AW_ALLOCATE_OP                  V$CLASS_CACHE_TRANSFER
V$AW_CALC                         V$CLASS_PING
V$AW_LONGOPS                      V$CLIENT_RESULT_CACHE_STATS
V$AW_OLAP                         V$CLIENT_STATS
V$AW_SESSION_INFO                 V$CLUSTER_INTERCONNECTS
V$BACKUP                          V$CONFIGURED_INTERCONNECTS
V$BACKUP_ARCHIVELOG_DETAILS       V$CONTEXT
V$BACKUP_ARCHIVELOG_SUMMARY       V$CONTROLFILE
V$BACKUP_ASYNC_IO                 V$CONTROLFILE_RECORD_SECTION
V$BACKUP_CONTROLFILE_DETAILS      V$COPY_CORRUPTION
```

```
NAME
------------------------------------------------------------------------------------
V$CORRUPT_XID_LIST                       V$FILESTAT
V$CPOOL_CC_INFO                          V$FILE_CACHE_TRANSFER
V$CPOOL_CC_STATS                         V$FILE_HISTOGRAM
V$CPOOL_CONN_INFO                        V$FILE_OPTIMIZED_HISTOGRAM
V$CPOOL_STATS                            V$FILE_PING
V$CR_BLOCK_SERVER                        V$FIXED_TABLE
V$CURRENT_BLOCK_SERVER                   V$FIXED_VIEW_DEFINITION
V$DATABASE                               V$FLASHBACK_DATABASE_LOG
V$DATABASE_BLOCK_CORRUPTION              V$FLASHBACK_DATABASE_LOGFILE
V$DATABASE_INCARNATION                   V$FLASHBACK_DATABASE_STAT
V$DATAFILE                               V$FLASHBACK_TXN_GRAPH
V$DATAFILE_COPY                          V$FLASHBACK_TXN_MODS
V$DATAFILE_HEADER                        V$FLASH_RECOVERY_AREA_USAGE
V$DATAGUARD_CONFIG                       V$FOREIGN_ARCHIVED_LOG
V$DATAGUARD_STATS                        V$FS_FAILOVER_HISTOGRAM
V$DATAGUARD_STATUS                       V$FS_FAILOVER_STATS
V$DATAPUMP_JOB                           V$GCSHVMASTER_INFO
V$DATAPUMP_SESSION                       V$GCSPFMASTER_INFO
V$DBFILE                                 V$GC_ELEMENT
V$DBLINK                                 V$GC_ELEMENTS_WITH_COLLISIONS
V$DB_CACHE_ADVICE                        V$GES_BLOCKING_ENQUEUE
V$DB_OBJECT_CACHE                        V$GES_ENQUEUE
V$DB_PIPES                               V$GLOBALCONTEXT
V$DB_TRANSPORTABLE_PLATFORM              V$GLOBAL_BLOCKED_LOCKS
V$DELETED_OBJECT                         V$GLOBAL_TRANSACTION
V$DETACHED_SESSION                       V$HM_CHECK
V$DIAG_CRITICAL_ERROR                    V$HM_CHECK_PARAM
V$DIAG_INFO                              V$HM_FINDING
V$DISPATCHER                             V$HM_INFO
V$DISPATCHER_CONFIG                      V$HM_RECOMMENDATION
V$DISPATCHER_RATE                        V$HM_RUN
V$DLM_ALL_LOCKS                          V$HS_AGENT
V$DLM_CONVERT_LOCAL                      V$HS_PARAMETER
V$DLM_CONVERT_REMOTE                     V$HS_SESSION
V$DLM_LATCH                              V$HVMASTER_INFO
V$DLM_LOCKS                              V$INCMETER_CONFIG
V$DLM_MISC                               V$INCMETER_INFO
V$DLM_RESS                               V$INCMETER_SUMMARY
V$DLM_TRAFFIC_CONTROLLER                 V$INDEXED_FIXED_COLUMN
V$DNFS_CHANNELS                          V$INSTANCE
V$DNFS_FILES                             V$INSTANCE_CACHE_TRANSFER
V$DNFS_SERVERS                           V$INSTANCE_LOG_GROUP
V$DNFS_STATS                             V$INSTANCE_RECOVERY
V$DYNAMIC_REMASTER_STATS                 V$IOFUNCMETRIC
V$EMON                                   V$IOFUNCMETRIC_HISTORY
V$ENABLEDPRIVS                           V$IOSTAT_CONSUMER_GROUP
V$ENCRYPTED_TABLESPACES                  V$IOSTAT_FILE
V$ENCRYPTION_WALLET                      V$IOSTAT_FUNCTION
V$ENQUEUE_LOCK                           V$IOSTAT_FUNCTION_DETAIL
V$ENQUEUE_STAT                           V$IOSTAT_NETWORK
V$ENQUEUE_STATISTICS                     V$IO_CALIBRATION_STATUS
V$EVENTMETRIC                            V$IR_FAILURE
V$EVENT_HISTOGRAM                        V$IR_FAILURE_SET
V$EVENT_NAME                             V$IR_MANUAL_CHECKLIST
V$EXECUTION                              V$IR_REPAIR
V$FAST_START_SERVERS                     V$JAVAPOOL
V$FAST_START_TRANSACTIONS                V$JAVA_LIBRARY_CACHE_MEMORY
V$FILEMETRIC                             V$JAVA_POOL_ADVICE
V$FILEMETRIC_HISTORY                     V$LATCH
V$FILESPACE_USAGE                        V$LATCHHOLDER
```

```
NAME
--------------------------------------------------------------------------------
V$LATCHNAME                             V$METRIC
V$LATCH_CHILDREN                        V$METRICGROUP
V$LATCH_MISSES                          V$METRICNAME
V$LATCH_PARENT                          V$METRIC_HISTORY
V$LIBCACHE_LOCKS                        V$MTTR_TARGET_ADVICE
V$LIBRARYCACHE                          V$MUTEX_SLEEP
V$LIBRARY_CACHE_MEMORY                  V$MUTEX_SLEEP_HISTORY
V$LICENSE                               V$MVREFRESH
V$LISTENER_NETWORK                      V$MYSTAT
V$LOADISTAT                             V$NFS_CLIENTS
V$LOADPSTAT                             V$NFS_LOCKS
V$LOBSTAT                               V$NFS_OPEN_FILES
V$LOCK                                  V$NLS_PARAMETERS
V$LOCKED_OBJECT                         V$NLS_VALID_VALUES
V$LOCKS_WITH_COLLISIONS                 V$OBJECT_DEPENDENCY
V$LOCK_ACTIVITY                         V$OBJECT_PRIVILEGE
V$LOCK_ELEMENT                          V$OBSOLETE_PARAMETER
V$LOCK_TYPE                             V$OFFLINE_RANGE
V$LOG                                   V$OPEN_CURSOR
V$LOGFILE                               V$OPTION
V$LOGHIST                               V$OSSTAT
V$LOGMNR_CALLBACK                       V$PARALLEL_DEGREE_LIMIT_MTH
V$LOGMNR_CONTENTS                       V$PARAMETER
V$LOGMNR_DBA_OBJECTS                    V$PARAMETER2
V$LOGMNR_DICTIONARY                     V$PARAMETER_VALID_VALUES
V$LOGMNR_DICTIONARY_LOAD                V$PERSISTENT_PUBLISHERS
V$LOGMNR_EXTENTS                        V$PERSISTENT_QMN_CACHE
V$LOGMNR_LATCH                          V$PERSISTENT_QUEUES
V$LOGMNR_LOGFILE                        V$PERSISTENT_SUBSCRIBERS
V$LOGMNR_LOGS                           V$PGASTAT
V$LOGMNR_OBJECT_SEGMENTS                V$PGA_TARGET_ADVICE
V$LOGMNR_PARAMETERS                     V$PGA_TARGET_ADVICE_HISTOGRAM
V$LOGMNR_PROCESS                        V$POLICY_HISTORY
V$LOGMNR_REGION                         V$PQ_SESSTAT
V$LOGMNR_SESSION                        V$PQ_SLAVE
V$LOGMNR_STATS                          V$PQ_SYSSTAT
V$LOGMNR_SYS_DBA_SEGS                   V$PQ_TQSTAT
V$LOGMNR_SYS_OBJECTS                    V$PROCESS
V$LOGMNR_TRANSACTION                    V$PROCESS_GROUP
V$LOGSTDBY                              V$PROCESS_MEMORY
V$LOGSTDBY_PROCESS                      V$PROCESS_MEMORY_DETAIL
V$LOGSTDBY_PROGRESS                     V$PROCESS_MEMORY_DETAIL_PROG
V$LOGSTDBY_STATE                        V$PROPAGATION_RECEIVER
V$LOGSTDBY_STATS                        V$PROPAGATION_SENDER
V$LOGSTDBY_TRANSACTION                  V$PROXY_ARCHIVEDLOG
V$LOG_HISTORY                           V$PROXY_ARCHIVELOG_DETAILS
V$MANAGED_STANDBY                       V$PROXY_ARCHIVELOG_SUMMARY
V$MAP_COMP_LIST                         V$PROXY_COPY_DETAILS
V$MAP_ELEMENT                           V$PROXY_COPY_SUMMARY
V$MAP_EXT_ELEMENT                       V$PROXY_DATAFILE
V$MAP_FILE                              V$PWFILE_USERS
V$MAP_FILE_EXTENT                       V$PX_BUFFER_ADVICE
V$MAP_FILE_IO_STACK                     V$PX_INSTANCE_GROUP
V$MAP_LIBRARY                           V$PX_PROCESS
V$MAP_SUBELEMENT                        V$PX_PROCESS_SYSSTAT
V$MAX_ACTIVE_SESS_TARGET_MTH            V$PX_SESSION
V$MEMORY_CURRENT_RESIZE_OPS             V$PX_SESSTAT
V$MEMORY_DYNAMIC_COMPONENTS             V$QMON_COORDINATOR_STATS
V$MEMORY_RESIZE_OPS                     V$QMON_SERVER_STATS
V$MEMORY_TARGET_ADVICE                  V$QMON_TASKS
```

NAME

V$QMON_TASK_STATS
V$QUEUE
V$QUEUEING_MTH
V$RECOVERY_AREA_USAGE
V$RECOVERY_FILE_DEST
V$RECOVERY_FILE_STATUS
V$RECOVERY_LOG
V$RECOVERY_PROGRESS
V$RECOVERY_STATUS
V$RECOVER_FILE
V$REDO_DEST_RESP_HISTOGRAM
V$REPLPROP
V$REPLQUEUE
V$REQDIST
V$RESERVED_WORDS
V$RESOURCE
V$RESOURCE_LIMIT
V$RESTORE_POINT
V$RESULT_CACHE_DEPENDENCY
V$RESULT_CACHE_DR
V$RESULT_CACHE_MEMORY
V$RESULT_CACHE_OBJECTS
V$RESULT_CACHE_RD
V$RESULT_CACHE_RR
V$RESULT_CACHE_STATISTICS
V$RESUMABLE
V$RFS_THREAD
V$RMAN_BACKUP_JOB_DETAILS
V$RMAN_BACKUP_SUBJOB_DETAILS
V$RMAN_BACKUP_TYPE
V$RMAN_COMPRESSION_ALGORITHM
V$RMAN_CONFIGURATION
V$RMAN_ENCRYPTION_ALGORITHMS
V$RMAN_OUTPUT
V$RMAN_STATUS
V$ROLLSTAT
V$ROWCACHE
V$ROWCACHE_PARENT
V$ROWCACHE_SUBORDINATE
V$RSRCMGRMETRIC
V$RSRCMGRMETRIC_HISTORY
V$RSRC_CONSUMER_GROUP
V$RSRC_CONSUMER_GROUP_CPU_MTH
V$RSRC_CONS_GROUP_HISTORY
V$RSRC_PLAN
V$RSRC_PLAN_CPU_MTH
V$RSRC_PLAN_HISTORY
V$RSRC_SESSION_INFO
V$RULE
V$RULE_SET
V$RULE_SET_AGGREGATE_STATS
V$SCHEDULER_RUNNING_JOBS
V$SECUREFILE_TIMER
V$SEGMENT_STATISTICS
V$SEGSTAT
V$SEGSTAT_NAME
V$SERVICEMETRIC
V$SERVICEMETRIC_HISTORY
V$SERVICES
V$SERVICE_EVENT

V$SERVICE_STATS
V$SERVICE_WAIT_CLASS
V$SERV_MOD_ACT_STATS
V$SESSION
V$SESSION_BLOCKERS
V$SESSION_CLIENT_RESULT_CACHE
V$SESSION_CONNECT_INFO
V$SESSION_CURSOR_CACHE
V$SESSION_EVENT
V$SESSION_FIX_CONTROL
V$SESSION_LONGOPS
V$SESSION_OBJECT_CACHE
V$SESSION_WAIT
V$SESSION_WAIT_CLASS
V$SESSION_WAIT_HISTORY
V$SESSMETRIC
V$SESSTAT
V$SESS_IO
V$SESS_TIME_MODEL
V$SES_OPTIMIZER_ENV
V$SGA
V$SGAINFO
V$SGASTAT
V$SGA_CURRENT_RESIZE_OPS
V$SGA_DYNAMIC_COMPONENTS
V$SGA_DYNAMIC_FREE_MEMORY
V$SGA_RESIZE_OPS
V$SGA_TARGET_ADVICE
V$SHARED_POOL_ADVICE
V$SHARED_POOL_RESERVED
V$SHARED_SERVER
V$SHARED_SERVER_MONITOR
V$SORT_SEGMENT
V$SORT_USAGE
V$SPPARAMETER
V$SQL
V$SQLAREA
V$SQLAREA_PLAN_HASH
V$SQLCOMMAND
V$SQLFN_ARG_METADATA
V$SQLFN_METADATA
V$SQLPA_METRIC
V$SQLSTATS
V$SQLSTATS_PLAN_HASH
V$SQLTEXT
V$SQLTEXT_WITH_NEWLINES
V$SQL_BIND_DATA
V$SQL_BIND_METADATA
V$SQL_CS_HISTOGRAM
V$SQL_CS_SELECTIVITY
V$SQL_CS_STATISTICS
V$SQL_CURSOR
V$SQL_FEATURE
V$SQL_FEATURE_DEPENDENCY
V$SQL_FEATURE_HIERARCHY
V$SQL_HINT
V$SQL_JOIN_FILTER
V$SQL_MONITOR
V$SQL_OPTIMIZER_ENV
V$SQL_PLAN

```
NAME
-----------------------------------------------------------------------------------
V$SQL_PLAN_MONITOR                    V$TEMPFILE
V$SQL_PLAN_STATISTICS                 V$TEMPORARY_LOBS
V$SQL_PLAN_STATISTICS_ALL             V$TEMPSTAT
V$SQL_REDIRECTION                     V$TEMP_CACHE_TRANSFER
V$SQL_SHARED_CURSOR                   V$TEMP_EXTENT_MAP
V$SQL_SHARED_MEMORY                   V$TEMP_EXTENT_POOL
V$SQL_WORKAREA                        V$TEMP_PING
V$SQL_WORKAREA_ACTIVE                 V$TEMP_SPACE_HEADER
V$SQL_WORKAREA_HISTOGRAM              V$THREAD
V$SSCR_SESSIONS                       V$THRESHOLD_TYPES
V$STANDBY_EVENT_HISTOGRAM            V$TIMER
V$STANDBY_LOG                         V$TIMEZONE_FILE
V$STATISTICS_LEVEL                    V$TIMEZONE_NAMES
V$STATNAME                            V$TOPLEVELCALL
V$STREAMS_APPLY_COORDINATOR          V$TRANSACTION
V$STREAMS_APPLY_READER                V$TRANSACTION_ENQUEUE
V$STREAMS_APPLY_SERVER                V$TRANSPORTABLE_PLATFORM
V$STREAMS_CAPTURE                     V$TSM_SESSIONS
V$STREAMS_MESSAGE_TRACKING           V$TYPE_SIZE
V$STREAMS_POOL_ADVICE                 V$UNDOSTAT
V$STREAMS_POOL_STATISTICS            V$UNUSABLE_BACKUPFILE_DETAILS
V$STREAMS_TRANSACTION                 V$VERSION
V$SUBCACHE                            V$VPD_POLICY
V$SUBSCR_REGISTRATION_STATS          V$WAITCLASSMETRIC
V$SYSAUX_OCCUPANTS                    V$WAITCLASSMETRIC_HISTORY
V$SYSMETRIC                           V$WAITSTAT
V$SYSMETRIC_HISTORY                   V$WAIT_CHAINS
V$SYSMETRIC_SUMMARY                   V$WALLET
V$SYSSTAT                             V$WLM_PCMETRIC
V$SYSTEM_CURSOR_CACHE                 V$WLM_PCMETRIC_HISTORY
V$SYSTEM_EVENT                        V$WLM_PC_STATS
V$SYSTEM_FIX_CONTROL                  V$WORKLOAD_REPLAY_THREAD
V$SYSTEM_PARAMETER                    V$XML_AUDIT_TRAIL
V$SYSTEM_PARAMETER2                   V$_LOCK
V$SYSTEM_PARAMETER4                   V$_LOCK1
V$SYSTEM_WAIT_CLASS                   V$_SEQUENCES
V$SYS_OPTIMIZER_ENV
V$SYS_TIME_MODEL                      525 rows selected.
V$TABLESPACE
```

Oracle 11g Scripts for the X$ Tables Used to Create the V$ Views

Because of the number of views in 11g, it's no longer possible to list all queries in this book. I have, however, listed several that pertain primarily to performance tuning. You can run your own query to see a specific one. There are several new SQL_ID and HASH_VALUE columns as well as other nice surprises. Here is the Oracle 11gR2 query to get a listing of *all* X$ queries for the V$ views:

```
select 'View Name: '||view_name,
       substr(substr(view_definition,1,3900),1,(instr(view_definition,'from')-1)) def1,
       substr(substr(view_definition,1,3900),(instr(view_definition,'from')))||';' def2
from    v$fixed_view_definition
order   by view_name;
```

View Name: GV$BH

```
select bh.inst_id, file#, dbablk, class, decode(state,0,'free',1,'xcur',2,
       'scur',3,'cr', 4,'read',5,'mrec',6,'irec',7,'write',8,'pi',
```

```
          9,'memory',10,'mwrite',11,'donated', 12,'protected',13,'securefile',
          14,'siop',15,'recckpt', 16, 'flashfree',  17, 'flashcur', 18, 'flashna'),
          0, 0, 0, bh.le_addr, le_id1, le_id2, decode(bitand(flag,1), 0, 'N', 'Y'),
          decode(bitand(flag,16), 0, 'N', 'Y'), decode(bitand(flag,1536), 0, 'N', 'Y'),
          decode(bitand(flag,16384), 0, 'N', 'Y'),
          decode(bitand(flag,65536), 0, 'N', 'Y'), 'N',
          obj, ts#, lobid,  bitand(OBJ_FLAG, 240)/16
from    x$bh bh, x$le le
where   bh.le_addr = le.le_addr (+);
```

View Name: V$BH

```
select  file#,block#,class#,status,xnc,forced_reads,forced_writes,lock_element_addr,
        lock_element_name,lock_element_class,dirty,temp,ping,stale,direct,new,objd,ts#,
        lobid, cachehint
from    gv$bh
where   inst_id = USERENV('Instance');
```

View Name: GV$BUFFER_POOL

```
select  inst_id,bp_id,bp_name,bp_blksz,decode(bp_state, 0, 'STATIC',1,'ALLOCATING',
        2,'ACTIVATING',3,'SHRINKING'),bp_currgrans * bp_gransz,bp_size,bp_tgtgrans *
        bp_gransz,bp_tgtgrans * bp_bufpergran,bp_prevgrans * bp_gransz,bp_prevgrans *
        bp_bufpergran,0,0,bp_lo_sid,bp_hi_sid,bp_set_ct
from    x$kcbwbpd
where   bp_id > 0 and bp_currgrans > 0 and bp_tgtgrans > 0;
```

View Name: V$BUFFER_POOL

```
select  id,name,block_size,resize_state,current_size,buffers,target_size,
        target_buffers,prev_size,prev_buffers,lo_bnum,hi_bnum,lo_setid,hi_setid,
        set_count
from    gv$buffer_pool
where   inst_id = USERENV('Instance');
```

View Name: GV$BUFFER_POOL_STATISTICS

```
select  kcbwbpd.inst_id,kcbwbpd.bp_id,kcbwbpd.bp_name,kcbwbpd.bp_blksz,
        sum(kcbwds.cnum_set),sum(kcbwds.cnum_repl),sum(kcbwds.cnum_write),
        sum(kcbwds.cnum_set),sum(kcbwds.buf_got),sum(kcbwds.sum_wrt),
        sum(kcbwds.sum_scn),sum(kcbwds.fbwait),sum(kcbwds.wcwait),
        sum(kcbwds.bbwait),sum(kcbwds.fbinsp),sum(kcbwds.dbinsp),
        sum(kcbwds.dbbchg),sum(kcbwds.dbbget),sum(kcbwds.conget),sum(kcbwds.pread),
        sum(kcbwds.pwrite)
from    x$kcbwds kcbwds,x$kcbwbpd kcbwbpd
where   kcbwds.set_id >= kcbwbpd.bp_lo_sid and kcbwds.set_id <= kcbwbpd.bp_hi_sid
        and kcbwbpd.bp_size != 0 group by kcbwbpd.inst_id,kcbwbpd.bp_id,
        kcbwbpd.bp_name,kcbwbpd.bp_blksz;
```

View Name: V$BUFFER_POOL_STATISTICS

```
select  id,name,block_size,set_msize,cnum_repl,cnum_write,cnum_set,buf_got,
        sum_write,sum_scan,free_buffer_wait,write_complete_wait,buffer_busy_wait,
        free_buffer_inspected,dirty_buffers_inspected,db_block_change,db_block_gets,
        consistent_gets,physical_reads,physical_writes
from    gv$buffer_pool_statistics
where   inst_id = USERENV('Instance');
```

View Name: GV$DB_CACHE_ADVICE

```
select    A.inst_id,A.bpid,B.bp_name,A.blksz,decode (A.status,2,'ON','OFF'),A.poolsz,
          round((A.poolsz / A.actual_poolsz),4),A.nbufs,decode(A.base_preads,0,
          to_number(null),round((A.preads / A.base_preads),4)),decode(A.base_preads,0,
          A.preads,round((A.preads * (A.actual_preads / A.base_preads)),0)),
          A.estd_time_for_disk_reads, decode (A.total_db_time, 0,
          A.estd_time_for_disk_reads,round((100 *
          A.estd_time_for_disk_reads / A.total_db_time), 1)),
          A.estd_rac_reads, A.estd_rac_time
from      x$kcbsc A, x$kcbwbpd B
where     A.bpid = B.bp_id and A.inst_id = B.inst_id
order by A.inst_id,A.bpid,A.poolsz;
```

View Name: V$DB_CACHE_ADVICE

```
select id,name,block_size,advice_status,size_for_estimate,size_factor,
       buffers_for_estimate,estd_physical_read_factor,estd_physical_reads,
       estd_physical_read_time, estd_pct_of_db_time_for_reads,
       estd_cluster_reads, estd_cluster_read_time
from   gv$db_cache_advice
where  inst_id = userenv('instance');
```

View Name: GV$DB_OBJECT_CACHE

```
select inst_id,kglnaown,kglnaobj,kglnadlk,kglhdnsd,kglobtyd,
       kglobhs0+kglobhs1+kglobhs2+kglobhs3+kglobhs4+kglobhs5+kglobhs6,
       kglhdldc,kglhdexc,kglhdlkc,kglobpc0,decode(kglhdkmk,0,'NO','YES'),
       kglhdclt, kglhdivc, kglnahsh, decode(kglhdlmd,0,'NONE',1, 'NULL',
       2,'SHARED', 3, 'EXCLUSIVE', 'UNKOWN'), decode(kglhdpmd,0,'NONE',1,'NULL',
       2,'SHARED', 3, 'EXCLUSIVE', 'UNKOWN'), decode(kglobsta,1, 'VALID',
       2, 'VALID_AUTH_ERROR', 3, 'VALID_COMPILE_ERROR', 4, 'VALID_UNAUTH',
       5, 'INVALID_UNAUTH', 6, 'INVALID', 'UNKOWN'),
       substr(to_char(kglnatim,'YYYY-MM-DD/HH24:MI:SS'),1,19),
       substr(to_char(kglnaptm,'YYYY-MM-DD/HH24:MI:SS'),1,19), kglobt23, kglobt24

from x$kglob;
```

View Name: V$DB_OBJECT_CACHE

```
select OWNER,NAME,DB_LINK,NAMESPACE,TYPE,SHARABLE_MEM,LOADS,EXECUTIONS,LOCKS,PINS,KEPT,
       CHILD_LATCH, INVALIDATIONS, HASH_VALUE, LOCK_MODE, PIN_MODE,

       STATUS, TIMESTAMP, PREVIOUS_TIMESTAMP, LOCKED_TOTAL, PINNED_TOTAL
from   GV$DB_OBJECT_CACHE
where  inst_id = USERENV('Instance');
```

View Name: GV$DLM_ALL_LOCKS

```
select USERENV('Instance'),HANDLE,GRANT_LEVEL,REQUEST_LEVEL,RESOURCE_NAME1,
       RESOURCE_NAME2,PID,TRANSACTION_ID0,TRANSACTION_ID1,GROUP_ID,OPEN_OPT_DEADLOCK,
       OPEN_OPT_PERSISTENT,OPEN_OPT_PROCESS_OWNED,OPEN_OPT_NO_XID,CONVERT_OPT_GETVALUE,
       CONVERT_OPT_PUTVALUE,CONVERT_OPT_NOVALUE,CONVERT_OPT_DUBVALUE,
       CONVERT_OPT_NOQUEUE,CONVERT_OPT_EXPRESS,CONVERT_OPT_NODEADLOCKWAIT,
       CONVERT_OPT_NODEADLOCKBLOCK,WHICH_QUEUE,STATE,AST_EVENT0,OWNER_NODE,BLOCKED,
       BLOCKER
from   V$GES_ENQUEUE;
```

View Name: **V$DLM_ALL_LOCKS**

```
select LOCKP,GRANT_LEVEL,REQUEST_LEVEL,RESOURCE_NAME1,RESOURCE_NAME2,PID,
       TRANSACTION_ID0,TRANSACTION_ID1,GROUP_ID,OPEN_OPT_DEADLOCK,OPEN_OPT_PERSISTENT,
       OPEN_OPT_PROCESS_OWNED,OPEN_OPT_NO_XID,CONVERT_OPT_GETVALUE,CONVERT_OPT_PUTVALUE,
       CONVERT_OPT_NOVALUE,CONVERT_OPT_DUBVALUE,CONVERT_OPT_NOQUEUE,CONVERT_OPT_EXPRESS,
       CONVERT_OPT_NODEADLOCKWAIT,CONVERT_OPT_NODEADLOCKBLOCK,WHICH_QUEUE,LOCKSTATE,
       AST_EVENT0,OWNER_NODE,BLOCKED,BLOCKER
from   GV$DLM_ALL_LOCKS
where  INST_ID = USERENV('Instance');
```

View Name: **GV$DLM_LATCH**

```
select USERENV('Instance'),addr,latch#,level#,name,gets,misses,sleeps,immediate_gets,
       immediate_misses,waiters_woken,waits_holding_latch,spin_gets,sleep1,sleep2,
       sleep3,sleep4,sleep5,sleep6,sleep7,sleep8,sleep9,sleep10,sleep11,wait_time
from   V$LATCH
where  NAME like 'ges %' or NAME like 'gcs %';
```

View Name: **V$DLM_LATCH**

```
select addr,latch#,level#,name,gets,misses,sleeps,immediate_gets,immediate_misses,
       waiters_woken,waits_holding_latch,spin_gets,sleep1,sleep2,sleep3,sleep4,sleep5,
       sleep6,sleep7,sleep8,sleep9,sleep10,sleep11,wait_time
from   GV$DLM_LATCH
where  INST_ID = USERENV('Instance');
```

View Name: **GV$DLM_LOCKS**

```
select USERENV('Instance'),HANDLE,GRANT_LEVEL,REQUEST_LEVEL,RESOURCE_NAME1,
       RESOURCE_NAME2,PID,TRANSACTION_ID0,TRANSACTION_ID1,GROUP_ID,OPEN_OPT_DEADLOCK,
       OPEN_OPT_PERSISTENT,OPEN_OPT_PROCESS_OWNED,OPEN_OPT_NO_XID,CONVERT_OPT_GETVALUE,
       CONVERT_OPT_PUTVALUE,CONVERT_OPT_NOVALUE,CONVERT_OPT_DUBVALUE,
       CONVERT_OPT_NOQUEUE,CONVERT_OPT_EXPRESS,CONVERT_OPT_NODEADLOCKWAIT,
       CONVERT_OPT_NODEADLOCKBLOCK,WHICH_QUEUE,STATE,AST_EVENT0,OWNER_NODE,BLOCKED,
       BLOCKER
from   V$GES_BLOCKING_ENQUEUE;
```

View Name: **V$DLM_LOCKS**

```
select LOCKP,GRANT_LEVEL,REQUEST_LEVEL,RESOURCE_NAME1,RESOURCE_NAME2,PID,
       TRANSACTION_ID0,TRANSACTION_ID1,GROUP_ID,OPEN_OPT_DEADLOCK,OPEN_OPT_PERSISTENT,
       OPEN_OPT_PROCESS_OWNED,OPEN_OPT_NO_XID,CONVERT_OPT_GETVALUE,CONVERT_OPT_PUTVALUE,
       CONVERT_OPT_NOVALUE,CONVERT_OPT_DUBVALUE,CONVERT_OPT_NOQUEUE,CONVERT_OPT_EXPRESS,
       CONVERT_OPT_NODEADLOCKWAIT,CONVERT_OPT_NODEADLOCKBLOCK,WHICH_QUEUE,LOCKSTATE,
       AST_EVENT0,OWNER_NODE,BLOCKED,BLOCKER
from   GV$DLM_LOCKS
where  INST_ID = USERENV('Instance');
```

View Name: **GV$ENQUEUE_LOCK**

```
select s.inst_id,l.addr,l.ksqlkadr,s.ksusenum,r.ksqrsidt,r.ksqrsid1,
       r.ksqrsid2, l.ksqlkmod, l.ksqlkreq,l.ksqlkctim,l.ksqlklblk
from   x$ksqeq l,x$ksuse s,x$ksqrs r
where  l.ksqlkses=s.addr
```

```
and     bitand(l.kssobflg,1)!=0
and     (l.ksqlkmod!=0 or l.ksqlkreq!=0)
and     l.ksqlkres=r.addr;
```

View Name: V$ENQUEUE_LOCK

```
select ADDR,KADDR,SID,TYPE,ID1,ID2,LMODE,REQUEST,CTIME,BLOCK
from    GV$ENQUEUE_LOCK
where   inst_id = USERENV('Instance');
```

View Name: GV$ENQUEUE_STAT

```
select inst_id, ksqsttyp, sum(ksqstreq), sum(ksqstwat), sum(ksqstsgt),
        sum(ksqstfgt), sum(ksqstwtm)
from    X$KSQST
group by inst_id, ksqsttyp having sum(ksqstreq) > 0;
```

View Name: V$ENQUEUE_STAT

```
select INST_ID,EQ_TYPE,TOTAL_REQ#,TOTAL_WAIT#,SUCC_REQ#,FAILED_REQ#,CUM_WAIT_TIME
from    GV$ENQUEUE_STAT
where   inst_id = USERENV('Instance');
```

View Name: GV$EVENT_NAME

```
select inst_id, indx, ksledhash, kslednam, ksledp1, ksledp2, ksledp3,
        ksledclassid, ksledclass#, ksledclass
from    x$ksled;
```

View Name: V$EVENT_NAME

```
select event#, event_id, name,parameter1,parameter2,parameter3,
        wait_class_id, wait_class#, wait_class
from    gv$event_name
where   inst_id = USERENV('Instance');
```

View Name: GV$EXECUTION

```
select inst_id,pid,val0,func,decode(id,1,'call',2,'return',3,'longjmp'),nvals,val2,
        val3,seqh,seql
from    x$kstex where op=10;
```

View Name: V$EXECUTION

```
select PID,DEPTH,FUNCTION,TYPE,NVALS,VAL1,VAL2,SEQH,SEQL
from    GV$EXECUTION
where   inst_id = USERENV('Instance');
```

View Name: GV$FILESTAT

```
select k.inst_id,k.kcfiofno,k.kcfiopyr,k.kcfiopyw,k.kcfiopbr, k.kcfiofbr,
        k.kcfiopbw,k.kcfiosbr, round(k.kcfioprt / 10000),
```

```
         round(k.kcfiopwt / 10000), round(k.kcfiosbt / 10000),round(k.kcfioavg / 10000),
         round(k.kcfiolst / 10000),round(k.kcfiomin / 10000),
         round(k.kcfiormx / 10000),round(k.kcfiowmx / 10000)
from     x$kcfio k,x$kccfe f
where    f.fedup <> 0
and      f.fenum=k.kcfiofno;
```

View Name: **V$FILESTAT**

```
select FILE#,PHYRDS,PHYWRTS,PHYBLKRD, OPTIMIZED_PHYBLKRD,
       PHYBLKWRT,SINGLEBLKRDS,READTIM,WRITETIM,
       SINGLEBLKRDTIM,AVGIOTIM,LSTIOTIM,MINIOTIM,MAXIORTM,MAXIOWTM
from    GV$FILESTAT
where   inst_id = USERENV('Instance');
```

View Name: **GV$FILE_CACHE_TRANSFER**

```
select x.inst_id, kcfiofno, 0, 0, 0, 0, 0, 0, 0, 0, 0, 0, 0, 0, 0, 0, 0
from    x$kcfio x, x$kccfe fe
where   x.kcfiofno = fe.fenum;
```

View Name: **V$FILE_CACHE_TRANSFER**

```
select file_number,x_2_null,x_2_null_forced_write,x_2_null_forced_stale,x_2_s,
       x_2_s_forced_write,s_2_null,s_2_null_forced_stale,rbr,rbr_forced_write,
       rbr_forced_stale,null_2_x,s_2_x,null_2_s,cr_transfers,cur_transfers
from    gv$file_cache_transfer
where   inst_id = USERENV('Instance');
```

View Name: **GV$FIXED_TABLE**

```
select inst_id,kqftanam,kqftaobj,'TABLE',indx
from    x$kqfta union all
        select inst_id,kqfvinam,kqfviobj,'VIEW',65537
        from    x$kqfvi union all
            select inst_id,kqfdtnam, kqfdtobj, 'TABLE', 65537
            from    x$kqfdt;
```

View Name: **V$FIXED_TABLE**

```
select NAME,OBJECT_ID,TYPE,TABLE_NUM
from    GV$FIXED_TABLE
where   inst_id = USERENV('Instance');
```

View Name: **GV$FIXED_VIEW_DEFINITION**

```
select i.inst_id,kqfvinam,kqftpsel
from    x$kqfvi i,x$kqfvt t
where   i.indx = t.indx;
```

View Name: V$FIXED_VIEW_DEFINITION

```
select VIEW_NAME,VIEW_DEFINITION
from   GV$FIXED_VIEW_DEFINITION
where  inst_id = USERENV('Instance');
```

View Name: GV$GES_BLOCKING_ENQUEUE

```
select USERENV('Instance'),HANDLE,GRANT_LEVEL,REQUEST_LEVEL,RESOURCE_NAME1,
       RESOURCE_NAME2,PID,TRANSACTION_ID0,TRANSACTION_ID1,GROUP_ID,
       OPEN_OPT_DEADLOCK,OPEN_OPT_PERSISTENT,OPEN_OPT_PROCESS_OWNED,OPEN_OPT_NO_XID,
       CONVERT_OPT_GETVALUE,CONVERT_OPT_PUTVALUE,CONVERT_OPT_NOVALUE,
       CONVERT_OPT_DUBVALUE,CONVERT_OPT_NOQUEUE,CONVERT_OPT_EXPRESS,
       CONVERT_OPT_NODEADLOCKWAIT,CONVERT_OPT_NODEADLOCKBLOCK, WHICH_QUEUE,
       STATE,AST_EVENT0,OWNER_NODE,BLOCKED,BLOCKER
from   V$GES_ENQUEUE
where (REQUEST_LEVEL != 'KJUSERNL')
and   (BLOCKED = 1 or BLOCKER = 1);
```

View Name: V$GES_BLOCKING_ENQUEUE

```
select HANDLE,GRANT_LEVEL,REQUEST_LEVEL,RESOURCE_NAME1,RESOURCE_NAME2,PID,
       TRANSACTION_ID0,TRANSACTION_ID1,GROUP_ID,OPEN_OPT_DEADLOCK,
       OPEN_OPT_PERSISTENT,OPEN_OPT_PROCESS_OWNED,OPEN_OPT_NO_XID,
       CONVERT_OPT_GETVALUE,CONVERT_OPT_PUTVALUE,CONVERT_OPT_NOVALUE,
       CONVERT_OPT_DUBVALUE,CONVERT_OPT_NOQUEUE,CONVERT_OPT_EXPRESS,
       CONVERT_OPT_NODEADLOCKWAIT,CONVERT_OPT_NODEADLOCKBLOCK,WHICH_QUEUE,STATE,
       AST_EVENT0,OWNER_NODE,BLOCKED,BLOCKER
from   GV$GES_BLOCKING_ENQUEUE
where  INST_ID = USERENV('Instance');
```

View Name: GV$GES_ENQUEUE

```
select inst_id,kjilkftlkp,kjilkftgl,kjilkftrl,kjilkftrn1,kjilkftrn2,kjilkftpid,
       kjilkftxid0,kjilkftxid1,kjilkftgid,kjilkftoodd,kjilkftoopt,kjilkftoopo,
       kjilkftoonxid,kjilkftcogv,kjilkftcopv,kjilkftconv,kjilkftcodv,kjilkftconq,
       kjilkftcoep,kjilkftconddw,kjilkftconddb,kjilkftwq,kjilkftls,kjilkftaste0,
       kjilkfton,kjilkftblked,kjilkftblker
from   x$kjilkft union all
          select inst_id, kjbllockp, kjblgrant, kjblrequest,kjblname,
                 kjblname2,0,0,0,0,0,1,0,1,0,0,0,0,0,0,0,0,kjblqueue,kjbllockst,0,
                 kjblowner,kjblblocked,kjblblocker
          from   x$kjbl;
```

View Name: V$GES_ENQUEUE

```
select HANDLE,GRANT_LEVEL,REQUEST_LEVEL,RESOURCE_NAME1,RESOURCE_NAME2,PID,
       TRANSACTION_ID0,TRANSACTION_ID1,GROUP_ID,OPEN_OPT_DEADLOCK,
       OPEN_OPT_PERSISTENT,OPEN_OPT_PROCESS_OWNED,OPEN_OPT_NO_XID,
       CONVERT_OPT_GETVALUE,CONVERT_OPT_PUTVALUE,CONVERT_OPT_NOVALUE,
       CONVERT_OPT_DUBVALUE,CONVERT_OPT_NOQUEUE,CONVERT_OPT_EXPRESS,
```

```
        CONVERT_OPT_NODEADLOCKWAIT,CONVERT_OPT_NODEADLOCKBLOCK,WHICH_QUEUE,STATE,
        AST_EVENT0,OWNER_NODE,BLOCKED,BLOCKER
from    GV$GES_ENQUEUE
where   INST_ID = USERENV('Instance');
```

View Name: **GV$GLOBAL_BLOCKED_LOCKS**

```
select USERENV('instance'),addr,kaddr,sid,type,id1,id2,lmode,request,ctime
from   v$lock l
where exists
  (select *
   from   v$dlm_locks d
   where  substr(d.resource_name2,1,instr(d.resource_name2, ',',1,1)-1) = id1
   and    substr(d.resource_name2,instr(d.resource_name2,',',1,1)+1,
          instr(d.resource_name2, ',',1,2)-instr(d.resource_name2,',',1,1)-1) = id2
   and    substr(d.resource_name2,instr(d.resource_name2,',',-1,1)+1,2) = type);
```

View Name: **V$GLOBAL_BLOCKED_LOCKS**

```
select ADDR,KADDR,SID,TYPE,ID1,ID2,LMODE,REQUEST,CTIME
from   gv$global_blocked_locks
where  inst_id = userenv('instance');
```

View Name: **GV$GLOBAL_TRANSACTION**

```
select inst_id,K2GTIFMT,K2GTITID_EXT,K2GTIBID,K2GTECNT,K2GTERCT,K2GTDPCT,
       decode (K2GTDFLG,0,'ACTIVE',1,'COLLECTING',2,'FINALIZED',4,'FAILED',8,
       'RECOVERING',16,'UNASSOCIATED',32,'FORGOTTEN',64,'READY FOR RECOVERY',
       128, 'NO-READONLY FAILED',
       256, 'SIBLING INFO WRITTEN',
       512,      '[ORACLE COORDINATED]ACTIVE',
       512+1,    '[ORACLE COORDINATED]COLLECTING',
       512+2,    '[ORACLE COORDINATED]FINALIZED',
       512+4,    '[ORACLE COORDINATED]FAILED',
       512+8,    '[ORACLE COORDINATED]RECOVERING',
       512+16,   '[ORACLE COORDINATED]UNASSOCIATED',
       512+32,   '[ORACLE COORDINATED]FORGOTTEN',
       512+64,   '[ORACLE COORDINATED]READY FOR RECOVERY',
       512+128,  '[ORACLE COORDINATED]NO-READONLY FAILED',
       1024,     '[MULTINODE]ACTIVE',
       1024+1,   '[MULTINODE]COLLECTING',
       1024+2,   '[MULTINODE]FINALIZED',
       1024+4,   '[MULTINODE]FAILED',
       1024+8,   '[MULTINODE]RECOVERING',
       1024+16,  '[MULTINODE]UNASSOCIATED',
       1024+32,  '[MULTINODE]FORGOTTEN',
       1024+64,  '[MULTINODE]READY FOR RECOVERY',
       1024+128, '[MULTINODE]NO-READONLY FAILED',
       1024+256, '[MULTINODE]SIBLING INFO WRITTEN',
       'COMBINATION'),K2GTDFLG,decode (K2GTETYP,0,'FREE',1,'LOOSELY COUPLED',2,
       'TIGHTLY COUPLED')
from   X$K2GTE2;
```

View Name: **V$GLOBAL_TRANSACTION**

```
select FORMATID,GLOBALID,BRANCHID,BRANCHES,REFCOUNT,PREPARECOUNT,STATE,FLAGS,
       COUPLING
```

```
from    GV$GLOBAL_TRANSACTION
where   INST_ID = USERENV('Instance');
```

View Name: GV$INDEXED_FIXED_COLUMN

```
select c.inst_id,kqftanam,kqfcoidx,kqfconam,kqfcoipo
from   x$kqfco c,x$kqfta t
where  t.indx = c.kqfcotab
and    kqfcoidx != 0;
```

View Name: V$INDEXED_FIXED_COLUMN

```
select TABLE_NAME,INDEX_NUMBER,COLUMN_NAME,COLUMN_POSITION
from   GV$INDEXED_FIXED_COLUMN
where  inst_id = USERENV('Instance');
```

View Name: GV$INSTANCE

```
select ks.inst_id,ksuxsins,ksuxssid,ksuxshst,ksuxsver,ksuxstim,
       decode(ksuxssts,0,'STARTED',1,'MOUNTED',2,'OPEN',3,'OPEN MIGRATE','UNKNOWN'),
       decode(ksuxsshr,0,'NO',1,'YES',2,NULL),ksuxsthr,
       decode(ksuxsarc,0,'STOPPED',1,'STARTED','FAILED'),
       decode(ksuxslsw,0,NULL,2,'ARCHIVE LOG',3,'CLEAR LOG',4,'CHECKPOINT',
       5,'REDO GENERATION'),
       decode(ksuxsdba,0,'ALLOWED','RESTRICTED'),
       decode(ksuxsshp,0,'NO','YES'),
       decode(kvitval,0,'ACTIVE',2147483647,'SUSPENDED','INSTANCE RECOVERY'),
       decode(ksuxsrol,1,'PRIMARY_INSTANCE',2,'SECONDARY_INSTANCE','UNKNOWN'),
       decode(qui_state,0,'NORMAL',1,'QUIESCING',2,'QUIESCED','UNKNOWN'),
       decode(bitand(ksuxsdst, 1), 0, 'NO', 1, 'YES', 'NO')
from   x$ksuxsinst ks, x$kvit kv, x$quiesce qu
where  kvittag = 'kcbwst';
```

View Name: V$INSTANCE

```
select INSTANCE_NUMBER,INSTANCE_NAME,HOST_NAME,VERSION,STARTUP_TIME,STATUS,PARALLEL,
       THREAD#,ARCHIVER,LOG_SWITCH_WAIT,LOGINS,SHUTDOWN_PENDING,DATABASE_STATUS,
       INSTANCE_ROLE,ACTIVE_STATE, BLOCKED
from   GV$INSTANCE
where  inst_id = USERENV('Instance');
```

View Name: GV$LATCH

```
select lt.inst_id,lt.kslltaddr,lt.kslltnum,lt.kslltlvl,lt.kslltnam, lt.ksllthsh,
       lt.kslltwgt,lt.kslltwff,lt.kslltwsl,lt.kslltngt,lt.kslltnfa,lt.kslltwkc,
       lt.kslltwth,lt.ksllthst0,lt.ksllthst1,lt.ksllthst2,lt.ksllthst3,lt.ksllthst4,
       lt.ksllthst5,lt.ksllthst6,lt.ksllthst7, lt.ksllthst8,lt.ksllthst9,
       lt.ksllthst10, lt.ksllthst11, lt.kslltwtt
from   x$kslltr lt;
```

View Name: V$LATCH

```
select addr,latch#,level#,name,hash,gets,misses,sleeps,immediate_gets,immediate_misses,
       waiters_woken,waits_holding_latch,spin_gets,sleep1,sleep2,sleep3,sleep4,
       sleep5,sleep6,sleep7,sleep8,sleep9,sleep10,sleep11,wait_time
```

```
from    gv$latch
where   inst_id = USERENV('Instance');
```

View Name: **GV$LATCHHOLDER**

```
select  inst_id,ksuprpid,ksuprsid,ksuprlat,ksuprlnm,ksulagts
from    x$ksuprlat;
```

View Name: **V$LATCHHOLDER**

```
select  PID,SID,LADDR,NAME,GETS
from    GV$LATCHHOLDER
where   inst_id = USERENV('Instance');
```

View Name: **GV$LATCHNAME**

```
select  inst_id,indx,kslldnam,kslldhsh
from    x$kslld;
```

View Name: **V$LATCHNAME**

```
select  latch#,name,hash
from    gv$latchname
where   inst_id = userenv('Instance');
```

View Name: **GV$LATCH_CHILDREN**

```
select  t.inst_id,t.kslltaddr,t.kslltnum,t.kslltcnm,t.kslltlvl,t.kslltnam,
        t.ksllthsh,t.kslltwgt,t.kslltwff,t.kslltwsl,t.kslltngt,t.kslltnfa,
        t.kslltwkc,t.kslltwth,t.kslltbst0,t.kslltbst1,t.kslltbst2,t.kslltbst3,
        t.kslltbst4,t.kslltbst5,t.kslltbst6,t.kslltbst7,t.kslltbst8,t.kslltbst9,
        t.kslltbst10, t.kslltbst11,t.kslltwtt
from    x$kslltr_children t;
```

View Name: **V$LATCH_CHILDREN**

```
select  ADDR,LATCH#,CHILD#,LEVEL#,NAME,HASH,GETS,MISSES,SLEEPS,IMMEDIATE_GETS,
        IMMEDIATE_MISSES,WAITERS_WOKEN,WAITS_HOLDING_LATCH,SPIN_GETS,SLEEP1,SLEEP2,
        SLEEP3,SLEEP4,SLEEP5,SLEEP6,SLEEP7,SLEEP8,SLEEP9,SLEEP10,SLEEP11,
        WAIT_TIME
from    GV$LATCH_CHILDREN
where   inst_id = USERENV('Instance');
```

View Name: **GV$LATCH_MISSES**

```
select  t1.inst_id,t1.ksllasnam,t2.ksllwnam,t1.kslnowtf,t1.kslsleep,t1.kslwscwsl,
        t1.kslwsclthg,t2.ksllwnam
from    x$ksllw t2,x$kslwsc t1
where   t2.indx = t1.indx;
```

View Name: V$LATCH_MISSES

```
select PARENT_NAME,LOCATION,NWFAIL_COUNT,SLEEP_COUNT,WTR_SLP_COUNT,LONGHOLD_COUNT,
       LOCATION
from   GV$LATCH_MISSES
where  inst_id = USERENV('Instance');
```

View Name: GV$LATCH_PARENT

```
select t.inst_id,t.kslltaddr,t.kslltnum,t.kslltlvl,t.kslltnam,t.ksllthsh,
       t.kslltwgt,t.kslltwff,t.kslltwsl,t.kslltngt,t.kslltnfa,t.kslltwkc,
       t.kslltwth,t.ksllthst0,t.ksllthst1,t.ksllthst2,t.ksllthst3,
       t.ksllthst4,t.ksllthst5,t.ksllthst6,t.ksllthst7,t.ksllthst8,
       t.ksllthst9,t.ksllthst10, t.ksllthst11,t.kslltwtt
from   x$kslltr_parent t;
```

View Name: V$LATCH_PARENT

```
select ADDR,LATCH#,LEVEL#,NAME,HASH,GETS,MISSES,SLEEPS,IMMEDIATE_GETS,IMMEDIATE_MISSES,
       WAITERS_WOKEN,WAITS_HOLDING_LATCH,SPIN_GETS,SLEEP1,SLEEP2,SLEEP3,SLEEP4,
       SLEEP5,SLEEP6,SLEEP7,SLEEP8,SLEEP9,SLEEP10,SLEEP11,WAIT_TIME
from   GV$LATCH_PARENT
where  inst_id = USERENV('Instance');
```

View Name: GV$LIBRARYCACHE

```
select inst_id, kglstdsc, kglstget, kglstght,
       decode(kglstget,0,1,kglstght/kglstget),kglstpin,kglstpht,
       decode(kglstpin,0,1,kglstpht/kglstpin),kglstrld,kglstinv,
       kglstlrq, kglstprq, kglstprq, kglstmiv, kglstmiv
from   x$kglst
where  kglsttyp = 'NAMESPACE'
and    kglstget != 0
and    LENGTH(kglstdsc) <= 15 ;
```

View Name: V$LIBRARYCACHE

```
select NAMESPACE,GETS,GETHITS,GETHITRATIO,PINS,PINHITS,PINHITRATIO,RELOADS,
       INVALIDATIONS,DLM_LOCK_REQUESTS,DLM_PIN_REQUESTS,DLM_PIN_RELEASES,
       DLM_INVALIDATION_REQUESTS,DLM_INVALIDATIONS
from   GV$LIBRARYCACHE
where  inst_id = USERENV('Instance');
```

View Name: GV$LIBRARY_CACHE_MEMORY

```
select inst_id,decode(kglsim_namespace,0,'SQL AREA',1,'TABLE/PROCEDURE',2,
       'BODY',3,'TRIGGER',4,'INDEX',5,'CLUSTER',6,'OBJECT',7,'PIPE',13,
       'JAVA SOURCE',14,'JAVA RESOURCE',32,'JAVA DATA','?'),kglsim_pincnt,
       kglsim_pinmem,kglsim_unpincnt,kglsim_unpinmem
from   x$kglmem
where  kglsim_namespace<8
```

```
or      kglsim_namespace=13
or      kglsim_namespace=14
or      kglsim_namespace=32
union
select  inst_id,'OTHER/SYSTEM',sum(kglsim_pincnt)sum_pincnt,
        sum(kglsim_pinmem)sum_pinmem,sum(kglsim_unpincnt) sum_unpincnt,
        sum(kglsim_unpinmem) sum_unpinmem
from    x$kglmem
where   not (kglsim_namespace<8
or      kglsim_namespace=13
or      kglsim_namespace=14
or      kglsim_namespace=32)
group   by   inst_id;
```

View Name: V$LIBRARY_CACHE_MEMORY

```
select lc_namespace,lc_inuse_memory_objects,lc_inuse_memory_size,
       lc_freeable_memory_objects,lc_freeable_memory_size
from   gv$library_cache_memory
where  inst_id = USERENV('Instance');
```

View Name: GV$LOCK

```
select s.inst_id,l.laddr,l.kaddr,s.ksusenum,r.ksqrsidt,r.ksqrsid1,
       r.ksqrsid2,l.lmode,l.request,l.ctime,decode(l.lmode,0,0,l.block)
from   v$_lock l,x$ksuse s,x$ksqrs r
where  l.saddr=s.addr
and    l.raddr=r.addr;
```

View Name: V$LOCK

```
select ADDR,KADDR,SID,TYPE,ID1,ID2,LMODE,REQUEST,CTIME,BLOCK
from   GV$LOCK
where  inst_id = USERENV('Instance');
```

View Name: GV$LOCKED_OBJECT

```
select x.inst_id,x.kxidusn,x.kxidslt,x.kxidsqn,l.ktadmtab,s.indx,s.ksuudlna,
       s.ksuseunm,s.ksusepid,l.ksqlkmod
from   x$ktcxb x,x$ktadm l,x$ksuse s
where  x.ktcxbxba = l.kssobown
and    x.ktcxbses = s.addr;
```

View Name: V$LOCKED_OBJECT

```
select xidusn,xidslot,xidsqn,object_id,session_id,oracle_username, os_user_name,
       process,locked_mode
from   gv$locked_object
where  inst_id = USERENV('Instance');
```

View Name: GV$LOCKS_WITH_COLLISIONS

```
select    USERENV('Instance'),lock_element_addr
from      v$bh
where     (forced_writes + forced_reads) > 10
group by lock_element_addr having count(*) >= 2;
```

View Name: V$LOCKS_WITH_COLLISIONS

```
select    lock_element_addr
from      v$bh
where     (forced_writes + forced_reads) > 10
group by lock_element_addr having count(*) >= 2;
```

View Name: GV$LOCK_ACTIVITY

```
Select    0, 'NULL', 'S', 'Lock buffers for read', 0
from      dual;
```

View Name: V$LOCK_ACTIVITY

```
select FROM_VAL,TO_VAL,ACTION_VAL,COUNTER
from    GV$LOCK_ACTIVITY
where   INST_ID = USERENV('INSTANCE');
```

View Name: GV$LOCK_ELEMENT

```
select inst_id,le_addr,indx, le_id2, le_id1,
       le_mode,le_blks,le_rls,le_acq,0,le_flags
from   x$le;
```

View Name: V$LOCK_ELEMENT

```
select lock_element_addr,indx,class,lock_element_name,mode_held,block_count,
       releasing,acquiring,invalid,flags
from   gv$lock_element
where  inst_id = USERENV('Instance');
```

View Name: GV$MYSTAT

```
select inst_id,ksusenum,ksusestn,ksusestv
from   x$ksumysta
where  bitand(ksspaflg,1)!=0
and    bitand(ksuseflg,1)!=0
and    ksusestn<
          (select ksusgstl
            from x$ksusgif);
```

View Name: **V$MYSTAT**

```
select  SID,STATISTIC#,VALUE
from    GV$MYSTAT
where   inst_id = USERENV('Instance');
```

View Name: **GV$OBSOLETE_PARAMETER**

```
select  inst_id,kspponm,decode(ksppoval,0,'FALSE','TRUE')
from    x$ksppo;
```

View Name: **V$OBSOLETE_PARAMETER**

```
select  NAME,ISSPECIFIED
from    GV$OBSOLETE_PARAMETER
where   inst_id = USERENV('Instance');
```

View Name: **GV$OPEN_CURSOR**

```
select inst_id,kgllkuse,kgllksnm,user_name,kglhdpar,kglnahsh,kgllksqlid,kglnaobj,
       kgllkest,decode(kgllkexc, 0, to_number(NULL), kgllkexc), kgllkctp
from   x$kgllk
where  kglhdnsp = 0
and    kglhdpar != kgllkhdl;
```

View Name: **V$OPEN_CURSOR**

```
select  SADDR,SID,USER_NAME,ADDRESS,HASH_VALUE,SQL_ID,SQL_TEXT,
        LAST_SQL_ACTIVE_TIME, SQL_EXEC_ID, CURSOR_TYPE

from    GV$OPEN_CURSOR
where   inst_id = USERENV('Instance');
```

View Name: **GV$OPTION**

```
select  inst_id,parameter,value
from    x$option;
```

View Name: **V$OPTION**

```
select  PARAMETER,VALUE
from    GV$OPTION
where   inst_id = USERENV('Instance');
```

View Name: **GV$PARAMETER**

```
select  x.inst_id,x.indx+1,ksppinm,ksppity,ksppstvl, ksppstdvl, ksppstdf,
        decode(bitand(ksppiflg/256,1),1,'TRUE','FALSE'),
        decode(bitand(ksppiflg/65536,3),1,'IMMEDIATE',2,'DEFERRED',
        3,'IMMEDIATE','FALSE'),decode(bitand(ksppiflg,4),4,'FALSE',
```

```
        decode(bitand(ksppiflg/65536,3), 0, 'FALSE', 'TRUE')),
        decode(bitand(ksppstvf,7),1,'MODIFIED',4,'SYSTEM_MOD','FALSE'),
        decode(bitand(ksppstvf,2),2,'TRUE','FALSE'),
        decode(bitand(ksppilrmflg/64, 1), 1, 'TRUE', 'FALSE'),
        decode(bitand(ksppilrmflg/268435456, 1), 1, 'TRUE', 'FALSE'),
        ksppdesc, ksppstcmnt, ksppihash
from    x$ksppi x, x$ksppcv y
where   (x.indx = y.indx)
and     bitand(ksppiflg,268435456) = 0
and     ((translate(ksppinm,'_','#') not like '##%')
and     ((translate(ksppinm,'_','#') not like '#%')
or      (ksppstdf = 'FALSE') or (bitand(ksppstvf,5) > 0)));
```

View Name: V$PARAMETER

```
select  NUM,NAME,TYPE,VALUE,DISPLAY_VALUE,ISDEFAULT,ISSES_MODIFIABLE,
        ISSYS_MODIFIABLE,ISINSTANCE_MODIFIABLE,ISMODIFIED,ISADJUSTED,
        ISDEPRECATED, ISBASIC, DESCRIPTION, UPDATE_COMMENT, HASH
from    GV$PARAMETER
where   inst_id = USERENV('Instance');
```

View Name: GV$PARAMETER2

```
select  x.inst_id,kspftctxpn,ksppinm,ksppity,kspftctxvl,kspftctxdvl, kspftctxdf,
        decode(bitand(ksppiflg/256,1),1,'TRUE','FALSE'),
        decode(bitand(ksppiflg/65536,3),1,'IMMEDIATE',2,'DEFERRED',
        3,'IMMEDIATE','FALSE'),
        decode(bitand(ksppiflg,4),4,'FALSE',
        decode(bitand(ksppiflg/65536,3), 0, 'FALSE', 'TRUE')),
        decode(bitand(kspftctxvf,7),1,'MODIFIED',4,'SYSTEM_MOD','FALSE'),
        decode(bitand(kspftctxvf,2),2,'TRUE','FALSE'),
        decode(bitand(ksppilrmflg/64, 1), 1, 'TRUE', 'FALSE'),
        decode(bitand(ksppilrmflg/268435456, 1), 1, 'TRUE', 'FALSE'),
        ksppdesc, kspftctxvn, kspftctxct
from    x$ksppi x, x$ksppcv2 y
where   ((x.indx+1) = kspftctxpn)
and     ((translate(ksppinm,'_','#') not like '##%')
and     ((translate(ksppinm,'_','#') not like '#%')
or      (kspftctxdf = 'FALSE') or (bitand(kspftctxvf,5) > 0)));
```

View Name: V$PARAMETER2

```
select  NUM,NAME,TYPE,VALUE,DISPLAY_VALUE,ISDEFAULT,ISSES_MODIFIABLE,
        ISSYS_MODIFIABLE,ISINSTANCE_MODIFIABLE,ISMODIFIED,ISADJUSTED,
        ISDEPRECATED, ISBASIC, DESCRIPTION,ORDINAL,UPDATE_COMMENT
from    GV$PARAMETER2
where   inst_id = USERENV('Instance');
```

View Name: **GV$PGASTAT**

```
select INST_ID,QESMMSGANM,
       decode(QESMMSGAUN,3,(QESMMSGAVL*QESMMSGAMU)/100,QESMMSGAVL*QESMMSGAMU),
       decode(QESMMSGAUN,0,'bytes',1,'microseconds',3,'percent','')
from   X$QESMMSGA
where  QESMMSGAVS = 1;
```

View Name: **V$PGASTAT**

```
select NAME,VALUE,UNIT
from   GV$PGASTAT
where  INST_ID = USERENV('Instance');
```

View Name: **GV$PGA_TARGET_ADVICE**

```
select INST_ID,PAT_PRED * 1024,round(PAT_PRED/PAT_CURR,4),
       decode(status,0,'OFF','ON'),BYTES_PROCESSED * 1024, ESTD_TIME,
       EXTRA_BYTES_RW * 1024,round(decode(BYTES_PROCESSED+EXTRA_BYTES_RW,0,0,
       (BYTES_PROCESSED*100)/(BYTES_PROCESSED+EXTRA_BYTES_RW))), OVERALLOC
from   X$QESMMAPADV;
```

View Name: **V$PGA_TARGET_ADVICE**

```
select PGA_TARGET_FOR_ESTIMATE,PGA_TARGET_FACTOR,ADVICE_STATUS,BYTES_PROCESSED,
       ESTD_TIME,ESTD_EXTRA_BYTES_RW,ESTD_PGA_CACHE_HIT_PERCENTAGE,ESTD_OVERALLOC_COUNT
from   GV$PGA_TARGET_ADVICE
where  INST_ID = USERENV('Instance');
```

View Name: **GV$PGA_TARGET_ADVICE_HISTOGRAM**

```
select INST_ID,PAT_PRED * 1024,round(PAT_PRED/PAT_CURR, 4),
       decode(status,0,'OFF','ON'),LOWBND * 1024,(HIBND * 1024)-1,
       OPTIMAL,ONEPASS,MPASS,MPASS+ONEPASS+OPTIMAL,IGNORED
from   X$QESMMAHIST;
```

View Name: **V$PGA_TARGET_ADVICE_HISTOGRAM**

```
select PGA_TARGET_FOR_ESTIMATE,PGA_TARGET_FACTOR,ADVICE_STATUS,LOW_OPTIMAL_SIZE,
       HIGH_OPTIMAL_SIZE,ESTD_OPTIMAL_EXECUTIONS,ESTD_ONEPASS_EXECUTIONS,
       ESTD_MULTIPASSES_EXECUTIONS,ESTD_TOTAL_EXECUTIONS,IGNORED_WORKAREAS_COUNT
from   GV$PGA_TARGET_ADVICE_HISTOGRAM
where  INST_ID = USERENV('Instance');
```

View Name: **GV$PROCESS**

```
select inst_id,addr,indx,ksuprpid, ksuprpname,
       ksuprunm,ksuprser,ksuprtid,ksuprpnm,ksuprtfi, ksuprtfn,
       decode(bitand(ksuprflg,2),0,null,1), decode(ksllawat,hextoraw('00'),
       null,ksllawat),decode(ksllaspn,hextoraw('00'),null,ksllaspn),
       ksuprpum,ksuprpnam+ksuprpram,ksuprpfm,
```

```
case
  when ksuprpnam+ksuprpram > ksuprpmm
  then ksuprpnam+ksuprpram
  else ksuprpmm end
from   x$ksupr
where  bitand(ksspaflg,1)!=0;
```

View Name: V$PROCESS

```
select  addr,pid,spid,pname,username,serial#,terminal,program,
        traceid, tracefile,background,latchwait,
        latchspin,pga_used_mem,pga_alloc_mem,pga_freeable_mem,pga_max_mem
from    gv$process
where   inst_id = USERENV('Instance') ;
```

View Name: GV$QUEUE

```
select  inst_id,kmcqspro,decode(bitand(kmcqstyp,1),1,'COMMON','DISPATCHER'),
        kmcqsncq,kmcqswat,kmcqstnc
from    x$kmcqs
where   bitand(kmcqsflg,1) = 1
and     bitand(kmcqstyp,3) != 0
and    (bitand(kmcqstyp,8) = 8 or bitand(kmcqstyp,2) = 2 or kmcqstnc > 0);
```

View Name: V$QUEUE

```
select  PADDR,TYPE,QUEUED,WAIT,TOTALQ
from    GV$QUEUE
where   inst_id = USERENV('Instance');
```

View Name: GV$RESULT_CACHE_STATISTICS

```
select  INST_ID,INDX + 1,QESRCSTA_NAM,decode(QESRCSTA_VLO, QESRCSTA_VHI,
        to_char(QESRCSTA_VLO),QESRCSTA_VLO||'-'||QESRCSTA_VHI)
from    x$qesrcsta;
```

View Name: V$RESULT_CACHE_STATISTICS

```
select  ID, NAME, VALUE
from    GV$RESULT_CACHE_STATISTICS
where   inst_id=USERENV('Instance');
```

View Name: GV$ROLLSTAT

```
select inst_id,kturdusn,kturdlat,kturdext,kturdsiz,kturdwrt,kturdnax,kturdget,
       kturdwat,decode(kturdopt, -1,to_number(null),kturdopt),kturdhwm,kturdnsh,
       kturdnwp,kturdnex,kturdash,kturdaae,
       decode(bitand(kturdflg,7),0,'ONLINE',2,'PENDING OFFLINE',3,'OFFLINE',4,
       'FULL','UNKNOWN'),kturdcex, kturdcbk
from   x$kturd
where  kturdsiz != 0
and    bitand(kturdflg,7) != 3;
```

View Name: **V$ROLLSTAT**

```
select USN,LATCH,EXTENTS,RSSIZE,WRITES,XACTS,GETS,WAITS,OPTSIZE,HWMSIZE,SHRINKS,
       WRAPS,EXTENDS,AVESHRINK,AVEACTIVE,STATUS,CUREXT,CURBLK
from   GV$ROLLSTAT
where  inst_id = USERENV('Instance');
```

View Name: **GV$ROWCACHE**

```
select inst_id,kqrstcid,decode(kqrsttyp,1,'PARENT','SUBORDINATE'),
       decode(kqrsttyp,2,kqrstsno,null),kqrsttxt,kqrstcsz,kqrstusg,kqrstfcs,
       kqrstgrq,kqrstgmi,kqrstsrq,kqrstsmi,kqrstsco,kqrstmrq,kqrstmfl,
       kqrstilr,kqrstifr,kqrstisr
from   x$kqrst;
```

View Name: **V$ROWCACHE**

```
select cache#,type,subordinate#,parameter,count,usage,fixed,gets,getmisses,scans,
       scanmisses,scancompletes,modifications,flushes,dlm_requests,dlm_conflicts,
       dlm_releases
from   gv$rowcache
where  inst_id = USERENV('Instance');
```

View Name: **GV$ROWCACHE_PARENT**

```
select inst_id,indx,kqrfphsh,kqrfpadd,kqrfpcid,kqrfpcnm,
       decode(bitand(kqrfpflg,1),0,'Y','N'),kqrfpmod,kqrfpreq,kqrfptxn,kqrfpses,
       kqrfpirq, kqrfpirl,kqrfpity, kqrfpii1,kqrfpii2,kqrfpkey
from   x$kqrfp;
```

View Name: **V$ROWCACHE_PARENT**

```
select indx,hash,address,cache#,cache_name,existent,lock_mode,lock_request,
       txn,saddr,inst_lock_request,inst_lock_release,inst_lock_type,inst_lock_id1,
       inst_lock_id2,key
from   gv$rowcache_parent
where  inst_id = USERENV('Instance');
```

View Name: **GV$ROWCACHE_SUBORDINATE**

```
select inst_id,indx,kqrfshsh,kqrfsadd,kqrfscid,kqrfssid,kqrfssnm,
       decode(bitand(kqrfsflg,1),0,'Y','N'),kqrfspar,kqrfskey
from x$kqrfs;
```

View Name: **V$ROWCACHE_SUBORDINATE**

```
select indx,hash,address,cache#,subcache#,subcache_name,existent,parent,key
from   gv$rowcache_subordinate
where  inst_id = USERENV('Instance');
```

View Name: V$SESSION

```
select SADDR,SID,SERIAL#,AUDSID,PADDR,USER#,USERNAME,COMMAND,OWNERID,TADDR,
       LOCKWAIT,STATUS,SERVER,SCHEMA#,SCHEMANAME,OSUSER,PROCESS,MACHINE,PORT,TERMINAL,
       PROGRAM,TYPE,SQL_ADDRESS,SQL_HASH_VALUE, SQL_ID, SQL_CHILD_NUMBER,SQL_EXEC_START,
       SQL_EXEC_ID, PREV_SQL_ADDR,PREV_HASH_VALUE,PREV_SQL_ID, PREV_CHILD_NUMBER,
       PREV_EXEC_START , PREV_EXEC_ID , PLSQL_ENTRY_OBJECT_ID,
       PLSQL_ENTRY_SUBPROGRAM_ID, PLSQL_OBJECT_ID, PLSQL_SUBPROGRAM_ID,
       MODULE,MODULE_HASH,ACTION,ACTION_HASH,CLIENT_INFO,FIXED_TABLE_SEQUENCE,
       ROW_WAIT_OBJ#,ROW_WAIT_FILE#,ROW_WAIT_BLOCK#,ROW_WAIT_ROW#,TOP_LEVEL_CALL#,
       LOGON_TIME,LAST_CALL_ET,PDML_ENABLED,FAILOVER_TYPE,FAILOVER_METHOD,FAILED_OVER,
       RESOURCE_CONSUMER_GROUP,PDML_STATUS,PDDL_STATUS,PQ_STATUS,
       CURRENT_QUEUE_DURATION,CLIENT_IDENTIFIER,BLOCKING_SESSION_STATUS,
       BLOCKING_INSTANCE,BLOCKING_SESSION, FINAL_BLOCKING_SESSION_STATUS,
       FINAL_BLOCKING_INSTANCE,FINAL_BLOCKING_SESSION,SEQ#,EVENT#,EVENT,P1TEXT,P1,P1RAW,
       P2TEXT,P2,P2RAW, P3TEXT,P3,P3RAW,WAIT_CLASS_ID, WAIT_CLASS#,WAIT_CLASS,
       WAIT_TIME, SECONDS_IN_WAIT,STATE, WAIT_TIME_MICRO,TIME_REMAINING_MICRO,
       TIME_SINCE_LAST_WAIT_MICRO,SERVICE_NAME, SQL_TRACE, SQL_TRACE_WAITS,
       SQL_TRACE_BINDS, SQL_TRACE_PLAN_STATS, SESSION_EDITION_ID,
       CREATOR_ADDR, CREATOR_SERIAL#, ECID
from   GV$SESSION
where  inst_id = USERENV('Instance');
```

View Name: GV$SESSION_CONNECT_INFO

```
select inst_id,ksusenum, ksuseser,decode(ksuseaty,0,'DATABASE',1,'OS',2,'NETWORK',3,
       'PROXY',4,'SERVER',5,'PASSWORD',6,'EXTERNAL ADAPTERS',7,'INTERNAL',8,
       'GLOBAL',9,'EXTERNAL',10,'PASSWORD BASED GLOBAL USER','?'),ksuseunm,ksuseban,
       decode(ksusecsid,0,'Unknown',nls_charset_name(ksusecsid)),
       decode(bitand(ksuseflags,1), 0, 'Heterogeneous', 'Homogeneous'),
       decode(ksusecllib,1,'Home-based',2,'Full Instant Client',3,
       'XE Instant Client',4,'Light Weight Instant Client',5,'OCI','Unknown'),
       SYS_OP_VERSION(ksuseclvsn), ksusecldrv,
       decode(bitand(ksusecllbf,1), 1, 'ClientTemp Lob Rfc On',
       'Client Temp Lob Rfc Off'),ksuseclregid
from   x$ksusecon
where  bitand(ksuseflg,1)!=0
and bitand(ksuseflg,16)=0;
```

View Name: V$SESSION_CONNECT_INFO

```
select sid, serial#,authentication_type,osuser,network_service_banner,
       client_charset,client_connection,client_oci_library,
       client_version,  client_driver, client_lobattr, client_regid
from   gv$session_connect_info
where  inst_id = USERENV('Instance');
```

View Name: GV$SESSION_CURSOR_CACHE

```
select inst_id,kgscugmax,kgscugcnt,kgscugopn,kgscughit,
       decode(kgscugopn,0,1,kgscughit/kgscugopn)
from x$kgscc;
```

View Name: **V$SESSION_CURSOR_CACHE**

```
select MAXIMUM,COUNT, OPENS,HITS,HIT_RATIO
from   GV$SESSION_CURSOR_CACHE
where  inst_id = USERENV('Instance');
```

View Name: **GV$SESSION_EVENT**

```
select s.inst_id, s.kslessid, d.kslednam, s.ksleswts, s.kslestmo,
       round(s.kslestim / 10000),
       round(s.kslestim / (10000 * s.ksleswts), 2),
       round(s.kslesmxt / 10000),  s.kslestim, d.ksledhash,
       d.ksledclassid, d.ksledclass#, d.ksledclass
from   x$ksles s, x$ksled d
where  s.ksleswts != 0 and s.kslesenm = d.indx;
```

View Name: **V$SESSION_EVENT**

```
select sid,event,total_waits,total_timeouts,time_waited,average_wait,max_wait,
       time_waited_micro,event_id, wait_class_id,wait_class#, wait_class
from   gv$session_event
where  inst_id = USERENV('Instance');
```

View Name: **GV$SESSION_LONGOPS**

```
select inst_id,ksulosno,ksulosrn,ksulopna,ksulotna,ksulotde,ksulosfr,ksulotot,
       ksulouni,to_date(ksulostm,'MM/DD/RR HH24:MI:SS','NLS_CALENDAR=Gregorian'),
       to_date(ksulolut,'MM/DD/RR HH24:MI:SS','NLS_CALENDAR=Gregorian'),
       to_date(ksuloinft, 'MM/DD/RR HH24:MI:SS','NLS_CALENDAR=Gregorian'),
       decode(ksulopna, 'Advisor', ksuloif2,
       decode(sign(ksulotot-ksulosfr),-1,to_number(NULL),
       decode(ksulosfr,0,to_number(NULL),
       round(ksuloetm*((ksulotot-ksulosfr)/ksulosfr))))),ksuloetm,ksuloctx,ksulomsg,
       ksulounm,ksulosql,ksulosqh,ksulosqi, ksulosqph, ksulosqesta,
       decode(ksulosqeid, 0, to_number(NULL), ksulosqeid),
       decode(ksulosqplid, 0, to_number(NULL), ksulosqplid),
       ksulosqplop,ksulosqplnm,ksuloqid
from   x$ksulop;
```

View Name: **V$SESSION_LONGOPS**

```
select SID,SERIAL#,OPNAME,TARGET,TARGET_DESC,SOFAR,TOTALWORK,UNITS,START_TIME,
       LAST_UPDATE_TIME,TIMESTAMP,
TIME_REMAINING,ELAPSED_SECONDS,CONTEXT,MESSAGE,USERNAME,
       SQL_ADDRESS,SQL_HASH_VALUE,SQL_ID, SQL_PLAN_HASH_VALUE,
       SQL_EXEC_START, SQL_EXEC_ID, SQL_PLAN_LINE_ID,
       SQL_PLAN_OPERATION, SQL_PLAN_OPTIONS, QCSID
from   GV$SESSION_LONGOPS
where  inst_id = USERENV('Instance');
```

View Name: GV$SESSION_OBJECT_CACHE

```
select inst_id,kocstpin,kocsthit,kocsttht,decode(kocstpin,0,1,kocsthit/kocstpin),
       decode(kocstpin,0,1,kocsttht/kocstpin),kocstorf,kocstrfs,kocstofs,
       kocstfls,kocstshr,kocstcnt,kocstpnd,kocstsiz,kocstopt,kocstmax
from   x$kocst;
```

View Name: V$SESSION_OBJECT_CACHE

```
select pins,hits,true_hits,hit_ratio,true_hit_ratio,object_refreshes,
       cache_refreshes,object_flushes,cache_flushes,cache_shrinks,
       cached_objects,pinned_objects,cache_size,optimal_size,maximum_size
from gv$session_object_cache
where inst_id=userenv('Instance');
```

View Name: GV$SESSION_WAIT

```
select s.inst_id,s.kslwtsid,s.kslwtseq,e.kslednam,e.ksledp1,s.kslwtp1,
       s.kslwtp1r,e.ksledp2, s.kslwtp2,s.kslwtp2r,e.ksledp3,s.kslwtp3,
       s.kslwtp3r, e.ksledclassid,e.ksledclass#, e.ksledclass,
       decode(s.kslwtinwait,0,decode(bitand(s.kslwtflags,256),0,-2,
       decode(round(s.kslwtstime/10000),0,-1,round(s.kslwtstime/10000))),0),
       decode(s.kslwtinwait,0,round((s.kslwtstime+s.kslwtltime)/1000000),
       round(s.kslwtstime/1000000)), decode(s.kslwtinwait,1,'WAITING',
       decode(bitand(s.kslwtflags,256),0,'WAITED UNKNOWN TIME',
       decode(round(s.kslwtstime/10000),0,'WAITED SHORT TIME','WAITED KNOWN TIME'))),
       s.kslwtstime, decode(s.kslwtinwait,0,to_number(null),
       decode(bitand(s.kslwtflags,64),64,0,s.kslwttrem)), s.kslwtltime
from   x$kslwt s, x$ksled e
where  s.kslwtevt=e.indx;
```

View Name: V$SESSION_WAIT

```
select sid,seq#,event,p1text,p1,p1raw,p2text,p2,p2raw,p3text, p3,p3raw,
       wait_class_id, wait_class#,wait_class,wait_time,
       seconds_in_wait,state,wait_time_micro,time_remaining_micro,
       time_since_last_wait_micro
from   gv$session_wait
where  inst_id = USERENV('Instance');
```

View Name: GV$SESSION_WAIT_CLASS

```
select s.inst_id,s.kslcssid,s.kslcsser,s.kslcsclsid,s.kslcscls,s.kslcsclsname,
       s.kslcswts, round(s.kslcstim / 10000)
from   x$kslcs s
where  s.kslcswts != 0;
```

View Name: V$SESSION_WAIT_CLASS

```
select sid,serial#,wait_class_id, wait_class#,wait_class,total_waits,
time_waited
from   gv$session_wait_class
where  inst_id = USERENV('Instance');
```

View Name: **GV$SESSION_WAIT_HISTORY**

```
select  s.inst_id,s.kslwhsid,s.kslwhridx,s.kslwhevt,
s.kslwhetext,s.kslwhp1text,
        s.kslwhp1,s.kslwhp2text,s.kslwhp2, s.kslwhp3text,s.kslwhp3,
        round(s.kslwhstime/10000),s.kslwhstime,s.kslwhltime
from    x$kslwh s;
```

View Name: **V$SESSION_WAIT_HISTORY**

```
select  sid,seq#,event#,event,p1text,p1,p2text,p2,p3text,p3,wait_time,
        wait_time_micro,time_since_last_wait_micro
from    gv$session_wait_history
where   inst_id = USERENV('Instance');
```

View Name: **GV$SESSMETRIC**

```
SELECT  inst_id, begtime, endtime, intsize_csec, sessid, sernum, cpu,
        phyrds, logrds, pga_memory, hard_parses, soft_parses, phyrds_pct,
        logrds_pct
FROM    x$kewmsemv
WHERE   flag1 = 1;
```

View Name: **V$SESSMETRIC**

```
SELECT  begin_time, end_time, intsize_csec, session_id, serial_num, cpu,
        physical_reads, logical_reads, pga_memory, hard_parses, soft_parses,
        physical_read_pct, logical_read_pct
FROM    gv$sessmetric
WHERE   inst_id = USERENV('INSTANCE');
```

View Name: **GV$SESSTAT**

```
select  inst_id,ksusenum,ksusestn,ksusestv
from    x$ksusesta
where   bitand(ksspaflg,1)!=0
and     bitand(ksuseflg,1)!=0
and     ksusestn<
   (select ksusgstl
    from x$ksusgif);
```

View Name: **V$SESSTAT**

```
select  SID,STATISTIC#,VALUE
from    GV$SESSTAT
where   inst_id = USERENV('Instance');
```

View Name: **GV$SESS_IO**

```
select  inst_id,indx,ksusesbg,ksusescg,ksusespr,ksusesbc,ksusescc,ksusesor
from    x$ksusio
```

```
where   bitand(ksspaflg,1)!=0
and     bitand(ksuseflg,1)!=0;
```

View Name: V$SESS_IO

```
select SID,BLOCK_GETS,CONSISTENT_GETS,PHYSICAL_READS,BLOCK_CHANGES,
       CONSISTENT_CHANGES, OPTIMIZED_PHYSICAL_READS
from   GV$SESS_IO
where  inst_id = USERENV('Instance');
```

View Name: GV$SGA

```
select inst_id,ksmsdnam,ksmsdval
from   x$ksmsd;
```

View Name: V$SGA

```
select NAME,VALUE
from   GV$SGA
where  inst_id = USERENV('Instance');
```

View Name: GV$SGASTAT

```
select inst_id,'',ksmssnam,ksmsslen
from   x$ksmfs
where  ksmsslen>1
union all
select inst_id,'shared pool',ksmssnam,sum(ksmsslen)
from x$ksmss
where ksmsslen>1
group by inst_id,'shared pool',ksmssnam
union all
select inst_id,'large pool',ksmssnam, sum(ksmsslen)
from x$ksmls
where ksmsslen>1
group by inst_id, 'large pool', ksmssnam
union all
select inst_id,'java pool',ksmssnam, sum(ksmsslen)
from   x$ksmjs
where  ksmsslen>1
group by inst_id, 'java pool', ksmssnam
union all
select inst_id,'numa pool',ksmnsnam, sum(ksmnslen)
from   x$ksmns
where  ksmnslen>1
group by inst_id, 'numa pool', ksmnsnam
union all
select inst_id,'streamspool',ksmssnam, sum(ksmsslen)
from   x$ksmstrs
where  ksmsslen>1
group by inst_id, 'streams pool', ksmssnam;
```

View Name: V$SGASTAT

```
select POOL,NAME,BYTES
from   GV$SGASTAT
where  inst_id = USERENV('Instance');
```

View Name: GV$SHARED_POOL_ADVICE

```
select inst_id,sp_size,round(sp_size / basesp_size, 4),kglsim_size,kglsim_objs,
       kglsim_timesave,decode(kglsim_basetimesave,0,to_number(null),
       round(kglsim_timesave / kglsim_basetimesave,4)), kglsim_parsetime,
       decode(kglsim_baseparsetime,0,to_number(null),
       round(kglsim_parsetime / kglsim_baseparsetime, 4)),kglsim_hits
from   x$kglsim;
```

View Name: V$SHARED_POOL_ADVICE

```
select shared_pool_size_for_estimate,shared_pool_size_factor,estd_lc_size,
       estd_lc_memory_objects,estd_lc_time_saved,estd_lc_time_saved_factor,
       estd_lc_load_time,  estd_lc_load_time_factor, estd_lc_memory_object_hits
from   gv$shared_pool_advice
where  inst_id = USERENV('Instance');
```

View Name: GV$SHARED_POOL_RESERVED

```
select p.inst_id, p.free_space, p.avg_free_size, p.free_count,
p.max_free_size, p.used_size, p.avg_used_size, p.used_count, p.max_used_size,
s.requests, s.request_misses, s.last_miss_size, s.max_miss_size,
s.request_failures, s.last_failure_size, s.aborted_request_threshold,
s.aborted_requests, s.last_aborted_size
from (select avg(x$ksmspr.inst_id) inst_id,
             sum(decode(ksmchcls,'R-free',ksmchsiz,0)) free_space,
             avg(decode(ksmchcls,'R-free',ksmchsiz,0)) avg_free_size,
             sum(decode(ksmchcls,'R-free',1,0)) free_count,
             max(decode(ksmchcls,'R-free',ksmchsiz,0)) max_free_size,
             sum(decode(ksmchcls,'R-free',0,ksmchsiz)) used_size,
             avg(decode(ksmchcls,'R-free',0,ksmchsiz)) avg_used_size,
             sum(decode(ksmchcls,'R-free',0,1)) used_count,
             max(decode(ksmchcls,'R-free',0,ksmchsiz)) max_used_size
      from   x$ksmspr
      where  ksmchcom not like '%reserved sto%') p,
             (select sum(kghlurcn) requests, sum(kghlurmi) request_misses,
                     max(kghlurmz) last_miss_size,
                     max(kghlurmx) max_miss_size,
                     sum(kghlunfu) request_failures,
                     max(kghlunfs) last_failure_size,
                     max(kghlumxa) aborted_request_threshold,
                     sum(kghlumer) aborted_requests,
                     max(kghlumes) last_aborted_size
              from x$kghlu) s;
```

View Name: V$SHARED_POOL_RESERVED

```
select FREE_SPACE,AVG_FREE_SIZE,FREE_COUNT,MAX_FREE_SIZE,USED_SPACE,AVG_USED_SIZE,
       USED_COUNT,MAX_USED_SIZE,REQUESTS,REQUEST_MISSES,LAST_MISS_SIZE,
       MAX_MISS_SIZE,REQUEST_FAILURES,LAST_FAILURE_SIZE,ABORTED_REQUEST_THRESHOLD,
       ABORTED_REQUESTS,LAST_ABORTED_SIZE
from   GV$SHARED_POOL_RESERVED
where  inst_id = USERENV('Instance');
```

View Name: GV$SORT_SEGMENT

```
select inst_id,tablespace_name,segment_file,segment_block,extent_size,
       current_users,total_extents,total_blocks,used_extents,used_blocks,
       free_extents,free_blocks,added_extents,extent_hits,freed_extents,
       free_requests,max_size,max_blocks,max_used_size,max_used_blocks,
       max_sort_size,max_sort_blocks,relative_fno
from   x$ktstssd;
```

View Name: V$SORT_SEGMENT

```
select TABLESPACE_NAME,SEGMENT_FILE,SEGMENT_BLOCK,EXTENT_SIZE,CURRENT_USERS,
       TOTAL_EXTENTS,TOTAL_BLOCKS,USED_EXTENTS,USED_BLOCKS,FREE_EXTENTS,FREE_BLOCKS,
       ADDED_EXTENTS,EXTENT_HITS,FREED_EXTENTS,FREE_REQUESTS,MAX_SIZE,MAX_BLOCKS,
       MAX_USED_SIZE,MAX_USED_BLOCKS,MAX_SORT_SIZE,MAX_SORT_BLOCKS,RELATIVE_FNO
from   GV$SORT_SEGMENT
where  inst_id = USERENV('Instance');
```

View Name: GV$SORT_USAGE

```
select x$ktsso.inst_id,username,username,ktssoses,ktssosno,prev_sql_addr,

prev_hash_value,prev_sql_id,ktssotsn,decode(ktssocnt,0,'PERMANENT',1,'TEMPORARY'),
       decode(ktssosegt,1,'SORT',2,'HASH',3,'DATA',4,'INDEX',5,
       'LOB_DATA',6,'LOB_INDEX','UNDEFINED'),ktssofno,ktssobno,ktssoexts,
       ktssoblks,ktssorfno
from   x$ktsso,v$session
where  ktssoses = v$session.saddr
and    ktssosno = v$session.serial#;
```

View Name: V$SORT_USAGE

```
select USERNAME,"USER",SESSION_ADDR,SESSION_NUM,SQLADDR,SQLHASH,SQL_ID,
TABLESPACE,CONTENTS,SEGTYPE,SEGFILE#,SEGBLK#,EXTENTS,BLOCKS,SEGRFNO#
from   GV$SORT_USAGE
where  inst_id = USERENV('Instance');
```

View Name: GV$SPPARAMETER

```
select INST_ID, KSPSPFFTCTXSPSID, KSPSPFFTCTXSPNAME,
       decode(KSPSPFFTCTXPARTYP,1,'boolean',2,'string', 3,'integer',
       4,'file',5,'number',6,'big integer','unknown'),KSPSPFFTCTXSPVALUE,
       KSPSPFFTCTXSPDVALUE, KSPSPFFTCTXISSPECIFIED, KSPSPFFTCTXORDINAL,
       KSPSPFFTCTXCOMMENT
```

```
from    x$kspspfile
WHERE   ((translate(KSPSPFFTCTXSPNAME,'_','#') not like '##%')
and     ((translate(KSPSPFFTCTXSPNAME, '_', '#') not like '#%')
OR      KSPSPFFTCTXISSPECIFIED = 'TRUE'));
```

View Name: V$SPPARAMETER

```
select SID,NAME, TYPE,VALUE,DISPLAY_VALUE,ISSPECIFIED,ORDINAL,UPDATE_COMMENT
from   GV$SPPARAMETER
where  INST_id = USERENV('Instance');
```

View Name: GV$SQL

```
select inst_id,kglnaobj,kglfnobj,kglobt03, kglobhs0+kglobhs1+kglobhs2+
       kglobhs3+kglobhs4+kglobhs5+kglobhs6+kglobt16, kglobt08+kglobt11,
       kglobt10, kglobt01, decode(kglobhs6,0,0,1), decode(kglhdlmd,0,0,1),
       kglhdlkc, kglobt04, kglobt05, kglobt48, kglobt35, kglobpc6, kglhdldc,
       substr(to_char(kglnatim,'YYYY-MM-DD/HH24:MI:SS'),1,19), kglhdivc,
       kglobt12, kglobt13, kglobwdw, kglobt14, kglobwap, kglobwcc,
       kglobwcl, kglobwui, kglobt42, kglobt43, kglobt15, kglobt02,
       decode(kglobt32,0,'NONE',1,'ALL_ROWS',2,'FIRST_ROWS',3,'RULE',
       4,'CHOOSE','UNKNOWN'), kglobtn0, kglobcce, kglobcceh, kglobt17,
       kglobt18, kglobts4, kglhdkmk, kglhdpar, kglobtp0, kglnahsh, kglobt46,
       kglobt30, kglobt09, kglobts5, kglobt48, kglobts0, kglobt19, kglobts1,
       kglobt20, kglobt21, kglobts2, kglobt06, kglobt07,
       decode(kglobt28, 0, to_number(NULL), kglobt28), kglhdadr, kglobt29,
       decode(bitand(kglobt00,64),64,'Y', 'N'), decode(kglobsta,
       1,'VALID',2,'VALID_AUTH_ERROR',3,'VALID_COMPILE_ERROR',
       4,'VALID_UNAUTH',5,'INVALID_UNAUTH',6,'INVALID'), kglobt31,
       substr(to_char(kglobtt0,'YYYY-MM-DD/HH24:MI:SS'),1,19),
       decode(kglobt33, 1, 'Y', 'N'),decode(bitand(kglobacs, 1), 1, 'Y', 'N'),
       decode(bitand(kglobacs, 2), 2, 'Y', 'N'),
       decode(bitand(kglobacs, 4), 4, 'Y', 'N'),  kglhdclt,
       kglobts3, kglobts7, kglobts6, kglobt44, kglobt45,  kglobt47, kglobt49,
       kglobcla,  kglobcbca, kglobt22, kglobt52, kglobt53, kglobt54, kglobt55,
       kglobt56, kglobt57, kglobt58, kglobt23, kglobt24, kglobt59,
       kglobt53 - ((kglobt55+kglobt57) - kglobt52)
from   x$kglcursor_child;
```

View Name: V$SQL

```
select SQL_TEXT,SQL_FULLTEXT, SQL_ID,SHARABLE_MEM,PERSISTENT_MEM,RUNTIME_MEM,SORTS,
       LOADED_VERSIONS,OPEN_VERSIONS,USERS_OPENING,FETCHES,EXECUTIONS,
       PX_SERVERS_EXECUTIONS,END_OF_FETCH_COUNT,USERS_EXECUTING,LOADS,FIRST_LOAD_TIME,
       INVALIDATIONS,PARSE_CALLS,DISK_READS,DIRECT_WRITES,
       BUFFER_GETS,APPLICATION_WAIT_TIME,
       CONCURRENCY_WAIT_TIME, CLUSTER_WAIT_TIME, USER_IO_WAIT_TIME, PLSQL_EXEC_TIME,
       JAVA_EXEC_TIME, ROWS_PROCESSED , COMMAND_TYPE , OPTIMIZER_MODE , OPTIMIZER_COST,
       OPTIMIZER_ENV, OPTIMIZER_ENV_HASH_VALUE, PARSING_USER_ID , PARSING_SCHEMA_ID,
       PARSING_SCHEMA_NAME, KEPT_VERSIONS , ADDRESS , TYPE_CHK_HEAP , HASH_VALUE,
       OLD_HASH_VALUE, PLAN_HASH_VALUE, CHILD_NUMBER, SERVICE, SERVICE_HASH, MODULE,
       MODULE_HASH , ACTION , ACTION_HASH ,  SERIALIZABLE_ABORTS , OUTLINE_CATEGORY,
       CPU_TIME, ELAPSED_TIME, OUTLINE_SID, CHILD_ADDRESS, SQLTYPE, REMOTE,
       OBJECT_STATUS, LITERAL_HASH_VALUE, LAST_LOAD_TIME, IS_OBSOLETE,
```

```
                 IS_BIND_SENSITIVE, IS_BIND_AWARE, IS_SHAREABLE, CHILD_LATCH,
                 SQL_PROFILE, SQL_PATCH, SQL_PLAN_BASELINE, PROGRAM_ID,PROGRAM_LINE#,
                 EXACT_MATCHING_SIGNATURE,FORCE_MATCHING_SIGNATURE, LAST_ACTIVE_TIME,
                 BIND_DATA TYPECHECK_MEM, IO_CELL_OFFLOAD_ELIGIBLE_BYTES, IO_INTERCONNECT_BYTES,
                 PHYSICAL_READ_REQUESTS, PHYSICAL_READ_BYTES, PHYSICAL_WRITE_REQUESTS,
                 PHYSICAL_WRITE_BYTES, OPTIMIZED_PHY_READ_REQUESTS, LOCKED_TOTAL,
                 PINNED_TOTAL, IO_CELL_UNCOMPRESSED_BYTES, IO_CELL_OFFLOAD_RETURNED_BYTES
   from     GV$SQL
   where    inst_id = USERENV('Instance');
```

View Name: GV$SQLAREA

```
select  inst_id, kglnaobj, kglfnobj, kglobt03, kglobhs0+kglobhs1+
        kglobhs2+kglobhs3+kglobhs4+kglobhs5+kglobhs6, kglobt08+kglobt11,
        kglobt10, kglobt01, kglobccc, kglobclc, kglhdlmd, kglhdlkc, kglobt04,
        kglobt05, kglobt48, kglobt35, kglobpc6, kglhdldc,
        substr(to_char(kglnatim,'YYYY-MM-DD/HH24:MI:SS'),1,19), kglhdivc,
        kglobt12, kglobt13, kglobwdw, kglobt14, kglobwap, kglobwcc, kglobwcl,
        kglobwui, kglobt42, kglobt43, kglobt15, kglobt02, decode(kglobt32, 0,
        'NONE',1,'ALL_ROWS',2,'FIRST_ROWS',3,'RULE',4, 'CHOOSE', 'UNKNOWN'),
        kglobtn0, kglobcce, kglobcceh, kglobt17, kglobt18, kglobts4, kglhdkmk,
        kglhdpar, kglnahsh, kglobt46, kglobt30, kglobts0, kglobt19, kglobts1,
        kglobt20, kglobt21, kglobts2, kglobt06, kglobt07,
        decode(kglobt28, 0, NULL, kglobt28), kglhdadr,
        decode(bitand(kglobt00,64),64, 'Y', 'N'),
        decode(kglobsta,1,'VALID',2,'VALID_AUTH_ERROR',3, 'VALID_COMPILE_ERROR',
        4,'VALID_UNAUTH',5,'INVALID_UNAUTH',6,'INVALID'), kglobt31, kglobtt0,
        decode(kglobt33, 1, 'Y', 'N'),   decode(bitand(kglobacs, 1), 1, 'Y', 'N'),
        decode(bitand(kglobacs, 2), 2, 'Y', 'N'),kglhdclt,kglobts3,
        kglobts7, kglobts6,kglobt44,kglobt45,kglobt47,kglobt49,kglobcla,
        kglobcbca,kglobt22,kglobt52,kglobt53,kglobt54,kglobt55,kglobt56,kglobt57,
        kglobt58,kglobt23,kglobt24,kglobt59,kglobt53 - ((kglobt55+kglobt57) - kglobt52)
   from   x$kglcursor_child_sqlid
   where  kglobt02 != 0;
```

View Name: V$SQLAREA

```
select SQL_TEXT, SQL_FULLTEXT, SQL_ID,SHARABLE_MEM,
       PERSISTENT_MEM,RUNTIME_MEM,SORTS,VERSION_COUNT,
       LOADED_VERSIONS,OPEN_VERSIONS,USERS_OPENING,FETCHES,EXECUTIONS,
       PX_SERVERS_EXECUTIONS, END_OF_FETCH_COUNT, USERS_EXECUTING,LOADS,FIRST_LOAD_TIME,
       INVALIDATIONS,PARSE_CALLS,DISK_READS,DIRECT_WRITES,
       BUFFER_GETS, APPLICATION_WAIT_TIME,CONCURRENCY_WAIT_TIME,CLUSTER_WAIT_TIME,
       USER_IO_WAIT_TIME, PLSQL_EXEC_TIME, JAVA_EXEC_TIME, ROWS_PROCESSED,
       COMMAND_TYPE,OPTIMIZER_MODE, OPTIMIZER_COST, OPTIMIZER_ENV,
       OPTIMIZER_ENV_HASH_VALUE, PARSING_USER_ID,PARSING_SCHEMA_ID,
       PARSING_SCHEMA_NAME, KEPT_VERSIONS,ADDRESS,HASH_VALUE,OLD_HASH_VALUE,
       PLAN_HASH_VALUE, MODULE,MODULE_HASH,ACTION,ACTION_HASH,SERIALIZABLE_ABORTS,
       OUTLINE_CATEGORY, CPU_TIME,ELAPSED_TIME, OUTLINE_SID,LAST_ACTIVE_CHILD_ADDRESS,
       REMOTE, OBJECT_STATUS, LITERAL_HASH_VALUE, LAST_LOAD_TIME, IS_OBSOLETE,
       IS_BIND_SENSITIVE, IS_BIND_AWARE, CHILD_LATCH, SQL_PROFILE,SQL_PATCH,
       SQL_PLAN_BASELINE, PROGRAM_ID, PROGRAM_LINE#, EXACT_MATCHING_SIGNATURE,
       FORCE_MATCHING_SIGNATURE, LAST_ACTIVE_TIME, BIND_DATA, TYPECHECK_MEM,
       IO_CELL_OFFLOAD_ELIGIBLE_BYTES, IO_INTERCONNECT_BYTES,PHYSICAL_READ_REQUESTS,
       PHYSICAL_READ_BYTES, PHYSICAL_WRITE_REQUESTS, PHYSICAL_WRITE_BYTES,
       OPTIMIZED_PHY_READ_REQUESTS, LOCKED_TOTAL, PINNED_TOTAL,
       IO_CELL_UNCOMPRESSED_BYTES, IO_CELL_OFFLOAD_RETURNED_BYTES
  from     GV$SQLAREA
  where    inst_id = USERENV('Instance');
```

View Name: GV$SQLAREA_PLAN_HASH

```
select inst_id, kglnaobj, kglfnobj, kglhdpar, kglobt46, kglobt03, kglobt30,
       kglobccc, kglhdadr, kglobhs0+kglobhs1+kglobhs2+kglobhs3+kglobhs4+
       kglobhs5+kglobhs6, kglobt08+kglobt11, kglobt10, kglobt01, kglobclc,
       kglhdlmd, kglhdlkc, kglobpc6, kglobt04, kglobt05, kglobt48, kglobt35,
       kglhdldc, kglnatim, kglobtt0, kglobcla, kglhdivc, kglobt12, kglobt13,
       kglobwdw, kglobt14, kglobt06, kglobt07, kglobwap, kglobwcc, kglobwcl,
       kglobwui, kglobt42, kglobt43, kglobt15, kglobt02,
       decode(kglobt32, 0, 'NONE', 1, 'ALL_ROWS',2, 'FIRST_ROWS',3, 'RULE',
       4, 'CHOOSE', 'UNKNOWN'), kglobtn0, kglobcce, kglobcceh, kglobt17,
       kglobt18, kglobts4, kglhdkmk, kglobts0, kglobt19, kglobts1, kglobt20,
       kglobt21, kglobts2, decode(kglobt28, 0, NULL, kglobt28),
       decode(bitand(kglobt00,64),64, 'Y', 'N'), decode(kglobsta, 1, 'VALID',
       2, 'VALID_AUTH_ERROR', 3, 'VALID_COMPILE_ERROR', 4, 'VALID_UNAUTH',
       5, 'INVALID_UNAUTH', 6, 'INVALID'), kglobt31, kglobts3, kglobt44,
       kglobt45, kglobt47, kglobt49, kglobcbca , kglobt22, kglobt52,
       kglobt53, kglobt54, kglobt55, kglobt56, kglobt57, kglobt58,
       kglobt59, kglobt53 - ((kglobt55+kglobt57) - kglobt52)
from   x$kglcursor_child_sqlidph;
```

View Name: V$ SQLAREA_PLAN_HASH

```
select  SQL_TEXT, SQL_FULLTEXT, ADDRESS, HASH_VALUE, SQL_ID, PLAN_HASH_VALUE,
        VERSION_COUNT, LAST_ACTIVE_CHILD_ADDRESS, SHARABLE_MEM, PERSISTENT_MEM,
        RUNTIME_MEM, SORTS, LOADED_VERSIONS, OPEN_VERSIONS,USERS_OPENING,
        USERS_EXECUTING, FETCHES, EXECUTIONS, PX_SERVERS_EXECUTIONS,
        END_OF_FETCH_COUNT, LOADS, FIRST_LOAD_TIME, LAST_LOAD_TIME,
        LAST_ACTIVE_TIME, INVALIDATIONS, PARSE_CALLS, DISK_READS,
        DIRECT_WRITES, BUFFER_GETS, CPU_TIME, ELAPSED_TIME,
        APPLICATION_WAIT_TIME, CONCURRENCY_WAIT_TIME, CLUSTER_WAIT_TIME,
        USER_IO_WAIT_TIME, PLSQL_EXEC_TIME, JAVA_EXEC_TIME, ROWS_PROCESSED,
        COMMAND_TYPE, OPTIMIZER_MODE, OPTIMIZER_COST, OPTIMIZER_ENV,
        OPTIMIZER_ENV_HASH_VALUE, PARSING_USER_ID, PARSING_SCHEMA_ID,
        PARSING_SCHEMA_NAME, KEPT_VERSIONS, MODULE, MODULE_HASH, ACTION,
        ACTION_HASH, SERIALIZABLE_ABORTS, OUTLINE_CATEGORY, OUTLINE_SID,
        REMOTE, OBJECT_STATUS, LITERAL_HASH_VALUE, SQL_PROFILE, PROGRAM_ID,
        PROGRAM_LINE#, EXACT_MATCHING_SIGNATURE, FORCE_MATCHING_SIGNATURE,
        BIND_DATA, TYPECHECK_MEM, IO_CELL_OFFLOAD_ELIGIBLE_BYTES,
        IO_INTERCONNECT_BYTES, PHYSICAL_READ_REQUESTS, PHYSICAL_READ_BYTES,
        PHYSICAL_WRITE_REQUESTS, PHYSICAL_WRITE_BYTES, OPTIMIZED_PHY_READ_REQUESTS,
        IO_CELL_UNCOMPRESSED_BYTES, IO_CELL_OFFLOAD_RETURNED_BYTES
from    GV$SQLAREA_PLAN_HASH
where   inst_id = USERENV('Instance');
```

View Name: GV$SQLSTATS

```
select INST_ID, SQL_TEXT, SQL_FULLTEXT, SQL_ID, LAST_ACTIVE_TIME,
       LAST_ACTIVE_CHILD_ADDRESS, PLAN_HASH_VALUE, PARSE_CALLS, DISK_READS,
       DIRECT_WRITES, BUFFER_GETS, ROWS_PROCESSED, SERIALIZABLE_ABORTS,
       FETCHES, EXECUTIONS, END_OF_FETCH_COUNT, LOADS, VERSION_COUNT,
       INVALIDATIONS, PX_SERVERS_EXECUTIONS, CPU_TIME, ELAPSED_TIME,
       AVG_HARD_PARSE_TIME, APPLICATION_WAIT_TIME,CONCURRENCY_WAIT_TIME,
       CLUSTER_WAIT_TIME, USER_IO_WAIT_TIME, PLSQL_EXEC_TIME, JAVA_EXEC_TIME,
```

```
         SORTS, SHARABLE_MEM, TOTAL_SHARABLE_MEM, TYPECHECK_MEM,
         IO_CELL_OFFLOAD_ELIGIBLE_BYTES, IO_INTERCONNECT_BYTES,
         PHYSICAL_READ_REQUESTS, PHYSICAL_READ_BYTES, PHYSICAL_WRITE_REQUESTS,
         PHYSICAL_WRITE_BYTES, EXACT_MATCHING_SIGNATURE, FORCE_MATCHING_SIGNATURE,
         IO_CELL_UNCOMPRESSED_BYTES, IO_INTERCONNECT_BYTES -
         ((PHYSICAL_READ_BYTES+PHYSICAL_WRITE_REQUESTS)-IO_CELL_OFFLOAD_ELIGIBLE_BYTES)
FROM    x$kkssqlstat;
```

View Name: V$SQLSTATS

```
select SQL_TEXT, SQL_FULLTEXT, SQL_ID,LAST_ACTIVE_TIME, LAST_ACTIVE_CHILD_ADDRESS,
       PLAN_HASH_VALUE, PARSE_CALLS, DISK_READS, DIRECT_WRITES, BUFFER_GETS,
       ROWS_PROCESSED, SERIALIZABLE_ABORTS, FETCHES, EXECUTIONS,
       END_OF_FETCH_COUNT, LOADS, VERSION_COUNT, INVALIDATIONS,
       PX_SERVERS_EXECUTIONS,CPU_TIME,ELAPSED_TIME,AVG_HARD_PARSE_TIME,
       APPLICATION_WAIT_TIME, CONCURRENCY_WAIT_TIME, CLUSTER_WAIT_TIME,
       USER_IO_WAIT_TIME, PLSQL_EXEC_TIME, JAVA_EXEC_TIME, SORTS, SHARABLE_MEM,
       TOTAL_SHARABLE_MEM, TYPECHECK_MEM, IO_CELL_OFFLOAD_ELIGIBLE_BYTES,
       IO_INTERCONNECT_BYTES, PHYSICAL_READ_REQUESTS, PHYSICAL_READ_BYTES,
       PHYSICAL_WRITE_REQUESTS, PHYSICAL_WRITE_BYTES, EXACT_MATCHING_SIGNATURE,
       FORCE_MATCHING_SIGNATURE, IO_CELL_UNCOMPRESSED_BYTES,
       IO_CELL_OFFLOAD_RETURNED_BYTES
FROM   gv$sqlstats
where inst_id=USERENV('Instance');
```

View Name: GV$SQLTEXT

```
select inst_id,kglhdadr,kglnahsh, kglnasqlid, kgloboct,piece,name
from   x$kglna where kgloboct != 0;
```

View Name: V$SQLTEXT

```
select ADDRESS,HASH_VALUE,SQL_ID,COMMAND_TYPE,PIECE,SQL_TEXT
from   GV$SQLTEXT
where  inst_id = USERENV('Instance');
```

View Name: GV$SQLTEXT_WITH_NEWLINES

```
select inst_id,kglhdadr,kglnahsh,kglnasqlid,kgloboct,piece,name
from   x$kglna1 where kgloboct != 0;
```

View Name: V$SQLTEXT_WITH_NEWLINES

```
select ADDRESS,HASH_VALUE,SQL_ID,COMMAND_TYPE,PIECE,SQL_TEXT
from   GV$SQLTEXT_WITH_NEWLINES
where  inst_id = USERENV('Instance');
```

View Name: GV$SQL_BIND_DATA

```
select inst_id,kxsbdcur,kxsbdbnd,kxsbddty,kxsbdmxl,kxsbdpmx,kxsbdmal,kxsbdpre,
       kxsbdscl,kxsbdof1,kxsbdof2,kxsbdbfp,kxsbdbln,kxsbdavl,kxsbdbfl,kxsbdind,
       kxsbdval
from   x$kxsbd;
```

View Name: **V$SQL_BIND_DATA**

```
select CURSOR_NUM,POSITION,DATATYPE,SHARED_MAX_LEN,PRIVATE_MAX_LEN,ARRAY_SIZE,
       PRECISION,SCALE,SHARED_FLAG,SHARED_FLAG2,BUF_ADDRESS,BUF_LENGTH,VAL_LENGTH,
       BUF_FLAG,INDICATOR,VALUE
from   GV$SQL_BIND_DATA
where  inst_id = USERENV('Instance');
```

View Name: **GV$SQL_BIND_METADATA**

```
select inst_id,kglhdadr,position,kkscbndt,kkscbndl,kkscbnda,kksbvnnam
from   x$kksbv;
```

View Name: **V$SQL_BIND_METADATA**

```
select ADDRESS,POSITION,DATATYPE,MAX_LENGTH,ARRAY_LEN,BIND_NAME
from   GV$SQL_BIND_METADATA
where  inst_id = USERENV('Instance');
```

View Name: **GV$SQL_CURSOR**

```
select inst_id,kxscccur,kxscccfl,
       decode(kxsccsta,0,'CURNULL',1,'CURSYNTAX',2,'CURPARSE',3,'CURBOUND',4,
       'CURFETCH',5,'CURROW','ERROR'),kxsccphd,kxsccplk, kxsccclk, kxscccpn,
       kxscctbm,kxscctwm,kxscctbv,kxscctdv,kxsccbdf,kxsccflg,kxsccfl2,kxsccchd
from   x$kxscc;
```

View Name: **V$SQL_CURSOR**

```
select CURNO,FLAG,STATUS,PARENT_HANDLE,PARENT_LOCK,CHILD_LOCK,CHILD_PIN,

PERS_HEAP_MEM,WORK_HEAP_MEM,BIND_VARS,DEFINE_VARS,BIND_MEM_LOC,INST_FLAG,
       INST_FLAG2,CHILD_HANDLE
from   GV$SQL_CURSOR
where  inst_id = USERENV('Instance');
```

View Name: **GV$SQL_JOIN_FILTER**

```
SELECT  INST_ID, QCSID, QCINSTID, SQLHASHV, LEN, NSET, FLT, TOT, ACTIVE
FROM    X$QESBLSTAT;
```

View Name: **V$SQL_JOIN_FILTER**

```
SELECT qc_session_id, qc_instance_id, sql_plan_hash_value, length,
       bits_set, filtered, probed, active
FROM   GV$SQL_JOIN_FILTER
WHERE  inst_id = USERENV('INSTANCE');
```

View Name: GV$SQL_OPTIMIZER_ENV

```
select INST_ID, KQLFSQCE_PHAD, KQLFSQCE_HASH, KQLFSQCE_SQLID, KQLFSQCE_HADD,
       KQLFSQCE_CHNO, KQLFSQCE_PNUM, KQLFSQCE_PNAME,
       decode(bitand(KQLFSQCE_FLAGS, 2), 0, 'NO', 'YES'), KQLFSQCE_PVALUE
from   X$KQLFSQCE
where  bitand(KQLFSQCE_FLAGS, 8) = 0
and    (bitand(KQLFSQCE_FLAGS, 4)= 0
or     bitand(KQLFSQCE_FLAGS, 2) = 0);
```

View Name: V$SQL_OPTIMIZER_ENV

```
select ADDRESS, HASH_VALUE, SQL_ID, CHILD_ADDRESS, CHILD_NUMBER, ID, NAME,
       ISDEFAULT, VALUE
from   GV$SQL_OPTIMIZER_ENV
where  INST_ID = USERENV('Instance');
```

View Name: GV$SQL_PLAN

```
select inst_id,kqlfxpl_phad,kqlfxpl_hash,kqlfxpl_sqlid,kqlfxpl_plhash,
       kqlfxpl_hadd,kqlfxpl_chno,kqlfxpl_timestamp,substr(kqlfxpl_oper, 1, 30),
       substr(kqlfxpl_oopt, 1, 30),substr(kqlfxpl_tqid, 1, 40),
       to_number(decode(kqlfxpl_objn, 0, NULL, kqlfxpl_objn)),
       kqlfxpl_objowner,kqlfxpl_objname,kqlfxpl_alias,
       substr(kqlfxpl_objtype, 1, 20),substr(kqlfxpl_opti, 1, 20),
       kqlfxpl_opid,to_number(decode(kqlfxpl_opid,0,NULL,kqlfxpl_paid)),
       kqlfxpl_depth,to_number(decode(kqlfxpl_pos, 0,
       decode(kqlfxpl_cost,4294967295,NULL,kqlfxpl_cost),kqlfxpl_pos)),
       kqlfxpl_scols,to_number(decode(kqlfxpl_cost, 4294967295, NULL,
       kqlfxpl_cost)), to_number(decode(kqlfxpl_card, 0, NULL, kqlfxpl_card)),
       to_number(decode(kqlfxpl_size, 0, NULL, kqlfxpl_size)),
       substr(kqlfxpl_otag, 1, 35),substr(kqlfxpl_psta, 1, 64),
       substr(kqlfxpl_psto, 1, 64),
       to_number(decode(kqlfxpl_pnid, 0, NULL, kqlfxpl_pnid)),
       kqlfxpl_other,substr(kqlfxpl_dist, 1, 20),
       to_number(decode(kqlfxpl_cpuc, 4294967295, NULL, kqlfxpl_cpuc)),
       to_number(decode(kqlfxpl_ioct, 4294967295, NULL, kqlfxpl_ioct)),
       to_number(decode(kqlfxpl_temp, 0, NULL, kqlfxpl_temp)),kqlfxpl_keys,
       kqlfxpl_filter, kqlfxpl_proj,
       to_number(decode(kqlfxpl_time, 0, NULL, kqlfxpl_time)),
       kqlfxpl_qblock, kqlfxpl_remark, kqlfxpl_other_xml
from   x$kqlfxpl p ;
```

View Name: V$SQL_PLAN

```
select ADDRESS, HASH_VALUE, SQL_ID, PLAN_HASH_VALUE, CHILD_ADDRESS,
       CHILD_NUMBER, TIMESTAMP, OPERATION, OPTIONS, OBJECT_NODE, OBJECT#,
       OBJECT_OWNER, OBJECT_NAME, OBJECT_ALIAS, OBJECT_TYPE, OPTIMIZER,
       ID, PARENT_ID, DEPTH, POSITION, SEARCH_COLUMNS, COST, CARDINALITY,
       BYTES, OTHER_TAG, PARTITION_START, PARTITION_STOP, PARTITION_ID, OTHER,
       DISTRIBUTION, CPU_COST, IO_COST, TEMP_SPACE, ACCESS_PREDICATES,
       FILTER_PREDICATES, PROJECTION, TIME, QBLOCK_NAME, REMARKS, OTHER_XML
```

```
from    GV$SQL_PLAN
where   inst_id = USERENV('Instance');
```

View Name: GV$SQL_PLAN_STATISTICS

```
select  inst_id,PHADD_QESRS,HASHV_QESRS,SQLID_QESRS,PLHASH_QESRS,HADDR_QESRS,
        CHILDNO_QESRS,OPERID_QESRS,EXECS_QESRS,LSTARTS_QESRS,STARTS_QESRS,
        LOUTROWS_QESRS,OUTROWS_QESRS,LCRGETS_QESRS,CRGETS_QESRS,LCUGETS_QESRS,
        CUGETS_QESRS,LDREADS_QESRS,DREADS_QESRS,LDWRITES_QESRS,DWRITES_QESRS,
        LELAPTIME_QESRS,ELAPTIME_QESRS
from    X$QESRSTAT;
```

View Name: V$SQL_PLAN_STATISTICS

```
select  ADDRESS, HASH_VALUE, SQL_ID, PLAN_HASH_VALUE, CHILD_ADDRESS,
        CHILD_NUMBER,OPERATION_ID,EXECUTIONS,LAST_STARTS,STARTS,
        LAST_OUTPUT_ROWS,OUTPUT_ROWS,LAST_CR_BUFFER_GETS,CR_BUFFER_GETS,
        LAST_CU_BUFFER_GETS,CU_BUFFER_GETS,LAST_DISK_READS,DISK_READS,
        LAST_DISK_WRITES,DISK_WRITES,LAST_ELAPSED_TIME,ELAPSED_TIME
from    GV$SQL_PLAN_STATISTICS
where   inst_id = USERENV('Instance');
```

View Name: GV$SQL_PLAN_STATISTICS_ALL

```
select  inst_id, PHADD_QESRS, HASHV_QESRS, SQLID_QESRS, PLHASH_QESRS,
        HADDR_QESRS,  CHILDNO_QESRS, TIMESTAMP_QESRS, substr(oper_qesrs, 1, 30),
        substr(oopt_qesrs, 1, 30), substr(tqid_qesrs, 1, 40),
        to_number(decode(objn_qesrs, 0, NULL, objn_qesrs)), objowner_qesrs,
        objname_qesrs,  alias_qesrs, substr(objtype_qesrs, 1, 20),
        substr(opti_qesrs, 1, 20), opid_qesrs,
        to_number(decode(opid_qesrs, 0, NULL, paid_qesrs)), depth_qesrs,
        to_number(decode(pos_qesrs,0,decode(cost_qesrs,4294967295,NULL,cost_qesrs),
        pos_qesrs)),  scols_qesrs, to_number(decode(cost_qesrs, 4294967295,
        NULL, cost_qesrs)),  to_number(decode(card_qesrs, 0, NULL, card_qesrs)),
        to_number(decode(size_qesrs, 0, NULL, size_qesrs)),
        substr(otag_qesrs, 1, 35), substr(psta_qesrs, 1, 64),
        substr(psto_qesrs, 1, 64), to_number(decode(pnid_qesrs, 0, NULL, pnid_qesrs)),
        other_qesrs,  substr(dist_qesrs, 1, 20),
        to_number(decode(cpuc_qesrs, 4294967295, NULL, cpuc_qesrs)),
        to_number(decode(ioct_qesrs, 4294967295, NULL, ioct_qesrs)),
        to_number(decode(temp_qesrs, 0, NULL, temp_qesrs)),  KEYS_QESRS,
        FILTER_QESRS,PROJ_QESRS,to_number(decode(time_qesrs, 0, NULL, time_qesrs)),
        QBLOCK_QESRS,   REMARK_QESRS,   OTHER_XML_QESRS,   EXECS_QESRS,
        to_number(decode(LSTARTS_QESRS, 4294967295, NULL, LSTARTS_QESRS)),
        to_number(decode(LSTARTS_QESRS, 4294967295, NULL, STARTS_QESRS)),
        to_number(decode(LSTARTS_QESRS, 4294967295, NULL, LOUTROWS_QESRS)),
        to_number(decode(LSTARTS_QESRS, 4294967295, NULL, OUTROWS_QESRS)),
        to_number(decode(LSTARTS_QESRS, 4294967295, NULL, LCRGETS_QESRS)),
        to_number(decode(LSTARTS_QESRS, 4294967295, NULL, CRGETS_QESRS)),
        to_number(decode(LSTARTS_QESRS, 4294967295, NULL, LCUGETS_QESRS)),
        to_number(decode(LSTARTS_QESRS, 4294967295, NULL, CUGETS_QESRS)),
        to_number(decode(LSTARTS_QESRS, 4294967295, NULL, LDREADS_QESRS)),
        to_number(decode(LSTARTS_QESRS, 4294967295, NULL, DREADS_QESRS)),
        to_number(decode(LSTARTS_QESRS, 4294967295, NULL, LDWRITES_QESRS)),
        to_number(decode(LSTARTS_QESRS, 4294967295, NULL, DWRITES_QESRS)),
        to_number(decode(LSTARTS_QESRS, 4294967295, NULL, LELAPTIME_QESRS)),
```

```
         to_number(decode(LSTARTS_QESRS, 4294967295, NULL, ELAPTIME_QESRS)),
         substr(SIZEPOLICY_QESRS, 1, 10),
         to_number(decode(OPTIMAL_QESRS, 0, NULL, OPTIMAL_QESRS * 1024)),
         to_number(decode(OPTIMAL_QESRS, 0, NULL, ONEPASS_QESRS * 1024)),
         to_number(decode(OPTIMAL_QESRS, 0, NULL, LASTMEM_QESRS * 1024)),
         decode(OPTIMAL_QESRS, 0, NULL,
         substr(decode(LASTPASS_QESRS, 0, 'OPTIMAL',
         to_char(LASTPASS_QESRS)||' PASS'||decode(LASTPASS_QESRS, 1, '', 'ES')),1,10)),
         to_number(decode(LASTDOP_QESRS, 0, NULL, LASTDOP_QESRS)),
         to_number(decode(OPTIMAL_QESRS, 0, NULL, (OPTACTS_QESRS + SPAACTS_QESRS
         + MPAACTS_QESRS))),to_number(decode(OPTIMAL_QESRS,0,NULL,OPTACTS_QESRS)),
         to_number(decode(OPTIMAL_QESRS, 0, NULL, SPAACTS_QESRS)),
         to_number(decode(OPTIMAL_QESRS, 0, NULL, MPAACTS_QESRS)),
         to_number(decode(OPTIMAL_QESRS, 0, NULL, ATIME_QESRS)),
         to_number(decode(MAXTSEG_QESRS, 0, NULL, MAXTSEG_QESRS)),
         to_number(decode(LASTTSEG_QESRS, 0, NULL, LASTTSEG_QESRS))
from     X$QESRSTATALL p
where    p.haddr_qesrs != p.phadd_qesrs;
```

View Name: V$SQL_PLAN_STATISTICS_ALL

```
select ADDRESS, HASH_VALUE, SQL_ID, PLAN_HASH_VALUE, CHILD_ADDRESS,
       CHILD_NUMBER, TIMESTAMP, OPERATION, OPTIONS, OBJECT_NODE,
       OBJECT#, OBJECT_OWNER, OBJECT_NAME, OBJECT_ALIAS, OBJECT_TYPE,
       OPTIMIZER,ID, PARENT_ID, DEPTH, POSITION, SEARCH_COLUMNS, COST,
       CARDINALITY, BYTES, OTHER_TAG, PARTITION_START, PARTITION_STOP,
       PARTITION_ID, OTHER, DISTRIBUTION, CPU_COST, IO_COST, TEMP_SPACE,
       ACCESS_PREDICATES, FILTER_PREDICATES, PROJECTION,TIME, QBLOCK_NAME,
       REMARKS, OTHER_XML, EXECUTIONS, LAST_STARTS, STARTS, LAST_OUTPUT_ROWS,
       OUTPUT_ROWS, LAST_CR_BUFFER_GETS, CR_BUFFER_GETS, LAST_CU_BUFFER_GETS,
       CU_BUFFER_GETS, LAST_DISK_READS, DISK_READS, LAST_DISK_WRITES,
       DISK_WRITES, LAST_ELAPSED_TIME, ELAPSED_TIME, POLICY,
       ESTIMATED_OPTIMAL_SIZE, ESTIMATED_ONEPASS_SIZE, LAST_MEMORY_USED,
       LAST_EXECUTION, LAST_DEGREE, TOTAL_EXECUTIONS, OPTIMAL_EXECUTIONS,
       ONEPASS_EXECUTIONS, MULTIPASSES_EXECUTIONS, ACTIVE_TIME,
       MAX_TEMPSEG_SIZE, LAST_TEMPSEG_SIZE
from     GV$SQL_PLAN_STATISTICS_ALL
where    inst_id = USERENV('Instance');
```

View Name: GV$SQL_REDIRECTION

```
select c.inst_id,c.kglhdadr,c.kglhdpar,c.kglnahsh,C.kglobt03,c.kglobt09,
       c.kglobt17,c.kglobt18, c.kglobt02,
       decode(r.reason,1,'INVALID OBJECT',2,'ROWID',3,'QUERY REWRITE','READ ONLY'),
       r.error_code,r.position,r.sql_text_piece,r.error_msg
from     x$kglcursor_child c, x$kkssrd r
where    c.kglhdpar = r.parAddr
and      c.kglhdadr = r.kglhdadr;
```

View Name: V$SQL_REDIRECTION

```
select ADDRESS,PARENT_HANDLE,HASH_VALUE,SQL_ID,CHILD_NUMBER,PARSING_USER_ID,
       PARSING_SCHEMA_ID,COMMAND_TYPE,REASON,ERROR_CODE,POSITION,SQL_TEXT_PIECE,
       ERROR_MESSAGE
from     GV$SQL_REDIRECTION
where    inst_id = USERENV('Instance');
```

View Name: **V$SQL_SHARED_CURSOR**

```
select SQL_ID, ADDRESS, CHILD_ADDRESS, CHILD_NUMBER, UNBOUND_CURSOR,
       SQL_TYPE_MISMATCH, OPTIMIZER_MISMATCH, OUTLINE_MISMATCH, STATS_ROW_MISMATCH,
       LITERAL_MISMATCH, FORCE_HARD_PARSE, EXPLAIN_PLAN_CURSOR,
       BUFFERED_DML_MISMATCH, PDML_ENV_MISMATCH, INST_DRTLD_MISMATCH,
       SLAVE_QC_MISMATCH, TYPECHECK_MISMATCH, AUTH_CHECK_MISMATCH, BIND_MISMATCH,
       DESCRIBE_MISMATCH, LANGUAGE_MISMATCH,       TRANSLATION_MISMATCH,
       BIND_EQUIV_FAILURE, INSUFF_PRIVS, INSUFF_PRIVS_REM,
       REMOTE_TRANS_MISMATCH, LOGMINER_SESSION_MISMATCH, INCOMP_LTRL_MISMATCH,
       OVERLAP_TIME_MISMATCH, EDITION_MISMATCH, MV_QUERY_GEN_MISMATCH,
       USER_BIND_PEEK_MISMATCH, TYPCHK_DEP_MISMATCH, NO_TRIGGER_MISMATCH,
       FLASHBACK_CURSOR, ANYDATA_TRANSFORMATION, INCOMPLETE_CURSOR,
       TOP_LEVEL_RPI_CURSOR, DIFFERENT_LONG_LENGTH, LOGICAL_STANDBY_APPLY,
       DIFF_CALL_DURN, BIND_UACS_DIFF, PLSQL_CMP_SWITCHS_DIFF,
       CURSOR_PARTS_MISMATCH, STB_OBJECT_MISMATCH,CROSSEDITION_TRIGGER_MISMATCH,
       PQ_SLAVE_MISMATCH, TOP_LEVEL_DDL_MISMATCH, MULTI_PX_MISMATCH,
       BIND_PEEKED_PQ_MISMATCH, MV_REWRITE_MISMATCH, ROLL_INVALID_MISMATCH,
       OPTIMIZER_MODE_MISMATCH, PX_MISMATCH, MV_STALEOBJ_MISMATCH,
       FLASHBACK_TABLE_MISMATCH, LITREP_COMP_MISMATCH,
       PLSQL_DEBUG,LOAD_OPTIMIZER_STATS,ACL_MISMATCH,FLASHBACK_ARCHIVE_MISMATCH,
       LOCK_USER_SCHEMA_FAILED,REMOTE_MAPPING_MISMATCH,LOAD_RUNTIME_HEAP_FAILED,
       HASH_MATCH_FAILED, PURGED_CURSOR, BIND_LENGTH_UPGRADEABLE
from   GV$SQL_SHARED_CURSOR
where  inst_id = USERENV('Instance');
```

View Name: **GV$SQL_SHARED_MEMORY**

```
select /*+use_nl(h,c)*/ c.inst_id,kglnaobj,kglfnobj,kglnahsh, kglobt03,kglobhd6,
       rtrim(substr(ksmchcom,1,instr(ksmchcom, ':', 1, 1) - 1)),
       ltrim(substr(ksmchcom,-(length(ksmchcom) - (instr(ksmchcom,':',1,1)))),
       (length(ksmchcom) - (instr(ksmchcom,':',1,1)) + 1))),ksmchcom,ksmchptr,
       ksmchsiz,ksmchcls,ksmchtyp,ksmchpar
from   x$kglcursor c, x$ksmhp h
where  ksmchds = kglobhd6
and    kglhdadr != kglhdpar;
```

View Name: **V$SQL_SHARED_MEMORY**

```
select SQL_TEXT,SQL_FULLTEXT,HASH_VALUE,SQL_ID,HEAP_DESC,STRUCTURE,FUNCTION,
       CHUNK_COM,CHUNK_PTR,CHUNK_SIZE,ALLOC_CLASS,CHUNK_TYPE,SUBHEAP_DESC
from   GV$SQL_SHARED_MEMORY
where  inst_id = USERENV('Instance');
```

View Name: **GV$SQL_WORKAREA**

```
SELECT INST_ID,PHADD_QKSMM, HASHV_QKSMM, SQLID_QKSMM, CHILDNO_QKSMM, WADDR_QKSMM,
       substr(OPERTYPE_QKSMM, 1, 20),
       to_number(decode(OPERTID_QKSMM, 65535, NULL, OPERTID_QKSMM)),
       substr(SIZEPOLICY_QKSMM, 1, 10),OPTIMAL_QKSMM * 1024, ONEPASS_QKSMM * 1024,
       LASTMEM_QKSMM * 1024,substr(decode(LASTPASS_QKSMM, 0, 'OPTIMAL',
       to_char(LASTPASS_QKSMM) || 'PASS' || decode(LASTPASS_QKSMM,1,'','ES')),1,10),
       LASTDOP_QKSMM,(OPTACTS_QKSMM + SPAACTS_QKSMM + MPAACTS_QKSMM),OPTACTS_QKSMM,
       SPAACTS_QKSMM,MPAACTS_QKSMM,ATIME_QKSMM,
```

```
        to_number(decode(MAXTSEG_QKSMM,0,NULL,MAXTSEG_QKSMM*1024)),
        to_number(decode(LASTTSEG_QKSMM,0,NULL,LASTTSEG_QKSMM*1024))
from    X$QKSMMWDS;
```

View Name: V$SQL_WORKAREA

```
select ADDRESS,HASH_VALUE,SQL_ID,CHILD_NUMBER,WORKAREA_ADDRESS,OPERATION_TYPE,
       OPERATION_ID,POLICY,ESTIMATED_OPTIMAL_SIZE,ESTIMATED_ONEPASS_SIZE,
       LAST_MEMORY_USED,LAST_EXECUTION,LAST_DEGREE,TOTAL_EXECUTIONS,OPTIMAL_EXECUTIONS,
       ONEPASS_EXECUTIONS,MULTIPASSES_EXECUTIONS,ACTIVE_TIME,MAX_TEMPSEG_SIZE,
       LAST_TEMPSEG_SIZE
from   GV$SQL_WORKAREA
where  inst_id = USERENV('Instance');
```

View Name: GV$SQL_WORKAREA_ACTIVE

```
select INST_ID,SQLHASHV,SQLID,EXECSTA,
       decode(execid, 0, to_number(NULL), execid),
       WADDR,substr(OPER_TYPE,1,20),
       to_number(decode(OPID,65535,NULL,OPID)),
       substr(decode(bitand(MEM_FLAGS,1),0,'MANUAL','AUTO'),1,6),SID,
       to_number(decode(QCINSTID,65535,NULL,QCINSTID)),
       to_number(decode(QCSID,65535,NULL,QCSID)),ATIME,WA_SIZE * 1024,
       to_number(decode(bitand(MEM_FLAGS,1),0,NULL,EXP_SIZE*1024)),
       ACTUAL_MEM * 1024,MAX_MEM * 1024,PASSES,
       to_number(decode(KTSSOTSN,'',NULL,KTSSOSIZE*1024)),
       decode(KTSSOTSN,'',NULL,KTSSOTSN),
       to_number(decode(KTSSOTSN,'',NULL,KTSSORFNO)),
       to_number(decode(KTSSOTSN,'',NULL,KTSSOBNO))
from   x$qesmmiwt;
```

View Name: V$SQL_WORKAREA_ACTIVE

```
select SQL_HASH_VALUE,SQL_ID, SQL_EXEC_START, SQL_EXEC_ID,
       WORKAREA_ADDRESS,OPERATION_TYPE,OPERATION_ID,POLICY,SID,
       QCINST_ID,QCSID,ACTIVE_TIME,WORK_AREA_SIZE,EXPECTED_SIZE,ACTUAL_MEM_USED,
       MAX_MEM_USED,NUMBER_PASSES,TEMPSEG_SIZE,TABLESPACE,SEGRFNO#,SEGBLK#
from   GV$SQL_WORKAREA_ACTIVE
where  INST_ID = USERENV('Instance');
```

View Name: GV$STATISTICS_LEVEL

```
select inst_id,name,description,
       decode(session_status,0,'DISABLED',1,'ENABLED','UNKNOWN'),
       decode(system_status,0,'DISABLED',1,'ENABLED', 'UNKNOWN'),
       decode(activation_level,0,'BASIC',1,'TYPICAL','ALL'),
       view_name,decode(session_changeable,0,'NO','YES')
from   x$prmsltyx;
```

View Name: **V$STATISTICS_LEVEL**

```
select statistics_name,description,session_status,system_status,activation_level,
       statistics_view_name,session_settable
from   gv$statistics_level
where  inst_id = USERENV('Instance');
```

View Name: **GV$SUBCACHE**

```
select inst_id,kglnaown,kglnaobj,kglobtyp,kqlfshpn,kqlfscid,kqlfsscc,kqlfsesp,
       kqlfsasp, kqlfsusp
from   x$kqlset;
```

View Name: **V$SUBCACHE**

```
select OWNER_NAME,NAME,TYPE,HEAP_NUM,CACHE_ID,CACHE_CNT,HEAP_SZ,HEAP_ALOC,HEAP_USED
from   GV$SUBCACHE
where  inst_id = USERENV('Instance');
```

View Name: **GV$SYSSTAT**

```
select inst_id,indx,ksusdnam,ksusdcls,ksusgstv,ksusdhsh
from   x$ksusgsta;
```

View Name: **V$SYSSTAT**

```
select STATISTIC#,NAME,CLASS,VALUE,STAT_ID
from   GV$SYSSTAT
where  inst_id = USERENV('Instance');
```

View Name: **GV$SYSTEM_CURSOR_CACHE**

```
select inst_id,kgicsopn,kgicshit,decode(kgicsopn,0,1,kgicshit/kgicsopn)
from   x$kgics;
```

View Name: **V$SYSTEM_CURSOR_CACHE**

```
select OPENS,HITS,HIT_RATIO
from   GV$SYSTEM_CURSOR_CACHE
where  inst_id = USERENV('Instance');
```

View Name: **GV$SYSTEM_EVENT**

```
select d.inst_id, d.kslednam, (s.ksleswts_un + s.ksleswts_fg + s.ksleswts_bg),
       (s.kslestmo_un + s.kslestmo_fg + s.kslestmo_bg),
        round((s.kslestim_un + s.kslestim_fg + s.kslestim_bg)/10000),
        round((s.kslestim_un + s.kslestim_fg + s.kslestim_bg)/
       (10000 * (s.ksleswts_un + s.ksleswts_fg + s.ksleswts_bg)), 2),
       (s.kslestim_un + s.kslestim_fg + s.kslestim_bg), s.ksleswts_fg,
        s.kslestmo_fg, round(s.kslestim_fg/10000),
        round(s.kslestim_fg/decode(s.ksleswts_fg, 0, 1, 10000 * s.ksleswts_fg), 2),
        s.kslestim_fg, d.ksledhash, d.ksledclassid, d.ksledclass#,
        d.ksledclass
```

```
from    x$kslei s, x$ksled d
where (s.ksleswts_un > 0 or s.ksleswts_fg > 0 or s.ksleswts_bg > 0)
and     s.indx = d.indx;
```

View Name: V$SYSTEM_EVENT

```
select event,total_waits,total_timeouts,time_waited,average_wait,time_waited_micro,
       total_waits_fg, total_timeouts_fg, time_waited_fg,
       average_wait_fg, time_waited_micro_fg,
       event_id, wait_class_id, wait_class#, wait_class
from    gv$system_event
where  inst_id = USERENV('Instance');
```

View Name: GV$SYSTEM_PARAMETER

```
select x.inst_id,x.indx+1,ksppinm,ksppity,ksppstvl, ksppstdvl,ksppstdf,
       decode(bitand(ksppiflg/256,1),1,'TRUE','FALSE'),
       decode(bitand(ksppiflg/65536,3),1,'IMMEDIATE',
       2,'DEFERRED', 3,'IMMEDIATE','FALSE'),
       decode(bitand(ksppiflg,4),4,'FALSE', decode(bitand(ksppiflg/65536,3),
       0, 'FALSE', 'TRUE')), decode(bitand(ksppstvf,7),1,'MODIFIED','FALSE'),
       decode(bitand(ksppstvf,2),2,'TRUE','FALSE'),
       decode(bitand(ksppilrmflg/64, 1), 1, 'TRUE', 'FALSE'),
       decode(bitand(ksppilrmflg/268435456, 1), 1, 'TRUE', 'FALSE'),
       ksppdesc, ksppstcmnt, ksppihash
from    x$ksppi x, x$ksppsv y
where (x.indx = y.indx)
and    bitand(ksppiflg,268435456) = 0
and   ((translate(ksppinm,'_','#') not like '##%')
and   ((translate(ksppinm,'_','#') not like '#%')
or     (ksppstdf = 'FALSE')
or     (bitand(ksppstvf,5) > 0)));
```

View Name: V$SYSTEM_PARAMETER

```
select NUM,NAME,TYPE,VALUE,DISPLAY_VALUE,ISDEFAULT,ISSES_MODIFIABLE,
       ISSYS_MODIFIABLE,ISINSTANCE_MODIFIABLE,ISMODIFIED,ISADJUSTED,
       ISDEPRECATED, ISBASIC, DESCRIPTION,UPDATE_COMMENT,HASH
from    GV$SYSTEM_PARAMETER
where  inst_id = USERENV('Instance');
```

View Name: GV$SYSTEM_PARAMETER2

```
select x.inst_id,kspftctxpn,ksppinm,ksppity,kspftctxvl,   kspftctxdvl,
kspftctxdf,
       decode(bitand(ksppiflg/256,1),1,'TRUE','FALSE'),   decode(bitand
       (ksppiflg/65536,3),1,'IMMEDIATE',2,'DEFERRED', 3,'IMMEDIATE','FALSE'),
       decode(bitand(ksppiflg,4),4,'FALSE',
       decode(bitand(ksppiflg/65536,3), 0, 'FALSE', 'TRUE')),
       decode(bitand(kspftctxvf,7),1,'MODIFIED','FALSE'),
       decode(bitand(kspftctxvf,2),2,'TRUE','FALSE'),
       decode(bitand(ksppilrmflg/64, 1), 1, 'TRUE', 'FALSE'),
       decode(bitand(ksppilrmflg/268435456, 1), 1, 'TRUE', 'FALSE'),
       ksppdesc, kspftctxvn, kspftctxct
```

```
from    x$ksppi x, x$ksppsv2 y
where   ((x.indx+1) = kspftctxpn)
and     ((translate(ksppinm,'_','#') not like '##%')
and     (translate(ksppinm,'_','#') not like '#%'
or      (kspftctxdf = 'FALSE')
or      (bitand(kspftctxvf,5) > 0)));
```

View Name: V$SYSTEM_PARAMETER2

```
select NUM,NAME,TYPE,VALUE,DISPLAY_VALUE,ISDEFAULT,ISSES_MODIFIABLE,
        ISSYS_MODIFIABLE,ISINSTANCE_MODIFIABLE,ISMODIFIED,ISADJUSTED,ISDEPRECATED,
        ISBASIC, DESCRIPTION,ORDINAL,UPDATE_COMMENT
from    GV$SYSTEM_PARAMETER2
where   inst_id = USERENV('Instance');
```

View Name: GV$TABLESPACE

```
select inst_id,tstsn,tsnam,decode(bitand(tsflg, 1+2), 1, 'NO', 2,'NO','YES'),
        decode(bitand(tsflg, 4), 4,'YES','NO'),
        decode(bitand(tsflg, 8), 8,'NO','YES'),
        decode(bitand(tsflg, 16+32), 16, 'ON', 32, 'OFF', to_char(null))
from    x$kccts
where   tstsn != -1;
```

View Name: V$TABLESPACE

```
select TS#,NAME,INCLUDED_IN_DATABASE_BACKUP,BIGFILE,FLASHBACK_ON,ENCRYPT_IN_BACKUP
from    GV$TABLESPACE
where   inst_id = USERENV('Instance');
```

View Name: GV$TRANSACTION

```
select inst_id,ktcxbxba,kxidusn,kxidslt,kxidsqn,ktcxbkfn,kubablk,kubaseq,kubarec,
        decode(ktcxbsta,0,'IDLE',1,'COLLECTING',2,'PREPARED',3,'COMMITTED',4,
        'HEURISTIC ABORT',5,'HEURISTIC COMMIT',6,'HEURISTIC DAMAGE',7,'TIMEOUT',9,
        'INACTIVE',10,'ACTIVE',11,'PTX PREPARED',12,'PTX COMMITTED','UNKNOWN'),
        ktcxbstm,ktcxbssb,ktcxbssw,ktcxbsen,ktcxbsfl,ktcxbsbk,ktcxbssq,ktcxbsrc,
        ktcxbses,ktcxbflg, decode(bitand(ktcxbflg,16),0,'NO','YES'),
        decode(bitand(ktcxbflg,32),0,'NO','YES'),decode(bitand(ktcxbflg,64),0,
        'NO','YES'), decode(bitand(ktcxbflg,8388608),0,'NO','YES'),ktcxbnam,
        ktcxbpus,ktcxbpsl,ktcxbpsq,ktcxbpxu,ktcxbpxs,ktcxbpxq,ktcxbdsb,ktcxbdsw,
        ktcxbubk,ktcxburc,ktcxblio,ktcxbpio,ktcxbcrg,ktcxbcrc,
        to_date(ktcxbstm,'MM/DD/RR HH24:MI:SS','NLS_CALENDAR=Gregorian'),
        ktcxbdsb, ktcxbdsw,  ktcxbssc, ktcxbdsc, ktcxbxid, ktcxbpid, ktcxbpxi
from    x$ktcxb
where   bitand(ksspaflg,1)!=0
and     bitand(ktcxbflg,2)!=0;
```

View Name: V$TRANSACTION

```
select ADDR,XIDUSN,XIDSLOT,XIDSQN,UBAFIL,UBABLK,UBASQN,UBAREC,STATUS,START_TIME,
        START_SCNB,START_SCNW,START_UEXT,START_UBAFIL,START_UBABLK,START_UBASQN,
```

```
           START_UBAREC,SES_ADDR,FLAG,SPACE,RECURSIVE,NOUNDO,PTX,NAME,PRV_XIDUSN,
           PRV_XIDSLT,PRV_XIDSQN,PTX_XIDUSN,PTX_XIDSLT,PTX_XIDSQN,"DSCN-B","DSCN-W",
           USED_UBLK,USED_UREC,LOG_IO,PHY_IO,CR_GET,CR_CHANGE, START_DATE, DSCN_BASE,
           DSCN_WRAP, START_SCN, DEPENDENT_SCN, XID, PRV_XID, PTX_XID
from       gv$transaction
where      inst_id = USERENV('Instance');
```

View Name: GV$TRANSACTION_ENQUEUE

```
select s.inst_id,l.ktcxbxba,
       l.ktcxblkp,s.ksusenum,r.ksqrsidt,r.ksqrsid1,r.ksqrsid2,l.ksqlkmod,l.ksqlkreq,
       l.ksqlkctim,l.ksqlklblk
from    x$ktcxb l,x$ksuse s,x$ksqrs r
where   l.ksqlkses=s.addr
and     bitand(l.ksspaflg,1)!=0
and     (l.ksqlkmod!=0)
or      l.ksqlkreq!=0)
and     l.ksqlkres=r.addr;
```

View Name: V$TRANSACTION_ENQUEUE

```
select ADDR,KADDR,SID,TYPE,ID1,ID2,LMODE,REQUEST,CTIME,BLOCK
from    GV$TRANSACTION_ENQUEUE
where   inst_id = USERENV('Instance');
```

View Name: GV$VERSION

```
select inst_id,banner
from    x$version;
```

View Name: V$VERSION

```
select BANNER
from    GV$VERSION
where   inst_id = USERENV('Instance');
```

View Name: GV$WAITSTAT

```
select inst_id,decode(indx,1,'data block',2,'sort block',3,'save undo block',4,
       'segment header',5,'save undo header',6,'free list',7,'extent map',8,
       '1st level bmb',9,'2nd level bmb',10,'3rd level bmb', 11,'bitmap block',12,
       'bitmap index block',13,'file header block',14,'unused',15,
       'system undo header',16,'system undo block', 17,'undo header',18,
       'undo block'), count,time
from    x$kcbwait
where   indx!=0;
```

View Name: V$WAITSTAT

```
select class,count,time
from    gv$waitstat
where   inst_id = USERENV('Instance');
```

View Name: GV$_LOCK

```
select USERENV('Instance'),laddr,kaddr,saddr,raddr,lmode,request,ctime,block
from   v$_lock1
union all
select inst_id,addr,ksqlkadr,ksqlkses,ksqlkres,ksqlkmod,ksqlkreq,ksqlkctim,ksqlklblk
from   x$ktadm
where  bitand(kssobflg,1)!=0
and    (ksqlkmod!=0 or ksqlkreq!=0)
union all
select inst_id,addr,ksqlkadr,ksqlkses,ksqlkres,ksqlkmod,ksqlkreq,ksqlkctim,ksqlklblk
from   x$ktatrfil
where  bitand(kssobflg,1)!=0
and    (ksqlkmod!=0 or ksqlkreq!=0)
union all
select inst_id,addr,ksqlkadr,ksqlkses,ksqlkres,ksqlkmod,ksqlkreq,ksqlkctim,ksqlklblk
from   x$ktatrfsl
where  bitand(kssobflg,1)!=0
and    (ksqlkmod!=0 or ksqlkreq!=0)
union all
select inst_id,addr,ksqlkadr,ksqlkses,ksqlkres,ksqlkmod,ksqlkreq,ksqlkctim,ksqlklblk
from   x$ktatl
where  bitand(kssobflg,1)!=0
and    (ksqlkmod!=0 or ksqlkreq!=0)
union all
select inst_id,addr,ksqlkadr,ksqlkses,ksqlkres,ksqlkmod,ksqlkreq, ksqlkctim,ksqlklblk
from   x$ktstusc
where  bitand(kssobflg,1)!=0
and    (ksqlkmod!=0 or ksqlkreq!=0)
union all
select inst_id,addr,ksqlkadr,ksqlkses,ksqlkres,ksqlkmod,ksqlkreq, ksqlkctim,ksqlklblk
from   x$ktstuss
where  bitand(kssobflg,1)!=0
and    (ksqlkmod!=0 or ksqlkreq!=0)
union all
select inst_id,addr,ksqlkadr,ksqlkses,ksqlkres,ksqlkmod,ksqlkreq,ksqlkctim,ksqlklblk
from   x$ktstusg
where  bitand(kssobflg,1)!=0
and (ksqlkmod!=0 or ksqlkreq!=0)
union all
select inst_id,ktcxbxba,ktcxblkp,ksqlkses,ksqlkres,ksqlkmod,ksqlkreq,ksqlkctim,ksqlklblk
from   x$ktcxb
where  bitand(ksspaflg,1)!=0
and    (ksqlkmod!=0 or ksqlkreq!=0);
```

View Name: V$_LOCK

```
select LADDR,KADDR,SADDR,RADDR,LMODE,REQUEST,CTIME,BLOCK
from   GV$_LOCK
where  inst_id = USERENV('Instance');
```

View Name: GV$_LOCK1

```
select inst_id,addr,ksqlkadr,ksqlkses,ksqlkres,ksqlkmod,ksqlkreq,ksqlkctim,ksqlklblk
from   x$kdnssf
where  bitand(kssobflg,1)!=0
and    (ksqlkmod!=0 or ksqlkreq!=0)
union all
```

```
select inst_id,addr,ksqlkadr,ksqlkses,ksqlkres,ksqlkmod,ksqlkreq,ksqlkctim,ksqlklblk
from   x$ksqeq
where  bitand(kssobflg,1)!=0
and    (ksqlkmod!=0 or ksqlkreq!=0);
```

View Name: V$_LOCK1

```
select LADDR,KADDR,SADDR,RADDR,LMODE,REQUEST,CTIME,BLOCK
from   GV$_LOCK1
where  inst_id = USERENV('Instance');
```

APPENDIX
C

The X$ Tables (DBA)

T he X$ tables are usually not mentioned or talked about in many Oracle books or even in the Oracle user community. For this reason, I am including them in this book as one of the few references available (Chapter 13 contains *many* X$ queries). There are 945 X$ tables in 11gR2 (11.2.0.1.0). There were 613 X$ tables in 10gR2 (10.2.0.1) and only 394 in Oracle 9i Release 2 (9.2.0.1.0). The X$ tables vary in structure and number, depending on the database version and release used. Run the queries on your version of the database to get the number of views and structure for your specific version. Areas covered in this appendix include:

- A list of all Oracle 11gR2 (11.2.0.1.0) X$ tables (945 total)

- A list of all Oracle 11gR2 (11.2.0.1.0) X$ indexed columns (628 total)

- The Oracle 11gR2 (11.2.0.1.0) V$ views cross-referenced to the X$ tables

Oracle 11gR2 X$ Tables Ordered by Name

Here is the Oracle 11g query to get the following listing:

```
select      name
from        v$fixed_table
where       name like 'X%'
order by    name;
```

The following table contains the entire 945 Oracle 11gR2 11.2.0.1.0 X$ tables (ordered by name):

NAME		
X$ABSTRACT_LOB	X$DBKH_CHECK_PARAM	X$DIAG_HM_INFO
X$ACTIVECKPT	X$DBKINCMETCFG	X$DIAG_HM_MESSAGE
X$ASH	X$DBKINCMETINFO	X$DIAG_HM_RECOMMENDATION
X$BH	X$DBKINCMETSUMMARY	X$DIAG_HM_RUN
X$BUFFER	X$DBKINFO	X$DIAG_INCCKEY
X$BUFFER2	X$DBKRECO	X$DIAG_INCIDENT
X$BUFFERED_PUBLISHERS	X$DBKRUN	X$DIAG_INCIDENT_FILE
X$BUFFERED_QUEUES	X$DGLPARAM	X$DIAG_INC_METER_CONFIG
X$BUFFERED_SUBSCRIBERS	X$DGLXDAT	X$DIAG_INC_METER_IMPT_DEF
X$CELL_NAME	X$DIAG_ADR_CONTROL	X$DIAG_INC_METER_INFO
X$CKPTBUF	X$DIAG_ADR_INVALIDATION	X$DIAG_INC_METER_PK_IMPTS
X$CONTEXT	X$DIAG_ALERT_EXT	X$DIAG_INC_METER_SUMMARY
X$DBGALERTEXT	X$DIAG_AMS_XACTION	X$DIAG_INFO
X$DBGDIREXT	X$DIAG_DDE_USER_ACTION	X$DIAG_IPS_CONFIGURATION
X$DBGRICX	X$DIAG_DDE_USER_ACTION_DEF	X$DIAG_IPS_FILE_COPY_LOG
X$DBGRIFX	X$DIAG_DDE_USR_ACT_PARAM	X$DIAG_IPS_FILE_METADATA
X$DBGRIKX	X$DIAG_DDE_USR_ACT_PARAM_DEF	X$DIAG_IPS_PACKAGE
X$DBGRIPX	X$DIAG_DDE_USR_INC_ACT_MAP	X$DIAG_IPS_PACKAGE_FILE
X$DBKECE	X$DIAG_DDE_USR_INC_TYPE	X$DIAG_IPS_PACKAGE_HISTORY
X$DBKEFAFC	X$DIAG_DIAGV_INCIDENT	X$DIAG_IPS_PACKAGE_INCIDENT
X$DBKEFDEAFC	X$DIAG_DIR_EXT	X$DIAG_IPS_PKG_UNPACK_HIST
X$DBKEFEFC	X$DIAG_EM_DIAG_JOB	X$DIAG_IPS_REMOTE_PACKAGE
X$DBKEFIEFC	X$DIAG_EM_TARGET_INFO	X$DIAG_PICKLEERR
X$DBKFDG	X$DIAG_EM_USER_ACTIVITY	X$DIAG_PROBLEM
X$DBKFSET	X$DIAG_HM_FDG_SET	X$DIAG_RELMD_EXT
X$DBKH_CHECK	X$DIAG_HM_FINDING	X$DIAG_SWEEPERR

NAME

X$DIAG_VEM_USER_ACTLOG	X$GIMSA	X$KCBWH
X$DIAG_VEM_USER_ACTLOG1	X$GLOBALCONTEXT	X$KCCACM
X$DIAG_VHM_RUN	X$HOFP	X$KCCAGF
X$DIAG_VIEW	X$HS_SESSION	X$KCCAL
X$DIAG_VIEWCOL	X$INSTANCE_CACHE_TRANSFER	X$KCCBF
X$DIAG_VINCIDENT	X$IR_MANUAL_OPTION	X$KCCBI
X$DIAG_VINCIDENT_FILE	X$IR_REPAIR_OPTION	X$KCCBL
X$DIAG_VINC_METER_INFO	X$IR_REPAIR_STEP	X$KCCBLKCOR
X$DIAG_VIPS_FILE_COPY_LOG	X$IR_RS_PARAM	X$KCCBP
X$DIAG_VIPS_FILE_METADATA	X$IR_WF_PARAM	X$KCCBS
X$DIAG_VIPS_PACKAGE_FILE	X$IR_WORKING_FAILURE_SET	X$KCCCC
X$DIAG_VIPS_PACKAGE_HISTORY	X$IR_WORKING_REPAIR_SET	X$KCCCF
X$DIAG_VIPS_PACKAGE_MAIN_INT	X$IR_WR_PARAM	X$KCCCP
X$DIAG_VIPS_PACKAGE_SIZE	X$JOXDRC	X$KCCDC
X$DIAG_VIPS_PKG_FILE	X$JOXDRR	X$KCCDFHIST
X$DIAG_VIPS_PKG_INC_CAND	X$JOXFC	X$KCCDI
X$DIAG_VIPS_PKG_INC_DTL	X$JOXFD	X$KCCDI2
X$DIAG_VIPS_PKG_INC_DTL1	X$JOXFM	X$KCCDL
X$DIAG_VIPS_PKG_MAIN_PROBLEM	X$JOXFR	X$KCCFC
X$DIAG_VNOT_EXIST_INCIDENT	X$JOXFS	X$KCCFE
X$DIAG_VPROBLEM	X$JOXFT	X$KCCFLE
X$DIAG_VPROBLEM1	X$JOXMAG	X$KCCFN
X$DIAG_VPROBLEM2	X$JOXMEX	X$KCCIC
X$DIAG_VPROBLEM_BUCKET	X$JOXMFD	X$KCCIRT
X$DIAG_VPROBLEM_BUCKET1	X$JOXMIC	X$KCCLE
X$DIAG_VPROBLEM_BUCKET_COUNT	X$JOXMIF	X$KCCLH
X$DIAG_VPROBLEM_INT	X$JOXMMD	X$KCCNRS
X$DIAG_VPROBLEM_LASTINC	X$JOXMOB	X$KCCOR
X$DIAG_VSHOWCATVIEW	X$JOXOBJ	X$KCCPA
X$DIAG_VSHOWINCB	X$JOXREF	X$KCCPD
X$DIAG_VSHOWINCB_I	X$JOXRSV	X$KCCRDI
X$DIAG_VTEST_EXISTS	X$JOXSCD	X$KCCRL
X$DIAG_V_ACTINC	X$JSKJOBQ	X$KCCRM
X$DIAG_V_ACTPROB	X$JSKSLV	X$KCCRS
X$DIAG_V_INCCOUNT	X$K2GTE	X$KCCRSP
X$DIAG_V_INCFCOUNT	X$K2GTE2	X$KCCRSR
X$DIAG_V_INC_METER_INFO_PROB	X$KAUVRSTAT	X$KCCRT
X$DIAG_V_IPSPRBCNT	X$KCBBES	X$KCCSL
X$DIAG_V_IPSPRBCNT1	X$KCBBF	X$KCCTF
X$DIAG_V_NFCINC	X$KCBBHS	X$KCCTIR
X$DIAG_V_SWPERRCOUNT	X$KCBDBK	X$KCCTS
X$DNFS_CHANNELS	X$KCBFWAIT	X$KCFIO
X$DNFS_FILES	X$KCBKPFS	X$KCFIOFCHIST
X$DNFS_HIST	X$KCBKWRL	X$KCFIOHIST
X$DNFS_META	X$KCBLDRHIST	X$KCFISCAP
X$DNFS_SERVERS	X$KCBLSC	X$KCFISOSS
X$DNFS_STATS	X$KCBMMAV	X$KCFISOSSC
X$DRA_FAILURE	X$KCBOBH	X$KCFISOSSN
X$DRA_FAILURE_CHECK	X$KCBOQH	X$KCFISOSST
X$DRA_FAILURE_CHECK_MAP	X$KCBPRFH	X$KCFISTCAP
X$DRA_FAILURE_PARAM	X$KCBSC	X$KCFISTSA
X$DRA_FAILURE_PARENT_MAP	X$KCBSDS	X$KCFTIO
X$DRA_FAILURE_REPAIR	X$KCBSH	X$KCLCRST
X$DRA_FAILURE_REPAIR_MAP	X$KCBSW	X$KCLCURST
X$DRA_REPAIR	X$KCBTEK	X$KCLDELTAST
X$DRA_REPAIR_PARAM	X$KCBUWHY	X$KCLFX
X$DRC	X$KCBVBL	X$KCLLS
X$DRM_HISTORY	X$KCBWAIT	X$KCLQN
X$DUAL	X$KCBWBPD	X$KCLRCVST
X$ESTIMATED_MTTR	X$KCBWDS	X$KCPXPL

```
NAME
------------------------------------------------------------------------------------
X$KCRFDEBUG            X$KEWMAFMV             X$KFVACFSV
X$KCRFSTRAND           X$KEWMDRMV             X$KFVOL
X$KCRFWS               X$KEWMDSM              X$KFVOLSTAT
X$KCRFX                X$KEWMEVMV             X$KFZGDR
X$KCRMF                X$KEWMFLMV             X$KFZUAGR
X$KCRMT                X$KEWMGSM              X$KFZUDR
X$KCRMX                X$KEWMIOFMV            X$KGHLU
X$KCRRARCH             X$KEWMRMGMV            X$KGICS
X$KCRRASTATS           X$KEWMRSM              X$KGLAU
X$KCRRDSTAT            X$KEWMRWMV             X$KGLBODY
X$KCRRLNS              X$KEWMSEMV             X$KGLCLUSTER
X$KCRRNHG              X$KEWMSMDV             X$KGLCURSOR
X$KCTICW               X$KEWMSVCMV            X$KGLCURSOR_CHILD
X$KCTLAX               X$KEWMWCRMV            X$KGLCURSOR_CHILD_SQLID
X$KCVFH                X$KEWMWPCMV            X$KGLCURSOR_CHILD_SQLIDPH
X$KCVFHALL             X$KEWRATTRNEW          X$KGLDP
X$KCVFHMRR             X$KEWRATTRSTALE        X$KGLINDEX
X$KCVFHONL             X$KEWRSQLCRIT          X$KGLJMEM
X$KCVFHTMP             X$KEWRSQLIDTAB         X$KGLJSIM
X$KDLT                 X$KEWRTB               X$KGLLK
X$KDLU_STAT            X$KEWRTOPTENV          X$KGLMEM
X$KDNSSF               X$KEWRTSEGSTAT         X$KGLNA
X$KDXHS                X$KEWRTSQLPLAN         X$KGLNA1
X$KDXST                X$KEWRTSQLTEXT         X$KGLOB
X$KEACMDN              X$KEWSSESV             X$KGLOBXML
X$KEAFDGN              X$KEWSSMAP             X$KGLPN
X$KEAOBJT              X$KEWSSVCV             X$KGLRD
X$KECPDENTRY           X$KEWSSYSV             X$KGLSIM
X$KECPRT               X$KEWXOCF              X$KGLSN
X$KEHECLMAP            X$KEWX_LOBS            X$KGLST
X$KEHEVTMAP            X$KEWX_SEGMENTS        X$KGLTABLE
X$KEHF                 X$KFALS                X$KGLTR
X$KEHOSMAP             X$KFBH                 X$KGLTRIGGER
X$KEHPRMMAP            X$KFCBH                X$KGLXS
X$KEHR                 X$KFCCE                X$KGSCC
X$KEHRP                X$KFCLLE               X$KGSKASP
X$KEHR_CHILD           X$KFDAT                X$KGSKCFT
X$KEHSQT               X$KFDDD                X$KGSKCP
X$KEHSYSMAP            X$KFDFS                X$KGSKDOPP
X$KEHTIMMAP            X$KFDPARTNER           X$KGSKNCFT
X$KELRSGA              X$KFDSK                X$KGSKPFT
X$KELRTD               X$KFDSK_STAT           X$KGSKPP
X$KELRXMR              X$KFENV                X$KGSKQUEP
X$KELTGSD              X$KFFIL                X$KGSKSCS
X$KELTOSD              X$KFFOF                X$KGSKTE
X$KELTSD               X$KFFXP                X$KGSKTO
X$KESPLAN              X$KFGBRB               X$KGSKVFT
X$KESSPAMET            X$KFGBRW               X$KJBL
X$KESWXMON             X$KFGMG                X$KJBLFX
X$KESWXMON_PLAN        X$KFGRP                X$KJBR
X$KETCL                X$KFGRP_STAT           X$KJBRFX
X$KETOP                X$KFKID                X$KJCTFR
X$KETTG                X$KFKLIB               X$KJCTFRI
X$KEWAM                X$KFKLSOD              X$KJCTFS
X$KEWASH               X$KFMDGRP              X$KJDRHV
X$KEWECLS              X$KFNCL                X$KJDRMAFNSTATS
X$KEWEFXT              X$KFNSDSKIOST          X$KJDRMHVSTATS
X$KEWEPCS              X$KFRC                 X$KJDRMREQ
X$KEWESMAS             X$KFTMTA               X$KJDRPCMHV
X$KEWESMS              X$KFVACFS              X$KJDRPCMPF
                       X$KFVACFSS             X$KJICVT
```

```
NAME
----------------------------------------------------------------------------------
X$KJILFT                    X$KOCST                    X$KRVXOP
X$KJILKFT                   X$KPONESTAT                X$KRVXSV
X$KJIRFT                    X$KPOQSTA                  X$KRVXTHRD
X$KJISFT                    X$KPPLCC_INFO              X$KRVXTX
X$KJITRFT                   X$KPPLCC_STATS             X$KRVXWARNV
X$KJLEQFP                   X$KPPLCONN_INFO            X$KSBDD
X$KJMDDP                    X$KPPLCP_STATS             X$KSBDP
X$KJMSDP                    X$KQDPG                    X$KSBFT
X$KJPNPX                    X$KQFCO                    X$KSBSRVDT
X$KJREQFP                   X$KQFDT                    X$KSBTABACT
X$KJXM                      X$KQFOPT                   X$KSDAF
X$KJZNHANGS                 X$KQFP                     X$KSDAFT
X$KJZNHANGSES               X$KQFSZ                    X$KSDHNG_CACHE_HISTORY
X$KJZSIWTEVT                X$KQFTA                    X$KSDHNG_CHAINS
X$KKCNRSTAT                 X$KQFTVRTTST0              X$KSDHNG_SESSION_BLOCKERS
X$KKKICR                    X$KQFVI                    X$KSFDFTYP
X$KKOCS_HISTOGRAM           X$KQFVT                    X$KSFDSTCG
X$KKOCS_SELECTIVITY         X$KQLFBC                   X$KSFDSTCMP
X$KKOCS_STATISTICS          X$KQLFSQCE                 X$KSFDSTFILE
X$KKSAI                     X$KQLFXPL                  X$KSFDSTHIST
X$KKSBV                     X$KQLSET                   X$KSFDSTTHIST
X$KKSCS                     X$KQRFP                    X$KSFMCOMPL
X$KKSSQLSTAT                X$KQRFS                    X$KSFMELEM
X$KKSSQLSTAT_PLAN_HASH      X$KQRPD                    X$KSFMEXTELEM
X$KKSSRD                    X$KQRSD                    X$KSFMFILE
X$KLCIE                     X$KQRST                    X$KSFMFILEEXT
X$KLPT                      X$KRASGA                   X$KSFMIOST
X$KMCQS                     X$KRBAFF                   X$KSFMLIB
X$KMCVC                     X$KRBMCA                   X$KSFMSUBELEM
X$KMGSBSADV                 X$KRBMROT                  X$KSFQDVNT
X$KMGSBSMEMADV              X$KRBMRST                  X$KSFQP
X$KMGSCT                    X$KRBMSFT                  X$KSFVQST
X$KMGSOP                    X$KRBZA                    X$KSFVSL
X$KMGSTFR                   X$KRCBIT                   X$KSFVSTA
X$KMMDI                     X$KRCCDE                   X$KSIMAT
X$KMMDP                     X$KRCCDR                   X$KSIMAV
X$KMMHST                    X$KRCCDS                   X$KSIMSI
X$KMMNV                     X$KRCEXT                   X$KSIRESTYP
X$KMMRD                     X$KRCFBH                   X$KSIRGD
X$KMMSAS                    X$KRCFDE                   X$KSKPLW
X$KMMSG                     X$KRCFH                    X$KSLCS
X$KMMSI                     X$KRCGFE                   X$KSLECLASS
X$KMPCMON                   X$KRCSTAT                  X$KSLED
X$KMPCP                     X$KRDEVTHIST               X$KSLEI
X$KMPCSO                    X$KRFBLOG                  X$KSLEMAP
X$KMPSRV                    X$KRFGSTAT                 X$KSLES
X$KNGFL                     X$KRFSTHRD                 X$KSLHOT
X$KNGFLE                    X$KRSSMS                   X$KSLLCLASS
X$KNLAROW                   X$KRSTALG                  X$KSLLD
X$KNLASG                    X$KRSTAPPSTATS             X$KSLLTR
X$KNSTACR                   X$KRSTDEST                 X$KSLLTR_CHILDREN
X$KNSTANR                   X$KRSTDGC                  X$KSLLTR_PARENT
X$KNSTASL                   X$KRSTPVRS                 X$KSLLW
X$KNSTCAP                   X$KRVSLV                   X$KSLPO
X$KNSTCAPS                  X$KRVSLVPG                 X$KSLSCS
X$KNSTMT                    X$KRVSLVS                  X$KSLSESHIST
X$KNSTMVR                   X$KRVSLVST                 X$KSLWH
X$KNSTRPP                   X$KRVSLVTHRD               X$KSLWSC
X$KNSTRQU                   X$KRVXDKA                  X$KSLWT
X$KNSTTXN                   X$KRVXDTA                  X$KSMDD
```

```
NAME
--------------------------------------------------------------------------------
X$KSMDUT1               X$KSUPR               X$KTSLCHUNK
X$KSMFS                 X$KSUPRLAT            X$KTSPSTAT
X$KSMFSV                X$KSURLMT             X$KTSSO
X$KSMGE                 X$KSURU               X$KTSTFC
X$KSMHP                 X$KSUSD               X$KTSTSSD
X$KSMJCH                X$KSUSE               X$KTSTUSC
X$KSMJS                 X$KSUSECON           X$KTSTUSG
X$KSMLRU                X$KSUSECST           X$KTSTUSS
X$KSMLS                 X$KSUSESTA           X$KTTEFINFO
X$KSMMEM                X$KSUSEX              X$KTTETS
X$KSMNIM                X$KSUSGIF            X$KTTVS
X$KSMNS                 X$KSUSGSTA           X$KTUCUS
X$KSMPGDP               X$KSUSIO             X$KTUGD
X$KSMPGDST              X$KSUSM              X$KTUQQRY
X$KSMPGST               X$KSUTM              X$KTURD
X$KSMPP                 X$KSUVMSTAT          X$KTURHIST
X$KSMSD                 X$KSUXSINST          X$KTUSMST
X$KSMSGMEM              X$KSWSAFTAB          X$KTUSMST2
X$KSMSP                 X$KSWSASTAB          X$KTUSUS
X$KSMSPR                X$KSWSCLSTAB         X$KTUXE
X$KSMSP_DSNEW          X$KSWSEVTAB          X$KUPVA
X$KSMSP_NWEX           X$KSXAFA             X$KUPVJ
X$KSMSS                 X$KSXPCLIENT         X$KVII
X$KSMSST               X$KSXPIA             X$KVIS
X$KSMSTRS             X$KSXPIF             X$KVIT
X$KSMUP                 X$KSXPPING           X$KWDDEF
X$KSOLSFTS             X$KSXPTESTTBL        X$KWQBPMT
X$KSOLSSTAT           X$KSXP_STATS         X$KWQDLSTAT
X$KSPPCV               X$KSXRCH             X$KWQITCX
X$KSPPCV2             X$KSXRCONQ           X$KWQMNC
X$KSPPI               X$KSXRMSG            X$KWQMNJIT
X$KSPPO               X$KSXRREPQ           X$KWQMNSCTX
X$KSPPSV               X$KSXRSG             X$KWQMNTASK
X$KSPPSV2             X$KTADM              X$KWQMNTASKSTAT
X$KSPSPFH             X$KTATL              X$KWQPD
X$KSPSPFILE          X$KTATRFIL           X$KWQPS
X$KSPVLD_VALUES      X$KTATRFSL           X$KWQSI
X$KSQDN               X$KTCNCLAUSES        X$KWRSNV
X$KSQEQ               X$KTCNINBAND         X$KXFPBS
X$KSQEQTYP           X$KTCNQROW           X$KXFPCDS
X$KSQRS               X$KTCNQUERY          X$KXFPCMS
X$KSQST               X$KTCNREG            X$KXFPCST
X$KSRCCTX             X$KTCNREGQUERY       X$KXFPDP
X$KSRCDES             X$KTCSP              X$KXFPIG
X$KSRCHDL             X$KTCXB              X$KXFPINSTLOAD
X$KSRMPCTX           X$KTFBFE             X$KXFPNS
X$KSRMSGDES          X$KTFBHC             X$KXFPPFT
X$KSRMSGO            X$KTFBUE             X$KXFPPIG
X$KSRPCIOS           X$KTFTBTXNGRAPH      X$KXFPSDS
X$KSTEX               X$KTFTBTXNMODS       X$KXFPSMS
X$KSUCF               X$KTFTHC             X$KXFPSST
X$KSUCPUSTAT         X$KTFTME             X$KXFPYS
X$KSUINSTSTAT        X$KTIFB              X$KXFQSROW
X$KSULL               X$KTIFF              X$KXFRSVCHASH
X$KSULOP             X$KTIFP              X$KXSBD
X$KSULV               X$KTIFV              X$KXSCC
X$KSUMYSTA           X$KTPRHIST           X$KYWMCLTAB
X$KSUNETSTAT         X$KTPRXRS            X$KYWMNF
X$KSUPGP             X$KTPRXRT            X$KYWMPCTAB
X$KSUPGS             X$KTRSO              X$KYWMWRCTAB
X$KSUPL               X$KTSKSTAT           X$KZDOS
```

```
NAME
-----------------------------------------------------------------------------------
X$KZEKMENCWAL              X$LOGMNR_SEG$              X$QESRSTAT
X$KZEKMFVW                 X$LOGMNR_SESSION          X$QESRSTATALL
X$KZPOPR                   X$LOGMNR_SUBCOLTYPE$      X$QKSBGSES
X$KZRTPD                   X$LOGMNR_TAB$             X$QKSBGSYS
X$KZSPR                    X$LOGMNR_TABCOMPART$      X$QKSCESES
X$KZSRO                    X$LOGMNR_TABPART$         X$QKSCESYS
X$KZSRT                    X$LOGMNR_TABSUBPART$      X$QKSFM
X$LE                       X$LOGMNR_TS$              X$QKSFMDEP
X$LOBSEGSTAT               X$LOGMNR_TYPE$            X$QKSFMPRT
X$LOBSTAT                  X$LOGMNR_UET$             X$QKSHT
X$LOBSTATHIST              X$LOGMNR_UNDO$            X$QKSMMWDS
X$LOGBUF_READHIST          X$LOGMNR_USER$            X$QUIESCE
X$LOGMNR_ATTRCOL$          X$MESSAGES                X$RFAFO
X$LOGMNR_ATTRIBUTE$        X$MUTEX_SLEEP             X$RFAHIST
X$LOGMNR_CALLBACK          X$MUTEX_SLEEP_HISTORY     X$RFMP
X$LOGMNR_CDEF$             X$NFSCLIENTS              X$RFMTE
X$LOGMNR_CLU$              X$NFSLOCKS                X$RULE
X$LOGMNR_COL$              X$NFSOPENS                X$RULE_SET
X$LOGMNR_COLTYPE$          X$NLS_PARAMETERS          X$SKGXPIA
X$LOGMNR_CONTENTS          X$NSV                     X$SKGXP_CONNECTION
X$LOGMNR_DICTIONARY        X$OBJECT_POLICY_STATISTICS X$SKGXP_MISC
X$LOGMNR_DICTIONARY_LOAD   X$OCT                     X$SKGXP_PORT
X$LOGMNR_ENC$              X$OPARG                   X$TARGETRBA
X$LOGMNR_ENCRYPTED_OBJ$    X$OPDESC                  X$TEMPORARY_LOB_REFCNT
X$LOGMNR_ENCRYPTION_PROFILE$ X$OPERATORS             X$TIMEZONE_FILE
X$LOGMNR_FILE$             X$OPTION                  X$TIMEZONE_NAMES
X$LOGMNR_IND$              X$OPVERSION               X$TRACE
X$LOGMNR_INDCOMPART$       X$ORAFN                   X$TRACE_EVENTS
X$LOGMNR_INDPART$          X$PERSISTENT_PUBLISHERS   X$UGANCO
X$LOGMNR_INDSUBPART$       X$PERSISTENT_QUEUES       X$VERSION
X$LOGMNR_KOPM$             X$PERSISTENT_SUBSCRIBERS  X$VINST
X$LOGMNR_KTFBUE            X$POLICY_HISTORY          X$XML_AUDIT_TRAIL
X$LOGMNR_LATCH             X$PRMSLTYX                X$XPLTON
X$LOGMNR_LOB$              X$QERFXTST                X$XPLTOO
X$LOGMNR_LOBFRAG$          X$QESBLSTAT               X$XSAGGR
X$LOGMNR_LOG               X$QESMMAHIST              X$XSAGOP
X$LOGMNR_LOGFILE           X$QESMMAPADV              X$XSAWSO
X$LOGMNR_LOGS              X$QESMMIWH                X$XSLONGOPS
X$LOGMNR_NTAB$             X$QESMMIWT                X$XSOBJECT
X$LOGMNR_OBJ$              X$QESMMSGA                X$XSOQMEHI
X$LOGMNR_OPQTYPE$          X$QESRCDEP                X$XSOQOJHI
X$LOGMNR_PARAMETERS        X$QESRCDR                 X$XSOQOPHI
X$LOGMNR_PARTOBJ$          X$QESRCMEM                X$XSOQOPLU
X$LOGMNR_PROCESS           X$QESRCMSG                X$XSOQSEHI
X$LOGMNR_PROPS$            X$QESRCOBJ                X$XSSINFO
X$LOGMNR_REFCON$           X$QESRCRD                 X$XS_SESSION_ROLES
X$LOGMNR_REGION            X$QESRCRR
X$LOGMNR_ROOT$             X$QESRCSTA                945 rows selected.
```

Oracle 11g X$ Indexes

Here is the Oracle 11g query to get the following listing:

```
select     table_name, column_name, index_number
from       v$indexed_fixed_column
order by   table_name, index_number;
```

Following are the Oracle 11gR2 X$ indexed columns ordered by table name (628 total):

TABLE_NAME	COLUMN_NAME	INDEX_NUMBER
X$ASH	NEED_AWR_SAMPLE	1
X$ASH	SAMPLE_ADDR	1
X$ASH	SAMPLE_ID	1
X$BUFFER	OBJNO	1
X$BUFFER2	OBJNO	1
X$DIAG_ADR_CONTROL	COLA	3
X$DIAG_ADR_INVALIDATION	ADR_PATH_IDX	3
X$DIAG_ALERT_EXT	ADR_PATH_IDX	3
X$DIAG_AMS_XACTION	ADR_PATH_IDX	3
X$DIAG_DDE_USER_ACTION	ADR_PATH_IDX	3
X$DIAG_DDE_USER_ACTION_DEF	ADR_PATH_IDX	3
X$DIAG_DDE_USR_ACT_PARAM	ADR_PATH_IDX	3
X$DIAG_DDE_USR_ACT_PARAM_DEF	ADR_PATH_IDX	3
X$DIAG_DDE_USR_INC_ACT_MAP	ADR_PATH_IDX	3
X$DIAG_DDE_USR_INC_TYPE	ADR_PATH_IDX	3
X$DIAG_DIAGV_INCIDENT	ADR_PATH_IDX	3
X$DIAG_DIR_EXT	ADR_PATH_IDX	3
X$DIAG_EM_DIAG_JOB	ADR_PATH_IDX	3
X$DIAG_EM_TARGET_INFO	ADR_PATH_IDX	3
X$DIAG_EM_USER_ACTIVITY	ADR_PATH_IDX	3
X$DIAG_HM_FDG_SET	ADR_PATH_IDX	3
X$DIAG_HM_FINDING	ADR_PATH_IDX	3
X$DIAG_HM_INFO	ADR_PATH_IDX	3
X$DIAG_HM_MESSAGE	ADR_PATH_IDX	3
X$DIAG_HM_RECOMMENDATION	ADR_PATH_IDX	3
X$DIAG_HM_RUN	ADR_PATH_IDX	3
X$DIAG_INCCKEY	ADR_PATH_IDX	3
X$DIAG_INCIDENT	ADR_PATH_IDX	3
X$DIAG_INCIDENT_FILE	ADR_PATH_IDX	3
X$DIAG_INC_METER_CONFIG	ADR_PATH_IDX	3
X$DIAG_INC_METER_IMPT_DEF	ADR_PATH_IDX	3
X$DIAG_INC_METER_INFO	ADR_PATH_IDX	3
X$DIAG_INC_METER_PK_IMPTS	ADR_PATH_IDX	3
X$DIAG_INC_METER_SUMMARY	ADR_PATH_IDX	3
X$DIAG_IPS_CONFIGURATION	ADR_PATH_IDX	3
X$DIAG_IPS_FILE_COPY_LOG	ADR_PATH_IDX	3
X$DIAG_IPS_FILE_METADATA	ADR_PATH_IDX	3
X$DIAG_IPS_PACKAGE	ADR_PATH_IDX	3
X$DIAG_IPS_PACKAGE_FILE	ADR_PATH_IDX	3
X$DIAG_IPS_PACKAGE_HISTORY	ADR_PATH_IDX	3
X$DIAG_IPS_PACKAGE_INCIDENT	ADR_PATH_IDX	3
X$DIAG_IPS_PKG_UNPACK_HIST	ADR_PATH_IDX	3
X$DIAG_IPS_REMOTE_PACKAGE	ADR_PATH_IDX	3
X$DIAG_PICKLEERR	ADR_PATH_IDX	3
X$DIAG_PROBLEM	ADR_PATH_IDX	3
X$DIAG_RELMD_EXT	ADR_PATH_IDX	3
X$DIAG_SWEEPERR	ADR_PATH_IDX	3
X$DIAG_VEM_USER_ACTLOG	ADR_PATH_IDX	3
X$DIAG_VEM_USER_ACTLOG1	ADR_PATH_IDX	3
X$DIAG_VHM_RUN	ADR_PATH_IDX	3
X$DIAG_VIEW	ADR_PATH_IDX	3
X$DIAG_VIEWCOL	ADR_PATH_IDX	3
X$DIAG_VINCIDENT	ADR_PATH_IDX	3
X$DIAG_VINCIDENT_FILE	ADR_PATH_IDX	3
X$DIAG_VINC_METER_INFO	ADR_PATH_IDX	3
X$DIAG_VIPS_FILE_COPY_LOG	ADR_PATH_IDX	3
X$DIAG_VIPS_FILE_METADATA	ADR_PATH_IDX	3

TABLE_NAME	COLUMN_NAME	INDEX_NUMBER
X$DIAG_VIPS_PACKAGE_FILE	ADR_PATH_IDX	3
X$DIAG_VIPS_PACKAGE_HISTORY	ADR_PATH_IDX	3
X$DIAG_VIPS_PACKAGE_MAIN_INT	ADR_PATH_IDX	3
X$DIAG_VIPS_PACKAGE_SIZE	ADR_PATH_IDX	3
X$DIAG_VIPS_PKG_FILE	ADR_PATH_IDX	3
X$DIAG_VIPS_PKG_INC_CAND	ADR_PATH_IDX	3
X$DIAG_VIPS_PKG_INC_DTL	ADR_PATH_IDX	3
X$DIAG_VIPS_PKG_INC_DTL1	ADR_PATH_IDX	3
X$DIAG_VIPS_PKG_MAIN_PROBLEM	ADR_PATH_IDX	3
X$DIAG_VNOT_EXIST_INCIDENT	ADR_PATH_IDX	3
X$DIAG_VPROBLEM	ADR_PATH_IDX	3
X$DIAG_VPROBLEM1	ADR_PATH_IDX	3
X$DIAG_VPROBLEM2	ADR_PATH_IDX	3
X$DIAG_VPROBLEM_BUCKET	ADR_PATH_IDX	3
X$DIAG_VPROBLEM_BUCKET1	ADR_PATH_IDX	3
X$DIAG_VPROBLEM_BUCKET_COUNT	ADR_PATH_IDX	3
X$DIAG_VPROBLEM_INT	ADR_PATH_IDX	3
X$DIAG_VPROBLEM_LASTINC	ADR_PATH_IDX	3
X$DIAG_VSHOWCATVIEW	ADR_PATH_IDX	3
X$DIAG_VSHOWINCB	ADR_PATH_IDX	3
X$DIAG_VSHOWINCB_I	ADR_PATH_IDX	3
X$DIAG_VTEST_EXISTS	ADR_PATH_IDX	3
X$DIAG_V_ACTINC	ADR_PATH_IDX	3
X$DIAG_V_ACTPROB	ADR_PATH_IDX	3
X$DIAG_V_INCCOUNT	ADR_PATH_IDX	3
X$DIAG_V_INCFCOUNT	ADR_PATH_IDX	3
X$DIAG_V_INC_METER_INFO_PROB	ADR_PATH_IDX	3
X$DIAG_V_IPSPRBCNT	ADR_PATH_IDX	3
X$DIAG_V_IPSPRBCNT1	ADR_PATH_IDX	3
X$DIAG_V_NFCINC	ADR_PATH_IDX	3
X$DIAG_V_SWPERRCOUNT	ADR_PATH_IDX	3
X$DRA_FAILURE	ADDR	1
X$DRA_FAILURE	INDX	2
X$DRA_FAILURE_CHECK	ADDR	1
X$DRA_FAILURE_CHECK	INDX	2
X$DRA_FAILURE_CHECK_MAP	ADDR	1
X$DRA_FAILURE_CHECK_MAP	INDX	2
X$DRA_FAILURE_PARAM	ADDR	1
X$DRA_FAILURE_PARAM	INDX	2
X$DRA_FAILURE_PARENT_MAP	ADDR	1
X$DRA_FAILURE_PARENT_MAP	INDX	2
X$DRA_FAILURE_REPAIR	ADDR	1
X$DRA_FAILURE_REPAIR	INDX	2
X$DRA_FAILURE_REPAIR_MAP	ADDR	1
X$DRA_FAILURE_REPAIR_MAP	INDX	2
X$DRA_REPAIR	ADDR	1
X$DRA_REPAIR	INDX	2
X$DRA_REPAIR_PARAM	ADDR	1
X$DRA_REPAIR_PARAM	INDX	2
X$DUAL	ADDR	1
X$DUAL	INDX	2
X$JOXFM	OBN	1
X$JOXFT	JOXFTOBN	1
X$KAUVRSTAT	ADDR	1
X$KAUVRSTAT	INDX	2
X$KCBBF	INDX	1
X$KCBBHS	ADDR	1
X$KCBBHS	INDX	2
X$KCBDBK	ADDR	1
X$KCBDBK	INDX	2

TABLE_NAME	COLUMN_NAME	INDEX_NUMBER
X$KCBFWAIT	ADDR	1
X$KCBFWAIT	INDX	2
X$KCBKWRL	ADDR	1
X$KCBKWRL	INDX	2
X$KCBLDRHIST	ADDR	1
X$KCBLDRHIST	INDX	2
X$KCBLSC	ADDR	1
X$KCBLSC	INDX	2
X$KCBPRFH	ADDR	1
X$KCBPRFH	INDX	2
X$KCBSDS	ADDR	1
X$KCBSDS	INDX	2
X$KCBSW	ADDR	1
X$KCBSW	INDX	2
X$KCBUWHY	ADDR	1
X$KCBUWHY	INDX	2
X$KCBWAIT	ADDR	1
X$KCBWAIT	INDX	2
X$KCBWBPD	ADDR	1
X$KCBWBPD	INDX	2
X$KCBWDS	INDX	1
X$KCBWH	ADDR	1
X$KCBWH	INDX	2
X$KCCACM	ACMREC	1
X$KCCAL	ALRID	1
X$KCCBF	BFRID	1
X$KCCBI	BIRID	1
X$KCCBL	BLRID	1
X$KCCBLKCOR	BLKRID	1
X$KCCBP	BPRID	1
X$KCCBS	BSRID	1
X$KCCCC	CCRID	1
X$KCCCP	CPTNO	1
X$KCCDC	DCRID	1
X$KCCDFHIST	DFHRID	1
X$KCCDL	DLRID	1
X$KCCFC	FCRID	1
X$KCCFE	FENUM	1
X$KCCFLE	FLENUM	1
X$KCCFN	FNNUM	1
X$KCCIC	ICRID	1
X$KCCLE	LENUM	1
X$KCCLH	LHRID	1
X$KCCNRS	NRSRID	1
X$KCCOR	ORRID	1
X$KCCPA	PCRID	1
X$KCCPD	PCRID	1
X$KCCRL	RLRID	1
X$KCCRM	RMRNO	1
X$KCCRSR	RSRRID	1
X$KCCRT	RTNUM	1
X$KCCTF	TFNUM	1
X$KCCTIR	TIRNUM	1
X$KCCTS	TSRNO	1
X$KCFIO	INDX	1
X$KCFISOSS	CELLNAME	1
X$KCFISOSS	STATTYPE	2
X$KCFISOSSC	CELLNAME	1
X$KCFISOSSC	CONFTYPE	2
X$KCFISOSSN	CELLNAME	1

TABLE_NAME	COLUMN_NAME	INDEX_NUMBER
X$KCFISOSST	CELLNAME	1
X$KCFISTSA	TSID	1
X$KCFTIO	INDX	1
X$KCLCRST	ADDR	1
X$KCLCRST	INDX	2
X$KCLCURST	ADDR	1
X$KCLCURST	INDX	2
X$KCLRCVST	ADDR	1
X$KCLRCVST	INDX	2
X$KCPXPL	ADDR	1
X$KCPXPL	INDX	2
X$KCRFDEBUG	ADDR	1
X$KCRFDEBUG	INDX	2
X$KCRFWS	ADDR	1
X$KCRFWS	INDX	2
X$KCVFH	HXFIL	1
X$KCVFHTMP	HTMPXFIL	1
X$KDNSSF	ADDR	1
X$KDNSSF	INDX	2
X$KDXHS	ADDR	1
X$KDXHS	INDX	2
X$KDXST	INDX	1
X$KEACMDN	ADDR	1
X$KEACMDN	INDX	2
X$KEAFDGN	ADDR	1
X$KEAFDGN	INDX	2
X$KEAOBJT	ADDR	1
X$KEAOBJT	INDX	2
X$KEHF	ADDR	1
X$KEHF	INDX	2
X$KEHR	ADDR	1
X$KEHR	INDX	2
X$KEHRP	ADDR	1
X$KEHRP	INDX	2
X$KEHSQT	ADDR	1
X$KEHSQT	INDX	2
X$KELRSGA	ADDR	1
X$KELRSGA	INDX	2
X$KELRTD	ADDR	1
X$KELRTD	INDX	2
X$KELRXMR	HNUM	1
X$KELTGSD	ADDR	1
X$KELTGSD	INDX	2
X$KELTOSD	ADDR	1
X$KELTOSD	INDX	2
X$KELTSD	ADDR	1
X$KELTSD	INDX	2
X$KESSPAMET	ADDR	1
X$KESSPAMET	INDX	2
X$KESWXMON	KEY_KESWXMON	1
X$KESWXMON	EXECID_KESWXMON	2
X$KESWXMON	SQLID_KESWXMON	2
X$KESWXMON	EXECSTART_KESWXMON	2
X$KESWXMON_PLAN	KEY_KESWXMONP	1
X$KESWXMON_PLAN	EXECID_KESWXMONP	2
X$KESWXMON_PLAN	EXECSTART_KESWXMONP	2
X$KESWXMON_PLAN	SQLID_KESWXMONP	2
X$KETCL	ADDR	1
X$KETCL	INDX	2

TABLE_NAME	COLUMN_NAME	INDEX_NUMBER
X$KETOP	ADDR	1
X$KETOP	INDX	2
X$KETTG	ADDR	1
X$KETTG	INDX	2
X$KEWAM	ADDR	1
X$KEWAM	INDX	2
X$KEWASH	IS_AWR_SAMPLE	1
X$KEWECLS	CLSPOS	1
X$KEWEPCS	PCKEY	1
X$KEWEPCS	PCSPOS	2
X$KEWESMAS	STATPOS	1
X$KEWESMS	STATPOS	1
X$KEWMAFMV	GROUPID	1
X$KEWMDRMV	GROUPID	1
X$KEWMEVMV	GROUPID	1
X$KEWMFLMV	GROUPID	1
X$KEWMGSM	ADDR	1
X$KEWMGSM	INDX	2
X$KEWMIOFMV	GROUPID	1
X$KEWMRMGMV	GROUPID	1
X$KEWMRWMV	GROUPID	1
X$KEWMSEMV	GROUPID	1
X$KEWMSMDV	GROUPID	1
X$KEWMSVCMV	GROUPID	1
X$KEWMWCRMV	GROUPID	1
X$KEWMWPCMV	GROUPID	1
X$KEWRTB	ADDR	1
X$KEWRTB	INDX	2
X$KEWSSESV	KSUSENUM	1
X$KEWSSESV	KEWSNUM	2
X$KEWSSMAP	EXTID	1
X$KEWSSVCV	SVCHSH	1
X$KEWSSVCV	KEWSOFF	2
X$KEWSSYSV	ADDR	1
X$KEWSSYSV	INDX	2
X$KFALS	GROUP_KFALS	1
X$KFALS	ENTNUM_KFALS	2
X$KFALS	REFER_KFALS	3
X$KFALS	PARENT_KFALS	4
X$KFDAT	GROUP_KFDAT	1
X$KFDAT	NUMBER_KFDAT	2
X$KFDAT	COMPOUND_KFDAT	3
X$KFDDD	GRPNUM_KFDDD	1
X$KFDFS	GROUP_KFDFS	1
X$KFDFS	NUMBER_KFDFS	2
X$KFDFS	COMPOUND_KFDFS	3
X$KFDPARTNER	GRP	1
X$KFDPARTNER	DISK	2
X$KFDPARTNER	COMPOUND	3
X$KFDSK	GRPNUM_KFDSK	1
X$KFDSK	NUMBER_KFDSK	2
X$KFDSK	COMPOUND_KFDSK	3
X$KFDSK_STAT	GRPNUM_KFDSK	1
X$KFDSK_STAT	NUMBER_KFDSK	2
X$KFDSK_STAT	COMPOUND_KFDSK	3
X$KFENV	GROUP_KFENV	1
X$KFENV	ENTNUM_KFENV	2
X$KFFIL	GROUP_KFFIL	1
X$KFFIL	NUMBER_KFFIL	2
X$KFFIL	COMPOUND_KFFIL	3

TABLE_NAME	COLUMN_NAME	INDEX_NUMBER
X$KFFOF	GROUP_KFFOF	1
X$KFFOF	NUMBER_KFFOF	2
X$KFFOF	COMPOUND_KFFOF	3
X$KFFXP	GROUP_KFFXP	1
X$KFFXP	NUMBER_KFFXP	2
X$KFFXP	COMPOUND_KFFXP	3
X$KFGBRB	NUMBER_KFGBRB	1
X$KFGBRW	NUMBER_KFGBRW	1
X$KFGMG	NUMBER_KFGMG	1
X$KFGRP	NUMBER_KFGRP	1
X$KFGRP_STAT	NUMBER_KFGRP	1
X$KFTMTA	GROUP_KFTMTA	1
X$KFTMTA	ENTRY_KFTMTA	2
X$KFTMTA	COMPOUND_KFTMTA	3
X$KFVOL	GROUP_KFVOL	1
X$KFVOL	ENTRY_KFVOL	2
X$KFVOL	COMPOUND_KFVOL	3
X$KFVOLSTAT	COMPOUND_KFVOLSTAT	3
X$KFZGDR	GROUP_KFZGDR	1
X$KFZGDR	ENTNUM_KFZGDR	2
X$KFZGDR	REFER_KFZGDR	3
X$KFZUAGR	GROUP_KFZUAGR	1
X$KFZUDR	GROUP_KFZUDR	1
X$KFZUDR	ENTNUM_KFZUDR	2
X$KFZUDR	REFER_KFZUDR	3
X$KGICS	ADDR	1
X$KGICS	INDX	2
X$KGLDP	KGLNAHSH	1
X$KGLLK	KGLNAHSH	1
X$KGLLK	KGLLKSQLID	2
X$KGLNA	KGLNAHSH	1
X$KGLNA	KGLNASQLID	2
X$KGLNA1	KGLNAHSH	1
X$KGLNA1	KGLNASQLID	2
X$KGLOB	KGLNAHSH	1
X$KGLOB	KGLOBT03	2
X$KGLOBXML	KGLNAHSH	1
X$KGLPN	KGLNAHSH	1
X$KGLRD	KGLNACHV	1
X$KGSCC	ADDR	1
X$KGSCC	INDX	2
X$KGSKASP	ADDR	1
X$KGSKASP	INDX	2
X$KGSKCP	ADDR	1
X$KGSKCP	INDX	2
X$KGSKDOPP	ADDR	1
X$KGSKDOPP	INDX	2
X$KGSKPP	ADDR	1
X$KGSKPP	INDX	2
X$KGSKQUEP	ADDR	1
X$KGSKQUEP	INDX	2
X$KGSKTE	ADDR	1
X$KGSKTE	INDX	2
X$KGSKTO	ADDR	1
X$KGSKTO	INDX	2
X$KJDRMAFNSTATS	ADDR	1
X$KJDRMAFNSTATS	INDX	2
X$KJDRMHVSTATS	ADDR	1
X$KJDRMHVSTATS	INDX	2

TABLE_NAME	COLUMN_NAME	INDEX_NUMBER
X$KJMDDP	INDX	1
X$KJMSDP	INDX	1
X$KKOCS_HISTOGRAM	HASHV_KKOCS	1
X$KKOCS_HISTOGRAM	SQLID_KKOCS	2
X$KKOCS_SELECTIVITY	HASHV_KKOCS	1
X$KKOCS_SELECTIVITY	SQLID_KKOCS	2
X$KKOCS_STATISTICS	HASHV_KKOCS	1
X$KKOCS_STATISTICS	SQLID_KKOCS	2
X$KKSCS	SQL_ID	1
X$KKSSQLSTAT	SQL_ID	1
X$KMMDI	ADDR	1
X$KMMDI	INDX	2
X$KMMDP	INDX	1
X$KMMHST	ADDR	1
X$KMMHST	INDX	2
X$KMMRD	ADDR	1
X$KMMRD	INDX	2
X$KMMRD	KMMRDBUC	3
X$KMMSAS	ADDR	1
X$KMMSAS	INDX	2
X$KMMSG	ADDR	1
X$KMMSG	INDX	2
X$KMMSI	ADDR	1
X$KMMSI	INDX	2
X$KNSTRQU	ADDR	1
X$KNSTRQU	INDX	2
X$KOCST	ADDR	1
X$KOCST	INDX	2
X$KQDPG	ADDR	1
X$KQDPG	INDX	2
X$KQFDT	ADDR	1
X$KQFDT	INDX	2
X$KQFOPT	ADDR	1
X$KQFOPT	INDX	2
X$KQFP	ADDR	1
X$KQFP	INDX	2
X$KQFSZ	ADDR	1
X$KQFSZ	INDX	2
X$KQFVI	ADDR	1
X$KQFVI	INDX	2
X$KQFVT	ADDR	1
X$KQFVT	INDX	2
X$KQLFBC	KQLFBC_HASH	1
X$KQLFBC	KQLFBC_SQLID	2
X$KQLFSQCE	KQLFSQCE_HASH	1
X$KQLFSQCE	KQLFSQCE_SQLID	2
X$KQLFXPL	KQLFXPL_HADD	1
X$KQLFXPL	KQLFXPL_PHAD	2
X$KQLFXPL	KQLFXPL_HASH	3
X$KQLFXPL	KQLFXPL_SQLID	4
X$KQRFP	KQRFPHSH	1
X$KQRFS	KQRFSHSH	1
X$KQRPD	ADDR	1
X$KQRPD	INDX	2
X$KQRSD	ADDR	1
X$KQRSD	INDX	2
X$KQRST	ADDR	1
X$KQRST	INDX	2
X$KRBAFF	FNO	1
X$KRCSTAT	ADDR	1

TABLE_NAME	COLUMN_NAME	INDEX_NUMBER
X$KRCSTAT	INDX	2
X$KRVXDKA	ADDR	1
X$KRVXDKA	INDX	2
X$KRVXDTA	ADDR	1
X$KRVXDTA	INDX	2
X$KSBDD	ADDR	1
X$KSBDD	INDX	2
X$KSBDP	INDX	1
X$KSBFT	ADDR	1
X$KSBFT	INDX	2
X$KSBSRVDT	ADDR	1
X$KSBSRVDT	INDX	2
X$KSFDFTYP	ADDR	1
X$KSFDFTYP	INDX	2
X$KSFDSTCG	ADDR	1
X$KSFDSTCG	INDX	2
X$KSFDSTCMP	ADDR	1
X$KSFDSTCMP	INDX	2
X$KSFDSTFILE	INDX	1
X$KSFMIOST	FILE_IDX	1
X$KSFQP	SID	1
X$KSIMAT	ADDR	1
X$KSIMAT	INDX	2
X$KSIRESTYP	ADDR	1
X$KSIRESTYP	INDX	2
X$KSLCS	KSLCSSID	1
X$KSLECLASS	ADDR	1
X$KSLECLASS	INDX	2
X$KSLED	ADDR	1
X$KSLED	INDX	2
X$KSLEMAP	ADDR	1
X$KSLEMAP	INDX	2
X$KSLES	KSLESSID	1
X$KSLHOT	ADDR	1
X$KSLHOT	INDX	2
X$KSLLCLASS	ADDR	1
X$KSLLCLASS	INDX	2
X$KSLLW	ADDR	1
X$KSLLW	INDX	2
X$KSLPO	ADDR	1
X$KSLPO	INDX	2
X$KSLWH	KSLWHSID	1
X$KSLWSC	ADDR	1
X$KSLWSC	INDX	2
X$KSLWT	KSLWTSID	1
X$KSMDD	INDX	1
X$KSMDUT1	ADDR	1
X$KSMDUT1	INDX	2
X$KSMDUT1	ARR1_INDX	3
X$KSMFSV	ADDR	1
X$KSMFSV	INDX	2
X$KSMHP	KSMCHDS	1
X$KSMMEM	ADDR	1
X$KSMMEM	INDX	2
X$KSMSP_DSNEW	ADDR	1
X$KSMSP_DSNEW	INDX	2
X$KSOLSFTS	FTS_OBJD	1
X$KSPVLD_VALUES	PARNO_KSPVLD_VALUES	1
X$KSQDN	ADDR	1
X$KSQDN	INDX	2

TABLE_NAME	COLUMN_NAME	INDEX_NUMBER
X$KSQEQ	ADDR	1
X$KSQEQ	INDX	2
X$KSQEQTYP	ADDR	1
X$KSQEQTYP	INDX	2
X$KSQRS	ADDR	1
X$KSQRS	INDX	2
X$KSQST	ADDR	1
X$KSQST	INDX	2
X$KSRCCTX	ADDR	1
X$KSRCCTX	INDX	2
X$KSRCDES	ADDR	1
X$KSRCDES	INDX	2
X$KSRMPCTX	ADDR	1
X$KSRMPCTX	INDX	2
X$KSRMSGDES	ADDR	1
X$KSRMSGDES	INDX	2
X$KSRPCIOS	INDX	1
X$KSUCF	ADDR	1
X$KSUCF	INDX	2
X$KSUCF	KSUPLSTN	3
X$KSUPL	ADDR	1
X$KSUPL	INDX	2
X$KSUPL	KSUPLSTN	3
X$KSUPR	INDX	1
X$KSURU	INDX	1
X$KSURU	KSURIND	3
X$KSUSE	INDX	1
X$KSUSECST	INDX	1
X$KSUSESTA	KSUSENUM	1
X$KSUSESTA	KSUSESTN	2
X$KSUSEX	SID	1
X$KSUSGIF	ADDR	1
X$KSUSGIF	INDX	2
X$KSUSIO	INDX	1
X$KSUSM	INDX	1
X$KSUTM	ADDR	1
X$KSUTM	INDX	2
X$KSXPCLIENT	ADDR	1
X$KSXPCLIENT	INDX	2
X$KSXPPING	ADDR	1
X$KSXPPING	INDX	2
X$KSXP_STATS	KSXPTESTF1	3
X$KSXP_STATS	KSXPTESTF5	4
X$KSXRCH	ADDR	1
X$KSXRCH	INDX	2
X$KSXRCONQ	ADDR	1
X$KSXRCONQ	INDX	2
X$KSXRMSG	ADDR	1
X$KSXRMSG	INDX	2
X$KSXRREPQ	ADDR	1
X$KSXRREPQ	INDX	2
X$KSXRSG	ADDR	1
X$KSXRSG	INDX	2
X$KTATL	ADDR	1
X$KTATL	INDX	2
X$KTATRFIL	ADDR	1
X$KTATRFIL	INDX	2
X$KTATRFSL	ADDR	1
X$KTATRFSL	INDX	2

TABLE_NAME	COLUMN_NAME	INDEX_NUMBER
X$KTFBFE	KTFBFETSN	1
X$KTFBHC	KTFBHCAFNO	1
X$KTFBUE	KTFBUESEGBNO	1
X$KTFBUE	KTFBUESEGFNO	1
X$KTFBUE	KTFBUESEGTSN	1
X$KTFTHC	KTFTHCTFNO	1
X$KTFTHC	KTFTHCTSN	2
X$KTFTME	KTFTMETSN	1
X$KTIFP	KTIFPNO	1
X$KTIFV	KTIFVPOOL	1
X$KTSKSTAT	KTSKSTATOBJD	1
X$KTSLCHUNK	KTSLCHUNKTSN	1
X$KTSLCHUNK	KTSLCHUNKSEGFNO	1
X$KTSLCHUNK	KTSLCHUNKSEGBLKNO	1
X$KTSTFC	KTSTFCTSN	1
X$KTSTUSC	ADDR	1
X$KTSTUSC	INDX	2
X$KTSTUSG	ADDR	1
X$KTSTUSG	INDX	2
X$KTSTUSS	ADDR	1
X$KTSTUSS	INDX	2
X$KTTVS	ADDR	1
X$KTTVS	INDX	2
X$KTUGD	ADDR	1
X$KTUGD	INDX	2
X$KTUQQRY	XID	1
X$KTUSUS	KTUSUSTSN	1
X$KTUXE	KTUXEUSN	1
X$KVII	ADDR	1
X$KVII	INDX	2
X$KVIS	ADDR	1
X$KVIS	INDX	2
X$KVIT	ADDR	1
X$KVIT	INDX	2
X$KWQITCX	ADDR	1
X$KWQITCX	INDX	2
X$KWQMNSCTX	ADDR	1
X$KWQMNSCTX	INDX	2
X$KWQMNTASKSTAT	ADDR	1
X$KWQMNTASKSTAT	INDX	2
X$KWQSI	KWQSIQID	1
X$KWRSNV	ADDR	1
X$KWRSNV	INDX	2
X$KXFPCDS	ADDR	1
X$KXFPCDS	INDX	2
X$KXFPCMS	ADDR	1
X$KXFPCMS	INDX	2
X$KXFPCST	ADDR	1
X$KXFPCST	INDX	2
X$KXFPSDS	ADDR	1
X$KXFPSDS	INDX	2
X$KXFPSMS	ADDR	1
X$KXFPSMS	INDX	2
X$KXFPSST	ADDR	1
X$KXFPSST	INDX	2
X$KYWMNF	INDX	1
X$KYWMPCTAB	KYWMPCTABHASH	1
X$KZDOS	ADDR	1
X$KZDOS	INDX	2
X$KZRTPD	KZRTPDPH	1

TABLE_NAME	COLUMN_NAME	INDEX_NUMBER
X$KZSRO	ADDR	1
X$KZSRO	INDX	2
X$MESSAGES	ADDR	1
X$MESSAGES	INDX	2
X$OCT	ADDR	1
X$OCT	INDX	2
X$OPVERSION	ADDR	1
X$OPVERSION	INDX	2
X$ORAFN	ADDR	1
X$ORAFN	INDX	2
X$QESMMIWH	ADDR	1
X$QESMMIWH	INDX	2
X$QESRCRD	QESRCRD_KEY	1
X$QESRSTAT	HADDR_QESRS	1
X$QESRSTAT	PHADD_QESRS	2
X$QESRSTAT	HASHV_QESRS	3
X$QESRSTAT	SQLID_QESRS	4
X$QESRSTATALL	HADDR_QESRS	1
X$QESRSTATALL	PHADD_QESRS	2
X$QESRSTATALL	HASHV_QESRS	3
X$QESRSTATALL	SQLID_QESRS	4
X$QKSMMWDS	HASHV_QKSMM	1
X$QKSMMWDS	SQLID_QKSMM	2
X$QUIESCE	ADDR	1
X$QUIESCE	INDX	2
X$RFMP	ADDR	1
X$RFMP	INDX	2
X$SKGXPIA	ADDR	1
X$SKGXPIA	INDX	2
X$XPLTON	XPLTON_ID	1
X$XPLTOO	XPLTOO_ID	1
X$XSAWSO	ADDR	1
X$XSAWSO	INDX	2
X$XSOBJECT	AW_XSOBJFT	1

628 rows selected.

Oracle 11g V$ Views Cross-Referenced to the X$ Tables

The Oracle 11g V$ views are the same as the GV$ views without the INSTANCE_ID. I show the X$ table mapped back to the V$ view. Because of the number of views in 11g, it's no longer possible to list all cross-references here. I have, however, listed several that pertain primarily to performance tuning. You can run your own query to see a specific query associated with the GV$ or V$ views, as shown in Appendix B. You must go through the GV$ view to make this inference. Here are the referenced X$ tables, ordered by the selected V$ view names:

Fixed View	Underlying Base X$ Tables and/or Fixed Views
V$BH	xbh, xle
V$BUFFER_POOL	x$kcbwbpd
V$BUFFER_POOL_STATISTICS	x$kcbwds, kcbwds,x$kcbwbpd kcbwbpd
V$DATABASE	x$kccdi, x$kccdi2
V$DATAFILE	x$kccfe, x$kccfn, x$kccfn, x$kcvfh
V$DB_CACHE_ADVICE	x$kcbsc, x$kcbwbpd
V$DB_OBJECT_CACHE	x$kglob

Fixed View	Underlying Base X$ Tables and/or Fixed Views
V$DLM_ALL_LOCKS	V$GES_ENQUEUE
V$DLM_LATCH	V$LATCH
V$DLM_LOCKS	V$GES_BLOCKING_ENQUEUE
V$ENQUEUE_LOCK	x$ksqeq, x$ksuse, x$ksqrs
V$ENQUEUE_STAT	x$ksqst
V$EVENT_NAME	x$ksled
V$EXECUTION	x$kstex
V$FILESTAT	x$kcfio, x$kccfe
V$FILE_CACHE_TRANSFER	x$kcfio, x$kccfe
V$FIXED_TABLE	x$kqfta, x$kqfvi, x$kqfdt
V$FIXED_VIEW_DEFINITION	x$kqfvi, x$kqfvt
V$GES_BLOCKING_ENQUEUE	V$GES_BLOCKING_ENQUEUE
V$GES_ENQUEUE	x$kjilkft, x$kjbl
V$GLOBAL_BLOCKED_LOCKS	v$lock, v$dlm_locks
V$GLOBAL_TRANSACTION	x$k2gte2
V$INDEXED_FIXED_COLUMN	x$kqfco, x$kqfta
V$INSTANCE	x$ksuxsinst, x$kvit, x$quiesce
V$LATCH	x$kslltr
V$LATCHHOLDER	x$ksuprlat
ult1V$LATCHNAME	x$kslld
V$LATCH_CHILDREN	x$kslltr_children
V$LATCH_MISSES	x$ksllw, x$kslwsc
V$LATCH_PARENT	x$kslltr_parent
V$LIBRARYCACHE	x$kglst
V$LIBRARY_CACHE_MEMORY	x$kglmem
V$LOCK	v$_lock, x$ksuse, x$ksqrs
V$LOCKED_OBJECT	x$ktcxb, x$ktadm, x$ksuse
V$LOCKS_WITH_COLLISIONS	v$bh
V$LOCK_ACTIVITY	Dual
V$LOCK_ELEMENT	x$le
V$MTTR_TARGET_ADVICE	x$kcbmmav
V$MUTEX_SLEEP	x$mutex_sleep
V$_MUTEX_SLEEP_HISTORY	x$mutex_sleep_history
V$MVREFRESH	x$knstmvr, v$session
V$MYSTAT	x$ksumysta, x$ksusgif
V$OBSOLETE_PARAMETER	x$ksppo
V$OPEN_CURSOR	x$kgllk
V$OPTION	x$option
V$PARAMETER	x$ksppi, x$ksppcv
V$PARAMETER2	x$ksppi, x$ksppcv2
V$PGASTAT	x$qesmmsga
V$PGA_TARGET_ADVICE	x$qesmmapadv
aV$PGA_TARGET_ADVICE_HISTOGRAM	x$qesmmahist
V$PROCESS	x$ksupr
V$QUEUE	x$kmcqs
V$ROLLSTAT	x$kturd
V$ROWCACHE	x$kqrst
V$ROWCACHE_PARENT	x$kqrfp
V$ROWCACHE_SUBORDINATE	x$kqrfs
V$SEGMENT_STATISTICS	obj$, user$, x$ksolsfts, ts$, ind$
V$SEGSTAT	x$ksolsfts
V$SEGSTAT_NAME	x$ksolsstat
V$SESSION	x$ksuse, x$ksled
V$SESSION_CONNECT_INFO	x$ksusecon
V$SESSION_CURSOR_CACHE	x$kgscc
V$SESSION_EVENT	x$ksles, x$ksled
V$SESSION_LONGOPS	x$ksulop
V$SESSION_OBJECT_CACHE	x$kocst
V$SESSION_WAIT	x$kslwt, x$ksled
V$SESSION_WAIT_CLASS	x$kslcs

Fixed View	Underlying Base X$ Tables and/or Fixed Views
V$SESSION_WAIT_HISTORY	x$kslwh
V$SESSMETRIC	x$kewmsemv
V$SESSTAT	x$ksusesta, x$ksusgif
V$SESS_IO	x$ksusio
V$SGA	x$ksmsd
V$SGASTAT	x$ksmfs, x$ksmss, x$ksmls, x$ksmjs, x$ksmns, x$ksmstrs
V$SHARED_POOL_ADVICE	x$kglsim
V$SHARED_POOL_RESERVED	x$ksmspr, x$kghlu
V$SORT_SEGMENT	x$ktstssd
V$SORT_USAGE	x$ktsso, v$session
V$SPPARAMETER	x$kspspfile
V$SQL	x$kglcursor_child
V$SQLAREA	x$kglcursor_child_sqlid
V$SQLAREA_PLAN_HASH	x$kglcursor_child_sqlidph
V$SQLSTATS	x$kkssqlstat
V$SQLTEXT	x$kglna
V$SQLTEXT_WITH_NEWLINES	x$kglna1
V$SQL_BIND_CAPTURE	x$kqlfbc
V$SQL_BIND_DATA	x$kxsbd
V$SQL_BIND_METADATA	x$kksbv
0V$SQL_CURSOR	x$kxscc
V$SQL_JOIN_FILTER	x$qesblstat
V$SQL_OPTIMIZER_ENV	x$kqlfsqce
V$SQL_PLAN	x$kqlfxpl
V$SQL_PLAN_STATISTICS	x$qesrstat
V$SQL_PLAN_STATISTICS_ALL	x$qesrstatall
V$SQL_REDIRECTION	x$kglcursor_child, x$kkssrd
V$SQL_SHARED_CURSOR	x$kkscs
V$SQL_SHARED_MEMORY	x$kglcursor, x$ksmhp
V$SQL_WORKAREA	x$qksmmwds
V$SQL_WORKAREA_ACTIVE	x$qesmmiwt
V$STATISTICS_LEVEL	x$prmsltyx
V$SUBCACHE	x$kqlset
V$SYSSTAT	x$ksusgsta
apdefaultV$SYSTEM_CURSOR_CACHE	x$kgics
V$SYSTEM_EVENT	x$kslei, x$ksled
V$SYSTEM_PARAMETER	x$ksppi, x$ksppsv
V$SYSTEM_PARAMETER2	x$ksppi, x$ksppsv2
V$TABLESPACE	x$kccts
V$TEMPFILE	x$kcctf, x$kccfn, x$kcvfhtmp
V$TEMPSTAT	x$kcftio, x$kcctf
V$TEMP_CACHE_TRANSFER	x$kcftio, x$kcctf
V$TEMP_EXTENT_MAP	ts$, x$ktftme
V$TEMP_EXTENT_POOL	ts$,x$ktstfc
V$TEMP_PING	x$kcftio, x$kcctf
V$TEMP_SPACE_HEADER	ts$, x$ktfthc
V$THREAD	x$kccrt, x$kcctir, x$kcccp
V$TRANSACTION	x$ktcxb
V$TRANSACTION_ENQUEUE	x$ktcxb, x$ksuse, x$ksqrs
V$UNDOSTAT	x$ktusmst
V$VERSION	x$version
V$WAITSTAT	x$kcbwait
V$_LOCK	v$_lock1, x$ktadm, x$ktatrfil, x$ktatrfsl, x$ktatl, x$ktstusc, x$ktstuss, x$ktstusg, x$ktcxb,
V$_LOCK1	x$kdnssf, x$ksqeq
O$SQL_BIND_CAPTURE	x$kqlfbc

Thanks to Jacob Niemiec for testing the queries and providing the new listings for 11gR2.

Index

I

GET YOUR FREE SUBSCRIPTION TO *ORACLE MAGAZINE*

Oracle Magazine is essential gear for today's information technology professionals. Stay informed and increase your productivity with every issue of *Oracle Magazine*. Inside each free bimonthly issue you'll get:

- Up-to-date information on Oracle Database, Oracle Application Server, Web development, enterprise grid computing, database technology, and business trends
- Third-party news and announcements
- Technical articles on Oracle and partner products, technologies, and operating environments
- Development and administration tips
- Real-world customer stories

If there are other Oracle users at your location who would like to receive their own subscription to *Oracle Magazine*, please photo-copy this form and pass it along.

Three easy ways to subscribe:

① Web
Visit our Web site at **oracle.com/oraclemagazine**
You'll find a subscription form there, plus much more

② Fax
Complete the questionnaire on the back of this card
and fax the questionnaire side only to **+1.847.763.9638**

③ Mail
Complete the questionnaire on the back of this card
and mail it to **P.O. Box 1263, Skokie, IL 60076-8263**

ORACLE

Want your own FREE subscription?

To receive a free subscription to *Oracle Magazine*, you must fill out the entire card, sign it, and date it (incomplete cards cannot be processed or acknowledged). You can also fax your application to +1.847.763.9638. **Or subscribe at our Web site at oracle.com/oraclemagazine**

O **Yes, please send me a FREE subscription** *Oracle Magazine*.   O No.

O From time to time, Oracle Publishing allows our partners exclusive access to our e-mail addresses for special promotions and announcements. To be included in this program, please check this circle. If you do not wish to be included, you will only receive notices about your subscription via e-mail.

O Oracle Publishing allows sharing of our postal mailing list with selected third parties. If you prefer your mailing address not to be included in this program, please check this circle.

If at any time you would like to be removed from either mailing list, please contact Customer Service at +1.847.763.9635 or send an e-mail to oracle@halldata.com. If you opt in to the sharing of information, Oracle may also provide you with e-mail related to Oracle products, services, and events. If you want to completely unsubscribe from any e-mail communication from Oracle, please send an e-mail to: unsubscribe@oracle-mail.com with the following in the subject line: REMOVE [your e-mail address]. For complete information on Oracle Publishing's privacy practices, please visit oracle.com/html/privacy/html

X

signature (required) _____   date _____

name _____   title _____

company _____   e-mail address _____

street/p.o. box _____

city/state/zip or postal code _____   telephone _____

country _____   fax _____

Would you like to receive your free subscription in digital format instead of print if it becomes available? O Yes   O No

---

YOU MUST ANSWER ALL 10 QUESTIONS BELOW.

① WHAT IS THE PRIMARY BUSINESS ACTIVITY OF YOUR FIRM AT THIS LOCATION? (check one only)

- □ 01 Aerospace and Defense Manufacturing
- □ 02 Application Service Provider
- □ 03 Automotive Manufacturing
- □ 04 Chemicals
- □ 05 Media and Entertainment
- □ 06 Construction/Engineering
- □ 07 Consumer Sector/Consumer Packaged Goods
- □ 08 Education
- □ 09 Financial Services/Insurance
- □ 10 Health Care
- □ 11 High Technology Manufacturing, OEM
- □ 12 Industrial Manufacturing
- □ 13 Independent Software Vendor
- □ 14 Life Sciences (biotech, pharmaceuticals)
- □ 15 Natural Resources
- □ 16 Oil and Gas
- □ 17 Professional Services
- □ 18 Public Sector (government)
- □ 19 Research
- □ 20 Retail/Wholesale/Distribution
- □ 21 Systems Integrator, VAR/VAD
- □ 22 Telecommunications
- □ 23 Travel and Transportation
- □ 24 Utilities (electric, gas, sanitation, water)
- □ 98 Other Business and Services _____

② WHICH OF THE FOLLOWING BEST DESCRIBES YOUR PRIMARY JOB FUNCTION? (check one only)

CORPORATE MANAGEMENT/STAFF
- □ 01 Executive Management (President, Chair, CEO, CFO, Owner, Partner, Principal)
- □ 02 Finance/Administrative Management (VP/Director/ Manager/Controller, Purchasing, Administration)
- □ 03 Sales/Marketing Management (VP/Director/Manager)
- □ 04 Computer Systems/Operations Management (CIO/VP/Director/Manager MIS/IS/IT, Ops)

IS/IT STAFF
- □ 05 Application Development/Programming Management
- □ 06 Application Development/Programming Staff
- □ 07 Consulting
- □ 08 DBA/Systems Administrator
- □ 09 Education/Training
- □ 10 Technical Support Director/Manager
- □ 11 Other Technical Management/Staff
- □ 98 Other

③ WHAT IS YOUR CURRENT PRIMARY OPERATING PLATFORM (check all that apply)

- □ 01 Digital Equipment Corp UNIX/VAX/VMS
- □ 02 HP UNIX
- □ 03 IBM AIX
- □ 04 IBM UNIX
- □ 05 Linux (Red Hat)
- □ 06 Linux (SUSE)
- □ 07 Linux (Oracle Enterprise)
- □ 08 Linux (other)
- □ 09 Macintosh
- □ 10 MVS
- □ 11 Netware
- □ 12 Network Computing
- □ 13 SCO UNIX
- □ 14 Sun Solaris/SunOS
- □ 15 Windows
- □ 16 Other UNIX
- □ 98 Other
- □ 99 None of the Above

④ DO YOU EVALUATE, SPECIFY, RECOMMEND, OR AUTHORIZE THE PURCHASE OF ANY OF THE FOLLOWING? (check all that apply)

- □ 01 Hardware
- □ 02 Business Applications (ERP, CRM, etc.)
- □ 03 Application Development Tools
- □ 04 Database Products
- □ 05 Internet or Intranet Products
- □ 06 Other Software
- □ 07 Middleware Products
- □ 99 None of the Above

⑤ IN YOUR JOB, DO YOU USE OR PLAN TO PURCHASE ANY OF THE FOLLOWING PRODUCTS? (check all that apply)

SOFTWARE
- □ 01 CAD/CAE/CAM
- □ 02 Collaboration Software
- □ 03 Communications
- □ 04 Database Management
- □ 05 File Management
- □ 06 Finance
- □ 07 Java
- □ 08 Multimedia Authoring
- □ 09 Networking
- □ 10 Programming
- □ 11 Project Management
- □ 12 Scientific and Engineering
- □ 13 Systems Management
- □ 14 Workflow

HARDWARE
- □ 15 Macintosh
- □ 16 Mainframe
- □ 17 Massively Parallel Processing

- □ 18 Minicomputer
- □ 19 Intel x86(32)
- □ 20 Intel x86(64)
- □ 21 Network Computer
- □ 22 Symmetric Multiprocessing
- □ 23 Workstation Services

SERVICES
- □ 24 Consulting
- □ 25 Education/Training
- □ 26 Maintenance
- □ 27 Online Database
- □ 28 Support
- □ 29 Technology-Based Training
- □ 30 Other
- □ 99 None of the Above

⑥ WHAT IS YOUR COMPANY'S SIZE? (check one only)

- □ 01 More than 25,000 Employees
- □ 02 10,001 to 25,000 Employees
- □ 03 5,001 to 10,000 Employees
- □ 04 1,001 to 5,000 Employees
- □ 05 101 to 1,000 Employees
- □ 06 Fewer than 100 Employees

⑦ DURING THE NEXT 12 MONTHS, HOW MUCH DO YOU ANTICIPATE YOUR ORGANIZATION WILL SPEND ON COMPUTER HARDWARE, SOFTWARE, PERIPHERALS, AND SERVICES FOR YOUR LOCATION? (check one only)

- □ 01 Less than $10,000
- □ 02 $10,000 to $49,999
- □ 03 $50,000 to $99,999
- □ 04 $100,000 to $499,999
- □ 05 $500,000 to $999,999
- □ 06 $1,000,000 and Over

⑧ WHAT IS YOUR COMPANY'S YEARLY SALES REVENUE? (check one only)

- □ 01 $500, 000, 000 and above
- □ 02 $100, 000, 000 to $500, 000, 000
- □ 03 $50, 000, 000 to $100, 000, 000
- □ 04 $5, 000, 000 to $50, 000, 000
- □ 05 $1, 000, 000 to $5, 000, 000

⑨ WHAT LANGUAGES AND FRAMEWORKS DO YOU USE? (check all that apply)

- □ 01 Ajax
- □ 02 C
- □ 03 C++
- □ 04 C#
- □ 05 Hibernate
- □ 06 J++/J#
- □ 07 Java
- □ 08 JSP
- □ 09 .NET
- □ 10 Perl
- □ 11 PHP
- □ 12 PL/SQL
- □ 13 Python
- □ 14 Ruby/Rails
- □ 15 Spring
- □ 16 Struts
- □ 17 SQL
- □ 18 Visual Basic
- □ 98 Other

⑩ WHAT ORACLE PRODUCTS ARE IN USE AT YOUR SITE? (check all that apply)

ORACLE DATABASE
- □ 01 Oracle Database 11*g*
- □ 02 Oracle Database 10*g*
- □ 03 Oracle9*i* Database
- □ 04 Oracle Embedded Database (Oracle Lite, Times Ten, Berkeley DB)
- □ 05 Other Oracle Database Release

ORACLE FUSION MIDDLEWARE
- □ 06 Oracle Application Server
- □ 07 Oracle Portal
- □ 08 Oracle Enterprise Manager
- □ 09 Oracle BPEL Process Manager
- □ 10 Oracle Identity Management
- □ 11 Oracle SOA Suite
- □ 12 Oracle Data Hubs

ORACLE DEVELOPMENT TOOLS
- □ 13 Oracle JDeveloper
- □ 14 Oracle Forms
- □ 15 Oracle Reports
- □ 16 Oracle Designer
- □ 17 Oracle Discoverer
- □ 18 Oracle BI Beans
- □ 19 Oracle Warehouse Builder
- □ 20 Oracle WebCenter
- □ 21 Oracle Application Express

ORACLE APPLICATIONS
- □ 22 Oracle E-Business Suite
- □ 23 PeopleSoft Enterprise
- □ 24 JD Edwards EnterpriseOne
- □ 25 JD Edwards World
- □ 26 Oracle Fusion
- □ 27 Hyperion
- □ 28 Siebel CRM

ORACLE SERVICES
- □ 28 Oracle E-Business Suite On Demand
- □ 29 Oracle Technology On Demand
- □ 30 Siebel CRM On Demand
- □ 31 Oracle Consulting
- □ 32 Oracle Education
- □ 33 Oracle Support
- □ 98 Other
- □ 99 None of the Above